Tips for Studying with This Book

This textbook has been designed to help you succeed in your U.S. history course. Follow these steps to get the most out of reading and studying from *The American Promise: A Compact History,* Third Edition.

- **PREVIEW: Before You Read**

    a. *Orient Yourself:* Look at the chapter title and study the chapter outline to preview the topics in the chapter and the order in which they will be covered.

    b. *Skim "Reviewing the Chapter":* Look at the Reviewing the Chapter section at the end of the chapter. The Who and What lists contain key terms to look for while you read. The Review Questions and Making Connections alert you to topics you should pay close attention to as you read.

- **FOCUS: While You Read**

    a. *Follow the Story:* Read the opening story carefully. It previews topics that will be important in the chapter. Pay attention to section headings as you continue to read; they alert you to what is to come and help you keep track of where the chapter is heading.

    b. *Pay Attention to the Context:* Look at the maps, tables, and figures in the chapter, which can help you understand the national and regional contexts of the story.

    c. *Check Your Reading:* After you read each major section, try to answer the review question at the end. If you have trouble, skim the section again for the answer.

- **REVIEW: After You Read**

    a. *Test Your Knowledge:* Turn to the Reviewing the Chapter section at the end of the chapter and review the list of Key Terms. Can you identify them and explain why they are important to the chapter? If not, flip back to the page number indicated and skim to refresh your memory.

    b. *Review the Timeline:* Review the order of events in the Timeline to make sure you understand the relationships between events in the chapter and their sequence.

    c. *Place the Specifics in the Big Picture:* Answer the Review Questions and Making Connections questions, citing evidence from the text to make sure you understand the important developments in the chapter.

- **TAKE PRACTICE QUIZZES: Online Study Guide**
  bedfordstmartins.com/roarkcompact

    a. *See What You've Learned:* To determine what you know and what you need to review, visit the Online Study Guide, which provides self-assessment quizzes for each chapter with instantly graded results.

    b. *Deepen Your Knowledge:* Develop a rich understanding of the period covered in the chapter and hone your interpretive skills by exploring other online features such as Reading Historical Documents and Visual Activity.

THE CONTEMPORARY WORLD

80 N

60 N

40 N

20 N

0 Equator

20 S

40 S

60 S

80 S

160 W   140 W   120 W   100 W   80 W   60 W   40 W   20 W

PACIFIC OCEAN

ATLANTIC OCEAN

ATLANTIC OCEAN

Alaska

Greenland (Den.)

ICELAND

UNITED KINGDOM

IRELAND

FRANCE

SPAIN

PORTUGAL

CANADA

UNITED STATES

Azores (Port.)

MOROCCO

Canary Is. (Sp.)

Western Sahara (Mor.)

MEXICO

Hawaii

BAHAMAS
DOMINICAN
HAITI REPUBLIC
CUBA
Puerto Rico (U.S.)
JAMAICA
BELIZE
ST. KITTS AND NEVIS
ANTIGUA AND BARBUDA
Guadeloupe (Fr.) DOMINICA
Martinique (Fr.)
ST. LUCIA
GRENADA
TRINIDAD AND TOBAGO
BARBADOS
ST. VINCENT AND THE GRENADINES

MAURITANIA

CAPE
VERDE

SENEGAL

MALI

GAMBIA

GUINEA-BISSAU

GUINEA

SIERRA LEONE

LIBERIA

CÔTE D'IVOIRE

BURKINA FASO

GHANA

GUATEMALA
EL SALVADOR
HONDURAS
NICARAGUA
COSTA RICA
PANAMA

VENEZUELA
GUYANA
SURINAME
French Guiana (Fr.)

COLOMBIA

ECUADOR

Galápagos Is. (Ec.)

PERU

BRAZIL

BOLIVIA

PARAGUAY

SAMOA

TONGA

Easter I. (Chile)

CHILE

URUGUAY

ARGENTINA

Falkland Is. (U.K.)

0   1,500   3,000 miles

0   1,500   3,000 kilometers

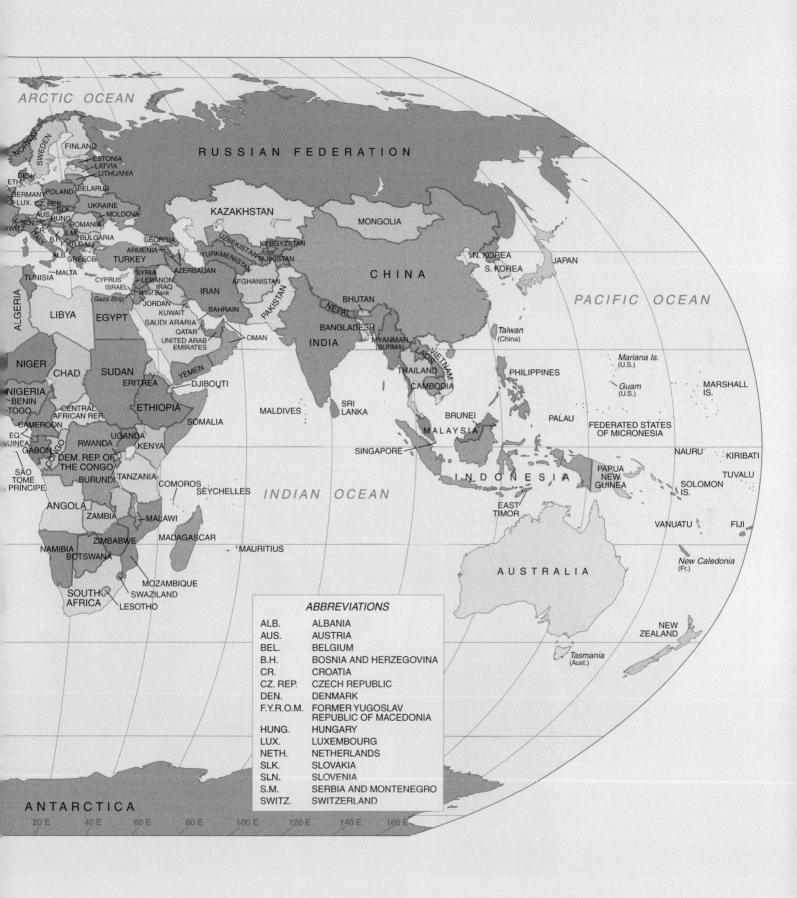

ARCTIC OCEAN

NORWAY
SWEDEN
FINLAND
ESTONIA
LATVIA
LITHUANIA
DEN.
ETH.
GERMANY
LUX. CZ. REP.
POLAND
BELARUS
AUS.
HUNG.
SLN.
SWITZ.
CR.
ITALY
B.H.
S.M.
F.Y.R.O.M.
ALB.
GREECE
BULGARIA
UKRAINE
MOLDOVA
ROMANIA
GEORGIA
ARMENIA
AZERBAIJAN
TURKEY
TUNISIA
MALTA
CYPRUS
ISRAEL
SYRIA
LEBANON
West Bank
Gaza Strip
JORDAN
IRAQ
KUWAIT
SAUDI ARABIA
QATAR
BAHRAIN
UNITED ARAB EMIRATES
OMAN
YEMEN
DJIBOUTI

RUSSIAN FEDERATION

KAZAKHSTAN
UZBEKISTAN
KYRGYZSTAN
TURKMENISTAN
TAJIKISTAN
AFGHANISTAN
IRAN
PAKISTAN

MONGOLIA

CHINA

N. KOREA
S. KOREA
JAPAN

PACIFIC OCEAN

ALGERIA
LIBYA
EGYPT

NIGER
CHAD
SUDAN
ERITREA

NIGERIA
BENIN
TOGO
CENTRAL AFRICAN REP.
CAMEROON
EQ. GUINEA
GABON
CONGO
DEM. REP. OF THE CONGO
SÃO TOMÉ PRÍNCIPE
RWANDA
UGANDA
KENYA
BURUNDI
TANZANIA
ETHIOPIA
SOMALIA
COMOROS
SEYCHELLES

NEPAL
BHUTAN
BANGLADESH
INDIA
MYANMAR (BURMA)
LAOS
VIETNAM
THAILAND
CAMBODIA

MALDIVES
SRI LANKA

Talwan (China)

Mariana Is. (U.S.)
Guam (U.S.)
MARSHALL IS.

PHILIPPINES

BRUNEI
MALAYSIA
SINGAPORE
PALAU

FEDERATED STATES OF MICRONESIA

NAURU
KIRIBATI
TUVALU

ANGOLA
ZAMBIA
MALAWI
NAMIBIA
ZIMBABWE
BOTSWANA
MADAGASCAR
MOZAMBIQUE
SWAZILAND
SOUTH AFRICA
LESOTHO
MAURITIUS

INDIAN OCEAN

INDONESIA
EAST TIMOR

PAPUA NEW GUINEA

SOLOMON IS.

VANUATU
FIJI

New Caledonia (Fr.)

AUSTRALIA

NEW ZEALAND

Tasmania (Aust.)

ABBREVIATIONS

ALB.	ALBANIA
AUS.	AUSTRIA
BEL.	BELGIUM
B.H.	BOSNIA AND HERZEGOVINA
CR.	CROATIA
CZ. REP.	CZECH REPUBLIC
DEN.	DENMARK
F.Y.R.O.M.	FORMER YUGOSLAV REPUBLIC OF MACEDONIA
HUNG.	HUNGARY
LUX.	LUXEMBOURG
NETH.	NETHERLANDS
SLK.	SLOVAKIA
SLN.	SLOVENIA
S.M.	SERBIA AND MONTENEGRO
SWITZ.	SWITZERLAND

ANTARCTICA

20 E   40 E   60 E   80 E   100 E   120 E   140 E   160 E

NEYSA McMEIN, THE POPULAR ILLUSTRATOR AND PORTRAIT ARTIST AT AGE TWENTY-NINE, CARRYING THE FLAG IN 1917
The New York Times Photo Archives.

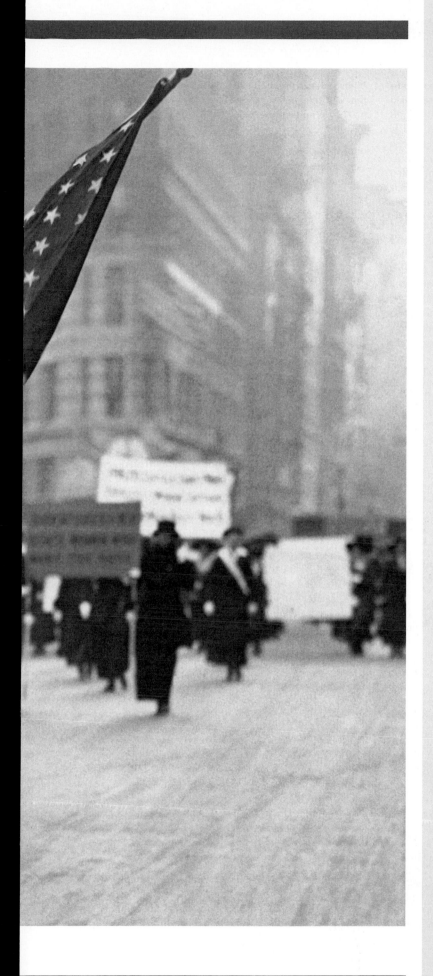

The American Promise

A COMPACT HISTORY

Third Edition

James L. Roark
Emory University

Michael P. Johnson
Johns Hopkins University

Patricia Cline Cohen
University of California, Santa Barbara

Sarah Stage
Arizona State University

Alan Lawson
Boston College

Susan M. Hartmann
The Ohio State University

BEDFORD/ST. MARTIN'S
Boston ◆ New York

FOR BEDFORD/ST. MARTIN'S

Executive Editor for History: Mary Dougherty
Director of Development for History: Jane Knetzger
Senior Developmental Editor: Heidi L. Hood
Senior Production Editor: Karen S. Baart
Production Supervisor: Jennifer Wetzel
Executive Marketing Manager: Jenna Bookin Barry
Associate Editor: Shannon Hunt
Editorial Assistant: Daniel Cole
Production Assistants: Katherine Caruana and Lindsay DiGianvittorio
Copyeditor: Patricia Herbst
Text Design: Wanda Kossak
Photo Research: Pembroke Herbert/Sandi Rygiel, Picture Research Consultants & Archives, Inc.
Indexer: Anne Harbour
Cover Design: Billy Boardman
Cartography: Mapping Specialists Ltd.
Composition: Techbooks
Printing and Binding: R.R. Donnelley & Sons Company

President: Joan E. Feinberg
Editorial Director: Denise B. Wydra
Director of Marketing: Karen Melton Soeltz
Director of Editing, Design, and Production: Marcia Cohen
Managing Editor: Elizabeth M. Schaaf

Library of Congress Control Number: 2005938010

Manufactured in the United States of America.

1 0 9 8 7 6
f e d c b a

For information, write: Bedford/St. Martin's, 75 Arlington Street, Boston, MA 02116 (617-399-4000)

ISBN-10: 0–312–44165–7   ISBN-13: 978–0–312–44165–4 (combined edition)
ISBN-10: 0–312–44841–4   ISBN-13: 978–0–312–44841–7 (Vol. I)
ISBN-10: 0–312–44842–2   ISBN-13: 978–0–312–44842–4 (Vol. II)
ISBN-10: 0–312–45643–3   ISBN-13: 978–0–312–45643–6 (high school edition)

Cover Art: *Neysa McMein, the Popular Illustrator and Portrait Artist at Age Twenty-nine, Carrying the Flag in 1917.* The New York Times Photo Archives.

BRIEF CONTENTS

CONTENTS

CHAPTER 1

Ancient America: Before 1492   3

CHAPTER 8
Building a Republic,
1775–1789   185

CHAPTER 9
The New Nation Takes Form,
1789–1800   211

CHAPTER 18
The West in the Gilded Age, 1870–1900   453

CHAPTER 19
The City and Its Workers, 1870–1900   477

MAPS, FIGURES, AND TABLES

MAPS, FIGURES, AND TABLES

MAPS, FIGURES, AND TABLES

SPECIAL FEATURES

THE THIRD EDITION of *The American Promise: A Compact History* is an occasion for celebration. As authors, we are deeply gratified that our book has become one of the best selling and most popular texts for the U.S. history survey, and we continue to take pride in the book's distinctly useful format, one which combines a brief narrative with all of the art, maps, features, and pedagogical tools of a full-length text. With this particular revision, we feel we have reached a new milestone in our ongoing efforts to present the most teachable and readable book available on the market.

In this edition we not only did our own abridgement to make the book 30 percent shorter, as we have done in the past, but we also created a new in-text study guide. At the end of each major section of a chapter, students will find review questions that also form part of the comprehensive chapter review appearing at each chapter's end. These new Reviewing the Chapter sections offer step-by-step guidance that leads students from basic comprehension to questions for analysis. These elements of the revision derive from our commitment to making this book accessible to students, and they were strengthened by the insights of our adopters and reviewers. We are grateful for their suggestions and confident the resulting text will be even more useful to students and instructors.

From the beginning, *The American Promise* has been shaped by our firsthand knowledge that the survey course is the most difficult to teach and the most difficult to take. Collectively, we have logged more than a century in introductory American history classrooms in institutions that range from small community colleges to large research universities. Drawing on our practical experience, we set an ambitious goal, one that we continue to focus on in the third compact edition: to produce the most teachable and readable introductory American history textbook available. Our experience as teachers informs every aspect of our text, beginning with its framework. Many survey texts emphasize either a social or a political approach to history, and by focusing on one, they inevitably slight the other. In our classrooms, we have found that students need **both** the structure a political narrative provides and the insights gained from examining social and cultural experience. To write a comprehensive, balanced account of American history we have focused on the public arena — the place where politics intersects social and cultural developments — to show how Americans confronted the major issues of their day and created far-reaching historical change.

We also thought hard about the concerns most frequently voiced by instructors: that students often find history boring, unfocused, and difficult and their textbooks lifeless and overwhelming. Getting students to open the book is one of the biggest hurdles instructors face. We asked ourselves how our text could address these concerns and engage students in ways that would help them understand and remember the main developments in American history. To make the political, social, economic, and cultural changes vivid and memorable and to portray fully the diversity of the American experience, we stitch into our narrative the voices of hundreds of contemporaries—from presidents to pipefitters, sharecroppers to suffragists—whose ideas and actions shaped their times and whose efforts still affect our lives. By incorporating a rich selection of authentic American voices, we seek to capture history as it happened and to create a narrative that compels students' interest and sparks their historical imagination.

Our title, *The American Promise,* reflects our emphasis on human agency and our conviction that American history is an unfinished story. For millions, the nation held out the promise of a better life, unfettered worship, representative government, democratic politics, and other freedoms seldom found elsewhere around the world. But none of these promises has come with guarantees. And promises fulfilled for some have meant promises denied to others. As we see it, much of American history is a continuing struggle over the definition and realization of the nation's promise. Abraham Lincoln, in the midst of what he termed the "fiery trial" of the Civil War, pronounced the nation "the last best hope of Earth." Kept alive by countless sacrifices, that hope has been marred by compromises, disappointments, and denials, but it still lives. We believe that *The American Promise: A Compact History,* Third Edition, with its attention to making history come alive, will help students become aware of the legacy of hope bequeathed to them by previous generations of Americans stretching back nearly four centuries, a legacy that is theirs to preserve and build on.

Features

From the beginning, readers have proclaimed this textbook a visual feast, richly illustrated in ways that extend and reinforce the narrative. The third compact edition offers more than 460 contemporaneous **illustrations**, a visual program usually found only in a full-sized text, and many are in full color and large enough to study in detail. Over 250 **artifacts** make the past tangible. Full-page **chapter-opening artifacts** and other captioned artifacts throughout the text emphasize the importance of material culture in the study of the past and enrich the historical account. **New embedded artifacts** (small images of material culture)—from boots and political buttons to guns and sewing machines—are folded into the narrative. Similarly, **new illustrated chapter timelines** provide thumbnail-size images from the chapter to reinforce the narrative and stimulate students' power of recall. A striking **new design** highlights the illustration program and makes the most of our **comprehensive captions** while enticing students to delve deeper into the text itself.

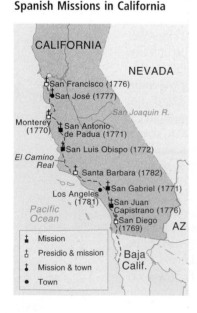

Spanish Missions in California

CALIFORNIA

NEVADA

San Francisco (1776)
San José (1777)

San Joaquin R.

Monterey (1770)
San Antonio de Padua (1771)

San Luis Obispo (1772)

El Camino Real

Santa Barbara (1782)

Los Angeles (1781)
San Gabriel (1771)

San Juan Capistrano (1776)

San Diego (1769)

AZ

Pacific Ocean

Baja Calif.

‡ Mission
⚓ Presidio & mission
‡ Mission & town
● Town

We have expanded our highly regarded **map program** to offer the most effective set of maps available in a compact survey text. More than 160 **full-color maps**—far more than in most full-length books—help students learn geography and its role in history. Each chapter offers, on average, three to four **full-sized maps** showing major developments in a wide range of areas, from environmental and technological issues to political, social, cultural, and diplomatic matters. New maps reflect our increased attention to Native American peoples and to the West in particular. In addition, each chapter includes two or three **spot maps**, small, single-concept maps embedded in the narrative to strengthen students' grasp of crucial issues. Unique to *The American Promise*, new spot maps highlight such topics as Spanish missions in California, frontier land opened by Indian removal in the 1830s, the Mexican cession, selected Indian relocations from 1950 to 1970, contemporary Israel, and the recent conflict in Afghanistan. Finally, each chapter includes a **critical-thinking map exercise**, almost all of which are new.

As part of our ongoing efforts to make this the most teachable and readable survey text available, we paid renewed attention to imaginative and effective pedagogy. Thus, this third compact edition has increased its reach, lending greater in-text help to all levels of students. All chapters are constructed to preview, reinforce, and review the narrative in the most memorable and engaging way possible. To prepare students for the reading to come, each chapter begins with a **new chapter outline** to accompany the vivid **opening vignette** that invites students into the narrative with lively accounts of individuals or groups who embody the central themes of the chapter. New vignettes in this edition include, among others, Roger Williams being banished from Puritan Massachusetts, runaway slave William Gould enlisting in the Union navy, Native American boarding school students celebrating Indian Citizenship Day, Henry Ford putting America on wheels, Colonel Paul Tibbets dropping the bomb on Hiroshima, Phyllis Schlafly promoting conservatism, and Colin Powell adjusting to the post–cold war world. Each vignette ends with a **narrative overview** of the chapter's main topics. To further prepare students as they read, major sections within each chapter begin with **introductory paragraphs** that preview the subsections that follow and conclude with **new review questions** to help students absorb main points and build confidence in their mastery as they read. Throughout each chapter, **two-tiered running heads** with dates and topical headings remind students where the sections they are reading fall chronologically. In addition, **new thematic chronologies** reinforce and extend points in the narrative, and a **new Glossary of Historical Vocabulary** aids students' comprehension by defining terms that some may find hard to grasp, such as *covenant, laissez-faire,* and *progressivism*. At the end of each chapter, a **conclusion** critically reexamines central ideas and provides a bridge to the next chapter.

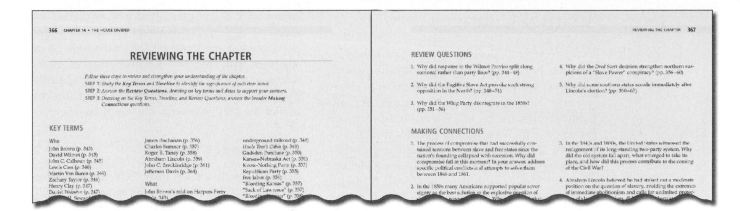

Perhaps the most notable new way this edition reaches out to students is through a substantial **new Reviewing the Chapter** section at the end of each chapter that provides step-by-step study plans to ensure student success. These two-page chapter review guides start with clear **study instructions** that lead students through an incremental approach to reviewing the chapter. Lists of **Key Terms** with page numbers highlight important people, events, and concepts, while illustrated chapter **Timelines** give clear chronological overviews of key events. Two sets of questions prompt students to think critically and make use of the facts they have mastered. The focused **Review Questions** are repeated from within the chapter for reinforcement, while **Making Connections** questions ask students about broad developments in preparation for essay examinations. Finally, the chapter review ends with an **Online Study Guide cross-reference** pointing students to free self-assessment quizzes and other study aids for further help.

Special features reinforce the narrative and offer teachers more points of departure for assignments and discussion. Because students live in an increasingly global world and need help making connections with the world outside the United States, we added ten essays in our **new Beyond America's Borders** feature. These essays seek to widen students' perspectives, to help them see that this country did not develop in isolation. Essays as varied as "American Tobacco and European Consumers," "Filibusters: The Underside of Manifest Destiny," "Transnational Feminisms," and "Jobs in a Globalizing Era" consider the reciprocal connections between the United States and the wider world and challenge students to think about the effects of transnational connec-

tions over time. A broader notion of American history will help students understand more fully the complex development of their nation's history and help prepare them to live in the twenty-first century.

Fresh topics in our three enduring special features further enrich this compact edition. Each **Documenting the American Promise** feature juxtaposes three or four primary documents to dramatize the human dimension of major events and show varying perspectives on a topic or issue. Feature introductions and document headnotes contextualize the sources, while Questions for Analysis and Debate promote critical thinking about primary sources. New topics include "Missionaries Report on California Missions" and "Voices of Protest." **Historical Question** essays pose and interpret historical questions of continuing interest to demonstrate the depth and variety of possible answers, thereby countering the belief of many beginning students that historians simply gather facts and string them together in a chronological narrative. New questions in this edition include "How Long Did the Seven Years' War Last in Indian Country?" and "Why Did the ERA Fail?" **The Promise of Technology** essays examine the social, economic, and cultural ramifications —positive and negative—of technological innovations. New topics in this edition include "Stoves Transform Cooking" and "Better Living through Electricity."

BEYOND AMERICA'S BORDERS

Transnational Feminisms

When large numbers of American women began to protest sex discrimination in the 1960s, most were unaware that they belonged to a movement stretching more than one hundred years back in history and across oceans. In 1850, Ernestine Rose, who had been born in Poland and lived in Berlin, Paris, and London, told a women's rights convention in Massachusetts, "We are not contending here for the rights of the women of New England, or of old England,

assumption of superiority or of patronage on the part of Europe or America . . . will alienate . . . the womanhood of Asia and Africa." White, Christian women from the United States and Europe dominated the organization and all too readily assumed that they could speak for all women. But oppression and discrimination looked quite different to women in other parts of the world. For example, in **colonized** countries such as India and Egypt, feminism arose alongside movements for inde-

Textual Changes

In our ongoing effort to offer a comprehensive text that braids all Americans into the national narrative, we give particular attention to diversity and the influence of class, religion, race, ethnicity, gender, and region. For example, increased coverage of the West and its peoples from the beginning of American history means fresh material throughout the text and a new post–Civil War chapter, "The West in the Gilded Age." We also give more coverage to the environment, Native Americans, Mexicans, Latinos, and other topics closely related to the history of the West. To strengthen coverage and increase clarity and accessibility, we have reorganized certain chapters. In particular, organizational changes in the chapters on antebellum America and the Gilded Age provide clearer themes with smoother transitions and place the West firmly in the national narrative. We also provide stronger post-1945 chapters, reorganized to make themes more compelling and chronology clearer. These post-1945 chapters also include a fresh array of voices, pay greater attention to the West and related topics, and, of course, present up-to-date coverage of the George W. Bush administration, the Middle East, and the war on terrorism.

Staying abreast of current scholarship is important to us, and this edition reflects that keen interest. We incorporated a wealth of new scholarship to benefit students. Readers will note that we made good use of the latest works on the Spanish borderlands, Native Americans in the Seven Years' War, the role of political wives in the early Republic, the social history of the Gold Rush, the active participation of blacks in their own liberation during the Civil War, mining and commercial farming in the Gilded Age West, race and Americanization, Mexican migration into the American Southwest and how it compares to black migration into the North, the story of the atomic bomb, and the rise of contemporary conservatism.

Supplements

Developed with our guidance and thoroughly revised to reflect the changes in the third edition, the comprehensive collection of print and electronic resources accompanying the textbook represents a host of practical learning and teaching aids. Again, we learned much from the book's community of adopters, and we broadened the scope of the supplements to create a learning package that responds to the real needs of instructors and students. Cross-references in the textbook to the Online Study Guide and to the primary source reader signal the tight integration of the core text with the supplements.

For Students

Reading the American Past: Selected Historical Documents, **Third Edition.** Edited by Michael P. Johnson (Johns Hopkins University), one of the authors of *The American Promise,* and designed to complement the textbook, *Reading the American Past* provides a broad selection of over 150 primary source documents as well as editorial apparatus to help students understand the sources. Emphasizing the important social, political, and economic themes of U.S. history courses, 31 new documents (one per chapter) were added to provide a multiplicity of perspectives on environmental, western, ethnic, and gender history and to bring a global dimension to the anthology. Available free when packaged with the text.

Online Study Guide at bedfordstmartins.com/ roarkcompact**.** The popular Online Study Guide for *The American Promise* is a free and uniquely personalized learning tool to help students master

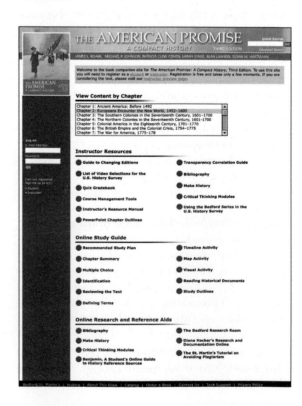

themes and information presented in the textbook and improve their historical skills. Assessment quizzes let students evaluate their comprehension and provide them with customized plans for further study through a variety of activities. Instructors can monitor students' progress through the online Quiz Gradebook or receive e-mail updates.

The Bedford Glossary for U.S. History. This handy supplement for the survey course gives students clear, concise definitions of the political, economic, social, and cultural terms used by historians and contemporary media alike. The terms are historically contextualized to aid comprehension. Available free when packaged with the text.

History Matters: A Student Guide to U.S. History Online. This new resource, written by Alan Gevinson, Kelly Schrum, and Roy Rosenzweig (all of George Mason University), provides an illustrated and annotated guide to 250 of the most useful Web sites for student research in U.S. history as well as advice on evaluating and using Internet sources. This essential guide is based on the acclaimed "History Matters" Web site developed by the American History Social Project and the Center for History and New Media. Available free when packaged with the text.

NEW *Maps in Context: A Workbook for American History.* Written by historical cartography expert Gerald A. Danzer (University of Illinois, Chicago), this skill-building workbook helps students comprehend essential connections between geographic literacy and historical understanding. Organized to correspond to the typical U.S. history survey course, *Maps in Context* presents a wealth of map-centered projects and convenient pop quizzes that give students hands-on experience working with maps. Available free when packaged with the text.

Bedford Series in History and Culture. Over 100 titles in this highly praised series combine first-rate scholarship, historical narrative, and important primary documents for undergraduate courses. Each book is brief, inexpensive, and focused on a specific topic or period. Package discounts are available.

Historians at Work Series. Brief enough for a single assignment yet meaty enough to provoke thoughtful discussion, each volume in this series examines a single historical question by combining unabridged selections by distinguished historians, each with a different perspective on the issue, with helpful learning aids. Package discounts are available.

NEW **Trade Books.** Titles published by sister companies Farrar, Straus and Giroux; Henry Holt and Company; Hill and Wang; Picador; and St. Martin's Press are available at deep discounts when packaged with the text.

Online Bibliography at bedfordstmartins.com/roarkcompact. Organized by book chapter and topic, the online bibliography provides an authoritative and comprehensive list of references to jump-start student research.

Critical Thinking Modules at bedfordstmartins.com/historymodules. This Web site offers over two dozen online modules for interpreting maps, audio, visual, and textual sources, centered on events covered in the U.S. history survey. An online guide correlates modules to textbook chapters.

A Student's Online Guide to History Reference Sources at bedfordstmartins.com/benjamin. This Web site provides links to history-related databases, indexes, and journals, plus contact information for state, provincial, local, and professional history organizations.

Research and Documentation Online at bedfordstmartins.com/resdoc. This Web site provides clear advice on how to integrate primary and secondary sources into research papers, how to cite sources correctly, and how to format in MLA, APA, *Chicago*, or CBE style.

The St. Martin's Tutorial on Avoiding Plagiarism at bedfordstmartins.com/plagiarismtutorial. This online tutorial reviews the consequences of plagiarism and explains what sources to acknowledge, how to keep good notes, how to organize research, and how to integrate sources appropriately. The tutorial includes exercises to help students practice integrating sources and recognize acceptable summaries.

Bedford Research Room at bedfordstmartins.com/researchroom. The Research Room, drawn from Mike Palmquist's *The Bedford Researcher,* offers a wealth of resources—including interactive tutorials, research activities, student writing samples, and links to hundreds of other places online—to support students in courses across the disciplines. The site also offers instructors a library of helpful instructional tools.

Telecourse Guides for *Shaping America: U.S. History to 1877* **and** *Transforming America: U.S. History since 1877.* These guides by Kenneth G. Alfers (Dallas County Community College District) are designed for students using *The American Promise* in conjunction with the Dallas Tele-Learning telecourses *Shaping America* and *Transforming America.* Lesson overviews, assignments, objectives, and focus points provide structure for distance learners, while enrichment ideas, suggested readings, and brief primary sources extend the unit lessons. Practice tests help students evaluate their mastery of the material.

For Instructors

Instructor's Resource Manual. This popular manual by Sarah E. Gardner (Mercer University) and Catherine A. Jones (Johns Hopkins University) offers both experienced and first-time instructors tools for presenting textbook material in exciting and engaging ways—learning objectives, annotated chapter outlines, model answers to review questions, lecture strategies, tips for helping students with common misconceptions and difficult topics, and suggestions for in-class activities, including using film and video, ways to start discussions, topics for debate, and analyzing primary sources. The new edition also features a chapter-by-chapter guide to all of the supplements available with *The American Promise: A Compact History*, an extensive guide for first-time teaching assistants, sample syllabi, and a brief guide for using the book companion site.

Transparencies. This set of over 160 full-color acetate transparencies of full-size maps and many other images from both the full and compact editions of *The American Promise* helps instructors present lectures and teach students important map-reading skills.

Book Companion Site at bedfordstmartins.com/ roarkcompact. The companion Web site gathers all the electronic resources for *The American Promise: A Compact History*, including the Online Study Guide and related Quiz Gradebook, at a single Web address, providing convenient links to lecture, assignment, and research materials such as PowerPoint chapter outlines and the digital libraries at Make History.

Computerized Test Bank. This test bank by Bradford Wood (Eastern Kentucky University), Peter Lau (University of Rhode Island), and Sondra Cosgrove (Community College of Southern Nevada) contains easy-to-use software to create tests. Over 80 exercises are provided per chapter, including multiple-choice, fill-in-the-blank, map analysis, short essay, and full-length essay questions. Instructors can customize quizzes, add or edit both questions and answers, and export questions and answers to a variety of formats, including WebCT and Blackboard. The disc includes correct answers and essay outlines as well as separate test banks for the associated telecourses *Shaping America* and *Transforming America.*

Instructor's Resource CD-ROM. This disc provides instructors with ready-made and customizable PowerPoint multimedia presentations built around chapter outlines, maps, figures, and selected images from the textbook. The disc also includes selected images from the textbook in jpeg format, the *Instructor's Resource Manual*, outline maps in pdf format for quizzing or handouts, and a quick-start guide to the Online Study Guide.

NEW Make History at bedfordstmartins.com/ makehistory. Comprising the content of our five acclaimed online libraries—Map Central, the U.S. History Image Library, DocLinks, HistoryLinks, and PlaceLinks, Make History provides one-stop access to relevant digital content including maps, images, documents, and Web links. Students and instructors alike can search this free, easy-to-use database by keyword, topic, date, or specific chapter of *The American Promise* and can download any content they find. Instructors using *The American Promise* can also create entire collections of content and store them online for later use or post their collections to the Web to share with students.

Using the Bedford Series in History and Culture in the U.S. History Survey at bedfordstmartins .com/usingseries. This online guide helps instructors integrate volumes from the highly regarded Bedford Series in History and Culture into their U.S. history survey course. The guide not only correlates themes from each series book with the survey course but also provides ideas for classroom discussions.

Course Management Content. E-content is available for this book in Blackboard, WebCT, Angel, and Desire2Learn course management systems. This e-content includes nearly all of the offerings from the book's Online Study Guide as well as the book's test bank and the test banks from the associated telecourses *Shaping America* and *Transforming America*.

Videos and Multimedia. A wide assortment of videos and multimedia CD-ROMs on various topics in American history is available to qualified adopters. Also available are 59 short clips from the telecourses *Shaping America* and *Transforming America* in DVD and VHS formats for presentation during lectures.

***The American Promise* for Distance Learning via Telecourse.** We are pleased to announce that *The American Promise* has been selected as the textbook for the award-winning U.S. history telecourses *Shaping America: U.S. History to 1877* and *Transforming America: U.S. History since 1877* by Dallas TeleLearning at the LeCroy Center for Educational Telecommunications, Dallas County Community College District. Guides for students and instructors fully integrate the narrative of *The American Promise* into each telecourse. For more information on these distance-learning opportunities, visit the Dallas TeleLearning Web site at http://telelearning.dcccd.edu, e-mail tlearn@dcccd.edu, or call 972-669-6650.

Acknowledgments

We gratefully acknowledge all of the helpful suggestions from those who have read and taught from the previous editions of *The American Promise*, and we hope that our many classroom collaborators will be pleased to see their influence in the third compact edition. In particular, we wish to thank the talented scholars and teachers who gave generously of their time and knowledge to review this book; their critiques and suggestions contributed greatly to the published work: Troy Bickham, *Texas A&M University*; Vincent Clark, *Johnson County Community College*; James Denton, *University of Colorado at Boulder*; Andy DeRoche, *Front Range Community College*; Mark Ellis, *University of Nebraska*; James Good, *North Harris College*; Larry Hartzell, *Brookdale Community College*; Donald Heidenreich, *Lindenwood University*; Adam Howard, *George Mason University*; Jerome Rodnitzky, *University of Texas at Arlington*; Jeffrey Smith, *Lindenwood University*; Richard Sorrell, *Brookdale Community*

College; Richard Ulibarri, *Weber State University*; and Keith Zahniser, *Ohio State University*.

In addition, we wish to thank the reviewers of the full-length third edition of this textbook, whose comments about organization and content informed the compact edition as well: Eric Arnesen, *University of Illinois, Chicago*; Carl H. Boening, *Shelton State Community College*; Tommy L. Bynum, *Georgia Perimeter College*; Lawrence Cebula, *Missouri Southern State College*; Michael Connolly, *Tidewater Community College*; Gary Darden, *Rutgers University*; David Engerman, *Brandeis University*; Maurine W. Greenwald, *University of Pittsburgh*; David Igler, *University of Utah*; Peter F. Lau, *University of Rhode Island*; Charles H. Martin, *University of Texas, El Paso*; April Masten, *State University of New York, Stony Brook*; Jim R. McClellan, *Northern Virginia Community College*; Constance McGovern, *Frostburg State University*; Karen Merrill, *Williams College*; Peggy Renner, *Glendale Community College*; Steven Reschly, *Truman State University*; Leo Ribuffo, *The George Washington University*; Christine Sears, *University of Delaware*; Michael Sherry, *Northwestern University*; Steven Stoll, *Yale University*; Diana Turk, *New York University*; Elliott West, *University of Arkansas*; Jon A. Whitfield, *Central Texas College, Fort Knox*; Thomas Winn, *Austin Peay State University*; and Thomas Zeiler, *University of Colorado at Boulder*.

A project as complex as this requires the talents of many individuals. First, we would like to acknowledge our families for their support, forbearance, and toleration of our textbook responsibilities. Pembroke Herbert and Sandi Rygiel of Picture Research Consultants, Inc., contributed their unparalleled knowledge and diligent research to make possible the extraordinary illustration program.

We would also like to thank the many people at Bedford/St. Martin's who have been crucial to this project. No one contributed more than senior editor Heidi L. Hood, who managed the entire revision and oversaw the development of each chapter. We thank as well associate editor Shannon Hunt for her help with portions of the manuscript. Thanks also go to editorial assistant Daniel Cole, who provided invaluable editorial support and who coordinated the supplements. We are also grateful to Jane Knetzger, director of development for history, and Mary Dougherty, executive editor, for their support and guidance. For their imaginative and tireless efforts to promote the book, we want to thank Jenna Bookin Barry, marketing manager, and Amanda Byrnes, marketing associate. With great skill and professionalism, senior production editor Karen Baart juggled and monitored the many pieces related to copyediting, design, and typesetting. Karen was ably assisted by production intern Lindsay DiGianvittorio and by Katherine Caruana, production assistant; Katherine also saw to the production of the *Instructor's Resource Manual.* Managing editor Elizabeth Schaaf and assistant managing editor John Amburg offered their customary expert guidance. Production supervisor Jennifer Wetzel oversaw the manufacturing of the book. Page makeup artist DeNee Skipper, copyeditor Patricia Herbst, and proofreaders Janet Cocker and Barbara Price attended to the myriad details that help make the book shine. Anne Harbour provided an especially useful index. Associate new media editor Danielle Slevens and new media production coordinator Coleen O'Hanley made sure that *The American Promise* remains at the forefront of technological support for students and instructors. Editorial director Denise Wydra provided helpful advice throughout the course of the project. Finally, president Joan E. Feinberg and former president Charles H. Christensen took a personal interest in *The American Promise* from the start, for which we are grateful.

JAMES L. ROARK

Born in Eunice, Louisiana, and raised in the West, James L. Roark received his B.A. from the University of California, Davis, in 1963 and his Ph.D. from Stanford University in 1973. His dissertation won the Allan Nevins Prize. He has taught at the University of Nigeria, Nsukka; the University of Nairobi, Kenya; the University of Missouri, St. Louis; and, since 1983, Emory University, where he is Samuel Candler Dobbs Professor of American History. In 1993, he received the Emory Williams Distinguished Teaching Award, and in 2001–2002 he was Pitt Professor of American Institutions at Cambridge University. He has written *Masters without Slaves: Southern Planters in the Civil War and Reconstruction* (1977). With Michael P. Johnson, he is author of *Black Masters: A Free Family of Color in the Old South* (1984) and editor of *No Chariot Let Down: Charleston's Free People of Color on the Eve of the Civil War* (1984). He has received research assistance from the American Philosophical Society, the National Endowment for the Humanities, and the Gilder Lehrman Institute of American History. Active in the Organization of American Historians and the Southern Historical Association, he is also a fellow of the Society of American Historians.

MICHAEL P. JOHNSON

Born and raised in Ponca City, Oklahoma, Michael P. Johnson studied at Knox College in Galesburg, Illinois, where he received a B.A. in 1963, and at Stanford University in Palo Alto, California, earning a Ph.D. in 1973. He is currently professor of history at Johns Hopkins University in Baltimore, having previously taught at the University of California, Irvine, San Jose State University, and LeMoyne (now LeMoyne-Owen) College in Memphis. His publications include *Toward a Patriarchal Republic: The Secession of Georgia* (1977); with James L. Roark, *Black Masters: A Free Family of Color in the Old South* (1984) and *No Chariot Let Down: Charleston's Free People of Color on the Eve of the Civil War* (1984); *Abraham Lincoln, Slavery, and the Civil War: Selected Speeches and Writings* (2001); *Reading the American Past: Selected Historical Documents*, the documents reader for *The American Promise*; and articles that have appeared in the *William and Mary Quarterly*, the *Journal of Southern History, Labor History,* the *New York Review of Books,* the *New Republic,* the *Nation,* and other journals. Johnson has been awarded research fellowships by the American Council of Learned Societies, the National Endowment for the Humanities, and the Center for Advanced Study in the Behavioral Sciences and Stanford University, and the Times Mirror Foundation Distinguished Research Fellowship at the Huntington Library. He has directed a National Endowment for the Humanities Summer Seminar for College Teachers and has been honored with the University of California, Irvine, Academic Senate Distinguished Teaching Award and the University of California, Irvine, Alumni Association Outstanding Teaching Award. He won the *William and Mary Quarterly* award for best article in 2002 and the Organization of American Historians ABC-CLIO *America: History and Life* Award for best American history article in 2002. He is an active member of the American Historical Association, the Organization of American Historians, and the Southern Historical Association.

PATRICIA CLINE COHEN

Born in Ann Arbor, Michigan, and raised in Palo Alto, California, Patricia Cline Cohen earned a B.A. at the University of Chicago in 1968 and a Ph.D. at the University of California, Berkeley in 1977. In 1976, she joined the history faculty at the University of California, Santa Barbara. In 2005–2006 she received the university's Distinguished Teaching Award. Cohen has written *A Calculating People: The Spread of Numeracy in Early America* (1982; reissued 1999) and *The Murder of Helen Jewett: The Life and Death of a Prostitute in Nineteenth-Century New York* (1998). She has also published articles on quantitative literacy, mathematics education, prostitution, and murder in journals including the *Journal of Women's History, Radical History Review,* the *William and Mary Quarterly,* and the *NWSA Journal.* Her scholarly work has received support from the National Endowment for the Humanities, the National Humanities Center, the University of California President's Fellowship in the Humanities, the Mellon Foundation, the American Antiquarian Society, the Schlesinger Library, and the

Newberry Library. She is an active associate of the Omohundro Institute of Early American History and Culture, sits on the advisory council of the Society for the History of the Early American Republic, and is past president of the Western Association of Women Historians. She has served as chair of the history department, as chair of the Women's Studies Program, and as acting dean of the humanities and fine arts at the University of California at Santa Barbara. In 2001–2002 she was the Distinguished Senior Mellon Fellow at the American Antiquarian Society. Currently she is working on a book about women's health advocate Mary Gove Nichols.

SARAH STAGE

Sarah Stage was born in Davenport, Iowa, and received a B.A. from the University of Iowa in 1966 and a Ph.D. in American studies from Yale University in 1975. She has taught U.S. history for more than twenty-five years at Williams College and the University of California, Riverside. Currently she is professor of Women's Studies at Arizona State University at the West campus in Phoenix. Her books include *Female Complaints: Lydia Pinkham and the Business of Women's Medicine* (1979) and *Rethinking Home Economics: Women and the History of a Profession* (1997), which has been translated for a Japanese edition. Among the fellowships she has received are the Rockefeller Foundation Humanities Fellowship, the American Association of University Women dissertation fellowship, a fellowship from the Charles Warren Center for the Study of History at Harvard University, and the University of California President's Fellowship in the Humanities. She is at work on a book entitled *Women and the Progressive Impulse in American Politics, 1890–1914.*

ALAN LAWSON

Born in Providence, Rhode Island, Alan Lawson received his B.A. from Brown University in 1955 and his M.A. from the University of Wisconsin in 1956. After Army service and experience as a high school teacher, he earned his Ph.D. from the University of Michigan in 1967. Since winning the Allan Nevins Prize for his dissertation, Lawson has served on the faculties of the University of California, Irvine, Smith College, and, currently, Boston College. He has written *The Failure of Independent Liberalism* (1971) and coedited *From*

Revolution to Republic (1976). While completing the forthcoming *Ideas in Crisis: The New Deal and the Mobilization of Progressive Experience,* he has published book chapters and essays on political economy, the cultural legacy of the New Deal, multiculturalism, and the arts in public life. He has served as editor of the *Review of Education* and the *Intellectual History Newsletter* and contributed articles to those journals as well as to the *History of Education Quarterly.* He has been active in the field of American studies as director of the Boston College American studies program and as a contributor to the *American Quarterly.* Under the auspices of the United States Information Agency, Lawson has been coordinator and lecturer for programs to instruct faculty from foreign nations in the state of American historical scholarship and teaching.

SUSAN M. HARTMANN

Professor of history at Ohio State University, Susan M. Hartmann received her B.A. from Washington University and her Ph.D. from the University of Missouri. After specializing in the political economy of the post–World War II period and publishing *Truman and the 80th Congress* (1971), she expanded her interests to the field of women's history, publishing many articles and three books: *The Home Front and Beyond: American Women in the 1940s* (1982); *From Margin to Mainstream: American Women and Politics since 1960* (1989); and *The Other Feminists: Activists in the Liberal Establishment* (1998). Her work has been supported by the Truman Library Institute, the Rockefeller Foundation, the National Endowment for the Humanities, and the American Council of Learned Societies. At Ohio State she has served as director of women's studies, and in 1995 she won the Exemplary Faculty Award in the College of Humanities. Hartmann has taught at the University of Missouri, St. Louis, and Boston University, and she has lectured on American history in Australia, Austria, France, Germany, Greece, Japan, Nepal, and New Zealand. She is a fellow of the Society of American Historians, has served on award committees of the American Historical Association, the Organization of American Historians, the American Studies Association, and the National Women's Studies Association, and currently is on the Board of Directors at the Truman Library Institute. Her current research is on gender and the transformation of politics since 1945.

The American Promise

A COMPACT HISTORY

Third Edition

ANASAZI EFFIGY

Ancient North Americans crafted human likenesses in stone, clay, and wood, as well as depicting human forms on canyon walls, pottery, and elsewhere. An Anasazi Indian in the Southwest carved this artifact from stone sometime around AD 1200. The unmistakably human features of the object tempt us to believe that it might be an ancient American self-portrait. Certainly the carver took care to give the object a recognizably human face, neck, arms, hands, legs, and feet. The brightly colored pigments suggest clothing or body decorations. The Anasazi who painted the object had a clear idea of what should be painted orange, turquoise, and red. Red belonged on wrists, not on lips. This color code that made perfect sense to the Anasazi remains obscure to us, a hint that the carver may have intended to depict a deity or supernatural being who had some human features. For example, the artifact lacks ears and sexual organs. The polished tip of the nose contrasts with the rough surface of the torso and legs, suggesting that Anasazi often rubbed the nose. Experts refer to this artifact and others like it as effigies, that is, objects that presumably had ritualistic or spiritual significance. Instead of showing us what the Anasazi considered a self-portrait, this effigy probably depicts one of their many gods. Yet, since the Anasazi—like other human beings—probably created gods in their own image, the effigy may somewhat resemble Anasazi people.

Jerry Jacka Photography.

1

Ancient America

Before 1492

GEORGE MCJUNKIN, the manager of the Crowfoot Ranch near Folsom, New Mexico, rode out to mend fences and to look for missing cattle after a violent rainstorm in August 1908. An American of African descent, McJunkin had been born a slave in Texas and had been riding horses since he was a boy. After he became free at the end of the Civil War in 1865, McJunkin worked as a cowboy in Colorado and New Mexico before becoming the Crowfoot manager in 1891. Now, as he rode across the ranch land he knew so well to survey damage caused by the recent storm, McJunkin noticed that floodwater had washed away the bank of a gulch called Wild Horse Arroyo and exposed a deposit of stark white bones. Curious, he dismounted and chipped away at the deposit until he uncovered an entire fossilized bone. The bone was much larger than the parched skeletons of range cattle and buffalo that McJunkin often saw, so he saved it, hoping someday to identify it.

Four years later, in 1912, McJunkin met Carl Schwachheim, a white man in Raton, New Mexico. Schwachheim, a blacksmith, shared McJunkin's curiosity about fossils, and the two men became friends. McJunkin told Schwachheim about the fossil deposit he had discovered. Ten years later, a few months after McJunkin's death, Schwachheim finally drove out to Wild Horse Arroyo and dug out several bones. But, like McJunkin, he could not identify any animal that had such big bones.

In 1926, Schwachheim delivered cattle to the stockyards in Denver, and he took some of the fossilized bones to the Denver Museum of Natural History and showed them to J. D. Figgins, a paleontologist who was an expert on fossils of ancient animals. Figgins immediately recognized the significance of the bones and a few months later began an excavation of the Folsom site that revolutionized knowledge about the first Americans.

When Figgins began his dig at Folsom, archaeologists (individuals who examine **artifacts** left by long-vanished peoples as part of the study of **archaeology**) believed that Native Americans had arrived relatively recently in the Western Hemisphere, probably no more than three or four thousand years earlier when, experts assumed, they had paddled small boats across the icy waters of the Bering Strait from what is now Siberia. At Folsom, Figgins learned that the bones McJunkin had first spotted belonged to twenty-three giant bison, a species known to have been extinct for at least 10,000 years. Far more startling, Figgins found among the bones nineteen flint spear points (Folsom points, they have since been called), proof that human beings had been alive at the same time as the giant bison. One spear point remained stuck

George McJunkin

This photo shows McJunkin a few years after he discovered the Folsom site but about fifteen years before anyone understood the significance of his find. He appears here in his work clothes on horseback, as he probably was when he made the discovery. The fossilized bones he discovered belonged to an extinct bison species that was much larger than modern bison; the horns of the ancient animal often spanned six feet, wide enough for McJunkin's horse to have stood sideways between the horns.

Eastern New Mexico University, Blackwater Draw Site, Portales, New Mexico 88130.

between two ribs of a giant bison, where a Stone Age hunter had plunged it more than 10,000 years earlier. No longer could anyone doubt that human beings had inhabited North America for at least ten millennia.

The Folsom discovery sparked other major finds of ancient artifacts that continue to this day. Since the 1930s, archaeologists have tried to reconstruct the history of ancient Americans, to understand the hunters who killed giant bison with flint-tipped spears as well as their ancestors who first arrived in North America and their descendants who built southwestern pueblos and eastern burial mounds, and *their* descendants who encountered Europeans in 1492. Although the long history of ancient Americans is incomplete and controversial, scholars have learned the identity of ancient Americans, where they came from, and some basic features of the complex cultures they created and passed along to their descendants who eventually came face-to-face with Europeans.

Archaeology and History

Archaeologists and historians share the desire to learn about people who lived in the past, but they usually employ different methods to obtain information. Both archaeologists and historians study artifacts as clues to the activities and ideas of the humans who created them. They concentrate, however, on different kinds of artifacts. Archaeologists tend to focus on physical objects such as bones, stones, pots, baskets, jewelry, textiles, clothing, graves, and buildings. Historians direct their attention mostly to writings, which encompass personal and private jottings such as diary entries and love letters, official and public pronouncements such as laws and speeches, as well as an enormous variety of other documents. Although historians are interested in other artifacts and archaeologists do not neglect written sources if they exist, the characteristic concentration of historians on writings and archaeologists on other physical objects denotes a rough cultural and chronological boundary between the human beings studied by the two groups of scholars, a boundary marked by the use of writing.

Writing is defined as a system of symbols that record spoken language. Writing originated among ancient peoples in China, Egypt, and Central America about 8,000 years ago, within the most recent 2 percent of the 400 millennia that modern human beings (*Homo sapiens*) have existed. Writing came into use even later in most other places in the world. The ancient Americans who inhabited North America in 1492, for example, possessed many forms of symbolic representation, but not writing.

The people who lived during the millennia before writing were biologically nearly identical to us. Their DNA was the template for ours. But unlike us, they did not use writing to communicate across space and time. They invented hundreds of spoken languages; they learned to survive and even to thrive in almost every natural environment; they chose and honored leaders; they traded, warred, and worshiped; and, above all, they learned from and taught each other. Much of what we would like to know about their experiences remains unknown because it took place before writing existed. The absence of writing forever muffles their words and thus their history.

Archaeologists specialize in learning about people who did not document their history in writing. They study the millions of artifacts created by these people. They also scrutinize soil,

Anasazi Pictograph
This unusual pictograph was painted about AD 1300 on the wall of an Anasazi dwelling in what is now Canyonlands National Park in Utah. The colorful design presumably had a specific meaning for the Anasazi who created it, but that meaning remains indecipherable to experts today.
J. Q. Jacobs.

geological strata, pollen, climate, and other environmental features to reconstruct the history of ancient peoples. Although no documents chronicle ancient Americans' lives, archaeologists have learned to make artifacts tell a great deal about the people who made them.

Since ancient America was the long first phase of the history of the United States, this chapter relies on the work of archaeologists to sketch a brief overview of this important era. Ancient Americans and their descendants resided in North America for thousands of years before Europeans arrived. They created societies and cultures of remarkable diversity and complexity. Because they did not use written records, their history cannot be reconstructed with the detail and certainty made possible by writing. But it is better to abbreviate and oversimplify their history than to ignore it.

REVIEW Why do historians rely on the work of archaeologists to write the history of ancient America?

The First Americans

The first human beings to arrive in the Western Hemisphere emigrated from Asia. They brought with them hunting skills, weapon- and tool-making techniques, and a full range of other forms of human knowledge developed millennia earlier in Africa, Europe, and Asia. These first Americans specialized in hunting mammoths, giant elephant-like creatures they had learned in Europe and Asia to kill, butcher, and process for food, clothing, building materials, and many other purposes. Most likely, these first Americans wandered into the Western Hemisphere more or less accidentally, hungry and in pursuit of their prey.

African and Asian Origins

Human beings lived elsewhere in the world for hundreds of thousands of years before they reached the Western Hemisphere. Millions of years before humans evolved anywhere on the globe, North and South America became detached from the gigantic common landmass scientists now call Pangaea. About 240 million years ago, powerful forces deep within the earth fractured Pangaea and slowly pushed the continents apart to approximately their present positions (Map 1.1). This process of continental drift encircled the land of the Western Hemisphere with large oceans that isolated it from the other continents, long before early human beings (*Homo erectus*) first appeared in Africa about 2 million years ago. (Hereafter in this chapter, the abbreviation *BP*—archaeologists' notation for "years before the present"—is used to indicate dates earlier than 2,000 years ago. Dates more recent than 2,000 years ago are indicated with the common and familiar notation *AD*—for example, AD 1492.)

More than a million and a half years after *Homo erectus* appeared, or about 400,000 BP, modern humans (*Homo sapiens*) evolved in Africa. All human beings throughout the world today are descendants of these ancient Africans. Slowly, over many millennia, *Homo sapiens* migrated out of Africa and into Europe and Asia. Unlike North and South America, Europe and Asia retained land connections to Africa, making migration possible for *Homo sapiens*. The vast oceans encircling North and South America kept human beings away for roughly 97 percent of the time *Homo sapiens* have been on earth.

Two major developments made it possible for human beings to migrate to the Western

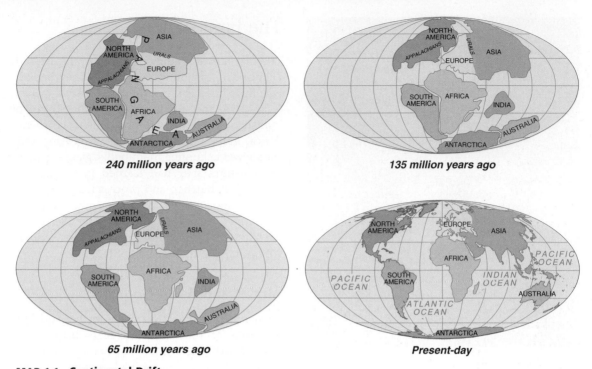

240 million years ago

135 million years ago

65 million years ago

Present-day

MAP 1.1 Continental Drift
Massive geological forces separated North and South America from other continents eons before human beings evolved in Africa in the last 1.5 million years.

Hemisphere. First, humans successfully adapted to the frigid environment near the Arctic Circle. Second, changes in the earth's climate reconnected North America to Asia.

By about 25,000 BP, *Homo sapiens* had spread from Africa throughout Europe and Asia. People, presumably women, had learned to use bone needles to sew animal skins into warm clothing that permitted them to become permanent residents of extremely cold regions like northeastern Siberia. Ancient Siberians walked to North America on land that now lies submerged beneath sixty miles of water that separates easternmost Siberia from westernmost Alaska. During the last global cold spell—the Wisconsin glaciation, which endured from about 80,000 BP to about 10,000 BP—the sea level dropped as much as 350 feet below its current level, exposing what experts refer to as a land bridge between Asian Siberia and American Alaska. This land bridge, which scientists call Beringia, opened a pathway about a thousand miles wide between the Eastern and Western Hemispheres.

Beringia

Siberian hunters presumably roamed into Beringia for centuries in search of game animals. (See "Beyond America's Borders," page 8.) Grasses and small shrubs that covered Beringia supported herds of mammoth, bison, and numerous smaller animals. As the hunters ventured farther and farther east, they became pioneers of human life in the Western Hemisphere. Unbeknownst to them, their migrations revolutionized the history of the world.

Archaeologists speculate that these Siberian hunters traveled in small bands of no more than 25 people. How many such bands arrived in North America before Beringia once again disappeared beneath the sea will never be known. When they came is hotly debated by experts. The first migrants probably arrived sometime after 15,000 BP. Scattered and inconclusive evidence suggests that they may have arrived several thousand years earlier. Certainly humans inhabited the Western Hemisphere by 13,000 BP.

Archaeologists refer to these first migrants and their

descendants for the next few millennia as Paleo-Indians. While the date of their arrival is somewhat uncertain, they certainly originated in Asia. Some archaeologists have speculated that the Paleo-Indians may have sailed across the South Pacific from Polynesia or across the North Atlantic from Europe, but no evidence conclusively supports such views. Instead, detailed analyses of Native American languages, blood proteins, and DNA patterns, along with extensive archaeological discoveries, provide conclusive evidence of ancient Americans' Asian origins.

Paleo-Indian Hunters

When humans first arrived in the Western Hemisphere, massive glaciers covered most of present-day Canada. A narrow corridor not entirely obstructed by ice ran along the eastern side of Canada's Rocky Mountains, and most archaeologists believe that Paleo-Indians migrated through the ice-free passageway in pursuit of game. They may also have traveled along the coast in small boats, hopscotching from one desirable landing spot to another. At the southern edge of the glaciers, Paleo-Indians entered a hunters' paradise.

North, Central, and South America teemed with wildlife that had never before confronted wily two-legged predators armed with razor-sharp spears. The abundance of game presumably made hunting relatively easy. Ample food permitted the Paleo-Indian population to grow. Within a thousand years or so, Paleo-Indians lived throughout the Western Hemisphere.

Paleo-Indians used a distinctively shaped spearhead known now as a Clovis point, named for the place in New Mexico where it was first excavated. Archaeologists' discovery of Clovis points throughout North and Central America in sites occupied between 11,500 BP and 11,000 BP provides evidence that these nomadic hunters shared a common ancestry and way of life. Paleo-Indians probably hunted smaller animals, but most of the artifacts that have survived from this era indicate that they specialized in hunting mammoths. One mammoth kill supplied meat for weeks or, if dried, for months. Mammoth hide and bones provided clothing, shelter, tools, and much more.

About 11,000 BP, Paleo-Indians confronted a major crisis. The mammoths and other big-game animals they hunted became extinct.

FIGURE 1.1 Human Habitation of the World and the Western Hemisphere
These clock faces illustrate the long global history of modern humans (left) and of human history in the Western Hemisphere since the arrival of the first ancient Americans (right). If the total period of human life on earth is considered, American history since the arrival of Columbus in 1492 comprises less than one minute (or one-tenth of 1 percent) of modern human existence. And if the total period of human life in the New World is converted from millennia to a 12-hour clock, then ancient American history makes up the first 11½ hours, and all history since the arrival of the Europeans in 1492 occupies only the last half hour.

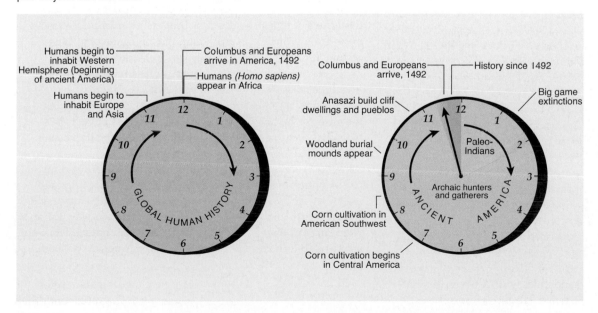

Nature's Immigrants

Like the first human beings who came to the New World, most of the large animals in ancient America were descendants of migrants from elsewhere on the globe. Mammoths, the signature prey of the Clovis hunters of ancient America, illustrate the persistent immigration of animals from Asia to North America. The ancestors of the mammoths that Clovis hunters stalked about 12,000 years ago had emigrated from Asia about 1.7 million years earlier. The first mammoth migrants from Asia followed in the tracks of hundreds of other animal species that had made their way across Beringia to North America for more than 60 million years. These immigrants and their descendants populated the natural environment of America that ancient Americans first encountered. Clearly, America was a land of immigrants long before the first humans arrived.

An extraterrestrial event created the basic precondition for these animal migrations. Scientists have discovered convincing evidence that about 65 million years ago a meteorite about six miles in diameter slammed into the Yucatán peninsula in

Mexico. Experts estimate that the meteorite sped toward Yucatán at about 54,000 miles an hour and cratered into the earth with an explosion equivalent to trillions of atomic bombs. Coming in at a low angle to the curvature of the earth from the direction of the Southern Hemisphere, the meteorite incinerated almost all the exposed animals and plants in North America with a blast of heat a thousand times hotter than that reaching the earth from the sun. The plume of dust and smoke propelled into the atmosphere by the impact of the meteorite darkened skies, reduced or eliminated photosynthesis, and showered the earth with sulfuric acid. These catastrophic changes in the global environment caused the extinction of many animals worldwide, including dinosaurs who had ruled the earth for more than 100 million years. But outside the fiery blast zone that extended thousands of miles north from ground zero in Yucatán, many animals survived the mass extinction and became the ancestors of animals that eventually migrated to North America.

Among the animals that survived the great extinction were small ratlike creatures, the ances-

tors of mammals that began to multiply and remultiply, ultimately filling many of the environmental niches previously occupied by dinosaurs and other extinct species. For example, a tiny hoofed mammal now called Procerberus made the trek across Beringia from Asia to North America and within about 4 million years spawned dozens of new species of hoofed mammals in the New World, the largest the size of a small pony. Procerberus became the ancient ancestor of both horses and camels, species that evolved first in North America.

In the millions of years that followed ancestor species' initial migration from Asia, distinctive North American descendants evolved, just as horses and camels did. The ancestor of North American cats migrated from Asia about 17 million years ago, but within a few million years, North America had evolved distinctive cat species, including lions roughly twice as large as the largest male African lions today. Similarly, nature's migrants from Asia developed into distinctive North American elephants (including mammoths), rhinoceroses, and pigs, as well as many smaller creatures such as beavers, skunks, and weasels. Although the migration of ancient birds is less well known because of the scarcity of fossil remains, the ancestor of today's common raven made the colossal journey to North America over millions of years by flying through Asia from its starting point in Australia.

Some animals that evolved in North America eventually migrated back to Asia and beyond. Horses and camels illustrate this two-way traffic on the Beringian land bridge. Horses evolved in North America for about

Meteor Impact in North America, 65 Million Years Ago

Saber-Toothed Cat Skeleton
Saber-toothed cats ranged throughout North America when the first Americans arrived. This fossilized skeleton came from the La Brea tar pits in present-day Los Angeles, California. For millennia before the arrival of human beings in the New World, these cats and 660 other animal species became bogged down in the tar pits, which ultimately served to preserve their remains. Hundreds of thousands of saber-toothed cat bones have been recovered from the tar pit deposits. The cats probably used their huge incisors to tear open the throats or abdomens of their prey. Unlike the swift-footed big cats of today, saber-toothed cats did not chase down their prey. Since they weighed about twice as much as modern lions, they crouched in ambush and leaped on unsuspecting victims. This mode of attack probably accounts for the many fossils in the tar pits. Cats who attacked prey mired in the sticky tar probably became trapped themselves sometimes. Like many other big mammals that inhabited North America during the Paleo-Indian era, the saber-toothed cat became extinct about 11,000 BP.

George C. Page Museum.

migrants was in the other direction, from Asia to North America. The greater variety of well-established species in the larger Asian landmass made it difficult for many North American species to get a foothold there. Conversely, migrants from Asia more readily carved out an environmental niche for themselves in the New World.

On the eve of the arrival of ancient Americans in the New World, the large mammals they would prey upon—and in some cases compete with for prey—were the descendants of migrants who had preceded the first Americans millions of years earlier. The giant bison who roamed the plains—and whose fossilized remains George McJunkin excavated early in the twentieth century—descended from Asian migrants. So did the giant sloths that measured eighteen feet from nose to tail and weighed three tons. So did the massive short-faced bear that ran down its prey despite weighing the better part of a ton. So did the saber-toothed cat that, fossil deposits prove, feasted on young mammoths. And so did the mammoths themselves. The human beings who first set foot in the New World were pioneers of human migration to North America, but they were only the latest of latecomers among the thousands of nature's migrants from Asia that had been pioneering in North America for more than 60 million years.

20 million years before they first wandered across the land bridge to Asia. They didn't stop there. Modern-day zebras on the plains of Africa are the descendants of those ancient American migrant horses. Camels were much more recent out-migrants, wending their way from North America to Asia only about 4 million years ago. Dogs, evidently one of the few native North American mammals, also migrated to Asia, along with other distinctive species. But the dominant stream of nature's

Scientists are not completely certain why the extinction occurred, although the changing environment probably contributed to it. About this time the Wisconsin glacial period came to an end, glaciers melted, and sea levels rose. Some large mammals probably had difficulty adapting to the warmer climate. Many archaeologists also believe, however, that Paleo-Indians contributed to the extinctions in the Western Hemisphere by killing these animals more rapidly than they could reproduce. Within just a few thousand years of their arrival in the New World (the term that Europeans eventually coined for the Western Hemisphere), Paleo-Indian hunters helped bring about a radical change in the natural environment—namely the extinction of large mammals that had existed for millions of years and whose presence had initially drawn hunters west across Beringia.

Paleo-Indians adapted to the drastic environmental change of the big-game extinctions by making at least two important changes in their way of life. First, hunters began to prey more intensively on smaller animals. Second, Paleo-Indians devoted more energy to foraging, that is, to collecting wild plant foods such as roots, seeds, nuts, berries, and fruits. When Paleo-Indians made these changes, they replaced the apparent uniformity of the big-game-oriented Clovis culture* with great cultural diversity. This diversity arose because ancient Americans adapted to the many natural environments throughout the hemisphere, ranging from icy tundra to steamy jungles.

Post-Clovis adaptations to local environments resulted in the astounding variety of Native American cultures that existed when Europeans arrived in AD 1492. By then, more than three hundred major tribes and hundreds of lesser groups inhabited North America alone. Hundreds more lived in Central and South America. These peoples spoke different languages, practiced different religions, lived in different dwellings, followed different subsistence strategies, and observed different rules of kinship and inheritance. Hundreds of other ancient American cultures had disappeared or transformed themselves as their people constantly adapted to environmental and other changes.

> **REVIEW**   Why were humans able to migrate into North America after 15,000 BP?

Archaic Hunters and Gatherers

Archaeologists use the term **Archaic** to describe both the many different hunting and gathering cultures that descended from Paleo-Indians and the long period of time when those cultures dominated the history of ancient America, roughly from 10,000 BP to somewhere between 4000 BP and 3000 BP. The term usefully describes the era in the history of ancient America that followed the Paleo-Indian big-game hunters and preceded the development of agriculture. It denotes a hunter-gatherer way of life that persisted in North America long after European colonization.

Archaic Indians hunted with spears; but they also took smaller game with traps, nets, and hooks. Unlike their Paleo-Indian predecessors, most Archaic peoples used a variety of stone tools to prepare food from wild plants. A characteristic Archaic artifact is a grinding stone used to pulverize seeds into edible form. Most Archaic Indians migrated from place to place to harvest plants and hunt animals. They usually did not establish permanent villages, although they

---

* The word *culture* is used here to connote what is commonly called "way of life." It refers not only to how a group of people supplied themselves with food and shelter but also to their family relationships, social groupings, religious ideas, and other features of their lives. For most prehistoric cultures—as for the Clovis people—more is known about food and shelter because of the artifacts that have survived. Ancient Americans' ideas, assumptions, hopes, dreams, and fantasies were undoubtedly important, but we know very little about them.

Clovis Spear Straightener
Clovis hunters used this bone spear straightener about 11,000 BP at a campsite in Arizona where archaeologists discovered it lying among the butchered remains of two mammoth carcasses and thirteen ancient bison. Similar objects often appear in ancient sites in Eurasia, but this is the only bone artifact yet discovered in a Clovis-era site in North America. Presumably Clovis hunters stuck their spear shafts through the opening and then grasped the handle of the straightener and moved it back and forth along the length of the shaft to remove imperfections and make the spear a more effective weapon.
Arizona State Museum, University of Arizona.

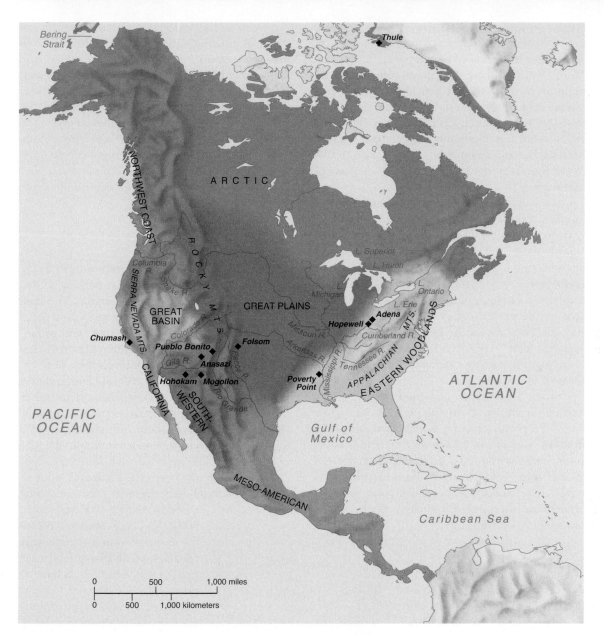

MAP 1.2 Native North American Cultures

Environmental conditions defined the boundaries of the broad zones of cultural similarity among ancient North Americans.

READING THE MAP: What crucial environmental features set the boundaries of each cultural region? (The topography indicated on Map 1.3, "Native North Americans about 1500," may be helpful.)

CONNECTIONS: How did environmental factors and variations affect the development of different groups of Native American cultures? Why do you think historians and archaeologists group cultures together by their regional positions?

FOR MORE HELP ANALYZING THIS MAP, see the map activity for this chapter in the Online Study Guide at bedfordstmartins.com/roarkcompact.

often returned to the same river valley or fertile meadow from year to year. In certain regions with especially rich resources—such as present-day California and the Pacific Northwest—they developed permanent settlements. Many groups became highly proficient basket makers in order to collect and store plant food. Instead of depending on agriculture, they gathered wild plants and hunted wild animals. Archaic peoples followed these practices in distinctive ways in the different environmental regions of North America (Map 1.2).

Great Plains Bison Hunters

After the extinction of large game such as mammoths, some hunters began to concentrate on huge herds of bison that grazed the grassy, arid plains stretching for hundreds of miles east of the Rocky Mountains. For almost a thousand years after the big-game extinctions, Archaic Indians hunted bison with Folsom points like those found at the site discovered by George McJunkin.

Like their nomadic predecessors, Folsom hunters moved constantly to maintain contact with their prey. Often two or three hunters from a band of several families would single out a few bison from a herd and creep up close enough to spear them. Great Plains hunters also developed trapping techniques that made it easier to kill large numbers of animals. At the original Folsom site, careful study of the bones McJunkin found suggests that early one winter hunters drove bison into the narrow gulch and speared twenty-three of them.

Bows and arrows reached Great Plains hunters from the north about AD 500. They largely replaced spears, which had been the hunters' weapon of choice for millennia. Bows permitted hunters to wound an animal from farther away, and arrows made it easy to shoot repeatedly. But these new weapons did not otherwise alter age-old techniques of bison hunting.

Great Basin Cultures

Archaic peoples in the Great Basin between the Rocky Mountains and the Sierra Nevada inhabited a region of great environmental diversity. Some Great Basin Indians lived along the shores of large marshes and lakes that formed during rainy periods. They ate fish of every available size and type, catching them with bone hooks and nets. Other cultures survived in the foothills of mountains between the blistering heat on the desert floor and the cold, treeless mountain heights. Hunters killed deer, antelope, and sometimes bison, as well as smaller game like rabbits, rodents, and snakes.

Despite the variety and occasional abundance of animals, Great Basin peoples relied on plants for their most important food source. Unlike meat and fish, plant food could be collected and stored for long periods to protect against shortages caused by the fickle rainfall. By diversifying their food sources and migrating to favorable locations to collect and store them, Great Basin peoples adapted to the severe environmental challenges of the region and maintained their Archaic hunter-gatherer way of life for centuries after AD 1492.

Pacific Coast Cultures

The richness of the natural environment made present-day California the most densely settled area in all of ancient North America. The land and ocean offered such ample food that California peoples remained hunters and gatherers for hundreds of years after AD 1492. The diversity of California's environment also encouraged corresponding diversity among native peoples. The mosaic of Archaic settlements in California included about five hundred separate tribes speaking some ninety languages, each with local dialects. No other region of comparable size in North America exhibited such cultural variety.

The Chumash, one of the many California cultures, emerged in the region surrounding what is now Santa Barbara about 5000 BP. Comparatively plentiful food resources—especially acorns—permitted Chumash people to establish relatively permanent villages. Conflict frequently broke out among the villages, evidently caused by competition for valuable acorn-gathering territory. Although few other California cultures achieved the population density and village settlements of the Chumash, all shared the hunter-gatherer way of life and reliance on acorns as a major food source.

Another rich natural environment lay along the Pacific Northwest coast. Like the Chumash, Northwest peoples built more or less permanent villages. After about 5500 BP, they concentrated on catching large quantities of salmon, halibut, and other fish, which they dried

Ancient California

Chumash Necklace

Long before the arrival of Europeans, ancient Chumash people in southern California made this elegant necklace of abalone shell. The carefully formed, polished, and assembled pieces of shell illustrate the artistry of the Chumash and their access to the rich and diverse marine life of the Pacific coast. Since living abalone cling stubbornly to submerged rocks along the coast, Chumash divers presumably pried abalone from their rocky perches to obtain their delicious flesh; then one or more Chumash artisans recycled the inedible shell to make this necklace. Its iridescent splendor demonstrates that Chumash people wore beautiful as well as useful adornments.

Natural History Museum of Los Angeles County.

to last throughout the year and to trade with people who lived hundreds of miles from the coast. Fishing also freed Northwest peoples to develop sophisticated woodworking skills. They fashioned elaborate wood carvings that denoted wealth and status as well as huge canoes for fishing, hunting, and conducting warfare against neighboring tribes. Much of the warfare among Archaic northwesterners grew out of attempts to defend or gain access to prime fishing sites.

Eastern Woodland Cultures

East of the Mississippi River, Archaic peoples adapted to a forest environment that included many local variants, such as the major river valleys of the Mississippi, Ohio, Tennessee, and Cumberland; the Great Lakes region; and the Atlantic coast (see Map 1.2). Throughout these diverse locales, Archaic peoples followed similar survival strategies.

Woodland hunters stalked deer as their most important prey. Deer supplied Woodland peoples with food as well as hides and bones that they crafted into clothing, weapons, needles, and many other tools. Like Archaic peoples elsewhere, Woodland Indians gathered edible plants, seeds, and nuts. About 6000 BP, some Woodland groups established more or less permanent settlements of 25 to 150 people, usually near a river or lake that offered a wide variety of plant and animal resources. The existence of such settlements has permitted archaeologists to locate numerous Archaic burial sites that suggest Woodland people had a life expectancy of about eighteen years.

Around 4000 BP, Woodland cultures added two important features to their basic hunter-gatherer lifestyles: agriculture and pottery. Gourds and pumpkins that were first cultivated thousands of years earlier in Mexico spread to Woodland peoples through trade and migration. Woodland peoples also began to cultivate local species such as sunflowers, as well as small quantities of tobacco, another import from South America. Corn, the most important plant food in Mexico, became a significant Woodland food crop around 2500 BP. These cultivated crops added to the quantity, variety, and predictability of Woodland food sources, but they did not alter Woodland peoples' dependence on gathering wild plants, seeds, and nuts.

Like agriculture, pottery also probably originated in Mexico. Traders and migrants probably brought pots into North America along with Central and South American seeds. Pots were more durable than baskets for cooking and storage of food and water, but they were also much heavier. The permanent settlements of Woodland peoples made the heavy weight of pots much less important than their advantages compared to leaky and fragile baskets. While pottery and agriculture introduced changes in Woodland cultures, ancient Woodland Americans retained the other basic features of their Archaic hunter-gatherer lifestyle, which persisted in most areas to 1492 and beyond.

REVIEW Why did post-Clovis Native Americans shift from big-game hunting to foraging and smaller-game hunting?

Agricultural Settlements and Chiefdoms

Among Eastern Woodland peoples and most other Archaic cultures, agriculture supplemented hunter-gatherer subsistence strategies. Reliance on wild animals and plants required most Archaic groups to remain small and mobile. But beginning about 4000 BP, distinctive southwestern cultures slowly began to depend on agriculture and to build permanent settlements. Later, around 2500 BP, Woodland peoples in the vast Mississippi valley began to construct burial mounds and other earthworks that suggest the existence of social and political hierarchies that archaeologists term chiefdoms. Although the hunter-gatherer lifestyle never entirely disap-

peared, the development of agricultural settlements and chiefdoms represented important innovations to the Archaic way of life.

Southwestern Cultures

Ancient Americans in present-day Arizona, New Mexico, and southern portions of Utah and Colorado developed cultures characterized by agriculture and multiunit dwellings called pueblos. All southwestern peoples confronted the challenge of a dry climate and unpredictable fluctuations in rainfall that made the supply of wild plant food very unreliable. These ancient Americans probably adopted agriculture in response to this basic environmental condition.

About 3500 BP southwestern hunters and gatherers began to cultivate their signature

Ancient Agriculture
Dropping seeds into holes punched in cleared ground by a pointed stick, known as a "dibble," this ancient American farmer sows a new crop while previously planted seeds—including the corn and beans immediately opposite him—bear fruit for harvest. Created by a sixteenth-century European artist, the drawing misrepresents who did the agricultural work in many ancient American cultures—namely women rather than men. However, the three-foot dibble would have been used as shown here.
The Pierpont Morgan Library/Art Resource, NY; Jerry Jacka Photography.

food crop, corn, which had been grown in Central and South America since about 7000 BP. During the next 3,000 years, corn became the most important cultivated crop for ancient Americans throughout North America. In the Southwest, the demands of corn cultivation encouraged hunter-gatherers to restrict their migratory habits in order to tend the crop. A vital consideration was access to water. Southwestern Indians became irrigation experts, conserving water and distributing it to thirsty crops.

About AD 200, small farming settlements began to appear throughout southern New Mexico, marking the emergence of the Mogollon culture.

Southwestern Cultures

much like their neighbors to the south. Beginning around AD 1000 (again, it is not known why), Anasazi began to move to large, multistory cliff dwellings whose spectacular ruins still exist at Mesa Verde, Colorado, and elsewhere. Other Anasazi communities—like the one whose impressive ruins can be visited at Chaco Canyon, New Mexico—erected huge, stone-walled pueblos with enough rooms to house everyone in the settlement. Anasazi pueblos and cliff dwellings typically contained one or more kivas used for secret ceremonies, restricted to men, that sought to communicate with the supernatural world.

Typically, a Mogollon settlement included a dozen pit houses, made by digging out a rounded pit about fifteen feet in diameter and a foot or two deep and then erecting poles to support a roof of branches or dirt. Larger villages usually had one or two bigger pit houses that may have been the predecessors of the circular kivas, the ceremonial rooms that became a characteristic of nearly all southwestern settlements. About AD 1000, Mogollon culture began to decline, for reasons that remain obscure.

Around AD 500, while the Mogollon culture prevailed in New Mexico, other ancient people migrated from Mexico to southern Arizona and established the distinctive Hohokam culture. Hohokam settlements used sophisticated grids of irrigation canals to plant and harvest crops twice a year. Hohokam culture reflected the continuing influence of its origins in Mexico. The people built sizable platform mounds and ball courts characteristic of many Mexican cultures to the south. Hohokam culture declined about AD 1400, for reasons that remain a mystery.

North of the Hohokam and Mogollon cultures, in a region that encompassed southern Utah and Colorado and northern Arizona and New Mexico, the Anasazi culture began to flourish about AD 100. The early Anasazi built pit houses on mesa tops and used irrigation

Drought began to plague the region about AD 1130, and it lasted for more than half a century,

Hohokam "Cigarettes"
Ancient Hohokam smokers in present-day Arizona stuffed these reeds (which probably grew near their irrigation canals) with shredded tobacco. They wrapped cotton thread around each reed to protect their fingers from heat while they inhaled the smoke of the burning tobacco. When hunting or tending their crops, Hohokam smokers probably found these "cigarettes" more convenient than their heavier and more cumbersome stone or ceramic pipes, which were better suited for sedentary occasions.
Jerry Jacka Photography.

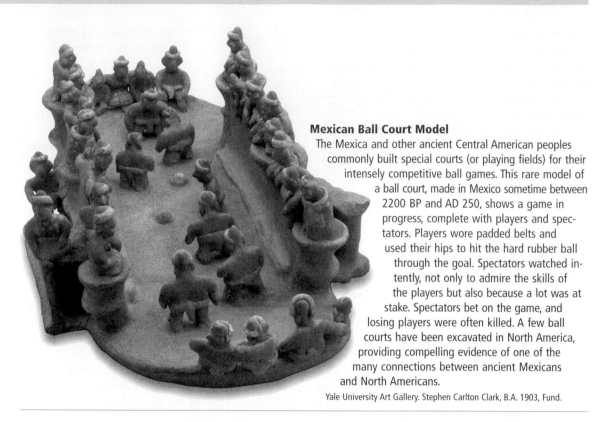

Mexican Ball Court Model

The Mexica and other ancient Central American peoples commonly built special courts (or playing fields) for their intensely competitive ball games. This rare model of a ball court, made in Mexico sometime between 2200 BP and AD 250, shows a game in progress, complete with players and spectators. Players wore padded belts and used their hips to hit the hard rubber ball through the goal. Spectators watched intently, not only to admire the skills of the players but also because a lot was at stake. Spectators bet on the game, and losing players were often killed. A few ball courts have been excavated in North America, providing compelling evidence of one of the many connections between ancient Mexicans and North Americans.

Yale University Art Gallery. Stephen Carlton Clark, B.A. 1903, Fund.

Pueblo Bonito, Chaco Canyon, New Mexico

About AD 1000, Pueblo Bonito stood at the center of Chacoan culture that extended over more than 20,000 square miles in the region at the intersection of present-day Utah, Colorado, Arizona, and New Mexico. The numerous circular kivas show the significance of ceremonies and rituals to the people of Chaco Canyon. Major buildings appear to have been aligned to mark the spring and winter solstices and the phases of the lunar cycle, suggesting that the ceremonies at Chaco Canyon may have symbolized the potent connections between earth and sky, between humans and the omnipotent celestial ruler.

Richard Alexander Cooke III.

triggering the disappearance of Anasazi culture. By AD 1200, the large Anasazi pueblos had been abandoned. The prolonged drought probably intensified conflict among pueblos and made it impossible to depend on the techniques of irrigated agriculture that had worked for centuries. Some Anasazi migrated toward regions with more reliable rainfall and settled in Hopi, Zuñi, and Acoma pueblos that their descendants in Arizona and New Mexico have occupied ever since.

Woodland Burial Mounds and Chiefdoms

No other ancient Americans created dwellings similar to pueblos, but around 2500 BP, Woodland cultures throughout the vast area drained by the Mississippi River began to build burial mounds. The size of the mounds, the labor and organization required to erect them, and differences in the artifacts buried with certain individuals suggest the existence of a social and political hierarchy that archaeologists term a chiefdom. Experts do not know the name of a single chief, nor do they know the organizational structure a chief headed. But the only way archaeologists can account for the complex and labor-intensive burial mounds and artifacts found in them is to assume that one person—whom scholars term a chief— had the ability to command the labor and obedience of very large numbers of other people, who comprised the chief's chiefdom.

Between 2500 BP and 2100 BP, Adena people built hundreds of burial mounds radiating from central Ohio. In the mounds, the Adena usually accompanied burials with grave goods that included spear points and stone pipes as well as thin sheets of mica (a glasslike mineral) crafted into shapes of birds, beasts, and human hands. Over the body and grave goods Adena people piled dirt into a mound. Sometimes burial mounds were constructed all at once, but often they were built up slowly over many years.

About 2100 BP, Adena culture evolved into the more elaborate Hopewell culture, which lasted about 500 years. While centered in Ohio, Hopewell culture extended throughout the drainage of the Ohio and Mississippi rivers. Hopewell people built larger mounds and filled them with more

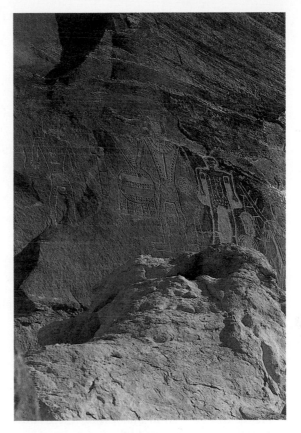

Ashley Creek Petroglyph
Ancient Americans incised this large petroglyph on a rock wall in present-day Utah. The elaborate shield and regalia (the headdress, breastplate, belt, and skirt) suggest that the larger figure depicts a chief or a warrior (who may also have been a chief). Experts do not know the meaning of these and other petroglyphs, although the care with which they were rendered proves that they were significant to the ancient Southwestern artists who made them.
J. Q. Jacobs.

FOR MORE HELP ANALYZING THIS IMAGE, see the visual activity for this chapter in the Online Study Guide at bedfordstmartins.com/roarkcompact.

magnificent grave goods than had their Adena predecessors.

Burial was probably reserved for the most important members of Hopewell groups. Most people were cremated. Burial rituals appear to have brought many people together to honor the dead person and to help build the mound. Hopewell mounds were often 100 feet in diameter and 30 feet high. Grave goods at Hopewell sites testify to the high quality of Hopewell crafts and to the existence of a thriving trade network that ranged from Wyoming to Florida. Archaeologists believe that Hopewell chiefs probably played an important role in this sprawling interregional trade.

Hopewell culture declined about AD 400 for reasons that are obscure. Archaeologists speculate that bows and arrows, along with increasing reliance on agriculture, made small settlements more self-sufficient and, therefore, less dependent on the central authority of the Hopewell chiefs who were responsible for the burial mounds.

Four hundred years later, another mound-building culture flourished. The Mississippian culture emerged in the floodplains of the major southeastern river systems about AD 800 and lasted until about AD 1500. Major Mississippian sites included huge mounds with platforms on top for ceremonies and for the residences of great chiefs. The largest Mississippian site was Cahokia, whose remnants can be seen in Illinois near the confluence of the Mississippi and Missouri rivers.

At Cahokia, more than one hundred mounds were grouped around large open plazas. Monk's Mound, the largest, covered sixteen acres at its base and was one hundred feet tall. Dwellings may have housed as many as thirty thousand inhabitants, easily qualifying Cahokia as the largest settlement in ancient North America. One Cahokia burial mound suggests the authority a great chief exercised. One man—presumably the chief—was buried with the bodies of more than sixty people who had been killed at the time of burial, including fifty young women who had been strangled. Such a mass sacrifice illustrates the coercive power of a Cahokia chief.

Cahokia and other Mississippian cultures had dwindled by AD 1500. When Europeans arrived, most of the descendants of Mississippian cultures, like those of the Hopewell culture, lived in small dispersed villages supported by hunting and gathering supplemented by agriculture.

> **REVIEW**   How did the availability of food influence the distribution of Native American population across the continent?

Major Mississippian Mounds, AD 800–1500

Native Americans in the 1490s

About thirteen millennia after Paleo-Indians first migrated to the Western Hemisphere, a new migration—this time from Europe—began in 1492 with the journey of Christopher Columbus. In the decades before the arrival of Columbus, Native Americans continued to employ their ancestors' time-tested survival strategies of hunting, gathering, and agriculture. Those strategies succeeded in both populating and shaping the new world Europeans encountered.

By the 1490s, Native Americans lived throughout North America, but their total population is a subject of heated debate among scholars. Some experts claim Native Americans numbered 18 million to 20 million, while others place the population at no more than a million. A prudent estimate is about 4 million. On the eve of European colonization, the small island nation of England had about the same number of people as all of North America. Compared to England and elsewhere in Europe, Native Americans were spread thin across the land, an outgrowth of their survival strategies of hunting, gathering, and agriculture.

Regions in North America with abundant resources had relatively high population. About one-fifth of Native Americans lived along the West Coast in food-rich California and the Pacific Northwest, where the population density was, respectively, six times greater and four times greater than the average for the whole continent. The food-scarce vastness of the Great Plains, Great Basin, and Arctic regions held about one-quarter of Native Americans, but the population density was extremely low, roughly one-tenth the continental average. About a quarter of Native Americans resided in the arid Southwest, where irrigation and intensive agriculture permitted a population density about twice the continental average. But even in California, the most densely inhabited region of North America, population density was just one-twentieth of England's.

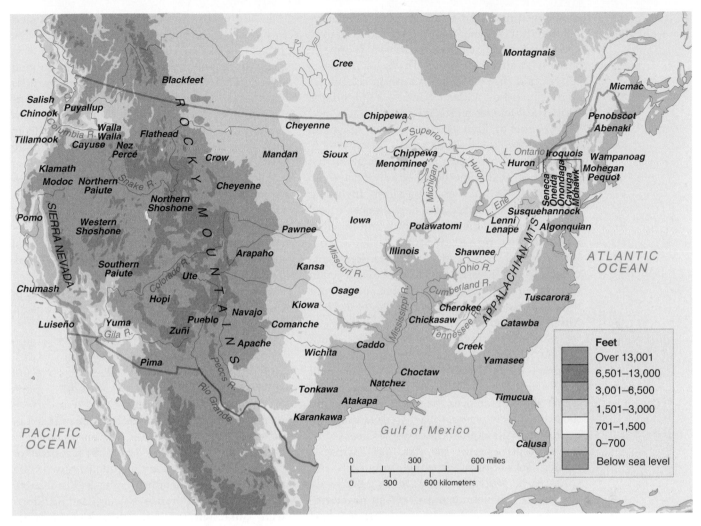

MAP 1.3 Native North Americans about 1500

Distinctive Native American peoples resided throughout the area that, centuries later, would become the United States. This map indicates the approximate location of some of the larger tribes about 1500. In the interest of legibility, many other peoples who inhabited North America at the time are omitted from the map.

The enormous Woodland region east of the Mississippi River was home to about one-third of Native Americans, whose population density approximated the continental average of one person per square mile. Eastern Woodland peoples clustered into three broad linguistic and cultural groups: Algonquian, Iroquoian, and Muskogean.

Algonquian tribes inhabited the Atlantic seaboard, the Great Lakes region, and much of the upper Midwest (Map 1.3). The relatively mild climate along the Atlantic permitted the coastal Algonquians to grow corn and other crops as well as to hunt and fish. Around the Great Lakes and in northern New England, however, cool summers and severe winters made agriculture impractical. Instead, the Abenaki, Penobscot, Chippewa, and other tribes concentrated on hunting and fishing, using canoes both for transportation and for gathering wild rice.

Inland from the Algonquian region, Iroquoian tribes occupied territories centered in Pennsylvania and upstate New York, as well as the hilly upland regions of the Carolinas and Georgia. Three features distinguished Iroquoian tribes from their neighbors. First, their success in cultivating corn and other crops allowed them to build permanent settlements, usually consisting of several bark-covered longhouses up to one hundred feet long and housing five to ten families. Second, Iroquoian societies adhered to matrilineal rules of descent. Property of all sorts belonged to women. Women headed family clans and even selected the chiefs (normally men) who governed tribes. Third, for purposes of war and diplomacy, an Iroquoian confederation—including the Seneca, Onondaga, Mohawk, Oneida, and Cayuga tribes—formed the League of Five Nations, which remained powerful well into the eighteenth century.

Muskogean peoples spread throughout the woodlands of the Southeast, south of the Ohio River and east of the Mississippi. Including Creek, Choctaw, Chickasaw, and Natchez tribes, Muskogeans inhabited a bountiful natural environment that provided abundant food from hunting, gathering, and agriculture. Remnants of the earlier Mississippian culture still existed in Muskogean religion. The Natchez even built temple mounds modeled after those of their Mississippian ancestors.

Great Plains peoples accounted for about one out of seven Native Americans. Inhabiting the huge region west of the Eastern Woodland people and east of the Rocky Mountains, many tribes had migrated to the Great Plains within the last century or two, forced westward by Iroquoian and Algonquian tribes. Some Great Plains tribes—especially the Mandan and Pawnee—farmed successfully, growing both corn and sunflowers. But the Teton Sioux, Blackfeet, Comanche, Cheyenne, and Crow on the northern plains and the Apache and other nomadic tribes on the southern plains depended on buffalo (American bison) for subsistence.

Southwestern cultures included about a quarter of all native North Americans. These descendants of the Mogollon, Hohokam, and Anasazi cultures lived in settled agricultural communities, many of them pueblos. They continued to grow corn, beans, and squash with methods they had refined for centuries. However, their communities came under attack by a large number of warlike Athapascan tribes who invaded the Southwest beginning around AD 1300. The Athapascans—principally Apache and Navajo—were skillful warriors who preyed on the sedentary pueblo Indians, reaping the fruits of agriculture without the work of farming.

About a fifth of all native North Americans resided along the Pacific coast. In California, abundant acorns and nutritious marine life supported high population densities but retarded the development of agriculture. Similar dependence on hunting and gathering persisted along the Northwest coast, where fishing reigned supreme. Salmon was so abundant that at the Dalles site on the Columbia River, Northwest peoples caught millions of pounds of salmon every summer and traded it as far away as California and the Great Plains. Although important trading centers existed throughout North America, particularly in the Southwest, it is likely that the Dalles site was the largest Native American trading center in North America.

While trading was common, all native North Americans in the 1490s still depended on hunting and gathering for a major portion of their food. Most of them also practiced agriculture. People throughout North America used bows, arrows, and other weapons for hunting and warfare. None of them employed writing, expressing themselves instead in many other ways: drawings sketched on stones, wood, and animal skins; patterns woven in baskets and textiles; designs painted on pottery, crafted into beadwork, or carved into effigies; as well as in song, dance, religious ceremonies, and burial rites.

These rich and varied cultural resources of Native Americans did not include features of life common in Europe during the 1490s. Native Americans did not use wheels; sailing ships were unknown to them; they had no large domesticated animals such as horses, cows, or oxen; their use of metals was restricted to copper. However, the absence of these European conveniences mattered less to native North Americans than their own cultural adaptations to the natural environment local to each tribe and to the social environment among neighboring peoples. That great similarity—adaptation to natural and social environments—underlay all the cultural diversity among native North Americans.

It would be a mistake, however, to conclude that native North Americans lived in blissful harmony with nature and each other. Archaeological sites provide ample evidence of violent conflict among Native Americans. Skeletons bear the marks of wounds as well as of ritualistic human sacrifice and even cannibalism. In general, fear and anxiety must have been at least as common among Native Americans as feelings of peace and security.

Native Americans not only adapted to the natural environment; they also changed it in many ways. They built thousands of structures, from small dwellings to massive pueblos and enormous mounds, permanently altering the landscape. Their gathering techniques selected productive and nutritious varieties of plants, thereby shifting the balance of local plants toward useful varieties. The first stages of North American agriculture, for example, probably resulted from Native Americans gathering wild seeds and then sowing them in a meadow for later harvest. It is almost certain that fertile and hardy varieties of corn were developed in this way, first in Mexico and later in North America.

Native Americans also altered the natural environment by setting fires. Great Plains hunters often used fires to force buffalo together and make them easy to slaughter. Eastern Woodland, Southwest, and Pacific coast Indians also set fires to hunt deer and other valuable prey. Over thousands of square miles throughout North America, Indians started fires along the edges of woods to burn off shrubby undergrowth and encroaching tree seedlings. These burns encouraged the growth of tender young plants that attracted deer and other game animals, bringing them within convenient range of hunters' weapons.

Because fires usually burned until they ran out of fuel or were extinguished by rain or wind, enormous regions of North America were burned over. In the long run, fires created and maintained light-dappled meadows for hunting and agriculture, cleared entangling underbrush from forests, and promoted a diverse and productive natural environment. Fires, like other activities of Native Americans, shaped the landscape of North America long before Europeans arrived in 1492.

> **REVIEW** Why did some Native Americans set fire to the land?

The Mexica: A Meso-American Culture

The indigenous population of the New World (the Western Hemisphere) numbered roughly 80 million in the 1490s, about the same as the population of Europe. Almost all these people lived in Mexico and Central and South America.

Like their much less numerous North American counterparts, they too lived in a natural environment of tremendous diversity. They too developed hundreds of cultures, far too numerous to catalog here. But among all these cultures, the Mexica stood out. (Europeans often called these people Aztecs, a name the Mexica did not use.) Their empire stretched from coast to coast across central Mexico, encompassing as many as 25 million people. We know more about the Mexica than about any other Native American society of the time, principally because of their massive monuments and their Spanish conquerors' well-documented interest in subduing them. Their significance in the history of the New World after 1492 dictates a brief discussion of their culture and society.

The Mexica began their rise to prominence about 1325 when small bands settled on a marshy island in Lake Texcoco, the site of the future city of Tenochtitlán, the capital of the Mexican empire. Resourceful, courageous, and cold-blooded warriors, the Mexica often hired out as mercenaries for richer, more settled tribes. By 1430, the Mexica succeeded in asserting their dominance over their former allies and leading their own military campaigns in an ever-widening arc of empire building. Despite pockets of resistance, by the 1490s the Mexica ruled an empire that covered more land than Spain and Portugal combined and contained almost three times as many people.

The empire exemplified the central values of Mexican society. The Mexica worshipped the war god Huitzilopochtli. Warriors held the most exalted positions in the Mexican social hierarchy, even above the priests who performed the sacred ceremonies that won Huitzilopochtli's favor. In the almost constant battles necessary to defend and extend the empire, young Mexican men exhibited the courage and daring that would allow them to rise in the carefully graduated ranks of warriors. The Mexica considered capturing prisoners the ultimate act of bravery. Warriors usually turned over the captives to Mexican priests, who sacrificed them to Huitzilopochtli by cutting out their hearts.

The empire contributed far more to Mexican society than victims for sacrifice. At the most basic level, the empire functioned as a military and political system that collected tribute from subject peoples. The Mexica forced conquered tribes to pay tribute in goods, not money. Tribute redistributed to the Mexica as much as one-third of the goods produced by conquered tribes. It included everything from candidates for human sacrifice to textiles and basic food products such as corn and beans as well as exotic luxury items such as gold, turquoise, and rare bird feathers.

Tribute reflected the fundamental relations of power and wealth that pervaded the Mexican empire. The relatively small nobility of Mexican warriors, supported by a still smaller priesthood, possessed the military and religious power to command the obedience of thousands of non-noble Mexicans and of millions of other non-Mexicans in subjugated provinces. The Mexican elite exercised their power to obtain tribute and thereby to redistribute wealth from the conquered to the conquerors, from the commoners to the nobility, from the poor to the rich. This redistribution of wealth made possible the achieve-

ments of Mexican society that eventually amazed Spaniards: the huge cities, fabulous temples, teeming markets, and luxuriant gardens, not to mention the storehouses stuffed with gold and other treasures.

On the whole, the Mexica did not interfere much with the internal government of conquered regions. Instead, they usually permitted the traditional ruling elite to stay in power—so long as they paid tribute. The conquered provinces received very little in return from the Mexica, except immunity from punitive raids. Subjugated communities felt exploited by the constant payment of tribute to the Mexica. By depending on military conquest and constant collection of tribute, the Mexica failed to create among their subjects a belief that Mexican domination was, at some level, legitimate and equitable. The high level of discontent among subject peoples constituted the soft, vulnerable underbelly of the Mexican empire, a fact Spanish intruders exploited after AD 1492 to conquer the Mexica.

> **REVIEW**   Why were the Mexica able to build monumental cities and structures?

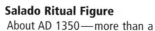

Salado Ritual Figure
About AD 1350—more than a century before Columbus arrived in the Western Hemisphere—this figure was carefully wrapped in a reed mat with other items and stored in a cave in a mountainous region of New Mexico by people of the Salado culture, descendants of the Mimbres, who had flourished three centuries earlier. The face of this figure is as close to a self-portrait of ancient Americans on the eve of their encounter with Europeans as we are ever likely to have. Adorned with vivid pigments, cotton string, bright feathers, and stones, the effigy testifies to the human complexity of all ancient Americans, a complexity visible in artifacts that have survived the millennia before the arrival of Europeans.
© 2000 The Art Institute of Chicago.

Conclusion: The World of Ancient Americans

Ancient Americans shaped the history of human beings in the New World for more than twelve thousand years. They established continuous human habitation in the Western Hemisphere from the time the first big-game hunters crossed Beringia until 1492 and beyond. Much of their history remains irretrievably lost because they relied on oral rather than written communication. But much can be pieced together from artifacts they left behind, like the Folsom points among the bones discovered by George McJunkin. Ancient Americans achieved their success through resourceful adaptation to the hemisphere's many and ever-changing natural environments. They also adapted to social and cultural changes caused by human beings—such as marriages, deaths, political struggles, and warfare—but the sparse evidence that has survived renders those adaptations almost entirely unknowable. Their creativity and artistry are unmistakably documented in the artifacts they left at kill sites, camps, and burial mounds. Those artifacts sketch the only likenesses of ancient Americans we will ever have—blurred, shadowy images that are indisputably human but forever silent.

In the five centuries after 1492—just 4 percent of the time human beings have inhabited the Western Hemisphere—Europeans and their descendants began to shape and eventually to dominate American history. Native American peoples continued to influence major developments of American history for centuries after 1492. But the new wave of strangers that at first trickled and then flooded into the New World from Europe and Africa forever transformed the peoples and places of ancient America.

Suggestions for Further Reading

Karen Olsen Bruhns and Karen R. Stothert, *Women in Ancient America* (1999). An informative account of ancient American women, who are often neglected in other books.

Colin G. Calloway, *One Vast Winter Count: The Native American West before Lewis and Clark* (2003). A fascinating overview of Native Americans in the West.

Michael D. Coe and Rex Koontz, *Mexico: From the Olmecs to the Aztecs* (5th ed., 2002). An authoritative survey of ancient Mexico.

Brian M. Fagan, *Ancient North America: The Archaeology of a Continent* (1991). The compelling story of the role of archaeological evidence in piecing together the history of ancient North America.

Tim Flannery, *The Eternal Frontier: An Ecological History of North America and Its Peoples* (2001). A sweeping ecological history of North American plants and animals covering millions of years.

▶ **For more books about topics in this chapter,** see the Online Bibliography at **bedfordstmartins.com/roarkcompact**.

▶ **For additional firsthand accounts of this period,** see Chapter 1 in Michael Johnson, ed., *Reading the American Past,* Third Edition.

▶ **For Web sites and documents related to topics and places in this chapter,** see "HistoryLinks," "DocLinks," and "PlaceLinks" at **bedfordstmartins.com/roarkcompact**.

REVIEWING THE CHAPTER

Follow these steps to review and strengthen your understanding of the chapter.

STEP 1: *Study the* **Key Terms** *and* **Timeline** *to identify the significance of each item listed.*

STEP 2: *Answer the* **Review Questions,** *drawing on key terms and dates to support your answers.*

STEP 3: *Drawing on the Key Terms, Timeline, and Review Questions, answer the broader* **Making Connections** *questions.*

KEY TERMS

Who

George McJunkin (p. 3)
Carl Schwachheim (p. 3)
J. D. Figgins (p. 3)
Paleo-Indians (p. 7)
Folsom hunters (p. 12)
Great Basin peoples (p. 12)
California peoples (p. 12)
Chumash (p. 12)
Northwest peoples (p. 12)
Woodland peoples (p. 13)
Southwestern peoples (p. 14)
Mogollon (p. 15)
Hohokam (p. 15)
Anasazi (p. 15)
Adena (p. 17)
Hopewell peoples (p. 17)
Mississippian peoples (p. 18)
Algonquian peoples (p. 19)

Iroquoian peoples (p. 19)
Muskogean peoples (p. 20)
Great Plains peoples (p. 20)
Athapascans (p. 20)
Mexica (p. 21)

What

Wild Horse Arroyo (p. 3)
artifacts (p. 3)
Folsom points (p. 3)
Pangaea (p. 5)
continental drift (p. 5)
Homo erectus (p. 5)
Homo sapiens (p. 5)
Wisconsin glaciation (p. 6)
Beringia (p. 6)
Clovis points (p. 7)
Clovis culture (p. 10)
Archaic era (p. 10)

hunter-gatherer (p. 10)
Great Basin (p. 12)
agriculture (p. 13)
pottery (p. 13)
pueblo (p. 14)
kiva (p. 15)
agricultural settlements (p. 15)
burial mounds (p. 17)
chiefdoms (p. 17)
interregional trade (p. 18)
Cahokia (p. 18)
matrilineal rules of descent (p. 20)
League of Five Nations (p. 20)
Dalles site (p. 20)
Tenochtitlán (p. 21)
Huitzilopochtli (p. 21)
warriors (p. 21)
Mexican empire (p. 21)
tribute (p. 21)

TIMELINE

NOTE: Major events are depicted below in chronological order, but the time scale between events varies from millennia to centuries.

(*BP* is an abbreviation used by archaeologists for "years before the present.")

◄ **c. 80,000–10,000 BP** • Wisconsin glaciation exposes Beringia.

c. 13,000 BP • First humans arrive in North America.

c. 11,500–11,000 BP • Paleo-Indians use Clovis points to hunt big game.

c. 11,000 BP • Mammoths become extinct.

c. 10,000–3000 BP • Archaic cultures dominate ancient America.

c. 4000 BP • Some Eastern Woodland peoples grow gourds and pumpkins and begin making pottery.

c. 3500 BP
• Southwestern cultures begin corn cultivation.
• Stone pipes for tobacco smoking appear in Eastern Woodland regions.

c. 2500 BP
• Eastern Woodland cultures start to build burial mounds.

REVIEW QUESTIONS

1. Why do historians rely on the work of archaeologists to write the history of ancient America? (pp. 4–5)

2. Why were humans able to migrate into North America after 15,000 BP? (pp. 5–10)

3. Why did post-Clovis Native Americans shift from big-game hunting to foraging and smaller-game hunting? (pp. 10–13)

4. How did the availability of food influence the distribution of Native American population across the continent? (pp. 14–18)

5. Why did some Native Americans set fire to the land? (pp. 18–21)

6. Why were the Mexica able to build monumental cities and structures? (pp. 21–22)

MAKING CONNECTIONS

1. Explain the different approaches historians and archaeologists bring to studying people in the past. How do the different sources they draw on shape their accounts of the human past? In your answer, cite specific examples from the history of ancient America.

2. Discuss Native Americans' strategies for surviving in the varied climates of North America. How did their different approaches to survival contribute to the diversity of Native American cultures?

3. For over twelve thousand years Native Americans successfully adapted to environmental changes in North America; they also produced significant changes in the environments around them. In your answer, discuss specific examples of how Native Americans changed the North American landscape.

4. Rich archaeological and manuscript sources have enabled historians to develop a detailed portrait of the Mexica on the eve of European contact. How did the Mexica establish and maintain their expansive empire?

► **FOR PRACTICE QUIZZES, A CUSTOMIZED STUDY PLAN, AND OTHER STUDY TOOLS,** see the Online Study Guide at bedfordstmartins.com/roarkcompact.

---

c. 2100 BP–AD 400 • Hopewell culture emerges in Mississippi and Ohio valleys.

c. AD 200–AD 900 • Mogollon culture emerges in New Mexico.

c. AD 500 • Bows and arrows appear in North America.
• Pacific Northwest cultures create elaborate wood carvings.

c. AD 500–AD 1400 • Hohokam culture develops in Arizona.

c. AD 800–AD 1500
• Mississippian culture flourishes in Southeast.

c. AD 1000–AD 1100 • Anasazi peoples build cliff dwellings.

c. AD 1325–AD 1500
• Mexica empire established.

AD 1492
• Christopher Columbus arrives in New World.

TAINO ZEMI BASKET
This basket is an example
of the effigies Tainos made
to represent *zemis,* their
deities. The effigy illustrates the
artistry of the basket maker, almost
certainly a Taino woman. Crafted sometime between
1492 and about 1520, the effigy demonstrates that Tainos readily incorporated goods obtained through contacts
with Europeans into their own traditional beliefs and practices. The basket maker used African ivory and European
mirrors as well as Native American fibers, dyes, and designs.

Archivio Fotogràfico del Museo Preistòrico Etnografico L. Pigorini, Roma.

Europeans Encounter the New World

1492–1600

A HALF HOUR BEFORE SUNRISE on August 3, 1492, Christopher Columbus commanded three ships to catch the tide out of a harbor in southern Spain and sail west. Just over two months later, in the predawn moonlight of October 12, 1492, Columbus glimpsed an island on the western horizon. At last, he believed, he had found what he had been looking for—the western end of a route across the Atlantic Ocean to Japan, China, and India. At daybreak, Columbus could see people on the shore who had spotted his ships. He rowed ashore and, as the curious islanders crowded around, he claimed possession of the land for Ferdinand and Isabella, king and queen of Spain, who had sponsored his voyage. He named the island San Salvador, in honor of the Savior, Jesus Christ.

A day or two afterward, Columbus described that first encounter with the inhabitants of San Salvador in an extensive diary he kept during his voyage. He called these people Indians, assuming that their island lay somewhere in the East Indies near Japan or China. The Indians were not dressed in the finery Columbus expected. "All of them go around as naked as their mothers bore them; and the women also," he observed. Their skin color was "neither black nor white." They were not familiar with the Spaniards' weapons. "I showed them swords," Columbus wrote, "and they took them by the edge and through ignorance cut themselves." This first encounter led Columbus to conclude, "They should be good and intelligent servants, for I see that they say very quickly everything that is said to them; and I believe that they would become Christians very easily, for it seemed to me that they had no religion."

The people Columbus called Indians called themselves Tainos, which to them meant "good" or "noble." They inhabited most of the Caribbean islands Columbus visited on his first voyage, as had their ancestors for more than two centuries. The Tainos were an agricultural people who grew cassava, a nutritious root, as well as sweet potatoes, corn, cotton, tobacco, and other crops. To fish and to travel from island to island, they built canoes from hollowed-out logs. The Tainos worshipped gods they called *zemis*, the spirits of ancestors and of natural objects like trees and stones. They made effigies of zemis and performed rituals to honor them. "It seemed to me that they were a people very poor in everything," Columbus wrote.

What the Tainos thought about Spaniards we can only surmise, since they left no written documents. At first, Columbus believed that the Tainos thought he and his men came from heaven. After six weeks of contact, Columbus

Cacique's Canoe
This sixteenth-century drawing of a large canoe carrying a cacique, or chief, and powered by twenty oarsmen probably resembles the canoes used by Tainos and the other Native Americans who paddled out to visit the ships of Columbus and other European explorers. The influence of such European contacts may be reflected in the flags flying from the corners of the leafy awning that shades the enthroned cacique and rowers.
The Pierpont Morgan Library / Art Resource, NY.

concluded that in fact he did not understand Tainos. Late in November 1492, he wrote that "the people of these lands do not understand me nor do I, nor anyone else that I have with me, them. And many times I understand one thing said by these Indians…for another, its contrary."

The confused communication between Europeans and Tainos suggests how different, how strange, each group seemed to the other. Columbus's perceptions of Tainos were shaped by European ideas, attitudes, and expectations, just as Tainos' perceptions of Europeans must have been colored by their own culture. Yet the word that Columbus coined for the Tainos— *Indians*, a word that originated in a colossal misunderstanding—hinted at the direction of the future. To Europeans, *Indians* came to mean all native inhabitants of the New World, the name they gave to the lands in the Western Hemisphere. After 1492, the perceptions, the cultures, and even the diseases of Europeans began to exert a transforming influence on the New World and its peoples.

Long before 1492, certain Europeans restlessly expanded the limits of the world known to them. Their efforts made possible Columbus's encounter with the Tainos. In turn, Columbus's

landfall in the Caribbean changed the history not only of the Tainos, but also of Europe and the rest of the world. Beginning in 1492, the promise of the New World lured more and more Europeans to venture their lives and fortunes on the western shores of the Atlantic, a promise realized largely at the expense of New World peoples like the Tainos.

Europe in the Age of Exploration

Historically, the East—not the West—attracted Europeans. Around the year 1000, Norsemen ventured west across the North Atlantic and founded a small fishing village at L'Anse aux Meadows on the tip of Newfoundland that lasted only a decade or so. Viking sagas memorialized the Norse "discovery," but it had virtually no other impact in the New World or in Europe. Instead, wealthy Europeans developed a taste for luxury goods from Asia and Africa, and merchants competed to satisfy that taste. As Europeans traded with the East and with one another, they acquired new information about the world they inhabited. A few people—sailors, merchants, and aristocrats—

took the risks of exploring beyond the limits of the world known to Europeans. Those risks were genuine and could be deadly. But sometimes they paid off in new information, new opportunities, and eventually in the discovery of a world entirely new to Europeans.

Mediterranean Trade and European Expansion

From the twelfth through the fifteenth centuries, spices, silk, carpets, ivory, gold, and other exotic goods traveled overland from Persia, Asia Minor, India, and Africa and then were funneled into continental Europe through Mediterranean trade routes (Map 2.1). Dominated primarily by the Italian cities of Venice, Genoa, and Pisa, this lucrative trade enriched Italian merchants and bankers, who fiercely defended their near-**monopoly** of

access to eastern goods. The vitality of the Mediterranean trade offered few incentives to look for alternatives. New routes to the East and the discovery of new lands were the stuff of fantasy.

Preconditions for turning fantasy into reality developed in fifteenth-century Europe. In the mid-fourteenth century, Europeans suffered a catastrophic epidemic of bubonic plague. The Black Death, as it was called, killed about a third of the European population. This devastating pestilence had major long-term consequences. By drastically reducing the population, it made Europe's limited supply of food more plentiful for survivors. Many survivors inherited property from plague victims, giving them new chances for advancement. The turmoil caused by the plague also prompted peasants to move away from their homes and seek opportunities elsewhere.

MAP 2.1   European Trade Routes and Portuguese Exploration in the Fifteenth Century

The strategic geographic position of Italian cities as a conduit for overland trade from Asia was slowly undermined during the fifteenth century by Portuguese explorers who hopscotched along the coast of Africa and eventually found a sea route that opened the rich trade of the East to Portuguese merchants.

Ivory Saltcellar

This exquisitely carved sixteenth-century ivory saltcellar combines African materials, craftsmanship, and imagery in an artifact for Portuguese tables. Designed to hold table salt in the central globe, the saltcellar portrays a victim about to be beheaded by the armed man who has already beheaded five others. To Portuguese eyes, the saltcellar dramatized African brutality and quietly suggested the superiority of Portuguese virtues and their beneficial influence in Africa.

Archivio Fotogràfico del Museo Preistòrico Etnografico L. Pigorini, Roma.

Understandably, most Europeans perceived the world as a place of alarming risks where the delicate balance of health, harvests, and peace could quickly be tipped toward disaster by epidemics, famine, and violence. Most people protected themselves from the constant threat of calamity by worshipping the supernatural, by living amid kinfolk and friends, and by maintaining good relations with the rich and powerful. But the insecurity and uncertainty of fifteenth-century European life also encouraged a few people to take greater risks, such as embarking on dangerous sea voyages through uncharted waters to points unknown.

Exploration promised fame and fortune in European societies to those who succeeded, whether they were kings or commoners. Monarchs hoped to enlarge their realms and enrich their dynasties. More territory meant more subjects who could pay more taxes, provide more soldiers, and participate in more commerce, magnifying monarchs' power and prestige. Voyages of exploration also could stabilize monarchs' regimes by diverting unruly noblemen toward distant lands. Some explorers, like Columbus, were commoners who hoped to be elevated to the aristocracy as a reward for their daring achievements.

Scientific and technological advances also helped set the stage for exploration. The invention of movable type made printing easier and cheaper, stimulating diffusion of information among literate Europeans, including news of discoveries. By 1400, crucial navigational aids employed by maritime explorers like Columbus were already available: compasses; hourglasses, which allowed calculation of elapsed time, useful in estimating speed; and the astrolabe and the quadrant, devices for determining latitude. Many people throughout fifteenth-century Europe knew about these and other technological advances. The Portuguese were the first to use them in a campaign to sail beyond the limits of the world known to Europeans.

A Century of Portuguese Exploration

Portugal had less than 2 percent of the population of Christian Europe, but it devoted far more energy and wealth to the geographical exploration of the world between 1415 and 1460 than all the other countries of Europe combined. Facing the Atlantic, the Portuguese lived on the margins of the thriving Mediterranean trade. As a Christian kingdom, Portugal cooperated with Spain in the Reconquest, the centuries-long drive to expel Muslims from the Iberian Peninsula.

The religious zeal that propelled the Reconquest also justified expansion into what the Portuguese considered heathen lands. The key victory came in 1415 when Portuguese forces conquered Ceuta, the Muslim bastion at the mouth of the Strait of Gibraltar that had blocked Portugal's access to the Atlantic coast of Africa.

The most influential advocate of Portuguese exploration was Prince Henry the Navigator, son of the Portuguese king. From 1415 until his death in 1460, Henry collected the latest information about sailing techniques and geography, supported new crusades against the Muslims, encouraged fresh sources of trade to fatten Portuguese pocketbooks, and pushed explorers to go farther still.

Neither the Portuguese nor anybody else in Europe knew the immensity of Africa or the length or shape of its coastline, which, in reality, fronted the Atlantic for more than 7,000 miles—about five times the considerable distance from Genoa, Columbus's hometown, to Lisbon, the Portuguese capital. By 1434, Portuguese mariners had sailed along the north African coast to reach the northern edge of the Sahara Desert, where strong westerly currents swept them out to sea. They soon learned to ride those currents far away from the coast before catching favorable winds that turned them back toward land, a technique that allowed them to reach Cape Verde by 1444 (see Map 2.1). To stow the supplies necessary for long periods at sea and to withstand the battering of waves in the open ocean, the Portuguese developed the caravel, a sturdy ship that became explorers' vessel of choice. In caravels, Portuguese mariners sailed into and around the Gulf of Guinea and as far south as the Congo by 1480.

Fierce African resistance confined Portuguese expeditions to coastal trading posts, where they bartered successfully for gold, slaves, and ivory. Portuguese merchants learned that relatively peaceful trading posts on the coast were far more profitable than attempts at violent conquest and **colonization** of inland regions. In the 1460s, the Portuguese used African slaves to develop sugar plantations on the Cape Verde Islands, inaugurating an association between enslaved Africans and plantation labor that would be transplanted to the New World in the centuries to come.

About 1480, Portuguese explorers began a conscious search for a sea route to Asia. In 1488, Bartolomeu Dias sailed around the Cape

Benin Queen Mother
Early in the sixteenth century, as the Portuguese began their forays along the African coast, the Oba (king) of Benin, in present-day Nigeria, introduced the notion of a queen mother who possessed the ability to communicate with supernatural deities. Brass castings of Benin queen mothers like the one shown here appeared on altars in royal palaces. The distinctive headdress apparently signified the queen mother's semidivine status.
The National Museums, Liverpool.

of Good Hope at the southern tip of Africa and hurried back to Lisbon with the exciting news that it appeared to be possible to sail on to India and China. In 1498, after ten years of careful preparation, Vasco da Gama commanded the first Portuguese fleet to sail to India. Portugal quickly capitalized on the commercial potential of da Gama's new sea route. By the early sixteenth century, the Portuguese controlled a far-flung commercial empire in India, Indonesia, and China (collectively referred to as the East Indies). Their new sea route to the East eliminated overland travel and allowed Portuguese merchants to charge much lower prices for the eastern goods they imported.

Portugal's African explorations during the fifteenth century broke the monopoly of the old Mediterranean trade with the East, dramatically expanded the world known to Europeans, established a network of Portuguese outposts in Africa and Asia, and developed methods of sailing the high seas that Columbus employed on his revolutionary voyage west.

REVIEW Why did European exploration expand dramatically in the fifteenth century?

A Surprising New World in the Western Atlantic

In retrospect, the Portuguese seemed ideally qualified to venture west across the Atlantic. They had pioneered the **frontiers** of seafaring, exploration, and geography for almost a century. However, the Portuguese and most other European experts believed that sailing west to landfall across the Atlantic was literally impossible. The European discovery of America required someone bold enough to believe that the experts were wrong. That person was Christopher Columbus. His explorations inaugurated a geographical revolution that forever altered Europeans' understanding of the world and its peoples, including themselves. Columbus's landfall in the Caribbean originated a thriving exchange between the people, ideas, cultures, and institutions of the Old and New Worlds that continues to this day.

Columbus's First Voyage to the New World, 1492–1493

The Explorations of Columbus

Born in 1451 into the family of an obscure master weaver in Genoa, Italy, Columbus went to sea when he was about fourteen. Sometime around 1476, he arrived in Lisbon and within a few years married Felipa Moniz. Felipa's father had been raised in the household of Prince Henry the Navigator, and her family retained close ties to the prince. Through Felipa, Columbus gained access to explorers' maps and papers crammed with information about the tricky currents and winds encountered in sailing the Atlantic. Columbus himself ventured into the Atlantic frequently and at least twice sailed all the way to the central coast of Africa.

Like other educated Europeans, Columbus believed that the earth was a sphere and that theoretically it was possible to reach the East Indies by sailing west. Most Europeans believed, however, that the earth was simply too big for anyone to sail west from Europe to Asia. Sailors would die of thirst and starvation long before they reached Asia.

Columbus rejected this conventional wisdom. With flawed calculations, he estimated that Asia was only about 2,500 miles from the westernmost boundary of the known world, a shorter distance than Portuguese ships routinely sailed between Lisbon and the Congo. In fact, the shortest distance to Japan from Europe's jumping-off point was nearly 11,000 miles. Convinced by his erroneous calculations, Columbus became obsessed with a scheme to prove he was right.

In 1492, after years of unsuccessful lobbying in Portugal, Spain, England, and France,

Columbus finally won financing for his journey from Spain's monarchs, Ferdinand and Isabella. The Spanish monarchs saw Columbus's venture as an inexpensive gamble: The potential loss was small while the potential gain was huge.

After scarcely three months of hurried preparation, Columbus and his small fleet—the *Niña* and *Pinta*, both caravels, and the *Santa María*, a larger merchant vessel—headed west. Six weeks after leaving the Canary Islands, where he stopped for supplies, Columbus landed on a tiny Caribbean island about three hundred miles north of the eastern tip of Cuba.

Columbus and his men understood that they had made a momentous discovery. Yet they found it frustrating. Although the Tainos proved friendly, they did not have the riches Columbus expected to find in the East Indies. For three months Columbus cruised from island to island, looking for the king of Japan and the Grand Khan of China. In mid-January 1493, he started back to Spain. When he reached Isabella and Ferdinand, they were overjoyed by his news. With a voyage that had lasted barely eight months, Columbus appeared to have catapulted Spain from a secondary position in the race for a sea route to Asia into that of a serious challenger to Portugal, whose explorers had not yet sailed to India or China. The Spanish monarchs elevated Columbus to the nobility and awarded him the title "Admiral of the Ocean Sea."

Soon after Columbus returned to Spain, the Portuguese and Spanish monarchs negotiated the Treaty of Tordesillas in 1494. The treaty drew an imaginary line eleven hundred miles west of the Canary Islands (Map 2.2). Land discovered west of the line belonged to Spain; Portugal claimed land to the east.

Before Columbus died in 1506, he returned to the New World three times without relinquishing his belief that the East Indies were there, someplace. Other explorers continued to search for a passage to the East or some other source of profit. Before long, however, prospects of beating the Portuguese to Asia began to dim along with the hope of finding vast hoards of gold. Nonetheless, Columbus's discoveries forced sixteenth-century Europeans to think about the world in new ways. He proved that it was possible to sail from Europe to the western rim of the Atlantic and return to

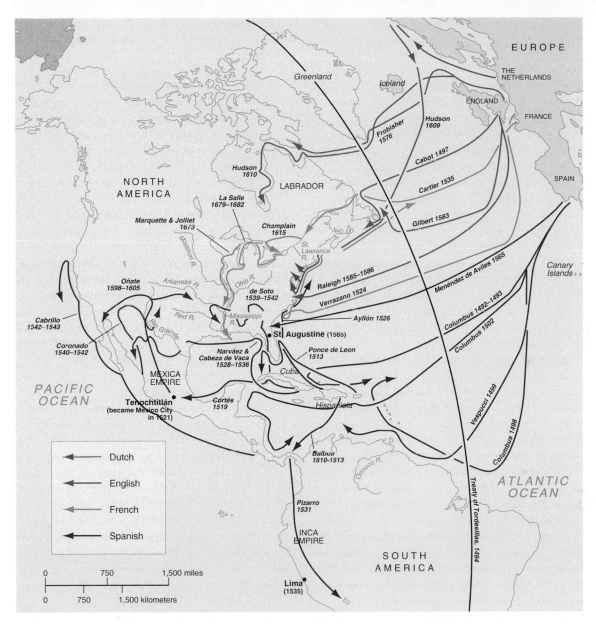

MAP 2.2 European Exploration in Sixteenth-Century America
This map illustrates the approximate routes of early European explorations of the New World.

Europe. Most important, Columbus made clear that beyond the western shores of the Atlantic lay lands entirely unknown to Europeans.

The Geographic Revolution and the Columbian Exchange

Within thirty years of Columbus's initial discovery, Europeans' understanding of world geography underwent a revolution. An elite of perhaps twenty thousand people with access to Europe's royal courts and trading centers learned the exciting news about global geography. But it took a generation of additional exploration before they could comprehend the larger contours of Columbus's discoveries.

European monarchs hurried to stake their claims to the newly discovered lands. In 1497, King Henry VII of England, who had spurned Columbus a decade earlier, sent John Cabot to look for a "Northwest Passage" to the Indies across the North Atlantic (see Map 2.2). Cabot reached the tip of Newfoundland, which he believed was part of Asia, and hurried back to

England, where he assembled a small fleet and sailed west again in 1498. But he was never heard from again. Three thousand miles to the south, a Spanish expedition landed on the northern coast of South America in 1499 accompanied by Amerigo Vespucci, an Italian businessman. In 1500, Pedro Álvars Cabral commanded a Portuguese fleet bound for the Indian Ocean that accidentally made landfall on the coast of Brazil as it looped westward into the Atlantic.

By 1500, European experts knew that several large chunks of land cluttered the western Atlantic. A few cartographers speculated that these chunks were connected to one another in a landmass that was not Asia. In 1507, Martin Waldseemüller, a German cartographer, published the first map that showed the New World separate from Asia; he named the land America, in honor of Amerigo Vespucci.

Two additional discoveries confirmed Waldseemüller's speculation. In 1513, Vasco Núñez de Balboa crossed the isthmus of Panama and reached the Pacific Ocean. Clearly, more water lay between the New World and Asia. How much water Ferdinand Magellan discovered when he led an expedition to circumnavigate the globe in 1519. Sponsored by King Charles I of Spain, Magellan's voyage took him first to the New World, around the southern tip of South America, and into the Pacific late in November 1520. Crossing the Pacific took almost four months. By the time he reached the Philippines, his crew had been decimated by starvation and thirst. Magellan himself was killed by Philippine tribesmen. A remnant of his expedition continued on to the Indian Ocean and managed to transport a cargo of spices back to Spain in 1522.

In most ways Magellan's voyage was a disaster. One ship and 18 men crawled back from an expedition that had begun with five ships and more than 250 men. But the geographic information it provided left no doubt that America was a continent separated from Asia by the enormous Pacific Ocean. The voyage made clear that Columbus was dead wrong about the identity of what he had discovered. It was possible to sail west to reach the East Indies, but that was a terrible way to go. After Magellan, most Europeans who sailed west set their sights on the New World, not on Asia.

Columbus's arrival in the Caribbean anchored the western end of what might be imagined as a sea bridge that spanned the Atlantic, connecting the Western Hemisphere to Europe.

That sea bridge ended the age-old separation of the hemispheres and initiated the **Columbian exchange**, a transatlantic exchange of goods, people, and ideas that has continued ever since.

Spaniards brought novelties to the New World that were commonplace in Europe, including Christianity, iron technology, sailing ships, firearms, wheeled vehicles, horses and other domesticated animals, and much else. Unknowingly, they also smuggled along many Old World viruses that caused epidemics of smallpox, measles, and other diseases that would kill the vast majority of Indian peoples during the sixteenth century and continue to decimate survivors in later centuries. European diseases made the Columbian exchange catastrophic for Native Americans. In the long term, these diseases were decisive in transforming the dominant peoples of the New World from descendants of Asians, who had inhabited the hemisphere for millennia, to descendants of Europeans and Africans, recent arrivals from the Old World by way of the newly formed sea bridge.

Ancient American goods, people, and ideas made the return trip across the Atlantic. Europeans were introduced to New World foods such as corn and potatoes as well as exotic fruits like pineapples, named for their resemblance to pinecones. Columbus's sailors became infected with syphilis in sexual encounters with New World women and then unwittingly carried the deadly parasite back to Europe, where it may already have had a foothold. New World tobacco created a European fashion for smoking that ignited quickly and has yet to be extinguished. But for almost a generation after 1492, this Columbian exchange did not reward Spaniards with the riches they yearned to find.

REVIEW   How did Columbus's landfall in the Caribbean help revolutionize Europeans' understanding of world geography?

Spanish Exploration and Conquest

During the sixteenth century, the New World helped Spain become the most powerful monarchy in both Europe and the Americas. Spaniards enslaved Caribbean islanders and put them to work growing crops and mining gold. But the profits from these early ventures barely covered

Columbian Exchange
The arrival of Columbus in the New World started an ongoing transatlantic exchange of goods, people, and ideas. Spaniards brought domesticated animals from the Old World, including horses, cattle, goats, chickens, cats, and sheep (left). The novelty of such animals is demonstrated by the Nahua words the Mexican people initially used to refer to these strange new beasts: for horses, they used the Nahua word for deer; a cow was "one with horns"; a goat was a "bearded one with horns"; a chicken was a "Spanish turkey hen"; a cat was a "little cougar"; a sheep was referred to with the word for cotton, linking the animal with its fibrous woolen coat. Spaniards brought many other alien items such as cannon, which the Mexica at first termed "fat fire trumpets," and guitars, which the Mexica called "rope drums." Spaniards also carried Old World microorganisms that caused devastating epidemics of smallpox, measles, and other diseases (center). Ancient American people, goods, and ideas made the return trip across the Atlantic. Columbus's sailors quickly learned to use Indian hammocks and became infected with syphilis in sexual encounters with Indian women; then they carried both hammocks and syphilis back to Europe. Smoking tobacco, like the cigar puffed by the ancient Mayan lord (right), became such a fashion in Europe that some came to believe, as a print of two men relaxing with their pipes was captioned, "Life Is Smoke." The strangeness of New World peoples and cultures also reinforced Europeans' notions of their own superiority. Although the Columbian exchange went in both directions, it was not a relationship of equality. Europeans seized and retained the upper hand.
University of California at Berkeley, The Bancroft Library; Arxiu Mas; Collection of Dr. Francis Robicsek.

the costs of maintaining the settlers. After almost thirty years of exploration, the promise of Columbus's discovery seemed illusory.

In 1519, however, that promise was fulfilled, spectacularly, by Hernán Cortés's march into the Mexican mainland. By about 1545, Spanish conquests extended from northern Mexico to southern Chile, and New World riches filled Spanish treasure chests. Cortés's expedition served as the model for Spaniards' and other Europeans' expectations that the New World could yield bonanza profits for its conquerors.

The Conquest of Mexico

Hernán Cortés, who became the richest and most famous conquistador (conqueror), arrived in the New World in 1504, an obscure nineteen-year-old Spaniard seeking adventure and the chance to make a name for himself. He fought in the conquest of Cuba and elsewhere in the Caribbean. In 1519, the governor of Cuba authorized Cortés to organize an expedition to investigate rumors of a fabulously wealthy kingdom somewhere in the interior of the mainland. A charming, charismatic

Cortés Arrives in Tenochtitlán
This portrayal of the arrrival of Cortés and his army in the Mexican capital illustrates the importance of Malinali, who stands at the front of the Spaniards' procession, serving as their translator and intermediary with Montezuma (not pictured), who has come out to greet the invaders. Painted by a Mexican artist after the conquest, the work contrasts Cortés—dressed as a Spanish gentleman, respectfully doffing his hat to Montezuma and accompanied by his horse and African groom—with his soldiers, who are armed and ready for battle. The painting displays the choices confronted by the Mexica: accepting the pacific overtures of Cortés or facing the lances, swords, and battle axes of the Spanish soldiers. Also notable is the importance of Indian porters who carried the Spaniards' food and other supplies. What do you think was the significance of the winged image on the flag?
Bibliothèque Nationale, Paris.

accompanied Cortés, "we would not have understood the language of New Spain and Mexico." With her help, Cortés talked and fought with Indians along the Gulf coast of Mexico, trying to discover the location of the fabled kingdom.

In the capital of the Mexican empire, Tenochtitlán, the emperor Montezuma heard rumors about some strange creatures sighted along the coast. (Montezuma and his people are often called Aztecs, but they called themselves Mexica.) Montezuma sent representatives to meet with the strangers and bring them gifts fit for gods. Before the Mexican messengers served food to the Spaniards, they sacrificed several hostages and soaked the food in their blood. This fare disgusted the Spaniards and might have been enough to turn them back to Cuba. But along with the food, the Mexica also brought the Spaniards another gift, a "disk in the shape of a sun, as big as a cartwheel and made of very fine gold," as one of the Mexica recalled. Here was conclusive evidence that the rumors of fabulous riches heard by Cortés had some basis in fact.

In August 1519, Cortés marched inland to find Montezuma. Leading about 350 men armed with swords, lances, and muskets and supported by ten cannons, four smaller guns, and sixteen horses, Cortés had to live off the land, establishing peaceful relations with indigenous tribes when he could and killing them when he thought necessary. On November 8, 1519, Cortés reached Tenochtitlán. Montezuma came out to welcome the Spaniards and showered them with lavish hospitality. Quickly, Cortés took Montezuma hostage and held him under house arrest, hoping to make him a puppet through which the Spaniards could rule the Mexican empire. This uneasy peace existed for several months until, after a brutal massacre of many Mexican nobles by one of Cortés's subordinates, the population of Tenochtitlán revolted, murdered Montezuma, and mounted a ferocious assault on the Spaniards. On June 30, 1520, Cortés and about a hundred other Spaniards fought their way out of Tenochtitlán and retreated toward the coast about one hundred miles to Tlaxcala, a stronghold of bitter enemies of the Mexica. The Tlaxcalans—who had long resented Mexican power—allowed Cortés to regroup, obtain reinforcements, and plan a strategy to conquer Tenochtitlán.

leader, Cortés quickly assembled a force of about six hundred men, loaded his ragtag army aboard eleven ships, and set out.

Cortés's confidence that he could talk his way out of most situations and fight his way out of the rest fortified the small band of Spaniards. But Cortés could not speak any Native American language. Landing first on the Yucatán peninsula, he had the good fortune to receive a gift from a chief of the Tobasco people: a fourteen-year-old girl named Malinali who spoke Mayan and Nahuatl, the language of the Mexica, the most powerful people in what is now Mexico and Central America (see chapter 1). Malinali, whom the Spaniards called Marina, soon learned Spanish and became Cortés's interpreter. "Without her help," wrote one of the Spaniards who

Cortés's Invasion of Tenochtitlán, 1519–1521

0   50   100 miles
0   50 100 kilometers

Gulf of Mexico

Otumba   Zautla   Jalapa
Texcoco
Tenochtitlán   Tlaxcala   Veracruz
Cholula

→ Cortés' original route, 1519
→ Cortés' retreat, 1520
→ Cortés' return route, 1520–1521

In the spring of 1521, Cortés mounted a complex campaign against the Mexican capital. The Spaniards and tens of thousands of Indian allies laid siege to the city. With a relentless, scorched-earth strategy, Cortés finally defeated the last Mexican defenders on August 13, 1521. The great capital of the Mexican empire "looked as if it had been ploughed up," one of Cortés's soldiers remembered. A defeated Mexica lamented, "The houses are roofless now, and their walls are red with blood."

The Search for Other Mexicos

Lured by their insatiable appetite for gold, conquistadors quickly fanned out from Tenochtitlán in search of other sources of treasure like Mexico. The most spectacular prize fell to Francisco Pizarro, who conquered the Incan empire in Peru. The Incas controlled a vast, complex region that contained more than nine million people and stretched along the western coast of South America for more than two thousand miles. In 1532, Pizarro and his army of fewer than two hundred men captured the Incan emperor Atahualpa and held him hostage. As ransom, the Incas gave Pizarro the largest treasure yet produced by the conquests: gold and silver equivalent to half a century's worth of precious-metal production in Europe. With the ransom in hand, the Spaniards executed Atahualpa. The Incan treasure spurred Spaniards to search for more.

Juan Ponce de León had sailed along the Florida coast in 1513. Encouraged by Cortés's success, he went back to Florida in 1521 to find riches, only to be killed in battle with Calusa Indians. A few years later, Lucas Vázquez de Ayllón explored the Atlantic coast north of Florida to present-day South Carolina. In 1526 he established a small, short-lived settlement on the Georgia coast that he named San Miguel de Gualdape, the first Spanish attempt to establish a foothold in what is now the United States. Pánfilo de Narváez surveyed the Gulf coast from Florida to Texas in 1528. The Narváez expedition ended disastrously with a shipwreck on the Texas coast near present-day Galveston.

In 1539, Hernando de Soto, a seasoned conquistador who had taken part in the conquest of Peru, set out to find another Peru in North America. Landing in Florida, de Soto literally slashed his way through much of southeastern North America for three years, searching for the rich, majestic civilizations he thought were there. After much brutality and hardship, de Soto died in

Mexican Warrior
Warriors held the most exalted status in Mexican society. This sixteenth-century Mexican painting of a warrior in full battle regalia illustrates the Mexica's careful attention to their magnificent, awe-inspiring costumes. The elaborate clothing and decorative adornments (notice the ornamental stone plug in the warrior's lower lip) expressed warriors' high status; they also were intended to intimidate enemies who dared oppose the fearsome Mexica. Spanish soldiers developed healthy respect for the military skills of the Mexica but were not intimidated by the costumes of Mexican warriors. They did not understand the meaning the costumes had for the Mexica—for example, the costumes' evocation of supernatural support. In addition, although Mexican wooden swords lined with sharp stones could inflict deadly wounds, they proved no match for Spanish body armor, steel swords, horses, and guns.
Bibliothèque Nationale, Paris.

1542. His men buried him in the Mississippi River before turning back to Mexico, disappointed.

Tales of the fabulous wealth of the mythical Seven Cities of Cíbola lured Francisco Vásquez de Coronado to search the Southwest and Great Plains of North America. In 1540, Coronado left

Zuñi Defend Pueblo against Coronado
This sixteenth-century drawing by a Mexican artist shows Zuñi bowmen fighting back against the arrows of Coronado's men and the entreaties of Christian missionaries. Intended to document the support some Mexican Indians gave to Spanish efforts to extend the conquest into North America, the drawing depicts the Zuñi defender at the bottom of the pueblo aiming his arrow at a Mexican missionary armed only with religious weaponry: a crucifix, a rosary, and a book—presumably the Bible.
Hunterian Museum Library, University of Glasgow. Glasgow University Library, Department of Special Collections.

northern Mexico with a large expedition and a priest who claimed to know the way to what he called "the greatest and best of the discoveries." Cíbola turned out to be a small Zuñi pueblo of about a hundred families. Convinced that the rich cities must lie somewhere over the horizon, Coronado kept moving all the way to central Kansas before deciding in 1542 that the rumors he had pursued were just that, nothing more.

Juan Rodríguez Cabrillo led a maritime expedition in 1542 that sailed along the coast of California. Cabrillo died on Santa Catalina Island, offshore from present-day Los Angeles, but his men sailed on to Oregon, where a ferocious storm forced them to turn back toward Mexico.

These probes into North America by de Soto, Coronado, and Cabrillo persuaded Spaniards

that enormous territories stretched northward, but their inhabitants had little to loot or exploit. After a generation of vigorous exploration, Spaniards concluded that there was only one Mexico and one Peru.

New Spain in the Sixteenth Century

For all practical purposes, Spain was the dominant European power in the Western Hemisphere during the sixteenth century (Map 2.3). Portugal claimed the giant territory of Brazil under the Tordesillas treaty but was far more concerned with exploiting its hard-won trade with the East Indies than with colonizing the New World. England and France were absorbed by domestic and diplomatic concerns in Europe and largely lost interest in America until late in the century. In the decades after 1519, Spaniards created the distinctive colonial society of New Spain that showed other Europeans how the New World could be made to serve the purposes of the Old.

The Spanish monarchy claimed ownership of most of the land in the Western Hemisphere and gave the conquistadors permission to explore and plunder. (See "Documenting the American Promise," page 40.) The crown took one-fifth, called the "royal fifth," of any loot confiscated and allowed the conquerors to divide the rest. In the end, most conquistadors received very little after the plunder was divided among leaders such as Cortés and his favorite officers. To compensate his disappointed, battle-hardened soldiers after the conquest of Tenochtitlán, Cortés gave them towns the Spaniards had subdued.

The distribution of conquered towns institutionalized the system of *encomienda*, which empowered conquistadors to rule the Indians and the lands in and around their towns. The concept of encomienda was familiar to the Spaniards, who had used it to govern regions recaptured from the Muslims during the Reconquest. In New Spain, encomienda allowed the Spanish *encomendero* (the man who "owned" the town) to collect the tribute goods that the town had previously paid to the Mexican empire.

In theory, encomienda involved a reciprocal relationship between the encomendero and "his" Indians. In return for the tribute and labor of the Indians, the encomendero was supposed to encourage the Indians to convert to Christianity, to be responsible for their material well-being, and to guarantee order and justice in the town. Catholic missionaries labored earnestly to convert Indians to Christianity. Missionaries fervently believed that

God expected them to save Indians' souls by convincing them to abandon their old, sinful beliefs and to embrace the one true Christian faith. After baptizing tens of thousands of Indians, the missionaries learned that many Indians continued to worship their own gods along with the Christian God. Most friars came to believe that the Indians were lesser beings inherently incapable of fully understanding the Christian faith.

In practice, encomenderos were far more interested in what the Indians could do for them than in what they or missionaries could do for the Indians. Encomenderos subjected Indians to chronic overwork, mistreatment, and abuse. As one Spaniard remarked, "Everything [the Indians] do is slowly done and by compulsion. They are malicious, lying, [and] thievish." Economically, however, encomienda recognized a fundamental reality of New Spain: The most important treasure the Spaniards could plunder from the New World was not gold but uncompensated Indian labor. To exploit that labor, New Spain's richest natural resource, encomienda gave encomenderos the right to force Indians to work when, where, and how the Spaniards pleased.

Encomienda engendered two groups of influential critics. A few of the missionaries were horrified at the brutal mistreatment of the Indians. "What will [the Indians] think about the God of the Christians," Father Bartolomé de Las Casas asked, when they see their friends "with their heads split, their hands amputated, their intestines torn open?…Would

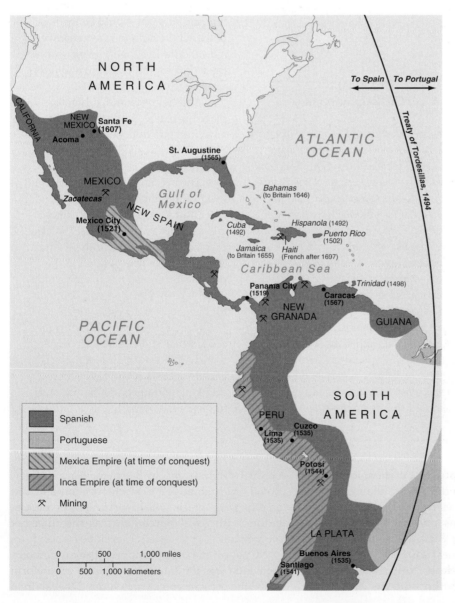

MAP 2.3   New Spain in the Sixteenth Century

Spanish control spread throughout Central and South America during the sixteenth century, with the important exception of Portuguese Brazil. North America, though claimed by Spain under the Treaty of Tordesillas, remained peripheral to Spain's New World empire.

READING THE MAP: Track Spain's efforts at colonization by date. How did political holdings, the physical layout of the land, and natural resources influence where the Spanish directed their energies?

CONNECTIONS: What was the purpose of the Treaty of Tordesillas? How might the location of silver and gold mines have affected Spain's desire to assert its claims over regions still held by Portugal after 1494, and Spain's interest in California, New Mexico, and Florida?

FOR MORE HELP ANALYZING THIS MAP, see the map activity for this chapter in the Online Study Guide at bedfordstmartins.com/roarkcompact.

Justifying Conquest

The immense riches Spain reaped from its New World empire came largely at the expense of Indians. A few individual Spaniards raised their voices against the brutal exploitation of Indians. Their criticisms prompted the Spanish monarchy to formulate an official justification of conquest that, in effect, blamed Indians for resisting Spanish dominion.

DOCUMENT 1
Montecino's 1511
Sermon

In 1511, a Dominican friar named Antón Montecino delivered a blistering sermon that astonished the Spaniards gathered in the church in Santo Domingo, headquarters of the Spanish Caribbean.

Your greed for gold is blind. Your pride, your lust, your anger, your envy, your sloth, all blind....You are in mortal sin. And you are heading for damnation....For you are destroying an innocent people. For they are God's people, these innocents, whom you destroyed. By what right do you make them die? Mining gold for you in your mines or working for you in your fields, by what right do you unleash enslaving wars upon them? They have lived in peace in this land before you came, in peace in their own homes. They did nothing to harm you to cause you to slaughter them wholesale.... Are you not under God's command to love them as you love yourselves? Are you out of your souls, out of your minds? Yes. And that will bring you to damnation.

SOURCE: Zvi Dor-Ner, *Columbus and the Age of Discovery* (New York: William Morrow, 1991), 220–21.

DOCUMENT 2
The Requerimiento

Montecino returned to Spain to bring the Indians' plight to the king's attention. In 1512 and 1513, King Ferdinand met with philosophers, theologians, and other advisers and concluded that the holy duty to spread the Christian faith justified conquest. To buttress this claim, the king had his advisers prepare the Requerimiento. *According to the* Requerimiento, *Indians who failed to welcome Spanish conquest and all its blessings deserved to die. Conquistadors were commanded to read the* Requerimiento *to Indians before any act of conquest. Beginning in 1514, they routinely did so, speaking in Spanish while other Spaniards brandishing unsheathed swords stood nearby.*

On the part of the King... [and] queen of [Spain], subduers of the barbarous nations, we their servants notify and make known to you, as best we can, that the Lord our God, living and eternal, created the heaven and the earth, and one man and one woman, of whom you and we, and all the men of the world, were and are descendants....

God our lord gave charge to one man called St. Peter, that he should be lord and superior to all the men in the world, that all should obey him, and that he should be the head of the whole human race, wherever men should live...and he gave him the world for his kingdom and jurisdiction.

And he commanded him to place his seat in Rome, as the spot most fitting to rule the world from.... This man was called Pope, as if to say, Admirable Great Father and Governor of men. The men who lived in that time obeyed that St. Peter and took him for lord, king, and superior of the universe. So also they have regarded the others who after him have been elected to the pontificate, and so has it been continued even till now, and will continue till the end of the world.

One of these pontiffs, who succeeded that St. Peter as lord of the world...made donation of these islands and mainland to the aforesaid king and queen [of Spain] and to their successors....

they want to come to Christ's sheepfold after their homes had been destroyed, their children imprisoned, their wives raped, their cities devastated, their maidens deflowered, and their provinces laid waste?" Las Casas and other outspoken missionaries softened few hearts among the encomenderos, but they did win some sympathy for the Indians from the Spanish monarchy and royal bureaucracy. Royal officials moved to abolish encomienda in an effort to replace swashbuckling old conquistadors with royal bureaucrats as the rulers of New Spain.

One of the most important blows to encomienda was the imposition in 1549 of a reform called the *repartimiento,* which limited the labor an

So their highnesses are kings and lords of these islands and mainland by virtue of this donation; and… almost all those to whom this has been notified, have received and served their highnesses, as lords and kings, in the way that subjects ought to do, with good will, without any resistance, immediately, without delay, when they were informed of the aforesaid facts. And also they received and obeyed the priests whom their highnesses sent to preach to them and to teach them our holy faith; and all these, of their own free will, without any reward or condition have become Christians, and are so, and the highnesses have joyfully and graciously received them, and they have also commanded them to be treated as their subjects and vassals; and you too are held and obliged to do the same. Wherefore, as best we can, we ask and require that you consider what we have said to you, and that you take the time that shall be necessary to understand and deliberate upon it, and that you acknowledge the Church as the ruler and superior of the whole world, and the high priest called Pope, and in his name the king and queen [of Spain] our lords, in his place, as superiors and lords and kings of these islands and this mainland by virtue of the said donation, and that you consent and permit that these religious fathers declare and preach to you….

If you do so…we…shall receive you in all love and charity, and shall leave you your wives and your children and your lands free without servitude, that you may do with them and with yourselves freely what you like and think best, and they shall not compel you to turn to Christians unless you yourselves, when informed of the truth, should wish to be converted to our holy Catholic faith.…And besides this, their highnesses award you many privileges and exemptions and will grant you many benefits.

But if you do not do this or if you maliciously delay in doing it, I certify to you that with the help of God we shall forcefully enter into your country and shall make war against you in all ways and manners that we can, and shall subject you to the yoke and obedience of the Church and of their highnesses; we shall take you and your wives and your children and shall make slaves of them, and as such shall sell and dispose of them as their highnesses may command; and we shall take away your goods and shall do to you all the harm and damage that we can, as to vassals who do not obey and refuse to receive their lord and resist and contradict him; and we protest that the deaths and losses which shall accrue from this are your fault, and not that of their highnesses, or ours, or of these soldiers who come with us.

Indians who heard the Requerimiento could not understand Spanish, of course. No native documents survive to record the Indians' thoughts upon hearing the Spaniards' official justification for conquest, even when it was translated into a language they recognized. But one conquistador reported that when the Requerimiento was translated for two chiefs in Colombia, they responded that if the pope gave the king so much territory that belonged to other people, "the Pope must have been drunk."

Source: Adapted from A. Helps and M. Oppenheim, eds., *The Spanish Conquest in America and Its Relation to the History of Slavery and to the Government of the Colonies,* 4 vols. (London and New York, 1900–1904), 1:264–67.

Questions for Analysis and Debate

1. How did the Requerimiento answer the criticisms of Montecino? According to the Requerimiento, why was conquest justified? What was the source of Indians' resistance to conquest?

2. What arguments might a critic like Montecino have used to respond to the Requerimiento's justification of conquest? What arguments might the Mexican leader Montezuma have made against those of the Requerimiento?

3. Was the Requerimiento a faithful expression or a cynical violation of Spaniards' Christian faith?

encomendero could command from his Indians to forty-five days per year from each adult male. The repartimiento, however, did not challenge the principle of forced labor, nor did it prevent encomenderos from continuing to mistreat their Indians. However, as the old encomenderos died, repartimiento slowly replaced encomienda as the basic system of exploiting Indian labor.

The practice of coerced labor in New Spain grew directly out of the Spaniards' assumption that they were superior to the Indians. As one missionary put it, the Indians "are incapable of learning.…The Indians are more stupid than asses and refuse to improve in anything." Therefore, most Spaniards assumed, Indians' labor should be organized by and for their

Testerian Catechism

After conquest, Catholic missiionaries tried to teach the Mexica the basic doctrines of Christianity by using pictures (pictographs) that resembled the symbols in preconquest Mexican codices (books composed of pictographs). Missionaries hoped to appeal to the Mexica's respect for the authority of the ancient texts. These Testerian catechisms demonstrate the missionaries' awareness that the Mexica often retained their faith in their preconquest gods. The catechism shown here incorporates symbols of both Christian and Mexican belief. Try to puzzle out the identity of the various figures and the meanings Catholic missionaries intended them to convey to the Mexica.

conquerors. Spaniards seldom hesitated to use violence to coerce Indians to work.

From the viewpoint of Spain, the single most important economic activity in New Spain after 1540 was silver mining. In the early decades of the century, Spain imported more New World gold than silver, but that changed with the discovery of major silver deposits at Potosí, Bolivia, in 1545 and Zacatecas, Mexico, in 1546. As these mines swung into large-scale production, an ever-growing stream of silver flowed from New Spain to Spain (Figure 2.1). Overall, exports of precious metals from New Spain during the sixteenth century were worth about twenty-five times more than hides, the next most important export. The mines required large capital investments and many miners. Typically, a few Spaniards supervised large groups of Indian miners, who were supplemented by African slaves later in the sixteenth century.

For Spaniards, life in New Spain was relatively easy. Only a few thousand Spaniards actually fought during the conquests. Although the riches they won fell far short of their expectations, the benefits of encomienda gave them a comfortable, leisurely life that was the envy of many Spaniards back in Europe. As one colonist wrote to his brother in Spain, "Don't hesitate [to come]....This land [New Spain] is as good as ours [in Spain], for God has given us more here than there, and we shall be better off."

During the century after 1492, about 225,000 Spaniards settled in the colonies. Virtually all of them were poor young men of common (non-noble) lineage who came directly from Spain. Laborers and **artisans** made up the largest proportion, but soldiers and sailors were also numerous. Throughout the sixteenth century, men vastly outnumbered women, although the proportion of women grew from about one in twenty before 1519 to one in three by the 1580s. The gender and number of Spanish settlers shaped two fundamental features of the society of New Spain. First, Europeans never made up more than 1 or 2 percent of the total population. Although Spaniards ruled New Spain, the population was almost wholly Indian. Second, the shortage of Spanish women meant that Spanish men frequently married Indian women or used them as concubines.

The tiny number of Spaniards, the masses of Indians, and the frequency of intermarriage created a steep social hierarchy defined by perceptions of national origin and race. Natives of Spain—*peninsulares* (people born on the Iberian Peninsula)—enjoyed highest social status in New Spain. Below them but still within the white elite were creoles, children born in the New World to Spanish men and Spanish women. Together, peninsulares and creoles made up barely 1 or 2 percent of the population. Below them on the social pyramid was a larger group of mestizos, the offspring of Spanish men and Indian women, who comprised 4 or 5 percent of the population. So many of the mestizos were born to unmarried parents that the term *mestizo* (after the Spanish word for "mixed") became almost synonymous with bastard in the sixteenth century. Some mestizos worked as artisans and labor overseers and lived well, and a few rose into the ranks of the elite, especially if their Indian ancestry was not obvious from their skin color. Most mestizos, however, were lumped with Indians, the enormous bottom mass of the population.

The society of New Spain established the precedent for what would become a pronounced pattern in the European colonies of the New World: a society stratified sharply by social origin and race. All Europeans of whatever social origin considered themselves superior to Native Americans; in New Spain, they were a dominant minority in both power and status.

The Toll of Spanish Conquest and Colonization

By 1560, the major centers of the Indians' civilization had been conquered, their leaders overthrown, their religion held in contempt, and their people forced to work for the Spaniards.

FIGURE 2.1 New World Gold and Silver Imported into Spain during the Sixteenth Century, in Pesos
Spain imported more gold than silver during the first three decades of the sixteenth century, but the total value of this treasure was quickly eclipsed during the 1530s and 1540s when rich silver mines were developed. Silver accounted for most of the enormous growth in Spain's precious-metal imports from the New World.

 = one million pesos

Español con India,
Mestizo.

Mestizo con Española,
Castizo.

Castizo con Española,
Español.

Español con Mora,
Mulato.

5

6

Mulato con Española,
Morisco.

Morisco con Española,
Chino.

7

Chino con India,
Salta atras.

Salta atras con Mulata,
Lobo.

Profound demoralization pervaded Indian society. As a Mexican poet wrote:

> Nothing but flowers and songs of sorrow
> are left in Mexico…
> where once we saw warriors and wise men.…
> We are crushed to the ground;
> we lie in ruins.
> There is nothing but grief and suffering
> in Mexico.

Adding to the culture shock of conquest and colonization was the deadly toll of European diseases. As conquest spread, Indians succumbed to virulent epidemics of measles, smallpox, and respiratory illnesses. Indians had built up no immunity to these diseases because they had not been exposed to them before the arrival of Europeans. By 1570, only a half century after Cortés entered Tenochtitlán, the Indian population of New Spain had fallen about 90 percent from what it was when Columbus arrived. The destruction of the Indian population was a catastrophe unequaled in human history. A Mayan Indian recalled that when sickness struck his village, "Great was the stench of the dead.…The dogs and vultures devoured the bodies. The mortality was terrible.…So it was that we became orphans.…We were born to die!" For most Indians, New Spain was a graveyard.

For Spaniards, Indian deaths meant that the most valuable resource of New Spain—Indian labor—dwindled. By the last quarter of the sixteenth century, Spanish colonists felt the pinch

Mixed Races
Residents of New Spain maintained a lively interest in each person's racial lineage. These eighteenth-century paintings illustrate forms of racial mixture common in the sixteenth century. In the first painting, a Spanish man and an Indian woman have a mestizo son; in the fourth, a Spanish man and a woman of African descent have a mulatto son; in the fifth, a Spanish woman and a mulatto man have a *morisco* daughter. The many racial permutations of parents led residents of New Spain to develop an elaborate vocabulary of ancestry. The child of a morisco and a Spaniard was a *chino;* the child of a chino and an Indian was a *salta abas;* the child of a salta abas and a mulatto was a *lobo;* and so on. Can you detect hints of some of the meanings of racial categories in the clothing depicted in these paintings?
Bob Schalkwijk / INAH.

FOR MORE HELP ANALYZING THIS IMAGE, see the visual activity for this chapter in the Online Study Guide at bedfordstmartins.com/roarkcompact.

of a labor shortage. To help redress the need for laborers, the colonists began to import African slaves. Some Africans had come to Mexico with the conquistadors. In the years before 1550 while Indian labor was still adequate, only 15,000 slaves were imported from Africa. Even after Indian labor began to decline, the relatively high cost of African slaves kept imports low, approximately 36,000 from 1550 to the end of the century. During the sixteenth century, New Spain continued to rely primarily on a diminishing number of Indians.

Spanish Outposts in Florida and New Mexico

After the explorations of de Soto, Coronado, and Cabrillo, officials in New Spain lost interest in America north of Mexico. The monarchy claimed that Spain owned all of North America and insisted that a few settlements be established in the northernmost borderlands of New Spain to give some tangible reality to its claims. Settlements in Florida would have the additional benefit of protecting Spanish ships from enemy ships that lurked along the southeastern coast to prey upon the Spanish treasure fleet sailing from Spanish colonies to Spain.

In 1565, the Spanish king sent Pedro Menéndez de Avilés to create settlements along the Atlantic coast of North America. In early September, Menéndez founded St. Augustine in Florida, the first permanent European settlement within what became the United States. By 1600, St. Augustine had a population of about five hundred, the remaining Spanish beachhead on the vast Atlantic shoreline of North America.

More than sixteen hundred miles west of St. Augustine, Spaniards founded another outpost in 1598. Juan de Oñate led an expedition of about five hundred people to settle northern Mexico, now called New Mexico, and claim the booty rumored to exist there. When Oñate and his companions reached pueblos near present-day Albuquerque and Santa Fe, he met with the pueblos' leaders and received their oath of loyalty to the Spanish king and the Christian God. Oñate sent out scouting parties to find the legendary treasures of the region and to locate the ocean, which he believed must be nearby. Meanwhile, relations with the Indians deteriorated. When the Acoma pueblo revolted against the Spaniards in 1599, Oñate ruthlessly suppressed the uprising, killing 800 Indians. Although

Catholic Feather Mosaic
In sixteenth-century Europe, Catholic churches conveyed religious messages in paintings, sculptures, and stained glass. The visual images both dramatized Christian stories and made religious doctrines accessible to the majority of Europeans who could not read. This feather mosaic produced by Mexican craftsmen in 1539 had a similar purpose. It follows European Christians' example of portraying a major event in Christian faith—Christ's resurrection after his death on the cross—in the distinctively Mexican medium of a mosaic of feathers collected from New World birds. Can you detect any other hints that the mosaic was designed to be understood by the Mexica?
The Mass of St. Gregory, 1539, feather mosaic, Auch, Musée des Jacobins, France (Gers).

Oñate reconfirmed the Spaniards' military superiority, he did not bring peace or stability to the region. After a second pueblo revolt occurred in 1599, many of Oñate's settlers returned to Mexico, leaving New Mexico as a small, dusty assertion of Spanish claims to the North American Southwest.

REVIEW Why did New Spain develop a society highly stratified by race and national origin?

A Sign of Conquest

This skull of an Indian man in his fifties was recently excavated from the site of a Native American village in southwestern Georgia visited by de Soto's expedition in 1540.
The skull shows that the man suffered a fatal sword
wound above his right eye. Combined with slashed and
severed arm and leg bones from the same site, the skull
demonstrates the brutality de Soto employed against
indigenous peoples on his voyage through the Southeast.
No native weapons could have inflicted the wounds in-
delibly left on this skull and the other bones.
Robert L. Blakely.

African Slaves Mining Gold

This sixteenth-century illustration depicts African slaves mining gold in New Spain.
Spaniards imported African slaves in substantial numbers after the Native American population had been decimated by conquest and disease. Here, the two slaves
on the right dig ore, from which the gold is separated by the slave in the center
and then washed in hot water over the fire. The clean nuggets are then given to
the Spaniard, who carefully weighs and saves them. How did the artist emphasize
the differences between the Spaniard and the slaves? Is it possible to detect the
artist's point of view about who was more "civilized"?
The Pierpont Morgan Library, New York. MA 3900, f.100.

The New World and Sixteenth-Century Europe

The riches of New Spain helped make the
sixteenth century the Golden Age of Spain. After
the deaths of Queen Isabella and King
Ferdinand, their sixteen-year-old grandson
became King Charles I of Spain in 1516. Three
years later, just as Cortés ventured into Mexico,
Charles I used judicious bribes to secure his
selection as Holy Roman Emperor Charles V. His
empire encompassed more than that of any other
European monarch. He used the wealth of New
Spain to protect his sprawling empire and to
defend orthodox Christianity from the insurgent
heresy of the **Protestant Reformation**. Spain's
power in sixteenth-century Europe spread the
message that a New World empire could bankroll
Old World ambitions.

The Protestant Reformation and the European Order

In 1517, Martin Luther, an obscure Catholic
priest in central Germany, initiated the
Protestant Reformation by publicizing his criticisms of the Catholic Church. Luther's ideas
won the sympathy of many Catholics, but they
were considered extremely dangerous by church
officials and monarchs like Charles V who
believed with total conviction that, just as the
church spoke for God, they ruled for God.

Luther preached a doctrine known as *justification by faith*: Individual Christians could obtain salvation and life everlasting only by having faith that God would save them. Giving offerings to the church, following the orders of priests, or participating in church rituals would not put believers one step closer to heaven. The only true source of information about God's will was the Bible, not the church. By reading the Bible, any Christian could learn as much about God's commandments as any priest. Indeed, Luther called for a "priesthood of all believers."

In effect, Luther charged that the Catholic Church was in many respects fraudulent. Luther insisted that priests were not necessary for salvation and that they encouraged Christians to violate God's will by promoting religious practices not specifically commanded by the Bible. The church, Luther declared, had neglected its true purpose of helping individual Christians understand the spiritual realm revealed in the Bible and had wasted its resources in worldly conflicts of politics and wars. Luther hoped his ideas would reform the Catholic Church, but instead they ruptured forever the unity of Christianity in western Europe.

Charles V pledged to exterminate Luther's **Protestant** heresies. The wealth pouring into Spain from the New World fueled his efforts to defend orthodox Catholic faith against Protestants as well as against Muslims in eastern Europe and any other nation bold enough to contest Spain's supremacy. As the wealthiest and most powerful monarch in Europe, Charles V, followed by his son and successor, Philip II, assumed responsibility for upholding the existing order of sixteenth-century Europe.

New World Treasure and Spanish Ambitions

Both Charles V and Philip II fought wars throughout the world during the sixteenth century. Mexican silver funneled through the royal treasury into the hands of military suppliers, soldiers, and sailors wherever Spain's forces fought. New World treasure was dissipated in military adventures that served the goals of the monarchy but did very little to benefit the average Spaniard.

In a sense, New World wealth made the Spanish monarchy too rich and too powerful among the states of Europe since it fueled grandiose Spanish ambitions. The ambitions of Charles V and Philip II were so great that the expenses of constant warfare far outstripped the revenues arriving from New Spain. To help meet military expenditures, both kings raised taxes in Spain more than fivefold during the sixteenth century. Since the nobility, by far the wealthiest class, was exempt from taxation, the burdensome new taxes fell mostly on poor peasants. The ambitions of the monarchy impoverished the vast majority of Spain's population and brought the nation to the brink of bankruptcy. When taxes proved insufficient, the monarchy borrowed heavily from European bankers. By the end of the sixteenth century, interest payments on royal debts swallowed two-thirds of the crown's annual revenues. In retrospect, the riches from New Spain proved a short-term blessing but a long-term curse.

But sixteenth-century Spaniards did not see it that way. As they looked at their accomplishments in the New World, they saw unmistakable signs of progress. They had added enormously to their knowledge and wealth. They had built mines, cities, Catholic churches, and even universities on the other side of the Atlantic. Their military, religious, and economic achievements gave them great pride and confidence.

Europe and the Spanish Example

The lessons of sixteenth-century Spain were not lost on Spain's European rivals. Spain proudly displayed the fruits of its New World conquests. In 1520, for example, Charles V exhibited some of the gifts Montezuma had given to Cortés. The objects astonished the German artist Albrecht Dürer, who wrote in his diary that he "marveled over the subtle ingenuity of the men in these distant lands" who created such "things which were brought to the King…[such as] a sun entirely of gold, a whole fathom [six feet] broad." But the most exciting news about "the men in these distant lands" was that they could serve the interests of Europeans as Spain had shown. With a few notable exceptions, Europeans saw the New World as a place for the expansion of European influence, a place where, as one Spaniard wrote, Europeans could "give to those strange lands the form of our own."

France and England tried to follow Spain's example. Both nations warred with Spain in Europe, preyed on Spanish treasure fleets, and ventured to the New World, where they too hoped to find an undiscovered passageway to the East Indies or another Mexico or Peru.

Algonquian Ceremonial Dance
When the English artist John White visited the coast of present-day North Carolina in 1585 as part of
Raleigh's expedition, he painted this watercolor portrait of an Algonquian ceremonial dance. This and
White's other portraits are the only surviving likenesses of sixteenth-century North American Indians
that were drawn from direct observation in the New World. White's portrait captures the individuality
of these Indians' appearances and gestures while depicting a ceremony that must have appeared
bizarre and alien to a sixteenth-century Englishman. The significance of this ceremonial dance is still a
mystery, although the portrait's obvious signs of order, organization, and collective understanding show
that the dancing Indians knew what it meant.
Copyright © The British Museum.

In 1524, France sent Giovanni da Verrazano to scout the Atlantic coast of North America from North Carolina to Canada, looking for a Northwest Passage (see Map 2.2). Eleven years later, France probed farther north with Jacques Cartier's voyage up the St. Lawrence River. Encouraged, Cartier returned to the region with a group of settlers in 1541, but the colony they established—like the search for a Northwest Passage—came to nothing.

English attempts to follow Spain's lead were slower but equally ill fated. Not until 1576, almost eighty years after John Cabot's voyages, did the English try again to find a Northwest Passage. This time Martin Frobisher sailed into the frigid waters of northern Canada. His sponsor was the Cathay Company, which hoped to open trade with China (see Map 2.2). Like many other explorers who preceded and followed him, Frobisher was mesmerized by the Spanish example and was sure he had found gold. But the tons of "ore" he hauled back to England proved worthless, the Cathay Company collapsed, and English interests shifted southward.

English explorers' attempts to establish North American settlements were no more fruitful than their search for a northern route to China. Sir Humphrey Gilbert led expeditions in 1578 and 1583 that made feeble efforts to found colonies in Newfoundland until Gilbert vanished at sea. Sir

Walter Raleigh organized an expedition in 1585 to settle Roanoke Island off the coast of present-day North Carolina. The first group of explorers left no colonists on the island, but two years later Raleigh sent a contingent of more than one hundred settlers to Roanoke under John White's leadership. White returned to England for supplies, and when he came back to Roanoke in 1590, the colonists had disappeared, leaving only the word *Croatoan* (whose meaning is unknown) carved on a tree. The Roanoke colonists most likely died from a combination of natural causes and unfriendly Indians. By the end of the century, England had failed to secure a New World beachhead.

Roanoke Settlement, 1585–1590

REVIEW   How did Spain's conquests in the New World shape Spanish influence in Europe?

Conclusion: The Promise of the New World for Europeans

The sixteenth century in the New World belonged to the Spaniards who employed Columbus and to the Indians who greeted him as he stepped ashore. Spaniards initiated the Columbian exchange between the New World and the Old that continues to this day. The exchange subjected Native Americans to the ravages of European diseases and Spanish conquest. Spanish explorers, conquistadors, and colonists forced Indians to serve the interests of Spanish settlers and the Spanish monarchy. The exchange illustrated one of the most important lessons of the sixteenth century: After millions of years, the Atlantic no longer was an impermeable barrier separating the Eastern and Western Hemispheres. After the voyages of Columbus, European sailing ships regularly bridged the Atlantic and carried people, products, diseases, and ideas from one shore to the other.

No European monarch could forget the seductive lesson taught by Spain's example: The New World could vastly enrich the Old.

Spain remained a New World power for almost four centuries, and its language, religion, culture, and institutions left a permanent imprint. By the end of the sixteenth century, however, other European monarchies had begun to contest Spain's dominion in Europe and to make forays into the northern fringes of Spain's New World preserve. To reap the benefits Spaniards enjoyed from their New World domain, other Europeans had to learn a difficult lesson: how to deviate from Spain's example. That discovery lay ahead.

Suggestions for Further Reading

Álvar Núñez Cabeza de Vaca, *Adventures in the Unknown Interior of America* (1993, and many other editions). A riveting account by a sixteenth-century Spaniard shipwrecked on the Gulf Coast who lived among Native Americans for years before returning to New Spain.

John L. Kessell, *Spain in the Southwest: A Narrative History of Colonial New Mexico, Arizona, Texas, and California* (2002). The story of the long legacy of New Spain in what is now the Southwest of the United States.

Diarmaid MacCulloch, *The Reformation: A History* (2004). A sweeping, authoritative overview of the historic rupture of Christianity.

Hugh Thomas, *Conquest: Montezuma, Cortés, and the Fall of Old Mexico* (2002). The amazing history of the conquest of Mexico.

Hugh Thomas, *Rivers of Gold: The Rise of the Spanish Empire from Columbus to Magellan* (2004). The fascinating history of the Spanish explorations that forged the connections between the Old and the New Worlds.

► FOR MORE BOOKS ABOUT TOPICS IN THIS CHAPTER, see the Online Bibliography at bedfordstmartins.com/roarkcompact.

► FOR ADDITIONAL FIRSTHAND ACCOUNTS OF THIS PERIOD, see Chapter 2 in Michael Johnson, ed., *Reading the American Past,* Third Edition.

► FOR WEB SITES AND DOCUMENTS RELATED TO TOPICS AND PLACES IN THIS CHAPTER, see "HistoryLinks," "DocLinks," and "PlaceLinks" at bedfordstmartins.com/roarkcompact.

REVIEWING THE CHAPTER

Follow these steps to review and strengthen your understanding of the chapter.

STEP 1: *Study the* **Key Terms** *and* **Timeline** *to identify the significance of each item listed.*

STEP 2: *Answer the* **Review Questions,** *drawing on key terms and dates to support your answers.*

STEP 3: *Drawing on the Key Terms, Timeline, and Review Questions, answer the broader* **Making Connections** *questions.*

KEY TERMS

Who

Christopher Columbus (p. 27)
Tainos (p. 27)
Prince Henry the Navigator (p. 31)
Vasco de Gama (p. 31)
John Cabot (p. 33)
Amerigo Vespucci (p. 34)
Martin Waldseemüller (p. 34)
Ferdinand Magellan (p. 34)
Hernán Cortés (p. 35)
Malinali (p. 36)
Montezuma (p. 36)
Mexica (p. 36)
Tlaxcalans (p. 36)
Francisco Pizarro (p. 37)
Atahualpa (p. 37)
Hernando de Soto (p. 37)
Francisco Vásquez de Coronado (p. 37)
Juan Rodríguez Cabrillo (p. 38)

Bartolomé de Las Casas (p. 39)
Juan de Oñate (p. 45)
Holy Roman Emperor Charles V (King Charles I of Spain) (p. 46)
Martin Luther (p. 46)
Philip II (p. 47)
Jacques Cartier (p. 48)
Martin Frobisher (p. 48)
Sir Walter Raleigh (p. 49)
John White (p. 49)

What

bubonic plague (p. 29)
the Reconquest (p. 30)
caravel (p. 31)
Treaty of Tordesillas (p. 32)
Northwest Passage (p. 33)
Columbian exchange (p. 34)
conquistador (p. 35)

conquest of Tenochtitlán (p. 36)
Incan empire (p. 37)
San Miguel de Gualdape (p. 37)
Seven Cities of Cíbola (p. 37)
New Spain (p. 38)
royal fifth (p. 38)
encomienda (p. 38)
repartimiento (p. 40)
Potosí, Bolivia (p. 42)
Zacatecas, Mexico (p. 42)
peninsulares (p. 43)
creoles (p. 43)
mestizos (p. 43)
St. Augustine (p. 45)
Acoma pueblo revolt (p. 45)
Protestant Reformation (p. 46)
justification by faith (p. 47)
Roanoke Island (p. 49)

TIMELINE

NOTE: Events are depicted chronologically, but the passage of time is not to exact scale.

◀ **1480** • Portuguese ships reach Congo.

1488 • Bartolomeu Dias rounds Cape of Good Hope.

1492 • Christopher Columbus lands on Caribbean island that he names San Salvador.

1493 • Columbus makes second voyage to New World.

1494 • Portugal and Spain negotiate Treaty of Tordesillas.

1497 • John Cabot searches for Northwest Passage.

1498 • Columbus makes third voyage to New World.
• Vasco da Gama sails to India.

1502 • Columbus makes fourth voyage to New World.

1513 • Vasco Núñez de Balboa crosses isthmus of Panama.

1517 • Protestant Reformation begins in Germany.

1519 • Hernán Cortés leads expedition to find wealth in Mexico.
• Ferdinand Magellan sets out to sail around the world.

1520 • Mexica in Tenochtitlán revolt against Spaniards.

1521 • Cortés conquers the Mexica at Tenochtitlán.

REVIEW QUESTIONS

1. Why did European exploration expand dramatically in the fifteenth century? (pp. 28–31)

2. How did Columbus's landfall in the Caribbean help revolutionize Europeans' understanding of world geography? (pp. 31–34)

3. Why did New Spain develop a society highly stratified by race and national origin? (pp. 34–45)

4. How did Spain's conquests in the New World shape Spanish influence in Europe? (pp. 46–49)

MAKING CONNECTIONS

1. The Columbian exchange exposed people on both sides of the Atlantic to surprising new people and goods. It also produced dramatic demographic and political transformations in the Old World and the New. How did the Columbian exchange lead to redistributions of power and population? Discuss these changes, being sure to cite examples from both contexts.

2. Despite inferior numbers, the Spaniards were able to conquer the Mexica and maintain control of the colonial hierarchy that followed. Why did the Spanish conquest of the Mexica succeed, and how did the Spaniards govern the conquered territory to maintain their dominance?

3. Spanish conquest in North America brought new peoples into constant contact. How did Spaniards' and Indians' perceptions of each other shape their interactions? In your answer, cite specific examples and consider how perceptions changed over time.

4. How did the astonishing wealth generated for the Spanish crown by its conquest of the New World influence European colonial exploration throughout the sixteenth century? In your answer, discuss the ways in which it both encouraged and limited interest in exploration.

▶ FOR PRACTICE QUIZZES, A CUSTOMIZED STUDY PLAN, AND OTHER STUDY TOOLS, see the Online Study Guide at bedfordstmartins.com/roarkcompact.

1532 • Francisco Pizarro begins conquest of Peru.

   1535 • Jacques Cartier explores St. Lawrence River.

      1539 • Hernando de Soto explores southeastern North America.

         1540 • Francisco Vásquez de Coronado starts to explore the Southwest and Great Plains.

           1542 • Juan Rodríguez Cabrillo explores California coast.

              1549 • *Repartimiento* reforms begin to replace *encomienda*.

                  1565 • St. Augustine, Florida, settled.

                        1576 • Martin Frobisher explores areas of northern Canadian waters.

                            1587 • English settle Roanoke Island.

                              1598
                                • Juan de Oñate explores New Mexico.

                              1599
                                • Pueblos revolt against Oñate.

ALGONQUIAN POUCH

This pouch belonged to an important Algonquian Indian, possibly even the chief Powhatan, whose people inhabited the region first settled by the Virginia colonists. One or more Algonquian women probably made the pouch. Dangling from each end are two arrow-shaped pendants decorated with nearly 6,000 beads made from shells collected from Virginia's beaches. Algonquians—again, probably women— cut beads from the shells and punctured each bead, creating a tiny hole through which they threaded sinew interwoven with strips of deer hide to make the elaborate beaded design. Only a powerful Algonquian dignitary could command the labor and materials necessary to produce such a pouch. In turn, the pouch signaled the dignitary's importance when he wore it. The wearer draped the pouch over a belt that passed through the fold at the top. The opening to the pouch is on the inside of the fold and not visible here. The wearer probably used the pouch to carry tobacco and ritualistic objects that symbolized his authority. Most likely, however, the main function of the pouch was to dazzle ordinary Algonquians with the wearer's magnificence.

Ashmolean Museum, Oxford, England.

3

The Southern Colonies in the Seventeenth Century

1601–1700

I N DECEMBER 1607, barely six months after arriving at Jamestown with the first English colonists, Captain John Smith was captured by warriors of Powhatan, the supreme chief of about fourteen thousand Algonquian people who inhabited the coastal plain of present-day Virginia, near the Chesapeake Bay. According to Smith, Powhatan "feasted him after their best barbarous manner." Then, Smith recalled, "two great stones were brought before Powhatan: then as many [Indians] as could layd hands on [Smith], dragged him to [the stones], and thereon laid his head, and being ready with their clubs, to beate out his braines." At that moment, Pocahontas, Powhatan's eleven-year-old daughter, rushed forward and "got [Smith's] head in her armes, and laid her owne upon his to save him from death." Pocahontas, Smith wrote, "hazarded the beating out of her owne braines to save mine, and…so prevailed with her father, that I was safely conducted [back] to James towne."

This romantic story of an Indian maiden rescuing a white soldier and saving Jamestown and ultimately English colonization of North America has been enshrined in the writing of American history since 1624 when Smith published his *Generall Historie of Virginia*. Historians believe that this episode happened more or less as Smith described it. But Smith did not understand why Pocahontas acted as she did. Many commentators have claimed that her love for Smith caused her to rebel against her father's authority. Pocahontas herself left no document that explains her motives; most likely, she could not write. Everything known about her comes from the pens of Smith or other Englishmen. When their writings are considered in the context of what is known about the Algonquian society Pocahontas was born into, her actions appear in an entirely different light.

Most likely, what Smith interpreted as Pocahontas's saving him from certain death was instead a ceremonial enactment of Powhatan's willingness to incorporate Smith and the white strangers at Jamestown into Powhatan's empire. The ceremony displayed Powhatan's power of life or death over a subordinate chief—Smith—and Powhatan's willingness to give protection to those who acknowledged his supremacy—in this case, the interlopers at Jamestown. By appearing to save Smith, Pocahontas was probably acting out Smith's new status as an adopted member of Powhatan's extended family. Rather than a rebellious, love-struck girl, Pocahontas was almost certainly a dutiful daughter playing the part prescribed for her by her father and her culture.

Smith went back to England about two years after the adoption ritual. In the meantime, Pocahontas frequently visited the English settlement and often brought gifts of food to the colonists from her father. Powhatan routinely attached his sons and daughters to subordinate tribes as an expression of his protection and his dominance. It appears that Pocahontas's attachment to the English colonists grew out of Powhatan's attempt to treat the tribe of white strangers at Jamestown as he did other tribes in his empire, an attempt that failed.

Pocahontas in England

Shortly after Pocahontas and her husband John Rolfe arrived in England in 1616, an engraver made this portrait of her dressed in English clothing suitable for a princess. The portrait captures the dual novelty of England for Pocahontas and of Pocahontas for the English. Ornate, courtly clothing probably signified to English observers that Pocahontas was royalty and to Pocahontas that the English were accepting her as befitted the "Emperor" Powhatan's daughter. The mutability of Pocahontas's identity is displayed in the engraving's identification of her as "Matoaka" or "Rebecca."

Library of Congress.

In 1613, after relations between Powhatan and the English colonists had deteriorated into bloody raids by both parties, the colonists captured Pocahontas and held her hostage at Jamestown. Within a year she converted to Christianity and married one of the colonists, a widower named John Rolfe. After giving birth to a son named Thomas, Pocahontas, her husband, and the new baby sailed for England in the spring of 1616. When John Smith heard that Pocahontas was in London, he went to see her. According to Smith, Pocahontas said, "You did promise Powhatan what was yours should bee his, and he the like to you; you called him father, being in his land a stranger, and by the same reason so must I doe you." It seems likely that Pocahontas believed her incorporation into English society was a counterpart of the adoption ritual Powhatan had staged for John Smith in Virginia back in 1607.

Pocahontas died in England in 1617. Her son, Thomas, ultimately returned to Virginia, and by the time of the American Revolution his descendants numbered in the hundreds. But the world Thomas Rolfe and his descendants inhabited was shaped by a reversal of the power ritualized when his mother "saved" John Smith. By the end of the seventeenth century, Native Americans no longer dominated the newcomers who arrived in the Chesapeake with John Smith.

During the seventeenth century, English colonists learned how to deviate from the example of New Spain (see chapter 2) by growing tobacco, a crop Native Americans had cultivated in small quantities for centuries. The new settlers, however, grew enormous quantities of tobacco and exported most of it to England. Instead of incorporating Powhatan's people into their new society, the settlers encroached on Indian lands and they built new societies on the foundation of tobacco agriculture and transatlantic trade.

To produce large crop surpluses for export required hard labor and people who were willing—or could be forced—to do it. For the most part, Native Americans refused to be conscripted into the colonists' fields. Instead, the settlers depended on the labor of family members, **indentured servants**, and—by the last third of the seventeenth century—African slaves. By the end of the century, the southern colonies had become sharply different both from the world dominated by Powhatan when the Jamestown settlers first arrived and from contemporary English society. In ways unimaginable to Powhatan, Pocahontas, and John Smith, the colonists paid homage to the international market and the English monarch by working mightily to make a good living growing crops for sale to the Old World.

An English Colony on the Chesapeake

When James I became king of England in 1603, he eyed North America as a possible location for English colonies that could supply profits similar to those Spanish colonies sent to Spain. In 1606, London investors organized the Virginia Company, a joint stock company that received from King James a grant of over six million acres in North America. In effect, the king's **land grant** was a royal license to poach on both Spanish claims and Powhatan's chiefdom.

The Virginia Company investors hoped to found an empire that would strengthen England both overseas and at home. Richard Hakluyt, a strong proponent of **colonization**, claimed that a colony would provide work for swarms of poor "valiant youths rusting and hurtfull by lack of employment" in England. Colonists could buy English goods and make products that England now had to import from other nations. Enthusiastic reports from explorers claimed that in Virginia "the earth bringeth foorth all things in aboundance ...without toile or labour." Maybe a valuable crop could be grown or perhaps rich lodes of gold and silver awaited discovery, as they had in New Spain. Such hopes failed to grapple with the difficulties of adapting European desires and expectations to the New World, already inhabited by Native Americans. Within two decades, the Jamestown settlement managed to survive, but royal government replaced the private Virginia Company, which never earned a penny for its investors.

The Fragile Jamestown Settlement

In December 1606, the ships *Susan Constant, Discovery,* and *Godspeed* carried 144 Englishmen toward Virginia. They arrived at the mouth of the Chesapeake Bay on April 26, 1607. That night while the colonists rested on shore, one of them later recalled, a band of Indians "creeping upon all foure, from the Hills like Beares, with their Bowes in their mouthes," attacked and dangerously wounded two men. The attack gave the colonists an early warning that the North American wilderness was not quite the paradise

Secotan Village

This engraving, published in 1612, was copied from an original drawing John White made in 1585 when he visited the village of Secotan on the coast of North Carolina. The drawing provides a schematic view of daily life in the village, which may have resembled one of Powhatan's settlements. White noted on the original that the fire burning behind the line of crouching men was "the place of solemne prayer." The large building in the lower left was a tomb where the bodies of important leaders were kept. Dwellings similar to those illustrated on John Smith's map of Virginia (see page 56) lined a central space, where men and women ate. Corn is growing in the fields along the right side of the village. The engraver included hunters shooting deer at the upper left. Hunting was probably never so convenient—no such hunters or deer appear in White's original drawing. This drawing conveys the message that Secotan was orderly, settled, religious, harmonious, and peaceful (notice the absence of fortifications), and very different from English villages.

Princeton University Libraries, Department of Rare Books and Special Collections.

FOR MORE HELP ANALYZING THIS IMAGE, see the visual activity for this chapter in the Online Study Guide at **bedfordstmartins.com/roarkcompact.**

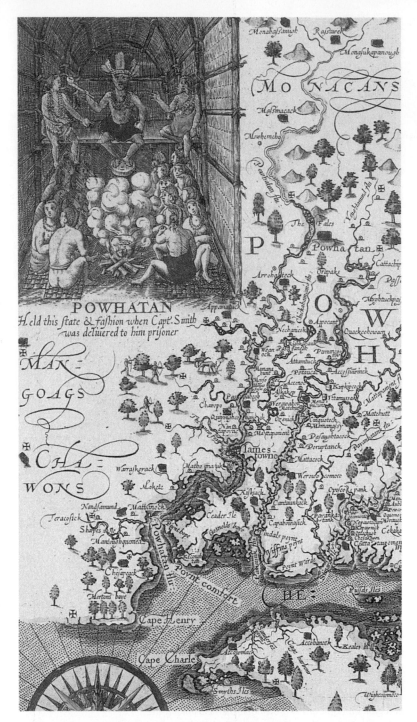

John Smith's Map of Virginia

In 1612, John Smith published a detailed map that showed not only geographic features of early Virginia but also the limits of exploration (indicated by small crosses), the locations of the houses of the Indian "kings" (indicated by red boxes), and "ordinary houses" of indigenous people (indicated by dots). The map shows the early settlers' intense interest in knowing where the Indians were—and were not. Notice the location of Jamestown (upriver from Point Comfort) and of Powhatan's residence at the falls (just to the right of the large *P* outside the hut on the upper left side). The drawing of Powhatan surrounded by some of his many wives was almost certainly made by an English artist who had never been to Virginia or seen Powhatan but tried to imagine the scene as described by John Smith.

Princeton University Libraries, Department of Rare Books and Special Collections.

described by the Virginia Company's publications in England. A few weeks later they went ashore on a small peninsula in the midst of Powhatan's chiefdom. With the memory of their first night in America fresh in their minds, they quickly built a fort, the first building in the settlement they named Jamestown.

The Jamestown fort showed the colonists' awareness that they needed to protect themselves from Indians and Spaniards. Spain employed spies to stay informed about the new English colony. Spain planned to wipe out Jamestown when the time was ripe, but that time never came. Powhatan's people defended Virginia as their own. The settlers and Powhatan's warriors skirmished repeatedly. English muskets and cannon repelled Indian attacks on Jamestown, but the Indians' superior numbers and knowledge of the Virginia wilderness made it risky for the settlers to venture far beyond the peninsula. Late in June 1607, Powhatan sensed a stalemate and made peace overtures.

The settlers soon confronted dangerous, invisible threats: disease and starvation. During the summer, many of the Englishmen lay "night and day groaning in every corner of the Fort most pittiful to heare," wrote George Percy, one of the settlers. The colonists increased their misery by bickering among themselves, leaving crops unplanted and food supplies shrinking. "For the most part [the settlers] died of meere famine," Percy wrote; "there were never Englishmen left in a forreigne Countrey in such miserie as wee were in this new discovered Virginia."

Powhatan's people came to the rescue of the weakened and demoralized Englishmen. Early in September 1607, they began to bring corn to the colony for barter. When that was insufficient to keep the colonists fed, the settlers sent Captain John Smith to trade (and plunder) for corn with Indians upriver from Jamestown. His efforts managed to keep 38 of the original settlers alive until a fresh supply of food and 120 more colonists arrived from England in January 1608.

It is difficult to exaggerate the fragility of the early Jamestown settlement. Although the Virginia Company sent hundreds of new settlers to Jamestown each year, few survived. During the "starving time" winter of 1609–10, food became so short that one or two famished settlers resorted to eating their recently deceased neighbors. The Virginia Company continued to pour people into the colony, promising in a 1609 pamphlet that "the place will make them rich." But most settlers went instead to an early grave.

Cooperation and Conflict between Natives and Newcomers

Powhatan's people stayed in contact with the English settlers but maintained their distance. The Virginia Company boasted that the settlers bought from the Indians "the pearles of earth [corn] and [sold] to them the pearles of heaven [Christianity]." In fact, few Indians converted to Christianity, and the English devoted scant effort to proselytizing. Marriage between Indian women and English men was also rare, despite the acute shortage of English women in Virginia in the early years.

Powhatan's people regarded the English with suspicion, for good reasons. While the settlers often made friendly overtures to the Indians, they did not hesitate to use their guns and swords to enforce English notions of proper Indian behavior. More than once the Indians refused to trade their corn to the settlers, evidently hoping to starve them out. Each time the English broke the boycott by attacking the uncooperative Indians, pillaging their villages, and confiscating their corn.

Powhatan's people retaliated against English violence, but for fifteen years they did not organize an all-out assault on the European intruders, probably for several reasons. Although Christianity held few attractions for the Indians, the power of the settlers' God impressed them. One chief told John Smith that "he did believe that our [English] God as much exceeded theirs as our guns did their bows and arrows." Powhatan probably concluded that these powerful strangers would make better allies than enemies. As allies, the English strengthened Powhatan's dominance over the tribes in the region. They also traded with his people, usually exchanging European goods for corn. Native Virginians had some copper weapons and tools before the English arrived, but they quickly recognized the superiority of the intruders' iron and steel knives, axes, and pots and traded eagerly to obtain them.

The trade that supplied Indians with European conveniences provided English settlers with a necessity: food. But why did the settlers prove unable to feed themselves for more than a decade? First, as the staggering death rate suggests, many settlers were too sick to be productive members of the colony. Second, very few farmers came to Virginia in the early years. Instead, most of the newcomers were gentlemen and their servants, men who, in John Smith's words, "never did know what a day's work was." Smith declared repeatedly that in Virginia "there is no country to pillage [as in New Spain]…all you can expect from [Virginia] must be by labor." For years, however, colonists clung to English notions that gentlemen should not work with their hands and tradesmen should work only in trades for which they had been trained, ideas about labor that made more sense in labor-rich England than in labor-poor Virginia. In the meantime, the colonists depended on the Indians' corn for food.

Powhatan died in 1618, and his brother Opechancanough replaced him as supreme chief. In 1622, Opechancanough organized an all-out assault on the English settlers. Striking on March 22, the Indians killed nearly a third of the English population. But the attack failed to dislodge the colonists. In the aftermath, the settlers unleashed a murderous campaign of Indian extermination that in a few years pushed Indians beyond the small circumference of white settlement. Before 1622, the settlers knew that the Indians, though dangerous, were necessary to keep the colony alive. After 1622, most colonists considered Indians their perpetual enemies.

From Private Company to Royal Government

The 1622 uprising prompted a royal investigation of affairs in Virginia. The investigators discovered that the appalling mortality among the colonists was caused more by disease and mismanagement than by Indian raids. In 1624, King James revoked the charter of the Virginia Company and made Virginia a royal colony, subject to the direction of the royal government rather than to the company's private investors, an arrangement that lasted until 1776.

Wolf Head Pendant
A Susquehanna man probably wore this pendant suspended from the deer hide necklace (dyed red) extending from the back of the wolf head. The Native American who made the pendant in the mid-seventeenth century took the jawbone and teeth of a wolf and skillfully stitched them into a head shaped from deer hide stuffed with deer hair, taking care to display the wolf's menacing teeth. Inside the wolf's jaws, the maker sewed a realistic tongue (not visible in the picture) made of blue cloth obtained in trade with European colonists. Whether a wolf's tongue crafted from a European textile conveyed Susquehanna interpretation of words spoken by Europeans is unknown.
Courtesy, Skokloster Castle, Uppland, Sweden.

Advertisement for Jamestown Settlers
While Virginia imported thousands of indentured servants to labor in tobacco fields, the colony advertised in 1631 for settlers like those pictured here. The notice features men and women equally, although men heavily outnumbered women among actual newcomers to the Chesapeake. How would the English experiences of the individuals portrayed in the advertisement be useful in Virginia? Why would such individuals want to leave England and go to Virginia? If indentured servants were pictured, how might they differ in appearance from these people?
Harvard Map Collection, Pusey Library, Harvard University.

The king now appointed the governor of Virginia and his council, but most other features of local government established under the Virginia Company remained intact. In 1619, for example, the company had inaugurated the House of Burgesses, an assembly of representatives (called burgesses) elected by the colony's inhabitants. Under the new royal government, laws passed by the burgesses had to be approved by the king's bureaucrats in England rather than by the company. Otherwise, the House of Burgesses continued as before, acquiring distinction as the oldest representative legislative assembly in the British colonies.

The demise of the Virginia Company marked the end of the first phase of colonization of the Chesapeake region. From the first 105 adventurers in 1607, the population had grown to about 1,200 by 1624. Despite mortality rates higher than during the worst epidemics in London, new settlers still came. Their arrival and King James's willingness to take over the struggling colony reflected a fundamental change in Virginia. After years of fruitless experimentation, it was becoming clear that English settlers could make a fortune in Virginia by growing tobacco.

> **REVIEW**   Why did Powhatan pursue largely peaceful relations with the Jamestown settlement?

A Tobacco Society

Tobacco grew wild in the New World, and Native Americans used it for thousands of years before Europeans arrived. During the sixteenth century, Spanish colonists in the New World sent tobacco to Europe, where it was an expensive luxury used sparingly by a few. During the next century, English colonists in North America sent so much tobacco to European markets that it became an affordable indulgence used often by many people. (See "Beyond America's Borders," page 60.)

John Rolfe—Pocahontas's husband-to-be—planted West Indian tobacco seeds in 1612 and learned that they flourished in Virginia. By 1617, the colonists had grown enough tobacco to send the first commercial shipment to England, where it sold for a high price. After that, Virginia pivoted from a colony of rather aimless adventurers into a society of dedicated tobacco **planters**.

Dedicated they were. By 1700, nearly 100,000 colonists lived in the Chesapeake region (encompassing Virginia, Maryland, and northern North Carolina), and they exported over 35 million pounds of tobacco. Chesapeake colonists mastered the demands of tobacco agriculture, and the "Stinkinge Weede" (a seventeenth-century Marylander's term for tobacco) also mastered the

colonists. Settlers lived by the rhythms of tobacco agriculture, and their endless need for labor attracted droves of English indentured servants to work in Chesapeake tobacco fields (Map 3.1).

Tobacco Agriculture

A demanding crop, tobacco required close attention and a great deal of hand labor year-round. Primitive tools and methods made this intensive cycle of labor taxing. Like the Indians, colonists "cleared" fields by cutting a ring of bark from trees (a procedure known as girdling), thereby killing them. Girdling brought sunlight to clearings but left fields studded with tree stumps, making the use of plows impractical. Instead, colonists tilled their tobacco fields with heavy hoes. To plant, a visitor observed, colonists "just make holes [with a stick] into which they drop the seeds," much as the Indians did.

MAP 3.1   Chesapeake Colonies in the Seventeenth Century

The intimate association between land and water in the settlement of the Chesapeake in the seventeenth century is illustrated by this map. The fall line indicates the limit of navigable water, where rapids and falls prevented farther upstream travel. Although Delaware had excellent access to navigable water, it was claimed and defended by the Dutch colony at New Amsterdam (discussed in chapter 4) rather than by the English settlements in Virginia and Maryland shown on this map.

Reading the map: Using the notations on the map, create a chronology of the establishment of towns and settlements. What physical features correspond to the earliest habitation by English settlers?

Connections: Why was access to navigable water so important? Given the settlers' need for defense against native tribes, what explains the distance between settlements?

For more help analyzing this map, see the map activity for this chapter in the Online Study Guide at **bedfordstmartins.com/roarkcompact**.

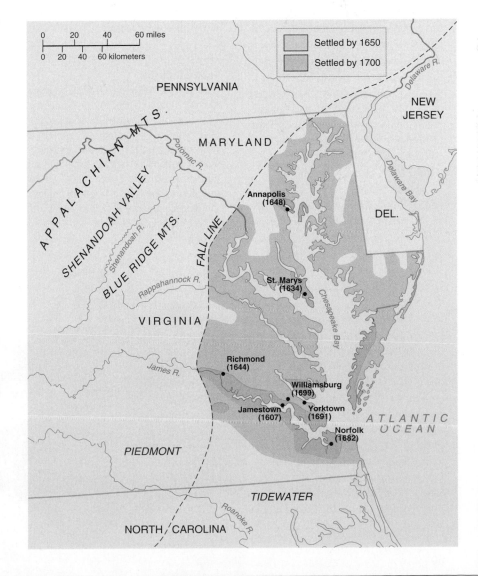

American Tobacco and European Consumers

English colonies in the Chesapeake were "wholly built upon smoke," King Charles I remarked. The king's shrewd comment highlighted the fundamental reason why the seventeenth-century Chesapeake colonies prospered by growing ever-increasing crops of tobacco: because people on the eastern side of the Atlantic were willing to buy ever-increasing quantities of tobacco to smoke—and to sniff, chew, and drink, and even to use for enemas. Europeans' desire for tobacco was the only reason it had commercial value. If Europeans had considered tobacco undesirable, the history of both the British North American colonies and the rest of the world would have been very different.

Some Europeans did hate tobacco, England's King James I foremost among them. In *A Counterblaste to Tobacco*, a pamphlet published in 1611, James declared that smoking was "A custome lothsome to the eye, hatefull to the Nose, harmefull to the braine, dangerous to the Lungs, and in the blacke stinking fume thereof, neerest resembling the horrible…smoke of the pit that is bottomelesse." James pulled out all the stops in attacking smoking. "What honour or policie can moove us to imitate the barbarous and beastly manners of the wilde, godlesse, and slavish Indians, especially in so vile and stinking a custome?" he asked. "Why doe we not as well imitate them in walking naked as they doe? in preferring glasses, feathers, and such toyes, to golde and precious stones, as they do? yea why do we not denie God and adore the Devill, as they doe?" James reviled the "filthy smoke," the "stinking Suffumigation," the "spitting," the "lust," the "shameful imbecilitie," and the "sin" of tobacco. James's fulminations acknowledged that "the generall use of Tobacco" was "daily practiced…by all sorts and complexions of people." He noted, "The publike use [of tobacco], at all times, and in all places, hath now so farre prevailed that a man cannot heartily welcome his friend now, but straight they must bee in hand with Tobacco.…It is become…a point of good fellowship, and he that will refuse to take a pipe of Tobacco among his fellows…is accounted peevish and no good company." Clearly, James championed a lost cause.

When Spaniards first brought tobacco to Europe during the sixteenth century, physicians praised it as a wonder drug. One proclaimed that "to seek to tell the virtues and greatness of this holy herb, the ailments which can be cured by it, and have been, the evils from which it has saved thousands would be to go on to infinity…this precious herb is so general a human need [that it is] not only for the sick but for the healthy." Such strong recommendations from learned men were reinforced by everyday experiences of commoners. Sailors returning from the New World "suck in as much smoke as they can," one Spaniard observed, "[and] in this way they say that their hunger and thirst are allayed, their strength is restored and their spirits are refreshed; [and]… their brains are lulled by a joyous intoxication." That joyous intoxication—"a bewitching quality" King James called it—made tobacco irresistible to most Europeans. And, as we know all too well today, the bewitching intoxication of tobacco was highly addictive.

Feeding that habit was expensive at the beginning of the seventeenth century because tobacco was scarce. In 1603, for

---

Tobacco Cutter

Tobacconists in Europe used this machine to chop tobacco leaves into small pieces. Then they often flavored the chopped tobacco with oils, herbs, and spices much as coffeehouse baristas today add hazelnut, mocha, or vanilla flavors to lattes and cappucinos. The picture on the side of the cutter refers to the Native American origins of the tobacco processed by the cutter's screws, clamps, and blades.

Niemeyer Nederlands Tabacologisch Museum.

Smoking Club

In Europe, tobacco smokers congregated in clubs to enjoy the intoxicating weed. This seventeenth-century print satirizes smokers' promiscuous gatherings of fashionable men, women, and children who indulged their taste for tobacco. Emblems of the tobacco trade adorn the wall; pipes, spittoons, and other smoking implements are close at hand; and the dog cleans up after those who cannot hold their smoke.

Koninklijke Bibliotheek, The Hague.

example, England imported only about 25,000 pounds of tobacco, all from New Spain. By 1700, England imported nearly 40 million pounds of tobacco, almost all from the Chesapeake colonies. The huge increase in tobacco supply caused prices to plummet. A quantity of tobacco that sold for a dollar in 1600 cost less than two and a half cents by 1700.

The low prices made possible by bumper crops harvested by planters in the Chesapeake transformed tobacco consumption in England and elsewhere in Europe. Per capita tobacco use in England grew over 200-fold during the seventeenth century, from less than a fifth of an ounce in the 1620s to 2.3 pounds by 1700.

American tobacco became the first colonial product of mass consumption by Europeans, blazing a trail followed by New World sugar, coffee, and chocolate.

Tobacco altered European culture. It spawned new industries, new habits, and new forms of social life. Smoking was the most common form of tobacco consumption in the seventeenth century, and smokers needed far more than tobacco to light up. They needed pipes, and hundreds of pipe makers supplied them with millions of ceramic pipes. They needed boxes or tins to hold their tobacco and a container to hold the embers they used to light the tobacco, or a flint and steel to strike

sparks; they needed pipe cleaners; they needed spittoons if they were smoking in a respectable place that disapproved of spitting on the floor. European merchants and manufacturers supplied all these needs, along with tobacco itself, which had to be graded, chopped, flavored, packaged, stored, advertised, and sold. Men and women smoked in taverns, in smoking clubs, around dinner tables, and in bed. A visitor to London noted that tobacco was not only in "frequent use…at every hour of the day but even at night [smokers] keep the pipe and steel at their pillows and gratify their longings."

The somewhat cumbersome paraphernalia of smoking caused many tobacco users to shift to snuff, which became common in the eighteenth century. Snuff use eliminated smoke, fire, and spitting with the more refined arts of taking a pinch of powdered, flavored tobacco from a snuffbox and sniffing it into one or both nostrils, which produced a fashionable sneeze followed by a genteel wipe with a dainty handkerchief. Sneezing induced by snuff was considered not only fashionable but healthful. One snuff taker explained that "by its gently pricking and stimulating the membranes, [snuff] causes Sneezing or Contractions, whereby the Glands like so many squeezed Sponges, dismiss their Seriosities and Filth."

Whether consumed by smoking, by sniffing, or in other ways, tobacco profoundly changed European habits, economies, and societies. It is no exaggeration to conclude that planters, servants, and eventually slaves in the Chesapeake made it possible for Europeans to become hooked on tobacco.

English settlers worked hard because their labor promised greater rewards in the Chesapeake region than in England. One colonist proclaimed that "the dirt of this Province affords as great a profit to the general Inhabitant, as the Gold of Peru doth to…the Spaniard." Although he exaggerated, it was true that a hired man could expect to earn two or three times more in Virginia tobacco fields than in England. Better still, in Virginia land was so abundant that it was extremely cheap, compared to land in England. By the mid-seventeenth century, common laborers could buy a hundred acres for less than their annual wages—an impossibility in England. New settlers who paid their own transportation to the Chesapeake received a grant of fifty acres of free land (termed a headright). The Virginia Company initiated the headright policy to encourage settlement, and the royal government continued it for the same reason.

A Servant Labor System

Headrights, cheap land, and high wages gave poor English folk powerful incentives to immigrate to the New World. Yet many potential immigrants could not scrape together the fare to cross the Atlantic. Their poverty and the colonists' crying need for labor formed the basic context for the creation of a servant labor system.

About 80 percent of the immigrants to the Chesapeake during the seventeenth century were indentured servants. Twenty Africans arrived in Virginia in 1619, and they probably were enslaved, although scanty records make it impossible to be certain. For the next fifty years, however, only a small number of slaves labored in Chesapeake tobacco fields. (Large numbers of slaves came in the eighteenth century, as chapter 5 explains.) Instead of a slave society, the seventeenth-century Chesapeake region was fundamentally a society of servants and ex-servants.

To buy passage aboard a ship bound for the Chesapeake, an English immigrant had to come up with about £5, roughly a year's wages for an English servant or laborer. Earning wages at all was difficult in England since job opportunities were shrinking. Unemployed people drifted into seaports like Bristol, Liverpool, and London, where they learned about the plentiful jobs in North America.

Unable to pay for their trip across the Atlantic, poor immigrants agreed to a contract called an indenture, which functioned as a form of credit. By signing an indenture, an immigrant borrowed the cost of transportation to the Chesapeake from a merchant or ship captain in England. To repay this loan, the indentured person agreed to work as a servant for four to seven years in North America. Once the indentured person arrived in the colonies, the merchant or ship captain sold his right to the immigrant's labor to a local tobacco planter. To obtain the servant's labor, the planter paid about twice the cost of transportation and agreed to provide the servant with food and shelter during the term of the indenture. When the indenture expired, the planter owed the former servant "freedom dues," usually a few barrels of corn and a suit of clothes.

Ideally, indentures allowed poor immigrants to trade their most valuable assets—their freedom and their ability to work—for a trip to the New World and a period of servitude followed by freedom in a land of opportunity. Planters reaped more immediate benefits. Servants meant more hands to grow more tobacco. A planter expected a servant to grow enough tobacco in one year to cover the price the planter paid for the indenture. Servants' labor during the remainder of the indenture promised a handsome profit for the planter. But roughly half of all servants became sick and died before serving out their indentures, reducing planters' gains. Planters also received a headright of fifty acres of land from the colonial government for every newly purchased servant.

About three out of four servants were men between the ages of fifteen and twenty-five when they arrived in the Chesapeake. Typically they shared the desperation of sixteen-year-old Francis Haires, who indentured himself for seven years because "his father and mother and All friends [are] dead and he [is] a miserable wandering boy." Like Francis, most servants had no special training or skills, although the majority had some experience with agricultural work. "Hunger and fear of prisons bring to us onely such servants as have been brought up to no Art or Trade," one Virginia planter complained. A skilled craftsman could obtain a shorter indenture, but few risked coming to the colonies since their prospects were better at home.

Women were almost as rare as skilled craftsmen in the Chesapeake and more ardently desired. In the early days of the tobacco boom, the Virginia Company shipped young single women servants to the colony as prospective wives for male settlers willing to pay "120 weight [pounds] of the best leaf tobacco for each of them," in effect getting both a wife and a servant. The company reasoned that, as one official wrote in 1622, "the plantation can never flourish till families be planted, and the respect of wives and children fix the people on the soil." The company's efforts as a marriage broker proved no more successful than its other ventures. Women remained a small minority of the Chesapeake population until late in the seventeenth century. The servant labor system perpetuated the gender imbalance. Although female servants cost about the same as males and generally served for the same length of time, only about one servant in four was a woman. Planters preferred male servants for fieldwork, although many servant women hoed and harvested tobacco fields. Most women servants also did household chores such as cooking, washing, cleaning, gardening, and milking.

Servant life was harsh by the standards of seventeenth-century England and even by the **frontier** standards of the Chesapeake. Unlike servants in England, Chesapeake servants had no control over who purchased their labor—and thus them—for the period of their indenture. Many servants were bought and sold several times before their indenture expired. A Virginia servant protested in 1623 that his master "hath sold me for £150 sterling like a damnd slave." But tobacco planters' need for labor muffled such complaints about treating servants as property.

Severe laws aimed to keep servants in their place. Punishments for petty crimes stretched servitude far beyond the original terms of indenture. Christopher Adams, for example, had to serve three extra years for running away for six months. Richard Higby received six extra years of servitude for killing three hogs. After midcentury, the Virginia legislature added three or more years to the indentures of most servants by requiring them to serve until they were twenty-four years old.

Women servants were subject to special restrictions and risks. They were prohibited from marrying until their servitude had expired. A servant woman, the law assumed, could not serve two masters at the same time: one who owned her indentured labor and another who was her husband. However, the predominance of men in the Chesapeake population inevitably pressured women to engage in sexual relations.

Indenture Contract

Indenture contracts were so common that forms were printed with blank spaces for details to be written in. In mid-November 1698, fifteen-year-old Matthew Evans, a friendless boy from Harfordshire, agreed to serve mariner Thomas Graves, or anybody to whom Graves sold his rights, for four years in Virginia. The contract specifies that Graves will carry Evans to Virginia and provide during the term of the indenture "all necessary Cloathes, Meat, Drink, Washing, Lodging and other necessaryes, fit and convenient for him according to the Custom of the said Plantation, as other Servants in such Cases are usually Provided for...." The Library of Virginia.

As a rule, if a woman servant gave birth to a child, she had to serve two extra years and pay a fine. However, for some servant women, premarital pregnancy was a path out of servitude: The father of an unborn child sometimes purchased the indenture of the servant mother-to-be, freed, and married her.

Such punishments reflected four fundamental realities of the servant labor system. First, planters' hunger for labor caused them to demand as much labor as they could get from their servants, including devising legal ways to extend the period of servitude. Second, servants hoped to survive their servitude and use their freedom to obtain land and start a family. Third, servants' hopes frequently conflicted with planters' demands. Since servants saw themselves as free people in a temporary status of servitude, they often made grudging, half-hearted workers. Finally, both servants and planters put up with this contentious arrangement because the alternatives were less desirable.

Planters could not easily hire free men and women because land was readily available and free people preferred to work on their own land, for themselves. Nor could planters depend on much labor from family members. The preponderance of men in the population meant that families were few, were started late, and thus had few children. And, until the 1680s and 1690s, slaves were expensive and hard to come by. Before then, masters who wanted to expand their labor force and grow more tobacco had few alternatives to buying indentured servants.

Cultivating Land and Faith

Villages and small towns dotted the rural landscape of seventeenth-century England, but in the Chesapeake acres of wilderness were interrupted here and there by tobacco farms. Tobacco was such a labor-intensive crop that one fieldworker could tend only about two acres of the plants in a year (an acre is slightly smaller than a football field), plus a few more acres for food crops. A successful farmer needed a great deal more land, however, because tobacco quickly exhausted the fertility of the soil. Since each farmer cultivated only 5 or 10 percent of his land at any one time, a "settled" area comprised swatches of cultivated land surrounded by forest. Arrangements for marketing tobacco also contributed to the dispersion of settlements. Tobacco planters sought land that fronted

Settlement Patterns along the James River

a navigable river in order to minimize the work of transporting the heavy barrels of tobacco onto ships.

Most Chesapeake colonists were nominally **Protestants**. Attendance at Sunday services and conformity to the doctrines of the Church of England were required of all English men and women. Few clergymen migrated to the Chesapeake, however, and too few of those who did come were models of righteousness and piety. Certainly some colonists took their religion seriously. But on the whole, religion did not awaken the zeal of Chesapeake settlers, certainly not as it did the zeal of New England settlers in these same years (see chapter 4). The religion of the Chesapeake colonists was Anglican, but their faith lay in the turbulent, competitive, high-stakes gamble of survival as tobacco planters.

The situation was similar in the Catholic colony of Maryland. In 1632, England's King Charles I granted his Catholic friend Lord Baltimore about six and a half million acres in the northern Chesapeake region. In return, the king specified that Lord Baltimore pay him the token rent of "two Indian arrowheads" a year. Lord Baltimore intended to create a refuge for Catholics, who suffered severe discrimination in England. He fitted out two ships, the *Ark* and the *Dove,* gathered about 150 settlers, and sent them to the new colony, where they arrived on March 25, 1634. However, Maryland failed to live up to Baltimore's hopes. The colony's population grew very slowly for twenty years, and most settlers were Protestants rather than Catholics. The religious turmoil of the **Puritan** Revolution in England (discussed in chapter 4) spilled across the Atlantic, creating conflict between Maryland's few Catholics—most of them wealthy and prominent—and the Protestant majority, most of them neither wealthy nor prominent. During the 1660s, Maryland began to attract settlers as readily as Virginia, mostly Protestants. Although Catholics and the Catholic faith continued to exert influence in Maryland, the colony's society, economy, politics, and culture became nearly indistinguishable from Virginia's. Both colonies shared a devotion to tobacco, the true faith of the Chesapeake.

REVIEW Why did the vast majority of European immigrants to the Chesapeake come as indentured servants?

The Evolution of Chesapeake Society

The system of indentured servitude sharpened inequality in Chesapeake society by the mid-seventeenth century, propelling social and political polarization that culminated in 1676 with Bacon's Rebellion. The rebellion prompted reforms that stabilized relations between elite planters and their lesser neighbors and paved the way for a social hierarchy based less overtly on land and wealth than on race. Amid this social and political evolution, one thing did not change: the dedication of Chesapeake colonists to growing tobacco.

Social and Economic Polarization

The first half of the seventeenth century in the Chesapeake was the era of the **yeoman**—a farmer who owned a small plot of land sufficient to support a family and tilled largely by servants and a few family members. A small number of elite planters had larger estates and commanded ten or more servants. But for the first several decades, few men lived long enough to accumulate a fortune sufficient to set them much apart from their neighbors. Until midcentury, the principal division in Chesapeake society was less between rich and poor planters than between free farmers and unfree servants. While these two groups contrasted sharply in their legal and economic status, their daily lives had many similarities. Servants looked forward to the time when their indentures would expire and they would become free and eventually own land. On the whole, a rough, frontier equality characterized free families in the Chesapeake until about 1650.

Three major developments splintered that equality during the third quarter of the century. First, as planters grew more and more tobacco, the ample supply depressed tobacco prices in European markets. Cheap tobacco reduced planters' profits and made it more difficult for freed servants to save enough to become landowners. Second, because the mortality rate in the Chesapeake colonies declined, more and more servants survived their indentures, and landless freemen became more numerous and grew more discontented. Third, declining mortality also encouraged the formation of a planter elite. By living longer, the most successful planters compounded their success. The wealthiest planters also began to serve as merchants, marketing crops for their less successful neighbors, importing English goods for sale, and giving credit to hard-pressed customers.

By the 1670s, the society of the Chesapeake had become polarized. Landowners—the planter elite and the more numerous yeoman planters—clustered around one pole. Landless colonists, mainly freed servants, gathered at the other. Each group eyed the other with suspicion and mistrust. For the most part, planters saw landless freemen as a dangerous rabble rather than as fellow colonists with legitimate grievances. Governor William Berkeley feared the political threat to the governing elite posed by "six parts in seven [of Virginia colonists who]…are poor, indebted, discontented, and armed."

Tobacco Plantation
This print illustrates the processing of tobacco on a seventeenth-century plantation. Workers cut the mature plants and put the leaves in piles to wilt (left foreground and center background). After the leaves dry somewhat, they are suspended from poles in a drying barn (right foreground), where they are seasoned before being packed in casks for shipping. Sometimes, tobacco leaves are left to dry in the fields (center background). The print suggests the labor demands of tobacco by showing twenty-two individuals, all but two of them actively at work with the crop. The one woman, hand in hand with a man in the left foreground, may be on her way to work on the harvested leaves, but it is more likely that she and the man are overseeing the labor of their servants or employees.
From "About Tobacco," Lehman Brothers.

Government Policies and Political Conflict

In general, government and politics strengthened the distinctions in Chesapeake society. The most vital distinction separated servants and masters, and the colonial government enforced it with an iron fist. Poor men like William Tyler complained that "nether the Governor nor Counsell could or would doe any poore men right, but that they would shew favor to great men and wronge the poore." Most Chesapeake colonists, like most Europeans, assumed that "great men" should bear the responsibilities of government. Until 1670, all freemen could vote, and they routinely elected prosperous planters to the legislature. No former servant served in either the governor's council or the House of Burgesses after 1640. Yet Tyler and other poor Virginians believed that the "great men" used their government offices to promote their selfish personal interests, rather than governing impartially.

As discontent mounted among the poor during the 1660s and 1670s, colonial officials tried to keep political power in safe hands. Beginning in 1661, for example, Governor Berkeley did not call an election for the House of Burgesses for fifteen years. In 1670, the House of Burgesses outlawed voting by poor men, permitting only men who headed a household and were landowners to vote.

The king also began to tighten the royal government's control of trade and to collect substantial revenue from the Chesapeake. A series of navigation acts funneled the colonial trade exclusively into the hands of English merchants and shippers. Navigation Acts of 1650 and 1651 specified that colonial goods had to be transported in English ships with predominantly English crews. A 1660 act required all colonial products to be sent only to English ports, and a 1663 law stipulated further that all goods sent to the colonies must pass through English ports and be carried in English ships manned by English sailors. Taken together, these navigation acts reflected the English government's **mercantilist** assumptions about the colonies: What was good for England should determine colonial policy.

Assumptions about mercantilism also underlay the import duty on tobacco inaugurated by the 1660 Navigation Act. The law assessed an import tax of two pence on every pound of colonial tobacco brought into England, about the price a Chesapeake tobacco farmer received. The tax gave the king a major financial interest in the size of the tobacco crop. During the 1660s, these tobacco import taxes yielded about a quarter of all English customs revenues.

Bacon's Rebellion

Colonists, like residents of European monarchies, accepted social hierarchy and inequality as long as they believed government officials ruled for the general good. When rulers violated that precept, ordinary people felt justified in rebelling. In 1676, Bacon's Rebellion erupted as a dispute over Virginia's Indian policy. Before it was over, the rebellion convulsed Chesapeake politics and society, leaving in its wake death, destruction, and a legacy of hostility between the great planters and their poorer neighbors.

Opechancanough, the Algonquian chief who had led the Indian uprising of 1622 in Virginia, mounted another surprise attack in 1644 and killed about 500 Virginia colonists in two days. During the next two years of bitter fighting, the colonists eventually gained the upper hand, capturing and murdering the old chief. The treaty that concluded the war established policies toward the Indians that the government tried to maintain for the next thirty years. The Indians relinquished all claims to land already settled by the English. Wilderness land beyond the fringe of English settlement was supposed to be reserved exclusively for Indian use. The colonial government hoped to minimize contact between settlers and Indians and thereby maintain the peace.

Had the Chesapeake population remained constant, the policy might have worked. But the number of land-hungry colonists, especially poor, recently freed servants, continued to multiply. In their quest for land, they pushed beyond the treaty limits of English settlement and encroached steadily on Indian land. During the 1660s and 1670s, violence between colonists and Indians repeatedly flared along the advancing frontier. The government, headquartered in the tidewater region near the coast, far from the danger of Indian raids, took steps to calm the disputes and reestablish the peace. Frontier settlers thirsted for revenge against what their leader, Nathaniel Bacon, termed "the protected and Darling Indians." Indians were not the only enemies Bacon and his men singled out. Bacon charged that "Grandees," or elite planters, operated the government for their private gain, a charge that made sense to many colonists. Bacon crystallized the grievances of the small planters and poor farmers against both the Indians and the colonial rulers in Jamestown.

Hoping to maintain the fragile peace on the frontier in 1676, Governor Berkeley pronounced Bacon a rebel, threatened to punish him for treason, and called for new elections of burgesses who, Berkeley believed, would endorse his get-tough policy. To Berkeley's surprise, the elections backfired. Almost all the old burgesses were voted out of office, their places taken by local leaders, including Bacon. The legislature was now in the hands of minor grandees who, like Bacon, chafed at the rule of the elite planters.

In June 1676, the new legislature passed a series of reform measures known as Bacon's Laws. Among other changes, the laws gave local settlers a voice in setting tax levies, forbade officeholders from demanding bribes or other extra fees for carrying out their duties, placed limits on holding multiple offices, and restored the vote to all freemen. Under pressure, Berkeley pardoned Bacon and authorized his campaign of Indian warfare. But elite planters soon convinced Berkeley that Bacon and his men were a greater threat than Indians.

When Bacon learned that Berkeley had once again branded him a traitor, he declared war against Berkeley and the other grandees. For three months, Bacon's forces fought the Indians, sacked the grandees' plantations, and attacked Jamestown. Berkeley's loyalists retaliated by plundering the homes of Bacon's supporters. The fighting continued until late October, when Bacon unexpectedly died, most likely from dysentery, and several English ships arrived to bolster Berkeley's strength. With the rebellion crushed, Berkeley hanged several of Bacon's allies and destroyed farms that belonged to Bacon's supporters.

The rebellion did nothing to dislodge the grandees from their positions of power. If anything, it strengthened their position. When the king learned of the turmoil in the Chesapeake and its devastating effect on tobacco exports and customs duties, he ordered an investigation. Royal officials replaced Berkeley with a governor more attentive to the king's interests, nullified Bacon's Laws, and instituted an export tax on every hogshead of tobacco as a way of paying the expenses of government without having to

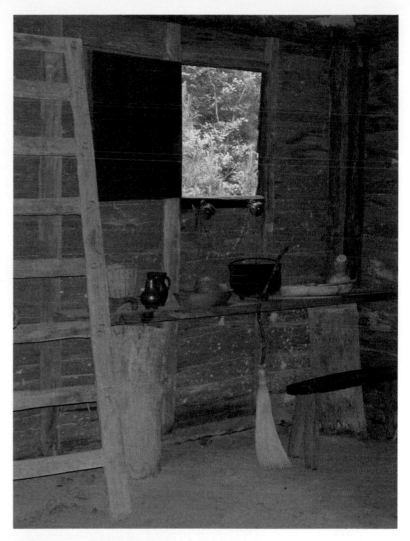

Inside a Poor Planter's House
The houses of seventeenth-century Chesapeake settlers were typically "earth-fast": The structural timbers that framed the house were simply placed in holes in the ground, and the floor was packed dirt. No seventeenth-century house was substantial enough to survive until today. This photo shows a carefully documented historical reconstruction of the interior of a poor planter's house at St. Mary's City, Maryland. The wall of this one-room dwelling with a loft features a window with a shutter but no glass; when the shutter was closed, the only source of light was a candle or a fire. Notice the rustic, unfinished bench, table, and walls. These meager furnishings were usually accompanied by a storage chest and some bedding but not a bed. If and when planters became more prosperous, a bed was likely to be their first acquisition, suggesting that the lack of a good night's sleep was one of their major discomforts.
Image courtesy of Historic St. Mary's City.

obtain the consent of the tightfisted House of Burgesses.

In the aftermath of Bacon's Rebellion, tensions between great planters and small farmers gradually lessened. Bacon's Rebellion showed, a governor of Virginia said, that it was necessary "to steer between…either an Indian or a civil war." The ruling elite concluded that it was safer for colonists to fight Indians rather than each other, and the government made little effort to restrict settlers' encroachment on Indian lands. Tax cuts were another policy welcomed by all freemen. The export duty on tobacco imposed by the king allowed the colonial government to reduce taxes by 75 percent between 1660 and 1700. In the long run, however, the most important contribution to political stability was the declining importance of the servant labor system. During the 1680s and 1690s, fewer servants arrived in the Chesapeake, partly because of improving economic conditions in England. Accordingly, the number of poor, newly freed servants also declined, reducing the size of the lowest stratum of free society. In 1700, as many as one-third of the free colonists still worked as tenants on land owned by others, but the social and political distance between them and the great planters did not seem as important as it had been in 1660. The main reason was that by 1700 the Chesapeake was in the midst of transition to a slave labor system that minimized the differences between poor farmers and rich planters and magnified the differences between whites and blacks.

> **REVIEW**   Why did Chesapeake colonial society become increasingly polarized between 1650 and 1670?

Religion and Revolt in the Spanish Borderland

While English colonies in the Chesapeake grew and prospered with the tobacco trade, the northern outposts of the Spanish empire in New Mexico and Florida stagnated. Instead of attracting settlers and growing crops for export, New Mexico and Florida appealed to Spanish missionaries seeking to harvest Indian souls. The missionaries baptized thousands of Indians in Spanish North America during the seventeenth century, but they also planted the seeds of Indian uprisings against Spanish rule.

Few Spaniards came to New Spain's northern borderland during the seventeenth century. Only about 1,500 Spaniards lived in Florida and roughly twice as many inhabited New Mexico. One royal governor complained that "no

[Spaniard] comes…to plow and sow [crops], but only to eat and loaf." In both colonies, Indians outnumbered Spaniards ten or twenty to one.

Royal officials seriously considered eliminating both colonies because their costs greatly exceeded their benefits. Every three years a caravan from Mexico brought wagons full of goods to outposts in New Mexico. Florida required even larger subsidies because it housed a garrison of soldiers as well as missionaries who persuaded the Spanish government that, instead of being losing propositions, the colonies represented golden opportunities to convert heathen Indians to Christianity. Stirrups adorned with Christian crosses on soldiers' saddles proclaimed the faith behind Spaniards' swords, and vice versa. Royal officials hoped that the missionaries' efforts would pacify Indians and be a relatively cheap way to preserve Spanish footholds in North America.

Dozens of missionaries came to Florida and New Mexico to teach Indians that their religious beliefs and rituals were idolatrous devil worship and that their way of life was barbaric. Missionaries followed royal instructions that Indians should be taught "to live in a civilized manner, clothed and wearing shoes…[and] given the use of…bread, linen, horses, cattle, tools, and weapons, and all the rest that Spain has had." In effect, missionaries sought to convert Indians not just into Christians but also into surrogate Spaniards.

Missionaries supervised the building of scores of Catholic churches across Florida and New Mexico. Typically, they conscripted Indian women and men to do the construction labor. Adopting practices common elsewhere in New Spain, missionaries forced Indians both to work and to pay tribute in the form of food, blankets, and other goods. While missionaries congratulated themselves on the many Indians they converted, their coercive methods subverted their goals. A missionary reported that an Indian in New Mexico asked him, "if we [missionaries] who are Christians caused so much harm and violence [to Indians], why should they [i.e., Indians] become Christians?"

Indians retaliated repeatedly against Spanish exploitation, but Spaniards suppressed the violent uprisings by taking advantage of the disunity among Indians much as Cortés did in the conquest of Mexico (see chapter 2). In 1680, however, Pueblo Indians organized a unified revolt under the leadership of Popé, who ordered his followers, as one recounted, to "break up and burn the images of the holy Christ, the Virgin Mary, and the other saints, the crosses, and everything pertaining to Christianity." During the Pueblo Revolt, Indians desecrated churches, killed two-thirds of Spanish missionaries, and drove Spaniards out of New Mexico to present-day El Paso, Texas. Spaniards managed to return to New Mexico by the end of the seventeenth century, but only by curtailing missionaries and reducing labor exploitation. Florida Indians never mounted a unified attack on Spanish rule, but they too organized sporadic uprisings and resisted conversion.

REVIEW Why did the Pueblo Indians revolt against Spanish missionaries in 1680?

Toward a Slave Labor System

During the sixteenth century, Spaniards and Portuguese supplemented Indian laborers in the New World with enslaved Africans. On this foundation, European colonizers built African slavery into the most important form of coerced labor in the New World. During the seventeenth century, British colonies in the West Indies followed the Spanish and Portuguese examples and developed sugar plantations with slave labor. In the British North American colonies, however, a slave labor system did not emerge until the last quarter of the seventeenth century. During the 1670s, settlers from Barbados brought slavery to the new English mainland colony of Carolina, where the imprint of the West Indies remained strong for decades. In

Sugar Mill
This seventeenth-century drawing of a Brazilian sugar mill highlights the heavy equipment needed to extract the juice from sugarcane. A vertical waterwheel turns a large horizontal gear that exerts force on the jaws of the press that squeezes the cane. Workers remove crushed cane from the press and replace it with freshly harvested cane as it is unloaded from an oxcart. Except for the overseer (just to the right of the waterwheel), all of the workers are black, presumably slaves from Africa, as suggested by their clothing. All of the mill workers appear to be men, a hint of the predominance of men among newly imported African slaves.
Musées Royaux des Beaux-Arts de Belgique.

Chesapeake tobacco fields at about the same time, slave labor began to replace servant labor, marking the transition toward a society of freedom for whites and slavery for Africans.

The West Indies: Sugar and Slavery

The most profitable part of the British New World empire in the seventeenth century lay in the Caribbean (Map 3.2). The tiny island of Barbados, colonized in the 1630s, was the jewel of the British West Indies. During the 1640s, Barbadian planters began to grow sugarcane with such success that a colonial official proclaimed Barbados "the most flourishing Island in all those American parts, and I verily beleive in all the world for the production of sugar." Sugar commanded high prices in England, and planters rushed to grow as much as they could. By midcentury, annual sugar exports from the British Caribbean totaled about 150,000 pounds; by 1700, exports reached nearly 50 million pounds.

Sugar transformed Barbados and other West Indian islands. Poor farmers could not afford the expensive machinery that extracted and refined sugarcane juice. Planters with the necessary capital to grow sugar got rich. By 1680, the wealthiest Barbadian sugar planters were, on average, four times richer than tobacco grandees in the Chesapeake. The sugar grandees differed from their Chesapeake counterparts in another crucial way: The average sugar baron in Barbados in 1680 owned 115 slaves.

African slaves planted, cultivated, and harvested the sugarcane that made West Indian planters wealthy. Beginning in the 1640s, Barbadian planters purchased thousands of slaves to work their plantations, and the African population on the island mushroomed. During the 1650s, when blacks made up only 3 percent of the Chesapeake population, they had already become the majority on Barbados. By 1700, slaves constituted more than three-fourths of the island's population.

For slaves, work on a sugar plantation was a life sentence to brutal, unremitting labor. Slaves suffered high death rates. Since slave men outnumbered slave women two to one, few slaves could form families and have children. These grim realities meant that in Barbados and elsewhere in the West Indies, the slave population did not grow by natural reproduction.

Instead, planters continually purchased enslaved Africans. Although sugar plantations did not gain a foothold in North America in the seventeenth century, the West Indies nonetheless exerted a powerful influence on the development of slavery in the mainland colonies.

Carolina: A West Indian Frontier

The early settlers of what became South Carolina were immigrants from Barbados. In 1663, a Barbadian planter named John Colleton and a group of seven other men obtained a charter from England's King Charles II to establish a colony south of the Chesapeake and north of the Spanish territories in Florida. The men, known as "proprietors," hoped to siphon settlers from Barbados and other colonies and encourage them to develop a profitable export crop comparable to West Indian sugar and Chesapeake tobacco. Following the Chesapeake example, the proprietors offered headrights of up to 150 acres of land for each settler. In 1670, they established the colony's first permanent English settlement, Charles Towne (later spelled Charleston) (see Map 3.2).

As the proprietors had planned, most of the early settlers were from Barbados. In fact, Carolina was the only seventeenth-century English colony to be settled principally by colonists from other colonies rather than from England. The Barbadian immigrants brought their slaves with them. More than a fourth of the early settlers were slaves, and as the colony continued to attract settlers from Barbados, the black population multiplied. By 1700, slaves made up about half the population of Carolina. The new colony's close association with Barbados caused English officials to refer routinely to "Carolina in ye West Indies."

The Carolinians experimented unsuccessfully to match their semitropical climate with profitable export crops of tobacco, cotton, indigo, and olives. In the mid-1690s, colonists identified a hardy strain of rice and took advantage of the knowledge of rice cultivation among their many African slaves to build rice plantations. Settlers also sold livestock and timber to the West Indies, as well as another "natural resource": They captured and enslaved several thousand local Indians and sold them to Caribbean planters. Both economically and socially, seventeenth-century Carolina was a frontier outpost of the West Indian sugar economy.

Slave Labor Emerges in the Chesapeake

By 1700, more than eight out of ten people in the southern colonies of British North America lived in the Chesapeake. Until the 1670s, almost all Chesapeake colonists were white people from England. By 1700, however, one out of eight people in the region was a black person from Africa. Between 1670 and 1700 hundreds of tobacco planters made the transition from servant to slave labor. For planters, slaves had several obvious advantages over servants. Although slaves cost three to five times more than servants, slaves never became free. Since the mortality rate had declined by the 1680s, planters could reasonably expect slaves to live longer than a servant's period of indenture. Slaves also promised to be a perpetual labor force, since children of slave mothers inherited the status of slavery.

For planters, slaves had another important advantage over servants: They could be con-trolled politically. Bacon's Rebellion had demonstrated how disruptive former servants could be when their expectations were not met. Slavery kept discontented laborers in permanent servitude, and their color was a badge of their bondage.

The slave labor system polarized Chesapeake society along lines of race and status: All slaves were black, and nearly all blacks were slaves; almost all free people were white, and all whites were free or only temporarily bound in indentured servitude. Unlike Barbados, however, the Chesapeake retained a vast white majority. Among whites, huge differences of wealth and status still existed. By 1700, more than three-quarters of white families had neither servants nor slaves. Nonetheless, poor white farmers enjoyed the privileges of free status. By emphasizing the privileges of freedom shared by all white people, the slave labor system reduced the tensions between poor folk and grandees that had plagued the Chesapeake region in the 1670s.

MAP 3.2 The West Indies and Carolina in the Seventeenth Century
Although Carolina was geographically close to the Chesapeake colonies, it was culturally closer to the West Indies in the seventeenth century because its early settlers—both blacks and whites—came from Barbados. South Carolina retained strong ties to the West Indies for more than a century, long after the arrival of many of its subsequent settlers from England, Ireland, France, and elsewhere.

Bell of Slave Ship
The English slave ship *Henrietta Marie* sailed from England to the west African coast in 1699, loaded a cargo of slaves, made the **Middle Passage** to the West Indies, where the slaves were sold, then started back to England but sank with all aboard off the Florida Keys. Centuries later, this bronze bell was recovered from the wreckage.

© 1991 Mel Fisher Maritime Heritage Society, Key West, FL. Photo: Dylan Kibler.

In contrast to slaves in Barbados, most slaves in the seventeenth-century Chesapeake colonies had frequent and close contact with white people. Slaves and white servants performed the same tasks on tobacco plantations, often working side by side in the fields. Slaves took advantage of every opportunity to slip away from white supervision and seek out the company of other slaves. Planters often feared that slaves would turn such seemingly innocent social pleasures to political ends, either to run away or to conspire to strike against their masters. Slaves often ran away, but they usually were captured or returned after a brief absence. Despite planters' nightmares, slave insurrections did not occur.

While slavery resolved the political unrest caused by the servant labor system, it created new political problems. By 1700, the bedrock political issue in the southern colonies was keeping slaves in their place, at the end of a hoe. The slave labor system in the southern colonies stood roughly midway between the sugar plantations and black majority of Barbados to the south and the small farms and homogeneous villages that developed in seventeenth-century New England to the north (see chapter 4).

REVIEW Why had slave labor largely displaced indentured servant labor by 1700 in Chesapeake tobacco production?

Conclusion: The Growth of English Colonies Based on Export Crops and Slave Labor

By 1700, the colonies of Virginia, Maryland, and Carolina were firmly established. The staple crops they grew for export provided a livelihood for many, a fortune for a few, and valuable revenues for shippers, merchants, and the English monarchy. Their societies differed markedly from English society in most respects, yet the colonists considered themselves English people who happened to live in North America. They claimed the same rights and privileges as English men and women while they denied those rights and privileges to Native Americans and African slaves.

The English colonies also differed from the example of New Spain. Settlers and servants flocked to English colonies, in contrast to Spaniards who trickled into New Spain. Few English missionaries sought to convert Indians to Protestant Christianity, unlike the numerous Catholic missionaries in New Mexico and Florida. Large quantities of gold and silver never materialized in British North America. English colonists never adopted the system of *encomienda* (see chapter 2) because Indians were too few and too hostile and their communities too small and decentralized compared with those of the Mexica. Yet forms of coerced labor and racial distinction that developed in New Spain had North American counterparts, as English colonists employed servants and slaves and defined themselves as superior to Indians and Africans.

By 1700, the remnants of Powhatan's people still survived. As English settlement pushed north, west, and south of the Chesapeake Bay, Indians faced the new colonial world that Powhatan and Pocahontas had encountered when John Smith and the first colonists arrived at Jamestown. By 1700, the many descendants of Pocahontas's son, Thomas, as well as other colonists and Native Americans, understood that the English had come to stay.

Suggestions for Further Reading

James F. Brooks, *Captives and Cousins: Slavery, Kinship, and Community in the Southwest Borderlands* (2002). A detailed study of relationships among Native Americans in the Southwest Borderlands.

David Eltis, *The Rise of African Slavery in the Americas* (2001). An authoritative economic and cultural overview of the rise of slavery in the New World.

Jason Hughes, *Learning to Smoke: Tobacco Use in the West* (2003). The surprising history of how Europeans learned to consume tobacco by smoking.

Karen Kupperman, *Indians and English: Facing Off in Early America* (2002). An expert survey of encounters between Native Americans and English colonists.

Edmund S. Morgan, *American Slavery, American Freedom: The Ordeal of Colonial Virginia* (1975). Classic account of seventeenth-century Virginia by an eminent historian.

Helen C. Rountree, *Pocahontas, Powhatan, Opechancanough: Three Indian Lives Changed by Jamestown* (2005). The compelling story of how English settlement changed the lives of three important Native Americans.

► **FOR MORE BOOKS ABOUT TOPICS IN THIS CHAPTER,** see the Online Bibliography at bedfordstmartins.com/roarkcompact.

► **FOR ADDITIONAL FIRSTHAND ACCOUNTS OF THIS PERIOD,** see Chapter 3 in Michael Johnson, ed., *Reading the American Past,* Third Edition.

► **FOR WEB SITES AND DOCUMENTS RELATED TO TOPICS AND PLACES IN THIS CHAPTER,** see "HistoryLinks," "DocLinks," and "PlaceLinks" at bedfordstmartins.com/roarkcompact.

REVIEWING THE CHAPTER

Follow these steps to review and strengthen your understanding of the chapter.

STEP 1: *Study the* **Key Terms** *and* **Timeline** *to identify the significance of each item listed.*

STEP 2: *Answer the* **Review Questions**, *drawing on key terms and dates to support your answers.*

STEP 3: *Drawing on the Key Terms, Timeline, and Review Questions, answer the broader* **Making Connections** *questions.*

KEY TERMS

Who

Captain John Smith (p. 53)
Algonquian Indians (p. 53)
Powhatan (p. 53)
Pocahontas (p. 53)
John Rolfe (p. 54)
James I (p. 55)
Opechancanough (p. 57)
Charles I (p. 64)
Lord Baltimore (p. 64)
William Berkeley (p. 65)
Nathaniel Bacon (p. 66)
Pueblo Indians (p. 69)
Charles II (p. 70)

What

Virginia Company (p. 55)
joint stock company (p. 55)
colonization (p. 55)
Jamestown (p. 56)
royal colony (p. 57)
House of Burgesses (p. 58)
tobacco (p. 58)
headright (p. 62)
indentured servants (p. 62)
yeoman (p. 65)
Navigation Acts (p. 66)
mercantilism (p. 66)
Bacon's Rebellion (p. 66)

grandees (p. 67)
Bacon's Laws (p. 67)
Barbados (p. 70)

TIMELINE

NOTE: Events are depicted chronologically, but the passage of time is not to exact scale.

◀ **1588** • England defeats Spanish Armada.

1606 • Virginia Company receives royal charter.

1607 • English colonists found Jamestown settlement;
Pocahontas "rescues" John Smith.

1609 • Starvation plagues Jamestown.

1612 • John Rolfe begins to plant tobacco in Virginia.

1617 • First commercial tobacco shipment leaves Virginia for England.
• Pocahontas dies in England.

1618 • Powhatan dies; Opechancanough becomes
chief of the Algonquians.

1619 • First Africans arrive in Virginia.
• House of Burgesses begins to meet in Virginia.

1622 • Opechancanough leads Indian uprising
against Virginia colonists.

1624 • Virginia becomes royal colony.

1632 • King Charles I grants
Lord Baltimore land for
colony of Maryland.

REVIEW QUESTIONS

1. Why did Powhatan pursue largely peaceful relations with the Jamestown settlement? (pp. 55–58)

2. Why did the vast majority of European immigrants to the Chesapeake come as indentured servants? (pp. 58–64)

3. Why did Chesapeake colonial society become increasingly polarized between 1650 and 1670? (pp. 65–68)

4. Why did the Pueblo Indians revolt against Spanish missionaries in 1680? (pp. 68–69)

5. Why had slave labor largely displaced indentured servant labor by 1700 in Chesapeake tobacco production? (pp. 69–72)

MAKING CONNECTIONS

1. Given the extraordinary vulnerability of the Jamestown settlement in its first two decades, why did its sponsors and settlers not abandon it? In your answer, discuss the challenges the settlement faced and the benefits different participants in England and the New World hoped to derive from their efforts.

2. Tobacco dominated European settlement in the seventeenth-century Chesapeake. How did tobacco agriculture shape the region's development? In your answer, be sure to address the demographic and geographic features of the colony.

3. Bacon's Rebellion highlighted significant tensions within Chesapeake society. What provoked the rebellion, and what did it accomplish? In your answer, be sure to consider causes and results in the colonies and in England.

4. In addition to making crucial contributions to the economic success of seventeenth-century English colonies, Native Americans and enslaved Africans influenced colonial politics. Describe how European colonists' relations with these populations contributed to political friction and harmony within the colony.

> ▶ FOR PRACTICE QUIZZES, A CUSTOMIZED STUDY PLAN, AND OTHER STUDY TOOLS, see the Online Study Guide at bedfordstmartins.com/roarkcompact.

1634 • Colonists begin to arrive in Maryland.

    1640s • Barbados colonists begin to grow sugarcane with labor of African slaves.

        1644 • Opechancanough leads Indian uprising against Virginia colonists.

        1660 • Navigation Act requires colonial tobacco to be shipped to English ports.

          1663 • Royal charter is granted for Carolina colony.

          1670
           • Charles Towne, South Carolina, founded.

          1670–1700
           • Slave labor system emerges in Carolina and Chesapeake colonies.

            1676
             • Bacon's Rebellion.

              1680
               • Pueblo Revolt.

AMERICA'S FIRST BOOK

The first book printed in what is now the United States, this well-thumbed copy of *The Whole Booke of Psalmes Faithfully Translated into English Metre* was published in Cambridge, Massachusetts, in 1640. Puritan services banned musical instruments and other diversions from God's holy word. Worshippers used this book and others to sing psalms, celebrating with a chorus of voices the wonders of God's Truth. The famous Twenty-third Psalm begins near the bottom of the left-hand page and concludes on the facing page. Read the psalm aloud to re-create the experience of seventeenth-century New England Puritan congregations.

Roger Foley / Library of Congress.

The Northern Colonies in the Seventeenth Century

1601–1700

ROGER WILLIAMS AND HIS WIFE MARY arrived in Massachusetts in February 1631. Fresh from a superb education at Cambridge University, the twenty-eight-year-old Williams was "a godly [Puritan] minister," noted Governor John Winthrop. Winthrop's Boston church asked Williams to become its minister, but he refused because the church had not openly rejected the corrupt Church of England. New England's premier Puritan church was not pure enough for Williams.

Williams and his wife moved to Plymouth colony for two years, where he spent a great deal of time among the Narragansett Indians. Williams believed that "Nature knows no difference between Europeans and Americans in blood, birth, [or] bodies...God having made of one blood all mankind." He sought to learn about their language, their religion, and their culture, without trying to convert them to Christianity. Williams insisted that Indians' religion and culture should be respected since all human beings should live according to their consciences as revealed to them by God. His respect for Indians led him to condemn English colonists for their "sin of unjust usurpation" of Indian lands.

Massachusetts officials defended colonists' settlement on Indian land. If land "lies common, and hath never been replenished or subdued, [it] is free to any that possess or improve it," Governor Winthrop explained. Besides, he said, "if we leave [the Indians] sufficient [land] for their use, we may lawfully take the rest, there being more than enough for them and us." Winthrop's arguments prevailed, but Williams refused to knuckle under. "God Land," he said, "[is] as great a God with us English as God Gold was with the Spaniards." Such views ultimately caused him to be banished from the colony.

Williams became the minister at Salem, Massachusetts, in 1633. Like other New England Puritans, the members of the Salem church had solemnly agreed to "**Covenant** with the Lord and one with another; and doe bynd our selves in the presence of God, to walke together in all his waies, according as he is pleased to reveale himself unto us in his Blessed word of truth [the Bible]." Most New England Puritans believed churches and governments should enforce both godly belief and behavior according to biblical rules. They claimed that "the Word of God is...clear." In contrast, Williams believed the

Bible shrouded the word of God in "mist and fog." Williams pointed out that devout and pious Christians could and did differ about what the Bible said. That observation led him to denounce the emerging New England order as impure, ungodly, and tyrannical.

Williams also disagreed with the New England government's requirement that everyone attend church service. He argued that forcing people who were not Christians to attend church was wrong in four major ways. First, Williams preached, it was akin to requiring "a dead child to suck the breast, or a dead man [to] feast." The only way for any person to become a true Christian was by God's gift of faith revealed to the person's conscience. Second, churches should separate "holy from unholy…[and] godly from ungodly." He said requiring everybody to attend church was "False Worshipping" that promoted "spiritual drunkenness and whoredom, a soul sleep and a soul sickness." Third, the government had no business ruling on spiritual matters. Williams termed New England's regulation of religious behavior "spiritual rape" that inevitably would lead governments to use coercion and violence to enforce the government's misguided way. Finally, Williams believed that governments should tolerate all religious beliefs because only God knows the truth; no person and no religion can understand God with absolute certainty. "I commend that man," Williams wrote, "that steers no otherwise than his conscience dares." In Williams's view, toleration of religious belief and liberty of conscience were the only paths to religious purity and political harmony.

New England's leaders denounced Williams's arguments. One minister wrote that Williams sought "liberty to enfranchise all false Religions," which was "the greatest impiety in the World." Genuine **liberty**, he said, was "to contend earnestly for the Truth; to preserve unity of Spirit, Faith, ordinances, to be all like minded, of one accord." Like-minded New Englanders banished Williams for his "extreme and dangerous" opinions. He escaped from an attempt to ship him back to England and in the winter of 1636 spent fourteen weeks walking south to Narragansett Bay. There he founded the colony of Rhode Island, which enshrined "Liberty of Conscience" as a fundamental ideal and became a refuge for other dissenters.

Although New England's leaders expelled Williams from their holy commonwealth, his dissenting ideas arose from orthodox Puritan doctrines. By urging believers to search for evidence of God's grace, **Puritanism** encouraged the faithful to listen for God's whisper of truth and faith. Puritanism combined rigid insistence on conformity to God's law and aching uncertainty about how to identify and act upon it. Despite the best efforts of New England's leaders to define their way as God's way, Puritanism inspired believers like Roger Williams to draw their own conclusions and stick to them.

During the seventeenth century, New England's Puritan zeal—exemplified by Roger Williams and his persecutors—cooled. The goal of founding a holy New England faded. Late in the century, new "middle" colonies—New York, New Jersey, and Pennsylvania—featuring greater religious and ethnic diversity than New England were founded. Religion remained important throughout all the colonies, but it competed with the growing faith that the promise of a better life required less focus on salvation and more attention to worldly concerns of family, work, and trade.

As settler populations increased throughout the British mainland colonies, settlements encroached on Indian lands, causing violent conflict to flare up repeatedly. Political conflict also arose among colonists, particularly in response to major political upheavals in England. By the end of the seventeenth century, the English monarchy exerted greater control over its North American empire. The lifeblood of the empire, however, remained the continual flow of products, people, and ideas that pulsed between England and the colonies, energizing both.

Puritan Origins: The English Reformation

The religious roots of the Puritans who founded New England reached back to the Protestant **Reformation**, which arose in Germany in 1517 (see chapter 2). The Reformation spread quickly to other countries, but the English church initially remained within the Catholic fold and continued its allegiance to the pope in Rome. King Henry VIII, who reigned from 1509 to 1547, understood that the Reformation offered him an opportunity to break with Rome and take control of the church in England. In 1534, Henry formally initiated the English Reformation. At his insistence, Parliament passed the Act of Supremacy, which outlawed the Catholic Church and proclaimed the king "the only supreme head on earth of the Church of England."

In the short run, the English Reformation allowed Henry VIII to achieve his political goal of controlling the church. In the long run, however, the Reformation brought to England the political and religious turmoil that Henry had hoped to avoid. Henry himself sought no more than a halfway Reformation. Protestant doctrines held no attraction for Henry; in almost all matters of religious belief and practice he remained an orthodox Catholic. Many English Catholics wanted to revoke the English Reformation; they hoped to return the Church of England to the pope and to restore Catholic doctrines and ceremonies. But many other English people insisted on a genuine, thoroughgoing Reformation; these people came to be called Puritans.

During the sixteenth century, Puritanism was less an organized movement than a set of ideas and religious principles that appealed strongly to many dissenting members of the Church of England. They sought to purify the Church of England by eliminating what they considered the offensive features of Catholicism. For example, they demanded that the church hierarchy be abolished and that ordinary Christians be given greater control over religious life. They wanted to do away with the rituals of Catholic worship and instead emphasize an individual's relationship with God developed through Bible study, prayer, and introspection. Although there were many varieties and degrees of Puritanism, all Puritans shared a desire to make the English church thoroughly Protestant.

The fate of **Protestantism** waxed and waned under the monarchs who succeeded Henry VIII. Elizabeth I assumed the throne in 1558 and tried to position the English church between the extremes of Catholicism and Puritanism. Like her father, she was less concerned with theology than with politics. Above all, she desired a church that would strengthen the monarchy and the nation. By the time Elizabeth died in 1603, many people in England looked on Protestantism as a defining feature of national identity.

When her successor, James I, became king, English Puritans petitioned for further reform of the Church of England. James authorized a new

Persecution of English Protestants

This sixteenth-century drawing shows Protestant prisoners being marched to London to be tried for heresy during the reign of Queen Mary I, a staunch Catholic. The artist emphasizes the severity of the Catholic persecutors by depicting the use of four well-armed guards, two on horseback, to escort some fifteen prisoners, including at least five women who are roped together but not because they appear menacing or likely to run away. The guards seem to be necessary less to maintain order among the prisoners than to discourage sympathetic citizens from rushing forward and freeing the prisoners. The artist seems to assume that most citizens opposed the queen's persecution of Protestants. The Bible verse from the book of Matthew underscores the Protestants' fealty to Christ rather than to mere "Princes and rulers" like Queen Mary.

Folger Shakespeare Library.

translation of the Bible, known ever since as the King James version. However, neither James I nor his son Charles I, who became king in 1625, was receptive to the ideas of Puritan reformers. James and Charles moved the Church of England away from Puritanism. They enforced conformity to the Church of England and punished dissenters, both ordinary Christians and ministers. In 1629, Charles I dissolved Parliament—where Puritans were well represented—and initiated aggressive anti-Puritan policies. Many Puritans despaired about continuing to defend their faith in England and began to make plans to emigrate. Some left for Europe, others for the West Indies. The largest number set out for America.

REVIEW Why did Henry VIII initiate the English Reformation?

Puritans and the Settlement of New England

Puritans who emigrated aspired to escape the turmoil and persecution of England and to build a new, orderly, Puritan version of England. Puritans established the first small settlement in New England in 1620, followed a few years later by additional settlements by the Massachusetts Bay Company. Allowed self-government through royal charter, these Puritans were in a unique position to direct the new colonies according to their faith. Their faith shaped the colonies they established in almost every way. Although many New England colonists were not Puritans, Puritanism remained a paramount influence in New England's religion, politics, and community life during the seventeenth century.

The Pilgrims and Plymouth Colony

One of the first Protestant groups to emigrate, later known as Pilgrims, espoused a heresy known as separatism. These Separatists sought to withdraw—separate—from the Church of England, which they considered hopelessly corrupt. In 1608, they moved to Holland; by 1620, they realized that they could not live and worship there as they had hoped. The Separatists formed a joint stock company and obtained permission to settle in the lands granted to the Virginia Company (see chapter 3). In August 1620, Pilgrim families boarded the *Mayflower* and, after eleven weeks at sea, all but one of the 102 migrants arrived at the outermost tip of Cape Cod, in present-day Massachusetts.

The Pilgrims realized immediately that they had landed far north of the Virginia grants and had no legal authority to settle in the area. To provide order and security as well as a claim to legitimacy, they drew up the Mayflower Compact on the day they arrived. They pledged to "covenant and combine ourselves together into a civil Body Politick, for our better Ordering and Preservation." The signers (all men) agreed to enact and obey necessary and just laws.

The Pilgrims settled at Plymouth and elected William Bradford their governor. That first winter "was most sad and lamentable," Bradford wrote later. "In two or three months' time half of [our] company died…being the depth of winter, and wanting houses and other comforts [and] being infected with scurvy and other diseases."

In the spring, Wampanoag Indians rescued the floundering Plymouth settlement. With the Indians' guidance in how to cultivate corn, the Pilgrims managed to harvest enough food to guarantee their survival through the coming winter, an occasion they celebrated in the fall of 1621 with a feast of thanksgiving attended by the Wampanoags.

The Plymouth colony remained precarious, but the Pilgrims lived quietly and simply, coexisting in relative peace with the Indians. They paid the Wampanoags when settlers gradually encroached on Indian lands. By 1630, Plymouth had become a permanent settlement, but it failed to attract many other English Puritans.

The Founding of Massachusetts Bay Colony

In 1629, shortly before Charles I dissolved Parliament, a group of Puritan merchants and country gentlemen obtained a royal charter for the Massachusetts Bay Company. The charter provided the usual privileges granted to joint stock companies, including land for **colonization**. In addition, a unique provision of the charter permitted the government of the Massachusetts Bay Company to be located in the colony rather than in England. This provision allowed Puritans to exchange their position as a harassed minority in England for self-government in Massachusetts.

To lead the emigrants, the stockholders of the Massachusetts Bay Company elected John Winthrop, a prosperous lawyer and landowner, to serve as governor. In March 1630, eleven ships crammed with seven hundred passengers sailed for Massachusetts; six more ships and another five hundred emigrants followed a few months later. Winthrop's fleet arrived in Massachusetts Bay in early June. Unlike the Separatists, Winthrop's Puritans aspired to reform the corrupt Church of England (rather than separate from it) by setting an example of godliness in the New World. Winthrop and a small group chose to settle on the peninsula that became Boston, and other settlers clustered at promising locations nearby.

In a sermon to his companions aboard the *Arbella* while they were still at sea—probably the most famous sermon in American history—Winthrop explained the cosmic significance of their journey. The Puritans had "entered into a covenant" with God to "work out our salvation under the power and purity of his holy ordinances," Winthrop proclaimed. This sanctified agreement with God meant that the Puritans had to make "extraordinary" efforts to "bring into fa-miliar and constant practice" religious principles that most people in England merely preached. "We must be knit together in this work as one man," Winthrop declared. "We must delight in each other, make others' conditions our own, re-joice together, mourn together, labor and suffer to-gether." The stakes could not be higher, Winthrop told his listeners: "We must consider that we shall be as a city upon a hill. The eyes of all people are upon us."

That belief shaped seventeenth-century New England as profoundly as tobacco shaped the Chesapeake. Winthrop's vision of a city on a hill fired the Puritans' fierce determination to keep their covenant and live according to God's laws, unlike the backsliders and compromisers who accommodated to the Church of England. Their determination to adhere strictly to God's plan charged nearly every feature of life in sev-enteenth-century New England with a distinc-tive, high-voltage piety.

The new colonists, as Winthrop's son John wrote later, had "all things to do, as in the begin-ning of the world." Unlike the early Chesapeake settlers, the first Massachusetts Bay colonists encountered few Indians because the local popu-lation had been almost entirely exterminated by an epidemic more than a decade earlier. Still, as in the Chesapeake, the colonists fell victim to deadly ailments. More than 200 settlers died during the first year, including one of Winthrop's sons and eleven of his servants. But each year from 1630 to 1640, ship after ship followed in the wake of Winthrop's fleet. In all, more than 20,000 new set-tlers came, their eyes focused on the Puritans' city on a hill.

Often, when the Church of England cracked down on a Puritan minister in England, he and many of his followers uprooted and moved to-gether to New England. By 1640, New England had one of the highest ratios of preachers to population in all of Christendom. A few minis-ters sought to carry the message of Christianity to Indians, accompanied by instructions replac-ing what missionary John Eliot termed Indians' "unfixed, confused, and ungoverned…life, un-civilized and unsubdued to labor and order." (See "Documenting the American Promise," page 82.) For the most part, however, the colonists focused on saving Indians' souls less than on saving their own.

The occupations of New England immi-grants reflected the social origins of English Puritans. On the whole, the immigrants came from the middle ranks of English society. The vast majority of immigrants were either farmers or tradesmen, including carpenters, tailors, and textile workers. Servants, whose numbers domi-nated the Chesapeake settlers, accounted for only about a fifth of those headed for New England. Most New England immigrants paid their way to Massachusetts, even though the

Seal of Massachusetts Bay Colony
In 1629, the Massachusetts Bay Company designed this seal depicting an Indian man inviting English set-tlers to "Come Over And Help Us." Of course, such an invitation was never issued. The seal was an attempt to lend an aura of altruism to the Massachusetts Bay Company's colonization efforts. In English eyes, the Indian man obviously needed help. The only signs that he was more civilized than the pine trees flank-ing him were his girdle of leaves, his bow and arrow, and his miraculous use of English. In reality, colonists in Massachusetts and elsewhere were far less inter-ested in helping Indians than in helping themselves. For the most part, that suited the Indians, who wanted no "help" from the colonists.
Courtesy of Massachusetts Archives.

FOR MORE HELP ANALYZING THIS IMAGE, see the visual activity for this chapter in the Online Study Guide at bedfordstmartins .com/roarkcompact.

King Philip Considers Christianity

*B*eginning in 1646, the Puritan minister John Eliot served as a missionary to New England's Indians, trying to teach the doctrines of Christianity and proper English behavior. During his half-century tenure as leader of the Puritan congregation in Roxbury, Massachusetts, Eliot studied the languages, customs, and beliefs of Native Americans, hoping to help them along the path to Christian piety and to strengthen them against colonists' unscrupulous encroachment on their lands. The efforts of Eliot and other missionaries convinced some Indians to leave their own communities and settle in "praying towns" populated by Native Americans who had agreed to live in conformity with English ways. Most Indians, however, did not move into praying towns or adopt the faith or manners of the colonists.

In Indian Dialogues, *a book published in 1671, Eliot illustrated the challenge he and other missionaries confronted as they tried to convince Native Americans of the errors of their ways. Based on his decades of missionary experience, Eliot created imaginary conversations between converted Indians and those who resisted Christianity. Eliot's invented conversations echoed arguments he and other missionaries had encountered repeatedly. The following selection from an imaginary dialogue between two praying Indians, Anthony*

and William, and King Philip (or Metacomet), the chief (or sachem) of the powerful Wampanoags, documents Eliot's perception of the attractions of Christianity and one Indian leader's doubts about it, doubts that ultimately prevailed when King Philip led the Wampanoags in an all-out attack against the settlers in 1675.

Anthony: Sachem, we salute you in the Lord, and we declare unto you, that we are sent by the church, in the name of our Lord Jesus Christ, to call you, and beseech you to turn from your vain conversation unto God, to pray unto God, and to believe in Jesus Christ for the pardon of your sins, and for the salvation of your soul....So we are come this day unto you, in the name of Jesus Christ, to call you to come unto the Lord, and serve him....We hear that many of your people do desire to pray to God, only they depend on you. We pray you to consider that your love to your people should oblige you to do them all the good you can....You will not only yourself turn from sin unto God..., but all your people will turn to God with you, so that you may say unto the Lord, oh Lord Jesus, behold here am I, and all the people which thou hast given me. We all come unto thy service, and promise to pray unto God so long as

we live....Oh how happy will all your people be....It will be a joy to all the English magistrates, and ministers, and churches, and good people of the land, to hear that Philip and all his people are turned to God, and become praying Indians....

Philip: Often have I heard of this great matter of praying unto God, and hitherto I have refused....Mr. Eliot himself did come unto me. He was in this town, and did persuade me. But we were then in our sports, wherein I have much delighted, and in that temptation, I confess, I did neglect and despise the offer, and lost that opportunity. Since that time God hath afflicted and chastised me, and my heart doth begin to break. And I have some serious thoughts of accepting the offer, and turning to God, to become a praying Indian, I myself and all my people. But I have some great objections, which I cannot tell how to get over, which are still like great rocks in my way, over which I cannot climb. And if I should, I fear I shall fall down the precipice on the further side, and be spoiled and undone. By venturing to climb, I shall catch a deadly fall to me and my posterity.

The first objection that I have is this, because you praying Indians do reject your sachems, and refuse to pay them tribute, in so much that if any of my people turn to pray unto God, I do reckon that I have lost him. He will no longer own me for his sachem, nor pay me any tribute. And hence it will come to pass, that if I should pray to God, and all my people with me, I must become as a common man among them, and so lose all my power and authority over them. This is such a temptation as… I, nor any of the other great sachems, can tell how to get over. Were this temptation removed, the way would be more easy and open for me to turn praying Indian. I begin to have some good likance of the way, but I am loth to buy it at so dear a rate.

William: …I say, if any of the praying Indians should be disobedient (in lawful things) and refuse to pay tribute unto their sachems, it is not their religion and praying to God that teaches them so to do, but their corruptions. …I am sure the word of God commandeth all to be subject to the higher powers, and pay them tribute…. And therefore, beloved sachem, let not your heart fear that praying to God will alienate your people from you…for the more beneficent you are unto them, the more obligation you lay upon them. And what greater beneficence can you do unto them than to further them in religion, whereby they may be converted, pardoned, sanctified, and saved?…

Philip: I have another objection stronger than this, and that is, if I pray to God, then all my men that are willing to pray to God will (as you say) stick to me, and be true to me. But all such as love not and care not to pray to God, especially such as hate praying to God, all these will forsake me, yea will go and adjoin themselves unto other sachems that pray not to God. And so it will come to pass, that if I be a praying sachem, I shall be a poor and weak one, and easily trod

upon by others, who are like to be more potent and numerous. And by this means my tribute will be small, and my people few, and I shall be a great loser by praying to God. In the way I am now, I am full and potent, but if I change my way and pray to God, I shall be empty and weak….

William: …Suppose all your subjects that hate praying to God should leave you. What shall you lose by it? You are rid of such as by their sins vitiate others, and multiply transgression, and provoke the wrath of God against you and yours. But consider what you shall gain by praying to God…. All the praying Indians will rejoice at it, and be your friends, and they are not a few…. [And] you shall gain a more intimate love of the Governor, and Magistrates…. They will more honor, respect, and love you, than ever they did…. The Governor and Magistrates of the Massachusetts will own you, and be fatherly and friendly to you…. Yea more, the King of England, and the great peers who… yearly send over means to encourage and promote our praying to God, they will take notice of you.

Philip: I perceive that in your praying to God, and in your churches, all are brought to an equality. Sachems and people they are all fellow brethren in your churches. Poor and rich are equally privileged. The vote of the lowest of the people hath as much weight as the vote of the sachem. Now I doubt [worry] that this way will lift up the heart of the poor to too much boldness, and debase the

rulers to[o] low. This bringing all to an equality will bring all to a confusion…. [T]here is yet another thing that I am much afraid of, and that is your church admonitions and excommunications. I hear that your sachems are under that yoke. I am a sinful man as well as others, but if I must be admonished by the church, who are my subjects, I know not how I shall like that. I doubt [worry] it will be a bitter pill, too hard for me to get down and swallow…. I feel your words sink into my heart and stick there. You speak arrows…. I desire to ponder and consider of these things…. I am willing they should still lie soaking in my heart and mind.

Source: John Eliot, *Indian Dialogues* (Cambridge, 1671), in Henry W. Bowden and James P. Ronda, eds., *John Eliot's Indian Dialogues: A Study in Cultural Interaction*, 120–31. Copyright © 1980. Reproduced with permission of Greenwood Publishing Group, Inc., Westport, CT.

Questions for Analysis and Debate

1. To what degree is Eliot's dialogue a reliable guide to Philip's doubts about the wisdom of becoming a praying Indian?
2. According to Eliot, was Philip's religion a stumbling block to his acceptance of Christianity? What made Philip fear that he would "fall down the precipice"?
3. If Philip had written a dialogue proposing that Eliot convert to the Wampanoag way of life, what arguments might he have made?

journey often took their life savings. In contrast to the Chesapeake newcomers, New England immigrants usually arrived as families. In fact, more Puritans came with family members than did any other group of immigrants in all of American history.

As Winthrop reminded the first settlers in his *Arbella* sermon, each family was a "little commonwealth" that mirrored the hierarchy among all God's creatures. Just as humankind was subordinate to God, so young people were subordinate to their elders, children to their parents, and wives to their husbands. The immi-grants' family ties reinforced their religious beliefs with universally understood notions of hierarchy and mutual dependence. While immigrants to the Chesapeake were disciplined mostly by the coercions of servitude and the caprices of the tobacco market, immigrants to New England entered a social order defined by the interlocking institutions of family, church, and community.

REVIEW Why did the Puritans immigrate to North America?

New England Great Chair

This thronelike chair belonged to Michael Metcalf, a teacher in seventeenth-century Dedham, Massachusetts. The oldest known piece of New England furniture inscribed with a date, 1652, the chair was made in Dedham specifically for Metcalf (notice the initials flanking the date), who turned sixty-six in that year. Metcalf stored books, presumably including a Bible, in the enclosed compartment under the seat. No overstuffed recliner, the chair is suited less for a relaxing snooze than for alert concentration. The panels under the arms served to block chilly drafts. Otherwise, the chair shows few concessions to comfort or ease. The carved chair back—rigidly upright—displays motifs often found on Puritan tombstones. The grand austerity of the chair hints at the importance of serious Bible study and unflinching introspection in Puritan New England.

Dedham Historical Society / photo by Forrest Frazier.

European Throne Chair

In contrast to the New England great chair, this late-sixteenth-century European throne chair is embellished on every surface with elaborate carvings proclaiming the worldly magnificence of the chair's owner. This chair illustrates the ostentatious display of luxury and refinement that disgusted Puritans considered signs of the vanity and false pride that distracted people from seeking and following God's Truth.

Courtesy of Huntington Antiques Ltd., Gloucestershire, England.

MAP 4.1 New England Colonies in the Seventeenth Century

New Englanders spread across the landscape town by town during the seventeenth century. (For the sake of legibility, only a few of the more important towns are shown on the map.)

READING THE MAP: Using the notations on the map, create a chronology of the establishment of towns in New England. What physical features correspond to the earliest habitation by English settlers?

CONNECTIONS: Why were towns so much more a feature of seventeenth-century New England than of the Chesapeake (see also chapter 3)? How did Puritan dissent influence the settlement of New England colonies?

FOR MORE HELP ANALYZING THIS MAP, see the map activity for this chapter in the Online Study Guide at bedfordstmartins.com/roarkcompact.

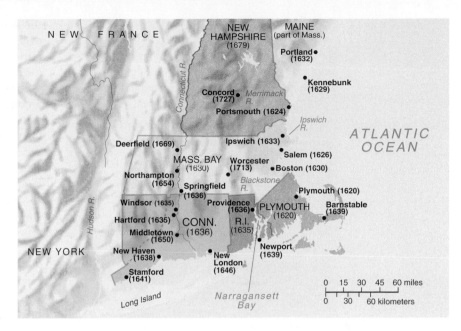

The Evolution of New England Society

The New England colonists, unlike their counterparts in the Chesapeake, settled in small towns, usually located on the coast or by a river (Map 4.1). Massachusetts Bay colonists founded 133 towns during the seventeenth century, each with one or more churches. Church members' fervent piety, buttressed by the institutions of local government, enforced remarkable religious and social conformity in the small New England settlements. During the century, tensions within the Puritan faith and changes in New England communities splintered religious orthodoxy and weakened Puritan zeal. By 1700, however, Puritanism still maintained a distinctive influence in New England.

Church, Covenant, and Conformity

Puritans believed that the church consisted of men and women who had entered a solemn covenant with one another and with God. Winthrop and three other men signed the original covenant of the first Boston church in 1630. Each new member of the covenant had to persuade existing members that she or he had fully experienced conversion. By 1635, the Boston church had added more than 250 names to the covenant.

Puritan views on religion and church membership derived from **Calvinism**, the doctrines of John Calvin, a sixteenth-century Swiss Protestant theologian who insisted that Christians strictly discipline their behavior to conform to certain religious ideas. As followers of Calvin's ideas, the Puritans believed in **predestination**—the idea that all-powerful God, before the creation of the world, decided which few human souls would receive eternal life. Only God knows the identity of these fortunate, predestined individuals—the "elect" or "saints." Nothing a person did in his or her lifetime could alter God's inscrutable choice or provide assurance that the person was predestined for salvation with the elect or damned to hell with the doomed multitude.

Despite this looming uncertainty, Puritans believed that if a person lived a rigorously godly life—constantly winning the daily battle against sinful temptations—his or her behavior was likely to be a hint, a visible sign, that he or she was one of the elect. Puritans thought that "sainthood" would become visible in individuals' behavior, especially if they were privileged to know God's Word as revealed in the Bible.

The connection between sainthood and saintly behavior, however, was far from certain. Some members of the elect, Puritans believed, had not heard God's word as revealed in the Bible, and therefore their behavior did not necessarily signal their sainthood. One reason Puritans required all town residents to attend church services was to enlighten anyone who was ignorant of God's Truth. The slippery relationship between saintly behavior—observable by anybody—and God's

THE
World turn'd upside down:
OR,
A briefe defcription of the ridiculous Fafhions
of thefe diftracted Times.

By T.J. a well-willer to King, Parliament and Kingdom.

London : Printed for John Smith. 1647.

The Puritan Challenge to the Status Quo

This title page of "The World Turn'd Upside Down" satirizes the Puritan notion that the contemporary world was deeply flawed. Printed in London in 1647, the pamphlet refers to the "distracted Times" of the Puritan Revolution in England. The drawing ridicules criticisms of English society that were also common among New England Puritans. The drawing shows at least a dozen examples of the conventional world of seventeenth-century England turned upside down. Can you identify them? Puritans, of course, would claim that the artist had it wrong—that the conventional world turned God's order upside down. How might the drawing have been different if a devout Puritan had drawn it?

By permission of The British Library.

predestined election—invisible and unknowable to anyone—caused Puritans to worry constantly that individuals who acted like saints were fooling themselves and others. Nevertheless, Puritans thought that "visible saints"—persons who passed their demanding tests of conversion and church membership—probably, though not certainly, were among God's elect.

Members of Puritan churches ardently hoped that God had chosen them to receive eternal life and tried to demonstrate saintly behavior. Their covenant bound them to help each other attain salvation and to discipline the entire community by saintly standards. Church members kept an eye on the behavior of everybody in town. Infractions of morality, order, or propriety were reported to Puritan elders, who summoned the wayward to a church inquiry. By overseeing every aspect of life, the visible saints enforced a remarkable degree of righteous conformity in Puritan communities. Total conformity, however, was never achieved. Ardent Puritans differed among themselves; non-Puritans shirked orthodox rules. But Puritan doctrine spelled out the fiery punishment for failure to conform: A servant in Roxbury declared that "if hell were ten times hotter, [I] had rather be there than [I] would serve [my] master."

Despite the central importance of religion, churches played no direct role in the civil government of New England communities. Puritans did not want to mimic the Church of England, which they considered a puppet of the king rather than an independent body that served the Lord. They were determined to insulate New England churches from the contaminating influence of the civil state and its merely human laws. Although ministers were the most highly respected figures in New England towns, they were prohibited from holding government office.

Puritans had no qualms, however, about their religious beliefs influencing New England governments. As much as possible, the Puritans tried to bring public life into conformity with their view of God's law. For example, fines were issued for Sabbath-breaking activities such as working, traveling, playing a flute, smoking a pipe, and visiting neighbors.

Puritans mandated other purifications of what they considered corrupt English practices. They refused to celebrate Christmas or Easter because the Bible did not mention either one. They outlawed religious wedding ceremonies; couples were married by a magistrate in a civil ceremony. Cards, dice, shuffleboard, and other games of chance were banned, as were music and dancing. The distinguished minister Increase Mather insisted that "Mixt or Promiscuous Dancing…of Men and Women" could not be tolerated since "the unchaste Touches and Gesticulations used by Dancers have a palpable tendency to that which is evil."

Government by Puritans for Puritanism

It is only a slight exaggeration to say that seventeenth-century New England was governed by Puritans for Puritanism. The charter of the Massachusetts Bay Company empowered the company's stockholders, known as freemen, to meet as a body known as the General Court and make the laws needed to govern the company's affairs. The colonists transformed this arrangement for running a joint stock company into a structure for governing the colony. Hoping to ensure that godly men would decide government policies, the General Court expanded the number of freemen in 1631 to include all male church members. Only freemen had the right to vote for governor, deputy governor, and other colonial officials. As new settlers were recognized as freemen, the size of the General Court grew too large to meet conveniently. So in 1634, the freemen in each town agreed to send two deputies to the General Court to act as the colony's legislative assembly. All other men were classified as "inhabitants," and they had the right to vote, hold office, and participate fully in town government.

A "town meeting," composed of a town's inhabitants and freemen, chose the selectmen and other officials who administered local affairs. New England town meetings routinely practiced a level of popular participation in political life that was unprecedented elsewhere during the seventeenth century. Almost every adult man could speak out in town meetings and fortify his voice with a vote. However, all women—even church members—were prohibited from voting, and towns did not permit "contrary-minded" men to become or remain inhabitants. Although town meeting participants wrangled from time to time, widespread political participation tended to reinforce conformity to Puritan ideals.

One of the most important functions of New England government was land distribution. Settlers who desired to establish a new town entered a covenant and petitioned the General Court for a grant of land. The court granted town sites to suitably pious petitioners but did not allow settlement until the Indians who inhabited a grant agreed to relinquish their claim to the land, usually in exchange for manufactured goods.

Having obtained their grant, town founders apportioned land among themselves and any newcomers they permitted to join them. Normally, each family received a house lot large enough for an adjacent garden as well as one or more strips of agricultural land on the perimeter of the town. Although there was a considerable difference between the largest and smallest family plots, most clustered in the middle range— roughly fifty to one hundred acres—resulting in a more nearly equal distribution of land in New England than in the Chesapeake.

Sabbath Breakers

These seventeenth-century prints show some of the punishments to which Sabbath breakers could be subjected by man and God. In the upper illustration, a person who gathered sticks on the Sabbath is stoned to death as Puritans believed the Bible commanded. In the lower print, three women who broke the Sabbath by preparing flax to be spun and woven into linen suffer God's retribution when they are burned to death. New Englanders differed about exactly when the Sabbath began. Some thought it started at sunset on Saturday evening, but John Winthrop believed the Sabbath began about three o'clock Saturday afternoon. Given the extreme punishments inflicted on Sabbath breakers, New Englanders needed to be careful about what they did between Saturday afternoon and Monday morning.

Divine Examples of God's Severe Judgements upon Sabbath-Breakers (London, 1671).

Joseph Capen House

This substantial house was built in 1683 for Joseph Capen, a Harvard graduate who had recently arrived in Topsfield, Massachusetts, to serve as the local minister. The town granted Capen twelve acres for a homesite, and he probably paid for the house with the dowry of his new wife, Priscilla Appleton, the daughter of a wealthy colonist in nearby Ipswich, Massachusetts. The plain but imposing house suggests the sturdy ties between preachers and their congregations and, more generally, between families, faith, and communities. Capen lived in the house and preached to the Topsfield church for more than forty years until his death in 1725. Now, more than three centuries after Capen built the house, it still stands, a monument to New England colonists' convictions that they were building a society to endure for the ages.

Picture Research Consultants & Archives.

The physical layout of New England towns encouraged settlers to look inward toward their neighbors, multiplying the opportunities for godly vigilance. Most people considered the forest that lay just beyond every settler's house an alien environment that was interrupted here and there by those oases of civilization, the towns. Footpaths connecting one town to another were so rudimentary that even John Winthrop once got lost within half a mile of his house and spent a sleepless night in the forest, circling the light of his small campfire and singing psalms.

The Splintering of Puritanism

Almost from the beginning, John Winthrop and other leaders had difficulty enforcing their views of Puritan orthodoxy. In England, persecution as a dissenting minority had unified Puritan voices in opposition to the Church of England. In New England, the promise of a godly society and the Puritans' emphasis on individual Bible study led New Englanders toward different visions of godliness. Puritan leaders, however, interpreted dissent as an error caused either by a misguided

believer or by the malevolent power of Satan. Whatever the cause, errors could not be tolerated. As one Puritan minister proclaimed, "The Scripture saith…there is no Truth but one."

Shortly after banishing Roger Williams, Winthrop confronted another dissenter, this time a devout Puritan woman steeped in Scripture and absorbed by religious questions: Anne Hutchinson. The mother of fourteen children, Hutchinson served her neighbors as a skilled midwife. After she settled into her new home in Boston in 1634, women gathered there to hear her weekly lectures on recent sermons. As one listener observed, she was a "Woman that Preaches better Gospell then any of your black-coates…[from] the Ninneversity." As the months passed, Hutchinson began to lecture twice a week, and crowds of sixty to eighty women and men gathered to listen to her.

Hutchinson expounded on the sermons of John Cotton, her favorite minister. Cotton stressed what he termed the "covenant of grace"—the idea that individuals could be saved only by God's grace in choosing them to be members of the elect. Cotton contrasted this familiar Puritan doctrine with the "covenant of works," the erroneous belief that a person's behavior—one's works—could win God's favor and ultimately earn a person salvation. Belief in the covenant of works and in the possibility of salvation for all was known as Arminianism. Cotton's sermons strongly hinted that many Puritans, including ministers, embraced Arminianism, which claimed—falsely, Cotton declared—that human beings could influence God's will. Anne Hutchinson agreed with Cotton. Her lectures emphasized her opinion that many of the colony's leaders affirmed the Arminian covenant of works. Like Cotton, she preached that only God's covenant of grace led to salvation.

The meetings at Hutchinson's house alarmed her nearest neighbor, John Winthrop, who believed that she was subverting the good order of the colony. In 1637, Winthrop had formal charges brought against Hutchinson and denounced her lectures as "not tolerable nor comely in the sight of God nor fitting for your sex." He told her, "You have stept out of your place, you have rather bine a Husband than a Wife and a preacher than a Hearer; and a Magistrate than a Subject."

In court, Winthrop interrogated Hutchinson, fishing for a heresy he could pin on her. Winthrop and other Puritan elders referred to Hutchinson and her followers as **antinomians**, people who believed that Christians could be saved by faith alone and did not need to act in accordance with God's law as set forth in the Bible and as interpreted by the colony's leaders. Hutchinson nimbly defended herself against the accusation of antinomianism. Yes, she acknowledged, she believed that men and women were saved by faith alone; but no, she did not deny the need to obey God's law. "The Lord hath let me see which was the clear ministry and which the wrong," she said. Finally, Winthrop had cornered her. How could she tell which ministry was which? "By an immediate revelation," she replied, "by the voice of [God's] own spirit to my soul." Winthrop spotted in this statement the heresy of prophecy, the view that God revealed his will directly to a believer instead of exclusively through the Bible, as every right-minded Puritan knew.

In 1638, the Boston church formally excommunicated Hutchinson. The minister decreed, "I doe cast you out and…deliver you up to Satan that you may learne no more to blaspheme to seduce and to lye." Banished, Hutchinson and her family moved first to Roger Williams's Rhode Island and then to present-day New York, where she and most of her family were killed by Indians.

The strains within Puritanism exemplified by Anne Hutchinson and Roger Williams caused it to splinter repeatedly during the seventeenth century. Thomas Hooker, a prominent minister, clashed with Winthrop and other leaders over the composition of the church. Hooker argued that men and women who lived godly lives should be admitted to church membership even if they had not experienced conversion. This issue, like most others in New England, had both religious and political dimensions, for only church members could vote in Massachusetts. In 1636, Hooker led an exodus of more than 800 colonists from Massachusetts to the Connecticut River valley, where they founded Hartford and neighboring towns. In 1639, the towns adopted the Fundamental Orders of Connecticut, a quasi-constitution that could be altered by the vote of freemen, who did not have to be church members, though nearly all of them were.

Other Puritan churches divided and subdivided throughout the seventeenth century as acrimony developed over doctrine and church government. Sometimes churches split over the appointment of a controversial minister. Sometimes families who had a long walk to the meetinghouse simply decided to form their own church nearer their houses. These schisms arose from ambiguities and tensions within Puritan belief. As the colonies matured, other tensions developed as well.

Religious Controversies and Economic Changes

A revolutionary transformation in the fortunes of Puritans in England had profound consequences in New England. Disputes between King Charles I and Parliament, dominated by Puritans, escalated in 1642 to civil war in England, a conflict known as the Puritan Revolution. Parliamentary forces led by the staunch Puritan Oliver Cromwell were victorious, executing Charles I in 1649 and proclaiming England a Puritan republic. From 1649 to 1660, England's rulers were not monarchs who suppressed Puritanism but believers who championed it. In a half century, English Puritans had risen from a harassed group of religious dissenters to a dominant power in English government.

When the Puritan Revolution began, the stream of immigrants to New England dwindled to a trickle, creating hard times for the colonists. They could no longer consider themselves a city on a hill setting a godly example for humankind.

David, Joanna, and Abigail Mason
This 1670 painting depicts the children of Joanna and Anthony Mason, a wealthy Boston baker. The artist lavished attention on the children's elaborate clothing. Fashionable slashed sleeves, fancy laces, silver-studded shoes, six-year-old Joanna's and four-year-old Abigail's necklaces, and nine-year-old David's silver-headed cane suggest not only the Masons' wealth but also their desire to display and memorialize their possessions and adornments. The painting hints that the children themselves were adornments, young sprouts of the Mason lineage, which could afford such finery. The portrait is unified not by signs of warm affection, innocent smiles, or familial solidarity but by trappings of wealth and sober self-importance. The painting expresses the growing respect for wealth and its worldly rewards in seventeenth-century New England.
Fine Arts Museums of San Francisco. Gift of Mr. and Mrs. John D. Rockefeller III.

English society was being reformed by Puritans in England, not New England. Furthermore, when immigrant ships became rare, the colonists faced sky-high prices for scarce English goods and few customers for their own colonial products. As they searched to find new products and markets, they established the enduring patterns of New England's economy.

New England's rocky soil and short growing season ruled out cultivating the southern colonies' crops of tobacco and rice that found a ready market in Atlantic ports. Exports that New Englanders could not get from the soil they took instead from the forest and the sea. During the first decade of settlement, colonists traded with Indians for animal pelts, which were in demand in Europe. By the 1640s, fur-bearing animals had become scarce unless traders ventured far beyond the **frontiers** of

English settlement. Trees from the seemingly limitless forests of New England proved a longer-lasting resource. Masts for ships and staves for barrels of Spanish wine and West Indian sugar were crafted from New England timber.

But the most important New England export was fish. Dried, salted codfish found markets in southern Europe and the West Indies. The fish trade also stimulated colonial shipbuilding and trained generations of fishermen, sailors, and merchants, creating a commercial network that endured for more than a century. But this export economy remained peripheral to most New England colonists. Their lives revolved around their farms, their churches, and their families.

Although immigration came to a standstill in the 1640s, the population continued to boom, doubling every twenty years. In New England, almost everyone married and women often had eight or nine children. Long, cold winters prevented the warm-weather ailments of the southern colonies and reduced New England mortality. The descendants of the immigrants of the 1630s multiplied and remultiplied, boosting the New England population to roughly equal that of the southern colonies (Figure 4.1).

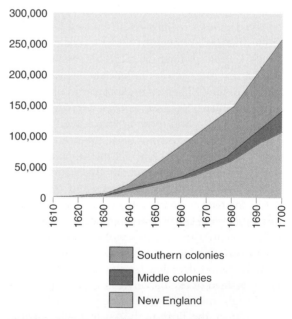

FIGURE 4.1   Population of the British North American Colonies in the Seventeenth Century
The colonial population grew at a steadily accelerating rate during the seventeenth century. New England and the southern colonies each composed about half the total colonial population until after 1680, when growth in Pennsylvania and New York contributed to a surge in the population of the middle colonies.

During the last half of the seventeenth century, under the pressures of steady population growth and integration into the Atlantic economy, the white-hot piety of the founders cooled. After 1640, the population grew faster than church membership. All residents attended sermons on pain of fines and punishment, but many could not find seats in the meetinghouses. By the 1680s, women were the majority of church members throughout New England. In some towns, only 15 percent of the adult men were members. A growing fraction of New Englanders, especially men, embraced what one historian has termed "horse-shed Christianity": They attended sermons but loitered outside near the horse shed, gossiping about the weather, fishing, their crops, or the scandalous behavior of neighbors. This slackening of piety led Puritan minister Michael Wigglesworth to ask, in verse,

How is it that I find
   In stead of holiness Carnality,
In stead of heavenly frames an Earthly mind,
   For burning zeal luke-warm Indifferency,
For flaming love, key-cold Dead-heartedness,
   For temperance (in meat, and drinke, and cloaths) excess?
Whence cometh it, that Pride, and Luxurie
   Debate, Deceit, Contention, and Strife,
False-dealing, Covetousness, Hypocrisie
   (With such Crimes) amongst them are so rife,
That one of them doth over-reach another?
   And that an honest man can hardly trust his
Brother?

Most alarming to Puritan leaders, many of the children of the visible saints of Winthrop's generation failed to experience conversion and attain full church membership. Puritans tended to assume that sainthood was inherited—that the children of visible saints were probably also among the elect. Acting on this premise, churches permitted saints to baptize their infant sons and daughters, symbolically cleansing them of their contamination with original sin. As these children grew up during the 1640s and 1650s, however, they seldom experienced the inward transformation that signaled conversion and qualification for church membership. The problem of declining church membership and the watering-down of Puritan orthodoxy became urgent during the 1650s when the children of saints, who had grown to adulthood in New England but had not experienced conversion, began to have children

themselves. Their sons and daughters—the grandchildren of the founders of the colony—could not receive the protection that baptism afforded against the terrors of death because their parents had not experienced conversion.

Puritan churches debated what to do. To allow anyone, even the child of a saint, to become a church member without conversion was an unthinkable retreat from fundamental Puritan doctrine. In 1662, a synod of Massachusetts ministers reached a compromise known as the **Halfway Covenant.** Unconverted children of saints would be permitted to become "halfway" church members. Like regular church members, they could baptize their infants. But unlike full church members, they could not participate in communion or have the voting privileges of church membership. The Halfway Covenant generated a controversy that sputtered through Puritan churches for the remainder of the century. With the Halfway Covenant, Puritan churches came to terms with the lukewarm piety that had replaced the founders' burning zeal.

Nonetheless, New England communities continued to enforce piety with holy rigor. Beginning in 1656, small bands of Quakers—or members of the Society of Friends, as they called themselves—began to arrive in Massachusetts. Many of their beliefs were at odds with orthodox Puritanism. Quakers believed that God spoke directly to each individual through an "inner light," and that individuals needed neither a preacher nor the Bible in order to discover God's Word. Maintaining that all human beings were equal in God's eyes, Quakers refused to conform to mere temporal powers such as laws and governments unless God requested otherwise.

New England communities treated Quakers with ruthless severity. Some Quakers were branded on the face "with a red-hot iron with [an] H. for heresie." When Quakers refused to leave Massachusetts, Boston officials sentenced two men and a woman to be hanged in 1659.

New Englanders' partial success in realizing the promise of a godly society ultimately undermined the intense appeal of Puritanism. In the pious Puritan communities of New England, leaders tried to eliminate sin. In the process, they diminished the sense of utter human depravity that was the wellspring of Puritanism. By 1700, New Englanders did not doubt that human beings sinned, but they were more concerned with the sins of others than with their own.

Witches Show Their Love for Satan
Mocking pious Christians' humble obeisance to God, witches willingly debased themselves by standing in line to kneel and kiss Satan's buttocks—or so it was popularly believed. This seventeenth-century print portrays Satan with clawlike hands and feet, the tail of a rodent, the wings of a bat, and the head of a lustful ram attached to the torso of a man. Notice that women predominate among the witches eager to express their devotion to Satan and to do his bidding.
UCSF Library / Center for Knowledge Management.

Witch trials held in Salem, Massachusetts, were signs of the erosion of religious confidence and assurance. In 1692, the frenzied Salem proceedings accused more than 100 people of witchcraft, a capital crime. Most of the accused were middle-aged women who, according to their accusers, were in thrall to Satan, who tortured and bedeviled the accusers. Usually accusers had suffered a misfortune that they believed must have been caused by a witch. One woman claimed, for example, that her cow was bewitched because it gave discolored milk. Seventeenth-century New Englanders found such claims plausible since they believed supernatural power—whether God's or Satan's—influenced everything, even the color of a cow's milk. When something bad happened, an unhappy God may have caused it to show his displeasure, or a diabolical Satan acting through a witch might be to blame. If misfortunes could be pinned on a witch in thrall to Satan, then the accuser was absolved of responsibility and guilt. Witches helped New Englanders explain the disorder that crept into their communities: It was caused by Satan's minions, not by godly good folk. The Salem court executed 19 accused witches, signaling enduring belief in the supernatural origins of evil and gnawing doubt about the strength of Puritan New Englanders' faith.

REVIEW Why did Massachusetts Puritans adopt the Halfway Covenant?

The Founding of the Middle Colonies

South of New England and north of the Chesapeake, a group of middle colonies were founded in the last third of the seventeenth century. Before the 1670s, few Europeans settled in the region. For the first two-thirds of the seventeenth century, the most important European outpost in the area was the relatively small Dutch colony of New Netherland. By 1700, however, the English monarchy had seized New Netherland, renamed it New York, and encouraged the creation of a Quaker colony led by William Penn. Unlike the New England colonies, the middle colonies of New York, New Jersey, and Pennsylvania originated as **land grants** by the English monarch to one or more proprietors, who then possessed both the land and the extensive, almost monarchical, powers of government (Map 4.2). These middle colonies attracted settlers of more diverse European origins and religious faiths than were found in New England.

From New Netherland to New York

In 1609, the Dutch East India Company dispatched Henry Hudson to search for a Northwest Passage to the Orient. Hudson sailed along the Atlantic coast and ventured up the large river that now bears his name until it dwindled to a stream that obviously did not lead to China. A decade later, the Dutch government granted the West India Company—a group of Dutch merchants and shippers—exclusive rights to trade with the Western Hemisphere.

In 1626, Peter Minuit, the resident director of the company, purchased Manhattan Island from the Manhate Indians for trade goods worth the equivalent of a dozen beaver pelts. New Amsterdam, the small settlement established at the southern tip of Manhattan Island, became the

MAP 4.2 The Middle Colonies in the Seventeenth Century
For the most part, the middle colonies in the seventeenth century were inhabited by settlers who clustered along the Hudson or Delaware rivers. The vast geographic extent of the colonies shown in this map reflects land grants authorized in England. Most of this area was inhabited by Native Americans rather than settled by colonists.

principal trading center in New Netherland and the colony's headquarters.

Unlike the English colonies, New Netherland did not attract many European immigrants. Although few in number, New Netherlanders were remarkably diverse, especially compared with the homogeneous English settlers to the north and south. Religious dissenters and immigrants from Holland, Sweden, France, Germany, and elsewhere made their way to the colony. A minister of the Dutch Reformed Church complained to his superiors in Holland that several groups of Jews had recently arrived, adding to the religious mixture of "Papists, Mennonites and Lutherans among the Dutch [and] many Puritans...and many other atheists...who conceal themselves under the name of Christians."

The West India Company struggled to govern the motley colonists. Peter Stuyvesant, governor from 1647 to 1664, tried to enforce conformity to the Dutch Reformed Church, but the company declared that "the consciences of men should be free and unshackled," making a virtue of New Netherland necessity. The company never permitted the colony's settlers to form a representative government. Instead, the company appointed government officials who set policies, including taxes, which many colonists deeply resented.

In 1664, New Netherland became New York. Charles II, who became king of England in 1660 when Parliament restored the monarchy, gave his brother James, the Duke of York, an enormous grant of land that included New Netherland. The duke quickly organized a small fleet of warships, which appeared off Manhattan Island in late summer 1664, and demanded that Stuyvesant surrender. With little choice, he did.

As the new proprietor of the colony, the Duke of York exercised almost the same unlimited authority over the colony as had the West India Company. The duke never set foot in New York, but his governors struggled to impose order on the unruly colonists. Like the Dutch, the duke permitted "all persons of what Religion soever, quietly to inhabit...provided they give no disturbance to the publique peace, nor doe molest or disquiet others in the free exercise of their religion." This policy of religious toleration was

New Amsterdam
In the background of this 1673 Dutch portrait of New Amsterdam appears the settlement on Manhattan Island—complete with a windmill. Wharves connect Manhattan residents to the seaborne commerce of the Atlantic world. In the foreground, the Dutch artist placed native inhabitants of the mainland, drawing them in such a way that they resemble Africans rather than Lenni Lenape (Delaware) Indians. Dutch merchants carried tens of thousands of African slaves to New World ports, New Amsterdam among them. Probably, the artist had never seen Indians, had never been to New Amsterdam, and depended on well-known artistic conventions about the appearance of Africans to create his Native Americans. The portrait contrasts orderly, efficient, businesslike New Amsterdam with the exotic natural environment of America, to which the native woman clings as if she is refusing to succumb to the culture represented by those neat rows of rectangular houses across the river.
© Collection of the New-York Historical Society.

less an affirmation of liberty of conscience than a recognition of the reality of the most heterogeneous colony in seventeenth-century North America.

New Jersey and Pennsylvania

The creation of New York led indirectly to the founding of two other middle colonies, New Jersey and Pennsylvania (see Map 4.2). In 1664, the Duke of York subdivided his grant and gave the portion between the Hudson and Delaware rivers to two of his friends. The proprietors of this new colony, New Jersey, quarreled, and called in a prominent English Quaker, William Penn, to arbitrate their dispute. Penn eventually worked out a settlement that continued New Jersey's proprietary government. In the process, Penn became intensely interested in what he

William Penn
This portrait was drawn about a decade after the founding of Pennsylvania. At a time when extravagant clothing and fancy wigs proclaimed that their wearer was an important person, Penn is portrayed informally, lacking even a coat, his natural hair neat but undressed — all a reflection of his Quaker faith. Penn's full face and double chin show that his faith did not make him a stranger to the pleasures of the table. No hollow-cheeked ascetic or wild-eyed enthusiast, Penn appears sober and observant, as if sizing up the viewer and reserving judgment. The portrait captures the calm determination — anchored in faith — that inspired Penn's hopes for his new colony.
Historical Society of Pennsylvania.

termed a "holy experiment" of establishing a genuinely Quaker colony in America.

Unlike most Quakers, William Penn came from an eminent family. His father had served both Cromwell and Charles II and had been knighted. Born in 1644, the younger Penn trained for a military career, but the ideas of dissenters from the reestablished Church of England appealed to him, and he became a devout Quaker.

The Quakers' concept of an open, generous God who made his love equally available to all people manifested itself in behavior that continually brought them into conflict with the English government. Quaker leaders were ordinary men and women, not specially trained preachers. Quakers allowed women to assume positions of religious leadership. "In souls there is no sex," they said. Since all people were equal in the spiritual realm, Quakers considered social hierarchy false and evil. They called everyone "friend" and shook hands instead of curtsying or removing their hats — even when meeting the king. These customs enraged many non-Quakers and provoked innumerable beatings and worse. Penn was jailed four times for such offenses, once for nine months.

Despite his many run-ins with the government, Penn remained on good terms with Charles II. Partly to rid England of the troublesome Quakers, Charles made Penn the proprietor in 1681 of a new colony called Pennsylvania.

Toleration and Diversity in Pennsylvania

Quakers flocked to Pennsylvania; between 1682 and 1685, nearly 8,000 immigrants arrived, most of them from England, Ireland, and Wales. They represented a cross section of the **artisans**, farmers, and laborers who predominated among English Quakers. Quaker missionaries also encouraged immigrants from the European continent, and many came, giving Pennsylvania greater ethnic diversity than any other English colony except New York. The Quaker colony prospered, and the capital city, Philadelphia, soon rivaled New York as a center of commerce. By 1700, the city's 5,000 inhabitants participated in a thriving trade exporting flour and other food products to the West Indies and importing English textiles and manufactured goods.

Penn was determined to live in peace with the Indians who inhabited the region. His Indian policy expressed his Quaker ideals and contrasted sharply with the hostile policies of the other English colonies. Penn instructed his agents to obtain the Indians' consent by purchasing their land, respecting their claims, and dealing with them fairly.

Penn declared that the first principle of government was that every settler would "enjoy the free possession of his or her faith and exercise of worship towards God." Accordingly, Pennsylvania tolerated Protestant sects of all kinds as well as Roman Catholics. All voters and officeholders had to be Christians, but the government did not compel settlers to attend religious services, as in Massachusetts, or to pay taxes to maintain a state-supported church, as in Virginia.

Despite its toleration and diversity, Pennsylvania was as much a Quaker colony as New England was a stronghold of Puritanism. Penn had no hesitation about using civil government to enforce religious morality. One of the colony's first laws provided severe punishment for "all such offenses against God, as swearing, cursing, lying, profane talking, drunkenness, drinking of healths, [and] obscene words... which excite the people to rudeness, cruelty, looseness, and irreligion."

As proprietor, Penn had extensive powers, subject only to review by the king. He appointed a governor who maintained the proprietor's power to veto any laws passed by the colonial council, which was elected by property owners who possessed at least one hundred acres of land or who paid taxes. The council had the power to originate laws and administer all the affairs of government. A popularly elected assembly served as a check on the council; its members had the authority to reject or approve laws framed by the council.

Penn stressed that the exact form of government mattered less than the men who served in it. In Penn's eyes, "good men" staffed Pennsylvania's government because Quakers dominated elective and appointive offices. Quakers, of course, differed among themselves. Members of the assembly struggled to win the right to debate and amend laws, especially tax laws. They finally won the battle in 1701 when a new Charter of Privileges gave the proprietor the power to appoint the council and in turn stripped the council of all its former powers and gave them to the assembly, which became the only single-house legislature in all the British colonies.

REVIEW How did Quaker ideals shape the colony of Pennsylvania?

The Colonies and the British Empire

Proprietary grants to faraway lands had been a cheap way for the king to reward friends. As the colonies grew, however, the grants became more valuable. After 1660, the king took initiatives to channel colonial trade through English hands and to consolidate royal authority over colonial governments. These initiatives defined the basic relationship between the colonies and England that endured until the American Revolution (Map 4.3).

Royal Regulation of Colonial Trade

English economic policies toward the colonies were designed to yield customs revenues for the monarchy and profitable business for English merchants and shippers. Also, the policies were intended to divert the colonies' trade from England's enemies, especially the Dutch and the French.

The Navigation Acts of 1650, 1651, 1660, and 1663 (see chapter 3) set forth two fundamental rules governing colonial trade. First, goods shipped to and from the colonies had to be transported in English ships using primarily English crews. Second, the Navigation Acts listed ("enumerated," in the language of the time) specific colonial products that could be shipped only to England or to other English colonies. While these regulations prevented Chesapeake **planters** from shipping their tobacco directly to the European continent, they interfered less with the commerce of New England and the middle colonies, whose principal exports—fish, lumber, and flour—were not enumerated and could legally be sent directly to their most important markets in the West Indies.

By the end of the seventeenth century, colonial commerce was defined by regulations that subjected merchants and shippers to royal supervision and gave them access to markets throughout the British empire. In addition, colonial commerce received protection from the British navy. By 1700, colonial goods (including those from the West Indies) accounted for one-fifth of all British imports and for two-thirds of all goods reexported from England to the European continent. In turn, the colonies absorbed more than one-tenth of British exports. The commercial regulations gave economic value to England's proprietorship of American colonies.

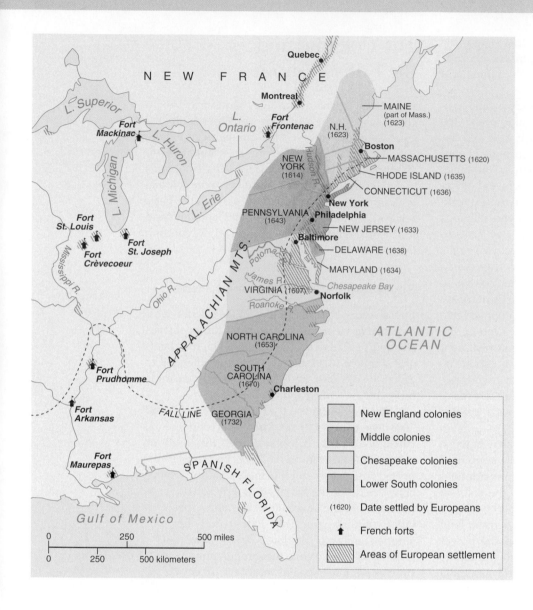

MAP 4.3 American Colonies at the End of the Seventeenth Century

By the end of the seventeenth century, settlers inhabited a narrow band of land that stretched more or less continuously from Boston to Norfolk, with pockets of settlement farther south. The colonies' claims to enormous tracts of land to the west were contested by Native Americans as well as by France and Spain.

Pine Tree Shilling

Currency was in short supply in the colonies. Since England prohibited the export of its coins, the precious currency circulating in the North American colonies tended to be Spanish, Dutch, French, or Portuguese. In violation of English rules that forbade colonies from issuing their own currency, John Hull, a wealthy Boston merchant and shipowner, began to mint coins in 1652. Shown here is one of his pine tree shillings, both sides boldly announcing its Massachusetts origins. A shilling was worth twelve pennies; twenty shillings equaled a pound sterling. Despite Hull's attempt to ease the currency shortage, the legal tender most colonists used consisted of such commonly available items as bushels of corn or wheat, skins of beaver or deer, and, following Native American practice, wampum.

Courtesy of the Museum of the American Numismatic Association.

King Philip's War and the Consolidation of Royal Authority

The monarchy also took steps to exercise greater control over colonial governments. Virginia had been a royal colony since 1624; Maryland, South Carolina, and the middle colonies were proprietary colonies with close ties to the crown. The New England colonies possessed royal charters, but they had developed their own distinctively Puritan governments. Charles II, whose father, Charles I, had been executed by Puritans in England, took a particular interest in harnessing the New England colonies more firmly to the British empire. The occasion was a royal investigation following King Philip's War.

In 1675, warfare between Indians and colonists erupted in the Chesapeake and New England. Massachusetts settlers had massacred hundreds of Pequot Indians in 1637, but they had established relatively peaceful relations with the more potent Wampanoags. In the decades that followed, New Englanders steadily encroached on Indian lands, and, in 1675, the Wampanoags struck back with attacks on settlements in western Massachusetts. Metacomet—whom the colonists called King Philip—probably neither planned the attacks nor masterminded a conspiracy with the Nipmucks and the Narragansetts, as the colonists feared. But when militias from Massachusetts and other New England colonies counterattacked all three tribes, a deadly sequence of battles killed over a thousand colonists and thousands more Indians. The Indians utterly destroyed thirteen English settlements and partially burned another half dozen. The colonists finally defeated the Indians, principally with a scorched-earth policy of burning their food supplies. King Philip's War left the New England colonists with an enduring hatred of Indians, a large war debt, and a devastated frontier. And in 1676, an agent of the king arrived to investigate whether New England was abiding by English laws.

Not surprisingly, the king's agent found all sorts of deviations from English rules, and the monarchy decided to govern New England more directly. In 1684, an English

King Philip (Metacomet)
No portrait of Metacomet, or King Philip, was made during his lifetime. The artist of this likeness imagines him as a proud warrior wrapped in a shawl and armed with a musket, which indicates both his adoption of this European weapon and his willingness to use it against English colonists.
Library of Congress.

King Philip's War, 1675

Pennacook
Pocumtuck
Peskeompscut
Deerfield (Turner's Falls)
MASSACHUSETTS
Northampton   Boston
Nipmuck   Deer Island
Springfield   Plymouth
Hartford   Pocasset
CONNECTICUT   Wampanoag
Mount   Nauset
New Haven   Hope
Great Swamp Fight   Sakonnet
Dec. 1675   Kingston
Mohegan
RHODE   Narragansett
ISLAND   Fort

♦ Indian settlements
● English settlements attacked

court revoked the Massachusetts charter, the foundation of the distinctive Puritan government. Two years later, royal officials incorporated Massachusetts and the other colonies north of Maryland into the Dominion of New England. To govern the dominion, the English sent Sir Edmund Andros to Boston. Some New England merchants cooperated with Andros, but most colonists were offended by his flagrant disregard of such Puritan traditions as keeping the Sabbath. Worst of all, the Dominion of New England invalidated all land titles, confronting every landowner in

King Philip's Sash
This woolen sash belonged to Wampanoag chief Metacomet, or King Philip. Small white glass beads, obtained through trade with Europeans, are stitched into the sash in the shape of a serpent.
Peabody Museum of Archaeology and Ethnology, Harvard University.

New England with the horrifying prospect of losing his or her land.

Events in England, however, permitted Massachusetts colonists to overthrow Andros and retain title to their property. When Charles II died in 1685, he was succeeded by his brother James II, a zealous Catholic. James's aggressive campaign to appoint Catholics to government posts engendered such unrest that in 1688 a group of Protestant noblemen in Parliament invited the Dutch ruler William III of Orange, James's son-in-law, to claim the English throne. When William III landed in England at the head of a large army, James fled to France and William III and his wife Mary II (James's daughter) became co-rulers in the relatively bloodless "Glorious Revolution," reasserting Protestant influence in England and its empire.

Rumors of the revolution raced across the Atlantic and emboldened colonial uprisings against royal authority in Massachusetts, New York, and Maryland. In Boston in 1689, rebels tossed Andros and other English officials in jail, destroyed the Dominion of New England, and re-established the former charter government. New Yorkers followed the Massachusetts example. Under the leadership of Jacob Leisler, rebels seized the royal governor in 1689 and ruled the colony for more than a year. That same year in Maryland, the Protestant Association, led by John Coode, overthrew the colony's pro-Catholic government, fearing it would not recognize the new Protestant king.

But these rebel governments did not last. When King William III's governor of New York arrived in 1691, he executed Leisler for treason. Coode's men ruled Maryland until the new royal governor arrived in 1692 and ended both Coode's rebellion and Lord Baltimore's proprietary government. In Massachusetts, John Winthrop's city on a hill became another royal colony in 1691. The new charter said that the governor of the colony would be appointed by the king rather than elected by the colonists' representatives. But perhaps the most unsettling change was the new qualification for voting. Possession of property replaced church membership as a prerequisite for voting in colony-wide elections. Wealth replaced God's grace as the defining characteristic of Massachusetts citizenship.

Much as colonists chafed under increasing royal control, they still valued English protection from hostile neighbors. While the northern colonies were distracted by the Glorious Revolution, French forces from the fur-trading regions along the Great Lakes and in Canada attacked villages in New England and New York. Known as King William's War, the conflict with the French was a colonial outgrowth of William's war against France in Europe. The war dragged on until 1697 and ended inconclusively in both Europe and the colonies. But it made clear to many colonists that along with English royal government came a welcome measure of military security.

REVIEW   Why did the "Glorious Revolution" in England lead to uprisings in the American colonies?

Conclusion: An English Model of Colonization in North America

By 1700, the diverse English colonies in North America had developed along lines quite different from the example New Spain had set in 1600. In the North American colonies, English immigrants and their descendants created societies of settlers unlike the largely Indian societies in New Spain ruled by a tiny group of Spaniards. Although many settlers came to North America from other parts of Europe and a growing number of Africans arrived in bondage, English laws, habits, ideas, and language dominated all the colonies.

Economically, the English colonies thrived on agriculture and trade instead of mining silver and exploiting Indian labor as in New Spain. Southern colonies grew huge crops of tobacco and rice with the labor of indentured servants and slaves, while farmers in the middle colonies planted wheat and New England fishermen harvested the sea. Although servants and slaves could be found throughout the North American colonies, many settlers depended principally on the labor of family members. Relations between settlers and Native Americans often exploded in bloody warfare, but Indians seldom served as an important source of labor for settlers, as they did in New Spain.

Protestantism prevailed in the North American settlements, relaxed in some colonies and straitlaced in others. The convictions of Puritanism that motivated John Winthrop and others to build a new England in the colonies became muted as the New England colonies matured and dissenters like Roger Williams multiplied. Catholics, Quakers, Anglicans (members of the Church of England), Jews, and others settled in the middle and southern colonies, creating considerable religious toleration, especially in Pennsylvania and New York.

Politics and government differed from colony to colony, although the imprint of English institutions and practices existed everywhere. And everywhere, local settlers who were free adult white men had an extraordinary degree of political influence, far beyond that of colonists in New Spain or ordinary citizens in England. A new world of settlers that Columbus could not have imagined, that Powhatan only glimpsed, had been firmly established in English North America by 1700. During the next half century, that English colonial world would undergo surprising new developments built on the achievements of the seventeenth century.

Suggestions for Further Reading

Virginia DeJohn Anderson, *Creatures of Empire: How Domestic Animals Transformed Early America* (2004). An innovative study of the influence of domestic animals on humans and the natural environment in early America.

Colin G. Calloway, *New Worlds for All: Indians, Europeans, and the Remaking of Early America* (1998). A sweeping overview of encounters between European settlers and Native Americans.

David D. Hall, *Worlds of Wonder, Days of Judgment: Popular Religious Belief in Early New England* (1989). A fascinating survey of popular religious belief in the context of Puritan New England.

Eve LaPlante, *American Jezebel: The Uncommon Life of Anne Hutchinson, the Woman Who Defied the Puritans* (2005). A compelling biography of the Puritan woman who challenged early New England orthodoxy.

Mary Beth Norton, *In the Devil's Snare: The Salem Witchcraft Crisis of 1692* (2002). An authoritative analysis of the cultural cross-currents that influenced the Salem witchcraft crisis.

Russell Shorto, *The Island at the Center of the World: The Epic Story of Dutch Manhattan and the Forgotten Colony That Shaped America* (2004). A vivid account of the Dutch colony that became New York.

▶ FOR MORE BOOKS ABOUT TOPICS IN THIS CHAPTER, see the Online Bibliography at bedfordstmartins.com/roarkcompact.

▶ FOR ADDITIONAL FIRSTHAND ACCOUNTS OF THIS PERIOD, see Chapter 4 in Michael Johnson, ed., *Reading the American Past*, Third Edition.

▶ FOR WEB SITES AND DOCUMENTS RELATED TO TOPICS AND PLACES IN THIS CHAPTER, see "HistoryLinks," "DocLinks," and "PlaceLinks" at bedfordstmartins.com/roarkcompact.

REVIEWING THE CHAPTER

Follow these steps to review and strengthen your understanding of the chapter.

STEP 1: *Study the* **Key Terms** *and* **Timeline** *to identify the significance of each item listed.*

STEP 2: *Answer the* **Review Questions,** *drawing on key terms and dates to support your answers.*

STEP 3: *Drawing on the Key Terms, Timeline, and Review Questions, answer the broader* **Making Connections** *questions.*

KEY TERMS

Who

Roger Williams (p. 77)
Henry VIII (p. 78)
Elizabeth I (p. 79)
James I (p. 79)
Charles I (p. 79)
Pilgrims (p. 80)
William Bradford (p. 80)
Wampanoag Indians (p. 80, 97)
John Winthrop (p. 80)
John Calvin (p. 85)
"visible saints" (p. 86)
Anne Hutchinson (p. 88)
John Cotton (p. 88)
antinomians (p. 89)
Thomas Hooker (p. 89)
Oliver Cromwell (p. 89)
Quakers (p. 91)
Peter Minuit (p. 92)
Manhate Indians (p. 92)
Peter Stuyvesant (p. 93)
Charles II (p. 93)
Duke of York (p. 93)

William Penn (p. 94)
Pequot Indians (p. 97)
Metacomet (p. 97)
Edmund Andros (p. 97)
James II (p. 98)
William III of Orange (p. 98)
Mary II (p. 98)
Jacob Leisler (p. 98)
John Coode (p. 98)

What

Rhode Island (p. 78)
English Reformation (p. 79)
Act of Supremacy (p. 79)
Church of England (p. 79)
Puritanism (p. 79)
separatism (p. 80)
Mayflower Compact (p. 80)
Plymouth (p. 80)
royal charter (p. 80)
Massachusetts Bay Company (p. 80)
Boston (p. 80)
Arbella (p. 80)

Calvinism (p. 85)
predestination (p. 85)
General Court (p. 87)
town meeting (p. 87)
covenant of grace (p. 88)
covenant of works (p. 89)
Arminianism (p. 89)
Fundamental Orders of Connecticut
   (p. 89)
Puritan Revolution (p. 89)
Halfway Covenant (p. 91)
Dutch East India Company
   (p. 92)
Manhattan Island (p. 92)
Philadelphia (p. 94)
Charter of Privileges (p. 95)
Navigation Acts (p. 95)
King Philip's War (p. 97)
Dominion of New England
   (p. 97)
Glorious Revolution (p. 98)
Protestant Association (p. 98)
King William's War (p. 98)

TIMELINE

◄ **1534** • King Henry VIII breaks with Roman Catholic Church.

1609 • Henry Hudson searches for Northwest Passage.

1620 • Plymouth colony is founded.

1626 • Manhattan Island is purchased and New Amsterdam founded.

1629 • Massachusetts Bay Company receives royal charter.

1630 • John Winthrop leads Puritan settlers to Massachusetts Bay.

1636 • Rhode Island colony is established.
       • Connecticut colony is founded.

1638 • Anne Hutchinson is excommunicated.

1642 • Puritan Revolution inflames England.

1649
       • English Puritans win civil war and execute Charles I.

REVIEW QUESTIONS

1. Why did Henry VIII initiate the English Reformation? (pp. 78–79)

2. Why did the Puritans immigrate to North America? (pp. 80–84)

3. Why did Massachusetts Puritans adopt the Halfway Covenant? (pp. 85–92)

4. How did Quaker ideals shape the colony of Pennsylvania? (pp. 92–95)

5. Why did the "Glorious Revolution" in England lead to uprisings in the American colonies? (pp. 95–98)

MAKING CONNECTIONS

1. How did the religious dissenters who flooded into the northern colonies address the question of religious dissent in their new homes? Comparing two colonies, discuss their different approaches and the implications of those approaches for colonial development.

2. In his sermon aboard the *Arbella*, John Winthrop spoke of the Massachusetts Bay Colony as "a city upon a hill." What did he mean? How did this expectation influence life in New England during the seventeenth century? In your answer, be sure to consider the relationship between religious and political life in the colony.

3. Religious conflict and political turmoil battered England in the seventeenth century. How did political developments in England affect life in the colonies? In your answer, consider the establishment of the colonies and the crown's attempts to exercise authority over them.

4. Although both were settled by the English, colonial New England was dramatically different from the colonial Chesapeake. How did they differ and why? In your answer, consider the economies, systems of governance, and patterns of settlement in each colony.

► FOR PRACTICE QUIZZES, A CUSTOMIZED STUDY PLAN, AND OTHER STUDY TOOLS, see the Online Study Guide at **bedfordstmartins.com/roarkcompact**.

1656 • Quakers arrive in Massachusetts and are persecuted there.

   1660 • Monarchy restored in England; Charles II becomes king.
        • Navigation Act.

    1662 • Many Puritan congregations adopt Halfway Covenant.

     1663 • Staple Act.

      1664 • English seize Dutch colony, rename it New York.
          • Colony of New Jersey created.

          1675 • King Philip's War.

            1681 • William Penn receives a charter for colony of Pennsylvania.

              1686 • Dominion of New England created.

               1688 • England's "Glorious Revolution"; William III and Mary II become the new rulers.

                 1692 • Salem witch trials.

COLONIAL SLAVE DRUM

An African in Virginia made this drum sometime around the beginning of the eighteenth century. The maker of the drum was probably a man who had been enslaved in Africa, transported across the Atlantic in the hold of a slave ship, and sold to a tobacco planter in the Chesapeake. The drum combines deerskin and cedar wood from North America with African skills and designs the maker had mastered before enslavement. The drum signifies the millions of enslaved African men, women, and children who were among the many goods bought and sold in the booming transatlantic trade of the eighteenth century. At a time when Benjamin Franklin and other whites—both native-born and immigrants from Europe—were finding opportunities to better their lives in America, tens of thousands of Africans were arriving in the British North American colonies in hereditary, lifetime bondage. The drum embodies slaves' use of African cultural resources in the alien and oppressive environment of New World slavery. During moments of respite from work, slaves played drums to accompany dances learned in Africa. They also drummed out messages from plantation to plantation. Whites knew slaves used drums for communication, but they could not decipher the meanings of the rhythms and sounds. Fearful that drums signaled rebellious up-risings, whites outlawed drumming but could not eliminate it. Most likely, the messages expressed by the hands that struck this drumhead included lamentations about a life of bondage in America.

Colonial America in the Eighteenth Century
1701–1770

EARLY ON A SUNDAY MORNING in October 1723, young Benjamin Franklin stepped from a wharf along the Delaware River onto the streets of Philadelphia. As he recalled in his autobiography, "I was dirty from my Journey; my Pockets were stuff'd out with Shirts and Stockings; I knew no Soul, nor where to look for Lodging. I was fatigu'd with Travelling, Rowing and Want of Rest. I was very hungry."

Born in 1706, Benjamin Franklin grew up in Boston, where his father, Josiah, worked making soap and candles. At the age of twelve, Benjamin signed a contract to serve for nine years as an apprentice to his brother James, a printer. In James's shop, Benjamin learned the printer's trade and had access to the latest books and pamphlets, which he read avidly. In 1721, James inaugurated the *New England Courant*, avowing to "expose the Vice and Follies of Persons of all Ranks and Degrees" with articles written "so that the meanest ploughman…may understand them."

Benjamin's responsibilities in the print shop grew quickly, but "My Brother was passionate and had often beaten me," he remembered. Benjamin resolved to escape from his apprenticeship "to assert my Freedom" and to run away to New York, nearly three hundred miles from anyone he knew. When he could not find work there, he talked his way aboard a small boat heading toward Philadelphia. After rowing half the night, Franklin arrived in the city and went straight to a bakery where he purchased "three great Puffy Rolls." Then he set off for the wharf, "with a Roll under each Arm," to wash down the bread with "a Draught of the River Water." After quenching his thirst, Franklin followed "many clean dress'd People…to the great Meeting House of the Quakers.…I sat down among them, and…I fell fast asleep, and continu'd so till the Meeting broke up."

Franklin's account of his life in Boston and his arrival in Philadelphia illustrates everyday experiences shared by many other colonists: long hours of labor subject to the authority of a parent, relative, or employer; and a restless quest for escape from the ties that bound, for freedom. Franklin's account hints at other, less tangible trends: ambition to make something of oneself in this world rather than worry too much about the hereafter; eagerness to subvert orthodox opinion by publishing dissenting views expressed in simple, clear language understandable by "the meanest ploughman"; confidence that, with a valued skill and a few coins, a young man could make his way in the world; and a slackening of religious fervor displayed, for example, in Franklin's quiet snooze during the Quaker meeting he wandered into on his first day in Philadelphia.

Mrs. Charles Willing

This portrait of Mrs. Charles Willing of Philadelphia illustrates the prosperity achieved by numerous women and men in the eighteenth-century colonies. Painted by the Philadelphia artist Robert Feke in 1746, the portrait depicts the close connections between Europe and the North American colonies made possible by thriving transatlantic commerce. Scholars have discovered that Anna Maria Garthwaite, an established textile designer in Spitalfields — a silk-weaving center near London — designed the silk used to make Mrs. Willing's dress in 1743. A Spitalfields weaver, Simeon Julins, then wove the fabric in the months between the fall of 1743 and the spring of 1744 and sold it to a merchant who exported it to Philadelphia in 1744. Mrs. Willing must have spotted the silk in a shop much like the one Benjamin Franklin eventually ran with his wife Deborah after he had become more established in Philadelphia. Mrs. Willing would have purchased enough to have this fashionable gown sewn and fitted for her portrait, only three years after Anna Garthwaite first sketched the design in Spitalfields. The portrait demonstrates that, like other prosperous colonists, Mrs. Willing kept abreast of the latest London fashions available in the shops of colonial merchants.

Courtesy, Winterthur Museum, gift of Mrs. George P. Bissell Jr.

Franklin's story introduces some of the major changes that affected all the British colonies in eighteenth-century North America. Social and economic changes tended to reinforce the differences among New England, the middle colonies, and the southern colonies, while important cultural and political developments tugged in the opposite direction, creating common experiences, aspirations, and identities. In 1776, when *E Pluribus Unum* (Latin meaning "From Many, One") was adopted as the motto for the Great Seal of the United States, the changes in eighteenth-century America that strengthened *Pluribus* also planted the seeds of *Unum*.

In contrast to the British colonies' economic growth and political maturation, the Spanish and French colonies in North America remained thinly populated outposts of European empires interested principally in maintaining a toehold in the vast North American territories they claimed. The social, cultural, and religious developments that tended to unify the British North American colonies were unique to what would soon become the United States of America.

A Growing Population and Expanding Economy in British North America

The most important fact about eighteenth-century British America is its phenomenal population growth: In 1700, colonists numbered about 250,000; by 1770, they tallied well over 2 million. An index of the emerging significance of colonial America is that in 1700 there were 19 people in England for every American colonist, but by 1770 there were only 3. The eightfold growth of the colonial population signaled the maturation of a distinctive colonial society. That society was by no means homogeneous. Colonists of different ethnic groups, races, and religions lived in varied environments under thirteen different colonial governments, all of them part of the British empire.

In general, the growth and diversity of the eighteenth-century colonial population derived from two sources: immigration and natural increase (growth through reproduction). Natural increase contributed about three-fourths of the population growth, immigration about one-fourth. Immigration shifted the ethnic and racial balance among the colonists, making them by

1770 less English and less white than ever before. Fewer than 10 percent of eighteenth-century immigrants came from England; about 36 percent were Scots-Irish, mostly from northern Ireland; 33 percent arrived from Africa, almost all of them slaves; nearly 15 percent had left the many German-language principalities (the nation of Germany did not exist until 1871); and almost 10 percent came from Scotland. In 1670, more than 9 out of 10 colonists were of English ancestry, and only 1 out of 25 was of African ancestry. By 1770, only about half the colonists were of English descent, while more than 20 percent descended from Africans. By 1770, the people of the colonies had a distinctive colonial—rather than English—profile (Map 5.1).

The booming population of the colonies hints at a second major feature of eighteenth-century colonial society: an expanding economy. In 1700, after almost a century of settlement, nearly all the colonists lived within fifty miles of the Atlantic coast. The almost limitless wilderness stretching westward made land relatively cheap. Land in the colonies commonly sold for a fraction of its price in the Old World. The abundance of land in the colonies made labor precious, and the colonists always needed more. The colonists' insatiable demand for labor was the fundamental economic environment that sustained the mushrooming population. Economic historians estimate that free colonists (those who were not **indentured servants** or slaves) had a higher standard of living than the majority of people elsewhere in the Atlantic world. The unique achievement of the eighteenth-century colonial economy was the modest economic welfare of the vast bulk of the free population.

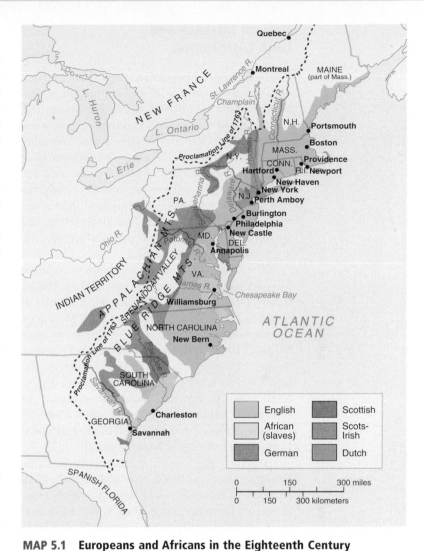

MAP 5.1   Europeans and Africans in the Eighteenth Century
This map illustrates regions where Africans and certain immigrant groups clustered. It is important to avoid misreading the map. Predominantly English and German regions, for example, also contained colonists from other places. Likewise, regions where African slaves resided in large numbers also included many whites, slave masters among them. The map suggests the polyglot diversity of eighteenth-century colonial society.

REVIEW   How did the North American colonies achieve the remarkable population growth of the eighteenth century?

New England: From Puritan Settlers to Yankee Traders

The New England population grew sixfold during the eighteenth century but lagged behind the growth in the other colonies. Why did New England fail to keep pace? Most immigrants chose other destinations because of New England's relatively densely settled land and because Puritan orthodoxy made these colonies comparatively inhospitable to religious dissenters and those indifferent to religion. As the population grew, many settlers in search of farmland dispersed from towns, and Puritan communities lost much of their cohesion. Nonetheless, networks of economic exchange laced New Englanders to their neighbors, to Boston merchants, and to the broad currents of Atlantic commerce. In many ways, trade became a faith that competed strongly with the traditions of **Puritanism**.

Natural Increase and Land Distribution

The New England population grew mostly by natural increase, much as it had during the seventeenth century. Nearly every adult woman married. Most married women had children—often many children, thanks to the relatively low mortality rate in New England. The perils of childbirth gave wives a shorter life expectancy than husbands, but wives often lived to have six, seven, or eight babies. When a wife died, her husband usually remarried quickly. Benjamin Franklin's father had seven children with his first wife and ten (including Benjamin) with his second.

The burgeoning New England population pressed against a limited amount of land. The interior of New England was smaller than that of colonies farther south (see Map 5.1). Moreover, as the northernmost group of colonies, New England had a contested northern and western frontier. Powerful Indian tribes, especially the Iroquois and Mahicans, jealously guarded their territories. When provoked by colonial or European disputes, the French (and Catholic) colony of Quebec also menaced the English (and **Protestant**) colonies of New England.

During the seventeenth century, New England towns parceled out land to individual families. In most cases, the original settlers practiced partible inheritance (they subdivided land more or less equally among sons). By the eighteenth century, the original land allotments had to be further subdivided to accommodate grandsons and great-grandsons, and many plots of land became too small for subsistence. Sons who could not hope to inherit sufficient land to farm had to move away from the town where they were born.

During the eighteenth century, colonial governments in New England abandoned the seventeenth-century policy of granting land to towns. Needing revenue, the governments of both Connecticut and Massachusetts sold land directly to individuals, including speculators. Now money, rather than membership in a community bound by a church **covenant**, determined whether a person could obtain land. The new land policy eroded the seventeenth-century pattern of settlement. As colonists moved, they tended to settle on individual farms rather than in the towns and villages that characterized the seventeenth century. New Englanders still depended on their relatives and neighbors for help in clearing land, raising a house, worshipping God, and having a good time. But far more than in the seventeenth century, they regulated their behavior in newly settled areas by their own individual dictates.

Farms, Fish, and Trade

A New England farm was a place to get by, not to get rich. New England farmers did not produce a huge marketable surplus. Instead of one big crop, farmers grew many small ones. If they had extra, they sold to or traded with neighbors. Poor roads made travel difficult, time-consuming, and expensive, especially with bulky and heavy agricultural goods. The one major agricultural product the New England colonies exported—livestock—walked to market on its own legs. By 1770, New Englanders had only one-fourth as much wealth as free colonists in the southern colonies.

As consumers, New England farmers were the foundation of a diversified commercial economy that linked remote farms to markets throughout the world. Merchants large and small stocked imported goods—English textiles, ceramics, and metal goods; Chinese tea; West Indian sugar; and Chesapeake tobacco. Larger towns, especially Boston, housed skilled tradesmen such as cabinetmakers and silversmiths, along with printers like Benjamin Franklin's brother. Shipbuilders tended to do better than other **artisans** because they served the most dynamic sector of the New England economy.

Many New Englanders made their fortunes at sea, as they had since the seventeenth century. Fish accounted for more than a third of New England's eighteenth-century exports; livestock and timber made up another third. The West Indies absorbed two-thirds of all New England's exports. Slaves on Caribbean sugar plantations ate dried, salted codfish caught by New England fishermen, filled barrels crafted from New England timber with molasses and refined sugar, and loaded those barrels aboard ships bound ultimately for Europeans with a sweet tooth (Map 5.2). Almost all the rest of New England's exports went to England and continental Europe.

Merchants dominated this Atlantic commerce. The largest and most successful merchants lived in Boston, where they not only bought and sold imported goods but also owned and insured the ships that carried the merchandise. The luxurious homes of Boston's merchants

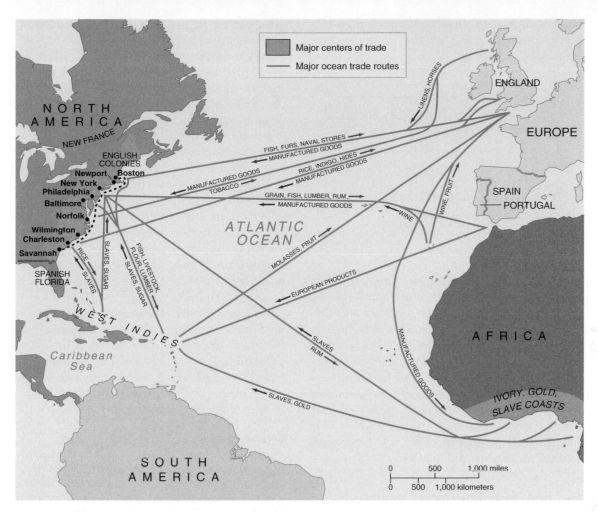

MAP 5.2   Atlantic Trade in the Eighteenth Century
This map illustrates the economic outlook of the colonies in the eighteenth century—east toward the Atlantic world rather than west toward the interior of North America. The long distances involved in the Atlantic trade and the uncertainties of seaborne travel suggest the difficulties Britain experienced governing the colonies and regulating colonial commerce.

contrasted with the modest dwellings of other New Englanders, an indication of the polarization of wealth that occurred in Boston and other seaports during the eighteenth century. By 1770, the richest 5 percent of Bostonians owned about half the city's wealth; the poorest two-thirds of the population owned less than one-tenth.

Although the rich got richer and everybody else had a smaller share of the total wealth, the incidence of genuine poverty did not change much. Overall, colonists were better off than most people in England. A Connecticut traveler wrote from England in 1764, "We in New England know nothing of poverty and want, we have no idea of the thing, how much better do our poor people live than 7/8 of the people on this much famed island."

The contrast with English poverty had meaning because the overwhelming majority of New Englanders traced their ancestry to England; New England was more homogeneous than any other region. People of African ancestry (almost all of them slaves) barely diluted the region's 97 percent white majority. New Englanders had no hesitation about acquiring slaves, and many Puritan ministers owned one or two. But New England's family farms were unsuited for slave labor. Instead, slaves concentrated in towns, especially Boston, where most of them worked as domestic servants and laborers.

By 1770, the population, wealth, and commercial activity of New England differed from what they had been in 1700. Ministers still enjoyed high status, but Yankee traders had replaced Puritan saints as the symbolic New Englanders.

> **REVIEW**   Why did settlement patterns in New England change from the seventeenth to the eighteenth century?

The Middle Colonies: Immigrants, Wheat, and Work

In 1700, almost twice as many people lived in New England as in the middle colonies of Pennsylvania, New York, New Jersey, and Delaware. But by 1770, the population of the middle colonies had multiplied tenfold—mainly from an influx of German, Irish, Scottish, and other immigrants—and nearly equaled the population of New England. Immigrants made the middle colonies a uniquely diverse society. By 1800, barely one-third of Pennsylvanians and less than half the total population of the middle colonies traced their ancestry to England.

German and Scots-Irish Immigrants

Germans made up the largest contingent of migrants from the European continent to the middle colonies. By 1770, about 85,000 Germans had arrived in the colonies. Their fellow colonists often referred to them as "Pennsylvania Dutch," an English corruption of *Deutsch,* the word the immigrants used to describe themselves.

Most German immigrants came from what is now southwestern Germany, where, one observer noted, peasants were "not as well off as cattle elsewhere." Devastating French invasions of Germany during Queen Anne's War (1702–1713) made bad conditions worse and triggered the first large-scale migration. German immigrants included numerous artisans and a few merchants, but the great majority were farmers and laborers. Economically, they represented "middling" folk, neither the poorest (who could

not afford the trip) nor the better off (who did not want to leave).

By the 1720s, Germans who had established themselves in the colonies wrote back to their friends and relatives, as one reported, "of the civil and religious liberties [and] privileges, and of all the goodness I have heard and seen." Such letters prompted still more Germans to pull up stakes and embark for America, to exchange the miserable certainties of their lives in Europe for the uncertain attractions of life in the colonies.

Similar motives propelled the Scots-Irish, who considerably outnumbered German immigrants. The term *Scots-Irish* was another misleading label coined in the colonies. Immigrants labeled "Scots-Irish" actually hailed from the north of Ireland, Scotland, and northern England. Like the Germans, the Scots-Irish were Protestants, but with a difference. Most German immigrants worshipped in Lutheran or German Reformed churches; many others belonged to dissenting sects such as the Mennonites, Moravians, and Amish, whose adherents sought

German Hymnal

This manuscript hymnal contains words and music created by Johann Conrad Beissel, the founder of the Seventh-Day Baptists and among the earliest musical composers in the colonies. A German sect that migrated to Pennsylvania in 1732, the Seventh-Day Baptists, like many other German immigrants, continued to worship in their native German long after arriving in the British colonies. Once owned by Benjamin Franklin, this book expresses on its title page the hymns' evocation of the Seventh-Day Baptists' vision of this world and the next: "The Bitter good, or the song of the turtledove, the Christian church here on earth, in the valley of sadness, where it bemoans its 'widowhood'; and at the same time sings of another future reunion [with God]." Roger Foley/Library of Congress.

relief from persecution they had suffered in Europe for their refusal to bear arms and to swear oaths, practices they shared with Quakers. In contrast, the Scots-Irish tended to be militant Presbyterians who seldom hesitated to bear arms or swear oaths. Like German settlers, however, Scots-Irish immigrants were clannish, residing when they could among relatives or neighbors from the old country.

In the eighteenth century, wave after wave of Scots-Irish immigrants arrived, beginning in 1717, cresting every twelve or fifteen years thereafter, and culminating in a flood of immigration in the years just before the American Revolution. Deteriorating economic conditions in northern Ireland, Scotland, and England pushed many toward America. Most of the immigrants were farm laborers or tenant farmers fleeing droughts, crop failures, high food prices, or rising rents. They came, they told British officials, because of "poverty," "tyranny of landlords," and the desire to "do better in America."

Both Scots-Irish and Germans probably heard the common saying that "Pennsylvania is heaven for farmers [and] paradise for artisans," but they almost certainly did not fully understand the risks of their decision to leave their native lands. Ship captains, aware of the hunger for labor in the colonies, eagerly signed up the penniless emigrants as "redemptioners," a variant of indentured servants. A captain would agree to provide transportation to Philadelphia, where redemptioners would obtain the money to pay for their passage by borrowing it from a friend or relative who was already in the colonies or, as most did, by selling themselves as servants. Impoverished Scots-Irish emigrants, especially the majority who traveled alone rather than with families, typically paid for their passage by contracting as indentured servants before they sailed to the colonies.

Redemptioners and indentured servants were packed aboard ships "as closely as herring," one migrant observed. Seasickness compounded by exhaustion, poverty, poor food, bad water, inadequate sanitation, and tight quarters encouraged the spread of disease. On the sixteen immigrant ships arriving in Philadelphia in 1738, over half the passengers died en route. When one ship finally approached land, a traveler wrote, "everyone crawls from below to the deck…and people cry for joy, pray, and sing praises and thanks to God." Unfortunately, their troubles were far from over. Redemptioners and indentured servants had to stay on board until somebody came to purchase their labor. Unlike indentured servants, redemptioners negotiated independently with their purchasers about their period of servitude. Typically, a healthy adult redemptioner agreed to four years of labor. Indentured servants commonly served five, six, or seven years.

Pennsylvania: "The Best Poor [White] Man's Country"

New settlers, whether free or in servitude, poured into the middle colonies because they perceived unparalleled opportunities, particularly in Pennsylvania, "the best poor Man's Country in the World," as an indentured servant wrote in 1743. Although the servant reported that "the Condition of bought Servants is very hard" and masters often failed to live up to their promise to provide decent food and clothing, opportunity abounded because there was more work to be done than workers to do it.

Most servants toiled in Philadelphia, New York City, or one of the smaller towns or villages. Artisans, small manufacturers, and shopkeepers prized the labor of male servants. Female servants made valuable additions to households, where nearly all of them cleaned, washed, cooked, or minded children. From the masters' viewpoint, servants were a bargain. A master could purchase five or six years of a servant's labor for approximately the wages a common laborer would earn in four months.

Since a slave cost at least three times as much as a servant, only affluent colonists could afford the long-term investment in slave labor. After Benjamin Franklin became prosperous, he purchased five slaves. But most farmers in the middle colonies used family labor, not slaves. Consequently, the population of African ancestry (almost all slaves) comprised only about 7 percent of the total population.

Enough slaves arrived to prompt colonial assemblies to pass laws that punished slaves much more severely than servants for the same transgressions. "For the least trespass," servant Moraley reported, slaves "undergo the severest Punishment." In practice, both servants and slaves were governed more by their masters than by the laws. But in cases of abuse, servants could and did charge masters with violating the terms of their indenture contracts. The terms of a slave's bondage were set forth in a master's commands, not in a written contract.

Small numbers of slaves managed to obtain their freedom, but free African Americans did not escape whites' firm convictions about black inferiority and white supremacy. Whites' racism and blacks' lowly social status made African Americans scapegoats for European Americans' suspicions and anxieties. In 1741, when arson and several unexplained thefts plagued New York City, officials suspected a murderous slave conspiracy. On the basis of little more than evidence of slaves' "insolence" (refusal to conform fully to whites' expectations of servile behavior), city authorities had thirteen slaves burned at the stake and eighteen others hanged. Although slaves were certifiably poor, they were not included among the poor for whom the middle colonies were reputed to be the best country in the world.

Immigrants swarmed to the middle colonies because of the availability of land. The Penn family encouraged immigration to bring in potential buyers for their enormous tracts of land in Pennsylvania. From the beginning, Pennsylvania followed a policy of negotiating with Indian tribes to purchase additional land. This policy reduced the violent frontier clashes more common elsewhere in the colonies.

The price of farmland depended on soil quality, access to water, distance from a market town, and the extent of improvements. One hundred acres of improved land that had been cleared, plowed, fenced, and ditched, and perhaps had a house and barn built on it, cost three or four times more than the same acreage of uncleared, unimproved land. Since the cheapest land always lay at the margin of settlement, would-be farmers tended to migrate to promising areas just beyond already improved farms. By midcentury, settlement had reached the eastern slopes of the Appalachian Mountains, and newcomers spilled south down the fertile valley of the Shenandoah River into western Virginia and the Carolinas. Thousands of settlers migrated from the middle colonies through this back door to the South.

Farmers made the middle colonies the breadbasket of North America. They planted a wide variety of crops to feed their families, but they grew wheat in abundance. Flour milling was the number-one industry and flour the number-one export, constituting nearly three-fourths of all exports from the middle colonies. Pennsylvania flour fed residents in other colonies, in southern Europe, and, above all, in the West Indies (see Map 5.2).

The standard of living in rural Pennsylvania was probably higher than in any other agricultural region of the eighteenth-century world. The comparatively widespread prosperity of all the middle colonies permitted residents to indulge in a half-century shopping spree for English imports. The middle colonies' per capita consumption of imported goods from England more than doubled between 1720 and 1770, far outstripping the per capita consumption of English goods in New England and the southern colonies.

At the crossroads of trade in wheat exports and English imports stood Philadelphia. By 1776, Philadelphia had a larger population than any other city in the entire British empire except London. Merchants occupied the top stratum of Philadelphia society. In a city where only 2 percent of the residents owned enough property to qualify to vote, merchants built grand homes and dominated local government. Many of Philadelphia's wealthiest merchants were Quakers. Quaker traits of industry, thrift, honesty, and sobriety encouraged the accumulation of wealth. A colonist complained that a Quaker "prays for his neighbor on First Days [the Sabbath] and then preys on him the other six."

The ranks of merchants reached downward to aspiring tradesmen like Benjamin Franklin. After he started to publish the *Pennsylvania Gazette* in 1728, Franklin opened a shop, run mostly by his wife, Deborah, that sold a little bit of everything: cheese, codfish, coffee, goose feathers, sealing wax, soap, and now and then a slave. In 1733, Franklin began to publish *Poor Richard's Almanack*, which preached the likelihood of long-term rewards for tireless labor. The *Almanack* sold thousands of copies, quickly becoming Franklin's most profitable product.

The popularity of *Poor Richard's Almanack* suggests that many Pennsylvanians thought less about the pearly gates than about their pocketbooks. Poor Richard's advice that "God

Patterns of Settlement, 1700–1770

Bethlehem, Pennsylvania
This view of the small community of Bethlehem, Pennsylvania, in 1757 dramatizes the profound transformation of the natural landscape wrought in the eighteenth century by highly motivated human labor. Founded
by Moravian immigrants in 1740, Bethlehem must have appeared at first like the dense woods on the upper
left horizon. In fewer than twenty years, precisely laid-out orchards and fields replaced forests and glades. By
carefully penning their livestock (lower center right) and fencing their fields (lower left), farmers safeguarded
their livelihoods from the risks and disorders of untamed nature. Individual farmsteads (lower center) and impressive multistory brick town buildings (upper center) integrated the bounty of the land with the delights of
community life. Few eighteenth-century communities were as orderly as Bethlehem, but many effected a comparable transformation of the environment.
Print Collection, Miriam and Ira D. Wallack Division of Art, Prints and Photographs, The New York Public Library. Astor, Lenox, and Tilden
Foundations.

FOR MORE HELP ANALYZING THIS IMAGE, see the visual activity for this chapter in the Online Study Guide at
bedfordstmartins.com/roarkcompact.

gives all Things to Industry" might be considered the motto for the middle colonies. The
promise of a worldly payoff made work a secular faith. Poor Richard advised, "Work as if you
were to live 100 years, Pray as if you were to die
Tomorrow."

William Penn's Quaker utopia became a
center of worldly affluence whose most famous
citizen, Franklin, was neither a Quaker nor a
utopian. Quakers remained influential, but
Franklin spoke for most colonists with his

aphorisms of work, discipline, and thrift that
echoed Quaker rules for outward behavior.
Franklin's maxims did not look to the Quakers'
divine inner light for guidance. They depended
instead on the spark of ambition and the glow
of gain.

REVIEW   Why did German immigrants flood into
Pennsylvania during the eighteenth century?

The Southern Colonies: Land of Slavery

Between 1700 and 1770, the population of the southern colonies of Virginia, Maryland, North Carolina, South Carolina, and Georgia grew almost ninefold. By 1770, about twice as many people lived in the South as in either the middle colonies or New England. As elsewhere, natural increase and immigration accounted for the rapid population growth. Many Scots-Irish and German immigrants funneled from the middle colonies into the southern backcountry. Other immigrants were indentured servants (mostly English and Scots-Irish) who followed their seventeenth-century predecessors. But slaves made the most striking contribution to the booming southern colonies, transforming the racial composition of the population. Slavery became the defining characteristic of the southern colonies during the eighteenth century, shaping the region's economy, society, and politics.

The Atlantic Slave Trade and the Growth of Slavery

The number of southerners of African ancestry (nearly all of them slaves) rocketed from just over 20,000 in 1700 to well over 400,000 in 1770. The black population increased nearly three times faster than the South's briskly growing white population. Consequently, the proportion of southerners who were black grew from 20 percent in 1700 to 40 percent in 1770.

Southern colonists clustered into two distinct geographic and agricultural zones. The colonies in the upper South, surrounding the Chesapeake Bay, specialized in growing tobacco, as they had since the early seventeenth century. Throughout the eighteenth century, nine out of ten southern whites and eight out of ten southern blacks lived in the Chesapeake region. The upper South retained a white majority during the eighteenth century.

In the lower South, a much smaller cluster of colonists inhabited the coastal region and specialized in the production of rice and indigo (a plant used to make blue dye). Lower South colonists made up only 5 percent of the total population of the southern colonies in 1700 but inched upward to 15 percent by 1770. South Carolina was the sole British colony along the southern Atlantic coast until 1732, when Georgia

was founded. (North Carolina, founded in 1711, was largely an extension of the Chesapeake region.) Blacks in South Carolina, in contrast to every other British mainland colony, outnumbered whites almost two to one; in some low-country districts, the ratio of blacks to whites exceeded ten to one.

The enormous growth in the South's slave population occurred through natural increase and the flourishing Atlantic slave trade (Map 5.3 and Table 5.1). Slave ships brought almost 300,000 Africans to British North America between 1619 and 1780. Of these Africans, 95 percent arrived in the South and 96 percent arrived during the eighteenth century. Unlike indentured servants or redemptioners, these Africans did not choose to come to the colonies. Most of them had been born into free families in villages located within a few hundred miles of the West African coast. Although they shared African origins, they came from many different African cultures, including Akan, Angolan, Asante, Bambara, Gambian, Igbo, Mandinga, and others.

The most important experience they had in common was enslavement. Captured in war, kidnapped, or sold into slavery by other Africans, they were brought to the coast, sold to African traders who assembled slaves for resale, and sold again to European or colonial slave traders or ship captains, who packed two to three hundred or more aboard ships that carried them on the **Middle Passage** across the Atlantic and then sold them yet again to a colonial slave merchant or a southern **planter**.

In 1789, Olaudah Equiano published an account of his own enslavement that hints at the stories that might have been told by the millions of other Africans swept up in the slave trade. Equiano was born in 1745 in the interior of what is now Nigeria. "I had never heard of white men or Europeans, nor of the sea," he recalled. One

TABLE 5.1	SLAVE IMPORTS, 1451–1870
Estimated Slave Imports to the Western Hemisphere	
1451–1600	275,000
1601–1700	1,341,000
1701–1810	6,100,000
1811–1870	1,900,000

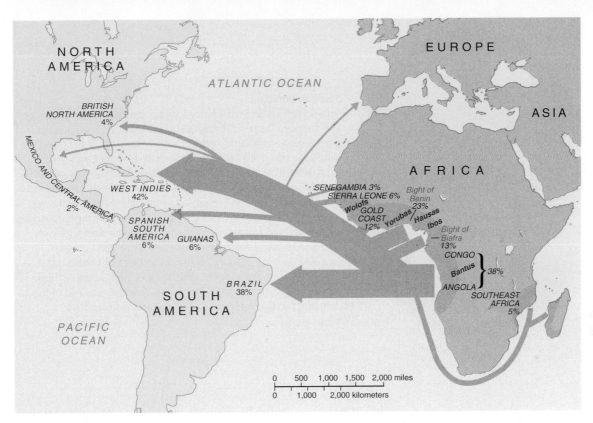

MAP 5.3   The Atlantic Slave Trade
Although the Atlantic slave trade lasted from about 1450 to 1870, its peak occurred during the eighteenth century, when more than six million African slaves were imported to the New World. Only a small fraction of the African slaves imported to the Western Hemisphere were taken to British North America; most went to sugar plantations in Brazil and the Caribbean.

READING THE MAP: From where in Africa did most slaves originate? Approximately how far was the trip from the busiest ports of origin to the two most common New World destinations?
CONNECTIONS: Why were so many more African slaves sent to the West Indies and Brazil than to British North America?

FOR MORE HELP ANALYZING THIS MAP, see the map activity for this chapter in the Online Study Guide at
bedfordstmartins.com/roarkcompact.

day when Equiano was eleven years old, he was kidnapped by Africans, who sold him to other Africans, who in turn eventually sold him to a slave ship on the coast. Equiano feared he would be "eaten by those white men with horrible looks." Once the ship set sail, many slaves died from sickness, crowded together in suffocating heat fouled by filth of all descriptions. "The shrieks of the women and the groans of the dying rendered the whole a scene of horror almost inconceivable," Equiano recalled. Most of the slaves on the ship were sold in Barbados, but Equiano and other leftovers were shipped off to Virginia, where Equiano "saw few or none of our native Africans and not one soul who could talk to me."

Only about 15 percent of the slaves brought into the southern colonies came as Equiano did, aboard ships from the West Indies. All the other slaves brought into the southern colonies came directly from Africa, and almost all the ships that brought them (roughly 90 percent) belonged to British merchants. Most slaves on board were young adults, men usually outnumbering women two to one. Children under the age of fourteen, like Equiano, were typically no more than 10 or 15 percent of a cargo.

Mortality during the Middle Passage varied considerably from ship to ship. On average, about 15 percent of the slaves died, but sometimes half or more perished. The average mortality among

Olaudah Equiano

This portrait shows Equiano more than a decade after he had bought his freedom. The portrait evokes Equiano's successful acculturation to the customs of eighteenth-century England. His clothing and hairstyle reflect the fashions of respectable young Englishmen. In his *Interesting Narrative*, Equiano explained that he had learned to speak and understand English while he was a slave. He wrote that he "looked upon [the English]…as men superior to us [Africans], and therefore I had the stronger desire to resemble them, to imbibe their spirit and imitate their manners; I therefore embraced every occasion of improvement, and every new thing that I observed I treasured up in my memory." Equiano's embrace of English culture did not cause him to forsake his African roots. He honored his dual identity by campaigning against slavery. His *Narrative* was one of the most important and powerful antislavery documents of the time.
Library of Congress.

the white crew of slave ships was often nearly as bad. In general, the longer the voyage lasted, the larger was the number of deaths.

Normally an individual planter purchased at any one time a relatively small number of newly arrived Africans, or "new Negroes," as they were called. Planters preferred to purchase small groups of slaves to permit their other slaves—either those born into slavery in the colonies (often called "country-born" or "creole" slaves) or Africans who had arrived earlier—to help new Negroes become accustomed to their strange new surroundings.

Planters' preferences for slaves from specific regions of Africa aided slaves' acculturation (or "seasoning," as it was called) to the routines of bondage in the southern colonies. Chesapeake planters preferred slaves from Senegambia, the Gold Coast, or—like Equiano—the Bight of Biafra, the origin of 40 percent of all Africans imported to the Chesapeake. South Carolina planters favored slaves from the central African Congo and Angola regions, the origin of about 40 percent of the African slaves they imported (see Map 5.3). Although slaves within each of these regions spoke many different languages, enough linguistic and cultural similarities existed that they could usually communicate with other Africans from the same region.

Seasoning acclimated new Africans to the physical as well as the cultural environment of the

southern colonies. Slaves who had just endured the Middle Passage were poorly nourished, weak, and sick. In this vulnerable state they encountered the alien diseases of North America without having developed a biological arsenal of acquired immunities. As many as 10 or 15 percent of newly arrived Africans, sometimes more, died during their first year in the southern colonies.

While newly enslaved Africans poured into the southern colonies, slave mothers birthed babies who caused the slave population in the South to grow rapidly. Slave owners encouraged these births. Thomas Jefferson explained, "I consider the labor of a breeding [slave] woman as no object, that a [slave] child raised every 2 years is of more profit than the crop of the best laboring [slave] man." The growing number of slave babies set the southern colonies apart from other New World slave societies, which experienced a natural decrease of the slave population (slave deaths exceeded births). The high rate of natural increase in the southern colonies meant that by the 1740s the majority of southern slaves were country-born.

Slave Labor and African American Culture

Southern planters expected slaves to work from sunup to sundown and beyond. George Washington wrote that his slaves should "be at their work as soon as it is light, work til it is dark,

The African Slave Trade

The African slave trade existed to satisfy the New World's demand for labor and Europe's voracious appetite for such New World products as sugar, tobacco, and rice. African men, women, and children were kidnapped or captured in wars—typically by other Africans—and enslaved. Uprooted from their homes and kin, they were usually taken to coastal enclaves where African traders and European ship captains negotiated prices, made deals, and often branded the newly enslaved people. The collaboration between Europeans and their African trading partners is evident in the seventeenth-century Benin bronze box in the shape of a royal palace in Nigeria guarded by massive predatory birds and two Portuguese soldiers. Jammed into the holds of slave ships, enslaved Africans made the dreaded Middle Passage to the New World. The model of a slave ship shown here was used in parliamentary debates by antislavery leaders in Britain to demonstrate the inhumanity of shipping people as if they were just so much tightly packed cargo. The model does not show another typical feature of slave ships: weapons. Slaves vastly outnumbered the crews aboard the ships, and crew members justifiably feared slave uprisings.

Benin bronze box: Staatliche Museen Zu Berlin, Preussischer Kulturbesitz; slave ship model: Wilberforce House, Hull City Museums and Art Galleries, UK/Bridgeman Art Library.

and be diligent while they are at it." The conflict between the masters' desire for maximum labor and the slaves' reluctance to do more than necessary made the threat of physical punishment a constant for eighteenth-century slaves. Masters preferred black slaves to white indentured servants, not just because slaves served for life but also because colonial laws did not limit the force masters could use against slaves. As a traveler observed in 1740, "A new negro…[will] let a hundred men show him how to hoe, or drive a wheelbarrow; he'll still take the one by the bottom and the other by the wheel and…often die before [he] can be conquered." Slaves, the traveler noted, resisted their masters' demands because of their "greatness of soul," their stubborn unwillingness to conform to their masters' definition of them as merely slaves.

Some slaves escalated their acts of resistance to direct physical confrontation with the master, the mistress, or an overseer. But a hoe raised in anger, a punch in the face, or a desperate swipe with a knife led to swift and predictable retaliation by whites. Throughout the southern colonies, the balance of physical power rested securely in the hands of whites.

Rebellion occurred, however, at Stono, South Carolina, in 1739. Before dawn on a September Sunday, a group of about twenty slaves attacked a country store, killed the two storekeepers, and confiscated the store's guns, ammunition, and powder. Enticing other rebel slaves to join, the group plundered and burned more than a half dozen plantations and killed more than twenty white men, women, and children. A mounted force of whites quickly suppressed the rebellion. The Stono rebellion illustrated that eighteenth-century slaves had no chance of overturning slavery and very little chance of defending themselves in any bold strike for freedom.

Slaves maneuvered constantly to protect themselves and to gain a measure of autonomy within the boundaries of slavery. In Chesapeake tobacco fields, most slaves were subject to close supervision by whites. In the lower South, the task system gave slaves some control over the pace of their work and some discretion in the use of the rest of their time. A "task" was typically defined as a certain area of ground to be cultivated or a specific job to be completed. A slave who completed the assigned task might use the remainder of the day, if any, to work in a garden, fish, hunt, spin, weave, sew, or cook.

Eighteenth-century slaves also planted the roots of African American lineages that branch out to the present. Slaves valued family ties and, as in West African societies, kinship structured slaves' relations with one another. Newly imported African slaves usually arrived alone, like Equiano, without kin. Often slaves who had traversed the Middle Passage on the same ship adopted one another as "brothers" and "sisters." Likewise, as new Negroes were seasoned and incorporated into existing slave communities, established families often adopted them as "fictive" kin.

When possible, slaves expressed many other features of their West African origins in their lives on New World plantations. They gave their children traditional dolls and African names such as Cudjo or Quash, Minda or Fuladi. They grew food crops they had known in Africa, such as yams and okra. They constructed huts with mud walls and thatched roofs similar to African residences. They fashioned banjos, drums, and other musical instruments, held dances, and observed funeral rites that echoed African practices. In these and many other ways, slaves drew upon their African heritages as much as the oppressive circumstances of slavery permitted.

Tobacco, Rice, and Prosperity

Slaves' labor bestowed prosperity on their masters, British merchants, and the monarchy. The southern colonies supplied 90 percent of all North American exports to England. Rice exports from the lower South exploded from less than half a million pounds in 1700 to eighty million pounds in 1770, nearly all of it grown by slaves. Exports of indigo also boomed. Together, rice and indigo made up three-fourths of lower South exports, nearly two-thirds of them going

to England and most of the rest to the West Indies, where sugar-growing slaves ate slave-grown rice. Tobacco was by far the most important export from British North America; by 1770, it represented almost one-third of all colonial exports and three-fourths of all Chesapeake exports. And under the provisions of the Navigation Acts (see chapter 4), nearly all of it went to England, where the monarchy collected a lucrative tax on each pound. British merchants then reexported more than 80 percent of the tobacco to the European continent, pocketing a nice markup for their troubles.

These products of slave labor made the southern colonies by far the richest in North America. The per capita wealth of free whites in the South was four times greater than that in New England and three times that in the middle colonies. At the top of the wealth pyramid stood the rice grandees of the lower South and the tobacco gentry of the Chesapeake. These elite families commonly resided on large estates in handsome mansions adorned by luxurious gardens, maintained and supported by slaves.

The vast differences in wealth among white southerners engendered envy and occasional tension between rich and poor, but remarkably little open hostility. In private, the planter elite spoke disparagingly of humble whites but in public acknowledged their lesser neighbors as equals, at least in belonging to the superior—in their minds—white race. Looking upward, white **yeomen** and tenants (who owned neither land nor slaves) sensed the gentry's condescension and veiled contempt. But they also appreciated the gentry for granting favors, upholding white supremacy, and keeping slaves in their place. While racial slavery made a few whites much richer than others, it also gave those who did not get rich a powerful reason to feel similar (in race) to those who were so different (in wealth).

The slaveholding gentry dominated the politics and economy of the southern colonies. In Virginia, only adult white men who owned at least one hundred acres of unimproved land or twenty-five acres of land with a house could vote. This property-holding requirement prevented about 40 percent of white men in Virginia from voting for representatives to the House of Burgesses. In South Carolina, only fifty acres of land were required to vote, and most adult white men qualified. But in both colonies, voters elected members of the gentry to serve in the colonial legislature. The gentry passed elected political offices from generation to generation, almost as if they were hereditary. Politically, the gentry built a self-perpetuating oligarchy—rule by the elite few—with the votes of their many humble neighbors.

The gentry also set the cultural standard in the southern colonies. They entertained lavishly, gambled regularly, and attended Anglican (Church of England) services more for social than for religious reasons. Above all, they cultivated the leisurely pursuit of happiness. They did not condone idleness, however. Their many pleasures and responsibilities as plantation owners kept them busy. Thomas Jefferson, a phenomenally productive member of the gentry, recalled that his earliest childhood memory was of being carried on a pillow by a family slave—a powerful image of the slave hands supporting the gentry's leisure and achievement.

REVIEW Why did the Stono rebellion fail?

Unifying Experiences

While the societies of New England, the middle colonies, and the southern colonies became more sharply differentiated during the eighteenth century, colonists throughout British North America shared certain unifying experiences that eluded settlers in Spanish and French colonies. The first was economic. Colonists sold their distinctive products in markets that, in turn, offered to consumers throughout British North America a more or less uniform array of goods. A second unifying experience was a decline in the importance of religion. Some settlers called for a revival of religious intensity, but most people focused less on religion and more on the affairs of the world than they had in the seventeenth century. Third, white inhabitants throughout British North America became aware that they shared a distinctive identity as British colonists. Royal officials who expected loyalty from the colonists often had difficulty obtaining obedience. The British colonists asserted their prerogatives as British subjects to defend their special colonial interests.

Commerce and Consumption

Eighteenth-century commerce whetted the appetite to consume. Colonial products spurred the development of mass markets throughout the Atlantic world (Figure 5.1). Huge increases in the supply of colonial tobacco and sugar brought the price of these small luxuries within reach of most free whites. Colonial goods brought into focus an important lesson of eighteenth-century commerce: Ordinary people, not just the wealthy elite, would buy the things that they desired in addition to what they absolutely needed. Even news, formerly restricted mostly to a few people through face-to-face conversations or private letters, became an object of public consumption through the innovation of newspapers. With the appropriate stimulus, market demand seemed unlimited.

The Atlantic commerce that took colonial goods to markets in England brought objects of consumer desire back to the colonies. English merchants and manufacturers recognized that colonists made excellent customers, and the Navigation Acts gave English exporters privileged access to the colonial market. Most English exports went to the vast European market, where potential customers outnumbered those in the colonies by more than one hundred to one. But as European competition stiffened, colonial markets became increasingly important. English exports to North America multiplied eightfold between 1700 and 1770, outpacing the rate of population growth after midcentury (see Figure 5.1). When the colonists' eagerness to consume exceeded their ability to pay, English exporters willingly extended credit, and colonial debts soared.

Imported mirrors, silver plate, spices, bed and table linens, clocks, tea services, wigs, books, and more infiltrated parlors, kitchens, and bedrooms throughout the colonies. Despite the many differences among the colonists, the consumption of English exports built a certain material uniformity across region, religion, class, and status. Consumption of English exports made the colonists look and feel more British even though they lived at the edge of a wilderness an ocean away from England.

The rising tide of colonial consumption had other less visible but no less important consequences. Consumption presented women and men with a novel array of choices. In many respects, the choices might appear trivial: whether to buy knives and forks, teacups, or a clock. But such small choices confronted eighteenth-century consumers with a big question: "What do you want?" As colonial consumers defined and expressed their desires with greater frequency during the eighteenth century, they became accustomed to thinking of themselves as individuals who had the power to make decisions that influenced the quality of their lives—attitudes

FIGURE 5.1
Colonial Exports, 1768–1772

These pie charts provide an overview of the colonial export economy in the 1760s. The first two show that almost two-thirds of colonial exports came from the South and that the majority of the colonies' exports went to Great Britain. The remaining charts illustrate the distinctive patterns of exports in each colonial region. Fish, livestock, and wood products were New England's most important exports; they were sent primarily to the West Indies, only a small fraction going to Great Britain. From the colonial breadbasket in the middle colonies, grain products made up three-fourths of all exports, most of which went to the West Indies or to southern Europe. The Chesapeake also exported some grain, but tobacco accounted for three-fourths of the region's export trade, nearly all of it bound for Great Britain as mandated by the Navigation Acts. Rice and indigo comprised three-fourths of the exports from the lower South, the bulk of which was sent to Great Britain. Taken together, these charts reveal Britain's economic interest in the exports of the North American colonies.

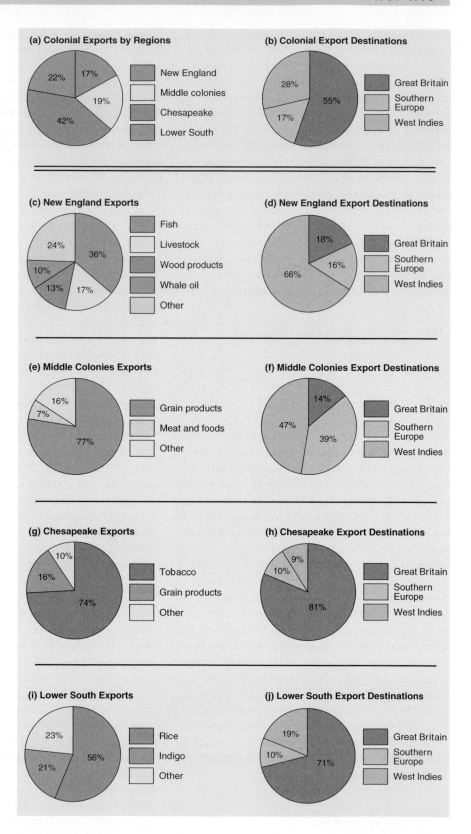

of significance in the hierarchical world of eighteenth-century British North America.

Religion, Enlightenment, and Revival

Eighteenth-century colonists could choose from almost as many religions as consumer goods. Virtually all of the bewildering variety of religious denominations represented some form of Christianity, almost all of them Protestant. Slaves made up the largest group of non-Christians. A few slaves converted to Christianity in Africa or after they arrived in North America, but most continued to embrace elements of indigenous African religions. Roman Catholics concentrated in Maryland as they had since the seventeenth century, but even there they were outnumbered by Protestants.

The varieties of Protestant faith and practice ranged across a broad spectrum. The middle colonies and the southern backcountry included militant Baptists and Presbyterians. In New England, old-style Puritanism splintered into strands of Congregationalism that differed over fine points of theological doctrine. The Congregational Church was the official established church in New England, and all residents paid taxes for its support. Throughout the plantation South and in urban centers like Charleston, New York, and Philadelphia, prominent colonists belonged to the Anglican Church, which received tax support in the South. But dissenting faiths grew everywhere, and in most colonies their adherents won the right to worship publicly, although the established churches retained official support.

Many educated colonists became deists, looking for God's plan in nature more than in the Bible. Deists shared the ideas of eighteenth-century European **Enlightenment** thinkers who tended to agree that science and reason could disclose God's laws in the natural order. In the colonies as well as in Europe, Enlightenment ideas encouraged people to study the world around them, to think for themselves, and to ask whether the disorderly appearance of things masked the principles of a deeper, more profound natural order. The American Philosophical Society, founded in 1769, fostered communication among leading colonial thinkers; Benjamin Franklin was its first president. Franklin's interest in electricity, stoves, and eyeglasses exemplified the shift of focus among many eighteenth-century colonists from heaven to the here and now.

Most eighteenth-century colonists went to church seldom or not at all, although they probably considered themselves Christians. In the leading colonial cities, church members were a small minority of eligible adults, no more than 10 to 15 percent. Anglican parishes in the South rarely claimed more than one-fifth of eligible adults as members. In some regions of rural New England and the middle colonies, church membership embraced two-thirds of eligible adults, while in other areas only one-quarter of the residents belonged to a church. As a late-eighteenth-century traveler observed, "Religious indifference is imperceptibly disseminated from one end of the continent to the other."

The spread of religious indifference, of deism, of denominational rivalry, and of comfortable backsliding profoundly concerned many Christians. A few despaired that, as one wrote, "religion…lay a-dying and ready to expire its last breath of life." Some ministers set out to convert nonbelievers and to revive the piety of the faithful with a new style of preaching that appealed more to the heart than to the head. Historians have termed this wave of revivals the **Great Awakening**. In Massachusetts during the mid-1730s, the fiery Puritan minister Jonathan Edwards reaped a harvest of souls by reemphasizing traditional Puritan doc-trines of humanity's utter depravity and God's vengeful omnipotence. The title of Edwards's most famous sermon, "Sinners in the Hands of an Angry God," conveys the flavor of his message. In Pennsylvania and New Jersey, William Tennent led revivals that dramatized spiritual rebirth with accounts of God's miraculous powers, such as raising Tennent's son from the dead.

The most famous revivalist in the eighteenth-century Atlantic world was George Whitefield. An Anglican, Whitefield preached well-worn messages of sin and salvation to large audiences in England using his spellbinding, unforgettable voice. Whitefield visited the North American colonies seven times, staying for more than three years during the mid-1740s and attracting tens of thousands to his sermons, including Benjamin Franklin. Whitefield's preaching transported many in his audience to emotion-choked states of religious ecstasy.

The revivals awakened and refreshed the spiritual energies of thousands of colonists struggling with the uncertainties and anxieties of eighteenth-century America. The revivals communicated that every soul mattered, that men and women could choose to be saved, that individuals had

George Whitefield
An anonymous artist portrayed George Whitefield preaching, emphasizing the power of his sermons to transport his audience to a revived awareness of divine spirituality. Light from above gleams off Whitefield's forehead. His crossed eyes and faraway gaze suggest that he spoke in a semihypnotic trance. Notice the absence of a Bible at the pulpit. Rather than elaborating on God's word as revealed in Scripture, Whitefield speaks from his own inner awareness. The young woman bathed in light below his hands appears transfixed, her focus not on Whitefield but on some inner realm illuminated by his words. Her eyes and Whitefield's do not meet, yet the artist's use of light suggests that she and Whitefield see the same core of holy Truth. The other people in Whitefield's audience appear not to have achieved this state. They remain intent on Whitefield's words, failing so far to be ignited by the divine spark.
National Portrait Gallery, London.

the power to make a decision for everlasting life or death. Colonial revivals expressed in religious terms many of the same democratic and egalitarian values expressed in economic terms by colonists' patterns of consumption. One colonist noted the analogy by referring to itinerant revivalists as "Pedlars in divinity." Like consumption, revivals contributed to a set of common experiences that bridged colonial divides of faith, region, class, and status.

> **REVIEW** Why did religious revivals flourish during the 1730s and 1740s?

Bonds of the British Empire

The plurality of peoples, faiths, and communities that characterized the North American colonies arose from the somewhat haphazard policies of the eighteenth-century British empire. Since the mid-seventeenth century, British monarchs had valued the colonies' contributions to trade and encouraged their growth and development. Unlike Spain and France—whose policies of excluding Protestants and foreigners kept the population of their North American colonial territories tiny—Britain kept the door to its colonies open to anyone, and tens of thousands of non-British immigrants settled in the North American colonies and raised families. The open door did not extend to trade, however, as the seventeenth-century Navigation Acts restricted colonial trade to British ships and traders. These policies evolved because they served the interests of the monarchy and of influential groups in England and the colonies. The policies also gave the colonists a common framework of political expectations and experiences.

At a minimum, British power defended the colonists from foreign enemies. Each colony organized a militia, but the British navy and army bore responsibility for colonial defense. Royal officials warily eyed the small North American settlements of New France and New Spain for signs of threats to the colonies. Alone, neither New France nor New Spain jeopardized British North America, but with Indian allies they could become a potent force that kept colonists on their guard.

Defending the Borderlands of Empire: Indians and French and Spanish Outposts

All along the ragged edge of settlement, colonists encountered Indians. Native Americans' impulse to defend their territory from colonial incursions warred with their desire for trade, which tugged them toward the settlers. As a colonial official observed in 1761, "A modern Indian cannot subsist without Europeans…[the European goods that were] only conveniency at first [are] now become necessity." To obtain such necessities as guns, ammunition, clothing, sewing utensils, and much more that was manufactured largely by the British, Indians trapped beaver, deer, and other fur-bearing animals throughout the interior.

Colonial traders and their respective empires competed to control the fur trade (Map 5.4). British, French, Spanish, and Dutch officials monitored the trade to prevent their competitors from deflecting the flow of furs toward their own markets. Indians took advantage of this competition to improve their own prospects, playing one trader and empire off against another. Indian tribes and confederacies also competed among themselves for favored trading rights with one colony or another, a competition colonists encouraged.

The shifting alliances and complex dynamics of the fur trade struck a fragile balance along the frontier. The threat of violence from all sides was ever present, and the threat became reality often enough for all parties to be prepared for the worst. In the Yamasee War of 1715, Yamasee and Creek Indians—with French encouragement—mounted a coordinated attack against colonial settlements in South Carolina and inflicted heavy casualties. The Cherokees, traditional enemies of the Creeks, refused to join the attack. Instead, they protected their access to British trade goods by allying with the colonists and turning the tide of battle, thus triggering a murderous rampage of revenge by the colonists against the Creeks and Yamasees.

Relations between Indians and the colonists differed from colony to colony and from year to year. But the colonists' nagging perceptions of menace on the frontier kept them continually hoping for help from the British in keeping the Indians at bay and in maintaining the essential flow of trade. In 1754, the colonists' endemic competition with the French flared into the Seven Years' War (also known as the French and Indian War), which would inflame the frontier for years (see chapter 6). Before the 1760s, neither the colonists nor the British developed a coherent policy toward Indians. But both agreed that Indians made deadly enemies, profitable trading partners, and powerful allies. As a result, the British and the colonists kept an eye on the Spanish empire to the west and relations with the Indians there.

Indians' potential as allies prompted officials in New Spain to mount a campaign to block Russian access to present-day California by building forts (called *presidios*) and missions. Russian hunters in search of seals and sea otters ventured along the California coast and threatened to become a permanent presence on New Spain's northern frontier.

In 1769, an expedition headed by a military man, Gaspar de Portolá, and a Catholic priest, Junípero Serra, traveled north from Mexico to present-day San Diego, where they founded the first California mission, San Diego de Alcalá. They soon journeyed all the way to Monterey, which became the capital of Spanish California. There Portolá established a presidio in 1770 "to defend us from attacks by the Russians," he wrote. By 1772, Serra had founded other missions along the path from San Diego to Monterey.

For Indians, the Spaniards' California missions had horrendous consequences, as they had elsewhere in the Spanish borderlands. European diseases decimated Indian populations, Spanish soldiers raped Indian women, and missionaries beat Indians and subjected them to near slavery. Indian uprisings against the Spaniards occurred repeatedly (see "Documenting the American Promise," page 124), but the presidios and missions endured as feeble projections of the Spanish empire along the Pacific coast.

Spanish Missions in California

Monterey Presidio
This eighteenth-century portrait of the Monterey Presidio illustrates the military significance of the Spanish outposts in California. The walled enclosure and proximity to the bay (in the background) served defensive purposes, principally against Russian expansion but also against British and French interlopers. The Indian men and women working in the fields and hanging out laundry served to support the soldiers in the presidio. Notice that no Spaniard is pictured at work. At Monterey and elsewhere in Spanish California, the presidios and missions focused on maintaining outposts of empire rather than on developing booming settlements or producing goods for export.
University of California at Berkeley, Bancroft Library.

Colonial Politics in the British Empire

British attempts to exercise political power in their colonial governments met with success so long as British officials were on or very near the sea. Colonists acknowledged—although they did not always readily comply with—British authority to collect customs duties, inspect cargoes, and enforce trade regulations. But when royal officials tried to wield their authority on land, in the internal affairs of colonies, they invariably encountered colonial resistance. A governor appointed by the king in each of the nine royal colonies (Rhode Island and Connecticut selected their own governors) or by the proprietors in Maryland and Pennsylvania headed the government of each colony. The British envisioned colonial governors as mini-monarchs able to exert influence in the colonies much as the king did in England. But colonial governors were not kings, and the colonies were not England.

◀ **MAP 5.4   Zones of Empire in Eastern North America**
British colonies extending westward from the Atlantic coast were much more densely settled than the zones under French, Spanish, or Indian control. The comparatively large number of settlers made British colonists more secure than the relatively few colonists in the vast regions claimed by France and Spain or settlers among the many Indian peoples in the huge area between the Mississippi River and the Appalachian Mountains. Yet British colonists were not powerful enough to dominate the French, Spanish, or Indians. Instead, British colonists had to guard against powerful Indian groups who allied with either the French or the Spanish, since such alliances threatened settlers in the region under British control.

Missionaries Report on California Missions

Catholic missionaries sent regular reports to their superiors in Mexico City, New Spain's capital city. The reports described what the missionaries considered their successes in converting pagan Indians—whom they called gentiles—as well as the difficulties caused by the behavior of both Spaniards and Indians.

DOCUMENT 1
Father Luis Jayme
Describes Conditions
at Mission San Diego
de Alcalá, 1772

Father Luis Jayme, a Franciscan missionary, reported on the deplorable behavior of some of the Spanish soldiers at Mission San Diego, who frequently raped Indian women, causing many Indians to resist the efforts of the missionaries.

With reference to the Indians, I wish to say that great progress [in converting Indians] would be made if there was anything to eat and the soldiers would set a good example. We cannot give them anything to eat because what Don Pedro [the governor] has given is not enough to last half a year for the Indians from the Californias who are here. Thus little progress will be made under present conditions. As for the example set by the soldiers, no doubt some of them are good exemplars and deserve to be treated accordingly, but very many of them deserve to be hanged on account of the continuous outrages which they are committing in seizing and raping the women. There is not a single mission where all the gentiles have not been scandalized, and even on the roads, so I have been told. Surely, as the gentiles themselves state, they [the soldiers] are committing a thousand evils, particularly of a sexual nature....

At one of these Indian villages near this mission of San Diego, which said village is very large, and which is on the road to Monterey, the gentiles therein many times have been on the point of coming here to kill us all, and the reason for this is that some soldiers went there and raped their women, and other soldiers who were carrying the mail to Monterey turned their animals into their fields and they ate up their crops. Three other Indian villages...[near] here have reported the same thing to me several times. For this reason on several occasions when...I have gone to see these Indian villages, as soon as they saw us they fled from their villages and fled to the woods or other remote places....They do this so that the soldiers will not rape their women as they have already done so many times in the past.

No wonder the Indians here were bad when the mission was first founded. To begin with, they did not know why [the Spaniards] had come, unless they wanted to take their lands away from them. Now they all want to be Christians because they know that there is a God who created the heavens and earth and all things, that there is a Hell and Glory, that they have souls, etc., but when the mission was first founded...they thought they were like animals, and ...they were very loath to pray, and they did not want to be Christians at all....[Now] they all know the natural law, which, so I am informed, they have observed as well or better than many Christians elsewhere. They do not have idols; they do not go on drinking sprees; they do not marry relatives; and they have but one wife. The married men sleep with their wives only....Some of the first adults whom we baptized, when we pointed out to them that it was wrong to have sexual intercourse with a woman to whom they were not married, told me that they already knew that, and that among them it was considered to be very bad, and so they do not do so at all. "The soldiers," they told me, "are Christians and, although they know that God will punish them in Hell, do so, having sexual intercourse

Eighty percent of colonial governors had been born in England, not in the colonies. Some governors stayed in England, close to the source of royal patronage, and delegated the grubby details of colonial affairs to subordinates. Even the best-intentioned colonial governors had difficulty developing relations of trust and respect with influential colonists because their terms of office averaged just five years and could be terminated at any time. In obedience to England, colonial with our wives." "We," they said, "although we did not know that God would punish us for that in Hell, considered it to be very bad, and we did not do it, and even less now that we know that God will punish us if we do so." When I heard this, I burst into tears to see how these gentiles were setting an example for us Christians.

DOCUMENT 2
Father Junípero Serra Describes the Indian Revolt at Mission San Diego de Alcalá, 1775

Father Junípero Serra, the founder of many of the California missions, reported to his superiors in Mexico City that an Indian uprising had destroyed Mission San Diego. He recommended rebuilding and urged officials to provide additional soldiers to defend the missions, but not to punish the rebellious Indians.

As we are in the vale of tears, not all the news I have to relate can be pleasant. And so I make no excuses for announcing…the tragic news that I have just received of the total destruction of the San Diego Mission, and of the death of the senior of its two religious ministers, called Father Luis Jayme, at the hand of the rebellious gentiles and of the Christian neophytes [Indians who lived in the mission]. All this happened, November 5th, about one or two o'clock at night. The gentiles came together from forty rancherías, according to information given me,

and set fire to the church, after sacking it. They then went to the storehouse, the house where the Fathers lived, the soldiers' barracks, and all the rest of the buildings. They killed a carpenter…and a blacksmith.… They wounded with their arrows the four soldiers, who alone were on guard at the…mission.…

And now, after the Father has been killed, the Mission burned, its many and valuable furnishings destroyed, together with the sacred vessels, its paintings, its baptismal, marriage, and funeral records, and all the furnishings for the sacristy, the house, and the farm implements—now the forces [of soldiers] of both presidios [nearby] come together to set things right.…What happened was that before they set about reestablishing the Mission, they wanted to…lay hands on the guilty ones who were responsible for the burning of the Mission, and the death of the Fathers, and chastise them. The harassed Indians rebelled anew and became more enraged.…And so the soldiers there are gathered together in their presidios, and the Indians in their state of heathenism.…

While the missionary is alive, let the soldiers guard him, and watch over him, like the pupils of God's very eyes. That is as it should be.… But after the missionary has been killed, what can be gained by campaigns [against the rebellious Indians]? Some will say to frighten them and prevent them from killing others. What I say is that, in order to

prevent them from killing others, keep better guard over them than they did over the one who has been killed; and, as to the murderer, let him live, in order that he should be saved—which is the very purpose of our coming here, and the reason which justifies it.

SOURCES: Maynard Geiger, trans. and ed., *Letter of Luís Jayme, O.F.M.: San Diego, October 17, 1772* (Los Angeles, 1970), 38–42. Antonine Tibesar, O.F.M., ed., *The Writings of Junípero Serra.* © 1956. Reprinted by permission of the American Academy of Franciscan History.

QUESTIONS FOR ANALYSIS AND DEBATE

1. In what ways did Jayme and Serra agree about the motivations of Indians in and around Mission San Diego? In what ways did they disagree? How would Serra's recommendations for rebuilding the mission address the problems identified by Jayme that caused the revolt?

2. How did the goals and activities of the Spanish soldiers compare with those of the Catholic missionaries? What accounts for the differences and similarities?

3. How did the religious convictions of Jayme and Serra influence their reports? What might Spanish soldiers or Indians have said about these events? What might they have said about missionaries like Jayme and Serra?

governors fought incessantly with the colonial assemblies. They battled over governors' vetoes of colonial legislation, removal of colonial judges, creation of new courts, dismissal of the representative assemblies, and other local issues. Some

governors developed a working relationship with the assemblies. But during the eighteenth century, the assemblies gained the upper hand.

Since British policies did not clearly define the powers of colonial assemblies, they made

Ambush of Spanish Expedition

This detail from a remarkable hide painting depicts an ambush of a Spanish expedition by French soldiers and their Pawnee and Oto allies in August 1720. Two and a half months earlier, the governor of New Mexico had sent forty-three Spanish soldiers along with sixty Pueblo Indian allies to expel French intruders from the northern border-lands of New Spain. When the expedition reached the confluence of the Platte and Loup rivers in present-day Nebraska, they were surprised by an attack by French, Pawnees, and Otos, who killed thirty-three Spaniards and twelve Pueblos and drove the expedition back to New Mexico. Shortly afterward, an artist—whether Indian or Spanish is unknown—recorded the disastrous ambush of the Spaniards in this painting. The priest in the center of the detail shown here was Father Juan Minguez, the first priest assigned to Albuquerque; he was killed in the ambush. The Indian directly in front of the priest was Joseph Naranjo, who was also killed; he came from the Santa Clara Pueblo. He was the leader of the Spaniards' Pueblo allies and was the son of Domingo Naranjo, a leader of the Pueblo Revolt against the Spaniards in 1680. Courtesy of the Museum of New Mexico, Neg. No. 149804.

many of their own rules and established a strong tradition of representative government analogous, in their eyes, to the English Parliament. Voters often returned the same representatives to the assemblies year after year, building continuity in power and leadership that far exceeded that of the governor. By 1720, colonial assemblies had won the power to initiate legislation, including tax laws and authorizations to spend public funds. Although all laws passed by the assemblies (except in Maryland, Rhode Island, and Connecticut) had to be approved by the governor and then by the Board of Trade in England, the difficulties in communication about complex subjects over long distances effectively ratified the assemblies' decisions.

The heated political struggles between royal governors and colonial assemblies that occurred throughout the eighteenth century taught colonists a common set of political lessons. They learned to employ traditionally British ideas of representative government to defend their own interests. They learned that power in the British colonies rarely belonged to the British government.

> **REVIEW** Why did the Spanish expand and fortify their presence in California in the eighteenth century?

Conclusion: The Dual Identity of British North American Colonists

During the eighteenth century, a society that was both distinctively colonial and distinctively British emerged in British North America. Tens of thousands of immigrants and slaves gave the colonies an unmistakably colonial complexion and contributed to the colonies' growing population and expanding economy. People of different ethnicities and faiths sought their fortunes in the colonies, where land was cheap, labor was dear, and—as Benjamin Franklin preached—work promised to be rewarding. Indentured servants and redemptioners risked a temporary period of bondage for the potential reward of better opportunities than on the Atlantic's eastern shore. Slaves endured lifetime servitude that they neither chose nor desired but from which their masters greatly benefited.

Identifiably colonial products from New England, the middle colonies, and the southern colonies flowed across the Atlantic. Back came unquestionably British consumer goods along with fashions in ideas, faith, and politics. The bonds of the British empire required colonists to think of themselves as British subjects and, at the same time, encouraged them to consider their status as colonists.

People of European origin in the North American colonies of Spain and France did not share in the emerging political identity of the British colonists. They also did not participate in the cultural, economic, social, and religious changes experienced by their counterparts in British North America. Unlike the much more numerous colonists in British North America, North American Spanish and French colonists did not develop societies that began to rival the European empires that sponsored and supported them.

By 1750, British colonists in North America could not imagine that their distinctively dual identity—as British and as colonists—would soon become a source of intense conflict. But by 1776, colonists in British North America had to choose whether they were British or American.

Suggestions for Further Reading

Ira Berlin, *Generations of Captivity: A History of African-American Slaves* (2003). An expert overview of the rise of slavery in British North America.

George M. Marsden, *Jonathan Edwards: A Life* (2003). A thoughtful biography of the leading minister of the Great Awakening.

Kerby A. Miller, et al., eds., *Irish Immigrants in the Land of Canaan: Letters and Memoirs from Colonial and Revolutionary America* (2003). A rich treasury of contemporary accounts of eighteenth-century American through the eyes of Irish immigrants.

Simon P. Newman, *Embodied History: The Lives of the Poor in Early Philadelphia* (2003). A revealing look at the poor in the "best poor man's country."

Randy J. Sparks, *Two Princes of Calabar: An Eighteenth-Century Odyssey* (2004). The amazing saga of two brothers, both Africans involved in the slave trade, who become enslaved and, like Equiano, eventually freed, but unlike Equiano, they return to Africa and continue slave trading.

David Waldstreicher, *Runaway America: Benjamin Franklin, Slavery, and the American Revolution* (2004). A fascinating study of Benjamin Franklin and slavery.

▶ **For more books about topics in this chapter,** see the Online Study Guide at bedfordstmartins.com/roarkcompact.

▶ **For additional firsthand accounts of this period,** see Chapter 5 in Michael Johnson, ed., *Reading the American Past,* Third Edition.

▶ **For Web sites and documents related to topics and places in this chapter,** see "HistoryLinks," "DocLinks," and "PlaceLinks" at bedfordstmartins.com/roarkcompact.

REVIEWING THE CHAPTER

Follow these steps to review and strengthen your understanding of the chapter.

STEP 1: *Study the* **Key Terms** *and* **Timeline** *to identify the significance of each item listed.*

STEP 2: *Answer the* **Review Questions,** *drawing on key terms and dates to support your answers.*

STEP 3: *Drawing on the Key Terms, Timeline, and Review Questions, answer the broader* **Making Connections** *questions.*

KEY TERMS

Who

Benjamin Franklin (p. 103)
Iroquois (p. 106)
Mahican Indians (p. 106)
Pennsylvania Dutch (p. 108)
middling folk (p. 108)
Scots-Irish (p. 108)
redemptioners (p. 109)
Olaudah Equiano (p. 112)
"new Negroes" (p. 114)
Jonathan Edwards (p. 119)
George Whitefield (p. 119)
Yamasee (p. 121)
Creek Indians (p. 121)
Cherokee (p. 121)
Gaspar de Portolá (p. 121)
Junípero Serra (p. 121)

What

natural increase (p. 104)
partible inheritance (p. 106)
Queen Anne's War (p. 108)
Poor Richard's Almanack (p. 110)
Middle Passage (p. 112)
creole (p. 114)
"seasoning" (p. 114)
Senegambia (Gold Coast) (p. 114)
Bight of Biafra (p. 114)
African Congo (p. 114)
Angola (p. 114)
Stono rebellion (p. 115)
task system (p. 116)
gentry (p. 116)
property-holding requirement (p. 116)
mass markets (p. 117)

Congregational Church (p. 119)
deism (p. 119)
Enlightenment (p. 119)
American Philosophical Society (p. 119)
Great Awakening (p. 119)
fur trade (p. 121)
Yamasee War of 1715 (p. 121)
Seven Years' War (p. 121)
presidios (p. 121)
San Diego de Alcalá (p. 121)

TIMELINE

1702 • Queen Anne's War triggers German migration to North America.

   1711 • North Carolina founded.

      1715 • Yamasee War.

         1717 • Scots-Irish immigration increases.

            1721 • *New England Courant* begins publication.

               1730s • Jonathan Edwards leads "Great Awakening."

                  1732 • Georgia founded.

                     1733 • Benjamin Franklin begins to publish *Poor Richard's Almanack.*

                        1739
                        • Stono rebellion.

REVIEW QUESTIONS

1. How did the North American colonies achieve the remarkable population growth of the eighteenth century? (pp. 104–05)

2. Why did settlement patterns in New England change from the seventeenth to the eighteenth century? (pp. 105–08)

3. Why did German immigrants flood into Pennsylvania during the eighteenth century? (pp. 108–11)

4. Why did the Stono rebellion fail? (pp. 112–17)

5. Why did religious revivals flourish during the 1730s and 1740s? (pp. 117–20)

6. Why did the Spanish expand and fortify their presence in California in the eighteenth century? (pp. 120–26)

MAKING CONNECTIONS

1. Colonial products such as tobacco and sugar transformed consumption patterns on both sides of the Atlantic in the eighteenth century. How did consumption influence the relationship between the American colonies and Britain? In your answer, consider how it might have strengthened and weakened connections.

2. Why did the importance of religion decline throughout the colonies from the seventeenth to the eighteenth century? How did American colonists respond to these changes?

3. Surging population expanded British colonial frontiers and the potential for conflict with Indians and other Europeans in the eighteenth century. How did different colonies attempt to manage relations with Indians? How did Indians attempt to manage relationships with Europeans? In your answer, consider disputes over territory *and* trade.

4. Varied immigration patterns contributed to important differences between the British colonies. Compare and contrast patterns of immigration to the middle and southern colonies. Who came and how did they get there? How did they shape the economic, cultural, and political character of each colony?

▶ **For practice quizzes, a customized study plan, and other study tools,** see the Online Study Guide at bedfordstmartins.com/roarkcompact.

1740s • George Whitefield preaches religious revival.
　　　• Majority of southern slaves are colonial-born.

1741 • New York slave conspiracy trials.

1745 • Olaudah Equiano born.

1750s • Colonists begin to move down Shenandoah Valley.

1754 • Seven Years' War begins.

1769 • American Philosophical Society founded.

1770 • Mission and presidio established at Monterey, California.
　　　• British North American colonists number over 2 million.

1775 • Indians destroy San Diego mission.

PATRICK HENRY'S MAP DESK

Like many of the leading gentry of 1760s Virginia, Patrick Henry pursued land speculation as a way to gain wealth. From 1767 to 1773, he engaged in a half-dozen land ventures, buying up thousands of acres of frontier land in regions now part of Kentucky—purchases that would soon figure in the emerging crisis of empire. This odd little table was Henry's map desk. Its fold-out extensions provided support for the large maps required to represent Virginia's vast western land claims, and its light weight allowed Henry to position it near the best light source in his law office. As is often the case with speculative purchases, Henry's land deals entailed risk: Many of his properties were occupied by the Cherokee, who did not recognize his claim of ownership. The British government, fearing war between Indians and settlers, tried to choke off risky land speculation in 1763 by establishing an imaginary line along the crest of the Appalachian Mountains beyond which settlement was prohibited. But men like Henry continued to buy land cheap in the hopes of selling dear at a later time. As a leading planter and powerful orator, Patrick Henry quickly became a spokesman in the growing imperial struggle with Britain. When he gained election to the Virginia House of Burgesses in 1765, he skillfully maneuvered that assembly into the startling repudiation of British power known as the Virginia Resolves. By 1775 he favored independence from England, a position that eventually would unleash settlers looking to buy land in the West. In 1776, he was elected the first governor of the Commonwealth of Virginia. Patrick Henry ultimately had seventeen children, fourteen of whom survived to adulthood. Through astute land purchases, he managed to establish each with a landed estate.

Courtesy of Scotchtown, photo by Katherine Wetzel.

6

The British Empire and the Colonial Crisis
1754–1775

I N 1771, THOMAS HUTCHINSON became the royal governor of the colony of Massachusetts. Unlike most royal governors, who were British aristocrats sent over by the king for short tours of duty, Hutchinson was a fifth-generation American. A Harvard-educated member of the Massachusetts elite, from a family of successful merchants, Hutchinson had served two decades in the Massachusetts general assembly. In 1758 he was appointed lieutenant governor, and in 1760 he also became chief justice of the colony's highest court. He lived in the finest mansion in Boston. Wealth, power, and influence were his in abundance. He was proud of his connection to the British empire and loyal to his king.

Hutchinson had the misfortune to be a loyal colonial leader during the two very tumultuous decades leading up to the American Revolution. He worked hard to keep the British and colonists aligned in interests, even promoting a plan to unify the colonies into a single defensive unit (the Albany Plan of Union) to ward off Indian wars. The plan of union failed, and a major war ensued—the Seven Years' War, pitting the British and colonists against the French and their Indian allies in the backcountry of the American colonies. When the war ended and the British government began to think about taxing colonists to pay for it, Hutchinson had no doubt that the new British policies were legitimate. Unwise, perhaps, in their specific formulation, but certainly legitimate.

Not everyone in Boston shared his opinion. Fervent, enthusiastic crowds protested against a succession of British taxation policies enacted after 1763—the Sugar Act, the Stamp Act, the Townshend duties, the Tea Act, all landmark events on the road to the American Revolution. But Hutchinson maintained his steadfast loyalty to England. His love of order and tradition inclined him to unconditional support of the British empire, and he was, by nature, a measured and cautious man. "My temper does not incline to enthusiasm," he once wrote.

Privately, he lamented the stupidity of the British acts that provoked trouble, but his sense of duty required him to defend the king's policies, however misguided. Quickly, he became an inspiring villain to the emerging revolutionary movement. Governor Hutchinson came to personify all that was wrong with British and colonial relations. The man not inclined to enthusiasm unleashed popular enthusiasm all around him. He never appreciated that irony.

In another irony, Thomas Hutchinson was actually one of the first Americans to recognize the difficulties of maintaining full rights and privileges for colonists so far from their supreme government, the king and

Thomas Hutchinson
The only formal portrait of Thomas Hutchinson still in existence shows an assured young man in ruffles and hair ribbons. Decades of turmoil in Boston failed to puncture his self-confidence. Doubtless he sat for several portraits, as did all the Boston leaders in the 1760s to 1780s, but no other likeness has survived. One portrait hung in his summer house outside Boston, but a revolutionary crowd mutilated it and stabbed out the eyes. In 1775, Hutchinson fled to England, the country he had regarded as his cultural home, only to realize how very American he was.
Courtesy of the Massachusetts Historical Society.

Parliament in England. In 1769, when British troops occupied Boston in an effort to provide civil order, he wrote privately to a friend in England, "There must be an abridgement of what are called English liberties.... I doubt whether it is possible to project a system of government in which a colony three thousand miles distant from the parent state shall enjoy all the liberty of the parent state." What he could not imagine was the possibility of giving up the parent state and creating an independent government closer to home.

Thomas Hutchinson was a loyalist; in the 1750s, most English-speaking colonists were affectionately loyal to England. But the Seven Years' War, which England and its colonies fought together as allies, shook that affection, and imperial policies in the decade following the war (1763–1773) shattered it completely. Over the course of that decade, colonists insistently raised serious questions about American liberties and rights, especially over the issues of taxation and representation. Many came to believe what Thomas Hutchinson could never credit, that a tyrannical Britain had embarked on a course to enslave the colonists by depriving them of their traditional English liberties.

The opposite of **liberty** was slavery, a condition of nonfreedom and of coercion. Political rhetoric about liberty, tyranny, and slavery heated up emotions of white colonists during the many crises of the 1760s and 1770s. But this rhetoric turned out to be a two-edged sword. The call for an end to tyrannical slavery meant one thing when sounded by Boston merchants whose commercial shipping rights had been revoked; the same call meant something quite different in 1775 when sounded by black Americans locked in the bondage of slavery.

All of this was set in motion by the Seven Years' War. The British victory at first fortified loyalty to England, but its aftermath, taxation, stirred up discussions of rights, fueled white colonists' fear of enslavement by king and Parliament, and produced a potent political vocabulary with unexpected consequences.

The Seven Years' War, 1754–1763

For the first fifty years of the eighteenth century, England was at war intermittently with France or Spain. Often the colonists in America experienced reverberations from these conflicts, most acutely along the French **frontier** in northern New England. In the 1750s, international tensions mounted again, but this time over events originating in America. The conflict centered on contested land in the Ohio Valley, variously claimed by Virginians, Pennsylvanians, the French in Canada, and the Indians already living on the land. The result was the costly Seven Years' War, which spread in 1756 to encompass much of Europe, the Caribbean, and even India. Many thousands of British and American soldiers shared the hardships of battle and the glory of victory over the French and their Indian allies. But the immense costs of the war—in money, death, and desires for revenge by losers and even winners—laid the groundwork for the imperial crisis of the 1760s between the British and Americans.

French-British Rivalry in the Ohio Country

For several decades, French traders had cultivated alliances with the Indian tribes in the Ohio Country, a frontier region encompassing present day western Pennsylvania and eastern Ohio. Cementing their relationships with gifts, they established a profitable trade of manufactured goods for beaver furs. But in the 1740s, aggressive Pennsylvanians began to poach on their business, underselling French goods and threatening to reorient Indian loyalties. Virginians too advanced on the same land, obtaining a charter to settle it from the British king in 1747. A group of enterprising Virginians, including the brothers Lawrence and Augustine Washington, formed the Ohio Company; their hope for profit lay not in the fur trade but in land speculation, fueled by the exploding English-American population.

In response to these incursions, the French sent soldiers to build a series of military forts to secure their trade routes and to create a western barrier to British-American population expansion. In 1753, the royal governor of Virginia, Robert Dinwiddie, himself a shareholder in the Ohio Company, sent a messenger to warn the French that they were trespassing on Virginia land.

The messenger on this dangerous mission was George Washington, younger half-brother of the Ohio Company leaders. Although only twenty-one, Washington was an ambitious youth whose imposing height (six feet two) and air of silent competence convinced the governor he could do the job. The middle child in a family of eight, Washington did not stand to inherit great wealth, so he sought to gain public reputation and impress the Virginia elite by volunteering for this perilous duty.

Washington returned from his mission with crucial intelligence about French military plans. Impressed, Dinwiddie appointed the youth to lead a small military expedition west to assert and, if need be, defend Virginia's claim. Imperial officials in London, concerned by the French fortifications, had authorized the governor "to repel force by force," but only if the French attacked first. By early 1754, the French had built Fort Duquesne at the forks of the Ohio River; Washington's assignment was to chase the French away without being the aggressor.

In spring of 1754, Washington set out with 160 Virginians along with Indian allies of the Mingo tribe. The first engagement with the French occurred early one May morning when the Mingo chief Tanaghrisson led a detachment of Washington's soldiers to a small French encampment in the woods. A brief skirmish left fourteen Frenchmen wounded. While Washington struggled to communicate with the injured French commander, Tanaghrisson and his men intervened to kill and then scalp the wounded soldiers, including the commander, probably with the aim of enflaming hostilities between the French and colonists.

This sudden massacre violated Washington's instructions to avoid being the aggressor and

Washington's Journal, 1754

When George Washington returned from his first mission to the French, Governor Dinwiddie asked him to write a full report of what he had seen of the western countryside, of the Indians, and of French troop strength. Washington obliged, writing about 7,000 words in less than two days (about equivalent to a 25-page double-spaced paper). He coolly narrated scenes of personal danger: of traveling in deep snow, of falling off a raft into an icy river, of being shot at by a lone Indian. Dinwiddie printed Washington's report, along with his own letter and the French commander's defiant answer, in a 32-page pamphlet; shortly thereafter it was reprinted in London. The governor's aim was to inform Virginians and British leaders about the French threat to the west. But the pamphlet suited Washington's aims as well: At age twenty-two, he became known on both sides of the Atlantic for resolute and rugged courage.

The Huntington Library and Art Collections, San Marino, California.

Ohio River Valley, 1753

- British fort
- French fort

The brave old Hendrick the great SACHEM or Chief of the Mohawk Indians one of the Six Nations now in Alliance with & Subject to the King of Great Britain

Chief Hendrick and John Caldwell

What might it mean when a Mohawk chief dresses in English clothes and a British soldier goes native? Dress is a symbol system that conveys status and self-presentation to viewers. Might it also change the way the dresser thinks about himself or herself? Chief Hendrick (top) worked closely with the British in New York to maintain the trade alliance known as the Covenant Chain. At age sixty, he traveled to England and sat for this portrait. His red coat, ruffled shirt, and three-cornered hat are all signs of the well-dressed British gentleman; but he holds a tomahawk in one hand and wampum in the other, and his long white hair is conspicuously uncurled, unlike an eighteenth-century gent's wig. John Caldwell (bottom) holds a tomahawk and sports Indian garb: feather headdress, blankets, leggings, and moccasins. During the Revolutionary War, Caldwell was stationed at Fort Detroit, a British garrison that provided aid to tribes in the Ohio Valley battling Americans. Caldwell acquired this Indian outfit for a diplomatic mission to the Shawnee in 1780; he took the clothes back to England and wore them for this portrait. Do you think these instances of imitation indicate a willingness to cross cultural boundaries and try to be like, think like, or experience the other culture? Is the co-opting just play or a sign of something deeper?

raised the stakes considerably. Fearing retaliation, Washington ordered his men to fortify their position; the flimsy "Fort Necessity" was the result. Reinforcements amounting to several hundred more Virginians arrived; but the Mingos, sensing disaster and displeased by Washington's style of command, fled. (Tanaghrisson later said: "The Colonel was a good-natured man, but had no experience; he took upon him to command the Indians as his slaves, [and] would by no means take advice from the Indians.") In early July, over 600 French soldiers aided by Indians attacked Fort Necessity, killing or wounding a third of Washington's men. The message was clear: The French would not depart from the disputed territory.

The Albany Congress and Intercolonial Defense

Even as Virginians, Frenchmen, and Indians fought and died in the Ohio Country, British imperial leaders hoped to prevent a larger war. One obvious strategy was to strengthen British alliances with seemingly neutral Indian tribes. To this end, British authorities directed the governor of New York to convene a colonial conference.

In June and July of 1754, twenty-four delegates from seven colonies met in Albany, New York. Also attending were Iroquois Indians of the Six Nations, a confederacy of tribes inhabiting the central and western parts of present-day New York. Albany was the traditional meeting place of the Covenant Chain, a trade alliance first created in 1692 between New York leaders and Mohawk Indians, the most easterly of the Six Nations. In 1753, the aged Mohawk leader, Hendrick, accused the English of breaking the Covenant Chain, so a prime goal of the Albany Congress was to repair trade relations with the Mohawk and secure their help—or at least their neutrality—against the French threat.

Two delegates at the congress had more ambitious plans. Benjamin Franklin of Pennsylvania and Thomas Hutchinson of Massachusetts, both rising political stars in their home colonies, coauthored the Albany Plan of Union, a proposal for a government unifying the colonies but limited to war and defense policies. In the course of the meeting, the Albany delegates learned of Washington's defeat at Fort Necessity and understood instantly the escalating risk of war with France; they approved the plan. Key features included a president general appointed by the crown and a grand council, meeting annually to consider questions of war, peace, and trade with the Indians. The writers of the Albany Plan humbly reaffirmed Parliament's authority; this was no bid for enlarged autonomy of the colonies.

To Franklin's surprise, not a single colony approved the Albany Plan. The Massachusetts assembly feared it was "a Design of gaining power over the Colonies," especially the power of taxation. Others objected that it would be impossible to agree on unified policies toward scores of quite different Indian tribes. The British government never backed the Albany Plan either, and soon after it appointed two superintendents of Indian affairs, one for the northern and another for the southern colonies, each with exclusive powers to negotiate with tribes.

The Indians at the Albany Congress were not impressed with the Albany Plan either. The Covenant Chain alliance with the Mohawk tribe was reaffirmed, but the other nations left without pledging to help the British battle the French. At this very early point in the Seven Years' War, the Iroquois figured that the French military presence around the Great Lakes would discourage the westward push of American colonists and therefore better serve their interests.

The War and Its Consequences

By 1755, Washington's frontier skirmish had turned into a major mobilization of British and American troops against the French. At first, the British hoped for quick victory on three fronts. General Edward Braddock, recently arrived from England, marched his army toward Fort Duquesne in western Pennsylvania. In Massachusetts, Governor William Shirley aimed his soldiers at Fort Niagara, critically located between Lakes Erie and Ontario. And William Johnson, a New Yorker recently appointed superintendent of Indian affairs, led forces north toward Lake Champlain, intending to push the French back to Canada (Map 6.1).

Unfortunately for the British, the French had cemented respectful alliances with many Indian tribes. In July 1755, General Braddock's force of 2,000 British and Virginia troops was aided by just eight Oneida Indians. One day short of Fort Duquesne, they were ambushed by 250 French soldiers and 640 Indian warriors, including Ottawas, Ojibwas, Potawatomis, Shawnees, and Delawares. In the bloody battle nearly a thousand on the British side were killed or wounded. Washington was unhurt, though two horses in succession were shot out from under him; General Braddock was killed.

News of Braddock's defeat caused the other two British armies, then hacking their way through the dense forests of northern New York, to retreat from action. For the next two years, the British stumbled badly on the American front. What finally turned the war around was the rise to power in 1757 of William Pitt, England's prime minister, a man willing to commit massive resources to fight France and its ally Spain worldwide. In America, British and American troops captured Forts Duquesne, Niagara, and Ticonderoga and then the French cities of Quebec and Montreal, all from 1758 to 1760.

American colonists rejoiced, but the worldwide war was not over yet. Battles continued in the Caribbean, where the French sugar islands Martinique and Guadeloupe fell to the British, as did Spain's Cuba. After further fighting in Europe and India, France and Spain capitulated, and the Treaty of Paris was signed in 1763.

The triumph of victory was sweet but short-lived. The complex peace negotiations reorganized the map of North America but stopped short of providing England with the

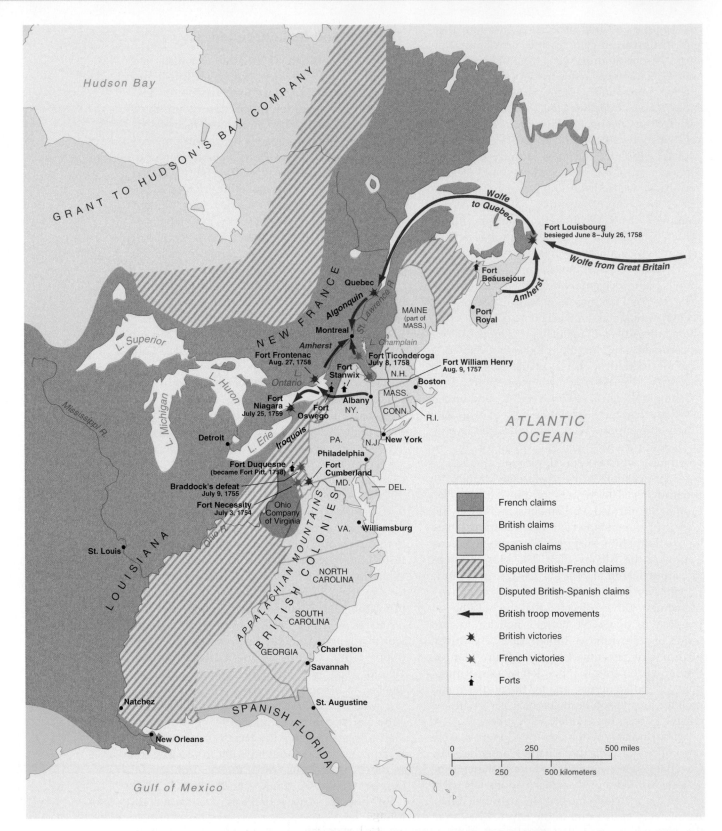

MAP 6.1   European Areas of Influence and the Seven Years' War, 1754–1763
In the mid-eighteenth century, France, England, and Spain claimed vast areas of North America, many of them already inhabited by various Indian peoples. The early flash points of the Seven Years' War were in regions of disputed claims where the French had allied with powerful native groups—the Iroquois and the Algonquian—to put pressure on the westward-moving English.

MAP 6.2 North America after the Seven Years' War
In the peace treaty of 1763, France ceded its interior lands but retained fishing rights and islands in the far north and several sugar islands in the Caribbean. Much of France's claim to the area called Louisiana went not to England but to Spain.

full spoils of victory. England gained control of Canada, eliminating the French threat from the north and west. English and American title to the eastern half of North America, precisely what England had claimed before the war, was confirmed. But all French territory west of the Mississippi River, including New Orleans, was transferred to Spain as compensation for Spain's assistance to France during the war. Stranger still, Cuba was returned to Spain, and Martinique and Guadeloupe were returned to France (Map 6.2).

In truth, the French islands in the Caribbean were hardly a threat to Americans, for they provided a profitable trade in smuggled molasses. The main threat to the safety of colonists came instead from Indians, ignored by the Treaty of Paris. With the French gone, the Indians lost the advantage of having two opponents to play off against each other, and they now had to cope with the westward-moving Americans. Indian policy would soon become a serious point of contention between the British government and the colonists.

England's version of the victory of 1763 awarded all credit to the mighty British army, inadequately supported by ungrateful colonists. Worse still, the colonists had engaged in smug-

gling—notably a lively trade in beaver pelts with French fur traders and an illegal molasses trade in the Caribbean. American traders, grumbled the British leaders, were really traitors. William Pitt was convinced that the illegal trade "principally, if not alone, enabled France to sustain and protract this long and expensive war."

Colonists read the lessons of the war differently. American colonial soldiers had turned out in force, they claimed, but had been relegated to grunt work by arrogant British leaders and subjected to unexpectedly harsh military discipline, ranging from floggings to executions. General Braddock had foolishly bragged to Benjamin Franklin that "these savages may, indeed, be a formidable enemy to your raw American militia, but upon the king's regular and disciplined troops, sir, it is impossible they should make any impression." Braddock's defeat "gave us Americans," Franklin wrote, "the first suspicion that our exalted ideas of the prowess of British regulars had not been well founded."

The human costs of the war were etched especially sharply in the minds of New England colonists. About one-third of all Massachusetts men between fifteen and thirty had seen service. Many families lost loved ones, a cost not soon forgotten. The enormous expense of the war caused

Silver Medal to Present to Indians

After Pontiac's uprising ended, the British attempted to mend relations with Indian tribes by honoring them with gifts. This silver medal, minted in 1766, displays a profile of King George III on the front and a cozy depiction on the back of an Indian and Briton sharing a smoking peace pipe. The Latin words on the front announce George's name, title, and kingly dominions; the English words on the back would have been equally unintelligible to the recipients of the gift. Imagine a conversation between an Indian chief and an English translator who tries to explain what the slogan "happy while united" might mean. The scene depicted—two men with relaxed, friendly body language—illustrates "happy" and "united." The "while," rooted in a sense of time, temporariness, and contingency, might be tricky to explain. Why?

The American Numismatic Society.

by Pitt's no-holds-barred military strategy cast another huge shadow over the victory. By 1763, England's national debt, double what it had been when Pitt took office, posed a formidable challenge to the next decade of leadership in England.

British Leadership, Indians, and the Proclamation of 1763

In 1760, in the middle of the Seven Years' War, twenty-two-year-old George III came to the British throne. Timid and insecure, the new king trusted only his Scottish tutor, the Earl of Bute, an outsider to power circles in London, and made him head of his cabinet of ministers. Bute made blunders and did not last long, but he made one significant decision—to keep a standing army in the colonies after the last battle was over in 1760. In both financial and political terms, this was a costly move.

The ostensible reason for stationing British troops in America was to maintain the peace between the colonists and the Indians. This was not a misplaced concern. The defeat and withdrawal of the French from North America had left their Indian allies—who did not accept defeat—in a state of alarm. Just three months after the Treaty of Paris was signed in 1763, Pontiac, chief of the Ottawa tribe in the northern Ohio region, attacked the British garrison near Detroit. Six more attacks on forts quickly followed, and frontier settlements were also raided by nearly a dozen tribes from western New York, the Ohio Valley, and the Great Lakes region.

By fall, more than 400 British soldiers were dead and another 2,000 colonists killed or taken captive. Pontiac's uprising was quelled in December 1763 by the combined efforts of British and colonial soldiers, but tensions remained high. (See "Historical Question," page 140.)

To minimize violence, the British government issued the Proclamation of 1763, forbidding colonists to settle west of the Appalachian Mountains. The Proclamation chiefly aimed to separate Indians and settlers, but it also limited trade with Indians to traders licensed by colonial governors, and it forbade private sales of Indian land. The Proclamation's language took care not to identify western lands as belonging to the Indians. Instead, it spoke of Indians "who live under our protection" on "such parts of our Dominions and Territories as, not having been ceded to or purchased by Us, are reserved to them, as their Hunting Grounds." Other parts of the Proclamation of 1763 referred to American and even French colonists in Canada as "our loving subjects" entitled to English rights and privileges. The Indians were not described as British subjects.

The 1763 boundary proved impossible to enforce. Surging population growth had already sent many hundreds of settlers west of the Appalachians, and land speculators, such as those of Virginia's Ohio Company, had no desire to lose opportunities for profitable resale of their land grants. Bute's decision to post a standing army in the colonies was thus a cause for concern for western settlers, eastern speculators, and Indian tribes alike.

REVIEW   How did the Seven Years' War erode relations between colonists and Britain?

Pontiac's Uprising, 1763

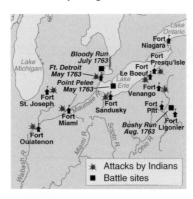

The Sugar and Stamp Acts, 1763–1765

Lord Bute lost power in 1763, and the young King George turned to a succession of leaders throughout the 1760s, searching for a prime minister he could trust. A half dozen ministers in seven years took turns dealing with one basic, underlying British reality: A huge war debt, amounting to £123 million and growing due to interest, needed to be serviced, and the colonists, as British subjects, should help to pay it off. To many Americans, however, that proposition seemed in deep violation of what they perceived to be their rights and liberties as British subjects, and it created resentment that eventually erupted in rebellion. The first provocative revenue acts were the work of Sir George Grenville, prime minister from 1763 to 1765.

Paper Currency of the 1750s to 1770s
Colonists generally used coins of valued metal for money (British shillings, Spanish doubloons) or else engaged in barter. But during the upheaval of the Seven Years' War, several colonies printed paper money. The currency shown here is laden with words stipulating the legality and value of the money. To discourage counterfeiting, each paper had an elaborate design, a unique handwritten number, and the signature of some authority who vouched for its authenticity. London merchants did not like accepting colonial paper money and prevailed on Parliament to pass a Currency Act in 1764 prohibiting the colonies from printing any, which put a crimp in the colonial economy, always short of coinage. In 1775, the newly established Continental Congress began printing paper money to finance the war. Notice the three-dollar paper at the lower left.
Courtesy of the Decorative & Industrial Arts Collection of the Chicago Historical Society.

Grenville's Sugar Act

To find revenue, George Grenville scrutinized the customs service, which collected all import and export duties. Grenville found that the salaries of customs officers cost the government four times what was collected in revenue. The shortfall was due in part to bribery and smuggling, so Grenville began to insist on rigorous attention to paperwork and a strict accounting of collected duties.

The hardest duty to enforce was the one imposed by the Molasses Act of 1733—a stiff tax of six pence per gallon on any molasses purchased from non-British sources. The purpose of the tax was to discourage trade with French Caribbean islands and redirect the molasses trade to British sugar islands. But it did not work: French molasses remained cheap and abundant because French **planters** on Martinique and Guadeloupe had no use for it. A by-product of sugar production, molasses was a key ingredient in rum, a drink the French scorned. Rum-loving Americans were eager to buy French molasses, and they had ignored the tax law for decades.

Grenville's ingenious solution was the Revenue Act of 1764, popularly dubbed the "Sugar Act." It lowered the duty on French molasses to three pence, making it more attractive for shippers to obey the law, and at the same time raised penalties for smuggling. The act appeared to be in the tradition of navigation acts meant to regulate trade, but Grenville's actual intent was

to raise revenue. He was using an established form of law for new ends and accomplishing his goal by the novel means of lowering a duty.

The Sugar Act toughened enforcement policies. From now on, all British naval crews could act as impromptu customs officers, boarding suspicious ships and seizing cargoes found to be in violation. Smugglers caught without proper paperwork would be prosecuted, not in a friendly civil court with a local jury but in a vice-admiralty court located in Halifax, Nova Scotia, where a single judge presided. The implication was that justice would be sure and severe.

Grenville hoped that the new Sugar Act would reform American smugglers into law-abiding shippers and in turn generate income for

How Long Did the Seven Years' War Last in Indian Country?

France was defeated on the North American continent in 1760, and the Treaty of Paris officially ended the global war between France and England in 1763. But there was no lasting peace for the Indian nations of the Ohio Valley and Great Lakes region. In 1761, a Chippewa chief named Minavavana clearly explained why in an ominous speech delivered to a British trader at Fort Michilimackinac, a British outpost guarding the straits of Mackinaw where Lakes Huron and Michigan meet: "Englishman, although you have conquered the French, you have not yet conquered us! We are not your slaves. These lakes, these woods and mountains were left to us by our ancestors. They are our inheritance; and we will part with them to none." Furthermore, Minavavana pointedly noted, "your king has never sent us any presents, nor entered into any treaty with us, wherefore he and we are still at war; and until he does these things we must consider that we have no other father, nor friend, among the white men than the King of France."

Minavavana and other Indians of the region had cause to be alarmed. With the exit of the French, British regiments took over the French-built forts all over the Northwest. Fort Duquesne, renamed Fort Pitt in honor of the British leader who authorized the war-winning strategy, underwent two years of fortification. No one could mistake the new walls—sixty feet

thick at their base, ten at the top—for the external facade of a friendly fur trading post. Nonmilitary Americans were moving into Fort Pitt's neighborhood too, just as Indians had feared they would, crowding out native inhabitants and relying on the military protection of the fort.

Minavavana's complaint about the lack of British presents was a far more serious problem than the British military leaders figured. Gifts exchanged in Indian culture cemented social relationships; they symbolized honor and established obligation. The French over many decades had mastered the subtleties of gift exchange, distributing clothing, textiles, and hats, and receiving calumets (ornamented ceremonial pipe stems) as symbols of friendship. New to the practice, British military leaders often discarded the calumets as trivial trinkets, thereby insulting the givers. Major General Jeffrey Amherst was sometimes willing to offer gifts to particular Indian leaders, positioning the "gift" as a bribe in the British frame of reference. But Amherst saw extensive gift exchange as demeaning to the British, forcing them to pay tribute to people whom he considered inferior. "It is not my intention ever to attempt to gain the friendship of Indians by presents," Amherst declared. The Indian view was the opposite: Generous givers expressed dominance and protection, not subordination, in the act of giving. William Johnson, superintendent of northern Indian affairs, warned

Amherst that he was insulting the Indians, but the imperious Amherst did not listen.

A religious revival in 1760–1761, fueled by the prophetic visions of an Indian leader named Neolin, greatly enhanced the prospects of frontier war in the Northwest. Neolin, of the Delaware tribe, predicted a swift decline for all tribes unless they altered their ways, gave up quarreling with each other, shunned trade in guns, alcohol, and other trade goods, and curbed their overkill of animals for the pelt trade. His preachings spread quickly, gaining credence as the British bungled diplomacy and American settlers continued to penetrate western lands.

A renewal of commitment to Indian ways and the formation of tribal alliances led to open warfare in 1763, called (by the British) Pontiac's War. (The Indians would not have credited Pontiac with sole leadership; the coordination of the uprising was the work of many men.) Jeffrey Amherst, never a shrewd observer of Indian relations, flatly declared in April 1763 that reports of impending attack were "Meer Bugbears." But by mid-May, the British commander at Detroit knew the threat was real. Pontiac, chief of the Ottawa, along with Potawatomi and Huron warriors, attacked Fort Detroit and laid siege for two months. In late May, within two weeks of Pontiac's first move, Indians captured four more forts in Ohio, through ruses in which Indians pretending to have peaceful business gained entry to the garrisons. A fifth fort, at Michilimackinac, fell to Ojibwas who seemed to be playing a game of lacrosse near the fort. After several hours of strenuous play, the ball landed near the fort's open gate, and the enthralled British spectators realized too late that the convergence of players on the ball was really a rush

Plan of the New Fort at Pittsburgh

The French Fort Duquesne sat at the strategic forks of the Ohio River on a triangle of land formed by the Allegheny and Monongahela rivers rushing together to create the mighty Ohio. Built in 1754, Fort Duquesne provided a supply depot and a meeting place for the Indian allies of the French. It was the intended target of General Braddock's English army in 1755, but Braddock was forced into battle and soundly defeated a day before his planned attack. In 1758, the British captured an English-speaking man named Johnson along with some Indians taken prisoner. Johnson, an apparent traitor, saved his life by yielding information that Fort Duquesne was greatly undermanned and an easy hit. British and colonial troops sped to attack it; once taken, the fort was blown into rubble. In 1759, this plan for a new fort, named for Prime Minister William Pitt, showed a grand and imposing stronghold with room enough to house 1,000 soldiers inside the thick protective walls. By 1762, the fort was finished, fulfilling Pitt's mandate to "maintain His Majesty's subjects in undisputed possession of the Ohio."

of warriors into the fort. The players seized tomahawks that had been hidden under blankets worn by Indian women on the sidelines. The Ojibwas took the fort.

By the end of June, thirteen British garrisons had either fallen or been evacuated under threat of attack. Yet the British managed to hold on to the three most important forts—Detroit, Niagara, and Pitt—besieged by Indians. At Fort Pitt, two ostensibly friendly Delaware Indians showed up at the end of May to suggest that the British leave to avoid attack. Pitt's commander thanked them but declined their suggestion and sent them on their way with his idea of a gift: two blankets and a handkerchief used by British smallpox patients in the fort. "We hope it will have the desired effect," wrote a militiaman in his diary. Two months later, Jeffrey Amherst suggested to a subordinate that spreading smallpox—a practice akin to later germ warfare—should be considered as a method of war: "We must use Every Strategem in our Power to Reduce them." There is no evidence that the infected blankets actually propagated smallpox or that Amherst's war strategem was put into greater practice.

From late summer of 1763 into the early months of 1764, Indian country was the scene of tremendous bloodshed. Indians targeted British supply routes and civilian settlements, resulting in several thousand deaths. Two thousand British troops were moved west from points in upper New York and Canada to join the fray. In December, Pennsylvania civilians went on the offensive. Some fifty vigilantes known as the Paxton Boys decided to make war on any Indians they could find. They descended on a peaceful village of friendly Conestoga Indians and murdered and scalped twenty of them. The vigilantes, numbers swelling to 500, next marched on Philadelphia to try to capture and murder some Christian Indians held in protective custody. British troops prevented that, but the unruly Paxton Boys escaped all punishment for their murderous attack on the Conestoga.

In 1764, the rebellion faded. The Indians were short on ammunition; the British were tired and broke. Amherst's superiors in Britain blamed him for mishandling the conflict, and when he was recalled home, his own soldiers toasted his leaving. Thomas Gage took command and soon distributed gifts profusely among the Indians.

Was the Seven Years' War finally over for the Indians, ten years after it started? If 1764 represents an end, it was only a brief one. Periodic raids and killings punctuated the rest of the 1760s and early 1770s, climaxing in the late 1770s as Indians joined the British to fight the Americans in the Revolutionary War. Warfare and massacres occurred in New England and New York, down to South Carolina and Georgia, and especially in the Ohio Country. The American Revolution eventually ended as well, but the frontier war between Americans and Indians continued on and off—mostly on—until 1815, the end of the War of 1812. Perhaps the Seven Years' War could be called the Sixty-One Years' War, from the Indian point of view.

the empire. Unfortunately, the decrease in duty was not sufficient to offset the attractions of smuggling. The vigilant customs officers made bribery harder to accomplish, and several ugly confrontations occurred in port cities. Reaction to the Sugar Act foreshadowed questions about England's right to tax Americans, but in 1764 objections to the act came principally from Americans in the shipping trades inconvenienced by the law.

From the British point of view, the Proclamation of 1763 and the Sugar Act seemed to be reasonable efforts to administer the colonies. To the Americans, however, the British supervision appeared to be a disturbing intrusion into colonial practices.

The Stamp Act

By his second year in office, Grenville had made almost no dent in the national debt. So in February 1765, he escalated his revenue program with the Stamp Act, precipitating a major conflict between England and the colonies over Parliament's right to tax. The Stamp Act imposed a tax on all paper used for official documents—newspapers, pamphlets, court documents, licenses, wills, ships' cargo lists—and required an affixed stamp as proof the tax had been paid. Unlike the Sugar Act, which regulated trade, the Stamp Act was designed plainly and simply to raise money. It affected nearly everyone who used any taxed paper, but most of all those in the business and legal communities, heavily reliant on official documents.

Grenville was no fool. Anticipating that the stamp tax would be unpopular—Thomas Hutchinson had forewarned him—he delegated the administration of the act to Americans, to avoid the problem of hostility to British enforcers. In each colony, local stamp distributors would be hired at a handsome salary of 8 percent of the revenue collected.

British tradition held that taxes were a gift of the people to their monarch, granted by the people's representatives. This view of taxes as a freely given gift preserved an essential concept of English political theory: the idea that citizens have the liberty to enjoy and use their property without fear of confiscation. The king could not demand money; only the House of Commons could grant it. Grenville quite agreed with the notion of taxation by consent, but he argued that the colonists were

already "virtually" represented in Parliament. The House of Commons, he insisted, represented all British subjects, wherever they were.

Colonial leaders emphatically rejected this view, arguing that **virtual representation** could not withstand the stretch across the Atlantic. The stamp tax itself, levied by a distant Parliament on unwilling colonies, illustrated the problem. "The MINISTER'S virtual representation in Support of the TAX on us is fantastical and frivolous," Maryland inhabitants complained.

Resistance Strategies and Crowd Politics

News of the Stamp Act arrived in the colonies in April 1765, seven months before it was to take effect on November 1. There was time therefore to object. Governors were unlikely to challenge the law, for most of them owed their office to the king. Instead, the colonial assemblies took the lead; eight of them held discussions on the Stamp Act.

Virginia's assembly, the House of Burgesses, was the first. At the end of its May session, after two-thirds of the members had left, Patrick Henry, a young political newcomer, presented a series of resolutions on the Stamp Act that were debated and passed, one by one. They became known as the Virginia Resolves.

Henry's resolutions inched the assembly toward radical opposition to the Stamp Act. The first three stated the obvious: that Virginians were British citizens, that they enjoyed the same rights and privileges as Britons, and that self-taxation was one of those rights. The fourth resolution noted that Virginians had always taxed themselves, through their representatives in the House of Burgesses. The fifth took a radical leap by pushing the other four unexceptional statements to one logical conclusion—that the Virginia assembly alone had the right to tax Virginians.

Two more fiery resolutions were debated as Henry pressed the logic of his case to the extreme. The sixth resolution denied legitimacy to any tax law originating outside Virginia, and a seventh boldly called anyone who disagreed with these propositions an enemy of Virginia. This was too much for the other representatives. They voted down resolutions six and seven and later rescinded their vote on number five as well.

Their caution hardly mattered, however, because newspapers in other colonies printed all seven Virginia Resolves, creating the impression that a daring first challenge to the Stamp Act had occurred. Consequently, other assemblies were willing to consider even more radical questions, such as: By what authority could Parliament legislate for the colonies without also taxing them? No one disagreed, in 1765, that Parliament had legislative power over the colonists, who were, after all, British subjects. Several assemblies advanced the argument that there was a distinction between *external* taxes, imposed to regulate trade, and *internal* taxes, such as a stamp tax or a property tax, which could only be self-imposed.

Reaction to the Stamp Act ran far deeper than political debate in assemblies. Every person whose livelihood required official paper had to decide whether to comply with the act. Local communities strategized their responses. Should they boycott all paper use? A boycott would keep noncompliance within the law but would be highly inconvenient, crippling newspapers as well as legal and business paperwork. Should communities defy the law and conduct business as usual on unstamped paper, running the risk of fines or jail? A third strategy promised the surest success: preventing distribution of the stamps at the source, before the law took effect, thus ensuring universal noncompliance.

The first organized resistance to the Stamp Act began in Boston, under the leadership of Samuel Adams, a town politician with a history of opposition to Lieutenant Governor Thomas Hutchinson. Unlike Hutchinson, Adams cared nothing for status, high office, or fine material goods. He was the Harvard-educated son of a Boston brewer, a man with shrewd political instincts and a gift for organizing. He mobilized shopkeepers, master craftsmen, dockworkers, and laborers into a group of protesters who called themselves the Sons of Liberty.

The plan hatched by the Boston Sons of Liberty called for a large street demonstration highlighting a ritualized mock execution, designed to convince Andrew Oliver, the stamp distributor, to resign. On August 14, 1765, a crowd of two to three thousand demonstrators hung an effigy of Oliver in a tree and then paraded it around town before finally beheading and burning it. The flesh-and-blood Oliver stayed in hiding; the next day he resigned his office in a well-publicized announcement.

The demonstration provided lessons for everyone. Oliver learned that stamp distributors would be very unpopular people. Francis Bernard, the royal governor, learned the limitations of his power to govern, with no police to call on. The demonstration's leaders learned that street action was effective. And hundreds of laborers, sailors,

Andrew Oliver
This portrait shows Bostonian Andrew Oliver at age twenty-two, just a few years after his graduation from Harvard College. The powdered wig and stern look add years to his face; the blousy clothing adds substance to his body. He was fifty-nine and probably even more imposing in appearance when he ran afoul of the Stamp Act rioters in Boston in 1765.
Collection of the Oliver Family, photo by Clive Russ.

and apprentices not only learned what the Stamp Act was all about but also gained pride in their ability to have a decisive impact on politics.

Twelve days later, another crowd action showed how well these lessons had been learned. On August 26, a crowd visited the houses of three detested customs and court officials, breaking windows and raiding wine cellars. A fourth target was the finest dwelling in Massachusetts, owned by the stiff-necked Thomas Hutchinson. Rumors abounded that Hutchinson had urged Grenville to adopt the Stamp Act. Although he had done the opposite, Hutchinson refused to set the record straight, saying curtly, "I am not obliged to give an answer to all the questions that may be put me by every lawless person." The crowd attacked his house, and by daybreak only the exterior walls were standing.

The destruction of Hutchinson's house brought a temporary halt to crowd activities in

Boston. The Boston town meeting issued a statement of sympathy, but a large reward for the arrest and conviction of rioters failed to produce a single lead. The Sons of Liberty denied involvement. Essentially, the opponents of the Stamp Act in Boston had triumphed; no one volunteered to replace Oliver as distributor. When the Stamp Act took effect on November 1, customs officers were unable to prevent ships lacking properly stamped clearance papers from passing through the harbor.

Liberty and Property

Boston's crowd actions of August sparked similar eruptions by groups calling themselves Sons of Liberty in nearly fifty towns throughout the colonies, and stamp distributors everywhere hastened to resign. One Connecticut distributor was forced by a crowd to throw his hat and powdered wig in the air while shouting a cheer for "Liberty and property!" This man fared better than another Connecticut stamp agent, who was nearly buried alive by Sons of Liberty. Only when the thuds of dirt sounded on his coffin did he have a sudden change of heart, shouting out his resignation to the crowd above. Luckily, he was heard. In Charleston, South Carolina, the stamp distributor resigned after crowds burned effigies and chanted "Liberty! Liberty!"

Some colonial leaders, disturbed by the riots, sought a more moderate challenge to parliamentary authority. Twenty-seven delegates representing nine colonial assemblies met in New York City in October 1765 as the Stamp Act Congress. For two weeks, the men hammered out a petition about taxation addressed to the king and Parliament. Their statement closely resembled the first five Virginia Resolves, claiming taxes were "free gifts of the people" that only the people's representatives could give. They dismissed virtual representation: "The people of these colonies are not, and from their local circumstances, cannot be represented in the House of Commons." But the delegates carefully affirmed their subordination to Parliament and monarch in deferential language. Nevertheless, the Stamp Act Congress, by the mere fact of its meeting, advanced a radical potential, the notion of intercolonial political action.

The rallying cry of "Liberty and property" made perfect sense to many white Americans of all social ranks, who feared that the Stamp Act threatened their traditional right to liberty as British subjects. In this case the liberty in question was the right to be taxed only by representative government. "Liberty and property" came from a trinity of concepts—"life, liberty, property"—that had come to be regarded as the birthright of freeborn British subjects since at least the seventeenth century. A powerful tradition of British political thought invested representative government with the duty to protect individual lives, liberties, and property (possessions or money) against potential abuse by royal authority. Up to 1765, Americans consented to accept Parliament as a body that in some way represented them. But now, in this matter of taxation via stamps, Parliament seemed a distant body that had failed to protect Americans' liberty and property against royal authority.

Alarmed, some Americans began to speak and write about a plot by British leaders to enslave them. The opposite of liberty was slavery, the condition of being under the control of someone else. A Maryland writer warned that if the colonies lost "the right of exemption from all taxes without their consent," that loss would "deprive them of every privilege distinguishing freemen from slaves." The opposite meanings of liberty and slavery were utterly clear to white Americans, but they stopped short of applying similar logic to the half million black Americans they held in bondage. Many blacks, however, could see the contradiction. When a crowd of Charleston blacks paraded with shouts of "Liberty!" just a few months after white Sons of Liberty had done the same, the town militia turned out to break up the demonstration.

Politicians and merchants in England reacted with alarm to the American demonstrations and petitions. Merchants particularly feared trade disruptions and pressured Parliament to repeal the Stamp Act. By late 1765, yet another new minister, the Marquess of Rockingham, headed the king's cabinet and sought a way to repeal the act without losing face. The solution came in March 1766: The Stamp Act was repealed, but with it came the Declaratory Act, which asserted Parliament's right to legislate for the colonies "in all cases whatsoever." Perhaps the stamp tax had been inexpedient, but the power to tax—one prime case of a legislative power—was stoutly upheld.

> **REVIEW** Why did the Sugar and Stamp acts draw fierce opposition from colonists?

The Townshend Acts and Economic Retaliation, 1767–1770

Rockingham was soon out of government, replaced by William Pitt, who then appointed Charles Townshend to be chancellor of the exchequer, the chief financial minister. Facing both the old war debt and the continuing cost of stationing British troops in America, Townshend turned again to taxation. But his simple yet naive idea to raise revenue touched off a year of coordinated boycotts of British goods in the colonies. Even women were politicized as self-styled "Daughters of Liberty." Boston led the uproar, causing the British to send peacekeeping soldiers to assist the royal governor. The stage was thus set for the first fatalities in the brewing revolution.

The Townshend Duties

Townshend proposed new taxes in the old form of a navigation act. Officially called the Revenue Act of 1767, it established new duties on tea, glass, lead, paper, and painters' colors imported into the colonies, to be paid by the importer but passed on to consumers in the retail price. A year before, the duty on French molasses had been reduced from three pence to one pence per gallon, and finally the Sugar Act was pulling in a tidy revenue of about £45,000 annually. So it was not unreasonable to suppose that duties on additional trade goods might also improve the cash flow. Townshend assumed that external taxes on transatlantic trade would be more acceptable to Americans than internal taxes, such as the stamp tax.

The Townshend duties were not especially burdensome, but the principle they embodied—taxation through trade duties—looked different to the colonists in the wake of the Stamp Act crisis. Although Americans once distinguished between external and internal taxes, that distinction was wiped out by an external tax meant only to raise money. John Dickinson, a Philadelphia lawyer, articulated this view in a series of articles titled *Letters from a Farmer in Pennsylvania*, widely reprinted in the winter of 1767–68. "We are taxed without our consent.... We are therefore—SLAVES," Dickinson wrote, calling for "a total denial of the power of Parliament to lay upon these colonies any 'tax' whatever."

A controversial provision of the Townshend duties directed that some of the revenue generated would pay the salaries of royal governors. Before 1767, local assemblies set the salaries of their own officials, giving them significant influence over crown-appointed officeholders. Townshend wanted to strengthen the governors' position as well as to curb the growing independence of the assemblies.

The Massachusetts assembly took the lead in protesting the Townshend duties. Samuel Adams, a member from Boston, argued that any form of parliamentary taxation was unjust because Americans were not represented in Parliament. Further, he argued that the new way to pay governors' salaries subverted the proper relationship between the people and their rulers. The assembly circulated a letter with Adams's arguments to other colonial assemblies for their endorsement. As with the Stamp Act Congress of 1765, colonial assemblies were starting to coordinate their protests.

In response to Adams's letter, the new man in charge of colonial affairs in Britain, Lord Hillsborough, instructed the Massachusetts governor, Francis Bernard, to dissolve the assembly if it refused to repudiate the letter. The assembly refused and Governor Bernard carried out his instruction. In the summer of 1768, Boston was in an uproar.

Nonconsumption and the Daughters of Liberty

The Boston town meeting had already passed resolutions, termed "nonconsumption agreements," calling for a boycott of all British-made goods. Dozens of other towns passed similar resolutions in 1767 and 1768. For example, prohibited purchases in the town of New Haven, Connecticut, included carriages, furniture, hats, clothing, lace, clocks, and textiles. The idea was to encourage home manufacture and to hurt trade, causing London merchants to pressure Parliament for repeal of the duties.

Nonconsumption agreements were very hard to enforce. With the Stamp Act, there was one hated item, a stamp, and a limited number of official distributors. In contrast, an agreement to boycott all British goods required serious personal sacrifice. Some merchants were wary of nonconsumption because it hurt their pocketbooks, and a few continued to import in readiness for the end of nonconsumption (or to sell on the side to people choosing to ignore nonconsumption). In Boston, such merchants found themselves blacklisted in newspapers and broadsides.

A more direct blow to trade came from nonimportation agreements, but it proved more difficult to get merchants to agree to these. There was always the risk that merchants in other colonies might continue to trade and thus receive handsome profits if neighboring colonies prohibited trade. Not until late 1768 could Boston merchants agree to suspend trade through a nonimportation agreement lasting one year starting January 1, 1769. Sixty signed the agreement. New York merchants soon followed suit, as did Philadelphia and Charleston merchants in 1769.

Doing without British products, whether luxury goods, tea, or textiles, no doubt was a hardship. But it also presented an opportunity, for many of the British products specified in nonconsumption agreements were household goods traditionally under the control of the "ladies." By 1769, male leaders in the patriot cause clearly understood that women's cooperation in nonconsumption and home manufacture was beneficial to their cause. The Townshend duties thus provided an unparalleled opportunity for encouraging

female patriotism. During the Stamp Act crisis, Sons of Liberty took to the streets in protest. During the difficulties of 1768–69, the concept of "Daughters of Liberty" emerged to give shape to a new idea—that women might play a role in public affairs.

Any woman could express affiliation with the colonial protest through conspicuous boycotts of British-made goods. In Boston, over three hundred women signed a petition to abstain from tea, "sickness excepted," in order to "save this abused Country from Ruin and Slavery." A nine-year-old girl visiting the royal governor's house in New Jersey took the tea she was offered, curtsied, and tossed the beverage out a nearby window.

Homespun cloth became a prominent symbol of patriotism. A young Boston girl learning to spin called herself "a daughter of liberty," noting that "I chuse to wear as much of our own manufactory as pocible." In the boycott period of 1768–1770, newspapers reported on spinning matches or bees in some sixty New England towns, in which women came together in public to make yarn. Nearly always, the bee was held at the local minister's house, and the yarn produced was charitably handed over to him for distribution to the poor. Newspaper accounts variously called the spinners "Daughters of Liberty" or "Daughters of Industry."

This surge of public spinning was related to the politics of the boycott, which infused traditional women's work with new political purpose. But the women spinners were not equivalents of the Sons of Liberty. The Sons marched in streets, burned effigies, threatened hated officials, and celebrated anniversaries of their successes with raucous drinking and feasting in taverns. The Daughters manifested their patriotism quietly, in

Spinning Wheel

A lot of skill was needed to spin high-quality thread and yarn. This wheel was used for spinning flax (a plant with a long fibrous stem) into linen thread; it is likely the type used in the politicized 1769 spinning bees in which "Daughters of Liberty" proclaimed their boycott of British textiles. A foot treadle controls the turning of the wheel, and a spindle holds the thread produced. The art of spinning was all in the spinster's hand, which controlled the tension on the thread and the speed of the twisting. The spinning Daughters of Liberty were praised for their virtuous industry. Responding to such praise, one young woman complained, in a Rhode Island newspaper, that young male patriots were deficient in virtue: "Alas! We hear nothing of their working matches, nothing of their concern for the honor of their King or for the safety or liberties of their country"; instead the news is of "nocturnal Carousals and Exploits; of their drinking, gaming & whoring matches; and how they disturb the quiet of honest people."

Smithsonian Institution, Washington, D.C.

ways marked by piety, industry, and charity. The difference was due in part to cultural ideals of gender, which prized masculine self-assertion but feminine selflessness. It also was due to class: The Sons were a cross-class alliance, with leaders from the middling orders reliant on men and boys of the lower ranks to fuel their crowds. The Daughters, dusting off spinning wheels and shelving their teapots, were genteel ladies used to buying British goods. The difference between the Sons and Daughters also speaks to two views of how best to challenge authority. Was resistance to British policy most effectively communicated through violent threats and street actions? Or were self-discipline and self-sacrifice the better strategies?

On the whole, the anti-British boycotts were a success. Imports fell by more than 40 percent; British merchants felt the pinch and let Parliament know it. In Boston, the Hutchinson family also endured losses, but even more alarming to the rigid and orderly lieutenant governor, Boston seemed overrun with anti-British sentiment. The Sons of Liberty staged annual rollicking celebrations of the Stamp Act riot, and Hutchinson along with Governor Bernard concluded that British troops were necessary to restore order.

Military Occupation and "Massacre" in Boston

In the fall of 1768, three thousand uniformed troops arrived to occupy Boston. The soldiers drilled conspicuously on the Common, played loud music on the Sabbath, and in general grated on the nerves of Bostonians. Although the situation was frequently tense, no major troubles occurred during that winter and through most of 1769. But as January 1, 1770, approached, marking the end of the nonimportation agreement, it was clear that some merchants—the Hutchinsons, for example—would no longer engage in the boycott.

Trouble began in January, when the door of the Hutchinson brothers' shop was defaced by "Hillsborough paint," a potent mixture of human excrement and urine. In February, a crowd surrounded the house of customs official Ebenezer Richardson, who panicked and fired a musket, accidentally killing a young boy passing on the street. The Sons of Liberty mounted a massive funeral procession to mark this first instance of violent death in the struggle with England.

For the next week, tension gripped Boston. The climax came on Monday evening, March 5,

1770, when a crowd taunted eight British soldiers guarding the customs house, throwing snowballs and rocks and daring the soldiers to fire; finally one did. After a short pause, during which someone yelled "Fire!" the other soldiers shot into the crowd, hitting eleven men, five of them fatally.

The Boston Massacre, as the event quickly became called, was over in minutes. In the immediate aftermath, Hutchinson (now acting governor after Bernard's recall to England) showed courage in addressing the crowd from the balcony of the statehouse. He quickly removed the regiments to an island in the harbor to prevent further bloodshed, and he jailed Captain Thomas Preston and his eight soldiers, a protective move, promising they would be held for trial.

The Sons of Liberty staged elaborate martyrs' funerals for the five victims. Significantly, the one nonwhite victim shared equally in the public's veneration: Crispus Attucks, a sailor and ropemaker in his forties, son of an African man and a Natick Indian woman, a slave in his youth but at the time of his death a free laborer at the Boston docks. Attucks was possibly the first American partisan to die in the American Revolution, and certainly the first African American.

The trial of the eight soldiers came in the fall of 1770. They were defended by two young Boston attorneys, Samuel Adams's cousin John Adams and Josiah Quincy. Because Adams and Quincy had direct ties to the leadership of the Sons of Liberty, their decision to defend the British soldiers at first seems odd. But John Adams was deeply committed to the idea that even unpopular defendants deserve a fair trial. Samuel Adams respected his cousin's decision to take the case, for there was a tactical benefit as well. It showed that the Boston leadership was not lawless but could be seen as defenders of British liberty and law.

The five-day trial, with dozens of witnesses, resulted in acquittal for Preston and for all but two of the soldiers, who were convicted of manslaughter, branded on the thumbs, and released. Nothing materialized in the trial to indicate a conspiracy or concerted plan to provoke trouble, either by the British or by the Sons of Liberty. To this day, the question of responsibility for the Boston Massacre remains obscure.

REVIEW   Why did Britain send troops to occupy Boston in the fall of 1768?

The Tea Party and the Coercive Acts, 1770–1774

In the same week as the Boston Massacre, a new British prime minister, Frederick North, recommended repeal of the Townshend duties. A skillful politician, Lord North took office in 1770 and kept it for twelve years; at last King George had stability at the helm. Seeking peace with the colonies and prosperity for British merchants, North persuaded Parliament to remove all the duties except the tax on tea, kept as a symbol of Parliament's power.

The renewal of trade and the return of cooperation between England and the colonies gave men like Thomas Hutchinson hope that the worst of the crisis was behind them. For nearly two years, peace seemed possible, but tense incidents in 1772 followed by a renewed struggle over the tea tax in 1773 precipitated a full-scale crisis that by 1775 resulted in war.

The Calm before the Storm

Repeal of the Townshend duties brought an end to nonimportation, despite the tax on tea. Trade boomed in 1770 and 1771. Moreover, the leaders of the popular movement seemed to be losing their power. Samuel Adams, for example, ran for a minor local office in Boston and lost to a conservative merchant.

Then in 1772, several incidents again brought the conflict with England into sharp focus. One was the burning of the *Gaspée*, a Royal Navy ship pursuing suspected smugglers off the coast of Rhode Island. A British investigating commission failed to arrest anyone but announced that it would send suspects, if any were found, to England for trial on charges of high treason. This ruling seemed to fly in the face of the traditional English right to trial by a jury of one's peers.

When news of the *Gaspée* investigation spread, it was greeted with disbelief in other colonies. Patrick Henry, Thomas Jefferson, and Richard Henry Lee in the Virginia House of Burgesses proposed that a network of standing committees be established to link the colonies and pass along alarming news. By mid-1773, every colonial assembly except Pennsylvania's had a "committee of correspondence."

Another British action in 1772 further spread the communications network. Lord North proposed to pay the salaries of superior court justices out of the tea revenue, similar to Townshend's plan for paying royal governors.

The Bloody Massacre Perpetrated in King Street, Boston, on March 5, 1770
This mass-produced engraving by Paul Revere sold for six pence a copy. In this patriot version of events, British soldiers fire on an unarmed crowd under orders of their captain. The tranquil dog is an artistic device to signal the crowd's peaceful intent. Crispus Attucks, a black sailor, was among the five killed, but Revere shows only whites among the casualties.
Anne S. K. Brown Military Collection, Brown University Library.

FOR MORE HELP ANALYZING THIS IMAGE, see the visual activity for this chapter in the Online Study Guide at bedfordstmartins.com/roarkcompact.

Tossing the Tea
This colored engraving appeared in an English book published in 1789, recounting the history of
North America from its earliest settlement to "becoming united, free, and independent states."
Men on the ship break into the chests and dump the contents; a few are depicted in Indian dis-
guise, with feathers on their heads or topknots of hair. A large crowd on the shore looks on. The
red rowboat is clearly stacked with tea chests, suggesting that some of the raiders were stealing
rather than destroying the tea. However, the artist, perhaps careless, shows the rowboat heading
toward the ship instead of away. This event was not dubbed the "Tea Party" until the 1830s,
when a later generation celebrated the illegal destruction of the tea and made heroes out of the
few surviving participants, by then men in their eighties and nineties.
Library of Congress.

The Boston town meeting, fearful that judges
would now be in the pockets of their new pay-
masters, urged all Massachusetts towns to establish a committee of correspondence. The first
vital message, circulated in December 1772, attacked the judges' salary policy as the latest proof
of a British plot to undermine traditional "liberties": unjust taxation, military occupation, massacre, now capped by the subversion of justice.
By spring 1773, half the towns in Massachusetts
had set up committees of correspondence, providing local forums for debate. These committees
politicized ordinary townspeople and bypassed
the official flow of power and information
through the colony's royal government.

The final incident shattering the relative
calm of the early 1770s was the Tea Act of 1773.
Americans had resumed buying the taxed British
tea, but they were also smuggling large quantities of Dutch tea, cutting into the sales of Britain's
East India Company. So Lord North proposed

legislation giving favored status to the East India
Company, allowing it to sell tea directly to government agents rather than through public auction to independent merchants. The hope was to
lower the price of the East India tea, including the
duty, below that of the smuggled Dutch tea, mo-
tivating Americans to obey the law.

Tea in Boston Harbor

In the fall of 1773, news of the Tea Act reached the
colonies. Parliamentary legislation to make tea inexpensive struck many colonists as an insidious
plot to trick Americans into buying large quantities of the duties tea. The real goal, some argued,
was the increased revenue, which would be used
to pay the royal governors and judges. The Tea Act
was thus a painful reminder of Parliament's claim
to the power to tax and legislate for the colonies.

But how to resist the Tea Act? Nonimportation
was not viable, because the tea trade was too

lucrative to expect all merchants to give it up willingly. Consumer boycotts were ineffective, because it was impossible to distinguish between dutied tea (the object of the boycott) and smuggled tea (illegal but politically clean) once it was in the teapot. The appointment of tea agents, parallel to the stamp act distributors, suggested one solution. In every port city, revived Sons of Liberty pressured tea agents to resign, and tea cargoes either landed without paperwork or were sent on their way home.

But Boston under Hutchinson was different. Three ships bearing tea arrived in November 1773. They cleared customs and unloaded their other cargoes but not the tea. Sensing the town's extreme tension, the captains wished to return to England, but Hutchinson would not grant them clearance to leave without paying the tea duty. Also, there was a time limit on the stay allowed in the harbor. After twenty days, the duty had to be paid or local authorities would confiscate the tea. Hutchinson refused to bend any rules.

For the full twenty days, pressure built in Boston. Daily mass meetings energized citizens from Boston and surrounding towns, alerted by the committees of correspondence. On the final day, December 16, a large crowd gathered at Old South Church to hear Samuel Adams declare, "This meeting can do nothing more to save the country." This was a signal to adjourn to the harbor, where between 100 and 150 men, thinly disguised as Indians, boarded the ships and dumped thousands of pounds of tea into the water while a crowd of 2,000 watched.

The Coercive Acts

Lord North's response was swift and stern; he persuaded Parliament to issue the Coercive Acts, four laws meant to punish Massachusetts. In America those laws, along with a fifth one, the Quebec Act, were soon known as the Intolerable Acts.

The Boston Port Act closed Boston harbor to all shipping as of June 1, 1774, until the destroyed tea was paid for. England's objective was to halt the commercial life of the city. The second act, called the Massachusetts Government Act, altered the colony's charter, underscoring Parliament's claim to supremacy over Massachusetts. The royal governor's powers were greatly augmented, and the council became an appointive, not elective, body. No town meeting beyond the annual spring election of town selectmen could be held unless the governor expressly permitted it.

Not only Boston but every Massachusetts town felt the punitive sting.

The third Coercive Act, the Impartial Administration of Justice Act, stipulated that any royal official accused of a capital crime—for example, Captain Preston and his soldiers at the Boston Massacre—would be tried in a court in England. It did not matter that Preston got a fair trial in Boston. What this act ominously suggested was that down the road more Captain Prestons and soldiers might be firing into unruly crowds.

The fourth act amended the 1765 Quartering Act and permitted military commanders to lodge soldiers wherever necessary, even in private households. In a related move, Lord North appointed General Thomas Gage, commander of the Royal Army in New York, governor of Massachusetts. Thomas Hutchinson was out, relieved at long last of his duties. Military rule, including soldiers, returned once more to Boston.

Ill-timed, the fifth act—the Quebec Act—had nothing to do with the four Coercive Acts, but it fed American fears. It confirmed the continuation of French civil law, government form, and Catholicism for Quebec—all an affront to **Protestant** New Englanders denied their own representative government. The act also gave Quebec control of disputed lands (and control of the lucrative fur trade) throughout the Ohio Valley, lands also claimed by Virginia, Pennsylvania, and a number of Indian tribes.

The five Intolerable Acts spread alarm in all the colonies. If England could squelch Massachusetts—change its charter, suspend government, inaugurate military rule, and on top of that give Ohio to Catholic Quebec—then what liberties were secure? Fearful royal governors in a half-dozen colonies suspended the sitting assemblies, adding to the sense of urgency; some suspended assemblies defiantly continued to meet in new locations. Through the committees of correspondence, colonial leaders arranged to meet in Philadelphia in the fall of 1774 to respond to the crisis.

The First Continental Congress

Every colony except Georgia sent delegates to Philadelphia to the First Continental Congress in September 1774. The gathering included notables such as Samuel Adams and John Adams from Massachusetts and George Washington and Patrick Henry from Virginia. A few colonies purposely sent men who opposed provoking a crisis with England, such as Pennsylvania's

Joseph Galloway, to keep the congress from becoming too radical.

Delegates sought to identify their liberties as British subjects and the powers Parliament held over them, and they debated possible responses to the Coercive Acts. Some wanted a total ban on trade with England to force repeal, while others, especially southerners dependent on tobacco and rice exports, opposed halting trade. Samuel Adams and Patrick Henry were eager for a ringing denunciation of all parliamentary control. The conservative Joseph Galloway proposed a plan (quickly defeated) to create a secondary parliament in America to assist the British Parliament in ruling the colonies.

The congress met for seven weeks and produced a declaration of rights couched in traditional language: "We ask only for peace, liberty and security. We wish no diminution of royal prerogatives, we demand no new rights." But, from England's point of view, the rights assumed already to exist were radical. Chief among them was the claim that Americans were not represented in Parliament and so each colonial government had the sole right to govern and tax its own people. The one slight concession to England was a carefully worded agreement that the colonists would "cheerfully consent" to trade regulations for the larger good of the empire—so long as trade regulation was not a covert means of raising revenue.

To put pressure on England, the delegates agreed to a staggered and limited boycott of trade—imports prohibited this year, exports the following, and rice totally exempted (to keep South Carolinians happy). To enforce the boycott, they called for a Continental Association, with chapters in each town variously called committees of public safety or of inspection, to monitor all commerce and punish suspected violators of the boycott (sometimes with a bucket of tar and a bag of feathers). Its work done, the congress disbanded in October 1774, with agreement to reconvene the following May.

The committees of public safety, the committees of correspondence, the regrouped and defiant colonial assemblies, and the Continental Congress were all political bodies functioning without any constitutional authority. British officials did not recognize them as legitimate, but many Americans who supported the patriot cause instantly accepted them. A key reason for the stability of such unauthorized governing bodies was that they were composed of generally the same men who had held elective office before.

Tarring and Feathering Cartoon
In 1774, a Boston crowd tarred and feathered customs collector John Malcolm as punishment for extorting money from shippers. This ritualized humiliation involved stripping a man, painting him with hot tar, and dipping him in chicken feathers. Local committees of public safety often used threats of this treatment as a weapon to enforce boycotts; actual tarring and feathering was not a common occurrence. This cartoon, of British origin, is hostile to Americans, who are shown with cruelly gleeful faces, forcing tea down Malcolm's throat. The Liberty Tree has become a gallows; posted to it is the Stamp Act, upside down. The dumping of tea in the harbor is shown in the background.
Courtesy of the John Carter Brown Library at Brown University.

England's severe reaction to Boston's destruction of the tea finally succeeded in making many colonists from New Hampshire to Georgia realize that the problems of British rule went far beyond questions of taxation. The Coercive Acts infringed on liberty and denied self-government; they could not be ignored. With one colony already subordinated to military rule and a British army at the ready in Boston, the threat of a general war was at the doorstep.

REVIEW   Why did Parliament pass the Coercive Acts in 1774?

Domestic Insurrections, 1774–1775

Before the Second Continental Congress could meet, war broke out in Massachusetts. General Thomas Gage, military commander and the new royal governor, at first thought he faced a domestic insurrection that could be quieted with only a show of force. But the rebels saw things differently: They were defending their homes and liberties against an intrusive power bent on enslaving them. To the south, a different and inverted version of the same story began to unfold, as thousands of enslaved black men and women seized an unprecedented opportunity to mount a different kind of insurrection—against planter-patriots who looked over their shoulders uneasily whenever they called out for liberty from the British.

Lexington and Concord

Over the winter of 1774–75 Americans pressed on with boycotts. Optimists hoped to effect a repeal of the Coercive Acts; pessimists started stockpiling arms and ammunition. In Massachusetts, gunpowder and shot were secretly stored, and militia units known as minutemen prepared to respond on a minute's notice to any threat from the British troops in Boston.

Thomas Gage soon realized how desperate the British position was. The people, Gage wrote Lord North, were "numerous, worked up to a fury, and not a Boston rabble but the freeholders and farmers of the country." Gage requested twenty thousand reinforcements. He also

British Troops in Concord Center

In this contemporary engraving by Amos Doolittle, based on a painting done on the spot by Ralph Earl, two British officers seek the high ground of the cemetery in Concord, Massachusetts, to orient themselves to the unfamiliar town at around 9 A.M. on April 19, 1775. Their troops march in formation, fresh from the skirmish at Lexington. American militiamen had amassed at the Old North Bridge, off to the right about a mile from the town center. The officer with the telescope is undoubtedly scanning for them.

Miriam and Ira D. Wallah Division of Art, Prints and Photographs, The New York Public Library. Astor, Lenox and Tilden Foundations.

strongly advised repeal of the Coercive Acts, but leaders in England could not admit failure. Instead, they ordered Gage in mid-April 1775 to arrest the trouble-makers immediately, before the Americans got better organized.

Gage quickly planned a surprise attack on a suspected ammunition storage site at Concord, a village eighteen miles west of Boston (Map 6.3). Near midnight on April 18, 1775, British soldiers moved west across the Charles River. Boston silversmith Paul Revere and William Dawes, a tanner, raced ahead to alert the minutemen. When the soldiers got to Lexington, a village five miles east of Concord, they were met by some seventy armed men assembled on the village green. The British commander barked out, "Lay down your arms, you damned rebels, and disperse." The militiamen hesitated and began to comply, turning to leave the green, but then someone—unknown—fired. In the next two minutes, more firing left eight Americans dead and ten wounded.

The British units continued their march to Concord, any pretense of surprise gone. Three companies of minutemen nervously occupied the town center but offered no challenge to the British as they searched in vain for the ammunition. Finally, at Old North Bridge in Concord, troops and minutemen exchanged shots, killing two Americans and three British soldiers.

By now both sides were very apprehensive. The British had failed to find the expected arms storage, and the Americans had failed to stop their raid. As the British returned to Boston along a narrow road, militia units in hiding attacked from the sides of the road in the bloodiest fighting of the day. In the end, 273 British soldiers were wounded or dead; the toll for the Americans stood at about 95. It was April 19, 1775, and the war had begun.

Rebelling against Slavery

News of the battles of Lexington and Concord spread rapidly. Within eight days, Virginians had heard of the fighting, and, as Thomas Jefferson reflected, "A phrenzy of revenge seems to have seized all ranks of people." The royal governor of Virginia, Lord Dunmore, removed a large quantity of gunpowder from the Williams-

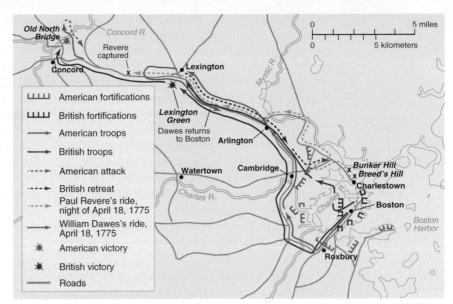

MAP 6.3   Lexington and Concord, April 1775

Under pressure from England, some 900 British forces at Boston staged a raid on a suspected rebel arms supply in Concord, Massachusetts, starting the first battle of the Revolutionary War. The routes of two early warning scouts are marked. Paul Revere went by boat from Boston to Charlestown and then continued by horse through Medford to Lexington, while William Dawes casually passed British sentries guarding the only land route out of Boston, a land bridge called the Neck, and then rode his horse full speed to Lexington. Re-vere and Dawes reached Samuel Adams and John Hancock, guests in a Lexington home, and urged them to flee to avoid capture. The two then went on to Concord, to warn residents of the impending attack.

READING THE MAP: William Dawes was, like Paul Revere, a messenger who raced ahead of British troops to warn the minutemen of British plans for raiding their supply of weapons. How did Dawes's route differ from Revere's? What kinds of terrain and potential dangers did each man face during his ride, according to the map?

CONNECTIONS: Why might it matter who shot first on the Lexington Green? What is at stake for each side in claiming the other shot first?

FOR MORE HELP ANALYZING THIS MAP, see the map activity for this chapter in the Online Study Guide at bedfordstmartins.com/roarkcompact.

burg powder house and put it on a ship in the dead of night, out of reach of any frenzied Virginians. Next, he threatened to arm slaves, if necessary, to ward off attacks by colonists.

This was an effective threat; Dunmore understood full well how to produce panic among the planters. He did not act on his warning until November 1775, when he issued an official proclamation promising freedom to defecting able-bodied slaves who would fight for the British. Although Dunmore wanted to scare the planters, he had no intention of liberating all slaves or of starting a real slave rebellion. Female, young, and elderly slaves were not welcome behind British lines, and many were sent back to face irate masters. Astute blacks noticed that Dunmore neglected to free his own slaves. A Virginia barber named Caesar declared that "he did not know any one foolish enough to believe him [Dunmore], for if he intended to do so, he ought first to set his own free."

By December 1775, around 1,500 slaves in Virginia had fled to Lord Dunmore, who armed them and called them his "Ethiopian Regiment." Camp diseases quickly set in: dysentery, typhoid fever, and worst of all, smallpox. When Dunmore sailed for England in mid-1776, he took just 300 black survivors with him. But the association of freedom with the British authorities had been established, and throughout the war, thousands more southern slaves made bold to run away as soon as they heard the British army was approaching.

In the northern colonies as well, slaves clearly recognized the evolving political struggle with England as an ideal moment to bid for freedom. A twenty-one-year-old Boston domestic slave employed biting sarcasm in a 1774 newspaper essay to call attention to the hypocrisy of local slave owners: "How well the Cry for Liberty, and the reverse Disposition for exercise of oppressive Power over others agree,—I humbly think it does not require the Penetration of a Philosopher to Determine." This extraordinary young woman, Phillis Wheatley, had already gained international recognition through a book of poems, endorsed by Governor Thomas Hutchinson and Boston merchant John Hancock and published in London in 1773. Possibly neither man fully appreciated the irony of his endorsement, however, for Wheatley's poems spoke of "Fair Freedom" as the "Goddess long desir'd" by Africans enslaved in America. At the urging of his wife, Wheatley's master freed the young poet in 1775.

Wheatley's poetic ideas about freedom found concrete expression among other discontented groups. Some slaves in Boston petitioned Thomas Gage, promising to fight for the British if he would liberate them. Gage turned them down. In Ulster County, New York, along the Hudson River, two blacks were overheard discussing gunpowder, and thus a plot unraveled that involved at least twenty slaves in four villages discovered to have ammunition stashed away.

In Maryland, soon after the news of the Lexington battle arrived, blacks exhibited impatience with their status as slaves, causing one Maryland planter to report that "the insolence of the Negroes in this county is come to such a height, that we are under a necessity of disarming them.…We took about eighty guns, some bayonets, swords, etc." In North Carolina, a planned uprising was uncovered and scores of slaves were arrested; ironically, it was the revolutionary committee of public safety that ordered the whippings to punish this quest for liberty.

By 1783, when the Revolutionary War ended, as many as 20,000 blacks had voted against slavery with their feet by seeking refuge with the British army. Most failed to achieve the liberation they were seeking. The British generally used them for menial labor; and disease, especially smallpox, devastated encampments of runaways. But some eight to ten thousand persisted through the war and later, under the protection of the British army, left America to start new lives of freedom in Canada's Nova Scotia or Africa's Sierra Leone.

> **REVIEW** How did enslaved people in the colonies react to the stirrings of revolution?

Conclusion: How Far Does Liberty Go?

The Seven Years' War set the stage for the imperial crisis of the 1760s and 1770s by creating distrust between England and its colonies and by running up a huge deficit in the British treasury. The years from 1763 to 1775 brought repeated attempts by the British government to subordinate the colonies into taxpaying partners in the larger scheme of empire.

American resistance grew slowly but steadily over those years. In 1765, loyalist Thomas Hutchinson shared with patriot Samuel Adams the belief that it was exceedingly unwise for England to assert a right to taxation, because Parliament did not adequately represent Americans. But by temperament and office, Hutchinson had to uphold British policy; Adams, in contrast, protested the policy and made political activists out of thousands in the process.

By 1775, events propelled many Americans to the conclusion that a concerted effort was afoot to deprive them of all their liberties, the most important of which were the right to self-taxation, the right to live free of an occupying army, and the right to self-rule. Hundreds of minutemen converged on Concord, prepared to die for these American liberties. April 19 marked the start of their rebellion.

Another rebellion under way in 1775 was doomed to be short-circuited. Black Americans who had experienced actual slavery listened to shouts of "Liberty!" from white crowds and appropriated the language of revolution swirling around them that spoke to their deepest needs and hopes. Defiance of authority was indeed contagious.

The emerging leaders of the patriot cause were mindful of a delicate balance they felt they had to strike. To energize the American public about the crisis with England, they had to politicize masses of men—and eventually women too—and infuse them with a keen sense of their rights and liberties. But in so doing, they became fearful of the unintended consequences of teaching a vocabulary of rights and liberties. They worried that the rhetoric of enslavement might go too far.

The question of how far the crisis could be stretched before something snapped was largely unexamined in 1765. Patriot leaders in that year wanted a correction, a restoration of an ancient liberty of self-taxation that Parliament seemed to be ignoring. But events from 1765 to 1775 convinced many that a return to the old ways was impossible. Challenging Parliament's right to tax had led, step by step, to challenging Parliament's right to legislate over the colonies in any matter. If Parliament's sovereignty was set aside, then who actually had authority over the American colonies? By 1775, with the outbreak of fighting and the specter of slave rebellions, American leaders turned to the king for the answer to that question.

Suggestions for Further Reading

Fred Anderson, *Crucible of War: The Seven Years' War and the Fate of Empire in British North America, 1754–1766* (2000). A gripping and richly detailed account of the world war that precipitated the American Revolution.

Bernard Bailyn, *The Ordeal of Thomas Hutchinson* (1974). A sympathetic portrait of an unyielding man caught in a revolution he could not countenance.

Robert A. Gross, *The Minutemen and Their World* (25th anniversary ed., 2001). The American Revolution in microcosm, built on a social history of the sleepy village of Concord, Massachusetts.

Woody Holton, *Forced Founders: Indians, Debtors, Slaves, and the Making of the American Revolution in Virginia* (1999). An account of how debt crisis, land speculation, and fears of Indian raids and slave rebellions shaped the political actions of the Virginia gentry on the eve of the Revolution.

Robert Middlekauff, *The Glorious Cause: The American Revolution, 1763–1789* (rev. ed., 2005). A classic panoramic history of the American Revolution.

Alfred F. Young, *The Shoemaker and the Tea Party: Memory and the American Revolution* (1999). An exploration of the life of the last surviving participant in the Boston Tea Party.

▶ **For more books about topics in this chapter,** see the Online Study Guide at bedfordstmartins.com/roarkcompact.

▶ **For additional firsthand accounts of this period,** see Chapter 6 in Michael Johnson, ed., *Reading the American Past,* Third Edition.

▶ **For Web sites and documents related to topics and places in this chapter,** see "HistoryLinks," "DocLinks," and "PlaceLinks" at bedfordstmartins.com/roarkcompact.

REVIEWING THE CHAPTER

Follow these steps to review and strengthen your understanding of the chapter.

STEP 1: *Study the **Key Terms** and **Timeline** to identify the significance of each item listed.*

STEP 2: *Answer the **Review Questions,** drawing on key terms and dates to support your answers.*

STEP 3: *Drawing on the Key Terms, Timeline, and Review Questions, answer the broader **Making Connections** questions.*

KEY TERMS

Who

Thomas Hutchinson (p. 131)
Robert Dinwiddie (p. 133)
George Washington (p. 133)
Tanaghrisson (p. 133)
Benjamin Franklin (p. 135)
Edward Braddock (p. 135)
William Pitt (p. 135)
George III (p. 138)
Pontiac (p. 138)
George Grenville (p. 139)
Patrick Henry (p. 142)
Samuel Adams (p. 143)
Andrew Oliver (p. 143)
Charles Townshend (p. 145)
Thomas Preston (p. 147)
Frederick North (p. 148)
Thomas Gage (p. 152)

minutemen (p. 152)
Paul Revere (p. 153)
Lord Dunmore (p. 153)
Phillis Wheatley (p. 154)

What

Seven Years' War (p. 132)
Ohio Company (p. 133)
Fort Duquesne (p. 133)
"Fort Necessity" (p. 134)
Covenant Chain (p. 135)
Albany Plan of Union (p. 135)
Treaty of Paris (p. 135)
Proclamation of 1763 (p. 138)
Molasses Act of 1733 (p. 139)
Sugar Act (Revenue Act of 1764) (p. 139)
Stamp Act (p. 142)
virtual representation (p. 142)

Virginia Resolves (p. 142)
Sons of Liberty (p. 143)
Stamp Act Congress (p. 144)
Declaratory Act (p. 144)
Revenue Act of 1767 (p. 145)
nonconsumption agreements (p. 145)
nonimportation agreements (p. 146)
Daughters of Liberty (p. 146)
Boston Massacre (p. 147)
Gaspée (p. 148)
committees of correspondence (p. 149)
Tea Act of 1773 (p. 149)
Coercive Acts (p. 150)
First Continental Congress (p. 150)
Continental Association (p. 151)
committees of public safety (p. 151)

TIMELINE

◀ **1747** • Ohio Company of Virginia formed.

1754 • Seven Years' War begins in North America.
   • Albany Congress proposes Plan of Union (never implemented).

1755 • Braddock's defeat in western Pennsylvania.

   1757 • William Pitt fully commits England to war effort.

      1759 • Quebec falls to British.

         1760 • Montreal falls to British.
            • George III becomes British king.

            1763 • Treaty of Paris ends Seven Years' War.
               • Pontiac's uprising.
               • Paxton Boys massacre friendly Indians in Pennsylvania.
               • Proclamation of 1763.

               1764 • Parliament enacts Revenue (Sugar) Act.

                  1765 • Parliament enacts Stamp Act.
                     • Virginia Resolves challenge Stamp Act.
                     • Dozens of crowd actions by Sons of Liberty.
                     • Stamp Act Congress meets.

REVIEW QUESTIONS

1. How did the Seven Years' War erode relations between colonists and Britain? (pp. 132–38)

2. Why did the Sugar and Stamp acts draw fierce opposition from colonists? (pp. 139–44)

3. Why did Britain send troops to occupy Boston in the fall of 1768? (pp. 145–47)

4. Why did Parliament pass the Coercive Acts in 1774? (pp. 148–51)

5. How did enslaved people in the colonies react to the stirrings of revolution? (pp. 152–54)

MAKING CONNECTIONS

1. In the mid-eighteenth century, how did Native Americans influence relations between European nations? Between Britain and the colonists?

2. Why did disputes over taxation figure so prominently in the deteriorating relations between Britain and the colonies? In your answer, refer to specific disputed British attempts to raise revenue and the colonial response.

3. How did the colonists organize to oppose British power so effectively? In your answer, discuss the role of communications in facilitating the colonial resistance, being sure to cite specific examples.

> ▶ FOR PRACTICE QUIZZES, A CUSTOMIZED STUDY PLAN, AND OTHER STUDY TOOLS, see the Online Study Guide at bedfordstmartins.com/roarkcompact.

1766 • Parliament repeals Stamp Act and passes Declaratory Act.

1767 • Parliament enacts Townshend duties.

1768 • British station troops in Boston.

1769 • Merchants sign nonimportation agreements.

1770 • Boston Massacre.
• Parliament repeals Townshend duties.

1772 • British navy ship *Gaspée* burned.
• Committees of correspondence formed.

1773 • Parliament passes Tea Act.
• Dumping of tea in Boston Harbor.

1774 • Parliament passes Coercive Acts (Intolerable Acts).
• First Continental Congress meets; Continental Association formed.

1775 • Battles of Lexington and Concord.
• Lord Dunmore promises freedom to defecting slaves.

CONTINENTAL ARMY UNIFORM WORN AT THE SIEGE OF FORT STANWIX, 1777

In 1775, the Continental Congress faced the daunting prospect of fielding an army to fight the largest military force in the world. Money was scarce, soldiers were hastily trained and short of equipment, and uniforms were hard to come by. (Many were purchased from France.) At the start of the war, ordinary enlisted men often wore brown work clothes, and while this outfit gave them a unified look, it did not allow for easy categorization of soldiers by their units. When General Washington finally issued dress specifications, he chose the color already preferred by many officers—dark blue—and then specified the variety of colors to be used for the facings and linings of the coat to establish the rank and the unit of each soldier. Officers especially needed distinctive clothing to distinguish them from ordinary soldiers and from other officers, so that the military hierarchy could be maintained at all times. The coat pictured here belonged to a brigadier general, Peter Gansevoort, who was twenty-eight in 1777 and in command of Fort Stanwix in the Mohawk Valley of New York. The coat has a buff-colored lining (seen inside the coattails) and bright red facings on the collar, the lapel, and the cuffs, marking him as a New York soldier. The color of the shoulder ribbons reveals Gansevoort's rank; the ribbons could be easily replaced with a new color, enabling a man to ascend in rank without having to get a new coat. Young Gansevoort became a celebrated hero when he successfully defended Fort Stanwix against an attack by British and Indians; his grandson, the author Herman Melville, named his second son Stanwix to honor the event.

National Museum of American History, Smithsonian Institution, Washington, D.C.

The War for America
1775–1783

ABIGAIL ADAMS WAS IMPATIENT for American independence. While her husband, John, was away in Philadelphia as a member of the Second Continental Congress, Abigail tended house and farm in Braintree, Massachusetts, just south of British-occupied Boston. She had four young children to look after, and in addition to her feminine duties, such as cooking, sewing, and making soap, she also had to shoulder masculine duties in her husband's absence—hiring farm help, managing rental property, selling the crop. John wrote to her often, approving of the fine "Farmeress" who was conducting his business so well. She replied, conveying news of the family along with shrewd commentary on revolutionary politics. In December 1775, she chastised the congress for being too timid and urged that independence be declared. A few months later, she astutely observed to John that southern slave owners might shrink from a war in the name of **liberty**: "I have sometimes been ready to think that the passion for Liberty cannot be Equally strong in the Breasts of those who have been accustomed to deprive their fellow Creatures of theirs."

"I long to hear that you have declared an independency," she wrote in March 1776. "And by the way in the new Code of Laws which I suppose it will be necessary for you to make I desire you would Remember the Ladies, and be more generous and favourable to them than your ancestors." If Abigail was politically precocious in favoring independence and questioning slave owners' devotion to liberty, she was positively visionary in this extraordinary plea to her husband to "Remember the Ladies." "Do not put such unlimited power into the hands of the Husbands," she advised. "Remember all Men would be tyrants if they could." Abigail had put her finger on another form of tyranny that was rarely remarked on in her society: that of men over women. "If particular care and attention is not paid to the Ladies," she jokingly threatened, "we are determined to foment a Rebellion, and will not hold ourselves bound by any Laws in which we have no voice, or Representation."

John Adams dismissed his wife's provocative idea as a "saucy" suggestion: "As to your extraordinary Code of Laws, I cannot but Laugh." The Revolution had perhaps unleashed discontent among other dependent groups, he allowed; children, apprentices, students, Indians, and blacks had grown "disobedient" and "insolent." "But your Letter was the first Intimation that another Tribe more numerous and powerful than all the rest were grown discontented." Men were too smart to repeal their "Masculine Systems," John assured her, for otherwise they would find themselves living under a "despotism of the petticoat."

This clever exchange between husband and wife in 1776 says much about the cautious, limited radicalism of the American Revolution. Both John and Abigail Adams understood (Abigail probably far more than John) that ungluing the hierarchical bond between the king and his subjects potentially unglued

Abigail Adams

Abigail Smith Adams was twenty-two when she sat for this pastel portrait in 1766. A wife for two years and a mother for one, Adams exhibits a steady, intelligent gaze. Pearls and a lace collar anchor her femininity, while her facial expression projects a confidence and maturity not often credited to young women of the 1760s.

Courtesy of the Massachusetts Historical Society ©.

tion, had their hands full in 1775 and 1776. The war had already begun, and the congress had to raise an army, finance it, and explore diplomatic alliances with foreign countries. In part a classic war with professional armies and textbook battles, the Revolutionary War was also a civil war in America, at times even a brutal **guerrilla war**, of committed rebels versus loyalists.

In one glorious moment, the congress issued a ringing statement about how social hierarchy would be rearranged in America after submission to the king was undone. That was on July 4, 1776, when the Declaration of Independence asserted that "all men are created equal." But this striking phrase went completely unremarked in the two days of congressional debate spent tinkering with the language of the Declaration. The solvent to dissolve social inequalities in America was created at that moment, but none of the men at the congress, or even Abigail Adams up in Braintree, fully realized it at the time.

The Second Continental Congress

On May 10, 1775, nearly one month after the fighting at Lexington and Concord, the Second Continental Congress assembled in Philadelphia. The congress immediately set to work on two crucial and seemingly contradictory tasks: to raise and supply an army and to explore reconciliation with England. To do the former, they needed soldiers and a commander to come to the aid of the Massachusetts militiamen, they needed money, and they needed to work out a declaration of war. To do the latter, however, they needed diplomacy to approach the king. But the king was not receptive, and by 1776, as the war progressed and hopes of reconciliation faded, delegates at the congress began to ponder the treasonous act of declaring independence—said by some to be plain common sense.

Assuming Political and Military Authority

Like members of the First Continental Congress (see chapter 6), the delegates to the second were well-established figures in their home colonies, but they still had to learn to know and trust each other; they did not always agree. The Adams cousins John and Samuel defined the radical end of the spectrum, favoring independence. John

other kinds of social inequalities. John was surely joking in listing the groups made unruly in the spirit of a challenge to authority, for children, apprentices, and students were hardly rebellious in the 1770s. But it would soon prove to be an uncomfortable joke, because Indians and blacks did strike for their own liberty during the Revolution, and the great majority of them saw their liberty best served by joining the British side in the war.

Though Abigail Adams was impatient for independence, many other Americans feared separation from Britain. What kind of civilized country had no king? Who, if not Britain, would protect Americans from the French and Spanish? How could the colonies possibly win a war against the most powerful military machine on the globe? Reconciliation, not independence, was favored by many.

Members of the Continental Congress, whether they were pro-independence like John Adams or more cautiously hoping for reconcilia-

Dickinson of Pennsylvania, no longer the eager revolutionary who had dashed off *Letters from a Farmer* back in 1767, was now a moderate, seeking reconciliation with England. Benjamin Franklin, fresh off a ship from an eleven-year residence in England, was feared by some to be a British spy. Mutual suspicions flourished easily when the undertaking was so dangerous, opinions were so varied, and a misstep could spell disaster.

Most of the delegates were not yet prepared to break with England. Several legislatures instructed their delegates to oppose independence. Some felt that government without a king was unworkable, while others feared it might be suicidal to lose England's protection against the traditional enemies, France and Spain. Colonies that traded actively with England feared undermining their economies. Probably the vast majority of ordinary Americans were unable to envision independence. From the Stamp Act of 1765 to the Coercive Acts of 1774 (see chapter 6), the constitutional struggle with England had turned on the issue of parliamentary power. During that decade, almost no one had questioned the legitimacy of the monarchy.

The few men at the Continental Congress who did think that independence was desirable were, not surprisingly, from Massachusetts. Their colony had been stripped of civil government under the Coercive Acts, and their capital was occupied by the British army. Even so, those men knew that it was premature to push for a break with England. John Adams wrote to Abigail in June 1775: "America is a great, unwieldy body. Its progress must be slow. It is like a large fleet sailing under convoy. The fleetest sailors must wait for the dullest and slowest."

As slow as the American colonies were in sailing toward political independence, they needed to take swift action to coordinate a military defense, for the Massachusetts countryside was under threat of further attack. Even the hesitant moderates in the congress agreed that a military buildup was necessary. Around the country, militia units from New York to Georgia collected arms and drilled on village greens in anticipation. (See "The Promise of Technology," page 162.) On June 14, the congress voted to create the Continental army. Choosing the commander in chief offered an opportunity to demonstrate that this was no local war of a single rebellious colony. The congress bypassed Artemas Ward from Massachusetts, a veteran of the Seven Years' War, then already commanding the soldiers massed around Boston, and instead chose a southerner, George Washington.

Washington's appointment sent the clear message to England that there was widespread commitment to war beyond New England.

Next the congress drew up a document titled "A Declaration on the Causes and Necessity of Taking Up Arms," which rehearsed familiar arguments about the tyranny of Parliament and the need to defend English liberties. This declaration was first drafted by a young Virginia **planter**, Thomas Jefferson, a newcomer to the congress and a radical on the question of independence. The moderate John Dickinson, fearing that the declaration would offend England and rule out reconciliation, was allowed to rewrite it; however, he still left much of Jefferson's highly charged language about choosing "to die freemen rather than to live slaves." Even a man as reluctant for independence as Dickinson acknowledged the necessity of military defense against an invading army.

To pay for the military buildup, the congress authorized a currency issue of $2 million. The Continental dollars were merely paper; they did not represent gold or silver, for the congress owned no precious metals. The delegates somewhat naively expected that the currency would be accepted as valuable on trust as it spread in the population through the hands of soldiers, farmers, munitions suppliers, and beyond.

In just two months, the Second Continental Congress had created an army, declared war, and issued its own currency. It had taken on the major functions of a legitimate government, both military and financial, without any legal basis for its authority, for it had not—and would not for a full year—declare independence from the authority of the king.

Pursuing Both War and Peace

Three days after the congress approved a Continental army, one of the bloodiest battles of the Revolution occurred. The British commander in Boston, Thomas Gage, had recently received troop reinforcements, three talented generals (William Howe, John Burgoyne, and Henry Clinton), and new instructions to root out the rebels around Boston. But before Gage could take the offensive, the Americans fortified the hilly terrain of Charlestown, a peninsula just north of Boston, on the night of June 16, 1775.

The British generals could have nipped off the peninsula where it met the mainland, to box in the Americans. But General Howe insisted on a bold frontal assault, sending his 2,500 soldiers across the water and up the hill in an intimidating but

Arming the Soldiers: Muskets and Rifles

How combat-ready was the American side in the Revolutionary War? Were there adequate numbers of firearms along with men trained in their use? These lively and important questions have recently generated sharp debate among historians. A book published in 2000 argued that gun ownership was surprisingly rare in the 1770s, occurring in only one out of seven households. This finding did not square with historians' largely untested assumption that a militia-based defense system implied that nearly all households contained a gun. The ensuing controversy quickly became a firestorm, involving activists on both sides of the modern gun-control debate as well as historians. In consequence, the examination of evidence and methods to evaluate gun ownership has been considerably sharpened.

What were eighteenth-century guns like? Guns called fowling pieces fired shot (small pellets) and were useful for hunting ducks and wild turkeys and small game such as raccoons and squirrels. For larger game and for warfare, muskets, a sixteenth-century invention, were the preferred weapon. By the mid-eighteenth century, the musket had an improved flintlock ignition system: The trigger released a spring-held cock that caused a hammer to strike a flint, creating sparks; the sparks set off a small charge in a priming pan, producing a larger explosion in the gun barrel. To load a musket, the shooter first put the hammer on half cock to prevent an accidental firing. He next put a small quantity of gunpowder (carried in a powder horn) in the priming pan and closed it, poured more gunpowder down the smooth gun barrel, dropped in the projectile—usually a one-ounce lead ball—and with a ramrod wadded paper down the gun barrel to hold the loose ball in place. He then raised the gun to firing position, put the hammer on full cock, and fired. The whole procedure took highly experienced shooters from 45 to 90 seconds.

The range of muskets extended only about 50 to 100 yards. They were notoriously inaccurate because of the poor fit between ball and barrel and the considerable kick produced by firing, which interfered with aiming. Far more accurate were the longer-barreled rifles, used in frontier regions where big-game hunting was more common. Spiral grooves inside the rifle barrel imparted spin to the lead ball as it traversed the barrel, stabilizing and lengthening its flight and enabling expert marksmen to hit small targets at 150 or 200 yards. Yet militiamen preferred muskets. Rifles took twice as long to load and fire, and their longer barrels made them unwieldy for soldiers on the march. Inaccurate muskets were quite deadly enough when fired by a group of soldiers in unison at targets 50 yards away.

How many American men actually owned fowling pieces, muskets, or rifles? A partial answer can be gleaned from probate inventories, many thousands of which exist in state archives. Inventories listed a decedent's possessions to facilitate settling the estate and to make sure creditors were paid off. Yet these sources are fraught with thorny problems. For one thing, many inventories are not complete: If few of them itemized clothing, can we conclude the decedents went nude? If no firearm is listed, can we conclude the decedent *never* owned a gun? Clearly not. Probate inventories were made for only a subset of dead property owners, primarily for the use of creditors and heirs, so they are biased by age (older), sex (male), and wealth (more).

Despite complexities, scholars have worked with probate inventories to establish a baseline figure for gun ownership. It takes sophistication with statistical sampling technique as well as ability to read old handwriting to use the evidence, since the thousands of inventories cannot all be tallied. Recent careful studies based on this source yield estimates on overall gun ownership that range from 40 to 50 percent of all probated estates in the 1770s.

A second way to assess gun ownership is to look at the arms procurement experiences of state legislatures and the Continental Congress as they geared up for war. In the early months of 1775, New England patriot leaders had a keen interest to know how many armed soldiers could be mobilized in the event of war. One scholar has located militia returns from thirty towns in Massachusetts, New Hampshire, and Rhode Island. Scattered returns from other states exist in archives. At their most complete, these records form a census of soldiers and equipment taken on a militia training day. A particularly detailed list from Salem, Massachusetts, notes against each man's name his ownership of a firelock, a bayonet, a sword, a pouch, a cartouche box, a cartridge, a flint, lead balls, gunpowder, a knapsack, and priming wires. Salem's list appears to support the conclusion that 100 percent of adult men owned guns, yet the scholar seeking to calculate gun ownership must ask: Who is not on this list? Who failed to report to the muster exercise? This careful study concludes that in 1775, probably three-quarters of all men ages sixteen to sixty in New England owned guns.

These high rates of ownership, however, are not matched by a final kind of evidence: reports from militia officers to state legislatures complaining of being underarmed. A New Hampshire captain complained of his unit's plight in June 1775: "We are in want of both arms and ammunition. There is but very little, nor none worth mentioning— perhaps one pound of powder to twenty men, and not one-half our men have arms." A militia officer in Pennsylvania noted that men who owned high-quality muskets and rifles were often reluctant to report for active duty with them unless assured they would be reimbursed in the event of loss of the valuable possession. A Prussian general who volunteered his expertise to the Continental army arrived at Valley Forge in 1778 and was shocked to find "muskets, carbines, fowling pieces, and rifles" all in the same company of troops. Lack of uniformity in guns posed considerable problems for supplying appropriate ammunition. While this evidence seems to point to an underarmed soldiery, the opposite evidence— militia captains who failed to register complaints—did not leave a corresponding paper trail for historians. Historians must take care not to be misled by stray documents or quotations that may be atypical.

The Continental Congress knew more guns were needed, certainly. Before 1774, American artisans imported British-made gunlocks, the central firing mechanism, and added the wooden stock and iron barrel to produce muskets. But in October 1774, the British Parliament, anticipating trouble, prohibited all gunlock and firearm exports to the colonies. Congress then turned to French and Dutch suppliers to purchase gunlocks, gunpowder, and finished muskets.

Muskets and even fowling pieces worked well enough for the Revolutionary War, where similarly armed combatants engaged in massed, synchronized firing at close range. In individual use, however, muskets were clumsy, inaccurate, and not highly lethal. High rates of musket ownership did not translate to high rates of successful homicide or accidental deaths by shooting. Sixty years after the Revolution, all that changed with the advent of machine-tooled firearms such as the Colt revolver and the Remington rifle. Those new repeat-fire weapons were cheaper, more accurate, and far more deadly. Comparing ownership rates of muskets and of revolvers—or assault weapons—across time may not be the most meaningful path to understanding this country's historic relationship with guns.

Powder Horn

James Pike, a twenty-three-year-old New England militiaman, made and then personalized this powder horn, a hollow cow's horn capped on both ends with leather. The stopper was designed to be pulled off by the teeth so the hands of the user would be free to hold the musket barrel and pour the powder. Pike's carvings suggest his motivation for fighting. Above his name he depicts a scene dated April 19, 1775, in which British soldiers, labeled "the Aggressors," fire through the Liberty Tree at "Provincials, Defending." Pike was not at Lexington or Concord; his first combat experience came two months later at the battle of Bunker Hill, where he saw his brother killed and was himself wounded in the shoulder.

Chicago Historical Society.

Committee of Safety Musket

This gun was one of the small number of American-made muskets produced in 1775 in a German region of Pennsylvania where blacksmith shops were numerous. The smithy forged and fashioned the gun barrel and attached it to an imported gunlock, the mechanism over the trigger. A wooden stock completed the design.

York County Historical Society.

potentially costly attack. The American troops, 1,400 strong, listened to the British drummers pacing the uphill march and held their fire until the British were about twenty yards away. At that distance, the musket volley was sure and deadly, and the British turned back. Twice more General Howe sent his men up the hill and received the same blast of firepower; each time they had to step around the bodies of men felled in the previous attempts.

On the third assault, the British took the hill, mainly because the American ammunition supply gave out, and the defenders quickly retreated. The battle of Bunker Hill was thus a British victory, but an expensive one. The dead numbered 226 on the British side, with more than 800 wounded; the Americans suffered 140 dead, 271 wounded, and 30 captured. As General Clinton later remarked, "It was a dear bought victory; another such would have ruined us."

Instead of pursuing the fleeing Americans, Howe pulled his army back to Boston, unwilling to risk more raids into the countryside. If the British had had any grasp of the basic instability of the American units gathered around Boston, they might have pushed westward and perhaps decisively defeated the Americans. Instead they lingered in Boston, abandoning it without a fight nine months later. Howe used the time in Boston to inoculate his army against smallpox, because a new epidemic of the deadly disease was spreading in port cities along the Atlantic. Inoculation worked by producing a light but real (and therefore risky) case of smallpox, followed by lifelong immunity. Howe's instinct here was right: From 1775 to 1782, the years coinciding with the American Revolution, some 130,000 people on the American continent, most of them Indians, died of smallpox.

A week after Bunker Hill, when General Washington arrived to take charge of the new Continental army, he found enthusiastic but undisciplined troops. Sanitation was an unknown concept, drunkenness on duty was common, and soldiers came and went at will. The amazed general attributed the disarray to the New England custom of letting militia units elect their own officers, a custom he felt undermined deference. Washington quickly imposed more hierarchy and authority.

While military plans moved forward, the Second Continental Congress pursued its second,

Battle of Bunker Hill, 1775

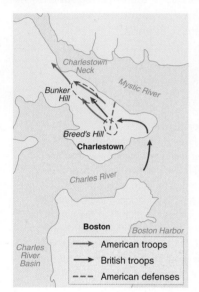

contradictory objective, reconciliation with England. Delegates from the middle colonies (Pennsylvania, Delaware, and New York), whose merchants depended on trade with England, urged that channels for negotiation remain open. In July 1775, congressional moderates led by John Dickinson engineered an appeal to the king called the Olive Branch Petition. The petition affirmed loyalty to the monarchy and blamed all the troubles on the king's ministers and on Parliament. It proposed that the American colonial assemblies be recognized as individual parliaments, under the umbrella of the monarchy. By late fall 1775, however, reconciliation was out of the question. King George III rejected the Olive Branch Petition and heatedly condemned the Americans, calling them rebels and traitors. Thereafter it was hard to blame only ministers and not the king himself for the conflict.

Thomas Paine and the Case for Independence

Pressure for independence started to mount in January 1776, when a pamphlet titled *Common Sense* appeared in Philadelphia. Thomas Paine, its author, was an English **artisan** and coffeehouse intellectual who had come to America in the fall of 1774. He landed a job with the *Pennsylvania Magazine* and soon met delegates from the Second Continental Congress. With their encouragement, he wrote *Common Sense* to lay out a lively and compelling case for complete independence.

In simple yet forceful language, Paine elaborated on the absurdities of the British monarchy. Why should one man, by accident of birth, claim extensive power over others? he asked. A king might be foolish or wicked. "One of the strongest natural proofs of the folly of hereditary right in kings," Paine wrote, "is that nature disapproves it; otherwise she would not so frequently turn it into ridicule by giving mankind *an ass for a lion*." Calling the king of England an ass broke through the automatic deference most Americans still had for the monarchy. To replace monarchy, he advocated **republican** government, based on the consent of the people. Rulers, according to Paine, were only representatives of the people, and the best form of government relied on frequent elections to achieve the most direct **democracy** possible.

Paine's pamphlet sold more than 150,000 copies in a matter of weeks. Newspapers reprinted it; men read it aloud in taverns and coffeehouses; John Adams sent a copy to Abigail Adams, who passed it around to neighbors. New

An Exact View of the Late Battle at Charlestown, June 17th 1775

This dramatic panorama is the earliest visual representation of the battle of Bunker Hill. On sale to the public six weeks after the battle, the engraving shows Charlestown in flames (center back) and British and American soldiers in fixed formation firing muskets at each other. The Americans, to the left, are dug in along the crest of the hill; British casualties have begun to mount up. The artist, Bernard Romans, was a noted cartographer, military engineer, linguist, and mathematician. Born in the Netherlands, he came to America as a British-paid surveyor, but he took the American side in the Revolution. His maps of war zones were bought by Americans eager to track the geography of war. His large depiction of Bunker Hill, produced in multiple copies, some of them hand-colored like this one, likely decorated many a patriot's wall. It was advertised for sale in newspapers in Philadelphia and Virginia, and a half-size copy was engraved and inserted in an issue of *The Pennsylvania Magazine,* a monthly periodical edited by Thomas Paine. One ad for the picture promised that "Every well-wisher to this country cannot but delight in seeing a plan of the ground on which our brave American Army conquered the British Ministerial Forces." Technically the British won the battle by taking the hill, but that was not the story told by this picture.

Colonial Williamsburg Foundation.

George Washington's Camp Chest

This portable camp chest (or mess kit) belonged to George Washington during the Revolutionary War. The wooden box, covered in leather and lined with wool fabric, held an elaborate setup neatly collapsed into a small space: four tin pots with detached handles, five tin plates, three tin platters, two tin boxes, two knives, three forks, eight glass bottles with cork stoppers, salt and pepper shakers, and a woolen sack with six compartments. The chest also contained a tinder box, which held kindling and a flint for starting a fire, and a gridiron (or grate) with collapsed legs for cooking over the fire. Washington—or, more likely, a subordinate preparing his food—would have used this chest when the army was on the move. It was an officer's chest, presented to the general by a Philadelphia merchant in 1776; enlisted men would have had something much more basic, if anything. Washington saved the chest for two decades after the war. After his death it was auctioned off and donated to the federal government by the new owner. It is now owned by the Smithsonian Institution in Washington, D.C.

National Museum of American History, Smithsonian Institution, Behring Center.

Englanders desired independence, but other colonies, under no immediate threat of violence, remained cautious. But by May, all but four colonies favored independence. Two of the holdouts were Pennsylvania and South Carolina, both with large loyalist populations.

In early June, the Virginia delegation introduced a resolution calling for independence. The moderates still commanded enough support to postpone a vote on the measure until July, so they could go home and consult about this extreme step. In the meantime, the congress appointed a committee, with Thomas Jefferson and others, to draft a longer document setting out the case for independence.

On July 2, after intense politicking, all but one state voted for independence; New York abstained. The congress then turned to the document drafted by Jefferson and his committee. Jefferson began with a preamble that articulated philosophical principles about natural rights, equality, the right of revolution, and the consent of the governed as the only true basis for government. He then listed more than two dozen grievances against King George. The congress merely glanced at the political philosophy, finding nothing exceptional in it; the ideas about natural rights and the consent of the governed were seen as "self-evident truths," just as the document claimed. In itself, this absence of comment showed a remarkable transformation in political thinking since the end of the Seven Years' War. The single phrase declaring the natural equality of "all men" was also passed over without comment; no one elaborated on its radical implications.

For two days, the congress wrangled over the list of grievances, especially the issue of slavery. Jefferson had included an impassioned statement blaming the king for slavery, which delegates from Georgia and South Carolina struck out. They had no intention of denouncing their labor system as an evil practice. But the congress let stand another of Jefferson's fervent grievances, blaming the king for mobilizing "the merciless Indian Savages" into bloody **frontier** warfare, a reference to Pontiac's uprising (see chapter 6).

On July 4, the amendments to Jefferson's text were complete and the congress formally adopted the document. (See appendix I, page A-1.) A month later, the delegates gathered to sign the official parchment copy, handwritten by an exacting scribe. Four men, including John Dickinson, declined to sign; several others "signed with regret…and with many doubts," according to John Adams. The document was then printed, widely distributed, and read aloud in celebrations everywhere. A crowd in New York listened to a public reading of it and then toppled a lead statue of George III on horseback to melt it down for bullets. On July 15, the New York delegation switched from abstention to endorsement, making the vote on independence unanimous.

> **REVIEW**   Why were many Americans reluctant to pursue independence from Britain?

The First Year of War, 1775–1776

Both sides approached the war for America with uneasiness. The Americans, with inexperienced militias, opposed the mightiest military power in the world. Also, their country was not unified; many remained loyal to Britain. The British faced serious obstacles as well. Their disdain for the fighting abilities of the Americans required reassessment in light of the Bunker Hill battle. The logistics of supplying an army with food across three thousand miles of water were daunting. And since the British goal was to regain allegiance, not to destroy and conquer, the army was often constrained in its actions. These patterns— undertrained American troops, British troops strangely unwilling to press their advantage— played out repeatedly in the first year of war when the Americans invaded Canada, the British invaded New York, and the two sides chased each other up and down the length of New Jersey.

The American Military Forces

Americans claimed that the initial months of war were purely defensive, triggered by the British army's invasion. But quickly the war also became a rebellion, an overthrowing of long-established authority. As both defenders and rebels, Americans were generally highly motivated to fight, and the potential manpower that could be mobilized was in theory very great.

Local defense in the colonies had long rested with a militia requiring participation from able-bodied men over age sixteen. When the main threat to public safety was the occasional Indian attack, the local militia made sense. But such attacks were now mostly limited to the frontier. Southern militias trained with potential slave rebellions in mind, but these too were rare. The annual muster day in most communities had evolved into a holiday of drinking, marching, and shooting practice with small fowling guns or muskets.

Militias were best suited to limited engagements and not for extended wars requiring military campaigns far from home. In forming the Continental army, the congress set enlistment at one year, but army leaders soon learned that was inadequate time to train soldiers and carry out campaigns. A three-year enlistment earned a new soldier a $20 bonus, while men who committed for the duration of the war were promised a postwar **land grant** of one hundred acres. For this inducement to be effective, of course, recruits had to believe that the Americans would win.

Women also served in the Continental army, cooking, washing, and nursing the wounded. The British army established a ratio of one woman to every ten men; in the Continental army, the ratio was set at one woman to fifteen men. Close to 20,000 women served during the war, probably most of them wives of men in service. Children tagged along as well, and babies were born in the camps and on the road.

Black Americans were at first excluded from the Continental army, by George Washington's orders. But as manpower needs increased, the northern states welcomed free blacks into service; slaves in some states could serve, with their masters' permission. About 5,000 black men served in the Revolutionary War on the rebel side, nearly all from the northern states. Black Continental soldiers sometimes were segregated into separate units; two battalions from Rhode Island were entirely black. Just under three hundred blacks joined regiments from Connecticut. While some of these were **draftees**, others were clearly inspired by the ideals of freedom being voiced in a war against tyranny. For example, twenty-three blacks gave "Liberty," "Freedom," or "Freeman" as their surname at the time of enlistment.

Military service helped to politicize Americans during the early stages of the war. In early 1776, independence was a risky idea, potentially treasonous. But as the war heated up and recruiters demanded commitment, some Americans discovered that apathy had its dangers as well. Anyone who refused to serve ran the risk of being called a traitor to the cause. Military service became a prime way of defining and demonstrating political allegiance.

The American army was at times raw and inexperienced and much of the time woefully undermanned. It never had the precision and discipline of European professional armies. But it was never as bad as the British continually

Black Revolutionary War Sailor
From the beginning of the war, the fledgling American navy recruited blacks from the pool of experienced free black sailors in northern maritime cities. Most were hired as ordinary seamen, but a few served as ship pilots. The names of these men are preserved in crew lists; rarely, however, were their likenesses preserved. This 1780 portrait by an unknown artist shows an unnamed man in dress uniform, sword and scabbard at hand, with a ship in view to establish his naval connection.
Collection of A. A. McBurney.

assumed. The British were to learn that it was a serious mistake to underrate the enemy.

The British Strategy

The American strategy was straightforward—to repulse and defeat an invading army. The British strategy was not nearly so clear. England wanted to put down a rebellion and restore monarchical power in the colonies, but the question was how to accomplish this. A decisive defeat of the Continental army was essential but not sufficient to end the rebellion, for the British would still have to contend with an armed and motivated insurgent population.

Furthermore, there was no single political nerve center whose capture would spell certain victory. The Continental Congress moved from place to place, staying just out of reach of the

British. During the course of the war, the British captured and occupied every major port city, but that brought no serious loss to the Americans, 95 percent of whom lived in the countryside.

England's delicate task was to restore the old governments, not to destroy an enemy country. Hence, the British generals were reluctant to ravage the countryside, confiscate food, or burn villages and towns. There were thirteen distinct political entities to capture, pacify, and then restore to the crown, and they stretched in a long line from New Hampshire to Georgia. Clearly a large land army was required for the job. Without the willingness to seize food from the locals, the British needed hundreds of supply ships bringing food for storage. The British strategy also assumed that many Americans remained loyal to the king and would come to their aid. Without substantial numbers of loyal subjects, the plan to restore old royal governments made no sense.

The overall British plan was a divide-and-conquer approach, focusing first on New York, the state judged to harbor the greatest number of loyal subjects. New York offered a geographic advantage as well: Control of the Hudson River would allow the British to isolate those troublesome New Englanders. British armies could descend from Canada and move up from New York City along the Hudson River into western Massachusetts. Squeezed between a naval blockade on the eastern coast and army raids in the west, Massachusetts could be driven to surrender. New Jersey and Pennsylvania would fall in line, the British thought, due to loyalist strength. Virginia was a problem, like Massachusetts, but the British were confident that the Carolinas would help them isolate and subdue Virginia.

Quebec, New York, and New Jersey

In late 1775, an American expedition was swiftly launched to capture the British cities Montreal and Quebec before British reinforcements could arrive. This offensive was a clear sign that the war was not purely a reaction to the invasion of Massachusetts. A force of New York Continentals commanded by General Richard Montgomery took Montreal easily in September 1775 and then advanced on Quebec. Meanwhile, a second contingent of Continentals led by Colonel Benedict Arnold moved north through Maine to Quebec, a punishing trek through freezing rain with woefully inadequate supplies; many men died. Arnold's determination to get to Quebec was heroic, but in human costs the campaign was a

tragedy. Arnold and Montgomery jointly attacked Quebec in December but failed to take the city (Map 7.1). Worse yet, they encountered smallpox, which killed more men than had been felled by the British.

The main action of the first year of war came not in Canada, however, but in New York, so crucial to England. In August 1776, some 45,000 British troops (including 8,000 German mercenaries, called Hessians) landed south of New York City, under the command of General Howe. General Washington had anticipated that New York would be Howe's target and had moved his army, numbering about 20,000, south from Massachusetts. The battle of Long Island, in late August 1776, pitted the well-trained British "redcoats" (common slang referring to the red British uniforms) against a very green Continental army. Howe attacked, inflicting many casualties (1,500 dead and wounded) and spreading panic among the American soldiers, who fled to the eastern edge of Long Island. Howe failed to press forward, however, perhaps remembering the costly victory of Bunker Hill, and Washington evacuated his troops to Manhattan Island in the dead of a foggy night.

Washington knew it would be hard to hold Manhattan, so he further withdrew north to two forts on either side of the Hudson River. For two months, the armies engaged in limited skirmishing, but in November, Howe finally captured Fort Washington and Fort Lee, taking thousands of prisoners. Washington retreated quickly across New Jersey into Pennsylvania. Yet again Howe unaccountably failed to press his advantage. Had

MAP 7.1   The War in the North, 1775–1778 ▶
After the early battles in Massachusetts in 1775, rebel forces invaded Canada but failed to capture Quebec. A large British army landed in New York in August 1776, turning New Jersey into a continual site of battle in 1777 and 1778. Burgoyne arrived to secure Canada and made his attempt to pinch off New England along the Hudson River line, but he was stopped at Saratoga in 1777 in the key battle of the early war years.

READING THE MAP: Which general's troops traveled the farthest in each of these years: 1775, 1776, and 1777? How did the availability of water routes affect British and American strategy?
CONNECTIONS: Why did the French wait until early 1778 to join American forces against the British? What did they hope to gain from participating in the war?

FOR MORE HELP ANALYZING THIS MAP, see the map activity for this chapter in the Online Study Guide at bedfordstmartins.com/roarkcompact.

he attacked Washington's army at Philadelphia, he probably would have taken the city. Instead he parked his German troops in winter quarters along the Delaware River. Perhaps he knew that many of the Continental soldiers' enlistment periods ended on December 31, so he felt confident that the Americans would not attack him. But he was wrong. On December 25 near midnight, as a storm of sleet and hail rained down, Washington stealthily moved his large army across the icy Delaware River and in the early morning made a quick capture of the unsuspecting German soldiers encamped at Trenton. This impressive victory lifted the sagging morale of the patriot side. For the next two weeks, Washington remained on the offensive, capturing supplies in a clever attack on British units at Princeton on January 3. Soon he was safe in Morristown, in northern New Jersey, settled in for the winter, finally with time enough to administer mass smallpox inoculations and see his men through the abbreviated course of the disease. Future recruits would also face inoculation.

All in all, in the first year of declared war, the rebellious Americans had a few isolated moments to feel proud of but also much to worry about. The very inexperienced Continental army had barely hung on in the New York campaign. Washington had shown exceptional daring as well as admirable restraint, but what really saved the Americans may have been the repeated reluctance of the British to follow through militarily when they had the advantage.

> **REVIEW** Why did the British exercise restraint in their efforts to recapture the colonies?

The Home Front

Battlefields alone did not determine the outcome of the war. Struggles on the home front were equally important. In 1776, each community contained small numbers of highly committed people on both sides and far larger numbers who were uncertain about whether independence was worth a war. Both persuasion and force were used to gain the allegiance of the many neutrals. Revolutionaries who took control of local government often used it to punish loyalists and intimidate neutrals, while loyalists worked to reestablish British authority. The struggle to secure political allegiance was complicated greatly by a shaky wartime economy. The creative financing of the fledgling government brought hardships as well as opportunities, forcing Americans to confront new manifestations of virtue and corruption.

Patriotism at the Local Level

Committees of correspondence, of public safety, and of inspection dominated the political landscape in patriot communities. These committees took on more than customary local governance; they enforced boycotts, picked army draftees, and policed suspected traitors. They sometimes invaded homes to search for contraband goods such as British tea or textiles.

Loyalists were dismayed by what seemed to them to be arbitrary power taken on by patriots. A man in Westchester, New York, described his response to intrusions by committees: "Choose your committee or suffer it to be chosen by a half dozen fools in your neighborhood—open your doors to them—let them examine your tea-cannisters and molasses-jugs, and your wives' and daughters' petty coats—bow and cringe and tremble and quake—fall down and worship our sovereign lord the mob.…Should any pragmatical committee-gentleman come to my house and give himself airs, I shall show him the door." Oppressive or not, the local committees were rarely challenged. Their persuasive powers convinced many middle-of-the-road citizens that neutrality was not a comfortable option.

Another group new to political life—white women—increasingly demonstrated a capacity for patriotism as wartime hardships dramatically altered their work routines. Like Abigail Adams on her farm, many wives with husbands away on military or political service took on masculine duties. Their competence to tend farms and make business decisions encouraged some to assert competence in politics as well. Eliza Wilkinson managed a South Carolina plantation and talked revolutionary politics with women friends. "None were greater politicians than the several knots of ladies who met together," she remarked, alert to the unusual turn female conversations had taken. "We commenced perfect statesmen."

Women from prominent Philadelphia families took more direct action, forming the Ladies Association in 1780 to collect money for Continental soldiers. A published broadside, "The Sentiments of an American Woman," defended their female patriotism. "The time is arrived to display the same sentiments which animated us at the beginning of the Revolution, when we renounced the use of teas [and] when our republican and laborious hands spun the flax."

The Loyalists

Between 20 and 30 percent of the American population remained loyal to the crown in 1776, and another 20 to 40 percent were probably neutral. With proper cultivation, this large base might have sustained the British empire in America (Map 7.2). In general, loyalists had strong cultural and economic ties to England; they thought that social stability depended on a government anchored by monarchy and aristocracy. Perhaps most of all, they feared democratic tyranny. Like Abigail Adams, they understood that dissolving the automatic respect that subjects had for their king could lead to a society in which hierarchy came unglued. Adams welcomed this chance to identify tyranny in unequal power relations, as between men and women; loyalists feared it. Patriots seemed to them to be unscrupulous, violent, self-interested men who simply wanted power for themselves.

The most visible loyalists (called Tories by their enemies) were royal officials, not only governors like Thomas Hutchinson but also local judges and customs officers. Wealthy merchants gravitated toward loyalism to maintain the trade protections of navigation acts and the British navy. Conservative urban lawyers admired the stability of British law and order. Some colonists chose loyalism simply to oppose traditional adversaries. For example, backcountry farmers in the Carolinas tended to be loyalists out of resentment over the political and economic power of the lowlands gentry. And of course southern slaves had their own resentments against the white slave-owning class and looked to Britain for hope of freedom.

Many Indian tribes hoped to remain neutral at the war's start, seeing the conflict as a civil war between English and American brothers. But eventually most were drawn in, many taking the British side. The powerful Iroquois confederacy divided: Mohawk, Cayuga, Seneca, and Onondaga peoples lined up with the British; the Oneida and Tuscarora aided Americans. One young Mohawk leader, Thayendanegea (known also by his English name, Joseph Brant), traveled to England in 1775 to complain to King George about American settlers cheating his people of land. "It is very hard when we have let the King's subjects have so much of our lands for so little value," he wrote, "they should want to cheat us in this manner of the small spots we have left for our women and children to live on. We are tired out in making complaints & getting no redress." Brant pledged Indian support for the king in exchange for protection from encroaching settlers. In the Ohio Country, parts of the Shawnee and Delaware tribes started out pro-American but shifted to the British side by 1779 in the face of repeated betrayals by American settlers and soldiers.

Pockets of loyalism thus existed everywhere—in the middle colonies, in the backcountry of

Joseph Brant
The Mohawk leader Thayendanegea, called Joseph Brant by Americans, had been educated in English ways at Eleazar Wheelock's New England school (which became Dartmouth College in 1769). In 1775, the thirty-four-year-old Brant traveled to England with another warrior to negotiate Mohawk support for the British. While there, he had his portrait painted by the English artist George Romney. Notice that Brant wears a metal gorget around his neck over his English shirt, along with Indian armbands, sash, and headdress. A gorget was a symbolic piece of armor, a shrunken version of a throatpiece from the feudal days of metal-clad knights. Many military men, both white and Indian, wore gorgets when they dressed formally for portraits—or for war.
National Gallery of Canada.

the southern colonies, and out beyond the Appalachian Mountains in Indian country. Even New England towns at the heart of turmoil, like Concord, Massachusetts, had a small and increasingly silenced core of loyalists who refused to countenance armed revolution.

Loyalists were most vocal between 1774 and 1776, when the possibility of a full-scale rebellion against England was still uncertain. Loyalists challenged the emerging patriot side in pamphlets and newspapers. In New York City, some loyalists circulated a broadside titled "A Declaration of Dependence," in rebuttal to the congress's July 4 declaration, denouncing this

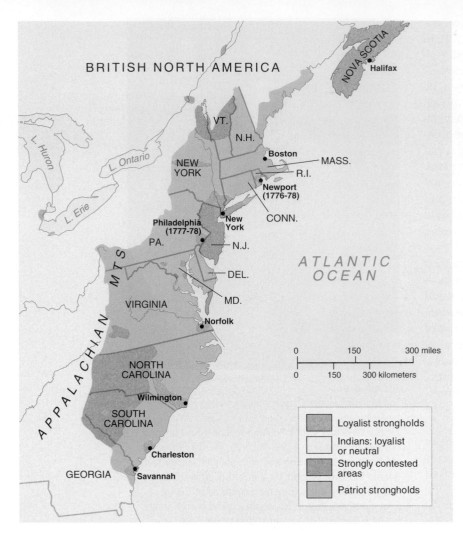

MAP 7.2 Loyalist Strength and Rebel Support
The exact number of loyalists can never be known. No one could have made an accurate count at the time; in addition, political allegiance often shifted with the winds. This map shows the regions of loyalist strength on which the British relied—most significantly the lower Hudson River Valley and the Carolina piedmont.

ized loyalists, raiding their houses or tarring and feathering them.

Were wives of loyalists also traitors? When loyalist families fled the country, property controlled by the husband was typically confiscated. But if the wife stayed, courts usually allowed her to keep one-third of the property, the amount due her if widowed, and confiscated the rest. A wife who fled with her husband might have little choice in the matter. After the Revolution, descendants of refugee loyalists filed several lawsuits to regain property that had entered the family through the mother's inheritance. In one well-publicized Massachusetts case in 1805, the outcome confirmed the traditional view of women as political blank slates. The American son of loyalist refugee Anna Martin recovered her property on the grounds that she had no independent will to be a loyalist.

Tarring and feathering, property confiscation, deportation, terrorism—to the loyalists, such denials of liberty of conscience and of freedom to own private property proved that democratic tyranny was more to be feared than the monarchical variety. A Boston loyalist, Mather Byles, aptly expressed this point: "They call me a brainless Tory, but tell me... which is better—to be ruled by one tyrant three thousand miles away, or by three thousand tyrants not a mile away?" Byles was soon sentenced to deportation.

Throughout the war, probably 7,000 to 8,000 loyalists fled to England, and 28,000 found closer haven in Canada. But many chose to remain in the new United States and tried to swing with the changing political winds. In some instances, that proved difficult. In New Jersey, for example, 3,000 Jerseyites felt protected (or scared) enough by the occupying British army in 1776 to swear an oath of allegiance to the king. But then General Howe drew back to New York City, leaving them to the mercy of local patriot committees. British strategy depended on using loyalists to hold occupied territory, but the New Jersey experience showed how poorly that strategy was carried out.

"most unnatural, unprovoked Rebellion that ever disgraced the annals of Time."

Who Is a Traitor?

In June 1775, the First Continental Congress declared loyalists to be traitors. Over the next year, state laws defined as treason acts such as joining or provisioning the British army, saying or printing anything that undermined patriot morale, or discouraging men from enlisting in the Continental army. Punishments ranged from house arrest and suspension of voting privileges to confiscation of property and deportation. And sometimes self-appointed committees of Tory-hunters bypassed the judicial niceties and terror-

Financial Instability and Corruption

Wars cost money—for arms and ammunition, for food and uniforms, for soldiers' pay. The Continental Congress printed money, but its value quickly deteriorated because the congress held no reserves of gold or silver to back the currency. In practice, it was worth only what buyers and sellers agreed it was worth; the dollar eventually bottomed out at one-fortieth of its face value. States too were printing paper money to pay for wartime expenses, further complicating the economy.

As the currency depreciated, the congress turned to other means to procure supplies and labor. One method was to borrow **hard money** (gold or silver coins) from wealthy men in exchange for certificates of debt (public securities) promising repayment with interest. The certificates of debt were similar to present-day **government bonds**. To pay soldiers, the congress issued land grant certificates, written promises of acreage usually located in frontier areas such as central Maine or eastern Ohio. Both the public securities and the land grant certificates quickly became forms of negotiable currency. A soldier with no cash, for example, could sell his land grant certificate to get food for his family. These certificates soon depreciated too.

Depreciating currency inevitably led to rising prices, as sellers compensated for the falling value of the money. The wartime economy of the late 1770s, with its unreliable currency and price inflation, was extremely demoralizing to Americans everywhere. In 1778, in an effort to impose stability, local committees of public safety began to fix prices on essential goods like flour. Inevitably, some turned this unstable situation to their advantage. Money that fell fast in value needed to be spent quickly; being in debt was suddenly advantageous because the debt could be repaid in devalued currency. A brisk black market sprang up in prohibited luxury imports, such as tea, sugar, textiles, and wines, even though these items came from Britain. A New Hampshire delegate to the congress denounced the violation of the homespun association agreements of just a few years before: "We are a crooked and perverse generation, longing for the fineries and follies of those Egyptian task masters from whom we have so lately freed ourselves."

REVIEW How did the patriots promote support for their cause in the colonies?

The Campaigns of 1777–1779: The North and West

In early 1777, the Continental army faced bleak choices. General Washington had skillfully avoided outright defeat, but the minor victories in New Jersey lent only faint optimism to the American side. Meanwhile, British troops moved south from Quebec, aiming to isolate New England from the rest of the colonies by taking control of the Hudson River. Their presence drew the Continental army up into central New York, polarizing Indian tribes of the Iroquois nation and turning the Mohawk Valley into a bloody war zone. By 1779, tribes in western New York and in Indian country in the Ohio Valley were fully involved in the Revolutionary War; most sided with the British and against the Americans. The Americans had some success in this period, such as the victory at Saratoga, but the involvement of Indians and the continuing strength of the British forced the American government to look toward France for help.

Burgoyne's Army and the Battle of Saratoga

In 1777, British general John Burgoyne assumed command of an army of 7,800 soldiers in Canada and began the northern squeeze on the Hudson River valley. His goal was to capture Albany, near the intersection of the Hudson and Mohawk rivers (see Map 7.1). Accompanied by a thousand "camp followers" (cooks, laundresses, musicians) and some 400 Indian warriors, Burgoyne's army did not travel light. In addition to food and supplies for 9,200 people, the army carried food for the 400 horses hauling heavy artillery. Burgoyne also carted thirty trunks of personal belongings, including fine wines and elegant clothing.

In July, Burgoyne captured Fort Ticonderoga with ease. Some 3,000 American troops stationed there spotted the approaching British and abandoned the fort without a fight. The British continued to move south, but the large army moved slowly on primitive roads through heavily forested land.

The logical second step in isolating New England should have been to advance troops up the Hudson from New York City to meet Burgoyne. American surveillance indicated that General Howe in Manhattan was readying his men for a major move in August 1777. George Washington, watching from New Jersey, was astonished to see Howe's men sail south; Howe had decided to try to capture Philadelphia.

The third prong of the British strategy involved troops moving east from the Great Lakes and down the Mohawk River, aided by Mohawks and Senecas of the Iroquois confederacy. The British counted on help from Palatine Germans living in the Mohawk Valley, assumed to be loyalist. But a hundred miles west of Albany, they encountered American Continental soldiers at Fort Stanwix, reinforced by Palatine German militiamen and Oneida Indians. Led by the Mohawk Joseph Brant, the Senecas and Mohawks ambushed the Germans and the Oneidas in a narrow ravine called Oriskany and inflicted heavy losses, killing 500 out of 800 of them. On Brant's side, some 90 warriors were killed. But Fort Stanwix repelled the British and Seneca and forced them to retreat (see Map 7.1). The Oriskany and Fort Stanwix battles were very deadly; they were also complexly multiethnic, pitting Indians against Indians, German Americans against German mercenaries, New York patriots against neighboring New York loyalists, and English Americans against the British.

The British retreat at Fort Stanwix deprived General Burgoyne of the additional troops he expected. Camped at a small village called Saratoga, he was isolated with food supplies dwindling and men deserting. His adversary at Albany, General Horatio Gates, began moving 7,000 Continental soldiers toward him. Burgoyne decided to attack first because every day his army weakened. In this first attack, the British prevailed, but at the great cost of 600 dead or wounded redcoats. Three weeks later, an American attack on Burgoyne's forces at Saratoga cost the British another 600 men and most of their cannons. Burgoyne finally surrendered to the American forces at Saratoga on October 17, 1777.

General Howe, meanwhile, had succeeded in occupying Philadelphia in September 1777. Figuring that the Saratoga loss was balanced by the capture of Philadelphia, the British government proposed a negotiated settlement—not including independence—to end the war. The American side refused.

Battle of Saratoga, 1777

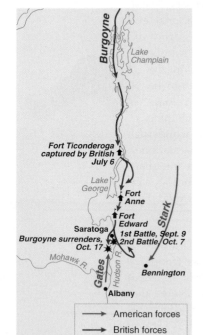

Patriot optimism was not well founded. Spirits ran high, but supplies of arms and food ran precariously low. Washington moved his troops into winter quarters at Valley Forge, just west of Philadelphia. Quartered in drafty huts, the men lacked blankets, boots, stockings, and food. Some 2,000 men at Valley Forge died of disease; another 2,000 deserted over the bitter six-month encampment.

Washington blamed the citizenry for lack of support, and indeed, evidence of corruption and profiteering was abundant. Army suppliers too often provided defective food, clothing, and gunpowder. A shipment of blankets turned out to be a quarter of their customary size. Preserved meat in barrels arrived rotten because brine had been drained to ease transport costs. Selfishness and greed seemed to infect the American side. As one Continental officer said, "The people at home are destroying the Army by their conduct much faster than Howe and all his army can possibly do by fighting us."

The War in the West: Indian Country

Burgoyne's defeat in the fall of 1777 and Washington's long stay at Valley Forge up to June 1778 might suggest that the war paused for a time; and it did, on the Atlantic coast. But in the interior western areas—the Mohawk Valley, the Ohio Valley, and Kentucky—the war was heating up. For native tribes, the struggle was not about taxation, representation, or monarchical rule; it was about independence, freedom, and land.

The ambush and slaughter at Oriskany in August 1777 marked the beginning of three years of terror for the inhabitants of the Mohawk Valley. Loyalists and Indians together engaged in many raids on farms throughout 1778, capturing or killing the residents. In retaliation, American militiamen destroyed Joseph Brant's home village, Onaquaga. A month later, Brant's warriors attacked the town of Cherry Valley, killing 32 townspeople and 16 soldiers and taking 71 people captive.

The following summer, General Washington authorized a campaign to wreak "total destruction and devastation" on all the Iroquoian villages of central New York. Some 4,500 troops commanded by General John Sullivan carried out a deliberate campaign of terror in the fall of 1779. Forty Indian towns met with total obliteration; the soldiers looted and torched the dwellings, then burned cornfields and orchards. In a few towns, women and children were slaughtered; but in most, the inhabitants managed to escape, fleeing to the British at Fort Niagara. Thousands of Indian refugees, sick and starving, camped around the fort in one of the most miserable winters on record.

Much farther to the west, beyond Fort Pitt, another complex story unfolded, of alliances and betrayals between American militiamen and Indians. Some 150,000 native peoples lived between the Appalachian Mountains and the Mississippi River, and by 1779, neutrality was no longer an option. Most sided with the British, who maintained a major garrison at Fort Detroit, but a portion of the Shawnee and Delaware tribes at first sought peace with the Americans. In mid-1778, the Delaware chief White Eyes negotiated a treaty at Fort Pitt, pledging Indian support in the war in exchange for supplies and trade goods. But escalating violence undermined the agreement. That fall, when American soldiers killed two friendly Shawnee chiefs, Cornstalk and Red Hawk, the Continental Congress hastened to apologize, as did the governors of Pennsylvania and Virginia, but the soldiers who stood trial for the murders were acquitted. Two months later, White Eyes, still nominally an ally and informant for the Americans, died under mysterious circumstances, almost certainly murdered by militiamen, who repeatedly had trouble honoring distinctions between allied and enemy Indians.

In Tennessee, the frontier war zone in the South, militias attacked Cherokee settlements, destroying thirty-six villages and burning fields and livestock. Indian raiders from north of the Ohio River in alliance with the British repeatedly attacked white settlements like Boonesborough in Kentucky (Map 7.3). In retaliation, a young Virginian, George Rogers Clark, led Kentucky militiamen into what is now Illinois, his men attacking and taking the British fort at Kaskaskia. Clark's men wore hunting shirts and breech cloths, native clothing, but their native dress was not a sign of solidarity with Indians. When they attacked British-held Fort Vincennes in 1779, Clark's troops tomahawked Indian captives and threw their still-live bodies in the river in a gory spectacle witnessed by the redcoats. "To excel them in barbarity is the only way to make war upon Indians," Clark announced. And, he might have added, a good way to terrorize the British soldiers as well.

By 1780, very few Indians remained neutral. Violent raids by Americans drove Indians into the arms of the British at Detroit and Niagara, or

A Soldier's Canteen

This wooden canteen belonged to Noah Allen, whose name and regiment number are carved into the side. Allen was from the Sixth Continental Regiment from Massachusetts. Almost no piece of equipment surpassed in importance the soldier's canteen.
Fort Ticonderoga Museum.

into the arms of the Spanish, who still held much of the land west of the Mississippi River. Said one officer on the Sullivan campaign, "Their nests are destroyed but the birds are still on the wing." For those who stayed near their native lands, chaos and confusion prevailed. Rare as it was, Indian support for the American side occasionally emerged out of a strategic sense that the Americans were unstoppable in their westward pressure and that it was better to work out an alliance than to lose in a war. But American treatment of even friendly Indians showed that for the Indians there was no winning strategy.

The French Alliance

On their own, the Americans could not have defeated Britain, and the western pressure from hostile Indians magnified their task. Essential help arrived as a result of the victory at Saratoga, which convinced the French to enter the war; a formal alliance was signed in February 1778. France recognized the United States as an independent nation and promised full military and commercial support throughout the war. Most crucial was the French navy, which could challenge England's transatlantic shipment of supplies and troops.

Although France had been waiting for a promising American victory to justify a formal declaration of war, since 1776 the French had been providing aid to the Americans in the form of cannons, muskets, gunpowder, and highly trained military advisers. Still, monarchical France was understandably cautious about endorsing a democratic revolution attacking the principles of kingship. For France, the main attraction of an alliance was the opportunity it provided to defeat archrival Britain. A victory would also open pathways to trade and perhaps result in France acquiring the coveted British West Indies. Even American defeat would not be

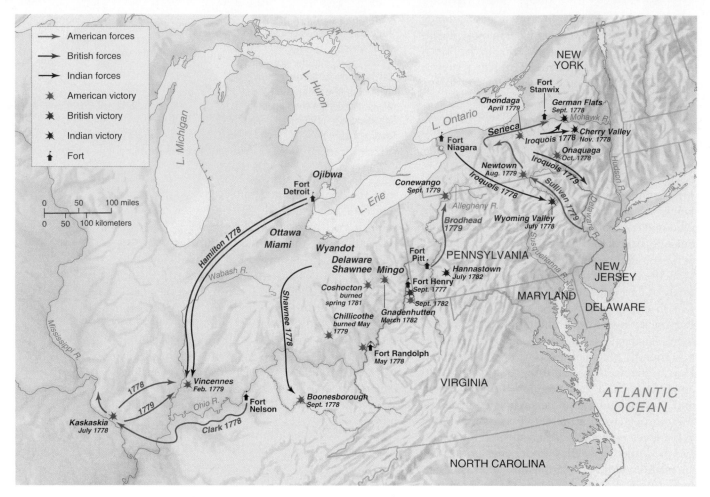

MAP 7.3   The War in the West, 1778–1782
The American Revolution involved many Indian tribes, most of them supporting the British side. Iroquois with British aid attacked American towns in New York's Mohawk Valley throughout 1778. In 1779 the Continental army marched on 40 Iroquois villages in central New York and destroyed them. The Shawnee and Delaware to the west of Fort Pitt tangled with American militia units in 1779, while tribes supported by the British at Fort Detroit conducted raids on Kentucky settlers who hit back with raids of their own. George Rogers Clark led Kentucky militiamen against Indians in the Illinois region. Sporadic fighting continued in the West through 1782, ending with Indian attacks on Hannastown, Pennsylvania, and Fort Henry on the Ohio River. By the late 1780s, occasional fighting resumed, sparked by American settlers pressing west onto Indian lands.

a full disaster for France if the war lasted many years and drained England of men and money.

French support materialized slowly. The navy arrived off the Virginia coast in July 1778 but then sailed south to the West Indies to defend the French sugar-producing islands. French help would prove indispensable to the American victory, but the alliance's first months brought no dramatic victories, and some Americans grumbled that the partnership would prove worthless.

REVIEW   Why did the Americans need assistance from the French to ensure victory?

The Southern Strategy and the End of the War

When France joined the war, some British officials wondered whether the fight was worth continuing. A troop commander, arguing for an immediate negotiated settlement, shrewdly observed that "we are far from an anticipated peace, because the bitterness of the rebels is too widespread, and in regions where we are masters the rebellious spirit is still in them. The land is too large, and there are too many people. The more land we win, the weaker our army gets in the field." The commander of the British navy argued for abandoning the war, and even Lord North, the prime minister, agreed. But the king was determined to crush the rebellion, and he encouraged a new strategy for victory focusing on the southern colonies, thought to be more persuadably loyalist. It was a brilliant but desperate plan, and ultimately unsuccessful. Southern colonists were not all that loyal and in fact were willing to engage in guerrilla warfare against the British. The southern strategy thus led to a British defeat at Yorktown and the end of the war.

Georgia and South Carolina

The new strategy called for British forces to abandon New England and focus on the South, with its valuable crops— tobacco, rice, and indigo—and its large slave population, potentially a powerful destabilizing factor that might keep rebellious white southerners in line. Georgia and the Carolinas appeared to hold large numbers of loyalists, providing a base for the British to recapture the southern colonies one by one, moving north to the more problematic middle colonies and saving prickly New England for last.

Georgia, the first target, fell at the end of December 1778 (Map 7.4). A small army of British soldiers occupied Savannah and Augusta, and a new royal governor and loyalist assembly were quickly installed. Taking Georgia was easy because the bulk of the Continental army was in New York and New Jersey, keeping an eye on General Henry Clinton, Howe's replacement as commander in chief, and the French were in the West Indies. The British in Georgia quickly organized twenty loyal militia units, and 1,400 Georgians swore an oath of allegiance to the king. So far, the southern strategy looked as if it might work.

Next came South Carolina. The Continental army put ten regiments into the port city of Charleston to defend it from attack by British troops shipped south from New York under the command of General Clinton. For five weeks in early 1780, the British laid siege to the city and took it in May 1780, sending 3,300 American soldiers, a tremendous loss, into British captivity. Again, the king's new strategy seemed to be on target.

Clinton returned to New York, leaving the pacification of South Carolina to General Charles Cornwallis and 4,000 troops. A bold commander, Lord Cornwallis quickly chased out the remaining Continentals and established military rule of South Carolina by midsummer. He purged rebels from government office and disarmed rebel militias. The export of South Carolina's main crop, rice, resumed, and as in Georgia, pardons were offered to Carolinians who swore loyalty oaths to the crown and took up arms for the British.

By August, American troops arrived from the North to strike back at Cornwallis. General Gates, the hero of the battle of Saratoga, led 3,000

MAP 7.4 The War in the South, 1780–1781

After taking Charleston in May 1780, the British advanced into South Carolina and the foothill region of North Carolina, leaving a bloody civil war in their wake. When the American general Horatio Gates and his men fumbled and fled from the humiliating battle of Camden, Gates was replaced by General Nathanael Greene and General Daniel Morgan, who pulled off major successes at King's Mountain and Cowpens. The British general Cornwallis then moved north and invaded Virginia but was bottled up and finally overpowered at Yorktown in the fall of 1781.

Benedict Arnold
This portrait shows Benedict Arnold in 1776, when he was the hero of the Quebec campaign. Probably the final straw for Arnold came when he failed to earn a promotion while men he considered inferior were elevated to higher rank.
Anne S. K. Brown Military Collection, Providence, R.I.

men, some of them experienced soldiers and others newly recruited militiamen, into battle against Cornwallis at Camden, South Carolina, on August 16 (see Map 7.4). Gates's militiamen panicked at the sight of the approaching enemy cavalry and fled. When regiment leaders tried to regroup the next day, only 700 showed up; the rest were dead, captured, or still in flight. Camden was a devastating defeat; prospects seemed very grim for the Americans.

The British gained help in 1780 from an unexpected source: An American general, Benedict Arnold, furnished them with valuable information about American troop movements. The hero of several American battles, Arnold was a brilliant military talent but also a deeply insecure man who never felt he got his due in either honor or financial reward. Sometime in 1779, he

opened secret negotiations with General Clinton in New York, trading information for money and hinting that he could deliver far more of value. When General Washington made him commander of West Point, a new fort sixty miles north of New York City on the Hudson River, Arnold's plan crystallized. West Point controlled the Hudson; its easy capture by the British might well have meant victory in the war.

Arnold's plot to sell a West Point victory to the British was foiled when Americans captured the man carrying plans of the fort's defense from Arnold to Clinton. News of Arnold's treason created shock waves. Arnold represented all of the patriots' worst fears about themselves: greedy self-interest like that of the war profiteers, the unprincipled abandonment of war aims like that of turncoat southern Tories, panic like that of the terrified soldiers at Camden. But instead of symbolizing all that was troubling about the American side of the war, the treachery of Arnold was publicly and ritually denounced in a kind of displacement of the anxieties of the moment. Vilifying Arnold allowed Americans to stake out a wide distance between themselves and dastardly conduct. It inspired a renewal of patriotism at a particularly low moment.

The Other Southern War: Guerrillas

Shock over Gates's defeat at Camden and Arnold's treason revitalized rebel support in western South Carolina, an area that Cornwallis believed to be pacified and loyal. The backcountry of the South soon became the site of guerrilla warfare. In hit-and-run attacks, both sides burned and ravaged not only opponents' property but the property of anyone claiming to be neutral. Loyalist militia units organized by the British were met by fierce rebel militia units who figured they had little to lose. In South Carolina, some six thousand rebels met loyalist units in bloody engagements. Some were classic battles, but on other occasions the fighters were more like bandits than soldiers. Guerrilla warfare soon spread to Georgia and North Carolina. Both sides committed murders and atrocities and plundered property, clear deviations from standard military practice.

The British southern strategy depended on sufficient loyalist strength to hold reconquered territory as the army moved north. The backcountry civil war proved this assumption false. The Americans won few major battles in the

South, but they ultimately succeeded by harassing the British forces and preventing them from foraging for food. Cornwallis moved the war into North Carolina in the fall of 1780, not because he thought South Carolina was secure—it was not—but because the North Carolinians were supplying the South Carolina rebels with arms and men (see Map 7.4). Then news of a brutal massacre of loyalist units in western South Carolina at King's Mountain, at the hands of 1,400 frontier riflemen, sent him hurrying back. The British were stretched too thin to hold on to even two of their onetime colonies.

Surrender at Yorktown

In 1781, Cornwallis moved back to North Carolina again and thence to Virginia, where he captured Williamsburg in June. A raiding party proceeded to Charlottesville, the seat of government, capturing members of the Virginia assembly but not Governor Thomas Jefferson, who escaped the soldiers by a mere ten minutes. (More than a dozen of Jefferson's slaves chose this moment to seek refuge with the British.) These minor victories allowed Cornwallis to imagine that he was gaining the upper hand in Virginia. He next marched to Yorktown, near Chesapeake Bay, to await arrival of back-up troops by ship from New York City, still held by the British.

At this juncture, the French-American alliance came into play. Already French regiments commanded by the Comte de Rochambeau had joined General Washington in Rhode Island in mid-1780, and now in 1781 warships under the Comte de Grasse sailed from France. Washington, Rochambeau, and de Grasse fixed their attention on the Chesapeake Bay in Virginia. The French fleet got there ahead of the British troop ships from New York; a five-day naval battle left the French navy in clear control of the Virginia coast. This proved to be the decisive factor in ending the war, because it eliminated the possibility of reinforcements for Cornwallis's army, dug in at Yorktown, and made rescue by the British navy impossible.

On land, General Cornwallis and his 7,500 troops faced a combined French and American army numbering over 16,000. For twelve days, the Americans and French bombarded the British fortifications at Yorktown; Cornwallis ran low on food and ammunition. An American observer keeping a diary noted that "the enemy, from want of forage, are killing off their horses in great numbers. Six or seven hundred of these valuable animals have been killed, and their carcasses are almost continually floating down the river." Realizing escape was impossible, Cornwallis signaled his intention to surrender. On October 19, 1781, he formally capitulated.

What began as a promising southern strategy in 1778 turned into a discouraging defeat by 1781. British attacks in the South had energized American resistance, as did the timely exposure of Benedict Arnold's treason. The arrival of the French fleet sealed the fate of Cornwallis at Yorktown, and the military war quickly came to a halt.

Siege of Yorktown, 1781

The Losers and the Winners

The surrender at Yorktown proved to be the end of the war with England, but it took some time for the principals to realize that. Frontier areas in Kentucky, Ohio, and Illinois still blazed with Indian warfare. The British army still occupied three coastal cities, and the Continental army remained in the field, in case the treaty process failed.

The peace treaty was two years in the making. Commissioners from America, Britain, and France met in Paris and worked out eighty-two articles of peace. The first article went to the heart of the matter: "His Britannic Majesty acknowledges the said United States to be free Sovereign and independent States." Other articles set the western boundary of the new country at the Mississippi River and guaranteed that creditors on both sides could collect debts owed them in sterling money, a provision especially important to British merchants. England agreed to withdraw its troops quickly; more than a decade later, this promise still had not been fully kept. The Treaty of Paris was signed on September 2, 1783.

Like the treaty ending the Seven Years' War, this treaty failed to recognize the Indians as players in the conflict. As one American told the Shawnee people, "Your Fathers the English have made Peace with us for themselves, but forgot you their Children, who Fought with them, and neglected you like Bastards." Indian lands were assigned to the victors as though they were uninhabited. Some Indian refugees fled west

"The Ballance of Power," 1780

This cartoon was published in England soon after Spain and the Netherlands declared an alliance with France to support the war in America. On the left, Britannia, a female figure representing Great Britain, cannot be moved by all the lightweights combined on the right side of the scale. France wears a ruffled shirt, Spain has a feather in his hat, and a Dutch boy has just hopped on, saying, "I'll do anything for money." The forlorn Indian maiden, the standard icon representing America in the eighteenth century, sits on the scale, head in hand, wailing, "My Ingratitude is Justly Punished." The poem printed below the cartoon predicts that "The Americans too will with Britons unite." This fanciful prediction was punctured nine months after it appeared, when the British surrendered to the Americans and the French at Yorktown in 1781.

Print Collection, Miriam and Ira D. Wallach Division of Art, Prints, and Photographs, the New York Public Library. Astor, Lenox and Tilden Foundations.

FOR MORE HELP ANALYZING THIS IMAGE, see the visual activity for this chapter in the Online Study Guide at **bedfordstmartins.com/roarkcompact**.

into present-day Missouri and Arkansas, and others, such as Joseph Brant's Mohawks, relocated to Canada. But significant numbers remained within the new United States, occupying their traditional homelands in areas west and north of the Ohio River. For them, the Treaty of 1783 brought no peace at all; their longer war against the Americans would extend at least until 1795 and for some to 1813. Their ally, Britain, conceded defeat, but the Indians did not.

With the treaty finally signed, the British began their evacuation of New York, Charleston, and Savannah, a process complicated by the sheer numbers involved—soldiers, fearful loyalists, and runaway slaves by the thousands. In New York City, more than 27,000 soldiers and 30,000 loyalists sailed on hundreds of ships for England in late fall 1783. In a final act of mischief, on the November day when the last ships left, the losing side raised the British flag at the southern tip of Manhattan, cut away the ropes used to hoist it, and greased the flagpole.

REVIEW   Why did the British southern strategy ultimately fail?

Conclusion: Why the British Lost

The British began the war for America convinced that they could not lose. They had the best-trained army and navy in the world; they were familiar with the landscape from the Seven Years' War; they had the willing warrior-power of most of the native tribes of the backcountry; and they easily captured every port city of consequence in America. Probably one-fifth of the population was loyalist, and another two-fifths were undecided. Why, then, did the British lose?

One continuing problem the British faced was the uncertainty of supplies. Unwilling to ravage the countryside, the army depended on supply ships from England. Insecurity about food helps explain their reluctance to pursue the Continental army aggressively. A further obstacle was their continual misuse of loyalist energies. Any plan to repacify the colonies required the co-operation of the loyalists, but repeatedly, the British left them to the mercy of vengeful rebels.

French aid looms large in any explanation of the British defeat. Even before the formal alliance, French artillery and ammunition proved vital for the underarmed Continental army. After 1780, the French army brought a new infusion of troops to a war-weary America, and the French navy made the Yorktown victory possible. Finally, the British abdicated civil power in the colonies in 1775 and 1776, when royal officials fled to safety, and they never really regained it. For seven years, the Americans created their own government structures, from the Continental Congress to local committees and militias. Staffed by many who before 1775 had been the political elites, these new government agencies had remarkably little trouble establishing their authority to rule. The basic British goal—to turn back the clock to imperial rule—receded into impossibility as the war dragged on.

The war for America had lasted just over five years, from Lexington to Yorktown; negotiations and the evacuation took two more. It profoundly disrupted the lives of Americans everywhere. It was a war for independence from England, but it was more. It was a war that required men and women to think about politics and the legitimacy of authority. The precise disagreement with England about representation and political participation had profound implications for the kinds of governance the Americans would adopt, both in the moment of emergency and in the longer run of the late 1770s and early 1780s when states began to write their constitutions. The rhetoric employed to justify the revolution against England put words such as *liberty, tyranny, slavery, independence,* and *equality* into common usage. These words carried far deeper meanings than a mere complaint over taxation without representation. As Abigail Adams and others saw, the Revolution unleashed a dynamic of equality and liberty. That it was largely unintended and unwanted by the revolutionary leaders of 1776 made it all the more potent a force in American life in the decades to come.

Suggestions for Further Reading

Carol Berkin, *Revolutionary Mothers: Women in the Struggle for America's Independence* (2005). A lively account of the many ways women participated in the war for independence, including camp followers, generals' wives, loyalists, slaves, and Indians.

Clare Brandt, *The Man in the Mirror: A Life of Benedict Arnold* (1994). A highly readable account of a man whose very name became synonymous with treachery.

Piers Mackesy, *The War for America, 1775–1783* (1964). A classic that presents the Revolution from the point of view of the British.

Pauline Maier, *American Scripture: Making the Declaration of Independence* (1997). Meticulous and fascinating scholarship showing the context and precursors to the famous document of 1776.

Ray Raphael, *A People's History of the American Revolution: How Common People Shaped the Fight for Independence* (2001). A look at the Revolution from the bottom up.

Charles Royster, *A Revolutionary People at War: The Continental Army and American Character, 1775–1783* (1979). A prize-winning social history exploring how the long war tested the ideals and beliefs of the American soldiers.

▶ For more books about topics in this chapter, see the Online Study Guide at bedfordstmartins.com/roarkcompact.

▶ For additional firsthand accounts of this period, see Chapter 7 in Michael Johnson, ed., *Reading the American Past*, Third Edition.

▶ For Web sites and documents related to topics and places in this chapter, see "HistoryLinks," "DocLinks," and "PlaceLinks" at bedfordstmartins.com/roarkcompact.

REVIEWING THE CHAPTER

Follow these steps to review and strengthen your understanding of the chapter.

STEP 1: *Study the* **Key Terms** *and* **Timeline** *to identify the significance of each item listed.*

STEP 2: *Answer the* **Review Questions**, *drawing on key terms and dates to support your answers.*

STEP 3: *Drawing on the Key Terms, Timeline, and Review Questions, answer the broader* **Making Connections** *questions.*

KEY TERMS

Who

Abigail Adams (p. 159)
John Dickinson (p. 161)
George Washington (p. 161)
Thomas Jefferson (p. 161)
Thomas Gage (p. 161)
William Howe (p. 161)
George III (p. 164)
Thomas Paine (p. 164)
Richard Montgomery (p. 168)
Benedict Arnold (pp. 168, 178)
Hessians (p. 168)
redcoats (p. 168)
Tories (p. 171)
Joseph Brant (Thayendanegea) (p. 171)

John Burgoyne (p. 173)
Horatio Gates (p. 174)
John Sullivan (p. 174)
White Eyes (p. 175)
Henry Clinton (p. 177)
Charles Cornwallis (p. 177)
Comte de Rochambeau (p. 179)

What

Second Continental Congress (p. 160)
Continental army (p. 161)
battle of Bunker Hill (p. 164)
smallpox (p. 164)
Olive Branch Petition (p. 164)
Common Sense (p. 164)

battle of Long Island (p. 168)
Ladies Association (p. 170)
Fort Ticonderoga (p. 173)
Fort Stanwix (p. 174)
battle of Oriskany (p. 174)
battle of Saratoga (p. 174)
Valley Forge (p. 174)
Mohawk Valley (p. 174)
Fort Niagara (p. 175)
Fort Pitt (p. 175)
southern strategy (p. 177)
battle of Camden (p. 178)
battle of King's Mountain (p. 179)
battle of Yorktown (p. 179)
Treaty of Paris (p. 179)

TIMELINE

1775 • Second Continental Congress convenes.
• British win battle of Bunker Hill.
• King George rejects Olive Branch Petition.

    1776 • Americans lose battle of Quebec.
    • *Common Sense* published.
    • British evacuate Boston.
    • **July 4.** Congress adopts Declaration of Independence.
    • British forces take Manhattan.

        1777 • British take Fort Ticonderoga.
        • Ambush at Oriskany.
        • Americans hold Fort Stanwix.
        • British occupy Philadelphia.
        • British surrender at Saratoga.
        • Continental army endures winter in Valley Forge.

            1778 • France enters war on American side.
            • American militiamen destroy Mohawk Joseph Brant's village.
            • White Eyes negotiates a treaty with Americans; later mysteriously dies.

REVIEW QUESTIONS

1. Why were many Americans reluctant to pursue independence from Britain? (pp. 160–66)

2. Why did the British exercise restraint in their efforts to recapture the colonies? (pp. 166–70)

3. How did the patriots promote support for their cause in the colonies? (pp. 170–73)

4. Why did the Americans need assistance from the French to ensure victory? (pp. 173–76)

5. Why did the British southern strategy ultimately fail? (pp. 176–80)

MAKING CONNECTIONS

1. Even before the colonies had committed to independence, they faced the likelihood of serious military conflict. How did they mobilize for war? In your answer, discuss specific challenges they faced, noting any unintended consequences of their solutions.

2. Congress's adoption of the Declaration of Independence confirmed a decisive shift in the conflict between the colonies and Britain. Why did the colonies make this decisive break in 1776? In your answer, discuss some of the arguments for and against independence.

3. The question of whether colonists' loyalty would be to the new government or to the old king was pivotal during the Revolutionary War. Discuss the importance of loyalty to the outcome of the conflict. In your answer, consider both military and political strategy.

4. American colonists and British soldiers were not the only participants in the Revolutionary War. Discuss the role of Native Americans in the war. How did they shape the conflict? What benefits did they hope to gain? Did they succeed?

▶ **FOR PRACTICE QUIZZES, A CUSTOMIZED STUDY PLAN, AND OTHER STUDY TOOLS,** see the Online Study Guide at bedfordstmartins.com/roarkcompact.

1779 • Militias attack Cherokee settlements in North Carolina and Tennessee.
• Americans destroy 40 Indian towns in New York.
• Americans take Forts Kaskaskia and Vincennes.

   1780 • Philadelphia Ladies Association raises money for soldiers.
   • British take Charleston, South Carolina.
   • French army arrives at Newport.
   • British win battle of Camden.
   • Benedict Arnold exposed as traitor.
   • Americans win battle of King's Mountain.

      1781 • British forces invade Virginia.
      • French fleet blockades Chesapeake Bay.
      • Cornwallis surrenders at Yorktown; concedes British defeat.

         1783 • Treaty of Paris ends war; United States gains all land to the Mississippi River.

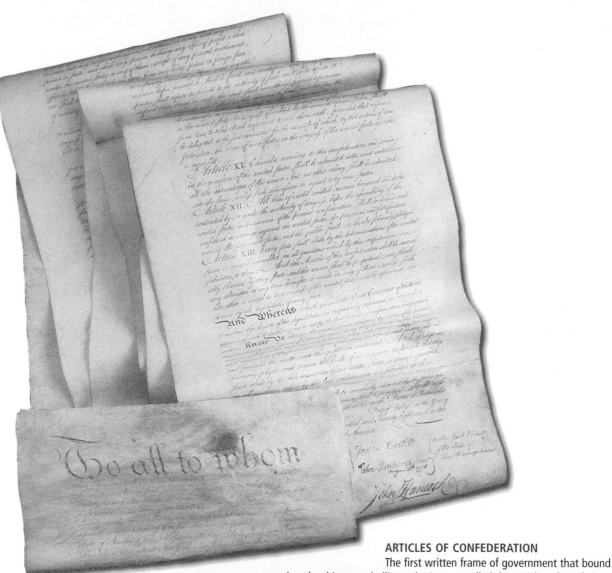

ARTICLES OF CONFEDERATION

The first written frame of government that bound together the thirteen rebelling colonies was called the Articles of Confederation. Delegates to the Second Continental Congress hammered out the plan over many months in 1776 and 1777, working on it when there was time free from the more pressing problems of pursuing the war. Once the congress agreed on it, the plan was printed and distributed to state legislatures for ratification, a process that took nearly five years because it required the assent of all thirteen. After ratification, in February 1781, this parchment copy became the official original version. As was often done with significant manuscript documents, a professional scribe wrote the opening words of the Articles in very large print, to proclaim the news. How does "To all to whom" compare with such famous opening words as "In Congress, July 4, 1776" (the start of the Declaration of Independence) and "We the people" (the start of the U.S. Constitution, which replaced the Articles in 1788)? Do you think "To all to whom" would have become a slogan or catchphrase had the Articles persisted as the country's sacred text? Why or why not?

National Archives.

Building a Republic
1775–1789

JAMES MADISON GRADUATED from Princeton College in New Jersey in 1771, not knowing what to do next with his life. Certainly the twenty-year-old had an easy fallback position. As the firstborn son of a wealthy plantation owner, he could return home to the foothills of Virginia and wait to inherit substantial land and a large force of slaves. But James was an intensely studious young man, uninterested in farming and reluctant to leave the collegiate environment. Five years at boarding school had given him fluency in Greek, Latin, French, and mathematics, and three years at Princeton acquainted him with the great thinkers, both ancient and modern. Driven by a thirst for learning, young Madison slept only five hours a night, perhaps undermining his health. Protesting that he was too ill to travel, he hung around Princeton six months after graduation.

In 1772, he returned home, still adrift. He tried studying law, but his unimpressive oratorical talents discouraged him. Instead he swapped reading lists and ideas about political theory by letter with a Princeton classmate, prolonging his student life. While Madison struggled for direction, the powerful winds before the storm of the American Revolution swirled through the colonies; the youth's drifting would abruptly end. In May 1774, Madison traveled north to deliver his brother to boarding school and was in Philadelphia when the startling news broke that Britain had closed the port of Boston in retaliation for the destruction of the tea. Turbulent protests over the Coercive Acts turned him into a committed revolutionary.

Back in Virginia, Madison joined his father on the newly formed committee of public safety. For a few days in early 1775, the twenty-four-year-old took up musket practice, but his continued poor health ruled out the soldier's life. His special talent lay in the science of politics, and in the spring of 1776, he gained election to the Virginia Convention, a revolutionary assembly replacing the defunct royal government. The convention's main task was to hammer out a state constitution with innovations like frequent elections and a limited executive power. Shy, self-effacing, and still learning the ropes, Madison mostly stayed on the sidelines, but Virginia's elder statesmen noted the young man's logical, thoughtful contributions. When his county failed to return him to the assembly in the next election, he was appointed to the governor's council, where he spent two years gaining experience in a wartime government.

In early 1780, Madison represented Virginia in the Continental Congress. Not quite twenty-nine, unmarried, and supported by his father's money, Madison was free of the burdens that made distant political service difficult for so many others. He stayed in the North for three years, working with men such as Alexander Hamilton of New York and Robert Morris of Pennsylvania as the congress wrestled with the chaotic economy and the ever-precarious war effort. In one crisis Madison's negotiating skills proved crucial: He broke the deadlock over the ratification of the Articles of Confederation by arranging for the cession of Virginia's vast western lands. Those lands would soon appear on maps as the Northwest Territory, calling forth a series of western land ordinances planned out by Madison's friend Thomas Jefferson that were the shining example of promise and high hopes for the future of the new confederation government. But more often, service in the congress proved frustrating to Madison because the confederation government seemed to lack essential powers, chief among them the power to tax.

Madison resumed a seat in the Virginia state assembly in 1784. But he did not retreat to a local point of view as so many other state politicians of the decade did. The difficult economic hardships created by heavy state taxation programs—which in Massachusetts led to a full-fledged rebellion against state government—spurred Madison to pursue means to strengthen the government of the thirteen new states. He worked hard to bring about an all-state convention in Philadelphia in the late spring of 1787, where he took the lead in steering the delegates to a complete rewrite of the structure of the national government, investing it with considerably greater powers. True to form,

Madison spent the months before the convention in feverish study of the great thinkers he had read in college, searching out the best way to constitute a government on **republican** principles. His lifelong passion for scholarly study, seasoned by a dozen years of energetic political experience, paid off handsomely. The United States Constitution was the result.

By the end of the 1780s, James Madison had had his finger in every kind of political pie, on the local, state, confederation, and finally national level. He had transformed himself from a directionless and solitary youth into one of the leading political thinkers of the Revolutionary period. His personal history over the 1780s was deeply entwined with the path of the emerging United States.

The Articles of Confederation

For five years after declaring independence, the Second Continental Congress continued to meet in Philadelphia and other cities without any formal constitutional basis. Delegates first had to work out a plan of government that embodied Revolutionary principles. With monarchy gone, where would sovereignty lie? What would be the nature of representation? Who would hold the power of taxation? Who should vote; who

James Madison, by Charles Willson Peale
A short and slight man, James Madison appeared younger than he was. This miniature portrait, made in 1783 when he was thirty-two, shows him with natural hair (no wig) and a boyishly smooth face. Madison commissioned the portrait on the occasion of his first serious romance. The Philadelphia artist Charles Willson Peale painted matching miniatures of Madison and his fiancée, Kitty Floyd, the sixteen-year-old daughter of a New York delegate to the Continental Congress. Madison and his Virginia friend Thomas Jefferson both boarded with the Floyd family while the congress met in Philadelphia. Jefferson, a very recent widower, encouraged the shy Madison and assured him that Kitty "will render you happier than you can possibly be in a single state." Madison's portrait was mounted in a brooch (note the pin sticking out on the right) so that his lady love might wear it on her person; the back of the brooch held a neatly plaited lock of Madison's hair. The companion miniature of Kitty no longer holds a lock of her hair, if it ever did, for Kitty soon jilted Madison for a suave younger man and returned the Madison miniature to the grieving bachelor. Eleven years later, Madison tried romance again when New York congressman Aaron Burr introduced him to a Virginia widow named Dolley Payne Todd, seventeen years his junior. Madison was forty-three and Dolley was twenty-six; they married four months after meeting.
Library of Congress.

should rule? The resulting plan, called the Articles of Confederation, proved to be surprisingly difficult to implement, mainly because the thirteen states had serious disagreements about how to manage lands to the west whose political ownership was contested. Once the Articles were finally ratified and the confederation was formally constituted, that arena of government seemed to many to be far less relevant or interesting than the state governments.

Congress, Confederation, and the Problem of Western Lands

Only after declaring independence did the Continental Congress turn its attention to creating a written document that would specify what powers the congress had and by what authority it existed. There was widespread agreement on key government powers: pursuing war and peace, conducting foreign relations, regulating trade, and running a postal service. But there was serious disagreement about the powers of the congress over the western boundaries of the states. Virginia and Connecticut, for example, had old colonial charters that located their western boundaries at the Mississippi River. States without extensive land claims insisted on redrawing those colonial boundaries.

For over a year, the congress tinkered with drafts of the Articles of Confederation, reaching agreement only in November 1777. The Articles defined the union as a loose confederation of states, characterized as "a firm league of friendship" existing mainly to foster a common defense. The structure of the government paralleled that of the existing Continental Congress. There was no national executive (that is, no president) and no national judiciary. The congress was composed of two to seven delegates from each state, selected annually by the state legislatures and prohibited from serving more than three years out of any six. The actual number of delegates was not critical, since each state delegation cast a single vote.

Routine decisions in the congress required a simple majority of seven states; for momentous decisions, such as declaring war, nine states needed to agree. To approve or amend the Articles required the unanimous consent both of the thirteen state delegations and of the thirteen state legislatures. The congressional delegates undoubtedly thought they were guaranteeing that no individual state could be railroaded by the other twelve in fundamental constitutional matters. But what this requirement really did was to hamstring the government. One state could—and did—hold the rest of the country hostage to its demands.

On the delicate question of taxes, needed to finance the war, the Articles provided an ingenious but ultimately troublesome solution. Each state was to contribute in proportion to the property value of the state's land. Large and populous states would give more than small or sparsely populated states. The actual taxes would be levied by the state legislatures, not by the congress, to preserve the Revolution's principle of taxation only by direct representation. However, no mechanism was created to compel states to contribute their fair share.

The lack of centralized authority in the confederation government was exactly what many state leaders wanted in the late 1770s. A league of states with rotating personnel, no executive branch, no power of taxation, and a requirement of unanimity for any major change seemed to be a good way to avoid the potential tyranny of government. But right away, the inherent weaknesses of these features became apparent.

The requirement for unanimous approval, for example, stalled the acceptance of the Articles for five years. The key dispute involved the problem of lands west of the existing states. Five states, all lacking land claims, insisted that the congress control western lands as a national domain that would eventually constitute new states. The other eight states refused to yield their colonial-era claims and opposed giving the congress power to alter boundaries (Map 8.1). In all the heated debate, few seemed to remember that those same western lands were inhabited by many thousands of Indians not party to the disputes.

The eight land-claiming states were ready to sign the Articles of Confederation in 1777. Three states without claims, Rhode Island, Pennsylvania, and New Jersey, eventually capitulated and signed, "not from a Conviction of the Equality and Justness of it," said a New Jersey delegate, "but merely from an absolute Necessity there was of complying to save the Continent." But Delaware and Maryland continued to hold out, insisting on a national domain policy. In 1779, the disputants finally compromised: Any land a state volunteered to

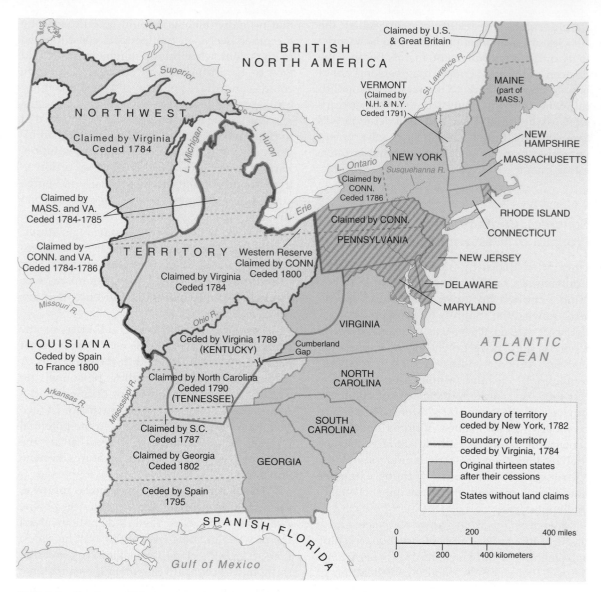

MAP 8.1   Cession of Western Lands, 1782–1802
The thirteen new states found it hard to ratify the Articles of Confederation without settling their conflict-ing land claims in the West, an area larger than the original states and occupied by Indian tribes. The five states objecting to the Articles' silence over western lands policy were Maryland, Delaware, New Jersey, Rhode Island, and Pennsylvania.

relinquish would become the national domain. When James Madison and Thomas Jefferson ceded Virginia's huge land claim in 1781, the Articles were at last unanimously approved.

The western lands issue demonstrated that powerful interests divided the thirteen new states. The apparent unity of purpose inspired by fighting the war against England papered over sizable cracks in the new confederation.

Running the New Government

No fanfare greeted the long-awaited inaugura-tion of the new government. The congress continued to sputter along, its problems far from solved by the signing of the Articles. Lack of a quorum often hampered day-to-day activi-ties. The Articles required representation from seven states to conduct business, and a mini-mum of two men from each state's delegation.

But some days, fewer than fourteen men in total showed up. State legislatures were slow to select delegates, and many of those appointed were reluctant to attend, especially if they had wives and children at home. Consequently, some of the most committed delegates were young bachelors like James Madison and men in their fifties and sixties whose families were grown, like Samuel Adams. Many politicians preferred to devote their energies to state governments, especially during the creative burst of state constitution writing in the late 1770s. Often the Continental Congress seemed deadlocked or, worse, irrelevant.

It also did not help that the congress had no permanent home. During the war, when the British army threatened Philadelphia, the congress relocated to small Pennsylvania towns such as Lancaster and York and then to Baltimore. After hostilities ceased, the congress moved from Trenton to Princeton to Annapolis to New York City.

To address the difficulties of an inefficient congress, executive departments of war, finance, and foreign affairs were created to handle purely administrative functions. When the department heads were ambitious—as was Robert Morris, a wealthy Philadelphia merchant who served as superintendent of finance—they could exercise considerable executive power. The Articles of Confederation had deliberately refrained from setting up an executive branch, but a modest one was being invented by necessity.

> **REVIEW** Why was the confederation government's authority so limited?

The Sovereign States

In the first decade of independence, the states were sovereign and all-powerful. Relatively few functions, like that of declaring war and peace, had been transferred to the confederation government. As Americans discarded their British identity, they thought of themselves instead as Virginians or New Yorkers or Rhode Islanders. Familiar and close to home, state government claimed the allegiance of citizens and became the arena in which the Revolution's innovations would first be tried. States defined who was a voter, and they also defined who would be free.

The question of slavery quickly became a front-burner issue, as all the states were forced to grapple with squaring revolutionary ideals with lifelong bondage for African Americans. Northern states had more success with this than did the southern, where slavery was deeply entrenched in the economy.

The State Constitutions

In May 1776, the congress recommended that all states draw up constitutions based on "the authority of the people." By 1778, ten had done so, and three more (Connecticut, Massachusetts, and Rhode Island) adopted and updated their original colonial charters. Having been denied unwritten British **liberties**, Americans wanted written contracts that guaranteed basic principles.

A shared feature of all the state constitutions was the conviction that government ultimately rests on the consent of the governed. Political writers in the late 1770s embraced the concept of republicanism as the underpinning of the new governments. Republicanism meant more than popular elections and representative institutions. For some, republicanism invoked a way of thinking about who leaders should be: autonomous, virtuous citizens who placed civic values above private interests. For others, it suggested direct **democracy**, with nothing standing in the way of the will of the people. For all, it meant government that promoted the people's welfare.

Widespread agreement about the virtues of republicanism went hand in hand with the idea that republics could succeed only in relatively small units, so the people could make sure their interests were being served. Nearly every state continued the colonial practice of a two-chamber assembly but greatly augmented the powers of the lower house. Two states, Pennsylvania and Georgia, abolished the more elite upper house altogether, and most states severely limited the powers and terms of the governor. Instead, real power resided with the lower houses, constituted to be very responsive to popular majorities, with annual elections and guaranteed rotation in office. If a representative displeased his constituents, he could be out of office in a matter of months.

Six of the state constitutions included bills of rights, lists of basic individual liberties that governments could not abridge. Virginia debated and passed the first bill of rights in June 1776, and many of the other states borrowed from it. Its language bears a close resemblance to the wording of the Declaration of Independence, which Thomas Jefferson was drafting that same June in Philadelphia: "That all men are by nature equally free and independent, and have certain inherent rights, of which, when they enter into a state of society, they cannot by any compact deprive or divest their posterity; namely, the enjoyment of life and liberty, with the means of acquiring and possessing property, and pursuing and obtaining happiness and safety." Along with these inherent rights went more specific rights to freedom of speech, freedom of the press, and trial by jury.

Who Are "the People"?

When the Continental Congress called for state constitutions based on "the authority of the people," and when the Virginia bill of rights granted "all men" certain rights, who was meant by "the people"? Who exactly were the citizens of this new country, and how far would the principle of democratic government extend? Different people answered these questions differently, but in the 1770s certain limits to full political participation by all Americans were widely agreed upon.

One limit was defined by property. In nearly every state, candidates for the highest offices had to meet substantial property qualifications. In Maryland, a candidate for governor had to be worth £5,000, a large sum of money. Voters in Maryland had to own fifty acres of land or £30, a barrier to one-third of adult white males. In the most democratic state, Pennsylvania, voters and candidates needed to be taxpayers, owning enough property to owe taxes. Only property owners were presumed to possess the necessary independence of mind to make wise political choices. Are not propertyless men, asked John Adams, "too little acquainted with public affairs to form a right judgment, and too dependent upon other men to have a will of their own?"

Property qualifications probably disfranchised from one-quarter to one-half of adult white males in all the states. Not all of them took their nonvoter status quietly. One Maryland man wondered what was so special about being worth £30: "Every poor man has a life, a personal liberty, and a right to his earnings; and is in danger of being injured by government in a variety of ways." Why then restrict such a man from voting? Others pointed out that propertyless men were fighting and dying in the Revolutionary War; surely they were expressing an active concern about politics. Finally, a few radical voices challenged the notion that owning property transformed men into good citizens. Perhaps it did the opposite: The richest men might well be greedy and selfish and therefore bad citizens. But ideas like this were clearly outside the mainstream. The writers of the new constitutions, themselves men of property, viewed the right to own and preserve property as a central principle of the Revolution.

Another exclusion from voting—women—was so ingrained that few stopped to question it. Yet the logic of allowing propertied females to vote did occur to at least two well-placed women. Abigail Adams wrote to John in 1782 that "Even in the freest countrys our property is subject to the controul and disposal of our partners, to whom the Laws have given a sovereign Authority. Deprived of a voice in Legislation, obliged to submit to those Laws which are imposed upon us, is it not sufficient to make us indifferent to the publick Welfare?" A wealthy Virginia widow named Hannah Corbin wrote to her brother, Richard Henry Lee, to complain of her taxation without the corresponding representation. Her letter no longer exists, but his reply does: "You complain that widows are not represented, and that being temporary possessors of the estates, ought not to be liable to the tax." Yet, he continued, women would be "out of character... to press into those tumultuous assemblies of men where the business of choosing representatives is conducted."

Only three states specified that voters had to be male, so powerful was the unspoken assumption that only men could vote. Still, in one state, small numbers of women began to turn out at the polls in the 1780s. New Jersey's constitution of 1776 enfranchised all free inhabitants worth over £50, language that in theory opened the door to free blacks as well as unmarried women, if propertied. (Married women owned no property, for by law their husbands held title to everything.) Little fanfare accompanied this radical shift, and some historians have inferred that the inclusion of unmarried women and blacks was an oversight. Yet other parts of the **suffrage** clause pertaining to residency and property were extensively debated when it was put in the state constitution, and no objections were raised at that time to its gender- and race-free language. Thus other historians have concluded that the law was intentionally inclusive. In 1790, a revised election law used the words *he* or *she* in reference to voters, making woman suffrage explicit. As one New Jersey legislator declared, "Our Constitution gives this right to maids or widows *black* or *white*."

In 1790, only about 1,000 free black adults of both sexes lived in New Jersey, a state with a population of 184,000. The number of unmarried adult white women was probably also small, mainly widows. In view of the property requirement, the voter bloc enfranchised under this law could not have been decisive in elections. Still, this highly unusual situation lasted until 1807, when a new state law specifically disfranchised both blacks and women. Henceforth, independence of mind, that essential precondition of voting, was redefined to be sex- and race-specific.

In the 1780s, voting everywhere was class-specific, due to the property restrictions. John Adams urged the framers of the Massachusetts constitution not even to discuss the scope of suffrage but simply to adopt the traditional colonial property qualifications. If suffrage is brought up for debate, he warned, "there will be no end of it. New claims will arise; women will demand a vote; lads from twelve to twenty-one will think their rights not enough attended to; and every man who has not a farthing, will demand an equal voice with any other." Adams was astute enough to anticipate complaints about excluding women, youth, and poor men from political life, but it did not even occur to him to worry about another group: slaves.

Equality and Slavery

Restrictions on political participation did not mean that propertyless people enjoyed no civil rights and liberties. The various state bills of rights applied to all individuals who had, as the Virginia bill so carefully phrased it, "enter[ed] into a state of society." No matter how poor, a free person was entitled to life, liberty, property, and freedom of conscience. Unfree people, however, were another matter.

The author of the Virginia bill of rights was George Mason, a plantation owner with 118 slaves. When he penned the sentence "all men are

A Possible Voter in Essex County, New Jersey
Mrs. Elizabeth Alexander Stevens was married to John Stevens, a New Jersey delegate to the Continental Congress in 1783. Widowed in 1792, she would have then been eligible to vote in state elections according to New Jersey's unique enfranchisement of property-holding women. Mrs. Stevens's family was a prominent one. Her father had been surveyor general of New Jersey and New York; her husband was active in politics and was secretary to the governor of New York. Her son, John Stevens, was the inventor of steamboat and locomotive innovations; her daughter Mary married Robert R. Livingston of New York, also a delegate to the Continental Congress and a man who later built a fortune in steamboating. Essex County, where Elizabeth Stevens lived, was said to be the place where female suffrage was exercised most actively. This portrait, done around 1793–1794, represents the most likely face of that rare bird, the eighteenth-century female voter. The widow Stevens died in 1799, before suffrage was redefined to be the exclusive right of males.
New Jersey Historical Society.

by nature equally free and independent," he did not have slaves in mind; he meant that Americans were the equals of the British and could not be denied the liberties of British citizens. Other Virginia legislators, worried about misinterpretations, added the phrase specifying that rights belonged only to people who had entered civil society. As one wrote, with relief, "Slaves, not being constituent members of our society, could never pretend to any benefit from such a maxim."

One month later, the Declaration of Independence used essentially the same phrase about equality, this time without the modifying clause about entering society. Two state constitutions, for Pennsylvania and Massachusetts, also picked it up. In Massachusetts, one town suggested rewording the draft constitution to read "All men, whites and blacks, are born free and equal." The suggestion fell on deaf ears.

Nevertheless, after 1776 the ideals of the Revolution about natural equality and liberty began to erode the institution of slavery. Sometimes enslaved blacks led the challenge. (See "Documenting the American Promise," page 194.) In 1777, several Massachusetts slaves petitioned the state legislature, claiming a "natural & unalienable right to that freedom which the great Parent of the Universe hath bestowed equally on all mankind." They modestly asked for freedom for their children at age twenty-one and were turned down. In 1779, similar petitions in Connecticut and New Hampshire met with no success. Seven Massachusetts freemen, including the mariner brothers Paul and John Cuffe, refused to pay taxes for three years on the grounds that they could not vote and so were not represented. The Cuffe brothers landed in jail in 1780 for tax evasion, but their petition to the state legislature soon spurred the extension of suffrage to taxpaying free blacks in that state.

Another way to bring the issue before lawmakers was to sue in court. In 1781, a Massachusetts slave named Quok Walker charged his master with assault and battery, arguing that he was a free man under the state constitution's assertion that "all men are born free and equal." Walker won and was set free, a decision confirmed in an appeal to the state's superior court in 1783. Several similar cases followed, and by 1789 slavery had been effectively abolished by judicial decision in Massachusetts.

Legal Changes to Slavery, 1777–1804

In other northern states, untold numbers of blacks simply ran away from owners and claimed their freedom, sometimes with the help of sympathetic whites. One estimate holds that more than half of young slave men in Philadelphia took flight in the 1780s and joined the ranks of free blacks. By 1790, free blacks outnumbered slaves in Pennsylvania by nearly a factor of two.

Pennsylvania ended slavery by a gradual **emancipation** law in 1780. Only infants born to a slave mother on or after March 1, 1780, would be freed, but not until age twenty-eight. Thus no current slave in Pennsylvania would gain freedom until 1808; well into the nineteenth century those blacks born before 1780 would still be slaves. (Not until 1847 did Pennsylvania fully abolish slavery.) Rhode Island and Connecticut adopted gradual emancipation laws in 1784. In 1785, New York expanded the terms under which individual owners could free slaves, but only in 1799 did the state adopt a gradual emancipation law; New Jersey followed suit in 1804. These were the two northern states with the largest number of slaves: New York in 1800 with 20,000, New Jersey with more than 12,000. In contrast, slaves in Pennsylvania numbered just 1,700. Gradual emancipation illustrates the tension between radical and conservative implications of republican ideology. Republican government protected people's liberties and property, yet slaves were both people and property. Gradual emancipation balanced the civil rights of blacks and the property rights of their owners by delaying the promise of freedom.

South of Pennsylvania, in Delaware, Maryland, and Virginia, where slavery was so important to the economy, emancipation bills were rejected. All three states, however, eased legal restrictions and allowed individual acts of emancipation for adult slaves below the age of forty-five, under new manumission laws passed in 1782 (Virginia), 1787 (Delaware), and 1790 (Maryland). By 1790, close to 10,000 newly freed Virginia slaves had formed local free black communities complete with schools and churches.

In the deep South—the Carolinas and Georgia—freedom for slaves was unthinkable for whites. Yet several thousands had defected to the British during the war, and between three and four thousand shipped out of Savannah and Charleston, destined for freedom. Adding northern blacks evacuated from New York City in 1783, the probable total of emancipated blacks who left the United States was between eight and ten thousand. Some went to Canada, some to England, and some to Sierra Leone, on the west coast of Africa. Many hundreds took refuge with Seminole and Creek Indians, becoming permanent members of their communities in Spanish Florida and western Georgia.

Although all these instances of emancipation were gradual, small, and certainly incomplete, their symbolic importance was enormous. Every state from Pennsylvania northward acknowledged that slavery was fundamentally inconsistent with Revolutionary ideology; "all men are created equal" was beginning to acquire real force as a basic principle.

REVIEW How did states determine who would be allowed to vote?

The Critical Period

From 1781 to 1786, a sense of crisis gripped some of the Revolutionary leaders who feared the Articles of Confederation were too weak. But others defended the Articles as the best guarantee of individual liberty, because real governance occurred at the state level, closer to the people. Political theorizing about the proper relation among citizen, state, and confederation remained active and controversial throughout the decade as Americans confronted questions of finance, territorial expansion, and civil disorder.

Financial Chaos and Paper Money

Seven years of war produced a chaotic economy in the 1780s. The confederation and the individual states had run up huge war debts, financed

Black Loyalists in Canada
This rare sketch from 1788 shows an ordinary day laborer: a black woodcutter who came to Nova Scotia in the migration of black loyalists. Over 3,000 black refugees from the American Revolution arrived in northeastern Canada between 1783 and 1785. Very few were able to acquire land, and after 1786 the British authorities stopped provisioning them. Most, like the man pictured here, were forced to become servants or day laborers for whites. Low wages created dissatisfaction, and racial tensions broke loose in a riot. In 1791–1792, nearly a third of the black refugees in Nova Scotia left for Sierra Leone in West Africa, where British officials promised them landownership and opportunities for self-rule. In 1798, a refugee from South Carolina named Boston King published a memoir of his experiences joining the British during the Revolution, living in Nova Scotia, and traveling on to Sierra Leone; his rich account is one of the few existing personal narratives of black loyalism.
William Booth, National Archives of Canada C-401621.

by printing paper money and borrowing from private sources. Some $400 to $500 million in paper currency had been injected into the economy, and prices and wages fluctuated wildly. Private debt and rapid expenditure flourished, and jails became crowded with debtors. A serious postwar

Blacks Petition for Freedom and Rights

In the 1780s, a language of rights and liberty was in the air and on many lips. Extraordinary times encouraged extraordinary actions, and enslaved as well as newly freed African Americans everywhere felt emboldened to make bids to enlarge their own liberty. Brand-new state governments held out the potential for revolutionary change in legal and social relations, encouraging some blacks to petition for various freedoms. To be effective, petitions generally needed to beg or persuade rather than assert. Notice the kinds of arguments made by these petitioners, the ways they describe themselves, and the promises they make about how they will use their hoped-for freedom.

DOCUMENT 1
Four Men Petition the Massachusetts Assembly for Their Freedom, 1773

Massachusetts law in the 1770s allowed even slaves to present petitions to the government. These four enslaved men printed their petition and sent a copy to each representative instead of submitting a single petition to the assembly, a shrewd strategy to maximize its impact.

Boston, April 20th, 1773
Sir, The efforts made by the legislative of this province in their last sessions to free themselves from slavery, gave us, who are in that deplorable state, a high degree of satisfaction. We expect great things from men who have made such a noble stand against the designs of their fellow-men to enslave them. We cannot but wish and hope Sir, that you will have the same grand object, we mean civil and religious liberty, in view in your next session. The divine spirit of freedom, seems to fire every humane breast on this continent, except such as are bribed to assist in executing the execrable plan.

We are very sensible that it would be highly detrimental to our present masters, if we were allowed to demand all that of right belongs to us for past services; this we disclaim. Even the Spaniards, who have not those sublime ideas of freedom that English men have, are conscious that they have no right to all the services of their fellow-men, we mean the Africans, whom they have purchased with their money; therefore they allow them one day in a week to work for themselves, to enable them to earn money to purchase the residue of their time.... We acknowledge our obligations to you for what you have already done, but as the people of this province seem to be actuated by the principles of equity and justice, we cannot but expect your house will again take our deplorable case into serious consideration, and give us that ample relief which, as men, we have a natural right to.

But since the wise and righteous governor of the universe, has permitted our fellow men to make us slaves, we bow in submission to him, and determine to behave in such a manner as that we may have reason to expect the divine approbation of, and assistance in, our peaceable and lawful attempts to gain our freedom.

We are willing to submit to such regulations and laws, as may be made relative to us, until we leave the province, which we determine to do as soon as we can, from our joynt labours procure money to transport ourselves to some part of the Coast of Africa, where we propose a settlement. We are very desirous that you should have instructions relative to us, from your town, therefore we pray you to communicate this letter to them, and ask this favor for us.

In behalf of our fellow slaves in this province, and by order of their Committee.

Peter Bestes,   Felix Holbrook,
Sambo Freeman,   Chester Joie.

SOURCE: Herbert Aptheker, ed., *A Documentary History of the Negro People in the United States* (New York: Citadel Press, 1968), 1:7–8. Copyright © by Citadel Press. Reprinted with permission.

DOCUMENT 2
Paul and John Cuffe Protest Taxation in Massachusetts, 1780

After judicial emancipation in Massachusetts, Paul and John Cuffe, together with five other freed men from the town of Dartmouth, sent this petition to the Massachusetts legislature.

To the Honouerable Councel and House of Representatives in General Court assembled for the State of the Massachusetts Bay in New England—March 14th AD 1780—
The petition of several poor Negroes & molattoes who are Inhabitant of the Town of Dartmouth

Humbly Sheweth—That we being Chiefly of the African Extract and by Reason of Long Bondag and hard Slavery we have been deprived of Injoying the Profits of our Labouer or the advantage of Inheriting Estates from our Parents as our Neighbouers the white peopel do haveing some of us not long Injoyed our own freedom & yet of late, Contrary to the invariable Custom & Practice of the Country we have been & now are Taxed both in our Polls and that small Pittance of Estate which through much hard Labour & Industry we have got together to Sustain our selves & families withal—We apprehand it therefore to be hard usag and will doubtless if Continued will Reduce us to a State of Beggary whereby we shall become a Berthan to others if not timely prevented by the Interposition of your Justice & power & yor Petitioners farther sheweth that we apprehand ourselves to be Aggreeved, in that while we are not allowed the Privilage of freemen of the State having no vote or Influence in the Election of those that Tax us yet many of our Colour (as is well known) have cheerfully Entered the field of Battle in the defence of the Common Cause and that (as we conceive) against a similar Exertion of Power (in Regard to taxation) too well Known to need a recital in this place—

That these the Most honouerable Court we Humbley Beseech they would take this into Considerration and Let us aside from Paying tax or taxes or cause us to Be Cleaired for we ever have Been a people that was fair from all these thing ever since the days of our four fathers and therefore we take it as aheard ship that we should be so delt By now in these Difficulty times for there is not to exceed more then five or six that hath a cow in this town and theirfore in our Distress we send unto the peaceableness of thee people and the mercy of God that we may be Releaved for we are not alowed in voating in the town meating in nur to chuse an oficer Neither their was not one ever heard in the active Court of the General Asembly the poor Dispised miserable Black people, & we have not an equal chance with white people neither by Sear nur by Land therefore we take it as a heard ship that poor old Negroes should be Rated which have been in Bondage some thirty some forty and some fifty years and now just got their Liberty some by going into the serviese and some by going to Sea and others by good fortan and also poor Distressed mungrels which have no larning and no land.... Neither where to put their head but some shelter them selves into an old rotten hut which thy dogs would not lay in.

Therefore we pray that these may give no offence at all ... therefore we Humbley Beg and pray thee to plead our Case for us with thy people O God; that those who have the rule in their hands may be mercyfull unto the poor and needy give unto those who ask of thee and he that would Borrow of thee turn not away empty.... Neither with lieing Lips therefore we think that we may be clear from being called tories tho some few of our Colour hath Rebelled and Done Wickedly however we think that there is more of our Collour gone into the wars according to the Number of them into the Respepiktive towns then any other nation here.... We most humbley Request therefore that you would take our unhappy Case into your serious Consideration and in your wisdom and Power grant us Relief from Taxation while under our Present depressed Circumstances and your poor Petioners as in duty bound shall ever pray &c.

Source: Herbert Aptheker, ed., *A Documentary History of the Negro People in the United States* (New York: Citadel Press, 1968), 1:15–16. Copyright © 1968 by Citadel Press. Reprinted with permission.

Questions for Analysis and Debate

1. What do the four Massachusetts petitioners mean when they congratulate the state legislators for their recent efforts "to free themselves from slavery"? Are they contradictory when they claim a natural right "as men" to relief from slavery but then also "bow in submission" to the "governor of the universe" who has allowed their slavery? What is it they "disclaim" out of consideration to their present masters? Why do they raise the case of a Spanish version of slavery?

2. Is the Cuffe petition essentially a call for "no taxation without representation"? Does it differ from the Revolutionaries' stand on taxation in relation to Britain? Do the petitioners want representation or relief from taxation? Why do they mention their military service?

3. What can you conclude about the options available to northern blacks to secure freedom or rights under law? Are the petitioners confident about their rights or about the outcome they expect? How have they had to shape their petitions to appeal to an all-white legislature? Do you see instances of subtle irony or sarcasm?

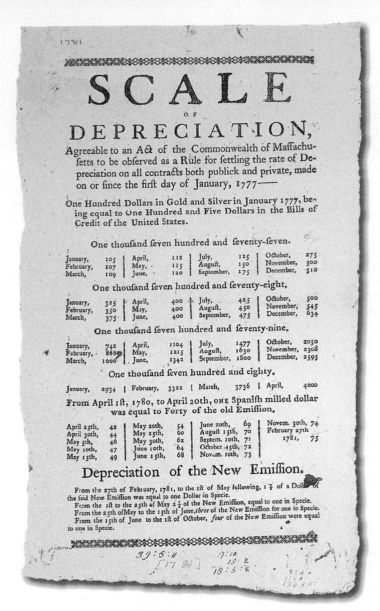

Scale of Depreciation

This chart shows the monthly value of U.S. Continental dollars from January 1777 to February 1781 as stipulated by the government of Massachusetts. For example, in March 1780, 3,736 Continental dollars equaled the buying power of $100 in gold or silver based on values of the dollar in January 1777. By April 1780, the same value of hard money required $4,000 Continentals. Such a chart was needed when debtors and creditors settled accounts contracted at one time and paid off later in greatly depreciated dollars. How easy would you find it to keep your head above water in an economy with such fast currency depreciation? What level of arithmetic and chart-reading skills were required? Notice the handwritten figuring at the bottom of the chart. Do these arithmetic operations look familiar to you?

Courtesy, American Antiquarian Society.

depression settled in by the mid-1780s and did not lift until the 1790s.

The confederation government itself was in a terrible financial fix. Continental dollars had lost almost all value: It took 146 of them to buy what one dollar had bought in 1775. Desperate times required desperate measures. The congress chose Robert Morris, Philadelphia merchant and newly reelected delegate, to be superintendent of finance. Morris had a gift for financial dealings but had resigned from the congress in 1778 amid accusations of enriching his firm while engaged in public service. Now his talents were again needed, and from 1781 to 1784 he took charge of the confederation's economic problems.

To augment the government's revenue, Morris first proposed a 5 percent impost (an import tax). Since the Articles of Confederation did not authorize taxation, an amendment was needed; but unanimous agreement proved impossible. Rhode Island and New York, whose bustling ports provided ample state revenue, preferred to keep their money and simply refused to agree to a national impost.

Morris's next idea was the creation of the Bank of North America. This private bank would enjoy a special relationship with the confederation, holding the government's **hard money** as well as private deposits, and providing it with short-term loans. The bank's contribution to economic stability came in the form of banknotes, pieces of paper inscribed with a dollar value. Unlike paper money, banknotes were backed by hard money in the bank's vaults and thus would not depreciate. Morris hoped this form of money would retain value; Congress agreed and voted to approve the bank in 1781. But the bank had limited success curing the confederation's economic woes because it issued very little currency; its charter was allowed to expire in 1786.

If Morris could not resuscitate the economy in the 1780s, probably no one could have done it. Because the Articles of Confederation reserved most economic functions to the states, the congress was helpless to tax trade, control inflation, curb the flow of state-issued paper money, or pay the mounting public debt. But the confederation had acquired one source of enormous potential wealth: the huge territory ceded by Virginia, which in 1784 became the national domain.

Land Ordinances and the Northwest Territory

The Continental Congress appointed Thomas Jefferson to draft a national domain policy. Jefferson proposed dividing the territory north of the Ohio River and east of the Mississippi—called the Northwest Territory—into ten new states consisting of townships ten miles square. He at first advocated giving the land to settlers, rather than selling it, arguing that future property taxes on the improved lands would be payment enough. Jefferson's aim was to encourage rapid and democratic settlement, to build a nation of freeholders (as opposed to renters), and to avoid land speculation. Jefferson also insisted on representative governments in the new states; they would not become colonies of the older states. Finally, Jefferson's draft prohibited slavery in the ten new states.

The congress adopted parts of Jefferson's plan in the Ordinance of 1784: the rectangular grid, the ten states, and the guarantee of self-government and eventual statehood. What the congress found too radical was the proposal to

give away the land; the national domain was the confederation's only source of independent wealth. The slavery prohibition also failed, by a vote of seven to six states.

A year later, the congress revised the legislation with procedures for mapping and selling the land. The Ordinance of 1785 called for three to five states divided into townships six miles square, further divided into thirty-six sections of 640 acres, each section enough for four family farms. Property was thus reduced to easily mappable squares. Land would be sold by public auction, at a minimum price of one dollar an acre, with highly desirable land bid up for more. Two further restrictions applied: The minimum purchase was 640 acres, and payment must be in hard money or in certificates of debt from Revolutionary days. This effectively meant that the land's first owners would be prosperous speculators. The grid of invariant squares further enhanced speculation, allowing buyers and sellers to operate without ever setting foot on the acreage. The commodification of land had been taken to a new level.

Speculators usually held the land for resale rather than inhabiting it. Thus they avoided direct contact with the most serious obstacle to settlement: the dozens of Indian tribes that

Thomas Jefferson, **by John Trumbull**

This miniature shows Thomas Jefferson at age forty-five, during his years as a diplomat in Paris. The American artist John Trumbull visited France in 1788 and painted Jefferson's likeness in this five-by-four-inch format so he could later copy it into his planned large canvas depicting the signing of the Declaration of Independence. Jefferson requested three replicas of the miniature to bestow as gifts. One went to his daughter Martha, another to an American woman in London, and the third to Maria Cosway, a British artist with whom Jefferson shared an intense infatuation during his stay in France. A widower, Jefferson never remarried, but a scandal over his private life erupted in 1802, when a journalist charged that he had fathered several children by his slave Sally Hemings. In 1998, a careful DNA study concluded that uniquely marked Jefferson Y-chromosomes were common to male descendants in both the Hemings and Jefferson lines. The DNA evidence, when combined with historical evidence about Jefferson's whereabouts at the start of each of Hemings's six pregnancies, makes it nearly certain that Jefferson fathered some or perhaps all of her children. What cannot be known is the nature of the relationship between the two. Was it coerced or voluntary, or somewhere in between? In all his voluminous writings, Jefferson left no comment about Sally Hemings, and the record on her side is entirely mute.

Monticello / Thomas Jefferson Memorial Foundation, Inc.

Jefferson's Map of the Northwest Territory
Thomas Jefferson sketched out borders for ten new states in his initial plan for the Northwest Territory in 1784. Straight lines and right angles held a strong appeal for him. But such regularity ignored inconvenient geographic features such as rivers and even more inconvenient political features such as Indian territorial claims, most unlikely to be ceded by treaty in orderly blocks. Jefferson also submitted ten distinctive names for the states. Number 9, for example, was Polypotamia, "land of many rivers" in Greek. William L. Clements Library.

For more help analyzing this image, see the visual activity for this chapter in the Online Study Guide at **bedfordstmartins.com/roarkcompact.**

claimed the land as their own. Treaties signed at Fort Stanwix in 1784 and Fort McIntosh in 1785 coerced partial cessions of land from Iroquois, Delaware, Huron, and Miami tribes. Then in 1786, a united Indian meeting near Detroit issued an ultimatum: No cession would be valid without unanimous consent. The Indians advised the United States to "prevent your surveyors and other people from coming upon our side of the Ohio river." For two more decades, violent Indian wars in Ohio and Indiana would continue to impede white settlement (see chapter 9).

In 1787, a third land act, called the Northwest Ordinance, set forth a three-stage process by which settled territories would advance to statehood. First, congress would appoint officials for a sparsely populated territory who would adopt a legal code and appoint local magistrates to administer justice. When the free male population of voting age and landowning status (fifty acres) reached 5,000, the territory could elect its own legislature and send a nonvoting delegate to the congress. When the population of voting citizens reached 60,000, they could write a state constitution and apply for full admission to the Union. At all three territorial stages, the inhabitants were subject to taxation to support the Union, in the same manner as were the original states.

The Northwest Ordinance of 1787 was perhaps the most important legislation passed by the confederation government. It ensured that the new United States, so recently released from colonial dependency, would not itself become a colonial power—at least not with respect to white citizens. The mechanism it established allowed for the successful and orderly expansion of the United States across the continent in the next century.

Nonwhites were not forgotten or neglected in the 1787 ordinance. The brief document acknowledged the Indian presence in the Northwest Territory and promised that "the utmost good faith shall always be observed towards the Indians; their lands and property shall never be taken from them without their consent; and, in their property, rights, and liberty, they shall never be invaded or disturbed, unless in just and lawful wars authorized by Congress." The 1787 ordinance further pledged that "laws founded in justice and humanity, shall from time to time be made for preventing wrongs being done to them, and for preserving peace and friendship with them." These promises were full of noble intentions, but they were not generally honored in the decades to come.

Jefferson's original and remarkable suggestion to prohibit slavery in the Northwest Territory resurfaced in the 1787 ordinance, passing this time without any debate. Probably the addition of a fugitive slave provision in the act set southern congressmen at ease: Escaped slaves caught north of the Ohio River would be returned south. The ordinance thus acknowledged and supported slavery. Further, abundant territory south of the Ohio was still available for the spread of slavery. Still, the prohibition of slavery in the Northwest Territory perpetuated the dynamic of gradual emancipation in the North: North-South sectionalism based on slavery was slowly taking shape.

Shays's Rebellion, 1786–1787

Without an impost amendment, and with public land sales projected but not yet realized, the confederation turned to the states in the 1780s to contribute revenue voluntarily. Struggling with their own war debts, most state legisla-

tures were reluctant to tax their constituents too heavily. Massachusetts, however, had a fiscally conservative legislature, dominated by the coastal commercial centers. For four years, the legislature passed tough tax laws that called for payment in hard money, not cheap paper. Farmers in the western two-thirds of the state found it increasingly difficult to comply and repeatedly petitioned against what they called oppressive taxation. In July 1786, when the legislature adjourned having yet again ignored their complaints, dissidents held a series of conventions and called for revisions to the state constitution to promote democracy, eliminate the elite upper house, and move the capital farther west in the state.

Still unheard in Boston, the dissidents targeted the county courts, the local symbol of state authority. In the fall of 1786, several thousand armed men marched on courthouses in six Massachusetts counties and forced bewildered judges to close their courts until the state constitution was revised. Sympathetic local militias did not intervene. The insurgents were not predominantly poor or debt-ridden farmers; they included veteran soldiers and officers in the Continental army as well as town leaders. One was a farmer and one-time army captain, Daniel Shays, from the town of Pelham.

The governor of Massachusetts, James Bowdoin, who had once organized protests against British taxes, now characterized the western dissidents as illegal rebels. He vilified Shays as the chief leader, and a Boston newspaper claimed Shays planned to burn Boston to the ground and overthrow the government, clearly an overreaction. Another former radical, Samuel Adams, took the extreme position that "the man who dares rebel against the laws of a republic ought to suffer death." Those aging revolutionaries had given little thought to the possibility that popular majorities, embodied in a state legislature, could seem to be just as oppressive as monarchs. The dissidents challenged the assumption that popularly elected governments would always be fair and just.

Members of the Continental Congress worried that the Massachusetts insurgency was spinning out of control. In October, the congress attempted to triple the size of the federal army, calling for 660 new recruits from Massachusetts and another 560 from New England; but fewer than 100 enlisted in the troubled state. So Governor Bowdoin raised a

Silver Bowl for an Anti-Shays General
Members of the militia of Springfield in western Massachusetts presented their leader, General William Shepard, with this silver bowl to honor his victory over the insurgents in Shays's Rebellion. Presentational silver conveyed a double message. It announced gratitude and praise in engraved words, and it transmitted considerable monetary value in the silver itself. General Shepard could display his trophy on a shelf, use it as a punch bowl, will it to descendants to keep his famous moment alive in memory, or melt it down in hard times. Shepard's is not the only name commemorated on the bowl; Shays's name appears in the last line, there for the ages to remember.
Yale University Art Gallery, Mabel Brady Garvan Collection.

private army, gaining the services of some 3,000 by paying them bounties provided by wealthy and fearful Boston merchants (and later repaid by the state).

In January 1787, the insurgents learned of the private army marching their way, and 1,500 of them moved swiftly to capture a federal armory in Springfield to gain weapons. But a militia band loyal to the state government beat them to the weapons facility and met their attack with gunfire; four rebels were killed and another twenty wounded. The final and bloodless encounter came at Petersham, where Bowdoin's army surprised the rebels on a freezing February morning and took 150 prisoners; the others fled into the woods. Shays took off for Canada and other leaders left the state, but more than 1,000 dissidents were rounded up and jailed.

In the end, two men were executed for rebellion; sixteen more sentenced to hang were reprieved at the last moment on the gallows.

Shays's Rebellion, 1786–1787

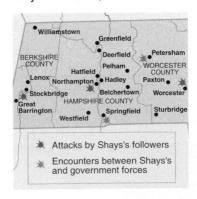

✳ Attacks by Shays's followers

✳ Encounters between Shays's and government forces

Some 4,000 men gained leniency by confessing their misconduct and swearing an oath of allegiance to the state. A special Disqualification Act prohibited the penitent rebels from voting, holding public office, serving on juries, working as schoolmasters, or operating taverns for up to three years.

Shays's Rebellion caused leaders throughout the country to worry about the confederation's ability to handle civil disorder. Inflammatory Massachusetts newspapers wrote about bloody mob rule; perhaps, some feared, similar "combustibles" in other states were awaiting the spark that would set off a dreadful political conflagration. New York lawyer John Jay wrote to George Washington, "Our affairs seem to lead to some crisis, some revolution—something I cannot foresee or conjecture. I am uneasy and apprehensive; more so than during the war." Benjamin Franklin, in his eighties, shrewdly observed that in 1776 Americans had feared "an excess of power in the rulers" but now the problem was "a defect of obedience" in the subjects. Among such leaders, the sense of crisis in the confederation had greatly deepened.

> **REVIEW** Why did farmers in western Massachusetts revolt against the state legislature?

The United States Constitution

Shays's Rebellion provoked an odd mixture of fear and hope that the government under the Articles of Confederation was losing its grip on power. A small circle of Virginians decided to try one last time to augment the powers granted to the government by the Articles. Their call for a meeting to discuss trade regulation led, more quickly than they could have imagined in 1786, to a total reworking of the national government.

From Annapolis to Philadelphia

The Virginians, led by James Madison, convinced the congress to allow a meeting of delegates at Annapolis, Maryland, in September

1786, to try again to revise the trade regulation powers of the Articles. But only five states participated, and they rescheduled the meeting for Philadelphia in May 1787. The congress reluctantly endorsed the Philadelphia meeting and limited its scope to "the sole and express purpose of revising the Articles of Confederation." But at least one representative at the Annapolis meeting had more ambitious plans. Alexander Hamilton of New York hoped the Philadelphia meeting would do whatever was necessary to strengthen the federal government. Hamilton got his wish as the meeting soon turned into a constitutional convention.

Alexander Hamilton by character was suited for such bold steps. The illegitimate son of a poor mother in the West Indies, at age sixteen the bright lad greatly impressed an American trader, who sent him to New York City for a college education. Hamilton soon got swept up in the military enthusiasm of 1776 and by 1777 had joined George Washington's staff, serving at the general's side through much of the Revolution. After the war, he studied law, married into a New York merchant family, and sat in the Continental Congress for two years. Despite his stigmatized and impoverished childhood, the aspiring Hamilton identified with the elite classes and their fear of democratic disorder.

The fifty-five men who assembled at Philadelphia in May 1787 were generally those most concerned about weaknesses in the Articles of Confederation. Few attended who were opposed to revising the Articles. Patrick Henry, author of the Virginia Resolves in 1765 and more recently state governor, refused to go, saying he "smelled a rat." Rhode Island refused to send delegates. Two New York representatives left in dismay in the middle of the convention, leaving Hamilton as the sole New York delegate.

This gathering of white men included no **artisans** or day laborers or even farmers of middling wealth. Two-thirds of the delegates were lawyers. The majority had served in the confederation congress and knew its strengths and weaknesses; half had been officers in the Continental army. Seven men had been governors of their states and knew firsthand the frustrations of thwarted executive power. A few elder statesmen attended, such as Benjamin Franklin and George Washington, but on the whole, the delegates were young, like Madison and Hamilton.

The Virginia and New Jersey Plans

The convention worked in secrecy, so the men could freely explore alternatives without fear that their honest opinions would come back to haunt them. The Virginia delegation first laid out a fifteen-point plan for a complete restructuring of the government. This Virginia Plan

City Tavern

Philadelphia's City Tavern, built in 1773, became a favorite gathering place for members of the Continental Congress. Taverns provided important public meeting spaces for business and social functions; they were critical nodes on the information network of the day, the place to learn news from travelers, newspapers, or local gossip. John Adams called the City Tavern "the most genteel one in America." In the Long Room on the second floor, delegates toasted each other on the anniversary of the Declaration of Independence on July 4, 1777. The men who wrote the Constitution in the summer of 1787 took meals and drinks there. This engraving and others like it aided in the complete reconstruction of the tavern on its original site in the 1970s; today it is open to the public as a period restaurant, complete with staff in costume.

Rare Book Department, The Free Library of Philadelphia.

was a total repudiation of the principle of a confederation of states. Largely the work of Madison, the plan set out a three-branch government composed of a two-chamber legislature, a powerful executive, and a judiciary. It practically eliminated the voices of the smaller states by pegging representation in both houses of the congress to population. The theory was that government operated directly on people, not on states. Among the breathtaking powers assigned to the congress were the rights to veto state legislation and to coerce states militarily to obey national laws. To prevent the congress from having absolute power, the executive and judiciary could jointly veto its actions.

In mid-June, delegates from New Jersey, Connecticut, Delaware, and New Hampshire—all small states—unveiled an alternative proposal.

The Pennsylvania Statehouse

The constitutional convention assembled at the Pennsylvania statehouse to sweat out the summer of 1787. Despite the heat, the delegates nailed the windows shut to eliminate the chance of being heard by eavesdroppers, so intent were they on secrecy. The statehouse, built in the 1740s to house the colony's assembly, accommodated the Continental Congresses at various times in the 1770s and 1780s. The building is now called Independence Hall, in honor of the signing of the Declaration of Independence within its walls in 1776.

Historical Society of Pennsylvania.

The New Jersey Plan, as it was called, maintained the existing single-house congress of the Articles of Confederation in which each state had one vote. Acknowledging the need for an executive, it created a plural presidency to be shared by three men elected by the congress from among its membership. Where it sharply departed from the existing government was in the sweeping powers it gave to the congress: the right to tax, to regulate trade, and to use force on unruly state governments. In favoring national power over **states' rights**, it aligned itself with the Virginia Plan. But the New Jersey Plan retained the confederation principle that the national government was to be an assembly of states, not of people.

For two weeks, delegates debated the two plans, focusing on the key issue of representation. The small-state delegates conceded that one house in a two-house legislature could be apportioned by population, but they would never agree that both houses could be. Madison was equally vehement about bypassing representation by state, which he viewed as the fundamental flaw in the Articles.

The debate seemed deadlocked, and for a while the convention was "on the verge of dissolution, scarce held together by the strength of a hair," according to one delegate. Only in mid-July did the so-called Great Compromise break the stalemate and produce the basic structural features of the emerging United States Constitution. Proponents of the competing plans agreed on a bicameral legislature. Representation in the lower house, the House of Representatives, would be apportioned by population, and representation in the upper house, the Senate, would come from all the states equally. Instead of one vote per state in the upper house, as in the New Jersey Plan, the compromise provided two senators who voted independently.

Representation by population turned out to be an ambiguous concept once it was subjected to rigorous discussion. Who counted? Were slaves, for example, people or property? As people, they would add weight to the southern delegations in the House of Representatives, but as property they would add to the tax burdens of those states. What emerged was the compromise known as the three-fifths clause: All free persons plus "three-fifths of all other Persons" constituted the numerical base for the apportionment of representatives. Using "all other Persons" as a substitute for "slaves" indicates the discomfort delegates felt in acknowledging in the Constitution the existence of slavery. But though slavery was nowhere named, nonetheless it was recognized, guaranteed, and thereby perpetuated by the U.S. Constitution.

Democracy versus Republicanism

The delegates in Philadelphia made a distinction between *democracy* and *republicanism* new to American political vocabulary. Pure democracy was now taken to be a dangerous thing. As a Massachusetts delegate put it, "the evils we experience flow from the excess of democracy." The delegates still favored republican institutions, but they created a government that gave direct voice to the people only in the House and that granted a check on that voice to the Senate, a body of men elected not by direct popular vote but by the state legislatures. Senators served for six years, with no limit on reelection; they were protected from the whims of democratic majorities, and their long terms fostered experience and maturity in office.

Similarly, the presidency evolved into a powerful office out of the reach of direct democracy. The delegates devised an electoral college whose only function was to elect the president and vice president. Each state's legislature would choose the electors, whose number was the sum of representatives and senators for the state, an interesting melding of the two principles of representation. The president thus would owe his office not to the Congress, the states, or the people, but to a temporary assemblage of distinguished citizens who could vote their own judgment on the candidates.

The framers had developed a far more complex form of federal government than that provided by the Articles of Confederation. To curb the excesses of democracy, they devised a government with limits and checks on all three branches of government. They set forth a powerful president who could veto Congress, but they gave Congress power to override presidential vetoes. They set up a national judiciary to settle disputes between states and citizens of different states. They separated branches of government not only by functions and by reciprocal checks but by deliberately basing the election of each branch on different universes of voters—voting citizens (the House), state legis-

lators (the Senate), and the electoral college (the presidency).

The convention carefully listed the powers of Congress and of the president. The president could initiate policy, propose legislation, and veto acts of Congress; he could command the military and direct foreign policy; and he could appoint the entire judiciary, subject to Senate approval. Congress held the purse strings: the power to levy taxes, to regulate trade, and to coin money and control the currency. States were expressly forbidden to issue paper money. Two more powers of Congress—to "provide for the common defence and general Welfare" of the country and "to make all laws which shall be necessary and proper" for carrying out its powers—provided elastic language that came closest to Madison's wish to grant sweeping powers to the new government.

While no one was entirely satisfied with every line of the Constitution, only three dissenters refused to sign the document. The Constitution specified a mechanism for ratification that avoided the dilemma faced earlier by the confederation government: Nine states, not all thirteen, had to ratify it, and special ratifying conventions elected only for that purpose, not state legislatures, would make the crucial decision.

> **REVIEW** Why did the government proposed by the constitutional convention employ multiple checks on each branch?

Ratification of the Constitution

Had a popular vote been taken on the Constitution in the fall of 1787, it would probably have been rejected. In the three most populous states—Virginia, Massachusetts, and New York—substantial majorities opposed a powerful new national government. North Carolina and Rhode Island refused to call ratifying conventions. Seven of the eight remaining states were easy victories for the Constitution, but securing the approval of the ninth proved difficult. Pro-Constitution forces, called Federalists, had to strategize very shrewdly to defeat anti-Constitution forces, who were called Antifederalists.

The Federalists

Proponents of the Constitution moved into action swiftly. To silence the criticism that they had gone beyond their charge (which indeed they had), they sent the document to the congress. Congress withheld explicit approval but resolved to send the Constitution to the states for their consideration. The pro-Constitution forces shrewdly secured another advantage by calling themselves "Federalists." By all logic, this label was more suitable for the backers of the confederation concept, because the Latin root of the word *federal* means "league." Their opponents became known as "Antifederalists," a label that made them sound defensive and negative, lacking a program of their own.

To gain momentum, the Federalists targeted the states most likely to ratify quickly. Delaware provided unanimous ratification by early December, before the Antifederalists had even begun to campaign. Pennsylvania, New Jersey, and Georgia followed within a month (Map 8.2). Delaware and New Jersey were small states surrounded by more powerful neighbors; a government that would regulate trade and set taxes according to population was an attractive proposition. Georgia sought the protection that a stronger national government would afford against hostile Indians and Spanish Florida to the south.

Another three easy victories came in Connecticut, Maryland, and South Carolina. As in Pennsylvania, merchants, lawyers, and urban artisans in general favored the new Constitution, as did large landowners and slaveholders. This tendency for the established political elite to be Federalist enhanced the prospects of victory, for Federalists already had power disproportionate to their numbers. Antifederalists in these states tended to be rural, western, and noncommercial, men whose access to news was limited and whose participation in state government was tenuous.

Massachusetts was the only early state that gave the Federalists difficulty. The vote to select the ratification delegates decidedly favored the Antifederalists, whose strength lay in the western areas of the state, home to Shays's Rebellion. One rural delegate from Worcester County

voiced widely shared suspicions: "These lawyers and men of learning and money men that talk so finely, and gloss over matters so smoothly, to make us poor illiterate people swallow down the pill, expect to get into Congress themselves; they expect to be the managers of the Constitution and get all the power and all the money into their own hands, and then they will swallow up all us little folks." Nevertheless, the Antifederalist lead was slowly eroded by a vigorous newspaper campaign. In the end, the Federalists won by a very slim margin and only with promises that amendments to the Constitution would be taken up in the first Congress.

By May 1788, eight states had ratified; only one more was needed. North Carolina and Rhode Island were hopeless for the Federalist cause, and New Hampshire seemed nearly as bleak. More worrisome was the failure to win over the largest and most important states, Virginia and New York.

The Antifederalists

Antifederalists were a composite group, united mainly in their desire to block the Constitution. Although much Antifederalist strength came from backcountry areas long suspicious of eastern elites, many Antifederalist leaders came from the same social background as Federalist leaders; economic class alone did not differentiate them. Antifederalism also drew strength in states already on sure economic footing, like New York, that could afford to remain independent. Probably the biggest appeal of antifederalism lay in the long-nurtured fear that distant power might infringe on people's liberties. The language of the earlier revolutionary movement was not easily forgotten.

For example, in the proposed House of Representatives, the only directly democratic element of the Constitution, one member represented some 30,000 people. How could that member really know or communicate with his whole constituency, the Antifederalists wondered. In contrast, one wrote, "The members of our state legislatures are annually elected—they are subject to instructions—they are chosen within small circles—they are sent but a small distance from their respective homes. Their conduct is constantly known to their constituents. They frequently see, and are seen, by the men whose servants they are."

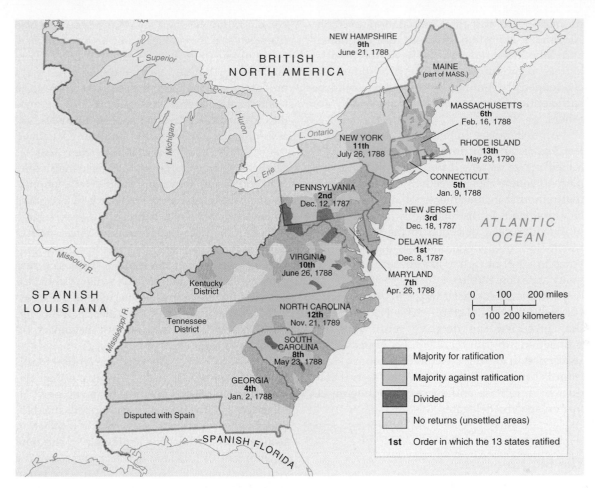

NEW HAMPSHIRE
9th
June 21, 1788

BRITISH
NORTH AMERICA

MAINE
(part of MASS.)

MASSACHUSETTS
6th
Feb. 16, 1788

NEW YORK
11th
July 26, 1788

RHODE ISLAND
13th
May 29, 1790

CONNECTICUT
5th
Jan. 9, 1788

PENNSYLVANIA
2nd
Dec. 12, 1787

NEW JERSEY
3rd
Dec. 18, 1787

*ATLANTIC
OCEAN*

DELAWARE
1st
Dec. 8, 1787

VIRGINIA
10th
June 26, 1788

MARYLAND
7th
Apr. 26, 1788

Kentucky
District

SPANISH
LOUISIANA

Tennessee
District

NORTH CAROLINA
12th
Nov. 21, 1789

SOUTH
CAROLINA
8th
May 23, 1788

GEORGIA
4th
Jan. 2, 1788

Disputed with Spain

SPANISH FLORIDA

0   100   200 miles

0   100 200 kilometers

Majority for ratification

Majority against ratification

Divided

No returns (unsettled areas)

1st   Order in which the 13 states ratified

MAP 8.2   Ratification of the Constitution, 1788–1790
Populated areas cast votes for delegates to state ratification conventions. This map shows Antifederalist strength generally concentrated in backcountry, noncoastal, and nonurban areas, but with significant exceptions (for example, Rhode Island).

READING THE MAP: Where was Federalist opinion concentrated? How did the distribution of Federalist and Antifederalist sentiment affect the order of state ratifications of the Constitution?
CONNECTIONS: What objections did Antifederalists have to the new United States Constitution? How did their locations affect their view of the Federalist argument?

FOR MORE HELP ANALYZING THIS MAP, see the map activity for this chapter in the Online Study Guide at **bedfordstmartins.com/roarkcompact.**

The Antifederalists also worried that elected representatives would always be members of the elite. Such men "will be ignorant of the sentiments of the middling and much more of the lower class of citizens, strangers to their ability, unacquainted with their wants, difficulties, and distress," worried a Maryland man. None of this would be a problem under a confederation system, according to the Antifederalists, because real power would continue to reside in the state governments.

The Federalists generally agreed that the elite would be favored for election to the House of Representatives, not to mention the Senate and the presidency. That was precisely what they hoped. Federalists wanted power to flow to intelligent, virtuous, public-spirited leaders like themselves. They did not envision a government constituted of every class of people. "Fools and knaves have voice enough in government already," argued a New York Federalist, without being guaranteed representation in proportion to the total population of fools. Alexander Hamilton claimed that mechanics and laborers preferred to have their social betters represent them. The Antifederalists challenged the notion that any class could be sufficiently selfless to rule disinterestedly for others.

Antifederalists fretted over many specific features of the Constitution. It prohibited state-issued paper money. It regulated the time and place of congressional elections, leading to fears that only one inconvenient polling place might be authorized, to disfranchise rural voters. The most widespread objection to the Constitution was its lack of any guarantees of individual liberties in a bill of rights, like those contained in many state constitutions.

Despite Federalist campaigns in the large states, it was a small state—New Hampshire—that provided the decisive ninth vote for ratification, on June 21, 1788. Federalists there succeeded in getting the convention postponed from February to June and in the interim conducted an intense and successful lobbying effort on specific delegates.

The Big Holdouts: Virginia and New York

Four states still remained outside the new union, and a glance at a map demonstrated the necessity of pressing the Federalist case in the two largest, Virginia and New York. Though Virginia was home to Madison and Washington, an influential Antifederalist group led by Patrick Henry and George Mason made the outcome uncertain. The Federalists finally but barely won ratification by proposing twenty specific amendments that the new government would promise to consider.

New York voters tilted toward Antifederalism out of a sense that a state so large and powerful need not relinquish so much authority to the new federal government. But New York was also home to some of the most persuasive Federalists. Starting in October 1787, Alexander Hamilton collaborated with James Madison and

New York lawyer John Jay on a series of eighty-five essays on the political philosophy of the new Constitution, published in New York newspapers and later republished as *The Federalist*. The essays brilliantly set out the failures of the Articles of Confederation and offered an analysis of the complex nature of federalism. In one of the most compelling essays, number 10, Madison challenged the Antifederalists' heartfelt conviction that republican government had to be small-scale. Madison argued that a large and diverse population was itself a guarantee of liberty. In a national government, no single faction could ever be large enough to subvert the freedom of other groups. "Extend the sphere, and you take in a greater variety of parties and interests; you make it less probable that a majority of the whole will have a common motive to invade the rights of other citizens," Madison asserted. He called it "a republican remedy for the diseases most incident to republican government."

At New York's ratifying convention, Antifederalists predominated, but impassioned debate and lobbying—plus the dramatic news of Virginia's ratification—finally tipped the balance to the Federalists. New York's ratification assured the solidity and legitimacy of the new government. It took another year and a half for Antifederalists in North Carolina to come around. Fiercely independent Rhode Island held out until May 1790, and even then it ratified by only a two-vote margin.

In less than twelve months, the U.S. Constitution was both written and ratified. (See appendix I, page A-3.) An amazingly short time by twentieth-century standards, it is even more remarkable for the late eighteenth century, with its horse-powered transportation and hand-printed communications. The Federalists had faced a formidable task, but by building momentum and assuring consideration of a **Bill of Rights**, they did indeed carry the day.

REVIEW   Why did Antifederalists oppose the Constitution?

Conclusion: The "Republican Remedy"

Thus ended one of the most intellectually tumultuous and creative decades in American history. American leaders experimented with ideas and drew up plans to embody their evolving and conflicting notions of how a society and a government ought to be formulated. There was widespread agreement that government should derive its power and authority from the people, but there was fierce disagreement over the degree of democracy—the amount of direct control of government by the people—that would be workable in American society.

The decade began in 1776 with a confederation government that could barely be ratified because of its requirement of unanimity, but there was no reaching unanimity on the western lands, on the impost amendment, or on the proper way to respond to unfair taxation in a republican state. The new Constitution offered a different approach to these problems by loosening the grip of impossible unanimity and by embracing the ideas of a heterogeneous public life and a carefully balanced government that together would prevent any one part of the public from tyrannizing another. The genius of James Madison was to anticipate that diversity of opinion was not only an unavoidable reality but a hidden strength of the new society beginning to take shape. This is what he meant in his tenth *Federalist* essay when he spoke of the "republican remedy" for the troubles most likely to befall a government where the people are the source of authority.

Despite Madison's optimism, political differences remained keen and worrisome to many. The Federalists still hoped for a society in which leaders of exceptional wisdom would discern the best path for public policy. They looked backward to a society of hierarchy, rank, and benevolent rule by an aristocracy of talent, but they created a government with forward-looking **checks and balances** as a guard against corruption, which they figured would most likely emanate from the people. The Antifederalists also looked backward, but to an old order of small-scale direct democracy and local control, where virtuous people kept a close eye on potentially corruptible rulers. Antifederalists feared a national government led by distant, self-interested leaders who needed to be held in check. In the 1790s, these two conceptions of republicanism and of leadership would be tested in real life.

Suggestions for Further Reading

Lance Banning, *The Sacred Fire of Liberty: James Madison and the Founding of the Federal Republic* (1995). An eloquent biography detailing Madison's passionate involvement in the politics of the 1780s.

Saul Cornell, *The Other Founders: Anti-Federalism and the Dissenting Tradition in America, 1788–1828* (1999). Nuances of Antifederalism illuminated by the fascinating histories of those who opposed the Constitution.

Joanne Pope Melish, *Disowning Slavery: Gradual Emancipation and "Race" in New England, 1780–1860* (1998). A fine-grained study of gradual emancipation in New England.

Jack N. Rakove, *Original Meanings: Politics and Ideas in the Making of the Constitution* (1996). A prize-winning book on the political theory of the framers in Philadelphia.

Leonard L. Richards, *Shays's Rebellion: The American Revolution's Final Battle* (2002). A new interpretation of the Massachusetts insurgency based on a social profile of the arrested men.

Rosemarie Zagarri, *A Woman's Dilemma: Mercy Otis Warren and the American Revolution* (1995). A short, highly readable account of the life of the foremost political woman of the 1780s.

▶ **For more books about topics in this chapter,** see the Online Study Guide at bedfordstmartins.com/roarkcompact.

▶ **For additional firsthand accounts of this period,** see Chapter 8 in Michael Johnson, ed., *Reading the American Past,* Third Edition.

▶ **For Web sites and documents related to topics and places in this chapter,** see "HistoryLinks," "DocLinks," and "PlaceLinks" at bedfordstmartins.com/roarkcompact.

REVIEWING THE CHAPTER

Follow these steps to review and strengthen your understanding of the chapter.

STEP 1: *Study the **Key Terms** and **Timeline** to identify the significance of each item listed.*

STEP 2: *Answer the **Review Questions**, drawing on key terms and dates to support your answers.*

STEP 3: *Drawing on the Key Terms, Timeline, and Review Questions, answer the broader **Making Connections** questions.*

KEY TERMS

Who

James Madison (p. 185)
Abigail Adams (p. 190)
John Adams (p. 191)
George Mason (p. 191)
Paul and John Cuffe (p. 192)
Quok Walker (p. 192)
Robert Morris (p. 196)
Iroquois (p. 198)
Delaware (p. 198)
Huron (p. 198)
Miami (p. 198)
Daniel Shays (p. 199)
James Bowdoin (p. 199)
Federalists (p. 204)
Antifederalists (p. 204)

What

Virginia Convention (p. 185)
Continental Congress (p. 186)
Articles of Confederation (p. 187)
republicanism (p. 189)
bills of rights (p. 189)
manumission law (p. 192)
gradual emancipation (p. 193)
impost (p. 196)
Bank of North America (p. 196)
Northwest Territory (p. 197)
Ordinance of 1784 (p. 197)
Ordinance of 1785 (p. 197)
Fort Stanwix (p. 198)
Fort McIntosh (p. 198)
Northwest Ordinance (p. 198)

Disqualification Act (p. 200)
U.S. Constitution (p. 200)
constitutional convention (p. 201)
Virginia Plan (p. 201)
New Jersey Plan (p. 202)
Great Compromise (p. 202)
three-fifths clause (p. 202)
The Federalist (p. 206)

TIMELINE

NOTE: Events are depicted chronologically, but the passage of time is not to exact scale.

1775 • Second Continental Congress meets.

   1776 • Virginia adopts state bill of rights.

      1777 • Articles of Confederation sent to states.

         1778 • State constitutions completed.

           1780 • Pennsylvania institutes gradual emancipation.

               • Massachusetts extends suffrage to taxpaying free blacks.

              1781 • Articles of Confederation ratified.

                  • Creation of executive departments.

                  • Bank of North America chartered.

                  • Slave Quok Walker successfully sues for freedom.

                1782 • Virginia relaxes state manumission law.

                  1783 • Treaty of Paris signed, ending the Revolutionary War.

                    1784 • Gradual emancipation laws passed in Rhode Island and Connecticut.

                      • Treaty of Fort Stanwix.

REVIEW QUESTIONS

1. Why was the confederation government's authority so limited? (pp. 186–89)

2. How did states determine who would be allowed to vote? (pp. 189–93)

3. Why did farmers in western Massachusetts revolt against the state legislature? (pp. 193–200)

4. Why did the government proposed by the constitutional convention employ multiple checks on each branch? (pp. 200–03)

5. Why did Antifederalists oppose the Constitution? (pp. 203–06)

MAKING CONNECTIONS

1. Leaders in the new nation held that voting should be restricted to citizens who possessed independence of mind. Why? What did they mean by independence of mind? How did this principle limit voters in the early republic?

2. Why did many Revolutionary leaders shaping the government of the new nation begin to find the principle of democracy troubling? How did they attempt to balance democracy with other concerns in the new government?

3. Twenty-first-century Americans see a profound tension between the revolutionary ideals of liberty and equality, and the persistence of American slavery. Did Americans in the late eighteenth century see a tension? In your answer, be sure to discuss factors that might have shaped varied responses, such as region, race, and class.

4. The Northwest Territory was the confederation's greatest asset. Discuss the proposals to manage settlement of the new territory. How did they shape the nation's expansion? Which proposals succeeded and which failed?

▶ FOR PRACTICE QUIZZES, A CUSTOMIZED STUDY PLAN, AND OTHER STUDY TOOLS, see the Online Study Guide at bedfordstmartins.com/roarkcompact.

1786 • Virginia adopts Statute of Religious Freedom.
 • Shays's Rebellion begins.
 1787 • Shays's Rebellion crushed.
 • Northwest Ordinance.
 • Delaware provides manumission law.
 • Constitutional convention meets in Philadelphia.
 1788 • U.S. Constitution ratified.
 1790 • Maryland provides manumission law.
 1799 • Gradual emancipation law passed in New York.
 1804 • Gradual emancipation law passed in New Jersey.

WASHINGTON STANDS OUTSIDE OF TIME

A French clockmaker and artist produced this piece of Washington memorabilia after the death of the president. Washington's trim figure, rendered in gilt bronze, sports a spiffy uniform complete with fringed epaulets. One gloved hand rests on a sword; the other holds a rolled parchment, offered up in front of an eagle, the symbol of America's strength. Below the eagle a familiar motto is inscribed: "E Pluribus Unum" — "Out of many, one" — a reference to the political unity of the sovereign states. Below the clock is a motto about Washington that was first uttered in his funeral eulogy: "First in War, First in Peace, and First in the Hearts of his Countrymen." Death elevated Washington to celebrity status, and Americans immortalized him in many souvenirs.

The Warner Collection of Gulf States Paper Corporation.

9

The New Nation Takes Form

1789–1800

ALEXANDER HAMILTON, the first secretary of the United States Treasury, faced a challenge in June 1790. The new Constitution, with its power to raise taxes, explicitly promised to honor the Revolutionary War debt, and it fell to Hamilton to propose an implementation plan. Hamilton's controversial solution was to roll over the nearly worthless federal debt certificates of the 1770s and 1780s into new certificates having the same dollar amount with interest payments guaranteed by the new government. Hamilton also proposed adding to the federal debt all the states' still-outstanding debts. This large-scale debt consolidation (called *assumption* at the time) struck critics as expensive, unnecessary, unfair, and, worse, a power grab by the new government to subordinate the states. Hamilton's bold plan became deadlocked in Congress.

Hamilton's chief opponent on the debt question was James Madison, now a member of the first federal Congress sitting in New York City. Together, these former allies had written *The Federalist* essays during ratification, brilliantly creating the intellectual underpinnings of federalism. But the trust between them had eroded. Madison feared that Virginians, who had responsibly paid down their state's debt, would be taxed to pay the debts of other states. He also objected to the windfall profits to be realized by speculators who bought old debt certificates at a fraction of their face value. Greedy speculators, Madison claimed, "are still exploring the interior & distant parts of the Union in order to take advantage of the holders." Through strenuous politicking, Madison had stalled out Hamilton's plan.

At this first crisis point—one of many to come in the 1790s—a solution arrived thanks to the hospitality of Thomas Jefferson, the secretary of state. Deeply worried about the stability of the Union, Jefferson invited Hamilton and Madison to dinner at his New York residence. Over good food and candlelight, Hamilton secured the reluctant Madison's promise to restrain his opposition. In return, Hamilton pledged to back efforts to locate the nation's new capital city in the South, along the Potomac River, an outcome that was sure to please Virginians. In early July, Congress voted for the Potomac site, and in late July, Congress passed the debt package, assumption and all.

This tense political transaction both revealed and perpetuated the fragility of the new government in its first years of existence. Jefferson and Madison feared that Hamilton's funding plan would not only reward the wrong sort of men but dangerously bind them by financial ties to the government. Jefferson

***Alexander Hamilton,* by John Trumbull**
Hamilton was brash, confident, handsome, and audacious. Through force of personality, he overcame what was for his era and culture a double obstacle in life, being born in obscurity and bastardy on the small West Indies island of Nevis. His mother died when he was thirteen, and five years later he made his way to the mainland colony of New York and managed to charm his way into elite circles. He attended college, served in the Continental army, earned George Washington's uncommon admiration, and helped to write and ratify the Constitution. Along the way, he married Betsey Schuyler, whose father was one of the richest men in New York. He posed for this portrait in 1792, at the age of thirty-seven and at the height of his power.
Yale University Art Gallery.

later wrote that the deal "was unjust, and was acquiesced in merely from a fear of disunion, while our government was still in its infant state." They feared "disunion" when fellow Virginians compared Hamilton's assumption plan to the parlia-

mentary taxation that had sparked the Revolution. Their solution was to do what it took to get the capital city situated in their own region, the better to watch and influence it.

From 1790 to 1800, the "Founding Fathers" of the Revolution and Constitution era became competitors and even bitter rivals. Personalities clashed: Hamilton's charm no longer worked with Madison, and it had never worked with John Adams, the new vice president, who privately called Hamilton "the bastard brat of a Scotch pedlar" motivated by "disappointed Ambition and unbridled malice and revenge." Abigail Adams thought Hamilton a second Napoleon Bonaparte, an uncomplimentary reference to the belligerent leader of war-torn France. Years later, when asked why he deserted Hamilton, Madison replied, "Colonel Hamilton deserted me."

Rivalry also sprang from serious differences in political philosophy. Hamilton assumed that government was safest when in the hands of "the rich, the wise, and the good"—in other words, America's commercial elite. For Hamilton, economic and political power naturally belonged together, creating an energetic force for economic growth. In contrast, Jefferson and Madison trusted most those whose livelihood was tied to the land. Agrarian values ran deep with them, and they were suspicious of get-rich-quick speculators and financiers.

And finally, the 1780s Federalist alliance broke up over differing views of and policies toward European powers. Hamilton was an unabashed admirer of everything British, while Jefferson was enchanted by France, where he had lived in the 1780s. These loyalties governed foreign relations in the late 1790s, when the United States was in a war or near war with both of these overseas rivals.

The personal and political antagonisms of this first generation of American leaders left their marks on the young country. No one was prepared for the intense and passionate polarization that emerged over economic and foreign policy. The disagreements were articulated around particular events and policies: taxation and the public debt, a new farmers' rebellion in a western region, policies favoring commercial development, a treaty with England, a rebellion in Haiti, and a quasi-war with France that led to severe strictures on ideas of sedition and free speech. But at their heart, these disagreements arose out of opposing ideological stances on the value of **democracy**, the nature of leadership, and the limits of federal power. About the only major policy development that did not replicate or intensify these antagonisms among political leaders was Indian policy in the new republic.

By 1800, the oppositional politics ripening between Hamiltonian and Jeffersonian politicians would begin to crystallize into political parties, the Federalists and the Republicans. To the men of that day, this appeared to be an unhappy development.

The Search for Stability

Political parties were not part of the Constitution's plan for government. James Madison had argued in *The Federalist* in 1788 that a superior feature of the national government was precisely that the country's extensive size would prevent small, selfish factions from becoming dangerously dominant. Parties were thought of as destructive political forces, and their development was unanticipated and unwelcome. Only in future decades would American politicians come to realize that parties serve to organize conflict, legitimize disagreement, and mediate among competing political strategies.

Leaders in the early 1790s instead sought ways to heal divisions of the 1780s and maximize unity. Widespread veneration for President Washington promoted political stability. People trusted him to exercise the untested and perhaps elastic powers of the presidency. Congress quickly agreed on a **Bill of Rights**, which answered concerns of many Antifederalists. And the private virtue of women was mobilized to bolster the public virtue of male citizens; **republicanism** was forcing a rethinking of women's relation to the state.

Washington Inaugurates the Government

The election of George Washington in February 1789 was quick work, the tallying of the unanimous votes by the electoral college a mere formality. Everyone's first choice, Washington, perfectly embodied the republican ideal of disinterested, public-spirited leadership. Indeed, he cultivated that image through astute ceremonies such as the dramatic surrender of his sword to the Continental Congress at the end of the war, symbolizing the subservience of military power to the law.

Once in office, Washington calculated his moves, knowing that every step set a precedent and any misstep could be dangerous for the fragile government. How kingly should a president be? Congress debated a range of titles, such as "His Highness, the President of the United States of America and Protector of Their Liberties" and "His Majesty, the President"; Washington was known to favor "His High Mightiness." But in the end, republican simplicity prevailed. The final title was simply "President of the United States of America," and the established form of address became "Mr. President," a subdued yet dignified title in a society where only property-owning adult white males could presume to be called "Mister."

Washington's genius in establishing the presidency lay in his capacity for implanting his own reputation for integrity into the office itself.

Liverpool Souvenir Pitcher, 1789
A British pottery manufacturer produced this commemorative pitcher for the American market to capture sales at the time of George Washington's inauguration in 1789. The design shows Liberty as a woman dressed in a golden gown, her liberty cap on a pole, holding a laurel wreath (signifying classical honors) over Washington's head. Fifteen labeled links encircle the scene, representing the states, although in 1789, Rhode Island and North Carolina had not yet ratified the Constitution, and two more—Vermont and Kentucky—were merely anticipated states. The Liverpool manufacturer was looking ahead. Commemorative pitchers, jugs, and mugs were commonplace articles of consumer culture produced in Britain for specialized markets.
Smithsonian Institution, Washington, D.C.

He was not a brilliant thinker or a shrewd political strategist. He was not even a particularly congenial man. In the political language of the day, he was *virtuous*, meaning that he took pains to elevate the public good over private interest and projected honesty and honor over ambition. He remained aloof, resolute, and dignified, to the point of appearing wooden at times. He encouraged pomp and ceremony to create respect for the office, traveling with six horses to pull his coach, hosting formal balls, and surrounding himself with uniformed servants. He even held weekly levees, as European monarchs did, hourlong audiences granted to distinguished visitors (and including women), at which Washington appeared attired in black velvet, with a feathered hat and a polished sword. The president and his guests bowed, avoiding the egalitarian familiarity of handshakes. But he always managed, perhaps just barely, to avoid the extreme of royal splendor.

Washington chose talented and experienced men to preside over the newly created departments of war, treasury, and state. Yet deep philosophical differences separated key appointees. For the Department of War, Washington chose General Henry Knox, former secretary of war in the confederation government. For the Treasury—an especially tough job in view of revenue conflicts during the confederation (see chapter 8)—the president picked Alexander Hamilton, known for his general brilliance and financial astuteness. To lead the Department of State, the foreign policy arm of the executive branch, Washington chose Thomas Jefferson, a master of diplomatic relations and the current minister to France. For attorney general, Washington picked Edmund Randolph, a Virginian who had attended the Constitutional Convention but had turned Antifederalist during ratification. For chief justice of the Supreme Court, Washington designated John Jay, a New York lawyer who, along with Madison and Hamilton, had vigorously defended the Constitution in *The Federalist*.

Soon Washington began to hold regular meetings with these men, thereby establishing the precedent of a presidential cabinet. (Vice President John Adams was not included; his only official duty, to preside over the Senate, he found "a punishment" because he could not participate in legislative debates. To his wife he complained, "My country has in its wisdom contrived for me the most insignificant office.") No one anticipated that two decades of party turbu-

lence would emerge from the brilliant but explosive mix of Washington's first cabinet.

The Bill of Rights

An early order of business in the First Congress was the passage of a Bill of Rights. Seven states had ratified the Constitution on the condition that guarantees of individual liberties and limitations to federal power be swiftly incorporated. Federalists of 1787 had thought an enumeration of rights unnecessary, but in 1789 Congressman James Madison understood that healing the divisions of the 1780s was of prime importance. "It will be a desirable thing to extinguish from the bosom of every member of the community, any apprehensions that there are those among his countrymen who wish to deprive them of the liberty for which they valiantly fought and honorably bled."

Madison pulled much of his wording of rights directly from various state constitutions with bills of rights. He enumerated guarantees of freedom of speech, press, and religion, the right to petition and assemble, the right to be free from unwarranted searches and seizures. One amendment asserted the right to keep and bear arms in support of a "well-regulated militia," to which Madison added, "but no person religiously scrupulous of bearing arms, shall be compelled to render military service in person." That provision for what a later century would call "conscientious objector" status failed to gain acceptance in Congress.

In September 1789, Congress approved a set of twelve amendments and sent them to the states for approval; ten were eventually ratified. Amendments One through Eight dealt with individual liberties, and Nine and Ten concerned the boundary between federal and state authority. (See the amendments to the U.S. Constitution in appendix I, page A-8.) One proposal that failed of passage suggested a formula for finetuning the ratio of representation as population grew; the other required that any congressional pay raise voted in would not take effect until after the next election (not until 1992 did this amendment—the Twenty-seventh—pass). The process of state ratification took another two years, but there was no serious doubt about the outcome.

Still, not everyone was entirely satisfied. State ratifying conventions had submitted some eighty proposed amendments. Congress never considered proposals to change structural features of the new government, and Madison had no intention of reopening debates about the length of the president's term or the power to levy excise taxes.

Significantly, no one complained about one striking omission in the Bill of Rights: the right to vote. Only much later was voting seen as a fundamental **liberty** requiring protection by constitutional amendment—indeed, by four amendments. The Constitution deliberately left the definition of voters to the states, because of the existing wide variation in local voting practices, most based on property qualifications but some touching on religion and, in one unusual case, New Jersey, on sex and race (see chapter 8, page 190).

The Republican Wife and Mother

The exclusion of women from political activity did not mean they had no civic role or responsibility. A flood of periodical articles in the 1790s by both male and female writers reevaluated courtship, marriage, and motherhood in light of republican ideals. Tyrannical power in the ruler, whether king or husband, was now declared a thing of the past. Affection, not duty, bound wives to their husbands and citizens to their government. In republican marriages, the writers claimed, women had the capacity to reform the morals and manners of men. One male author promised women that "the solidity and stability of the liberties of your country rest with you; since Liberty is never sure, 'till Virtue reigns triumphant.... While you thus keep our country virtuous, you maintain its independence."

Until the 1790s, public virtue was strictly a masculine quality. But another sort of virtue loomed in importance: sexual chastity, a private asset prized as a feminine quality. Essayists of the 1790s explicitly advised young women to use sexual virtue to increase public virtue in men. "Love and courtship...invest a lady with more authority than in any other situation that falls to the lot of human beings," one male essayist proclaimed. If women spurned selfish suitors, they could promote good morals more than any social institution could, essayists promised.

Republican ideals also cast motherhood in a new light. Throughout the 1790s, advocates for female education, still a controversial proposition, argued that education would produce better mothers, who in turn would produce better

Republican Womanhood: Judith Sargent Murray
The twenty-one-year-old in this portrait became known eighteen years later as America's foremost public spokeswoman for the idea of woman's equality to man. Judith Sargent Murray frequently wrote essays for *Massachusetts Magazine* under the pen name "Constantia." In "On the Equality of the Sexes," published in 1790, she confidently asserted that women had "natural powers" of mind fully the equal of men's. Murray, the wife of a Universalist minister, also wrote plays that were performed on the Boston stage. In 1798 she published her collected "Constantia" essays in a book titled *The Gleaner;* George Washington and John Adams each bought a copy. Her indexed letter book contains copies of nearly two thousand letters that she wrote during her lifetime.
John Singleton Copley, *Portrait of Mrs. John Stevens* (Judith Sargent, later Mrs. John Murray), 1770–1772, oil on canvas, 50 × 40 inches, Terra Foundation for the Arts, Daniel J. Terra Art Acquisition Endowment Fund, 2000.6; photograph courtesy of Terra Foundation for the Arts, Chicago.

citizens. Benjamin Rush, a Pennsylvania physician and educator, called for female education because "our ladies should be qualified...in instructing their sons in the principles of liberty and government." A series of published essays by Judith Sargent Murray of Massachusetts favored education that would remake women into self-confident, rational beings, poised to become the equals of men. But even Murray had to dress her advanced ideas in the cloak of republican motherhood, justifying female education in the context of family duty.

Although women's obligations as wives and mothers were now infused with political meaning, traditional gender relations remained unaltered. (For the relatively few American voices that raised questions about what rights women might have, see "Beyond America's Borders," page 218.) The analogy between marriage and civil society worked precisely because of the self-subordination inherent in the term *virtue*. Men should put the public good first, before selfish desires, just as women must put their husbands and families first, before themselves. Women might gain literacy and knowledge, but only in the service of improved domestic duty. In Federalist America, wives and citizens alike should feel affection for their rulers; neither should ever rebel.

> **REVIEW**   How did political leaders in the 1790s attempt to overcome the divisions of the 1780s?

Hamilton's Economic Policies

The new government had the lucky break to be launched in flush economic times. Compared to the severe financial instability of the 1780s, the 1790s brimmed with opportunity and prosperity, as seen in increased agricultural trade, transportation, and banking improvements. In 1790, the federal government moved from New York City to Philadelphia, a more central location with a substantial mercantile class. There, Alexander Hamilton, secretary of the treasury, embarked on his innovative and controversial plan to solidify the government's economic base.

Agriculture, Transportation, and Banking

Dramatic increases in international grain prices motivated American farmers to boost agricultural production for the export trade. Europe's rising population needed grain, and the French Revolutionary and Napoleonic Wars that engulfed Europe for a dozen years after 1793 severely compromised production there. From the Connecticut River valley to the Chesapeake, farmers planted more wheat,

Major Roads in the 1790s

generating new jobs for millers, coopers, dockworkers, and ship and wagon builders.

Cotton production also underwent a boom, spurred by market demand and a mechanical invention. Limited amounts of smooth-seed cotton had long been grown in the coastal areas of the South, but this variety of cotton did not prosper in the drier, inland regions. Green-seed cotton grew well inland, but its rough seeds stuck to the cotton fibers and were difficult to remove. In 1793, Yale graduate Eli Whitney visited Georgia and devised a machine called a gin that separated out the seeds. Cotton planting soared, the cleaned cotton shipped to English factories to be made into textiles.

A surge of road building stimulated the economy. Before 1790, a series of bumpy Post Roads connected the miles from Maine to Georgia, but with the establishment of the U.S. Post Office in 1792, six times as many miles of road were quickly constructed to facilitate the transport of mail. Privately chartered companies also built roads; the first toll road in the nation was the Lancaster Turnpike of 1794, connecting Philadelphia with Lancaster, Pennsylvania. Another turnpike linked Boston with Albany, New York. Farther inland, a major road extended southwest down the Shenandoah Valley, while another joined Richmond, Virginia, with the Tennessee towns of Knoxville and Nashville.

By 1800, a dense network of dirt, gravel, or plank roadways connected cities and towns in southern New England and the Middle Atlantic states, spurring commercial stage companies to regularize and speed up passenger traffic. A trip from New York to Boston took four days; from New York to Philadelphia, less than two (Map 9.1). In 1790, Boston had only three stagecoach companies; by 1800 there were twenty-four. Transport of goods by road was still expensive per mile compared to water transport on navigable rivers or along the coast, but at least it was possible.

A third development signaling economic resurgence was the growth of commercial bank-

MAP 9.1 Travel Times from New York City in 1800

Notice that travel out of New York extends over a much greater distance in the first week than in subsequent weeks. River corridors in the West and East speeded up travel—but only if one were going downriver. Also notice that travel by sea (north and south along the coast) was much faster than land travel.

READING THE MAP: Compare this map to the map of "Major Roads in the 1790s" (page 216) and to Map 9.2. What physical and cultural elements account for the slower travel times west of Pittsburgh?

CONNECTIONS: Why did Americans in the 1790s become so interested in traveling long distances? How did travel times affect the American economy?

FOR MORE HELP ANALYZING THIS MAP, see the map activity for this chapter in the Online Study Guide at bedfordstmartins.com/roarkcompact.

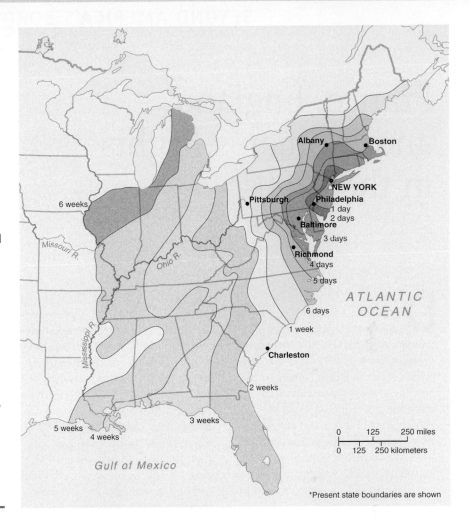

*Present state boundaries are shown

ing. During the 1790s, the number of banks nationwide multiplied tenfold, from three to twenty-nine in 1800. Banks drew in money chiefly through the sale of stock. They then made loans in the form of banknotes, paper currency backed by the gold and silver that stockholders paid in. Because banks issued two or three times as much money in banknotes as they held in **hard money**, they were creating new money for the economy.

The Public Debt and Taxes

The upturn in the economy suggested that the government might soon repay its wartime debts, amounting to some $52 million owed to foreign and domestic creditors. But Hamilton had a different plan. He issued a *Report on Public Credit* in January 1790, recommending that the debt be funded—but not repaid immediately—at full value. This meant that old certificates of debt would be rolled over into new bonds, which would earn interest until they were retired several years later. There would still be a public debt, but it would be secure, supported by citizens' presumed confidence in the new government. The bonds would circulate, injecting new valuable money into the economy. "A national debt if not excessive will be to us a national blessing; it will be a powerfull cement of our union," Hamilton wrote to a financier.

A large part of the old debt had been bought up cheaply by speculators in the late 1780s. (Hamilton himself held no certificates, but his father-in-law had certificates with a face value of $60,000.) These investors would have a direct financial stake in the new government, support that Hamilton regarded as essential to the country's stability. They would also own some $40 million in secured bonds, ready for new investment.

This funding plan was controversial, but Hamilton further proposed adding to the federal debt another $25 million that some state governments still owed to individuals. During the war, all the states had obtained supplies by issuing IOUs to farmers, merchants, and moneylenders. Some states, such as Virginia and New

France, England, and Woman's Rights in the 1790s

During the 1770s and 1780s in America, only rarely did anyone wonder about rights for women. Abigail Adams's letter to husband John in 1776, asking him to "remember the ladies" when writing new laws, stayed a private document for a century. Boycotts by Daughters of Liberty did not challenge gender hierarchy, nor did New Jersey's handful of women voters. Simply replacing a monarchy with a republic did not, in America, lead to an immediate or substantial challenge to women's subordinate status. It was influence from abroad, not at home, that initially sparked Americans' ideas about women's place in society.

In France between 1789 and 1793, the revolution against monarchy enlarged ideas about citizenship and led some women to argue for the concept of the *citoyenne*, the female citizen. Women's political clubs such as the Society of Republican Revolutionary Women in Paris sent petitions and gave speeches to the National Assembly, demanding education, voting rights, and a curbing of the paternal and marital powers of men over women. In 1791, Frenchwoman Olympe de Gouges rewrote the male revolutionaries' document

The Rights of Man into *The Rights of Woman,* asserting that "All women are born free and remain equal to men in rights." Another prominent woman, Théroigne de Méricourt, held a feminist salon, marched around Paris in masculine riding attire, and took part in an attack on a palace. Her vision went beyond political rights to the social customs that dictated women's subordination: "It is time for women to break out of the shameful incompetence in which men's ignorance, pride, and injustice have so long held us captive."

While voting rights for French women never passed in that era, the male National Assembly reformed French civil and family law in the early 1790s. Marriage was removed from the control of the church, divorce was legalized, and the age of majority for women was lowered. A far-reaching advance in inheritance law required division of a patriarch's estate among all his children, regardless of age, sex, and even legitimacy. Henceforth daughters could inherit along with sons; no longer did a woman from a family of means need to marry money—or indeed, to marry at all. In contrast, most American states imported traditional English family

law virtually unchanged into their lawbooks.

French **feminism** traveled across the channel to England and directly inspired a talented woman named Mary Wollstonecraft. In 1792 she published *A Vindication of the Rights of Woman,* arguing for the intellectual equality of the sexes, economic independence for women, and participation in representative government. Most radically, she called marriage legalized prostitution.

Wollstonecraft's book created a sensation in America. Excerpts appeared immediately in Philadelphia and Boston periodicals, bookstores stocked the London edition, and by 1795 there were three American reprints. Some women readers were cautious. A sixty-year-old Philadelphian, Elizabeth Drinker, reflected in her diary that "In very many of her sentiments, she, as some of our friends say, speaks my mind; in some others, I do not altogether coincide with her. I am not for quite so much independence." Other women embraced Wollstonecraft's ideas. A woman much younger than Drinker, Priscilla Mason, gave a biting commencement address at the new Young Ladies' Academy in Philadelphia in 1794 and took Wollstonecraft as her departure for a rousing speech condemning "the high and mighty lords"—men—who had denied women education and professional opportunities in church, law, and politics. "Happily, a more liberal way of thinking begins to prevail....Let us by suitable education, qualify ourselves for those high departments," and, she concluded with unwarranted optimism, "they will open before us." Many women's letters report lively debates stimulated by *A Vindication of the Rights of Woman.*

Male readers' responses were varied as well. Aaron Burr, a senator from New York, called the book "a work of genius." A Fourth of July speaker in New Jersey in 1793 proclaimed that "the Rights of Woman are no longer strange sounds to an American ear," and he hoped they would soon be embedded in state law codes. A more negative orator on that same holiday in New York argued that woman's rights really meant a woman's duty "to submit to the control of that government she has voluntarily chosen," namely the government of a husband. And a New Hampshire July Fourth orator advanced this tart joke: "Every man, by the Constitution, is born with an equal right to be elected to the highest office. And every woman is born with an equal right to be the wife of the most eminent man." For some, it was clearly hard to think seriously about gender equality.

The notion of equal rights for women had a long incubation period in the United States. In the 1790s, ideas of equality were too closely associated with the radicalism of the French Revolution, a divisive topic in America; and soon revelations of Wollstonecraft's unconventional personal life as an unwed mother dampened enthusiasm for her pioneering book. Not until the 1830s and 1840s would there be a new generation of women, led by Sarah Grimké, raising questions of sex equality anew (see chapter 11, page 272, and chapter 12, page 308). Most Americans of the 1790s preferred a moderate stance, praising women's contribution to civil society through their influence on family—the "Republican motherhood" concept, historians have called it. While this fell far short of an egalitarian claim to rights, it did justify—and this was no small gain—women's formal education. A young woman speaker at a Fourth of July picnic in Connecticut in 1799 summed it up perfectly to her all-female audience: "As mothers, wives, sisters, and daughters, we may all be important, [and] teach our little boys, the inestimable value of Freedom, how to blend and harmonize the natural and social rights of man, and as early impressions are indelible, thus assist our dear country, to be as glorious in maintaining, as it was great in gaining her immortal independence."

FRONTISPIECE.

Thackara & Vallance sculp.

Publish'd at Philad.ª Dec.ʳ 1ˢᵗ 1792.

Woman's Rights in the *Lady's Magazine* of 1792

This frontispiece, appearing in the first volume of the Philadelphia periodical the *Lady's Magazine and Repository of Entertaining Knowledge,* accompanied excerpts from Mary Wollstonecraft's *Vindication.* (The editor was a literary man, Charles Brockden Brown.) The caption identified the kneeling figure as "the Genius of the *Lady's Magazine,*" accompanied by "the Genius of Emulation" carrying a trumpet and a laurel wreath. (*Genius* here meant a spirit; *emulation* meant ambition to excel, now an obsolete usage. Thus the genius of emulation was the spirit of ambition—women's ambition in this case.) The spirit representing the *Lady's Magazine* kneels before Liberty, identified by her liberty cap on a pole, and presents a paper titled "rights of woman." Study the objects arranged below Liberty: two books, a musical instrument, artist's paints, a globe, and a page of geometrical shapes. The kneeling figure seems to gesture toward them. What do they suggest about the nature of the "rights of woman" that this picture endorses?

Library Company of Philadelphia.

RATE OF TOLL

	Cts
Each foot passenger	3
Each rider	8
Two wheeled Pleasure carriage	20
Four wheeled do do	50
Curricle	30
Cart or waggon by one beast	10
Drawn by two beasts	15
Loaded do	25
By three do empty	20
Loaded do	30
By four do empty	25
Loaded do	37½
Each additional beast	5
Sleigh drawn by one beast	10
By two do	15
Sled by one do	6½
By two do	12½
By four do	25
Each additional beast	5
Horse jack or mule	4
Neat cattle	3
Sheep & swine each	1

Bridge Toll Sign, 1796
This sign lists an amazing variety of tolls charged for crossing a bridge over the Connecticut River between Cornish, New Hampshire, and Windsor, Vermont, in 1796. Owners of bridges and toll roads collected fees from users of their privately built rights-of-way. Can you deduce any principle of pricing in this list? Is the list exhaustive? What if a boy with a dog attempted to cross the bridge? Do you imagine there were traffic jams at the tollgate?
New Hampshire Historical Society.

proposals. "No man is more ardently intent to see the public debt soon and sacredly paid off than I am. This exactly marks the difference between Colonel Hamilton's views and mine, that I would wish the debt paid tomorrow; he wishes it never to be paid, but always to be a thing where with to corrupt and manage the legislature." Eventually, Madison, Jefferson, and Hamilton worked out a compromise at that fateful dinner party in June 1790 (see chapter opening). Hamilton got his way on the federal assumption of state debts, and in exchange, a decision favoring Virginians was reached to locate the nation's capital on the banks of the Potomac River, on the border shared by Virginia and Maryland.

The First Bank of the United States and the *Report on Manufactures*

The second and third major elements of Hamilton's economic plan were his proposal to create a national Bank of the United States and his program to encourage domestic manufacturing. Believing that banks were the "nurseries of national wealth," Hamilton modeled his bank plan on the Bank of England, a private corporation that worked primarily for the public good. According to Hamilton's plan, the federal government would buy 20 percent of the bank's stock. In effect, the bank would become the government's fiscal agent, holding its revenues derived from import duties, land sales, and various other taxes. The other 80 percent of the bank's capital would come from private investors, who could buy stock in the bank with either hard money (silver or gold) or federal securities. Because of its size and the privilege of being the only national bank, the bank would help stabilize the economy by exerting prudent control over credit, interest rates, and the value of currency.

Concerned that a few rich bankers might have undue influence over the economy, Madison tried but failed to stop the plan in Congress. Jefferson advised President Washington that the Constitution did not permit Congress to charter banks. Hamilton, however, pointed out that the Constitution gave Congress specific powers to regulate commerce and a broad right "to make all laws which shall be necessary and proper for carrying into execution the foregoing powers." Washington sided with Hamilton and signed the Bank of the United States into law in February 1791, with a charter allowing it to operate for twenty years.

York, had paid off these debts entirely. Others, like Massachusetts, had partially paid them through heavy taxation of the inhabitants. About half the states had made little headway. Hamilton called for the federal government to assume these state debts and combine them with the federal debt, in effect consolidating federal power over the states.

Congressman James Madison objected to putting windfall profits in the pockets of speculators. He proposed instead a complex scheme to pay both the original holders of the federal debt and the speculators, each at fair fractions of the face value. He also strenuously objected to assumption of all the states' debts. A large debt was dangerous, Madison warned, especially because it would lead to high taxation. Secretary of State Jefferson also was fearful of Hamilton's

When the bank's privately held stock went on sale in New York City in July, it sold out in a few hours, touching off an immediate mania of speculation in resale. A discouraged Madison reported that "the Coffee House is an eternal buzz with the gamblers," some of them self-interested congressmen intent on "public plunder."

The third component of Hamilton's plan was issued in December of 1791 in the *Report on Manufactures*, a proposal to encourage the production of American-made goods. Domestic manufacturing (chiefly iron products) was in its infancy, the result of years of dependence on British imports. Hamilton aimed to mobilize the new powers of the federal government to grant subsidies to manufactures and to impose moderate tariffs on those same products from overseas. This would protect the nascent industries at home and give them extra incentive to get established. Because the treasury secretary was cautious about tariff hikes, not wanting to undercut his important merchant allies, the proposed protective tariffs only covered goods in competition with domestic production. The *Report on Manufactures*, however, was not approved by Congress.

The Whiskey Rebellion

Hamilton's plan to restore public credit required new taxation to pay the interest on the large national debt. Hamilton did not propose a general increase in import duties, in deference to the merchant class, nor did he propose land taxes, which would have fallen hardest on the nation's wealthiest landowners. Instead, he convinced Congress in 1791 to pass a 25 percent excise tax on whiskey, to be paid by farmers when they brought their grain to the distillery, then passed on to individual whiskey consumers in the form of higher prices. Members of Congress from eastern areas favored the tax—especially those from New England, where the favorite drink was rum. A New Hampshire representative observed that the country would be "drinking down the national debt," an idea he evidently found acceptable.

Not surprisingly, the new excise tax proved unpopular with cash-short grain farmers in the western regions and whiskey drinkers everywhere. In 1791, farmers in the western parts of Pennsylvania, Virginia, Maryland, and the Carolinas and throughout Kentucky forcefully conveyed to Congress their resentment of Hamilton's tax. Congress responded with modest modifications to the tax in 1792; but even so, dis-content was rampant, and the tax proved hard to collect. Simple evasion of the law was the most common response. In some places, crowds threatened to tar and feather federal tax collectors, and some distilleries underreported their production. With embarrassment, Hamilton admitted to Congress that the revenue was far less than anticipated, but instead of abandoning the law, he tightened up the prosecution of tax evaders.

In western Pennsylvania, Hamilton had one ally, a stubborn tax collector named John Neville, who refused to quit even after a group of spirited farmers burned him in effigy. In May 1794, Neville filed charges against seventy-five farmers and distillers for tax evasion. In July, he and a federal marshal were ambushed in Allegheny County by a group of forty men; then Neville's house was burned to the ground by a crowd estimated at five hundred, and one man in the crowd was killed. At the end of July, 7,000 Pennsylvania farmers planned a march—or perhaps an attack, some thought—on Pittsburgh to protest the hated tax.

In response, President Washington nationalized the Pennsylvania militia and set out, with Hamilton at his side urging him on, at the head of 13,000 soldiers. A worried Philadelphia newspaper criticized the show of force: "Shall Pennsylvania be converted into a human slaughter house because the dignity of the United States will not admit of conciliatory measures? Shall torrents of blood be spilled to support an odious excise system?" But in the end, no blood was spilled. By the time the army arrived in late September, the demonstrators had dispersed. No battles were fought, and no shots were exchanged. Twenty men were rounded up as rebels and charged with high treason, but only two were convicted, and both were soon pardoned by Washington.

Had the federal government overreacted? Thomas Jefferson thought so; he saw the event as a replay of Shays's Rebellion of 1786, when a protest against government taxation had been met with unreasonable government force (see chapter 8). The rebel farmers agreed; they felt entitled to protest oppressive taxation. Hamilton and Washington, however, thought laws passed by a republican government must be obeyed. The Whiskey Rebellion presented an opportunity for the new federal government to flex its muscles and stand up to civil disorder.

REVIEW Why were Hamilton's economic policies controversial?

Conflicts West, East, and South

While the whiskey rebels challenged federal leadership from within the country, disorder threatened the United States from external sources as well. From 1790 onward, serious trouble brewed in three directions. To the west, a powerful confederation of Indian tribes in the Ohio Country resisted white encroachment, resulting in a brutal war. At the same time, conflicts between the major European powers forced Americans to take sides and nearly thrust the country into another war, this time

across the Atlantic. And to the south, a Caribbean slave rebellion raised fears that racial war would be imported to the United States. Despite these conflicts, and the grave threats they posed to the young country, Washington won reelection to the presidency unanimously in the fall of 1792.

To the West: The Indians

By the Treaty of Paris of 1783, England had given up all land east of the Mississippi River to the United States—but without consulting its onetime allies, the Indian tribes who inhabited 25,000 square miles of that territory. When the Indians learned of the treaty terms, they expressed astonishment. "They told me they never could believe that our king could pretend to cede to America what was not his own to give," the British commander at Fort Niagara wrote of the Iroquois. In Ohio, British Indian agents assured the Shawnee and Delaware peoples that England had relinquished only political control to the United States and the Indians still had the right to occupy the land. Also, British troops still occupied a half dozen forts in the northwest. Such confusion and misrepresentation aggravated an already volatile situation.

The doubling of the American population from two million in 1770 to nearly four million in 1790 greatly intensified the pressure for western land. Several thousand settlers a year moved down the Ohio River in the mid-1780s. Most headed for Kentucky on the south bank of the river, but some eyed the forests to the north, in Indian country. By the late 1780s, government land sales in eastern Ohio had commenced (Map 9.2), though actual settlement lagged.

Meanwhile, the U.S. army entered the western half of Ohio, where white settlers did not dare to go. Fort Washington, built on the Ohio River in 1789 at the site of present-day Cincinnati, became the command post for three major invasions of Indian country. General Josiah Harmar, under orders to subdue the Indians of western Ohio, marched with 1,400 men into Ohio's northwest region in the fall of 1790, burning Indian villages. His inexperienced troops were ambushed by Miami and Shawnee Indians led by their chiefs Little Turtle and Blue Jacket, and one in eight of Harmar's men was killed.

Harmar's defeat—so humiliating that Harmar was court-martialed—spurred efforts to clear Ohio for permanent American settlement. General Arthur St. Clair, the military gov-

Washington's Proclamation Protecting Indian Territory
The president's name, in bold print, prefaces a warning that American citizens were forbidden to injure Indians or trespass on their lands in the Northwest Territory. When the federal government signed treaties with tribes ceding land, it often guaranteed protections for land not ceded. This poster of 1793, designed to be tacked up on trees, announced federal protection for Indians around the Eel River in Ohio. Such warnings were not very effective. Washington wrote in 1796, "I believe scarcely any thing short of a Chinese Wall, or line of Troops will restrain Land Jobbers, and the Incroachment of Settlers, upon Indian Territory."
The Huntington Library and Art Collections, San Marino, California.

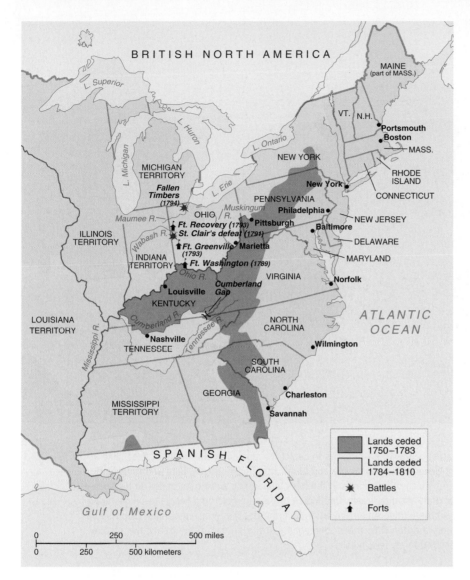

MAP 9.2 Western Expansion and Indian Land Cessions to 1810 By the first decade of the nineteenth century, intense Indian wars had resulted in significant cessions of land to the U.S. government by treaty.

ernor of the Northwest Territory, had pursued peaceful tactics in the 1780s, signing treaties with Indians for land in eastern Ohio—dubious treaties, as it happened, since the Indian negotiators were not authorized to yield land. In the wake of Harmar's bungled operation, St. Clair geared up for military action, and in the fall of 1791 he led 2,000 men (accompanied by 200 women camp followers) north from Fort Washington to engage in battle with the Miami and Shawnee. The Indians attacked at daybreak on November 4, at the headwaters of the Wabash River. Before noon, 55 percent of the Americans were dead or wounded; only three of the women escaped alive. The Indians scalped and dismembered the dying and pursued fleeing survivors for miles. With more than 900 lives lost, this was the most stunning American loss in the entire history of the U.S.-Indian wars.

Grisly tales of St. Clair's defeat became instantly infamous, increasing the level of sheer terror that Americans brought to their confrontations with the Indians.

President Washington doubled the U.S. military presence in Ohio and appointed a new commander, General Anthony Wayne of Pennsylvania, nicknamed "Mad Anthony" for his headstrong, hard-drinking style of leadership. About the Ohio natives Wayne wrote, "I have always been of the opinion that we never should have a permanent peace with those Indians until they were made to experience our superiority." With some 3,500 men, Wayne established two new military camps, Fort Greenville and Fort Recovery, deep in Indian territory in western Ohio.

Throughout 1794 Wayne's army engaged in skirmishes with Shawnee, Delaware, and Miami Indians. Chief Little Turtle of the Miami tribe

Treaty of Greenville, 1795
This painting by an unknown artist of the 1790s purports to depict the signing of the Treaty of Greenville in 1795. The treaty was signed by General Anthony Wayne and Chief Little Turtle of the Miami and Chief Tarhe the Crane of the Wyandot. An American officer kneels in the front, apparently writing on paper on his knee—not a likely posture in which to draft a formal treaty. One Indian of the three pictured seems to be gesturing with emphasis, as if to dictate to the writing American, but in fact, the treaty's terms were most favorable to the Americans. Many Indians from a dozen Ohio tribes congregated at the signing of the treaty; this picture shows unrealistically open spaces and very few Indians.
Chicago Historical Society.

advised negotiation; in his view, Wayne's large army looked overpowering. But Blue Jacket of the Shawnees counseled continued warfare, and his view prevailed. The decisive action came in August 1794 at the battle of Fallen Timbers, near the Maumee River where a recent tornado had felled many trees. The confederated Indians—mainly Ottawa, Potawatomi, Shawnee, and Delaware, numbering around 800—ambushed the Americans but were underarmed, and Wayne's troops made effective use of their guns and bayonets. The Indians withdrew and sought refuge at nearby Fort Miami, still held by the British. Their former allies, however, locked the gate and refused protection. Surviving Indians fled to the woods, their ranks decimated.

Fallen Timbers was a major defeat for the Indians. The Americans had destroyed corn-fields and villages on the march north, and with winter approaching, the Indians' confidence was sapped. They reentered negotiations in a much less powerful bargaining position. In 1795, about a thousand Indians representing nearly a dozen tribes met with Wayne and other American emissaries to work out the Treaty of Greenville. The Americans offered treaty goods (calico shirts, axes, knives, blankets, kettles, mirrors, ribbons, thimbles, and abundant wine and liquor casks) worth $25,000 and promised additional shipments every year. The government's idea was to create a dependency on American goods to keep the Indians friendly. In exchange, the Indians ceded most of Ohio to the Americans; only the northwest part of the territory was reserved solely for the Indians.

The treaty brought temporary peace to the region, but it did not restore a peaceful life to the Indians. The annual allowance from the United States too often came in the form of liquor. "More of us have died since the Treaty of Greenville than we lost by the years of war before, and it is all owing to the introduction of liquor among us," said Chief Little Turtle in 1800. "This liquor that they introduce into our country is more to be feared than the gun and tomahawk."

Across the Atlantic: France and England

While Indian battles engaged the American military, another war overseas had to be closely watched. Since 1789, revolution had been raging in France. At first, the general American reaction was positive, for it was flattering to think that the American Revolution had inspired imitation in France. Monarchy and privilege were overthrown in the name of republicanism; towns throughout America celebrated the victory of the French people with civic feasts and public festivities.

But news of the beheading of King Louis XVI quickly dampened the uncritical enthusiasm for everything French. Those who fondly remembered the excitement and risk of the American Revolution were still likely to regard France with optimism. However, the reluctant revolutionaries of the 1770s and 1780s, who had worried about excessive democracy and social upheaval in America, deplored the far greater violence occurring in the name of republicanism as France in 1793 moved into the Reign of Terror, with its surge of executions.

Support for the French Revolution could remain a matter of personal conviction until 1793, when England and France went to war and French versus British loyalty became a critical foreign policy question. France had helped America substantially during the American Revolution, and the confederation government had signed an alliance in 1778 promising aid if France were ever under attack. Americans optimistic about the eventual outcome of the French Revolution wanted to deliver on that promise. But others, including those shaken by the guillotining of thousands of French people as well as those with strong commercial ties to England, sought ways to stay neutral.

In May 1793, President Washington issued a Neutrality Proclamation with friendly assurances to both sides. But tensions at home flared in response to official neutrality. "The cause of France is the cause of man, and neutrality is de-

sertion," wrote H. H. Brackenridge, a western Pennsylvanian, voicing the sentiments of thousands. Dozens of pro-French political clubs called Democratic or Republican Societies sprang up around the country. The societies mobilized farmers and mechanics, issued circular letters, injected pro-French and anti-British feelings into local elections, and in general heightened popular participation and public interest in foreign policy. The activities of these societies disturbed Washington and Hamilton intensely, for they encouraged opposition to the policies of the president.

The Neutrality Proclamation fit Washington's goal of staying out of European wars. Yet American ships continued to trade between the French West Indies and France, and in late 1793 and early 1794, the British expressed their displeasure by capturing more than three hundred of these vessels near the West Indies. Clearly, something had to be done to assert American power.

President Washington sent John Jay, the chief justice of the Supreme Court and a man of strong pro-British sentiments, to England to negotiate commercial relations in the British West Indies and secure compensation for the seizure of American ships. In addition, Jay was supposed to resolve several long-standing problems. Southern **planters** wanted reimbursement for the slaves lured away by the British army during the war, and western settlers wanted England to vacate the frontier forts still occupied because of their proximity to the Indian fur trade.

Jay returned from his diplomatic mission in 1795 with a treaty that no one could love. First, the treaty failed to address the captured cargoes or the lost property in slaves. Second, it granted the British eighteen months to withdraw from the frontier forts along with continued rights in the fur trade. (Even with the delay, the provision disheartened the Indians just then negotiating the Treaty of Greenville out in Ohio; it was a significant factor in their decision to make peace.) Finally, the Jay Treaty called for repayment with interest of the debts that some American planters still owed to British firms dating from the Revolutionary War. In exchange for such generous terms, Jay secured limited trading rights in the West Indies and agreement that some issues—boundary disputes with Canada, the damage and loss claims of the shipowners—would be decided later by arbitration commissions.

When newspapers published the terms of the treaty, powerful opposition emerged from Maine to Georgia. In Massachusetts, graffiti read: "Damn John Jay!…Damn everyone who won't stay up all night damning John Jay!" Nevertheless, the treaty passed the Senate in 1795 by a vote of twenty to ten. Some representatives in the House, led by Madison, tried to undermine the Senate's approval by insisting on a separate vote on the funding provisions of the treaty, on the grounds that the House controlled all money bills. Finally, in 1796, the House approved funds to implement the various commissions mandated by the treaty, but by only a three-vote margin. The cleavage of votes in both houses of Congress divided along the same lines as the Hamilton-Jefferson split on economic policy.

To the South: The Haitian Revolution

In addition to the Indian wars in Ohio and the European wars across the Atlantic, a third bloody conflict to the south polarized and even terrorized many Americans in the 1790s. The western third of the large Caribbean island of Hispaniola, just to the east of Cuba, became engulfed in revolution starting in 1791. The eastern portion of the island was a Spanish colony called Santo Domingo; the western part, in bloody conflagration, was the French Saint Domingue. War raged in Saint Domingue for over a decade, resulting in the birth of the Republic of Haiti in 1804, distinguished as the first and only independent black state to arise out of a successful slave revolution.

The Haitian Revolution was a complex event involving many participants, including the diverse local population and, eventually, three European countries. Some 30,000 whites ruled the island in 1790, running sugar and coffee plantations with close to half a million slaves, two-thirds of them of African birth. The white French colonists were not the only plantation owners, however. About 28,000 free coloreds (*gens de couleur*) of mixed race also lived in Saint Domingue; they owned one-third of the island's plantations and nearly a quarter of the slave

Haitian Revolution, 1790–1804

Beginning of slave revolt, 1791

Border of Saint Domingue/ Santo Domingo, 1790

Border of Haiti/ Santo Domingo, 1820

labor force. Despite their economic status, the free coloreds were barred from political power, but they aspired to it.

The French Revolution of 1789 was the immediate catalyst for rebellion in this already tense society. First, white colonists challenged the white royalist government in an effort to link Saint Domingue with the new revolutionary government in France. Next the free coloreds rebelled in 1791, demanding equal civil rights with the whites. No sooner was this revolt viciously suppressed than another part of the island exploded as thousands of slaves armed with machetes and torches wreaked devastation and slaughter. In 1793, the civil war escalated to include French, Spanish, and British troops fighting the inhabitants and also each other. Slaves led by Toussaint L'Ouverture in alliance with Spain occupied the northern regions of the island, leaving a thousand plantations in ruins and tens of thousands of people dead. Thousands of whites and free coloreds, along with some of their slaves, fled to Spanish Louisiana and southern cities of the United States.

White Americans followed the revolution in fascinated horror through newspapers and refugees' accounts. A few sympathized with the impulse for liberty, but many more shuddered at the violent atrocities. Many black American slaves also followed the revolution, for the amazing news of the success of a first-ever, massive revolution by slaves traveled quickly in this oral culture. Whites complained of behaviors that might prefigure plots and conspiracies, such as increased insolence and higher runaway rates among slaves.

The Haitian Revolution provoked naked fear in white Americans. Jefferson, agonizing over the contagion of liberty in 1797, wrote another Virginia slaveholder that "if something is not done, and soon done, we shall be the murderers of our own children…; the revolutionary storm, now sweeping the globe, will be upon us, and happy if we make timely provision to give it an easy passage over our land. From the present state of things in Europe and America, the day which brings our combustion must be near at hand; and only a single spark is wanting to make that day tomorrow."

REVIEW Why did the United States feel vulnerable to international threats in the 1790s?

Federalists and Republicans

By the mid-1790s, polarization over the French Revolution, Haiti, the Jay Treaty, and Hamilton's economic plans had led to two distinct and consistent rival political groups: Federalists and Republicans. Politicians and newspapers adopted these labels, words that summarized conflicting ideologies and principles; they did not yet describe full-fledged political parties. Washington's decision not to seek a third term led to serious partisan electioneering in the presidential and congressional elections of 1796. Federalist John Adams won the presidency, but party strife accelerated over failed diplomacy in France, bringing the United States to the brink of war. Pro-war and antiwar antagonism created a major crisis over political free speech, militarism, and fears of sedition and treason.

The Election of 1796

Washington struggled to appear to be above party politics, and in his farewell address he stressed the need to maintain a "unity of government" reflecting a unified body politic. He also urged the country to "steer clear of permanent alliances with any portion of the foreign world." The leading contenders for his position, John Adams of Massachusetts and Thomas Jefferson of Virginia, in theory agreed with him, but around them raged a party contest split along pro-English versus pro-French lines.

The leading Federalists informally caucused and chose Adams as their candidate, with Thomas Pinckney of South Carolina to run with him; the Republicans settled on Aaron Burr of New York to pair with Jefferson. The Constitution did not anticipate parties and tickets. Instead, each electoral college voter could cast two votes for any two candidates, but on only one ballot. The top vote-getter became president and the next highest assumed the vice presidency. (This procedural flaw was corrected by the Twelfth Amendment, adopted in 1804.) With only one ballot, careful maneuvering was required to make sure the chief rivals for the presidency did not land in the top two spots.

Into that maneuverable moment stepped Alexander Hamilton. No longer in the cabinet, Hamilton had returned to his law practice in

Washington's Farewell Address Printed on a Textile, 1806
This small square of fabric, suitable for framing or tacking to the wall, was one of many items that served to immortalize Washington as the benevolent savior of the young Republic. Known well by close associates as a man with ordinary human failings—one Federalist member of his last cabinet complained that he was "vain and weak and ignorant"—Washington in death became a demigod, a genius of inspired leadership and faultless integrity. This 1806 textile features the final paragraph of Washington's 1796 farewell address, one highlighting his modesty and self-deprecation. At the bottom, the American eagle and the British lion flank two sailing ships (one close, one far off) under the words "Commercial Union." The textile picture, then, was an implicit criticism of the new president, Thomas Jefferson, whose leadership was producing deteriorating relations with Britain that would finally result in the War of 1812.
Collection of Janice L. and David J. Frent.

1795, but he kept a firm hand on political developments. Hamilton did not trust Adams; he preferred Pinckney, and he tried to influence electors to throw their support to the South Carolinian. But his plan backfired: Adams was elected president with 71 electoral votes, and Jefferson came in second with 68 and thus became vice president. Pinckney got 59 votes, while Burr trailed with 30.

Adams's inaugural speech pledged neutrality in foreign affairs and respect for the French people, which made Republicans hopeful. To please Federalists, Adams retained three

***John Adams*, by John Trumbull**
In 1793, a year after painting a portrait of the youthful secretary of the treasury Alexander Hamilton (see page 212), Trumbull painted Vice President John Adams, then age fifty-eight. A friend once listed Adams's shortcomings as a politician: "He can't dance, drink, game, flatter, promise, dress, swear with gentlemen, and small talk and flirt with the ladies."
National Portrait Gallery, Smithsonian Institution/Art Resources, NY.

cabinet members from Washington's administration—the secretaries of state, treasury, and war. But the three were Hamilton loyalists, passing on Hamilton's judgments and advice as their own to the unwitting Adams. Vice President Jefferson expected to work closely with Adams, but the Hamiltonian cabinet ruined the honeymoon. Jefferson's advice was spurned, and he withdrew from active counsel of the president.

The XYZ Affair

From the start, Adams's presidency was in crisis. France retaliated for the British-friendly Jay Treaty by abandoning its 1778 alliance with the United States. French privateers—armed private vessels—started detaining American ships carrying British goods; by March 1797, more than 300 American vessels had been seized. To avenge these insults, Federalists started murmuring openly about war with France. Adams preferred negotiations and dispatched a three-man commis-

sion to France in the fall of 1797. When the three commissioners arrived in Paris, French officials would not receive them. Finally the French minister of foreign affairs, Talleyrand, sent three French agents, unnamed and later known to the American public as X, Y, and Z, to the American commissioners with the information that $250,000 might grease the wheels of diplomacy and a $12 million loan to the French government would be the price of a peace treaty. Incensed, the commissioners brought news of the bribery attempt to the president.

Americans reacted to the XYZ affair with shock and anger. Even staunch pro-French Republicans began to reevaluate their allegiance. The Federalist-dominated Congress appropriated money for an army of 10,000 soldiers and repealed all prior treaties with France. In 1798 twenty naval warships launched the United States into its first undeclared war, called the Quasi-War by historians to underscore its uncertain legal status. The main scene of action was the Caribbean, where over 100 French ships were captured.

There was no home-front unity in this time of undeclared war; antagonism only intensified between Federalists and Republicans. Republican newspapers heaped abuse on Adams. Pro-French mobs roamed the capital city, and Adams, fearing for his personal safety, stocked weapons in his presidential quarters. Federalists too went on the offensive. In Newburyport, Massachusetts, they lit a huge bonfire and burned issues of the state's Republican newspapers. One Federalist editor ominously declared that "he who is not for us is against us."

The Alien and Sedition Acts

With tempers so dangerously high, and fears that political dissent was perhaps akin to treason, Federalist leaders moved to muffle the opposition. In mid-1798, Congress hammered out a Sedition Act that made not only conspiracy and revolt illegal, but also penalized speaking or writing anything that defamed the president or Congress. Criticisms of government leaders became criminal utterances. In all, twenty-five men, almost all Republican newspaper editors, were charged with sedition; twelve were convicted.

Congress also passed two Alien Acts. The first extended the waiting period for an alien to achieve citizenship from five to fourteen years and required all aliens to register with the federal government. The second empowered the presi-

Cartoon of the Matthew Lyon Fight in Congress

The political tensions of 1798 were not merely intellectual. A February session in Congress degenerated from name-calling to a brawl. Roger Griswold, a Connecticut Federalist, called Matthew Lyon, a Vermont Republican, a coward. Lyon responded with some well-aimed spit, the first departure from the gentleman's code of honor. Griswold responded by raising his cane to Lyon, whereupon Lyon grabbed nearby fire tongs to beat back his assailant. Madison wrote to Jefferson that the two should have dueled: "No man ought to reproach another with cowardice, who is not ready to give proof of his own courage" by negotiating a duel, the honorable way to avenge insults in Virginia's planter class. But Lyon, a Scots-Irish immigrant, did not come from a class or culture that cultivated the art of the duel; rough-and-tumble fighting was his first response to insult. What is the picture on the back wall?
Library of Congress.

FOR MORE HELP ANALYZING THIS IMAGE, see the visual activity for this chapter in the Online Study Guide at **bedfordstmartins.com/roarkcompact**.

dent in time of war to deport or imprison without trial any foreigner suspected of being a danger to the United States. The clear intent of the alien laws was to harass French immigrants already in the United States and discourage others from coming.

Republicans strongly opposed the Alien and Sedition Acts on the grounds that they were in conflict with the Bill of Rights, but they did not have the votes to revoke the acts in Congress, nor could the federal judiciary, dominated by Federalist judges, be counted on to challenge them. Jefferson and Madison turned to the state legislatures, the only other competing political

arena, to press their opposition. Each man drafted a set of resolutions condemning the acts and had the legislatures of Virginia and Kentucky present them to the federal government in late fall 1798. The Virginia and Kentucky Resolutions tested the novel argument that state legislatures have the right to judge the constitutionality of federal laws and to **nullify** laws that infringe on the liberties of the people as defined in the Bill of Rights. The resolutions made little dent in the Alien and Sedition Acts, but the idea of a state's right to nullify federal law did not disappear. It surfaced several times in decades to come, most notably in a major tariff dispute in

1832 and in the sectional arguments that led to the Civil War.

Amid all the war hysteria and sedition fears in 1798, President Adams regained his balance. He was uncharacteristically restrained in pursuing opponents under the Sedition Act, and he finally refused to declare war on France, as extreme Federalists wished. No doubt he was beginning to realize how much he had been the dupe of Hamilton. He also shrewdly realized that France was not in fact eager for war and that a peaceful settlement might be close at hand. In January 1799, a peace initiative from France arrived in the form of a letter assuring Adams that diplomatic channels were open again and that new commissioners would be welcomed in France. Adams accepted this overture and appointed new negotiators. By late 1799, the Quasi-War with France had subsided, and in 1800 the negotiations resulted in a treaty declaring "a true and sincere friendship" between the United States and France. But Federalists were not pleased; Adams lost the support of a significant part of his own party and sealed his fate as the first one-term president of the United States.

The election of 1800 was openly organized along party lines. The self-designated national leaders of each group met to handpick their candidates for president and vice president. Adams's chief opponent was Thomas Jefferson. When the election was finally over, President Jefferson mounted the inaugural platform to announce, "We are all republicans, we are all federalists," an appealing rhetoric of harmony appropriate to an inaugural address. But his formulation perpetuated a denial of the validity of party politics, a denial that ran deep in the founding generation of political leaders.

> **REVIEW** Why did Congress pass the Alien and Sedition Acts in 1798?

Conclusion: Parties Nonetheless

American political leaders began operating the new government in 1789 with great hopes to unify the country and to overcome selfish factionalism. The enormous trust in President Washington was the central foundation for that hope, and Washington did not disappoint, becoming a model

Mr. President with a blend of integrity and authority. Stability was further aided by easy passage of the Bill of Rights (to appease Antifederalists) and by attention to cultivating a virtuous citizenry of upright men supported and rewarded by republican womanhood. Yet the hopes of the honeymoon period soon turned to worries and then fears as major political disagreements flared up.

At the core of the conflict was a group of talented men—Hamilton, Madison, Jefferson, and Adams—so recently allies but now opponents. They diverged over Hamilton's economic program, over relations with the British and the Jay Treaty, over the French and Haitian revolutions, and over preparedness for war abroad and free speech rights at home. Hamilton was perhaps the driving force in these conflicts, but the antagonism was not about mere personality. Parties were taking shape, not around individuals but around principles, such as ideas about what constitutes enlightened leadership, how powerful should the federal government be, who is the best ally in Europe, and when does oppositional political speech turn into treason. The Federalists were pro-British, pro-commerce, and ever alarmed about the potential excesses of democracy. The Republicans celebrated, up to a point, the radical republicanism of France and opposed the Sedition Act as an alarming example of an overbearing government cutting off freedom of speech.

When Jefferson, then, in his inaugural address of 1800 offered his conciliatory assurance that Americans were at the same time "all republicans" and "all federalists," he probably mystified some listeners. Possibly he meant to suggest that both groups shared two basic ideas—the value of republican government, in which power derived from the people, and the value of the unique federal system of shared governance structured by the Constitution. But by 1800, these two words defined competing philosophies of government. To at least some of his listeners, Jefferson's assertion of harmony across party lines could only have seemed bizarre. For the next two decades, these two parties would battle each other, each fearing that the success of the other might bring the demise of the country. And for the next two decades, leaders continued to worry that party spirit itself was a bad thing.

Suggestions for Further Reading

Susan Branson, *These Fiery Frenchified Dames: Women and Political Culture in Early National Philadelphia* (2001). A study of 1790s women in the capital city and their developing relationship to print culture, literacy, and political thought.

Ron Chernow, *Alexander Hamilton* (2004). An intimate biography of the financial genius of the 1790s.

Stanley Elkins and Eric McKitrick, *The Age of Federalism: The Early American Republic, 1788–1800* (1993). The authoritative and exhaustive account of the 1790s.

Joseph J. Ellis, *Founding Brothers: The Revolutionary Generation* (2000). Captivating chapters illuminate the complex rivalries of the 1790s leaders.

David McCullough, *John Adams* (2001). John Adams glorified *and* humanized by a superb storyteller.

Henry Wiencek, *An Imperfect God: George Washington, His Slaves, and the Creation of America* (2003). A close exploration of Washington's words and personal actions regarding slavery.

▶ FOR MORE BOOKS ABOUT TOPICS IN THIS CHAPTER, see the Online Study Guide at bedfordstmartins.com/roarkcompact.

▶ FOR ADDITIONAL FIRSTHAND ACCOUNTS OF THIS PERIOD, see Chapter 9 in Michael Johnson, ed., *Reading the American Past*, Third Edition.

▶ FOR WEB SITES AND DOCUMENTS RELATED TO TOPICS AND PLACES IN THIS CHAPTER, see "HistoryLinks," "DocLinks," and "PlaceLinks" at bedfordstmartins.com/roarkcompact.

REVIEWING THE CHAPTER

Follow these steps to review and strengthen your understanding of the chapter.

STEP 1: *Study the **Key Terms** and **Timeline** to identify the significance of each item listed.*

STEP 2: *Answer the **Review Questions**, drawing on key terms and dates to support your answers.*

STEP 3: *Drawing on the Key Terms, Timeline, and Review Questions, answer the broader **Making Connections** questions.*

KEY TERMS

Who

Alexander Hamilton (pp. 211, 214, 217)
James Madison (pp. 211, 214, 220)
Thomas Jefferson (pp. 211, 214)
George Washington (p. 213)
John Jay (pp. 214, 225)
Judith Sargent Murray (p. 215)
Eli Whitney (p. 216)
Josiah Harmar (p. 222)
Arthur St. Clair (p. 222)
Anthony Wayne (p. 223)
Little Turtle (p. 223)
Blue Jacket (p. 224)
Toussaint L'Ouverture (p. 226)

What

Revolutionary War debt (p. 211)
Bill of Rights (p. 214)
Report on Public Credit (p. 217)
Bank of the United States (p. 220)
Report on Manufactures (p. 221)
Whiskey Rebellion (p. 221)
Fort Washington (p. 222)
Fort Greenville (p. 223)
Fort Recovery (p. 223)
battle of Fallen Timbers (p. 224)
Treaty of Greenville (p. 224)

Neutrality Proclamation (p. 225)
Jay Treaty (p. 225)
Haitian Revolution (p. 226)
Federalists (p. 227)
Republicans (p. 227)
XYZ affair (p. 228)
Quasi-War (p. 228)
Sedition Act (p. 228)
Alien Acts (p. 228)
Virginia and Kentucky Resolutions (p. 229)

TIMELINE

1789 • George Washington inaugurated first president.
• French Revolution begins.
• First Congress meets.
• Fort Washington erected in western Ohio.

1790 • Congress approves Hamilton's debt plan.
• Judith Sargent Murray publishes "On the Equality of the Sexes."
• Shawnee and Miami Indians in Ohio defeat General Josiah Harmar.

1791 • States ratify Bill of Rights.
• Congress charters Bank of the United States.
• Ohio Indians defeat General Arthur St. Clair.
• Congress passes whiskey tax.
• Haitian Revolution begins.
• Hamilton issues *Report on Manufactures*.

1793 • Napoleonic Wars break out between France and England.
• Washington issues Neutrality Proclamation.
• Eli Whitney invents cotton gin.

REVIEW QUESTIONS

1. How did political leaders in the 1790s attempt to overcome the divisions of the 1780s? (pp. 213–16)

2. Why were Hamilton's economic policies controversial? (pp. 216–21)

3. Why did the United States feel vulnerable to international threats in the 1790s? (pp. 222–26)

4. Why did Congress pass the Alien and Sedition Acts in 1798? (pp. 227–30)

MAKING CONNECTIONS

1. Why did the Federalist alliance fracture in the 1790s? Why was this development troubling to the nation? In your answer, cite specific ideological and political developments that compromised cooperation.

2. What provoked the Whiskey Rebellion? How did the government respond? In your answer, discuss the foundations and precedents of the conflict as well as the significance of the government's response.

3. Americans held that virtue was pivotal to the success of their new nation. What did they mean by virtue? How did they hope to ensure that their citizens and their leaders possessed virtue?

4. The domestic politics of the new nation were profoundly influenced by conflicts beyond the nation's borders. Discuss how conflicts abroad contributed to domestic political developments in the 1790s.

▶ For practice quizzes, a customized study plan, and other study tools, see the Online Study Guide at bedfordstmartins.com/roarkcompact.

1794 • Whiskey Rebellion.
• Battle of Fallen Timbers.
   1795 • Treaty of Greenville.
   • Jay Treaty.
      1796 • Federalist John Adams elected second president, Thomas Jefferson vice president.
         1797 • XYZ affair.
            1798 • Quasi-War with France erupts.
            • Alien and Sedition Acts.
            • Virginia and Kentucky Resolutions.
               1800 • Republican Thomas Jefferson elected third president.

A JEFFERSON FAN

Ladies' fans became increasingly popular fashion accessories in the late eighteenth and early nineteenth centuries, equally useful for communication and cooling. This folding fan of vellum and carved ivory, made in the early 1800s, features a medallion portrait of President Thomas Jefferson. Carried by the ribbon on a woman's wrist, the fan could be flicked open to announce a partisan political statement. Fans and other handheld articles such as parasols and handkerchiefs expanded the repertoire of nonverbal expression for women, who by the custom and training of the time were expected to be less assertive than men in mixed-sex conversation. Many emotions and messages—from modesty, coyness, and flirtatiousness to anger, irritability, and boredom—could be communicated by the expert deployment of this delicate emblem of femininity. Women learned the conventions of fluttering the fan by close observation and perhaps by explicit training.

Collection of David J. and Janice L. Frent.

Republicans in Power

1800–1824

THE NAME TECUMSEH translates to "Shooting Star," a fitting name for the Shawnee chief who reached meteoric heights of fame among Indians during Thomas Jefferson's presidency. From Canada to Georgia and west to the Mississippi, Tecumseh was accounted a charismatic leader of Indians, for which white Americans praised (and feared) him. Graceful, eloquent, compelling, astute: Tecumseh was all these and more, a gifted natural commander, equal parts politician and warrior.

The Ohio Country, where Tecumseh was born in 1768, was home to some dozen Indian tribes, including the Shawnee, recently displaced from the South. During the Revolutionary War, the region became a battleground with the Big Knives, as the Shawnee people called the Americans. Tecumseh's childhood was marked by repeated violence and the loss of his father and two brothers in battle. The Revolution's end in 1783 brought no peace to the Indians' country; American settlers pushed west, and the youthful Tecumseh honed his warrior skills by ambushing pioneers flatboating down the Ohio River. He fought at the battle of Fallen Timbers, a major Indian defeat, but avoided the 1795 negotiations of the Treaty of Greenville, in which a half dozen dispirited tribes ceded much of Ohio to the Big Knives. With frustration he watched as seven additional treaties between 1802 and 1805 whittled away more Indian land.

Some Indians, resigned and tired, looked for ways to accommodate to new realities, taking up farming, trade, and even intermarriage with the Big Knives. Others spent their treaty payments on deadly alcohol. Tecumseh's younger brother Tenskwatawa led an embittered life of idleness and drink. But Tecumseh rejected assimilation and inebriation and instead campaigned for a return to ancient ways. Donning traditional animal-skin garb, he traveled around the Great Lakes area in the years after 1805, persuading tribes to join his pan-Indian confederacy. The American territorial governor of Indiana, William Henry Harrison, reported, "For four years he has been in constant motion. You see him today on the Wabash, and in a short time hear of him on the shores of Lake Erie or Michigan, or on the banks of the Mississippi, and wherever he goes he makes an impression favorable to his purpose." In 1811, the leader named Shooting Star traveled among tribes in the South, while an especially brilliant comet illuminated the night sky.

Even his once-dissolute brother was born anew. After a near-death experience in 1805, Tenskwatawa revived and recounted a startling vision of meeting the Master of Life. Renaming himself the Prophet, Tenskwatawa urged Indians everywhere to regard the white Americans as children of the Evil Spirit, destined to be destroyed. Tecumseh and the Prophet established a new village called Prophetstown, located in present-day Indiana, offering a potent blend of spiritual regeneration and political unity that attracted thousands of

Tecumseh
Several portraits of Tecumseh exist, but they all present a different visage, and none of them enjoys verified authenticity. This one perhaps comes closest: It is an 1848 engraving adapted from an earlier drawing that no longer exists, sketched by a French trader in Indiana named Pierre Le Dru in a live sitting with the Indian leader in 1808. The engraver has given Tecumseh a British army officer's uniform, showing that he fought on the British side in the War of 1812. Notice the head covering and the medallion around the neck, marking Tecumseh's Indian identity.
Library of Congress.

followers. Governor Harrison admired and feared Tecumseh, calling him "one of those uncommon geniuses which spring up occasionally to produce revolutions." President Jefferson had great reason to worry about an organized Indian opposition, and more, its potential for a renewed Indian alliance with the British in Canada.

Those worries became a reality in Jefferson's second term in office. Although his first term brought notable successes, such as the Louisiana Purchase and the Lewis and Clark expedition, his second term was consumed by the threat of war with either Britain or France, in a replay of the late-1790s tensions. When war came, in 1812, the enemy was Britain, bolstered by a reenergized Indian-British alliance. Among the causes of the war were insults over international shipping rights, the capture of American vessels, and

the impressment of American sailors, but the war also derived compelling strength from Tecumseh's confederacy, now pledged to help the British in Canada. Significant battles pitted American soldiers against Indians in the Great Lakes, Tennessee, and Florida.

In the end, the War of 1812 settled little between the Americans and the British, but it was tragically conclusive for the Indians. Eight hundred warriors led by Tecumseh helped defend Canada against American attacks, but the British did not reciprocate when Indians were under threat. Tecumseh died on Canadian soil at the battle of the Thames in the fall of 1813. No Indian leader with the star power of Tecumseh would emerge again east of the Mississippi.

The briefly unified Indian confederacy under Tecumseh had no counterpart in the young Republic's confederation of states, where widespread unity and enthusiasm behind a single leader proved impossible to achieve. Republicans did battle with Federalists during the Jefferson and Madison administrations, but then Federalists doomed their party by opposing the War of 1812 and after 1815 ceased to be a major force in political life. The next two presidents, James Monroe and John Quincy Adams, congratulated themselves on the Federalists' demise and Republican unity, but in fact divisions within their own party were extensive. Wives of politicians increasingly inserted themselves into this dissonant mix, managing men's politicking and jockeying for power in the Capitol, enabling their husbands to appear above the fray and maintain the fiction of a nonfactionalized state. That it was a fiction became sharply apparent in the most serious political crisis of this period, the Missouri Compromise of 1820.

Jefferson's Presidency

The nerve-wracking election of 1800, decided in the House of Representatives, enhanced fears that party divisions would ruin the country. A panicky Federalist newspaper in Connecticut predicted that Jefferson's victory would produce bloody civil war and usher in an immoral reign of "murder, robbery, rape, adultery and incest." Similar fears were expressed in the South, where a frightful slave uprising seemed a possible outcome of Jefferson's victory. But nothing nearly so drastic occurred. Jefferson later called his election the "revolution of 1800," referring to his repudiation of monarchical practices, his undoing of Federalist judicial appointments, and his cut-backs in military spending and taxes.

Jefferson indeed did radically transform the presidency, away from the Federalists' vision of a powerful executive branch to **republican** simplicity and limited government. Yet even Jefferson found that circumstances sometimes required him to draw on the expansive powers of the presidency. The rise of Napoleon to power in France brought France and England into open warfare again in 1803, creating unexpected opportunities and challenges for Jefferson's administration. One major opportunity arrived in the spectacular purchase from France of the Louisiana Territory; on the challenge side, British and French naval forces nipped at American ships—and American honor—in the Atlantic Ocean.

Turbulent Times: Election and Rebellion

The result of the election of 1800 remained uncertain from polling time in November to repeated roll-call votes in the House of Representatives in February 1801. Federalist John Adams, never secure in his leadership of the Federalist Party, was no longer in the presidential race once it got to the House. Instead, the contest was between Jefferson and his own running mate, Senator Aaron Burr of New York. Republican voters in the electoral college slipped up, giving Jefferson and Burr equal numbers of votes, an outcome possible because of the single balloting to choose both president and vice president. (The Twelfth Amendment to the Constitution, adopted four years later, provided for distinct ballots for the two offices to fix this problem.) The vain and ambitious Burr declined to concede, so the sitting Federalist-dominated House of Representatives got to choose the president.

Each state delegation commanded one vote, and the winner needed nine votes. Some Federalists preferred Burr, believing his character flaws made him especially susceptible to Federalist pressure. But the influential Alexander Hamilton, though no friend to Jefferson, recognized that the high-strung Burr would be more dangerous than Jefferson in the presidency. Jefferson was a "contemptible hypocrite" in Hamilton's opinion, but at least he was not corrupt. (In 1804, Burr shot and killed Hamilton in a formal but illegal dual, bearing out Hamilton's intuition that Burr was a dangerous man.) Jefferson got the votes of eight states on the first ballot. Thirty-six ballots and six days later he got the critical ninth vote (and also a tenth). This election demonstrated a remarkable

feature of the new constitutional government: No matter how hard fought the campaign, the leadership of the nation could shift from one group to a distinctly different group in a peaceful transfer of power effected by ballots, not bullets.

As the country struggled over its white leadership crisis, news of a plotted rebellion of slaves surfaced in Virginia. A twenty-four-year-old blacksmith named Gabriel, the slave of Thomas Prossor, was said to be organizing a thousand slaves to march on the state capital at Richmond and take the governor, James Monroe, hostage. On the appointed day, however, a few nervous slaves went to the authorities, and within days, scores of implicated conspirators were jailed and brought to trial.

One of the jailed rebels compared himself to the most venerated icon of the early Republic: "I have nothing more to offer than what General Washington would have had to offer, had he been taken by the British and put to trial by them." Such talk invoking the specter of a black George Washington worried white Virginians, and in September and October 1801, 27 black men were hanged for contemplating rebellion. Finally, President Jefferson advised Governor Monroe that the hangings had gone far enough: "The world at large will forever condemn us if we indulge a principle of revenge," Jefferson wrote.

The Jeffersonian Vision of Republican Simplicity

Jefferson sidestepped the problem of slavery and turned his attention to establishing his administration in clear contrast to the Federalists. For his inauguration, held in the village optimistically called Washington City, he dressed in everyday clothing, to strike a tone of republican simplicity, and he walked to the Capitol building for the modest swearing-in ceremony. Once in office, he continued to emphasize unfussy frugality. He scaled back on Federalist building plans for Washington and cut the government budget. He wore plain clothes, appearing "neglected but not slovenly," according to one onlooker. He cultivated a casual style, wearing slippers to greet important guests, avoiding the formality of state parties and liveried servants. Jefferson's studied carelessness was very deliberate.

Martha Washington and Abigail Adams had received the wives of government figures at weekly teas, thereby creating and cementing social relations in the governing class. But Jefferson, a long-term widower, disdained female gatherings

Jefferson's Red Waistcoat

During his presidency, Jefferson often wore this red silk waistcoat as informal daywear. The garment had a velvet collar, woolen sleeves, and a thick lining made from recycled cotton and wool stockings. The thrifty Jefferson preferred to conserve firewood by wearing layers of warm clothes. A senator visiting in 1802 reported in dismay that the president was "dressed, or rather undressed, with an old brown coat, red waistcoat, old corduroy small clothes, much soiled, woolen hose, and slippers without heels." Another guest in 1804 found him wearing the red waistcoat, green velveteen breeches with pearl buttons, and "slippers down at the heels" that made him look like an ordinary farmer. Such colorful clothing in silk and velveteen carries dressy or feminine connotations in the twenty-first century, but it did not in 1800. Jefferson put on silk stockings and clean linen for fancy dinner parties; and when he lived in Paris in the 1780s, he wore an elaborately embroidered silk waistcoat under a greatcoat trimmed with gold lace. But in the 1800s, he used simple, colorful clothes to make a point about republican manners.

Courtesy of Monticello. Photo by Colonial Williamsburg.

and avoided the women of Washington City. He abandoned George Washington's practice of weekly formal receptions, scaling back these drop-in gatherings to just two a year. His preferred social event was the small dinner party with carefully chosen politicos, either all Republicans or all Federalists (and all male). At these intimate dinners, the president demonstrated his version of statecraft, exercising influence and strengthening informal relationships that would help him to govern.

Jefferson's paramount goal was to scale back federal power. Jefferson was no Antifederalist. He had supported the Constitution in 1788, although he had qualms about the unrestricted reelection allowed to the president. But events of the 1790s had caused him to worry about the stretching of powers in the executive branch. Jefferson had watched with distrust as Hamiltonian policies refinanced the public debt, established a national bank, and secured commercial ties with England (see chapter 9). These policies seemed to Jefferson to promote the interests of greedy speculators at the expense of the rest of the country. Jefferson was not at all anticommerce. But financial schemes that seemed merely to allow rich men to become richer were corrupt and worthless, he believed, and their promotion by the federal government was not authorized by the Constitution. In Jefferson's vision, the source of true **liberty** in America was the independent farmer, someone who owned and worked his land both for himself and for the market.

Jefferson set out to dismantle Federalist innovations. He reduced the size of the army by a third, leaving only three thousand soldiers, and he cut back the navy from twenty-five to seven ships. Peacetime defense, he felt, should rest with "a well-disciplined militia," not a standing army. With the consent of Congress, he abolished all federal internal taxes based on population or on whiskey. A national tax on population had been tried just once, in 1798, and proved as burdensome and expensive as taking a census. Government revenue would now derive solely from customs duties and from the sale of western lands. This strategy was of particular benefit to the South, because the three-fifths clause of the Constitution counted slaves for both representation and taxation. The South could exercise its extra influence in the House of Representatives without the threat of extra taxes. By the end of his first term, Jefferson had deeply reduced Hamilton's cherished national debt.

A properly limited federal government, according to Jefferson, was responsible merely for running a postal system, maintaining the federal courts, staffing lighthouses, collecting customs duties, and conducting a census once every ten years. Government jobs were kept to a minimum. The president had just one private secretary, a young man named Meriwether Lewis, to help with his correspondence, and Jefferson paid him out of his own pocket. The Department of State employed only 8 people: Secretary James Madison, 6 clerks, and a messenger. The Treasury Department was by far the largest unit, with 73 revenue commissioners, auditors, and clerks, plus 2 watchmen. The entire payroll of the executive branch amounted to a mere 130 people in 1801.

The Judiciary and the Midnight Judges

There was one set of government workers not under Jefferson's control to appoint. His predecessor, John Adams, seized the few weeks between his election defeat and Jefferson's inauguration to appoint 217 Federalist men to various judicial, diplomatic, and military posts.

Most of this windfall of appointments came to Adams as a result of the Judiciary Act of 1801, passed in the final month of his presidency. Its predecessor, the Judiciary Act of 1789, had established a six-man Supreme Court and six circuit courts. The new law authorized sixteen circuit courts, each headed by a new judge. If he acted quickly, Adams could appoint sixteen circuit court judges with lifetime tenure, plus dozens more attorneys, marshals, and clerks for each court. The 1801 act also reduced the Supreme Court from six to five justices. Prior to its passage, however, Adams appointed solidly Federalist Virginian John Marshall to a vacant sixth seat. After the 1801 act became law, a future president would not be able to fill the next empty seat.

In the last weeks of February 1801, Adams and Marshall worked feverishly to secure agreements from the new appointees. In view of the slowness of mail, achieving 217 acceptances was astonishing. The two men were at work until 9 p.m. on the last night Adams was president, signing and delivering commissions (appointment papers) to the new officeholders.

The appointment of the "midnight judges" infuriated the Republicans. Jefferson, upon taking office, immediately canceled the appointments of the nontenured men and refused to honor the few appointments that had not yet been delivered. One of them was addressed to William Marbury, who soon decided to sue the new secretary of state, James Madison, for failure to make good on the appointment. This action gave rise to a landmark Supreme Court case, *Marbury v. Madison*, decided in 1803. The Court, presided over by John Marshall, ruled that although Marbury's commission was valid and the new president should have delivered it, the Court could not compel him to do so. What made the case significant was little noted at the time: The Court found that the grounds of Marbury's suit, resting in the Judiciary Act of 1789, were in conflict with the Constitution. For the first time, the Court acted to disallow a law on the grounds that it was unconstitutional. John Marshall quietly established the concept of judicial review; the Supreme Court in effect assumed the legal authority to **nullify** acts judged in conflict with the Constitution.

The Promise of the West: The Louisiana Purchase and the Lewis and Clark Expedition

The reach of the *Marbury* decision went largely unnoticed in 1803 because the president and Congress were preoccupied with other major issues, among them the acquisition of the Louisiana Territory. Up through the Seven Years' War (see chapter 6), France claimed but only lightly settled a large expanse of land west of the Mississippi River, only to lose it to Spain in the 1763 Treaty of Paris. Spain never sent adequate forces to control or settle the land, and Spanish power in North America remained precarious everywhere outside New Orleans. Meanwhile, American farming families were settling Kentucky and Tennessee, along rivers emptying into the upper Mississippi, and for a time, the Spanish allowed them to ship their agricultural produce downriver and even encouraged American settlements across the river, in an effort to augment the population. By 1801, Americans made up a sizable minority of the population around the lower Mississippi.

In 1802, rumors reached Jefferson that Spain had struck a secret bargain with France to hand over a large part of Spain's trans-Mississippi territory to Napoleon in exchange for some land in Italy. Spain had proved a weak western neighbor, but France was another story. Jefferson was so alarmed that he instructed Robert R. Livingston, America's minister in France, to try to buy New Orleans. At first the French denied they owned the city, but when Livingston hinted that the United States might simply seize it if buying was not an option, the French negotiator suddenly asked him to name his price for the entire Louisiana Territory, from the Gulf of Mexico north to Canada. Livingston stalled, and the Frenchman made suggestions: $125 million? $60 million? Livingston shrewdly stalled some more, and within days the French sold the entire territory for the bargain price of $15 million (Map 10.1).

Jefferson and most of Congress were delighted with the outcome of the diplomatic mission. Still, Jefferson had some qualms about the Louisiana Purchase. The price was right, and the enormous territory fulfilled Jefferson's dream of abundant farmland for future generations. But by what authority expressed in the Constitution could he justify the purchase? His frequent criticism of Hamilton's stretching of the Constitution came back to haunt him. His legal reasoning told him he needed a constitutional amendment to

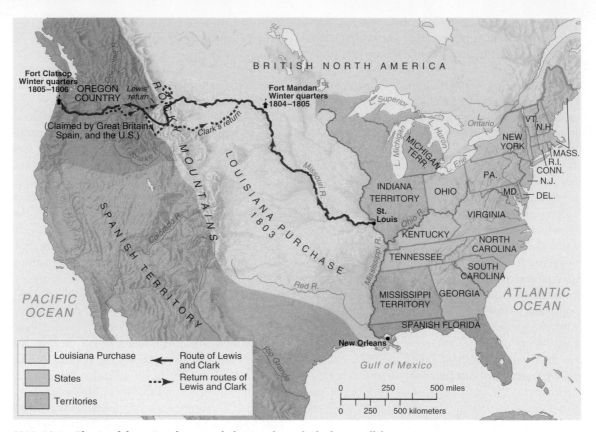

MAP 10.1   The Louisiana Purchase and the Lewis and Clark Expedition
Robert Livingston's bargain buy of 1803 far exceeded his initial assignment, to acquire the city of New Orleans. New England Federalists, worried that their geographically based power in the federal government would someday be eclipsed by the West, voted against the purchase. The Indians who inhabited the vast region, unaware that their land had been claimed by either the French or the Americans, got their first look at Anglo-American and African American men when the Lewis and Clark expedition came exploring in 1804–1806.

READING THE MAP: What natural boundaries defined the Louisiana Purchase? How did the size of the newly acquired territory compare to the existing land area of American states and territories?
CONNECTIONS: What political events in Europe created the opportunity for the Jefferson administration to purchase Louisiana? What constitutional obstacles to expansion did Jefferson have to contend with? How did the American acquisition of the Louisiana territory affect Spain's hold on North America?

FOR MORE HELP ANALYZING THIS MAP, see the map activity for this chapter in the Online Study Guide at
bedfordstmartins.com/roarkcompact.

authorize the addition of territory; more expedient minds told him the treaty-making powers of the president were sufficient. Expediency won out. In late 1803, the American army took formal control of the Louisiana Territory, and the United States grew by 828,000 square miles.

Even before the Louisiana Purchase, Jefferson had eyed the trans-Mississippi West with intense curiosity. In early 1803, he had arranged congressional funding for a secret scientific and military mission into Spanish and Indian territory. Jefferson appointed twenty-eight-year-old Meriwether Lewis, his personal secretary, to head the expedition, instructing him to investigate Indian cultures, to collect plant and animal specimens, and to chart the geography of the West. Congress had more traditional goals in mind: The expedition was to scout locations for military posts, open commercial agreements for the fur trade, and locate any possible waterway between the east and west coasts.

For his co-leader, Lewis chose Kentuckian William Clark, a veteran of the 1790s Indian wars. Together they handpicked a crew of forty-five, including expert rivermen, gunsmiths, hunters, interpreters, a cook, and a slave named York,

Grizzly Bear Claw Necklace

Lewis and Clark collected hundreds of Indian artifacts on their expedition, but until December 2003 only six were known to still exist. Then this grizzly bear claw necklace unexpectedly turned up at Harvard University's Peabody Museum of Archaeology and Ethnology, stored by mistake in a South Pacific collection. Curators instantly recognized it as a necklace missing since 1899 that had been part of a Lewis and Clark museum exhibit in the mid-nineteenth century. In their expedition journal, the famed explorers noted seeing bear claw necklaces on Shoshone warriors in the Rocky Mountains; possibly one of these warriors gave his necklace to the travelers. The 38 impressive claws, each 3 to 4 inches long, are strung together by rawhide thongs; the necklace required at least two four-pawed grizzly bears. Male grizzlies are large—6 to 7 feet tall, 500 to 900 pounds—and aggressive. What would it be like to wear this necklace? Whether spiritual or physical, it seems certain that a sense of power was bestowed on the wearer.

Peabody Museum of Archaeology and Ethnology, Harvard University.

who belonged to Clark. The explorers left St. Louis in the spring of 1804, working their way northwest up the Missouri River. They camped for the winter at a Mandan village in what is now central North Dakota.

The following spring, the explorers headed west, aided by a French trapper accompanied by a sixteen-year-old Indian woman named Sacajawea and their baby. Sacajawea's presence was to prove unexpectedly helpful, and not only for her translating abilities. Indian tribes encountered en route withdrew their suspicion that the Americans were hostile because, as Lewis wrote in his journal, "no woman ever accompanies a war party of Indians in this quarter."

The Lewis and Clark expedition reached the Pacific Ocean at the mouth of the Columbia River in November 1805. When Lewis and Clark returned home the following year, they were greeted as national heroes. They had established favorable relations with dozens of Indian tribes; they had collected invaluable information on the peoples, soils, plants, animals, and geography of the West; and they had inspired a nation of restless explorers and solitary imitators.

Transatlantic Troubles: Impressment and Embargo

The excitement of the Lewis and Clark expedition was balanced by dismaying and escalating tensions with France and England. Each European rival, embroiled in war, repeatedly warned America not to aid the other. Britain acted on these threats in 1806,

stopping American ships, inspecting cargoes for military aid to France, and seizing suspected deserters from the British navy, along with not a few Americans. Ultimately, 2,500 sailors were swept up—impressed—by the British. In retaliation, Jefferson convinced Congress to pass nonimportation laws banning a select list of British-made goods.

One incident made the usually cautious Jefferson nearly belligerent. In June 1807, an American ship, the *Chesapeake*, harboring some British deserters, was ordered to stop by a British frigate, the *Leopard*. The *Chesapeake* refused, and the *Leopard* opened fire, killing three Americans—right at the mouth of Chesapeake Bay, well within U.S. territory. In response Congress passed a total embargo in December 1807, banning all importation of British goods into the country. Though surely a drastic measure, the embargo was meant to forestall war. The goal was to make Britain suffer, and all foreign ports were declared off-limits, to discourage illegal trading through secondary ports. Jefferson was convinced that England needed America's agricultural products far more than America needed British goods. He also was wary of Federalist shipowners who might circumvent the ban.

The Embargo Act of 1807 was a total disaster. From 1790 to 1807, U.S. exports had increased

The *Chesapeake* Incident, June 22, 1807

fivefold; the embargo brought commerce to a standstill. In New England, the heart of the shipping industry, unemployment rose. Grain plummeted in value, river traffic halted, tobacco rotted in the South, and cotton went unpicked. Protest petitions flooded Washington. The federal government suffered too, for import duties were a significant source of revenue. Jefferson paid political costs as well. The Federalist Party, in danger of fading away after its weak showing in the elections of 1804, began to revive.

> **REVIEW**   How did Jefferson attempt to undo the Federalist innovations of earlier administrations?

The Madisons in the White House

In mid-1808, Jefferson indicated that he would not run for a third term. Secretary of State James Madison got the nod from Republican caucuses — informal political groups that orchestrated the selection of candidates for state and local elections. Federalist caucuses chose Charles Cotesworth Pinckney, their candidate also in 1804. Madison won, but Pinckney received 47 electoral votes, nearly half Madison's total. Support for the Federalists remained centered in New England, but Republicans still held the balance of power nationwide.

As president, Madison continued Jefferson's policy of economic pressure on Britain and France with a modified embargo, but he broke new ground in the domestic management of the executive office, with the aid of his astute and talented wife, Dolley Madison. Under her leadership, the president's house was designated the White House — something close to a palace, but a palace many Americans were welcome to visit. Under his leadership, the country went to war in 1812 with Britain and with Tecumseh's warrior confederacy. In 1814, British forces burned the White House and Capitol building nearly to the ground.

Women in Washington City

During in her first eight years in Washington, as wife of the highest-ranking cabinet officer, Dolley Madison developed elaborate social networks that, in the absence of any Mrs. Jefferson, constituted the top level of female politicking in the highly political city. Though women could not vote and supposedly left politics to men, the women of Washington took on several overtly political functions that greased the wheels of the affairs of state. They networked through dinners, balls, receptions, and the intricate custom of "calling," in which men and women paid brief visits and left calling cards at each other's houses. Webs of friendship and influence in turn facilitated female political lobbying. It was not uncommon for women in this social set to write letters of recommendation for men seeking government work. Hostessing was therefore no trivial or leisured business: It influenced the patronage system of the federal government.

When James Madison became president, Dolley Madison, called by some the "presidentress," struck a balance between queenliness and republican openness. She dressed the part in resplendent clothes, choosing a plumed velvet turban for her headdress at her husband's inaugura-

Dolley Madison, **by Gilbert Stuart**
The "presidentress" of the Madison administration sat for this official portrait in 1804. Mrs. Madison here wears an empire-style dress, at the height of French fashion in 1804 and worn by many women at the coronation of the emperor Napoleon in Paris. The hallmarks of an empire dress were light fabric in muslin or chiffon, short sleeves, a high waistline from which the fabric fell straight to the ground, and usually a low open neckline as shown here. The artist made a companion likeness of James Madison, and the two portraits hung in the drawing room of Madison's Virginia estate, Montpelier.
Courtesy of the Pennsylvania Academy of the Fine Arts, Philadelphia.

tion. She opened three large and newly elegant rooms in the executive mansion to evening parties once a week. George and Martha Washington's receptions had been stiff, brief affairs with few guests accomplishing little more than bows and curtsies. In contrast, the Madisons' parties went on for hours with scores and even hundreds of guests milling about, talking, and eating. Attendance at the weekly party, nicknamed "Mrs. Madison's crush" or "squeeze," required an invitation or letter of introduction if one did not already know the Madisons. Evidently invitations were not difficult to obtain. Members of Congress, cabinet officers, distinguished guests, envoys from foreign countries, all these and their womenfolk attended with regularity. Even people who hated parties—or these gatherings in particular—attended. Mrs. Madison's "squeeze" was an essential event for gaining political access and establishing informal channels that would smooth the governing process.

In 1810–1811, Dolley Madison's house acquired its present name, the "White House," probably a reference to its light sandstone exterior. The many guests at the weekly parties experienced simultaneously the splendor of the executive mansion and the atmosphere of republicanism that made it accessible to so many. Dolley Madison, ever an enormous political asset to her rather shy husband, understood well the symbolic function of inventing this new White House to enhance the power and legitimacy of the presidency.

Indian Troubles in the West

While the Madisons cemented alliances at home, difficulties with Britain and France overseas and with Indians in the old Northwest continued to increase. The Shawnee chief Tecumseh actively solidified his confederacy, while far northern tribes renewed ties with supportive British agents and fur traders in Canada, a potential source of food and weapons. If the United States went to war with Britain, there would clearly be serious repercussions on the **frontier**.

Shifting demographics raised the stakes for both sides. The 1810 census counted some 230,000 Americans living in Ohio, only seven years after statehood. Another 40,000 Americans inhabited the territories of Indiana, Illinois, and Michigan. The Indian population of the entire region (the old Northwest Territory) was much smaller, probably about 70,000, a number unknown (because uncounted) to the Americans but certainly gauged by Tecumseh during his extensive travels.

***Tenskwatawa*, by George Catlin**
Tenskwatawa, the Shawnee Prophet, and his brother Tecumseh led the spiritual and political efforts of a number of Indian tribes to resist land-hungry Americans moving west in the decade before the War of 1812. George Catlin portrays the Prophet wearing beaded necklaces, metal arm- and wristbands, and earrings. Compare the metal gorget here with the one worn by Joseph Brant (page 171). National Museum of American Art, Washington, D.C. / Art Resource, NY.

Up to 1805, Indiana's territorial governor, William Henry Harrison, had negotiated a series of treaties in a divide-and-conquer strategy extracting Indian lands for paltry payments. But with the rise to power of Tecumseh and his brother Tenskwatawa, the Prophet, Harrison's strategy faltered. A fundamental part of Tecumseh's message was the assertion that all Indian lands were held in common by all the tribes: "No tribe has the right to sell, even to each other, much less to strangers.... Sell a country! Why not sell the air, the great sea, as well as the earth? Didn't the Great Spirit make them all for the use of his children?" Taking advantage of Tecumseh's absence on a recruiting trip, Harrison assembled leaders of the Potawatomi, Miami, and Delaware tribes to negotiate the Treaty of Fort Wayne in 1809. After promising (falsely) that this was the last cession of land the United States would seek, Harrison secured three million acres at about two cents per acre.

When he returned, Tecumseh was furious with both Harrison and the tribal leaders. Leaving his

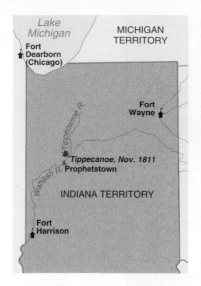

Battle of Tippecanoe, 1811

brother in charge at Prophetstown on Tippecanoe Creek, the Shawnee chief left on a trip to seek alliances in the South. Harrison then decided to attack Prophetstown with one thousand men. The two-hour battle resulted in the deaths of 62 Americans and 40 Indians before the Prophet's forces fled the town, which Harrison's men set on fire. The November 1811 battle of Tippecanoe was heralded as a glorious victory for the Americans. But Tecumseh was now more ready than ever to make war on the Americans.

The War of 1812

The Indian conflicts in the Northwest Territory in 1811 soon merged into the wider conflict with England now known as the War of 1812. Between 1809 and 1812, President Madison teetered between declaring England or France the prime enemy, as attacks by both countries on American ships continued. In 1809, Congress had replaced Jefferson's stringent embargo with the Non-Intercourse Act, which prohibited trade only with England and France and their colonies, thus opening up other trade routes to diminish somewhat the anguish of shippers, farmers, and **planters**. By 1811, the country was seriously divided and in a deep quandary. To some, the United States seemed, appropriately, on the verge of war — though with France or England was not clear. To others, war with either meant disaster for commerce.

A new Congress arrived in Washington in March 1811. Several dozen of the younger Republican members were eager to avenge the insults from abroad. Henry Clay, thirty-four, from Kentucky, and John C. Calhoun, twenty-nine, from South Carolina, became the center of a group informally known as the **War Hawks**. They saluted Harrison's Tippecanoe victory and urged the country to war. Mostly lawyers by profession, they came from the West and South, and they welcomed a war with England both to legitimize attacks on the Indians and to bring an end to impressment. Many were also expansionists, looking to occupy Florida and threaten Canada. Clay was elected Speaker of the House, an extraordinary honor for a young newcomer; Calhoun won a seat on the Foreign Relations Committee. The War Hawks approved major defense expenditures, and the army soon quadrupled in size.

In June 1812, Congress declared war on Great Britain in a vote divided on sectional lines: New England and some Middle Atlantic states opposed the war, while the South and West were strongly for it. Ironically, Great Britain had just announced it would stop the search and seizure of American ships, but the war momentum would not be slowed. The Foreign Relations Committee issued an elaborate justification titled *Report on the Causes and Reasons for War*, written mainly by Calhoun and containing extravagant language about Britain's "lust for power," "unbounded tyranny," and "mad ambition." These were fighting words in a war that was in large measure about insult and honor.

The War Hawks proposed an invasion of Canada, confidently predicting victory in four weeks. Instead, the war lasted two and a half years, and Canada never fell. The northern invasion turned out to be a series of blunders that revealed the grave unpreparedness of the United States for war. The combined British and Indian forces were unexpectedly powerful, and the United States made no attempt at the outset to create a naval presence on the Great Lakes. Detroit quickly fell, as did Fort Dearborn (site of the future Chicago). By the fall of 1812, the outlook was grim.

Worse, the New England states dragged their feet in raising troops, and some New England merchants carried on illegal trade with Great Britain. President Madison fumed in Washington about Federalist disloyalty while Bostonians drank India tea in Liverpool cups. The fall presidential election pitted Madison against DeWitt Clinton of New York, nominally a Republican but able to attract the Federalist vote. Clinton picked up all of New England's electoral votes, with the exception of Vermont's, and also took New York, New Jersey, and part of Maryland. Madison won in the electoral college, 128 to 89, but his margin of victory was considerably smaller than in 1808.

In late 1812 and early 1813, the tide began to turn in the Americans' favor. First came some reassuring victories at sea. Then Americans attacked York (now Toronto), the capital of Upper Canada, and burned it in April 1813. A few months later, Commodore Oliver Hazard Perry defeated the British fleet at the western end of Lake Erie. Emboldened, General Harrison drove an army into Canada from Detroit and in October 1813 defeated the British and Indians at the battle of the Thames, where Tecumseh met his death (Map 10.2).

Indians in the South who had allied with Tecumseh's confederacy were also plunged into

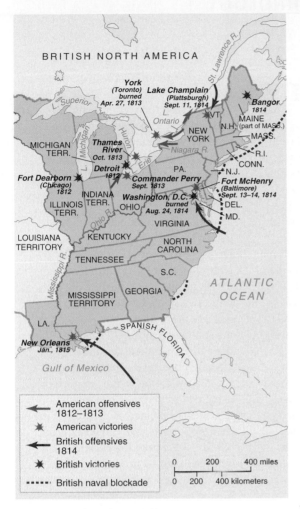

MAP 10.2 The War of 1812
During the War of 1812, battles were fought along the border of Canada and in the Chesapeake region. The most important American victory came in New Orleans two weeks after peace had been agreed to in England.

all-out war. Some fifty villages containing around 10,000 Creek Indians in the southern region of Mississippi Territory put up a spirited fight against American militia troops for ten months in 1813–1814. Even without Tecumseh's recruitment trip of 1811 or the War of 1812, the Creeks had grievances aplenty, sparked by American settlers moving into their territory. Using guns obtained in the panhandle of Spanish Florida, the Creeks mounted a strong defense. But the Creek War was suddenly over in March 1814, when a general named Andrew Jackson led 2,500 Tennessee militiamen in a bloody attack called the Battle of Horseshoe Bend. More than 550 Indians were killed, and several hundred more died trying to escape across a river. Later that year, General

Jackson extracted from the defeated Creeks a treaty relinquishing thousands of square miles of their land to the United States.

Washington City Burns: The British Offensive

In August 1814, British ships sailed into Chesapeake Bay, throwing the capital into a panic. Families evacuated, banks hid their money, and government clerks carted away boxes of important papers. Dolley Madison, with dinner for guests cooking on the fire (see "The Promise of Technology," page 246), fled with her husband's papers and a portrait of George Washington. Five thousand British troops entered the city and burned the White House, the Capitol, a newspaper office, and a well-stocked arsenal. Instead of trying to hold the city, the British headed north and attacked Baltimore, but a fierce defense by the Maryland militia thwarted that effort.

In another powerful offensive, British troops marched from Canada into New York State, but a series of mistakes cost them a naval skirmish at Plattsburgh on Lake Champlain and also cost them their nerve, and they retreated to Canada. The withdrawal was a decisive military event, for British leaders in England, hearing of the retreat, concluded that incursions by land into the United States would be expensive and difficult.

This point was confirmed when a large British army landed in lower Louisiana and encountered General Andrew Jackson and his militia just outside New Orleans in early January 1815. Jackson's forces dramatically carried the day. The British suffered between 2,000 and 3,000 casualties, the Americans fewer than 80. Jackson became an instant hero. The battle of New Orleans was the most glorious victory the Americans had experienced, allowing some Americans to boast that the United States had won a second war of independence from England. No one in the United States knew that negotiators in Europe had signed a peace agreement two weeks earlier.

The Treaty of Ghent, signed in December 1814, settled few of the surface issues that had led to war. Neither country could claim victory, and no land changed hands. Instead, the treaty reflected a mutual agreement to give up certain goals. The Americans yielded on impressment and gave up any claim to Canada; and the British agreed to abandon aid to Indians. Nothing was said about shipping rights. The most concrete result was a plan for a commission to determine the exact boundary between the United States and Canada.

Stoves Transform Cooking

The cookstove, one of the most underrated achievements of the technology of daily life, fundamentally changed the way men and women labored to put food on the table. Its slow development can be traced in the nearly one thousand patents registered between 1815 and 1850 by inventors tinkering to control heat, devise convenient cooking surfaces, and improve fuel efficiency.

Before 1815, nearly all household cooking was accomplished in wood-burning fireplaces. Daily fires used for cooking and heating consumed immense amounts of wood; in cold climates, a household might require 40 cords of wood per year. Supplying each cord (a pile measuring 4-by-4-by-8 feet) was laborious men's work; the difficult and dangerous tasks of cooking and maintaining the fire fell to women. Great skill was needed to time the peak heat to coordinate with the varying temperature needs of baking, stewing, and roasting. Muscles and stamina were required to hoist 20-pound iron pots and cauldrons onto the hooks that suspended them over the fire. Cooks worked dangerously close to open flames when tending a roasting joint of meat on a spit or raking smaller fires out of the large one to heat frying skillets set on trivets on the hearth. Women wearing long skirts risked clothing fires, and children running about sometimes collided with hot pots and burning logs at floor level. The heavy lifting and exposure to the blasting heat, especially uncomfortable on hot summer days, exacted a toll on every cook.

In 1744, Benjamin Franklin developed a heating stove that enclosed a wood fire on three sides in a small cast-iron box, which radiated heat to the room. (The open fourth side allowed a pleasing view of the dancing flames.) The Franklin stove cut fuel costs, but it did not catch on for another half century as an alternative to heating by fireplace. Its inadequate venting of smoke was one problem, not fixed until the 1790s. Further, cast iron was expensive and wood was cheap, and the Franklin stove offered no provision for cooking. As long as wood remained affordable, Americans preferred the look of a log fire and the taste of food cooked over one.

Then, between 1800 and 1815, a serious fuel shortage driven by the depletion of forests caused wood prices to double along the eastern coast. At the same time, domestic iron manufacturing started to flourish, encouraged by Jefferson's shipping embargo and the War of 1812. With wood rising and iron falling in price, the conditions were right for the start of serious cookstove manufacture. Many inventors got to work.

The cast iron contraptions advertised around 1815 were larger than the Franklin stove and had a flat surface on top where pots and pans could be heated by the fire burning below. One challenge was to find a simple way to modulate the fire by varying the amount of air feeding it, through better design of the damper system. Dampers were valves or movable plates that controlled the draft of air to the fire and hence the rate of combustion. A related challenge was to manage the temperatures of the cooking spaces and surfaces. This could be done by moving pots around, by raising and lowering the grate that held the logs inside the firebox, or even by using cranks to rotate the fire.

Most of the new stoves raised the cooking surface nearly to waist level, offering relief from the backbreaking labor required by fireplace cookery. They fully enclosed the fire, minimizing the risk of clothing fires; they prevented sparks from jumping on floors and carpets; and they piped sooty air with combustion pollutants out of the house. For all these reasons, stove cooking was a great advance in safety.

New stoves changed not only the way people cooked but the way they ate. On a hearth, separate dishes required separate fires, so cooks generally limited meals to one-pot stews. Using the new stoves, cooks could prepare several different dishes with

---

Antiwar New England Federalists could not gloat over the war's ambiguous conclusion, because of an ill-timed and seemingly unpatriotic move on their part. The region's leaders had convened a secret meeting in Hartford, Connecticut, in December 1814, to discuss dramatic measures to curb the South's power. They proposed amending the Constitution to abolish the three-fifths clause as a basis of representation; to specify that congressional powers to pass embargoes, admit states, or declare war should require a two-thirds vote instead of a simple majority; and to limit the president to one term and prohibit the election of successive presidents

An Early Cookstove

A stove of the 1820s, patented by W. T. James, sits in this reconstructed historical site adjacent to the fireplace it has replaced. A stovepipe vents combustion fumes out the old chimney; a large flat surface over the fire provides a cooktop, shown here with a copper pot and a teakettle whose extremely large base speeds water to a boil. The round container on the lower ledge of the stove is a reflector oven, called a "tin kitchen," first used with fireplaces and then adapted for cookstoves. A spit inside held meat, and a crank (visible on the end) was used to turn the food. Put against the fire, the tin oven cooked its contents by direct and reflected heat, while the round bottom preserved the meat juices. In this scene, the old fireplace is bricked up and used for storing wood for the stove. Householders of the 1820s would have seen this setup as a highly modern convenience offering improvements in safety, fuel efficiency, and heat control.

Old Sturbridge Village.

The cookstove changed home labor for both men and women. It shrank men's role in meal preparation by curtailing the work of procuring wood. No such reduction occurred for women. Replacing the hours of careful fire-tending that women had once done were hours spent maintaining and cleaning stoves—removing ashes, cleaning soot from flues and dampers, and blacking the entire stove weekly with a thick paste to keep it from rusting.

From 1815 to the mid-nineteenth century, the cookstove was a work in progress; the many imperfections in the initial designs sent inventors back to the workbench again and again to try to perfect this new cooking system. Nonetheless, women wanted stoves for their safety and convenience, and men liked them for their fuel efficiency. In the late 1840s, the widespread popularity of cookstoves became evident along wagon trails heading west. Many families had packed up their stoves for the trip—evidence they embraced the new style of cooking—but had to abandon them along the way when forced to lighten their loads. One traveling teenager wrote that "we heard great talk of things being thrown away on the road but we saw little that was any good excepting stoves and there were plenty of them." Cookstoves had become America's first popular "consumer durable."

just one fire, and meals became more varied. However, not everyone was pleased. Many complained that the convenience of stoves came at the price of food quality. Oven-baked meat was nearly universally regarded as less savory than meat roasted over a fire, and in flavor and crustiness oven-baked bread did not measure up to bread baked in the brick chamber of a fireplace wall. Nonetheless, convenience triumphed.

from the same state. The cumulative effect of these proposals would have been to reduce the South's political power and break the lock of the Virginia dynasty on national office. New England wanted to assure that no one sectional party could again lead the country into war against the clear interests of another. The Federalists at Hartford even discussed secession from the Union but rejected that path. Coming just as peace was achieved, however, the Hartford Convention suddenly looked very unpatriotic. The Federalist Party never recovered its grip, and within a few years its presence even in New England was reduced to a shadow.

No one really won the War of 1812. Americans celebrated as though they had, however, with parades and fireworks. The war gave rise to a new spirit of **nationalism**. The paranoia over British tyranny evident in the 1812 declaration of war was laid to rest, replaced by pride in a more equal relationship with the old mother country. Indeed, in 1817 the two countries signed the Rush-Bagot disarmament treaty (named after its two negotiators), which limited each country to a total of four naval vessels, each with just a single cannon, to patrol the vast watery border between them. The Rush-Bagot treaty was perhaps the most successful disarmament treaty for a century to come.

The biggest winners in the War of 1812 were the young men, once called War Hawks, who took up the banner of the Republican Party and carried it in new, expansive directions. These young politicians favored trade, western expansion, internal improvements, and the energetic development of new economic markets. The biggest losers of the war were the Indians. Tecumseh was dead, the Prophet discredited, the prospects of an Indian confederacy dashed, the Creeks' large homeland seized, and the British protectors gone.

> **REVIEW**   Why did Congress declare war on Great Britain in 1812?

Women's Status in the Early Republic

With the model of "presidentress" Dolley Madison before the public, and the 1790s debate over education for motherhood still fresh (see chapter 9), it might be expected that the early nineteenth century would post advances in the status of women. And in one area, female education, marked improvement did occur: Both boys and girls profited from the spread of basic public schooling, seen as vital to the production of citizens in a **democratic** state. By 1830, female literacy and numeracy were rapidly rising. Adolescent girls from genteel families could pursue higher learning at any of the 400 new female academies founded between 1790 and 1830. But other arenas and institutions central to the shaping of women's lives—laws, marriage, and church—showed either no change or only incremental change. State legislatures and the courts grappled with the legal dependency of married white women in a country whose defining char-

acteristic was independence, while religious organizations struggled to redefine the role of women in church governance. If, in the end, there was no giant step forward for women in these decades, it is still significant that these questions were raised at all.

Women and the Law

The Anglo-American view of women, implanted in British common law, was that wives had no independent legal or political personhood. The legal doctrine of *feme covert* (covered woman) held that a wife's civic life was completely subsumed by her husband's. A wife was obligated to obey her husband; her property was his, her domestic and sexual services were his, and even their children were legally his. Women had no right to keep their wages, to make contracts, or to sue or be sued. State legislatures generally passed up the opportunity to rewrite the laws of domestic relations even though they redrafted other British laws in light of republican principles. Lawyers never paused to defend, much less to challenge, the assumption that unequal power relations lay at the heart of marriage.

The one aspect of family law that changed in the early Republic was divorce. Before the Revolution, only New England jurisdictions recognized a limited right to divorce; by 1820, every state except South Carolina did so. However, divorce was uncommon and difficult and in many states could be obtained only by petition to the state's legislature, a daunting obstacle for many ordinary people. A mutual wish to terminate a marriage was never sufficient grounds for legal divorce. A New York judge affirmed that "it would be aiming a deadly blow at public morals to decree a dissolution of the marriage contract merely because the parties requested it. Divorces should never be allowed, except for the protection of the innocent party, and for the punishment of the guilty." States upheld the institution of marriage both to protect persons they thought of as naturally dependent (women and children) and to regulate the use and inheritance of property. (Unofficial self-divorce, desertion, and bigamy were remedies that ordinary people sometimes chose to get around the strictness of marriage law. But powerful social sanctions against such behavior usually prevailed.) Legal enforcement of marriage as an unequal relationship played a major role in maintaining gender inequality in the nineteenth century.

Single adult women could own and convey property, make contracts, initiate lawsuits, and pay taxes. They could not vote (except in New Jersey before 1807), serve on juries, or practice law, so their civil status was limited. Single women's economic status was often limited as well, by custom as much as by law. Unless they had inherited adequate property or could live with married siblings, single adult women in the early Republic were very often poor.

None of the legal institutions that structured white gender relations applied to black slaves. As property themselves, slaves could not freely consent to any contractual obligations, including marriage. The protective features of state-sponsored unions were thus denied to black men and women in slavery, who were controlled by a more powerful authority: the slave owner. But this also meant that slave unions did not establish unequal power relations between partners, backed by the force of law, as did marriages among the free.

Women and Church Governance

In most **Protestant** denominations around 1800, white women made up the majority of congregants, as they had for some time. Yet the church hierarchy—ordained ministers and elders—was exclusively male, and the governance of most denominations rested in men's hands.

There were some exceptions, however. In Baptist congregations in New England, women served along with men on church governance committees, deciding on admissions of new members, voting on hiring ministers, and even debating doctrinal points. Quakers, too, had a history of recognizing women's spiritual talents. Quaker women who felt a special call were accorded the status of minister, which meant they were capable of leading and speaking in Quaker meetings.

Between 1790 and 1820, a small and highly unusual set of women emerged who actively engaged in open preaching. Most were from Freewill Baptist groups centered in New England and upstate New York. Others came from small Methodist sects, and yet others rejected any formal religious affiliation. Probably fewer than a hundred such women existed, but several dozen traveled beyond their local communities, creating converts and controversy. They spoke from the heart, without prepared speeches, often exhibiting trances and claiming to exhort (counsel or warn) rather than to preach. None of these women were ordained ministers with official credentials to preach or perform baptisms.

Perhaps the most well-known exhorting woman was Jemima Wilkinson, who called herself the "Publick Universal Friend." After a near-death experience from high fever in 1776, Wilkinson proclaimed her body no longer female or male but the incarnation of the "Spirit of Light." She dressed in men's clothes, wore her hair in a masculine style, shunned gender-specific pronouns, and preached openly in Rhode Island and Philadelphia. In the early nineteenth century, Wilkinson withdrew to a settlement called New Jerusalem in western New York with some 250 followers.

The decades from 1790 to the 1820s marked a period of unusual confusion, ferment, and creativity in American religion. New denominations blossomed, new styles of religiosity gripped adherents, and an extensive periodical press devoted to religion popularized all manner of theological

Women and the Church: Jemima Wilkinson
Jemima Wilkinson, the "Publick Universal Friend," in an early woodcut, wears a clerical collar and body-obscuring robe, in keeping with the claim that the former Jemima was now a person without sex or gender. Her hair is pulled back tight on her head and curled at the neck in a masculine style of the 1790s. Did she become masculinized, or did she truly transcend gender?
Rhode Island Historical Society.

and institutional innovations. Congregations increasingly attracted vibrant female participation, often eclipsing the percentage of male congregants. In such a climate, the age-old tradition of gender subordination came into question here and there among the most radically democratic of the churches. But the presumption of male authority over women was deeply entrenched in American culture. Even denominations that had allowed women to participate in church governance began to pull back, and most churches reinstated patterns of hierarchy along gender lines.

REVIEW   How did the civil status of American women and men differ in the decades of the early Republic?

Monroe and Adams

With the elections of 1816 and 1820, Virginians continued their long hold on the presidency. In 1816, James Monroe beat Federalist Rufus King of New York by 183 electoral votes to 34. In 1820, Monroe was reelected with all but one electoral vote, but that near unanimity did not necessarily reflect voter satisfaction, for barely one-quarter of eligible voters went to the polls.

After Monroe's first victory, the collapse of the Federalist Party led one over-optimistic newspaper to proclaim the arrival of an "Era of Good Feelings," as though a period of one-party government was destined to be harmonious. The harmony did not last long. Monroe and his aloof wife Elizabeth sharply curtailed social gatherings in the White House, driving the hard work of social networking into different and competing channels. Ill feelings were stirred by a sectional crisis over the admission of Missouri to the Union, and foreign policy questions animated sharp disagreements as well. The election of 1824 brought forth an abundance of candidates, all claiming to be Republicans. The winner was John Quincy Adams, in an election decided by the House of Representatives and, many believed, by a backroom bargain. Put to the test of practical circumstances, the one-party political system failed and then fractured.

The Missouri Compromise

In February 1819, Missouri applied for statehood. Since 1815, four other states had joined the Union (Indiana, Mississippi, Illinois, and Alabama),

following the blueprint laid out by the Northwest Ordinance of 1787. But Missouri posed a problem. Although much of its area was on the same latitude as the free state of Illinois, its territorial population included 10,000 slaves brought there by southern white planters.

Missouri's unusual combination of geography and demography led a New York congressman, James Tallmadge Jr., to propose two amendments to the statehood bill. The first stipulated that slaves born in Missouri after statehood would be free at age twenty-five, and the second declared that no new slaves could be imported into the state. Tallmadge modeled the first amendment on New York's gradual **emancipation** law of 1799. It did not strip slave owners of their current property, and it allowed them full use of the labor of newborn slaves well into their prime productive years. Still, Southerners in Congress objected, because in the long run the amendments would make Missouri a free state, and presumably one no longer allied with southern economic and political interests. Just as southern economic power rested on slave labor, southern political power drew extra strength from the slave population because of the three-fifths rule. In 1820, the South owed seventeen of the region's seats in the House of Representatives to its slave population.

Tallmadge's amendments passed in the House by a close and sharply sectional vote of North against South. The ferocious debate led a Georgia representative to observe that the question had started "a fire which all the waters of the ocean could not extinguish. It can be extinguished only in blood." The Senate voted down the amendments, and Missouri statehood was postponed for the next congressional term.

In 1820, a compromise emerged. Maine, once a part of Massachusetts, applied for statehood as a free state, balancing against Missouri as a slave state. The Senate further agreed that the southern boundary of Missouri—latitude 36°30′—extended west, would become the permanent line dividing slave from free states, guaranteeing the North a large area where slavery was banned (Map 10.3). The House also approved the compromise, thanks to expert deal brokering by Kentucky's Henry Clay, who earned the nickname the "Great Pacificator" for his superb negotiating skills. The whole package passed because seventeen northern congressmen decided that minimizing sectional conflict was the best course and voted with the South.

President Monroe and former president Jefferson at first worried that the Missouri crisis

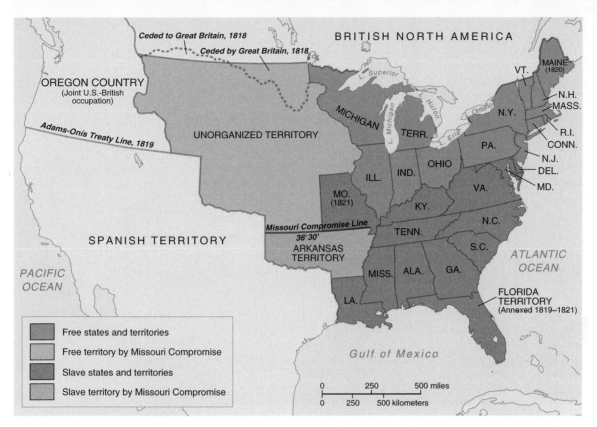

Free states and territories

Free territory by Missouri Compromise

Slave states and territories

Slave territory by Missouri Compromise

MAP 10.3   The Missouri Compromise, 1820
After a difficult battle in Congress, Missouri entered the Union in 1821 as part of a package of compromises. Maine was admitted as a free state to balance slavery in Missouri, and a line drawn at latitude 36°30' put most of the rest of the Louisiana Territory off limits to slavery in the future.

would reinvigorate the Federalist Party as the party of the North. But even ex-Federalists agreed that the split between free and slave states was too dangerous a fault line to be permitted to become a shaper of national politics. When new parties did develop in the 1830s, they took pains to bridge geography, each party developing a presence in both North and South. Monroe and Jefferson also worried about the future of slavery. Each understood slavery to be deeply problematic, but, as Jefferson said, "We have the wolf by the ears, and we can neither hold him, nor safely let him go. Justice is in one scale, and self-preservation in the other."

The Monroe Doctrine

New foreign policy challenges arose even as Congress struggled with the slavery issue. In 1816, American troops led by General Andrew Jackson invaded Spanish Florida in search of Seminole Indians harboring escaped slaves. Once there, Jackson declared himself the commander of northern Florida, demonstrating his power in

1818 by executing two British men who he claimed were dangerous enemies. In asserting rule over the territory, and surely in executing the two British subjects on Spanish land, Jackson had gone too far. Privately, President Monroe was distressed and pondered court-martialing Jackson, prevented only by Jackson's immense popularity as the hero of the battle of New Orleans. Instead, John Quincy Adams, the secretary of state, negotiated with Spain the Adams-Onís Treaty, which delivered Florida to the United States in 1819. In exchange, the Americans agreed to abandon any claim to Texas or Cuba.

Spain at that moment was preoccupied with its colonies in South America. One after another— Chile, Colombia, Peru, and finally Mexico— declared itself independent in the early 1820s. To discourage Spain or France from reconquering these colonies, Monroe formulated a declaration of principles on South America. Incorporated into his annual message to Congress in December 1823, the declaration became known in later years as the **Monroe Doctrine**. The president warned that

A View of St. Louis from an Illinois Town, 1835

Just fifteen years after the Missouri Compromise, St. Louis was already a booming city, having gotten its start in the eighteenth century as a French fur-trading village. It was incorporated as a town in 1809 and chartered as a city in 1822. In this 1835 view, commercial buildings and steamships line the riverfront; a ferry on the Illinois shore prepares to transport travelers across the Mississippi River. Black laborers (in the foreground) handle loading tasks. The Illinois side is a free state; Missouri, where the ferry lands, is a slave state.

A View of St. Louis from an Illinois Town, 1835: Private collection.

FOR MORE HELP ANALYZING THIS IMAGE, see the visual activity for this chapter in the Online Study Guide at **bedfordstmartins.com/roarkcompact**.

"the American Continents, by the free and independent condition which they have assumed and maintain, are henceforth not to be considered as subjects for future colonization by any European power." Any attempt to interfere in the Western Hemisphere would be regarded as "the manifestation of an unfriendly disposition towards the United States." In exchange for noninterference by Europeans, Monroe pledged that the United States would stay out of European struggles.

The Election of 1824

Monroe's nonpartisan administration was the last of its kind, a throwback to eighteenth-century ideals, led by the last president to wear a powdered wig and knee breeches. Monroe's cabinet contained men of sharply different philosophies. Secretary of State John Quincy Adams repre-sented the urban Northeast; South Carolinian John C. Calhoun spoke for the planter aristocracy as secretary of war; and William H. Crawford of Georgia, secretary of the treasury, was a proponent of Jeffersonian **states' rights** and limited federal power. Even before the end of Monroe's first term, these men and others began to maneuver for the election of 1824.

Crucially helping them to maneuver were their wives, who accomplished some of the work of modern campaign managers by courting of men—and women—of influence. The parties not thrown by Mrs. Monroe were now given all over town by women whose husbands were jockeying for political favor. Louisa Catherine Adams remodeled her house and had parties every Tuesday night for guests numbering in the hundreds. The somber Adams lacked charm—"I am a man of reserved, cold, austere, and forbidding manners" he once wrote—but his abundantly charming (and hardworking) wife made up for that. She attended to the etiquette of social calls, sometimes making two dozen in a morning, and counted sixty-eight members of Congress as her regular Tuesday guests.

Since 1800, the congressional caucus of each party had met to identify and lend its considerable but still informal support to its party's leading candidate. In 1824, with only one party alive—and alive with five serious candidates—the caucus system splintered. Since such a large number of candidates reduced the chance of anyone securing a majority in the electoral college, many expected that the final election would be decided by the House of Representatives. Having sixty-eight members of Congress on one's regular guest list was thus smart politics.

John Quincy Adams (and Louisa Catherine) very much wanted the presidency, an ambition fed by John's sense of rising to his father's accomplishment. Henry Clay, Speaker of the House, declared his candidacy; a man of vast congressional experience, he had engaged in high-level diplomacy in negotiating the Treaty of Ghent in 1814 with Britain. Clay promoted his "American System," a package of protective tariffs to encourage manufacturing and federal expenditures for extensive internal improvements such as roads and canals. Treasurer William Crawford was a favorite of Republicans from Virginia and New York; despite suffering an incapacitating stroke in mid-1824, he remained their favorite. Calhoun was another serious contender, having served in Congress and in several cabinets. Like Clay, he favored internal improvements and protective tariffs, which gained him support in northern states.

The final candidate was an outsider and a latecomer: General Andrew Jackson of Tennessee. Jackson had much less national political experience than the others, having served one year in the House and two in the Senate. His fame derived from his reputation as a military leader. In 1824, on the anniversary of the battle of New Orleans, the Adamses threw a spectacular ball with five hundred guests in honor of General Jackson. No doubt Adams hoped that some of Jackson's charisma would rub off on him; he was not yet thinking of Jackson as a rival for office. But later in 1824, Jackson supporters put his name in play, and voters in the West and South reacted with enthusiasm. Calhoun soon dropped out of the race and shifted his attention to winning the vice presidency.

The 1824 election was the first presidential contest in which candidates' popularity with

Election Sewing Box from 1824
The female owner of this sewing box displayed her presidential preference for John Quincy Adams. His picture adorns the interior surface of the lid; the top of the box, not visible here, carries a velvet pincushion emblazoned with the slogan "BE FIRM FOR ADAMS." Thousand of souvenir campaign boxes were manufactured for the leading candidates using a new lithographic process just coming into wide use in the 1820s.
Collection of Janice L. and David J. Frent.

ordinary voters could be measured. Recent changes in state constitutions gave voters in all but six states the power to choose electors for the electoral college. (Before, state legislatures had held this power.) Jackson was by far the most popular candidate with voters, winning 153,000 votes. Adams was second with 109,000, Clay won 47,000 votes, and the debilitated Crawford garnered 46,600. This was not a large voter turnout, probably amounting to only a quarter of adult white males. Many more voters participated regularly in local and state elections, where the real political action generally lay.

In the electoral college, Jackson received 99 votes, Adams 84, Crawford 41, and Clay 37 (Map 10.4). Jackson did not have a majority, so the election went to the House of Representatives, for the second (and last) time in American history. Each state delegation had one vote; according to the Twelfth Amendment to the Constitution, passed in 1804, only the top three candidates could enter the runoff. Thus Henry Clay was out of the race and in a position to bestow his support on another candidate.

Jackson's supporters later characterized the election of 1824 as the "corrupt bargain." Clay backed Adams, and Adams won by one vote in the House, in a vote in February 1825. Clay's support made sense on several levels. Despite strong mutual dislike, he and Adams agreed on issues such as federal support to build roads and canals, and Clay was uneasy with Jackson's volatile temperament and unstated political views and with Crawford's diminished capacity. What made Clay's decision look "corrupt" was that immediately after the election, Adams offered to appoint Clay secretary of state—and Clay accepted.

In the weeks before the vote in the House, rumors of such a deal had been denied by Adams and Clay supporters, confident that the two archenemies could never cooperate. There probably was no concrete bargain; Adams's subsequent cabinet appointments demonstrated his lack of political astuteness. But Andrew Jackson felt that the election had been stolen from him, and he wrote bitterly that "the Judas of the West has closed the contract and will receive the thirty pieces of silver."

The Adams Administration

John Quincy Adams, like his father, was a one-term president. His career had been built on diplomacy, not electoral politics, and, despite his wife's deft experience in the art of political influence, his own political horse sense was not well developed. His cabinet choices welcomed his opposition into his inner circle. He asked Crawford to stay on in the Treasury. He retained an openly pro-Jackson postmaster general even though that position controlled thousands of nationwide patronage appointments. He even asked Jackson to become secretary of war. With Calhoun as vice president (elected without opposition by the electoral college) and Clay at the State Department, the whole argumentative crew would have been thrust into the executive branch. Crawford and Jackson had the good sense to decline the appointments.

Adams had lofty ideas for federal action during his presidency, and the plan he put before Congress was so sweeping that it took Henry Clay aback. Adams called for federally built roads, canals, and harbors. He proposed a national university in Washington as well as government-sponsored scientific research. He wanted to build observatories to advance astronomical knowledge and to promote precision in timekeeping, and he backed a

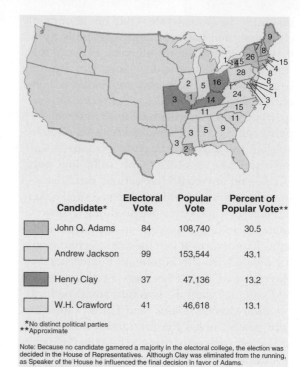

Candidate*	Electoral Vote	Popular Vote	Percent of Popular Vote**
John Q. Adams	84	108,740	30.5
Andrew Jackson	99	153,544	43.1
Henry Clay	37	47,136	13.2
W.H. Crawford	41	46,618	13.1

*No distinct political parties
**Approximate

Note: Because no candidate garnered a majority in the electoral college, the election was decided in the House of Representatives. Although Clay was eliminated from the running, as Speaker of the House he influenced the final decision in favor of Adams.

MAP 10.4   The Election of 1824

decimal-based system of weights and measures. In all these endeavors, Adams believed he was continuing the Jefferson and Madison legacy, using the powers of government to advance knowledge. But his opponents feared he was too Hamiltonian, using federal power inappropriately to advance commercial interests.

Whether he was more truly Federalist or Republican was a moot point, however. Lacking the give-and-take political skills required to gain congressional support, Adams was unable to implement much of his program. He scorned the idea of courting voters to gain support and using the patronage system to enhance his power. He often made appointments (to posts such as customs collectors) to placate enemies rather than reward friends. A story of a toast offered to the president may well have been mythical, but as humorous folklore it made the rounds during his term and came to summarize Adams's precarious hold on leadership. A dignitary raised a glass and said, "May he strike confusion to his foes…," to which another voice scornfully chimed in, "as he has already done to his friends."

> **REVIEW**   How did the collapse of the Federalist Party influence the administrations of James Monroe and John Quincy Adams?

Conclusion: Republican Simplicity Becomes Complex

Jeffersonian Republicans tried at first to undo much of what Federalists had created in the 1790s, but their promise of a simpler government gave way to the complexities of domestic and foreign issues. The sudden acquisition of the Louisiana Purchase promised land and opportunity to settlers but also complicated the country's political future with the issues central to the Missouri Compromise. Antagonism from both foreign and Indian nations led to complex and costly policies such as embargoes, treaties, and military action, culminating in the War of 1812, a war motivated less by concrete economic or political issues than by questions of honor. Its conclusion at the battle of New Orleans allowed Americans the illusion that they had fought a second war of independence.

The War of 1812 was the Indians' second *lost* war for independence. Tecumseh's vision of an unprecedentedly large confederacy of Indian tribes that would halt western expansion by white Americans was cut short by the war and by his death. Without British support, the Indians probably could not have successfully challenged for long the westward dynamic of American settlement. But British support came at a time when Canada was under attack, and the British valued their own defense more than they valued their promises to help the Indians.

The war elevated to national prominence General Andrew Jackson, whose sudden popularity with voters in the 1824 election surprised traditional politicians—and their politically astute wives—and threw the one-party rule of Republicans into a tailspin. John Quincy Adams had barely occupied his office in 1825 before the election campaign of 1828 was off and running. Appeals to the people—the mass of white male voters—would be the hallmark of all elections after 1824. It was a game Adams could not easily play.

Politics in this entire period was a game that women could not play either. Except for the political wives of Washington, women, whether white or free black, had no place in government. Male legislatures maintained women's *feme covert* status, keeping wives dependent on husbands. A few women found a pathway to greater personal autonomy through religion. Meanwhile, the routine inclusion of girls in public schools and the steady spread of female academies planted seeds that would blossom into a major transformation of gender in the 1830s and 1840s.

The War of 1812 started another chain of events that would prove momentous in later decades. Jefferson's long embargo and Madison's wartime trade stoppages gave strong encouragement to American manufacturing, momentarily protected from competition with British factories. When peace returned in 1815, the years of independent development burst forth into a period of sustained economic growth that continued nearly unabated into the mid-nineteenth century.

Suggestions for Further Reading

Catherine Allgor, *Parlor Politics: In Which the Ladies of Washington Help Build a City and a Government* (2000). A subtle study of the capital's female culture that supported and shaped national politics from Jefferson to Jackson.

George Dangerfield, *The Era of Good Feelings* (1952). An unmatched classic that takes the reader deep into politics from the Treaty of Ghent to the inauguration of Jackson.

David Edmunds, *Tecumseh and the Quest for Indian Leadership* (1984). An interesting, short biography of the great Shawnee leader.

Joseph J. Ellis, *American Sphinx: The Character of Thomas Jefferson* (1997). An astute psychological portrait of the sentimental third president.

Joanne B. Freeman, *Affairs of Honor: National Politics in the New Republic* (2001). A study of honor in the new nation that situates slander and dueling in the culture of politics.

Jon Kukla, *A Wilderness So Immense: The Louisiana Purchase and the Destiny of America* (2003). A gripping story of the country's greatest real estate purchase.

▶ **FOR MORE BOOKS ABOUT TOPICS IN THIS CHAPTER**, see the Online Study Guide at bedfordstmartins.com/roarkcompact.

▶ **FOR ADDITIONAL FIRSTHAND ACCOUNTS OF THIS PERIOD**, see Chapter 10 in Michael Johnson, ed., *Reading the American Past*, Third Edition.

▶ **FOR WEB SITES AND DOCUMENTS RELATED TO TOPICS AND PLACES IN THIS CHAPTER**, see "HistoryLinks," "DocLinks," and "PlaceLinks" at bedfordstmartins.com/roarkcompact.

REVIEWING THE CHAPTER

Follow these steps to review and strengthen your understanding of the chapter.

STEP 1: *Study the* **Key Terms** *and* **Timeline** *to identify the significance of each item listed.*

STEP 2: *Answer the* **Review Questions***, drawing on key terms and dates to support your answers.*

STEP 3: *Drawing on the Key Terms, Timeline, and Review Questions, answer the broader* **Making Connections** *questions.*

KEY TERMS

Who

Tecumseh (p. 235)
Tenskwatawa (the Prophet) (p. 235)
Thomas Jefferson (p. 236)
Aaron Burr (p. 237)
John Marshall (p. 239)
James Madison (pp. 239, 242)
Meriwether Lewis (p. 240)
William Clark (p. 240)
Sacajawea (p. 241)
Dolley Madison (p. 242)
William Henry Harrison (p. 243)
Henry Clay (pp. 244, 250)
John C. Calhoun (p. 244)

Andrew Jackson (p. 245)
Jemima Wilkinson (p. 249)
James Monroe (p. 250)
James Tallmadge Jr. (p. 250)
John Quincy Adams (p. 254)

What

Treaty of Greenville (p. 235)
Gabriel's rebellion (p. 237)
Judiciary Act of 1801 (p. 239)
Marbury v. Madison (p. 239)
Louisiana Purchase (p. 239)
impressment (p. 241)
the *Chesapeake* (p. 241)

Embargo Act of 1807 (p. 241)
Treaty of Fort Wayne (p. 243)
battle of Tippecanoe (p. 244)
War of 1812 (p. 244)
Creek War (p. 245)
battle of New Orleans (p. 245)
Treaty of Ghent (p. 245)
Hartford Convention (p. 247)
Rush-Bagot disarmament treaty (p. 248)
feme covert (p. 248)
"Era of Good Feelings" (p. 250)
Missouri Compromise (p. 250)
Adams-Onís Treaty (p. 251)
Monroe Doctrine (p. 251)

TIMELINE

◀ **1789** • Judiciary Act establishes six Supreme Court justices.

1800 • Republicans Thomas Jefferson and Aaron Burr tie in electoral college.
• Fears of slave rebellion led by Gabriel in Virginia lead to 27 executions.

1801 • Judiciary Act reduces Supreme Court justices to five, increases circuit courts.
• House of Representatives elects Jefferson president after 36 ballots.

1803 • *Marbury v. Madison.*
• England and France place embargoes on American shipping.
• United States purchases Louisiana Territory.

1804– • Lewis and Clark expedition goes to the Pacific.
1806

1807 • British attack and search *Chesapeake.*
• Embargo Act.

1808 • Republican James Madison elected president; Dolley Madison soon dubbed "presidentress."

1809 • Treaty of Fort Wayne.
• Non-Intercourse Act.

1811 • Battle of Tippecanoe.

REVIEW QUESTIONS

1. How did Jefferson attempt to undo the Federalist innovations of earlier administrations? (pp. 236–42)

2. Why did Congress declare war on Great Britain in 1812? (pp. 242–48)

3. How did the civil status of American women and men differ in the decades of the early Republic? (pp. 248–50)

4. How did the collapse of the Federalist Party influence the administrations of James Monroe and John Quincy Adams? (pp. 250–54)

MAKING CONNECTIONS

1. When Jefferson assumed the presidency following the election of 1800, he expected to transform the national government. Describe his Republican vision and his successes and failures in implementing it. Did subsequent Republican presidents advance the same objectives?

2. How did the United States expand and strengthen its control of territory in North America in the early nineteenth century? In your answer, discuss the roles of diplomacy, military action, and political leadership in contributing to this development.

3. Regional tensions emerged as a serious danger to the American political system in the early nineteenth century. Discuss specific conflicts that had regional dimensions. How did Americans resolve, or fail to resolve, these tensions?

4. Although the United States denied its female citizens equality in public life, some women were able to exert considerable influence. How did they do so? In your answer, discuss the legal and political status of women in the Republic.

► For practice quizzes, a customized study plan, and other study tools, see the Online Study Guide at bedfordstmartins.com/roarkcompact.

1812 • United States declares war on Great Britain.

1813 • Tecumseh dies at battle of the Thames.

1814 • British attack Washington, D.C.
• Treaty of Ghent.
• New England Federalists meet at Hartford Convention.

1815 • Battle of New Orleans.

1816 • Republican James Monroe elected president.

1819 • Adams-Onís Treaty.

1820 • Missouri Compromise.

1823 • Monroe Doctrine asserted.

1825 • John Quincy Adams elected president by House of Representatives.

SHIP'S FIGUREHEAD OF ANDREW JACKSON

Carved in 1834 and affixed to the bow of the revered navy frigate *Constitution,* this figurehead of Andrew Jackson symbolized national pride by putting "the image of the most popular man of the West upon the favorite ship of the East," according to the commodore who commissioned it. But when Jackson introduced a new, strict banking policy, his popularity in the urban East quickly plummeted. In Boston, where the *Constitution* was docked, protesters complained that the figurehead of a tyrant corrupted their ship. On the night of July 3, 1834, the eve of the national holiday, a twenty-seven-year-old mariner and ardent Whig stole on board and decapitated the figurehead, sawing it through just below the ears. Jackson deflected the insult with humor, declaring, "I never did like that image! Give the man a postmaster's job." The commodore, himself alert to symbolic actions, wrapped the headless statue in a flag and sent it to New York City, where woodworkers fashioned a new head in 1835. The figurehead was reattached to the ship in another port: Jackson's banking policies still rankled in urban financial centers, and naval authorities did not want to risk a second mutilation of the president's image. In 1990, the original head was recovered from a private collector in France and restored to view in the museum that now owns the figurehead.

Museum of the City of New York, Gift of the Seawanhaka Corinthian Yacht Club.

11

The Expanding Republic

1815–1840

PRESIDENT ANDREW JACKSON was the dominant figure of his age, yet his precarious childhood little foretold the fame, fortune, and influence he would enjoy in the years after 1815. Jackson was born in the Carolina backcountry in 1767. His Scots-Irish father had recently died, leaving a poor, struggling mother to support three small boys. During the Revolution, Andrew followed his brothers into the militia, where both died of disease, as did his mother. Orphaned at fourteen, Jackson drifted around, drinking, gambling, and brawling.

Then at seventeen, his prospects began to improve. He studied under a lawyer for three years and moved to Nashville, a **frontier** community full of opportunities for a young man with legal training and an aggressive temperament. He became a public prosecutor, married into a leading family, and acquired land and slaves. When Tennessee became a state in 1796, Jackson, then twenty-nine, was elected to Congress and served a single term. In 1802, he became major-general of the Tennessee militia, cultivating a fierce style of military leadership.

Jackson captured national attention in 1815 by leading the victory at the battle of New Orleans. With little else to celebrate about the War of 1812, many Americans seized on the Tennessee general as the champion of the day. Songs, broadsides, and an admiring biography set him up as the original self-made man, the parentless child magically responsible for his own destiny. Jackson seemed to have created himself, a gritty, forceful personality extracting opportunities from the dynamic, turbulent frontier.

Jackson was more than a man of action, however. He was also strong-willed, reckless, and quick to anger, impulsively challenging men to duels, sometimes on slight pretexts. In one legendary fight in 1806, Jackson deliberately let his opponent, an expert marksman, shoot first. The bullet hit him in a rib, but Jackson masked all sign of injury under a loose cloak and immobile face. He then took careful aim at the astonished man and killed him. Such steely courage chilled his political opponents.

Jackson's image as a tough frontier hero set him apart from the learned and privileged gentlemen from Virginia and Massachusetts who had occupied the presidency up to 1828. When he lost the 1824 election to John Quincy Adams, an infuriated Jackson vowed to fight a rematch. He won in 1828 and again in 1832, capturing large majorities. His appeal stretched across the urban working classes of the East, frontier voters of the West, and slaveholders in the South, who all saw something of themselves in Jackson. Once elected, he brought a combative style to politics and enlarged the powers of the presidency.

The confidence and even recklessness of Jackson's personality mirrored the new confidence of American society in the years after 1815. An entrepreneurial spirit gripped the country, producing a market revolution of unprecedented scale. Old social hierarchies eroded; ordinary men dreamed of moving high on the ladder of success, just as Jackson had done. Stunning advances in transportation and economic productivity fueled such dreams and propelled thousands to move west or to cities. Urban growth and technological change fostered the diffusion of a distinctive and vibrant public culture, spread mainly through increased circulation of newspapers, which allowed popular opinions to coalesce and intensify; Jackson's sudden nationwide celebrity was a case in point.

Expanded communication transformed politics dramatically. Sharp disagreements over the best way to promote individual **liberty**, economic opportunity, and national prosperity in the new market economy defined key differences between Jackson and Adams and the parties they gave rise to in the 1830s. The process of party formation brought new habits of political participation and party loyalty to many thousands more adult white males. Religion became democratized as well: A nationwide **evangelical** revival brought its adherents the certainty that salvation and perfection were now available to all.

As president from 1829 to 1837, Jackson presided over all these changes, fighting some and supporting others in his vigorous and volatile way. As with his own stubborn personality, there was a dark underside to the confidence and expansiveness of American society. Steamboats blew up, banks and businesses periodically collapsed, alcoholism rates soared, Indians were killed or relocated farther west, and slavery continued to expand. The brash confidence that turned some people into rugged, self-promoting, Jackson-like individuals inspired others to think about the human costs of rapid economic expansion and thus about reforming society in dramatic ways. The common denominator was a faith that people and societies could shape their own destinies.

The Market Revolution

The return of peace in 1815 unleashed powerful forces that revolutionized the organization of the economy. Spectacular changes in transportation facilitated the movement of commodities, information, and people, while textile mills and other factories created many new jobs, especially for young unmarried women. Innovations in banking, legal practices, and tariff policies promoted swift economic growth.

This was not yet an industrial revolution, as was beginning in Britain, but a market revolution, fueled by traditional sources—water, wood, beasts of burden, and human muscle. What was new was the accelerated pace of economic activity and the scale of distribution of goods. Men and women were drawn out of old patterns of rural self-sufficiency into the wider realm of national market relations. At the same time, the nation's money supply enlarged considerably, leading to speculative investments in commerce, manufacturing, transportation, and land. The new nature and scale of production and consumption changed Americans' economic behavior, attitudes, and expectations.

Improvements in Transportation

Before 1815, transportation in the United States was slow and expensive; it cost as much to ship a crate over thirty miles of domestic roads as it did to send it across the Atlantic Ocean. The fastest stagecoach trip from Boston to New York took four days. But between 1815 and 1840, networks of roads, canals, steamboats, and finally railroads dramatically raised the speed and lowered the cost of travel (Map 11.1). Andrew Jackson spent weeks riding to Nashville in the 1790s along old Indian trails, but in 1829, it took only days for the new president to get to Washington, D.C., by steamboat and turnpike.

Improved transportation moved goods into wider markets. It moved passengers too, broadening their horizons and allowing youth as well as adults to take up new employment in cities or factory towns. Transportation also facilitated the flow of political information through heavy traffic in newspapers, periodicals, books, and the U.S. mail.

Enhanced public transport was expensive and produced uneven economic benefits, so administrations from Jefferson to Monroe were reluctant to fund it with federal dollars. Only the National Road, begun in 1806, was government sponsored. By 1818, it linked Baltimore with Wheeling, in western Virginia. Instead, private investors pooled resources and chartered transport companies, receiving significant subsidies and **monopoly** rights from state governments.

MAP 11.1 Routes of Transportation in 1840

By the 1830s, transportation advances had cut travel times significantly. Goods and people could move from New York City to Buffalo, New York, in four days by way of the Erie Canal, a trip that took two weeks by road in 1800. A trip from New York to New Orleans that took four weeks in 1800 could be accomplished in less than half that time on steamboats in the western rivers.

READING THE MAP: In what parts of the country were canals built most extensively? Were most of them within a single state's borders, or did they encourage interstate travel and shipping? **CONNECTIONS:** What impact did the Erie Canal have on the development of New York City? How did improvements in transportation affect urbanization in other parts of the country?

FOR MORE HELP ANALYZING THIS MAP, see the map activity for this chapter in the Online Study Guide at bedfordstmartins.com/roarkcompact.

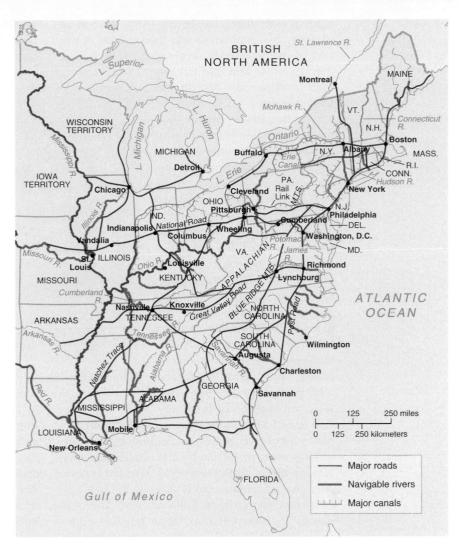

Turnpike and roadway mileage dramatically increased after 1815, reducing shipping costs. Stagecoach companies proliferated, and travel time on main routes was cut in half.

Water travel was similarly transformed. In 1807, Robert Fulton's steam-propelled boat, the *Clermont*, churned up the Hudson River from New York City to Albany, touching off a steamboat craze. In 1820, a dozen boats left New York City daily, and scores more operated on midwestern rivers and the Great Lakes. A voyager on one of the first steamboats to go down the Mississippi reported that the Chickasaw Indians called the vessel a "fire canoe" and considered it "an omen of evil." By the early 1830s, more than seven hundred steamboats were in operation on the Ohio and Mississippi rivers.

Steamboats were not benign advances, however. The urgency to cut travel time led to overstoked furnaces, sudden boiler explosions, and terrible mass fatalities. Another huge cost, to the environment, was the deforestation brought by steamboats, which had to load fuel—"wood up"—every twenty miles or so. By the 1830s the banks of main rivers were denuded of trees, and forests miles in from the rivers fell to the ax. Steamboats burned large amounts of wood, transferring the carbon stored in trees into the atmosphere, creating America's first significant air pollution.

Canals were another major innovation of the transportation revolution. These shallow highways of water allowed passage for barges and boats pulled by horses or mules trudging on a towpath. Travel speed was slow, under five miles per hour; the economy came from increased loads. The low-friction water allowed one horse to pull a fifty-ton barge. Pennsylvania in 1815 and New York in 1817 commenced major state-sponsored canal enterprises. Pennsylvania's Schuylkill Canal stretched 108 miles west from Philadelphia when it was completed in 1826. Much more impressive was the Erie Canal, finished in 1825, covering 350 miles between Albany and Buffalo and linking the port of New York City with the entire Great Lakes region. Wheat and flour moved east, household goods and tools moved west, and passengers went in both directions. By the 1830s, the cost of shipping by canal fell to less than a tenth of the cost of overland transport, and New York City quickly blossomed into the premier commercial city in the United States.

In the 1830s, private railroad companies began to give canals stiff competition, and by the mid-1840s the canal-building era was over. (However, use of the canals for freight continued well into the twentieth century.) The nation's first railroad, the Baltimore and Ohio, laid thirteen miles of track in 1829. During the 1830s, three thousand more miles of track materialized nationwide, the result of a speculative fever in railroad construction masterminded by bankers, locomotive manufacturers, and state legislators, who provided subsidies, charters, and land rights-of-way. Rail lines in the 1830s were generally short, on the order of twenty to one hundred miles. They did not yet provide an efficient distribution system for goods, but passengers flocked to experience the marvelous travel speeds of fifteen to twenty miles per hour. Railroads and other advances in transportation made possible enormous change by unifying the country culturally and economically.

Factories, Workingwomen, and Wage Labor

Transportation advances promoted expansion of manufacturing after 1815, creating a larger market for goods. The two leading industries, newly altering methods of production and labor relations, were textiles and shoes. Textile production was greatly spurred by the development of water-driven machinery, built near fast-coursing rivers. Shoe manufacturing, still using the power and skill of human hands, involved only a reorganization of production. Both mechanized and manual manufacturing pulled young women into the labor market for the first time.

The earliest factory, built by British immigrant Samuel Slater in Pawtucket, Rhode Island, in the 1790s, featured a mechanical spinning machine that produced thread and yarn. By 1815,

Cotton Textile Industry, 1839

nearly 170 spinning mills dotted lower New England. In British manufacturing cities, entire families worked in low-wage, health-threatening factories. American factories, in contrast, targeted young women as employees, cheap to hire because of their limited employment options. Mill girls would retire to marriage, replaced by fresh recruits earning a beginner's wage.

In 1821, a group of Boston entrepreneurs founded the town of Lowell, on the Merrimack River, centralizing all aspects of cloth production: combing, shrinking, spinning, weaving, and dyeing. By 1830, the eight mills in Lowell employed more than 5,000 young women, who lived in closely supervised company-owned boardinghouses. Corporation rules required church attendance and prohibited drinking and unsupervised courtship; dorm lockdown came at 10 p.m. Typical mill workers averaged $2 to $3 for a seventy-hour workweek, more than a seamstress or domestic servant could earn but less than a young man's wages. The job consisted of tending noisy power looms in rooms kept hot and humid, ideal for thread but not for people.

Despite the discomforts, young women left farms and flocked to factory towns in the hope of gaining more autonomy. They welcomed the unprecedented if still limited personal freedom of living in an all-female social space, away from parents and domestic tasks and with pay in their pockets. In evenings, the women could engage in self-improvement activities, such as attending lectures or writing for the company's periodical, *The Lowell Offering*.

In the mid-1830s, worldwide changes in the cotton market impelled mill owners to speed up work and lower wages. The workers protested, emboldened by their communal living arrangements and by their relative independence from the job as temporary employees. In 1834 and again in 1836, hundreds of women at Lowell went out on strike. All over New England, female mill workers led strikes and formed unions. Women at a mill in Dover, New Hampshire, in 1834 denounced their owners for trying to turn them into "slaves": "However freely the epithet of 'factory slaves' may be bestowed upon us, we

Mill Worker Tending a Power Loom, 1850
This daguerreotype—the earliest form of photograph—shows a young woman tending a power loom in a textile mill. Her main task was to replace the spindle when it ran out of thread, loading a new spindle into the shuttle. The close-up shows spindles of pink and blue thread next to a shuttle. The factory operative had to be constantly alert for sudden breaks in the warp yarn, which required a fast shutdown of the loom and a quick repair of the thread. In the 1830s, women weavers generally tended two machines at a time; in the 1840s, some companies increased the workload to four.
Mill worker: American Textile History Museum; shuttle with spindles: Picture Research Consultants & Archives.

will never deserve it by a base and cringing submission to proud wealth or haughty insolence." Their assertiveness surprised many; but ultimately their easy replaceability undermined their bargaining power, and owners in the 1840s began to shift to immigrant families as their labor source.

Other manufacturing enterprises of the 1820s and 1830s, such as shoemaking, employed women in ever larger numbers. New modes of organizing the work allowed the manufacturers to step up production, control wastage and quality, and lower wages by subdividing the tasks and by hiring women, including wives. Male workers cut leather and made soles. The stitching of the upper part of the shoe, called shoebinding, became women's work, performed at home so that it could mesh with domestic chores. Although their wages were lower than

men's, shoebinder wives contributed earned cash to family income.

In the economically turbulent 1830s, shoebinder wages fell. Unlike the mill workers, women shoebinders worked in isolation, a serious hindrance to organized protest. In Lynn, Massachusetts, a major shoemaking center, women used female church networks to organize resistance, communicating via religious newspapers. The Lynn shoebinders who demanded higher wages in 1834 built on a collective sense of themselves as women even though they did not share daily work lives. "Equal rights should be extended to all—to the weaker sex as well as the stronger," they wrote in a document forming the Female Society of Lynn.

In the end, the Lynn shoebinders' protests failed to achieve wage increases. Isolated workers all over New England continued to accept low wages, and even in Lynn, many women shied away from organized protest, preferring to situate their work in the context of family duty (helping their menfolk to finish shoes) instead of market relations.

Bankers and Lawyers

Entrepreneurs like the Lowell factory owners relied on innovations in the banking system to finance their ventures. The number of state-chartered banks in the United States more than doubled in the boom years 1814–1816, from fewer than 90 to 208. By 1830, there were 330; by 1840, hundreds more. Banks stimulated the economy by making loans to merchants and manufacturers and by enlarging the money supply. Borrowers were issued loans in the form of banknotes— certificates unique to each bank—which were used as money for all transactions. Neither federal nor state governments issued paper money, so banknotes became the currency of the country.

In theory, a note could always be traded in at a bank for its **hard-money** equivalent in gold or silver (in a transaction known as "specie payment"). A note from a solid local bank might be worth exactly what it was written for, but the face value of a note from a distant or questionable bank would be discounted by a fraction. Buying and selling banknotes in Jacksonian America required knowledge and caution. Not surprisingly, counterfeiting flourished.

Bankers exercised great power over the economy, deciding who would get loans and what the discount rates would be. The most powerful bankers sat on the board of directors for the second Bank of the United States, headquartered in Philadelphia. The twenty-year charter of the first Bank of the United States had expired in 1811. The second Bank of the United States, with eighteen branches throughout the country, opened for business in 1816 under another twenty-year charter. The rechartering of this bank would be a major issue in Andrew Jackson's reelection campaign in 1832.

Accompanying the market revolution was a revolution in commercial law, fashioned by politicians to enhance the prospects of private investment. In 1811, states started to rewrite laws of incorporation (allowing the chartering of businesses by states), and the number of corporations expanded rapidly, from about twenty in 1800 to eighteen hundred by 1817. Incorporation protected individual investors from being held liable for corporate financial debts. State lawmakers also wrote laws of eminent domain, empowering states to buy land for roads and canals, even from unwilling sellers. They drafted legislation on contributory negligence, relieving employers from responsibility for workplace injuries. In such ways, entrepreneurial lawyers of the 1820s and 1830s created the legal foundation for an economy that would give priority to ambitious individuals interested in maximizing their own wealth.

Not everyone applauded these developments. Andrew Jackson, himself a skillful lawyer-turned-politician, spoke for a large and mistrustful segment of the population when he warned about the abuses of power "which the moneyed interest derives from a paper currency which they are able to control, from the multitude of corporations with exclusive privileges which they have succeeded in obtaining in the different states, and which are employed altogether for their benefit." Jacksonians believed that ending government-granted privileges was the way to maximize individual liberty and economic opportunity.

Booms and Busts

One aspect of the economy that the lawyer-politicians could not control was the threat of financial collapse. The boom years from 1815 to 1818 exhibited a volatility that resulted in the first sharp, large-scale economic downturn in U.S. history, a depression that Americans called a "panic"; the pattern was repeated in the 1830s. Rapidly rising consumer demand stimulated price increases for goods, and speculative investment opportunities offering the possibility of high payoffs abounded— in bank stocks, western land sales, urban real estate, and commodities markets. High inflation made some people wealthy but created hardships for workers on fixed incomes.

When the bubble burst in 1819, the overnight rich suddenly became the overnight poor. Some blamed the panic of 1819 on the second Bank of the United States. The national bank had failed to exercise control over state banks, and many of them had suspended specie payments—the exchange of gold or silver for banknotes—in their eagerness to expand the economic bubble. In mid-1818, when the Bank of the United States started to call in its loans and insisted that state banks do likewise, the contracting of the money supply created tremors throughout the economy. The crunch was made worse by a financial crisis in Europe in the spring of 1819. Overseas, prices for

American cotton, tobacco, and wheat plummeted by more than 50 percent. Thus when the Bank of the United States and the state banks called in their outstanding loans, American debtors involved in the commodities trade could not come up with the money. The number of business and personal bankruptcies skyrocketed. The intricate web of credit and debt relationships meant that almost everyone with even a toehold in the new commercial economy was affected by the panic of 1819. Thousands of Americans lost their savings and property, and unemployment estimates suggest that a half million people lost their jobs.

Recovery took several years. Unemployment rates fell, but bitterness lingered, ready to be stirred up by politicians in the decades to come. The dangers of a system dependent on extensive credit were now clear: In one folksy formulation that circulated around 1820, a farmer compared credit to "a man pissing in his breeches on a cold day to keep his arse warm—very comfortable at first but I dare say … you know how it feels afterwards."

By the mid-1820s, the booming economy was back on track, driven by increases in productivity and consumer demand for goods, accelerating international trade, and a restless and calculating people moving goods, human labor, and investment capital in expanding circles of commerce. But an undercurrent of anxiety about rapid economic change continued to shape the political views of many Americans.

> **REVIEW**   Why did the United States experience a market revolution after 1815?

The Spread of Democracy

Just as the market revolution held out the promise, if not the reality, of economic opportunity for all who worked, the political transformation of the 1830s held out the promise of political opportunity for all who voted. During Andrew Jackson's presidency, 1829 to 1837, the second American party system took shape, although not until 1836 would the parties have distinct names and consistent programs that transcended the particular personalities running for office. Over those years, more men could and did vote, responding to new methods of arousing voter interest. In 1828, Jackson's charismatic personality

defined his party, and his election over John Quincy Adams turned on questions of character. Once in office, Jackson championed ordinary citizens against the power elite—**democracy** versus aristocracy in Jackson's terminology. A lasting contribution of the Jackson years was the notion that politicians needed to have the common touch in their dealings with voters.

Popular Politics and Partisan Identity

The election of 1828 was the first presidential contest in which popular votes determined the outcome. In twenty-two out of twenty-four states, voters—not state legislatures—now designated electors committed to a particular candidate. More than a million voters participated, three times the number in 1824 and nearly half the free male population, reflecting the high stakes that voters perceived in the Adams-Jackson rematch. Throughout the 1830s, voter turnout continued to rise, up to 70 percent in some localities, partly due to the disappearance of property qualifications in all but three states and partly due to heightened political interest.

The 1828 election inaugurated new campaign styles. State-level candidates routinely gave speeches at rallies, picnics, and banquets. Adams and Jackson still declined such activities as undignified; but Henry Clay of Kentucky, campaigning for Adams, earned the nickname "Barbecue Orator." Campaign rhetoric, under the necessity to create popular appeal, became more informal and even blunt. The Jackson camp established many Hickory Clubs, trading on Jackson's popular nickname, "Old Hickory," from a common Tennessee tree suggesting resilience and toughness. (Jackson was the first presidential candidate to have an affectionate and widely used nickname.)

Partisan newspapers in ever larger numbers defined issues and publicized political personalities as never before. Improved printing technology and rising literacy rates were fueling a great expansion of newspapers of all kinds (see Table 11.1).

TABLE 11.1	THE GROWTH OF NEWSPAPERS, 1820–1840			
	1820	*1830*	*1835*	*1840*
U.S. population (in millions)	9.6	12.8	15.0	17.1
Number of newspapers published	500	800	1,200	1,400
Daily newspapers	42	65	—	138

Party leaders dispensed subsidies and other favors to secure the loyalties of papers, even in remote towns and villages. In New York State, where party development was most advanced, a pro-Jackson group called the Bucktails controlled fifty weekly publications. Stories from the leading Jacksonian paper in Washington, D.C., were reprinted two days later in a Boston or Cincinnati paper, as fast as the mail stage could carry them. Presidential campaigns were now coordinated in a national arena.

Politicians at first identified themselves as Jackson or Adams men, honoring the fiction of Republican Party unity. By 1832 the terminology had evolved to National Republicans, favoring federal action to promote commercial development, and Democratic Republicans, who promised to be responsive to the will of the majority. Between 1834 and 1836, National Republicans shifted to the term Whig, while Jackson's party became simply the Democrats.

The Election of 1828 and the Character Issue

The campaign of 1828 was the first national election in which scandal and character questions reigned supreme. They became central issues because voters used them to comprehend the kind of public officer each man would make. Character issues conveyed in shorthand larger questions about morality, honor, and discipline. Jackson and Adams presented two radically different styles of masculinity.

John Quincy Adams was vilified by his opponents as an elitist, bookish academic, perhaps even a monarchist. Critics pointed to Adams's White House billiard table and ivory chess set as symbols of his aristocratic degeneracy along with the "corrupt bargain" of 1824, the alleged election deal between Adams and Henry Clay (see chapter 10). Adams's supporters returned fire with fire. They played on Jackson's fatherless childhood to portray him as the bastard son of a prostitute. Worse, the cloudy circumstances around his marriage to Rachel Donelson Robards in 1791 gave rise to the story that Jackson was a seducer and an adulterer, having married a woman whose divorce from her first husband was not entirely legal. Pro-Adams newspapers howled that Jackson was sinful and impulsive, while portraying Adams as pious, learned, and virtuous.

Editors in favor of Adams played up Jackson's notorious violent temper, evidenced by the many duels, brawls, and canings they could

recount. Jackson's supporters used the same stories to project Old Hickory as a tough frontier hero who knew how to command obedience. As for learning, Jackson's rough frontier education gave him a "natural sense," wrote a Boston editor, that "can never be acquired by reading books—it can only be acquired, in perfection, by reading men."

Jackson won a sweeping victory, 56 percent of the popular vote and 178 electoral votes to Adams's 83. Old Hickory took most of the South and West and carried Pennsylvania and New York as well; the loser carried the remainder in the East. Jackson's vice president was John C. Calhoun, who had just served as vice president under Adams but had broken with Adams's policies.

After 1828, national politicians no longer deplored the existence of political parties. They were coming to see that parties mobilized and delivered voters, sharpened candidates' differences, and created party loyalty that surpassed loyalty to individual candidates and elections. Adams and Jackson clearly symbolized and defined for voters the competing ideas of the emerging parties: Whigs—a moralistic, top-down party ready to make major decisions to promote economic growth; Democrats—a contentious, energetic party ready to embrace liberty-loving individualism.

Jackson's Democratic Agenda

Before the inauguration in March 1829, Rachel Jackson died. Certain that the ugly campaign had hastened her death, the president went into deep mourning, his depression worsened by constant pain from the 1806 bullet still lodged in his chest and by mercury poisoning from the medicines he took. Sixty-two years old, Jackson carried only 140 pounds on his six-foot-one frame. His adversaries doubted he would make it to a second term. His supporters, however, went wild at the inauguration. Thousands cheered his ten-minute inaugural address, the shortest in history. An open reception at the White House turned into a near riot as well-wishers jammed the premises, used windows as doors, stood on furniture for a better view of the great man, and broke thousands of dollars' worth of china and glasses.

During his presidency, Jackson continued to offer unprecedented hospitality to the public. Twenty spittoons newly installed in the East Room of the White House accommodated the

Campaign Posters from 1828

The poster on the left praises Andrew Jackson as a war hero and "man of the people" and reminds readers that Jackson, who won the largest popular vote in 1824, did not stoop to bargain for the presidency, as presumably John Quincy Adams had done in his dealings with Henry Clay. (What "two wars" does this poster refer to?) The poster with ominous tombstone and coffin graphics accuses Jackson of the unjustified killing of a Kentucky militiaman (one of six executed) during the Creek War in 1815. The text implores readers to think of the "hero" as a man capable of "bloody deeds."

Pro-Jackson broadside: © Collection of the New-York Historical Society; anti-Jackson broadside: Smithsonian Institute, Washington, D.C.

tobacco-chewers among the throngs that arrived daily to see the president. The courteous Jackson, committed to his image as president of the "common man," held audiences with unannounced visitors throughout his two terms.

Jackson's appointments marked a departure. Past presidents had tried to lessen party conflict by including men of different factions in their cabinets, but Jackson would have only Jackson loyalists. For secretary of state, the key job, he tapped New Yorker Martin Van Buren, one of the shrewdest politicians of the day. Throughout the federal government, from postal clerks to ambassadors, Jackson removed competent civil servants and installed party loyalists. "To the victor belong the spoils," said a Democratic senator from New York, expressing approval of patronage-driven appointments. Jackson's approach to civil service employment got tagged the **spoils system**; it was a concept the president strenuously defended.

Jackson's agenda quickly emerged. He favored a Jeffersonian limited federal government, fearing that intervention in the economy inevitably favored some groups at the expense of others. He therefore opposed federal support of transportation and grants of monopolies and charters that privileged wealthy investors. Like Jefferson, he anticipated rapid settlement of the country's interior, where land sales would spread economic democracy to settlers. Thus, establishing a federal policy to remove the Indians had high priority. Unlike Jefferson, however, Jackson exercised presidential veto powers over Congress. In 1830, he vetoed a highway project in Maysville, Kentucky—Henry Clay's home state—that Congress had voted to support with federal dollars. The Maysville Road veto articulated Jackson's principled stand that citizens' federal tax dollars could be spent only on projects of a "general, not local" character. In all, Jackson used the veto twelve times; all previous presidents had exercised that right a total of nine times.

REVIEW   Why did Jackson defeat John Quincy Adams so dramatically in the 1828 election?

Cultural Shifts, Religion, and Reform

Despite their differences about the best way to enhance commercial development, Jackson's Democratic Republicans and Henry Clay's National Republicans shared enthusiasm for the outcome—a growing, booming economy. For increasing numbers of families, especially in the commercialized Northeast, standards of living rose, consumption patterns changed, and the nature and location of work altered. All of these changes had a direct impact on the duties of men and women and on the training of youth for the economy of the future.

Along with economic change came an unprecedented revival of evangelical religion known as the **Second Great Awakening**. Just as universal male **suffrage** allowed all white men to vote, democratized religion offered salvation to all who chose to embrace it. Among the most serious adherents of evangelical **Protestantism** were men and women of the new merchant classes whose self-discipline in pursuing market ambitions meshed well with the message of self-discipline in pursuit of spiritual perfection. Not content with individual perfection, many of these men and women sought to perfect society as well, by defining excessive alcohol consumption, nonmarital sex, and slavery as three major evils of modern life in need of correction.

The Family and Separate Spheres

The centerpiece of new ideas about gender relations was the notion that husbands found their status and authority in the new world of work, leaving wives to tend the hearth and home. Sermons, advice books, periodicals, and novels reinforced the idea that men and women inhabited **separate spheres** and had separate duties. "To woman it belongs…to elevate the intellectual character of her household [and] to kindle the fires of mental activity in childhood," wrote Mrs. A. J. Graves in a popular book titled *Advice to American Women*. For men, in contrast, "the absorbing passion for gain, and the pressing demands of business, engross their whole attention." In particular, the home, now the exclusive domain of women, was sentimentalized as the source of intimacy, love, and safety, a refuge from the cruel and competitive world of market relations.

Some new aspects of society gave substance to this formulation of separate spheres. Men's work was undergoing profound change after 1815 and increasingly brought cash to the household, especially in the manufacturing and urban Northeast. Farmers and tradesmen sold products in a market, and bankers, bookkeepers, shoemakers, and canal diggers got pay envelopes. Furthermore, many men performed jobs outside of the home, at an office or store. For men who were not farmers, work indeed seemed newly disconnected from life at home.

A woman's domestic role was more complicated than the cultural prescriptions indicated. Although the vast majority of married white women did not hold paying jobs, the home continued to be a site of time-consuming labor. But the advice books treated household tasks as loving familial duties; housework as work was thereby rendered invisible in an economy that evaluated work by how much cash it generated. In reality, wives directly contributed to family income in many ways. Some took in boarders, while others engaged in outwork, earning pay for shoebinding, hatmaking, or needlework done at home. Wives in the poorer classes of society, including most free black wives, did not have the luxury of husbands earning adequate wages; for them, work as servants or laundresses helped augment family income.

The Education and Training of Youth

The market economy with its new expectations for men and women required fresh methods of training youth of both sexes. The generation that came of age in the 1820s and 1830s had opportunities for education and work unparalleled in previous eras, at least for white children in the middling classes and above. Northern states adopted public schooling between 1790 and the 1820s, and in the 1820s and 1830s southern states followed suit. The curriculum produced pupils who were able, by age twelve or fourteen, to read, write, and participate in marketplace calculations. Remarkably, girls usually received the same basic education as boys. Literacy rates for white females climbed dramatically, rivaling the rates for white males for the first time.

The fact that taxpayers paid for children's education created an incentive to seek an inexpensive teaching force. By the 1830s, school districts began replacing male teachers with young females. Like mill workers, teachers were in their late teens and regarded the work as temporary. Some were trained in private female academies, now numbering in the hundreds, while others attended teacher training schools ("normal" schools) for women students. With the exception of Oberlin College in Ohio, no colleges admitted women until after the Civil War, but a handful of private "female seminaries" established a rigorous curriculum that rivaled that of the best men's colleges. Two of the most prominent were the Troy Seminary in New York, founded by

Emma Willard in 1821, and Mount Holyoke in Massachusetts, founded by Mary Lyon in 1837.

Male youths leaving public school faced two paths. A small percentage continued at private boys' academies, and a far smaller number entered the country's two dozen colleges. More typically, boys left school at fourteen to apprentice in a specific trade or to seek business careers in entry-level clerkships, abundant in the growing urban centers. Young girls also headed for mill towns or for the cities in unprecedented numbers, seeking work in the expanding service sector as seamstresses and domestic servants.

Changes in patterns of youth employment meant that large numbers of youngsters in the 1830s and later escaped the watchful eyes of their families. Moralists fretted about the dangers of

Women Graduates of Oberlin College, Class of 1855

Oberlin College, founded in Ohio by evangelical and abolitionist activists in the 1830s, admitted men and women, both white and black. In the early years, the black students were all male, and the women students were all white. Instruction was not coeducational. The women attended classes in a separate Ladies' Department. By 1855, as this daguerreotype shows, black women had integrated the Ladies' Department. The two older women wearing bonnets were the principal and a member of the board. The students wear the latest fashion: dark taffeta dresses with sloping shoulders and a tight bodice topped by detachable white lace collars. Hair fashions were similarly uniform for women of all ages throughout the 1850s: a central part, hair dressed with oil and lustrously coiled over the ears. Compare these women with the mill woman pictured on page 263. What differences do you see?
Oberlin College Archives, Oberlin, Ohio.

unsupervised youth, and, following the lead of the Lowell mill owners, some established apprentices' libraries and uplifting lecture series to keep young people honorably occupied. Advice books published by the hundreds instructed youth in the virtues of hard work and delayed gratification.

The Second Great Awakening

A newly invigorated version of Protestantism gained huge momentum in the 1820s and 1830s as the economy reshaped gender and age relations. The earliest manifestations of this fervent piety appeared in 1801 in Kentucky, when a crowd of ten thousand people camped out on a hillside at Cane Ridge for a revival meeting that lasted several weeks. By the 1810s and 1820s, "camp meetings" had spread to the Atlantic seaboard states, finding especially enthusiastic audiences in western New York and Pennsylvania. The outdoor settings permitted huge attendance, which itself intensified the emotional impact of the experience. "For more than a half mile, I could see people on their knees before God in humble prayer," recalled one Cane Ridge worshipper.

The gatherings attracted women and men hungry for a more immediate access to spiritual peace, one not requiring years of soul-searching. One eyewitness at a revival reported that "some of the people were singing, others praying, some crying for mercy....At one time I saw at least five hundred swept down in a moment as if a battery of a thousand guns had been opened upon them, and then immediately followed shrieks and shouts that rent the very heavens."

From 1800 to 1820, church membership doubled in the United States, much of it among the evangelical groups. Methodists, Baptists, and Presbyterians formed the core of the new movement; Episcopalians, Congregationalists, Unitarians, Dutch Reformed, Lutherans, and Catholics maintained strong skepticism about the emotional enthusiasm. Women more than men were attracted to the evangelical movement, and wives and mothers typically recruited husbands and sons to join them.

The leading exemplar of the Second Great Awakening was a lawyer-turned-minister. Charles Grandison Finney lived in western New York, where the completion of the Erie Canal in 1825 fundamentally altered the social and economic landscape overnight. Towns swelled with new inhabitants who brought in remarkable prosperity along with other, less admirable side effects, such as prostitution, drinking, and gaming. Finney saw

New York canal towns as especially ripe for evangelical awakening. In Rochester, New York, he sustained a six-month revival through the winter of 1830, generating thousands of new converts.

Finney's message was directed primarily at women and men of the business classes. He argued that a reign of Christian perfection loomed, one that required public-spirited outreach to the less than perfect to foster their salvation. Evangelicals promoted Sunday schools to bring piety to children; they battled to end mail delivery, to stop public transport, and to close shops on Sundays to honor the Sabbath. Many women formed missionary societies, which distributed millions of Bibles and religious tracts. Through such avenues, evangelical religion offered women expanded spheres of influence. Finney adopted tactics of Jacksonian-era politicians—publicity, argumentation, rallies, and speeches—to sell his cause. His object, he said, was to get Americans to "vote in the Lord Jesus Christ as the governor of the Universe."

The Temperance Movement and the Campaign for Moral Reform

The evangelical disposition—a combination of faith, energy, self-discipline, and righteousness—animated vigorous campaigns to eliminate alcohol abuse and eradicate sexual sin. Millions of Americans took the temperance pledge to abstain from strong drink, and thousands became involved in efforts to end prostitution.

Alcohol consumption had risen steadily in the decades up to 1830, when the average person over age thirteen annually consumed an astonishing 9 gallons of hard liquor plus 30 gallons of hard cider, beer, and wine. All classes imbibed. A lively saloon culture fostered masculine camaraderie along with extensive alcohol consumption among laborers, while in elite homes, the after-dinner whiskey or sherry was commonplace. Colleges before 1820 routinely served students a pint of ale with meals, and the army and navy included rum in the standard daily ration.

Organized opposition to drinking first surfaced in the 1810s among health and religious reformers. In 1826, Lyman Beecher, a Connecticut minister of an "awakened" church, founded the American Temperance Society, which warned that drinking led to poverty, idleness, crime, and family violence. Adopting the methods of evangelical ministers, temperance lecturers traveled the country expounding the damage of drink; by 1833, some six thousand local affiliates of the

Charles G. Finney and His Broadway Tabernacle

The Reverend Charles G. Finney (shown here in a portrait done in 1834) took his evangelical movement to New York City in the early 1830s, operating first out of a renovated theater. In 1836, the Broadway Tabernacle was built for his pastorate. In its use of space, the tabernacle resembled a theater more than a traditional church, but in one respect it departed radically from one very theaterlike tradition of churches—the custom of charging pew rents. In effect, most churches required worshippers to purchase their seats. Finney, in contrast, insisted that all seats in his house were free, unreserved, and open to all.

Oberlin College Archives, Oberlin, Ohio.

FOR MORE HELP ANALYZING THIS IMAGE, see the visual activity for this chapter in the Online Study Guide at bedfordstmartins.com/roarkcompact.

American Temperance Society boasted more than a million members. Middle-class drinking began a steep decline.

In 1836, leaders of the **temperance movement** regrouped into a new society, the American Temperance Union, which demanded total abstinence of its adherents. The intensified war against alcohol moved beyond individual moral suasion into the realm of politics, as reformers sought to deny taverns liquor licenses. By 1845, temperance advocates had put an impressive dent in alcohol consumption, which diminished to one-quarter of the per capita consumption of 1830. In 1851, Maine became the first state to ban entirely the manufacture and sale of all alcoholic beverages.

More controversial than temperance was a social movement called "moral reform," which first aimed at public morals in general but quickly narrowed to a campaign to eradicate sexual sin, especially prostitution. In 1833, a group of Finneyite women started the New York Female Moral Reform Society. Its members insisted that uncontrolled male sexual expression posed a serious threat to society in general and to women in particular. The society's nationally distributed newspaper, the *Advocate of Moral Reform*, was the first major paper in the country that was written, edited, and typeset by women. In it they condemned men who visited brothels or who seduced innocent victims. Within five years, more than four thousand auxiliary groups of women members had sprung up, mostly in New England, New York, Pennsylvania, and Ohio.

In its analysis of the causes of licentiousness and its conviction that women had a duty to speak out about unspeakable things, the Moral Reform Society pushed the limits of what even the men in the evangelical movement could tolerate. Yet these women did not regard themselves as radicals. They were simply pursuing the logic of a gender system that defined home protection and morality as women's special sphere and a religious conviction that called for the eradication of sin.

Organizing against Slavery

More radical still was the movement in the 1830s to abolish the sin of slavery. The only previous antislavery organization, the American Colonization Society, had been founded in 1817 by some Maryland and Virginia **planters** to promote gradual individual **emancipation** of slaves followed by **colonization** in Africa. By the early 1820s, several thousand ex-slaves had been transported to Liberia on the West African coast. But not surprisingly, newly freed men and women were often not eager to emigrate; their African roots were three or more generations in the past. Colonization was too gradual (and expensive) to have much impact on American slavery.

Around 1830, northern challenges to slavery surfaced with increasing frequency and resolve, beginning in free black communities. In 1829, a Boston printer named David Walker published *An Appeal…to the Coloured Citizens of the World,* which condemned racism, invoked the egalitarian language of the Declaration of Independence, and hinted at racial violence if whites did not change their prejudiced ways. In 1830, at the inaugural National Negro Convention meeting in Philadelphia, forty blacks from nine states discussed the racism of American society and proposed emigration to Canada. In 1832, a twenty-eight-year-old black woman, Maria Stewart, delivered public lectures for black audiences in Boston on slavery and racial prejudice. While her arguments against slavery were welcomed, her voice—that of a woman—created problems even among her sympathetic audiences. Few American-born women had yet engaged in public speaking beyond theatrical performances or religious prophesizing; Stewart was breaking a social taboo. She retired from the platform in 1833 but took up writing and published her lectures in a national publication called the *Liberator,* giving them much wider circulation.

The *Liberator,* founded in 1831 in Boston, took antislavery agitation to new heights. Its founder and editor, an uncompromising twenty-six-year-old white printer named William Lloyd Garrison, advocated immediate abolition: "On this subject, I do not wish to think, or speak, or write, with moderation. No! No! Tell a man whose house is on fire to give a moderate alarm; tell him to moderately rescue his wife from the hands of the ravisher; tell the mother to gradually extricate her babe from the fire into which it has fallen;—but urge me not to use moderation in a cause like the present."

In 1832, Garrison supporters started the New England Anti-Slavery Society; similar groups were organized in Philadelphia and New York in 1833. Soon a dozen antislavery newspapers and scores of antislavery lecturers were spreading the word and inspiring the formation of new local societies, which numbered 1,300 by 1837. Entirely confined to the North, their membership totaled a quarter of a million men and women.

Many white Northerners were not prepared to embrace the abolitionist call for emancipation, immediate or gradual. They might oppose slavery as a blot on the country's ideals or as a rival to the **free-labor** system of the North, but at the same time most white Northerners remained antiblack and therefore antiabolition. From 1834 to 1838, there were more than a hundred eruptions of serious mob violence against abolitionists or free blacks. On one occasion, antislavery headquarters in Philadelphia and a black church and orphanage were burned to the ground; in another incident, Illinois abolitionist editor Elijah Lovejoy was killed by a rioting crowd attempting to destroy his printing press.

Women played a prominent role in abolition, just as they did in moral reform and evangelical religion. (See "Beyond America's Borders," page 274.) They formed women's auxiliaries and engaged in fund-raising to support lecturers in the field. They circulated antislavery petitions, presented to the U.S. Congress with tens of thousands of signatures. Garrison particularly welcomed women's activity. When a southern plantation daughter named Angelina Grimké wrote to him about her personal repugnance for slavery, Garrison published the letter in the *Liberator* and brought her overnight fame. In 1837, Grimké and her older sister Sarah became antislavery lecturers targeting women, but their powerful eyewitness speeches attracted men as well, causing leaders of the Congregational Church in Massachusetts to warn all ministers not to let the Grimké sisters use their pulpits. Like Maria Stewart, the Grimkés had violated a gender norm by presuming to instruct men.

In the late 1830s, the cause of abolition divided the nation as no other issue did. Even among the abolitionists, significant divisions emerged. The Grimké sisters, radicalized by the public reaction to their speaking tour, began to write and speak about woman's rights. They were opposed by moderate abolitionists who were unwilling to mix a new and controversial issue about women with their first cause, the rights of blacks. A few radical men, like Garrison, embraced women's rights fully, working to get women leadership positions in the national antislavery group.

The many men and women active in reform movements in the 1830s found their initial inspiration in evangelical Protestantism's dual message: Salvation was open to all, and society needed to be perfected. Their activist mentality squared well with the interventionist tendencies of the party forming in opposition to Andrew Jackson's Democrats. Generally, reformers gravitated to the Whig Party, the males as voters and the females as rallying supporters in the 1830s campaigns.

> **REVIEW** How did evangelical Protestantism contribute to the social reform movements of the 1830s?

Abolitionist Purses

Female antislavery societies raised many thousands of dollars to support the abolitionist cause by selling handcrafted items at giant antislavery fairs. Toys, infant clothes, quilts, caps and collars, purses, needlebooks, wax flowers, inlaid boxes: The list was endless. Items were often emblazoned with abolitionist mottoes, such as "Let My People Go," "Liberty," and "Loose the Bonds of Wickedness." These pink silk drawstring bags were decorated with pictures of the hapless slave woman, an object of compassion. Dollars raised at antislavery fairs supported the travels of abolitionist speakers as well as the publication and distribution of many antislavery books and articles.

The Daughters of the American Revolution Museum, Washington, D.C. Gift of Mrs. Erwin L. Broecker.

Jackson Defines the Democratic Party

As president, Andrew Jackson worked to implement his vision of a politics of opportunity for all white men. To open land for white settlement, he favored relocation of all eastern Indian peoples. He dramatically confronted John C. Calhoun and South Carolina when that state tried to nullify the tariff of 1828. Disapproving of all government-granted privilege, Jackson challenged what he called the "monster" Bank of the United States and took it down to defeat. Jackson's legacy to his successor, Martin Van Buren, was a Democratic Party strong enough to withstand the passing of Old Hickory. But another of his legacies was the most severe economic contraction yet to hit the U.S. economy. Although the panic of 1837 was not solely Jackson's doing, it was a fitting end to a decade of rambunctious speculation and expansion.

Indian Policy and the Trail of Tears

Probably nothing defined Jackson's presidency more than his efforts to "solve" what he saw as the Indian problem. Thousands of Indians lived in the South and the old Northwest, and some remained in New England and New York. Jackson, who rose to fame fighting the Creek and the Seminole tribes in the 1810s, declared in 1829 in his first message to Congress that removing Indians to territory west of the Mississippi was the only way to save them. White civilization destroyed Indian resources and thus doomed the Indians: "That this fate surely awaits them if they remain within the limits of the states does not admit of a doubt. Humanity and national honor demand that every effort should be made to avert so great a calamity." Jackson never publicly wavered from this seemingly noble theme, returning to it in his next seven annual messages.

Prior administrations had tried different policies. Starting in 1819, Congress granted $10,000 a year to various missionary associations eager to "civilize" native peoples by converting them to Christianity and encouraging English literacy and agricultural practices. Missionaries also promoted white gender customs, but Indian women were reluctant to embrace practices that accorded them less power than their tribal system did. The federal government had also pursued aggressive treaty making with many tribes, dealing with the Indians as if they were foreign nations. (See chapter 10, page 243.)

Transatlantic Abolition

Abolitionism blossomed in the United States in the 1830s, but its roots stretched back to the 1780s, both in the northern states and in Europe. Developments on both sides of the Atlantic reinforced each other, leading to a transatlantic antislavery movement with shared ideas and strategies, shared activists, shared songs, and, eventually, shared victories.

An important source of antislavery sentiment derived from the Quaker religion, with its deep convictions of human equality, so, not surprisingly, antislavery activism first spread along established Quaker networks in England, Ireland, and the United States, propelled by traveling ministers and religious pamphlet literature. In Pennsylvania, Quakers launched the Pennsylvania Society for Promoting the Abolition of Slavery, which non-Quakers Benjamin Franklin and Thomas Paine also joined. Founded in 1784, the Society worked to end slavery in that state and also petitioned the confederation congress—unsuccessfully—to put an end to American participation in the international slave trade. Quaker counterparts in the British cities of London and Plymouth formed antislavery societies that same year and embarked on a drive to ban Britain's transatlantic traffic in humans. A French group, the Société des Amis des Noirs (Society of the

Friends of Blacks) sprang up in Paris in 1788. All three groups agreed that ending the overseas commerce was the critical first step in ending slavery.

The English Quakers were initially the most successful in mounting a public campaign. From 1787 to 1791, the Society for Effecting the Abolition of the Slave Trade amassed thousands of signatures on petitions and organized a boycott of slave-produced sugar from the British West Indies, a boycott said to have involved 300,000 Britons. Women, the traditional cooks of English families, were essential to that effort. In 1789, the Society scored a publicity coup by publishing two chilling illustrations of cross-sectioned slaving ships stacked with human cargo, the dark, near-naked bodies packed like sardines in each ship's hold. These images, reprinted by the thousands, created a sensation. The Reverend Thomas Clarkson of the Society distributed them in Paris and in northern U.S. cities along with a book he wrote detailing the shipboard tortures inflicted on slaves by the use of shackles, handcuffs, whips, and branding irons. The Society mobilized the resulting groundswell of antislavery sentiment to pressure Parliament. A sympathetic member of that body, the Methodist William Wilburforce, brought the anti–slave trade issue to a debate and vote in 1791; it lost.

American Quakers approached the first federal Congress, meeting in New York in 1790, with petitions requesting an immediate end to the slave trade. This action caused some puzzlement at first, because the U.S. Constitution contained a clause prohibiting the federal government from banning the "Importation of Such Persons as any of the States now existing shall think proper to admit" (that is, slaves) before the year 1808. Congressmen banished the Quaker petitions to a committee. The next day, a bolder Quaker petition, endorsed by the venerated Benjamin Franklin, arrived requesting an end to slavery as well as to the slave trade and suggesting how to accomplish it. The petitioners urged Congress to invoke the constitutional provision that empowered the government to make all laws "necessary and proper" to ensure the "general welfare" of the country, arguing that "Liberty for all Negroes" was crucial to the general welfare. This petition triggered the first debate in the new government on slavery. As in Britain's Parliament, the outcome did not bode well for slaves: By a close vote (29 to 25), Congress not only rejected this move for emancipation but also clarified its view—in a precedent-setting resolution—that slavery was under the sole regulation of the states where it existed.

Over the next three decades, the antislavery cause in Britain and in America moved forward in piecemeal fashion. Efforts to ban the slave trade in England came to parliamentary votes in 1805 and again in 1807, when a law forbidding British ships to carry Africans into slavery finally passed. (The British law was not perfect, however; it levied a fine of £100 per slave on any British captain caught with illegal cargo, creating a grim incentive for captains to shove people overboard if they faced challenge by the British navy.) A year later, in 1808, the United States also banned the slave trade, meeting the constitutional time limit. What made passage relatively easy at this time was the burgeoning natural increase of the African American population. Older slave states supported the international ban because it increased the value of their native-born slaves, who could be sold and transported to points west in the interstate slave trade.

British antislavery opinion took a new tack in the 1820s, when women became active and pushed beyond the ban on trade. Quaker widow Elizabeth Heyrick authored *Immediate not Gradual Abolition* in 1824, triggering the formation of scores of all-women societies. A massive petition campaign again bombarded Parliament, and of the 1.3 million signatures submitted in 1833, 30 percent were women's. In 1833, Parliament finally passed the Abolition of Slavery Act, which freed all slave children under age six and gradually phased out slavery for everyone older during a four-year apprenticeship. The act also provided financial compensation for owners (£20 million), a key proviso made possible by the relatively small number of slave owners in the British slaveholding colonies.

American abolitionists were also heating up the struggle in the 1830s, and as in Britain, women's involvement was accelerating. The Grimké sisters were only the most visible part of women's new activism. Many hundreds of women joined female antislavery organizations and held fairs where they sold handmade goods to raise money to promote the abolitionist cause. Both women and men abolitionists from both sides of the Atlantic traveled overseas to meet their counterparts abroad. In one worrisome moment, a Boston crowd threatened to lynch British abolitionist George Thompson and his host, William Lloyd Garrison, the editor of the *Liberator*.

British and American abolitionists came together in full force at the World Antislavery Convention, held in London in 1840. Among the 409 delegates were Clarkson, who presided; Garrison; and Philadelphia Quaker Lucretia Mott, a lifelong antislavery activist. A half dozen French delegates attended; 53 others were Americans, and the rest were from Britain and the West Indies. Only about a quarter of the attendees were Quakers. Ten days of meetings produced speeches and fact-finding reports on slavery worldwide, captured in a 600-page book detailing the proceedings. Economic and religious strategies were debated, and a plan was hatched to inform America about how British emancipation had worked. Memorials were sent to governments, and each governor of a southern U.S. state was targeted with a letter condemning the interstate slave trade. The delegates closed their meeting, exhilarated by the idea of their international congress to move toward international solutions to an international problem.

Description of a Slave Ship

This powerful and often-reprinted image combined a precise technical rendering of a British ship (normally evoking pride in Britons) with the horrors of a crowded mass of dark human flesh.

Peabody Essex Museum, Salem, MA.

Privately, Andrew Jackson thought it was "absurd" to treat the Indians as foreigners; he saw them as subjects of the United States. Jackson also did not approve of assimilation; that way lay extinction, he said. In his 1833 annual message to Congress he wrote, "They have neither the intelligence, the industry, the moral habits, nor the desire of improvement which are essential.... Established in the midst of a superior race... they must necessarily yield to the force of circumstances and ere long disappear." Congress backed Jackson's goal and passed the Indian Removal Act of 1830, appropriating $500,000 to relocate eastern tribes west of the Mississippi. About 100 million acres of eastern land would be vacated for eventual white settlement under this act authorizing ethnic expulsion (Map 11.2).

For northern tribes, their numbers diminished by years of war, gradual removal was already well under way. But not all the Indians went quietly. In 1832 in western Illinois, Black Hawk, a leader of the Sauk and Fox Indians who had fought with Tecumseh in the War of 1812 (see chapter 10, pages 244–45), resisted. Volunteer militias attacked and chased the Indians into southern Wisconsin, where, after several skirmishes and a deadly battle (later called the Black Hawk War), Black Hawk was captured and some 400 of his people were massacred.

Southern tribes proved even more resistant to removal. The powerful Creek, Chickasaw, Choctaw, and Cherokee tribes refused to relocate. A second Seminole War in Florida broke out as the Indians there—a mixture of Seminoles and escaped black slaves who had intermarried with the tribe—took up arms against relocation in 1836–1837.

The Cherokee of Georgia responded with a unique legal challenge to being treated as subjects. More than any other southern tribe, the 17,000 Cherokee had incorporated white political and economic practices into their tribal life. Spurred by dedicated missionaries, they had adopted written laws, including a constitution of 1827 modeled on

MAP 11.2   Indian Removal and the Trail of Tears

The federal government under President Andrew Jackson pursued a vigorous policy of Indian removal in the 1830s. Tribes were forcibly moved west to land known as Indian Territory (in present-day Oklahoma). As many as a quarter of the Cherokee Indians died in 1838 on the route known as the Trail of Tears.

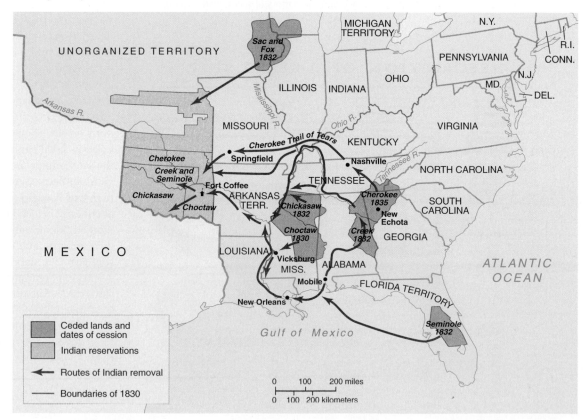

the U.S. Constitution. Two hundred of the wealthiest Cherokees had intermarried with whites and had adopted white styles of housing, dress, and cotton agriculture, including the ownership of a thousand slaves. They had developed a written alphabet and published a newspaper as well as Christian prayerbooks in their language.

In 1831, after Georgia announced it would subject the Indians to state law and seize their property, the Cherokee tribe appealed to the U.S. Supreme Court to restrain Georgia. Chief Justice John Marshall found for Georgia on the grounds that the Cherokee did not have standing to sue. When Georgia jailed two missionaries under an 1830 state law forbidding missionary aid to Indians without permission, the Cherokee brought suit again, fronting one of the missionaries as plaintiff. In the 1832 case, *Worcester v. Georgia,* the Supreme Court upheld the territorial sovereignty of the Cherokee, recognizing their existence as "a distinct community, occupying its own territory, in which the laws of Georgia can have no force." Ignoring the Supreme Court's decision, an angry President Jackson pressed the Cherokee for removal west. "If they now refuse to accept the liberal terms offered, they can only be liable for whatever evils and difficulties may arise. I feel conscious of having done my duty to my red children."

The Cherokee tribe remained in Georgia for two more years without significant violence. Then in 1835, a small, unauthorized part of the tribe signed a treaty selling all the tribal lands to the state, and Georgia rapidly resold the land to whites. But most Cherokees refused to move, so in May 1838, the deadline for voluntary evacuation, federal troops sent by Jackson's successor, Martin Van Buren, arrived to deport them. Under armed guard, the Cherokees embarked on a 1,200-mile journey west that came to be called the Trail of Tears. Nearly a quarter of the Cherokees died en route from the hardship. Survivors joined the fifteen thousand Creek, twelve thousand Choctaw, five thousand Chickasaw, and several thousand Seminole Indians also forcibly relocated to "Indian Territory" (which became, in 1907, the state of Oklahoma).

In his farewell address to the nation in 1837, Jackson again professed his belief about the benefit of Indian removal: "This unhappy race … are now placed in a situation where we may well hope that they will share in the blessings of civilization and be saved from the degradation and destruction to which they were rapidly hastening while they remained in the states." Possibly Jackson genuinely believed that exile to the West was necessary to save Indian cultures from destruction. But for the forcibly removed tribes, the costs of relocation were high.

The Tariff of Abominations and Nullification

Jackson's Indian policy happened to harmonize with the principle of **states' rights**: The president supported Georgia's right to ignore the Supreme

---

Cherokee Phoenix

Around 1820, Sequoyah, about forty-five years old and nephew of a Cherokee chief, invented written symbols to convey the Cherokee language. Each symbol represented a syllable of sound. In 1828, the Cherokees in New Echota, Georgia, ordered custom-made type embodying the new symbols and began printing a newspaper, the *Cherokee Phoenix,* the first newspaper published by Native Americans, printed in both English and Cherokee.

Special Collections Division, Georgetown University Library, Washington, D.C.

Court decision in *Worcester v. Georgia.* But in another pressing question of states' rights, Jackson contested South Carolina's attempt to ignore federal tariff policy.

Federal tariffs as high as 33 percent on imports such as textiles and iron goods had been passed in 1816 and again in 1824, in an effort to favor new American manufactures and shelter them from foreign competition as well as to raise federal revenue. Some southern congressmen opposed the steep tariffs, fearing they would decrease overseas shipping and hurt cotton exports. During John Quincy Adams's administration (1825–1829), tariff policy generated heated debate. In 1828, Congress passed a revised tariff that came to be known as the Tariff of Abominations. A bundle of conflicting duties—some as high as 50 percent—the legislation had provisions that pleased and angered every economic and sectional interest. Assembled mostly by southern congressmen, who loaded it with duties on raw materials needed by New England, it also contained protectionist elements favored by northern manufacturers.

South Carolina in particular suffered from the Tariff of Abominations. Worldwide prices for cotton had declined in the late 1820s, and the falloff in shipping caused by the high tariffs further hurt the South. In 1828, a group of South Carolina politicians headed by John C. Calhoun advanced a doctrine called **nullification**. The Union, they argued, was a confederation of states that had yielded some but not all power to the federal government. When Congress overstepped its powers, states had the right to nullify Congress's acts; as precedents they pointed to the Virginia and Kentucky Resolutions of 1798, which had attempted to invalidate the Alien and Sedition Acts (see chapter 9). Congress had erred in using tariff policy as an instrument to benefit specific industries, the South Carolinians claimed; tariffs should be used only to raise revenue.

On assuming the presidency in 1829, Jackson ignored the South Carolina statement of nullification and shut out Calhoun, his new vice president, from influence or power. Tariff revisions in early 1832 brought little relief to the South. Sensing futility, Calhoun resigned from the vice presidency in 1832 and accepted election by the South Carolina legislature to a seat in the U.S. Senate, where he could better argue his state's antitariff stance. Strained to their limit, the South Carolina leaders took the radical step of declaring the federal tariffs to be null and void in their state as of February 1,

1833. Finally, the constitutional crisis was out in the open.

Opting for a dramatic confrontation, Jackson sent armed ships to Charleston's harbor and threatened to invade the state. He pushed through Congress a bill, called the Force Bill, defining the Carolina stance as treason and authorizing military action to collect federal tariffs. At the same time, Congress moved quickly to pass a revised tariff more acceptable to the South. The conciliating Senator Henry Clay rallied support for a moderate bill that gradually reduced tariffs down to the 1816 level. On March 1, 1833, Congress passed both the new tariff and the Force Bill. South Carolina responded by withdrawing its nullification of the old tariff—and then nullifying the Force Bill. It was a symbolic gesture, since Jackson's show of muscle was no longer necessary. Both sides were satisfied with the immediate outcome. Federal power had prevailed over a dangerous assertion of states' rights, and South Carolina got the lower tariff it wanted.

Yet the question of federal power versus states' rights was far from settled. The implied threat behind nullification was secession, a position articulated in 1832 by some South Carolinians whose concerns went beyond tariff policy. The growing voice of antislavery activism in the North threatened the South's economic system. If and when a northern-dominated federal government decided to end slavery, the South Carolinians thought, the South must have the right to remove itself from the Union.

The Bank War and the Panic of 1837

Along with the tariff and nullification, President Jackson fought another political battle over the Bank of the United States. After riding out the panic of 1819, the bank finally prospered. It handled the federal government's deposits, extended credit and loans, and issued banknotes—by 1830 the most stable currency in the country. Now having twenty-nine branches, it benefited the whole nation. Jackson, however, did not find the bank's functions sufficiently valuable to offset his criticism of the concept of a national bank. In his first two annual messages to Congress, in 1829 and 1830, Jackson claimed that the bank concentrated undue economic power in the hands of a few.

National Republican (Whig) senators Daniel Webster and Henry Clay decided to force the issue. They convinced the bank to apply for charter renewal in 1832, well before the fall election, even though the existing charter ran until 1836. They fully expected that Congress's renewal would force Jackson to follow through on his rhetoric with a veto, that the unpopular veto would cause Jackson to lose the election, and that the bank would survive on an override vote from a new Congress swept into power on the anti-Jackson tide.

At first the plan seemed to work. The bank applied for rechartering, Congress voted to renew, and Jackson, angry over being manipulated, issued his veto. But it was a brilliantly written veto, full of fierce language about the privileges of the moneyed elite who oppress the democratic masses in order to enrich themselves. "Many of our rich men have not been content with equal protection and equal benefits, but have besought us to make them richer by act of Congress," Jackson wrote.

Clay and his supporters found Jackson's economic ideas so absurd and his language of class antagonism so shocking that they distributed thousands of copies of the bank veto as campaign material for their own party. A confident Henry Clay headed his party's ticket for the presidency. But the plan backfired. Jackson's translation of the bank controversy into a language of class antagonism and egalitarian ideals strongly resonated with many Americans. Old Hickory won the election easily, gaining 55 percent of the popular vote and a lopsided electoral college vote of 219 to 49. The Jackson party still controlled Congress, so no override was possible. The second Bank of the United States would cease to exist after 1836.

Jackson, however, wanted to destroy the bank sooner. Calling it a "monster," he ordered the sizable federal deposits to be removed from its vaults and redeposited into Democratic-inclined state banks. In retaliation, the Bank of the United States raised interest rates and called in loans. This action caused a brief decline in the economy in 1833 and actually enhanced Jackson's claim that the bank was too powerful for the good of the country.

Unleashed and unregulated, the economy in 1834 went into high gear. Perhaps only a small part of the problem arose from irresponsible banking practices. Just at this moment, an excess of silver from Mexican mines made its way into American banks, giving bankers license to print ever more banknotes. Inflation soared from 1834 to 1837; prices of basic goods rose more than 50 percent. States quickly chartered many hundreds of new private banks. Each bank issued its own banknotes and set interest rates as high as the market would bear. Entrepreneurs borrowed and invested money, much of it funneled into privately financed railroads and canals.

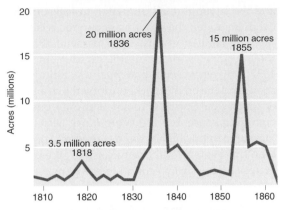

FIGURE 11.1   Western Land Sales, 1810–1860
Land sales peaked in the 1810s, 1830s, and 1850s as Americans rushed to speculate in western lands sold by the federal government. The surges in 1818 and 1836 demonstrate the volatile, speculative economy that suddenly collapsed in the panics of 1819 and 1837.

The market in western land sales heated up. In 1834, about 4.5 million acres of the public domain had been sold, the highest annual volume since the peak year 1819; by 1836, the total reached an astonishing 20 million acres (Figure 11.1). Some of this was southern land in Mississippi and Louisiana, which slave owners rushed to bring under cultivation, but much more was in the North, where land offices were deluged with buyers. The Jackson administration worried that the purchasers were overwhelmingly eastern capitalists, land speculators instead of self-reliant **yeoman** farmers who intended to settle on the land.

In one respect, the economy attained an admirable goal: The national debt disappeared, and, for the first and only time in American history, from 1835 to 1837, the government had a monetary surplus. But much of it consisted of questionable bank currencies—"bloated, diseased" currencies, in Jackson's vivid terminology.

Jackson decided to restrain the economy. In 1836, the Treasury Department issued the Specie Circular, an order that public land could be purchased only with hard money, federally coined gold and silver. In response, bankers started to reduce their loans, fearing a general contraction of the economy. Compounding the difficulty, the Bank of England also now insisted on hard-money payments for American loans, which had grown large since 1831 because of a trade imbalance. Failures in various crop markets, a downturn in cotton prices on the international market, and the silver glut, all unrelated to Jackson's fiscal policies, fed the growing economic crisis.

The familiar events of the panic of 1819 unfolded again, with terrifying rapidity. In April 1837, a wave of bank and business failures ensued, and the credit market tumbled like a house of cards. The Specie Circular was only one precipitating cause, but the Whig Party held it and Jackson responsible for the depression. For more than five years after the panic of 1837, the United States suffered from economic hard times.

Van Buren's One-Term Presidency

The election of 1836, which preceded the panic by six months, demonstrated the transformation of the Democrats from coalition to party. Jackson's personality had stamped the elections of 1824, 1828, and 1832. By 1836, the party apparatus was sufficiently developed to support itself. Local and state committees existed throughout the country. Democratic candidates ran in every state election, succeeding even in old Federalist states like Maine and New Hampshire. More than four hundred newspapers declared themselves Democratic. In 1836, the Democrats repeated an innovation begun in 1832: holding a national convention. They nominated Vice President Martin Van Buren of New York for president.

Sophisticated party organization was Martin Van Buren's specialty. Nicknamed the "Little Magician" for his consummate political skills, the New Yorker had built his career by pioneering many of the loyalty-enhancing techniques the Democrats used in the 1830s. After serving as senator and then governor, he became Jackson's secretary of state in 1828. Four years later he replaced Calhoun as Jackson's running mate. His eight years in the volatile Jackson administration required the full measure of his political deftness as he sought repeatedly to save Jackson from both his enemies and his own obstinacy.

Van Buren was a backroom politician, not a popular public figure, and the Whigs hoped that he might be defeatable. In many states, Whigs had captured high office in 1834, shedding the awkward National Republican label and developing statewide organizations to rival those of the Democrats. However, no figure commanded nationwide support, and so three regional candidates opposed Van Buren in 1836. Senator Daniel Webster of Massachusetts could deliver New England, home to reformers, merchants, and manufacturers; Senator Hugh Lawson White of Tennessee attracted proslavery (and thus anti–Van Buren) voters in the South; and the aging General William Henry Harrison of Indiana, memorable for his Indian war heroics in 1811, pulled in the western, anti-Indian vote. Not one of the three candidates could have won the presidency, but together they came close to denying Van Buren a majority vote. Their combined strength drew many Whigs into office at the state level. In the end, Van Buren had 170 electoral votes, while the other three received a total of 113.

Van Buren took office in March 1837, and a month later the panic hit. The new president called a special session of Congress to consider creating an independent treasury system to fulfill some of the functions of the defunct Bank of the United States. Such a system, funded by government deposits, would deal only in hard money, forcing commercial banks to restrict their issuance of paper currency, and it would not make loans, thus avoiding the danger of speculative meddling in the economy. In short, an independent treasury system could exert a powerful moderating influence on inflation and the credit market without itself being directly involved in the market. But Van Buren encountered strong resistance in Congress, even from Democrats. The treasury system finally won approval in 1840; by then, however, Van Buren's chances of a second term in office were virtually nil because of the tumultuous economy.

In 1840, the Whigs settled on William Henry Harrison, sixty-seven, to oppose Van Buren. The campaign drew on voter involvement as no presidential campaign ever had. The Whigs borrowed tricks from the Democrats: Harrison was touted as a common man born in a log cabin (in reality he was born on a Virginia plantation), and raucous campaign parades featured toy log cabins held aloft. His Indian-fighting days, now thirty years behind him, were played up to give him a Jacksonian aura. Whigs staged festive rallies all over the country, drumming up mass appeal with candlelight parades and song shows, and women participated in rallies as never before. Some 78 percent of eligible voters cast ballots—the highest percentage ever in American history. Harrison took 53 percent of the popular vote and won a resounding 234 electoral college votes to Van Buren's 60. A Democratic editor lamented, "We have taught them how to conquer us!"

REVIEW   How did Jackson's vision of democracy shape the policies of the Democratic Party?

Conclusion:
The Age of Jackson
or the Era of Reform?

Harrison's election closed a decade that had brought the common man and democracy to the forefront of American politics. Economic transformations loom large in explaining the fast-paced changes of the 1830s. Transportation advances put goods and people in circulation, augmenting urban growth and helping to create a national culture, and water-powered manufacturing began to change the face of wage labor. Trade and banking mushroomed, and western lands once occupied by Indians were auctioned off in a landslide of sales. Two economic downturns, the panics of 1819 and 1837, offered sobering lessons about speculative fever.

Andrew Jackson symbolized this age of opportunity for many. His fame as an aggressive general, Indian fighter, champion of the common man, and defender of slavery attracted growing numbers of voters to the emergent Democratic Party, which championed personal liberty, free competition, and egalitarian opportunity for all white men.

Jackson's constituency was challenged by a small but vocal segment of the population troubled by serious moral problems that Jacksonians preferred to ignore. Reformers drew sustenance from the message of the Second Great Awakening: that all men and women are free to choose salvation and that personal and societal sins can be overcome. Reformers targeted personal vices (illicit sex, intemperance) and social problems (prostitution, poverty, and slavery), and joined forces with evangelicals and wealthy lawyers and merchants North or South who appreciated a national bank and protective tariffs. The Whig Party was the party of activist moralism and state-sponsored entrepreneurship.

National politics in the 1830s were more divisive than at any other time since the 1790s. The new party system of Democrats and Whigs reached far deeper into the electorate than had the Federalists and Republicans. Stagecoaches and steamboats carried newspapers with their political coverage from the city to the backwoods, politicizing voters and creating party loyalty. Politics acquired immediacy and excitement, causing four out of five white men to cast ballots in 1840.

High rates of voter participation would continue into the 1840s and 1850s. Unprecedented urban growth, westward expansion, and early industrialism marked those decades, sustaining the Jacksonian-Whig split in the electorate. But critiques of slavery, concerns for free labor, and an emerging protest against women's second-class citizenship complicated the political scene of the 1840s, leading to third-party political movements. One of these third parties, called the Republican Party, would achieve dominance in 1860 with the election of an Illinois lawyer, Abraham Lincoln, to the presidency.

Suggestions for Further Reading

Patricia Cline Cohen, *The Murder of Helen Jewett: The Life and Death of a Prostitute in Nineteenth-Century New York* (1998). A true crime story of the underside of 1830s urban life, revealing in detail the sexual subculture protested by the Female Moral Reformers.

Daniel Feller, *The Jacksonian Promise: America, 1815–1840* (1995). An excellent one-volume narrative describing the energy and optimism of Jacksonian America's politics and society.

Paul E. Johnson and Sean Wilentz, *The Kingdom of Matthias: A Story of Sex and Salvation in Nineteenth-Century America* (1994). The bizarre but instructive tale of a self-proclaimed prophet operating at the margins of the Second Great Awakening.

Richard S. Newman, *The Transformation of American Abolitionism: Fighting Slavery in the Early Republic* (2002). An absorbing history of antislavery action in the United States from the 1780s to 1840, with close attention to race and gender.

Merrill D. Peterson, *The Great Triumvirate: Webster, Clay, and Calhoun* (1987). A vivid portrait of three powerful senators who also helped to define Jackson's decade.

Charles G. Sellers, *The Market Revolution: Jacksonian America, 1815–1846* (1991). A senior scholar's comprehensive synthesis of the economic, cultural, and political themes of the period.

▶ FOR MORE BOOKS ABOUT TOPICS IN THIS CHAPTER, see the Online Study Guide at bedfordstmartins.com/roarkcompact.

▶ FOR ADDITIONAL FIRSTHAND ACCOUNTS OF THIS PERIOD, see Chapter 11 in Michael Johnson, ed., *Reading the American Past*, Third Edition.

▶ FOR WEB SITES AND DOCUMENTS RELATED TO TOPICS AND PLACES IN THIS CHAPTER, see "HistoryLinks," "DocLinks," and "PlaceLinks" at bedfordstmartins.com/roarkcompact.

REVIEWING THE CHAPTER

Follow these steps to review and strengthen your understanding of the chapter.

STEP 1: *Study the **Key Terms** and **Timeline** to identify the significance of each item listed.*

STEP 2: *Answer the **Review Questions**, drawing on key terms and dates to support your answers.*

STEP 3: *Drawing on the Key Terms, Timeline, and Review Questions, answer the broader **Making Connections** questions.*

KEY TERMS

Who

Andrew Jackson (p. 259)
Robert Fulton (p. 261)
John Quincy Adams (p. 266)
Charles Grandison Finney (p. 270)
David Walker (p. 272)
Maria Stewart (p. 272)
William Lloyd Garrison (p. 272)
Angelina and Sarah Grimké (p. 272)
Black Hawk (p. 276)
John C. Calhoun (p. 278)
Henry Clay (p. 279)
Martin Van Buren (p. 280)
William Henry Harrison (p. 280)

What

Erie Canal (p. 261)
Baltimore and Ohio Railroad (p. 262)
Lowell mills (p. 262)
second Bank of the United States (p. 264)
panic of 1819 (p. 264)
Hickory Clubs (p. 265)
Bucktails (p. 266)
Whigs (p. 266)
Democrats (p. 266)
Maysville Road veto (p. 267)
Second Great Awakening (p. 268)
separate spheres (p. 268)
American Temperance Society (p. 270)
American Temperance Union (p. 271)
Female Moral Reform Society (p. 271)

American Colonization Society (p. 272)
National Negro Convention (p. 272)
Liberator (p. 272)
New England Anti-Slavery Society (p. 272)
Indian Removal Act of 1830 (p. 276)
Black Hawk War (p. 276)
second Seminole War (p. 276)
Worcester v. Georgia (p. 277)
Trail of Tears (p. 277)
Tariff of Abominations (p. 278)
nullification (p. 278)
Force Bill (p. 278)
Specie Circular (p. 279)
panic of 1837 (p. 280)

TIMELINE

◀ **1807** • Robert Fulton's boat *Clermont* sets off steamboat craze.

1816 • Second Bank of the United States chartered.

1817 • American Colonization Society founded.

1818 • National Road links Baltimore to western Virginia.

1819 • Economic panic.

1821 • Mill town of Lowell, Massachusetts, founded.

1825 • Erie Canal in New York completed.

1826 • American Temperance Society founded.
• Schuylkill Canal in Pennsylvania completed.

1828 • Congress passes Tariff of Abominations.
• Democrat Andrew Jackson elected president.

REVIEW QUESTIONS

1. Why did the United States experience a market revolution after 1815? (pp. 260–65)

2. Why did Jackson defeat John Quincy Adams so dramatically in the 1828 election? (pp. 265–68)

3. How did evangelical Protestantism contribute to the social reform movements of the 1830s? (pp. 268–73)

4. How did Jackson's vision of democracy shape the policies of the Democratic Party? (pp. 273–80)

MAKING CONNECTIONS

1. Andrew Jackson's presidency coincided with important changes in American politics. Discuss how Jackson benefited from, and contributed to, the vibrant political culture of the 1830s. Cite specific national developments in your answer.

2. Describe the market revolution that began in the 1810s. How did it affect Americans' work and domestic lives? In your answer, be sure to consider how gender contributed to these developments.

3. While a volatile economy buffeted the nation, some Americans in the 1830s looked to reform the nation. Discuss the objectives and strategies of two reform movements. What was the relationship of these reform movements to larger political and economic trends of the 1830s?

4. Describe Andrew Jackson's response to the "Indian problem" during his presidency. How did his policies revise or continue earlier federal policies toward Native Americans? How did Native Americans respond to Jackson's actions?

▶ For practice quizzes, a customized study plan, and other study tools, see the Online Study Guide at bedfordstmartins.com/roarkcompact.

1829 • David Walker's *Appeal . . . to the Coloured Citizens of the World* published.
  • Baltimore and Ohio Railroad begun.
  1830 • Indian Removal Act.
    1831 • William Lloyd Garrison starts the *Liberator*.
      • Charles G. Finney preaches in Rochester, New York.
      1832 • Massacre of Sauk and Fox Indians under Chief Black Hawk.
        • *Worcester v. Georgia*.
        • Jackson vetoes Bank of the United States charter.
        • New England Anti-Slavery Society founded.

        1833 • Nullification declared in South Carolina.
          • New York and Philadelphia antislavery societies founded.
          • New York Female Moral Reform Society founded.
          • Female mill workers strike in Lowell, Massachusetts.
          1836 • Jackson issues Specie Circular.
            • Democrat Martin Van Buren elected president.
            1837 • Economic panic.
              1838 • Trail of Tears: Cherokees forced to relocate west.
                1840 • Whig William Henry Harrison elected president.

GOLD NUGGETS
Gold! Nuggets like these scooped from a California river drove easterners crazy with excitement. A quarter of a million people joined the great rush for western riches in the five years after gold's discovery in 1848. Men from the East and around the world sought to escape routine jobs and mundane lives by "making their pile" in California. The carnival that was the gold rush fulfilled the hopes of only a few, but the rest participated in one of the great adventures of the nineteenth century and rarely regretted their experiences.

The Oakland Museum.

12

The New West and Free North

1840–1860

E ARLY IN NOVEMBER 1842, Abraham Lincoln and his new wife, Mary, moved into their first home in Springfield, Illinois, a rented room measuring eight by fourteen feet on the second floor of the Globe Tavern, the nicest place Abraham had ever lived. Mary Todd Lincoln had grown up in Lexington, Kentucky, attended by slaves in the elegant home of her father, a prosperous merchant, banker, and politician. The small room above the Globe Tavern was the worst place she had ever lived. Fewer than twenty years later, in March 1861, the Lincolns moved into what would prove to be their last home, the presidential mansion in Washington, D.C. Abraham Lincoln climbed from the Globe Tavern to the White House by relentless work, unslaked ambition, and immense talent, traits he had honed since boyhood.

Born in a Kentucky log cabin in 1809, Lincoln grew up on small, struggling farms as his family migrated westward. His father, Thomas, had left Virginia, where he had been born, and settled in Kentucky. Thomas Lincoln never learned to read or, as his son recalled, "never did more in the way of writing than to bunglingly sign his own name." Lincoln's mother, Nancy, could neither read nor write. In December 1816, Thomas Lincoln moved his young family from Kentucky to the Indiana wilderness. They lived for two frozen months in a crude lean-to while Thomas, a skilled carpenter, built a cabin. On the Indiana farmstead, Abraham learned the arts of agriculture practiced by families throughout the nation. Although only eight years old, he "had an axe put into his hands at once" and used it "almost constantly" for the next fifteen years. When he could be spared from work, the boy attended school, less than a year in all. "There was absolutely nothing to excite ambition for education," Lincoln recollected. In contrast, Mary Todd, his future wife, received ten years of schooling in Lexington's best academies for young women.

By 1830, Thomas Lincoln decided to move farther west and start over again. The Lincolns hitched up the family oxen and headed to central Illinois, where they built another log cabin. The next spring Thomas Lincoln moved yet again, but this time Abraham stayed behind and set out on his own, a "friendless, uneducated, penniless boy," as he described himself.

By dogged striving, Lincoln gained an education and the respect of his Illinois neighbors, although a steady income eluded him for years. He and Mary received help from her father, including eighty acres of land and an allowance of about $1,100 for six years that helped them move out of their room above the Globe Tavern. Lincoln eventually built a thriving law practice in Springfield

Abraham Lincoln's Hat
Abraham Lincoln wore this stovepipe hat, made of beaver pelt, during his years as president of the United States. Stovepipe hats were worn by established, respectable, middle-class men in the 1850s. Workingmen and farmers would have felt out of place wearing such a hat, except perhaps on special occasions like weddings or funerals. Growing up in Kentucky, Indiana, and Illinois, Lincoln may have seen stovepipe hats on the leading men of his community, but he probably never owned one until he became an aspiring Illinois lawyer and politician. Wearing such a hat was a mark that one had achieved a certain success in life, in Lincoln's case the enormous social distance he had traveled from his backwoods origins to the White House. But even as president he continued a backwoods practice he had begun as a young postmaster in New Salem, Illinois, using his hat as a place to store letters and papers. Lincoln's law partner William Herndon termed Lincoln's hat "an extraordinary receptacle [that] served as his desk and memorandum book."

Smithsonian Institution, Washington, D.C.

and served in the Illinois legislature and then in Congress. His political activity and hard-driving ambition ultimately propelled him into the White House, the first president born west of the Appalachian Mountains.

Like Lincoln, millions of Americans believed they could make something of themselves, whatever their origins, so long as they were willing to work. Individuals who refused to work—who were lazy, undisciplined, or foolish—had only themselves to blame if they failed. Work was a prerequisite for success, not a guarantee. The promise of rewards from hard work spurred efforts that shaped the contours of America, pushing the boundaries of the nation south to the Rio Grande, north to the Great Lakes, and ever west-ward to the Pacific Ocean. During his presidency, Lincoln talked about moving west to California at the end of his term. The economic, political, and geographic expansion that Lincoln exemplified raised anew the question of whether slavery should also move west, the question that Lincoln and other Americans confronted again and again following the Mexican-American War, yet another outgrowth of the nation's ceaseless westward movement.

The Westward Movement

The 1840s ushered in a new era of rapid westward movement. Until then, the overwhelming majority of Americans lived east of the Mississippi River. Native Americans inhabited the plains, deserts, and rugged coasts to the west. The British claimed Oregon Country, and the Mexicans held the Southwest. But by 1850, the boundaries of the United States stretched to the Pacific, and by 1860, the great migration had carried four million Americans west of the Mississippi River.

The nation's revolution in transportation and communication, its swelling population, and its booming economy propelled the westward surge. But the emigrants themselves conquered the continent. **Frontier** settlers craving land took the soil and then, with the exception of the Mormons, lobbied their government to acquire the territories they settled in. The human cost of westward expansion was high. The young Mexican nation lost half of its territory. Two centuries of Indian wars east of the Mississippi ended during the 1830s, but the old, fierce struggle between native inhabitants and invaders continued for another half century in the West.

Manifest Destiny

Most Americans believed that the superiority of their institutions and white culture bestowed on them a God-given right to spread their civilization across the continent. They imagined the West as a howling wilderness, empty and undeveloped. If they recognized Indians and Mexicans at all, they dismissed them as primitive drags on progress who would have to be redeemed, shoved aside, or exterminated. The sense of mission and superiority had been bolstered by the United States's amazing success. The West needed the civilizing power of the hammer and plow, the ballot box and pulpit, that had transformed the East, most Americans believed.

In 1845, New York journalist John L. O'Sullivan coined the term **manifest destiny** as the latest justification for white settlers to take the land they coveted. O'Sullivan called on Americans to resist any foreign power—British, French, or Mexican—that attempted to thwart "the fulfillment of our manifest destiny to overspread the continent allotted by Providence for the free development of our yearly multiplying millions…[and] for the development of the great experiment of liberty and federative self-government entrusted to us." Almost overnight, the magic phrase *manifest destiny* swept the nation and provided an ideological shield for conquering the West.

As important as national pride and racial arrogance were to manifest destiny, economic gain made up its core. Land hunger drew hundreds of thousands of average Americans westward. Some politicians, moreover, had become convinced that national prosperity depended on capturing the rich trade of the Far East. To trade with Asia, the United States needed the Pacific coast ports that stretched from San Diego to Puget Sound. No one was more eager to extend American trade in the Pacific than Missouri's Senator Thomas Hart Benton. "The sun of civilization must shine across the sea: socially and commercially," he declared. The United States and Asia must "talk together, and trade together. Commerce is a great civilizer." In the 1840s, American economic expansion came wrapped in the rhetoric of uplift and civilization.

Oregon and the Overland Trail

Oregon Country—a vast region bounded on the west by the Pacific, on the east by the Rockies, on the south by the forty-second parallel, and on the north by Russian Alaska—caused the pulse of American expansionists to race (Map 12.1). But the British also coveted the area. They argued their claim lay with Sir Francis Drake's discovery of the Oregon coast in 1579. Americans countered with historic claims of their own. Unable to agree, the United States and Great Britain decided in 1818 on "joint occupation" that would leave Oregon "free and open" to settlement by both countries. A handful of American fur traders and "mountain men" roamed the region in the 1820s, but in the 1830s and 1840s expansionists made Oregon Country an early target of manifest destiny.

By the late 1830s, settlers began to trickle along the Oregon Trail (see Map 12.1). The first wagon trains headed west in 1841, and by 1843 about 1,000 emigrants a year set out from Independence, Missouri. By 1869, when the first transcontinental railroad was completed, approximately 350,000 migrants had traveled west to the Pacific in wagon trains.

Emigrants encountered Plains Indians, a quarter of a million Native Americans who populated the area between the Rocky Mountains and the Mississippi River. Some were farmers who lived peaceful, sedentary lives, but a majority—the Sioux, Cheyenne, Shoshone, and Arapaho of the central Plains and the Kiowa, Wichita, and Comanche in the southern Plains—were horse-mounted, nomadic, nonagricultural peoples whose warriors symbolized the "savage Indian" in the minds of whites.

Horses, which had been brought to North America by Spaniards in the sixteenth century, permitted the Plains tribes to become highly mobile hunters of buffalo. They came to depend on buffalo for most of their food, clothing, shelter, and fuel. Competition for buffalo led to war between the tribes. Young men were introduced to warfare early, learning to ride ponies at breakneck speed while firing off arrows and, later, rifles with astounding accuracy. "A Comanche on his feet is out of his element," observed western artist George Catlin, "but the moment he lays his hands upon his horse, his *face* even becomes handsome, and he gracefully flies away like a different being."

Plains Indians struck fear in the hearts of whites on the wagon trains. But Native Americans had far more to fear from whites. Indians killed fewer than 400 emigrants on the trail between 1840 and 1860, while whites brought alcohol and deadly epidemics of smallpox, measles, cholera, and scarlet fever. Moreover, whites killed the buffalo, often slaughtering them

Plains Indians and Trails West in the 1840s and 1850s

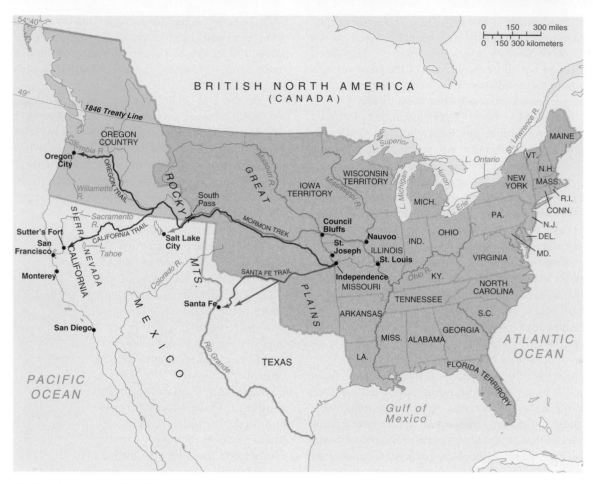

MAP 12.1   Trails to the West
In the 1830s, wagon trains began snaking their way to the Southwest and the Pacific coast. Deep ruts, some of which can still be seen today, soon marked the most popular routes.

for sport. Buffalo still numbered some twelve million in 1860, but the herds were shrinking rapidly, intensifying conflict among the Plains Indians.

Emigrants insisted that the federal government provide them more protection. The government responded by constructing a chain of forts along the Oregon Trail. More important, it adopted a new Indian policy: "concentration." First, the government rescinded the "permanent" buffer it had granted the Indians west of the ninety-fifth meridian. Then, in 1851, it called the Plains tribes to a conference at Fort Laramie, Wyoming. Some ten thousand Indians showed up, hopeful that something could be done to protect them from the ravages of the wagon trains. Instead, U.S. government negotiators

persuaded the chiefs to sign agreements that cleared a wide corridor for wagon trains by restricting Native Americans to specific areas that whites promised they would never violate. This policy of concentration became the seedbed for the subsequent policy of reservations. But whites would not keep out of Indian territory, and Indians would not easily give up their traditional ways of life. Competition meant warfare for decades to come.

Still, Indians threatened emigrants less than life on the trail did. The men, women, and children who headed west each spring could count on at least six months of grueling travel. With nearly two thousand miles to go and traveling no more than fifteen miles a day, the pioneers endured parching heat, drought, treacherous rivers, disease, physical and emotional exhaustion, and, if the snows closed the mountain passes before they got through, freezing and starvation. Women sometimes faced the dangers of trailside child-birth. It was said that a person could walk from Missouri to the Pacific stepping only on the graves of those who had died heading west. Such tribulations led one miserable woman, trying to keep her children dry in a rainstorm and to calm them as they listened to Indian shouts, to wonder "what had possessed my husband, anyway, that he should have thought of bringing us away out through this God forsaken country."

Men usually found Oregon "one of the greatest countries in the world." From "the Cascade mountains to the Pacific, the whole country can be cultivated," exclaimed one settler. When women reached Oregon, they found a wilderness. Things were in a "primitive state." One young wife set up housekeeping with her new husband with only one stew kettle and three knives. Necessity blurred the traditional division between men's and women's work. "I am maid of all traids," one busy woman remarked in 1853. Work seemed unending. "I am a very old woman," declared twenty-nine-year-old Sarah Everett. "My face is thin sunken and wrinkled, my hands bony withered and hard." Another settler observed, "A woman that can not endure almost as much as a horse has no business here." Despite the ordeal of the trail and the difficulties of starting from scratch, emigrants kept coming.

***Kee-O-Kuk, the Watchful Fox, Chief of the Tribe,* George Catlin, 1835**
In the 1830s, Pennsylvania-born artist George Catlin traveled the West painting Native American portraits, rituals, and landscapes. Although not the first artist to paint Indians, he was the first to portray them in their own environments and one of the few to present them as human beings, not savages. Convinced that western Indian cultures would soon disappear, Catlin sought to document Indian life through hundreds of paintings and prints. Keokuk, chief of the Sac and Fox, struggled with the warrior Black Hawk about the proper strategy for dealing with whites. Black Hawk fought American expansion; Keokuk believed war was fruitless and signed over land in Illinois, Missouri, and Wisconsin.
Smithsonian American Art Institution, Washington, D.C. Gift of Mrs. Joseph Harrison Jr.

The Mormon Exodus

Not every wagon train heading west was bound for the Pacific Slope. One remarkable group of religious emigrants halted near the Great Salt Lake in what was then Mexican territory. The Mormons deliberately chose the remote site as a refuge. After years of persecution in the East, they fled west to find religious freedom and communal security.

In 1830, Joseph Smith Jr., who was only twenty-four, published *The Book of Mormon* and founded the Church of Jesus Christ of Latter-Day Saints (the Mormons). A decade earlier, the upstate New York farm boy had begun to experience revelations that were followed, he said, by a visit from an angel who led him to golden tablets buried near his home. With the aid of magic stones, Smith translated the mysterious language on the tablets to produce *The Book of*

Mormon. It told the story of an ancient Christian civilization in the New World and predicted the appearance of an American prophet who would reestablish Jesus Christ's undefiled kingdom in America. Converts, attracted to the promise of a pure faith in the midst of **antebellum** America's social turmoil and rampant materialism, flocked to the new church.

Neighbors branded Mormons heretics and drove Smith and his followers from New York to Ohio, then to Missouri, and finally in 1839 to Nauvoo, Illinois, where they built a prosperous community. But dissenters within the church accused Smith of advocating plural marriage (polygamy). Non-Mormons caught wind of the controversy and eventually arrested Smith and his brother. On June 27, 1844, a mob stormed the jail and shot both men dead.

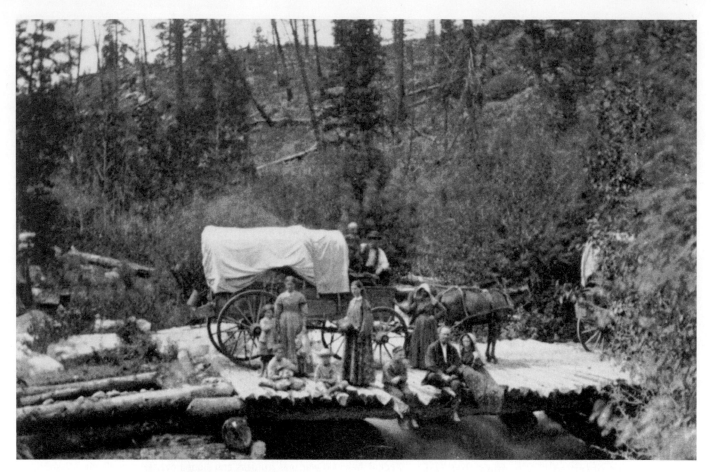

Pioneer Family on the Trail West
In 1860, W. G. Chamberlain photographed these unidentified travelers momentarily at rest by the upper Arkansas River in Colorado. We do not know their fates, but we can hope that they fared better than the Sager family: Henry, Naomi, and their six children, who set out from St. Joseph, Missouri, in 1844. "Father," one of Henry and Naomi's daughters remembered, "was one of those restless men who are not content to remain in one place long at a time. [He] had been talking of going to Texas. But mother, hearing much said about the healthfulness of Oregon, preferred to go there." Still far from Oregon, Henry Sager died of fever; twenty-six days later, Naomi died, leaving seven children, the last delivered on the trail. The Sager children, under the care of other families in the wagon train, pressed on. After traveling 2,000 miles in seven months, the migrants arrived in Oregon, where Marcus and Narcissa Whitman, whose own daughter had drowned, adopted all seven of the Sager children.
Denver Public Library, Western History Division # F3226.

FOR MORE HELP ANALYZING THIS IMAGE, see the visual activity for this chapter in the Online Study Guide at
bedfordstmartins.com/roarkcompact.

The embattled church turned to an extraordinary new leader, Brigham Young, who immediately began to plan a great exodus. In 1846, traveling in 3,700 wagons, 12,000 Mormons made their way to eastern Iowa; the following year they arrived at their new home beside the Great Salt Lake. Young described the region as a barren waste, "the paradise of the lizard, the cricket and the rattlesnake." Within ten years, however, the Mormons developed an irrigation system that made the desert bloom. They accomplished the feat through cooperative labor, not the individualistic and competitive enterprise common among most emigrants. Under Young's stern leadership, the Mormons built a thriving community.

In 1850, the Mormon kingdom was annexed to the United States as Utah Territory. The nation's attention focused on Utah in 1852 when Brigham Young announced that many Mormons practiced polygamy. Although only one Mormon man in five had more than one wife (Young had twenty-three), Young's statement caused a popular outcry that forced the U.S. government to establish its authority in Utah. In 1857, 2,500 U.S. troops invaded Salt Lake City in what was known as the Mormon War. The bloodless occupation illustrates that most Americans viewed the Mormons as a threat to American morality, law, and institutions. The invasion did not dislodge the Mormon Church from its central place in Utah, however, and for years to come most Americans perceived the Mormon settlement as strange and suitably isolated.

The Mexican Borderlands

In the Mexican Southwest, westward-moving Anglo-American pioneers confronted northern-moving Spanish-speaking frontiersmen. On this frontier as elsewhere, national cultures, interests, and aspirations collided. Since 1821, when Mexico won its independence from Spain, the Mexican flag had flown over the vast expanse that stretched from the Gulf of Mexico to the Pacific and from Oregon Country to Guatemala (Map 12.2). Mexico's borders remained ill defined, and its northern provinces were sparsely populated. Moreover, severe problems plagued the young nation: civil wars, economic crises, quarrels with the Roman Catholic Church, and devastating raids by the Comanche, Apache, and Kiowa. Mexico found it increasingly difficult to defend its borderlands, especially when faced with a northern neighbor convinced of its superiority and bent on territorial acquisition.

The American assault began quietly. In the 1820s, Anglo-American trappers, traders, and settlers drifted into Mexico's far northern provinces. Santa Fe, a remote outpost in the province of New Mexico, became a magnet for American enterprise. Each spring, American traders gathered at Independence, Missouri, for the long trek southwest along the Santa Fe Trail

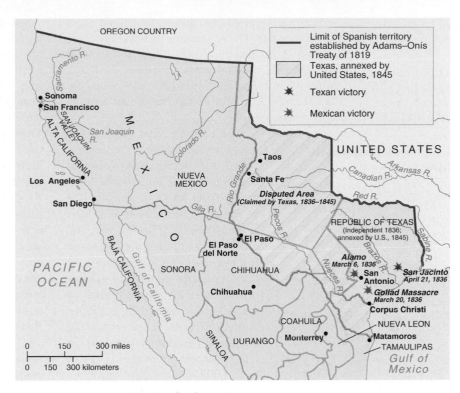

MAP 12.2 Texas and Mexico in the 1830s
As Americans spilled into lightly populated and loosely governed northern Mexico, Texas and then other Mexican provinces became contested territory.

(see Map 12.1). They crammed their wagons with inexpensive American manufactured goods and returned home with Mexican silver, furs, and mules.

The Mexican province of Texas attracted a flood of Americans who had settlement, not long-distance trade, on their minds (see Map 12.2). Wanting to populate and develop its northern territory, the Mexican government granted the American Stephen F. Austin a huge tract of land along the Brazos River. In the 1820s Austin became the first Anglo-American *empresario* (colonization agent) in Texas. Land was cheap—only ten cents an acre—and thousands of Americans poured across the border. Many brought cotton and slaves with them. By 1835, the settlers had established a thriving plantation economy in Texas. Americans numbered thirty-five thousand, while the *Tejano* (Spanish-speaking) population was less than eight thousand. Few Anglo-American settlers were Roman Catholic, spoke Spanish, or cared about assimilating into Mexican culture. In 1829, the Mexican government sought to halt further immigration by outlawing slavery, but the settlers sidestepped the decree by calling their slaves servants. The Americans increasingly complained about the puny voice they had in local government. General Antonio López de Santa Anna all but extinguished that voice when he seized political power and concentrated authority in Mexico City.

Faced with what they considered tyranny, the Texan settlers rebelled and declared the independent Republic of Texas. Santa Anna ordered the Mexican army northward and in February 1836 arrived at the outskirts of San Antonio. The rebels, who included the Tennessee frontiersman David Crockett and the Louisiana adventurer James Bowie, as well as a number of Tejanos, took refuge in a former Franciscan mission known as the Alamo. When Santa Anna's siege failed, he sent wave after wave of his 4,000-man army crashing against the walls until the attackers finally broke through and killed all 187 defenders. A few weeks later in the small town of Goliad, Mexican forces surrounded and captured a garrison of Texans. Following orders from Santa Anna, Mexican firing squads executed more than 300 of the men as "pirates." In April 1836 at San Jacinto, General Sam Houston's army adopted the massacre at Goliad as a battle cry and produced a crushing defeat of Santa Anna's troops. Texans had succeeded in establishing their Lone Star Republic, and the following year the United States recognized the independence of Texas from Mexico.

In California, the Mexican government sought to increase the number of Mexican immigrants. In 1824, it granted *ranchos*—huge estates devoted to cattle raising—to new settlers. *Rancheros* ruled over near-feudal empires worked by Indians whose condition sometimes approached that of slaves. Not satisfied, *rancheros* coveted the vast lands controlled by the Franciscan missions. In 1834, they persuaded the Mexican government to confiscate the missions and make their lands available to new settlement, a development that accelerated the decline of California Indians. Devastated by disease, the Indians, who numbered approximately 300,000

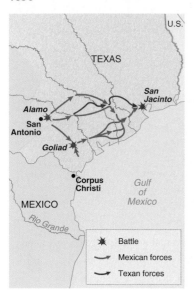

Texas War for Independence, 1836

when the Spanish arrived in 1769, declined to half that number by 1846.

Despite the efforts of the Mexican government, California in 1840 counted a population of only 7,000 Mexican settlers. Non-Mexican settlers numbered only 380, but among them were Americans who championed manifest destiny. They sought to woo American emigrants to California. Wagon after wagon left the Oregon Trail to head southwest on the California Trail in the 1840s (see Map 12.1). As the trickle of Americans became a river, Mexican officials grew alarmed, for as a New York newspaper put it in 1845, "Let the tide of emigration flow toward California and the American population will soon be sufficiently numerous to play the Texas game." Only a few Americans in California looked forward to war for independence, but many dreamed of living again under the American flag.

The U.S. government made no secret of its desire to acquire California. In 1835, President Andrew Jackson tried unsuccessfully to purchase it. In 1846, American settlers in the Sacramento Valley took matters into their own hands. Prodded by John C. Frémont, a former army captain and explorer who had arrived with a party of sixty buckskin-clad frontiersmen spoiling for a fight, the Californians raised an independence movement known as the Bear Flag Revolt. By then, James K. Polk, a champion of expansion, sat in the White House.

> **REVIEW** Why did westward migration expand dramatically in the mid-nineteenth century?

Expansion and the Mexican-American War

Although emigrants acted as the advance guard of American empire, there was nothing automatic about the U.S. annexation of territory in the West. Acquiring territory required political action. In the 1840s the politics of expansion became entangled with sectionalism and the slavery question. Texas, Oregon, and the Mexican borderlands thrust the United States into dangerous diplomatic crises with Great Britain and Mexico.

Aggravation between Mexico and the United States escalated to open antagonism in 1845 when the United States annexed Texas. Absorbing territory still claimed by Mexico ruptured diplomatic relations between the two countries and set the stage for war. But it was President James K. Polk's insistence on having Mexico's other northern provinces that made war certain. The war was not as easy as Polk anticipated, but it ended in American victory and the acquisition of a new American West.

The Politics of Expansion

Westward expansion ended up on the desk of John Tyler when he became president in April 1841. William Henry Harrison had been elected president in 1840 but died one month after taking office. The issue that stirred Tyler's blood, and that of much of the nation, was Texas. Texans had sought admission to the Union almost since winning their independence from Mexico in 1836. Tyler, an ardent expansionist, understood that Texas was a dangerous issue. Any suggestion of adding another slave state to the Union would enrage Northerners. Annexing Texas also risked precipitating war because Mexico had never relinquished its claim to its lost province.

Nevertheless, Tyler decided to risk annexing Texas. In April 1844, Secretary of State John C. Calhoun laid an annexation treaty before the Senate. But when Calhoun linked annexation to the defense of slavery, he doomed the treaty. Howls of protest erupted across the North. In Massachusetts, future senator Charles Sumner deplored the "insidious" plan to annex Texas and carve from it "great slaveholding states." The Senate soundly rejected the treaty, and it appeared that Tyler had succeeded only in inflaming sectional conflict.

The issue of Texas had not died down by the 1844 elections. In an effort to appeal to northern voters, Whig nominee for president Henry Clay came out against the immediate annexation of Texas. "Annexation and war with Mexico are identical," he declared. The Democrats chose Tennessean James K. Polk, who was as strong for the annexation of Texas as Clay was against it. To make Texas annexation palatable to Northerners, the Democrats shrewdly yoked Texas to Oregon, thus tapping the desire for expansion in the free states of the North as well as in the slave states of the South. The Democratic

Polk and Dallas Banner, 1844
In 1844, Democratic presidential nominee James K. Polk and vice presidential nominee George M. Dallas campaigned under this cotton banner. The extra star spilling over into the red and white stripes symbolizes Polk's vigorous support for annexing the huge slave republic of Texas, which had declared independence from Mexico eight years earlier. Henry Clay, Polk's Whig opponent, ran under a banner that was similar but conspicuously lacked the additional star.
Collection of Janice L. and David J. Frent.

platform called for the "reannexation of Texas" and the "reoccupation of Oregon." The suggestion that the United States was merely reasserting existing rights was poor history but good politics.

When Clay finally recognized the groundswell for expansion, he waffled, hinting that under certain circumstances he might accept the annexation of Texas. His retreat won little support in the South and succeeded only in alienating antislavery opinion in the North. James G. Birney, the candidate of the fledgling Liberty Party, picked up the votes of thousands of disillusioned Clay supporters. In the November election, Polk received 170 electoral votes and Clay 105. New York's 35 electoral votes proved critical to Clay's defeat. A shift of just one-third of Birney's 15,000 votes to Clay would have given Clay the state and the presidency.

On March 4, 1845, in his inaugural address, Polk confirmed his faith in America's manifest destiny. "This heaven-favored land," he declared, enjoyed the "most admirable and wisest system of well-regulated self-government...ever devised by human minds." And he asked, "Who shall assign limits to the achievements of free minds and free hands under the protection of this glorious Union?"

The nation did not have to wait for Polk's inauguration to see results from his victory. One month after the election, President Tyler announced that the triumph of the Democratic Party provided a mandate for the annexation of Texas "promptly and immediately." In February 1845, after a fierce debate between antislavery and proslavery forces, Congress approved a joint resolution offering the Republic of Texas admission to the United States. Texas entered as the fifteenth slave state.

Tyler delivered Texas, but Polk had promised Oregon, too. Westerners particularly demanded that the new president make good on the Democrats' pledge "Fifty-four Forty or Fight"— that is, all of Oregon, right up to Alaska (54°40′ was the southern latitude of Russian Alaska). But Polk was close to war with Mexico and could not afford a war with Britain over U.S. claims in Canada. After the initial bluster, therefore, Polk muted the all-of-Oregon refrain and renewed an old offer to divide Oregon along the forty-ninth parallel. When Britain accepted the compromise, some cried betrayal, but most Americans celebrated the agreement that gave the nation an enormous territory peacefully. Besides, when the Senate finally approved the treaty in June 1846, the United States and Mexico were already at war.

The Mexican-American War, 1846–1848

From the day he entered the White House, Polk craved Mexico's remaining northern provinces: California and New Mexico, land that today makes up California, Nevada, and Utah, most of New Mexico and Arizona, and parts of Wyoming and Colorado. Polk hoped to buy the territory, but when the Mexicans refused to sell, he concluded that military force would be needed to realize the United States's manifest destiny.

Polk had already ordered General Zachary Taylor to march his 4,000-man army from its position on the Nueces River, the southern boundary of Texas according to the Mexicans, 150 miles south, to the banks of the Rio Grande, the boundary claimed by Texans (Map 12.3). Viewing the American advance as aggression, the Mexican general in Matamoros ordered Taylor back to the Nueces. Taylor refused, and on April 25 Mexican cavalry attacked a party of American soldiers, killing or wounding sixteen and capturing the rest. Even before news of the battle arrived in Washington, Polk had already obtained his cabinet's approval of a war message.

On May 11, 1846, the president told Congress, "Mexico has passed the boundary of the United States, has invaded our territory, and shed American blood upon American soil." Thus "war exists, and, notwithstanding all our efforts to avoid it, exists by the act of Mexico herself." Congress passed a declaration of war and began raising an army. Despite years of saber rattling toward Mexico and Britain, the U.S. army was pitifully small, only 8,600 soldiers. Faced with the nation's first foreign war, against a Mexican army that numbered more than 30,000, Polk called for volunteers. Eventually, more than 112,000 white Americans (blacks were banned) rushed to the colors, eager to fight in Mexico.

Despite the flood of volunteers, the war divided the nation. Northern Whigs in particular condemned the war as the bullying of a weak neighbor. The Massachusetts legislature claimed that the war was being fought for the "triple object of extending slavery, of strengthening the slave power, and of obtaining control of the free states." On January 12, 1848, a gangly freshman Whig representative from Illinois rose from his back-row seat in the House of Representatives to deliver his first important speech in Congress. Before Abraham Lincoln sat down, he had questioned Polk's intelligence, honesty, and sanity. The president simply ignored the upstart representative, but antislavery, antiwar Whigs kept up the attack throughout the conflict. In their effort to undercut national support, they labeled it "Mr. Polk's War."

Since most Americans backed the war, it was not really Polk's war, but the president acted as if it were and directed the war personally. He planned a short war in which U.S. armies would occupy Mexico's northern provinces and defeat the Mexican army in a decisive battle or two, after which Mexico would sue for peace and the United States would keep the territory its armies occupied.

At first, Polk's strategy seemed to work. In May 1846, Zachary Taylor's troops drove south from the Rio Grande and routed the Mexican army, first at Palo Alto, then at Resaca de la Palma (see Map 12.3). "Old Rough and Ready,"

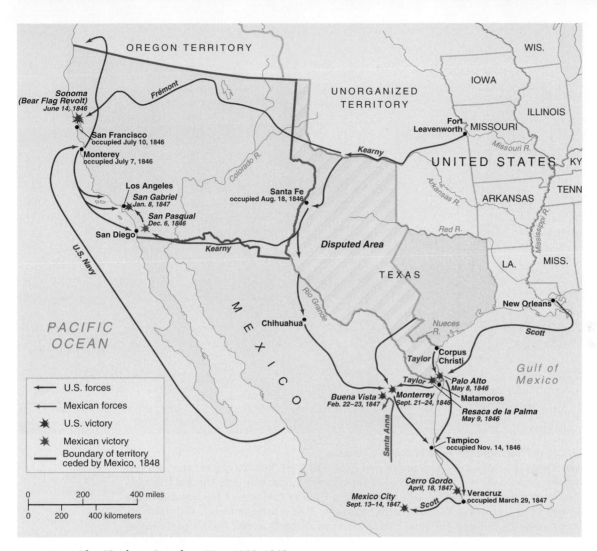

MAP 12.3   The Mexican-American War, 1846–1848
American and Mexican soldiers skirmished across much of northern Mexico, but the major battles took place between the Rio Grande and Mexico City.

as Taylor was affectionately known among his adoring troops, became an instant war hero. Polk rewarded Taylor for his victories by making him commander of the Mexican campaign.

A second prong of the campaign to occupy Mexico's northern provinces centered on Colonel Stephen Watts Kearny, who led a 1,700-man army from Missouri into New Mexico. Without firing a shot, U.S. forces took Santa Fe in August 1846. Polk then ordered Kearny to California. Pushing on with only 300 troops, Kearny three months later marched into San Diego and into a major Mexican rebellion against American rule. In January 1847, after several

clashes and severe losses, the U.S. forces occupied Los Angeles. California and New Mexico were in American hands.

By then, Taylor had driven deep into the interior of Mexico. In September 1846, after a five-day siege and house-to-house fighting, he took the fortified city of Monterrey. With reinforcements and fresh supplies, Taylor pushed his 5,000 troops southwest, where the Mexican hero of the Alamo, General Antonio López de Santa Anna, was concentrating an army of 21,000. On February 23, 1847, Santa Anna's troops attacked Taylor at Buena Vista. Superior American artillery and accurate musket fire won the day, but

Battala del Sacramento, Julio Michaud y Thomas

Most images of the Mexican-American War were created by artists from the United States, but Mexicans also recorded the war. In this hand-colored lithograph, Mexican artist Julio Michaud y Thomas offers his interpretation of the battle that took place in February 1847 when 1,100 American troops engaged 3,000 Mexicans on the banks of the Sacramento River in northern Mexico. Michaud accurately portrays the first moments of the bold Mexican cavalry charge at the American center, but he neglects to finish the story. American artillery forced the Mexican lancers to retreat, with "great confusion in their ranks." When the fighting ended, 700 Mexicans had been killed, wounded, or captured. American casualties amounted to one man killed and six wounded. The battle made a national hero of the American commander, Colonel Alexander Doniphan, who watched the battle with one leg hooked around his saddle horn, whittling a stick in full view of the enemy.

Yale Collection of Western Americana, Beinecke Rare Book and Manuscript Library.

the Americans suffered heavy casualties. The Mexicans suffered even greater losses (some 3,400 dead, wounded, and missing compared with 650 Americans). During the night Santa Anna withdrew his battered army from the battlefield, much to the "profound disgust of the troops," one Mexican officer remembered. "They are filled with grief that they were going to lose the benefit of all the sacrifices that they had made; that the conquered field would be abandoned, and that the victory would be given to the enemy." Retreat, he complained, fed the belief "that it was impossible to conquer the Americans."

The series of uninterrupted victories in northern Mexico certainly fed the American troops' sense of superiority. "No American force has ever thought of being defeated by any amount of Mexican troops," one soldier declared. The Americans worried about other hazards, however. "I can assure you that fighting is the least dangerous & arduous part of a soldier's life," one young man declared. Letters home told of torturous marches across arid wastes alive with tarantulas, scorpions, and rattlesnakes. Others recounted dysentery, malaria, smallpox, cholera, and yellow fever. Of the 13,000 American soldiers who died (some 50,000

Mexicans died), fewer than 2,000 fell to Mexican bullets and shells. Disease killed most of the others. Medicine was so primitive and conditions so harsh that as a Tennessee man observed, "nearly all who take sick die."

Victory in Mexico

Although Americans won battle after battle, President Polk's strategy misfired. Despite heavy losses on the battlefields, Mexico refused to trade land for peace. One American soldier captured the Mexican mood: "They cannot submit to be deprived of California after the loss of Texas, and nothing but the conquest of their Capital will force them to such a humiliation." Polk had arrived at the same conclusion. The president tapped another general to carry the war to Mexico City. While Taylor occupied the north, General Winfield Scott would land his army on the Gulf coast of Mexico and march 250 miles inland to the capital. Polk's plan entailed enormous risk because Scott would have to cut himself off from supplies and lead his men deep into enemy country against a much larger army.

After months of careful planning, an amphibious landing on March 9, 1847, near Veracruz put some 10,000 American troops ashore without the loss of a single life. After eighty-eight hours of furious shelling, Veracruz surrendered. In early April 1847, the U.S. army moved westward.

After the defeat at Buena Vista, Santa Anna had returned to Mexico City. He rallied his ragged troops and marched them east to set a trap for Scott in the mountain pass at Cerro Gordo. Knifing through Mexican lines, the Americans almost captured Santa Anna, who fled the field on foot. So complete was the victory that Scott gloated to Taylor, "Mexico no longer has an army." But Santa Anna, ever resilient, again rallied the Mexican army. Some 30,000 troops took up defensive positions on the outskirts of Mexico City and began melting down church bells to cast new cannon.

In August, Scott began his assault on the Mexican capital. The fighting proved the most brutal of the war. Santa Anna backed his army into the city, fighting each step of the way. At the battle of Churubusco, the Mexicans took 4,000 casualties in a single day and the Americans more than 1,000. At the castle of Chapultepec, American troops scaled the walls and fought the Mexican defenders hand to hand. After Chapultepec, Mexico City officials persuaded Santa Anna to evacuate the city to save it from destruction, and on September 14, 1847, General Winfield Scott rode in triumphantly. The ancient capital of the Aztecs had fallen once again to an invading army.

On February 2, 1848, American and Mexican officials signed the Treaty of Guadalupe Hidalgo in Mexico City. Mexico agreed to give up all claims to Texas north of the Rio Grande and to cede the provinces of New Mexico and California—more than 500,000 square miles—to the United States (see Map 12.3). The United States agreed to pay Mexico $15 million and to assume $3.25 million in claims that American citizens had against Mexico. In March 1848 the Senate ratified the treaty. The last American soldiers left Mexico a few months later.

Golden California

The American triumph had enormous consequences. Less than three-quarters of a century after its founding, the United States had achieved its self-proclaimed manifest destiny to stretch from the Atlantic to the Pacific (Map 12.4). It would enter the industrial age with vast new natural resources and a two-ocean economy, while Mexico faced a sharply diminished economic future. Moreover, with the northern half of Mexico in American hands, California gold would pour into American and not Mexican pockets.

On a cold January morning in 1848, just weeks before the formal transfer of territory, James Marshall discovered gold in the American River in the foothills of the Sierra Nevada. Marshall's discovery set off the California gold rush, one of the wildest mining stampedes in the world's history. Between 1849 and 1852, more than 250,000 "forty-niners," as the would-be miners were known, descended on the Golden State. In less than two years, Marshall's discovery transformed California from foreign territory to statehood.

News of gold quickly spread around the world. Soon a stream of races and nationalities bent on getting rich arrived in California, where the forty-niners remade the quiet world of Mexican ranches into a raucous, roaring mining and town economy. (See "Historical Question," page 300.) Forty-niners rarely had much money or mining experience, but as one witness observed, "No capital is required to obtain this gold, as the laboring man wants nothing but his pick, shovel, and tin pan, with which to dig and wash the gravel; and many frequently pick gold

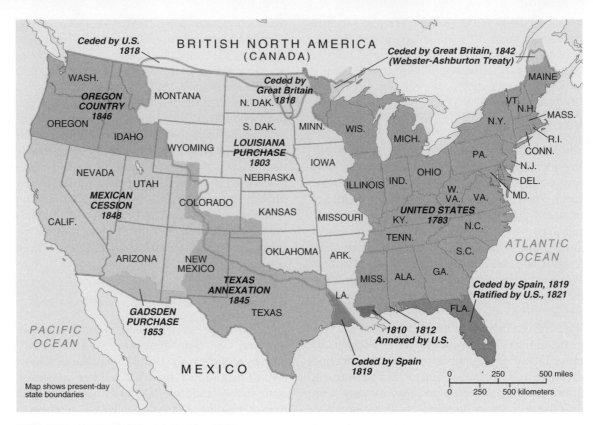

MAP 12.4   Territorial Expansion by 1860
Less than a century after its founding, the United States spread from the Atlantic seaboard
to the Pacific Ocean. War, purchase, and diplomacy had gained a continent.

out of the crevices of rock with their butcher knives in pieces from one to six ounces." Only a few struck it rich, and life in the gold fields was nasty, brutish, and often short. Men faced abysmal living conditions, sometimes living in holes and brush lean-tos. They also faced cholera and scurvy, exorbitant prices for food (eggs cost a dollar apiece), deadly encounters with claim jumpers, and endless backbreaking labor. Still, an individual with gold in his pocket could find temporary relief in the saloons, card games, dog fights, gambling dens, and brothels that flourished in the mining camps.

By 1853, San Francisco had grown into a raw, booming city of 50,000 that depended as much on gold as did the mining camps inland. It suffered from overcrowding, fire, crime, and violence, like all the towns that dotted the San Joaquin and Sacramento valleys, but enterprising individuals had learned that there was money to be made tending to the needs of the miners. Hotels, saloons, restaurants, laundries, and shops and stores of all kinds exchanged services and goods for miners' gold.

San Francisco was no tamer than the mining camps. In 1851, the "Committee of Vigilance" determined to bring order to the city. Members pledged that "no thief, burglar, incendiary or assassin shall escape punishment, either by the quibbles of the law, the insecurity of prisons, the carelessness or corruption of the police, or a laxity of those who pretended to administer justice." Lynchings proved that the Committee meant business. In time, merchants, **artisans**, and professionals made the city their home and brought their families from back east. Gradually, gunfights declined and theaters sprouted, but many years would pass before anyone pacified San Francisco.

Bigotry and efforts to establish civic order brought the Chinese special scrutiny. By 1851, 25,000 Chinese lived in California, and their religion, language, dress, queues (long pigtails), eating habits, and opium convinced many Anglos that they were not fit citizens of the

Golden State. As early as 1852, opponents demanded a halt to Chinese immigration. Chinese leaders in San Francisco fought back. Admitting deep cultural differences, they insisted that "in the important matters we are good men. We honor our parents; we take care of our children; we are industrious and peaceable; we trade much; we are trusted for small and large sums; we pay our debts; and are honest, and of course must tell the truth." Their protestations, however, offered little protection, and racial violence braided with forty-niner optimism and energy.

Westward expansion did not stop at the California shore. A vast network of trade soon connected California and the Pacific. American seafarers and merchants traded furs, hides and tallow, and lumber and engaged in whaling and the China trade. Still, as California's first congressional representative observed, this new West was separated "by thousands of miles of plains, deserts, and almost impossible mountains" from the rest of the Union. Dreamers imagined a railroad that would someday connect the Golden State with the booming agriculture and thriving industry of the East.

> **REVIEW** Why was the annexation of Texas such a controversial policy?

Economic and Industrial Evolution

During the 1840s and 1850s, Americans lived amid profound economic transformation that had been under way since the start of the nineteenth century. Since 1800, the total output of the U.S. economy had multiplied twelvefold. Four fundamental changes in American society fueled this phenomenal economic growth.

First, millions of Americans—Abraham Lincoln among them—moved from farms to urban areas, although farmers still made up 80 percent of the nation's population in 1860. Second, more Americans worked in factories, which contributed to economic growth because, in general, factory workers produced twice as much as agricultural workers. Third, the shift from water to steam as a source of energy raised productivity and sped transportation on rails and ships. Fourth, the underlying change propelling America's economic development was the rise in agricultural productivity, which nearly doubled during Lincoln's lifetime. While cities, factories, and steam engines multiplied throughout the nation—especially in the North and West—the roots of America's economic growth lay in agriculture.

Historians often refer to this transformation as an industrial revolution. However, the profound changes occurring in these years did not cause a revolutionary discontinuity in the economy or society. The United States remained overwhelmingly agricultural. Old methods of production continued alongside the new. The process that the American economy underwent before 1860 might best be termed "industrial evolution."

Agriculture and Land Policy

Forests impeded agriculture. The labor required for farmers to clear land for planting took time and energy that might instead have gone to growing crops, thereby limiting agricultural productivity. But as farmers pushed westward, they encountered the Midwest's comparatively treeless prairie, where they could spend less time with an ax and more time with a plow or hoe. Farmers like the Lincolns migrated to the Midwest by the tens of thousands between 1830 and 1860. The population of Indiana, Illinois, Michigan, Wisconsin, and Iowa exploded tenfold between 1830 and 1860, four times faster than the growth of the nation as a whole.

Labor-saving improvements in farm implements also hiked agricultural productivity. The cast-iron plow in use since the 1820s proved too weak for the thick turf and dense soil of the midwestern prairie. In 1837, John Deere patented a strong, smooth steel plow that sliced through prairie soil so cleanly that farmers called it the "singing plow." Deere's company became the leading plow manufacturer in the Midwest, turning out more than ten thousand plows a year by the late 1850s. Better plows permitted farmers to break more ground and plant more crops.

Improvements in wheat harvesting also multiplied farmers' productivity. In 1850, most farmers harvested wheat by hand, cutting two or three acres a day with backbreaking labor. Cyrus McCormick and others experimented with designs for mechanical reapers. By the 1850s, a McCormick

Who Rushed for California Gold?

When news of James Marshall's discovery reached the East in the fall of 1848, gold proved irresistible. Newspapers went crazy with stories about prospectors who extracted half a pan of gold from every pan of gravel they scooped from western streams. Soon, cities reverberated with men singing:

> Oh Susannah, don't you cry for me;
> I'm gone to California with my
> wash-bowl on my knee.

Scores of ships sailed from East Coast ports, headed either around South America to San Francisco or across the Gulf of Mexico to Panama, where the passengers made their way by foot and canoe to the Pacific coast and waited for a ship to carry them north. Even larger numbers of gold seekers took riverboats to the Missouri River and then set out in wagons, on horseback, or by foot for the West.

Young men everywhere contracted gold fever. As stories of California gold circled the globe, Chinese and Germans, Mexicans and Irish, Australians and French, Chileans and Italians, and people of dozens of other nationalities set out to strike it rich. Louisa Knapp Clappe, wife of a minister and one of the few women in gold country, remarked that when she walked through Indian Bar, the little mining town where she lived, she heard English, French, Spanish, German, Italian, Kanaka (Hawaiian), Asian Indian, and American Indian languages. Hangtown, Hell's Delight, Gouge Eye, and a hundred other crude mining camps became temporary home to a diverse throng of nationalities and peoples.

One of the largest groups of new arrivals was the Chinese. Between 1848 and 1854, Chinese men numbering 45,000 (but almost no Chinese women) arrived in California. Most considered themselves "sojourners," temporary residents who planned to return home as soon as their savings allowed. The majority came under a Chinese-controlled contract labor system in which each immigrant worked out the cost of his transportation. In the early years, most became wage laborers in mining. By the 1860s, they dominated railroad construction in the West. Ninety percent of the Central Pacific Railroad's 10,000 workers were Chinese. The Chinese also made up nearly half of San Francisco's labor force, working in the shoe, tobacco, woolen, laundry, and sewing trades. By 1870, the Chinese population had grown to 63,200, including 4,500 women. They constituted nearly 10 percent of the state's people and 25 percent of its wage-earning force.

The presence of peoples from around the world shattered the Anglo-American dream of a racially and ethnically homogeneous West, but ethnic diversity did nothing to increase the tolerance of Anglo-American prospectors. In their eyes, no "foreigner" had a right to dig for gold. In 1850, the California legislature passed the Foreign Miners' Tax Law, which levied high taxes on non-Americans to drive them from the gold fields, except as hired laborers working on claims owned by Americans. Stubborn foreign miners were sometimes hauled before "Judge Lynch." Among the earliest victims of lynching in the gold fields were a Frenchman and a Chilean.

Anglo-Americans considered the Chinese devious and unassimilable. They also feared that hardworking, self-denying Chinese labor would undercut white labor and drive it from the country. As a consequence, the Chinese were segregated residentially and occupationally and made ineligible for citizenship. Along with blacks and Indians, Chinese were denied public education and the right to testify in court. In addition to exclusion, they suffered from violence. Mobs drove them from Eureka, Truckee, and other mining towns.

American prospectors swamped the *Californios,* Spanish and Mexican settlers who had lived in California for generations. Soon after the American takeover, raging prejudice and discriminatory laws pushed Hispanic *rancheros*, professionals,

Gold Mountain
This hardworking young man is wearing the typical dress of Chinese laborers, a blue cotton shirt and baggy pants. We cannot tell if a queue is hanging down his back. He bears the heavy tools of his trade of placer (surface) mining but still manages a smile. Although he probably did not strike it rich in Gum Sam (Gold Mountain), he did find a new world and a new way of life.
Nevada Historical Society.

merchants, and artisans into the ranks of unskilled labor. Americans took their land even though the U.S. government had pledged to protect Mexican and Spanish land titles after the cession of 1848. Anglo forty-niners branded Spanish-speaking miners, even native-born Californios, "foreigners" and drove them from the diggings. Mariano Vallejo, a leading Californio, said of the forty-niners: "The good ones were few and the wicked many."

For Native Americans, the gold rush was a catastrophe. Numbering about 150,000 in 1848, the Indian population of California fell to 25,000 in 1856. Californios had exploited the Native peoples, but the forty-niners wanted to eradicate them. Starvation, disease, and a declining birthrate took a heavy toll. Indians also fell victim to wholesale murder. "That a war of extermination will continue to be waged between the two races until the Indian race becomes extinct must be expected," declared California governor Peter W. Burnett in 1851. The nineteenth-century historian Hubert Howe Bancroft described white behavior toward Indians during the gold rush as "one of the last human hunts of civilization, and the basest and most brutal of them all." To survive, Indians moved to the most remote areas of the state and tried to stay out of the way.

The forty-niners created dazzling wealth—in 1852, 81 million ounces of gold, nearly half of the world's production. Only a few prospectors—of whatever race and nationality—struck it rich, however.

The era of the prospector panning in streams quickly gave way to corporate-owned deep-shaft mining. The larger the scale of mining operations became, the smaller were the opportunities for individual miners. Most forty-niners eventually took up farming or opened small businesses or worked for wages for the corporations that pushed them out. But because of gold, an avalanche of people had roared into California. Anglo-Americans were most numerous, and Anglo dominance developed early. But the gold rush also brought a rainbow of nationalities. Anglo-American ascendancy *and* ethnic and racial diversity in the West both count among the most significant legacies of the gold rush. But because Anglo-Americans made the rules, not everyone shared equally.

Harvesting Grain with Cradles
This late-nineteenth-century painting shows the grain harvest during the mid-nineteenth century at Bishop Hill, Illinois, a Swedish community where the artist, Olof Krans, and his parents settled in 1850. The men swing cradles, slowly cutting a swath through the grain; the women gather the cut grain into sheaves to be hauled away later for threshing. Bishop Hill, a well-organized community, could call upon the labor of a large number of men and women at harvest time. Most farmers had only a few family members and a hired hand or two to help with the harvest. Notice that although the grain field appears level enough to be ideal for a mechanical reaper, all the work is done by hand; no machine is in sight.

Bishop Hill State Historic Site, Illinois Historic Preservation Agency.

reaper that cost between $100 and $150 allowed a farmer to harvest twelve acres a day. Although most farmers continued to cut their grain by hand, improved reapers and plows, mostly powered by horses or oxen, allowed farmers to cultivate more land, doubling the corn and wheat harvests between 1840 and 1860.

Federal land policy made possible the agricultural productivity that fueled the nation's economy. Up to 1860, the United States continued to be land-rich and labor-poor. During the nineteenth century, the nation became a great deal richer in land, acquiring more than a billion acres with the Louisiana Purchase (see chapter

10) and the annexation of Florida, Oregon, and vast territories following the Mexican-American War. The federal government made the land available for purchase to attract settlers and to generate revenues. Although a farmer could buy federal land for just $1.25 an acre, millions of Americans could not afford to pay $50 for a forty-acre farm. They squatted on unclaimed federal land and carved out a farm that they neither rented nor owned.

Government land policy also enriched wily speculators who found ways to claim large tracts of the most desirable plots and sell them to settlers at a generous markup. Nonetheless, by making land available to millions of ordinary people, the federal government achieved the goal of attracting settlers to the new territories in the West, which in due course joined the Union as new states. Above all, federal land policy created the basic precondition for the increase in agricultural productivity that underlay the nation's impressive economic growth.

Manufacturing and Mechanization

Changes in manufacturing arose from the nation's land-rich, labor-poor economy. England and other European countries had land-poor, labor-rich economies; there, meager opportunities in agriculture kept factory laborers plentiful and wages low. In the United States, western expansion and government land policies buoyed agriculture, keeping millions of people on the farm and thereby limiting the supply of workers for manufacturing and elevating wages. Because of this relative shortage of workers, manufacturers searched constantly for ways to save labor.

Mechanization allowed manufacturers to produce more with less labor. The practice of manufacturing and then assembling interchangeable parts spread from gun making to other industries and became known as the "American system." Mechanization became so integral to American manufacturing that some machinists specialized in what was called the machine tool industry, which made machines that made parts for other machines.

Manufacturing and agriculture meshed into a dynamic national economy. New England led the nation in manufacturing, shipping products such as clocks, guns, and axes west and south, while commodities such as wheat, pork, whiskey, tobacco, and cotton moved north and east. Manufacturers specialized in producing for the gigantic domestic market rather than for export. British goods dominated the international market and, on the whole, they were cheaper and better than American-made products. U.S. manufacturers supported tariffs to minimize British competition, but their best protection from British competitors was to strive harder to please their American customers.

Throughout American manufacturing, hand labor continued to be essential despite advances in mechanization. Even in heavily mechanized industries, factories remained fairly small; few had more than twenty or thirty employees. The industrial evolution under way before 1860 would quicken later in the nineteenth century; railroads were a harbinger of that future.

Railroads: Breaking the Bonds of Nature

Railroads incorporated the most advanced developments of the age. They seemed to break the bonds of nature. When canals and rivers froze in winter or became impassable during summer droughts, trains steamed ahead. When becalmed sailing ships went nowhere, locomotives kept on chugging, averaging over twenty miles an hour during the 1850s. Above all, railroads offered cities not blessed with canals or navigable rivers a way to compete for the trade of the countryside.

By 1850, trains steamed along nine thousand miles of track, almost two-thirds of it in New England and the Middle Atlantic states. By 1860, several railroads had crossed the Mississippi River to link frontier farmers to the nation's 30,000 miles of track, approximately as much as in all the rest of the world combined (Map 12.5). This massive expansion of railroads helped the United States catapult into position as the world's second leading industrial power, behind Great Britain.

In addition to speeding transportation, railroads propelled the growth of the iron and coal industries. Iron production grew five times faster than the population during the decades up to 1860, in part to meet the demand for rails, wheels, axles, locomotives, and heavy, gravity-defying iron bridges. Railroads also stimulated the fledgling telegraph industry. In 1844, Samuel F. B. Morse persuasively demonstrated the potential of his telegraph by transmitting a series of dots and dashes that instantly conveyed an electronic message along forty miles of wire strung between Washington and Baltimore. By 1861, more than fifty thousand miles of wire stretched across the continent to the Pacific, often alongside railroad tracks.

Almost all railroads were built and owned by private corporations rather than by governments. But privately owned railroads received massive government aid, especially federal **land grants**. Up to 1850, the federal government had

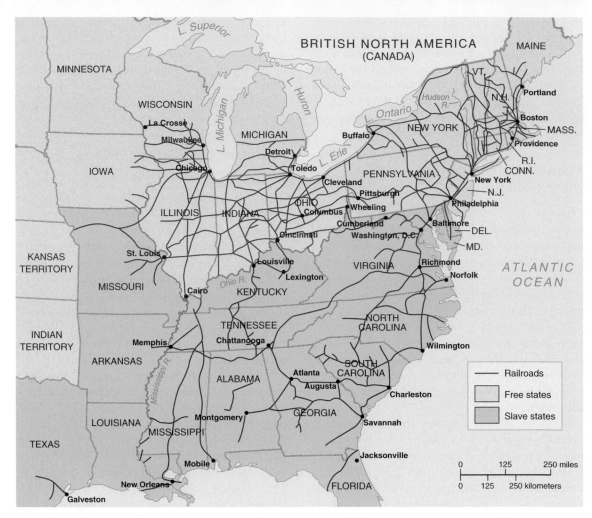

MAP 12.5   Railroads in 1860
Railroads were a crucial component of the revolutions in transportation and communications that transformed nineteenth-century America. The railroad system reflected the differences in the economies of the North and South.

READING THE MAP: In which sections of the country were most of the railroad tracks laid by the middle of the nineteenth century? What cities served as the busiest railroad hubs?
CONNECTIONS: How did the expansion of railroad networks affect the American economy? Why was the U.S. government willing to grant more than twenty million acres of public land to the private corporations that ran the railroads?

FOR MORE HELP ANALYZING THIS MAP, see the map activity for this chapter in the Online Study Guide at
bedfordstmartins.com/roarkcompact.

granted a total of seven million acres of federal land to various turnpike, highway, and canal projects. In 1850, Congress approved a precedent-setting grant to railroads of 6 square miles of federal land for each mile of track laid. By 1860, Congress had granted railroads more than twenty million acres of federal lands.

The railroad boom of the 1850s signaled the growing industrial might of the American econ-

omy. But railroads, like other industries, succeeded because they served farms as well as cities. And older forms of transportation remained significant. By 1857, for example, trains carried only about one-third of the mail; most of the rest still went by stagecoach or horseback. In 1860, most Americans were still far more familiar with four-legged horses than with iron horses.

The economy of the 1840s and 1850s linked an expanding, westward-moving population by muscles, animals, and farms as well as machines, steam, railroads, and cities. Abraham Lincoln split rails as a young man and defended railroad corporations as a successful attorney. His upward mobility illustrated the direction of economic change and the opportunities that change offered to enterprising individuals.

> **REVIEW** Why did the United States become a leading industrial power in the nineteenth century?

Free Labor: Promise and Reality

The nation's impressive economic performance did not reward all Americans equally. Native-born white men tended to do better than immigrants. With few exceptions, women were excluded from the opportunities open to men. Tens of thousands of women worked as seamstresses, laundresses, domestic servants, factory hands, and teachers but had little opportunity to aspire to higher-paying jobs. In the North and West, slavery was slowly eliminated in the half century after the American Revolution, but most free African Americans there found themselves relegated to dead-end jobs as laborers and servants. Discrimination against immigrants, women, and free blacks did not trouble most white men. With certain notable exceptions, they considered it proper and just.

The Free-Labor Ideal: Freedom plus Labor

During the 1840s and 1850s, leaders throughout the North and West emphasized a set of ideas that seemed to explain why the changes under way in their society benefited some more than others. They referred again and again to the advantages of what they termed **free labor**. (The word *free* referred to laborers who were not slaves; it did not mean laborers who worked for nothing.) By the 1850s, free-labor ideas described a social and economic ideal that accounted for both the successes and the shortcomings of the economy and society taking shape in the North and West.

Free-labor spokesmen celebrated hard work, self-reliance, and independence. They proclaimed that the door to success was open not just to those who inherited wealth or status but also to self-made men like Abraham Lincoln. The free-labor system, Lincoln argued, permitted farmers and artisans to enjoy the products of their own labor, and it also benefited wage workers. "The prudent, penniless beginner in the world," Lincoln asserted, "labors for wages awhile, saves a surplus with which to buy tools or land, for himself; then labors on his own account another while, and at length hires another new beginner to help him." Wage labor was the first rung on the ladder toward self-employment and, eventually, to hiring others.

The free-labor ideal affirmed an egalitarian vision of human potential. Lincoln and other spokesmen stressed the importance of universal education to permit "heads and hands [to] cooperate as friends." Throughout the North and West, communities supported public schools to make the rudiments of learning available to young children. By 1860, many cities and towns boasted that up to 80 percent of children ages seven to thirteen attended school at least for a few weeks each year. In rural areas, where the labor of children was more difficult to spare, schools typically enrolled no more than half the school-age children. Textbooks and teachers—most of whom were young women—drummed into students the lessons of the free-labor system: self-reliance, discipline, and, above all, hard work. "Remember that all the ignorance, degradation, and misery in the world is the result of indolence and vice," one textbook intoned. In school and out, free-labor ideology emphasized labor as much as freedom.

Economic Inequality

The free-labor ideal made sense to many Americans, especially in the North and West, because it seemed to describe their own experiences. Lincoln frequently referred to his humble beginnings as a hired laborer and implicitly invited his listeners to consider how far he had come. In 1860, his wealth of $17,000 easily placed him in the top 5 percent of the population. The opportunities presented by the expanding economy made a few men much, much richer. In 1860, the nation had about forty millionaires.

Most Americans, however, measured success in far more modest terms. The average wealth of adult white men in the North in 1860 barely topped $2,000. Nearly half of American men had no wealth at all; about 60 percent owned no land. Because property possessed by married women was normally considered to belong to their husbands, women had less wealth than men. Free African Americans had still less; 90 percent of them were propertyless.

Free-labor spokesmen considered these economic inequalities a natural outgrowth of freedom, the inevitable result of some individuals being more able, more willing to work, and luckier. These inequalities suggest, however, the gap between the promise and the performance of the free-labor ideal. Economic growth permitted many men to move from being landless squatters to landowning farmers and from being hired laborers to independent, self-employed producers. But many more Americans remained behind, landless and working for wages. Even those who realized their aspirations had a precarious hold on their independence. Bad debts, crop failure, sickness, or death could quickly eliminate a family's gains.

Seeking out new opportunities in pursuit of free-labor ideals created restless social and geographic mobility. Up to two-thirds of the residents of a rural area moved every decade, and the population turnover in cities was even greater. Such constant comings and goings weakened community ties to neighbors and friends and threw individuals even more on their own resources for help in times of trouble.

Immigrants and the Free-Labor Ladder

The risks and uncertainties of free labor did not deter millions of immigrants from entering the United States during the 1840s and 1850s. Almost 4.5 million immigrants arrived between 1840 and 1860, six times more than had come during the previous two decades (Figure 12.1). The half-million immigrants who came in 1854 accounted for nearly 2 percent of the entire U.S. population, a higher proportion than in any other single year of the nation's history. By 1860, foreign-born residents made up about one-eighth of the U.S. population, a fraction that held steady well into the twentieth century.

Nearly three out of four of the immigrants who arrived between 1840 and 1860 came from

FIGURE 12.1 Antebellum Immigration, 1820–1860
After increasing gradually for several decades, immigration shot up in the mid-1840s. Between 1848 and 1860, nearly 3.5 million immigrants entered the United States.

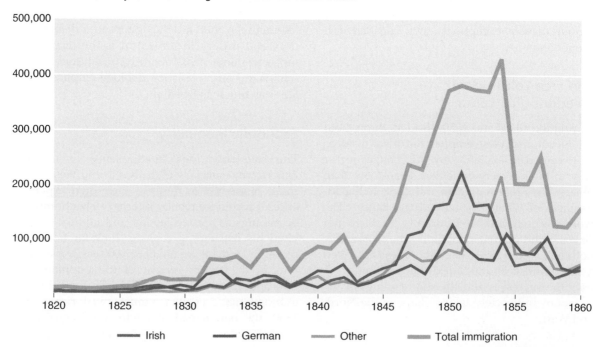

Germany or Ireland. The vast majority of the 1.4 million Germans who entered the United States during these years were skilled tradesmen and their families. They left Germany to escape deteriorating economic conditions, and they had little difficulty finding work in the expanding American economy. German butchers, bakers, beer makers, carpenters, shopkeepers, machinists, and others tended to congregate in cities, particularly in the Midwest. Roughly a quarter of German immigrants were farmers, most of whom scattered throughout the Midwest, although some settled in Texas. On the whole, German Americans settled into that middle stratum of sturdy independent producers celebrated by free-labor spokesmen; relatively few Germans occupied the bottom rung of the free-labor ladder as wage laborers or domestic servants.

Irish immigrants, in contrast, entered at the bottom of the free-labor ladder and had difficulty climbing up. Nearly 1.7 million Irish immigrants arrived between 1840 and 1860, nearly all of them desperately poor and often weakened by hunger and disease. Potato blight struck Ireland in 1845 and returned repeatedly in subsequent years, spreading a catastrophic famine throughout the island. Many of the lucky ones, half-starved, crowded into the holds of ships and set out for America, where they congregated in northeastern cities. As one immigrant group declared, "All we want is to get out of Ireland; we must be better anywhere than here."

Roughly three out of four Irish immigrants worked as laborers or domestic servants. Irish men dug canals, loaded ships, laid railroad track, and took what other work they could find. Irish women hired out to cook, wash and iron, mind children, and clean house. Almost all Irish immigrants were Catholic, a fact that set them apart from the overwhelmingly **Protestant** native-born residents. Many natives regarded the Irish as hard-drinking, obstreperous, half-civilized folk. Such views lay behind the discrimination reflected in job announcements that commonly stated, "No Irish need apply." Despite such prejudices, native residents hired Irish immigrants because they accepted low pay and worked hard.

In America's labor-poor economy, Irish laborers could earn far more than in Ireland. In America, one immigrant explained in 1853, there was "plenty of work and plenty of wages plenty to eat and no land lords thats enough what more does a man want." But some immigrants wanted more, especially respect and decent working conditions. One immigrant complained that he was "a slave for the Americans as the generality of the Irish…are."

Such testimony illustrates that the free-labor system, whether for immigrants or native-born laborers, often did not live up to the optimistic vision outlined by Abraham Lincoln and others. Many wage laborers could not realistically aspire to become independent, self-sufficient property holders, despite the claims of free-labor proponents.

> **REVIEW**   How did the free-labor ideal account for economic inequality?

Reforming Self and Society

The emphasis on self-discipline and individual effort at the core of the free-labor ideal pervaded America in the 1840s and 1850s. Many Americans believed that insufficient self-control caused the major social problems of the era. **Evangelical** Protestants struggled to control individuals' propensity to sin, and **temperance** advocates exhorted drinkers to control their urge for alcohol. In the midst of the worldly disruptions of geographic expansion and economic change, evangelicals brought more Americans than ever before into churches. Historians estimate that church members accounted for about one-third of the American population by midcentury. Most Americans remained outside churches, as did Abraham Lincoln. But the influence of evangelical religion reached far beyond those who belonged to churches. The evangelical temperament—a conviction of righteousness coupled with energy, self-discipline, and faith that the world could be improved—animated most reformers.

A few activists pointed out that certain fundamental injustices lay beyond the reach of individual self-control. Transcendentalists and utopians believed that perfection could be attained only by rejecting the competitive values of the larger society. Women's rights activists and abolitionists sought to reverse the subordination of women and to eliminate the enslavement of blacks by changing laws and social institutions as well as attitudes and customs. They confronted the daunting challenge of repudiating widespread assumptions about male supremacy and white supremacy and somehow subverting the entrenched institutions that reinforced those assumptions: the family and slavery.

The Pursuit of Perfection: Transcendentalists and Utopians

A group of New England writers that came to be known as transcendentalists believed that individuals should conform neither to the dictates of the materialistic world nor to the dogma of formal religion. Instead, people should look within themselves for truth and guidance. The leading transcendentalist, Ralph Waldo Emerson—an essayist, poet, and lecturer—proclaimed that the power of the solitary individual was nearly limitless. Henry David Thoreau, Margaret Fuller, and other transcendentalists agreed with Emerson that "if the single man plant himself indomitably on his instincts, and there abide, the huge world will come round to him." In many ways, transcendentalism represented less an alternative to the values of mainstream society than an exaggerated form of the rampant individualism of the age.

Unlike transcendentalists who sought to turn inward, a few reformers tried to change the world by organizing utopian communities as alternatives to prevailing social arrangements. Although these communities never attracted more than a few thousand people, the activities of their members demonstrated both dissatisfaction with the larger society and their efforts to realize their visions of perfection. Some communities functioned as retreats for those who did not want to sever ties with the larger society. Brook Farm, organized in 1841 in West Roxbury, Massachusetts, briefly provided a haven for a few literary and artistic New Englanders trying to balance bookish pursuits with manual labor.

Other communities set out to become models of perfection that they hoped would point the way toward a better life for everyone. During the 1840s, more than two dozen communities organized around the ideas of Charles Fourier, a French critic of contemporary society. Members of Fourierist phalanxes, as these communities were called, believed that individualism and competition were evils that denied the basic truth that "men…are brothers and not competitors." Fourierist phalanxes aspired to replace competition with harmonious cooperation based on communal ownership of property. But Fourierist communities failed to realize their lofty goals. Few survived more than two or three years.

The Oneida community went beyond the Fourierist notion of communalism. John Humphrey Noyes, the charismatic leader of Oneida, believed that American society's commitment to private property made people greedy and selfish. Noyes claimed that the root of private property lay in marriage, in men's conviction that their wives were their exclusive property. Drawing from a substantial inheritance, Noyes organized the Oneida community in New York in 1848 to abolish marital property rights through the practice of what he called "complex marriage." Sexual intercourse was not restricted to married couples but was permitted between any man and consenting woman in the community. Noyes also required all members to relinquish their economic property to the community, which developed a lucrative business manufacturing animal traps. Oneida's sexual and economic communalism attracted several hundred members, but most of their neighbors considered Oneidans adulterers, blasphemers, and worse. Yet the practices that set Oneida apart from its mainstream neighbors strengthened the community, and it survived long after the Civil War.

Women's Rights Activists

Women participated in the many reform activities that grew out of evangelical churches. Women church members outnumbered men two to one and worked to put their religious ideas into practice by joining peace, temperance, antislavery, and other societies. Involvement in reform organizations gave a few women activists practical experience in such political arts as speaking in public, running a meeting, drafting resolutions, and circulating petitions. Along with such experience came confidence. The abolitionist Lydia Maria Child pointed out in 1841 that "those who urged women to become missionaries and form tract societies…have changed the household utensil to a living energetic being and they have no spell to turn it into a broom again."

In 1848, about one hundred reformers led by Elizabeth Cady Stanton and Lucretia Mott gathered at Seneca Falls, New York, for the first national women's rights convention in the United States. The Seneca Falls Declaration of Sentiments proclaimed that "the history of mankind is a history of repeated injuries and usurpations on the part of man toward woman, having in direct object the establishment of an absolute tyranny over her." In the style of the Declaration of Independence (see appendix I, page A-1), the Seneca Falls Declaration demanded that women "have immediate admission to all the rights and privileges which belong to them as citizens of the United States," particularly the "inalienable right to the elective franchise."

Nearly two dozen other women's rights conventions assembled before 1860, repeatedly calling for **suffrage**. But they had difficulty receiving a respectful hearing, much less obtaining legislative action. No state came close to permitting women to vote. Politicians and editorialists sneered that a woman's place was in the home, rearing her children and civilizing her man. Nonetheless, the Seneca Falls Declaration served as a pathbreaking manifesto of dissent against male supremacy and of support for woman suffrage, which would become the focus of the women's rights movement during the next seventy years.

Abolitionists and the American Ideal

During the 1840s and 1850s, abolitionists continued to struggle to draw the nation's attention to the plight of slaves and the need for **emancipation**. Former slaves such as Frederick Douglass, Henry Bibb, and Sojourner Truth lectured to reform audiences throughout the North about the cruelties of slavery. Abolitionists published newspapers, held conventions, and petitioned Congress. But they never attracted a mass following among white Americans. Many white Northerners became convinced that slavery was wrong, but they still believed that blacks were inferior. Many other white Northerners shared the common view of white Southerners that slavery was necessary and even desirable. The geographic expansion of the nation during the 1840s offered abolitionists

Mary Cragin, Oneida Woman
A founding member of the Oneida community, Mary Cragin had a passionate sexual relationship with John Humphrey Noyes even before the community was organized. Within the bounds of complex marriage as practiced by the Oneidans, Cragin's magnetic sexuality made her a favorite partner of many men. In her journal, she confessed that "every evil passion was very strong in me from my childhood, sexual desire, love of dress and admiration, deceit, anger, pride." Oneida, however, transformed evil passion to holy piety. Cragin wrote, "In view of [God's] goodness to me and of his desire that I should let him fill me with himself, I yield and offer myself, to be penetrated by his spirit, and desire that love and gratitude may inspire my heart so that I shall sympathize with his pleasure in the thing, before my personal pleasure begins, knowing that it will increase my capability for happiness." Oneida's sexual practices were considered outrageous and sinful by almost all other Americans. Even Oneidans did not agree with all of Noyes's ideas about sex. "There is no reason why [sex] should not be done in public as much as music and dancing," he declared. It would display the art of sex, he explained, and watching "would give pleasure to a great many of the older people who now have nothing to do with the matter." Nonetheless, public sex never caught on among Oneidans.
Oneida Community Mansion House.

an opportunity to link their unpopular ideal to a goal that many white Northerners found much more attractive—limiting the geographic expansion of slavery, an issue that moved to the center of national politics during the 1850s (see chapter 14).

Abolitionist Meeting

This rare daguerreotype was made by Ezra Greenleaf Weld in August 1850 at an abolitionist meeting in Cazenovia, New York. Frederick Douglass, who had escaped from slavery in Maryland twelve years earlier, is seated on the platform next to the woman at the table. One of the nation's most brilliant and eloquent abolitionists, Douglass also supported equal rights for women. The man immediately behind Douglass gesturing with his outstretched arm is Gerrit Smith, a wealthy New Yorker and militant abolitionist whose funds supported many reform activities. Notice the two black women in similar clothing on either side of Smith and the white woman next to Douglass. Most white Americans considered such voluntary racial proximity scandalous and promiscuous. What messages did abolitionists attempt to convey by attending such protest meetings?

Collection of the J. Paul Getty Museum, Malibu, CA.

Black leaders rose to prominence in the abolitionist movement during the 1840s and 1850s. African Americans had actively opposed slavery for decades, but a new generation of leaders came to the forefront in these years. Frederick Douglass, Henry Highland Garnet, William Wells Brown, Martin R. Delany, and others became impatient with white abolitionists' appeals to the conscience of the white majority. Garnet proclaimed in 1843 that slaves should rise in insurrection against their masters, an idea that alienated almost all white people. To express their own uncompromising ideas, black abolitionists founded their own newspapers and held their own antislavery conventions, although they still cooperated with sympathetic whites.

The commitment of black abolitionists to battling slavery grew out of their own experiences with white supremacy. The 250,000 free African Americans in the North and West constituted less than 2 percent of the total population. They confronted the humiliations of racial discrimination in nearly every arena of daily life. Only Maine, Massachusetts, New Hampshire, and Vermont permitted black men to vote; New York imposed a special property-holding requirement on black—but not white—voters, effectively excluding most black men from the **franchise**. The pervasive racial discrimination both handicapped and energized black abolitionists. Some cooperated with the American Colonization Society's efforts to send freed slaves and other black Americans to Liberia in west Africa. Other black American leaders organized campaigns against segregation, particularly in transportation and education. Their most notable success came in 1855 when Massachusetts integrated public schools. Elsewhere white supremacy continued unabated.

Outside the public spotlight, free African Americans in the North and West contributed to the antislavery cause by quietly aiding fugitive slaves. Harriet Tubman escaped from slavery in Maryland in 1849 and repeatedly risked her freedom and her life to return to the South to escort slaves to freedom. When the opportunity arose, free blacks in the North provided fugitive slaves with food, a safe place to rest, and a helping hand. This "underground railroad" ran mainly through black neighborhoods, black churches, and black homes, an outgrowth of the antislavery sentiment and opposition to white supremacy that unified nearly all African Americans in the North.

> **REVIEW** Why were women especially prominent in many nineteenth-century reform efforts?

Conclusion: Free Labor, Free Men

In the 1840s, diplomacy and war handed the United States 1.2 million square miles and more than 1,000 miles of Pacific coastline. California almost immediately rewarded its new owners with mountains of gold. To most Americans, new territory and vast riches were appropriate accompaniments to the nation's stunning economic transformation. In the first half of the nineteenth century, a cluster of interrelated developments—steam power, railroads, and the growing mechanization of agriculture and manufacturing—meant greater productivity, a burst of output from farms and factories, and prosperity for many.

To Northerners, industrial evolution confirmed the choice they had made to eliminate slavery and to promote free labor as the key to independence, equality, and prosperity. Like Abraham Lincoln, millions could point to personal experience as evidence of the practical truth of the free-labor ideal. But millions of others had different stories to tell. They knew that in the free-labor system poverty and wealth continued to rub shoulders. By 1860, instead of social independence, more than half of the nation's free-labor workforce toiled for someone else. Free-labor enthusiasts denied that the problems were inherent in the system. They argued that most social ills—including poverty and dependency—sprang from individual deficiencies. Consequently, reformers focused on

the lack of self-control and discipline, on sin and alcohol. They denied that free labor meant exploitation. Slaves, not free workers, suffered, they argued.

By midcentury, the nation was half slave and half free, and each region was animated by economic interests, cultural values, and political aims that were contrary to those of the other. Not even the victory over Mexico could bridge the deepening differences between North and South.

Suggestions for Further Reading

David Dary, *The Oregon Trail: An American Saga* (2004). A narrative based on the diaries and journals of the travelers who used the Oregon Trail.

Steven Mintz, *Moralists and Modernizers: America's Pre–Civil War Reformers* (1995). An informative survey of the many Americans eager to reform their world.

Malcolm Rohrbough, *Days of Gold: The California Gold Rush and the American Nation* (1997). A rollicking history of the forty-niners and the broad consequences of western gold.

Scott A. Sandage, *Born Losers: A History of Failure in America* (2005). The fascinating story of those who lost in America's free-labor economy.

Richard Bruce Winders, *Mr. Polk's Army: The American Military Experience in the Mexican War* (1997). An account of the war from the U.S. soldier's perspective.

Kenneth J. Winkle, *The Young Eagle: The Rise of Abraham Lincoln* (2001). The surprising story of Lincoln's rise from log cabin to lawyer and politician.

> ► **FOR MORE BOOKS ABOUT TOPICS IN THIS CHAPTER,** see the Online Bibliography at bedfordstmartins.com/roarkcompact.
>
> ► **FOR ADDITIONAL FIRSTHAND ACCOUNTS OF THIS PERIOD,** see Chapter 12 in Michael Johnson, ed., *Reading the American Past,* Third Edition.
>
> ► **FOR WEB SITES AND DOCUMENTS RELATED TO TOPICS AND PLACES IN THIS CHAPTER,** see "HistoryLinks," "DocLinks," and "PlaceLinks" at bedfordstmartins.com/roarkcompact.

REVIEWING THE CHAPTER

Follow these steps to review and strengthen your understanding of the chapter.
STEP 1: *Study the* **Key Terms** *and* **Timeline** *to identify the significance of each item listed.*
STEP 2: *Answer the* **Review Questions**, *drawing on key terms and dates to support your answers.*
STEP 3: *Drawing on the Key Terms, Timeline, and Review Questions, answer the broader* **Making Connections** *questions.*

KEY TERMS

Who

Abraham Lincoln (p. 285)
John L. O'Sullivan (p. 287)
Joseph Smith Jr. (p. 289)
Brigham Young (p. 290)
Stephen F. Austin (p. 291)
Antonio López de Santa Anna (p. 292)
Sam Houston (p. 292)
John C. Frémont (p. 292)
James K. Polk (p. 293)
John Tyler (p. 293)
John C. Calhoun (p. 293)
Henry Clay (p. 293)
Zachary Taylor (p. 294)
Stephen Watts Kearny (p. 295)
Winfield Scott (p. 297)
John Deere (p. 299)
Cyrus McCormick (p. 299)
Samuel F. B. Morse (p. 303)
Ralph Waldo Emerson (p. 308)
Elizabeth Cady Stanton (p. 309)

Lucretia Mott (p. 309)
Frederick Douglass (p. 309)
Henry Highland Garnet (p. 310)
Harriet Tubman (p. 310)

What

manifest destiny (p. 287)
Oregon Trail (p. 287)
policy of concentration (p. 288)
Fort Laramie conference (p. 288)
The Book of Mormon (p. 289)
Church of Jesus Christ of Latter-Day Saints (p. 289)
Utah Territory (p. 291)
Mormon War (p. 291)
Santa Fe Trail (p. 291)
Republic of Texas (p. 292)
the Alamo (p. 292)
Goliad (p. 292)
San Jacinto (p. 292)
ranchos (p. 292)

California Trail (p. 292)
Bear Flag Revolt (p. 292)
Mexican-American War (p. 294)
Treaty of Guadalupe Hidalgo (p. 297)
California gold rush (p. 297)
industrial evolution (p. 299)
singing plow (p. 299)
mechanical reaper (p. 299)
American system (p. 303)
free-labor ideal (p. 305)
transcendentalism (p. 308)
utopian communities (p. 308)
Brook Farm (p. 308)
Fourierist phalanxes (p. 308)
Oneida community (p. 308)
Seneca Falls Declaration of Sentiments (p. 309)
American Colonization Society (p. 310)
underground railroad (p. 311)

TIMELINE

1836 • Texas declares independence from Mexico.

    1837 • John Deere patents his steel plow.

        1840s • Practical mechanical reapers are created.

           1841 • First wagon trains head west on Oregon Trail.
                 • Vice President John Tyler becomes president when William Henry Harrison dies.

                1844 • Democrat James K. Polk elected president.
                    • Samuel F. B. Morse invents telegraph.

                    1845 • Term *manifest destiny* coined.
                      • United States annexes Texas, which enters Union as slave state.

                        1846 • Bear Flag Revolt in California.
                          • Congress declares war on Mexico.
                          • United States and Great Britain agree to divide Oregon Country.

REVIEW QUESTIONS

1. Why did westward migration expand dramatically in the mid-nineteenth century? (pp. 286–92)

2. Why was the annexation of Texas such a controversial policy? (pp. 292–99)

3. Why did the United States become a leading industrial power in the nineteenth century? (pp. 299–305)

4. How did the free-labor ideal account for economic inequality? (pp. 305–07)

5. Why were women especially prominent in many nineteenth-century reform efforts? (pp. 307–11)

MAKING CONNECTIONS

1. How did the ideology of manifest destiny contribute to the mid-nineteenth-century drive for expansion? Discuss its implications for individual migrants and the nation. In your answer, consider how manifest destiny built on, or revised, earlier understandings of the nation's history and racial politics.

2. The Mexican-American War reshaped U.S. borders and more. Discuss the consequences of the war for national political and economic developments in subsequent decades. What resources did the new territory give the United States? How did debate over annexation revive older political disputes?

3. Varied political, economic, and technological factors promoted migration west in the mid-nineteenth century. Considering these factors, discuss migration to two different regions (e.g., Texas, Oregon, Utah, or California). What drew migrants to the region? How did the U.S. government contribute to their efforts?

4. Some nineteenth-century reform movements drew on the free-labor ideal, while others challenged it. Discuss the free-labor ideal in relation to two reform movements (abolitionism, utopian communalism, etc.). How did they draw on the ideal to pursue specific reforms? How did these minority movements try to influence national developments?

▶ FOR PRACTICE QUIZZES, A CUSTOMIZED STUDY PLAN, AND OTHER STUDY TOOLS, see the Online Study Guide at bedfordstmartins.com/roarkcompact.

1847 • Mormons settle in Utah.

    1848 • Treaty of Guadalupe Hidalgo.
        • Oneida community organized in New York.
        • First U.S. women's rights convention takes place at Seneca Falls, New York.

        1849 • California gold rush begins.

            1850 • Mormon community annexed to United States as Utah Territory.

                1851 • Conference in Laramie, Wyoming, marks the beginning of government policy of forcing Indians onto reservations.
                     • Massachusetts integrates public schools.

CLAY JUG

This ceramic water cooler, made in about 1840, is attributed to Thomas Chandler, a famous potter of Edgefield District, South Carolina. The relatively fine clothes of the African American man and woman portrayed on the vessel suggest that they are house servants. On the wall of the home of Alexander Stephens in Crawfordsville, Georgia, an intriguing letter from Stephens states that two of his favorite slaves are getting married and orders the plantation manager to butcher a hog for their wedding. This cooler, with its portrait of a couple, a hog, and a jug, may have been commissioned by Stephens to commemorate the union. Potters made vessels to be used—to hold water and food. Analysis of the form, decoration, and glazes of southern pottery suggests a blend of European, African, and Native American ceramic traditions. Some pottery went beyond the utilitarian and became art. The most renowned slave potter was an Edgefield man named Dave, who skillfully fashioned huge vessels, inscribed poems on their surfaces, and proudly and boldly signed them "Dave the potter."

CHAPTER

13

The Slave South
1820–1860

NAT TURNER WAS BORN A SLAVE in Southampton County, Virginia, in October 1800. People in his neighborhood claimed that he had always been different. His parents noticed special marks on his body, which they said were signs that he was "intended for some great purpose." His master said that he learned to read without being taught. As an adolescent, he adopted an austere lifestyle of Christian devotion and fasting. In his twenties, he received visits from the "Spirit," the same spirit, he believed, that had spoken to the ancient prophets. In time, Nat Turner began to interpret these things to mean that God had appointed him an instrument of divine vengeance for the sin of slaveholding.

In the early morning of August 22, 1831, he set out with six trusted friends—Hark, Henry, Sam, Nelson, Will, and Jack—to punish slave owners and free their suffering slaves. Turner struck the first blow, an ax to the head of his master, Joseph Travis. The rebels killed all of the white men, women, and children they encountered in each household they attacked. By noon, they had visited eleven farms and slaughtered fifty-seven whites and, along the way, added fifty or sixty men to their army. Word spread quickly, however, and soon the militia and hundreds of local whites gathered. By the next day, whites had captured or killed all of the rebels, except Nat Turner, who successfully hid out for about ten weeks before being captured in nearby woods. Within a week, he was tried, convicted, and executed. By then, forty-five slaves had stood trial, twenty had been convicted and hanged, and another ten had been transported from Virginia. Frenzied whites had killed another hundred or more blacks—insurgents and innocent bystanders—in their counterattack against the rebellion.

Virginia's governor John Floyd asked how Turner's band of "assassins and murderers" could have assaulted the "unsuspecting and defenseless" citizens of "one of the fairest counties in the Commonwealth." White Virginians prided themselves on having the "mildest" slavery in the South, but sixty black rebels on a rampage challenged the comforting theory of the contented slave. Nonetheless, whites found explanations that allowed them to feel safer. They placed the blame on outside agitators. In 1829, David Walker, a freeborn black man living in Boston, had published his *Appeal...to the Coloured Citizens of the World*, an invitation to slaves to rise up in bloody rebellion, and copies had fallen into the hands of Virginia slaves. Moreover, on January 1, 1831, in Boston, William Lloyd Garrison, the Massachusetts abolitionist, had published the first issue of the *Liberator*, his fiery newspaper. White Virginians also dismissed the rebellion's leader, Nat Turner, as insane. "He is a complete fanatic, or plays his part admirably," wrote Thomas R. Gray, the lawyer who was assigned to defend Turner.

Nat Turner

There are no known contemporary images of Nat Turner. This imagined portrait comes from William Still's *The Underground Railroad* (1872). Meeting secretly at night deep in a forest and thus well out of earshot of whites, an intense Turner passionately tries to convince four other slaves to join him in rebellion. What do their faces reveal? What considerations do you suppose entered their calculations about whether to join Turner? Significantly perhaps, they are holding work tools, not arms.

Library of Congress.

In the months following the insurrection, white Virginians debated the future of slavery in their state. While some expressed substantial doubts, the Virginia legislature reaffirmed the state's determination to preserve black bondage. Delegates passed a raft of laws strengthening the institution of slavery and further restricting free blacks. A thirty-year-old professor at the College of William and Mary, Thomas R. Dew, published a vigorous defense of slavery that became the bible of Southerners' proslavery arguments. More than ever, the nation was divided along the "Mason-Dixon line," the surveyors' mark that in colonial times had established the boundary between Maryland and Pennsylvania but half a century later divided the free North and slave South.

Black slavery increasingly molded the South into a distinctive region. In the decades after 1820, Southerners, like Northerners, raced westward, but unlike Northerners who spread small farms and free labor, Southerners spread slavery, cotton, and plantations. Geographic expansion meant that slavery became more vigor-

ous and profitable than ever, embraced more people, and increased the South's political power. **Antebellum** Southerners included diverse peoples who at times found themselves at odds with one another—not only slaves and free people but also women and men; Indians, Africans, and Europeans; and aristocrats and common folk. Nevertheless, beneath this diversity of people, there was also forming a distinctively southern society and culture. The South became a slave society, and most white Southerners were proud of it.

The Growing Distinctiveness of the South

From the earliest settlements, inhabitants of southern colonies had shared a great deal with northern colonists. Most whites in both sections were British and **Protestant**, spoke a common language, and shared an exuberant pride in their victorious revolution against British rule. The creation of the new nation under the Constitution in 1789 forged strong political ties that bound all Americans. The beginnings of a national economy fostered economic interdependence and communication across regional boundaries. White Americans everywhere celebrated the achievements of the prosperous young nation, and they looked forward to its seemingly boundless future.

Despite these national similarities, Southerners and Northerners grew increasingly different. The French political observer Alexis de Tocqueville believed he knew why. "I could easily prove," he asserted in 1831, "that almost all the differences which may be noticed between the character of the Americans in the Southern and Northern states have originated in slavery." Slavery made the South different, and it was the differences between the North and South, not the similarities, that came to shape antebellum American history.

Cotton Kingdom, Slave Empire

In the first half of the nineteenth century, legions of Americans migrated west. In the South, the stampede began after the Creek War of 1813–1814, which divested the Creek Nation of

24 million acres and initiated the government campaign to remove Indian people living east of the Mississippi River to the West (see chapters 10 and 11). Eager slaveholders seeking virgin acreage for new plantations, struggling farmers looking for patches of land for small farms, herders and drovers pushing their hogs and cattle toward fresh pastures—anyone who was restless and ambitious felt the pull of Indian land. Southerners pushed westward relentlessly, until by midcentury the South encompassed nearly a million square miles, much of it planted in cotton.

The South's climate and geography were ideally suited for the cultivation of cotton. Advancing Southerners encountered a variety of terrain, soil, and weather, but cotton's requirements are minimal: two hundred frost-free days from planting to picking and plentiful rain, conditions found in much of the South. By the 1830s, cotton fields stretched from southern Virginia to central Texas. Heavy southern and westward migration led to statehood for Arkansas in 1836 and for Texas and Florida in 1845. Production soared from 300,000 bales in 1830 to nearly 5 million in 1860, when the South produced three-fourths of the world's supply. The South—especially that tier of states from South Carolina west to Texas known as the Lower South—had become the cotton kingdom (Map 13.1).

The cotton kingdom was also a slave empire. The South's cotton boom rested on the backs of slaves, who grew 75 percent of the crop on plantations, toiling in gangs in broad fields under the direct supervision of whites. As cotton agriculture expanded westward, whites shipped more than 300,000 slaves out of the old seaboard states. Victims of this brutal but thriving domestic slave trade marched hundreds of miles to new plantations in the Lower South. Cotton, slaves, and plantations moved west together.

The slave population grew enormously. Southern slaves numbered fewer than 700,000 in 1790, about 2 million in 1830, and over 4 million by 1860, an increase of almost 600 percent in seven decades. By 1860, the South contained more

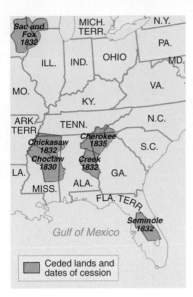

Frontier Land Opened by Indian Removal, 1830s

slaves than all the other slave societies in the New World combined. The extraordinary growth was not the result of the importation of slaves, which the federal government outlawed in 1808. Instead, the slave population grew through natural reproduction. By the nineteenth century, most slaves were native-born Southerners.

The South in Black and White

By 1860, one in every three Southerners was black (more than 4 million blacks and 8 million whites). In the Lower South states of Mississippi and South Carolina, blacks were the majority (Figure 13.1). The contrast with the North was striking: In 1860, only one Northerner in 76 was black (about 250,000 blacks to 19 million whites).

The presence of large numbers of African Americans had profound consequences for the South. Southern culture—language, food, music, religion, and even accents—was in part shaped by blacks. But the most direct consequence of the South's biracialism was southern whites' commitment to white supremacy. Northern whites believed in racial superiority, too, but they lived in a society in which blacks made up barely 1 percent of the population. Their dedication to white supremacy lacked the intensity and urgency increasingly felt by white Southerners who lived among millions of blacks. White Southerners despised blacks because they considered them members of an inferior race, further degraded by their status as slaves. They also feared blacks because they realized that slaves had every reason to hate them and to seek to end their oppression, as Nat Turner had, by any means necessary.

Attacks on slavery after 1820—from blacks and a handful of white antislavery advocates within the South and from abolitionists outside—jolted southern slaveholders into a distressing awareness that they lived in a dangerous and fragile world. In response, southern leaders initiated fresh efforts to strengthen slavery. State legislatures constructed slave codes (laws) that required the total submission of

MAP 13.1   Cotton Kingdom, Slave Empire: 1820 and 1860
As the production of cotton soared, the slave population increased dramatically. Slaves continued to toil in tobacco and rice fields along the Atlantic seaboard, but increasingly they worked on cotton plantations in Alabama, Mississippi, and Louisiana.

slaves to their masters and to white society in general. As the Louisiana code stated, a slave "owes his master…a respect without bounds, and an absolute obedience." The laws underlined the authority of all whites, not just masters. Any white could "correct" slaves who did not stay "in their place."

Intellectuals joined legislators in the campaign to strengthen slavery. The South's academics, writers, and clergy constructed a proslavery argument that sought to unify the region's whites around slavery and provide ammunition for the emerging war of words with northern abolitionists. With the intellectuals' guidance, white Southerners gradually moved away from defending slavery as a "necessary evil"—the halfhearted argument popular in Jefferson's day—and toward a full-throated, aggressive defense of slavery as a "positive good." John C. Calhoun declared that in the states where slavery had been abolished "the condition of the African, instead of being improved, has become

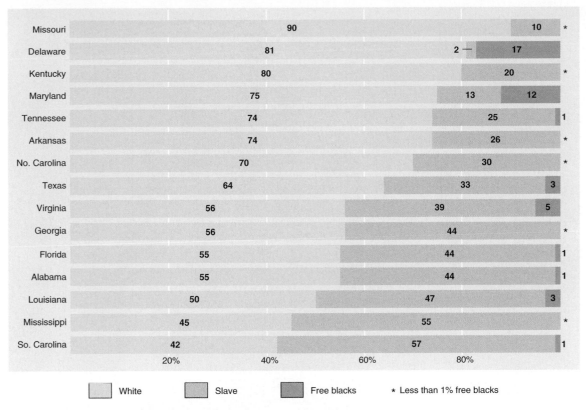

FIGURE 13.1   Black and White Populations in the South, 1860
Blacks represented a much larger fraction of the population in the South than in the North, but considerable variation existed from state to state. Only one Missourian in ten, for example, was black, while Mississippi and South Carolina had black majorities. States in the Upper South were "whiter" than states in the Lower South, despite the Upper South's greater number of free blacks.

worse," while in the slave states the Africans "have improved greatly in every respect."

Slavery's champions employed every imaginable defense. In the South slaves were legal property, and wasn't the security of property the bedrock of American **liberty**? History also endorsed slavery, they claimed. Weren't the great civilizations—such as those of the Hebrews, Greeks, and Romans—slave societies? They argued that the Bible, properly interpreted, also sanctioned slavery. Old Testament patriarchs owned slaves, they observed, and in the New Testament Paul returned the runaway slave Onesimus to his master. Some proslavery spokesmen went on the offensive and attacked the economy and society of the North. George Fitzhugh of Virginia argued that behind the North's grand slogan of **free labor** lay a heartless philosophy: "Every man for himself, and the devil take the hindmost." Gouging capitalists exploited wage workers unmercifully, Fitzhugh

declared, and he contrasted the North's vicious free-labor system with the humane relations that he claimed prevailed between masters and slaves because slaves were valuable capital that masters sought to protect.

But at the heart of the defense of slavery lay the claim of black inferiority. Black enslavement was both necessary and proper, antebellum defenders argued, because Africans were lesser beings. Rather than exploitative, slavery was a mass civilizing effort that lifted lowly blacks from barbarism and savagery, taught them disciplined work, and converted them to soul-saving Christianity. According to Virginian Thomas R. Dew, most slaves were grateful. He declared that "the slaves of a good master are his warmest, most constant, and most devoted friends."

Black slavery encouraged whites to unify around race. The grubbiest, most tobacco-stained white man could proudly proclaim his superiority

THE FRUITS OF AMALGAMATION.

The Fruits of Amalgamation

White Southerners and Northerners alike generally agreed that giving blacks equal rights would lead to miscegenation (also known as "amalgamation"). In this lithograph from 1839, Edward W. Clay of Philadelphia attacked abolitionists by imagining the outcome of their misguided campaign. He drew a beautiful white woman with her two black children, one suckling at her breast while her dark-skinned, ridiculously overdressed husband, resting his feet in his wife's lap, reads an abolitionist newspaper. The couple is attended by a white servant. Another interracial couple—perhaps the man is abolitionist William Lloyd Garrison himself—has come calling. Hanging on the wall is a picture entitled *Othello & Desdemona,* based on the popular play *Othello,* a tragic tale about a couple who crossed the color line. A black dog and a white dog play indiscriminately on the floor. Abolitionists denied the charge of amalgamation and pointed to the lasciviousness of southern slaveholders as the true source of miscegenation in antebellum America.

Courtesy, American Antiquarian Society.

to all blacks and his equality with the most refined southern patrician. Because of racial slavery, Georgia attorney Thomas R. R. Cobb observed, every white Southerner "feels that he belongs to an elevated class. It matters not that he is no slaveholder; he is not of the inferior race; he is a freeborn citizen." Consequently, the "poorest meets the richest as an equal; sits at his table with him; salutes him as a neighbor; meets him in every public assembly, and stands on the same social platform." In the South, Cobb boasted, "there is no war of classes."

In reality, slavery did not create perfect harmony among whites. But by providing every antebellum white Southerner membership in the ruling race, slavery helped whites bridge differences in wealth, education, and culture. Slavery meant white dominance, white superiority, and white equality.

The Plantation Economy

As important as slavery was in unifying white Southerners, only about a quarter of the white population lived in slaveholding families. Most slaveholders owned fewer than five slaves. Only about 12 percent of slave owners owned twenty or more, the number of slaves that historians consider necessary to distinguish a **planter** from a farmer. Although hugely outnumbered, planters nevertheless dominated the southern economy. In 1860, 52 percent of the South's slaves lived and worked on plantations. Plantation slaves produced more than 75 percent of the South's export crops, the backbone of the region's economy. Although slavery was dying elsewhere in the New World, slave plantations increasingly dominated southern agriculture.

The South's major cash crops—tobacco, sugar, rice, and cotton—grew on plantations (Map 13.2). Tobacco, the original plantation crop in North America, had shifted westward in the nineteenth century from the Chesapeake to Tennessee and Kentucky. Large-scale sugar production began in 1795, when Étienne de Boré built a modern sugar mill in what is today New Orleans, and sugar plantations were confined almost entirely to Louisiana. Commercial rice production began in the seventeenth century, and like sugar, rice was confined to a small geographic area, a narrow strip of coast stretching from the Carolinas into Georgia.

If tobacco, sugar, and rice were the princes of plantation agriculture, cotton was king. Cotton became commercially significant after the advent of Eli Whitney's cotton gin in 1793, which removed sticky cotton seeds and thus dramatically increased the production of raw cotton. Cotton was relatively easy to grow and took little capital to get started—just enough for land, seed,

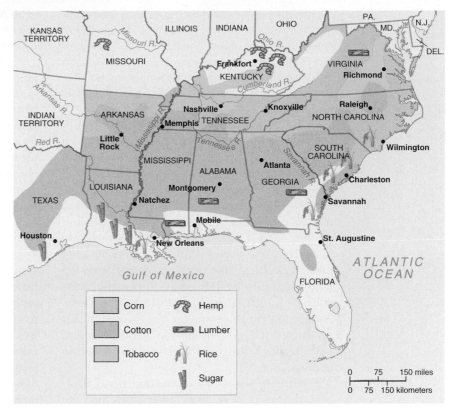

MAP 13.2 The Agricultural Economy of the South, 1860
Cotton dominated the South's agricultural economy, but the region grew a variety of crops and was largely self-sufficient in foodstuffs.

READING THE MAP: In what type of geographical areas were rice and sugar grown in 1860? After cotton, what crop commanded the greatest agricultural area in the South? In which region of the South was this crop predominantly found?
CONNECTIONS: What role did the South play in the U.S. economy in 1860? How did the economy of the South differ from that of the North?

FOR MORE HELP ANALYZING THIS MAP, see the map activity for this chapter in the Online Study Guide at bedfordstmartins.com/roarkcompact.

and simple tools. Thus, small farmers as well as planters grew the white fluffy stuff. But planters, whose fields were worked by slaves, produced three-quarters of the South's cotton. And cotton made planters rich.

Plantation slavery also enriched the nation. By 1840, cotton accounted for more than 60 percent of American exports. Much of the profit from sales of cotton overseas returned to planters, but some went to northern middlemen who bought, sold, insured, warehoused, and shipped cotton to the mills in Great Britain and elsewhere. As one New York merchant observed, "Cotton has enriched all through whose hands it has passed."

As middlemen invested their profits in the booming northern economy, industrial development received a burst of much-needed capital. Furthermore, southern plantations benefited northern industry by providing an important market for textiles, agricultural tools, and other manufactured goods.

The economies of the North and South steadily diverged. While the North developed a mixed economy—agriculture, commerce, and manufacturing—the South remained overwhelmingly agricultural. Since planters were earning healthy profits, they saw little reason to diversify. Year after year, they funneled the profits they earned from land and slaves back into more land and slaves. With its capital flowing into agriculture, the South did not develop many factories. By 1860, only 10 percent of the nation's industrial workers lived in the South. Some cotton mills sprang up, but the region that produced 100 percent of the nation's cotton manufactured less than 7 percent of its cotton textiles.

Without significant economic diversification, the South developed fewer cities than the North. In 1860, it was the least urban region in the country. While nearly 37 percent of New England's population lived in cities, less than 12 percent of Southerners were urban dwellers. Southern cities were mostly port cities on the periphery of the region and busy principally with exporting the agricultural products of plantations in the interior. Urban merchants provided agriculture with indispensable services, such as hauling, insuring, and selling cotton, rice, and sugar, but they were the tail on the plantation dog. Southern cities could claim something no northern city desired—140,000 slaves in 1860. In some cities, slaves made up half of the population, and they worked in nearly every conceivable occupation, helping the southern economy thrive.

Because the South had so few cities and industrial jobs, it attracted relatively small numbers of European immigrants. Seeking economic opportunity, not competition with slaves (whose labor would keep wages low), immigrants steered well north of the South's slave-dominated, agricultural economy. In 1860, 13 percent of all Americans were born abroad. But in nine of the fifteen slave states, only 2 percent or fewer were foreign-born.

Not every Southerner celebrated the region's plantation economy. Critics lambasted the excessive commitment to cotton and slaves and bemoaned what one called the "deplorable scarcity" of factories. Diversification, reformers promised, would make the South even more prosperous. State governments encouraged economic development by helping to create banking systems and by constructing railroads, but they also failed to create some of the essential services modern economies require. By the mid-nineteenth century, for example, no southern legislature had created a statewide public school system. Dominant slaveholders failed to see any benefit in educating small farmers, especially with their tax money. Despite the flurry of railroad building, the South's mileage in 1860 was less than half that of the North. Moreover, while railroads crisscrossed the North carrying manufactured goods as well as agricultural products, most railroads in the South ran from port cities back into farming areas and were built to export cotton (see Map 12.5, page 304).

Northerners claimed that slavery was a backward and doomed labor system, but few Southerners perceived economic weakness in their region. In fact, the planters' pockets were never fuller than in the 1850s. Compared with Northerners, Southerners invested less of their capital in industry, transportation, and public education. Planters' decisions to reinvest in agriculture ensured the momentum of the plantation economy and the political and social relationships rooted in it.

> **REVIEW** Why did the nineteenth-century southern economy remain primarily agricultural while the northern economy grew increasingly diversified?

Immigrants as a Percentage of State Populations, 1860

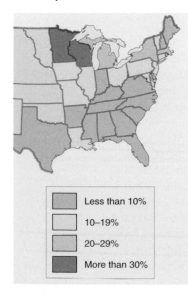

Less than 10%

10–19%

20–29%

More than 30%

Masters, Mistresses, and the Big House

Nowhere was the contrast between northern and southern life more vivid than on the plantations of the South. Located on a patchwork of cleared fields and dense forests, a plantation typically included a "big house" and a slave quarter. Scattered about were numerous outbuildings, each with a special function. Near the big house were the kitchen, storehouse, smokehouse (for curing and preserving meat), and hen coop. More distant were the barns, toolsheds, **artisans'** workshops, and overseer's house. Large plantations sometimes had additional buildings such as an infirmary and a chapel for slaves. Depending on the crop, there was a tobacco shed, a rice mill, a sugar refinery, or a cotton gin house. Lavish or plain, plantations everywhere had an underlying similarity.

The plantation was the home of masters, mistresses, and slaves. Slavery shaped the lives of all the plantation's inhabitants, from work to leisure activities, but it affected each differently. A hierarchy of rigid roles and duties governed relationships. Presiding was the master, who ruled his wife, children, and slaves, none of whom had many legal rights and all of whom were designated by the state as dependents under his dominion and protection.

Plantation Masters

While smaller planters supervised the labor of their slaves themselves, larger planters hired overseers who went to the fields with the slaves, leaving planters free to concentrate on marketing, finance, and general plantation affairs. Planters also found time to escape to town to discuss cotton prices, to the courthouse and legislature to debate politics, and to the woods to hunt and fish.

Increasingly in the nineteenth century, planters characterized their mastery in terms of what they called "Christian guardianship" and what historians have called **paternalism**. The concept of paternalism denied that the form of slavery practiced in the South was brutal and exploitative. Instead, it defined southern slavery as a set of reciprocal obligations between masters and slaves. In exchange for the slaves' labor and obedience, masters provided basic care and necessary guidance. As owners of blacks, masters argued, they had the heavy responsibility of caring for a childlike, dependent people. In 1814, Thomas Jefferson captured the essence of the advancing ideal: "We should endeavor, with those whom fortune has thrown on our hands, to feed & clothe them well, protect them from ill usage, require such reasonable labor only as is performed voluntarily by freemen, and be led by no repugnancies to abdicate them, and our duties to them." A South Carolina rice planter insisted, "I manage them as my children."

Paternalism was part propaganda and part self-delusion. But it was also economically

Southern Man with Children and Their Mammy
Obviously prosperous and looking like a man accustomed to giving orders and being obeyed, this patriarch poses around 1848 with his young daughters and their nurse. The black woman is clearly a servant, a status indicated by her race and her attire. Why does she appear in the daguerreotype? The absent mother may be dead. Her death might account for the inclusion of the African American woman in the family circle. In any case, her presence signals her importance in the household. Fathers left the raising of children to mothers and nurses.
Collection of the J. Paul Getty Museum, Malibu, CA.

shrewd. Masters increasingly recognized slaves as valuable assets to be maintained, and they realized that the expansion of the slave labor force could come only from natural reproduction. The rising price of slaves led one planter to declare in 1849 that "it behooves those who own them to make them last as long as possible." Another planter instructed his overseer to pay attention to "whatever tends to promote their health and render them prolific."

One consequence of this paternalism and economic self-interest was a small improvement in slaves' welfare. Diet improved, although nineteenth-century slaves still mainly ate fatty pork and cornmeal. Housing improved, although the cabins still had cracks large enough, slaves said, for cats to slip through. Clothing improved, although slaves seldom received much more than two crude outfits a year and perhaps a pair of cheap shoes. In the fields, workdays remained sunup to sundown, but planters often provided a rest period in the heat of the day. And most owners ceased the colonial practices of punishing slaves by branding and mutilation.

Paternalism should not be mistaken for "Ol' Massa's" kindness and goodwill. It encouraged better treatment because it made economic sense to provide at least minimal care for valuable slaves. Nor did paternalism require that planters put aside their whips. They could flail away and still claim that they were only fulfilling their responsibilities as guardians of their naturally lazy and at times insubordinate dependents. State laws gave masters nearly "uncontrolled authority over the body" of the slave, according to one North Carolina judge. Paternalism offered slaves some informal protection against the most brutal punishments, but whipping remained the planters' essential form of coercion. (See "Historical Question," page 326.)

With its notion that slavery imposed on masters a burden and a duty, paternalism provided slaveholders with a means of rationalizing their rule. But it also provided some slaves with leverage over the conditions of their lives. Slaves learned to manipulate a slaveholder's need to see himself as a good and decent master. To avoid a reputation as a cruel tyrant, planters sometimes negotiated with slaves, rather than just resorting to the whip. Masters sometimes granted slaves small garden plots in which they could work for themselves after their day in the fields or a few days off and a dance when they had gathered the last of the cotton.

The Virginia statesman Edmund Randolph argued that slavery created in white southern men a "quick and acute sense of personal liberty" and a "disdain for every abridgement of personal independence." Indeed, prickly individualism and aggressive independence became crucial features of the southern concept of honor. Social standing, political advancement, and even self-esteem rested on an honorable reputation. Defending honor became a male passion. Andrew Jackson's mother reportedly told her son, "Never tell a lie, nor take what is not your own, nor sue anybody for slander or assault and battery. Always settle them cases yourself." Southern boys were expected to master the "manly" arts, and among planters such advice sometimes led to duels. Dueling arrived from Europe in the eighteenth century. It died out in the North, but in the South, even after legislatures banned it, gentlemen continued to defend their honor with pistols at ten paces.

Slavery buttressed the power of white men, and planters brooked no opposition from any of their dependents, black or white. The master's absolute dominion sometimes led to **miscegenation**, the sexual mixing of the races. Laws prohibited interracial sex, and some masters practiced self-restraint. Others merely urged discretion. How many trips masters and their sons made to slave cabins is impossible to tell, but as long as slavery gave white men extraordinary power, slave women were forced to submit to the sexual appetites of the men who owned them.

Individualistic impulses were strong among planters, but duty to family was paramount. In time, as the children of one elite family married the children of another, ties of blood and kinship as well as economic interest and ideology linked planters to one another. Conscious of what they shared as slaveholders, planters worked together to defend their common interests. The values of the big house—slavery, honor, male domination—washed over the boundaries of plantations and flooded all of southern life.

Plantation Mistresses

Like their northern counterparts, southern ladies were expected to possess feminine virtues of piety, purity, chastity, and obedience within the context of marriage, motherhood, and domesticity. Southerners also expected ladies to mirror all that was best in plantation society. Countless toasts praised the southern lady as the perfect complement to her husband, the commanding patriarch. She was physically weak, "formed only for the less laborious occupations," and thus dependent on male protection. To gain this protection, she was naturally modest and delicate, possessed beauty and grace, and cultivated refinement and charm.

For women, this image of the southern lady was no blessing. Chivalry—the South's romantic ideal of male-female relationships—glorified the lady while it subordinated her. Chivalry's underlying assumptions about the weakness of women and the protective authority of men resembled the paternalistic defense of slavery. Indeed, the most articulate spokesmen for slavery also vigorously defended the subordination of women. George Fitzhugh insisted that "a woman, like children, has but one right and that is the right to protection. The right to protection involves the obligation to obey. A husband, a lord and master, nature designed for every woman....If she be

Bird Store, 626 Royal Street, **New Orleans**
Most elite white women in the antebellum South lived isolated existences on rural plantations. But some lived in cities, while others visited them from time to time, and going shopping was a prominent feature of such visits. Teenager Gertrude Clanton, who lived in Augusta, Georgia, wore store-bought clothes that she described endlessly in letters to her friends. Here a wealthy mother and daughter shop for a pet in a New Orleans bird store. The attentive proprietor and attractive shop provide everything they need—birds, cages, bird food, even an inviting couch and blanket in case they want to rest before moving on. Elite white women themselves were, in a way, like birds kept in golden cages. Could it be that they were attracted to the thought of owning birds of their own, something they could care for, train, and control?
Historic New Orleans Collection.

obedient she stands little danger of maltreatment." Just as the slaveholder's mastery was written into law, so too were the paramount rights of husbands. Once married, women found divorce almost impossible.

Daughters of planters confronted chivalry's demands at an early age. Their educations aimed at fitting them to become southern ladies. At their private boarding schools they read literature, learned languages, and studied the appropriate drawing-room arts. Elite women began courting at a young age and married early. Kate Carney exaggerated only slightly when she despaired in her diary: "Today, I am seventeen, getting quite old, and am not married." Yet marriage meant turning their fates over to their husbands, and making enormous efforts to live up to their region's lofty ideal.

Proslavery ideologues claimed that slavery freed white women from drudgery. Surrounded "by her domestics," declared Thomas R. Dew, "she ceases to be a mere beast of burden" and "becomes the cheering and animating center of the family circle." In reality, however, having servants required the plantation mistress to work long hours. Like her husband, she had managerial responsibilities. She managed the big house, directly supervising as many as a dozen slaves. But unlike her husband, the mistress had no overseer. All house servants

How Often Were Slaves Whipped?

As important as this question is to historians, and obviously was to slaves, we have very little reliable evidence on the frequency of whipping. We know from white sources that whipping was the prescribed method of physical punishment on most antebellum plantations. Masters' instructions to overseers authorized whippings and often set limits on the number of strokes an overseer could administer. Some planters allowed fifteen lashes, some fifty, and some one hundred. But slave owners' instructions, as revealing as they are, tell us more about the severity of beatings than about their frequency.

Remembrances of former slaves confirm that whipping was widespread and frequent. In the 1930s, a government program gathered testimony from more than 2,300 elderly African Americans about their experiences as slaves. Their accounts offered grisly evidence of the cruelty of slavery. "You say how did our Master treat his slaves?" asked one woman. "Scandalous, they treated them just like dogs." She was herself whipped "till the blood dripped to the ground." A few slaves remembered kind masters and never personally felt the sting of the lash. Bert Strong was one such slave, but he also recalled hearing slaves on other farms "hollering when

they get beat." He said, "They beat them till it a pity." Beatings occurred often, but how often?

A remarkably systematic record of whippings over a sustained period of time comes from the diary of Bennet H. Barrow, the master of Highland plantation in West Feliciana Parish, Louisiana. For a twenty-three-month period in 1840–1841, Barrow meticulously recorded every whipping he administered or ordered. On most large plantations, overseers handled the business of day-to-day management, but in 1838 Barrow concluded that overseers were "good for nothing" and "a perfect nuisance." He dismissed his white overseer and, assisted only by a black driver, began managing his own plantation.

What does the Barrow evidence show? In 1840, according to the federal census, Barrow owned 129 slaves. In the twenty-three-month period, Barrow recorded 160 whippings. That means that, on the average, a slave was whipped every four and a half days. Sixty of the 77 slaves who worked in the fields were whipped at least once. Most of the 17 field slaves who escaped being beaten were children and pregnant women. Eighty percent of male cotton pickers and 70 percent of female cotton pickers were whipped at least

once in this period. Dave Barley received eight floggings, more than any other Barrow slave, and Patience received six whippings, more than any other female slave.

In most instances, Barrow recorded not only the fact of a whipping but also its cause. All sorts of "misconduct," "rascallity," and "disorderly acts" made Barrow reach for his whip. The provocations included family quarrels in the slave quarters, impudence, running away, and failure to keep curfew. But nearly 80 percent of the acts he recorded were related to poor work. Barrow gave beatings for "not picking as well as he can," for picking "very trashy cotton," and for failing to pick the prescribed weight of cotton. One slave claimed to have lost his eyesight and for months refused to work until Barrow "gave him 25 cuts yesterday morning & ordered him to work Blind or not."

Whippings should not be mistaken for spankings. Some planters used whips that raised welts, caused blisters, and bruised. Others resorted to rawhide and cowhide whips that broke the skin, caused scarring, and sometimes permanently maimed. Occasionally, slaves were beaten to death. Whipping was not Barrow's only means of inflicting pain. His diary mentions confining slaves to a plantation jail, putting them in chains, shooting them, breaking a "sword cane" over one slave's head, having slaves mauled by dogs, placing them in stocks, "staking down" slaves for hours, "hand sawing" them, holding their heads under water, and a variety of punishments

answered directly to her. She assigned them tasks each morning, directed their work throughout the day, and punished them when she found fault. In addition to supervising a complex household, women also bore the dangers of childbearing and responsibilities of child rearing. Southern ladies did not often lead lives of leisure.

Whereas masters used their status as slaveholders as a springboard into public affairs, the intending to ridicule and to shame, including making men wear women's clothing and do "women's work," such as the laundry. Still, Barrow's preferred instrument of punishment was the whip.

On the Barrow plantation, as on many others, whipping was public. Victims were often tied to a stake in the quarter, and the other slaves were made to watch. In a real sense, the entire slave population on the plantation experienced a whipping every four and a half days. Even though some never felt the lash personally, all were familiar with its terror and agony.

Was whipping effective? Did it produce a hardworking, efficient, and conscientious labor force? Not according to Barrow's own record. No evidence indicates that whipping changed the slaves' behavior. What Barrow considered bad work continued. Unabated whipping is itself evidence of the failure of punishment to achieve the master's will. Slaves knew the rules, yet they continued to act "badly." And they continued to suffer. It was a gruesome drama—the master seeking from his slaves hard labor and slaves denying their master what he most wanted, day after day.

Did Barrow whip with the same frequency as other planters? We simply do not know. As much as we would like to answer the question precisely, because of the lack of quantifiable evidence we will never know exactly how often whippings occurred. Still, the Barrow evidence allows us to speculate profitably on the frequency of whipping by large

Gordon
This photograph of Gordon, a runaway slave from Baton Rouge, Louisiana, was taken on April 2, 1863, and sent home from the Civil War by Frederick W. Mercer, an assistant surgeon with the Forty-seventh Massachusetts Regiment. Mercer examined four hundred other runaways and found many "to be as badly lacerated." Masters claimed that they whipped only when they had to and only as hard as they had to, but slave testimony and photographic evidence refute their defense of slavery as a benign institution.
Courtesy of the Massachusetts Historical Society.

planters. We do know that Barrow did not consider himself a cruel man. He bitterly denounced his neighbor as "the most cruel Master i ever knew of" for castrating three of his slaves. Moreover, Barrow had dispensed with the overseers in part because of their "brutal feelings" toward slaves. Like most whites, he believed that the lash was essential to get work done. He used it no more than he believed absolutely necessary.

Most masters, including Barrow, tried to encourage work with promises of small gifts and brief holidays, but punishment was their most important motivator. We will

never know if the typical slave was beaten once a year as on the Barrow plantation, but the admittedly scanty evidence suggests that on large plantations the whip fell on someone's back every few days.

And former slaves remembered. More than a half century after emancipation, their sharpest recollections usually involved punishment. They remembered the pain, the injustice, and their bitter resentment. They evaluated their former masters according to how frequently they reached for the whip. According to one former slave, "some was good and some was bad, and about the most of them was bad."

---

mistress's life was circumscribed by the plantation. Masters left the plantation when they pleased, but plantation mistresses needed chaperones to travel. Women spent most days at home, where they often became lonely. In 1853,

Mary Kendall wrote how much she enjoyed her sister's letter: "For about three weeks I did not have the pleasure of seeing one white female face, there being no white family except our own upon the plantation."

The Price of Blood
This 1868 painting by T. S. Noble depicts a transaction between a slave trader and a rich planter. The trader nervously pretends to study the contract, while the planter waits impatiently for the completion of the sale. The planter's mulatto son, who is being sold, looks away. The children of white men and slave women were property and could be sold by the father/master. The tragedy of miscegenation, however, extended beyond the son shown here. Who is absent from the painting? Whose marriage has been betrayed? Who else's son is being sold away?
Morris Museum of Art, Augusta, GA.

For more help analyzing this image, see the visual activity for this chapter in the Online Study Guide at
bedfordstmartins.com/roarkcompact.

As members of slaveholding families, mistresses lived privileged lives. But they also had significant grounds for discontent. No feature of plantation life generated more rage and anguish among mistresses than miscegenation. Mary Boykin Chesnut of Camden, South Carolina, confided in her diary, "ours is a monstrous system, a wrong and iniquity. Like the patriarchs of old, our men live all in one house with their wives and their concubines; and the mulattos one sees in every family partly resemble the white children. Any lady is ready to tell you who is the father of all the mulatto children in everybody's household but her own. Those, she seems to think drop from the clouds."

But most planters' wives, including Mary Boykin Chesnut, accepted slavery. After all, the mistress's world rested on slave labor, just as the master's did. By acknowledging the realities of male power, mistresses enjoyed the rewards of their class and race. But these rewards came at a price. Still, the heaviest burdens of slavery fell not on those who lived in the big house but on those who toiled to support them.

REVIEW   Why did the ideology of paternalism gain currency among planters in the nineteenth century?

Slaves and the Quarter

On most plantations, only a few hundred yards separated the big house and the slave quarter. The distance was short enough to assure whites easy access to the labor of blacks, yet great enough to provide slaves with some privacy. Out of eyesight and earshot of the big house, slaves drew together and built lives of their own. They created families, worshipped God, and developed an African American community.

Despite the rise of plantations, a substantial minority of slaves lived and worked elsewhere. Most labored on small farms, where they wielded a hoe alongside another slave or two and perhaps their master. But by 1860, almost half a million slaves (one in eight) did not work in agriculture at all. Some were employed in towns and cities as domestics, day laborers, bakers, barbers, tailors, and more. Others, far from urban centers, toiled as fishermen, lumbermen, and railroad workers. Slaves could also be found in most of the South's factories. Nevertheless, a majority of slaves (52 percent) counted plantations as their homes and workplaces.

Work

Whites enslaved blacks for their labor, and all slaves who were capable of productive labor worked. Young children were introduced to the world of work as early as age five or six. Ex-slave Carrie Hudson recalled that children who were "knee high to a duck" were sent to the fields to carry water to thirsty workers or to protect ripening crops from hungry birds. Others helped in the slave nursery, caring for children even younger than themselves, or in the big house, where they swept floors or shooed flies in the dining room. When slave boys and girls reached the age of eleven or twelve, masters sent most of them to the fields, where they learned farm work by laboring alongside their parents. After a lifetime of labor, old women left the fields to care for the small children and spin yarn and old men moved on to mind livestock and clean stables.

The overwhelming majority of plantation slaves in 1860 worked as field hands. Planters sometimes assigned men and women to separate gangs, the women working at lighter tasks and the men doing the heavy work of clearing and breaking the land. But women also did heavy work. "I had to work hard," Nancy Boudry remembered, and "plow and go and split wood just like a man."

Haywood Dixon, Slave Carpenter
In this 1854 daguerreotype, Dixon (1826–c. 1889), a slave carpenter who worked in Greene County, North Carolina, poses with a symbol of his craft, the carpenter's square. When work was slow on the home plantation, masters could hire out their skilled artisans to neighbors who needed a carpenter, blacksmith, or mason.
Collection of William L. Murphy.

The backbreaking labor and the monotonous routines caused one ex-slave to observe, the "history of one day is the history of every day."

A few slaves (about one in ten) became house servants. And nearly all of those who did (nine of ten) were women. They cooked, cleaned house, babysat, washed clothes, and did the dozens of other tasks the master and mistress required. House servants enjoyed somewhat less physically demanding work than field hands, but they were constantly on call, with no time that was entirely their own. Since no servant could please constantly, most bore the brunt of white frustration and rage. Ex-slave Jacob Branch of Texas remembered, "My poor mama! Every washday old Missy give her a beating."

Even rarer than house servants were skilled artisans. In the cotton South, no more than one slave in twenty (almost all men) worked in a skilled trade. Most were blacksmiths and carpenters, but slaves also worked as masons, mechanics, millers, and shoemakers. Skilled slave fathers took pride in teaching their crafts to their sons. "My pappy was one of the black smiths and worked in the shop," John Mathews remembered. "I had to help my pappy in the shop when I was a child and I learnt how to beat out the iron and make wagon tires, and make plows."

Rarest of all slave occupations was that of slave driver. Probably no more than one male slave in a hundred worked in this capacity. These men were well named, for their primary task was driving other slaves to work harder in the fields. In some drivers' hands, the whip never rested. Ex-slave Jane Johnson of South Carolina called her driver the "meanest man, white or black, I ever see." But other drivers showed all the restraint they could. "Ole Gabe didn't like that whippin' business," West Turner of Virginia remembered. "When Marsa was there, he would lay it on 'cause he had to. But when old Marsa wasn't lookin', he never would beat them slaves."

Normally, slaves worked from what they called "can to can't," from "can see" in the morning to "can't see" at night. Even with a break at noon for a meal and rest, it made for a long day. For slaves, Lewis Young recalled, "work, work, work, 'twas all they do."

Family, Religion, and Community

From dawn to dusk, slaves worked for the master, but at night, when the labor was done, and all day Sundays and usually Saturday afternoons, slaves were left largely to themselves. Bone tired perhaps, they nonetheless used the time and space to develop and enjoy what mattered most: family, religion, and community.

In the quarter, slaves became husbands and wives, mothers and fathers, sons and daughters, preachers and singers, storytellers and conjurers. Over the generations, they created a community and a culture of their own that buoyed them up during long hours in the fields and brought them joy and hope in the few hours they had to themselves.

One of the most important consequences of the slaves' limited autonomy was the preservation and persistence of the family. Although severely battered, the black family survived slavery. No laws recognized slave marriage, and therefore no master or slave was legally obligated to honor the bond. Nevertheless, plantation records show that slave marriages were often long-lasting. Young men and women in the quarter fell in love, married, and set up housekeeping in cabins of their own. The primary cause of the ending of slave marriages was death, just as it was in white families. But the second most frequent cause of the end of slave marriages was the sale of the husband or wife, something no white family ever had to fear. Precise figures are unavailable, but in the years 1820 to 1860 sales destroyed

Slave Quarter, South Carolina

On large plantations, several score of African Americans lived in cabins that were often arranged along what slaves called "the street." The dwellings in this image by Civil War photographer George N. Barnard of a South Carolina plantation were better built than the typical rickety, one-room, dirt-floored slave cabin. Almost certainly posed, this photograph shows the inhabitants of the slave quarter—little children playing in the dirt, girls and women sitting on the steps talking and working at something, older boys and men driving carts and wagons. During the daylight hours of the workweek, when most men and women labored in the fields, the quarter was mostly empty. At night and on Sundays, it was a busy place.
Collection of the New-York Historical Society.

at least 300,000 slave marriages. Years after Moses Grandy was parted from his slave wife, he said, "I have never seen or heard of her from that day to this." And he added, "I loved her as I love my life."

Like families, religion also provided slaves with a refuge and a reason for living. Before the American Revolution, Baptists and Methodists began trying to convert slaves from their African beliefs. **Evangelicals** offered an emotional "religion of the heart" to which blacks (and many whites as well) responded enthusiastically. By the mid-nineteenth century, perhaps as many as one-quarter of all slaves claimed church membership, and many of the rest would not have objected to being called Christians.

Planters promoted Christianity in the quarter because they believed that the slaves' salvation was part of their obligation and that religion made slaves more obedient. South Carolina slaveholder Charles Colcock Jones, the leading missionary to the slaves, published his *Catechism for Colored Persons* in 1834. In it, he instructed blacks "to count their Masters 'worthy of all honour,' as those whom God has placed over them in this world." But slaves laughed up their sleeves at such messages. "That old white preacher just was telling us slaves to be good to our masters," one ex-slave chuckled. "We ain't cared a bit about that stuff he was telling us 'cause we wanted to sing, pray, and serve God in our own way."

Meeting in their cabins or secretly in the woods, slaves created an African American Christianity that served their needs, not the masters'. Laws prohibited teaching slaves to read, but a few could read enough to struggle with the Bible. They interpreted the Christian message themselves. Rather than obedience, their faith emphasized justice. Slaves believed that God kept score and that the accounts of this world would be settled in the next. "The idea of a revolution in the conditions of the whites and blacks is the corner-stone" of the slaves' religion, recalled one ex-slave. But the slaves' faith also spoke to their experiences in this world. In the Old Testament they discovered Moses, who delivered his people from slavery, and in the New Testament they found Jesus, who offered salvation to all. Jesus' message of equality provided a potent antidote to the planters' claim that blacks were an inferior people whom God condemned to slavery.

Christianity did not entirely drive out traditional African beliefs. Even slaves who were Christians sometimes continued to believe that conjurers, witches, and spirits possessed the power to injure and protect. Moreover, slaves' Christian music, preaching, and rituals reflected the influence of Africa, as did many of their secular activities, such as wood carving, quilt making, and storytelling. But by the mid-nineteenth century, black Christianity had assumed a central place in slaves' quest for freedom. In the words of one spiritual: "O my Lord delivered Daniel/O why not deliver me too?"

Gourd Fiddle

Found in St. Mary's County, Maryland, this slave-made gourd fiddle is an example of the many musical instruments that African Americans crafted and played throughout the South. Henry Wright, an ex-slave from Georgia, remembered: "I made a fiddle out of a large sized gourd—a long wooden handle was used as a neck, and the hair from a horse's tail was used for the bow. The strings were made of catgut." A hybrid of African and European elements, this fiddle offers material evidence of the cultural transformation of African slaves. Although Africans lost much in their forced journey to the Americas, Africa remained in their cultural memory. Black men and women drew on the traditions of their homeland and the South to create something new—an African American culture. Music, a crucial component of that sustaining culture, provided slaves with a creative outlet and relief from the rigors of slavery.

Smithsonian Institution / Aldo Tutino / Folio, Inc.

Resistance and Rebellion

Slaves did not suffer slavery passively. They were, as whites said, "troublesome property." Slaves understood that accommodation to what they could not change was the price of survival, but in a hundred ways they protested their bondage. Theoretically, the master was all-powerful and the slave powerless. But sustained by their families, religion, and community, slaves engaged in day-to-day resistance against their enslavers.

The spectrum of slave resistance ranged from mild to extreme. Telling a pointed story by the fireside in a slave cabin was probably the mildest form of protest. But when the weak got the better of the strong, as they did in tales of Br'er Rabbit and Br'er Fox (*Br'er* is a contraction of *Brother*), listeners could enjoy the thrill of a vicarious victory over their masters. Protest in the fields was riskier and included putting rocks in their cotton bags before having them weighed, feigning illness, and pretending to be so thickheaded that they could not understand the simplest instruction. Slaves broke so many hoes that owners outfitted hoes with oversized handles. Slaves so mistreated the work animals that masters switched from horses to mules, which could absorb more abuse. While slaves worked hard in the master's fields, they also sabotaged his interests.

Running away was a common form of protest. Some runaways sought the ultimate prize: freedom in the North or in Canada. Over the decades, thousands of slaves, almost all from the Upper South, made it. But escape from the Lower South was almost impossible, except in Texas, where several hundred slaves found freedom in Mexico. The overwhelming majority of runaways could hope only to escape for a few days. They usually stayed close to their plantation, keeping to the deep woods or swamps and slipping back into the quarter at night to get food. "Lying out," as it was known, usually ended when the runaway, worn out and ragged, gave up or was finally chased down by slave-hunting dogs.

While resistance was common, outright rebellion—a violent assault on slavery by large numbers of slaves—was very rare. The scarcity of revolts is not evidence of the slaves' contentedness, however. Rather, conditions gave rebels almost no chance of success. By 1860, whites in the South outnumbered blacks two to one and were heavily armed. Moreover, communication between plantations was difficult, and the South provided little protective wilderness into which rebels could retreat and defend themselves. Rebellion, as Nat Turner's experience showed, was virtual suicide.

Despite the rarity of slave revolts, whites believed that they were surrounded by conspiracies to rebel. In 1822, whites in Charleston accused Denmark Vesey, a free black carpenter, of conspiring with plantation slaves to slaughter Charleston's white inhabitants. The authorities rounded up scores of suspects, who, prodded by torture and the threat of death, implicated others in the plot "to riot in blood, outrage, and rapine." Although the city fathers never found any weapons and Vesey and most of the accused steadfastly denied the charges of conspiracy, officials hanged thirty-five black men, including Vesey, and banished another thirty-seven blacks from the state.

Masters boasted that their slaves were "instinctively contented," but steady resistance and occasional rebellion proved otherwise. Slaves did not have the power to end their bondage, but by asserting themselves, they affirmed their humanity and worth. By resisting their masters' will, slaves became actors in the plantation drama, helping to establish limits beyond which planters and overseers hesitated to go.

Still, slavery blunted and thwarted African Americans' hopes and aspirations. Slavery broke some and crippled others. But slavery's destructive power had to contend with the resiliency of the human spirit. Slaves fought back physically, culturally, and spiritually. They not only survived bondage, but they created in the quarter a vibrant African American culture and community that sustained them through more than two centuries of slavery and after.

REVIEW   Why did slave resistance rarely take the form of rebellion?

Black and Free: On the Middle Ground

Not every black Southerner was a slave. In 1860, some 260,000 (approximately 6 percent) of the region's 4.1 million African Americans were free (see Figure 13.1). What is surprising is not that their numbers were small but that they existed at all. "Free black" seemed increasingly a contradiction to most white Southerners. According to the emerging racial thinking, blacks were supposed to be slaves. Blacks who were free stood out, and whites made them more and more targets of oppression. Free blacks stood precariously between slavery and full freedom, on what a young free black artisan in Charleston in 1848 characterized as "a middle ground." But they made the most of their freedom, and a few found success despite the restrictions placed on them by white Southerners.

Precarious Freedom

The population of free blacks swelled after the Revolution, when the natural rights philosophy of the Declaration of Independence and the egalitarian message of evangelical Protestantism joined to challenge slavery. A brief flurry of **emancipation** visited the Upper South, where the ideological assault on slavery coincided with a deep depression in the tobacco economy. By 1810, free blacks in the South numbered more than 100,000, a fact that worried white Southerners, who, because of the cotton boom, wanted more slaves, not more free blacks.

In the 1820s and 1830s, state legislatures acted to stem the growth of the free black population and to shrink the liberty of those blacks who had already gained their freedom. Laws denied masters the right to free their slaves. Other laws humiliated and restricted free blacks by subjecting them to special taxes, requiring them to register annually with the state or to choose a white guardian, prohibiting them from interstate travel, denying them the right to have schools and to participate in politics, and requiring them to carry "freedom papers" to prove they were not slaves. Increasingly, whites subjected free blacks to the same laws as slaves. They could not testify under oath in a court of law or serve on juries. They were liable to whipping and the treadmill, like slaves. Free blacks were forbidden to strike whites, even to defend themselves. "Free negroes belong to a degraded caste of society," a South Carolina judge summed up in 1848. "They are in no respect on a perfect equality with the white man.... They ought, by law, to be compelled to demean themselves as inferiors."

The elaborate system of regulations confined most free African Americans to a constricted life of poverty and dependence. Typically, free blacks were rural, uneducated, unskilled agricultural

Freedom Paper
This legal document attests to the free status of the Rev. John F. Cook of Washington, D.C., his daughter Mary, and his son George. Cook was a free black man who kept his "freedom paper" in this watertight tin, which he probably carried with him at all times. Free blacks had to be prepared to prove their free status any time a white man challenged them, for southern law presumed that a black person was a slave unless he or she could prove otherwise. Without such proof, blacks risked enslavement.
Moorland-Spingarn Research Center, Howard University, Washington, D.C.

laborers and domestic servants. Opportunities of all kinds—for work, education, community— were slim. Planters looked on free blacks as degraded parasites, likely to set a bad example for slaves. They believed that free blacks subverted the racial subordination that was the essence of slavery.

Achievement despite Restrictions

Despite increasingly harsh laws and stepped-up persecution, free African Americans made the most of the advantages their status offered. Unlike slaves, free blacks could legally marry. They could protect their families from arbitrary disruption and pass on their heritage of freedom to their children. Freedom also meant that they could choose occupations and own property. For most, these economic rights proved only theoretical, for a majority of the South's free blacks remained propertyless.

Still, some free blacks escaped the poverty and degradation whites thrust on them. Particularly in urban areas—especially the cities of Charleston, Mobile, and New Orleans—a small elite of free blacks emerged. Urban whites enforced many of the restrictive laws only sporadically, allowing free blacks room to maneuver. The elite consisted overwhelmingly of light-skinned African Americans who worked at skilled trades, and their customers were prominent whites who appreciated their able, respectful service. The free black elite operated schools for their children and traveled in and out of their states, despite laws forbidding both activities. They worshipped with whites (in separate seating) in the finest churches and lived scattered about in white neighborhoods, not in ghettos. And like elite whites, some owned slaves. Blacks could own blacks because they had the right to own property, which in the South included human property. Of the 3,200 black slaveholders (barely 1 percent of the free black population), most owned only a few slaves, who were sometimes family members whom they could not legally free. But others owned slaves in large numbers and exploited them for labor.

One such free black slave owner was William Ellison of South Carolina. Ellison was born a slave in 1790, but in 1816 he bought his freedom and moved to a thriving plantation district about one hundred miles north of Charleston. He set up business as a cotton gin maker, a trade he had learned as a slave, and by 1835 he was prosperous enough to purchase the home of a former governor of the state. By the time of his death in 1861, he had become a cotton planter, with sixty-three slaves and an 800-acre plantation.

Most free blacks neither became slaveholders like Ellison nor sought to raise a slave rebellion, as whites accused Denmark Vesey of doing. Rather, most free blacks simply tried to preserve their freedom, which was under increasing attack. Free blacks clung to their precarious freedom by seeking to impress whites with their reliability, economic contribution, and good behavior.

> **REVIEW** Why did many state legislatures pass laws restricting free blacks' freedoms in the 1820s and 1830s?

The Plain Folk

Like most free blacks, most whites in the South did not own slaves, not even one. In 1860, more than 6 million of the South's 8 million whites lived in slaveless households. Most "plain folk" were small farmers. Perhaps three out of four were **yeomen**, small farmers who owned their own land. As in the North, farm ownership provided a family with an economic foundation, social respectability, and political standing. Unlike their northern counterparts, however, southern yeomen lived in a region whose economy and society were increasingly dominated by unfree labor.

In an important sense, the South had more than one white yeomanry. The huge southern landscape provided space enough for two yeoman societies, separated roughly along geographical lines. Yeomen throughout the South had much in common, but the life of a small farm family in the plantation belt—the flatlands that spread from South Carolina to east Texas—differed from the life of one in the upcountry—the area of hills and mountains.

Plantation Belt Yeomen

Plantation belt yeomen lived within the orbit of the planter class. Small farms actually outnumbered plantations in that great arc of fertile cotton land that spread from South Carolina to Texas, but they were dwarfed in importance. Small farmers grew mainly food crops, particularly corn, but they also devoted a portion of their land to cotton. With only family labor to draw upon, they produced only a few 400-pound bales each year, whereas large planters measured their crop in

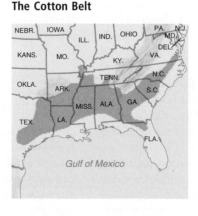

The Cotton Belt

hundreds of bales. The small farmers' cotton tied them to planters. Unable to afford cotton gins or baling presses of their own, they relied on helpful neighborhood slave owners to gin and bale their small crops. With no link to merchants in the port cities, plantation belt yeomen turned to better-connected planters to ship and sell their cotton.

A dense network of relationships laced small farmers and planters together in patterns of reciprocity and mutual obligation. Planters hired out surplus slaves to ambitious yeomen who wanted to expand cotton production. They sometimes chose overseers from among the sons of local farm families. Plantation mistresses sometimes nursed ailing neighbors. Family ties could span class lines, making rich and poor kin as well as neighbors. On Sundays, plantation dwellers and plain folk came together in church to worship and afterward lingered to gossip and to transact small business.

Plantation belt yeomen may have envied, and at times even resented, wealthy slaveholders, but in general small farmers learned to accommodate. Planters made accommodation easier by going out of their way to provide necessary services, behave as good neighbors, and avoid direct exploitation of slaveless whites in their community. As a consequence, rather than raging at the oppression of the planter regime, the typical plantation belt yeoman sought entry into it. He dreamed of adding acreage to his farm, buying a few slaves of his own, and retiring from exhausting fieldwork.

Upcountry Yeomen

By contrast, the hills and mountains of the South resisted the penetration of slavery and plantations. In the western parts of Virginia, North Carolina, and South Carolina, northern Georgia and Alabama, and eastern Tennessee and Kentucky, the higher elevation, colder climate, rugged terrain, and poor transportation made it difficult for commercial agriculture to make headway. As a result, yeomen dominated these isolated areas, and planters and slaves were scarce.

At the core of this distinctive upcountry society was the independent farm family working its own patch of land;

Upcountry of the South

raising hogs, cattle, and sheep; and seeking self-sufficiency and independence. Toward that end, all members of the family worked, their tasks depending on their sex and age. Husbands labored in the fields, and with their sons they cleared, plowed, planted, and cultivated primarily food crops. Although pressed into field labor at harvest time, wives and daughters of upcountry yeomen, like those of plantation belt yeomen, worked in and about the cabin most of the year. One upcountry farmer remembered that his mother "worked in the house cooking, spinning, weaving [and doing] patchwork." Women also tended the vegetable garden, kept a cow and some chickens, preserved foods, cleaned their homes, fed their families, and cared for their children. Male and female tasks were equally crucial to the farm's success, but as in other white southern households, the domestic sphere was subordinated to the will of the male patriarch.

The typical upcountry yeoman also grew a little cotton or tobacco, but production for home consumption was more important than production for the market. Not much currency changed hands in the upcountry. Barter was common. A yeoman might trade his cotton or tobacco to a country storeowner for a little salt, lead shot, needles, and nails. Or he might swap extra sweet potatoes with the blacksmith for a plow or with the tanner for leather. Networks of exchange and mutual assistance tied individual homesteads to the larger community. Farm families also joined together in logrolling, house- and barn-raising, and cornhusking.

Yeomen did not have the upcountry entirely to themselves. Even the hills had some plantations and slaves. But most upcountry counties were less than a quarter black, whereas counties in the plantation belt were more than half black. As a result, slaveholders had much less direct social and economic power, and yeomen had more. But yeoman domination did not mean that the upcountry opposed slavery. Yeomen there, like yeomen in the plantation belt, shared the planters' commitment to white supremacy and actively defended black subordination. In rural counties, nonslaveholding white men rode in slave patrols, which nightly scoured country roads for slaves who should have been in the quarter.

The Culture of the Plain Folk

Not all nonslaveholding farmers were yeomen who owned their own land. Perhaps one in four was landless and very poor. Some lived as tenants, renting land and struggling to make a go of it. Others strained to make a living by herding pigs and cattle or working as unskilled day laborers. Poor white men gained a reputation for unruly behavior and spontaneous violence. One visitor claimed that a "bowie-knife was a universal, and a pistol a not at all unusual companion." But most landless whites were ambitious people scratching to climb into the yeomanry. Many succeeded, but in the 1850s social mobility slowed. Profits from cotton allowed rich planters to expand their operations, often driving the price of land beyond the reach of poor families. Still, landless whites shared common cultural traits with yeoman farmers.

Situated on scattered farms and in tiny villages, rural plain folk lived isolated, local lives. Bad roads and a lack of newspapers meant that everyday life revolved around family, a handful of neighbors, the local church, and perhaps a country store. Work occupied most hours, but

plain folk still found time for pleasure. "Dancing they are all fond of," a visitor to North Carolina discovered, "especially when they can get a fiddle, or bagpipe." They also loved their tobacco. One visitor complained that the "use of tobacco is almost universal." Men smoked and chewed (and spat), while women dipped snuff. But the truly universal pastimes among men and boys were fishing and hunting. A traveler in Mississippi recalled that his host sent "two of his sons, little fellows that looked almost too small to shoulder a gun," for food. "One went off towards the river and the other struck into the forest, and in a few hours we were feasting on delicious venison, trout and turtle."

Plain folk did not usually associate "book learning" with the basic needs of life. A northern woman visiting the South in the 1850s observed, "Education is not extended to the masses here as at the North." Private academies charged fees that yeomen could not afford, and public schools were scarce. Although most people managed to pick up a basic knowledge of the "three R's," approximately one southern white man in five was illiterate in 1860, and the rate for white women was even higher. "People here prefer talking to reading," a Virginian remarked. Telling stories, reciting ballads, and singing hymns were important activities in yeoman culture.

Plain folk everywhere spent more hours in revival tents than in classrooms. Not all rural whites were religious, but many were, and the most characteristic feature of their evangelical Christian faith was the revival. The greatest of the early-nineteenth-century revivals occurred in 1801 at Cane Ridge, Kentucky, where some 20,000 people gathered to listen to a host of evangelical preachers who spoke day and night for a week. Ministers sought to save souls by bringing individuals to a personal conviction of sin. Revivalism crossed denominational lines, but Baptists and Methodists adopted it most readily and by midcentury had become the South's largest religious groups. By emphasizing free choice and individual worth, the plain folk's religion was hopeful and affirming. Hymns and spirituals provided guides to right and wrong—praising humility and steadfastness, condemning drunkenness and profanity.

A Baptising on the South Branch of the Potomac near Franklin, Virginia **(detail), 1844**
In 1844, noted painter William Thompson Russell Smith undertook a geological expedition to Virginia, and there he encountered a rural baptism. Primarily a landscape painter, Smith portrayed the human figures as minor characters. If one of the participants had sketched the baptism, he or she might have emphasized the human drama, the emotional pitch of what was for evangelical Christians throughout the South a profound religious moment.
The Charleston Renaissance Gallery, Robert M. Hicklin Jr., Inc., Charleston, South Carolina.

Above all, hymns spoke of eventual release from worldly sorrows and the assurance of eternal salvation.

> **REVIEW** Why did yeomen dominate the upcountry?

The Politics of Slavery

By the mid-nineteenth century, all southern white men—planters and plain folk alike—had gained the vote. But even after the South's politics became **democratic** for the white male population, political power remained unevenly distributed. The nonslaveholding white majority wielded less political power than their numbers indicated. The slaveholding white minority wielded more. Self-conscious, cohesive, and with a well-developed sense of class interest, slaveholders busied themselves with party politics, campaigns, and officeholding and made demands of state governments. As a result, they received significant benefits. Nonslaveholding whites were concerned mainly with preserving their liberties and keeping their taxes low. Collectively, they asked government for little of an economic nature, and they received little.

Slaveholders sometimes worried about non-slaveholders' loyalty to slavery, but since the eighteenth century, the majority of whites had accepted the planters' argument that the existing social order served all Southerners' interests. Slavery rewarded every white man—no matter how poor—with membership in the South's white ruling class. It also provided the means by which nonslaveholders might someday advance into the ranks of the planters. White men in the South fought furiously about many things, but they agreed that they should take land from Indians, promote agriculture, uphold white supremacy and masculine privilege, and defend slavery from its enemies.

The Democratization of the Political Arena

The political reforms that swept the nation in the first half of the nineteenth century reached deeply into the South. Southern politics became democratic politics—for white men. Southerners eliminated the wealth and property requirements

that had once restricted political participation. By the early 1850s, every state had extended **suffrage** to all adult white males. Most southern states also removed the property requirements for holding state offices. To be sure, undemocratic features lingered. Plantation districts still wielded disproportionate power in several state legislatures. Nevertheless, southern politics took place within an increasingly democratic political structure.

White male suffrage ushered in an era of vigorous electoral competition. Eager voters rushed to the polls to exercise their new rights. High turnouts—often approaching 80 percent—became a hallmark of southern electoral politics. As politics became aggressively democratic, it also grew fiercely partisan. From the 1830s to the 1850s, Whigs and Democrats battled for the electorate's favor. In the South, both parties presented themselves as the plain white folk's best friend. All candidates declared their fervent commitment to **republican** equality and pledged to defend the people's liberty. Each party sought to portray the other as a collection of rich, snobbish, selfish men who had antidemocratic designs up their silk sleeves. Each, in turn, claimed for itself the mantle of humble "servant of the people."

Planter Power

Whether Whig or Democrat, southern office-holders were likely to be slave owners. The power slaveholders exerted over slaves did not translate directly into political authority over whites, however. In the nineteenth century, political power could be won only at the ballot box, and almost everywhere nonslaveholders were in the majority. Yet year after year, proud and noisily egalitarian common men elected wealthy slaveholders (Table 13.1).

By 1860, the percentage of slave owners in state legislatures ranged from 41 percent in Missouri to nearly 86 percent in North Carolina. Legislators not only tended to own slaves—they often owned large numbers. The percentage of planters (individuals with twenty or more slaves) in southern legislatures in 1860 ranged from 5.3 percent in Missouri to 55.4 percent in South Carolina. In North Carolina, where only 3 percent of the state's white families belonged to the planter class, more than 36 percent of the legislature were planters. The democratization of politics in the nineteenth century meant that

TABLE 13.1	PERCENT OF SLAVEHOLDERS AND PLANTERS IN SOUTHERN LEGISLATURES, 1860	
Legislature	Slaveholders	Planters*
Virginia	67.3%	24.2%
Maryland	53.4	19.3
North Carolina	85.8	36.6
Kentucky	60.6	8.4
Tennessee	66.0	14.0
Missouri	41.2	5.3
Arkansas	42.0	13.0
South Carolina	81.7	55.4
Georgia	71.6	29.0
Florida	55.4	20.0
Alabama	76.3	40.8
Mississippi	73.4	49.5
Louisiana	63.8	23.5
Texas	54.1	18.1

*Planters: Owned 20 or more slaves.

Source: Adapted from Ralph A. Wooster, The People in Power: Courthouse and Statehouse in the Lower South, 1850–1860 (1969), 41; Wooster, Politicians, Planters, and Plain Folks: Courthouse and Statehouse in the Upper South (1975), 40. Courtesy of the University of Tennessee Press.

more ordinary citizens participated in elections, but yeomen and artisans remained rare sights in the halls of southern legislatures.

Upper-class dominance of southern politics reflected the elite's success in persuading the white majority that what was good for slaveholders was also good for them. In reality, the South had, on the whole, done well by the plain folk. Most had farms of their own. They participated as equals in a democratic political system. They enjoyed an elevated social status, above all blacks and in theory equal to all other whites. They commanded patriarchal authority over their households. And as long as slavery existed, they could dream of joining the planter class. Slaveless white men found much to celebrate in the slave South.

Most slaveholders took pains to win the plain folk's trust and to nurture their respect. One South Carolinian told his wealthy neighbor that he had a bright political future because he never thought himself "too good to sit down & talk to a poor man." South Carolinian Mary Boykin Chesnut complained about the fawning attention her slaveholding husband showed to poor men, including one who had "mud sticking up through his toes." Smart candidates found ways to convince wary plain folk of their democratic convictions and egalitarian sentiments,

whether they were genuine or not. When young John A. Quitman ran for a seat in the Mississippi legislature, he amazed a boisterous crowd of small farmers at one campaign stop by not only entering but winning contests in jumping, boxing, wrestling, and sprinting. For his finale he outshot the area's champion marksman. Then, demonstrating his deft political touch, he gave his prize, a fat ox, to the defeated rifleman. The electorate showed its approval by sending Quitman to the state capital.

Georgia politics illustrate how well planters protected their interests in state legislatures. In 1850, about half of the state's revenues came from taxes on slaves, the characteristic form of planter wealth. However, the tax rate on slaves was trifling, only about one-fifth the rate on land. Moreover, planters benefited far more than other groups from public spending. Financing railroads—which carried cotton to market—was the largest state expenditure. The legislature also established low tax rates on land, the characteristic form of yeoman wealth, which meant that the typical yeoman's annual tax bill was small. Still, relative to their wealth, large slaveholders paid less than did other whites. Relative to their numbers, they got more in return. A sympathetic slaveholding legislature protected planters' interests and gave the impression of protecting the small farmers' interests as well.

The South's elite defended slavery in other ways. In the 1830s, whites decided that slavery was too important to debate. "So interwoven is [slavery] with our interest, our manners, our climate and our very being," one man declared in 1833, "that no change can ever possibly be effected without a civil commotion from which the heart of a patriot must turn with horror." To end free speech on the slavery question, powerful whites dismissed slavery's critics from college faculties, drove them from pulpits, and hounded them from political life. Sometimes antislavery Southerners fell victim to vigilantes and mob violence. One could defend slavery; one could even delicately suggest mild reforms. But no Southerner could any longer safely call slavery evil or advocate its destruction.

In the South, therefore, the rise of the common man occurred alongside the continuing, even growing, power of the planter class. Rather than pitting slaveholders against nonslaveholders, elections remained an effective means of binding the region's whites together. Elections affirmed the sovereignty of white men, whether planter or plain folk, and the subordination of African Americans. Those twin themes played well among white women as well. Although unable to vote, white women supported equality for whites and slavery for blacks. In the antebellum South, the politics of slavery helped knit together all of white society.

> **REVIEW** How did planters benefit from their control of state legislatures?

Conclusion: A Slave Society

By the early nineteenth century, northern states had either abolished slavery or put it on the road to extinction while southern states were aggressively building the largest slave society in the New World. Regional differences increased over time, not merely because the South became more and more dominated by slavery, but also because developments in the North rapidly propelled it in a very different direction.

One-third of the South's population was enslaved by 1860. Bondage saddled blacks with enormous physical and spiritual burdens: hard labor, harsh treatment, broken families, and most important, the denial of freedom itself. Although degraded and exploited, they were not defeated. Out of African memories and New World realities, blacks created a life-affirming African American culture that sustained and strengthened them. Their families, religion, and community provided antidotes to white racist ideas and even to white power. Defined as property, they refused to be reduced to things. Perceived as inferior beings, they rejected the notion that they were natural slaves. Slaves engaged in a war of wills with masters who sought their labor while the slaves sought to live dignified, autonomous lives.

By the mid-nineteenth century, slavery was crucial to the South's distinctiveness and to the loyalty and regional identification of its whites. The South was not merely a society with slaves; it had become a slave society: Slavery shaped the region's economy, culture, social structure, and politics. Whites south of the Mason-Dixon line believed that racial slavery was necessary and just.

By making all blacks a pariah class, all whites gained a measure of equality and harmony.

Racism did not erase stress along class lines. Nor did the other features of southern life that helped confine class tensions: the wide availability of land, rapid economic mobility, the democratic nature of political life, and patriarchal power among white men. Anxious slaveholders continued to worry that yeomen would defect from the proslavery consensus. But during the 1850s, a far more ominous division emerged—between "slave states" and "free states."

Suggestions for Further Reading

Ira Berlin, *Generations of Captivity: A History of African-American Slaves* (2003). A modern synthesis of the slave experience that emphasizes geographical diversity and change over time.

Drew G. Faust, *James Henry Hammond and the Old South: A Design for Mastery* (1982). A lively biography of one of the South's most compelling planter/politicians.

Peter Kolchin, *American Slavery, 1619-1877* (1993). A masterful survey of the historiography of slavery and reflection upon slavery's meaning for southern history.

Stephanie McCurry, *Masters of Small Worlds: Yeoman Households, Gender Relations, and the Political Culture of the Antebellum South* (1995). An insightful analysis of yeoman households that argues the centrality of patriarchy to southern politics.

Willie Lee Rose, ed., *A Documentary History of Slavery in North America* (1976). A collection of contemporary documents that vividly illustrates slaves' responses to bondage.

Adam Rothman, *Slave Country: American Expansion and the Deep South* (2005). A dramatic account of how and why slavery spread west from the original coastal southern states.

> ► For more books about topics in this chapter, see the Online Bibliography at bedfordstmartins.com/roarkcompact.

> ► For additional firsthand accounts of this period, see Chapter 13 in Michael Johnson, ed., *Reading the American Past*, Third Edition.

> ► For Web sites and documents related to topics and places in this chapter, see "HistoryLinks," "DocLinks," and "PlaceLinks" at bedfordstmartins.com/roarkcompact.

REVIEWING THE CHAPTER

Follow these steps to review and strengthen your understanding of the chapter.
STEP 1: *Study the* **Key Terms** *and* **Timeline** *to identify the significance of each item listed.*
STEP 2: *Answer the* **Review Questions***, drawing on key terms and dates to support your answers.*
STEP 3: *Drawing on the Key Terms, Timeline, and Review Questions, answer the broader* **Making Connections** *questions.*

KEY TERMS

Who

Nat Turner (p. 315)
David Walker (p. 315)
William Lloyd Garrison (p. 315)
Eli Whitney (p. 321)
Mary Boykin Chesnut (p. 328)
Charles Colcock Jones (p. 331)
Denmark Vesey (p. 332)
William Ellison (p. 334)

What

Nat Turner's insurrection (p. 315)
Mason-Dixon line (p. 316)
Creek War of 1813–1814 (p. 316)
cotton kingdom (p. 317)
slave codes (p. 317)
planter (p. 321)
plantation (p. 321)
overseer (p. 323)
paternalism (p. 323)

miscegenation (p. 324)
chivalry (p. 324)
slave driver (p. 330)
slave resistance (p. 332)
Vesey conspiracy (p. 332)
"free black" (p. 333)
emancipation (p. 333)
yeomen (p. 334)
plantation belt (p. 334)
upcountry (p. 335)

TIMELINE

◀ **1808** • External slave trade outlawed.

1810s–1850s • Suffrage extended throughout South to white males.

1813–1814 • Creek War opens Indian land to settlement.

1820s–1830s • Southern legislatures enact slave codes to strengthen slavery.
• Southern legislatures enact laws to restrict growth of free black population.
• Southern intellectuals begin to fashion systematic defense of slavery.

1820–1860 • Cotton production soars.

1822 • Denmark Vesey executed.

1829 • *Appeal ... to the Coloured Citizens of the World* published.

1830 • Southern slaves number approximately 2 million.

REVIEW QUESTIONS

1. Why did the nineteenth-century southern economy remain primarily agricultural while the northern economy grew increasingly diversified? (pp. 316–22)

2. Why did the ideology of paternalism gain currency among planters in the nineteenth century? (pp. 322–28)

3. Why did slave resistance rarely take the form of rebellion? (pp. 329–32)

4. Why did many state legislatures pass laws restricting free blacks' freedoms in the 1820s and 1830s? (pp. 332–34)

5. Why did yeomen dominate the upcountry? (pp. 334–37)

6. How did planters benefit from their control of state legislatures? (pp. 337–39)

MAKING CONNECTIONS

1. By the mid-nineteenth century the South had become a "cotton kingdom." How did cotton's profitability shape the region's antebellum development? In your answer, discuss the region's distinctive demographic and economic features.

2. How did white southern legislators and intellectuals attempt to strengthen the institution of slavery in the 1820s? What prompted them to undertake this work? In your answer, be sure to explore regional and national influences.

3. Although bondage restricted slaves' autonomy and left slaves vulnerable to extreme abuse, they resisted slavery. Discuss the variety of ways in which slaves attempted to lessen the harshness of slavery. What were the short- and long-term effects of their efforts?

4. Despite vigorous political competition in the South, by 1860, legislative power was largely concentrated in the hands of a regional minority—slaveholders. Why were slaveholders politically dominant? In your answer, be sure to consider how the region's biracialism contributed to its politics.

► For practice quizzes, a customized study plan, and other study tools, see the Online Study Guide at bedfordstmartins.com/roarkcompact.

1831 • Nat Turner's slave rebellion.
• First issue of *Liberator* published.

    1834 • *Catechism for Colored Persons* published.

        1836 • Arkansas admitted to the Union as a slave state.

           1840 • Cotton accounts for more than 60 percent of the nation's exports.

                1845 • Texas and Florida admitted to the Union as slave states.

1860
• Southern slaves number nearly 4 million, one-third of the South's population.

JOHN BROWN'S PIKES

Scorning what he called "milk-and-water" abolitionists who only talked about slavery, John Brown favored "action!" In 1859 when he brought his abolitionist war to Virginia, he carried with him 950 pikes, handsome but deadly spears made by a Connecticut blacksmith, which he expected to put into the hands of rebelling slaves. Bloody pikes, he thought, would end slavery in America. After Brown's failure at Harpers Ferry, townspeople sold many of the weapons as souvenirs.

Chicago Historical Society.

14

The House Divided

1846–1861

OTHER THAN TWENTY CHILDREN, John Brown did not have much to show for his life in 1859. Grizzled, gnarled, and fifty-nine years old, he had for decades lived like a nomad, hauling his large family back and forth across six states as he tried desperately to better himself. He turned his hand to farming, raising sheep, running a tannery, and selling wool, but failure dogged him. The world had given John Brown some hard licks, but it had not budged his conviction that slavery was wrong and ought to be destroyed. He had learned to hate slavery at his father's knee, and in the wake of the fighting that erupted over the issue in Kansas in the 1850s, his beliefs turned violent. On May 24, 1856, he led an eight-man antislavery posse in the midnight slaughter of five allegedly proslavery men at Pottawatomie, Kansas. He told Mahala Doyle, whose husband and two oldest sons he killed, that if a man stood between him and what he thought right, he would take that man's life as calmly as he would eat breakfast.

After the killings, Brown slipped out of Kansas and reemerged in the East. More than ever, he was a man on fire for abolition. He spent thirty months begging money from New Englanders to support his vague plan for military operations against slavery. He captivated the genteel easterners, particularly the Boston elite. They were awed by his iron-willed determination and courage, but most could not accept violence. "These men are all talk," Brown declared. "What is needed is action—action!" But the hypnotic-eyed Brown convinced a handful that God had touched him for a great purpose, and they donated enough for him to gather a small band of antislavery warriors.

On the night of October 16, 1859, John Brown took his war against slavery into the South. With only twenty-one men, including five African Americans, he invaded Harpers Ferry, Virginia. His band quickly seized the town's armory and rifle works, but the invaders were immediately surrounded, first by local militia and then by Colonel Robert E. Lee, who commanded the U.S. troops in the area. When Brown refused to surrender, federal soldiers charged with bayonets. Seventeen men, two of whom were slaves, lost their lives. Although a few of Brown's raiders escaped, federal forces killed ten (including two of his sons) and captured seven, among them Brown.

"When I strike, the bees will begin to swarm," Brown told Frederick Douglass a few months before the raid. As slaves rushed to Harpers Ferry, Brown planned to arm them with the pikes he carried with him and with weapons stolen from the armory. They would then fight a war of liberation. Brown, however, neglected to inform the slaves that he had arrived in Harpers Ferry, and the few who knew of his arrival wanted nothing to do with his enterprise. "It was not a slave insurrection," Abraham Lincoln observed. "It was an attempt by white men to get up a revolt among slaves, in

John Brown

In this 1859 photograph, John Brown appears respectable, even statesmanlike, but contemporaries debated his mental state and moral character, and the debate still rages. Critics argue that he was a bloody terrorist, a religious fanatic who believed that he was touched by God for a great purpose, one for which he was willing to die. Admirers see a resolute and selfless hero, a rare white man who believed that black people were the equals of whites, a reformer who recognized that moral suasion would not end slavery in America.

National Portrait Gallery, Smithsonian Institution / Art Resource, NY.

which the slaves refused to participate. In fact, it was so absurd that the slaves, with all their ignorance, saw plainly enough it could not succeed."

Although Brown's raid ended in utter defeat, white Southerners viewed it as proof of their growing suspicion that Northerners actively sought to incite slaves in bloody rebellion. For more than a decade, Northerners and Southerners had accused one another of hostile intentions, and by 1859, emotions were raw. Sectional tension was as old as the Constitution, but hostility had escalated with the outbreak of war with Mexico in May 1846 (see chapter 12). Only three months after the war began, national expansion and the slavery issue intersected when Representative David Wilmot introduced a bill to prohibit slavery from any territory that might be acquired as a result of the war. After that, the problem of slavery in the territories became the principal wedge that divided the nation.

"Mexico is to us the forbidden fruit," South Carolina senator John C. Calhoun declared at the war's outset. "The penalty of eating it [is] to subject our institutions to political death." For a decade and a half, the slavery issue intertwined with the fate of former Mexican land, poisoning national political debate. Slavery proved powerful enough to transform party politics into sectional politics. Rather than Whigs and Democrats confronting one another across party lines, Northerners and Southerners eyed one another hostilely across the Mason-Dixon line. Sectional politics encouraged the South's separatist impulses. A fitful tendency before the Mexican-American War, southern separatism gained strength with each confrontation. As the nation lurched from crisis to crisis, southern disaffection and alienation mounted, and support for compromise and conciliation eroded. The era began with a crisis of Union and ended with the Union in even graver peril. As Abraham Lincoln predicted in 1858, "A house divided against itself cannot stand."

The Bitter Fruits of War

Between 1846 and 1848, the nation grew by 1.2 million square miles, an incredible two-thirds. By 1850, the gold rush had transformed the sleepy **frontier** of California into a booming, thriving economy (see chapter 12). The 1850s witnessed new "rushes," for gold in Colorado and silver in Nevada's Comstock Lode. People from around the world flocked to the West where they produced a vibrant agriculture as well as tons of gold and silver. But it quickly became clear that Northerners and Southerners had very different visions of the West, particularly the place of slavery in its future.

History provided contradictory precedents for handling slavery in the territories. In 1787, the Northwest Ordinance banned slavery north of the Ohio River. In 1803, slavery was allowed to remain in the newly acquired Louisiana Territory. The Missouri Compromise of 1820 prohibited slavery in part of that territory but allowed it in the rest. In 1846, when the war with Mexico suggested new territory for the United States, politicians offered various plans. But when the war ended in 1848, Congress had made no headway in solving the issue of slavery in the western territories. In 1850, Congress patched together a settlement, one that Americans hoped would be permanent.

The Wilmot Proviso and the Expansion of Slavery

Most Americans agreed that the Constitution had left the issue of slavery to the individual states to decide. Northern states had done away with slavery, while southern states had retained it. But what about slavery in the nation's territories? The Constitution states that "Congress shall have power to…make all needful rules and regulations respecting the territory…belonging to the United States." The debate about slavery, then, turned toward Congress.

In August 1846 the young Democratic representative from Pennsylvania, David Wilmot, proposed that Congress bar slavery from all lands acquired in the war with Mexico. The Mexicans had already abolished slavery in their country, and Wilmot declared, "God forbid that we should be the means of planting this institution upon it."

Regardless of party affiliation, Northerners lined up behind Wilmot's proviso. Many supported **free soil**, by which they meant territory from which slavery would be prohibited, on the basis of egalitarian principle. They wanted to preserve the West for **free labor**, for hard-working, self-reliant free men, not for slaveholders and slaves. But support also came from those who were simply anti-South. New slave territories would eventually mean new slave states, and they opposed magnifying the political power of Southerners. Wilmot himself said he saw his proposal as a means of blunting "the *power* of slaveholders" in the national government.

Additional support for free soil came from Northerners who were hostile to blacks and wanted to reserve new lands for whites. Wilmot understood what one Indiana man put bluntly: "The American people are emphatically a *Negro-hating* people." Wilmot himself blatantly encouraged racist support when he declared, "I would preserve for free white labor a fair country, a rich inheritance, where the sons of toil, of my own race and own color, can live without the disgrace which association with negro slavery brings upon free labor." It is no wonder that some called the Wilmot Proviso the White Man's Proviso.

The thought that slavery might be excluded outraged almost all white Southerners. They regarded the West as a ladder for economic and social opportunity. They also believed that the exclusion of slavery was a slap in the face to southern veterans of the Mexican-American War. "When the war-worn soldier returns home," one Alabaman asked, "is he to be told that he cannot carry his property to the country won by his blood?"

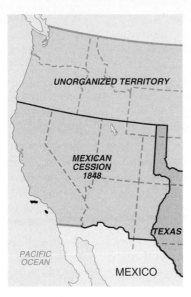

Mexican Cession, 1848

In addition, southern leaders understood the need for political parity with the North to protect the South's interests, especially slavery. James Henry Hammond of South Carolina predicted that ten new states would be carved from the acquired Mexican land. If free soil won, the North would "ride over us rough shod" in Congress, he claimed. "Our only safety is in *equality* of POWER."

The two sides squared off in the nation's capital. Because Northerners had a majority in the House, they easily passed the Wilmot Proviso. In the Senate, however, where slave states outnumbered free states fifteen to fourteen, Southerners defeated it. Senator John C. Calhoun of South Carolina denied that Congress had constitutional authority to

John C. Calhoun
Hollow-cheeked and dark-eyed in this 1850 daguerreotype by Mathew Brady, Calhoun had only months to live. Still, his passion and indomitable will come through. British writer Harriet Martineau once described the champion of southern rights as "the cast-iron man who looks as if he had never been born and could never be extinguished."
National Portrait Gallery, Smithsonian Institution / Art Resource, NY.

exclude slavery from the nation's territories. He argued that Congress could not justly deprive any state of equal rights in the territories and therefore could not bar citizens of one state from migrating with their property (including slaves) to the territories. Whereas Wilmot demanded that Congress slam shut the door to slavery, Calhoun called on Congress to hold the door wide open.

Senator Lewis Cass of Michigan offered a compromise through the doctrine of **popular sovereignty**, by which the people who settled the territories would decide for themselves slavery's fate. This solution, Cass argued, sat squarely in the American tradition of **democracy** and local self-government. It had the added attraction of removing the incendiary issue of the expansion of slavery from the nation's capital.

Popular sovereignty's most attractive feature was its ambiguity about the precise moment when settlers could determine slavery's fate. Northern advocates believed that the decision on slavery could be made as soon as the first territorial legislature assembled. With free-soil majorities likely because of the North's greater population, they would shut the door to slavery almost before the first slave arrived. Southern supporters declared that popular sovereignty guaranteed that slavery would be unrestricted throughout the entire territorial period. Only at the very end, when settlers in the territory drew up a constitution and applied for statehood, could they decide the issue of slavery. By then, slavery would have sunk deep roots. As long as the matter of timing remained vague, popular sovereignty gave hope to both sides.

When Congress ended its session in 1848, no plan had won a majority in both houses. Northerners who demanded no new slave territory anywhere, ever, and Southerners who demanded entry for their slave property into all territories, or else, staked out their extreme positions. Unresolved in Congress, the territorial question naturally became an issue in the presidential election of 1848.

The Election of 1848

When President Polk—worn out and ailing—chose not to seek reelection, the Democratic convention nominated Lewis Cass of Michigan, the man most closely associated with popular sovereignty. But in an effort to keep peace between their proslavery and antislavery factions, the Democrats adopted a platform that avoided a firm position on slavery in the territories. The

Whigs followed a different strategy and nominated a Mexican-American War hero, General Zachary Taylor. The Whigs bet that the combination of a military hero and total silence on the slavery issue would carry the day, and thus they declined to adopt a party platform. Taylor, who owned more than 100 slaves on plantations in Mississippi and Louisiana, was hailed by Georgia politician Robert Toombs as a "Southern man, a slaveholder, a cotton planter."

Antislavery Whigs balked and looked for an alternative. The time seemed ripe for a major political realignment. Senator Charles Sumner called for "one grand Northern party of Freedom," and in the summer of 1848 antislavery Whigs and antislavery Democrats founded the Free-Soil Party. Nearly 15,000 noisy Free-Soilers gathered in Buffalo, New York, where they nominated a Democrat, Martin Van Buren, for president and a Whig, Charles Francis Adams, for vice president. The platform boldly proclaimed, "Free soil, free speech, free labor, and free men."

The November election dashed the hopes of the Free-Soilers. Although they succeeded in making slavery the campaign's central issue, they did not carry a single state. The major parties went through contortions to present their candidates favorably in both North and South, and their evasions succeeded. Taylor won the all-important electoral vote, 163 to 127, carrying eight of the fifteen slave states and seven of the fifteen free states (Map 14.1). (Wisconsin had entered the Union earlier in 1848 as the fifteenth free state.) Northern voters proved they were not yet ready for Sumner's "one grand Northern party of Freedom," but the struggle over slavery in the territories had shaken the major parties badly.

Debate and Compromise

Southern slaveholder Zachary Taylor entered the White House in March 1849 and almost immediately shocked the nation by championing a free-soil solution to the Mexican cession. Believing that he could avoid further sectional strife if California and New Mexico skipped the territorial stage, he sent agents west to persuade the settlers to apply for admission to the Union as states. Predominately antislavery, the settlers began writing free-state constitutions. "For the first time," Mississippian Jefferson Davis

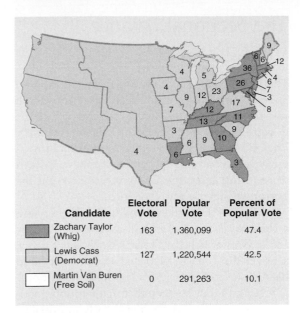

Candidate	Electoral Vote	Popular Vote	Percent of Popular Vote
Zachary Taylor (Whig)	163	1,360,099	47.4
Lewis Cass (Democrat)	127	1,220,544	42.5
Martin Van Buren (Free Soil)	0	291,263	10.1

MAP 14.1 The Election of 1848
When Congress convened in December 1849, anxious citizens packed the galleries, eager for the "Great Debate." They witnessed what proved to be one of the longest, most contentious, and most significant sessions in the history of Congress.

lamented, "we are about permanently to destroy the balance of power between the sections."

Congress convened in December 1849, beginning one of the most contentious and most significant sessions in its history. President Taylor urged Congress to admit California as a free state immediately and to admit New Mexico, which lagged behind a few months, as soon as it applied. Southerners exploded. In their eyes, Taylor had betrayed his region. Southerners who would "consent to be thus degraded and enslaved," a North Carolinian declared, "ought to be whipped through their fields by their own negroes."

In stepped Senator Henry Clay of Kentucky, the architect of Union-saving compromises in the Missouri and **nullification** crises. Clay offered a series of resolutions meant to answer and balance "all questions in controversy between the free and slave states, growing out of the subject of slavery." Admit California as a free state, he proposed, but organize the rest of the Southwest without restrictions on slavery. Require Texas to abandon its claim to parts of New Mexico, but compensate it by assuming its preannexation debt. Abolish the domestic slave trade in Washington, D.C., but confirm slavery itself in the nation's capital. Reassert Congress's lack of authority to interfere with the interstate

slave trade. And enact a more effective fugitive slave law.

Both antislavery advocates and "fire-eaters" (as radical Southerners who urged secession from the Union were called) savaged Clay's plan. Senator Salmon Chase of Ohio ridiculed it as "sentiment for the North, substance for the South." Senator Henry S. Foote of Mississippi denounced it as more offensive to the South than the speeches of abolitionists William Lloyd Garrison, Wendell Phillips, and Frederick Douglass combined. The most ominous response came from Calhoun, who argued that the fragile political unity of North and South depended on continued equal representation in the Senate, which Clay's plan for a free California destroyed. "As things now stand," he said in February 1850, the South "cannot with safety remain in the Union."

Senator Daniel Webster of Massachusetts then addressed the Senate. Like Clay, Webster sought to build a constituency for compromise. He appealed for an end to reckless proposals and, to the dismay of many Northerners, mentioned by name the Wilmot Proviso. A legal ban on slavery in the territories was unnecessary, he said, because the harsh climate effectively prohibited the expansion of cotton and slaves into the new American Southwest.

Free-soil forces recoiled from what they saw as Webster's desertion. In Boston, the clergyman and abolitionist Theodore Parker could only conclude that "the Southern men" must have offered Webster the presidency. In Washington, Senator William H. Seward of New York responded that Webster's and Clay's compromise with slavery was "radically wrong and essentially vicious." He flatly rejected Calhoun's argument that Congress lacked constitutional authority to exclude slavery from the territories. In any case, Seward said, in the most sensational moment in his address, there was a "higher law than the Constitution"—the law of God—to ensure freedom in all the public domain. Claiming that God was a Free-Soiler did nothing to cool the superheated political atmosphere.

In May, a Senate committee produced a bill that joined Clay's resolutions into a single comprehensive package, known as the Omnibus Bill because it was a vehicle on which "every sort of passenger" could ride. Clay bet that a majority of Congress wanted compromise and that each member would vote for the package to gain an overall settlement of sectional issues. But the omnibus strategy backfired. Free-Soilers and proslavery Southerners voted down the comprehensive plan.

Fortunately for those who favored a settlement, Senator Stephen A. Douglas, a rising Democratic star from Illinois, stepped in. He broke the bill into its various parts and skillfully ushered each through Congress. The agreement Douglas won in September 1850 was very much the one Clay had proposed in January. California entered the Union as a free state. New Mexico and Utah became territories where slavery would be decided by popular sovereignty. Texas accepted its boundary with New Mexico and received $10 million from the federal government. Congress ended the slave trade in the District of Columbia but enacted a more stringent fugitive slave law. In September, Millard Fillmore, who had become president when Zachary Taylor died suddenly in July, signed into law each bill, collectively known as the Compromise of 1850 (Map 14.2).

Actually, the Compromise of 1850 was not a true compromise at all. Douglas's parliamentary skill, not a spirit of conciliation, was responsible for the legislative success. Still, the nation breathed a sigh of relief, for the Compromise preserved the Union and peace for the moment.

> **REVIEW**   Why did response to the Wilmot Proviso split along sectional rather than party lines?

The Sectional Balance Undone

The Compromise of 1850 began to come apart almost immediately. The thread that unraveled it was not slavery in the Southwest, the crux of the disagreement, but runaway slaves in New England, a part of the settlement that had previously received relatively little attention. Instead of restoring calm, the Compromise brought the horrors of slavery into the North.

Millions of Northerners who had never seen a runaway slave confronted slavery in the early 1850s. Harriet Beecher Stowe's *Uncle Tom's Cabin*, a novel that vividly depicted the brutality and heartlessness of the South's "peculiar institution," aroused passions so deep that many found goodwill toward white Southerners nearly impossible. But no groundswell of antislavery sentiment compelled Congress to reopen the slavery controversy: Politicians did it themselves. Four years after Congress delicately stitched the sectional compromise together, it ripped the threads out. Once again it posed the question of slavery in the territories, the deadliest of all sectional issues.

The Fugitive Slave Act

The Fugitive Slave Act proved the most explosive of the Compromise measures. The issue of runaways was as old as the Constitution, which contained a provision for the return of any "person held to service or labor in one state" who escaped to another. In 1793, a federal law gave muscle to the provision by authorizing slave owners to enter other states to recapture their slave property. Proclaiming the 1793 law a license to kidnap free blacks, northern states in the 1830s began passing "personal liberty laws" that provided fugitives with some protection.

Some northern communities also formed vigilance committees to help runaways and to obstruct white Southerners who came north to reclaim them. Each year, a few hundred slaves escaped into free states and found friendly northern "conductors" who put them aboard the "underground railroad," which was not a railroad at all but a series of secret "stations" (hideouts) on the way to Canada. Harriet Tubman, an escaped slave from Maryland, returned to the South more

MAP 14.2   The Compromise of 1850
The patched-together sectional agreement was both clumsy and unstable. Few Americans—in either North or South—supported all five parts of the Compromise.

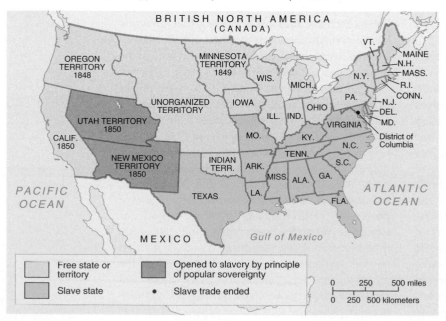

than a dozen times and guided more than 300 slaves to freedom in this way.

Furious about northern interference, Southerners in 1850 insisted on the stricter fugitive slave law that was passed as part of the Compromise. To seize an alleged slave, a slaveholder simply had to appear before a commissioner and swear that the runaway was his. The commissioner earned $10 for every black returned to slavery but only $5 for those set free. Most galling to Northerners, the law stipulated that all citizens were expected to assist officials in apprehending runaways.

In Boston in February 1851, an angry crowd overpowered federal marshals and snatched a runaway named Shadrach from a courtroom, put him on the underground railroad, and whisked him off to Canada. Three years later, when another Boston crowd rushed the courthouse in a failed attempt to rescue Anthony Burns, who had recently fled slavery in Richmond, a guard was shot dead. To white Southerners, it seemed that fanatics of the "higher law" creed had whipped Northerners into a frenzy of massive resistance. Such spectacular rescues were rare. The overwhelming majority of fugitives claimed before federal commissioners were reenslaved peacefully. But brutal enforcement of the unpopular law had a radicalizing effect in the North, particularly in New England. And to Southerners it seemed that Northerners had betrayed the Compromise. "The continued existence of the United States as one nation," warned the *Southern Literary Messenger,* "depends upon the full and faithful execution of the Fugitive Slave Bill."

Uncle Tom's Cabin

The spectacle of shackled African Americans being herded south seared the conscience of every Northerner who witnessed such a scene. But even more Northerners were turned against slavery by a fictional account, a novel. Harriet Beecher Stowe, a Northerner who had never seen a plantation, made the South's slaves into flesh-and-blood human beings almost more real than life.

A member of a famous clan of preachers, teachers, and reformers, Stowe despised the slave catchers and wrote to expose the sin of slavery. Published as a book in 1852, *Uncle Tom's Cabin, or Life among the Lowly* became a blockbuster hit and sold 300,000 copies in its first year and more than 2 million copies within ten years.

Stowe's characters leaped from the page. Here was the gentle slave Uncle Tom, a Christian saint who forgave those who beat him to death; the courageous slave Eliza, who fled with her child across the frozen Ohio River; and the fiendish overseer Simon Legree, whose Louisiana plantation was a nightmare of torture and death. Mother of seven children, Stowe aimed her most powerful blows at slavery's destructive impact on the family. Her character Eliza succeeds in keeping her son from being sold away, but other mothers are not so fortunate. When told that her infant has been sold, Lucy drowns herself. Driven half mad by the sale of a son and daughter, Cassy decides "never again [to] let a child live to grow up!" She gives her third child an opiate and watches as "he slept to death."

In the North, common people and literary giants alike shed tears and sang praises to *Uncle Tom's Cabin.* But what Northerners accepted as truth, Southerners denounced as slander. Virginian George F. Holmes proclaimed Stowe a member of the "Woman's Rights" and "Higher Law" schools and dismissed the novel as a work of "intense fanaticism." Although it is impossible to measure precisely the impact of a novel on public opinion, *Uncle Tom's Cabin* clearly helped to crystallize northern sentiment against slavery and to confirm white Southerners' suspicion that they no longer had any sympathy in the free states.

Uncle Tom's Cabin
The cover drawing on this early illustrated edition of Harriet Beecher Stowe's novel shows a runaway slave mother racing across ice floes to escape dogs and slave catchers. During the 1850s, at least ten individuals, including Harriet Beecher Stowe herself, dramatized the novel. Stowe's moral indictment of slavery translated well to the stage. Scenes of Eliza crossing the ice with bloodhounds in pursuit, the cruelty of Simon Legree, and Little Eva borne to heaven on puffy clouds gripped the imagination of audiences in America and Britain and fueled the growing antislavery crusade.
Picture Research Consultants & Archives.

Other writers—ex-slaves who knew life in slave cabins firsthand—also produced stinging indictments of slavery. Solomon Northup's compelling *Twelve Years a Slave* (1853) sold 27,000 copies in two years, and the powerful *Narrative of the Life of Frederick Douglass, as Told by Himself* (1845) eventually sold more than 30,000 copies. But no work touched the North's conscience like the novel by a free white woman. A decade after its publication, when Stowe visited Abraham Lincoln at the White House, he reportedly said, "So you are the little woman who wrote the book that made this great war."

The Kansas-Nebraska Act

As national elections approached in 1852, Democrats and Whigs sought to close the sectional rifts that had opened within their parties. For their presidential nominee, the Democrats turned to Franklin Pierce of New Hampshire. Pierce's most valuable asset was his well-known sympathy with southern views on public issues. His leanings caused northern critics to include him among the "doughfaces," northern men malleable enough to champion southern causes. The Whigs were less successful in bridging differences. Adopting the formula that had proved successful in 1848, they chose another Mexican-American War hero, General Winfield Scott of Virginia. But the Whigs were hopelessly divided between their northern and southern factions and suffered a humiliating defeat. The Democrat Pierce carried twenty-seven states to Scott's four, 254 electoral votes to 42. In the afterglow of the Compromise of 1850, the Free-Soil Party lost almost half of the voters who had turned to it in the tumultuous atmosphere of 1848.

Eager to leave the sectional controversy behind, the new president turned swiftly to foreign expansion. **Manifest destiny** remained robust. (See "Beyond America's Borders," page 352.) Pierce's major objective was Cuba, which was owned by Spain and in which slavery flourished, but his clumsy diplomatic efforts galvanized antislavery Northerners, who blocked Cuba's acquisition to keep more slave territory from entering the Union. Pierce's fortunes improved in Mexico. In 1853, he sent diplomat James Gadsden to negotiate a $15 mil-

lion purchase of some 30,000 square miles of territory south of the Gila River in present-day Arizona and New Mexico. The Gadsden Purchase stemmed from the dream of a transcontinental railroad to California and Pierce's desire for a southern route through Mexican territory. The booming population of the Pacific coast made it obvious that the vast, loose-jointed republic needed a railroad to bind it together. Talk of a railroad ignited rivalries in cities from New Orleans to Chicago as they maneuvered to become the eastern terminus. The desire for a transcontinental railroad evolved into a sectional contest, which by the 1850s inevitably involved slavery.

No one played the railroad game more enthusiastically than Illinois's Democratic senator Stephen A. Douglas. He badly wanted the transcontinental railroad for Chicago and his home state, and his chairmanship of the Senate Committee on Territories provided him with an opportunity. Any railroad that ran west from Chicago would pass through a region that Congress in 1830 had designated a "permanent" Indian reserve. Douglas proposed giving this vast area between the Missouri River and the Rocky Mountains an Indian name, Nebraska, and then throwing the Indians out. Once the region achieved territorial status, whites could survey and sell the land, establish civil government, and build a railroad.

Nebraska lay within the Louisiana Purchase and, according to the Missouri Compromise of 1820, was closed to slavery (see chapter 10). Since Douglas could not count on New England to back western economic development, he needed southern votes to pass his Nebraska legislation. But Southerners had no incentive to create another free territory or to help a northern city win the transcontinental railroad. Southerners, however, agreed to help organize Nebraska for a price: nothing less than repeal of the Missouri Compromise. Southerners insisted that Congress organize Nebraska according to popular sovereignty. That meant giving slavery a chance in the Nebraska Territory and reopening the dangerous issue of slavery expansion, which Douglas himself had so ably helped to resolve only four years earlier.

In January 1854, Douglas introduced his bill to organize the Nebraska Territory, leaving to the settlers themselves the decision

Gadsden Purchase, 1853

about slavery. At southern insistence, and even though he knew it would "raise a hell of a storm," Douglas added an explicit repeal of the Missouri Compromise. Indeed, the Nebraska bill raised a storm of controversy. Free-Soilers branded Douglas's plan "a gross violation of a sacred pledge" and an "atrocious plot" to transform free land into a "dreary region of despotism, inhabited by masters and slaves."

Undaunted, Douglas skillfully shepherded the explosive bill through Congress in May 1854. Nine-tenths of all southern members (Whigs and Democrats) and half of the northern Democrats cast votes in favor. In its final form, the Kansas-Nebraska Act divided the huge territory in two: Nebraska west of the free state of Iowa and Kansas west of the slave state of Missouri (Map 14.3). With this act, the government pushed the Plains Indians farther west, making way for farmers and railroads.

> **REVIEW** Why did the Fugitive Slave Act provoke such strong opposition in the North?

Realignment of the Party System

The Kansas-Nebraska Act marked a fateful escalation of the sectional conflict. Douglas's controversial measure had several consequences, none more crucial than the realignment of the nation's political parties. Since the rise of the Whigs in the early 1830s, Whigs and Democrats had organized and channeled political conflict in the nation. This party system dampened sectionalism and strengthened the Union. To achieve national political power, Whigs and Democrats had to retain strength in both North and South. Strong northern and southern wings required that each party compromise and find positions acceptable to both wings.

The Kansas-Nebraska controversy shattered this stabilizing political system. In place of two national parties with bisectional strength, the mid-1850s witnessed the development of one party heavily dominated by one section and another party entirely limited to the other section. Rather

than "national" parties, the country had what one critic disdainfully called "geographic" parties. Parties now sharpened ideological and policy differences between the sections and no longer muffled moral issues, like slavery. But the new party system also thwarted political compromise and instead promoted political polarization that further jeopardized the Union.

The Old Parties: Whigs and Democrats

Distress signals could be heard from the Whig camp as early as the Mexican-American War, when members clashed over the future of slavery in annexed Mexican lands. By 1852, the Whig Party could please its proslavery southern wing or its antislavery northern wing but not both. The Whigs' miserable showing in the election of 1852 made clear that they were no longer a strong national party. By 1856, after more than two decades of contesting the Democrats, they were hardly a party at all (Map 14.4).

The collapse of the Whig Party left the Democrats as the country's only national party. Although the Democrats were not immune to the

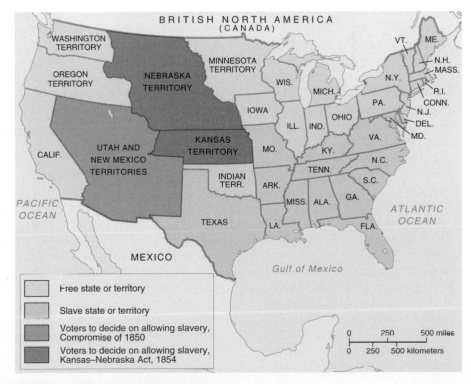

MAP 14.3 The Kansas-Nebraska Act, 1854
Americans hardly thought twice about dispossessing the Indians of lands guaranteed them by treaty, but many worried about the outcome of repealing the Missouri Compromise and opening up lands to slavery.

Filibusters: The Underside of Manifest Destiny

Each year the citizens of Caborca, Mexico, a small town in the northern state of Sonora, celebrate the defeat there in 1857 of an American army. The invaders did not wear the uniform of the U.S. army but marched as a private army, the "Arizona Colonization Company." Their commander, Henry A. Crabb, a Mississippian who followed the gold rush to California, saw fresh opportunity in the civil disorder that reigned south of the border. Fierce fighting between Mexicans and Apache and Yaqui Indians made life precarious in Sonora and divided the Mexicans. When the governor of Sonora faced an insurrection, he invited Crabb, who was married to a Sonoran woman, to help him repress his enemies in exchange for mineral rights and land.

Crabb marched his band of sixty-eight heavily armed ex-miners south from Los Angeles into Mexico. But by the time the Americans arrived, the governor had put down the insurgency, and he turned on the invaders. Every American except one died either in battle or at the hands of Mexican firing squads. Crabb's head was preserved in alcohol and placed on display as a symbol of victory.

Henry Crabb was one of thousands of American adventurers, known as "filibusters" (from Spanish *filibustero*, meaning "free-booter" or "pirate"), who in the mid-nineteenth century joined private armies that invaded foreign countries in North America, Central America, South America, and the Caribbean. Although these expeditions were illegal and violated the U.S. Neutrality Act of 1818, private American armies attacked Canada, Mexico, Ecuador, Honduras, Cuba, and Nicaragua and planned invasions of places as far away as the Hawaiian kingdom. The federal government occasionally winked at the actions of filibusters, but more often it cracked down, fearful that private invasions would jeopardize legitimate diplomatic efforts to promote trade and acquire territory.

Filibusters joined invading armies for a variety of reasons ranging from personal gain to validating manhood. Many saw themselves as carrying on the work of manifest destiny, extending America's reach beyond Texas, California, and Oregon, the prizes of the 1830s and 1840s. In addition, during the 1840s and 1850s when Northerners insisted on containing slavery's spread to the North and West, Southerners joined filibustering expeditions to expand slavery south beyond U.S. borders. Although filibusters came from all regions of the country, their greatest numbers and support came from the proslavery forces of the South. The leading proslavery ideologue, George Fitzhugh, sought to blunt criticism of filibustering by defending it through historical comparison: "They who condemn the modern filibuster, to be consistent, must also condemn the discoverers and settlers of America, of the East Indies of Holland, and of the Indian and Pacific Oceans." Such arguments, deeply rooted in manifest destiny, failed to convince many, including the ambassador from Costa Rica, who called filibustering America's "social cancer." Northerners claimed (with some justification) that filibustering was a southern campaign to extend "the empire of the lash."

One of the most vigorous filibusters to appeal to southern interests was not an American: Narciso Lopez was a Venezuelan-born Cuban who dedicated himself to the liberation of Cuba from Spanish rule. In his first attempt in 1849, he recruited an army of several hundred would-be liberators but got no farther than New York harbor, where U.S. marshals intercepted his fleet. Thereafter, he resolved to "rest his hopes on the men of the bold West and chivalric South." Lopez claimed that Spain was planning to free Cuba's slaves, and he told Southerners that "self-preservation" demanded that they seize the island. When Governor John Quitman of Mississippi joined his scheme, Lopez shifted his headquarters to New Orleans. Early in 1850, Lopez and an army of more than 500 landed on the northwest coast of Cuba, but Spanish troops quickly drove them off. Two months later, with 450 troops, he tried again. This

Filibustering in Nicaragua

In this image of a pitched battle in Nicaragua in 1856, Costa Ricans on foot fight American filibusters on horseback. Costa Rican soldiers and their Central American allies defeated William Walker's *filibusteros* in 1857, but before then the Pierce administration had extended diplomatic recognition to Walker's regime, and white Southerners had cheered Walker's attempt to "introduce civilization" in Nicaragua and to develop its rich resources "with slave labor."

London Illustrated Times, May 24, 1856.

time, the Spanish crushed the invasion, killing 200 filibusters, shipping 160 prisoners to Spain, executing 50 invaders by firing squad, and publicly garroting Lopez. John Quitman gathered another army of several thousand, but federal authorities seized one of his ships and ended the threat to Cuba.

The most successful of all filibusters was William Walker of Tennessee, a restless dreamer who longed for an empire of his own south of the border. Walker cut his filibustering teeth with expeditions to Baja California and Sonora, but when they failed, he turned to

Central America. He believed that Southerners paid too much attention to Kansas and that instead they should expand slavery in tropical America. In May 1855, Walker and an army of fifty-six men sailed from San Francisco to the west coast of Nicaragua. Two thousand reinforcements and a civil war in Nicaragua gave Walker his victory. He had himself proclaimed president, legalized slavery, and called on Southerners to come raise cotton, sugar, and coffee in "a magnificent country." Hundreds of Southerners took up **land grants**, but Walker's regime survived only until 1857, when a

coalition of Central American countries allied with the Nicaraguans and sent Walker packing. Walker doggedly launched four other attacks on Nicaragua; then in 1860, Honduran forces captured and shot him.

Filibustering had lost steam by 1861, but the battle-hardened adventurers found new employment in the armies of the Civil War, particularly in the service of the Confederate military. The Confederacy paid a diplomatic price for its association with filibustering, however. The Guatemalan minister Antonio Jose de Irisarri declared that there was "no foreign Nation which can have less cause for sympathy with the enemies of the American Union, than the Republics of Central America, because from the Southern States were set on foot those filibustering expeditions." No Central American nation recognized Confederate independence.

A century and more later, the peoples of Central America and the Caribbean, like the inhabitants of Sonora, harbor bitter memories of filibusters' private wars of **imperialism** and honor those who fought off American advances. When U.S. marines occupied Nicaragua in the 1920s, insurgents found inspiration in their country's defeat of William Walker's army of freebooters eighty years earlier. In 1851, on the centennial of Lopez's invasion, Cubans erected a monument at the very spot where his ill-fated army came ashore. Costa Ricans celebrate Juan Santamaria as their national martyr for his courage in battling William Walker. Memories of the invasions by nineteenth-century filibusters set the stage for anti-American sentiment in Latin America that lingers to this day.

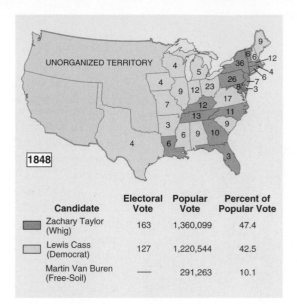

Candidate	Electoral Vote	Popular Vote	Percent of Popular Vote
Zachary Taylor (Whig)	163	1,360,099	47.4
Lewis Cass (Democrat)	127	1,220,544	42.5
Martin Van Buren (Free-Soil)	—	291,263	10.1

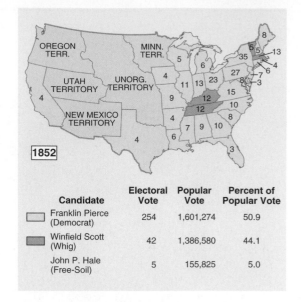

Candidate	Electoral Vote	Popular Vote	Percent of Popular Vote
Franklin Pierce (Democrat)	254	1,601,274	50.9
Winfield Scott (Whig)	42	1,386,580	44.1
John P. Hale (Free-Soil)	5	155,825	5.0

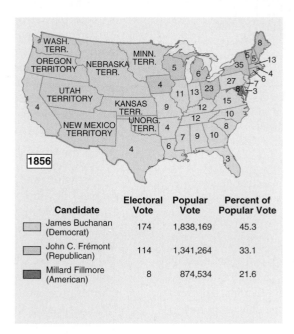

Candidate	Electoral Vote	Popular Vote	Percent of Popular Vote
James Buchanan (Democrat)	174	1,838,169	45.3
John C. Frémont (Republican)	114	1,341,264	33.1
Millard Fillmore (American)	8	874,534	21.6

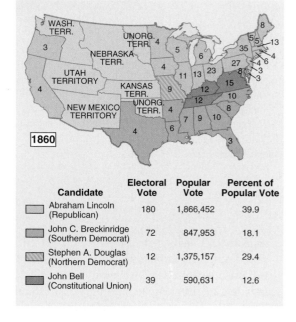

Candidate	Electoral Vote	Popular Vote	Percent of Popular Vote
Abraham Lincoln (Republican)	180	1,866,452	39.9
John C. Breckinridge (Southern Democrat)	72	847,953	18.1
Stephen A. Douglas (Northern Democrat)	12	1,375,157	29.4
John Bell (Constitutional Union)	39	590,631	12.6

MAP 14.4   Political Realignment, 1848–1860

In 1848, slavery and sectionalism began hammering the country's party system. The Whig Party was an early casualty. By 1860, national parties—those that contended for votes in both North and South—had been replaced by regional parties.

READING THE MAP: Which states did the Democrats pick up in the 1852 election over the previous election? Which of the states won in 1852 were lost to the Democrats in 1856? Compare the general geographical location of the states won by the Republicans in 1860 and in 1856.

CONNECTIONS: In the 1860 election, which party benefited the most from the addition of western and midwestern states added to the Union since 1848? Why would these states choose to back the Republicans over the Democrats?

FOR MORE HELP ANALYZING THIS MAP, see the map activity for this chapter in the Online Study Guide at bedfordstmartins.com/roarkcompact.

disruptive pressures of the territorial question, they discovered in popular sovereignty a doctrine that many Democrats could support. Even so, popular sovereignty very nearly undid the party. When Stephen Douglas applied the doctrine to the part of the Louisiana Purchase where slavery had been barred, he divided northern Democrats and destroyed the dominance of the Democratic Party in the free states. After 1854, the Democrats became a southern-dominated party. Nevertheless, the Democrats, unlike the Whigs, remained a national political organization. Gains in the South more than balanced Democratic losses in the North. During the 1850s, Democrats elected two presidents and won majorities in Congress in almost every election.

The breakup of the Whigs and the disaffection of significant numbers of northern Democrats set many Americans politically adrift. As they searched for new political harbors, Americans found that the death of the old party system created a multitude of fresh political alternatives. The question was which party would attract the drifters.

The New Parties: Know-Nothings and Republicans

Dozens of new political organizations vied for voters' attention. Out of the confusion two emerged as true contenders. One grew out of the slavery controversy, a spontaneous coalition of indignant antislavery Northerners. The other arose from an entirely different split in American society, between Roman Catholic immigrants and native **Protestants**.

The tidal wave of immigrants that broke over America from 1845 to 1855 produced a nasty backlash among Protestant Americans, who believed that the American Republic was about to drown in a sea of Roman Catholics from Ireland and Germany (see Figure 12.1, page 306). Most immigrants became Democrats because they perceived that party as more tolerant of newcomers than were the Whigs. But in the 1850s they met sharp political opposition when **nativists** (individuals who were anti-immigrant) began to organize, first into secret fraternal societies and then into a political party. Recruits swore never to vote for either foreign-born or Roman Catholic candidates and not to reveal any information about the organization. When questioned, they said: "I know nothing." Officially, they were named the American Party, but most Americans called them Know-Nothings.

The Know-Nothings exploded onto the political stage in 1854 and 1855 with a series of dazzling successes. They captured state legislatures in the Northeast, West, and South and claimed dozens of seats in Congress. Members of both traditional parties described the phenomenal success of the Know-Nothings as a "tornado," a "hurricane," and "a freak of political insanity." By 1855, an observer might reasonably have concluded that the Know-Nothings had emerged as the successor to the Whigs.

Know-Nothings were not the only new party making noise, however. One of the new antislavery organizations provoked by the Kansas-Nebraska Act called itself **Republican**. Republicans attempted to unite all the dissidents and political orphans—Whigs, Free-Soilers, anti-Nebraska Democrats, even Know-Nothings—who opposed the extension of slavery into any territory of the United States.

The Republican creed tapped into the basic beliefs and values of the northern public. Slavery, the Republicans argued, degraded the dignity of white labor by associating work with blacks and servility. They warned that the insatiable slaveholders of the South, whom antislavery Northerners called the "Slave Power," were

Know-Nothing Banner
Convinced that the incendiary issue of slavery had blinded Americans to the greater dangers of uncontrolled immigration and foreign influence, the Know-Nothing Party in 1856 ran Millard Fillmore for president. There is more than a little irony in this banner's appeal to "Native Americans" to stem the invasion from abroad. Know-Nothings meant native-born Americans, but bona fide Native Americans, American Indians, also faced an invasion and to them it made little difference whether the aggressors were fresh off the boat or born in the U.S.A.
Milwaukee County Historical Society.

conspiring through their control of the Democratic Party to expand slavery, subvert **liberty**, and undermine the Constitution. Only if slavery were restricted to the South, Republicans believed, could the system of free labor flourish elsewhere. The ideal of free labor respected the dignity of work and provided anyone willing to toil an opportunity for a decent living and for advancement (see chapter 12). These powerful images of liberty and opportunity attracted a wide range of Northerners to the Republican cause.

The Election of 1856

The election of 1856 revealed that the Republicans had become the Democrats' main challenger and slavery in the territories, not nativism, the election's principal issue. When the Know-Nothings insisted on a platform that endorsed the Kansas-Nebraska Act, most Northerners walked out and the party came apart. The few Know-Nothings who remained nominated ex-president Millard Fillmore.

The Republicans adopted a platform that focused almost exclusively on "making every territory free." When they labeled slavery a "relic of barbarism," Republicans signaled that they had written off the South. For president, they nominated the dashing soldier and California adventurer John C. Frémont, "Pathfinder of the West." Frémont lacked political credentials, but political know-how resided in his wife, Jessie, who, as a daughter of Senator Thomas Hart Benton of Missouri, knew the political map as well as her husband knew western trails. Although careful to maintain a proper public image, the vivacious young mother and antislavery zealot helped draw ordinary women into politics.

The Democrats chose another "doughface," James Buchanan of Pennsylvania. The Democrats took refuge in the ambiguity of popular sovereignty and portrayed Republicans as extremists ("Black Republican Abolitionists") whose support for the Wilmot Proviso risked pushing the South out of the Union.

The Democratic strategy carried the day for Buchanan, but Frémont did astonishingly well. Buchanan won 174 electoral votes against Frémont's 114 and Fillmore's 8. Campaigning under the banner "Free soil, Free men, Fremont," the Republican carried all but five of the states north of the Mason-Dixon line. The election made clear that the Whigs had disintegrated, the Know-Nothings would not ride nativism to national power, and the Republicans were a power to be reckoned with (see Map 14.4). Sectionalism had fashioned a new party system, one that spelled danger for the Republic (Figure 14.1). Indeed, war had already broken out between proslavery and antislavery forces in distant Kansas Territory.

> **REVIEW**   Why did the Whig Party disintegrate in the 1850s?

Freedom under Siege

Events in Kansas Territory in the mid-1850s provided the young Republican organization with an enormous boost and help explain its strong showing in the election of 1856. Republicans organized around the premise that the slaveholding South

John and Jessie Frémont Poster
The election of 1856 marked the first time a candidate's wife appeared on campaign items. Smart and ambitious, Jessie Benton Frémont made the breakthrough. In this poster—made from paper letters and figures cut from an English hunting print—Jessie and her husband, John C. Frémont, Republican Party presidential nominee, ride spirited horses. The scene emphasizes their youth (John was 43 and Jessie 31), their vigor, and their outdoor exuberance. Jessie helped plan Frémont's campaign, coauthored his election biography, and drew northern women into political activity as never before. "What a shame that women can't vote!" declared abolitionist Lydia Maria Child. "We'd carry 'our Jessie' into the White House on our shoulders, wouldn't we." Critics of Jessie's violation of women's traditional sphere ridiculed both Frémonts. A man who met the couple in San Francisco pronounced her "the better man of the two." Jessie Frémont was, as Abraham Lincoln observed ambivalently, "quite a female politician."
Museum of American Political Life.

provided a profound threat to "free soil, free labor, and free men," and now Kansas reeled with violence that Republicans argued was southern in origin. Kansas, Republicans claimed, opened a window to southern values and intentions. Republicans also pointed to the brutal beating by a Southerner of a respected northern senator on the floor of Congress. Even the Supreme Court, in the Republicans' view, reflected the South's drive toward tyranny and minority rule. Then, in 1858, the issues dividing North and South received an extraordinary airing in a senatorial contest in Illinois, when the nation's foremost Democrat debated a resourceful Republican.

"Bleeding Kansas"

Three days after the House of Representatives approved the Kansas-Nebraska Act in 1854, Senator William H. Seward of New York boldly challenged the South. "Come on then, Gentlemen of the Slave States," he cried, "since there is no escaping your challenge, I accept it in behalf of the cause of freedom. We will engage in competition for the virgin soil of Kansas, and God give the victory to the side which is stronger in numbers as it is in right." Because of Stephen Douglas, popular sovereignty would determine whether Kansas became slave or free. Free-state and slave-state settlers each sought majorities at the ballot box, claimed God's blessing, and kept their rifles ready.

In both North and South, emigrant aid societies sprang up to promote settlement from free states or slave states. Missourians, already bordered on the east by the free state of Illinois and on the north by the free state of Iowa, especially thought it important to secure Kansas for slavery. Thousands of rough frontiersmen, egged on by Missouri senator David Rice Atchison, invaded Kansas. "There are eleven hundred coming over from Platte County to vote," Atchison reported, "and if that ain't enough we can send five thousand—enough to kill every God-damned abolitionist in the Territory." Not surprisingly, proslavery candidates swept the elections in November 1854. When Kansas's first territorial legislature met, it enacted a raft of proslavery laws. Ever-pliant President Pierce endorsed the work of the fraudulently elected legislature. Free-soil Kansans did not. They elected their own legislature, which promptly banned both slaves and free blacks from the territory. Organized into two rival governments and armed to the teeth, Kansans verged on civil war.

Fighting broke out on the morning of May 21, 1856, when several hundred proslavery men

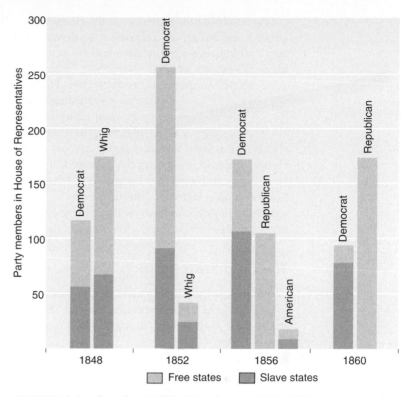

FIGURE 14.1   Changing Political Landscape, 1848–1860
The polarization of American politics between free states and slave states occurred in little more than a decade.

raided the town of Lawrence, the center of free-state settlement. Only one man died, but the "Sack of Lawrence," as free-soil forces called it, inflamed northern opinion. Elsewhere in Kansas, news of events in Lawrence provoked John Brown, a free-soil settler, to "fight fire with fire." He led the posse that massacred five allegedly proslavery settlers along the Pottawatomie Creek. After that, **guerrilla war** engulfed the territory.

Just as "Bleeding Kansas" gave the fledgling Republican Party fresh ammunition for its battle against the Slave Power, so, too, did an event that occurred in the national capital. In May 1856, Senator Charles Sumner of Massachusetts delivered a speech entitled "The Crime against Kansas" that included a scalding personal attack on the South Carolina senator Andrew P. Butler, whom Sumner described as a "Don Quixote" who had taken as his mistress "the harlot, slavery." Preston Brooks, a

"Bleeding Kansas," 1850s

young South Carolina member of the House and a kinsman of Butler, felt compelled to defend the honor of both his aged relative and his state. On May 22, Brooks entered the Senate, where he found Sumner working at his desk. He beat Sumner over the head with his cane until he lay bleeding and unconscious on the floor. Brooks resigned his seat in the House, only to be promptly reelected. In the North, the southern hero became an archvillain. Like "Bleeding Kansas," "Bleeding Sumner" provided the Republican Party with a potent symbol of the South's "twisted and violent civilization."

The *Dred Scott* Decision

Only the Supreme Court speaks definitively about the meaning of the Constitution, and in 1857, in the case of *Dred Scott v. Sandford,* the Court an-

nounced its judgment of the issue of slavery in the territories. The Court's decision demonstrated that it enjoyed no special immunity from the sectional and partisan passions that convulsed the land.

In 1833, John Emerson, an army doctor, bought the slave Dred Scott in St. Louis, Missouri, and took him as his personal servant to Fort Armstrong, Illinois. Two years later, Scott accompanied Emerson when he transferred to Fort Snelling in Wisconsin Territory. Emerson eventually returned Scott to St. Louis, where in 1846, Scott, with the help of white friends, sued to prove that he and his family were legally entitled to their freedom. Scott based his claim on his travels and residences in a free state and a free territory.

In 1857, the U.S. Supreme Court ruled in the case. Chief Justice Roger B. Taney hated Republicans and detested racial equality, and the Court's majority decision, which he wrote, reflected those prejudices. First, the Court ruled that Dred Scott could not legally claim violation of his constitutional rights because he was not a citizen of the United States. When the Constitution was written, Taney said, blacks "were regarded as beings of an inferior order…so far inferior, that they had no rights which the white man was bound to respect." Second, the laws of Dred Scott's home state, Missouri, determined his status, and thus his travels in free areas did not make him free. Third, Congress's power to

The Dred Scott Family

The *Dred Scott* case in 1857 not only produced a fierce political storm but also fueled enormous curiosity about the family suing for freedom. The correspondent for the popular *Frank Leslie's Illustrated Newspaper* met Dred Scott in St. Louis and reported: "We found him on examination to be a pure-blooded African, perhaps fifty years of age, with a shrewd, intelligent, good-natured face, of rather light frame, being not more than five feet six inches high." Northerners wanted to see all of the Scotts: Harriet, who was a slave when Dred Scott married her in Wisconsin Territory in about 1836; daughter Eliza, who was born in 1838 on board a ship traveling in free territory north of Missouri; and daughter Lizzie, born after the Scotts returned to St. Louis.
Library of Congress.

make "all needful rules and regulations" for the territories did not include the right to prohibit slavery. The Court explicitly declared the Missouri Compromise unconstitutional, even though it had already been voided by the Kansas-Nebraska Act.

The Taney Court's extreme proslavery decision outraged Republicans. By denying the federal government the right to exclude slavery in the territories, it cut the ground out from under the Republican Party. Moreover, as the *New York Tribune* lamented, the decision cleared the way for "all our Territories…to be ripened into Slave States." Particularly frightening to African Americans in the North was the Court's declaration that blacks were not citizens and had no rights.

The Republican rebuttal to the *Dred Scott* ruling relied heavily on the dissenting opinion of Justice Benjamin R. Curtis. Scott *was* a citizen of the United States, Curtis argued. At the time of the writing of the Constitution, free black men could vote in five states and participated in the ratification process. Scott *was* free. Because slavery was prohibited in Wisconsin, the "involuntary servitude of a slave, coming into the Territory with his master, should cease to exist." The Missouri Compromise *was* constitutional. The Founders had meant exactly what they said: Congress had the power to make "*all* needful rules and regulations" for the territories, including barring slavery.

Rejecting Curtis's arguments, a seven-to-two majority of the justices validated an extreme statement of the South's territorial rights. John C. Calhoun's claim that Congress had no authority to exclude slavery became the law of the land. White Southerners cheered, but the *Dred Scott* decision actually strengthened the young Republican Party. It provided dramatic evidence of the Republicans' claim that a hostile Slave Power conspired against northern liberties. Only the capture of the Supreme Court by the "slavocracy," Republicans argued, could explain the tortured and historically inaccurate decision.

Prairie Republican: Abraham Lincoln

By re-igniting the sectional flames, the *Dred Scott* case provided Republican politicians with fresh challenges and fresh opportunities. Abraham Lincoln had long since put behind him his hardscrabble log-cabin beginnings in Kentucky and Indiana. He lived in a fine two-story house in Springfield, Illinois, and earned good money as a lawyer. The law provided Lincoln's living, but politics was his life. "His ambition was a little engine that knew no rest," observed his law partner William Herndon. Lincoln had served as a Whig in the Illinois state legislature and in the House of Representatives, but he had not held public office since 1849.

The disintegration of the Whig Party meant that Lincoln had no political home. His credo—opposition to "the *extension* of slavery"—made the Republicans his only choice, and in 1856 Lincoln joined the party. Convinced that slavery was a "monstrous injustice," a "great moral wrong," and an "unqualified evil to the negro, the white man, and the State," Lincoln condemned Douglas's Kansas-Nebraska Act of 1854 for giving slavery a new life. He accepted that the Constitution permitted slavery in those states where it existed, but he believed that Congress could contain its spread. Penned in, Lincoln believed, plantation slavery would wither, and in time Southerners would end slavery themselves. By providing fresh land in the territories, Douglas had put slavery "on the high road to extension and perpetuity."

Lincoln held what were, for his times, moderate racial views. Like a majority of Republicans, Lincoln defended black humanity without challenging white supremacy. While he denounced slavery as immoral, he also viewed black equality as impractical and unachievable. "Negroes have natural rights…as other men have," he said, "although they cannot enjoy them here." Insurmountable white prejudice made it impossible to extend full citizenship and equality to blacks in America, he believed. In Lincoln's mind, social stability and black progress required that slavery end and that blacks leave the country.

Lincoln envisioned the western territories as "places for poor people to go to, and better their conditions." But slavery's expansion threatened free men's basic right to succeed. The Kansas-Nebraska Act and the *Dred Scott* decision persuaded him that slaveholders were engaging in a dangerous conspiracy to nationalize slavery. The next step, Lincoln warned, would be "another Supreme Court decision, declaring that the Constitution of the United States does not permit a State to exclude slavery from its limits." Unless the citizens of Illinois woke up, he warned, the Supreme Court would make "Illinois a slave State."

In Lincoln's view, the nation could not "endure, permanently half slave and half free." Either opponents of slavery would arrest its spread and place it on the "course of ultimate extinction," or its advocates would see that it became legal in "*all* the States, *old* as well as *new—North* as well as *South*." Lincoln's convictions that slavery was wrong, that Congress must stop its spread, and that it must be put on the road to extinction formed the core of the Republican ideology. Lincoln so impressed his fellow Republicans in Illinois that in 1858 they chose him to challenge the nation's premier Democrat, who was seeking reelection to the U.S. Senate.

The Lincoln-Douglas Debates

When Stephen Douglas learned that the Republican Abraham Lincoln would be his opponent for the Senate, he confided in a fellow Democrat: "He is the strong man of the party—full of wit, facts, dates—and the best stump speaker, with his droll ways and dry jokes, in the West. He is as honest as he is shrewd, and if I beat him my victory will be hardly won."

Not only did Douglas have to contend with a formidable foe, but he also carried the weight of a burden not of his own making. The previous year, the nation's economy experienced a sharp downturn. Prices plummeted, thousands of businesses failed, and unemployment rose. As a Democrat, Douglas had to go before the voters as a member of the party whose policies stood accused of causing the "panic of 1857."

Douglas's response to another crisis in 1857, however, helped shore up his standing in Illinois. Proslavery forces in Kansas met in the town of Lecompton, drafted a proslavery constitution, and applied for statehood. Everyone knew that Free-Soilers outnumbered proslavery settlers, but President Buchanan instructed Congress to admit Kansas as the sixteenth slave state. Republicans denounced the "Lecompton swindle." Senator Douglas broke with the Democratic administration and came out against the Lecompton constitution; Congress killed the Lecompton bill. (When Kansans reconsidered the Lecompton constitution in an honest election, they rejected it six to one. Kansas entered the Union in 1861 as a free state.) By denouncing the fraudulent proslavery constitution, Douglas declared his independence from the South and, he hoped, made himself acceptable at home.

A relative unknown and a decided underdog in the Illinois election, Lincoln challenged Douglas to debate him face-to-face. The two met in seven communities for what would become a legendary series of debates. Thousands stood straining to see and hear as they debated the central issues of the age—slavery and freedom. They showed the citizens of Illinois (and much of the nation because of widespread press coverage) the difference between an anti-Lecompton Democrat and a true Republican.

Lincoln badgered Douglas with the question of whether he favored the spread of slavery. He tried to force Douglas into the damaging admission that the Supreme Court had repudiated Douglas's own territorial solution, popular sovereignty. In the debate at Freeport, Illinois, Douglas admitted that settlers could not now pass legislation barring slavery, but he argued that they could ban slavery just as effectively by not passing protective laws, such as those found in slave states. Southerners condemned Douglas's "Freeport Doctrine" and charged him with trying to steal the victory they had gained with the *Dred Scott* decision. Lincoln chastised his opponent for his "don't care" attitude about slavery, for "blowing out the moral lights around us."

Douglas worked the racial issue. He called Lincoln an abolitionist and an egalitarian enamored with "our colored brethren." Put on the defensive, Lincoln came close to staking out positions on race that were as conservative as Douglas's. Lincoln reaffirmed his faith in white rule: "I will say, then, that I am not, nor ever have been, in favor of bringing about in any way the social and political equality of the white and black race." But unlike Douglas, who told racist jokes, Lincoln was no negrophobe. He tried to steer the debate back to what he considered the true issue: the morality and future of slavery. "Slavery is wrong," Lincoln repeated, because "a man has the right to the fruits of his own labor."

As Douglas predicted, the election was hard-fought and closely contested. Until the adoption of the Seventeenth Amendment in 1911, citizens voted for state legislators, who in turn selected U.S. senators. Since Democrats won a slight majority in the Illinois legislature, the members returned Douglas to the Senate. But the debates thrust Lincoln, the prairie Republican, into the national spotlight.

REVIEW   Why did the *Dred Scott* decision strengthen northern suspicions of a "Slave Power" conspiracy?

The Union Collapses

Lincoln's thesis that the "slavocracy" conspired to make slavery a national institution now seems exaggerated. But from the northern perspective, the

Kansas-Nebraska Act, the Brooks-Sumner affair, the *Dred Scott* decision, and the Lecompton constitution amounted to irrefutable evidence of the South's aggressiveness. White Southerners, of course, saw things differently. They were the ones who were under siege, they declared. Signs were everywhere, they believed, that the North planned to use its numerical advantage to attack slavery, and not just in the territories. Republicans had made it clear that they were unwilling to accept the *Dred Scott* ruling as the last word on the issue of slavery expansion. And John Brown's attempt to incite a slave insurrection in Virginia in 1859 proved that Northerners were unwilling to be bound by Christian decency and reverence for life.

Threats of secession increasingly laced the sectional debate. Talk of leaving the Union had been heard for years, but until the final crisis, Southerners had used secession as a ploy to gain concessions within the Union, not to destroy it. Then the 1850s delivered powerful blows to Southerners' confidence that they could remain Americans and protect slavery. When the Republican Party won the White House in 1860, many Southerners concluded that they would have to leave.

The Aftermath of John Brown's Raid

For his attack on Harpers Ferry, John Brown stood trial for treason, murder, and incitement of slave insurrection. "To hang a fanatic is to make a martyr of him and fledge another brood of the same sort," cautioned one newspaper, but on December 2, 1859, Virginia executed Brown. In life, Brown was a ne'er-do-well, but he died with courage and dignity. He told his wife that he was "determined to make the utmost possible out of a defeat." He told the court: "If it is deemed necessary that I should forfeit my life for the furtherance of the ends of justice, and mingle my blood further with the blood of…millions in this slave country whose rights are disregarded by wicked, cruel, and unjust enactments, I say, let it be done."

After Brown's heroic death, northern denunciation of Brown as a dangerous fanatic gave way to grudging respect. Some even celebrated his "splendid martyrdom." Abolitionist Lydia Maria Child likened Brown to Christ and declared that he made "the scaffold…as glorious as the Cross of Calvary." Some abolitionists explicitly endorsed Brown's resort to violence. Abolitionist William Lloyd Garrison, who usually professed pacifism, announced, "I am pre-

pared to say 'success to every slave insurrection at the South and in every country.'"

Most Northerners did not advocate bloody rebellion, however. Like Lincoln, they concluded that Brown's noble antislavery ideals could not "excuse violence, bloodshed, and treason." Still, when many in the North marked John Brown's execution with tolling bells, hymns, and prayer vigils, white Southerners contemplated what they had in common with people who "regard John Brown as a martyr and a Christian hero, rather than a murderer and robber." Georgia senator Robert Toombs announced solemnly that Southerners must "never permit this Federal government to pass into the traitorous hands of the black Republican party." At that moment, the presidential election was only months away.

Republican Victory in 1860

Events between Brown's hanging and the presidential election only heightened sectional hostility and estrangement. A southern business convention meeting in Nashville shocked the nation (including many Southerners) by calling for the reopening of the African slave trade. Chief Justice Taney provoked new indignation when the Supreme Court ruled northern personal liberty laws unconstitutional and reaffirmed the Fugitive Slave Act. Then, the normally routine business of electing a Speaker of the House threatened to turn bloody as Democrats and Republicans battled over control of the office. After two months of acrimonious debate left the House deadlocked, one congressman observed that the "only persons who do not have a revolver and a knife are those who have two revolvers." A last-minute compromise may have averted a shootout.

When Democrats converged on Charleston for their convention in April 1860, fire-eating Southerners denounced Stephen Douglas and demanded a platform that included federal protection of slavery in the territories. But northern Democrats knew that northern voters would not stomach a federal slave code. When the delegates approved a platform with popular sovereignty, representatives from the entire Lower South and Arkansas stomped out of the convention. The remaining Democrats adjourned to meet a few weeks later in Baltimore, where they nominated Douglas for president.

When southern Democrats met, they nominated Vice President John C. Breckinridge of Kentucky for president and approved a platform

John Brown Going to His Hanging, Horace Pippin, 1942
The grandparents of Horace Pippin, a Pennsylvania artist, were slaves. His grandmother witnessed the hanging of John Brown, and here Pippin recalls the scene she so often described to him. He uses a muted palette to establish the bleak setting and to tell the grim story, but he manages to convey a striking intensity nevertheless. Historically accurate, the painting depicts Brown tied and sitting erect on his coffin, passing resolutely before the silent, staring white men. The black woman in the lower right corner is presumably Pippin's grandmother.

Romare Bearden, a leading twentieth-century African American artist, recalled the central place of John Brown in black memory: "Lincoln and John Brown were as much a part of the actuality of the Afro-American experience, as were the domino games and the hoe cakes for Sunday morning breakfast. I vividly recall the yearly commemorations for John Brown and see my grandfather reading Brown's last speech to the court, which was a regular part of the ceremony at Pittsburgh's Shiloh Baptist Church."
Pennsylvania Academy of Fine Arts, Philadelphia. John Lambert Fund.

For more help analyzing this image, see the visual activity for this chapter in the Online Study Guide at **bedfordstmartins.com/roarkcompact**.

with a federal slave code. Southern moderates, however, refused to support Breckinridge. They formed a new party to provide voters a Unionist choice. Instead of adopting a platform and confronting the slavery question, the Constitutional Union Party merely approved a vague resolution pledging "to recognize no political principle other than _the Constitution...the Union...and the Enforcement of the Laws._" For president they picked former senator John Bell of Tennessee.

The Republicans smelled victory. But they estimated that they needed to carry nearly all the free states to win. To make their party more appealing, they expanded their platform beyond antislavery. They hoped that free homesteads, a protective tariff, a transcontinental railroad, and a guarantee of immigrant political rights would provide an economic and social agenda broad enough to unify the North. While reasserting their commitment to stop the spread of slavery, they also denounced John Brown's raid as "among the gravest of crimes" and confirmed the security of slavery in the South.

Republicans cast about for a moderate candidate to go with their evenhanded platform. The foremost Republican, William H. Seward, had made enemies with his radical "higher law" doctrine and "irrepressible conflict" speech. Lincoln, however, since bursting onto the national scene in 1858 had demonstrated his clear purpose, good judgment, and solid Republican credentials. That, and his residence in Illinois, a crucial state, made him attractive to the party. On the third ballot, the delegates chose Lincoln. Defeated by Douglas in a state contest less than two years earlier, Lincoln now stood ready to take him on for the presidency.

The election of 1860 was like none other in American politics. It took place in the midst of the nation's severest crisis. Four major candidates crowded the presidential field. Rather than a four-cornered contest, however, the election broke into two contests, each with two candidates. In the North, Lincoln faced Douglas; in the South, Breckinridge confronted Bell. Southerners did not even permit Lincoln's name to appear on the ballot in ten of the fifteen slave states, so outrageous did they consider the Republican Party.

On November 6, 1860, Lincoln swept all of the eighteen free states except New Jersey, which split its electoral votes between him and Douglas. While Lincoln received only 39 percent of the popular vote, he won easily in the electoral balloting, gaining 180 votes, 28 more than he needed for victory. Lincoln did not win because his opposition was splintered. Even if the votes of his three opponents had been combined, Lincoln would still have won. He won because his votes were concentrated in the free states, which contained a majority of electoral votes. Ominously, however, Breckinridge, running on a southern-rights platform, won the entire Lower South plus Delaware, Maryland, and North Carolina (Map 14.5).

Secession Winter

The telegraphs had barely stopped tapping out the news of Lincoln's victory when anxious Southerners began debating what to do. Although Breckinridge had carried the South, a vote for "southern rights" was not necessarily a vote for secession. Besides, slightly more than half of the Southerners who had voted cast ballots for Douglas and Bell, two stout defenders of the Union.

Abraham Lincoln
Lincoln actively sought the Republican presidential nomination in 1860. When in New York City to give a political address, he had his photograph taken by Mathew Brady. "While I was there I was taken to one of the places where they get up such things," Lincoln explained, sounding more innocent than he was, "and I suppose they got my shadow, and can multiply copies indefinitely." Multiply they did. Later, Lincoln credited his victory to his New York speech and to this dignified photograph by Brady.
The Lincoln Museum, Fort Wayne, Indiana. Photo: #0-17.

Southern Unionists tried to calm the fears that Lincoln's election triggered. Let the dust settle, they pleaded. Former congressman Alexander Stephens of Georgia asked what Lincoln had done to justify something as extreme as secession. Had he not promised to respect slavery where it existed? In Stephens's judgment, the fire-eater cure would be worse than the Republican disease. Secession might lead to war, which would loosen the hinges of southern society, possibly even open the door to slave insurrection. "Revolutions are much easier started

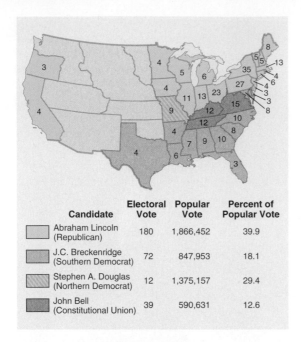

Candidate	Electoral Vote	Popular Vote	Percent of Popular Vote
Abraham Lincoln (Republican)	180	1,866,452	39.9
J.C. Breckenridge (Southern Democrat)	72	847,953	18.1
Stephen A. Douglas (Northern Democrat)	12	1,375,157	29.4
John Bell (Constitutional Union)	39	590,631	12.6

MAP 14.5   The Election of 1860

than controlled," he warned. "I consider slavery much more secure in the Union than out of it."

Secessionists emphasized the dangers of delay. "Mr. Lincoln and his party assert that this doctrine of equality applies to the negro," former Georgia governor Howell Cobb declared, "and necessarily there can exist no such thing as property in our equals." Lincoln's election without a single electoral vote from the South meant that Southerners were no longer able to defend themselves within the Union, Cobb argued. Why wait, he said, for Lincoln to send abolitionist emissaries to the South. As for war, there would be none. The Union was a voluntary compact, and Lincoln would not coerce patriotism. If Northerners did resist with force, secessionists argued, one southern woodsman could whip five of Lincoln's greasy mechanics.

For all their differences, southern whites were generally united in their determination to defend slavery. They disagreed about whether the mere presence of a Republican in the White House made it necessary to exercise what they considered a legitimate right to secede.

South Carolina seceded from the Union on December 20, 1860. By February 1861, the six other

Secession of the Lower South, December 1860–February 1861

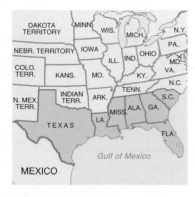

Lower South states marched in South Carolina's footsteps. In some states, the vote was close. In general, slaveholders spearheaded secession, while nonslaveholders in the Piedmont and mountain counties, where slaves were relatively few, displayed the greatest attachment to the Union. On February 4, representatives from South Carolina, Georgia, Florida, Alabama, Mississippi, Louisiana, and Texas met in Montgomery, Alabama, where three days later they celebrated the birth of the Confederate States of America. Jefferson Davis became president, and Alexander Stephens, who had spoken so eloquently about the dangers of revolution, became vice president.

Lincoln's election had split the Union. Now secession split the South. Seven slave states seceded during the winter, but the eight slave states of the Upper South rejected secession, at least for the moment. The fact was that the Upper South had a smaller stake in slavery. Just over half as many white families in the Upper South held slaves (21 percent) as did those in the Lower South (37 percent). Slaves represented twice as large a percentage of the population in the Lower South (48 percent) as in the Upper South (23 percent). Consequently, whites in the Upper South had fewer fears that Republican ascendancy meant economic catastrophe, social chaos, and racial war. Lincoln would need to do more than just be elected to provoke them into secession.

The nation had to wait until March 4, 1861, when Lincoln took office, to see what he would do. (Presidents-elect waited four months to take office until 1933, when the Twentieth Amendment to the Constitution shifted the inauguration forward to January 20.) After his election, Lincoln chose to stay in Springfield and to say nothing. "Lame-duck" president James Buchanan sat in Washington and did nothing. Buchanan demonstrated, William H. Seward said mockingly, that "it is the President's duty to enforce the laws, unless somebody opposes him." In Congress, efforts at cobbling together a peace-saving compromise came to nothing.

Lincoln began his inaugural address with reassurances to the South. He had "no lawful right" to interfere with slavery where it existed, he declared again, adding for emphasis that he had "no inclination to do so." Conciliatory about slavery, Lincoln proved inflexible about the Union. The Union, he declared, is "perpetual." Secession was "anarchy" and "legally void." The Constitution required him to execute the law "in all the States." He would hold federal property, collect federal duties, and deliver the mails.

The decision for civil war or peace rested in the South's hands, Lincoln declared. "You can have no conflict, without being yourselves the aggressors. *You* have no oath registered in Heaven to destroy the government, while *I* shall have the most solemn one to 'preserve, protect, and defend' it." What Confederates in Charleston held in their hands at that very moment were the cords for firing the cannons aimed at the federal garrison at Fort Sumter.

> **REVIEW** Why did some southern states secede immediately after Lincoln's election?

Conclusion: Slavery, Free Labor, and the Failure of Political Compromise

As their economies, societies, and cultures diverged in the nineteenth century, Northerners and Southerners expressed different concepts of the American promise and the role of slavery within it. Their differences crystallized into political form in 1846 when David Wilmot proposed banning slavery in any territory won in the Mexican-American War. "As if by magic," a Boston newspaper observed, "it brought to a head the great question that is about to divide the American people." Discovery of gold and other precious metals in the West added urgency to the controversy over slavery in the territories. Although Congress addressed the issue with the Compromise of 1850, the Fugitive Slave Act quickly brought conflict between free and slave states. Matters worsened with the 1852 publication of *Uncle Tom's Cabin*, which further hardened northern sentiments against slavery and confirmed southern suspicions of northern ill will. The bloody violence that erupted in Kansas in 1856 and the incendiary *Dred Scott* decision in 1857 further eroded hope for a solution to this momentous question.

During the extended crisis of the Union that stretched from 1846 to 1861, the slavery question braided with national politics. The traditional Whig and Democratic parties struggled to hold together, as new parties, most notably the Republican Party, emerged. Politicians fixed their attention on the expansion of slavery, but from the beginning the nation recognized that the controversy had less to do with slavery in the territories than with the future of slavery in America.

For more than seventy years, statesmen had found compromises that accepted slavery and preserved the Union. But as each section grew increasingly committed to its labor system and the promise it provided, Americans discovered that accommodation had limits. In 1859, John Brown's militant antislavery pushed white Southerners to the edge. In 1860, Lincoln's election convinced whites in the Lower South that slavery and the society they had built on it were at risk in the Union, and they seceded. In his inaugural, Lincoln pleaded, "We are not enemies but friends. We must not be enemies." By then, however, the seven southern states had ceased to sing what he called "the chorus of the Union." It remained to be seen whether disunion would mean war.

Suggestions for Further Reading

Charles B. Dew, *Apostles of Disunion: Southern Secession Commissioners and the Causes of the Civil War* (2001). An analysis that places slavery at the center of the decision to secede.

Don E. Fehrenbacher, *The Slaveholding Republic: An Account of the United States Government's Relations to Slavery* (2001). An insightful discussion of the federal government's changing relationship with slavery from the Constitution to the Civil War.

Eric Foner, *Free Labor, Free Soil, Free Men: The Ideology of the Republican Party before the Civil War* (1970). A probing analysis of the rise of the Republican Party.

Michael Holt, *Fate of Their Country: Politicians, Slavery Extension, and the Coming of the Civil War* (2004). A clear discussion of the political origins of the Civil War.

Bruce C. Levine, *Half Slave and Half Free: The Roots of the Civil War* (1992). A vivid narrative that describes the growing divergence between North and South.

David S. Reynolds, *John Brown, Abolitionist: The Man Who Killed Slavery, Sparked the Civil War, and Seeded Civil Rights* (2005). A provocative biography of one of the era's most controversial figures.

▶ **For more books about topics in this chapter,** see the Online Bibliography at bedfordstmartins.com/roarkcompact.

▶ **For additional firsthand accounts of this period,** see Chapter 14 in Michael Johnson, ed., *Reading the American Past*, Third Edition.

▶ **For Web sites and documents related to topics and places in this chapter,** see "HistoryLinks," "DocLinks," and "PlaceLinks" at bedfordstmartins.com/roarkcompact.

REVIEWING THE CHAPTER

Follow these steps to review and strengthen your understanding of the chapter.

STEP 1: *Study the* **Key Terms** *and* **Timeline** *to identify the significance of each item listed.*

STEP 2: *Answer the* **Review Questions**, *drawing on key terms and dates to support your answers.*

STEP 3: *Drawing on the Key Terms, Timeline, and Review Questions, answer the broader* **Making Connections** *questions.*

KEY TERMS

Who

John Brown (p. 343)
David Wilmot (p. 345)
John C. Calhoun (p. 345)
Lewis Cass (p. 346)
Martin Van Buren (p. 346)
Zachary Taylor (p. 346)
Henry Clay (p. 347)
Daniel Webster (p. 347)
William H. Seward (p. 347)
Stephen A. Douglas (p. 348)
Millard Fillmore (p. 348)
Harriet Beecher Stowe (p. 349)
Franklin Pierce (p. 350)
Winfield Scott (p. 350)
James Gadsden (p. 350)
John C. Frémont (p. 356)
Jessie Frémont (p. 356)

James Buchanan (p. 356)
Charles Sumner (p. 357)
Roger B. Taney (p. 358)
Abraham Lincoln (p. 359)
John C. Breckinridge (p. 361)
Jefferson Davis (p. 364)

What

John Brown's raid on Harpers Ferry (p. 343)
Wilmot Proviso (p. 345)
popular sovereignty (p. 346)
Democratic Party (pp. 346, 351)
Whig Party (pp. 346, 351)
Free-Soil Party (p. 346)
Omnibus Bill (p. 347)
Compromise of 1850 (p. 348)
Fugitive Slave Act (p. 348)

underground railroad (p. 348)
Uncle Tom's Cabin (p. 349)
Gadsden Purchase (p. 350)
Kansas-Nebraska Act (p. 351)
Know-Nothing Party (p. 355)
Republican Party (p. 355)
free labor (p. 356)
"Bleeding Kansas" (p. 357)
"Sack of Lawrence" (p. 357)
"Bleeding Sumner" (p. 358)
Dred Scott decision (p. 358)
panic of 1857 (p. 360)
Lecompton constitution (p. 360)
Lincoln-Douglas debates (p. 360)
Constitutional Union Party (p. 362)
Confederate States of America (p. 364)

TIMELINE

◄ **1820** • Missouri Compromise.

1846 • Wilmot Proviso introduced in Congress.

1847 • Wilmot Proviso defeated in Senate.
• Compromise of "popular sovereignty" offered.

1848 • Free-Soil Party founded.
• Whig General Zachary Taylor elected president.

1849 • California gold rush.

1850 • Taylor dies; Vice President Millard Fillmore becomes president.
• Compromise of 1850 becomes law.

1852 • *Uncle Tom's Cabin* published.
• Democrat Franklin Pierce elected president.

1853 • Gadsden Purchase.

1854 • American Party (Know-Nothings) emerges.
• Kansas-Nebraska Act.
• Republican Party emerges.

REVIEW QUESTIONS

1. Why did response to the Wilmot Proviso split along sectional rather than party lines? (pp. 344–48)

2. Why did the Fugitive Slave Act provoke such strong opposition in the North? (pp. 348–51)

3. Why did the Whig Party disintegrate in the 1850s? (pp. 351–56)

4. Why did the *Dred Scott* decision strengthen northern suspicions of a "Slave Power" conspiracy? (pp. 356–60)

5. Why did some southern states secede immediately after Lincoln's election? (pp. 360–65)

MAKING CONNECTIONS

1. The process of compromise that had successfully contained tensions between slave and free states since the nation's founding collapsed with secession. Why did compromise fail at this moment? In your answer, address specific political conflicts and attempts to solve them between 1846 and 1861.

2. In the 1850s many Americans supported popular sovereignty as the best solution to the explosive question of slavery in the western territories. Why was this solution so popular, and why did it ultimately prove inadequate? In your answer, be sure to address popular sovereignty's varied critics as well as champions.

3. In the 1840s and 1850s, the United States witnessed the realignment of its long-standing two-party system. Why did the old system fall apart, what emerged to take its place, and how did this process contribute to the coming of the Civil War?

4. Abraham Lincoln believed he had staked out a moderate position on the question of slavery, avoiding the extremes of immediate abolitionism and calls for unlimited protection of slavery. Why, then, did some southern states determine that his election necessitated the radical act of secession?

▶ FOR PRACTICE QUIZZES, A CUSTOMIZED STUDY PLAN, AND OTHER STUDY TOOLS, see the Online Study Guide at bedfordstmartins.com/roarkcompact.

1856 • "Bleeding Kansas."
     • Preston Brooks canes Charles Sumner.
     • Pottawatomie massacre.
     • Democrat James Buchanan elected president.
  1857 • *Dred Scott* decision.
       • Congress rejects Lecompton constitution.
       • Panic of 1857.
    1858 • Abraham Lincoln and Stephen A. Douglas debate slavery; Douglas wins Senate seat.
      1859 • John Brown raids Harpers Ferry, Virginia.
        1860 • Republican Abraham Lincoln elected president.
             • South Carolina secedes from Union.
          1861 • Six other deep South states secede.
               • The Confederate States of America is formed.
               • Lincoln takes office.

FORT SUMTER STARS AND STRIPES

This U.S. flag flew over Fort Sumter throughout the Confederate bombardment that started the Civil War on April 12, 1861. Shrapnel from thirty-three hours of cannon fire shredded the flag, but when the Union major Robert Anderson surrendered on April 13, he and his men marched out of the fort under this tattered banner. The governor of South Carolina cheered what he called the humbling of the flag of the United States. Northerners bridled at this insult, and within days flags sprouted across the Union. The Civil War stitched the flag and American nationalism together and made the Stars and Stripes the powerful symbol it is today. When Anderson returned to Fort Sumter in April 1865, he triumphantly raised this very flag.

Confederate Museum, United Daughters of the Confederacy.

15

The Crucible of War
1861–1865

O N THE RAINY NIGHT OF SEPTEMBER 21, 1862, in Wilmington, North Carolina, twenty-four-year-old William Gould and seven other black men crowded into a small boat on Cape Fear River and quietly pushed away from the dock. Knowing that the authorities would sound the alarm for eight runaway slaves at daybreak, they rowed hard throughout the night. By dawn, the runaways had traveled twenty-eight miles to where the river flowed into the Atlantic Ocean. They plunged into the swells and made for the Union navy patrolling offshore to disrupt the flow of goods in and out of Wilmington, a major Confederate port. At 10:30 that morning, the U.S.S. *Cambridge* took the men aboard.

Astonishingly, on the same day that Gould reached the federal ship, President Abraham Lincoln announced to his cabinet in Washington, D.C., that he intended to issue a proclamation of **emancipation** freeing slaves in the Confederate states. Because the proclamation would not take effect until January 1863, Gould was not legally free in the eyes of the U.S. government. But the U.S. navy, suffering from a shortage of sailors, cared little about the formal status of runaway slaves. Within days, all eight runaways became sailors "for three years," Gould said, "first taking the Oath of Allegiance to the Government of Uncle Samuel."

Unlike most slaves, William Gould could read and write, and he began making almost daily entries in a remarkable diary, apparently the only diary kept during the war by a sailor who had been a slave. In some ways, Gould's naval experience looked like that of white sailors. He found duty on a ship in the blockading squadron both boring and exhilarating. He often recorded "All hands painting, cleaning" and "Cruised as usual." But long days of tedious work were sometimes interrupted by a "period of daring exploit" as enemy ships engaged in combat. When Gould's ship closed in on one Confederate vessel, he declared that "we told them good morning in the shape of a shot." In a five-day period in 1862, his ship and two other block-aders captured four blockade runners and ran another aground. In October 1863, Gould transferred to the U.S.S. *Niagara* and sailed for European waters to search for Confederate cruisers abroad.

But Gould's Civil War experience was shaped by his race. Most whites fought to preserve their government and society, while most black men in the Union military saw service as an opportunity to fight slavery. From the be-ginning, Gould linked union and freedom, which he called "the holiest of all causes." Nevertheless, Gould witnessed a number of racial incidents on fed-eral ships. When a black regiment came aboard, "they were treated verry rough by the crew," he declared. White sailors "refused to let them eat off the mess pans and calld them all kinds of names[;]…in all they was treated

Newly Recruited Contrabands, 1862
The U.S. navy recruited men with little regard for status or color. Blacks initially served only as coal heavers, cooks, and stewards, but within a year, some black sailors joined their ships' gun crews. As this photograph of newly recruited ex-slaves reveals, naval service was not limited to young men.
Courtesy of the New Hampshire Historical Society.

shamefully." Recording another incident, Gould stated, "This Morning four or fiv[e] white fellows beat Jerry Jones (co[lored]). He was stabd in his left shoulder. Verry bad."

Still, Gould was proud of his service in the navy and monitored the progress of racial equality during the war. On shore leave in 1863, he cheered the "20th Regmt of U.S. (collard [colored]) Volunteers, the first collard Regement raised in New York pronounce[d] by all to be A splendid Regement." In March 1865, he celebrated the "passage of an amendment of the Con[sti]tution prohibiting slavery througho[ut] the United States." And a month later, he thrilled to the "Glad Tidings that the Stars and Stripe[s] had been planted over the Capital of the D—nd Confederacy by the invincible Grant." He added, we must not forget the "Mayrters to the cau[se] of Right and Equality."

Slaves like the eight runaways from Wilmington took the first steps toward making the war for union also a war for freedom. Early in the fighting, black abolitionist Frederick Douglass challenged the friends of freedom to *"be up and doing;—now is your time."* For the first eighteen months of the war, Union soldiers fought solely to uphold the Constitution and preserve the nation. But with the Emancipation Proclamation the northern war effort took on a dual purpose: to save the Union and to free the slaves.

Even if the Civil War had not touched slavery, the conflict still would have transformed America. As the world's first modern war, it mobilized the entire populations of North and South, harnessed the productive capacities of both economies, and produced battles that fielded 200,000 soldiers and created casualties in the tens of thousands. The carnage lasted four years and cost the nation an estimated 633,000 lives. The war helped mold the modern American nation-state and encouraged industrialization. The federal government emerged with new power and responsibility over national life. The war tore families apart and pushed women into new roles. But because the war for Union also became a war against slavery, the northern victory had truly revolutionary meaning. Defeat and emancipation destroyed the slave society of the Old South and gave birth to a different southern society.

Recalling the Civil War years, Frederick Douglass said, "It is something to couple one's name with great occasions." It *was* something—for William Gould and millions of other Americans. Whether they fought for the Confederacy or for the Union, whether they labored behind the lines to supply Yankee or rebel soldiers, whether they prayed for the safe return of Northerners or Southerners, all Americans experienced the crucible of war. But the war affected no group more than the four million African Americans who saw its beginning as slaves and emerged as free people.

"And the War Came"

Abraham Lincoln faced the worst crisis in the history of the nation: the threat of disunion. He revealed his strategy on March 4, 1861, in his inaugural address, firm yet conciliatory. First, he determined to avoid any act that would push the skittish Upper South (North Carolina, Virginia, Maryland, Delaware, Kentucky, Tennessee, Missouri, and Arkansas) out of the Union. Second, he reassured the Lower South (South Carolina, Georgia, Florida, Alabama, Mississippi, Louisiana, and Texas) that the Republicans would not abolish slavery. Lincoln believed that Unionists there would assert themselves and overturn the secession decision. Always, Lincoln denied the right of secession and upheld Union.

His counterpart, Jefferson Davis, fully intended to establish the Confederate States of America as an independent republic. To achieve permanence, Davis had to sustain the secession fever that had carried the Lower South out of the Union. Even if the Lower South held firm, however, the Confederacy would remain weak without additional states. Davis watched for opportunities to add new stars to the Confederate flag.

Neither man sought war. Both wanted to achieve their objectives peacefully. But as Lincoln later observed, "Both parties deprecated war, but one of them would *make* war rather than let the nation survive, and the other would *accept* war rather than let it perish. And the war came."

Attack on Fort Sumter

Major Robert Anderson and some eighty U.S. soldiers occupied Fort Sumter at the entrance to Charleston harbor. The fort with its American flag became a hated symbol of the nation that Southerners had abandoned, and they wanted federal troops out. Sumter was also a symbol to Northerners, a beacon affirming federal sovereignty in the seceded states.

Lincoln decided to hold Fort Sumter, but to do so, he had to provision it, for Anderson was running dangerously short of food. In the first week of April 1861, Lincoln authorized a peaceful expedition to bring supplies, but not military reinforcements, to the fort. The president understood that he risked war, but his plan honored his inaugural promises to defend federal property and to avoid using military force unless first attacked. Masterfully, Lincoln had shifted the fateful decision of war or peace to Jefferson Davis.

On April 9, Jefferson Davis and his cabinet met to consider the situation in Charleston harbor. The territorial integrity of the Confederacy demanded the end of the federal presence, Davis argued. But his secretary of state, Robert Toombs of Georgia, pleaded against military action. "Mr. President," he declared, "at this time it is suicide, murder, and will lose us every friend at the North. You will wantonly strike a hornet's nest which extends from mountain to ocean, and legions now

Fort Sumter after the Bombardment
Located on an artificial island inside the entrance to Charleston harbor, Fort Sumter had walls eight to twelve feet thick. The fort was so undermanned that when Confederate shells began raining down on April 12, U.S. troops could answer back with only a few of the fort's forty-eight guns. Confederate artillery lobbed more than 4,000 rounds. Cannonballs pulverized the walls, while hot shot ignited the wooden buildings inside.
Minnesota Historical Society.

quiet will swarm out and sting us to death." Davis rejected Toombs's prophecy and sent word to Confederate troops in Charleston to take the fort before the relief expedition arrived. Thirty-three hours of bombardment on April 12 and 13 reduced the fort to rubble. Miraculously, not a single Union soldier died. On April 14, with the fort ablaze, Major Anderson offered his surrender and lowered the U.S. flag. The Confederates had Fort Sumter, but they also had war.

On April 15, when Lincoln called for 75,000 militiamen to serve for ninety days to put down the rebellion, several times that number rushed to defend the flag. Democrats responded as fervently as Republicans. Stephen A. Douglas, the recently defeated Democratic candidate for president, pledged his support. "There are only two sides to the question," he said. "Every man must be for the United States or against it. There can be no neutrals in this war, *only patriots—or traitors.*" But the people of the Upper South found themselves torn.

The Upper South Chooses Sides

The Upper South faced a horrendous choice: either to fight against the Lower South or to fight against the Union. Many who only months earlier had rejected secession now embraced the Confederacy. To vote against southern independence was one thing, to fight fellow Southerners another. As one man concluded, "this is no time now to discuss the causes, but it is the duty of all who regard Southern institutions of value to side with the South, make common cause with the Confederate States and sink or swim with them."

One by one the states of the Upper South jumped off the fence. Within weeks, Virginia, Arkansas, Tennessee, and North Carolina had joined the Confederacy (Map 15.1). But in the border states of Delaware, Maryland, Kentucky, and Missouri, Unionism triumphed. Only in Delaware, where slaves accounted for less than 2 percent of the population, was the victory easy. In Maryland, Unionism needed a helping hand. Lincoln suspended the writ of habeas corpus, essentially setting aside constitutional guarantees that protect citizens from illegal and arbitrary arrest and detention, and he ordered U.S. troops into Baltimore. Maryland's legislature rejected secession.

The struggle turned violent in the West. In Missouri, Unionists won a narrow victory, but southern-sympathizing **guerrilla** bands roamed the state for the duration of the war, terrorizing civilians and soldiers alike. In Kentucky, Unionists also narrowly defeated secession, but a prosouthern minority claimed otherwise. The Confederacy, not especially careful about counting votes, eagerly made Missouri and Kentucky the twelfth and thirteenth stars on the Confederate flag.

Throughout the border states, but especially in Kentucky, the Civil War was truly a "brother's war." Seven of Henry Clay's grandsons fought: four for the Confederacy and three for the Union. Lincoln understood that the border states—particularly Kentucky—contained indispensable resources, population, and wealth and also controlled major rivers and railroads. "I think to lose Kentucky is nearly the same as to lose the whole game," Lincoln said. "Kentucky gone, we can not hold Missouri, nor, as I think, Maryland. These all against us,…we would as well consent to separation at once."

In the end, only eleven of the fifteen slave states joined the Confederate States of America. Moreover, the four seceding Upper South states contained significant numbers of people who felt little affection for the Confederacy.

MAP 15.1 Secession, 1860–1861
After Lincoln's election, the fifteen slave states debated what to do. Seven states quickly left the Union, four left after the firing on Fort Sumter, and four remained loyal to the Union.

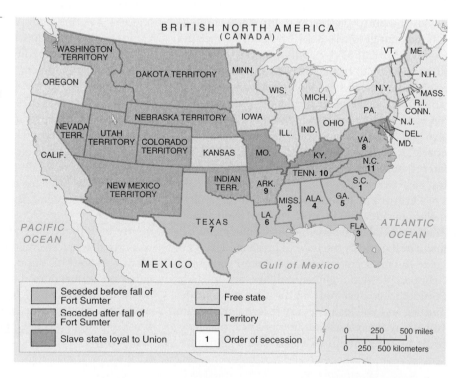

Dissatisfaction was so rife in the western counties of Virginia that in 1863 citizens there voted to create the separate state of West Virginia, loyal to the Union. Still, the acquisition of four new states greatly strengthened the Confederacy's drive for national independence.

> **REVIEW** Why did both the Union and the Confederacy consider control of the border states crucial?

The Combatants

Only slaveholders had a direct economic stake in preserving slavery (estimated at some $3 billion in 1860), but most whites in the Confederacy defended the institution, the way of life built on it, and the Confederacy itself. The degraded and subjugated status of blacks elevated the status of the poorest whites. Moreover, Yankee "aggression" was no longer a mere threat; it was real and at the South's door.

For Northerners, rebel "treason" threatened to destroy the best government on earth. The South's failure to accept the **democratic** election of a president and its firing on the nation's flag challenged the rule of law, the authority of the Constitution, and the ability of the people to govern themselves. As an Indiana soldier told his wife, a "good government is the best thing on earth. Property is nothing without it, because it is not protected; a family is nothing without it, because they cannot be educated."

While both sides claimed the lion's share of virtue, census figures show that the North's resources far surpassed the South's. Yankees took heart at their superior power, but the rebels believed they had advantages that nullified every northern strength. Both sides mobilized swiftly in 1861, and each devised what it believed would be a winning military and diplomatic strategy.

How They Expected to Win

The balance sheet of northern and southern resources reveals enormous advantages for the Union (Figure 15.1). The twenty-three states remaining in the

Union had a population of 22.3 million; the eleven Confederate states had a population of only 9.1 million, of whom 3.67 million (40 percent) were slaves. The North's economic advantages were even more overwhelming. So mismatched were Union and Confederacy that the question becomes why the South made war at all. Was not the South's cause lost before Confederates fired the first rounds at Fort Sumter? The answer quite simply is "no." Southerners expected to win—for some good reasons—and they came very close to doing so.

Southerners knew they bucked the military odds, but hadn't the **liberty**-loving colonists in 1776 also done so? "Britain could not conquer three million," a Louisianan proclaimed, and "the world cannot conquer the South." How could anyone doubt the outcome of a contest between lean, hard, country-born rebel warriors defending family, property, and liberty, and soft, flabby, citified Yankee mechanics waging an unconstitutional war?

The South's confidence also rested on its belief that northern prosperity depended on the

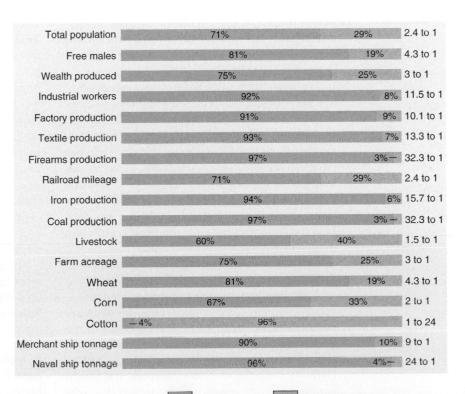

	Union	Confederacy	
Total population	71%	29%	2.4 to 1
Free males	81%	19%	4.3 to 1
Wealth produced	75%	25%	3 to 1
Industrial workers	92%	8%	11.5 to 1
Factory production	91%	9%	10.1 to 1
Textile production	93%	7%	13.3 to 1
Firearms production	97%	3%—	32.3 to 1
Railroad mileage	71%	29%	2.4 to 1
Iron production	94%	6%	15.7 to 1
Coal production	97%	3%—	32.3 to 1
Livestock	60%	40%	1.5 to 1
Farm acreage	75%	25%	3 to 1
Wheat	81%	19%	4.3 to 1
Corn	67%	33%	2 to 1
Cotton	—4%	96%	1 to 24
Merchant ship tonnage	90%	10%	9 to 1
Naval ship tonnage	96%	4%—	24 to 1

FIGURE 15.1 Resources of the Union and Confederacy
The Union's enormous statistical advantages failed to convince Confederates that their cause was doomed.

South's cotton. It followed then that without cotton, New England textile mills would stand idle. And without southern **planters** purchasing northern manufactured goods, northern factories would drown in their own unsold goods. A Virginian spoke for most Confederates when he declared that in the South's ability to "withhold the benefits of our trade, we hold a power over the North more powerful than a powerful army in the field."

Cotton would also make Europe a powerful ally of the Confederacy, Southerners reasoned. After all, they said, England's economy (and to a lesser degree France's) also depended on cotton. Of the 900 million pounds of cotton England imported annually, more than 700 million came from the South. If the supply were interrupted, sheer economic need would make England (and perhaps France) a Confederate ally. And because the British navy ruled the seas, the North would find Britain a formidable foe.

Southerners' confidence may seem naive today, but even tough-minded European military observers picked the South to win. Offsetting the Union's power was the Confederacy's expanse. The North, Europeans predicted, could not conquer the vast territory (750,000 square miles). To defeat the South, the Union would need to raise and equip a massive invading army and protect supply lines that would stretch farther than any in modern history.

Indeed, the South enjoyed major advantages, and the Confederacy devised a military strategy to exploit them. It recognized that a Union victory required the North to defeat and subjugate the South, but a Confederate victory required only that the South blunt invasions, avoid battles that risked annihilating its army, and outlast the North's will to fight. When an opportunity presented itself, the South would strike the invaders. Like the American colonists, the South could win independence by not losing the war.

If the North did nothing, the South would by default establish itself as a sovereign nation. The Lincoln administration therefore adopted an offensive strategy that applied pressure at many points. Lincoln declared a naval blockade of the Confederacy to deny the South the advantages offered by its most valuable commodity—cotton. Without the sale of cotton abroad, the South would have far fewer dollars to pay for war goods. Lincoln also ordered the Union army into Virginia, at the same time planning a march through the Mississippi valley that would cut the Confederacy in two. This ambitious strategy took advantage of the Union's superior resources.

Neither side could foresee the magnitude and duration of the war. Americans thought of war in terms of their most recent experience, the Mexican-American War of the 1840s. In Mexico, fighting had taken place between relatively small armies, had cost relatively few lives, and had inflicted only light damage on the countryside. On the eve of the Civil War, they could not know that four ghastly years of bloodletting lay ahead.

Lincoln and Davis Mobilize

Mobilization required effective political leadership, and at first glance the South appeared to have the advantage. Jefferson Davis brought to the Confederate presidency a distinguished political career, including experience in the U.S. Senate. He was also a West Point graduate, a combat veteran and authentic hero of the Mexican-American War, and a former secretary of war. In contrast, Abraham Lincoln brought to the White House one term in the House of Representatives, and his sole brush with anything military was as a captain in the militia in the Black Hawk War, a brief struggle in Illinois in 1832 in which whites expelled the last Indians from the state. The lanky, disheveled Illinois lawyer-politician looked anything but military or presidential in his bearing.

Davis, however, proved to be less than he appeared. Although he worked hard, Davis had no gift for military strategy yet intervened often in military affairs. He was an even less able political leader. Quarrelsome and proud, he had an acid tongue that made enemies the Confederacy could ill afford. He insisted on dealing with every scrap of paper that came across his desk, and he grew increasingly unbending and dogmatic.

With Lincoln, in contrast, the North got far more than met the eye. He proved himself a master politician and a superb leader. When forming his cabinet, Lincoln appointed the ablest men, no matter that they were often his chief rivals and critics. He appointed Salmon P. Chase secretary of the treasury, knowing that Chase had presidential ambitions. As secretary of state, he chose his chief opponent for the Republican nomination in 1860, William H. Seward. Despite his civilian background, Lincoln displayed an innate understanding of military strategy. No one was more crucial in mapping the Union war plan.

Minié Ball

The Union army was one of the best equipped armies in history. None of its weaponry proved more vital than a French innovation: Captain Claude Minié's new bullet. In 1848, Minié created an inch-long slug that was

rammed down a rifled barrel and would spin at great speed as it left the muzzle. The spin gave the bullet greater distance and accuracy than bullets fired from smoothbore weapons. When the war began, most soldiers carried smoothbore muskets; but by 1863, infantry on both sides fought with rifles. Bullets caused more than 90 percent of battle wounds, and minié balls proved extremely destructive to human bodies on impact.

Picture Research Consultants & Archives.

Further, Lincoln galvanized Union citizens in defense of the nation he called "the last best hope of earth."

Lincoln and Davis began gathering their armies. Confederates had to build almost everything from scratch, and Northerners had to channel their superior numbers and industrial resources to purposes of war. In 1860, the federal army numbered only 16,000 men, most of them scattered over the West subjugating Indians. One-third of the officers followed the example of the Virginian Robert E. Lee, resigning their commissions and heading south. The U.S. navy was in better shape. Forty-two ships were in service, and a large merchant marine would in time provide more ships and sailors for the Union cause. Possessing a much weaker navy, the South pinned its hopes on its armies.

The Confederacy made prodigious efforts to build new factories to produce tents, blankets, shoes, and its gray uniforms, but many rebel soldiers slept in the open air without proper clothes and sometimes without shoes. Even when factories managed to produce what the soldiers needed, southern railroads often could not deliver the goods. And each year more railroads were captured, destroyed, or left in disrepair. Food production proved less of a problem, but food sometimes rotted before it reached the soldiers. The one bright spot was the Confederacy's Ordnance Bureau, headed by Josiah Gorgas, a near miracle worker when it came to manufacturing gunpower, cannon, and rifles. In

April 1864, Gorgas proudly observed: "Where three years ago we were not making a gun, a pistol nor a sabre, no shot nor shell…—a pound of powder—we now make all these in quantities to meet the demands of our large armies."

Recruiting and supplying huge armies required enormous new revenues. At first, the Union and the Confederacy sold war bonds, which essentially were loans from patriotic citizens. In addition, both sides turned to taxes. The North raised one-fifth of its wartime revenue from taxes; the South raised only one-twentieth. Eventually, both began printing paper money. Inflation soared, but the Confederacy suffered more because it financed a greater part of its wartime costs through the printing press. Prices in the Union rose by about 80 percent during the war, while inflation in the Confederacy topped 9,000 percent.

Within months, both sides found men to fight and ways to supply and support them. But the underlying strength of the northern economy gave the Union the decided advantage. With their military and industrial muscles beginning to ripple, Northerners became itchy for action. They wanted an invasion that once and for all would smash the rebellion. Horace Greeley's *New York Tribune* began to chant: "Forward to Richmond! Forward to Richmond!"

> **REVIEW**   Why did the South believe it could win the war despite numerical disadvantages?

Battling It Out, 1861–1862

During the first year and a half of the war, armies fought major campaigns in both East and West. Because the rival capitals—Richmond and Washington, D.C.—were only ninety miles apart and each was threatened more than once with capture, the eastern campaign was especially dramatic. But the battles in the West proved more decisive. As Yankee and rebel armies pounded each other on land, the navies of each side fought on the seas and in the rivers of the South. In Europe, Confederate and U.S. diplomats competed for advantage in the corridors of power. All the while, casualty lists reached appalling lengths.

Stalemate in the Eastern Theater

Irvin McDowell, commanding general of the Union army assembling outside Washington, had no thought of taking his raw recruits into battle during the summer of 1861. Lincoln, however, ordered him to prepare his 35,000 troops for an attack on the 20,000 Confederates defending Manassas, a railroad junction in Virginia about thirty miles southwest of Washington. On July 21, the Union army forded Bull Run, a branch of the Potomac River, and engaged the southern forces effectively (Map 15.2). But fast-moving southern reinforcements blunted the Union attack and then counterattacked. What began as an orderly Union retreat turned into a panicky stampede. Demoralized federal troops ran over shocked civilians as the soldiers raced back to Washington.

By Civil War standards, casualties (wounded and dead) at Bull Run (or Manassas, as

MAP 15.2   The Civil War, 1861–1862

While eyes focused on the eastern theater, especially the 90-mile stretch of land between the U.S. capital at Washington and the Confederate capital at Richmond, Union troops were winning strategic victories in the West.

READING THE MAP: In which states did the Confederacy and the Union each win the most battles in this period? Which side used or followed water routes most for troop movements and attacks?

CONNECTIONS: Which major cities in the South and West fell to Union troops in 1862? Which strategic area did those Confederate losses place in Union hands? How did this outcome affect the later movement of troops and supplies?

FOR MORE HELP ANALYZING THIS MAP, see the visual activity for this chapter in the Online Study Guide at bedfordstmartins.com/roarkcompact.

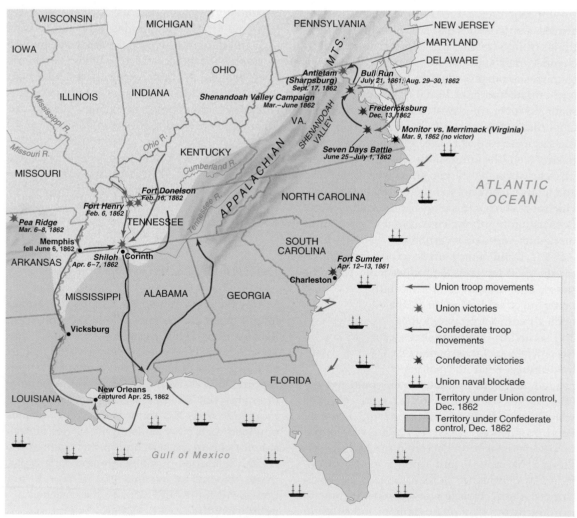

Southerners called the battle) were light. The significance of the battle lay in the lessons Northerners and Southerners drew from it. For Southerners, it confirmed the superiority of rebel fighting men and the inevitability of Confederate nationhood. Manassas was *"one of the decisive battles of the world,"* a Georgian proclaimed. It *"has secured our independence."* While victory elevated southern pride, defeat sobered Northerners. It was a major setback, admitted the *New York Tribune,* but "Let us go to work, then, with a will." Bull Run taught Lincoln that victory would be neither quick nor easy. Within four days of the disaster, the president authorized the enlistment of one million men for three years.

Lincoln also found a new general, replacing McDowell with young George B. McClellan. Born in Philadelphia of well-to-do parents,

The Battle of Savage's Station, Robert Knox Sneden, 1862
In 1862, thirty-year-old Robert Sneden joined the Fortieth New York Volunteers and soon found himself in Virginia, part of George McClellan's peninsula campaign. A gifted artist in watercolor as well as an eloquent writer, Sneden captures here an early Confederate assault in what became known as the Seven Days Battle. "The immense open space in front of Savage's [house] was densely thronged with wagon trains, artillery, caissons, ammunition trains, and moving troops," Sneden observed. The "storm of lead was continuous and deadly on the approaching lines of the Rebels. They bravely rushed up, however, to within twenty feet of our artillery, when bushels of grape and canister from the cannon laid them low in rows." Over the next three years, Sneden produced hundreds of vivid drawings and eventually thousands of pages of remembrance, providing one of the most complete accounts of a Union soldier's Civil War experience.
© 1996, Lora Robbins Collection of Virginia Art, Virginia Historical Society.

graduating from West Point second in his class, the thirty-four-year-old McClellan believed that he was a great soldier and that Lincoln was a dunce, the "original Gorilla." A superb administrator and organizer, McClellan came to Washington as commander of the newly named Army of the Potomac. McClellan energetically whipped his dispirited army into shape but was reluctant to send his soldiers into battle. For all his energy, McClellan lacked decisiveness. Lincoln wanted a general who would advance, take risks, and fight, but McClellan went into winter quarters. "If General McClellan does not want to use the army I would like to *borrow* it," Lincoln declared in frustration.

Finally, in May 1862, McClellan launched his long-awaited offensive. He transported his highly polished army, now 130,000 strong, to the mouth of the James River and began moving up the Yorktown peninsula toward Richmond. When he was within six miles of the Confederate capital, General Joseph Johnston hit him like a hammer. In the assault, Johnston was wounded and was replaced by Robert E. Lee, who would become the

South's most celebrated general. Lee named his command the Army of Northern Virginia.

The contrast between Lee and McClellan could hardly have been greater. McClellan brimmed with conceit and braggadocio; Lee was courteous and reserved. On the battlefield, McClellan grew timid and irresolute, and Lee became audaciously, even recklessly, aggressive. And Lee had at his side in the peninsula campaign military men of real talent: Thomas J. Jackson, nicknamed "Stonewall" for holding the line at Manassas, and James E. B. (Jeb) Stuart, a dashing twenty-nine-year-old cavalry commander who rode circles around Yankee troops.

Lee's assault initiated the Seven Days Battle (June 25–July 1)

Peninsula Campaign, 1862

and began McClellan's march back down the peninsula. By the time McClellan reached the safety of the Union navy, 30,000 men from both sides had died or been wounded. Although Southerners suffered twice the casualties of Northerners, Lee had saved Richmond and achieved a strategic success. Lincoln wired McClellan to abandon the peninsula campaign and replaced him with General John Pope.

In August, north of Richmond, at the second battle of Bull Run, Lee's smaller army battered Pope's forces and sent them scurrying back to Washington. Lincoln had not changed his mind about McClellan's capacity as a warrior, but he restored him to command. "If he can't fight himself, he excels in making others ready to fight," Lincoln admitted.

Sensing that he had the enemy on the ropes, Lee sought to land the knockout punch. He pushed his army across the Potomac and invaded Maryland. A victory on northern soil would dislodge Maryland from the Union, Lee reasoned, and might even cause Lincoln to sue for peace. On September 17, 1862, McClellan's forces engaged Lee's army at Antietam Creek (see Map 15.2). The Union army did severe damage. With "solid shot…cracking skulls like eggshells," according to one observer, the armies went after each other. By nightfall, 6,000 men lay dead or dying on the battlefield, and 17,000 more had been wounded. The battle of Antietam would be the bloodiest day of the war. Instead of being the war-winning fight Lee had anticipated when he came north, Antietam sent the battered Army of Northern Virginia limping back home. McClellan claimed to have saved the North, but Lincoln again removed him from command of the Army of the Potomac and appointed General Ambrose Burnside.

Although bloodied, Lee found an opportunity in December to punish the enemy at Fredericksburg, Virginia, where Burnside's 122,000 Union troops faced 78,500 Confederates dug in behind a stone wall on the heights above the Rappahannock River. Half a mile of open ground separated the armies. "A chicken could not live on that field when we open on it," a Confederate artillery officer predicted. Yet Burnside ordered a frontal assault. When the shooting ceased, the Federals counted nearly 13,000 casualties, the Confederates fewer than 5,000. The battle of Fredericksburg was one of the Union's worst defeats. As 1862 ended, the North seemed no nearer to ending the rebellion than it had been when the war began. Rather than checkmate, military struggle in the East had reached stalemate.

Union Victories in the Western Theater

While most eyes focused on events in the East, the decisive early encounters of the war were taking place between the Appalachian Mountains and the Ozarks (see Map 15.2). Confederates wanted Missouri and Kentucky, states they claimed but did not control. Federals wanted to split Arkansas, Louisiana, and Texas from the Confederacy by taking control of the Mississippi River and to occupy Tennessee, one of the Confederacy's main producers of food, mules, and iron—all vital resources.

Before Union forces could march on Tennessee, they needed to secure Missouri to the west. Union troops commanded by General Samuel R. Curtis swept across Missouri to the border of Arkansas, where in March 1862, they encountered General Earl Van Dorn's 16,000-man Confederate army, which included three regiments of Indians from the Five Civilized Nations in Indian Territory. Curtis's victory at the battle of Pea Ridge left Missouri free of Confederate troops, but Missouri was not free of Confederate guerrillas. Guerrilla bands led by the notorious William Clarke Quantrill and "Bloody Bill" Anderson burned, tortured, scalped, and murdered Union civilians and soldiers until the final year of the war.

Even farther west, Confederate armies sought to fulfill Jefferson Davis's vision of a slaveholding empire stretching all the way to the Pacific. Both sides recognized the immense value of the gold and silver mines of California, Nevada, and Colorado. A quick strike by Texas troops took Santa Fe, New Mexico, in the winter of 1861–62. Then in March 1862, a band of Colorado miners ambushed and crushed southern forces at Glorieta Pass, outside Santa Fe. Confederate military

Battle of Glorieta Pass, 1862

Native American Recruits

Both the Union and the Confederacy sought soldiers from tribes in Indian Territory. Here a Union recruiter swears in Indian recruits, but it was the Confederacy that signed treaties with the so-called Five Civilized Tribes—the Choctaw, Chickasaw, Creek, Seminole, and Cherokee—in 1861. Confederates promised to assume the financial obligations of the old treaties with the United States, guarantee slavery, respect the independence of the tribes, and permit the tribes to send delegates to Richmond. John Ross, chief of the Cherokee Nation, prayed that he had chosen the right side. "We are in the situation of a man standing upon a low naked spot of ground," he said, "with the water rising all around him.... The tide carries by him, in its mad course, a drifting log.... By refusing it he is a doomed man. By seizing hold of it he has a chance for his life." Several thousand Indians fought in blue and in gray uniforms. In some battles in Arkansas, Indians fought Indians.

Wisconsin Historical Society.

failures in the far West meant that there would be no Confederate empire beyond Texas.

The principal western battles took place in Tennessee, where General Ulysses S. Grant emerged as the key northern commander. Grant had graduated from West Point and served bravely in Mexico. When the Civil War began, he was a thirty-nine-year-old dry-goods clerk in Galena, Illinois. Gentle at home, he became pugnacious on the battlefield. "The art of war is simple," he said. "Find out where your enemy is, get at him as soon as you can and strike him as hard as you can, and keep moving on." Grant's philosophy of war as attrition would take a huge toll in human life, but it played to the North's strength: superiority in manpower. In his private's uniform and slouch hat, Grant did not look much like a general. But Lincoln, who did not look much like a president, learned his worth. Later, to critics who wanted the president to sack Grant because of his drinking, Lincoln would say: *"I can't spare this man. He fights."*

In February 1862, Grant captured Fort Henry on the Tennessee River and Fort Donelson on the Cumberland (see Map 15.2). Defeat forced the Confederates to withdraw from all of Kentucky and most of Tennessee, but Grant followed. On April 6, General Albert Sidney Johnston's army surprised him at Shiloh Church in Tennessee. Grant's troops were badly mauled the first day, but Grant remained cool and brought up reinforcements throughout the night. The next morning, the Union army counterattacked, driving the Confederates before it. The battle of Shiloh was terribly costly to both sides; there were 20,000 casualties, among them General Johnston. Grant later said that after Shiloh he "gave up all idea of saving the Union except by complete conquest."

Although no one knew it at the time, Shiloh ruined the Confederacy's bid to control the theater of operations in the West. In short order, the Yankees captured the strategic town of Corinth, Mississippi, the river city of Memphis, and the South's largest city, New Orleans. By the end of 1862, the far West and most—but not all—of the Mississippi valley lay in Union hands. At the same time, the outcome of the struggle in another theater of war was also becoming clearer.

Major Battles of the Civil War, 1861–1862

April 12–13, 1861	Attack on Fort Sumter
July 21, 1861	First battle of Bull Run (Manassas)
February 6, 1862	Battle of Fort Henry
February 16, 1862	Battle of Fort Donelson
March 9, 1862	Battle of the *Merrimack* (the *Virginia*) and the *Monitor*
March 26, 1862	Battle of Glorieta Pass
March 28, 1862	Battle of Pea Ridge
May–July 1862	McClellan's peninsula campaign
April 6–7, 1862	Battle of Shiloh
June 6, 1862	Fall of Memphis
June 25–July 1, 1862	Seven Days Battle
August 29–30, 1862	Second battle of Bull Run (Manassas)
September 17, 1862	Battle of Antietam
December 13, 1862	Battle of Fredericksburg

War and Diplomacy in the Atlantic Theater

At the beginning of the war, the U.S. navy's blockade fleet consisted of about three dozen ships to patrol more than 3,500 miles of southern coastline, and rebel merchant ships were able to slip in and out of southern ports nearly at will. Taking on cargoes in the Caribbean, sleek, fast Confederate blockade runners brought in vital supplies—guns and medicine. But with the U.S. navy commissioning a new blockader almost weekly, the naval fleet eventually numbered 150 ships on duty, and the Union navy dramatically improved its score.

Unable to build a conventional navy equal to the expanding U.S. fleet, Confederates experimented with a radical new maritime design: the ironclad warship. At Norfolk, Virginia, they layered the wooden hull of the frigate *Merrimack* with two-inch-thick armor plate. Rechristened *Virginia*, the ship steamed out in March 1862 and sank two large federal ships, killing at least 240 Union sailors (see Map 15.2). When the *Virginia* returned to finish off the federal blockaders, it was challenged by the *Monitor*, a federal ironclad of even more radical design, topped with a revolving turret holding two eleven-inch guns. On March 9, the two ships hurled shells at each other for two hours, but neither could penetrate the other's armor and the battle ended in a draw.

The Confederacy never found a way to break the Union blockade despite exploring many naval innovations including a new underwater vessel—the submarine. Each month the Union fleet tightened its noose. The growing effectiveness of the federal blockade, a southern naval officer observed, "shut the Confederacy out from the world, deprived it of supplies, weakened its military and naval strength." By 1865, the blockaders were intercepting about half of the southern ships attempting to break through.

What Confederates could not achieve on saltwater, they sought to achieve through foreign policy. In theory, King Cotton meant that cotton-starved European nations would have to break the Union blockade and recognize the Confederacy. Some European nations granted the Confederacy "belligerent" status, which enabled it to buy goods and build ships in European ports, but none challenged the blockade or recognized the Confederate States of America as a nation, a bold act that probably would have drawn them into war with the United States.

King Cotton diplomacy failed for several reasons. A bumper cotton crop in 1860 meant that the warehouses of British textile manufacturers bulged with surplus cotton throughout 1861. When a cotton shortage did occur, European manufacturers found new sources in Egypt and India. In addition, the development of a brisk trade between the Union and Britain—British war materiel for American grain and flour—helped offset the decline in textiles and encouraged Britain to remain neutral. Union military successes in the West also made Britain and France think twice about linking their fates to the Confederacy. Finally, in September 1862, five days after the Union victory at Antietam, Lincoln announced a new policy that made an alliance with the Confederacy an alliance with slavery, an alliance the French and British were not willing to make.

REVIEW   Why did King Cotton diplomacy fail?

Union *and* Freedom

For a year and a half, Lincoln insisted that the war was strictly to save the Union. But despite Lincoln's repeated pronouncements, the war for union became a war for African American freedom. Each month the conflict dragged on, it became clearer that the Confederate war machine depended heavily on slavery. Rebel armies used slaves to build fortifications, haul materiel, tend horses, and perform camp chores. On the home front, slaves labored in ironworks and shipyards, and they grew the food that fed both soldiers and civilians. Slavery undergirded the Confederacy as certainly as it had the Old South. Union military commanders and politicians alike gradually realized that to defeat the Confederacy, the North would have to destroy slavery. "I am a slow walker," Lincoln said, "but I never walk back."

From Slaves to Contraband

Lincoln detested human bondage, but as president he felt compelled to act prudently in the interests of the Union. He doubted his right under the Constitution to tamper with the "domestic institutions" of any state, even states in rebellion. An astute politician, Lincoln worked within the tight limits of public opinion. The issue of black freedom was particularly explosive in the loyal border states, where slaveholders threatened to jump into the arms of the Confederacy at even the hint of emancipation. Black freedom also raised alarms in the free states. The Democratic Party gave notice that emancipation would make the war strictly a Republican affair.

Moreover, many white Northerners were not about to risk their lives to satisfy abolitionist "fanaticism." "We Won't Fight to Free the Nigger," one popular banner read. They feared that emancipation would propel "two or three million semi-savages" northward, where they would crowd into white neighborhoods, compete for white jobs, and mix with white "sons and daughters." Thus, a surge of anti-emancipation, antiblack sentiment threatened to dislodge the loyal slave states from the Union, alienate the Democratic Party, deplete the armies, and perhaps even spark race warfare.

Yet proponents of emancipation pressed Lincoln as relentlessly as the anti-emancipation forces. Abolitionists argued that by seceding Southerners had forfeited their right to the protection of the Constitution, and that Lincoln could—as the price of their treason—legally confiscate their property in slaves. When Lincoln refused, abolitionists scalded him. Frederick Douglass labeled him "the miserable tool of traitors and rebels."

The Republican-dominated Congress declined to leave slavery policy entirely in Lincoln's hands. In August 1861, Congress approved the Confiscation Act, which allowed the seizure of any slave employed directly by the Confederate military. It also fulfilled the **free-soil** dream of prohibiting slavery in the territories and abolished slavery in Washington, D.C. Democrats and border-state representatives voted against even these mild measures, but Congress's attitude stiffened as it cast about for a just and practical slavery policy.

Slaves, not politicians, became the most insistent force for emancipation. By escaping their masters by the tens of thousands and running away to Union lines, they forced slavery on the North's wartime agenda. Runaways precipitated a series of momentous decisions. Were the runaways now free, or were they still slaves who, according to the fugitive slave law, had to be returned to their masters? At first, Yankee military officers sent the fugitives back. But Union armies needed laborers, and some officers accepted the runaways and put them to work. At Fort Monroe, Virginia, General Benjamin F. Butler refused to turn them over to their owners, calling them "contraband of war," meaning "confiscated property." Congress made Butler's practice national policy in March 1862 when it forbade returning fugitive slaves to their masters. Slaves were still not legally free, but there was a tilt toward emancipation.

Lincoln's policy of noninterference with slavery gradually crumbled. To calm Northerners' racial fears, Lincoln offered **colonization**, the deportation of African Americans from the United States to Haiti, Panama, or elsewhere. Congress voted a small amount of money to underwrite colonization, but after one miserable experiment on a small island in the Caribbean, practical limitations and black opposition sank further efforts.

While Lincoln was developing his own initiatives, he snuffed out actions that he believed would jeopardize northern unity. He was particularly alert to Union commanders who tried to dictate slavery policy from the field. In August 1861, when John C. Frémont freed the slaves belonging to Missouri rebels, Lincoln forced the general to revoke his edict and then removed him from command. The following May, when General David Hunter freed slaves in Georgia, South Carolina, and Florida, Lincoln countermanded his order. Events moved so rapidly, however, that Lincoln found it impossible to control federal policy on slavery.

From Contraband to Free People

On August 22, 1862, Lincoln replied to an angry abolitionist who demanded that he attack slavery. "My paramount objective in this struggle *is* to save the Union," Lincoln said deliberately, "and is *not* either to save or destroy slavery. If I could save the Union without freeing *any* slave I would do it, and if I could save it by freeing *all* the slaves I would do it; and if I could save it by freeing some and leaving others alone I would also do that." Instead of simply restating his old position that union was the North's sole objective, Lincoln now added that he would emancipate every slave if doing so would preserve the Union.

By the summer of 1862, events were tumbling rapidly toward emancipation. On July 17, Congress adopted a second Confiscation Act. The first had confiscated slaves employed by the Confederate military; the second declared all slaves of rebel masters "forever free of their servitude." In theory, this breathtaking measure freed most Confederate slaves, for slaveholders formed the backbone of the rebellion. Congress had traveled far since the war began.

Lincoln had, too. On July 21, the president informed his cabinet that he was ready "to take some definitive steps in respect to military action and slavery." The next day, he read a draft of a preliminary emancipation proclamation that promised to free *all* slaves in the seceding states on January 1, 1863. Lincoln described emancipation as an "act of justice," but it was the lengthening casualty lists that finally brought him around. Emancipation, he declared, was "a military necessity, absolutely essential to the preservation of the Union." On September 22, Lincoln issued his preliminary Emancipation Proclamation promising freedom to slaves in areas still in rebellion on January 1, 1863.

The limitations of the proclamation—it exempted the loyal border states and Union-occupied areas of the Confederacy—caused some to ridicule the act. The *London Times* observed cynically, "Where he has no power Mr. Lincoln will set the negroes free, where he retains power he will consider them as slaves." But Lincoln had no power to free slaves in loyal states, and invading Union armies would liberate slaves in the Confederacy as they advanced.

By presenting emancipation as a "military necessity," Lincoln hoped he had disarmed his **conservative** critics. Emancipation would deprive the Confederacy of valuable slave laborers, shorten the war, and thus save lives. Democrats, however, fumed that the "shrieking and howling abolitionist faction" had captured the White House and made it "a nigger war." Democrats made political hay out of Lincoln's action in the November 1862 elections, gaining thirty-four congressional seats. House Democrats quickly proposed a resolution branding emancipation "a high crime against the Constitution." The Republicans, who maintained narrow majorities in both houses of Congress, beat it back.

As promised, on New Year's Day 1863, Lincoln issued the final Emancipation Proclamation. In addition to freeing the slaves in the rebel states, the edict also committed the federal government to the fullest use of African Americans to defeat the Confederate enemy.

War of Black Liberation

Even before Lincoln proclaimed freedom a Union war aim, African Americans in the North had volunteered to fight. But the War Department, doubtful of their abilities and fearful of white reaction to serving side by side with them, refused to make black men soldiers. Instead, the army employed black men as manual laborers; black women sometimes found employment as laundresses and cooks. The navy, however, accepted blacks from the outset, including runaway slaves like William Gould.

As the Union experienced manpower shortages, Northerners gradually and reluctantly turned to African Americans to fill the Union army's blue uniforms. After the Emancipation Proclamation, whites—like it or not—were fighting and dying for black freedom, and few insisted that blacks remain out of harm's way behind the lines. Indeed, whites insisted that blacks share the danger, especially after March 1863, when Congress resorted to the **draft** to fill the Union army.

The military was far from color-blind. The Union army established segregated black regiments, paid black soldiers $10 per month rather than the $13 it paid to whites, refused blacks the opportunity to become commissioned officers, punished blacks as if they were slaves, and assigned blacks to labor battalions rather than to combat units. Still, when the war ended, 179,000 African American men—more than half ex-slaves—had served in the Union military, approximately 10 percent of the army total. An astounding 71 percent of black men ages eighteen to forty-five in the free states wore Union blue, a participation rate that was substantially higher than that of white men.

In time, whites allowed blacks to put down their shovels and to shoulder rifles. At the battles of Port Hudson and Milliken's Bend on the Mississippi River and at Fort Wagner in Charleston harbor, black courage under fire finally dispelled notions that African Americans could not fight. More than 38,000 black soldiers died in the Civil War, a mortality rate that was higher than that of white troops. Blacks played a crucial role in the triumph of the Union and the destruction of slavery in the South.

> **REVIEW** Why did the Union change policy in 1863 to allow black men to serve in the army?

The South at War

By seceding, Southerners brought on themselves a firestorm of unimaginable fury. Monstrous losses on the battlefields nearly bled the Confederacy to death. White Southerners on the home front also suffered, even at the hands of their own government. Efforts by the Davis administration in Richmond to centralize power to fight the war effectively convinced some men and women that the Confederacy had betrayed them. Wartime economic changes hurt everyone, some more than others. By 1863, planters and **yeomen** who had stood together began to drift apart. Most disturbing of all, slaves became open participants in the destruction of slavery and the Confederacy.

Revolution from Above

As one Confederate general observed, Southerners were engaged in a total war "in which the whole population and the whole production… are to be put on a war footing, where every institution is to be made auxiliary to war." Jefferson Davis faced the task of building an army and navy from scratch, supplying them from factories that were scarce and anemic, and paying for it all from a treasury that did not exist. Finding eager soldiers proved easiest. Very quickly, the Confederacy developed formidable striking power.

The Confederacy's economy and finances proved tougher problems. Because of the Union blockade, the government had no choice but to

Guard Detail of the 107th U.S. Colored Infantry, Arlington, Virginia, 1865
A white man's war when it began, the Civil War eventually gained color, as this photograph of the soldiers of the 107th U.S. Colored Infantry attests. The Lincoln administration was slow to accept black soldiers, in part because of lingering doubts about their ability to fight. Colonel Thomas W. Higginson, a white Massachusetts clergyman and abolitionist, commanded the First South Carolina Infantry, which was made up of former slaves. After his regiment's first skirmish with Confederate troops, Higginson celebrated his men's courage: "No officer in this regiment now doubts that the key to the successful prosecution of this war lies in the unlimited employment of black troops.…Instead of leaving their homes and families to fight they are fighting for their homes and families." After the spring of 1863, the federal government did all it could to maximize the number of black soldiers. Eventually, ex-slaves and free blacks filled 145 Union regiments. Throughout the war, however, policy required that blacks serve under white commissioned officers.
© Bettmann/Corbis.

build an industrial sector itself. Government-owned clothing and shoe factories, mines, arsenals, and powder works sprang up. The government also harnessed private companies to the war effort. Paying for the war became the most difficult task. A flood of paper money caused debilitating inflation. By 1863, Charlestonians paid ten times more for food than they had paid at the start of the war. By Christmas 1864, a Confederate soldier's monthly pay no longer bought a pair of socks. Despite bold measures, the Davis administration failed to transform the agricultural economy into a modern industrial one. The Confederacy never produced all that the South needed. Each month, the gap between the North's and the South's production widened.

Richmond's war-making effort brought unprecedented government intrusion into the private lives of Confederate citizens. In April 1862, the Confederate Congress passed the first **conscription** (draft) law in American history. All

Confederate Soldiers and Their Slaves
Soldiers of the Seventh Tennessee Cavalry pose with their slaves. Many slaveholders took "body servants" with them to war. These slaves cooked, washed, and cleaned for the white soldiers. In 1861, James H. Langhorne reported to his sister: "Peter…is charmed with being with me & 'being a soldier.' I gave him my old uniform overcoat & he says he is going to have his picture taken…to send to the servants." Do you think Peter was "puttin' on ol' massa" or just glad to be free of plantation labor?
Daguerreotype courtesy of Tom Farish. Photographed by Michael Latil.

FOR MORE HELP ANALYZING THIS IMAGE, see the visual activity for this chapter in the Online Study Guide at **bedfordstmartins.com/roarkcompact**.

able-bodied white males between the ages of eighteen and thirty-five (later seventeen and fifty) were liable to serve in the rebel army. The government adopted a policy of impressment, which allowed officials to confiscate food, horses, wagons, and whatever else they wanted from private citizens and to pay for them at below-market rates. After March 1863, the Confederacy legally impressed slaves, employing them as military laborers.

War necessitated much of the government's unprecedented behavior, but citizens found it arbitrary and inequitable. Richmond's centralizing efforts ran head-on into the South's traditional values of **states' rights** and unfettered individualism. The states lashed out at what Georgia governor Joseph E. Brown denounced as the "dangerous usurpation by Congress of the reserved right of the States." Richmond and the states struggled for control of money, supplies, and soldiers, with damaging consequences for the war effort. Individual citizens also remembered that Davis had promised to defend southern "liberty" against Republican "despotism."

Hardship Below

Hardships on the home front fell most heavily on the poor. Flour that cost three or four cents a pound in 1861 cost thirty-five cents in 1863. The draft stripped yeoman farms of men, leaving the women and children to grow what they ate. Government agents took 10 percent of farm

wives' harvests as a "tax-in-kind" on agriculture. Like inflation, shortages afflicted the entire population, but the rich lost luxuries while the poor lost necessities. In the spring of 1863, bread riots broke out in a dozen cities and villages across the South. In Richmond, a mob of nearly a thousand hungry women broke into shops and took what they needed.

"Men cannot be expected to fight for the Government that permits their wives & children to starve," a southern leader observed in November 1862. While a few wealthy individuals shared their bounty and the Confederate and state governments made efforts at social welfare, every attempt fell short. In late 1864, one desperate farm wife told her husband: "I have always been proud of you, and since your connection with the Confederate army, I have been prouder of you than ever before. I would not have you do anything wrong for the world, but before God, Edward, unless you come home, we must die." When the war ended, one-third of the soldiers had already gone home. A Mississippi deserter explained, "We are poor men and are willing to defend our country but our families [come] first."

Yeomen perceived a profound inequality of sacrifice. They called it "a rich man's war and a poor man's fight." The draft law permitted a man who had money to hire a substitute to take his place. Moreover, the "twenty-Negro law" exempted one white man on every plantation with twenty or more slaves. The government intended this law to provide protection for white women and to see that slaves tended the crops, but yeomen perceived it as rich men evading military service. A Mississippian complained that stay-at-home planters sent

Maria Isabella ("Belle") Boyd, Spy
Most white southern women, in addition to keeping their families fed and safe, served the Confederate cause by sewing uniforms, knitting socks, rolling bandages, and nursing the sick and wounded. But Belle Boyd became a spy. Only seventeen when the war broke out, she became in the words of a northern journalist "insanely devoted to the rebel cause." Her first act for the Confederacy came on July 3, 1861, when she shot a drunken federal soldier who barged into her Virginia home and insulted her mother. Her relations with occupying northern troops improved, and soon this compelling young woman was eavesdropping on officers' conversations and slipping messages to Confederate armies. Boyd's information handed Stonewall Jackson an easy victory at Front Royal, Virginia, in May 1862. "I thank you," the general wrote Boyd, "...for the immense service that you have rendered your country today." Imprisoned several times for spying, Boyd took up a theatrical career when the war ended.
Courtesy Warren Rifles Confederate Museum, Front Royal, VA.

off to war, but the extreme suffering of common folk and the relative immunity of planters fueled class animosity.

The Richmond government hoped that the crucible of war would mold a region into a nation. Officials and others worked to promote a southern **nationalism** that would "excite in our citizens an ardent and enduring attachment to our Government and its institutions." Clergymen assured their congregations that God had blessed slavery and the new nation. Patriotic songwriters, poets, authors, and artists extolled southern culture. But these efforts failed to win over thousands of die-hard Unionists. And friction between yeomen and planters increased rather than decreased. The war also threatened to rip the southern social fabric along its racial seam.

The Disintegration of Slavery

The legal destruction of slavery was the product of presidential proclamation, congressional legislation, and eventually constitutional amendment, but the practical destruction of slavery was the product of war, what Lincoln called war's "friction and abrasion." War exposed the illusion of slave contentment. Slaves took advantage of the upheaval to reach for freedom. Some half a million of the South's four million slaves ran away to northern military lines. More than 100,000 men fled bondage, took up arms as federal soldiers and sailors, and attacked slavery directly. Other men and women stayed in the slave quarter, where they staked their claim to more freedom.

War disrupted slavery in a dozen ways. Almost immediately, it called the master away, leaving white women to assume responsibility for the plantations. But mistresses could not maintain traditional standards of slave discipline in wartime, and the balance of power shifted. Slaves got to the fields late, worked indifferently, and quit early. Some slaveholders responded violently; most saw no alternative but to strike bargains—offering gifts or part of the crop—to keep slaves at home and at work. Slaveholders had believed that they "knew" their slaves but learned they did not. When the war began, a North Carolina woman praised her slaves as "diligent and respectful." When it ended, she said, "As to the idea of a *faithful servant, it is all a fiction.*"

As military action sliced through the South's farms and plantations, some slaveholders fled,

their slaves into the fields to grow cotton while in plain view "poor soldiers' wives are plowing with *their own* hands to make a subsistence for themselves and children—while their husbands are suffering, bleeding and dying for their country." In fact, most slaveholders went leaving their slaves behind. Many more took their slaves with them, but flight meant additional chaos and offered slaves new opportunities to resist bondage. But whites' greatest fear—retaliatory violence—rarely occurred. Slaves who stayed home steadily undermined white mastery and expanded control over their own lives.

> **REVIEW** How did wartime hardship in the South contribute to class animosity?

The North at War

While the North was largely untouched by the fighting, Northerners could not avoid being touched by war. Almost every family had a son, a husband, a brother in uniform. Moreover, total war blurred the distinction between home front and battlefield. As in the South, men marched off to fight, but preserving the country was also women's work. For civilians as well as soldiers, for women as well as men, war was transforming.

The need to build and fuel the Union war machine boosted the economy. The Union sent nearly 2 million men into the military and still increased production in almost every area. But because the rewards and burdens of patriotism were distributed unevenly, the North experienced sharp, even violent, divisions. Workers confronted employers, whites confronted blacks, and Democrats confronted Republicans. Still, Northerners on the home front remained fervently attached to the Union.

The Government and the Economy

When the war began, the United States had no national banking system, no national currency, and no federal income or excise taxes. But the secession of eleven slave states cut the Democrats' strength in Congress in half and destroyed their capacity to resist Republican economic programs. The Legal Tender Act of February 1862 created a national currency, paper money that Northerners called "greenbacks." With passage of the National Banking Act in February 1863, Congress created a system of national banks that by the 1870s had largely replaced the **antebellum** system of decentralized state banks. Congress also enacted a series of sweeping tax laws. By revolutionizing the country's banking, monetary, and tax structures, the Republicans generated enormous economic power.

The Republicans' wartime legislation also aimed at integrating the West more thoroughly into the Union. In May 1862, Congress approved the Homestead Act, which offered 160 acres of public land to settlers who would live and labor on it. The Homestead Act bolstered western loyalty and in time resulted in more than a million new farms. The Pacific Railroad Act in July 1862 provided massive federal assistance for building a transcontinental railroad that ran from Omaha to San Francisco when completed in 1869. Congress further bound East and West by subsidizing the Pony Express mail service and a transcontinental telegraph.

Two additional initiatives had long-term consequences for agriculture and industry. Congress created a Department of Agriculture and passed the Land-Grant College Act (also known as the Morrill Act after its sponsor, Representative Justin Morrill of Vermont), which set aside public lands to support universities that emphasized "agriculture and mechanical arts." The Lincoln administration immeasurably strengthened the North's effort to win the war, but its ideas also permanently changed the nation.

Women and Work on the Home Front

More than a million farm men were called to the military, so farm women added men's chores to their own. "I met more women driving teams on the road and saw more at work in the fields than men," a visitor to Iowa reported in the fall of 1862. Rising production figures testified to their success in plowing, planting, and harvesting. Rapid mechanization assisted farm women in their new roles. Cyrus McCormick sold 165,000 of his reapers during the war years. The combination of high prices for farm products and increased production ensured that war and prosperity joined hands in the rural North.

A few industries, such as textiles (which depended on southern cotton), declined during the war, but many more grew. Huge profits prompted one Pennsylvania ironmaster to remark, "I am in no hurry for peace." With orders pouring in and a million nonfarm workers at war, unemployment declined and wages often rose. The boom proved friendlier to owners than to workers, however. Inflation and taxes cut so deeply into workers' paychecks that their standard of living actually fell.

In cities, women stepped into jobs vacated by men, particularly in manufacturing, and also into essentially new occupations such as government secretaries and clerks. Women made up about one-quarter of the manufacturing workforce when the war began and one-third when it ended. But in 1864 New York seamstresses working fourteen-hour days earned only $1.54 a week. Urban workers resorted increasingly to strikes to wrench decent salaries from their employers, but their protests rarely succeeded. Nevertheless, tough times failed to undermine the patriotism of most workers.

Most middle-class white women stayed home and contributed to the war effort in traditional ways. They sewed, wrapped bandages, and sold homemade goods at local fairs to raise money to aid the soldiers. Other women expressed their patriotism in an untraditional way—as wartime nurses. Thousands of women on both sides defied prejudices about female delicacy and volunteered to nurse the wounded. Many northern female volunteers worked through the U.S. Sanitary Commission, a civilian organization that bought and distributed clothing, food, and medicine and recruited doctors and nurses.

Some volunteers went on to become paid military nurses. For example, Dorothea Dix, well known for her efforts to reform insane asylums, was named superintendent of female nurses in April 1861. Eventually, some 3,000 women served under her. Most nurses worked in hospitals behind the battle lines, but some, like Clara Barton, who later founded the American Red Cross, worked in battlefield units. At Antietam, as Barton was giving a wounded man a drink, a bullet ripped through her sleeve, striking and killing the soldier. Women who served in the war went on to lead the postwar movement to establish training schools for female nurses.

Union Ordnance, Yorktown, Virginia
As the North successfully harnessed its enormous industrial capacity to the needs of war, cannon, mortars, and shells poured out of its factories. A fraction of that abundance is seen here in 1862 at Yorktown, ready for transportation to Union troops in the field. Two years later, Abraham Lincoln observed that the Union was "gaining strength, and may if need be maintain the contest indefinitely.... Material resources are now more complete and abundant than ever.... The national resources are unexhausted, and, as we believe, inexhaustible."
Library of Congress.

Politics and Dissent

At first, the bustle of economic and military mobilization seemed to silence politics, but bipartisan unity did not last. Within a year, Democrats were labeling the Republican administration a "reign of terror," and Republicans were calling Democrats the party of "Dixie, Davis, and the Devil." Democrats denounced Republican policies— emancipating the slaves, subsidizing private business, and expanding federal power—as unconstitutional. In September 1862, in an effort to stifle opposition to the war, Lincoln placed under military arrest any person who discouraged enlistments, resisted the draft, or engaged in "disloyal" practices. Before the war ended, his administration imprisoned nearly 14,000 individuals, most in the border states. The campaign fell short of a reign of terror, for the majority of the prisoners were not northern Democratic opponents but Confederates, blockade runners, and citizens of foreign countries, and most of those arrested gained quick release. Still, the administration's heavy-handed tactics did suppress free speech.

When the Republican-dominated Congress enacted the draft law in March 1863, Democrats had another grievance. The law required that all men between the ages of twenty and forty-five enroll and make themselves available for a lottery that would decide who went to war. What poor men found particularly galling were provisions that allowed a draftee to hire a substitute or simply to pay a $300 fee and get out of his military obligation. As in the South, common folk could be heard chanting, "A rich man's war and a poor man's fight."

Linking the draft and emancipation, Democrats argued that Republicans employed an unconstitutional means (the draft) to achieve an unconstitutional end (emancipation). In the summer of 1863, antidraft, antiblack mobs went on rampages in northern cities. In New York City, Democratic Irish workingmen—crowded into filthy tenements, gouged by inflation, enraged by the draft, and dead set against fighting to free blacks—erupted in four days of rioting that killed at least 105 people, most of them black, and left the Colored Orphan Asylum a smoking ruin.

Racist mobs failed to achieve their purpose: the subordination of African Americans. Free black leaders had lobbied aggressively for emancipation, and after Lincoln's proclamation they fanned out over the North agitating for equality. They won few victories, however. Significant progress toward black equality would have to wait until the war ended.

REVIEW Why was the U.S. Congress able to pass such a bold legislative agenda during the war?

Vicksburg Campaign, 1863

Grinding Out Victory, 1863–1865

In the early months of 1863, the Union's prospects looked bleak, and the Confederate cause stood at high tide. Then in July 1863, the tide began to turn. The military man most responsible for this shift was Ulysses S. Grant. Lifted from obscurity by his successes in the West, Grant became the "great man of the day," one man observed in July 1864, "perhaps of the age." Elevated to supreme command, Grant knit together a powerful war machine that integrated a sophisticated command structure, modern technology, and complex logistics and supply systems. But the arithmetic of this plain man remained unchanged: Killing more of the enemy than he kills of you equaled "the complete overthrow of the rebellion."

The North ground out the victory, battle by bloody battle. The balance tipped in the Union's favor in 1863, but Southerners were not deterred. The fighting escalated in the last two years of the war. As national elections approached in the fall of 1864, Lincoln expected a war-weary North to reject him. Instead, northern voters declared their willingness to continue the war in the defense of the ideals of union and freedom.

Vicksburg and Gettysburg

Vicksburg, Mississippi, situated on the eastern bank of the Mississippi River, stood between Union forces and complete control of the river. Union forces under Grant attacked the city in May 1863, but when the Confederates beat back the assault, Grant decided to lay siege and starve out the enemy. Civilian residents of Vicksburg moved into caves to escape the incessant Union bombardment, and as the attack dragged on, they had to eat mules and rats to survive. After six weeks, on July 4, 1863, nearly 30,000 rebels marched out of Vicksburg, stacked their arms, and surrendered unconditionally. A Yankee captain wrote home to his wife: "The backbone of the Rebellion is this day broken. The Confederacy is divided.... Vicksburg is ours. The Mississippi

River is opened, and Gen. Grant is to be our next President."

On the same Fourth of July, word arrived that Union forces had crushed General Lee at Gettysburg, Pennsylvania (Map 15.3). Emboldened by his victory at Chancellorsville in May and hoping to relieve Virginia of the burden of the fighting, Lee and his 75,000-man army invaded Pennsylvania. On June 28, Union forces under General George G. Meade intercepted the Confederates at the small town of Gettysburg, where Union soldiers occupied the high ground. Three days of furious fighting involving 165,000 troops could not dislodge the Federals from the hills. Lee ached for a decisive victory, and on July 3 he ordered a major assault against the Union center on Cemetery Ridge. Open, rolling fields provided the dug-in Yankees with three-quarters of a mile of clear vision, and they raked the mile-wide line of Confederate soldiers under General George E. Pickett with cannon and rifle fire. Gettysburg cost Lee more than one-third of his army—28,000 casualties. "It's all my fault," he lamented. In a drenching rain on the night of July 4, 1863, he marched his battered army back to Virginia.

The twin disasters at Vicksburg and Gettysburg proved to be the turning point of the war. The Confederacy could not replace the nearly 60,000 soldiers who were captured, wounded, or killed. Lee never launched another major offensive north of the Mason-Dixon line. It is hindsight, however, that permits us to see the pair of battles as decisive. At the time, the Confederacy still controlled the heartland of the South, and Lee still had a vicious sting. War-weariness threatened to erode the North's will to win before Union armies could destroy the Confederacy's ability to go on.

Grant Takes Command

Toward the end of September 1863, Union general William Rosecrans placed his army in a dangerous situation in Chattanooga, Tennessee, where he had retreated after defeat at the battle of

Battle of Gettysburg, July 1–3, 1863

Chickamauga earlier in the month (see Map 15.3). Rebels surrounded the disorganized bluecoats and threatened to starve them into submission. Grant, now commander of Union forces between the Mississippi River and the Appalachians, arrived in Chattanooga in October. Within weeks, he opened an effective supply line, broke the siege, and routed the Confederate army. The victory at Chattanooga on November 25 opened the door to Georgia. It also confirmed Lincoln's estimation of Grant. In March 1864, the president asked Grant to come east to become the general in chief of all Union armies.

In Washington, Grant implemented his grand strategy for a war of attrition. He ordered a series of simultaneous assaults from Virginia to Louisiana. Two actions proved more significant than the others. In one, General William Tecumseh Sherman, whom Grant appointed his successor to command the western armies, plunged southeast toward Atlanta. In the other, Grant, who took control of the Army of the Potomac, went head-to-head with Lee for almost four straight weeks in Virginia.

Grant and Lee met in the first week of May 1864 in northern Virginia in a dense tangle of scrub oaks and small pines. Often unable to see more than ten paces, the armies pounded away at each other until approximately 18,000 Yankees and 11,000 rebels had fallen. The savagery of the Battle of the Wilderness did not compare with that at Spotsylvania Court House a few days later. Frenzied men fought hand to hand for eighteen hours in the rain. One veteran remembered men "piled upon each other in some places four layers deep, exhibiting every ghastly phase of mutilation." Spotsylvania cost Grant another 18,000 casualties and Lee 10,000, but the Yankee bulldog would not let go. Grant kept moving and tangled with Lee again at Cold Harbor, where he suffered 13,000 additional casualties to Lee's 5,000. (See "Historical Question," page 392.)

Twice as many Union soldiers as rebel soldiers died in four weeks of fighting in Virginia in May and June, but because Lee had only half as

Grant at Cold Harbor
Seated next to his chief of staff, John A. Rawlins, at his Cold Harbor, Virginia, headquarters, Ulysses S. Grant plots his next move against Robert E. Lee. On June 3, 1864, Grant ordered frontal assaults against entrenched Confederate forces, resulting in enormous Union losses. "I am disgusted with the generalship displayed," young Brigadier General Emory Upton exclaimed. "Our men have, in many cases, been foolishly and wantonly slaughtered." Years later, Grant said that he regretted the assault at Cold Harbor, but in 1864 he kept pushing toward Richmond.
Chicago Historical Society.

many troops as Grant, his losses were equivalent to Grant's. Grant knew that the South could not replace the losses. Moreover, the campaign carried Grant to the outskirts of Petersburg, just

south of Richmond, where he abandoned the costly tactic of the frontal assault and began a siege that immobilized both armies and dragged on for nine months.

Simultaneously, Sherman invaded Georgia. Grant instructed Sherman to "get into the interior of the enemy's country as far as you can, inflicting all the damage you can against their War resources." In early May, Sherman moved 100,000 men south against the 65,000 rebels. Skillful maneuvering, constant skirmishing, and one pitched battle, at Kennesaw Mountain, brought Sherman to Atlanta, which fell on September 2.

Intending to "make Georgia howl," Sherman marched out of Atlanta on November 15 with 62,000 battle-hardened veterans, heading for Savannah, 285 miles away on the Atlantic coast. One veteran remembered, "[We] destroyed all we could not eat, stole their niggers, burned their cotton & gins, spilled their sorghum, burned & twisted their R. Roads and raised Hell generally." Sherman's "March to the Sea" aimed at destroying the will of the southern people. A few weeks earlier, General Philip H. Sheridan had carried out his own scorched-earth campaign in the Shenandoah Valley, complying with Grant's order to turn the valley into "a barren waste...so that crows flying over it for the balance of this season will have to carry their provender [food] with them." When Sherman's troops entered an undefended Savannah in mid-December, the general telegraphed Lincoln that he had "a Christmas gift" for him. A month earlier, Union voters had bestowed on the president an even greater gift.

The Election of 1864

In the summer 1864, with Sherman temporarily checked outside Atlanta and Grant bogged down in the siege of Petersburg, the Democratic Party smelled victory in the fall elections. Rankled by inflation, the draft, the attack on civil liberties, and the commitment to blacks, Northerners appeared ready for a change. Lincoln himself concluded, "It seems exceedingly probable that this administration will not be re-elected."

Democrats were badly divided, however. "Peace" Democrats insisted on an armistice, while "war" Democrats supported the conflict but opposed Republican means of fighting it. The party tried to paper over the chasm by nominating a war

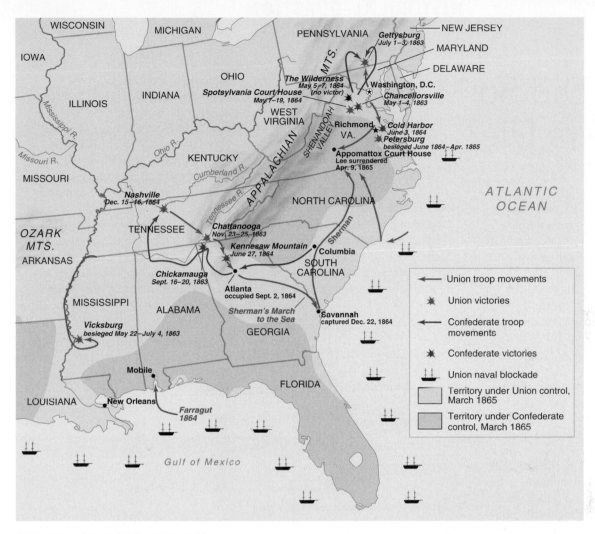

MAP 15.3   The Civil War, 1863–1865
Ulysses S. Grant's victory at Vicksburg divided the Confederacy at the Mississippi River. William Tecumseh Sherman's march from Chattanooga to Savannah divided it again. In northern Virginia, Robert E. Lee fought fiercely, but Grant's larger, better-supplied armies prevailed.

candidate, General George McClellan, but adopting a peace platform that demanded that "immediate efforts be made for a cessation of hostilities." Republicans denounced the peace plank as a sellout that "virtually proposed to surrender the country to the rebels in arms against us."

The capture of Atlanta on September 2 turned the political tide in favor of the Republicans. Lincoln received 55 percent of the popular vote, but his electoral margin was a whopping 212 to McClellan's 21. Republicans also gained large margins over the Democrats in the congressional elections. Lincoln's party won a resounding victory, one that gave him a mandate to continue the war until slavery and the Confederacy were dead.

The Confederacy Collapses

As 1865 dawned, military disaster littered the Confederate landscape. With the destruction of John B. Hood's army at Nashville in December 1864, the interior of the Confederacy lay in Yankee hands (see Map 15.3). Sherman's troops, resting momentarily in Savannah, eyed South Carolina hungrily. Farther north, Grant had Lee's army pinned down in Petersburg, a few miles from Richmond.

More and more Confederates turned their backs on the rebellion. News from the battlefields made it difficult not to conclude that the Yankees had beaten them. Soldiers' wives begged their husbands to return home to keep their families

Why Did So Many Soldiers Die?

From 1861 to 1865, Americans killed Americans on a scale never before seen. Not until the First World War, a half century later, would the world match (and surpass) the killing fields at Shiloh, Antietam, and Gettysburg (Figure 15.2). Why were the Civil War totals so horrendous? Why did 260,000 rebel soldiers and 373,000 Union soldiers die?

By the mid-nineteenth century, the balance between the ability to kill and the ability to save lives had tipped disastrously toward death. The sheer size of the armies—some battles involved more than 200,000 soldiers—ensured that battlefields would turn red with blood. Moreover, armies fought with antiquated Napoleonic strategy. In the generals' eyes, the ideal soldier was trained to advance with his comrades in a compact, close-order formation. Theory also emphasized frontal assaults. In classrooms at West Point and on the high plains of Mexico in the 1840s, men learned that infantry advancing shoulder to shoulder, supported by artillery, carried the day.

By the 1860s, modern technology had made such strategy appallingly deadly. Weapons with rifled barrels (that is, with spiral grooves cut into the bore) were replacing smoothbore muskets and cannon. Rifles propelled spinning bullets four times as far as muskets—about 320 yards. The rifle's greater range and accuracy,

and rifled cannons firing canisters filled with flesh-ripping, bone-breaking steel shot, made sitting ducks of charging infantry units and gave an enormous advantage to entrenched defensive forces. As a result,

battles took thousands of lives in a single day. On July 2, 1862, the morning after the battle at Malvern Hill in eastern Virginia, a Union officer surveyed the scene: "Over 5,000 dead and wounded men were on the ground…enough were alive and moving to give to the field a singular crawling effect."

Wounded soldiers often lay on battlefields for hours, sometimes days, without water or care of any kind. When the Civil War began, no one anticipated casualty lists with

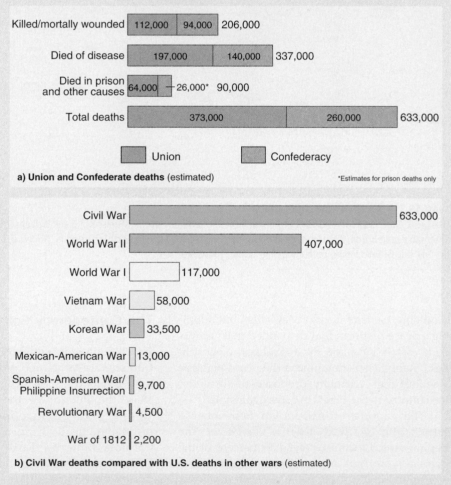

a) **Union and Confederate deaths** (estimated)   *Estimates for prison deaths only

b) **Civil War deaths compared with U.S. deaths in other wars** (estimated)

FIGURE 15.2 Civil War Deaths
The loss of life in the Civil War was almost equal to the losses in all other American wars.

thousands of names. Union and Confederate medical departments could not cope with skirmishes, much less large-scale battles. They had no ambulance corps to remove the wounded from the scene. They had no field hospitals. Early in the war, someone in the U.S. Quartermaster Department, which was responsible for constructing Union hospitals, responded to demands that it do something to improve the care of the wounded by saying: "Men need guns, not beds." Only the shock of massive casualties compelled reform. A lack of resources meant that the South lagged behind the North, but gradually both North and South organized effective ambulance corps, built hospitals, and hired trained surgeons and nurses.

Soldiers did not always count speedy transportation to a field hospital as a blessing. As one Union soldier said, "I had rather risk a battle than the Hospitals." Real danger lurked behind the lines. While the technology of killing advanced to very high standards, medicine remained primitive. Physicians gained a reputation as butchers, and soldiers dreaded the operating table more than they did entrenched riflemen. Serious wounds to a leg or an arm usually meant amputation, the best way doctors knew to save lives. After major battles, surgeons worked among piles of severed limbs.

A wounded man's real enemy was not doctors' callousness but medical ignorance. Physicians had almost no knowledge of the cause and transmission of disease or the benefits of antiseptics. Not aware of basic germ theory, they spread infection almost every time they operated.

Doctors wore the same bloody smocks for days and washed their hands and their scalpels and saws in buckets of dirty water. When they had difficulty threading their needles, they wet the thread with their own saliva. Soldiers often did not survive amputations, not because of the operation but because of the infection that inevitably followed. Of the Union soldiers whose legs were amputated above the knee, more than half died. A Union doctor discovered in 1864 that bromine (previously used in combination with other elements as a sedative) arrested gangrene, but the best that most amputees could hope for was maggots, which ate dead flesh on the stump and thus inhibited the spread of infection. During the Civil War, nearly one of every five wounded rebel soldiers died, and one of every six Yankees. A century later, in Vietnam, the proportion of deaths was one wounded American soldier in four hundred.

Soldiers who avoided battlefield wounds and hospital infections still faced sickness. Deadly diseases swept through crowded army camps, where latrines were often dangerously close to drinking-water supplies. The principal killers were dysentery and typhoid, but pneumonia and malaria also cut down thousands. Doctors did what they could, but often their treatments only added to the misery. They prescribed doses of turpentine for patients with typhoid, they fought respiratory problems with mustard plasters, and they attacked intestinal disorders by blistering the skin with sulfuric acid.

Thousands of female nurses, including Dorothea Dix, Clara Barton, and Juliet Ann Opie Hopkins, im-

Doctor's Surgical Kit
With simple instruments like these, not unlike the tools of the butcher's trade, northern and southern surgeons performed approximately 60,000 amputations. Approximately 45,000 of the amputees survived.
Chicago Historical Society.

proved the wounded men's odds and alleviated their suffering. Civilian relief agencies, such as the U.S. Sanitary Commission and the Women's Relief Society of the Confederacy, promoted hygiene in army camps and made some headway. Nevertheless, as Figure 15.2 shows, disease killed nearly twice as many soldiers as did combat. Many who died of disease were prisoners of war. Approximately 30,000 Northerners died in Confederate prisons, and approximately 26,000 Southerners died in Union prisons. No northern prison, however, could equal the horror of Andersonville in southern Georgia. In August 1864, about 33,000 emaciated men lived in unspeakable conditions in a 26-acre barren stockade with no shelter except what the prisoners were able to construct. More than 13,000 perished.

In the end, 633,000 northern and southern soldiers died, a staggering toll.

from starving, and the stream of deserters became a flood. In most cases, white Southerners lost the will to continue not so much because they lost faith in independence but because they had been battered into submission. They had demonstrated remarkable endurance for their cause. Half of the 900,000 Confederate soldiers had been killed or wounded, and ragged, hungry women and children had sacrificed throughout the bloodiest war then known to history.

The end came with a rush. On February 1, 1865, Sherman's troops stormed out of Savannah into South Carolina, the "cradle of the Confederacy." In Virginia, Lee abandoned Petersburg, and Richmond fell. Grant pursued Lee until he surrendered on April 9, 1865, at Appomattox Court House, Virginia. Grant offered generous peace terms. He allowed Lee's men to return home and to keep their horses to help "put in a crop to carry themselves and their families through the next winter." With Lee gone, the remaining Confederate armies lost hope and gave up within two weeks. After four years, the war was over.

No one was more relieved than Lincoln, but his celebration was restrained. He told his cabinet that his postwar burdens would weigh almost as heavily as those of wartime. Seeking

Ruins of Richmond
A Union soldier and a small boy wearing a Union cap contemplate the silence and devastation of the Confederacy's capital. On their way out of the city on the evening of April 2, 1865, Confederate demolition squads set fire to tobacco warehouses and ammunition dumps. Huge explosions tore holes in the city, and windswept fires destroyed much of what was left standing. As one Confederate observed, "The old war-scarred city seemed to prefer annihilation to conquest."
Library of Congress.

Major Battles of the Civil War, 1863–1865

May 1–4, 1863	Battle of Chancellorsville
July 1–3, 1863	Battle of Gettysburg
July 4, 1863	Fall of Vicksburg
September 16–20, 1863	Battle of Chickamauga
November 23–25, 1863	Battle of Chattanooga
May 5–7, 1864	Battle of the Wilderness
May 7–19, 1864	Battle of Spotsylvania Court House
June 3, 1864	Battle of Cold Harbor
June 27, 1864	Battle of Kennesaw Mountain
September 2, 1864	Fall of Atlanta
November–December 1864	Sheridan sacks Shenandoah Valley
	Sherman's "March to the Sea"
December 15–16, 1864	Battle of Nashville
December 22, 1864	Fall of Savannah
April 2–3, 1865	Fall of Petersburg and Richmond
April 9, 1865	Lee surrenders at Appomattox Court House

distraction, Lincoln attended Ford's Theatre on the evening of Good Friday, April 14, 1865. John Wilkes Booth, an actor with southern sympathies, slipped into the president's box and shot Lincoln in the head. He died at 7:22 the following morning. Vice President Andrew Johnson became president. The man who had led the nation through the war would not lead it during the postwar search for a just peace.

> **REVIEW** Why were the siege of Vicksburg and the battle of Gettysburg crucial to the outcome of the war?

Conclusion: The Second American Revolution

A transformed nation emerged from the crucible of war. Antebellum America was decentralized politically and loosely integrated economically. To accommodate Union victory, Congress enacted legislation that reshaped the nation's political and economic character. It created national currency and banking systems and turned to free land, a transcontinental railroad, and miles of telegraph lines to bind the West to the rest of the nation. Congress also established the sovereignty of the federal government and permanently increased its power. To most citizens before the war, Washington meant the post office and little more; during the war years, the federal government drafted, taxed, and judged Americans in unprecedented ways. The massive changes brought about by war—the creation of a national government, a national economy, and a national spirit—led one historian to call the American Civil War the "Second American Revolution."

The Civil War also had a profound effect on individual lives. When the war began in 1861, millions of men dropped their hoes, hammers, and pencils, put on blue or gray uniforms, and fought and suffered for what they passionately believed was right. The war disrupted families, leaving women at home with additional responsibilities while offering new opportunities to others for wartime work in factories, offices, and hospitals. It offered blacks new and more effective ways to resist slavery and agitate for equality.

The war devastated the South. Three-fourths of southern white men of military age served in the Confederate army, and at least half of them were captured, wounded, or killed or died of disease. The war destroyed two-fifths of the South's livestock, wrecked half of the farm machinery, and blackened dozens of cities and towns. The immediate impact of the war on the North was more paradoxical. The struggle cost the North a heavy price: 373,000 lives. But rather than devastating the land, war set the countryside and cities humming with business activity. The radical shift in power from South to North signaled a new direction in American development: the long decline of agriculture and the rise of industrial capitalism.

Most revolutionary of all, the war ended slavery. Ironically, the South's war to preserve slavery destroyed it. Ex-slaves like William Gould dedicated their wartime service to its eradication. Because slavery was both a labor and a racial system, the institution was entangled in almost every aspect of southern life. Slavery's uprooting inevitably meant fundamental change. But the full meaning of abolition remained unclear in 1865. Determining the new economic, political, and social status of four million ex-slaves would be the principal task of reconstruction.

Suggestions for Further Reading

Ira Berlin et al., eds., *Freedom: A Documentary History of Emancipation, 1861–1867*, 4 vols. (1982–1993). A monumental collection of contemporary documents that recount the black experience in the war.

Richard J. Carwardine, *Lincoln* (2003). A fresh biography of Lincoln as war leader.

Catherine Clinton and Nina Silber, eds., *Divided Houses: Gender and the Civil War* (1992). Essays that demonstrate that the Civil War was more than a "brother's war."

Gary W. Gallagher, *The Confederate War* (1997). A lively account of white Southerners' steadfast commitment to the Confederate cause.

William B. Gould IV, ed., *Diary of a Contraband: The Civil War Passage of a Black Sailor* (2002). A remarkable account of an ex-slave's service in the Union navy.

Margaret M. Storey, *Loyalty and Loss: Alabama's Unionists in the Civil War and Reconstruction* (2004). A new understanding of divided loyalties on the Confederate home front.

▶ For more books about topics in this chapter, see the Online Bibliography at bedfordstmartins.com/roarkcompact.

▶ For additional firsthand accounts of this period, see Chapter 15 in Michael Johnson, ed., *Reading the American Past*, Third Edition.

▶ For Web sites and documents related to topics and places in this chapter, see "HistoryLinks," "DocLinks," and "PlaceLinks" at bedfordstmartins.com/roarkcompact.

REVIEWING THE CHAPTER

Follow these steps to review and strengthen your understanding of the chapter.

STEP 1: *Study the* **Key Terms** *and* **Timeline** *to identify the significance of each item listed.*

STEP 2: *Answer the* **Review Questions**, *drawing on key terms and dates to support your answers.*

STEP 3: *Drawing on the Key Terms, Timeline, and Review Questions, answer the broader* **Making Connections** *questions.*

KEY TERMS

Who

Frederick Douglass (p. 370)
Abraham Lincoln (pp. 370, 374)
Jefferson Davis (pp. 371, 374)
Salmon P. Chase (p. 374)
William H. Seward (p. 374)
George B. McClellan (p. 377)
Joseph Johnston (p. 377)
Robert E. Lee (p. 377)
Ambrose Burnside (p. 378)
Samuel R. Curtis (p. 378)
William Clarke Quantrill (p. 378)
"Bloody Bill" Anderson (p. 378)
Ulysses S. Grant (p. 379)
Benjamin F. Butler (p. 381)
Dorothea Dix (p. 387)
Clara Barton (p. 387)
George G. Meade (p. 389)
George E. Pickett (p. 389)
William Tecumseh Sherman (p. 389)
Philip H. Sheridan (p. 390)

What

Fort Sumter (p. 371)
battle of Bull Run/Manassas (p. 376)
Virginia peninsula campaign (p. 377)
Seven Days Battle (p. 377)
battle of Antietam (p. 378)
battle of Fredericksburg (p. 378)
battle of Pea Ridge (p. 378)
Fort Henry (p. 379)
Fort Donelson (p. 379)
battle of Shiloh (p. 379)
Union blockade (p. 380)
Merrimack/Virginia (p. 380)
Monitor (p. 380)
King Cotton diplomacy (p. 380)
Confiscation Act (p. 381)
contraband of war (p. 381)
second Confiscation Act (p. 382)
Emancipation Proclamation (p. 382)
bread riots (p. 384)
National Banking Act (p. 386)

Homestead Act (p. 386)
Pacific Railroad Act (p. 386)
Land-Grant College Act (Morrill Act)
   (p. 386)
U.S. Sanitary Commission (p. 387)
American Red Cross (p. 387)
Union draft law (p. 388)
New York City draft riots (p. 388)
siege of Vicksburg (p. 388)
battle of Gettysburg (p. 389)
battle of Chattanooga (p. 389)
Battle of the Wilderness (p. 389)
Sherman's "March to the Sea" (p. 390)
"peace" Democrats (p. 390)

TIMELINE

1861 • **April.** Attack on Fort Sumter.

• **April–May.** Four Upper South states join Confederacy.

• **July.** Union forces routed in first battle of Bull Run.

• **August.** First Confiscation Act.

1862 • Grant captures Fort Henry and Fort Donelson.

• **March.** Confederates defeated at battle of Glorieta Pass.

• Union victory at battle of Pea Ridge.

• **April.** Battle of Shiloh in Tennessee ends Confederate bid to control Mississippi valley.

• Confederate Congress authorizes draft.

• **May.** Homestead Act.

• **May–July.** Union forces defeated during Virginia peninsula campaign.

• **July.** Second Confiscation Act.

• Militia Act.

• **September.** Battle of Antietam stops Lee's advance into Maryland.

REVIEW QUESTIONS

1. Why did both the Union and the Confederacy consider control of the border states crucial? (pp. 370–73)

2. Why did the South believe it could win the war despite numerical disadvantages? (pp. 373–75)

3. Why did King Cotton diplomacy fail? (pp. 375–80)

4. Why did the Union change policy in 1863 to allow black men to serve in the army? (pp. 380–83)

5. How did wartime hardship in the South contribute to class animosity? (pp. 383–86)

6. Why was the U.S. Congress able to pass such a bold legislative agenda during the war? (pp. 386–88)

7. Why were the siege of Vicksburg and the battle of Gettysburg crucial to the outcome of the war? (pp. 388–95)

MAKING CONNECTIONS

1. Despite loathing slavery, Lincoln embraced emancipation as a war objective late and with great caution. Why? In your answer, trace the progression of Lincoln's position, considering how legal, political, military, and moral concerns influenced his policies.

2. The Emancipation Proclamation did not accomplish the destruction of slavery on its own. How did a war over union bring about the end of slavery? In your answer, consider the direct actions of slaves and Union policymakers as well as indirect factors within the Confederacy.

3. In addition to restoring union and destroying slavery, what other significant changes did the war produce on the home front and in the nation's capital? In your answer, discuss economic, governmental, and social developments, being attentive to regional variations.

4. Brilliant military strategy alone did not determine the outcome of the war; victory also depended on generating revenue, material mobilization, diplomacy, and politics. In light of these considerations, explain why the Confederacy believed it would succeed, and why it ultimately failed.

▶ **For practice quizzes, a customized study plan, and other study tools,** see the Online Study Guide at bedfordstmartins.com/roarkcompact.

1863
- **January.** Emancipation Proclamation becomes law.
- **February.** National Banking Act.
- **March.** Congress authorizes draft.
- **July.** Fall of Vicksburg to Union forces.
- Lee defeated at battle of Gettysburg.
- New York City antidraft riots.

1864
- **March.** Grant appointed Union general in chief.
- **May–June.** The Wilderness campaign.
- **September.** Fall of Atlanta to Sherman.
- **November.** Lincoln reelected.
- **December.** Fall of Savannah to Sherman.

1865
- **April 2–3.** Fall of Petersburg and Richmond.
- **April 9.** Lee surrenders to Grant.
- **April 15.** Lincoln dies from bullet wound.
- Vice President Andrew Johnson becomes president.

CARPETBAG

A carpetbag was a nineteenth-
century suitcase made from carpet, often brightly
colored. Applied first to wildcat bankers on the western frontier, "carpetbagger" was a derogatory name for rootless and penniless adventurers
who could carry everything they owned in a single carpetbag. Critics of Republican administrations in the South hurled the name "carpetbaggers" at white Northerners who
moved South during reconstruction and became active in politics. According to white
Southerners, carpetbaggers exploited gullible ex-slaves to gain power and wealth. In
fact, many Northerners who came to the South joined with blacks and some southern
whites to form Republican state and local governments that were among the most
progressive anywhere in the nineteenth century.

Private Collection/Picture Research Consultants & Archives.

16

Reconstruction

1863–1877

"**Y**ORK DISAPPEARED on yesterday morning," David Golightly Harris noted in his journal on June 6, 1865. "I suppose that he has gone to the yankey. I wish they would give him a good whipping & hasten him back." York, a black field hand, had once belonged to Harris, a white slaveholder in Spartanburg District, South Carolina. When York disappeared, the war had been over for two months, and York was a free man. In Harris's mind, however, simply declaring York free did not make him so. In July, Harris noted that another field hand, Old Will, had left "to try to enjoy the freedom the Yankey's have promised the negroes." Two weeks later, black freedom still seemed in doubt. "There is much talk about freeing the negroes. Some are said already to have freed them," Harris declared. But Harris had not freed anyone. He did not inform his former slaves of their freedom until federal military authorities forced him to. "Freed the Negroes," he declared on August 16, four months after Appomattox and more than two and a half years after the Emancipation Proclamation.

Like many ex-slaveholders, Harris had trouble coming to grips with **emancipation**. "Family well, Horses well, Cattle well, Hogs well & everything else are well so far as I know, if it was not for the free negroes," Harris declared on September 17. "On their account everything is turned upside down. So much so that we do not know what to do with our land, nor who to hire if we want it worked.... We are in the midst of troublesome times & do not know what will turn up." Harris had owned ten slaves, and now he faced what seemed to him an insoluble problem. He needed blacks to cultivate his farm, but like most whites he did not believe that African Americans would work much when free. Some kind of compulsion would be needed, but slavery was gone, leaving the South upside down. White men in Harris's neighborhood sought to set it straight again. "In this district several negroes have been badly whipped & several have been hung by some unknown persons," he noted in November. "This has a tendency to keep them in their proper bounds & make them more humble." But the violence did not keep ex-slaves from acting like free people. On Christmas Day 1865, Harris recorded, "The negroes leave today to hunt themselves a new home while we will be left to wait upon ourselves."

Across the South, ex-masters predicted that emancipation would mean economic collapse and social anarchy. Carl Schurz, a Union general who undertook a fact-finding mission to the former Confederate states in the summer of 1865, encountered this dire prediction often enough to conclude that the Civil War was a "revolution but half accomplished." Northern victory had freed the slaves, but it had not changed former slaveholders' minds about the need for slavery. Left to themselves, Schurz believed, whites would "introduce some new system of forced labor, not perhaps exactly slavery in its old form but something similar to it." To defend their freedom, blacks would need federal protection, land of their own, and voting rights, Schurz concluded. Until whites "cut loose from the past, it will be a dangerous experiment to put Southern society upon its own legs." Schurz discovered that the end of the war did not mean the beginning of peace. Instead, the nation entered one of its most chaotic and violent eras—Reconstruction, an era that would define the status of the defeated South within the Union and the meaning of freedom for ex-slaves.

The status of the South and the contours of black freedom were determined in the nation's capital, where the federal government played an active role, but also in the state legislatures and county seats of the South. Moreover, on farms and plantations from Virginia to Texas, ex-slaves like York and Old Will, who were determined to become free people, battled with whites like David Golightly Harris, who clung to the Old South. In the midst of the racial flux and chaos, a small band of crusading women sought to achieve gender equality. The years of reconstruction witnessed an enormous struggle to determine the consequences of Confederate defeat and emancipation. Although white Southerners prevailed, their **New South** was a very different South from the one to which whites like David Golightly Harris wished to return.

Wartime Reconstruction

Reconstruction did not wait for the end of war. As the odds of a northern victory increased, thinking about reunification quickened. Immediately, a question arose: Who had authority to devise a plan for reconstructing the Union? Lincoln believed firmly that reconstruction was a matter of executive responsibility. Congress just as firmly asserted its jurisdiction. Fueling the argument about who had authority to set the terms of reconstruction were significant differences about the terms themselves. Lincoln's primary aim was the restoration of national unity, which he sought through a program of speedy, forgiving political reconciliation. Congress feared that the president's program amounted to restoring the old southern ruling class to power. It wanted greater assurances of white loyalty and greater guarantees of black rights.

Black Woman in Cotton Fields, Thomasville, Georgia
Few images of everyday black women during the Reconstruction era survive. This photograph was taken in 1895, but it nevertheless goes to the heart of the labor struggle after the Civil War. Before emancipation black women worked in the fields, and after emancipation white landlords wanted them to continue working there. Freedom allowed some women to escape field labor, but not this Georgian, who probably worked to survive. The photograph reveals a strong person with a clear sense of who she is. Though worn to protect her head and body from the fierce heat, her intricately wrapped headdress dramatically expresses her individuality. Her bare feet also reveal something about her life.
Courtesy, Georgia Department of Archives and History, Atlanta, Georgia.

In their eagerness to formulate a plan for political reunification, neither Lincoln nor Congress gave much attention to the South's land and labor problems. But as the war rapidly eroded slavery and traditional plantation agriculture, Yankee military commanders in the

Union-occupied areas of the Confederacy had no choice but to oversee the emergence of a new labor system.

"To Bind Up the Nation's Wounds"

On March 4, 1865, President Abraham Lincoln delivered his second inaugural address. He surveyed the history of the long, deadly war and then looked ahead to peace. "With malice toward none; with charity for all; with firmness in the right, as God gives us to see the right," Lincoln said, "let us strive on to finish the work we are in; to bind up the nation's wounds...to do all which may achieve and cherish a just, and a lasting peace." Lincoln had contemplated reunion for nearly two years. While deep compassion for the enemy guided his thinking about peace, his plan for reconstruction aimed primarily at shortening the war and ending slavery.

In his Proclamation of Amnesty and Reconstruction, issued in December 1863, Lincoln offered a full pardon to rebels willing to renounce secession and to accept emancipation. (Pardons were valuable because they restored all property, except slaves, and full political rights.) When merely 10 percent of a state's voting population had taken an oath of allegiance, the state could organize a new government. Lincoln's plan did not require ex-rebels to extend social or political rights to ex-slaves, nor did it anticipate a program of long-term federal assistance to freedmen. Clearly, the president looked forward to the speedy restoration of the broken Union.

Lincoln's easy terms enraged abolitionists like Bostonian Wendell Phillips, who charged that the president "makes the negro's freedom a mere sham." He "is willing that the negro should be free but seeks nothing else for him," Phillips declared. Phillips and other northern radicals called instead for a thorough overhaul of southern society. Their ideas proved to be too drastic for most Republicans during the war years, but Congress agreed that Lincoln's plan was inadequate. In July 1864, Congress put forward a plan of its own.

Congressman Henry Winter Davis of Maryland and Senator Benjamin Wade of Ohio jointly sponsored a bill that demanded that at least half of the voters in a conquered rebel state take the oath of allegiance before reconstruction could begin. Moreover, the Wade-Davis bill banned ex-Confederates from participating in the drafting of new state constitutions. Finally, the bill guaranteed the equality of freedmen before the law. When Lincoln exercised his right not to sign the bill and let it die instead, Wade and Davis published a manifesto charging the president with usurpation of power. They warned Lincoln to confine himself to "his executive duties—to obey and execute, not make the laws—to suppress by arms armed rebellion, and leave political organization to Congress."

Undeterred, Lincoln continued to nurture the formation of loyal state governments under his own plan. Four states—Louisiana, Arkansas, Tennessee, and Virginia—fulfilled the president's requirements, but Congress refused to seat representatives from the "Lincoln states." In his last public address in April 1865, Lincoln defended his plan but for the first time expressed publicly his endorsement of **suffrage** for southern blacks, at least "the very intelligent, and... those who serve our cause as soldiers." The announcement demonstrated that Lincoln's thinking about reconstruction was still evolving. Four days later, he was dead.

Land and Labor

Of all the problems raised by the North's victory in the war, none proved more critical than the South's transition from slavery to **free labor**. As federal armies invaded and occupied the Confederacy, hundreds of thousands of slaves became free workers. Union armies controlled vast territories in the South where legal title to land had become unclear. The wartime Confiscation Acts punished "traitors" by taking away their property. The question of what to do with federally occupied land and how to organize labor on it engaged former slaves, former slaveholders, Union military commanders, and federal government officials long before the war ended.

Up and down the Mississippi valley, occupying federal troops announced a new labor code. The code required slaveholders to sign contracts with ex-slaves and to pay wages. It obligated employers to provide food, housing, and medical care. It outlawed whipping, but it reserved to the army the right to discipline blacks who refused to work. The code required black laborers to enter into contracts, work diligently, and remain subordinate and obedient. Military leaders clearly had no intention of promoting a social or economic revolution. Instead, they sought to restore plantation agriculture with wage labor. The effort resulted in a hybrid system that one contemporary called "compulsory free labor," something that satisfied no one.

Planters complained because the new system fell short of slavery. Blacks could not be "transformed by proclamation," a Louisiana sugar planter warned. Yet under the new system, blacks "are expected to perform their new obligations without coercion, & without the fear of punishment which is essential to stimulate the idle and correct the vicious." Without the right to whip, he concluded, the new labor system did not have a chance.

African Americans found the new regime too reminiscent of slavery to be called free labor, and they lamented its failure to provide them land of their own. "What's the use of being free if you don't own land enough to be buried in?" one man asked. Freedmen believed they had a moral right to land because they and their ancestors had worked it without compensation for more than two centuries. Moreover, several wartime developments led them to believe that the federal government planned to undergird black freedom with landownership.

In January 1865, General William Tecumseh Sherman set aside part of the coast south of Charleston for black settlement. By June 1865, some 40,000 freedmen sat on 400,000 acres of "Sherman land." In addition, in March 1865, Congress passed a bill establishing the Bureau of Refugees, Freedmen, and Abandoned Lands. The Freedmen's Bureau, as it was called, distributed food and clothing to destitute Southerners and eased the transition of blacks from slaves to free persons. Congress also authorized the agency to divide abandoned and confiscated land into 40-acre plots, to rent them to freedmen, and eventually to sell them "with such title as the United States can convey." By June 1865, the bureau had situated nearly 10,000 black families on a half million acres abandoned by fleeing planters. Hundreds of thousands of other ex-slaves eagerly anticipated farms of their own.

Despite the flurry of activity, wartime reconstruction failed to produce agreement about whether the president or Congress had the authority to devise and direct policy or what proper policy should be. As Lincoln anticipated, the nation faced postwar dilemmas almost as trying as those of the war.

The African American Quest for Autonomy

Ex-slaves never had any doubt about what they wanted from freedom. They had only to contemplate what they had been denied as slaves. (See "Documenting the American Promise," page 404.) Slaves had to remain on their plantations; freedom allowed blacks to go wherever they pleased. Thus, in the first heady weeks after emancipation, freedmen often abandoned their plantations just to see what was on the other side of the hill. Slaves had to be at work in the fields by dawn; freedom permitted blacks to taste the formerly forbidden pleasure of sleeping through a sunrise. Freedmen also tested the etiquette of racial subordination. "Lizzie's maid passed me today when I was coming from church *without speaking to me*," huffed one plantation mistress.

To whites, emancipation looked like pure anarchy. Blacks, they said, had reverted to their natural condition: lazy, irresponsible, and wild. Actually, these former slaves were experimenting with freedom, but they could not long afford to roam the countryside, neglect work, and casually provoke whites. Soon, most were back at work in the kitchens and fields.

But other items on ex-slaves' agenda of freedom endured. They dreamed of land of their own. "The way we can best take care of ourselves is to have land," an ex-slave declared in 1865, "and turn it and till it by our own labor." Another explained that he wanted land, "not a Master or owner[,] Neither a driver with his Whip." In addition, freedmen wanted to learn to read and write. "I wishes the Childern all in School," a black Union army veteran asserted. "It is beter for them then to be their Sureving a mistes [mistress]."

Another persistent black aspiration was secure and complete families. Thousands of black men and women took to the roads in 1865 to look for kin who had been sold away or to free those who were being held illegally as slaves. A black soldier from Missouri wrote his daughters that he was coming for them. "I will have you if it cost me my life," he declared. "Your Miss Kitty said that I tried to steal you," he told them. "But I'll let her know that god never intended for a man to steal his own flesh and blood." And he swore that "if she meets me with ten thousand soldiers, she [will] meet her enemy."

Another hunger was for independent worship. Blacks greeted freedom with a mass exodus from white churches. Some joined the newly established southern branches of all-black northern churches, such as the African Methodist Episcopal Church. Others formed black versions of the major southern denominations, Baptists and Methodists. Freedmen interpreted the events of the Civil War and reconstruction as Christian people. One black woman thanked Lincoln for the Emancipation Proclamation, declaring, "When you are dead and in Heaven, in a thousand years that action of yours will make the Angels sing your praises I know it."

REVIEW   Why did Congress object to Lincoln's wartime plan for reconstruction?

Presidential Reconstruction

Abraham Lincoln died on April 15, 1865, just hours after John Wilkes Booth shot him at a Washington, D.C., theater. Chief Justice Salmon P. Chase immediately administered the oath of office to Vice President Andrew Johnson of Tennessee. Congress had adjourned in March, which meant that legislators were away from Washington when Lincoln was killed. They would not reconvene until December. Throughout the summer and fall, therefore, the "accidental president" made critical decisions about the future of the South without congressional input. Like Lincoln, Johnson believed that responsibility for restoring the Union lay with the president. With dizzying speed, he drew up and executed a plan of reconstruction.

Congress returned to the capital in December to find that, as far as the president and former Confederates were concerned, reconstruction was already decided. Most Republicans, however, thought Johnson's modest demands of ex-rebels made a mockery of the sacrifice of Union soldiers. It appeared to them that Johnson had acted as midwife to the rebirth of the Old South and the stillbirth of black liberty. To let his program stand, Republican legislators said, would mean that the North's dead had indeed died in vain. They proceeded to dismantle it and substitute a program of their own, one that southern whites found ways to resist.

Johnson's Program of Reconciliation

Born in 1808 in Raleigh, North Carolina, Andrew Johnson was the son of illiterate parents. Self-educated and ambitious, Johnson moved to Tennessee, where he worked as a tailor, accumu-

lated a fortune in land, acquired five slaves, and built a career in politics championing the South's common white people and assailing its "illegitimate, swaggering, bastard, scrub aristocracy." The only senator from a Confederate state to remain loyal to the Union, Johnson held the planter class responsible for secession. Less than two weeks before he became president, he made it clear what he would do to planters if he ever had the chance: "I would arrest them—I would try them—I would convict them and I would hang them."

Despite such statements, Johnson was no friend of the Republicans. A southern Democrat all his life, Johnson occupied the White House only because the Republican Party in 1864 had needed a vice presidential candidate who would appeal to loyal, Union-supporting Democrats. Johnson favored traditional Democratic causes, vigorously defending **states' rights** (but not secession) and opposing Republican efforts to expand the power of the federal government. A steadfast defender of slavery, Johnson had owned slaves until 1862, when Tennessee rebels, angry at his Unionism, confiscated them. He only grudgingly accepted emancipation. When he did, it was more because he hated planters than sympathized with slaves. "Damn the negroes," he said. "I am fighting those traitorous aristocrats, their masters." At a time when the nation confronted the future of black Americans, the new president harbored unshakable racist convictions. Africans, Johnson said, were "inferior to the white man in point of intellect—better calculated in physical structure to undergo drudgery and hardship."

Like Lincoln, Johnson stressed reconciliation between the Union and the defeated Confederacy and rapid restoration of civil government in the South. Like Lincoln, he promised to pardon most, but not all, ex-rebels. Johnson recognized the state governments created by Lincoln but set out his own requirements for restoring the other rebel states to the Union. All that the citizens of a state had to do was to renounce the right of secession, deny that the debts of the Confederacy were legal and binding, and ratify the Thirteenth Amendment abolishing slavery, which became part of the Constitution in December 1865. Johnson's plan ignored Lincoln's acceptance near the end of his life of some form of limited black voting.

Johnson's eagerness to restore relations with southern states and his lack of sympathy for blacks also led him to return to pardoned

The Meaning of Freedom

On New Year's Day 1863, President Abraham Lincoln issued the Emancipation Proclamation. It states that "all persons held as slaves" within the states still in rebellion "are, and henceforward shall be, free." Although the Proclamation in and of itself did not free any slaves, it transformed the character of the war. Despite often intolerable conditions, black people focused on the possibilities of freedom.

DOCUMENT 1
Letter from John Q. A. Dennis
to Edwin M. Stanton, July 26, 1864

John Q. A. Dennis, formerly a slave in Maryland, wrote to ask Secretary of War Edwin M. Stanton for help in reuniting his family.

Boston

Dear Sir I am Glad that I have the Honour to Write you afew line I have been in troble for about four yars my Dear wife was taken from me Nov 19th 1859 and left me with three Children and I being a Slave At the time Could Not do Anny thing for the poor little Children for my master it was took me Carry me some forty mile from them So I Could Not do for them and the man that they live with half feed them and half Cloth them & beat them like dogs & when I was admitted to go to see them it use to brake my heart & Now I say again I am Glad to have the honour to write to you to see if you Can Do Anny thing for me or for my poor little Children I was keap in Slavy untell last Novr 1863. then the Good lord sent the Cornel borne [federal Colonel William Birney?] Down their in Marland in worsester Co So as I have been recently freed I have but letle to live on but I am Striveing Dear Sir but what I went too know of you Sir is it possible for me to go & take my Children from those men that keep them in Savery if it is possible will you pleas give me a permit from your hand then I think they would let them go....

Hon sir will you please excuse my Miserable writeing & answer me as soon as you can I want get the little Children out of Slavery, I being Criple would like to know of you also if I Cant be permited to rase a Shool Down there & on what turm I Could be admited to Do so No more At present Dear Hon Sir

SOURCE: Ira Berlin, Joseph P. Reidy, and Leslie S. Rowland, eds., *Freedom: A Documentary History of Emancipation, 1861–1867*, ser. 1, vol. 1, *The Destruction of Slavery*, 386. Copyright © 1985. Reprinted with the permission of Cambridge University Press.

DOCUMENT 2
Report from Reverend
A. B. Randall, February 28, 1865

Freedom prompted ex-slaves to seek legal marriages, which under slavery had been impossible. Writing from Little Rock, Arkansas, to the adjutant general of the Union army, A. B. Randall, the white chaplain of a black regiment, affirmed the importance of marriage to freed slaves and emphasized their conviction that emancipation was only the first step toward full freedom.

Weddings, just now, are very popular, and abundant among the Colored People. They have just learned, of the Special Order No. 15. of Gen Thomas [Adjutant General Lorenzo Thomas] by which, they may not only be lawfully married, but have their Marriage Certificates, Recorded; in a book furnished by the Government. This is most desirable.... Those who were captured...at Ivy's Ford, on the 17th of January, by Col Brooks, had their Marriage Certificates, taken from them; and destroyed; and then were roundly cursed, for having such papers in their posession. I have married, during the month, at this Post; Twenty five couples; mostly, those, who have families; & have been living together for years. I try to dissuade single men, who are soldiers, from marrying, till their time of enlistment is out: as that course seems to me, to be most judicious.

The Colord People here, generally consider, this war not only; their exodus, from bondage; but the road, to Responsibility; Competency; and an honorable Citizenship—God grant that their hopes and expectations may be fully realized.

SOURCE: Ira Berlin, Joseph P. Reidy, and Leslie S. Rowland, eds., *Freedom: A Documentary History of Emancipation, 1861–1867*, ser. 2, vol. 1, *The Black Military Experience*, 712. Copyright © 1982. Reprinted with the permission of Cambridge University Press.

DOCUMENT 3
Petition "to the Union
Convention of Tennessee
Assembled in the Capitol at
Nashville," January 9, 1865

Early efforts at political reconstruction prompted petitions from former slaves

demanding civil and political rights. In January 1865, black Tennesseans petitioned a convention of white Unionists debating the reorganization of state government.

We the undersigned petitioners, American citizens of African descent, natives and residents of Tennessee, and devoted friends of the great National cause, do most respectfully ask a patient hearing of your honorable body in regard to matters deeply affecting the future condition of our unfortunate and long suffering race.

First of all, however, we would say that words are too weak to tell how profoundly grateful we are to the Federal Government for the good work of freedom which it is gradually carrying forward; and for the Emancipation Proclamation which has set free all the slaves in some of the rebellious States, as well as many of the slaves in Tennessee....

We claim freedom, as our natural right, and ask that in harmony and co-operation with the nation at large, you should cut up by the roots the system of slavery, which is not only a wrong to us, but the source of all the evil which at present afflicts the State. For slavery, corrupt itself, corrupted nearly all, also, around it, so that it has influenced nearly all the slave States to rebel against the Federal Government, in order to set up a government of pirates under which slavery might be perpetrated.

In the contest between the nation and slavery, our unfortunate people have sided, by instinct, with the former. We have little fortune to devote to the national cause, for a hard fate has hitherto forced us to live in poverty, but we do devote to its success, our hopes, our toils, our whole heart, our sacred honor, and our lives. We will work, pray, live, and, if need be, die for the Union, as cheerfully as ever a white patriot died for his country. The color of our skin does not lessen in the least degree, our love either for God or for the land of our birth....

We know the burdens of citizenship, and are ready to bear them. We know the duties of the good citizen, and are ready to perform them cheerfully, and would ask to be put in a position in which we can discharge them more effectually....

This is a democracy—a government of the people. It should aim to make every man, without regard to the color of his skin, the amount of his wealth, or the character of his religious faith, feel personally interested in its welfare. Every man who lives under the Government should feel that it is his property, his treasure, the bulwark and defence of himself and his family, his pearl of great price, which he must preserve, protect, and defend faithfully at all times, on all occasions, in every possible manner.

This is not a Democratic Government if a numerous, law-abiding, industrious, and useful class of citizens, born and bred on the soil, are to be treated as aliens and enemies, as an inferior degraded class, who must have no voice in the Government which they support, protect and defend, with all their heart, soul, mind, and body, both in peace and war....

The possibility that the negro suffrage proposition may shock popular prejudice at first sight, is not a conclusive argument against its wisdom and policy. No proposition ever met with more furious or general opposition than the one to enlist colored soldiers in the United States army. The opponents of the measure exclaimed on all hands that the negro was a coward; that he would not fight; that one white man, with a whip in his hand could put to flight a regiment of them; that the experiment would end in the utter rout and ruin of the Federal army. Yet the colored man has fought so well, on almost every occasion, that the rebel government is prevented, only by its fears and distrust of being able to force him to fight for slavery as well as he fights against it, from putting half a million of negroes into its ranks.

The Government has asked the colored man to fight for its preservation and gladly has he done it. It can afford to trust him with a vote as safely as it trusted him with a bayonet.

SOURCE: Ira Berlin, Joseph P. Reidy, and Leslie S. Rowland, eds., *Freedom: A Documentary History of Emancipation, 1861–1867*, ser. 2, vol. 1, *The Black Military Experience*, 811–16. Copyright © 1982. Reprinted with the permission of Cambridge University Press.

QUESTIONS FOR ANALYSIS AND DEBATE

1. How does John Q. A. Dennis interpret his responsibility as a father?

2. Why do you think ex-slaves wanted their marriages legalized?

3. Why, according to petitioners to the Union Convention of Tennessee, did blacks deserve voting rights?

ex-Confederates all confiscated and abandoned land, even if it was in the hands of freedmen. Reformers were shocked. They had expected the president's hatred of planters to mean the permanent confiscation of the South's plantations and the distribution of the land to loyal freedmen. Instead, his instructions canceled the promising beginnings made by General Sherman and the Freedmen's Bureau to settle blacks on land of their own. As one freedman observed, "Things was hurt by Mr. Lincoln getting killed."

White Southern Resistance and Black Codes

In the summer of 1865, delegates across the South gathered to draw up the new state constitutions required by Johnson's plan of reconstruction. Rather than take their medicine, delegates choked on even the president's mild requirements. Refusing to renounce secession, the South Carolina and Georgia conventions

merely "repudiated" their secession ordinances, preserving in principle their right to secede. South Carolina and Mississippi refused to disown their Confederate war debts. Mississippi rejected the Thirteenth Amendment outright, and Alabama rejected it in part. Despite these defiant acts, Johnson did nothing. By failing to draw a hard line, he rekindled southern resistance. White Southerners began to think that by standing up for themselves they—not victorious Northerners—would shape reconstruction. In the fall of 1865, newly elected southern legislators set out to reverse what they considered the "retreat into barbarism" that followed emancipation.

State governments across the South adopted a series of laws known as black codes, which made a travesty of black freedom. The codes sought to keep ex-slaves subordinate to whites by subjecting them to every sort of discrimination. Several states made it illegal for blacks to own a gun. Mississippi made insulting gestures and language by blacks a criminal offense. The codes barred blacks from jury duty. Not a single southern state granted any black—no matter how educated, wealthy, or refined—the right to vote.

At the core of the black codes, however, lay the matter of labor. Faced with the death of slavery, legislators sought to hustle freedmen back to the plantations. South Carolina attempted to limit blacks to either farmwork or domestic service by requiring them to pay annual taxes of $10 to $100 to work in any other occupation. Mississippi declared that blacks who did not possess written evidence of employment could be declared vagrants and be subject to involuntary plantation labor. Most states allowed judges to bind black children—orphans and others whose parents they deemed unable to support them—to white employers. Under these so-called apprenticeship laws, courts bound thousands of black children to work for planter "guardians."

Johnson refused to intervene. A staunch defender of states' rights, he believed that the citizens of every state should be free to write their own constitutions and laws. Moreover, since Johnson was as eager as other white Southerners to restore white supremacy and black subordination, the black codes did not offend him.

But Johnson also followed the path that he believed would offer him the greatest political return. A **conservative** Tennessee Democrat at the head of a northern Republican Party, he began to look southward for political allies.

The Black Codes
Titled "Selling a Freeman to Pay His Fine at Monticello, Florida," this 1867 drawing from a northern magazine equates the black codes with the reinstitution of slavery. The laws stopped short of reenslavement but sharply restricted blacks' freedom. In Florida, as in other southern states, certain acts, such as breaking a labor contract, were made criminal offenses, the penalty for which could be involuntary plantation labor for a year.
Library of Congress.

Despite tough talk about punishing traitors, he personally pardoned 14,000 wealthy or high-ranking ex-Confederates. By pardoning powerful whites, by acquiescing in the black codes, and by accepting governments even when they failed to satisfy his minimal demands, he won useful southern friends.

In the elections of 1865, white Southerners dramatically expressed their mood. To represent them in Congress, they chose former Confederates, not loyal Unionists. Of the eighty senators and representatives they sent to Washington, fifteen had served in the Confederate army, ten of them as generals. Another sixteen had served in civil and judicial posts in the Confederacy. Nine others had served in the Confederate Congress. One— Alexander Stephens—had been vice president of the Confederacy. In December, this remarkable group arrived on the steps of the nation's Capitol building to be seated in Congress. As one Georgian remarked, "It looked as though Richmond had moved to Washington."

Expansion of Federal Authority and Black Rights

Southerners had blundered monumentally. They had assumed that what Andrew Johnson was willing to accept Republicans would accept as well. But southern intransigence compelled even moderates to conclude that ex-rebels were a "generation of vipers," still untrustworthy and dangerous.

The black codes became a symbol of southern intentions to "restore all of slavery but its name." Northerners were hardly saints when it came to racial justice, but black freedom had become a hallowed war aim. "We tell the white men of Mississippi," the *Chicago Tribune* roared, "that the men of the North will convert the State of Mississippi into a frog pond before they will allow such laws to disgrace one foot of the soil in which the bones of our soldiers sleep and over which the flag of freedom waves."

The moderate majority of the Republican Party wanted only assurance that slavery and treason were dead. They did not champion black equality or the confiscation of plantations or black voting, as did the radicals, a minority within the party. But southern obstinacy had succeeded in forging unity (at least temporarily) among Republican factions. In December 1865, exercising Congress's right to determine the qualifications of its members, Republicans refused to seat the southern representatives. Rather than accept Johnson's claim that the "work of restoration" was done, Congress challenged his executive power. Congressional Republicans enjoyed a three-to-one majority over the Democrats, and if they could agree on a program of reconstruction, they could easily pass legislation and even override presidential vetoes.

Senator Lyman Trumbull of Illinois declared that the president's policy meant that the ex-slave would "be tyrannized over, abused, and virtually reenslaved without some legislation by the nation for his protection." Early in 1866, the moderates produced two bills that strengthened the federal shield. The first, the Freedmen's Bureau bill, prolonged the life of the agency established by the previous Congress. Since the end of the war, it had distributed food, supervised labor contracts, and sponsored schools for freedmen. Arguing that the Constitution never contemplated a "system for the support of indigent persons," President Andrew Johnson vetoed the bill. Congress failed by a narrow margin to override the president's veto.

The moderates designed their second measure, the Civil Rights Act, to nullify the black codes by affirming African Americans' rights to "full and equal benefit of all laws and proceedings for the security of person and property as is enjoyed by white citizens." The act boldly required the end of legal discrimination in state laws and represented an extraordinary expansion of black rights and federal authority. The president argued that the civil rights bill amounted to "unconstitutional invasion of states' rights" and vetoed it. In essence, he denied that the federal government possessed authority to protect the civil rights of blacks.

In April 1866, an incensed Republican Party again pushed the civil rights bill through Congress and overrode the presidential veto. In July, it passed another Freedmen's Bureau bill and overrode Johnson's veto. For the first time in American history, Congress had overridden presidential vetoes of major legislation. As a worried South Carolinian observed, Johnson had succeeded in uniting the Republicans and probably touched off "a fight this fall such as has never been seen."

REVIEW How did the North respond to the passage of black codes in the southern states?

Congressional Reconstruction

By the summer of 1866, President Andrew Johnson and Congress had dropped their gloves and stood toe to toe in a bare-knuckled contest unprecedented in American history. Johnson made it clear that he would not budge on either constitutional issues or policy. Moderate Republicans responded by amending the Constitution. But the obstinacy of Johnson and white Southerners pushed Republican moderates ever closer to the radicals and to acceptance of additional federal intervention in the South. In time, Congress debated whether to give the ballot to black men. Outside of Congress, blacks championed color-blind voting rights, while women sought to make voting sex-blind as well.

The Fourteenth Amendment and Escalating Violence

In June 1866, Congress passed the Fourteenth Amendment to the Constitution, and two years later it gained the necessary ratification of three-fourths of the states. The most important provisions of this complex amendment made all native-born or naturalized persons American citizens and prohibited states from abridging the "privileges and immunities" of citizens, depriving them of "life, liberty, or property without due process of law," and denying them "equal protection of the laws." By making blacks national citizens, the amendment provided a national guarantee of equality before the law. In essence, it protected blacks against violation by southern state governments.

The Fourteenth Amendment also dealt with voting rights. It gave Congress the right to reduce the congressional representation of states that withheld suffrage from some of its adult male population. In other words, white Southerners could either allow black men to vote or see their representation in Washington slashed.

Republicans stood to benefit from the Fourteenth Amendment. If southern whites granted voting rights to freedmen, Republicans, entirely a northern party, would gain valuable black votes, establish a wing in the South, and secure their national power. But if whites refused, representation of southern Democrats would plunge, and Republicans would still gain political power.

The Fourteenth Amendment's suffrage provisions completely ignored the small band of politicized and energized women who had emerged from the war demanding "the ballot for the two disenfranchised classes, negroes and women." Founding the American Equal Rights Association in 1866, Susan B. Anthony and Elizabeth Cady Stanton lobbied for "a government by the people, and the whole people; for the people and the whole people." They felt betrayed when their old antislavery allies, who now occupied positions of national power, proved to be fickle and refused to work for their goals. "It was the Negro's hour," Frederick Douglass later explained. Charles Sumner suggested that woman suffrage could be "the great question of the future."

The Fourteenth Amendment dashed women's expectations. It provided for punishment of any state that excluded voters on the basis of race but not on the basis of sex. The amendment also introduced the word *male* into the Constitution when it referred to a citizen's right to vote. Stanton predicted that "if that word 'male' be inserted, it will take us a century at least to get it out."

Tennessee approved the Fourteenth Amendment in July, and Congress promptly welcomed the state's representatives and senators back. Had Johnson counseled other southern states to ratify this relatively mild amendment and warned them that they faced the fury of an outraged Republican Party if they refused, they might have listened. Instead, Johnson advised Southerners to reject the Fourteenth Amendment and to rely on him to trounce the Republicans in the fall congressional elections.

Johnson had decided to make the Fourteenth Amendment the overriding issue of the 1866 congressional elections and to gather its white opponents into a new conservative party, the National Union Party. The president's strategy suffered a setback when whites in several southern cities went on rampages against blacks—an escalation of the violence that had never really ceased. When a mob in New Orleans assaulted delegates to a black suffrage convention, 34 blacks died. In Memphis, white mobs crashed through the black sections of town, killing at least 46 people. The slaughter shocked Northerners and renewed skepticism about Johnson's claim that southern whites could be trusted. "Who doubts that the Freedmen's Bureau ought to be abolished forthwith," a New Yorker observed sarcasti-

Susan B. Anthony

Like many outspoken suffragists, Anthony, depicted here in 1852, began her public career working on behalf of temperance and abolition. But she grew tired of laboring under the direction of male clergymen—"white orthodox little saints," she called them—who controlled the reform movements and routinely dismissed the opinions of women. Anthony's continued passion for other causes—improving working conditions for labor, for example—led some conservatives to oppose women's political rights because they equated the suffragist cause with radicalism in general. Women could not easily overcome such views, and the long struggle for the vote eventually drew millions of women into public life.

Susan B. Anthony House, Inc.

cally, "and the blacks remitted to the paternal care of their old masters, who 'understand the nigger, you know, a great deal better than the Yankees can.'"

The 1866 election resulted in an overwhelming Republican victory in which the party retained its three-to-one congressional majority. Johnson had bet that Northerners would not support federal protection of black rights and that a racist backlash would blast the Republican Party. But the war was still fresh in northern minds, and as one Republican explained, southern whites "with all their intelligence were traitors, the blacks with all their ignorance were loyal."

Radical Reconstruction and Military Rule

The elections of 1866 should have taught southern whites the folly of relying on Andrew Johnson to guide them through reconstruction. But when Johnson continued to urge Southerners to reject the Fourteenth Amendment, every southern state except Tennessee voted it down. "The last one of the sinful ten," thundered Representative James A. Garfield of Ohio, "has flung back into our teeth the magnanimous offer of a generous nation." After the South rejected the moderates' program, the radicals seized the initiative.

Each act of defiance by southern whites had boosted the standing of the radicals within the Republican Party. Except for freedmen themselves, no one did more to make freedom the "mighty moral question of the age." Radicals like Massachusetts senator Charles Sumner and Pennsylvania representative Thaddeus Stevens did not speak with a single voice, but they united in demanding civil and political equality. They insisted on extending to ex-slaves the same opportunities that northern working people enjoyed under the free-labor system. Southern states were "like clay in the hands of the potter," Stevens declared in January 1867, and he called on Congress to begin reconstruction all over again.

In March 1867, Congress overturned the Johnson state governments and initiated military rule of the South. The Military Reconstruction Act (and three subsequent acts) divided the ten unreconstructed Confederate states into five military districts. Congress placed a Union general in charge of each district and instructed him to "suppress insurrection, disorder, and violence" and to begin political reform. After the military had completed voter registration, which would include black men, voters in each state would elect delegates to conventions that would draw up new state constitutions. Each constitution would guarantee black suffrage. When the voters of each state had approved the constitution and the state legislature had ratified the Fourteenth Amendment, the state could submit its work to Congress. If Congress approved, the state's senators and representatives

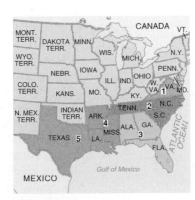

Reconstruction Military Districts, 1867

could be seated, and political reunification would be accomplished.

Radicals proclaimed the provision for black suffrage "a prodigious triumph," for it extended far beyond the limited suffrage provisions of the Fourteenth Amendment. Republicans united in the conviction that only the voting power of ex-slaves could bring about a permanent revolution in the South. Indeed, suffrage provided blacks with a powerful instrument of change and self-protection. When combined with the disfranchisement of thousands of ex-rebels, it promised to cripple any neo-Confederate resurgence and guarantee Republican state governments in the South.

Despite its bold suffrage provision, the Military Reconstruction Act of 1867 disappointed those who advocated the confiscation and redistribution of southern plantations to ex-slaves. Thaddeus Stevens, who believed that at bottom reconstruction was an economic problem, agreed with the freedman who said, "Give us our own land and we take care of ourselves, but without land, the old masters can hire us or starve us, as they please." But most Republicans believed they had already provided blacks with what they needed: equal legal rights and the ballot. If blacks were to get forty acres, they would have to gain the land themselves.

Declaring that he would rather sever his right arm than sign such a formula for "anarchy and chaos," Andrew Johnson vetoed the Military Reconstruction Act. Congress overrode his veto the very same day, dramatizing the shift in power from the executive to the legislative branch of government. With the passage of the Reconstruction Acts of 1867, congressional reconstruction was virtually completed. Congress left whites owning most of the South's land but, in a departure that justified the term "radical reconstruction," had given black men the ballot. In 1867, the nation began an unprecedented experiment in interracial democracy—at least in the South, for Congress's plan did not touch the North. But before the spotlight swung away from Washington to the South, the president and Congress had one more scene to play.

Impeaching a President

Despite his defeats, Andrew Johnson had no intention of yielding control of reconstruction. In a dozen ways he sabotaged Congress's will and encouraged white belligerence and resistance. He issued a flood of pardons to undermine efforts at political and economic change. He waged war against the Freedmen's Bureau by removing officers who sympathized too fully with ex-slaves. And he replaced Union generals eager to enforce Congress's Reconstruction Acts with conservative men eager to defeat them. Johnson claimed that he was merely defending the "violated Constitution." At bottom, however, the president subverted congressional reconstruction to protect southern whites from what he considered the horrors of "Negro domination."

Radicals argued that Johnson's abuse of constitutional powers and his failure to fulfill constitutional obligations were impeachable offenses, but moderates interpreted the constitutional provision to mean violation of criminal statutes. According to the Constitution, the House of Representatives can impeach and the Senate can try any federal official for "treason, bribery, or other high crimes and misdemeanors." As long as Johnson refrained from breaking a law, **impeachment** remained a faint hope.

Then in August 1867, Johnson suspended Secretary of War Edwin M. Stanton from office. As required by the Tenure of Office Act, which required the approval of the Senate for the removal of any government official who had been appointed with Senate approval, the president requested the Senate to consent to the dismissal. When the Senate balked, Johnson removed Stanton anyway. "Is the President crazy, or only drunk?" asked a dumbfounded Republican moderate. "I'm afraid his doings will make us all favor impeachment."

News of Johnson's open defiance of the law convinced every Republican in the House to vote for a resolution impeaching the president. Supreme Court Chief Justice Salmon Chase presided over the Senate trial, which lasted from March until May 1868. Chase refused to allow Johnson's opponents to raise broad issues of misuse of power and forced them to argue their case exclusively on the narrow legal grounds of Johnson's removal of Stanton. Johnson's lawyers argued that the president had not committed a criminal offense, that the Tenure of Office Act was unconstitutional, and that in any case it did not apply to Stanton, who had been appointed by Lincoln. When the critical vote came, 35 senators voted guilty and 19 not guilty. The impeachment forces fell one vote short of the two-thirds needed to convict.

Although Johnson survived, he did not come through the ordeal unscathed. After his trial he called a truce, and for the remaining ten months of his term congressional reconstruction proceeded unhindered by presidential interference. Without interference from Johnson, Congress revisited the suffrage issue.

The Fifteenth Amendment and Women's Demands

In February 1869, Republicans passed the Fifteenth Amendment to the Constitution, which prohibited states from depriving any citizen of the right to vote because of "race, color, or previous condition of servitude." The Reconstruction Acts of 1867 already required black suffrage in the South; the Fifteenth Amendment extended black voting nationwide. Partisan advantage played an important role in the amendment's passage. Gains by northern Democrats in the 1868 elections worried Republicans, and black voters now represented the balance of power in several northern states. By giving ballots to northern blacks, Republicans could lessen their political vulnerability. As one Republican congressman observed, "Party expediency and exact justice coincide for once."

Some Republicans, however, found the final wording of the Fifteenth Amendment "lame and halting." Rather than absolutely guaranteeing the right to vote, the amendment merely prohibited exclusion on grounds of race. The distinction would prove to be significant. In time, inventive white Southerners would devise tests of literacy and property and other apparently nonracial measures that would effectively disfranchise blacks yet not violate the Fifteenth Amendment. But an amendment that fully guaranteed the right to vote courted defeat outside the South. Rising antiforeign sentiment—against the Chinese in California and against European immigrants in the Northeast—caused states to resist giving up total control of suffrage requirements. In March 1870, after three-fourths of the states had ratified it, the Fifteenth Amendment became part of the Constitution. Republicans generally breathed a sigh of relief, confident that black suffrage was "the last great point that remained to be settled of the issues of the war."

Woman suffrage advocates, however, were sorely disappointed with the Fifteenth Amendment's failure to extend voting rights to women.

Major Reconstruction Legislation, 1865–1875

1865	
Thirteenth Amendment (ratified 1865)	Abolishes slavery.
1865 and 1866	
Freedmen's Bureau Acts	Establish the Freedmen's Bureau to distribute food and clothing to destitute Southerners and help freedmen with labor contracts and schooling.
Civil Rights Act of 1866	Affirms the rights of blacks to enjoy "full and equal benefit of all laws and proceedings for the security of person and property as is enjoyed by white citizens" and effectively requires the end of legal discrimination in state laws.
Fourteenth Amendment (ratified 1868)	Makes native-born blacks citizens and guarantees all citizens "equal protection of the laws." Threatens to reduce representatives of a state that denies suffrage to any of its male inhabitants.
1867	
Military Reconstruction Acts	Impose military rule in the South, establish rules for readmission of ex-Confederate states to the Union, and require those states to guarantee the vote to black men.
1869	
Fifteenth Amendment (ratified 1870)	Prohibits racial discrimination in voting rights in all states in the nation.
1875	
Civil Rights Act of 1875	Outlaws racial discrimination in transportation, public accommodations, and juries.

Although women fought hard to include the word *sex* (as they had fought hard to keep the word *male* out of the Fourteenth Amendment), the amendment denied states the right to forbid suffrage only on the basis of race. Elizabeth Cady Stanton and Susan B. Anthony condemned the Republicans' "negro first" strategy and concluded that woman "must not put her trust in man." The Fifteenth Amendment severed the early **feminist** movement from its abolitionist roots. Over the next several decades, women would establish an independent suffrage crusade that drew millions of women into political life.

Republicans took enough satisfaction in the Fifteenth Amendment to promptly scratch the "Negro question" from the agenda of national politics. Even that steadfast crusader for equality, Wendell Phillips, concluded that the black man now held "sufficient shield in his own hands.... Whatever he suffers will be largely now, and in future, his own fault." Northerners had no idea of the violent struggles that lay ahead.

> **REVIEW**   Why did Johnson urge southern states to reject the Fourteenth Amendment?

The Struggle in the South

Northerners believed they had discharged their responsibilities with the Reconstruction Acts and the amendments to the Constitution, but Southerners knew that the battle had just begun. Black suffrage established the foundation for the rise of the Republican Party in the South. Gathering together outsiders and outcasts, southern Republicans won elections, wrote new state constitutions, and formed new state governments. Challenging the established class for political control was dangerous business. Equally dangerous were the confrontations that took place on farms and plantations in the countryside, where blacks sought to give practical, everyday meaning to their newly won legal and political equality. Ex-masters like David Golightly Harris and other whites had their own ideas about the social and economic arrangements that should replace slavery. Freedom remained contested territory, and Southerners fought pitched battles with one another to determine the contours of their new world.

Freedmen, Yankees, and Yeomen

African Americans made up the majority of southern Republicans. After gaining voting rights in 1867, nearly every eligible black man registered to vote. Almost all registered as Republicans, grateful to the party that had freed them and granted them the **franchise**. Black women, like white women, remained disfranchised but mobilized along with black men. In the 1868 presidential election, they bravely wore buttons supporting the Republican candidate, former Union general Ulysses S. Grant. Southern

blacks did not have identical political priorities, but they united in their desire for education and equal treatment before the laws.

Northern whites who made the South their home after the war were a second element of the South's Republican Party. Conservative white Southerners called them "carpetbaggers," men so poor that they could stuff all their earthly belongings in a single carpet-sided suitcase and swoop southward like buzzards to "fatten on our misfortunes." But most Northerners who moved south were restless, relatively well-educated young men who looked upon the South as they did the West—as a promising place to make a living. They expected that the South without slavery would prosper, and they wanted to be part of it. Northerners in the southern Republican Party consistently supported programs that encouraged vigorous economic development along the lines of the northern free-labor model.

Southern whites made up the third element of the South's Republican Party. Approximately one out of four white Southerners voted Republican. The other three condemned the one who did as a traitor to his region and his race and called him a "scalawag," a term for runty horses and low-down, good-for-nothing rascals. **Yeoman** farmers accounted for the majority of southern white Republicans. Some were Unionists who emerged from the war with bitter memories of Confederate persecution. Others were small farmers who wanted to end state governments' favoritism toward plantation owners. Yeomen usually supported initiatives for public schools and for expanding economic opportunity in the South.

The South's Republican Party, then, was made up of freedmen, Yankees, and yeomen—an improbable coalition. The mix of races, regions, and classes inevitably meant friction as each group maneuvered to define the party. But Reconstruction represents an extraordinary moment in American politics: Blacks and whites joined together in the Republican Party to pursue political change. Formally, of course, only men participated in politics—casting ballots and holding offices—but women also played parts in the political struggle by joining in parades and rallies, attending stump speeches, and even campaigning.

Reconstruction politics was not for cowards. Activity on behalf of Republicans in particular took courage. Most whites in the South condemned reconstruction politics as illegitimate and felt justified in doing whatever they could to stamp out

Republicanism. Violence against blacks—the "white terror"—took brutal institutional form in 1866 with the formation in Tennessee of the Ku Klux Klan, a social club of Confederate veterans that quickly developed into a paramilitary organization supporting Democrats. The Klan went on a rampage of whipping, hanging, shooting, burning, and throat-cutting to restore white supremacy. Rapid demobilization of the Union army after the war left only 20,000 troops to patrol the entire South, a vast territory. Without effective military protection, southern Republicans had to take care of themselves.

Republican Rule

In the fall of 1867, southern states held elections for delegates to state constitutional conventions, as required by the Reconstruction Acts. About 40 percent of the white electorate stayed home because they had been disfranchised or because they had decided to boycott politics. Republicans won three-fourths of the seats. About 15 percent of the Republican delegates to the conventions were Northerners who had moved south, 25 percent were African Americans, and 60 percent were white Southerners. As a British visitor observed, the delegate elections reflected "the mighty revolution that had taken place in America." But Democrats described the state conventions as zoos of "baboons, monkeys, mules...and other jackasses." In fact, the conventions brought together serious, purposeful men who hammered out the legal framework for a new order.

The reconstruction constitutions introduced two broad categories of changes in the South: those that reduced aristocratic privilege and increased **democratic** equality and those that expanded the state's responsibility for the general welfare. In the first category, the constitutions adopted universal male suffrage, abolished property qualifications for holding office, and made more offices elective and fewer appointed. In the second category, they enacted prison reform; made the state responsible for caring for orphans, the insane, and the deaf and mute; and exempted debtors' homes from seizure.

These forward-looking state constitutions provided blueprints for a new South but stopped short of the specific reforms advocated by some. Despite the wishes of virtually every former slave, no southern constitution confiscated and redistributed land. And despite the prediction of Unionists that unless all former Confederates were banned from politics they would storm back and wreck reconstruction, no state constitution disfranchised ex-rebels wholesale.

Democrats, however, were blind to the limits of the Republican program. They thought they faced wild revolution. According to Democrats, Republican victories initiated "black and tan" (ex-slave and mulatto) governments across the South.

Congressman John R. Lynch

Although whites almost always maintained control of reconstruction politics, over 600 blacks served in legislatures in the South. Ex-slaves made up the majority of the black legislators. The Union army freed John R. Lynch of Mississippi, and he gained an education at a Natchez freedmen's school. Lynch (1847–1939) was only twenty-four when he became speaker of Mississippi's house of representatives. In 1872, he joined six other African Americans in Congress in Washington, D.C., where in support of civil rights legislation he described his personal experience of being forced to ride in railroad smoking cars with gamblers and drunks. After reconstruction ended, Lynch practiced law and wrote a history of the reconstruction legislatures, which, he argued, were the "best governments those States ever had." Natchez photographer Henry C. Norman took this powerful photograph, probably in the early 1870s.
Collection of Thomas H. Gandy and Joan W. Gandy.

But the claims of "Negro domination" had almost no validity. While four out of five Republican voters were black men, more than four out of five Republican officeholders were white. Southerners sent fourteen black congressmen and two black senators to Washington, but only 6 percent of Southerners in Congress during Reconstruction were black (Figure 16.1). With the exception of South Carolina, where blacks briefly held a majority in one house of the legislature, no state experienced "Negro rule," despite black majorities in the populations of some states.

In almost every state, voters ratified the new constitutions and swept Republicans into power. When the former Confederate states ratified the Fourteenth Amendment, Congress readmitted them. Southern Republicans then turned to a staggering array of problems. Wartime destruction—burned cities, shattered bridges, broken levees—still littered the landscape. The South's share of the nation's wealth had fallen from 30 to only 12 percent. Manufacturing limped along at a fraction of prewar levels, agricultural production remained anemic, and the region's railroads lay devastated. Without the efforts of the

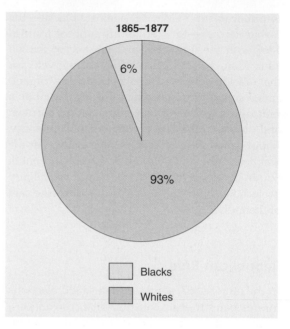

FIGURE 16.1 Southern Congressional Delegations, 1865–1877
The statistics contradict the myth of black domination of congressional representation during Reconstruction.

Freedmen's Bureau, black and white Southerners would have starved. Making matters worse, racial harassment and reactionary violence dogged Southerners who sought reform. In this desperate context, Republicans struggled to breathe life into their new state governments.

Republican activity focused on three areas—education, civil rights, and economic development. Every state inaugurated a system of public education. Before the Civil War, whites had deliberately kept slaves illiterate, and planter-dominated governments rarely spent tax money to educate

One-Cent Primer
"The people are hungry and thirsty after knowledge," a former slave observed after the Civil War. Future African American leader Booker T. Washington remembered "a whole race trying to go to school. Few were too young, and none too old, to make the attempt to learn." Inexpensive elementary textbooks (this eight-page primer cost a penny) offered ex-slaves the basic elements of literacy. For people long forbidden to learn to read and write, literacy symbolized freedom and allowed the deeply religious to experience the joy of Bible reading. It also permitted African Americans to understand labor agreements, sign contracts, and participate knowledgeably in politics.
Gladstone Collection.

the children of yeomen. By 1875, half of Mississippi's and South Carolina's eligible children (the majority of whom were black) were attending school. Despite underfunding and dilapidated facilities, literacy rates rose sharply. Although public schools were racially segregated, education remained for many blacks a tangible, deeply satisfying benefit of freedom and Republican rule.

State legislatures also attacked racial discrimination and defended civil rights. Republicans especially resisted efforts to segregate blacks from whites in public transportation. Mississippi levied fines of up to $1,000 and three years in jail for railroads, steamboats, hotels, and theaters that denied "full and equal rights" to all citizens. But passing color-blind laws was one thing; enforcing them another. Despite the law, segregation—later called **Jim Crow**—developed at white insistence and became a feature of southern life long before the end of the Reconstruction era.

Republican governments also launched ambitious programs of economic development. They envisioned a South of diversified agriculture, roaring factories, and booming towns. Republican legislatures chartered scores of banks and industrial companies, appropriated funds to fix ruined levees and to drain swamps, and went on a railroad-building binge. These efforts fell far short of solving the South's economic troubles, however. Republican spending to stimulate economic growth also meant rising taxes and enormous debt that drained funds from schools and other programs.

The southern Republicans' record, then, was mixed. To their credit, the biracial party took up an ambitious agenda to change the South under trying circumstances. Money was scarce, the Democrats continued their harassment, and factionalism threatened the Republican Party from within. However, corruption infected Republican governments in the South. Public morality reached new lows everywhere in the nation after the Civil War, and the chaos and disruption of the postwar South proved fertile soil for bribery, fraud, and influence peddling. Despite problems and shortcomings, however, the Republican Party made headway in its efforts to purge the South of aristocratic privilege and racist oppression. Republican governments had less success in overthrowing the long-established white oppression of black farm laborers in the rural South.

White Landlords, Black Sharecroppers

In the countryside, clashes occurred daily between ex-slaves who wished to escape slave labor and ex-masters who wanted to reinstitute old ways. Except for having to put down the whip and pay subsistence wages, planters had not been required to offer many concessions to emancipation. They continued to believe that African Americans were inherently lazy and would not work without coercion. Whites moved quickly to restore the antebellum world of work gangs, white overseers, field labor for black women and children, clustered cabins, minimal personal freedom, and even whipping whenever they could get away with it.

Ex-slaves resisted every effort to roll back the clock. They argued that if any class could be described as "lazy," it was the planters, who, as one ex-slave noted, "lived in idleness all their lives on stolen labor." Land of their own would anchor their economic independence, they believed, and end planters' interference in their personal lives. They could then, for example, make their own decisions about whether women and children would labor in the fields. Indeed, within months after the war, perhaps one-third of black women abandoned field labor to work on chores in their own cabins just as poor white women did. With freedom to decide how to use family time, hundreds of thousands of black children enrolled in school. But landownership proved to be beyond the reach of most blacks once the federal government abandoned plans to redistribute Confederate property. Without land, ex-slaves had little choice but to work on plantations.

Although they were forced to return to the planters' fields, freedmen resisted efforts to restore slavelike conditions. In his South Carolina neighborbood, David Golightly Harris discovered that few freedmen were "willing to hire by the day, month or year." Instead of working for wages, "the negroes all seem disposed to rent land," which would increase their independence from whites. By rejecting wage labor, by striking, and by abandoning the most reactionary employers, blacks sought to force concessions. Out of this tug-of-war between white landlords and black laborers emerged a new system of southern agriculture.

Sharecropping was a compromise that offered both ex-masters and ex-slaves something but satisfied neither. Under the new system, planters divided their cotton plantations into

Black Family, 1870s

"If a man got to go crost de riber, and he can't git a boat, he take a log," a South Carolina freedman declared after President Andrew Johnson allowed planters to repossess their land. "If I can't own de land, I'll hire or lease land, but I won't contract." Determined to "set up for himself," almost every freedman in the cotton South preferred the economic independence and personal freedom of sharecropping to the dependency of wage labor. The members of this black family posed in front of their dilapidated home are clearly proud and undefeated, but optimism was hard to sustain in the postwar rural South. "We thought we was goin' to be richer than the white folks," recalled a former slave in Texas, "cause we was stronger and knowed how to work, and the whites didn't and they didn't have us to work for them anymore. But it didn't turn out that way."

Roll, Jordan, Roll by Doris Ullmann 1933.

small farms of twenty-five to thirty acres that freedmen rented, paying with a share of each year's crop, usually half. Sharecropping gave blacks more freedom than the system of wages and labor gangs and released them from the day-to-day supervision of whites. Black families abandoned the old slave quarters and scattered over plantations, building separate cabins for themselves on the patches of land they rented (Map 16.1). Black families now decided who would work, for how long, and how hard. Still, most blacks remained dependent on white landlords, who had the power to expel them at the end of each growing season. For planters, sharecropping offered a way to resume agricultural production, but it did not allow them to restore the old slave plantation.

Sharecropping introduced a new figure—the country merchant—into the agricultural equation. Landlords supplied sharecroppers with land, mules, seeds, and tools, but blacks also needed credit to obtain essential food and clothing before they harvested their crops. Thousands of small crossroads stores sprang up to offer credit. Under an arrangement called a crop lien, a merchant would advance goods to a sharecropper in exchange for a lien, or legal claim, on the farmer's future crop. Some merchants charged exorbitant rates of interest, as much as 60 percent, on the goods they sold. At the end of the growing season, after the landlord had taken half of the farmer's crop for rent, the merchant took most of the rest. Sometimes, the farmer's debt to the merchant exceeded the income he received from his remaining half of the crop, and the farmer would have no choice but to borrow more from the merchant and begin the cycle all over again.

An experiment at first, sharecropping spread quickly and soon dominated the cotton South. Lien merchants forced tenants to plant cotton, which was easy to sell, instead of food crops. The result was excessive production of cotton and falling cotton prices, developments that cost thousands of small white farmers their land and pushed them into the great army of sharecroppers. The new sharecropping system of agriculture took shape just as the political power of Republicans in the South began to buckle under Democratic pressure.

REVIEW   Why was the Republican Party in the South a coalition party?

Reconstruction Collapses

By 1870, after a decade of war and reconstruction, Northerners wanted to turn to their own affairs and put "the southern problem" behind them. Increasingly, practical, business-minded men came to the forefront of the Republican Party, replacing the band of reformers and idealists who had been prominent in the 1860s. While northern commitment to defend black freedom eroded, southern commitment to white supremacy intensified. Without northern protection, southern Republicans were no match for the Democrats' economic coercion, political corruption, and bloody violence. One by one, Republican state governments fell in the South.

MAP 16.1   A Southern Plantation in 1860 and 1881

These maps of the Barrow plantation in Georgia illustrate some of the ways in which ex-slaves expressed their freedom. Freed men and women deserted the clustered living quarters behind the master's house, scattered over the plantation, built family cabins, and farmed rented land. The former Barrow slaves also worked together to build a school and a church.

READING THE MAP: Compare the number and size of the slave quarters in 1860 with the homes of the former slaves in 1881. How do they differ? Which buildings were prominently located along the road in 1860, and which could be found along the road in 1881?

CONNECTIONS: How might the former master feel about the new configuration of buildings on the plantation in 1881? In what ways did the new system of sharecropping replicate the old system of plantation agriculture? In what ways was it different?

FOR MORE HELP ANALYZING THIS MAP, see the map activity for this chapter in the Online Study Guide at bedfordstmartins.com/roarkcompact.

The election of 1876 both confirmed and completed the collapse of reconstruction.

Grant's Troubled Presidency

In 1868, the Republican Party's presidential nomination went to Ulysses S. Grant, the North's favorite general. Hero of the Civil War and a supporter of congressional reconstruction, Grant was the obvious choice. His Democratic opponent, Horatio Seymour of New York, ran on a platform that blasted congressional reconstruction as "a flagrant usurpation of power…unconstitu-tional, revolutionary, and void." The Republicans answered by "waving the **bloody shirt**"—that is, they reminded voters that the Democrats were "the party of rebellion." During the campaign, the Ku Klux Klan erupted in a reign of terror, murdering hundreds of southern Republicans. Violence in the South cost Grant votes, but he gained a narrow 309,000-vote margin in the popular vote and a substantial victory (214 votes to 80) in the electoral college (Map 16.2).

Grant hoped to forge a policy that secured both sectional reconciliation and justice for blacks. But he took office at a time when a majority of

Grant and Scandal

In this anti-Grant cartoon, Thomas Nast, the nation's most celebrated political cartoonist, shows the president falling headfirst into the barrel of fraud and corruption that tainted his administration. During Grant's eight years in the White House, many members of his administration failed him. Sometimes duped, sometimes merely loyal, Grant stubbornly defended wrongdoers, even to the point of perjuring himself to keep an aide out of jail.
Library of Congress.

FOR MORE HELP ANALYZING THIS IMAGE, see the visual activity for this chapter in the Online Study Guide at **bedfordstmartins.com/roarkcompact.**

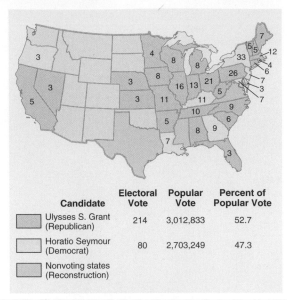

Candidate	Electoral Vote	Popular Vote	Percent of Popular Vote
Ulysses S. Grant (Republican)	214	3,012,833	52.7
Horatio Seymour (Democrat)	80	2,703,249	47.3
Nonvoting states (Reconstruction)			

MAP 16.2 The Election of 1868

white Northerners had grown weary of the "Southern Question" and were increasingly willing to let southern whites manage their own affairs. Moreover, Grant was not as good a president as he was a general. The talents he had demonstrated on the battlefield—decisiveness, clarity, and resolution—were less obvious in the White House. Able advisers might have helped, but he surrounded himself with fumbling kinfolk and old cronies from his army days. He also made a string of dubious appointments that led to a series of damaging scandals. Charges of corruption tainted his vice president, Schuyler Colfax, and brought down two of his cabinet officers. Grant's dogged loyalty to liars and cheats

only compounded the damage. While never personally implicated in any scandal, Grant was aggravatingly naive and his administration filled with rot.

In 1872 anti-Grant Republicans bolted and launched the Liberal Party. To clean up the graft and corruption, Liberals proposed ending the **spoils system**, by which victorious parties rewarded loyal workers with public office, and replacing it with a nonpartisan **civil service** commission that would oversee competitive examinations for appointment to office. Moreover, they demanded that the federal government remove its troops from the South and restore "home rule" (southern white control). Democrats liked the Liberals' southern policy and endorsed the Liberal presidential candidate, Horace Greeley, the longtime editor of the *New York Tribune*. However, the nation still felt enormous affection for the man who had saved the Union and reelected Grant with 56 percent of the popular vote.

Grant's ambitions for his administration extended beyond reconstruction, but not even foreign affairs could escape the problems of the South. The annexation of Santo Domingo in the Caribbean was Grant's greatest passion. He argued that the acquisition of this tropical land would permit the United States to expand its trade and also provide a new home for the South's blacks, who were so desperately harassed by the Klan. Aggressive foreign policy had not originated with the Grant administration.

Lincoln and Johnson's secretary of state, William H. Seward, had thwarted French efforts to set up a puppet empire under Maximilian in Mexico, and his purchase of Alaska ("Seward's Ice Box") from Russia in 1867 for only $7 million fired Grant's **imperialist** ambition. But in the end, Grant could not convince Congress to approve the treaty annexing Santo Domingo. The South preoccupied Congress and undermined Grant's initiatives.

Grant's Proposed Annexation of Santo Domingo

Northern Resolve Withers

While Grant genuinely wanted to see blacks' civil and political rights protected, he understood that most Northerners had grown weary of reconstruction. Average citizens wanted to shift their attention to other issues, especially after the nation slipped into a devastating economic depression in 1873. More than eighteen thousand businesses collapsed, leaving more than a million workers without jobs. Northern businessmen who wanted to invest in the South believed that recurrent federal intrusion was itself a major cause of instability in the region. Republican leaders began to question the wisdom of their party's alliance with the South's lower classes—its small farmers and sharecroppers. Grant's secretary of the interior, Jacob D. Cox of Ohio, proposed allying with the "thinking and influential native southerners…the intelligent, well-to-do, and controlling class."

Congress, too, wanted to leave reconstruction behind, but southern Republicans made that difficult. When the South's Republicans begged for federal protection from Klan violence, Congress enacted three laws in 1870 and 1871 that were intended to break the back of white terrorism. The severest of the three, the Ku Klux Klan Act (1871), made interference with voting rights a felony and authorized the use of the army to enforce it. Intrepid federal marshals arrested thousands of Klansmen, and the government came close to destroying the Klan but did not end terrorism against blacks. Congress also passed the Civil Rights Act of 1875, which boldly outlawed racial discrimination in transportation, public accommodations, and juries. But federal authorities never enforced the law aggressively, and segregated facilities remained the rule throughout the South.

By the early 1870s, the Republican Party had lost its principal spokesmen for African American rights to death or defeat at the polls. Others in Congress concluded that the quest for black equality was mistaken or hopelessly naive. In May 1872, Congress restored the right of officeholding to all but three hundred ex-rebels. In the opinion of many, traditional white leaders offered the best hope for honesty, order, and prosperity in the South.

Underlying the North's abandonment of reconstruction was unyielding racial prejudice. During the war, Northerners had learned to accept black freedom, but deep-seated prejudice prevented many from following freedom with equality. Even the actions they took on behalf of blacks often served partisan political advantage. Northerners generally supported Indiana senator Thomas A. Hendricks's harsh declaration that "this is a white man's Government, made by the white man for the white man."

The U.S. Supreme Court also did its part to undermine reconstruction. The Court issued a series of decisions that significantly weakened the federal government's ability to protect black Southerners under the Fourteenth and Fifteenth Amendments. In the *Slaughterhouse* cases (1873), the Court distinguished between national and state citizenship and ruled that the Fourteenth Amendment protected only those rights that stemmed from the federal government, such as voting in federal elections and interstate travel. Since the Court decided that most rights derived from the states, it sharply curtailed the federal government's authority to protect black citizens. Even more devastating, the *United States v. Cruikshank* ruling (1876) said that the reconstruction amendments gave Congress power to legislate against discrimination only by states, not by individuals. The "suppression of ordinary crime," such as assault, remained a state responsibility. The Supreme Court did not declare reconstruction unconstitutional but undermined its legal foundation.

The mood of the North found political expression in the election of 1874, when for the first time in eighteen years the Democrats gained control of the House of Representatives. As one Republican observed, the people had grown tired of the "negro question, with all its complications, and the reconstruction of Southern States, with all its interminable embroilments." Reconstruction had come apart. The people were tired of it. Grant grew increasingly unwilling to enforce it. Congress gradually abandoned it. The Supreme Court busily denied the constitutionality of significant parts of it. Rather than defend reconstruction from its southern enemies, Northerners steadily backed away from the challenge. After the early 1870s, southern blacks faced the forces of reaction largely on their own.

White Supremacy Triumphs

Republican state and local governments in the South attracted more bitterness and hatred than any other political regimes in American history. In the eyes of the majority of whites, Republican rule meant intolerable insults: Black militiamen patrolled town streets, black laborers negotiated contracts with former masters, black maids stood up to former mistresses, black voters cast ballots, and black legislators enacted laws. The northern retreat from reconstruction permitted southern Democrats to harness this white rage to politics. Taking the name "Redeemers," they promised to replace "bayonet rule" (some federal troops continued to be stationed in the South) with "home rule." They branded Republican governments a carnival of extravagance, waste, and fraud and promised that honest, thrifty Democrats would supplant the irresponsible tax-and-spend Republicans. Above all, Redeemers swore to save southern civilization from a descent into African "barbarism" and "negro rule." As one man put it, "We must render this either a white man's government, or convert the land into a Negro man's cemetery."

Southern Democrats adopted a two-pronged racial strategy to overthrow Republican governments. First, they sought to polarize the parties around color. They went about gathering all the South's white voters into the Democratic Party, leaving the Republicans to depend on blacks. The "straight-out" appeal to whites promised great advantage because whites made up a majority of the population in every southern state except Mississippi, South Carolina, and Louisiana.

To dislodge whites from the Republican Party, Democrats fanned the flames of racial prejudice. A South Carolina Democrat crowed that his party appealed to the "proud Caucasian race, whose sovereignty on earth God has proclaimed." Ostracism also proved effective. Local newspapers published the names of whites who kept company with blacks. So complete was the ostracism that one of its victims said, "No white man can live in the South in the future and act with any other than the Democratic party unless he is willing and prepared to live a life of social isolation."

Democrats also exploited the severe economic plight of small white farmers by blaming it on Republican financial policy. Government spending soared during reconstruction, and small farmers saw their tax burden skyrocket. "This is tax time," David Golightly Harris observed. "We are nearly all on our head about them. They are so high & so little money to pay with." Farmers without enough cash to pay their taxes began "selling every egg and chicken they can get." In 1871, Mississippi reported that one-seventh of the state's land—3.3 million acres—had been forfeited for nonpayment of taxes. The small farmers' economic distress had a racial dimension. Because few

"White Man's Country"
White supremacy emerged as a central tenet of the Democratic Party before the Civil War, and Democrats kept up a vicious racist attack on Republicans as long as reconstruction lasted. On this silk ribbon from the 1868 presidential election between Republican Ulysses S. Grant and his Democratic opponent, New York governor Horatio Seymour, the Democrats openly declare their racial goal. During the campaign, Democratic vice presidential nominee Francis P. Blair Jr. promised that a Seymour victory would restore "white people" to power by declaring the reconstruction governments in the South "null and void." The Democrats' promotion of white supremacy reached new levels of shrillness in the 1870s, when northern support for reconstruction began to waver.
Collection of Janice L. and David J. Frent.

freedmen succeeded in acquiring land, they rarely paid taxes. In Georgia in 1874, blacks made up 45 percent of the population but paid only 2 percent of the taxes. From the perspective of a small white farmer, Republican rule meant that he was paying more taxes and paying them to aid blacks. Democrats asked whether it was not time for hard-pressed yeomen to join the white man's party.

If racial pride, social isolation, and Republican financial policies proved insufficient to drive yeomen from the Republican Party, Democrats turned to terrorism. "Night riders" targeted white Republicans as well as blacks for murder and assassination. "A dead Radical is very harmless," South Carolina Democratic leader Martin Gary told his followers. By the 1870s, only a handful of white Republicans remained.

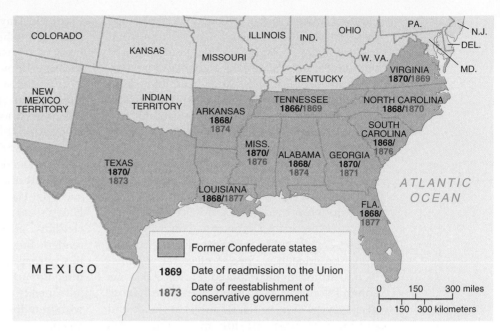

MAP 16.3   The Reconstruction of the South
Myth has it that Republican rule of the former Confederacy was not only harsh but long. In most states, however, conservative southern whites stormed back into power in a few months or a very few years. By the election of 1876, Republican governments could be found in only three states. And they soon fell.

The second prong of Democratic strategy aimed at the complete intimidation of black voters. Violence escalated to unprecedented levels. In 1873 a clash between black militiamen and gun-toting whites killed two white men and an estimated seventy black men in Louisiana. Whites slaughtered half of the black men after they surrendered. Although the federal government indicted more than one hundred white men, local juries failed to convict anyone.

Even before adopting the all-out white supremacist tactics of the 1870s, Democrats had already taken control of the governments of Virginia, Tennessee, and North Carolina. The new campaign brought fresh gains. The Redeemers retook Georgia in 1871, Texas in 1873, and Arkansas and Alabama in 1874. Mississippi became a scene of open, unrelenting, and often savage intimidation of black voters and their few remaining white allies. As the state election approached in 1876, Governor Adelbert Ames appealed to Washington for federal troops to control the violence, only to hear from the attorney general that the "whole public are tired of these annual autumnal outbreaks in the South." Abandoned, Mississippi Republicans succumbed to the Democratic onslaught in the fall elections.

By 1876, only three Republican state governments—in Florida, Louisiana, and South Carolina—survived (Map 16.3).

An Election and a Compromise

The centennial year of 1876 witnessed one of the most tumultuous elections in American history. Its chaos and confusion provided a fitting conclusion to the experiment known as reconstruction. The election took place in November, but not until March 2 of the following year did the nation know who would be inaugurated president on March 4.

The Democrats nominated New York's governor, Samuel J. Tilden, who immediately targeted the corruption of the Grant administration and the despotism of Republican reconstruction. The Republicans put forward Rutherford B. Hayes, governor of Ohio. Privately, Hayes considered "bayonet rule" a mistake but concluded that waving the "bloody shirt"—reminding voters that the Democrats were the "party of rebellion"—remained the Republicans' best political strategy.

On election day, Tilden tallied 4,300,000 votes to Hayes's 4,036,000. But in the all-important electoral college, Tilden fell one vote short of the majority required for victory. The electoral votes of three states—South Carolina, Louisiana, and Florida, the only remaining Republican governments in the South—remained in doubt because both Republicans and Democrats in those states claimed victory. To win, Tilden needed only one of the nineteen contested votes. Hayes had to have all of them.

Congress had to decide who had actually won the elections in the three southern states and thus who would be president. The Constitution provided no guidance for this situation. Moreover, Democrats controlled the House, and Republicans controlled the Senate. Congress created a special electoral commission to arbitrate the disputed returns. All of the commissioners voted their party affiliation, giving every state to the Republican Hayes and putting him over the top in electoral votes (Map 16.4).

Some outraged Democrats vowed to resist Hayes's victory. Rumors flew of an impending coup and renewed civil war. But the impasse was broken when negotiations behind the scenes between Hayes's lieutenants and some moderate southern Democrats resulted in an informal understanding, known as the Compromise of 1877. In exchange for a Democratic promise not to block Hayes's inauguration and to deal fairly with the freedmen, Hayes vowed to refrain from using the army to uphold the remaining Republican regimes in the South and to provide the South with substantial federal subsidies for internal improvements. Two days later, the nation celebrated Hayes's peaceful inauguration.

Stubborn Tilden supporters bemoaned the "stolen election" and damned "His Fraudulency," Rutherford B. Hayes. Old-guard radicals such as William Lloyd Garrison denounced Hayes's bargain as a "policy of compromise, of credulity, of weakness, of subserviency, of surrender." But the nation as a whole celebrated, for the country had weathered a grave crisis. The last three Republican state governments in the South fell quickly once Hayes abandoned them and withdrew the U.S. army. Reconstruction came to an end.

REVIEW   How did the Supreme Court undermine the Fourteenth and Fifteenth Amendments?

Conclusion: "A Revolution But Half Accomplished"

In 1865, when General Carl Schurz visited the South, he discovered "a revolution but half accomplished." White Southerners resisted the passage from slavery to free labor, from white racial despotism to equal justice, and from white political **monopoly** to biracial democracy. Ex-masters like David Golightly Harris had trouble seeing former slaves like York and Old Will as free people. The old elite wanted to get "things back as near to slavery as possible," Schurz reported, while ex-slaves and some whites were eager to exploit the revolutionary implications of defeat and emancipation.

The northern-dominated Republican Congress pushed the revolution along. Although it refused to provide for blacks' economic welfare, through constitutional amendments Congress required ex-Confederates to accept legal equality and share political power with black men. Congress was not willing to extend such power to women. Conservative southern whites fought

MAP 16.4   The Election of 1876

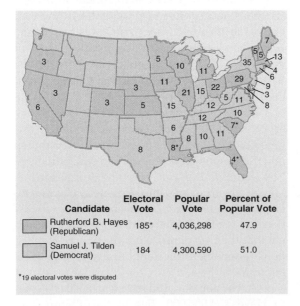

Candidate	Electoral Vote	Popular Vote	Percent of Popular Vote
Rutherford B. Hayes (Republican)	185*	4,036,298	47.9
Samuel J. Tilden (Democrat)	184	4,300,590	51.0

*19 electoral votes were disputed

ferociously to recover their power and privilege. When Democrats regained control of politics, whites used both state power and private violence to wipe out many of the gains of reconstruction, leading one observer to conclude that the North had won the war but the South had won the peace.

The Redeemer counterrevolution, however, did not mean a return to slavery. Northern victory in the Civil War ensured abolition, and ex-slaves gained the freedom to not be whipped or sold, to send their children to school, to worship in their own churches, and to work independently on their own rented farms. Even sharecropping, with all its hardships, provided more autonomy and economic welfare than bondage had. It was limited freedom, to be sure, but it was not slavery.

The Civil War and emancipation set in motion the most profound upheaval in the nation's history, and nothing whites did entirely erased its revolutionary impact. War destroyed the largest slave society in the New World. War also gave birth to a modern nation-state. For the first time sovereignty rested uncontested in the federal government, and Washington increased its role in national affairs. When the South returned to the Union, it did so as a junior partner. The victorious North now possessed the power to establish the nation's direction, and it set the nation's compass toward the expansion of industrial capitalism.

Despite massive changes, the Civil War remained only a "half accomplished" revolution. By not fulfilling the promises the nation seemed to hold out to black Americans at war's end, Reconstruction represents a tragedy of enormous proportions. The failure to protect blacks and guarantee their rights had enduring consequences. Almost a century after Reconstruction, the nation would embark on what one observer called a "second reconstruction." The solid achievements of the Thirteenth, Fourteenth, and Fifteenth Amendments to the Constitution would provide a legal foundation for the renewed commitment. It is worth remembering, though, that it was only the failure of the first reconstruction that made the modern civil rights movement necessary.

Suggestions for Further Reading

Jane Turner Censer, *The Reconstruction of White Southern Womanhood, 1865–1895* (2003). A lively investigation of the consequences of the Civil War for white southern women.

Eric Foner, *Reconstruction: America's Unfinished Revolution, 1863–1877* (1988). A masterful, comprehensive survey that makes African Americans the central actors in the Reconstruction era.

Stephen Kantrowitz, *Ben Tillman and the Reconstruction of White Supremacy* (2000). An eloquent biography of a leading white supremacist in South Carolina.

Philip N. Racine, ed., *Piedmont Farmer: The Journals of David Golightly Harris, 1855–1870* (1990). A skillfully edited journal that captures one slaveholder's confrontation with emancipation.

Brooks D. Simpson, *The Reconstruction Presidents* (1998). A thoughtful interpretation that emphasizes the differences between the policies and styles of presidents Lincoln, Johnson, Grant, and Hayes.

Michael Wayne, *The Reshaping of Plantation Society: The Natchez District, 1860–1880* (1983). A careful analysis of ex-slaves' and ex-masters' struggles to shape postwar economic and social relationships.

▶ **FOR MORE BOOKS ABOUT TOPICS IN THIS CHAPTER,** see the Online Bibliography at **bedfordstmartins.com/roarkcompact**.

▶ **FOR ADDITIONAL FIRSTHAND ACCOUNTS OF THIS PERIOD,** see Chapter 16 in Michael Johnson, ed., *Reading the American Past,* Third Edition.

▶ **FOR WEB SITES AND DOCUMENTS RELATED TO TOPICS AND PLACES IN THIS CHAPTER,** see "HistoryLinks," "DocLinks," and "PlaceLinks" at **bedfordstmartins.com/roarkcompact**.

REVIEWING THE CHAPTER

Follow these steps to review and strengthen your understanding of the chapter.

STEP 1: *Study the* **Key Terms** *and* **Timeline** *to identify the significance of each item listed.*

STEP 2: *Answer the* **Review Questions,** *drawing on key terms and dates to support your answers.*

STEP 3: *Drawing on the Key Terms, Timeline, and Review Questions, answer the broader* **Making Connections** *questions.*

KEY TERMS

Who

Carl Schurz (p. 399)
Abraham Lincoln (p. 401)
Wendell Phillips (p. 401)
Henry Winter Davis (p. 401)
Benjamin Wade (p. 401)
William Tecumseh Sherman (p. 402)
John Wilkes Booth (p. 403)
Salmon P. Chase (p. 403)
Andrew Johnson (p. 403)
Susan B. Anthony (p. 408)
Elizabeth Cady Stanton (p. 408)
Charles Sumner (p. 409)
Thaddeus Stevens (p. 409)
Edwin M. Stanton (p. 410)
Ulysses S. Grant (p. 417)
Horatio Seymour (p. 417)
Schuyler Colfax (p. 418)
Horace Greeley (p. 418)
William H. Seward (p. 419)
Jacob D. Cox (p. 419)

Redeemers (p. 420)
night riders (p. 421)
Samuel J. Tilden (p. 421)
Rutherford B. Hayes (p. 421)

What

Proclamation of Amnesty and
  Reconstruction (p. 401)
Wade-Davis bill (p. 401)
Confiscation Acts (p. 401)
compulsory free labor (p. 401)
Freedmen's Bureau (p. 402)
black codes (p. 406)
apprenticeship laws (p. 406)
Civil Rights Act of 1866 (p. 407)
Fourteenth Amendment (p. 408)
American Equal Rights Association
  (p. 408)
National Union Party (p. 408)
Memphis riots (p. 408)
Military Reconstruction Act (p. 409)

black suffrage (p. 409)
Reconstruction Acts of 1867 (p. 410)
impeachment (p. 410)
Tenure of Office Act (p. 410)
Fifteenth Amendment (p. 411)
woman suffrage (p. 411)
carpetbagger (p. 412)
scalawag (p. 412)
Ku Klux Klan (p. 413)
sharecropping (p. 415)
country merchant (p. 416)
crop lien (p. 416)
bloody shirt (p. 417)
Liberal Party (p. 418)
civil service commission (p. 418)
Ku Klux Klan Act (p. 419)
Civil Rights Act of 1875 (p. 419)
Slaughterhouse cases (p. 419)
United States v. Cruikshank (p. 419)
Compromise of 1877 (p. 422)

TIMELINE

1863 • Proclamation of Amnesty and Reconstruction.

1864 • Wade-Davis bill.

1865 • Freedmen's Bureau established.
  • Lincoln shot, dies on April 15, succeeded by Andrew Johnson.
  • Black codes enacted.
  • Thirteenth Amendment becomes part of Constitution.

1866 • Congress approves Fourteenth Amendment.
  • Civil Rights Act.
  • Equal Rights Association founded.
  • Ku Klux Klan founded.

1867 • Military Reconstruction Act.
  • Tenure of Office Act.

1868 • Impeachment trial of President Johnson.
  • Republican Ulysses S. Grant elected president.

1869 • Congress approves Fifteenth Amendment.

REVIEW QUESTIONS

1. Why did Congress object to Lincoln's wartime plan for reconstruction? (pp. 400–03)

2. How did the North respond to the passage of black codes in the southern states? (pp. 403–07)

3. Why did Johnson urge southern states to reject the Fourteenth Amendment? (pp. 408–12)

4. Why was the Republican Party in the South a coalition party? (pp. 412–16)

5. How did the Supreme Court undermine the Fourteenth and Fifteenth Amendments? (pp. 416–22)

MAKING CONNECTIONS

1. Reconstruction succeeded in advancing black civil rights but failed to secure them over the long-term. Why and how did the federal government retreat from defending African Americans' civil rights in the 1870s? In your answer, cite specific actions by Congress and the Supreme Court.

2. Why was distributing plantation land to former slaves such a controversial policy? In your answer, discuss why landownership was important to freedpeople and why Congress rejected redistribution as a general policy.

3. At the end of the Civil War, it remained to be seen exactly how emancipation would transform the South. How did emancipation change political and labor organization in the region? In your answer, discuss how ex-slaves exercised their new freedoms and how white southerners attempted to limit them.

4. The Republican Party shaped Reconstruction through its control of Congress and state legislatures in the South. How did the identification of the Republican Party with Reconstruction policy affect the party's political fortunes in the 1870s? In your answer, be sure to address developments on the federal and state levels.

▶ **For practice quizzes, a customized study plan, and other study tools,** see the Online Study Guide at bedfordstmartins.com/roarkcompact.

1871 • Ku Klux Klan Act.

    1872 • Liberal Party formed; calls for end of government corruption.
        • President Grant reelected.

        1873 • Economic depression sets in for remainder of decade.
            • *Slaughterhouse* cases.

            1874 • Democrats win majority in House of Representatives.

                1875 • Civil Rights Act.

                    1876 • *United States v. Cruikshank.*

                        1877 • Republican Rutherford B. Hayes elected president; Reconstruction era ends.

CLEVELAND AND BLAINE CAMPAIGN PINS, 1884
These gilt campaign pins from the election of 1884 show Republican candidate James G. Blaine, on the right, thumbing his nose at Democratic candidate Grover Cleveland. Considered "one of the vilest campaigns ever waged," the 1884 race pitted Cleveland, who had made his political reputation on his honest dealings, against Blaine, who was tainted with charges of corruption. However, when the *Buffalo Telegraph* revealed that the bachelor Cleveland had fathered an illegitimate child, the tables turned, and Cleveland and his followers lost the high moral ground. Perhaps this is why Blaine is portrayed in this mechanical pin as thumbing his nose at Cleveland. His gesture proved premature; Cleveland squeaked past Blaine in a close race. The gilt pins are a good symbol for Gilded Age politics, when corruption and party strife typified the nation's political life.
Collection of Janice L. and David J. Frent.

Business and Politics in the Gilded Age
1870–1895

O NE NIGHT OVER DINNER, the humorist and author Mark Twain and his friend Charles Dudley Warner teased their wives about the popular novels they read. When the two women challenged them to write something better, they set to work. Warner supplied the sentimental melodrama, while Twain "hurled in the facts." The result was a runaway best seller, uneven as fiction but offering a savage satire of the "get rich quick" era that forever after would be known by the book's title, *The Gilded Age* (1873).

Twain left no one unscathed in the novel—political hacks, Washington lobbyists, Wall Street financiers, small-town boosters, wildcat miners, and the "great putty-hearted public" that tolerated the plunder. Underneath the glitter of the Gilded Age, as Twain's title implied, lurked baser stuff. Twain had witnessed up close the corrupt partnership of business and politics in the administration of Ulysses S. Grant. Drawing on this experience, he described how a lobbyist could get an appropriation bill through Congress:

> Why the matter is simple enough. A Congressional appropriation costs money. Just reflect, for instance. A majority of the House Committee, say $10,000 apiece—$40,000; a majority of the Senate Committee, the same each—say $40,000; a little extra to one or two chairmen of one or two such committees, say $10,000 each—$20,000; and there's $100,000 of the money gone, to begin with. Then, seven male lobbyists, at $3,000 each—$21,000; one female lobbyist, $3,000; a high moral Congressman or Senator here and there—the high moral ones cost more, because they give tone to a measure—say ten of these at $3,000 each, is $30,000; then a lot of small fry country members who won't vote for anything whatever without pay—say twenty at $500 apiece, is $10,000 altogether; lot of jimcracks for Congressmen's wives and children—those go a long way—you can't spend too much money in that line—well, those things cost in a lump, say $10,000—along there somewhere;—and then comes your printed documents.... Oh, my dear sir, printing bills are destruction itself. Ours, so far amount to—let me see—...well, never mind the details, the total in clean numbers foots up $118,254.42 thus far!

In Twain's satire, Congress is for sale to the highest bidder. The unseemly intimacy between government and business meant that more often than not senators, representatives, and even members of the executive branch were on the payroll of business interests, if not in their pockets. This often corrupt interplay of business and politics raised serious questions about the health of American democracy.

The Gilded Age seemed to tarnish all who touched it. No one would learn that lesson better than Twain, who, even as he attacked it as an "era of incredible

Mark Twain and _The Gilded Age_
Popular author Mark Twain (Samuel Langhorne Clemens) wrote acerbically about the excesses of the Gilded Age in his novel of that name written with Charles Dudley Warner and published in 1873. No one knew the meretricious lure of the era better than Twain, who succumbed to a get-rich-quick scheme that left him bankrupt.
Left: Beinecke Rare Book and Manuscript Library, Yale University; right: Newberry Library.

rottenness," fell prey to its enticements. Born Samuel Langhorne Clemens, he grew up in a rough Mississippi River town where he first became a journeyman printer and then a riverboat pilot. Taking the pen name Mark Twain, he moved west and gained fame chronicling mining booms in California and Nevada. In 1866 he came east to launch a career as an author, public speaker, and itinerant humorist. Twain played to packed houses, but his work was judged too vulgar for the genteel tastes of the time because he wrote about common people and used common language. His masterpiece, _The Adventures of Huckleberry Finn,_ was banned in Boston when it appeared in 1884.

Huck Finn's creator eventually stormed the citadels of polite society, hobnobbing with the wealthy and living in increasingly expensive and elegant style. Succumbing to the money fever of his age, Twain plunged into one scheme after an-

other in the hope of making millions. The Paige typesetting machine proved his downfall. Twain invested heavily in this elaborate invention that promised to mechanize typesetting. The idea was a good one; a competing invention, the Linotype, eventually replaced hand type. The Paige machine, however, proved too temperamental to be practical. By the 1890s, Twain faced bankruptcy. Only the help of his friend Standard Oil millionaire Henry H. Rogers enabled him to begin his dogged climb out of debt.

Twain's tale was common in an age when the promise of wealth led as many to ruin as to riches. In the Gilded Age, fortunes were made and lost with dizzying frequency. Wall Street panics, like those in 1873 and 1893, periodically interrupted the boom times and plunged the country into economic depression. But with railroads and cities to be built and industry expanding on every level, the mood of the country remained buoyant.

The rise of industrialism in the United States and the interplay of business and politics strike the key themes in the Gilded Age. In the decades from 1870 to 1890, the transition from a rural, agricultural economy to urban industrialism transformed American society. The growth of old industries and the creation of new ones, along with the rise of big business, signaled the coming of age of industrial capitalism. With new times came new economic and political issues. Old divisions engendered by sectionalism and slavery still influenced politics. But increasingly new economic issues such as the tariff and monetary policy shaped party politics. And as concern grew over the power of big business and the growing chasm between the rich and the poor, many Americans looked to the government for solutions.

Perhaps nowhere were the hopes and fears that industrialism inspired more evident than in the public's attitude toward the great business moguls of the day, men like Jay Gould, Andrew Carnegie, John D. Rockefeller, and J. P. Morgan. These larger-than-life figures not only dominated business but also sparked the popular imagination as the heroes and villains in the high drama of industrialization. At no other period in U.S. history would the industrial giants and the businesses they built (and sometimes wrecked) loom so large in American life.

Old Industries Transformed, New Industries Born

In the years following the Civil War, the scale and scope of American industry expanded dramatically. Old industries like iron transformed into the modern steel industry, while discovery and invention stimulated new industries from oil refining to electric light and power. The expansion of the nation's rail system in the decades after the Civil War played the key role in the transformation of the American economy. The proliferation of new rail lines created a national market that enabled businesses to expand from a regional to a nationwide scale. The railroads became America's first big business.

Jay Gould, Andrew Carnegie, John D. Rockefeller, and other business leaders pioneered new strategies to seize markets and consolidate power in the rising railroad, steel, and oil industries. Always with an eye to the main chance, these business tycoons set the tone in the get-rich-quick era of freewheeling capitalism that came to be called the Gilded Age.

Railroads: America's First Big Business

In the decades following the Civil War, the United States built the greatest railroad network in the world. The first transcontinental railroad was completed in 1869 when the tracks of the Union Pacific and Central Pacific railroads came together at Promontory Point, Utah, linking new markets in the West to the nation's economy. Between 1870 and 1880, the amount of track in the country doubled, and it nearly doubled again in the following decade. By 1900, the nation boasted over 193,000 miles of railroad track, more than in all of Europe and Russia combined (Map 17.1).

To understand how the railroads developed and came to dominate American life, there is no better place to start than the career of Jay Gould, who pioneered the expansion of America's railway system and become the era's most notorious speculator. Jason "Jay" Gould bought his first railroad before he turned twenty-five. It was only sixty-two miles long, in bad repair, and on the brink of failure, but within two years he sold it at a profit of $130,000.

Gould, by his own account, knew little about railroads and cared less about their operation. The secretive Gould operated in the stock market like a shark, looking for vulnerable railroads, buying enough stock to take control, and threatening to undercut his competitors until they bought him out at a high profit. The railroads that fell into his hands fared badly and often went bankrupt; Gould's genius lay in cleverly buying and selling railroad stock, not in providing transportation. In the 1880s, he moved to put together a second transcontinental railroad. To defend their interests, his competitors had little choice but to adopt his strategy of expansion and consolidation, which in turn encouraged railroad building.

The dramatic growth of the railroads created the country's first big business. Before the Civil War, even the largest textile mill in New

Jay Gould as a Spider

In this 1885 political cartoon titled "Justice in the Web," artist Fredrick Burr Opper portrays Jay Gould as a hideous spider whose web, formed by Western Union telegraph lines, has entrapped "justice" through its monopoly of the telegraph industry. The telegraph, by transmitting coded messages across electric wire, formed the nervous system of the new industrial order. Gould, who controlled Western Union as well as the Erie Railroad, made his fortune by stock speculation. Images like this one fueled the public's distaste for him and made Gould, in his own words, "the most hated man in America."
Granger Collection.

JUSTICE IN THE WEB.

MAP 17.1   Railroad Expansion, 1870–1890

Railroad mileage nearly quadrupled between 1870 and 1890; the greatest growth occurred in the trans-Mississippi West. New transcontinental lines—the Great Northern, the Northern Pacific, the Southern Pacific, and the Atlantic and Pacific—were completed in the 1880s. Small feeder lines like the Oregon Short Line and the Atchison, Topeka, and Santa Fe fed into the great transcontinental systems, knitting the nation together.

READING THE MAP: Where were most of the railroad lines located in 1870? What cities were the major railroad centers? What was the end point of the only western route?

CONNECTIONS: Why were so many rails laid between 1870 and 1890? How did the railroads affect the nation's economy?

FOR MORE HELP ANALYZING THIS MAP, see the map activity for this chapter in the Online Study Guide at bedfordstmartins.com/roarkcompact.

England employed no more than 800 workers. In contrast, the Pennsylvania Railroad by the 1870s boasted a payroll of more than 55,000 workers. Capitalized at over $400 million, the Pennsylvania Railroad constituted the largest private enterprise in the world.

To encourage railroad building, the federal and state governments provided the railroad companies with generous cash subsidies and **land grants**. States and local communities clamored to offer inducements to railroad builders, knowing that towns and villages along the tracks would grow and flourish. The federal government held vast tracts of public land in the West, and

Congress did not hesitate to give it away to promote railroad building. The giveaway amounted to over 180 million acres, an area larger than Texas. The land grants diminished the amount of public land available to homesteaders and allowed the railroads to increase their profits by selling excess land to the settlers who followed the railroads west.

Lack of planning led to overbuilding. Already by the 1870s, the railroads competed fiercely for business on the eastern seaboard. A manufacturer who was fortunate enough to be in an area served by competing railroads could get substantially reduced shipping rates in return for promises of steady business. Because railroad owners lost money through this kind of competition, they tried to set up agreements, or "pools," to end cut-throat competition by dividing up territory and setting rates. These informal agreements invariably failed because men like Jay Gould, intent on undercutting all competitors, refused to honor the agreements.

The public's alarm at the control wielded by the new railroad magnates provided a barometer of attitudes toward big business itself. When Jay Gould died in 1892, the press described him as "the world's richest man," estimating his fortune at over $100 million. His competitor "Commodore" Cornelius Vanderbilt, who built the New York Central Railroad, judged Gould "the smartest man in America." But to the public, he was, as he himself admitted shortly before his death, "the most hated man in America."

Andrew Carnegie, Steel, and Vertical Integration

If Jay Gould was the man Americans loved to hate, Andrew Carnegie became one of America's heroes. Unlike Gould, for whom speculation was the game and wealth the goal, Carnegie turned his back on speculation and worked to build something enduring—Carnegie Steel, the biggest steel business in the world during the Gilded Age.

The growth of the steel industry proceeded directly from railroad building. The first railroads ran on iron rails, which cracked and broke with alarming frequency. Steel, both stronger and more flexible than iron, remained too expensive for use in rails until an Englishman named Henry Bessemer developed a way to make steel more cheaply from pig iron. Andrew Carnegie, among the first to champion the new "King Steel," came to dominate the emerging industry.

Carnegie, a Scottish immigrant, landed in New York in 1848 at the age of twelve. He rose from a job cleaning bobbins in a textile factory to become one of the richest men in America. Before he died, he gave away more than $300 million of his fortune, most notably to public libraries. His generosity, combined with his own rise from poverty, burnished his public image.

When Carnegie was a teenager, his skill as a telegraph operator caught the attention of Tom Scott, superintendent of the Pennsylvania Railroad. Scott hired Carnegie, soon promoted

him, and lent him the money for his first foray into Wall Street investment. A millionaire before his thirtieth birthday, Carnegie turned away from speculation and struck out on his own to reshape the iron and steel industry. "My preference was always manufacturing," he wrote. "I wished to make something tangible."

In 1872 Andrew Carnegie acquired 100 acres in Braddock, Pennsylvania, on the outskirts of Pittsburgh, convenient to two railroad lines and fronted by the Monongahela River, a natural highway up to Pittsburgh and the Ohio River and the coal fields farther north. There Carnegie built the most up-to-date Bessemer steel plant in the world and began turning out steel at a furious rate. He soon cut the cost of making rails by more than half. Carnegie turned steel into the nation's first manufacturing big business. His formula for success was simple: "Cut the prices, scoop the market, run the mills full; watch the costs and profits will take care of themselves." And they did. By 1900, Carnegie Steel earned $40 million a year.

To guarantee the lowest costs and the maximum output, Carnegie pioneered a system of business organization called **vertical integration**. All aspects of the business were under Carnegie's control—from the mining of iron ore, to its transport on the Great Lakes, to the production of steel. Vertical integration, in the words of one observer, meant that "from the moment these crude stuffs were dug out of the earth until they flowed in a stream of liquid steel in the ladles, there was never a price, profit, or royalty paid to any outsider."

Always Carnegie kept his eyes on the account books, looking for ways to cut costs. The great productivity Carnegie encouraged came at a high price. He deliberately pitted his managers against one another, firing the losers and rewarding the winners with a share in the company. Workers achieved the output Carnegie demanded by enduring long hours, low wages, and dangerous working conditions. One worker, commenting on the contradiction between Carnegie's generous philanthropy in endowing public libraries and his tight-fisted labor policy, observed, "After working twelve hours, how can a man go to a library?"

By 1900, Andrew Carnegie had become the best-known manufacturer in the nation, and the age of iron had yielded to an age of steel. Steel from Carnegie's mills supported the elevated trains in New York and Chicago, formed the skeleton of the Washington Monument, supported the first steel bridge to span the Mississippi, and girded America's first skyscrapers. As a captain of industry Carnegie had no rival but the titan of the oil industry, John D. Rockefeller.

John D. Rockefeller, Standard Oil, and the Trust

Edwin Drake's discovery of oil in Pennsylvania in 1859 sent thousands rushing to the oil fields in search of "black gold." In the days before the automobile and gasoline, crude oil was refined into lubricating oil for machinery and kerosene for lamps, the major source of lighting in nineteenth-century houses before the invention of gas lamps or electric lighting. The amount of capital needed to buy or build an oil refinery in the 1860s and 1870s remained relatively low: less

than $25,000, or roughly what it cost to lay one mile of railroad track. With start-up costs so low, the new petroleum industry experienced riotous competition among many small refineries. Ultimately, John D. Rockefeller and his Standard Oil Company succeeded in controlling nine-tenths of the oil-refining business.

Rockefeller grew up the son of a shrewd Yankee who peddled quack cures for cancer. Under his father's rough tutelage, he learned how to drive a hard bargain. "I trade with the boys and skin 'em and just beat 'em every time I can," Big Bill Rockefeller boasted. "I want to make 'em sharp." John D. learned his lessons well. In 1865, at the age of twenty-five, he controlled the largest oil refinery in Cleveland. Like a growing number of business owners, Rockefeller abandoned partnership or single proprietorship to embrace the

"What a Funny Little Government"

The power wielded by John D. Rockefeller and the Standard Oil Company is captured in this political cartoon, which appeared in the January 22, 1900, issue of *The Verdict*. Rockefeller is pictured holding the White House and the Treasury Department in the palm of his hand, while in the background the U.S. Capitol has been converted into an oil refinery. Rockefeller's influence could best be measured by his close relationship to Senate leader Nelson Aldrich, whose daughter married Rockefeller's son. Aldrich did not object to being called "the Senator from Standard Oil." Rockefeller and the company he ran held so much power that many feared democracy itself was threatened in the Gilded Age. Collection of The New-York Historical Society.

FOR MORE HELP ANALYZING THIS IMAGE, see the visual activity for this chapter in the Online Study Guide at bedfordstmartins.com/roarkcompact.

corporation as the business structure best suited to maximize profit and minimize personal liability. In 1870, he incorporated his oil business, founding the Standard Oil Company, a precursor of today's ExxonMobil Corporation.

As the largest refiner in Cleveland, Rockefeller demanded secret rebates from the railroads in exchange for his steady business. The railroads wanted Rockefeller's business so badly that they gave him a share of the rates that his competitors paid. These rebates enabled Rockefeller to undercut his competitors and pressure competing refiners to sell out or face ruin.

To gain legal standing for Standard Oil's secret deals, Rockefeller in 1882 pioneered a new form of corporate structure—the **trust**. The trust differed markedly from Carnegie's vertical approach in steel. Instead of attempting to control all aspects of the oil business, from the well to the consumer, Rockefeller moved horizontally to control only the refining process. Several trustees held stock in various refinery companies "in trust" for Standard's stockholders. This elaborate stock swap allowed the trustees to coordinate policy among the refineries, giving Rockefeller a virtual **monopoly** on the oil-refining business.

When the federal government threatened to outlaw the trust as a violation of free trade, Standard Oil changed tactics and reorganized as a **holding company**. Instead of stockholders in competing companies acting through trustees to set prices and determine territories, the holding company simply brought competing companies under one central administration. No longer technically separate businesses, they could act in concert without violating antitrust laws that forbade competing companies from forming "combinations in restraint of trade."

As Standard Oil's empire grew, Rockefeller ended the independence of the refinery operators and closed inefficient plants. Next he moved to control sources of crude oil and took charge of the transportation and marketing of petroleum products. By the 1890s, Standard Oil ruled more than 90 percent of the oil business, employed 100,000 people, and was the biggest, richest, most feared, and most admired business organization in the world.

John D. Rockefeller enjoyed enormous success in business, but he was not well liked by the public. Before he died in 1937 at the age of ninety-eight, Rockefeller had become the country's first billionaire. But despite his modest habits, his pious Baptist faith, and his many charitable gifts, he never shared in the public affection that

Carnegie enjoyed. Editor and journalist Ida M. Tarbell's *History of the Standard Oil Company,* which ran for three years (1902–1905) in serial form in *McClure's Magazine,* largely shaped the public's harsh view of Rockefeller. Tarbell's devastatingly thorough history chronicled the methods Rockefeller used to take over the oil industry. Publicly Rockefeller refused to respond to her allegations, although in private he dubbed her "Miss Tarball." "If I step on that worm I will call attention to it," he explained. "If I ignore it, it will disappear." Yet by the time Tarbell finished publishing her story, Rockefeller slept with a loaded revolver by his bed in fear of would-be assassins. Standard Oil and the man who created it had become the symbol of heartless monopoly. (See "Documenting the American Promise," page 434.)

New Inventions: The Telephone and Electricity

Although many Americans disliked industrial giants like Rockefeller, they admired inventors. The second half of the nineteenth century was an age of invention. Men like Thomas Alva Edison and Alexander Graham Bell became folk heroes. But no matter how dramatic the inventors or the inventions themselves, the new electric and telephone industries pioneered by Edison and Bell soon eclipsed their inventors and fell under the control of bankers and industrialists.

Alexander Graham Bell came to America from Scotland at the age of twenty-four with a passion to find a way to teach the deaf to speak (his wife and mother were deaf). Instead, he developed a way to transmit voice over wire—the telephone. Bell's invention astounded the world when he demonstrated it at the Philadelphia Centennial Exposition in 1876. Dumbfounded by the display, the emperor of Brazil cried out, "My God, it talks!" In 1880 Bell's company, American Bell, pioneered "long lines" (long-distance telephone service), creating American Telephone and Telegraph (AT&T) as a subsidiary. In 1900, AT&T became the parent company of the system as a whole, controlling Western Electric, which manufactured and installed the equipment, and coordinating the Bell regional divisions. This complicated organizational structure meant that Americans could communicate not only locally but across the country.

Even more than Alexander Graham Bell, inventor Thomas Alva Edison embodied the

Rockefeller and His Critics

*N*o one inspired the nation's fear of industrial consolidation more than John D. Rockefeller, creator of the Standard Oil trust. To many Americans, Rockefeller and "the sovereign state of Standard Oil" came to represent a danger to **democracy** itself because of the underhanded methods and enormous political influence of the corporation and its founder.

DOCUMENT 1
"The Smokeless Rebate," from Henry Demarest Lloyd's *Wealth against Commonwealth*, 1894

As early as 1881 Henry Demarest Lloyd introduced Rockefeller to a national audience by attacking Standard Oil and its founder in "The Story of a Great Monopoly," published in the February issue of Atlantic Monthly. *The public snapped up the exposé—the issue went through six printings. In 1894, Lloyd published* Wealth against Commonwealth, *a full-scale exposé of the company. To avoid charges of libel, Lloyd used no names, but readers knew he referred to Rockefeller and Standard Oil. Here Lloyd describes how Rockefeller used illegal railroad rebates to best his competitors.*

That entirely modern social arrangement—the private ownership of [railroads]—has introduced a new weapon into business warfare which means universal dominion to him who will use it with an iron hand.

This weapon is the rebate, smokeless, noiseless, invisible, of extraordinary range, and the deadliest gun known to commercial warfare. It is not a lawful weapon....It has to be used secretly. All the rates he got were a secret between himself and the railroads. "It has never been otherwise," testified one of the oil combination.

The smokeless rebate makes the secret of success in business to be not manufacture, but manufracture—breaking down with a strong hand the true makers of things. To those who can get the rebate it makes no difference who does the digging, building, mining, making, producing the million forms of wealth they covet for themselves. They need only get control of the roads....Builders, not of manufactories, but of privileges; inventors only of schemes..., contrivers, not of competition, but of ways to tax the property of their competitors into their pockets. They need not make money; they can take it from those who have made it.

SOURCE: Henry Demarest Lloyd, *Wealth against Commonwealth* (New York: Harper & Brothers, 1894), 474–75, 488.

DOCUMENT 2
Ida M. Tarbell, "The Oil War of 1872"

Editor and journalist Ida Minerva Tarbell, whose "History of the Standard Oil Company" ran for three years (1902–1905) in serial form in McClure's Magazine, *proved Rocke-feller's most damaging critic. Tarbell grew up in the Pennsylvania oil region; her father had owned a small refinery gobbled up by Standard Oil. In a devastatingly thorough history, she chronicled the underhanded methods Rockefeller used to gain control of the oil-refining industry. Here she portrays a critical chapter in the history of Standard Oil. In 1879, Rockefeller's first attempt to consolidate the oil industry through the use of illegal rebates had failed.*

If Mr. Rockefeller had been an ordinary man the outburst of popular contempt and suspicion which suddenly poured on his head would have thwarted and crushed him. But he was no ordinary man. He had the powerful imagination to see what might be done with the oil business if it could be centered in his hands—the intelligence to analyze the problem into its elements and to find the key to control. He had the essential element to all great achievement, a steadfastness to a purpose once conceived which nothing can crush. The Oil Regions might rage, call him a conspirator and those who sold to him traitors; the railroads might withdraw their contracts and the legislature annul his charter; undisturbed and unresting he kept at this great purpose....

He got a rebate....How much less a rate than $1.25 Mr. Rockefeller had before the end of April the writer does not know. Of course the rate was secret and he probably understood now, as he had not two months before, how essential it was that he keep it secret. His task was more difficult now, for he had an enemy active, clamorous, contemptuous, whose suspicions had reached that acute point where they could believe nothing but evil of him—the producers and independents of the Oil Regions....

They believed in independent effort—every man for himself and fair play for all. They wanted competition, loved open fight. They considered that all business should be done openly—that railways were bound as public carriers to give equal rates—that any combination which favored one firm or one locality at the expense of another was unjust and illegal....

Those theories which the body of oil men held as vital and fundamental Mr. Rockefeller and his associates either did not comprehend or were deaf to. This lack of comprehension by many men of what seems to other men to be the most obvious principles of justice is not rare. Many men who are widely known as good, share it. Mr. Rockefeller was "good." There was no more faithful Baptist in Cleveland than he. Every enterprise of that church he had supported liberally from youth. He gave to its poor. He visited its sick. He wept with its suffering. Moreover, he gave unostentatiously to many outside charities of whose worthiness he was satisfied. He was simple and frugal in his habits. He never went to the theater, never drank wine. He was a devoted husband, and he gave much time to the training of his children.... Yet he was willing to strain every nerve to obtain for himself special and illegal privileges from the railroads which were bound to ruin every man in the oil business not sharing them with him. Religious emotion and sentiments of charity, propriety and self-denial seem to have taken the place in him of notions of justice and regard for the rights of others.

SOURCE: Ida M. Tarbell, "The Oil War of 1872," in Ellen F. Fitzpatrick, ed., *Muckraking: Three Landmark Articles* (Boston: Bedford/St. Martin's, 1994), 77–79. Originally published in *McClure's Magazine,* January 1903.

DOCUMENT 3
Matthew Josephson, *The Robber Barons,* 1934

The historian Matthew Josephson, writing in 1934 in the trough of the Great Depression, took a dim view of the capitalists of the Gilded Age in his book The Robber Barons. *Josephson's portrait of the young John D. Rockefeller is a caricature of the bloodless miser.*

In his first position, bookkeeper to a produce merchant at the Cleveland docks, when he was sixteen, he distinguished himself by his composed orderly habits. Very carefully he examined each item on each bill before he approved it for payment. Out of a salary which began at $15 a month and advanced ultimately to $50 a month, he saved $800 in three years, the lion's share of his total earnings! This was fantastic parsimony....

He was given to secrecy; he loathed all display. When he married a few years afterward, he lost not a day from his business. His wife, Laura Spelman, proved an excellent mate. She encouraged his furtiveness, he relates, advising him always to be silent, to say as little as possible. His composure, his self-possession was excessive.... He was a hard man to best in a trade, he rarely smiled and almost never laughed, save when he struck a good bargain. Then he might clap his hands with delight, or he might even, if the occasion warranted, throw up his hat, kick his heels, and hug his informer. One time he was so overjoyed at a favorable piece of news that he burst out: "I'm bound to be rich! Bound to be rich!"

SOURCE: Excerpt (pp. 4, 48–49) from *The Robber Barons: The Great American Capitalists 1861–1901* by Matthew Josephson. Copyright © 1934 and renewed 1961 by Matthew Josephson. Reprinted by permission of Harcourt, Inc.

QUESTIONS FOR ANALYSIS AND DEBATE

1. Henry Demarest Lloyd and Ida Tarbell agree that Rockefeller gained control of the oil industry through illegal methods. What was his primary weapon, and how did it operate?

2. Compare Henry Demarest Lloyd's style to that of Ida Tarbell. Which is the more effective and why? Was either of these journalists an impartial observer?

3. Rockefeller never responded to his critics. Do you think Rockefeller's silence was a good strategy? Why or why not?

4. By the time Matthew Josephson wrote his unflattering portrait of Rockefeller, the oil titan was long retired, Standard Oil had been broken up by the Supreme Court, and oil discoveries in Texas and Oklahoma had eclipsed the oil regions in Pennsylvania and Ohio. What do you think motivated Josephson's attack on the "robber barons" in 1934?

old-fashioned virtues of Yankee ingenuity and rugged individualism that Americans most admired. A self-educated dynamo, he worked twenty hours a day in his laboratory in Menlo Park, New Jersey, vowing to turn out "a minor invention every ten days and a big thing every six months or so." He almost made good on his promise. At the height of his career, he averaged a patent every eleven days and invented such "big things" as the phonograph, the motion picture camera, and the filament for the incandescent lightbulb.

Edison, in competition with George W. Westinghouse, went on to pioneer the use of electricity as an energy source. By the late nineteenth century, electricity had become a part of American urban life. It powered trolley cars and lighted factories, homes, and office buildings. Indeed, electricity became so prevalent in urban life that it symbolized the city, whose bright lights contrasted with rural America, left largely in the dark.

While Americans thrilled to the new electric cities and the changes wrought by inventors, the day of the inventor quietly yielded to the heyday of the corporation. In 1892 the electric industry consolidated. Reflecting a nationwide trend in business, Edison General Electric dropped the name of its inventor, becoming General Electric, a behemoth that soon dominated the market.

REVIEW How did John D. Rockefeller gain control of 90 percent of the oil-refining business by 1890?

From Competition to Consolidation

Even as Rockefeller and Carnegie built their empires, the era of the "robber barons," as they were dubbed by their detractors, was drawing to a close. Increasingly, businesses replaced partnerships and sole proprietorships with the anonymous corporate structure that would come to dominate the twentieth century. At the same time, mergers led to the creation of huge new corporations.

Banks and financiers played a key role in this consolidation, so much so that the decades at the turn of the twentieth century can be characterized as a period of finance capitalism—investment sponsored by banks and bankers. As the depression following the panic of 1893 bankrupted many businesses, bankers stepped in to bring order and to reorganize major industries. During these years, a new social philosophy based on the theories of naturalist Charles Darwin helped to justify consolidation and to inhibit state or federal regulation of business. A **conservative** Supreme Court further frustrated attempts to control business by consistently declaring unconstitutional legislation designed to regulate railroad rates or to outlaw trusts and monopolies.

J. P. Morgan and Finance Capitalism

John Pierpont Morgan, the preeminent finance capitalist of the late nineteenth century, loathed competition and sought whenever possible to eliminate it by substituting consolidation and central control. Morgan's hatred of competition made him the architect of business mergers (Figure 17.1). Aloof and silent, Morgan looked down on the climbers and the speculators with a haughtiness that led his rivals to call him "Jupiter," after the ruler of the Roman gods. At the turn of the twentieth

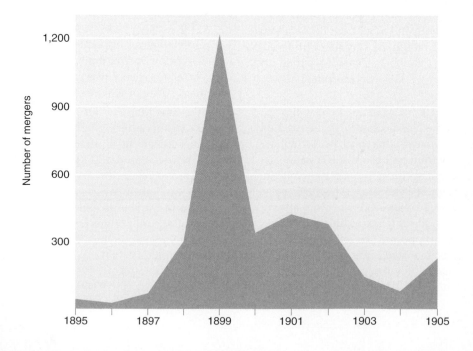

FIGURE 17.1 Merger Mania, 1895–1905
The depression that began with the panic of 1893 fueled a "merger mania," as businesses consolidated and reorganized, often at the prompting of finance capitalists like J. P. Morgan. The number of mergers peaked in 1899, but high rates of consolidation continued into the first decade of the twentieth century.

century, he dominated American banking, exerting an influence so powerful that his critics charged he controlled a vast "money trust."

Morgan acted as a power broker in the reorganization of the railroads and the creation of industrial giants like General Electric and U.S. Steel. When the railroads fell on hard times in the 1890s, Morgan, with his passion for order and his access to capital, emerged as the rescuer of embattled, wrecked, and ruined companies. He quickly moved to eliminate competition by creating what he called "a community of interest" among the managers he handpicked. By the time he finished reorganizing the railroads, Morgan had concentrated the nation's railroads in the hands of a few directors who controlled two-thirds of the nation's track.

Banker control of the railroads rationalized, or coordinated, the industry. But stability came at a high price. To keep investors happy and to guarantee huge profits from the sale of stock, Morgan heavily "watered" the stock of the railroads, issuing more shares than the assets of the company warranted. J. P. Morgan & Co. made millions of dollars from commissions and from blocks of stock acquired through reorganization. The flagrant overcapitalization created by the watered stock hurt the railroads in the long run, saddling them with enormous debts. Equally harmful was the management style of the Morgan directors, who aimed at short-term profit and discouraged the continued technological and organizational innovation needed to run the railroads effectively.

In 1898, Morgan moved into the steel industry, directly challenging Andrew Carnegie. Morgan supervised the mergers of several smaller steel companies, which soon expanded from the manufacture of finished goods into steel production. The pugnacious Carnegie cabled his partners in the summer of 1900: "Action essential: crisis has arrived...have no fear as to the result; victory certain."

The press trumpeted news of the impending fight between the feisty Scot and the haughty Wall Street banker, but what the papers called the "battle of the giants" in the end proved little more than the wily maneuvering of two businessmen so adept that even today it is difficult to say who won. For all his belligerence, the sixty-six-year-old Carnegie yearned to retire to Skibo castle, his home in Scotland. He may well have invited Morgan's bid for power. Morgan, who disdained haggling, agreed to pay Carnegie's asking price, $480 million (the equivalent of about $9.6 billion

J. P. Morgan, Photograph by Edward Steichen
Few photographs of J. P. Morgan exist. Morgan, who suffered from a skin condition that left him with a misshapen strawberry of a nose, rarely allowed his picture to be taken. But it was his eyes that people remembered—eyes so piercing that Edward Steichen, who took this photograph, observed that "meeting his gaze was a little like confronting the headlights of an express train."
George Eastman House. Reprinted with permission of Joanna T. Steichen.

in today's currency). According to legend, when Carnegie later teased Morgan, saying that he should have asked $100 million more, Morgan replied: "You would have got it if you had."

Morgan's acquisition of Carnegie Steel signaled the passing of one age and the arrival of another. Carnegie represented the old entrepreneurial order, Morgan the new corporate world. The banker quickly moved to pull together Carnegie's chief competitors to form a huge new steel corporation, United States Steel, known today as USX. Created in 1901 and capitalized at $1.4 billion, U.S. Steel was the largest corporation in the world. Yet for all its size, it did not hold a monopoly in the steel industry. Significant small competitors, such as Bethlehem Steel, remained independent, creating a competitive system called an **oligopoly**, in which several large companies control production and effectively blunt competition.

Homestead Steelworks

The Homestead steelworks, outside Pittsburgh, Pennsylvania, is pictured shortly after J. P. Morgan bought out Andrew Carnegie and created U.S. Steel, the precursor of today's USX. Try to count the smokestacks in the picture. Air pollution on this scale posed a threat to the health of citizens and made for a dismal landscape. Workers complained that trees would not grow in Homestead.

Hagley Museum & Library.

When J. P. Morgan died in 1913, his estate totaled $68 million, not counting an estimated $50 million in art treasures. Andrew Carnegie, who gave away more than $300 million before his death six years later, is said to have quipped, "And to think he was not a rich man!" But Carnegie's gibe missed the mark. The quest for power, not wealth, had motivated J. P. Morgan, and his power could best be measured not in the millions he owned but in the billions he controlled. Even more than Carnegie or Rockefeller, Morgan left his stamp on the twentieth century and formed the model for corporate consolidation that economists and social scientists soon justified with a new social theory known as **social Darwinism**.

Social Darwinism and the Gospel of Wealth

John D. Rockefeller Jr., the son of the founder of Standard Oil, once remarked to his Baptist Bible class that the Standard Oil Company, like the American Beauty rose, resulted from "pruning the early buds that grew up around it." The elim-ination of smaller, inefficient units, he said, was "merely the working out of a law of nature and a law of God." The comparison of the business world to the natural world formed the backbone of a theory of society based on the law of evolution formulated by British naturalist Charles Darwin. In his monumental work *On the Origin of Species* (1859), Darwin theorized that in the struggle for survival, the process of adaptation to environment triggered among species a natural selection process that led to evolutionary progress. Drawing on Darwin's work, Herbert Spencer in Britain and William Graham Sumner in the United States developed the theory of social Darwinism. Crudely applying Darwin's theory to human society, the social Darwinists concluded that progress came about as a result of relentless competition in which the strong survived and the weak died out.

In social terms, the idea of the survival of the fittest had profound significance, as Sumner, a professor of political economy at Yale University, made clear in his 1883 book, *What Social Classes Owe to Each Other*. "The drunkard in the gutter is just where he ought to be, according to the fitness and tendency of things," Sumner insisted. Conversely, "millionaires are the product of natural selection," and although "they get high wages and live in luxury," Sumner claimed, "the bargain is a good one for society."

Social Darwinists equated wealth and power with "fitness" and believed that the unfit should be allowed to die off to advance the progress of humanity. Any efforts by the rich to aid the poor would only tamper with the rigid laws of nature and slow evolution. Social Darwinism acted to curb social reform while at the same time it glorified great wealth. In an age when Rockefeller and Carnegie amassed hundreds of millions of dollars (billions in today's currency) and the average worker earned $500 a year (about $8,800), social Darwinism justified economic inequality.

Andrew Carnegie softened some of the harshness of social Darwinism in his essay "The Gospel of Wealth," published in 1889. The millionaire, Carnegie wrote, acted as a "mere trustee and agent for his poorer brethren, bringing to their service his superior wisdom, experience, and ability to administer, doing for them better than they could or would do for themselves." Carnegie preached philanthropy and urged the rich to "live unostentatious lives" and "administer surplus wealth for the good of the people." His **gospel of wealth** earned much praise but won few converts. Most millionaires followed the lead of J. P. Morgan, who contributed to charity but amassed private treasures in his marble library rather than living the unostentatious, philanthropic life Carnegie counseled.

Social Darwinism nicely suited an age in which the gross inequalities accompanying industrialization seemed to cry out for action. In an era noted for greed and crass materialism, social Darwinism reassured comfortable Americans that all was as it should be. And the gospel of wealth, which mitigated the harshest dictates of social Darwinism, did not challenge the basic order of industrial society.

Laissez-faire and the Supreme Court

Social Darwinism, with its emphasis on the free play of competition and survival of the fittest, encouraged the economic theory of **laissez-faire** (French for "let it alone"). Business argued that the government should not meddle in economic affairs, except to protect private property. The conservative Supreme Court agreed and used its power to protect business interests. During the 1880s and 1890s, the Court increasingly reinter-

preted the Constitution to protect business from taxation, regulation, labor organization, and antitrust legislation.

In a series of landmark decisions, the Court used the Fourteenth Amendment, originally intended to protect freed slaves from state laws violating their rights, to protect corporations. The Fourteenth Amendment declares that no state can "deprive any person of life, liberty, or property, without due process of law." By defining corporations as "persons" under the law, the Court determined that legislation designed to regulate corporations deprived them of "due process." Using this reasoning, the Court struck down state laws regulating railroad rates, declared income tax unconstitutional, and judged labor unions a "conspiracy in restraint of trade." The Court insisted on elevating the rights of property over all other rights. According to Justice Stephen J. Field, the Constitution "allows no impediments to the acquisition of property." Field, born into a wealthy New England family, spoke with the bias of the privileged class to whom property rights were sacrosanct. Imbued with this ideology, the Court refused to impede corporate consolidation and did nothing to curb the excesses of big business. Only in the arena of politics did Americans tackle the issues raised by corporate capitalism.

REVIEW Why did the ideas of social Darwinism appeal to many Americans in the late nineteenth century?

Politics and Culture

One could easily argue that politics constituted America's pastime in the Gilded Age. For many Americans, politics provided a source of identity, a means of livelihood, and a ready form of entertainment. No wonder voter turnout averaged a hefty 77 percent. A variety of factors contributed to the complicated interplay of politics and culture. Patronage provided an economic incentive for voter participation, but ethnicity, religion, sectional loyalty, race, and gender all influenced the political life of the period.

Political Participation and Party Loyalty

Patronage—the **spoils system**—proved a strong motivation for party loyalty among many voters. Political parties in power doled out federal, state, and local government jobs to their loyal supporters. With hundreds of thousands of jobs to be filled, the choice of party affiliation could mean the difference between a paycheck or an empty pocket. Money greased the wheels of the spoils system. Party bosses expected jobholders to kick back from 2 to 4 percent of their salaries to support the party's electoral campaigns. With their livelihoods tied to their party identity, government employees in particular had an incentive to vote in great numbers during the Gilded Age.

Political affiliation provided a powerful sense of group identity for many voters, proud of their loyalty to the Democrats or the Republicans. Democrats, who traced the party's roots back to Thomas Jefferson, called theirs "the party of the fathers." The Republican Party, founded in the 1850s, still claimed strong loyalties as a result of its alignment with the Union during the Civil War. Both Republicans in the North and Democrats in the South played to regional sentiments by a tactic called "waving the **bloody shirt**"—reminding voters which side they had fought for in the Civil War.

Politics also provided entertainment and spectacle for voters and nonvoters alike in an age before mass recreation and amusement, particularly in rural areas. Political parties sponsored parades, rallies, speeches, picnics, torchlight processions, and Fourth of July fireworks, attracting millions of Americans. Outside the big cities, only religious revivals and traveling shows could compete.

Religion and ethnicity also played a significant role in politics. In the North, **Protestants** from the old-line denominations, particularly Presbyterians and Methodists, flocked to the

Republican Party, which championed a series of moral reforms, including local laws requiring businesses to close in observance of the Sabbath. In the burgeoning cities, the Democratic Party courted immigrants and working-class Catholic and Jewish voters charging, rightly, that Republican moral crusades often masked attacks on immigrant culture.

Sectionalism and the New South

After the end of Reconstruction, voters in the former Confederate states remained loyal Democrats, voting for Democratic candidates in every presidential election for the next seventy years. Labeling the Republican Party the agent of "Negro rule," Democrats urged white Southerners to "vote the way you shot." Yet the so-called solid South proved far from solid on the state and local levels. The economic plight of the South led to shifting political alliances and to third-party movements that challenged Democratic attempts to define politics along race lines and maintain the Democratic Party as the white man's party.

The South's economy, devastated by the war, foundered at the same time the North experienced an unprecedented industrial boom. Soon an influential group of Southerners called for a **New South** modeled on the industrial North. Henry Grady, the ebullient young editor of the *Atlanta Constitution,* used his paper's substantial influence (it boasted the largest circulation of any weekly in the country) to extol the virtues of a new industrial South. Part bully, part booster, Grady exhorted the South to use its natural advantages—cheap labor and abundant natural resources—to go head-to-head in competition with northern industry.

Grady's message fell on receptive ears. Many Southerners, men and women, black and white, joined the national migration from farm to city, leaving the old plantations to molder and decay. With the end of military rule in 1877, southern Democrats took back state governments, calling themselves "Redeemers." Yet rather than restore the economy of the old **planter** class, they embraced northern promoters who promised prosperity and profits.

Hayes Campaign Lantern, 1876
Republicans carried this lantern in the campaign of 1876. Designed for nighttime rallies, the lantern featured paper transparencies that allowed light to shine through the stars and illuminate the portrait of the candidate, Rutherford B. Hayes. Marching men with lighted lanterns held aloft must have been a dramatic sight in small towns across the country. Politics constituted a major form of entertainment in nineteenth-century life.
Collection of Janice L. and David J. Frent.

The railroads came first, opening up the region for industrial development. Southern railroad mileage grew fourfold from 1865 to 1890 (see Map 17.1). The number of cotton spindles also soared, as textile mill owners abandoned New England in search of the cheap labor and proximity to raw materials promised in the South. By 1900 the South had become the nation's leading producer of cloth, and more than 100,000 Southerners, many of them women and children, worked in the region's textile mills.

The New South was proudest of its iron and steel industry, which grew up in the area surrounding Birmingham, Alabama. Andrew Carnegie toured the region in 1889 and observed, "The South is Pennsylvania's most formidable industrial enemy." But southern industry remained controlled by northern investors who had no intention of letting the South beat the North at its own game. Elaborate mechanisms rigged the price of southern steel, inflating it, as one northern insider confessed, "for the purpose of protecting the Pittsburgh mills and in turn the Pittsburgh steel users."

In only one industry did the South truly dominate—tobacco. Capitalizing on the invention of a machine for rolling cigarettes, the American Tobacco Company founded by the Duke family of North Carolina eventually dominated the industry. Cigarettes, which replaced chewing tobacco in popularity at the turn of the twentieth century, provided a booming market for Duke's "ready mades." Soon the company was selling 400,000 cigarettes a day.

In practical terms, the industrialized New South proved an illusion. Much of the South remained agricultural, caught in the grip of the insidious crop lien system (see chapter 16). White southern farmers, desperate to get out of debt, often joined with African Americans to pursue their goals politically. Southerners used this strategy in a variety of ways. Between 1865 and 1900, voters in every state south of the Mason-Dixon line experimented with political alliances that crossed the color line. In Virginia the "Readjusters," a coalition of blacks and whites determined to "readjust" (lower) the state debt and spend more money on public education, captured state offices from 1879 to 1883. In southern politics, the interplay of race and gender made coalitions like the Readjusters a potent threat to the status quo.

Gender, Race, and Politics

Gender—society's notion of what constitutes acceptable masculine or feminine behavior—influenced politics throughout the nineteenth century. From the early days of the Republic, citizenship had been defined in male terms. Citizenship and its prerogatives (voting and officeholding) served as a badge of manliness and rested on its corollary, patriarchy—the power and authority men exerted over their wives and families. With the advent of universal (white) male **suffrage** in the early nineteenth century, gender eclipsed class as the defining feature of citizenship; men's dominance over women provided the common thread that knit all white men together politically.

Gender permeated politics in other ways, especially in the tangled skein of the New South. Cross-racial alliances like the Readjusters rested on the belief that universal political rights (voting, officeholding, patronage) could be extended to black males in the public sphere without eliminating racial barriers in the private sphere. Democrats, for their part, fought back by trying to convince voters that black voting would inevitably lead to **miscegenation** (racial mixing). Black male political power and sexual power, they warned, went hand in hand. Ultimately their arguments prevailed, and many whites returned to the Democratic fold to protect "white womanhood" and with it white supremacy.

The notion that black men threatened white southern womanhood reached its most vicious form in the practice of lynching—the killing and mutilation of black men by white mobs. By 1892 the practice had become so prevalent that a courageous black woman, Ida B. Wells, launched an antilynching movement. That year a white mob lynched a friend of Wells's whose grocery store competed too successfully with a white-owned store. Wells shrewdly concluded that lynching served "as an excuse to get rid of Negroes who were acquiring wealth and property and thus keep the race terrorized." She began to collect data on lynching and discovered that in the decade between 1882 and 1892, lynching rose in the South by an overwhelming 200 percent; more than 241 people were killed. Wells struck back.

As the first salvo in her attack, Wells put to rest the "old threadbare lie that Negro men assault white women." As she pointed out, violations of black women by white men, which were much more frequent than black attacks on white

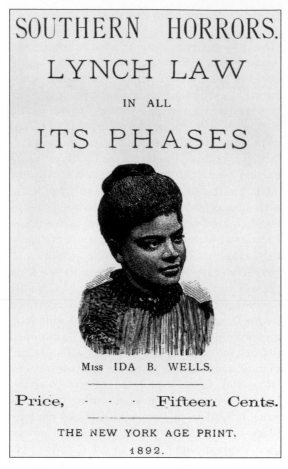

Ida B. Wells

Ida B. Wells began her antilynching campaign at the age of thirty after a friend's murder in 1892 led her to examine the extent of lynching in the South. She spread her message in lectures and pamphlets like this one distributed for fifteen cents. Wells brought the horror of lynching to a national and international audience and mobilized other African American women to undertake social action under the auspices of the National Association of Colored Women.

Manuscript, Archives and Rare Books Division, Schomburg Center for Research in Black Culture, The New York Public Library, Astor, Lenox, and Tilden.

women, went unnoticed and unpunished. Wells articulated lynching as a problem of race and gender. She insisted that the myth of black attacks on white southern womanhood masked the reality that mob violence had more to do with economics and the shifting social structure of the South than with rape. She demonstrated in a sophisticated way how the southern patriarchal system, having lost its control over blacks with the end of slavery, used its control over women to circumscribe the liberty of black men.

Wells's strong stance immediately resulted in reprisal. While she was traveling in the North, vandals ransacked her office in Tennessee and destroyed her printing equipment. Yet the warning that she would be killed on sight if she ever returned to Memphis only stiffened her resolve. As she wrote in her autobiography, *Crusader for Justice,* "Having lost my paper, had a price put on my life and been made an exile…, I felt that I owed it to myself and to my race to tell the whole truth now that I was where I could do so freely." Antilynching became a lifelong commitment that took Wells twice to Britain, where she placed lynching on the international agenda. As a reporter, first for the *New York Age* and later for the *Chicago Inter-Ocean,* she used every opportunity to hammer home her message.

Lynching did not end during Ida B. Wells's lifetime, nor did antilynching legislation gain passage in Congress; but Wells's forceful voice brought the issue to national prominence. At her funeral in 1931, black leader W. E. B. Du Bois eulogized Wells as the woman who "began the awakening of the conscience of the nation." Wells's determined campaign against lynching provided just one example of women's political activism during the Gilded Age. The suffrage and **temperance** movements also demonstrated how women refused to be relegated to a **"separate sphere"** that kept them out of politics by gendering it male.

Women's Politics: The Origins of the Suffrage and Temperance Movements

No one better recognized the potency of the gendered notion of political rights than Elizabeth Cady Stanton, who lamented the introduction of the word *male* into the Fourteenth Amendment (see chapter 16). The explicit linking of manhood with citizenship and voting rights in the Constitution marked a major setback for reformers who supported the vote for women. In 1869, Stanton along with Susan B. Anthony formed the National Woman Suffrage Association (NWSA), the first independent women's rights organization in the United States.

Women found ways to act politically long before they voted, as evidenced not only in the campaign for the vote but also in the temperance movement (the movement to end drunkenness). Temperance women adopted a new approach during the winter of 1873–74. Armed with Bibles and singing hymns, they marched on taverns and saloons and refused to leave until the proprietors signed a pledge to quit selling liquor. Known as the Woman's Crusade, the movement spread like a prairie fire through small towns in Ohio, Indiana, Michigan, and Illinois and soon moved east into New York, New England, and Pennsylvania. Before it was over, more than 100,000 women marched in over 450 cities and towns.

The Woman's Crusade dramatically brought the issue of temperance back into the national spotlight and led to the formation of a new organization, the Woman's Christian Temperance Union (WCTU) in 1874. Composed entirely of women, the WCTU advocated total abstinence from alcohol (see chapter 20). When the women of the WCTU joined with the Prohibition Party (formed in 1869 by a group of **evangelical** clergymen), one wag observed that "politics is a man's game, an' women, chidlhern, and prohyibitionists do well to keep out iv it." By sharing power with women, the Prohibitionist men violated the old political rules and risked such attacks on their honor and manhood.

Temperance, antilynching, and suffrage constituted only a few of women's political causes. Nevertheless, politics, particularly presidential politics, remained—like chewing tobacco—an exclusively male prerogative.

> **REVIEW** Why did New South promoters believe the region could compete with the North in industrialization?

Presidential Politics in the Gilded Age

Why do the great industrialists—Rockefeller, Morgan, Carnegie—jump vividly from the pages of the past while the presidents of that period remain so pallid? The presidents from Rutherford B. Hayes (1877–1881) to William McKinley (1897–1901) are indeed forgotten men, largely because so little was expected of them. Until the 1890s, few Americans thought the president or the national government had any role to play in addressing the problems accompanying the industrial transformation of the nation. The dominant creed of laissez-faire, coupled with the dictates of social Darwinism, warned government to leave business alone. Presidents in the Gilded Age grappled with corruption and party strife and struggled toward the creation of new political ethics designed to replace patronage with a

civil service system that promised to award jobs on the basis of merit, not party loyalty.

Corruption and Party Strife

The political corruption and party factionalism that characterized the administration of Ulysses S. Grant (1869–1877) continued to trouble the nation in the 1880s. The spoils system—awarding jobs for political purposes—remained the driving force in party politics at all levels of government in the Gilded Age. Reformers eager to replace the spoils system with civil service faced an uphill battle.

A small but determined group of reformers championed a new ethics that would preclude politicians from getting rich from public office. The selection of U.S. senators particularly concerned them. Under the Constitution, senators were selected by state legislatures, not directly elected by the voters. Powerful business interests often contrived to control state legislatures and through them U.S. senators. As journalist Henry Demarest Lloyd observed, Standard Oil "had done everything to the Pennsylvania legislature except to refine it." Nothing prevented a senator from collecting a paycheck from any of the great corporations. So many did that political cartoonists often portrayed senators as huge moneybags labeled with the names of the corporations they served. In this climate, a constitutional amendment calling for the direct election of senators faced opposition from entrenched interests.

Republican president Rutherford B. Hayes, whose disputed election in 1876 signaled the end of Reconstruction in the South, tried to steer a middle course between spoilsmen and reformers. Hayes wanted peace, prosperity, and an end to party strife. The Republican Party remained divided into factions led by strong party bosses who boasted that they could make or break a president.

Fiery and dynamic party bosses dominated politics on the national scene. Foremost among them stood Senator Roscoe Conkling of New York, a master spoilsman, who ridiculed civil service as "snivel service" and tried his best to get the Republicans to run Grant again for president in 1880. He and his followers were known as "Stalwarts." Conkling's archrival, Senator James G. Blaine of Maine, led a faction called the "Half Breeds." Not as openly corrupt as the Grant wing of the party, the Half Breeds and their champion were nevertheless tainted with charges of corruption. A third group, called the Mugwumps, consisted primarily of reform-minded Republicans from Massachusetts and New York who deplored

Civil Service Exams

In this 1890s photograph, prospective police officers in Chicago take the written civil service exam. Civil service meant that politicians and party bosses could no longer use jobs in the government to reward the party faithful. Many people worried that merit examinations would favor the educated elite at the expense of immigrant groups like the Irish, who had made a place for themselves in the political system by the late nineteenth century. The political cartoon (inset) underscores the point by showing an applicant sweating over the exam while in his pocket he carries a recommendation from his alderman. The cartoon implies that in the past this man would have received a job even though he couldn't answer simple questions.

Photo: Chicago Historical Society; inset: Chicago Historical Society.

the spoils system and advocated civil service reform. The name "Mugwump" came from the Algonquian word for *chief,* but critics used the term derisively, punning that the Mugwumps straddled the fence on issues of party loyalty, "with their mug on one side and wump on the other."

Despite his good intentions, President Hayes soon managed to alienate all factions in his party, and no one was surprised when he announced that he would not seek reelection in 1880. To avoid choosing among its factions, the Republican Party in 1880 nominated a "dark-horse" candidate, Representative James A. Garfield from Ohio. To appease Conkling, they picked Stalwart Chester A. Arthur as the vice presidential candidate. The Democrats made an

attempt to overcome sectionalism and establish a national party by selecting as their presidential standard-bearer an old Union general, Winfield Scott Hancock. But as one observer noted, "It is a peculiarly constituted party that sends rebel brigadiers to Congress because of their rebellion, and then nominates a Union General as its candidate for president because of his loyalty." Although the popular vote was close, Garfield won 214 electoral votes to Hancock's 155.

Garfield's Assassination and Civil Service Reform

"My God," Garfield swore after only a few months in office, "what is there in this place that a man should ever want to get into it?" Garfield, like Hayes, faced the difficult task of remaining independent while pacifying the party bosses and placating the reformers. As the federal bureaucracy grew to nearly 150,000 jobs, thousands of office seekers swarmed to the nation's capital, each clamoring for a position. In the days before Secret Service protection, the White House door stood open to all comers. Garfield took a fatalistic view. "Assassination," he told a friend, "can no more be guarded against than death by lightning, and it is best not to worry about either."

On July 2, 1881, less than four months after taking office, Garfield was fatally shot. His assassin, Charles Guiteau, though clearly insane, turned out to be a disappointed office seeker who claimed to be motivated by political partisanship. He told the police officer who arrested him, "I did it; I will go to jail for it; Arthur is president, and I am a Stalwart."

The press almost universally condemned Republican factionalism for creating the political climate that produced Guiteau. Stalwart Roscoe Conkling saw his hopes for the White House dashed. Attacks on the spoils system increased, and the public joined the chorus calling for reform. Reformers faced stiff opposition from those who recognized that civil service had class and ethnic biases. At a time when few men achieved more than a grammar school education, written civil service examinations threatened to undo political advances made by Irish Americans and return government to an educated Yankee elite.

Reform came with the passage of the Pendleton Civil Service Act in 1883. Both parties claimed credit for the act, which established a permanent Civil Service Commission of three members, appointed by the president. Some fourteen thousand jobs came under a merit system that required examinations for office and made it impossible to remove jobholders for political reasons. Half of the postal jobs and most of the customhouse jobs, the largest share of the spoils system's bounty, passed to the control of the Civil Service Commission. The new law also prohibited federal jobholders from contributing to political campaigns, thus drying up the major source of the party bosses' revenue. Soon business interests stepped in to replace officeholders as the nation's chief political contributors. Ironically, civil service reform thus gave business an even greater influence in political life.

Reform and Scandal: The Campaign of 1884

With Conkling's downfall, James G. Blaine assumed leadership of the Republican Party and at long last captured the presidential nomination in 1884. A magnetic Irish American politician, Blaine inspired such devotion that his supporters called themselves Blainiacs. But Mugwumps like editor Carl Schurz insisted that Blaine "wallowed in spoils like a rhinoceros in an African pool." They bolted the party and embraced the Democrats' presidential nominee, the stolid Grover Cleveland, reform governor of New York. The burly, beer-drinking Cleveland distinguished himself from an entire generation of politicians by the simple motto "A public office is a public trust." First as mayor of Buffalo and later as governor of New York, he built a reputation for honesty, economy, and administrative efficiency. The Democrats, who had not won the presidency since 1856, had high hopes for his candidacy, especially after the Mugwumps threw their support to Cleveland, insisting "the paramount issue this year is moral rather than political."

The Mugwumps soon regretted their words. The 1884 contest degenerated so far into scandal and nasty mudslinging that one disgusted journalist styled it "the vilest campaign ever waged." In July, Cleveland's hometown paper, the *Buffalo Telegraph,* dropped the bombshell that the bachelor candidate had fathered an illegitimate child in an affair with a local widow. Crushed by the scandal, the Mugwumps tried to argue the difference between public and private morality. But robbed of their moral righteousness, they lost much of their enthusiasm. "Now I fear it has resolved itself into a choice of two evils," one weary reformer confessed.

At public rallies, Blaine's partisans taunted Cleveland, chanting, "Ma, Ma, where's my Pa?" The stoic Cleveland accepted responsibility for the child and waged his campaign in the traditional fashion by staying home while Blaine broke precedent by making a national tour.

A campaign misstep by Blaine quickly revived Cleveland's chances. On a last-minute stop in New York City, the exhausted candidate overlooked a remark by a local clergyman that cast a slur on Catholic voters by styling the Democrats as the party of "Rum, Romanism, and Rebellion." By linking drinking (rum) and Catholicism (Romanism), the remark offended Irish Catholic voters, who had been counted on to desert the

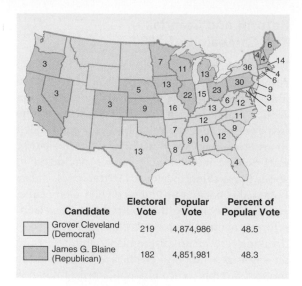

Candidate	Electoral Vote	Popular Vote	Percent of Popular Vote
Grover Cleveland (Democrat)	219	4,874,986	48.5
James G. Blaine (Republican)	182	4,851,981	48.3

MAP 17.2   The Election of 1884

Democratic Party and support Blaine because of his Irish background.

With less than a week to go until the election, Blaine had no chance to recover from the negative publicity. He lost New York State by fewer than 1,200 votes and with it the election. In the final tally, Cleveland defeated Blaine by a scant 29,214 votes nationwide but won 219 electoral votes to 182 (Map 17.2). Cleveland's followers had the last word. To the chorus of "Ma, Ma, where's my Pa?" they retorted, "Going to the White House, ha, ha, ha."

REVIEW   How did the question of civil service reform contribute to divisions within the Republican Party?

Economic Issues and Shifting Political Alliances

Four years later, in the election of 1888, fickle voters turned Cleveland out, electing Republican Benjamin Harrison, the grandson of President William Henry Harrison. Then, in the only instance in America's history when a president once defeated at the polls returned to office, the voters brought Cleveland back in the election of 1892. What factors account for such a surprising turnaround? The strengths and weaknesses of the men themselves partially determined the outcome. The stubborn Cleveland, newly mar-

ried, refused to campaign in 1888. Although he won more popular votes than Harrison, he lost in the electoral college. Once in office, Harrison proved to be a cold and distant leader, prompting critics to call him "the human iceberg."

But new issues as well as personalities increasingly swayed the voters. The 1880s witnessed a remarkable political realignment as a new set of economic concerns replaced appeals to Civil War sectional loyalties. The tariff, federal regulation of the railroads and trusts, and the campaign for **free silver** restructured American politics.

The Tariff and the Politics of Protection

The tariff became a potent political issue in the 1880s. The concept of a protective tariff to raise the price of imported goods and stimulate American industry dated back to Alexander Hamilton in the founding days of the Republic. Congress enacted the first tariff following the War of 1812. The Republicans turned the tariff to political ends in 1861 by enacting a measure that both raised revenues for the Civil War and rewarded their industrial supporters, who wanted protection from foreign competition. After the war, the Republicans continued to revise and enlarge the tariff at the prompting of northeastern industrialists. By the 1880s, the tariff was so high it posed a threat to prosperity. The huge surplus created by the tariff sat in the Treasury's vaults, depriving the country of money that might otherwise have been invested to create jobs and roads, while the government argued about how (or even whether) to spend it.

To many Americans, particularly southern and midwestern farmers who sold their crops in a world market yet had to buy goods priced artificially high because of the protective tariff, the answer was simple: Reduce the tariff. Advocates of free trade and moderates agitated for tariff reform. But those who benefited from the tariff—industrialists insisting that America's "infant industries" needed protection and some westerners producing protected raw materials such as wool, hides, and lumber—firmly opposed lowering the tariff. Many workers, too, believed that the tariff protected American wages by giving American products an edge over imported goods.

The Republican Party seized on the tariff question to forge a new national coalition. "Fold up the bloody shirt and lay it away," Blaine advised a colleague in 1880. "It's of no use to us. You want to shift the main issue to protection." By encouraging an alliance among industrialists, labor, and western producers of raw materials—groups who benefited from the tariff—Blaine hoped to solidify the North, Midwest, and West against the solidly Democratic South. Although the tactic failed for Blaine in the presidential election of 1884, it worked for the Republicans four years later. Cleveland, who had straddled the tariff issue in the election of 1884, startled the nation in 1887 by calling for tariff reform. The Republicans countered by arguing that "tariff tinkering" would only unsettle prosperous industries, drive down wages, and shrink the farmers' home market. Republican Benjamin Harrison, who supported the high tariff, ousted Cleveland from the White House in 1888, carrying all the western and northern states except Connecticut and New Jersey.

Back in power, the Republicans passed the highest tariff in the nation's history. The new tariff, sponsored by Republican representative William McKinley of Ohio and signed into law by Harrison, stirred a hornet's nest of protest across the United States. The American people had elected Harrison to preserve protection but not to enact a higher tariff.

Democrats condemned the McKinley tariff and labeled the Republican Congress that passed it the "Billion Dollar Congress" for its carnival of spending that depleted the nation's surplus by enacting a series of pork barrel programs shamelessly designed to bring federal money to congressmen's own constituents. In the congressional election of 1890, angry voters swept the hapless Republicans, including tariff sponsor McKinley, out of office. Two years later, Harrison himself was defeated. Grover Cleveland, whose call for tariff revision had lost him the election in 1888, triumphantly returned to the White House vowing to lower the tariff. Such were the changes in the political winds whipped up by the tariff issue.

Railroads, Trusts, and the Federal Government

American voters may have divided on the tariff, but increasingly they agreed on the need for federal regulation of the railroads and federal legislation against the "trusts" (a term loosely applied to all large business combinations). As early as the 1870s, angry farmers in the Midwest who suffered from the unfair shipping practices of the railroads organized to fight for railroad regulation. The Patrons of Husbandry, or the Grange, founded in 1867 as a social and educational organization for farmers, soon became an independent political movement. By electing Grangers to state office, farmers made it possible for several midwestern states to pass laws in the 1870s and 1880s regulating the railroads. At first the Supreme Court ruled in favor of state regulation (*Munn v. Illinois,* 1877). But in 1886, the Court reversed itself, ruling that because railroads crossed state boundaries, they fell outside state jurisdiction (*Wabash v. Illinois*). With more than three-fourths of railroads crossing state lines, the Supreme Court's decision effectively quashed the states' attempts at railroad regulation.

Anger over the *Wabash* decision finally led to the first federal law regulating the railroads, the Interstate Commerce Act, passed in 1887. The act established the nation's first federal regulatory agency, the Interstate Commerce Commission (ICC), to oversee the railroad industry. In its early years, the ICC was never strong enough to pose a serious threat to the railroads. It could not, for example, end rebates to big shippers. In its early decades, the ICC proved more important as a precedent than effective as a watchdog.

Concern over the growing power of the trusts led Congress to pass the Sherman Antitrust Act in 1890. The act outlawed pools and trusts, ruling that businesses could no longer enter into agreements to restrict competition. It did nothing to restrict huge holding companies like Standard Oil, however, and proved to be a weak sword against the trusts. In the decade after passing the Sherman Antitrust Act, the government successfully struck down only six trusts. And rather than acting solely as a check on big business, the act was used four times against labor by outlawing unions as a "conspiracy in restraint of trade." In 1895, the Supreme Court dealt the antitrust law a crippling blow in *United States v. E. C. Knight Company*. In its decision the Court ruled that "manufacture" did not constitute "trade." This semantic quibble drastically narrowed the law, in this case allowing the American Sugar Refining Company, which had bought out a number of other sugar companies (including E. C. Knight) and controlled 98 percent of the production of sugar, to continue its virtual monopoly.

Both the ICC and the Sherman Antitrust Act testified to the nation's concern about corporate abuses of power and to a growing willingness to use federal measures to intervene on behalf of the public interest. As corporate capitalism became more and more powerful, public pressure grew toward political intervention. Yet not until the twentieth century would more active presidents sharpen and use these weapons effectively against the large corporations.

The Fight for Free Silver

While the tariff and regulation of the trusts gained many backers, the silver issue stirred passions like no other issue of the day. On one side stood those who believed that gold constituted the only honest money. Although other forms of currency circulated, notably paper money like banknotes and greenbacks, the government's support of the **gold standard** meant that all currency could be redeemed for gold. Many who supported the gold standard were eastern creditors who did not wish to be paid in devalued dollars. On the opposite side stood a coalition of western silver barons and poor farmers from the West and South who called for free silver. The mining interests, who had seen the silver bonanza in the West drive down the price of the precious metal, wanted the government to buy silver and mint silver dollars. Farmers from the West and South who had suffered economically during the 1870s and 1880s hoped that increasing the money supply with silver dollars, thus causing inflation, would give them some relief by enabling them to pay off their debts with cheaper dollars.

Advocates of free silver pointed out that until 1873 the country had enjoyed a system of bimetalism—the minting of both silver and gold into coins. In that year, at the behest of those who favored gold, Congress voted to stop buying and minting silver, an act silver supporters denounced as the "crime of '73." In 1878 and again in 1890 with the Sherman Silver Purchase Act, Congress took steps to appease advocates of silver by passing legislation that required the government to buy silver and issue silver certificates. While good for the mining interests, the laws did little to promote the inflation desired by the farmers. Soon they began to call for "the free and unlimited coinage of silver," a plan whereby nearly all the silver mined in the West would be minted into coins circulated at the rate of sixteen ounces of silver to one ounce of gold.

The silver issue crossed party lines, but the Democrats hoped to use it to achieve a union between western and southern voters. Unfortunately for them, Grover Cleveland, a Democrat who was a staunch conservative in money matters and a strong supporter of the gold standard, sat in the White House. After a panic on Wall Street touched off a major depression in the spring of 1893, Cleveland called a special session of Congress and bullied the legislature into repealing the 1890 Silver Purchase Act. But repeal did not bring prosperity; it only divided the country. Angry farmers warned Cleveland not to travel west of the Mississippi River if he valued his life.

Panic and Depression

President Cleveland had scarcely begun his second term in office in 1893 when the nation fell into a deep economic depression, the worst the country had yet seen. In the winter of 1894–95, Cleveland walked the floor of the White House, sleepless over the prospect that the United States might go bankrupt. The Treasury's gold reserves had dipped so low that unless gold could be purchased abroad, the unthinkable might happen: The U.S. Treasury might not be able to meet its obligations.

At this juncture J. P. Morgan stepped in and suggested a plan. A group of bankers would purchase gold abroad and supply it to the Treasury. Cleveland knew that such a scheme would unleash a thunder of protest, yet to save the gold standard, the president had no choice but to turn to Morgan for help. A storm of controversy erupted over the deal. The press claimed that Cleveland had lined his own pockets and rumored that Morgan had made $8.9 million. Neither allegation was true. Cleveland had not profited a penny, and Morgan made about $300,000 on the deal—far less than the millions his critics claimed.

But if President Cleveland's action managed to salvage the gold standard, it did not save the country from hardship. The winter of 1894–95 was one of the hardest in American history. People faced unemployment, cold, and hunger. A firm believer in limited government, Cleveland insisted

U.S. Currency
Gold remained the nation's standard currency, but silver supporters, including farmers and western mining interests, demanded the minting of silver dollars and the issuance of silver certificates. In the center is a dollar gold piece.
The American Numismatic Assn.; Picture Research Consultants & Archives.

that nothing could be done to help. "I do not believe that the power and duty of the General Government ought to be extended to the relief of individual suffering which is in no manner properly related to the public service or benefit." Nor did it occur to Cleveland that his great faith in the gold standard prolonged the depression, favored creditors over debtors, and caused immense hardship for millions of Americans. Their discontent would touch off a Populist revolt and lead to one of the most hotly contested elections in the nation's history in 1896 (see chapter 20).

> **REVIEW**   Why were Americans split on the question of the tariff?

Conclusion: Business Dominates an Era

The deal between J. P. Morgan and Grover Cleveland underscored a dangerous reality: The federal government was so weak that its solvency depended on a private banker. This lopsided power relationship signaled the dominance of business in the era Mark Twain satirically but accurately characterized as the Gilded Age. Perhaps no other era in American history spawned greed, corruption, and vulgarity on so grand a scale—an era when speculators like Jay Gould not only built but wrecked businesses to turn paper profits; an era when business boasted openly of buying politicians, who in turn lined their pockets at the public's expense.

Nevertheless, the Gilded Age was not without its share of solid achievements. In these years, America made the leap into the industrial age. Factories and refineries poured out American steel and oil at unprecedented rates. Businessmen like Carnegie, Rockefeller, and Morgan developed new strategies to consolidate American industry. By the end of the nineteenth century, the country had achieved industrial maturity. It boasted the largest, most innovative, most productive economy in the world. Its citizens enjoyed the highest standard of living on the globe. No other era in the nation's history witnessed such a transformation.

Yet the changes that came with these developments worried many Americans and gave rise to much of the era's political turmoil. Race and gender profoundly influenced American politics, leading to new political alliances. Fearless activist Ida B. Wells fought racism in its most brutal form—lynching. Women's organizations championed suffrage and temperance, challenging prevailing views of woman's proper sphere. Reformers fought corruption by instituting civil service. And new issues—the tariff, the regulation of the trusts, and currency reform—restructured the nation's politics.

During the Gilded Age the country expanded west across the continent, displacing the Indians. Eight new states entered the Union, leaving only three territories in the continental United States. The problems and issues facing the nation—the growing power of corporations, corruption in business and politics, ethnic and racial animosities, and the exploitation of labor and natural resources—all had their western variations. Chapter 18 explores the way these themes played out in the West in the Gilded Age.

Suggestions for Further Reading

Ron Chernow, *Titan: The Life of John D. Rockefeller, Sr.* (1998). A lively portrait of the most ruthless capitalist of the Gilded Age.

Jane Dailey, Glenda Elizabeth Gilmore, and Bryant Simon, eds., *Jumpin' Jim Crow: Southern Politics from the Civil War to Civil Rights* (2000). A collection of essays that explore the evolution of Jim Crow segregation and underscore the interplay of race and gender in the politics of the New South.

Steven Hahn, *A Nation under Our Feet: Black Political Struggles in the Rural South from Slavery to the Great Migration* (2003). A Pulitzer Prize–winning study of the black political tradition that emerged out of slavery.

Jean Strouse, *Morgan, American Financier* (1999). This prize-winning biography of J. P. Morgan tells the engrossing story of the larger-than-life banker and the era he dominated.

Joseph Frazier Wall, *Andrew Carnegie* (1970). A model biography of the man who moved America from iron to steel.

> ▶ **FOR MORE BOOKS ABOUT TOPICS IN THIS CHAPTER,** see the Online Bibliography at bedfordstmartins.com/roarkcompact.

> ▶ **FOR ADDITIONAL FIRSTHAND ACCOUNTS OF THIS PERIOD,** see Chapter 17 in Michael Johnson, ed., *Reading the American Past,* Third Edition.

> ▶ **FOR WEB SITES AND DOCUMENTS RELATED TO TOPICS AND PLACES IN THIS CHAPTER,** see "HistoryLinks," "DocLinks," and "PlaceLinks" at bedfordstmartins.com/roarkcompact.

REVIEWING THE CHAPTER

Follow these steps to review and strengthen your understanding of the chapter.

STEP 1: *Study the* **Key Terms** *and* **Timeline** *to identify the significance of each item listed.*

STEP 2: *Answer the* **Review Questions**, *drawing on key terms and dates to support your answers.*

STEP 3: *Drawing on the Key Terms, Timeline, and Review Questions, answer the broader* **Making Connections** *questions.*

KEY TERMS

Who

Mark Twain (p. 427)
Jay Gould (p. 429)
Andrew Carnegie (p. 431)
John D. Rockefeller (p. 432)
Ida M. Tarbell (p. 433)
Alexander Graham Bell (p. 433)
Thomas Alva Edison (p. 433)
John Pierpont Morgan (p. 436)
Charles Darwin (p. 438)
William Graham Sumner (p. 438)
Ida B. Wells (p. 441)
Elizabeth Cady Stanton (p. 442)
Rutherford B. Hayes (p. 443)
Roscoe Conkling (p. 443)
James G. Blaine (p. 443)
James A. Garfield (p. 444)
Charles Guiteau (p. 445)
Grover Cleveland (p. 445)
Benjamin Harrison (p. 446)
William McKinley (p. 447)

What

The Gilded Age (p. 427)
Carnegie Steel (p. 431)
vertical integration (p. 431)
Standard Oil Company (p. 432)
trust (p. 433)
holding company (p. 433)
finance capitalism (p. 436)
United States Steel (p. 437)
oligopoly (p. 437)
On the Origin of Species (p. 438)
social Darwinism (p. 438)
What Social Classes Owe to Each Other (p. 438)
"The Gospel of Wealth" (p. 439)
laissez-faire (p. 439)
patronage (p. 439)
New South (p. 440)
Redeemers (p. 440)
Readjusters (p. 441)
antilynching movement (p. 441)

temperance movement (p. 442)
Woman's Christian Temperance Union (WCTU) (p. 443)
Stalwarts (p. 443)
Half Breeds (p. 443)
Mugwumps (p. 443)
civil service reform (p. 445)
Pendleton Civil Service Act (p. 445)
Grange (p. 447)
Wabash v. Illinois (p. 447)
Interstate Commerce Act (p. 447)
Sherman Antitrust Act (p. 447)
United States v. E. C. Knight Company (p. 447)
free silver (p. 448)
Sherman Silver Purchase Act (p. 448)
depression of 1893 (p. 448)

TIMELINE

1869 • Completion of first transcontinental railroad.

1870 • John D. Rockefeller incorporates Standard Oil Company.

1872 • Andrew Carnegie builds nation's largest Bessemer process steel plant.

1873 • U.S. government stops minting silver dollars.
• Wall Street panic leads to major economic depression.
• Woman's Crusade begins.

1874 • Woman's Christian Temperance Union founded.

1876 • Alexander Graham Bell demonstrates telephone.

1877 • Republican Rutherford B. Hayes sworn in as president.
• "Redeemers" come to power in the South.
• *Munn v. Illinois.*

1879 • Thomas Alva Edison perfects lightbulb.

1880 • Republican James A. Garfield elected president.

1880s • Jay Gould's profiteering encourages rapid railroad growth.

REVIEW QUESTIONS

1. How did John D. Rockefeller gain control of 90 percent of the oil-refining business by 1890? (pp. 429–36)

2. Why did the ideas of social Darwinism appeal to many Americans in the late nineteenth century? (pp. 436–39)

3. Why did New South promoters believe the region could compete with the North in industrialization? (pp. 439–43)

4. How did the question of civil service reform contribute to divisions within the Republican Party? (pp. 443–46)

5. Why were Americans split on the question of the tariff? (pp. 446–49)

MAKING CONNECTIONS

1. Late-nineteenth-century industrialization depended on developments in technology and business strategy. What were some of the key innovations in both arenas? How did they facilitate the maturation of American industry? In your answer, discuss the drawbacks and benefits of these developments.

2. By the 1870s, several new concerns had displaced slavery as the defining question of American politics. What were these new issues, and how did they shape new regional, economic, and racial alliances and rivalries? In your answer, consider the part political parties played in this process.

3. Energetic political activity characterized Gilded Age America, both within formal party politics and beyond. How did the activism of Americans denied the vote contribute to the era's electoral politics? In your answer, be sure to cite specific examples of political action.

4. The U.S. Congress and American courts facilitated the concentration of power in the hands of private business concerns during the Gilded Age. Citing specific policies and court decisions, discuss how government helped augment the clout of big business in the late nineteenth century.

▶ **FOR PRACTICE QUIZZES, A CUSTOMIZED STUDY PLAN, AND OTHER STUDY TOOLS,** see the Online Study Guide at bedfordstmartins.com/roarkcompact.

1881 • Garfield assassinated; Vice President Chester A. Arthur becomes president.

    1882 • Standard Oil develops the trust.

        1883 • Pendleton Act.

           1884 • Democrat Grover Cleveland elected president.

                1886 • *Wabash v. Illinois.*

                  1887 • Interstate Commerce Act.

                    1888 • Republican Benjamin Harrison elected president.

                      1890 • McKinley tariff.

                          • Sherman Antitrust Act.

                          1892 • Ida B. Wells launches antilynching campaign.

                            1893 • Wall Street panic touches off national depression.

                              1895 • J. P. Morgan bails out U.S. Treasury.

LAKOTA VEST
This Lakota vest belonged to Thomas American Horse, a member of the Oglala band of Lakota Sioux who lived on the Pine Ridge Reservation in South Dakota at the end of the nineteenth century. His initials are worked in beads across the shoulders. Made of tanned hide, with glass beads and tanned leather binding and lining, the vest shows how Native Americans adopted Euro-American articles of clothing and decorative motifs while employing materials that perpetuated native traditions. On the vest two mounted Indians in feathered headdresses face each other under American flags. The American flag as a decorative motif appeared frequently in Indian bead art and testifies to some of the great changes taking place in the Gilded Age West.

Private Collection, Photograph American Hurrah Archive, NYC.

18

The West in the Gilded Age

1870–1900

To CELEBRATE INDIAN CITIZENSHIP DAY in 1892, students at the Indian boarding school at Hampton Institute in Virginia staged a pageant honoring the four hundredth anniversary of the "discovery" of the New World. Students appeared dressed as the nation's heroes—among them Christopher Columbus, Miles Standish, and George Washington. Halfway through the program, the pageant finally honored some Native American heroes, but the Indians selected—Samoset, Pocahontas—all came from the distant past in lands east of the Appalachians. There was no mention of Crazy Horse, Sitting Bull, or Geronimo—Indians who resisted white encroachment and appropriation of their land in the West. Only two years earlier, the massacre of over 200 Miniconjou Sioux at Wounded Knee, South Dakota, marked the end of three decades of war against the Indians in the trans-Mississippi West. The Indian wars left the Native American population in the continental United States at 250,000, down from estimates as high as 15 million at the time of first contact with Europeans. Not only had the population been decimated by war and disease, but Indian lands had shrunk so much that by 1890 Euro-Americans controlled 97.5 percent of the territory formerly occupied by Native Americans.

The Hampton pageant could not entirely ignore catastrophe of this magnitude. Yet it managed to end on a note of reconciliation with a student proclaiming:

You have taken our rivers and fountains
    And the plains where we loved to roam,—
Banish us not to the mountains
    And the lonely wastes for home!
Our clans that were strongest and bravest,
    Are Broken and powerless through you:
Let us join the great tribe of the white men,
    As brothers to dare and to do!

How the actors felt about the lines they spoke we cannot know. But the pageant clearly reflected the values and beliefs that Indian boarding schools hoped to inculcate in their pupils at the end of the nineteenth century.

Indian schools constituted the cultural battleground of the Indian wars in the West, their avowed purpose "to destroy the Indian ... and save the man." In 1877 Congress appropriated funds for Indian education, reasoning "it was less expensive to educate Indians than to kill them." Hampton Institute, created in 1868 to school newly freed slaves, accepted its first Indian students in 1878.

Hampton Pageant, 1892

The Indian students in this picture are dressed for Columbia's Roll Call, a pageant at Hampton Institute honoring the nation's heroes on Indian Citizen Day, 1892. Front row, left to right—Thomas Last, Sioux, as Samoset, an Indian friend to the Pilgrims; David Hill, Onondaga, as Pilgrim Miles Standish. Middle row, left to right—Harry Kingman, Sioux, as White Mingo, an Iroquois killed by white settlers; Laura Face, Sioux, as Pocahontas, who saved the life of Captain John Smith; James Enouff, Potawatomi, as Christopher Columbus; Juanita Espinosa, Piegan, as Columbia, symbol of the Republic; Addie Stevens, Winnebago, as Puritan Priscilla Alden; Lucy Trudell, Sioux, as a Quaker woman. Back row, left to right—Frank Bazhaw, Potawatomi, as Pilgrim leader Captain John Smith; Ebenezer Kingsley, Winnebago, as Puritan John Eliot; William Moore, Sac and Fox, as the Herald of Fame; Frank Hubbard, Penobscot, as President George Washington; Adam Metoxen, Oneida, as William Penn, founder of Pennsylvania; Joseph Redhorse, Sioux, as Tamimend, an Indian friend of William Penn.

Courtesy of Hampton University Archives.

While many Indian schools operated on the reservations, authorities much preferred boarding facilities that isolated students from the "contamination" of tribal values.

Many parents resisted sending their children away. When all else failed, the military kidnapped the children and sent them off to school. An agent at the Mescalero Apache agency in Arizona Territory reported in 1886 how "it became necessary to visit the camps unexpectedly with a detachment of police, and seize such children as were proper and take them away to school, willing or unwilling." The parents put up a struggle. "Some hurried their children off to the mountains or hid them away in camp, and the police had to chase and capture them like so many wild rabbits," the agent observed. "This unusual proceeding created quite an outcry. The

men were sullen and muttering, the women loud in their lamentations, and the children almost out of their wits with fright."

Once at school, the children were stripped and scrubbed, their clothing and belongings confiscated, their hair hacked off and doused with kerosene to kill lice. Issued stiff new uniforms, shoes, and what one boy recalled as the "torture" of woolen long underwear, the children often lost not only their possessions but their names—Hehakaavita (Yellow Elk) became Thomas Goodwood, Polingaysi Qoyawayma became Elizabeth White.

The curriculum featured agricultural and manual arts for boys and domestic skills for girls, training designed to make Indians economically self-sufficient and no longer a burden on the government. The Carlisle Indian School in Pennsylvania, founded in 1879, became the model for later institutions. To encourage assimilation, Carlisle pioneered the "outing system"—sending students to live with white families during summer vacations. The policy reflected the school's slogan, "To civilize the Indian, get him into civilization. To keep him civilized, let him stay." Yet despite their education and acculturation, graduating students entered a dismal netherworld—never accepted in white society as equals but no longer at home on the reservation.

Merrill Gates, a member of the Board of Indian Commissioners, summed up the goal of Indian education: "To get the Indian out of the blanket and into trousers,—and trousers with a pocket in them, and with *a pocket that aches to be filled with dollars!*" Gilded Age preoccupation with the pursuit of the almighty dollar clearly did not stop at the Mississippi. In fact, it might be more accurate to say that the get-rich-quick mentality of the California gold fields produced a society addicted to gambling and speculation. In 1871, two years before he penned *The Gilded Age*, Mark Twain published *Roughing It*, his chronicle of days spent in mining towns in California and Nevada. There he found the same corrupt politics, vulgar display, and mania for speculation that he later skewered in his satire of life in the nation's capital.

The settlement of the West and the ensuing clash of cultures among Anglos, Native Americans, Hispanics, and others who followed the promise of land and riches into the West created many of the key issues facing Americans in the Gilded Age. Nor can the problems confronting the nation in the waning decades of the nineteenth century be fully understood without paying attention to the way they played out under western skies. The West witnessed the consolidation of business in mining, ranching, and commercial farming; corruption and cupidity in territorial government; vicious ethnic and racial animosity whether in the form of Indian wars or Chinese exclusion; and the exploitation of labor and natural resources that led to the decimation of the great bison herds, the pollution of rivers with mining wastes, and pitched battles between workers and bosses. The major themes of the era all had western variants, making the Gilded Age a truly national phenomenon.

Gold Fever and the Mining West

The four decades following California's 1849 gold rush witnessed equally frenzied rushes for gold and other metals, most notably on the Comstock Lode in Nevada and later in New Mexico, Colorado, the Dakotas, Montana, Idaho, Arizona, and Utah. Each rush built upon the last, producing new technologies and innovations in financing as hordes of miners, eager to strike it rich, moved from one boomtown to the next. (See "The Promise of Technology," page 456.) Mining in the Gilded Age West, however, was a story not only of boom and bust but also of community building and the development of territories into states (Map. 18.1). At first glance, the mining West may seem much different from the East, but by the 1870s "urban industrialism" described Virginia City, Nevada, as accurately as it did Pittsburgh or Cleveland. A close look at mining on the Comstock Lode indicates some of the patterns and paradoxes of western mining. And a look at territorial government uncovers striking parallels with Gilded Age politics east of the Mississippi.

Mining on the Comstock Lode

California's forty-niners proved a restless lot. By 1859, refugees from California's played-out mines flocked to the Washoe basin in Nevada. There they found the gold they sought mired in blackish sand they called "that blasted blue stuff." Eventually an enterprising miner had the stuff assayed, and it turned out that miners on the Washoe had stumbled on the richest vein of silver ore on the continent—the legendary Comstock Lode, named for prospector Henry Comstock.

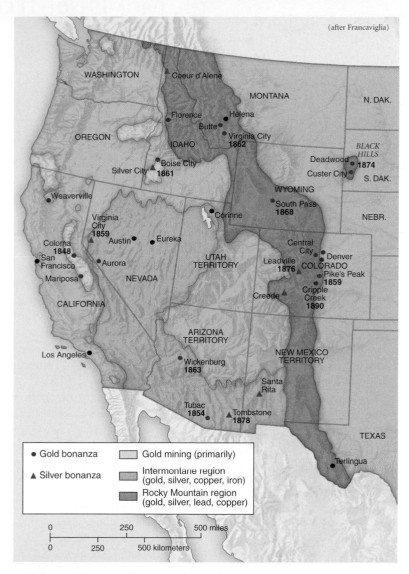

MAP 18.1 Western Mining, 1848–1890
Rich deposits of gold, silver, copper, lead, and iron larded the mountains of the West, from the Sierras of California to the Rockies of Colorado and the Black Hills of South Dakota. Beginning with the gold strike on Sutter's Creek in California in 1848 and continuing through the rush for gold in Cripple Creek, Colorado, in 1890, miners from all over the world flocked to the West in search of riches. Few struck it rich. Many more stayed on as paid workers in the increasingly mechanized corporate mines.

To exploit even potentially valuable silver claims required capital and expensive technology well beyond the means of the prospector. An active San Francisco stock market sprang up to finance operations on the Comstock. Shrewd businessmen soon recognized that the easiest way to get rich was not to mine at all but to sell their claims or to form mining companies and sell shares of stock. The most unscrupulous mined the wallets

Hydraulic Mining

Individual prospectors who made the first gold strikes in California in 1849 employed a simple process known as placer mining. "No capital is required to obtain this gold, as the laboring man wants nothing but his pick and shovel and tin pan with which to dig and wash the gravel." But when the easy pickings along the rivers and streams gave out, a good deal of gold still remained trapped in quartz or buried deep in the earth, extractable only by methods far beyond the means and capacity of the average prospector.

Soon technology and capital invaded the diggings. As early as 1853 a French Canadian sail maker, Antoine Chabot, hoping to avoid the cost and labor of digging a long feeder ditch to get water to his claim, stitched together heavy strips of canvas and made a 100-foot length of hose. Building on this invention, a Connecticut forty-niner named Edward Matteson marveled at the power of the new technology he called "hydraulicking." "Ten men who own a claim are enabled...by directing streams of water against the base of a high bank to cut away such an extent as to cause immense slides of earth which often bring with them large trees and heavy boulders." Tons of fallen earth "are carried away through the sluices with almost as much rapidity as if they were a bank of [melting] snow."

The speed and efficiency of hydraulic mining promised more gold in less time for less work. With water doing the labor formerly provided by pick and shovel, prospectors who came to the gold fields to make a fortune often ended up working for the big mines for $3 a day, a decent wage for the time but no way to get rich quick.

Hydraulic mining industrialized gold mining, introducing what amounted to a form of mass production that involved all the features of modern, capital-intensive industry: corporations trading shares on an international market, engineers in-stalling large and expensive works and equipment, and wage laborers replacing prospectors. By the 1880s, the Army Corps of Engineers estimated that some $100 million had been spent to build California's hydraulic mining system. The results proved worthwhile for the mine owners. Hydraulic mining produced 90 percent of California's gold.

Eager to make a quick profit, the purveyors of this new technology gave little thought to its impact on the environment. Hydraulic mining used prodigious amounts of water—two large nozzles could shoot out 1.7 million gallons a day. These huge water cannons washed away entire mountains, clogging streambeds and creating heaps of rubble. Thomas Starr King, a young Unitarian minister visiting hydraulic mining operations near Nevada City, California, was appalled by the sight that greeted him. Enormous nozzles blasted water, "tearing all the beauty out of the landscape and setting up 'the abomination of desolation' in its place." He grimly predicted, "If the hydraulic mining method is to be infinitely used, without restraint, upon all the surface that will yield a good return, then California of the future will be a waste more repulsive than any denounced in prophecy."

of gullible investors by selling shares in bogus mines to stockholders to whom the very word *Comstock* conjured up images of riches. In twenty years, more than $300 million poured from the earth in Nevada alone. A little stayed in Virginia City, but a great deal more went to speculators in California, some of whom got rich without ever leaving San Francisco.

The promise of gold and silver drew thousands to the mines of the West, the honest as well as the unprincipled. As Mark Twain observed, the Comstock attracted an international array of immigrants. "All the peoples of the earth had representative adventures in the Silverland," he wrote. Irish, Chinese, Germans, English, Scots, Welsh, Canadians, Mexicans, Italians, Scandinavians, French, Swiss, Chileans, and other South and Central Americans came to share in the bonanza. With them came a sprinkling of Russians, Poles, Greeks, Japanese, Spaniards, Hungarians, Portuguese, Turks, Pacific Islanders, Moroccans, as well as other North Americans, African Americans,

Angry farmers protested that hydraulic mines discharged tailings (debris) that filled channels and forced rivers out of their banks, causing devastating floods. Farms were swept away and cattle drowned. Millions of cubic yards of silt from the hydraulic tailings washed down and covered farms with a muddy sand (slickens) two to seven feet deep, destroying all hopes of vegetation. Orchards and fields disappeared each year under new layers of mining debris.

In 1875, farmers organized to stop the destruction. But after four years of litigation, the California Supreme Court ruled in favor of the miners. Gold remained king in California. Not until the mid-1880s, when California's economy tilted from mining to agriculture and wheat became California's new gold, did farmers finally succeed in winning a court injunction against hydraulic mining. Renegade miners continued to use hydraulic methods until the 1890s, when more aggressive enforcement finally silenced the great hoses. The sounds of nature eventually returned to the California foothills, and the rivers began to run clear.

Hydraulic Mining and the Environment
Hydraulic mining of California's gold ripped up the landscape, creating waterfalls, as seen in this picture. The pipes connected to huge hoses capable of washing away entire hills. The debris clogged rivers and caused devastating floods that wiped out entire farms.
California History Section, California State Library.

and American Indians. This polyglot population, typical of mining boomtowns, made Virginia City in the 1870s more cosmopolitan than New York or Boston.

Irish immigrants formed the largest ethnic group in the mining district. In Virginia City, fully one-third of the population claimed at least one parent from Ireland. In contrast, the Chinese community stood at 642 men in 1870. Virulent anti-Chinese sentiment barred them from work in the mines, but despite the violent anti-Asian rhetoric, the mining community came to depend on Chinese labor.

As was so often the case in the West, where white American ambitions clashed with Native American ways, the discovery of precious metals on the Comstock spelled disaster for the Native American population. No sooner had the miners struck pay dirt than they demanded army troops be dispatched to "hunt Indians" and establish forts to protect transportation to and from the diggings. This sudden and dramatic intrusion left

Nevada's native tribes—Northern Paiute and Bannock Shoshone—exiles in their own land. At first they resisted, but eventually they made peace with the invaders. Over time, Native Americans proved resourceful in finding ways to adapt and preserve their culture and identity despite the havoc wrought by western mining and settlement.

In 1873, Comstock miners uncovered a new vein of ore, a veritable cavern of gold and silver. This "Big Bonanza" speeded the transition from small-scale industry to corporate **oligopoly**, creating a radically new social and economic environment. The Comstock became a laboratory for new mining technology, a place of industry and engineers. Huge stamping mills pulverized rock, sucked water from the mine shafts, and circulated air in the underground chambers. Many of the mines were large, industrial operations. No backwoods mining camp, Virginia City was an industrial center, with more than 1,200 stamping mills working on average a ton of ore every day. Almost 400 men worked in milling, nearly 300 in manufacturing industries, and roughly 3,000 laborers worked in the mines.

New technology eliminated some of the dangers of mining but often created new ones. In the hard-rock mines of the West in the 1870s, accidents annually disabled one out of every thirty miners and killed one in eighty. Labor unions, which provided nursing care and death benefits, attracted many miners. In Nevada unions formed early and held considerable bargaining power. Comstock miners commanded $4 a day, the highest wage in the mining West.

The mining towns of the "Wild West" are often portrayed as lawless outposts, filled with saloons and rough gambling dens and populated almost exclusively by men, except for the occasional dance-hall floozy. The truth is more complex as Virginia City's development attests. An established community built to serve an industrial giant, Virginia City in its first decade boasted churches, schools, theaters, an opera house, and hundreds of families. By 1870, women composed 30 percent of the population, and 75 percent of the women listed their occupation in the census as housekeepers. Many of them made money on the side by providing lodging and by cooking, sewing, and doing laundry for bachelor miners.

By 1875, Virginia City boasted a population of 25,000 people, making it one of the largest cities between St. Louis and San Francisco. A "must see" stop on the way West, the Queen of the Comstock hosted American presidents as well as legions of lesser dignitaries. No rough outpost of the Wild West, Virginia City represented in the words of its most recent chronicler, "the distilled essence of America's newly established course—urban, industrial, acquisitive, and materialistic, on the move, 'a living polyglot' of cultures that collided and converged." In short, Virginia City made up an integral part of an America transformed in the Gilded Age.

Territorial Government

The federal government practiced a policy of benign neglect when it came to territorial government in the West. The president appointed a governor, a secretary, and two to four judges, along with an attorney and a marshal. In Nevada Territory that meant that a handful of officials governed an area the size of New England. Originally a part of the larger Utah Territory, Nevada, propelled by mining interests, moved on the fast track to statehood, entering the Union in 1864, long before its population or its development merited statehood. There as elsewhere in the West, gold and silver influenced politics.

More typical were the territories extant in 1870—New Mexico, Utah, Washington, Colorado, Dakota, Arizona, Idaho, Montana, and Wyoming. These areas remained territories for inordinately long periods ranging from twenty-three to sixty-two years. While awaiting statehood, they were subject to territorial governments that were underpaid, often unqualified, and largely ignored in Washington. The vast majority of territorial appointments fell under the **spoils system**. Most of the loyal party men who became governors had no knowledge of the areas they served, little notion of their duties, and limited ability to perform them.

In theory, territorial governors received adequate salaries, as high as $3,500 in an era when the average working man earned less than $500 a year. In practice, the funds rarely arrived in a timely fashion, and more than one governor found he had to pay government expenses out of his own pocket. As one cynic observed, "Only the rich or those having 'no visible means of support,' can afford to accept office." John C. Frémont, the governor of Arizona Territory, was so poor that he complained to Washington that he could not afford to travel within the territory and inspect the Grand Canyon because he didn't have enough money to keep a horse.

Territorial governors with few scruples accepted money from special-interest groups like mine owners or ranchers. Nearly all territorial appointees tried to make ends meet by maintaining business connections with the East or by taking advantage of investment opportunities in the West. Distance and the lack of funds made it difficult to summon officers from Washington to investigate charges of corruption. Those who ventured west often faced intimidation. One judge sent to New Mexico 1871 reported he "stayed three days, made up his mind that it would be dangerous to do any investigating,…and returned to his home without any action." Underfunded and overlooked, territorial government was rife with conflicts of interest and corruption, mirroring the political and economic values (or lack thereof) of Gilded Age America.

REVIEW How did industrial technology change mining in Nevada?

Land Fever

After the Civil War, Americans by the hundreds of thousands packed up and moved west, goaded if not by the hope of striking gold, then by the promise of owning land. In the three decades following 1870, more land was settled than in all the previous history of the country. Between 1876 and 1900, eight new western states entered the Union.

Even more than gold fever, the railroad spurred settlement in the West along with the Homestead Act of 1862. After the completion of the first transcontinental railroad in 1869, settlers abandoned the covered wagon, and by the 1880s they could choose from four competing rail lines and make the trip in a matter of days. The agrarian West shared with the mining West a persistent restlessness, an addiction to speculation, and a penchant for exploiting resources and labor.

Not all who wanted to own land achieved their goal. A growing number of Americans found themselves forced to work for wages on land they would never own. During the transition from the family farm to large commercial farming, small farms gave way to vast spreads worked by migrant labor or paid farmworkers. Just as industry corporatized and consolidated in the East, the Gilded Age witnessed the emergence of an industrial West.

Moving West: Homesteaders and Speculators

A Missouri homesteader remembered packing as her family pulled up stakes and headed west to Oklahoma in 1890. "We were going to God's Country," she wrote. "You had to work hard on that rocky country in Missouri. I was glad to be leaving it. We were going to God's Country.… We were going to a new land and get rich."

People who ventured west searching for "God's Country" faced hardship, loneliness, and deprivation. To carve a farm from the raw prairie of Iowa, the plains of Nebraska, or the forests of

Our Home
A mother and her children pose in front of their dugout near McCook, Nebraska, in the 1890s. With its real roof, glass windowpanes, and solid door, their dugout was more substantial than most. On the plains, where trees were scarce and lumber was often prohibitively expensive, settlers built with the materials at hand. The dugout was the most primitive dwelling, carved into a hillside. Other settlers built huts from blocks of sod cut from the earth. Homesteaders' lives were not easy. A homesteader in the Dakotas recalled, "Each day brought new, unexpected challenges and at times I wondered if I would be able to stay with it until the land was mine. Could any land be worth the lonely hours and hardships? The howling wind and driving snow, the mournful wail of the coyotes…did nothing to make the winter any more pleasant."
Nebraska State Historical Society.

the Pacific Northwest took more than fortitude and backbreaking toil. It took luck. Blizzards, tornadoes, grasshoppers, hailstorms, drought, prairie fires, accidental death, and disease were only a few of the catastrophes that could befall even the best farmer. Although the 1862 Homestead Act promised 160 acres to any hardy individual who settled on the land for five years, homesteaders still needed as much as $1,000 for a house, a team of farm animals, a well, fencing, and seed. Poor farmers called "sodbusters" did without even these basics, living in dugouts carved into the sod of hillsides and using muscle instead of machinery.

For women on the frontier, obtaining simple daily necessities such as water and fuel meant backbreaking labor. Out on the plains, where water was scarce, women often had to trudge to the nearest creek or spring. "A yoke was made to place across [Mother's] shoulders, so as to carry at each end a bucket of water," one daughter recollected, "and then water was brought a half mile from spring to house." Gathering fuel was another heavy chore. Without ready sources of coal or firewood, settlers on the plains turned to what substitutes they could scavenge—twigs, tufts of grass, corncobs, sunflower stalks. But by far the most prevalent fuel was "chips"—chunks of dried cattle and buffalo dung found in abundance on the plains.

For many the promise of the West failed to materialize. Already by the 1870s, much of the best land had been taken, given to the railroads as **land grants** or to the states to finance education. Too often, homesteaders found that only the least desirable tracts were left— poor land, far from markets, transportation, and society. Speculators took the lion's share of the land. "There is plenty of land for sale in California," one migrant complained in 1870, but "the majority of the available lands are held by speculators, at prices far beyond the reach of a poor man."

The railroads, flush from the land grants provided by the federal government, actively recruited settlers. Together the land grants totaled approximately 180 million acres—an area almost one-tenth the size of the United States (Map 18.2). Many farmers who went west ended up buying land from the railroads or from the speculators and land companies that quickly followed the railroads into the West. Of the 2.5 million farms established between 1860 and 1900, homesteading accounted for only one in five; the vast majority of farmland sold for a profit.

As land grew scarce on the prairie in the 1870s, farmers began to push farther west, moving into western Kansas, Nebraska, and eastern Colorado—the region called the Great American Desert by settlers who had passed over it on their way to California and Oregon. Many agricultural experts warned that the semiarid land (where less than twenty inches of rain fell annually) would not support a farm on the 160 acres allotted to homesteaders, but their words of caution were drowned out by the extravagant claims of western promoters, many employed by the railroads to sell off their land grants. "Rain follows the plow" became the slogan of western boosters, who insisted that cultivation would alter the climate of the region and bring more rainfall.

Instead, drought followed the plow. Droughts were a cyclical fact of life on the Great Plains. Plowed up, the dry topsoil blew away in the wind. A period of relatively good rainfall in the early 1880s encouraged farming; then a protracted drought in the late 1880s and early 1890s sent starving farmers reeling back from the plains. Some left in wagons carrying the slogan "In God we trusted, in Kansas we busted."

The fever for fertile land set off a series of spectacular land runs in Oklahoma. When former Indian territory opened for settlement in 1889, thousands of homesteaders massed on the border. At the opening pistol shot, "with a shout and a yell the swift riders shot out, then followed the light buggies or wagons," a reporter wrote. "Above all, a great cloud of dust hover[ed] like smoke over a battlefield." By nightfall, Oklahoma boasted two tent cities with more than 10,000 residents. In the last frenzied land rush in

Areas Settled before 1862

0   150   300 miles
0   150   300 kilometers

DAKOTA TERRITORY

MINN.   WIS.

IOWA

NEBRASKA TERRITORY

Western extent of settlement before Homestead Act of 1862

KANSAS

MO.

INDIAN TERRITORY

ARK.

TEXAS

LA.

1893, several settlers were killed in the stampede for free land.

Ranchers and Cowboys

Cattle ranchers followed the railroads onto the plains, establishing between 1865 and 1885 a cattle kingdom from Texas to Wyoming. Cowboys drove huge herds, as many as 3,000 head of cattle that grazed on public lands as they followed cattle tracks like the Chisholm Trail from Texas to railheads in Kansas. From there the cattle traveled by boxcar to Chicago, where they sold for as much as $45 a head.

Barbed wire revolutionized the cattle business and sounded the death knell for the open range in the 1870s. As the largest ranches in Texas began to fence, nasty fights broke out between the big ranchers and "fence cutters," who resented the end of the free range. One old-timer observed, "Those persons, Mexicans and Americans, without land but who had cattle were put out of business by fencing." Fencing forced small-time ranchers who could not afford to buy barbed wire or sink wells to sell out for the best price they could get. The displaced ranchers,

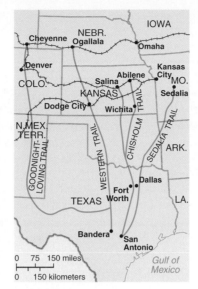

Cattle Trails, 1860–1890

many of them Mexicans, ended up as wageworkers on the huge spreads owned by Anglos or by European syndicates.

On the range, the cowboy gave way to the cattle king and, like the miner, became a wage laborer. Many cowboys were African Americans (as many as 5,000 in Texas alone). Writers of western literature chose to ignore the presence of black cowboys like Deadwood Dick (Nat Love), who was portrayed as a white man in the dime novels of the era. Cowboy life was hard and, like many other dissatisfied workers, cowboys organized labor unions in the 1880s and mounted strikes in both Texas and Wyoming.

By 1886, cattle overcrowded the range. Severe blizzards during the winters of 1886–87 and 1887–88 decimated the herds. "A whole generation of cowmen," wrote one chronicler, "went dead broke." Fencing worsened the situation. During blizzards, cattle stayed alive by keeping on the move. But when they ran up against the barbed wire fences, they froze to death. In the aftermath of the "Great Die Up," new labor-intensive forms of cattle ranching replaced the open range model.

Barbed Wire Machine and Soothing Liniment
The original working model of Joseph Glidden's barbing machine patented in 1874 consisted of an old-fashioned coffee mill with its casing cut away and its grinder altered to cut and coil small lengths of wire. The barbs were strung by hand between strands of plain wire. Despite its flimsiness, barbed wire could contain cattle, as master promoter John "Bet a Million" Gates demonstrated by corralling a herd of Texas longhorns in downtown San Antonio in 1879. With the invention of barbed wire, medicine makers cashed in by marketing products like the liniment shown in the photograph to soothe the cuts and scrapes made on man and beast by the barbed wire.
Barbed wire machine: Ellwood House Museum, De Kalb, Illinois; photo by Charles Philips; liniment: Kansas Barbed Wire Museum.

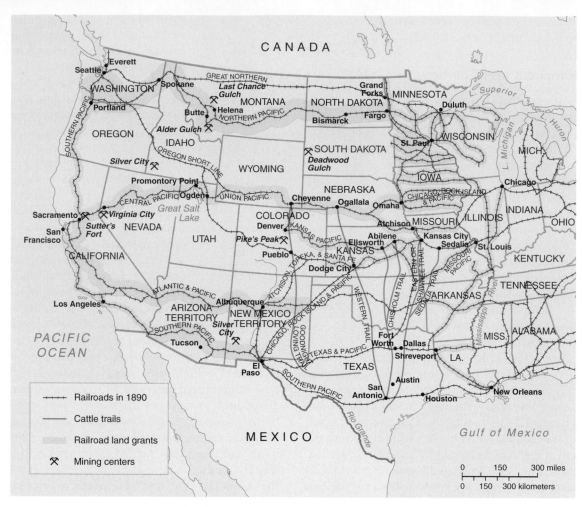

MAP 18.2   Federal Land Grants to Railroads and the Development of the West, 1850–1900
Generous federal land grants meant that railroads could sell the desirable land next to the track at a profit or hold it for speculation. Railroads received more than 180 million acres, an area as large as Texas. Notice how the cattle trails connect with major railheads in Dodge City, Abilene, and Kansas City and to mines in Montana, Nevada, Colorado, and New Mexico.

Tenants, Sharecroppers, and Migrants

Many who followed the American promise into the West prospered, but landownership proved an elusive goal for many others—freed slaves, immigrants from Europe and Asia, and Mexicans in California and on the Texas border. In the post–Civil War period, as agriculture became a big business tied to national and global markets, an increasing number of laborers worked land that they would never own.

In the southern United States, farmers labored under particularly heavy burdens (see chapter 16). The Civil War wiped out much of the region's capital, which had been invested in

slaves, and crippled the plantation economy. Newly freed slaves rarely obtained land of their own and often ended up as farm laborers. "The colored folks stayed with the old boss man and farmed and worked on the plantations," a black Alabama sharecropper observed bitterly. "They were still slaves, but they were free slaves." Some freed people did manage to pull together enough resources to go west. In 1879, over 15,000 black "Exodusters" moved from Mississippi and Louisiana to take up land in Kansas.

In California, Mexicans who held land grants from the former Spanish or Mexican governments found themselves in the aftermath of the Mexican-American War in the new state of California (1850), which demanded that they prove their claims in court. The process took on average seventeen years, and many *rancheros* (Mexican ranchers), discouraged by the wait, sold out to Anglos. Skilled horsemen, California's Mexican cowboys—*vaqueros*—commanded decent wages until the 1870s, when the coming of the railroads ended the long cattle drives in the state. The vaqueros ended up as migrant laborers, often on land their families had once owned.

After the heyday of cattle ranching ended in the late 1880s, cotton production rose in the southeastern regions of Texas. Ranchers turned their pastures into sharecroppers' plots and hired displaced cowboys, most of them Mexicans, as seasonal laborers for as little as seventy-five cents a day. Within ten years, ranch life in southern Texas gave way to a growing army of agricultural wageworkers.

In California, a pattern of land **monopoly** and large-scale farming fostered tenancy and migratory labor. By the 1870s, less than 1 percent of the population owned half the state's available agricultural land. The rigid economics of large-scale commercial agriculture and the seasonal nature of the crops spawned a ragged army of migratory agricultural laborers. Derisively labeled "blanket men" or "bindle stiffs," these transients worked the fields in the growing season and wintered in the flophouses of San Francisco. Wheat farming in California in the 1870s and 1880s exhausted the land and was replaced, with the introduction of irrigation, by fruit and sugar beet farming. Most of the California farm laborers were Chinese immigrants until the Chinese Exclusion Act of 1882 forced big growers to look to other groups, primarily Mexicans, Filipinos, and Japanese, for farm labor.

Commercial Farming and Industrial Cowboys

In the late nineteenth century, America's population remained overwhelmingly rural. The 1870 census showed that nearly 80 percent of the nation's people lived on farms and in villages of fewer than 8,000 inhabitants. By 1900, the figure had dropped to 66 percent. At the same time, the number of farms rose. Rapid growth in the West increased the number of the nation's farms from 2 million in 1860 to over 5.7 million in 1900.

New technology and farming techniques revolutionized American farm life. Mechanized plows and reapers halved the time and labor cost of production and made it possible to cultivate vast tracts of land. Urbanization provided farmers with expanding markets for their produce, and railroads carried crops to markets thousands of miles away. Even before the opening of the twentieth century, American agriculture had entered the era of what would come to be called **agribusiness**—farming as a big business.

As farming moved onto the prairies and plains, mechanization took command. Steel plows, reapers, mowers, harrows, seed drills, combines, and threshers replaced human muscle on the farm. Horse-drawn implements gave way to steam-powered machinery. By 1880, a single combine could do the work of twenty men. Mechanization spurred the growth of bonanza wheat farms, some over 100,000 acres, in California and the Red River Valley of North Dakota and Minnesota. This agricultural revolution meant that Americans raised more than four times the corn, five times the hay, and seven times the wheat and oats they had before the Civil War. Much of this new production went to feed people as far away as England and Germany.

Like the cotton farmer in the South, western grain and livestock farmers increasingly depended on foreign markets for their livelihood. A fall in market prices meant that a farmer's entire harvest went to pay off debts. In the depression that followed the panic of 1893, many heavily mortgaged farmers lost their land to creditors. As a Texas cotton farmer complained, "By the time the World Gets their Liveing out of the Farmer as we have to Feed the World, we the Farmer has nothing Left but a Bear Hard Liveing."

Commercial farming, along with mining, represented another way in which the West developed its own brand of Gilded Age industrialism. The far West's industrial economy sprang initially from California gold and the vast lands that came under American control following the Mexican-American War. In the ensuing rush on land and resources, environmental factors interacted with economic and social forces to produce enterprises as vast in scale and scope as anything found in the East. At the same time Carnegie consolidated the steel industry and Rockefeller monopolized oil refining, two Alsatian immigrants, Henry Miller and Charles Lux, pioneered the West's mix of agriculture and industrialism.

Beginning as meat wholesalers, Miller and Lux quickly expanded their business to encompass cattle, land, and land reclamation projects such as dams and irrigation systems. With a labor force of migrant workers, a highly coordinated corporate system, and large sums of investment capital, the firm of Miller & Lux became one of America's industrial behemoths. Already by 1870, Miller & Lux owned well over 300,000 acres of grazing land in California's central San Joaquin Valley, over half of it derived from former Mexican land grants. Its industrial-sized wheat operations in California bore little resemblance to any previous form of agriculture. Eventually these "industrial cowboys" grazed a herd of 100,000 cattle on 1.25 million acres of company land in three western states (California, Oregon, and Nevada) and employed over 1,200 migrant laborers on their corporate ranches. By 1900, Miller & Lux controlled capital and labor to a degree far surpassing most eastern manufacturing firms.

Miller & Lux developed remarkably dynamic investment strategies and corporate structures to control not only California land but water rights as well. The state's largest land speculators, Miller & Lux employed an army of lobbyists to serve its interests in Sacramento. Although the specifics of the Miller & Lux business may have differed from those in the East, the company nonetheless shared the main characteristics of other modern enterprises: corporate consolidation, **vertical integration**, and schemes to minimize labor costs and stabilize the workforce. Miller & Lux accomplished the last by offering free meals to migratory laborers. When the company's Chinese cooks rebelled at washing the dishes resulting from the free meals, the migrant laborers were forced to eat after the ranch hands and use their dirty plates. By the 1890s, over 800 migrants followed what came to be known as the "Dirty Plate Route" on Miller & Lux ranches throughout California.

Since the days of Thomas Jefferson, farming had been linked with the highest ideals of a democratic society. Now agrarianism itself had been transformed. The farmer was no longer the self-sufficient **yeoman** but often a businessman on the one hand or a wage laborer on the other, each tied to a global market. And even as farm production soared, industrialization outstripped it. More and more farmers left the fields for urban factories or found work in the "factories in the fields" of the new industrialized agribusiness. Now that the future seemed to lie not with the small farmer but with industrial enterprises, was **democracy** itself at risk? This question would ignite a farmers' revolt in the 1880s and dominate political debate in the 1890s.

> **REVIEW**   Why did many homesteaders find it difficult to acquire good land in the West?

A Clash of Cultures

In the movies, the American West is often portrayed in mythic terms as a picturesque landscape where strong-jawed heroes square off against villains. Often the bad guys are Indians—the name that Columbus mistakenly gave to Native Americans. In this masculine tableau, the setting is so timeless it is easy to forget that the action takes place at roughly the same time that waves of new immigrants sailed past the Statue of Liberty, engineers built the Brooklyn Bridge, and men like John D. Rockefeller consolidated their empires in emerging industrial America. Once the West is situated within its historical context, reality supersedes myth, and the West appears to be not so different from the rest of the country after all. The same racial antagonisms that marked the Gilded Age in the South and East flared up dramatically in the West and led to the exclusion of Chinese immigrants, the dispossession of Mexicans, and the decimation of Native Americans.

The Diverse Peoples of the West

"West" has always been a relative term. Until the gold rush of 1849 focused attention on California, the West for settlers lay beyond the Appalachians, east of the Mississippi in the lands drained by the Ohio River. But by 1870, "West" increasingly referred to the land across the Mississippi, from the Great Plains to the Pacific Ocean. The West of the late nineteenth century was a polyglot place, as much so as the big cities of the East.

The parade of peoples who came to the West included immigrants from Europe, Asia, and Canada, not to mention New Englanders, Mormons, African Americans, Mexicans, Latinos, and numerous Indian tribes removed by the government. The sheer number of peoples who mingled in the West produced a complex blend of racism and prejudice. One historian has noted, not entirely facetiously, that there were at least eight oppressed "races" in the West—Indians, Latinos, Chinese, Japanese, blacks, Mormons, strikers, and radicals.

African Americans who ventured out to the territories faced hostile settlers determined to keep the West "for whites only." Often they formed all-black communities like Nicodemas, Kansas, a settlement founded by thirty black Kentuckians in 1877, which grew to a community of 700 by 1880. Isolated and often separated by great distances, small black settlements grew up throughout the West, in Nevada, Utah, and the Pacific Northwest as well as in Kansas. Black soldiers who served in the West during the Indian wars often stayed on as settlers. Called "buffalo soldiers" because Native Americans thought their hair resembled that of the buffalo, these black troops numbered up to 25,000. They fought the Apaches in Arizona Territory and helped subdue the Sioux in the Dakotas.

Hispanic peoples had lived in Texas and the Southwest since Juan de Oñate led pioneer settlers up the Rio Grande in 1598. Hispanics had occupied the Pacific coast since San Diego was founded in 1769. Overnight they were reduced to a "minority" after the United States annexed Texas in 1845 and took lands stretching to California after the Mexican-American War ended in 1848. At first, the Hispanic owners of large *ranchos* in California, New Mexico, and Texas greeted conquest as an economic opportunity— new markets for their livestock and buyers for their lands. But racial prejudice soon ended their optimism. *Californios* (Mexican residents of California), who had been granted American citizenship by the Treaty of Guadalupe Hidalgo (1848), faced discrimination by Anglos who sought to keep them out of California's mines and commerce. Whites illegally squatted on rancho lands while protracted litigation over Spanish and Mexican land grants forced the *rancheros* into court. Although the U.S. Supreme Court eventually validated most of their claims, it took so long that many Californios sold their property to pay taxes and legal bills. The city of Oakland, California, sits on what was once a 19,000-acre ranch owned by the Peralta family, who lost the land to Anglos. Swindle, chicanery, and intimidation dispossessed scores of Californios. Many ended up segregated in urban barrios (neighborhoods) in their own homeland. Their percentage of California's population declined from 82 in 1850 to 19 percent by 1880 as Anglos immigrated into the state. In New Mexico and Texas, Mexicans remained a majority of the

Peralta Family
Don Antonio Peralta, grandson of Don Luis Peralta, whose vast landholdings once included most of Alameda County, California, is shown here in an 1870 photograph with his two sons, Nelson (left) and Vincente (right). The Peraltas and many other Californio families lost their land in protracted legal proceedings trying to prove the validity of their ancestors' Spanish land grants, which had gone unchallenged when Mexico ruled Alta California. The city of Oakland now sits on what was once the Peralta *rancho*. The Oakland Tribune.

population but became increasingly impoverished as Anglos dominated business and took the best jobs.

Like the Mexicans, the Mormons faced prejudice and hostility. The followers of Joseph Smith, the founder and prophet of the Church of Jesus Christ of Latter-Day Saints, fled west to avoid religious persecution. They believed that they had a divine right to the land, and their messianic militancy contributed to making them outcasts. The Mormons' polygamy (men taking more than one wife) became a convenient point of attack for those who hated and feared the group. After Smith was killed by an Illinois mob in 1844, Brigham Young led the flock, which numbered more than 20,000, over the Rockies to the valley of the Great Salt Lake in Utah Territory. The Mormons quickly set to work irrigating the desert land. They relied on cooperation and communalism, a strategy that excluded competition from those outside the faith. The church controlled water supplies, stores, insurance companies, and later factories and mining smelters. By 1882, the Mormons had built a thriving city of more than 150,000 residents—Salt Lake City. Not until 1896, however, when the church renounced polygamy and gave women the right to vote, did Congress grant Utah statehood.

The Chinese suffered brutal treatment at the hands of employers and other laborers. Drawn by the promise of gold, over 20,000 Chinese had joined the rush to California by 1852. Miners determined to keep "California for Americans" succeeded in passing prohibitive foreign license laws to keep the Chinese out of the mines. But Chinese immigration continued. In the 1860s when white workers rushed to find riches in the bonanza mines of Nevada, Chinese laborers took jobs abandonded by the white workers. Railroad magnate Charles Crocker hired Chinese gangs to work on the Central Pacific, reasoning that the race that built the Great Wall could lay tracks across the treacherous Sierras. Some 12,000 Chinese, representing 90 percent of Crocker's workforce, completed America's first transcontinental railroad in 1869.

By 1870, over 63,000 Chinese immigrants lived in America, 77 percent of them in California. A 1790 federal statute that limited naturalization to "white persons" was modified after the Civil War to extend naturalization to persons of African descent. But the Chinese and other Asians continued to be denied access to citizenship. As perpetual aliens they constituted a reserve army of transnational industrial laborers that many saw as a threat to American labor. For the most part, the Chinese did not displace white workers but instead found work as railroad laborers, cooks, servants, and farmhands while white workers sought out more lucrative fields. In the 1870s, when California and the rest of the nation weathered a major economic depression, the Chinese became easy scapegoats. California workingmen rioted and fought to keep the Chinese out of the state, claiming they were "coolie labor"—involuntary contract laborers recruited by business interests determined to keep wages at rock bottom.

In 1876, the Workingmen's Party formed to fight for Chinese exclusion. Racial and cultural animosities stood at the heart of anti-Chinese agitation. Denis Kearney, the fiery San Francisco leader of the movement, made clear this racist bent when he urged legislation to "expel every one of the moon-eyed lepers." Nor was California alone in its anti-immigrant **nativism**. As the country confronted growing ethnic and racial diversity with the rising tide of immigration, many in the nation questioned the principle of racial equality at the same time they argued against the assimilation of "nonwhite" groups. In this climate a Chinese Exclusion Act gained passage in 1882, effectively barring further Chinese immigration. The Exclusion Act led to a sharp drop in the Chinese population—from 105,465 in 1880 to 89,863 by 1900, because the Chinese immigrants, overwhelmingly male, did not have families to sustain their population. Eventually Japanese immigrants replaced the Chinese, particularly in agriculture. The Japanese immigrants included women as well as men. As "nonwhite"

Chinese Cook

This young Chinese cook and his helper prepare a meal in their woks for lumberjacks in a western lumber camp in the late 1880s. Barred from the mines, Chinese found work as cooks throughout the West. In the male enclave of a lumber or mining camp, a Chinese cook reinforced race and gender hierarchies. By giving Chinese men tasks such as cooking, laundry, and other domestic work, native white males feminized the Chinese, excluding them from men's work. Anti-Asian groups insisted that the Chinese drove down the pay of male workers, but the Chinese actually competed more directly with women, particularly in the laundry business, where in many places they replaced the Irish washerwoman.

University of California at Berkeley, Bancroft Library.

immigrants, they could not become naturalized citizens, but their children born in the United States claimed the rights of citizenship. Japanese parents, seeking to own land, purchased it in the names of their children. Although anti-Asian prejudice remained strong in California and elsewhere in the West, Asian immigrants formed an important part of the economic fabric of the western United States.

The American West in the nineteenth century witnessed more than its share of conflict and bloodshed. Violent prejudice against the Chinese and other Asian immigrants remained common. But violence also broke out between cattle ranchers and sheep ranchers, between ranchers and farmers, between striking miners and their bosses, among rival Indian groups, and between whites and Indians. At issue was who would control the vast resources of the emerging region. In the ensuing struggle, the biggest losers were those with the first and best claim to the land: the Native Americans, who had been living in the West before the arrival of European explorers, Spanish missionaries, or American settlers.

Indian Wars

From the early days of the Republic, Americans had advocated a policy of Indian removal. In the 1830s, President Andrew Jackson pushed the Cherokee, Choctaw, Chickasaw, Creek, and Seminole tribes off their lands in the southern United States. Jackson's Indian removal forced thousands of men, women, and children to leave their homes in Georgia and Tennessee and walk hundreds of miles to lands across the Mississippi River. So many died of hunger, exhaustion, and disease along the way that the Cherokee called their path "the trail on which we cried." At the end of this trail of tears stood the Great Plains. Here, the government promised the Indians, they could remain "as long as grass shall grow."

But in the 1840s, Oregon land fever, the Mexican-American War, and the gold rush in California put an end to the promise. Settlers repeatedly trespassed onto Indian land and then were surprised when they encountered hostility. Indignantly, they demanded protection from the U.S. army. The result was thirty years of Indian wars.

The Indian wars on the plains lasted from 1861 until 1890. To Americans filled with theories of racial superiority, the Indian constituted, in the words of a Colorado militia major, "an obstacle to civilization…[and] should be exterminated." The federal government, acting through the army, adopted a policy succinctly summed up by General William T. Sherman: "Remove all to a safe place and then reduce them to a helpless condition." The government herded the Indians onto reservations where the U.S. Bureau of Indian Affairs—a badly managed, weak agency, often acting through corrupt agents—supposedly ministered to their needs (Map 18.3).

On the plains and in the Southwest and Rocky Mountain region, the Sioux, Cheyenne, Arapaho, Nez Perce, Comanche, Kiowa, Ute, Apache, and Navajo nations put up a determined resistance. The Indian wars (which instead might be called settlers' wars since they began with "peaceful settlers," often miners, overrunning Native American lands) involved violence and atrocities on both sides. In 1864, Colonel John M. Chivington and his local Colorado militia slaughtered an entire village of Cheyenne, mostly women and children peacefully camped along Sand Creek. Chivington watched as his men mutilated their hapless victims and later justified the killing of Indian children with the terse remark "Nits make lice." The city of Denver treated Chivington and his men as heroes, but after a congressional inquiry revealed the shocking details of the Sand Creek massacre, he was forced to resign his commission to avoid court-martial.

The fever for gold fueled conflict with the Indians. In 1866, the Cheyenne united with the Sioux in Wyoming, where they fought to protect their lands from the building of the Bozeman Trail, connecting Fort Laramie with the goldfields in Montana. Captain William Fetterman, who had boasted that with eighty men he could ride through the Sioux Nation, died in an Indian attack along with all of his troops. The Sioux's impressive victories led to the Treaty of Fort Laramie in 1868, in which the United States agreed to abandon the Bozeman Trail and guaranteed Indians control of their sacred lands in the Black Hills. The government induced the Plains tribes to accept reservation lands, and the great chief Red Cloud led many of his people onto the new reservation. But several Sioux chiefs, among them Crazy Horse of the Oglala band and Sitting Bull of the Hunkpapa, refused to sign the treaty. Crazy Horse said that he wanted no part of the "piecemeal penning" of

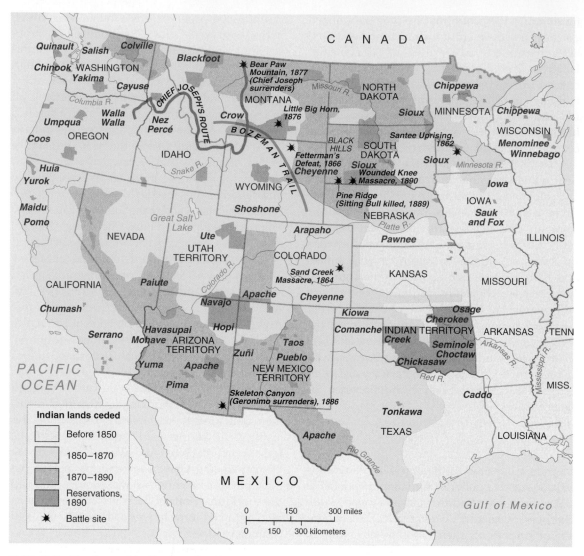

MAP 18.3   The Loss of Indian Lands, 1850–1890

By 1890, western Indians were isolated on small, scattered reservations. Native Americans had struggled to retain their land in major battles, from the Santee uprising in Minnesota in 1862 to the massacre at Wounded Knee, South Dakota, in 1890.

READING THE MAP: Where was the largest reservation located in 1890? Which states on this map show no reservations in 1890? Compare this map to Map 18.2, Federal Land Grants to Railroads and the Development of the West. Where do the contours of Indian lands ceded from 1850 to 1890 parallel the placement of the railroads?

CONNECTIONS: Why did the federal government force Native Americans onto reservations? What developments prompted these changes?

FOR MORE HELP ANALYZING THIS MAP, see the map activity for this chapter in the Online Study Guide at bedfordstmartins.com/roarkcompact.

his people. The army launched a series of campaigns to round up tribes who refused to accept confinement. Fights between the U.S. military and the Indians persisted into the 1870s, as bands of Sioux continued to roam the plains, hunting buffalo.

The coming of the transcontinental railroads and the eastern demand for buffalo hides led to the decimation of the great bison herds, spelling the ultimate disaster for Native Americans. To the Sioux and the Kiowa, the buffalo (American bison) constituted a way of life—the source of food, fuel, and shelter and a central part of religion and ritual. To the railroads, the buffalo were a nuisance, at best a target for sport and a source of cheap meat for their workers. In 1870, buffalo hunters hired by the railroads began to decimate the great herds; sport hunters fired at random from railroad cars just for the thrill of it. Trade in buffalo hides led to a heyday of buffalo hunting in the 1880s. In thirty years, more than sixty million animals were slaughtered. By 1895, fewer than a thousand bison survived. The army took credit for subduing the Indians, but their victory came about more as a result of the decimation of the great bison herds. General Philip Sheridan acknowledged as much when he applauded the hunters for "destroying the Indians' commissary." With their food supply gone, Indians had to choose between starvation and the reservations.

In 1874, gold fever jeopardized the Treaty of Fort Laramie. The discovery of gold in the Black Hills of the Dakotas led the government to break its promise to Red Cloud to preserve these lands sacred to the Indians. Miners began pouring into the area, and the Northern Pacific Railroad made plans to lay track. Lieutenant Colonel George Armstrong Custer, whose troopers found gold in the area, trumpeted news of the gold strike. At first the government offered to purchase the Black Hills, but the Indians refused to sell. The United States responded by ordering all Lakota Sioux and Northern Cheyenne bands onto the Pine Ridge Reservation. Under the leadership of Crazy Horse and Sitting Bull, the Sioux tribes massed to resist. In June 1876, Custer led 265 men of the Seventh Cavalry into the Indian camp on the Little Bighorn River in Montana Territory. Perhaps as many as 2,000 Sioux warriors set upon Custer and killed him along with all of his troops.

Their victory, however, proved short-lived. Within six years, the Indians suffered a series of defeats. Crazy Horse was killed in 1877 and Sitting Bull surrendered five years later in 1881. The government took the Black Hills and confined the Lakota to the Great Sioux Reservation. Chief Joseph of the Nez Perce resisted removal and fled toward Canada. In 1877 federal troops caught up with his band just forty miles from freedom. With his people cold and starving, the chief surrendered. His speech stands as an eloquent statement of the plight of the Indians:

> I am tired of fighting. Our chiefs are killed....It is cold and we have no blankets. The little children are freezing to death. My people, some of

them, have run away to the hills, and have no blankets, no food; no one knows where they are—perhaps freezing to death. I want to have time to look for my children and see how many I can find. Maybe I shall find them among the dead. Hear me, my chiefs, I am tired; my heart is sick and sad. From where the sun now stands, I will fight no more forever.

The Sioux never accepted the loss of the Black Hills. In 1923 they filed suit, demanding compensation for lands illegally taken from them. After a protracted court battle, the U.S. Supreme Court ruled in 1980 that the government had illegally abrogated the Treaty of Fort Laramie and upheld an award of $122.5 million in compensation to the tribes.

The Dawes Act and Indian Land Allotment

The practice of rounding up Indians and herding them onto reservations lost momentum in the 1880s in favor of allotment—a new policy designed to encourage assimilation through farming and the ownership of private property. Indian rights groups, often led by white Americans, mounted a campaign to dismantle the reservations, which in their judgment impeded full assimilation by preserving tribal culture. Believing they acted in the best interests of Native peoples, Indian rights groups called for a policy that would grant Indians full citizenship and give them farms. In 1887, Congress passed the Dawes Allotment Act to abolish reservations and allot lands to individual Indians as private property. Reformers hoped the elimination of reservations would push Indians toward individualism and self-sufficiency. Each Indian household received 160 acres of land from reservation property. Only those Indians who took allotments earned citizenship. Since Indian lands far surpassed the acreage needed for allotments, the government reserved the right to sell the "surplus" land. The act effectively reduced Indian lands from 138 million acres to a scant 48 million. The legislation, in the words of one critic, worked "to despoil the Indians of their lands and to make them vagabonds on the face of the earth." The opening of the "surplus" to white settlement set off the great land rushes in Oklahoma Territory in 1889 and 1893. Although the Indian Reorganization Act of 1934 restored the right of Native Americans to own land communally (see chapter 24), the Dawes Act dealt a damaging blow to traditional tribal culture.

The Last Acts of Indian Resistance

Faced with the extinction of their entire way of life, different groups of Indians responded in different ways in the waning decades of the nineteenth century. Apaches in the Southwest resorted to outright violence, while the Ghost Dance, a form of nonviolent resistance, swept across the Plains in 1889–1890. Both triggered brutal military repression by the U.S. army.

The Apache tribes who roamed the Sonoran desert of southern Arizona and northern Mexico never combined as the Plains Indians had done so successfully at the Little Bighorn. Instead they operated in small raiding parties, perfecting a hit-and-run **guerrilla warfare** that terrorized white settlers and bedeviled the army in the 1870s and 1880s. General George Crook combined a policy of dogged pursuit with judicious diplomacy. Crook relied on Indian scouts to track the raiding parties, recruiting nearly two hundred, including some Apaches along with Navajos and Paiutes. By 1882 Crook succeeded in persuading most of the Apaches to settle on the San Carlos Reservation in Arizona Territory. A desolate piece of desert inhabited by scorpions and rattlesnakes, San Carlos, in the words of one Apache, was "the worst place in all the great territory stolen from the Apaches."

Reservation life proved particularly difficult for the nomadic Apaches. Geronimo, a respected shaman (medicine man) of the fierce Chiricahua Apaches, repeatedly led raiding parties in the 1880s. His Apache warriors attacked ranches to get ammunition and horses, killing the ranchers and burning their homesteads. Among Geronimo's band was Lozen, a woman who rode with the male warriors, armed with a rifle and a cartridge belt. The sister of a great chief who described her as "Strong as a man, braver than most, and cunning in strategy," Lozen never married and remained a warrior in Geronimo's band even after her brother's death. In the spring of 1885, Lozen, along with Geronimo, went on a ten-month offensive, moving from the Apache sanctuary in the Sierra Madre to raid and burn ranches and towns on both sides of the Mexican border. General Crook caught up with Geronimo in the fall and persuaded him to return to San Carlos,

only to have him slip away with his small band on the way back to the reservation. Chagrined, Crook resigned his post. General Nelson Miles, Crook's replacement, adopted a policy of hunt and destroy.

Geronimo's band of thirty-three Apaches, including women and children, managed to elude Miles's troops for more than five months. Throughout the blistering summer, the Indians, constantly on the move, kept one step ahead of the army. In the end, this small band of Apaches fought two thousand soldiers to a stalemate.

After months of pursuit, Lieutenant Leonard Wood, a member of Crook's spit-and-polish cavalry, was reduced to wearing nothing "but a pair of canton flannel drawers, and an old blue blouse, a pair of moccasins and a hat without a crown." Eventually, the scouts tracked down Geronimo and his band. Caught between Mexican regulars and the U.S. army, in 1886 Geronimo agreed to march north with the soldiers and negotiate a settlement. "We have not slept for six months," Geronimo admitted, "and we are worn out." He met with General Miles to negotiate a peace, but, as in the past, the Indians did not get what they were promised. Fewer than three dozen Apaches had been hostile when General Miles induced them to surrender, yet the government gathered up nearly five hundred Apaches and sent them as prisoners to Florida, including the scouts who had helped track Geronimo. By 1889, more than a quarter of them had died, some by illness contracted in the damp, lowland climate and some by suicide. Their plight roused public opinion, and in 1892 they were moved to Fort Sill in Oklahoma and later to New Mexico.

Geronimo lived to become something of a celebrity. He appeared at the St. Louis Exposition in 1904, and he rode in President Theodore Roosevelt's inaugural parade in 1905. In a newspaper interview he confessed, "I want to go to my old home before I die.... Want to go back to the mountains again. I asked the Great White Father to allow me to go back, but he said no." None of the Apaches were permitted to return to Arizona; when Geronimo died in 1909, he was buried in Oklahoma.

On the plains many different tribes turned to a nonviolent form of resistance—a compelling new religion, the Ghost Dance. The Paiute shaman Wovoka, drawing on a cult that had developed in the 1870s, combined elements of

Ghost Dance Dress

An Arapaho woman wore this deerskin dress during the Ghost Dance fervor of 1889–1890 in Oklahoma. Decorated with stars and eagles, it was intended to protect its wearer. Ghost dancers believed that the clothing they wore made them impervious to army bullets. The symbols and the decoration on the garments evoked powerful magic. The men wore white Ghost Dance shirts; women and children dressed in more colorful garments like the one pictured here.

Division of Political History, Smithsonian Institution, Washington, D.C.

Christianity and traditional Indian religion to found the Ghost Dance religion in 1889. Wovoka claimed that he had received a vision in which the Great Spirit spoke through him to all Indians, urging them to unite and prophesying that whites would be destroyed in an apocalypse. The shaman promised that Indian warriors slain in battle would return to life and that buffalo once again would roam the land unimpeded. This religion of despair with its message of hope spread like wildfire over the plains. It was danced in Idaho, Montana, Utah, Wyoming, Colorado, Nebraska, Kansas, the Dakotas, and Oklahoma Territory by tribes as diverse as the Arapaho, Cheyenne, Pawnee, and Shoshone. Dances were held in a circle, and dancers often went into hypnotic trances, dancing until they dropped from exhaustion.

Ghost Dances were generally nonviolent, but among the Sioux the dance took on a more militant flavor. Sioux disciples of the Ghost Dance religion taught that wearing white ghost shirts made Indians immune to the bullets of the soldiers. Their message frightened whites, who began to fear an uprising. "Indians are dancing in the snow and are wild and crazy," wrote the Bureau of Indian Affairs agent at the Pine Ridge Reservation in South Dakota. Frantic, he pleaded for reinforcements. "We are at the mercy of these dancers. We need protection, and we need it now." President Benjamin Harrison dispatched several thousand federal troops to Sioux country to handle any outbreak.

In December 1890 when Sitting Bull joined the Ghost dancers, he was killed by Indian police as they tried to arrest him at his cabin on the Standing Rock Reservation. His people, fleeing the scene, joined with a larger group of Miniconjou Sioux who were apprehended by the Seventh Cavalry, Custer's old regiment, near Wounded Knee Creek, South Dakota. As the Indians laid down their arms, a shot rang out and the army opened fire. In the ensuing melee, Indian men, women, and children were mowed down in minutes by the army's brutally efficient Hotchkiss machine guns. More than 200 Sioux lay dead or dying in the snow. Settler Jules Sandoz surveyed the scene the day after the massacre. "Here in ten minutes an entire community was as the buffalo that bleached on the plains," he wrote. "There was something loose in the world that hated joy and happiness as it hated brightness and color, reducing everything to drab agony and gray."

Although the massacre at Wounded Knee did not end the story of Native Americans, it ended a way of life. The Indian population would gradually recover; the 2000 census showed 2.5 million Native Americans, compared to a scant 250,000 in 1890. But their culture sustained a crushing blow. In the words of the visionary Black Elk, "The nation's hoop is broken and scattered. There is no center any longer, and the sacred tree is dead." Not until the 1960s did Indians mount a protest movement to fight for tribal lands and recover Native American identity and cultural pride (see chapter 28).

The West of the Imagination

Even as the Old West was dying, the myth of the "Wild West" was being born. The dime novel, a precursor to today's paperback, capitalized on gun-slinging cowboy heroes like Kit Carson, Wild Bill Hickok, Calamity Jane, and Deadwood Dick to entertain readers seeking escapist fare. Published in the East and sometimes written by tenderfeet who had never ventured beyond the Hudson River, dime novels sold at a prodigious rate.

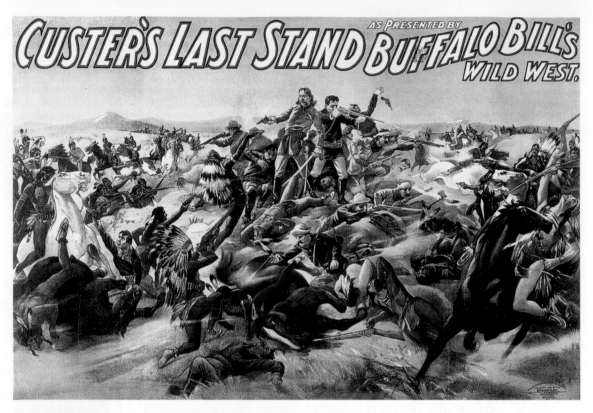

Buffalo Bill Poster

Buffalo Bill Cody used colorful posters to publicize his Wild West show during the 1880s and 1890s. One of his most popular features was the reenactment of Custer's Last Stand, which he performed for Queen Victoria in London and at the World's Columbian Exposition in Chicago. Cody hired Native Americans for his troop, including Sitting Bull, who had fought at the Battle of the Little Bighorn. Sitting Bull toured with the company in 1885 and traveled to England with the show.

Buffalo Bill Historical Center, Cody, Wyoming.

FOR MORE HELP ANALYZING THIS IMAGE, see the visual activity for this chapter in the Online Study Guide at **bedfordstmartins.com/roarkcompact**.

The prince of the dime novel heroes was Buffalo Bill, featured in more than two hundred titles. Born William F. Cody, the real-life Buffalo Bill had panned for gold, ridden for the Pony Express, scouted for the army, and earned his nickname hunting buffalo for the railroad. A masterful showman, he formed a touring Wild West company in 1883. Part circus, part theater, the Wild West extravaganza featured exhibitions of riding, shooting, and roping and presented dramatic reenactments of great moments in western U.S. history. The star of the show, Annie Oakley (Phoebe Moses), dubbed "Little Miss Sure Shot," delighted the crowd by shooting a dime out of her husband's hand. The centerpiece of Buffalo Bill's Wild West show was a reenactment of Custer's Last Stand, in which Indians wearing war paint and feathered headdresses massacred the hapless Custer and his men. At the end, Buffalo Bill galloped in through a cloud of dust and dramatically mouthed the words "Too late!" The Wild West that Buffalo Bill presented indiscriminately mixed the authentic with the romantic until reality itself blurred in the popular mind. Cody had not been at the Little Bighorn, but some of the Indians in his troupe, like Sitting Bull, who toured with the show in 1885, had been there and knew their parts firsthand. As history the Wild West show was dubious, but as spectacle it was unbeatable. The high drama of the struggle for the West had become little more than a thrilling but harmless entertainment.

REVIEW   How did the slaughter of bison contribute to Plains Indians' removal to reservations?

Conclusion:
The West, an Integral Part of Gilded Age America

Between 1870 and 1900, the United States filled out the map of the continent all the way to the Pacific Ocean as miners and settlers pushed into the trans-Mississippi West. Native Americans who resisted met defeat in the bloody Indian wars that raged from 1861 to 1890 and left the Indians dispossessed, forced onto reservations, and later put out to farm on 160-acre plots. At the same time, Indian boarding schools worked to erase tribal identity and force assimilation.

By 1900 eight new states had entered the Union, leaving only three territories. As settlers moved onto the plains, agriculture became increasingly mechanized and commercial; huge farms totaling thousands of acres were tilled by machine, not muscle. With its huge mining companies and burgeoning agribusiness, the West developed its own industrialism, paralleling industrial development in the East.

In the decades following the Civil War the American West, as much as the urban East, confronted the new problems of the Gilded Age that had replaced the old issues of slavery and sectionalism. The growing power of big business, the exploitation of labor and natural resources, corruption in politics, and ethnic and racial tensions exacerbated by unparalleled immigration dominated the debates of the day in both East and West. Industrialism changed the nature of the American promise, which for decades had been dominated by Jeffersonian agrarian ideals. Could such a promise exist in the new world of corporations, wage labor, and burgeoning cities?

As the nineteenth century ended, Americans had more questions than answers. But one thing was certain: The West with its mining companies and huge commercial farms, its displaced cowboys and migratory laborers, its corporate buccaneers and corrupt territorial officials, and the racial and ethnic tensions that beset its polyglot population was as much a part of the Gilded Age as any region east of the Mississippi. Neither out of place nor out of time, the West constituted an important part of Gilded Age America, tied to the rest of the nation not only by the get-rich-quick ethos and speculative mania of the era but by the reality of the thousands of miles of railway tracks crisscrossing the continent, linking the growing cities of the East to the mining towns of Nevada, the orange groves of California, and the cotton fields and cattle ranches of Texas—an integral part of an increasingly urban and industrial nation spanning the continent from sea to sea.

Suggestions for Further Reading

Najia Aarin-Heriot, *Chinese Immigrants, African Americans, and Racial Anxiety in the United States, 1848–1882* (2003). This work links the negative stereotypes and exclusionary laws that affected African Americans and Chinese immigrants in the nineteenth century.

David Wallace Adams, *Education for Extinction: American Indians and the Boarding School Experience, 1875–1928* (1995). A vivid and often heartbreaking study of the experiences of Indian youth sent to boarding schools.

Colin Calloway, *First Peoples: A Documentary Survey of American Indian History* (2nd ed., 2003). A good overview of American Indian history including historical narrative and significant documents.

David Igler, *Industrial Cowboys: Miller & Lux and the Transformation of the Far West, 1850–1920* (2001). A fascinating case study of how two neighborhood butchers became the West's leading industrialists.

Ronald M. James, *The Roar and the Silence: The History of Virginia City and the Comstock Lode* (1998). A lively account of life on the Comstock.

David M. Wrobel, *Promised Lands: Promotion, Memory, and the Creation of the American West* (2002). A study of how promoters and boosters lured settlers to the West and shaped the nation's perception of the region.

▶ FOR MORE BOOKS ABOUT TOPICS IN THIS CHAPTER, see the Online Bibliography at bedfordstmartins.com/roarkcompact.

▶ FOR ADDITIONAL FIRSTHAND ACCOUNTS OF THIS PERIOD, see Chapter 18 in Michael Johnson, ed., *Reading the American Past*, Third Edition.

▶ FOR WEB SITES AND DOCUMENTS RELATED TO TOPICS AND PLACES IN THIS CHAPTER, see "HistoryLinks," "DocLinks," and "PlaceLinks" at bedfordstmartins.com/roarkcompact.

REVIEWING THE CHAPTER

Follow these steps to review and strengthen your understanding of the chapter.

STEP 1: *Study the Key Terms and Timeline to identify the significance of each item listed.*

STEP 2: *Answer the Review Questions, drawing on key terms and dates to support your answers.*

STEP 3: *Drawing on the Key Terms, Timeline, and Review Questions, answer the broader Making Connections questions.*

KEY TERMS

Who

Deadwood Dick (pp. 461, 471)
Exodusters (p. 462)
buffalo soldiers (p. 465)
Joseph Smith (p. 465)
Charles Crocker (p. 466)
William T. Sherman (p. 467)
John M. Chivington (p. 467)
Red Cloud (p. 467)
Crazy Horse (p. 467)
Sitting Bull (p. 467)
George Armstrong Custer (p. 469)
Chief Joseph (p. 469)
George Crook (p. 470)
Geronimo (p. 470)
Nelson Miles (p. 470)
Wovoka (p. 470)
William F. Cody (p. 472)
Annie Oakley (p. 472)

What

Carlisle Indian School (p. 454)
California gold rush (p. 455)
Virginia City (p. 455)
Comstock Lode (p. 455)
Big Bonanza (p. 458)
Homestead Act of 1862 (p. 459)
Great American Desert (p. 460)
Chisholm Trail (p. 461)
free range (p. 461)
"Great Die Up" (p. 461)
agribusiness (p. 463)
Miller & Lux (p. 464)
Treaty of Guadalupe Hidalgo (1848) (p. 465)
Workingmen's Party (p. 466)
Chinese Exclusion Act (p. 466)
Indian removal (p. 467)
Indian wars (p. 467)

U.S. Bureau of Indian Affairs (p. 467)
Sand Creek massacre (p. 467)
Bozeman Trail (p. 467)
Treaty of Fort Laramie (p. 467)
Black Hills (p. 467)
Pine Ridge Reservation (p. 469)
Battle of Little Bighorn (p. 469)
Dawes Allotment Act (p. 469)
Indian Reorganization Act of 1934 (p. 469)
San Carlos Reservation (p. 470)
Ghost Dance (p. 470)
Massacre at Wounded Knee (p. 471)
Buffalo Bill's Wild West show (p. 472)

TIMELINE

◄ **1862** • Homestead Act.

1868 • Treaty of Fort Laramie.

1870 • Hunters begin to decimate bison herds.
• Henry Miller and Charles Lux develop agricultural empire in California.

1873 • Miners discover "Big Bonanza" on Comstock Lode.

1874 • Discovery of gold in Black Hills.

1876 • Battle of the Little Bighorn.

1877 • Chief Joseph surrenders.
• Crazy Horse surrenders and later is arrested and killed.

1878 • Indian students enroll at Hampton Institute in Virginia.

1879 • Carlisle Indian School opens.
• Over 15,000 Exodusters move to Kansas.

1881 • Sitting Bull surrenders.

1882 • Chinese Exclusion Act.

REVIEW QUESTIONS

1. How did industrial technology change mining in Nevada? (pp. 455–59)

2. Why did many homesteaders find it difficult to acquire good land in the West? (pp. 459–64)

3. How did the slaughter of bison contribute to Plains Indians' removal to reservations? (pp. 464–73)

MAKING CONNECTIONS

1. The economic and industrial developments characteristic of the East during the Gilded Age also made their mark on the West. How did innovations in business and technology transform mining and agriculture in the West? In your answer, be sure to consider effects on production *and* the consequences for the lives of miners and agricultural laborers.

2. Settlers from all over the world came to the American West seeking their fortune but found that opportunity was not equally available to all. In competition for work and land, why did Anglo-American settlers usually have the upper hand? How did legal developments contribute to this circumstance?

3. Westward migration brought settlers into conflict with Native Americans. How did the United States government attempt to subdue Indians in the West? How did Indians resist their actions? In your answer, discuss the cultural and military features of the conflict.

▶ FOR PRACTICE QUIZZES, A CUSTOMIZED STUDY PLAN, AND OTHER STUDY TOOLS, see the Online Study Guide at bedfordstmartins.com/roarkcompact.

1883 • Buffalo Bill Cody begins touring.

    1886 • Geronimo surrenders.

1886–1888 • Severe blizzards in Dakota Territory.

    1887 • Dawes Act.

      1889 • Rise of Ghost Dance religion.
         • 2 million acres in Oklahoma opened to settlement.

      1890 • Sitting Bull killed.
         • Massacre at Wounded Knee, South Dakota.
         • Gold discovered in Cripple Creek, Colorado.

        1893 • Last land rush takes place in Oklahoma Territory.

           1900
           • Census finds 66 percent of population lives in rural areas, compared to 80 percent in 1870.

BROOKLYN BRIDGE FAN

This commemorative fan celebrates the opening of the Brooklyn Bridge on May 24, 1883. A testament in stone and steel to the growing importance of urban America, the great bridge stood as a symbol not only of New York but of the era. The lithograph on the fan depicts a view of the bridge over the East River with ships in the foreground and the Manhattan skyline as well as commerce along the quays illustrated in detail in the background. Printed on the back are several facts about the design and construction of the bridge. Americans, proud of the great bridge, used it in advertising as a recurring motif. This fan doubles as an advertisement for the Cowperthwaits Furniture Company. The firm's sign is visible among the buildings on the front of the fan, and an image of the company's building, along with its address and telephone number, is printed on the back.

Museum of the City of New York.

The City and Its Workers

1870–1900

"A TOWN THAT CRAWLED now stands erect, and we whose backs were bent above the hearths know how it got its spine," boasted a steelworker surveying New York City. Where once wooden buildings stood rooted in the mire of unpaved streets, cities of stone and steel sprang up in the last decades of the nineteenth century. The labor of millions of workers, many of them immigrants, laid the foundations for urban America.

No symbol better represented the new urban landscape than the Brooklyn Bridge, opened in May 1883 and quickly hailed as "one of the wonders of the world." The great bridge soared over the East River in a single mile-long span connecting Brooklyn and Manhattan. Begun in 1869, the bridge was the dream of builder John Roebling, who did not live to see it completed.

The building of the Brooklyn Bridge took fourteen years and cost the lives of twenty men. Nearly 300 workers labored around the clock in three shifts, six days a week, most for $2 a day. To sink the foundation deep into the riverbed, common laborers tunneled down through mud and debris, working in reinforced wooden boxes called caissons, which were open at the bottom and pressurized to keep the water from flooding in. Before long the workers experienced a mysterious malady they called "bends" because it left them doubled over in pain after they came to the surface. (Scientists later discovered that nitrogen bubbles trapped in the bloodstream caused the condition and that it could be prevented if the men came up slowly to allow for decompression.) The first death occurred when the caisson reached a depth of seventy-one feet. On April 22, 1872, a heavy-set German immigrant named John Meyers complained he did not feel well and headed home to his boardinghouse. Before he could reach his bed, he collapsed and died. Eight days later another man dropped dead, and the entire workforce in the caissons went out on strike. Conditions had become so dangerous, so terrifying, that the workers demanded a higher wage for fewer hours of work.

One worker, Frank Harris, remembered the men's fear working in the caisson. As a scrawny, sixteen-year-old from Ireland, Harris started to work a few days after landing in America. He described how the men went into a coffin-like "air-lock" to acclimate to the pressure of the compressed air in the caissons:

> When the air was fully compressed, the door of the air-lock opened at a touch and we all went down to work with pick and shovel on the gravelly bottom. My headaches soon became acute. The six of us were working naked to the waist in the small iron chamber with the temperature of about 80 degrees

Fahrenheit: In five minutes the sweat was pouring from us, and all the while we were standing in icy water that was only kept from rising by the terrific pressure. No wonder the headaches were blinding.

Harris recalled the big Swede who headed the work gang saying to him that "I could stay as long as I liked, but he advised me to leave at the end of a month: It was too unhealthy." By the fifth day, Harris experienced terrible shooting pains in his ears, and fearing he might go deaf, he quit. Like Harris, many immigrant workers walked off the job, often as many as a hundred a week. But a ready supply of immigrants meant that the work never slowed or stopped; new workers eagerly entered the caissons, where they

Immigrant Couple

Wearing the clothing of the old country (cap and collarless shirt; apron and shawl), this immigrant couple carries their meager possessions—bedding in his bundle, food and utensils in her basket, and two umbrellas tied together. Notice how the man gazes confidently, almost defiantly, into the camera, while the woman, looking miserable, averts her eyes. What do their postures tell about who made the decision to come to America and about their individual hopes and apprehensions?

Wide World Photos.

could earn in a day more than they made in a week in Ireland or Italy.

Washington Roebling, who took over as chief engineer after his father's death, routinely worked twelve to fourteen hours, six days a week. Soon he too fell victim to the bends and ended up an invalid, directing the completion of the bridge from his window in Brooklyn Heights through a telescope. His wife, Emily Warren Roebling, acted as site superintendent and general engineer of the project. At the dedication of the bridge, Roebling turned to his wife and said, "I want the world to know that you, too, are one of the Builders of the Bridge."

Arching 130 feet above the East River, the bridge carried a roadway for vehicles and above it a pedestrian walkway. Together they pierced massive granite towers at each end through two huge Gothic arches. Roebling intended the bridge to stand as "a great work of art" as well as "a successful specimen of advanced Bridge engineering." Generations of artists and poets have testified to his success.

At the end of the nineteenth century the Brooklyn Bridge stood as a symbol of many things: the industrial might of the United States; the labor of the nation's immigrants; the ingenuity and genius of its engineers and inventors; the rise of iron and steel; and most of all, the ascendancy of urban America. Poised on the brink of the twentieth century, the nation was shifting inexorably from a rural, agricultural society to an urban, industrial nation. In the nation's cities tensions would erupt into conflict as workers squared off to fight for their right to organize into labor unions. And the explosive growth of the cities would foster political corruption as unscrupulous bosses and entrepreneurs found ways to cash in on the building boom. Immigrants, political bosses, middle-class managers, poor laborers, and the very rich populated the burgeoning cities, crowding the streets, laboring in the stores and factories, and taking their leisure at the new ballparks, amusement parks, dance halls, and municipal parks that dotted the urban landscape. As the new century dawned, the city and its workers moved to center stage in American life.

The Rise of the City

"We cannot all live in cities, yet nearly all seem determined to do so," New York editor Horace Greeley complained. The last three decades of the nineteenth century witnessed an urban explosion. Cities and towns grew more than twice as rapidly as the total population. Among the fastest-growing cities, Chicago expanded at a meteoric rate, from 100,000 in 1860 to over a million by 1890, doubling its population each decade. By 1900, the number of cities with more than 100,000 inhabitants had jumped from eighteen in 1870 to thirty-eight. Most of the nation's largest cities were east of the Mississippi, although St. Louis and San Francisco both ranked among the top ten urban areas in 1900. And in the far West, Los Angeles exploded from a sleepy village of 5,000 in 1870 to a metropolis of more than 100,000 a scant thirty years later. The United States boasted three cities with more than a million inhabitants in 1900—New York, Chicago, and Philadelphia.

Patterns of global migration contributed to the rise of the city. In the port cities of the East Coast, over 14 million people arrived, many from southern and eastern Europe, huddled together in dense urban ghettos. The word *slum* entered the American vocabulary and with it growing concern over the rising tide of newcomers. With immigration, the widening gap between rich and poor became more visible, exacerbated by changes in the city landscape brought about by transportation and technology.

The Urban Explosion, a Global Migration

The United States grew up in the country and moved to the city, or so it seemed by the end of the nineteenth century. Hundreds of thousands of farm boys and girls ran away to the city looking for jobs and adventure. But rural migrants to the cities were by no means limited to American farmers. Worldwide in scope, the movement from rural areas to urban industrial centers attracted millions of immigrants to American shores in the waning decades of the nineteenth century.

By the 1870s, the world could be conceptualized as three interconnected geographic regions (Map 19.1). At the center stood an industrial core bounded by Chicago and St. Louis in the west; Toronto, Glasgow, and Berlin in the north; Warsaw in the east; and Milan, Barcelona, Richmond, and

MAP 19.1   Economic Regions of the World, 1890s
The global nature of the world economy at the turn of the twentieth century is indicated by three interconnected geographic regions. At the center stands the industrial core—western Europe and the northeastern United States. The second region—the agricultural periphery—supplied immigrant laborers to the industries in the core. Beyond these two regions lay a vast area tied economically to the industrial core by colonialism.

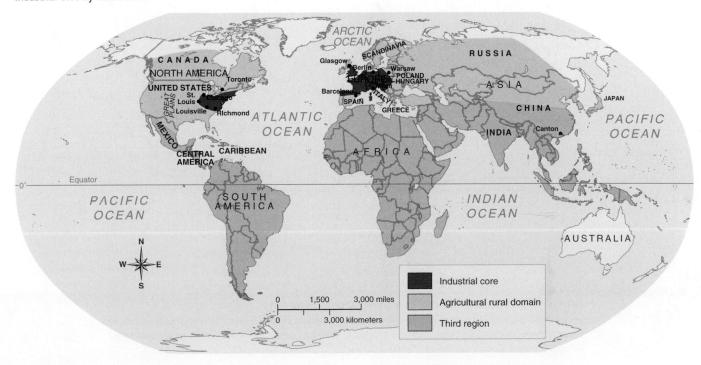

Louisville in the south. Surrounding this industrial core lay a vast agricultural domain encompassing Canada, much of Scandinavia, Russia and Poland, Hungary, Greece, Italy and Sicily, southern Spain, the South and the western plains of America, central and northern Mexico, the hinterlands of northern China, and the southern islands of Japan. Capitalist development in the late nineteenth century shattered traditional patterns of economic activity in this rural periphery. As old patterns broke down, these rural areas exported, along with other raw materials, new recruits for the industrial labor force.

Beyond this second circle lay an even larger third area including the Caribbean, Central and South America, the Middle East, Africa, India, and most of Asia. Ties between this part of the world and the industrial core strengthened in the late nineteenth century, but most of the people living there stayed put. They worked on planta-

tions and railroads, in mines and ports, as part of a huge export network managed by foreign powers that staked out spheres of influence and colonies in this vast region.

In the 1870s, railroad expansion and low steamship fares gave the world's peoples a newfound mobility that enabled industrialists to draw on a global population for cheap labor. When Andrew Carnegie opened his first steel mill in 1872, his superintendent hired workers he called "buckwheats"—young American boys just off the farm. By the 1890s, however, Carnegie's workforce was liberally sprinkled with other rural boys— Hungarians and Slavs who had migrated to the United States, willing to work for low wages.

European immigration to the United States in the nineteenth century came in two distinct waves that have been called the "old" and "new" immigration. Before 1880, the majority of immigrants came from northern and western Europe, with the

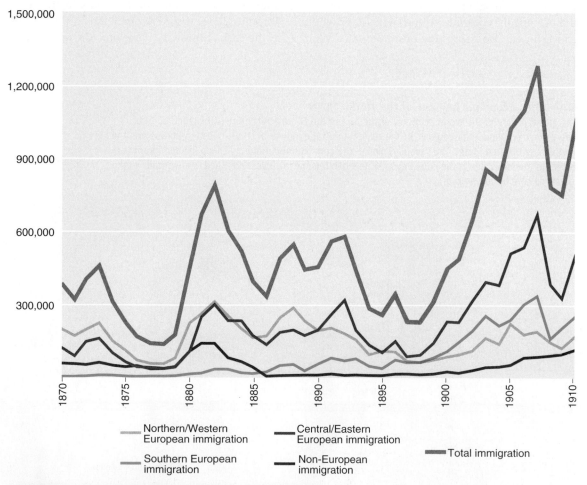

FIGURE 19.1   The Old and the New Immigration, 1870–1910
Before 1880, over 85 percent of immigrants came from western Europe—Germany, Ireland, England, and the Scandinavian countries. After 1880, 80 percent of the new arrivals came from Italy, Turkey, Hungary, Armenia, Poland, Russia, and other Slavic countries.

Germans, Irish, English, and Scandinavians making up approximately 85 percent of the newcomers. After 1880, the pattern shifted, with more and more ships carrying passengers from southern and eastern Europe. Italians, Hungarians, eastern European Jews, Turks, Armenians, Poles, Russians, and other Slavic peoples accounted for more than 80 percent of all immigrants by 1896 (Figure 19.1). Alongside the tide of new European immigrants streamed French Canadians flowing south to work in New England's mill towns and Mexicans and other Latin Americans heading north to settle in California and the Southwest, as well as Japanese and Chinese coming across the Pacific from Asia to ports on the West Coast (Map 19.2).

The "new" immigration resulted from a number of factors. While improved economic conditions in western Europe helped decrease the flow of immigration from northern and western Europe, economic depression in southern Italy, the religious persecution of Jews in eastern Europe, and a general desire to avoid **conscription** into the Russian army led many people from southern and eastern Europe to move to the United States. The need of America's industries for cheap, unskilled labor during prosperous years also stimulated immigration.

Steamship companies courted immigrants— a highly profitable, self-loading cargo. Agents from the large lines traveled throughout Europe drumming up business. Colorful pamphlets and

MAP 19.2 The Impact of Immigration, to 1910

Immigration flowed in all directions—south from Canada, north from Mexico, east from Asia to Seattle and San Francisco, and west from Europe to port cities like Boston and New York.

READING THE MAP: Which states have high percentages of immigrants? Which cities attracted the most immigrants? Which cities the fewest?

CONNECTIONS: Why did most immigrants gravitate toward the cities? Why do you think the South drew such a low percentage of immigrants?

FOR MORE HELP ANALYZING THIS MAP, see the map activity for this chapter in the Online Study Guide at bedfordstmartins.com/roarkcompact.

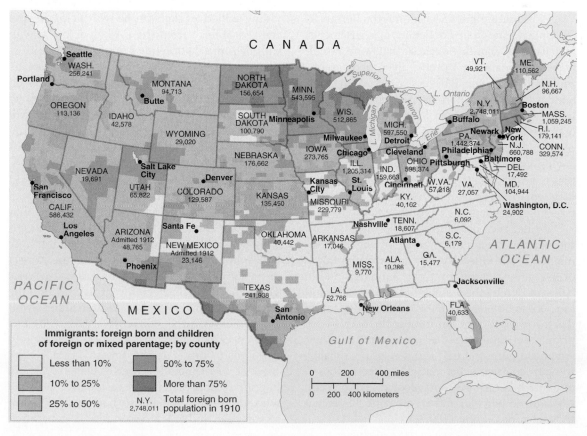

Immigrants: foreign born and children of foreign or mixed parentage; by county

- Less than 10%
- 10% to 25%
- 25% to 50%
- 50% to 75%
- More than 75%
- N.Y. 2,748,011 Total foreign born population in 1910

**Knife and Scissors
Sharpener Pushcart**
Joseph Antonucci, an Italian
immigrant, used this knife
and scissors sharpener cart on
Chicago's West Side in 1900. After a day's
work, Antonucci usually parked the cart in a fire
station or a customer's stable, then took the train home. He sometimes pushed his
cart for miles to ply his trade beyond the city limits in towns like Hammond, Indiana. For poor immigrants who could not afford rent, pushcarts provided a cheap
and portable means of livelihood. The cries of street peddlers, vendors, and scissors sharpeners like Antonucci added to the cacophony of the urban streets.
Chicago Historical Society.

Not all the newcomers came to stay. Perhaps eight million of the fourteen million European immigrants—most of them young men—worked for a year or a season and then returned to their homelands. Immigration officers called these young male immigrants, many of them Italians, "birds of passage" because they followed a regular pattern of migration to and from the United States. By 1900, almost 75 percent of the new immigrants were single young men.

Jews from eastern Europe most often came with their families and came to stay. In the 1880s, a wave of violent pogroms, or persecutions, in Russia and Poland prompted the departure of more than a million Jews in the next two decades. Most of the Jewish immigrants settled in the port cities of the East. New York City's Lower East Side soon replicated the Jewish ghettos of eastern Europe, teeming with street peddlers and pushcarts. Hester Street, at the heart of New York's Jewish section, rang with the calls of vendors hawking their wares, from pickles to feather beds.

Racism and the Cry for Immigration Restriction

Ethnic diversity and racism played a role in dividing skilled workers (those with a craft or specialized ability) from the unskilled (those who supplied muscle or tended machines). As industrialists mechanized to replace skilled workers with lower-paid, unskilled labor, they drew on immigrants from southern and eastern Europe who had come to the United States in the hope of bettering their lives. Skilled workers, usually members of older immigrant groups from northern or western Europe, criticized the newcomers. As one Irish worker complained, "There should be a law…to keep all the Italians from comin' in and takin' the bread out of the mouths of honest people."

The Irish worker's resentment of the new Italian immigrants brings into focus the impact of racism on America's immigrant laborers. Throughout the nineteenth century and into the twentieth, members of the educated elite as well as workers viewed ethnic and even religious differences as racial characteristics—referring to the Polish "race" or the Jewish "race." Each wave of newcomers was seen as being somehow inferior to the established residents. The Irish who judged the Italians so harshly had themselves been judged a lesser race a generation

posters advertised America as the land of promise. Would-be immigrants eager for information about the United States relied on letters, advertisements, and word of mouth—sources that were not always dependable or truthful. Even photographs proved deceptive: Workers dressed in their Sunday best looked more prosperous than they actually were to relatives in the old country, where only the very wealthy wore white collars or silk dresses. No wonder people left for America believing, as one Italian immigrant observed, "that if they were ever fortunate enough to reach America, they would fall into a pile of manure and get up brushing the diamonds out of their hair."

While the old immigrants had spread throughout the country, most of the new remained in the cities. By 1900, almost two-thirds of the nation's immigrant population resided in cities, drawn by the availability of jobs there and too poor to buy land in the West. Although rarely did the foreign-born outnumber the native-born population, taken together immigrants and their American-born children did constitute a majority, particularly in the nation's largest cities—Philadelphia, 55 percent; Boston, 66 percent; Chicago, 75 percent; and an amazing 80 percent in New York City by 1900.

earlier. Immigrants not only brought their own religious and racial prejudices to the United States but also absorbed the popular prejudices of American culture. **Social Darwinism**, with its strongly racist overtones, decreed that whites stood at the top of the evolutionary ladder. But who was "white"? The social construction of race is nowhere more apparent than in the testimony of an Irish dockworker who boasted that he hired only "white men" to load cargo, a category that he insisted excluded "Poles and Italians." For the new immigrants, Americanization and assimilation proved inextricably part of becoming "white."

For African Americans, the cities of the North promised not just economic opportunity but an end to segregation and persecution. **Jim Crow** laws—restrictions that segregated blacks—became common throughout the South in the decades following Reconstruction. Intimidation and lynching, excused by white Southerners as necessary to "keep the Negro in his place," terrorized blacks throughout the South (see chapter 17). "To die from the bite of frost is far more glorious than at the hands of a mob," proclaimed the *Defender*, Chicago's largest African American newspaper. In the 1890s, many blacks agreed and moved north, settling for the most part in the growing cities. New York, Philadelphia, and Chicago contained the largest black communities in the nation by 1900. Although the largest African American migration out of the South would occur during and after World War I, the great exodus was already under way.

On the West Coast, Asian immigrants, prohibited from owning land, flocked to the cities. San Francisco in 1870 housed a population estimated at 12,022, and it continued to grow until passage of the Chinese Exclusion Act in 1882 slowed immigration from China to a trickle (see chapter 18). Some Chinese managed to come to America, using a loophole that allowed relatives to join their families. But pressures to keep them out led in 1910 to the creation of an immigration station at Angel Island in San Francisco Bay. There Chinese immigrants were detained, sometimes for months, and many were deported as "undesirables."

In sheer numbers, the new immigration from Europe that began in the 1880s proved unprecedented. In 1888 alone, more than a half million Europeans landed in America, 75 percent of them arriving in New York City. The Statue of Liberty, a gift from the people of France erected in 1886, stood sentinel in the harbor. A young Jewish girl named Emma Lazarus penned the verse inscribed at Liberty's base:

> Give me your tired, your poor,
> Your huddled masses yearning to breathe free,
> The wretched refuse of your teeming shore,
> Send these, the homeless, tempest-tost to me,
> I lift my lamp beside the golden door!

The tide of immigrants to New York City soon swamped the immigration office at Castle Garden in lower Manhattan. An imposing new brick facility opened on Ellis Island in New York Harbor in 1900. Its overcrowded halls became the gateway to the United States for millions.

To many Americans, the new immigrants seemed uneducated, backward, and uncouth—impossible to assimilate. "These people are not Americans," editorialized the popular journal *Public Opinion*, "they are the very scum and offal of Europe." Terence Powderly, head of the Knights of Labor, complained that the newcomers "herded together like animals and lived like beasts."

Blue-blooded Yankees such as Senator Henry Cabot Lodge of Massachusetts formed an unlikely alliance with organized labor to press for immigration restriction. Lodge and his old-stock followers championed a literacy test, knowing that the vast majority of Italian and Slavic peasants were unable to read. In 1896, Congress approved a literacy test for immigrants, but President Grover Cleveland promptly vetoed it. "It is said," the president reminded Congress, "that the quality of recent immigration is undesirable. The time is quite within recent memory when the same thing was said of immigrants, who, with their descendants, are now numbered among our best citizens." Cleveland's veto forestalled immigration restriction but did not stop the forces seeking to close the gates. They would continue to press for restriction until they achieved their goal in the 1920s (see chapter 23).

The Social Geography of the City

During the Gilded Age, cities experienced demographic and technological changes that greatly altered the social geography of the city. Cleveland, Ohio, provides a good example. In the 1870s, Cleveland was a small city, in both population and area. Oil magnate John D. Rockefeller could, and often did, walk from his large brick house on Euclid Avenue to his office downtown. On his way he passed the small homes of his clerks and other middle-class families. Behind these homes ran miles of alleys crowded with the dwellings of Cleveland's working class. Farther out, on the shores of Lake Erie, close to the factories and foundries, clustered the shanties of the city's poorest laborers.

Within two decades, the Cleveland that Rockefeller knew no longer existed. The coming of mass transit transformed the walking city. In its place emerged a central business district surrounded by concentric rings of residences organized by ethnicity and income. First the horsecar in the 1870s and then the electric streetcar in the 1880s made it possible for those who could afford the five-cent fare to work downtown and flee after work to the "cool green rim" of the city with its single-family homes, lawns, gardens, and trees. By the early twentieth century, more than half of Cleveland's residents rode streetcars to work. Unable to afford even a few cents for streetcar fare, the city's poor crowded into the inner city or lived "back of the yards" near the factories where they worked. This pattern of development repeated throughout the country as urban congestion and suburban sprawl forever altered the social geography of the city.

Poverty, crowding, dirt, and disease constituted the daily reality of New York City's immigrant poor—a situation documented in photojournalist Jacob Riis's best-selling book, *How the Other Half Lives* (1890). Riis's audience shivered at his revelations about the "other half." But middle-class Americans worried equally about the excesses of the wealthy. They feared the class antagonism fueled by the growing chasm between rich and poor so visible in the nation's cities. Many people shared Riis's view that "the real danger to society comes not only from the tenements, but from the ill-spent wealth which reared them."

The excesses of the Gilded Age's newly minted millionaires were nowhere more visible than in the lifestyle of the Vanderbilts. "Commodore" Cornelius Vanderbilt, the uncouth ferryman who built the New York Central Railroad, died in 1877, leaving his son $90 million. William Vanderbilt doubled that sum, and his two sons proceeded to spend it on Fifth Avenue mansions and "cottages" in Newport, Rhode Island, which, with their marble and gold leaf, sought to rival the palaces of Europe. In 1883, Alva Vanderbilt (Mrs. William K. Vanderbilt I) launched herself in New York society by throwing a costume party so lavish that not even old New York society, which turned up its nose at the *nouveau riche* (new rich), could resist an invitation. The *New York World* speculated that Mrs. Vanderbilt's party cost over a quarter of a million dollars, more than $4 million in today's dollars.

Such ostentatious displays of wealth became especially alarming when they were coupled with disdain for the well-being of ordinary people. When a reporter in 1882 asked William Vanderbilt whether he considered the public good when running his railroads, he shot back, "The public be damned." The fear that America

How the Wealthy Lived

Shown here is Alice Vanderbilt as she appeared at the Vanderbilt costume ball in 1883, dressed as the "Spirit of Electricity." Her gown, by the French design house of Worth, was no doubt inspired by Thomas Edison's triumphant lighting of lower Manhattan six months earlier. Made of silk satin and trimmed with velvet, gilt metallic bullion, and diamonds, the gown epitomized what political economist Thorstein Veblen would call conspicuous consumption.

Collection of the New-York Historical Society.

FOR MORE HELP ANALYZING THIS IMAGE, see the visual activity for this chapter in the Online Study Guide at bedfordstmartins.com/roarkcompact.

had become a plutocracy—a society ruled by the rich—gained credence from the fact that the wealthiest 1 percent of the population owned more than half the real and personal property in the country (a century later, the top 1 percent controlled less than a quarter). As the new century dawned, reformers would form a **progressive movement** to address the problems of urban industrialism and the substandard living and working conditions it produced.

> **REVIEW** Why did American cities experience explosive growth in the late nineteenth century?

At Work in the City

Throughout the nineteenth century, America's urban industrial workers toiled in a variety of settings. Many skilled workers and **artisans** still earned a living in small workshops. But with the rise of corporate capitalism, large factories, mills, and mines increasingly dotted the landscape. Sweatshops and outwork, the contracting of piecework to be performed in the home, provided work experiences different from those of factory operatives (machine tenders) and industrial workers. Pick-and-shovel labor, whether on the railroads or in the building trades, constituted yet another kind of work. Managers and other white-collar employees as well as women "typewriters" and salesclerks formed a new white-collar segment of America's workforce. The best way to get a sense of the diversity of workers and workplaces is to look at the industrial nation at work.

America's Diverse Workers

Common laborers formed the backbone of the American labor force. They built the railroads and subways, tunneled under New York's East River to anchor the Brooklyn Bridge, and helped to lay the foundation of industrial America. These "human machines" stood at the bottom of the country's economic ladder and generally came from the most recent immigrant groups. Initially the Irish wielded the picks and shovels that built American cities, but by the turn of the century, as the Irish bettered their lot, Slavs and Italians took up their tools.

At the opposite end of labor's hierarchy stood skilled craftsmen like iron puddler James J.

Davis, a Welsh immigrant. Using brains along with brawn, puddlers took the melted pig iron in the heat of the furnace and, with long poles, formed the cooling metal into 200-pound balls, relying on eye and intuition to make each ball uniform. Possessing such a skill meant earning good wages, up to $7 a day, when there was work. But often no work could be found. Much industry and manufacturing in the nineteenth century remained seasonal; few workers could count on year-round pay. In addition, two major depressions only twenty years apart, beginning in 1873 and 1893, spelled unemployment and hardship for all workers. In an era before unemployment insurance, workers' compensation, or old-age pensions, even the best worker could not guarantee security for his family. "The fear of ending in the poor-house is one of the terrors that dog a man through life," Davis confessed.

New England's textile mills provide a classic example of the effects of mechanized factory labor in the nineteenth century. Mary, a weaver at the mills in Fall River, Massachusetts, told her story to the *Independent* magazine. She went to work in the 1880s at the age of twelve. By then, mechanization of the looms had reduced the job of the weaver to watching for breaks in the thread. "At first the noise is fierce, and you have to breathe the cotton all the time, but you get used to it," Mary told her interviewer. "When the bobbin flies out and a girl gets hurt, you can't hear her shout—not if she just screams, you can't. She's got to wait, 'till you see her....Lots of us is deaf."

The majority of factory operatives in the textile mills were young unmarried women like Mary. They worked from six in the morning to six at night, six days a week, and they took home about $1 a day. The seasonal nature of the work also drove wages down. "Like as not your mill will 'shut down' three months," and "some weeks you only get two or three days' work," Mary recounted. After twenty years of working in the mill, Mary's family had not been able to scrape together enough money to buy a house: "We saved some, but something always comes."

Mechanization transformed the garment industry as well. With the introduction of the foot-pedaled sewing machine in the 1850s and the use of mechanical cloth-cutting knives in the 1870s, independent tailors were replaced with workers hired by contractors to sew pieces of cloth into clothing. Working in sweatshops, small rooms hired for the season or even the contractor's own tenement, women and children formed an important segment of garment workers. Discriminated against in the marketplace, where they earned less than men, women generally worked only eight to ten years, until they married.

Sadie Frowne, a sixteen-year-old Polish Jew, went to work in a Brooklyn sweatshop in the 1890s. Frowne sewed for eleven hours a day in a room twenty feet long and fourteen feet wide containing fourteen machines. "The machines go like mad all day, because the faster you work the more money you get," she recalled. Paid by the piece, she earned about $4.50 a week and, by rigid economy, tried to save $2. Young and single, Frowne typified the woman wage earner in

Sweatshop Worker

Sweatshop workers endured crowded and often dangerous conditions. Most were young women, like the one shown here sewing pants in New York City. Young working girls earned little money but prided themselves on their independence. Notice the young woman's stylish hairdo, white shirtwaist, and necklace—indications that she did not turn over all the money in her pay envelope to her father, as was sometimes the case. Because most white women quit working when they married, spending money on finery to attract a husband could turn out to be a good investment in the long run.

George Eastman House.

the late nineteenth century. In 1890, the average working woman was twenty-two and had been working since the age of fifteen, laboring twelve hours a day, six days a week, and earning less than $6 a week.

The Family Economy: Women and Children

In 1890, the average male worker earned $500 a year, about $8,000 in today's dollars. Many working-class families, whether native-born or immigrant, lived in poverty or near poverty, their economic survival dependent on the contributions of all family members, regardless of sex or age. One statistician estimated that in 1900 as many as 64 percent of working-class families relied on income other than the husband's wages to make ends meet. The paid and unpaid work of women and children proved essential for family survival and economic advancement.

In the cities, boys as young as six years old plied their trades as bootblacks and newsboys. Often working under an adult contractor, these children earned as little as fifty cents a day. Many of them were homeless—orphaned or cast off by their families. "We wuz six, and we ain't got no father," a child of twelve told reporter Jacob Riis. "Some of us had to go." In New York City the Children's Aid Society tried to better the situation of these, the city's youngest workers, by establishing lodging houses. To encourage "self sufficiency and self respect," the boys were expected to pay their way—six cents for a bed, six for a breakfast of bread and coffee, and six for a supper of pork and beans. Lodged in dormitories that sometimes held more than a hundred berths, the boys had to be on good behavior. A sign at the entrance admonished, "Boys who swear and chew tobacco cannot sleep here."

Child labor increased decade by decade; the percentage of children under fifteen engaged in paid labor did not drop until after World War I. The 1900 census estimated that 1,750,178 children aged ten to fifteen were employed, an increase of more than a million since 1870. Children in this age range constituted over 18 percent of the industrial labor force. Many younger children not counted by the census worked in mills, in factories, and on the streets.

In the late nineteenth century, the number of women workers also rose sharply, with their most common occupation changing slowly from domestic service to factory work and then to office work. In 1870, the census listed 1.5 million women working for wages in nonagricultural occupations. By 1890, more than 3.7 million women earned wages. Women's working patterns varied considerably according to race and ethnicity. White married women, even among the working class, rarely labored outside the home. In 1890, only 3 percent were employed for wages. Nevertheless, married women found ways to contribute to the family economy. Families often took in boarders or lodgers, which meant extra housework. In many Italian families, piecework such as making artificial flowers allowed married women to contribute to the family economy without leaving their homes. Black women, married and unmarried, worked for wages in much greater numbers than white women. The 1890 census showed that 25 percent of African American married women worked for wages, often as domestics in the houses of white families.

Managers and White Collars

In the late nineteenth century, business expansion and consolidation led to a managerial revolution, creating a new class of managers. As skilled workers saw their crafts replaced by mechanization, some moved into management positions. "The middle class is becoming a salaried class," a writer for the *Independent* magazine observed, "and is rapidly losing the economic and moral independence of former days." As large business organizations consolidated, corporate development separated management from ownership, and the job of directing the firm became the province of salaried executives and managers, the majority of whom were white men drawn from the 8 percent of Americans who held high school diplomas. In 1880, the middle managers at the Chicago, Burlington, and Quincy Railroad earned between $1,500 and $4,000 a year; senior executives, generally recruited from the college-educated elite, took home $4,000 or more; and the company's general manager made $15,000 a year, approximately thirty times what the average worker earned.

Until late in the century, when engineering schools began to supply recruits, many skilled workers moved from the shop floor to positions of considerable responsibility. The career of Captain William "Billy" Jones provides a glimpse of a skilled ironworker turned manager. Jones,

the son of a Welsh immigrant, grew up in the heat of the blast furnaces, where he started working as an apprentice at the age of ten. When Andrew Carnegie opened his steelworks on the outskirts of Pittsburgh in 1872, he hired Jones as his plant superintendent. By all accounts, Jones was the best steel man in the industry. "Good wages and good workmen" was his motto. Carnegie constantly tried to force down workers' pay, but Jones succeeded in shortening the shift from twelve to eight hours a day by convincing Carnegie that shorter hours would reduce absenteeism and accidents. Jones himself demanded and received a "hell of a big salary." Carnegie paid him $25,000—the same salary as the president of the United States—a stupendous sum in the 1870s, which made Jones perhaps the most successful manager to move up from the shop floor.

"Typewriters" and Salesclerks

In the decades after the Civil War, as businesses became larger and more far-flung, the need for more elaborate and exact records as well as the greater volume of correspondence led to the hiring of more office workers. Mechanization transformed business as it had industry and manufacturing. The adding machine, the cash register, and the typewriter came into general use in the 1880s. Employers seeking literate workers soon turned to nimble-fingered women. Educated men had many other career choices, but for middle-class white women, secretarial work constituted one of very few areas where they could put their literacy to use for wages.

Sylvie Thygeson was typical of the young women who went to work as secretaries. Thygeson grew up in an Illinois prairie town. When her father died in 1884, she went to work as a country schoolteacher at the age of sixteen, immediately after graduating high school. Quickly learning that teaching school did not pay a living wage, she mastered typing and stenography and found work as a secretary to help support her family. According to her account, she made "a fabulous sum of money." Nevertheless, she gave up her job after a few years when she met and married her husband.

Called "typewriters," women workers like Thygeson were seen as indistinguishable from the machines they operated. Far from viewing their jobs as dehumanizing, women typewriters took pride in their work and relished the economic independence it afforded them. By the 1890s, secretarial work was the overwhelming choice of white, native-born women, who constituted over 90 percent of the female clerical force. Not only considered more genteel than factory work or domestic labor, office work also meant more money for shorter hours. Boston's clerical workers made more than $6 a week in 1883, compared with less than $5 for women working in manufacturing.

As a new **consumer culture** came to dominate American urban life in the late nineteenth century, department stores offered another employment opportunity for women in the cities. Boasting ornate facades, large plate-glass display windows, and marble and brass fixtures, stores like Macy's in New York, Wanamaker's in Philadelphia, and Marshall Field in Chicago stood as monuments to the material promise of the era. Within these palaces of consumption, cash girls, stock clerks, and wrappers earned as little as $3 a week while, at the top of the scale, buyers like Belle Cushman of the fancy goods department at Macy's earned $25 a week, an unusually high salary for a woman in the 1870s.

In all stores, saleswomen were subject to harsh and arbitrary discipline. Sitting was forbidden, and conversation with other clerks led to instant dismissal. Yet salesclerks counted themselves a cut above factory workers. Their work was neither dirty nor dangerous, and even when they earned less than factory workers, they felt a sense of superiority.

> **REVIEW**   How did business expansion and consolidation change workers' occupations in the late nineteenth century?

Workers Organize

By the late nineteenth century, industrial workers were losing ground in the workplace. In the fierce competition to lower prices and cut costs, industrialists like Andrew Carnegie invested heavily in new machinery that enabled managers to replace skilled workers with unskilled labor. The erosion of skill and the redefinition of labor as mere "machine tending" left the worker with a growing sense of individual helplessness that served as a spur to collective action. In the 1870s and 1880s labor unions grew, and the

Knights of Labor and the American Federation of Labor attracted many workers. The inflammatory rhetoric of some radical groups caused many Americans to equate the labor movement with the specter of violence and **anarchism**. In 1877, in the midst of a depression that left many workers destitute, labor flexed its muscle in the Great Railroad Strike and showed the power of collective action.

The Great Railroad Strike of 1877

Economic depression following the panic of 1873 threw as many as 3 million people out of work. Those who were lucky enough to keep their jobs watched as pay cuts eroded their wages until they could no longer feed their families. In the summer of 1877, the Baltimore and Ohio (B&O) Railroad announced a 10 percent wage reduction and at the same time declared a 10 percent dividend to its stockholders. Angry brakemen in West Virginia, whose wages had already fallen from $70 to $30 a month, walked out on strike. One B&O worker described the hardship that drove him to take such desperate action: "We eat our hard bread and tainted meat two days old on the sooty cars up the road, and when we come home, find our children gnawing bones and our wives complaining that they cannot even buy hominy and molasses for food."

The West Virginia brakemen's strike touched off the Great Railroad Strike of 1877, a nationwide uprising that spread rapidly to Pittsburgh and Chicago, St. Louis, and San Francisco (Map 19.3). Within a few days, nearly 100,000 railroad workers walked off the job. The spark of rebellion soon fired an estimated 500,000 laborers to join the train workers. In Reading, Pennsylvania, militiamen refused to fire on the strikers, saying, "We may be militiamen, but we are workmen first." Rail traffic ground to a halt; the nation lay paralyzed.

Violence erupted as the strike spread. In Pittsburgh, strikers clashed with militia brought in from Philadelphia, who arrogantly boasted they would clean up "the workingmen's town." Opening fire on the crowd, the militia killed twenty people. Angry workers retaliated by reducing an area two miles long beside the tracks to smoldering rubble. Before the day ended, twenty more workers had been shot, and the railroad had sustained property damage totaling $2 million.

Destruction from the Great Railroad Strike of 1877
Pictures of the devastation caused in Pittsburgh during the strike shocked many Americans. When militiamen fired on striking workers, killing more than 20 strikers, the mob retaliated by destroying a two-mile area along the track, reducing it to the smoldering rubble shown here. Property damage totaled $2 million. Curious pedestrians came out to view the destruction.
Carnegie Library of Pittsburgh.

Within eight days, the governors of nine states, acting at the prompting of the railroad owners and managers, defined the strike as an "insurrection" and called for federal troops. President Rutherford B. Hayes, after hesitating briefly, called out the army. By the time the troops arrived, the violence had run its course. Federal troops did not shoot a single striker in 1877. But they struck a blow against labor by acting as strikebreakers—opening rail traffic, protecting nonstriking "scab" train crews, and maintaining peace along the line.

Although the Great Railroad Strike was spontaneous and unorganized, it frightened the authorities and upper classes like nothing before in U.S. labor history, fueling their hostility to labor organization. They quickly tried to blame the tiny, radical Workingman's Party for the strike and predicted a bloody uprising. "Any hour the mob chooses it can destroy any city in the country—that is the simple truth," wrote future secretary of state John Hay to his wealthy father-in-law.

In three weeks the strike was over. "The strikes have been put down by force," President Hayes noted in his diary on August 5. "But now for the real remedy. Can't something be done by education of the strikers, by judicious control of the capitalists, by wise general policy to end or diminish the evil? The railroad strikers, as a

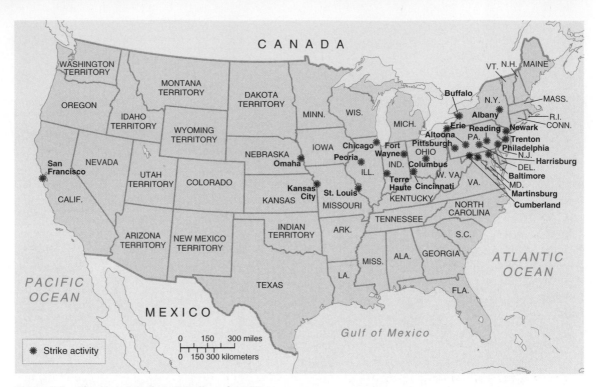

MAP 19.3   The Great Railroad Strike of 1877
Starting in West Virginia and Pennsylvania, the strike spread as far north as Buffalo and as far west as San Francisco, bringing rail traffic to a standstill.

rule, are good men, sober, intelligent, and industrious." While Hayes acknowledged the workers' grievances, most businessmen and industrialists did not and fought the idea of labor unions, arguing that workers and employers entered into contracts as individuals and denying the right of unions to bargain collectively for their workers. For their part, workers quickly recognized they held little power individually and flocked to join unions. As labor leader Samuel Gompers noted, the strike served as an alarm bell to labor "that sounded a ringing message of hope to us all."

The Knights of Labor and the American Federation of Labor

The Knights of Labor, the first mass organization of America's working class, proved the chief beneficiary of labor's newfound consciousness. The Noble and Holy Order of the Knights of Labor had been founded in 1869 by Uriah Stephens, a Philadelphia garment cutter.

A secret but peaceable society of workers, the Knights envisioned a "universal brotherhood" of all workers, from common laborers to master craftsmen. Although the Knights played no active role in the 1877 strike, membership swelled as a result of the growing interest in unionism that accompanied the strike. In 1878, the organization dropped the trappings of secrecy and launched an ambitious campaign to organize workers regardless of skill, sex, race, or nationality.

Under the direction of Grand Master Workman Terence V. Powderly, the Knights of Labor became the dominant force in labor during the 1880s. The Knights advocated a kind of workers' **democracy** that embraced reforms including public ownership of the railroads, an income tax, equal pay for women workers, and the abolition of child labor. The Knights sought to remove class distinctions and encouraged local assemblies to welcome all comers, employees and employers alike. "I hate the word 'class' and would drive it from the English language if I could," Powderly stated. Only the "parasitic" members of society—gamblers, stockbrokers, lawyers, bankers, and liquor dealers—were denied membership.

The Knights of Labor was not without rivals. Other trade unionists disliked the broad reform goals of the Knights and sought to focus on workplace issues. Samuel Gompers, a cigar maker born in London of Dutch Jewish ancestry, promoted what he called "pure and simple" unionism. Gompers founded the Organized Trades and Labor Unions in 1881 and reorganized it in 1886 into the American Federation of Labor (AFL), which coordinated the activities of craft unions throughout the United States. His plan was simple: Organize skilled workers like machinists and locomotive engineers—those with the most bargaining power—and use strikes to gain immediate objectives such as higher pay and better working conditions. Gompers at first drew few converts. The AFL had only 138,000 members in 1886, compared with 730,000 for the Knights of Labor. But events soon brought down the Knights and enabled Gompers to take control of the labor movement.

Haymarket and the Specter of Labor Radicalism

While the AFL and the Knights of Labor competed for members, radical socialists and anarchists, many of whom were immigrants steeped in the tradition of European **socialism**, believed that reform was futile and called instead for social revolution. Both groups, sensitive to criticism that they preferred revolution in theory to improvements here and now, rallied around the popular issue of the eight-hour day.

Since the 1840s, labor had sought to end the twelve-hour workday, which was standard in industry and manufacturing. By the mid-1880s, it seemed clear to many workers that labor shared too little in the new prosperity of the decade, and pressure mounted for the eight-hour day. The radicals seized on the popular issue and launched major rallies in cities across the nation. Supporters of the movement set May 1, 1886, as the date for a nationwide general strike in support of the eight-hour day.

All factions of the nascent labor movement came together in Chicago on May Day for what was billed as the largest demonstration to date. A group of radicals led by anarchist Albert Parsons, a *Mayflower* descendant, and August

Spies, a German immigrant, spearheaded the eight-hour movement in Chicago. Chicago's Knights of Labor rallied to the cause even though Powderly and the union's national leadership, worried by the increasing activism of the rank and file, refused to champion the movement for shorter hours. Samuel Gompers was on hand, too, to lead the city's trade unionists, although he privately urged the AFL assemblies not to participate in the general strike.

Gompers's skilled workers were labor's elite. Many still worked in small shops where negotiations between workers and employers took place in an environment tempered by personal relationships. Well dressed in their suits and starched shirts, the AFL's skilled workers stood in sharp contrast to the dispossessed workers out on strike across town at Chicago's huge McCormick reaper works. There strikers watched helplessly as the company brought in strikebreakers to take their jobs and marched the "scabs" to work under the protection of the Chicago police and security guards supplied by the Pinkerton Detective Agency. Cyrus McCormick Jr., son of the inventor of the mechanical reaper, viewed labor organization as a threat to his power as well as to his profits; he was determined to smash the union.

During the May Day rally, 45,000 workers paraded peacefully down Michigan Avenue in support of the eight-hour day, many singing the song that had become the movement's anthem:

> We mean to make things over;
>   we're tired of toil for naught
> But bare enough to live on: never
>   an hour for thought.
> We want to feel the sunshine; we
>   want to smell the flowers;
> We're sure that God has willed it,
>   and we mean to have eight hours.
> Eight hours for work, eight hours for rest,
>   eight hours for what we will!

Trouble came two days later, when strikers attacked scabs outside the McCormick works and police opened fire, killing or wounding six men. Angry radicals rushed out a circular urging workers to "arm yourselves and appear in full force" at a rally in Haymarket Square.

On the evening of May 4, the turnout at Haymarket was disappointing. No more than two or three thousand gathered in the drizzle to hear Spies, Parsons, and the other anarchist speakers. Mayor Carter Harrison, known as a friend of labor, mingled conspicuously in the crowd, pronounced the meeting peaceable, and went home to bed. A short time later, police captain John "Blackjack" Bonfield, who had made his reputation cracking skulls, marched his men into the crowd, by now fewer than three hundred people, and demanded that it disperse. Suddenly, someone threw a bomb into the police ranks. After a moment of stunned silence, the police drew their revolvers. "Fire and kill all you can," shouted a police lieutenant. When the melee ended, seven policemen and an unknown number of others lay dead. An additional sixty policemen and thirty or forty civilians suffered injuries.

News of the "Haymarket riot" provoked a nationwide convulsion of fear, followed by blind rage directed at anarchists, labor unions, strikers, immigrants, and the working class in general. Eight men went on trial in Chicago, although witnesses testified that none of them had thrown the bomb. From the start it was clear that the men were on trial for their ideas, not their actions. "Convict these men," thundered the state's attorney Julius S. Grinnell, "make examples of them, hang them, and you save our institutions." Although the state could not link any of the defendants to the Haymarket bomb, the jury nevertheless found them all guilty. Four were executed, one committed suicide, and three received prison sentences. On the gallows, August Spies spoke for the Haymarket martyrs: "The time will come when our silence will be more powerful than the voices you throttle today."

In 1893, Governor John Peter Altgeld, after a thorough investigation, pardoned the three remaining Haymarket anarchists. He denounced the trial as a shameless travesty of justice and concluded that Captain Bonfield was "the man really responsible for the death of the police officers." The governor's action brought on a storm of protest and cost him his political career.

The bomb blast at Haymarket had lasting repercussions. To commemorate the death of the Haymarket martyrs, labor made May 1 an annual international celebration of the worker. But the Haymarket bomb, in the eyes of one observer, proved "a godsend to all enemies of the labor movement." It effectively scotched the eight-hour-day movement and dealt a fatal blow to the Knights of Labor.

With the labor movement everywhere under attack, many skilled workers turned to the American Federation of Labor. Gompers's narrow economic strategy made sense at the time and enabled one segment of the workforce—the skilled—to organize effectively and achieve tangible gains. But the nation's unskilled workers remained untouched by the AFL's brand of trade unionism. The vast majority of America's workers would have to wait another forty years before a mainstream labor union, the Congress of Industrial Organizations (CIO), moved to organize the unskilled (see chapter 24).

"The Chicago Riot"

Inflammatory pamphlets like this one published in the wake of the Haymarket bombing presented a one-sided view of the incident and stirred public passion. In this charged atmosphere the anarchist speakers were tried and convicted for the bombing even though witnesses testified that none of them had thrown the bomb. The identity of the bomb thrower remains uncertain.

Chicago Historical Society.

THE CHICAGO RIOT

A RECORD OF THE
Terrible Scenes of May 4, 1886.

Chicago and New York:
BELFORD, CLARKE & CO.,
1886.

> **REVIEW**   Why did the fortunes of the Knights of Labor rise in the late 1870s and decline in the 1890s?

At Home and at Play

The growth of urban industrialism not only dramatically altered the workplace but also transformed home and family life and gave rise to new forms of commercialized leisure. Industrialization redefined the very concepts of work and home. Increasingly, men went out to work for wages, while most white married women stayed home, either working in the home without pay—cleaning, cooking, and rearing children—or supervising paid domestic servants who did the housework.

Domesticity and "Domestics"

The separation of the workplace and the home that marked the shift to industrial society redefined the home as a "haven in the heartless world," presided over by a wife and mother who made the household her **separate sphere**. The growing separation of workplace and home led to a new ideology, one that sentimentalized the home and women's role in it. The cultural ideology that dictated woman's place in the home has been called the **cult of domesticity**, a phrase used to prescribe an ideal of middle-class, white womanhood that dominated the period from 1820 to the end of the nineteenth century (see chapter 11).

In the decades after the Civil War, the typical middle-class dwelling became more embellished architecturally and its interiors more cluttered. Ownership of such a home, indeed of any home, marked the gulf between the working poor and the middle class. Homeowners constituted only 36 percent of the U.S. housing population in 1900, compared with 69 percent today.

The cult of domesticity and the elaboration of the middle-class home led to a major change in patterns of hiring household help. The live-in servant, or domestic, became a fixture in the North, replacing the hired girl of the previous century. (The South continued to rely on black female labor, first slave and later free.) In American cities by 1870, from 15 to 30 percent of all households included live-in domestic servants, more than 90 percent of them women. By the mid-nineteenth century, native-born women increasingly took up other work and left domestic service to immigrants. In the East the maid was so often Irish that "Bridget" became a generic term for female domestics.

Servants by all accounts resented the long hours and lack of privacy. "She is liable to be rung up at all hours," one study reported. "Her very meals are not secure from interruption, and even her sleep is not sacred." Furthermore, going into service carried a social stigma. As one young woman observed, "If a girl goes into the kitchen she is sneered at and called 'the Bridget,' but if she goes behind the counter she is escorted by gentlemen." Domestic service became the occupation of last resort, a "hard and lonely life" in the words of one servant girl.

For women of the white middle class, domestics were a boon, freeing them from household drudgery and giving them more time to spend with their children or to pursue club work or reform. Thus, while domestic service supported the cult of domesticity, it created for those women who could afford it opportunities that expanded their horizons outside the home.

Cheap Amusements

Growing class divisions manifested themselves in patterns of leisure as well as in work and home life. The poor and working class took their leisure, when they had any, not in the crowded tenements that housed their families, but increasingly in the cities' new dance halls, music houses, ballparks, and amusement arcades, which by the 1890s formed a familiar part of the urban landscape.

The growing anonymity of urban industrial society posed a challenge to traditional rituals of courtship. Adolescent working girls no longer met prospective husbands only through their families. Fleeing crowded tenements, the young sought each other's company in dance halls and other commercial retreats. Scorning proper introductions, working-class youth "picked up" partners at the dance halls, where drinking was part of the evening's entertainment. Young working women, who rarely could afford more than trolley fare when they went out, counted on being "treated" by men, a transaction that often implied sexual payback. Young women's need to negotiate sexual encounters if they wished to participate in commercial amusements blurred the line between respectability and promiscuity and made the dance halls a favorite target for reformers who feared they lured girls into prostitution.

For men, baseball became a national pastime in the 1870s—then, as now, one force in

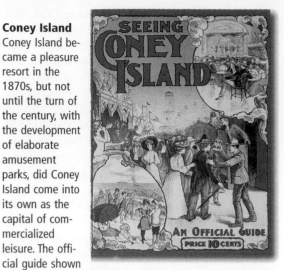

Coney Island
Coney Island became a pleasure resort in the 1870s, but not until the turn of the century, with the development of elaborate amusement parks, did Coney Island come into its own as the capital of commercialized leisure. The official guide shown here outlined highlights for visitors, including the beach, the vaudeville hall, and the midway with its rides and its risqué harem dancers.
Brooklyn Historical Society.

City Growth and City Government

Private enterprise, not planners, built the cities of the United States. Boosters, builders, businessmen, and politicians all had a hand in creating the modern metropolis. With a few notable exceptions, such as Washington, D.C., and Savannah, Georgia, there was no such thing as a comprehensive city plan. Cities simply mushroomed, formed by the dictates of private enterprise and the exigencies of local politics. With the rise of the city came the need for public facilities, transportation, and services that would tax the imaginations of America's architects and engineers and set the scene for the rough-and-tumble of big-city government, politics, and politicians.

urban life capable of uniting a city across class lines. Cincinnati mounted the first entirely paid team, the Red Stockings, in 1869. Soon professional teams proliferated in cities across the nation, and Mark Twain hailed baseball as "the very symbol, the outward and visible expression, of the drive and push and rush and struggle of the raging, tearing, booming nineteenth century."

The increasing commercialization of entertainment in the late nineteenth century can best be seen at Coney Island. A two-mile stretch of sand close to Manhattan by trolley or steamship, Coney Island in the 1870s and 1880s attracted visitors to its beaches, dance pavilions, and penny arcades— all connected by its famous boardwalk. In the 1890s, Coney Island was transformed into the site of some of the largest and most elaborate amusement parks in the country. Promoter George Tilyou built Steeplechase Park in 1897, advertising "10 hours of fun for 10 cents." With its mechanical thrills and funhouse laughs, the amusement park encouraged behavior that one schoolteacher aptly described as "everyone with the brakes off." By 1900 as many as a half million New Yorkers flocked to Coney Island on any given weekend, making the New York amusement park the unofficial capital of a new mass culture.

REVIEW   How did urban industrialism shape the world of leisure?

Building Cities of Stone and Steel

Skyscrapers and mighty bridges dominated the imagination and the urban landscape. Less imposing but no less significant were the paved streets, the parks and public libraries, and the subways and sewers. In the late nineteenth century, Americans rushed to embrace new technology of all kinds, making their cities the most modern in the world.

Structural steel made enormous advances in building possible. A decade after the completion of the Brooklyn Bridge, engineers used the new technology to construct the Williamsburg Bridge three miles to the north. More prosaic and utilitarian than its neighbor, the new bridge was never as acclaimed, but it was longer by four feet and completed in half the time. It became the model for future building as the age of steel supplanted the age of stone and iron.

Skyscrapers forever changed the cityscape. Competition for space in Manhattan pushed the city up into the air even before the use of steel. The invention of Elisha Otis's elevator (called a "safety hoister") in the 1850s led to the construction of cast-iron buildings with elevators that carried passengers as high as ten stories. But until the advent of structural steel in the 1880s, no building in Manhattan topped the spire of Wall Street's Trinity Church.

Chicago, not New York, gave birth to the modern skyscraper. Rising from the ashes of the Great Fire of 1871, which destroyed three square miles and left 18,000 homeless, Chicago offered a

Chicago Skyscraper Going Up
With the advent of structural steel, skyscrapers like this
one in progress in Chicago in 1894 became a feature of
the American urban landscape. Once the frame was up,
the walls could simply "hang" on the outside of the
building because they no longer had to support the
structure.
Culver Pictures.

generation of skilled architects and engineers the
chance to experiment with new technologies.
Commercial architecture became an art form at
the hands of a skilled group of architects who together constituted the "Chicago school." Men of
genius such as Louis Sullivan and John Wellborn
Root gave Chicago some of the world's finest
commercial buildings. Employing the dictum
"Form follows function," they built startlingly
modern structures.

Alongside the skyscrapers rose new residential apartments for the rich and middle class.
The "French flat"—apartments with the latest
plumbing and electricity—gained popularity in
the 1880s as affluent city dwellers overcame

their distaste for multifamily housing (which
carried the stigma of the tenement) and gave in
to "flat fever." Fashionable new apartments
boasted modern luxuries such as telephones,
central heating, and elevators. The convenience
of apartment living appealed particularly to
women. "Housekeeping isn't fun," cried one
New York woman. "Give us flats!" In 1883 alone,
more than 1,000 new apartments went up in
Chicago.

The flush toilets, bathtubs, and lavatories
of the new apartments would not have been possible without major improvements in city sewers
and water mains. In the absence of proper
sewage disposal, contaminated water wreaked
havoc in big cities. In 1882, an outbreak of typhoid fever caused by the city's polluted water
killed over 20,000 in Chicago. To end this
scourge, enlightened city engineers created and
expanded municipal sewage systems and devised ingenious ways to bring clean water to the
urban population. By the 1890s, the residents of American cities demanded and
received, at the twist of a faucet, water
for their bathtubs, toilets, and even their
lawn sprinklers. Those who could afford it
enjoyed a standard of living that was the envy of
civilization.

Across the United States municipal governments undertook public works on a scale never
before seen. They paved streets, built sewers and
water mains, replaced gas lamps with electric
lights, ran trolley tracks on the old horsecar lines,
and dug underground to build subways, tearing
down the unsightly elevated tracks that had
clogged the city streets. In San Francisco,
Andrew Smith Hallidie mastered the city's hills,
building a system of cable cars in 1873. Boston
completed the nation's first subway system
in 1897, and New York and Philadelphia soon
followed.

Cities became more beautiful with the creation of urban public parks to complement the
new buildings that quickly filled city lots. Much
of the credit for America's greatest parks goes to
one man—landscape architect Frederick Law
Olmsted. The indefatigable Olmsted designed
parks in Atlanta, Boston, Brooklyn, Hartford,
Detroit, Chicago, and Louisville, as well as the
grounds for the U.S. Capitol. But he is best remembered for the creation of New York City's
Central Park. Completed in 1873, it became the
first landscaped public park in the United States.
Olmsted and his partner, Calvert Vaux, directed
the planting of more than five million trees,

shrubs, and vines to transform the eight hundred acres between 59th and 110th Streets into an oasis for urban dwellers. We want a place, he wrote, where people "may stroll for an hour, seeing, hearing, and feeling nothing of the bustle and jar of the streets."

American cities did not overlook the mind in their efforts at improvement. They created a comprehensive free public school system that educated everyone from the children of the middle class to the sons and daughters of immigrant workers. The exploding urban population strained the system and led to crowded and inadequate facilities. In 1899, more than 544,000 pupils attended school in New York's five boroughs. Schools in Boston, New York, Chicago, and San Francisco as well as other cities and towns provided the only classrooms in the world where students could attend secondary school free of charge.

In addition to schools, the cities built libraries to educate their citizens. In the late nineteenth century, American cities created the most extensive free public library system in the world. In 1895, the Boston Public Library opened its bronze doors under the inscription "Free to All." Designed in the style of a Renaissance palazzo, with more than 700,000 books on the shelves ready to be checked out, the library earned the description "a palace of the people."

Despite the Boston Public Library's legend "Free to All," the poor did not share equally in the advantages of city life. The parks, the libraries, and even the subways and sewers benefited some city dwellers more than others. Few library cards were held by Boston's laborers, who worked six days a week and found the library closed on Sunday. And in the 1890s, there was nothing central about New York's Central Park. It was a four-mile walk from the tenements of Hester Street to the park's entrance at 59th Street and Fifth Avenue. Cities spent more money on plumbing improvements for affluent apartment dwellers than on public baths and lodging houses for the down-and-out. Even the uniform subway fare, which enabled Boston and New York riders to travel anywhere in the system for five cents, worked to the advantage of the middle-class commuter and not the downtown poor. Then, as now, the comfortable majority, not the indigent minority, reaped a disproportionate share of the benefits in the nation's big cities.

Any story of the American city, it seems, must be a tale of two cities—or, given the cities' great diversity, a tale of many cities within each metropolis. At the turn of the twentieth century a central paradox emerged: The enduring monuments of America's cities—the bridges, skyscrapers, parks, and libraries—stood as the undeniable achievements of the same system of municipal government that reformers dismissed as boss ridden, criminal, and corrupt.

City Government and the "Bosses"

The physical growth of the cities required the expansion of public services and the creation of entirely new facilities: streets, subways, elevated trains, bridges, docks, parks, sewers, and public utilities. There was work to be done and money to be made. The professional politician—the colorful big-city boss—became a phenomenon of urban growth. Though corrupt and often criminal, the boss saw to the building of the city and provided needed social services for the new residents. Yet not even the big-city boss could be said to rule the unruly city. The governing of America's cities resembled more a tug-of-war than boss rule.

The most notorious of all the city bosses was William Marcy Tweed of New York. At midcentury, Boss Tweed's Democratic Party "machine" held sway. A machine was really no more than a political party organized at the grassroots level. Its purpose was to win elections and reward its followers with jobs on the city's payroll. New York's citywide Democratic machine, Tammany Hall, commanded an army of party functionaries. At the bottom were district captains. In return for votes, they provided services for their constituents, everything from a scuttle of coal in the winter to housing for an evicted family. At the top were powerful ward bosses who distributed lucrative franchises for subways and streetcars. They formed a shadow government, more powerful than the city's elected officials. The only elected office Tweed ever held was alderman. But as chairman of the Tammany general committee, he wielded more power than the mayor. Through the use of bribery and graft, he kept the Democratic Party together and ran the city. "As long as I count the votes," he shamelessly boasted, "what are you going to do about it?"

The cost of Tweed's rule was staggering. The construction of New York City's courthouse, budgeted at $250,000, ended up costing the taxpayers $14 million. The inflated sum represented bribery, kickbacks, and the greasing of many palms. The excesses of the Tweed ring soon led to a clamor for reform and cries of "Throw the rascals out." Cartoonist Thomas Nast pilloried Tweed in the pages of *Harper's Weekly*. His cartoons, easily understood even by those who could not read, did the boss more harm than hundreds of outraged editorials. Eventually Tweed was tried and convicted and died in jail.

New York was not the only city to experience bossism and corruption. The British visitor James Bryce concluded in 1888, "There is no denying that the government of cities is the one conspicuous failure of the United States." More than 80 percent of the nation's thirty largest cities experienced some form of boss rule in the decades around the turn of the twentieth century.

Urban reformers and proponents of good government (derisively called "goo goos" by their rivals) challenged machine rule and sometimes succeeded in electing reform mayors. But the reformers rarely managed to stay in office for long. Their detractors called them "mornin' glories," observing that they "looked lovely in the mornin' and withered up in a short time." A few reform mayors managed to achieve success and longevity. Hazen S. Pingree of Detroit exemplified the successful reform mayor. A businessman who went into politics in the 1890s, Pingree, like most good-government candidates, promised to root out dishonesty and inefficiency. But when the depression of 1893 struck, Pingree emerged as a champion of the

working class and the poor. He hired the unemployed to build schools, parks, and public baths. By providing jobs and needed services, he built a powerful political organization based on working-class support. Detroit's voters kept him in the mayor's office for four terms and then helped elect him governor twice.

While most good-government candidates harped on the Sunday closing of saloons and attacked vice and crime, Pingree demurred. "The most dangerous enemies to good government are not the saloons, the dives, the dens of iniquity and the criminals," but "the temptations which are offered to city officials when franchises are sought by wealthy corporations, or contracts are to be let for public works." Through the skillful orchestration of rewards, an astute political operator could exert powerful leverage and line up support for his party from a broad range of constituents, from the urban poor to wealthy industrialists. In 1902, when journalist Lincoln Steffens began "The Shame of the Cities," a series of articles exposing city corruption, he found that business leaders who fastidiously refused to mingle socially with the bosses nevertheless struck deals with them. "He is a self-righteous fraud, this big businessman," Steffens concluded. "I found him buying boodlers [bribers] in St. Louis, defending grafters in Minneapolis, originating corruption in Pittsburgh, sharing with bosses in Philadelphia, deploring reform in Chicago, and beating good government with corruption funds in New York."

The complexity of big-city government, apparent in the many levels of corruption that Steffens uncovered, pointed to one conclusion: For all the color and flamboyance of the big-city boss, he was simply one of many actors in the drama of municipal government. The successful boss was not an autocratic ruler but a power broker. Old-stock aristocrats, new professionals, saloonkeepers, pushcart peddlers, and politicians all fought for their interests in the hurly-burly of city government. They didn't much like each other, and

Tammany Bank
This cast-iron bank, a campaign novelty, is named after the New York City Democratic machine. It tells its political reform message graphically: When you put a penny into the politician's hand, he puts it in his pocket. Tammany Hall dominated city politics for more than a century, dispensing contracts and franchises worth millions of dollars. Some of those dollars invariably found their way into the pockets of Tammany politicians.
Collection of Janice L. and David J. Frent.

The World's Columbian Exposition and Nineteenth-Century World's Fairs

Dedicated as much to commerce as to culture, the 1893 World's Columbian Exposition in Chicago and the other great world's fairs of the nineteenth century represented a unique phenomenon of industrial capitalism and a testament to the expanding global market economy. The Chicago fair, named to celebrate the four hundredth anniversary of Columbus's arrival in the New World, offered a cornucopia of international exhibits testifying to growing international influences ranging from cultural to technological exchange. Such a celebration of global commerce and influence seemed an appropriate way to honor Columbus, whose voyage in 1492 initiated one of the world's most significant international exchanges.

Beginning with London's Great Exhibition in 1851 with its famous Crystal Palace and continuing through the age of Western commercial and cultural expansion in the late nineteenth century, international exhibitions proliferated and flourished. By the time Chicago secured the right to host its celebration, world's fairs had evolved into monumental extravaganzas that showcased the products of the host country and city along with impressive international displays. Great cities vied to play host to world's fairs, as much to promote commercial growth as to demonstrate their cultural refinement. Each successive fair sought to outdo its predecessor. Chicago's fair followed upon the great success of the 1889 Universal Exposition in Paris commissioned to celebrate the hundredth anniversary of the French Revolution. The Paris Exposition featured as its crowning glory the 900-foot steel tower constructed by Alexander Gustav Eiffel. What could Chicago, a prairie upstart, do to top that?

The answer was the creation of the White City with its monumental architecture, landscaped grounds, and first Ferris wheel. Itself a tribute to the international style of architecture, the White City celebrated the classicism of the French Beaux Arts school, which borrowed heavily from the massive geometric styling and elaborate detailing of Greek and Renaissance architecture. With the exception of Louis Sullivan's Transportation Building, nothing hinted of the clean and simple lines of indigenous American design soon to be celebrated with the advent of Frank Lloyd Wright.

Beneath its Renaissance facade, the White City acted as an enormous emporium dedicated to the unabashed materialism of the Gilded Age. Participants from more than 100 states, territories, countries, and colonies, as well as thousands of concessionaires—from small businesses to the largest corporations—mounted exhibits to demonstrate their wares and compete for international attention. Fairgoers could view virtually every kind of manufactured product in the world inside the imposing Manufactures and Liberal Arts Building: Swiss glassware and clocks, Japanese lacquerware and bamboo ornaments, British woolen products, and French perfumes and linens. The German pavilion included fine wooden furniture as well as tapestries, porcelain, and jewelry belonging to the ruling family. As suited an industrial age, manufactured products and heavy machinery received privileged status, drawing the largest crowds. Displays introduced visitors to the latest mechanical and technological innovations, many the result of international influences. For five cents, fairgoers could put two hard rubber tubes into their ears and listen for the first time to a Gramophone playing the popular tune "The Cat Came Back." The Gramophone, which signaled the beginning of the recorded music industry, was itself the work of a German immigrant, Emile Berliner (although Thomas Edison later claimed credit for a similar invention, calling it the phonograph).

Such international influences were evident throughout the Columbian Exposition. At the

"All Nations Are Welcome"
Uncle Sam, flanked by the city of Chicago, welcomes representatives carrying the flags of many nations to the World's Columbian Exposition in 1893. In the background are the fairgrounds on the shores of Lake Michigan. Over one hundred nations participated in the fair by sending exhibits and mounting pavilions to showcase their cultures and products.
Chicago Historical Society.

Tiffany pavilion, one of the most popular venues at the fair, visitors oohed and aahed over the display of lamps, ornamental metalwork, and fine jewelry that Louis Comfort Tiffany credited to the influence of Japanese art forms. Juxtaposed with Tiffany's finery stood a display of firearms in the Colt gallery. Colt had been an international company since 1851 when it opened a factory in England. The company's revolvers enjoyed an international reputation—the best known firearms not only in America but in Canada, Mexico, and many European countries. And Colt's new automatic weapon, the machine gun, would soon play a major role on the world stage in both the Boxer uprising in China and the Spanish-American War.

All manner of foodstuffs—teas from India, Irish whiskey, and pastries and other confectionery from Germany and France—tempted fairgoers. American food products like Shredded Wheat, Aunt Jemima syrup, and Juicy Fruit gum debuted at the fair, where they competed for ribbons. Winners like Pabst "Blue Ribbon" Beer used the award in advertisements. And the fair introduced two new foods—carbonated soda and the hamburger—destined to become America's best-known contributions to international cuisine.

The Columbian Exposition also served as a testimony to American technological achievement and progress. By displaying technology in action, the White City tamed it and made it accessible to American and world consumers. The fair helped develop positive reactions to new technology, particularly electric light and power. With 90,000 electric lights, 5,100 arc lamps, electric fountains, an electric elevated railroad, and electric launches plying the lagoons, the White City provided a glowing advertisement for electricity. Indeed, an entire building was devoted to it. In the Electricity Building fairgoers visited the Bell Telephone Company exhibit, marveled at General Electric's huge dynamo (electric generator), and gazed into the future at the all-electric home and model demonstration kitchen.

Consumer culture received its first major expression and celebration at the Columbian Exposition. Not only did this world's fair anticipate the mass marketing, packaging, and advertising of the twentieth century, but the vast array of products on display cultivated the urge to consume. Thousands of concessionaires with products for sale sent a message that tied enjoyment inextricably to spending money and purchasing goods, both domestic and foreign. The Columbian Exposition set a pattern for the twentieth-century world's fairs that followed it, making a powerful statement about the possibilities of urban life in an industrial age and encouraging the rise of a new middle-class consumer culture. As G. Brown Goode, head of the Smithsonian Institution in 1893, observed, the Columbian Exposition was in many ways "an illustrated encyclopedia of civilization."

they sometimes fought savagely. But they learned to live with one another. Compromise and accommodation—not boss rule—best characterized big-city government by the turn of the twentieth century, although the cities' reputation for corruption left an indelible mark on the consciousness of the American public.

White City or City of Sin?

Americans in the late nineteenth century, like Americans today, were of two minds about the city. They liked to boast of its skyscrapers and bridges, its culture and sophistication, and they prided themselves on its bigness and bustle. At the same time they feared it as the city of sin, the home of immigrant slums, the center of vice and crime. Nowhere did the divided view of the American city take form more graphically than in Chicago in 1893.

In that year Chicago hosted the Columbian Exposition, the grandest world's fair in the nation's history. The fairground, called the White City and built on the shores of Lake Michigan to honor the four hundredth anniversary of Columbus's first voyage to America, offered a lesson in what Americans on the eve of the twentieth century imagined a city might be. Only five miles down the shore from Chicago, the White City seemed light-years away. Its very name celebrated a harmony and pristine beauty unknown in Chicago, with its stockyards, slums, and bustling terminals. Frederick Law Olmsted and architect Daniel Burnham supervised the transformation of a swampy wasteland into a paradise of lagoons, fountains, wooded islands, gardens, and imposing buildings.

"Sell the cookstove and come," the novelist Hamlin Garland wrote to his parents on the farm. And come they did, in spite of the panic and depression that broke out only weeks after the fair opened in May 1893. In six months fairgoers purchased more than 27 million tickets, turning a profit of nearly a half million dollars for promoters. Visitors from home and abroad strolled the elaborate grounds, visited the exhibits—everything from a model of the Brooklyn Bridge carved in soap to the latest goods and inventions. (See "Beyond America's Borders," page 498.) Half

carnival, half culture, the great fair offered something for everyone. On the Midway Plaisance, crowds thrilled to the massive wheel built by Mr. Ferris and watched agog as Little Egypt danced the hootchy-kootchy.

In October the fair closed its doors in the midst of the worst depression the country had yet seen. During the winter of 1894, Chicago's unemployed and homeless took over the grounds, vandalized the buildings, and frightened the city's comfortable citizens out of their wits. When reporters asked Daniel Burnham what should be done with the moldering remains of the White City, he responded, "It should be torched." And it was. In July 1894, in a clash between federal troops and striking railway workers, incendiaries set fire and leveled the fairgrounds.

In the end, the White City remained what it had always been, a dreamscape. Buildings that looked like marble were actually constructed of staff, a plaster of paris substance that began to crumble even before fire destroyed the fairgrounds. The White City was a fantasy never destined to last. Perhaps it was not so strange, after all, that the legacy of the White City could be found on Coney Island, where two new amusement parks, Luna and Dreamland, sought to combine, albeit in a more tawdry form, the beauty of the White City and the thrill of the Midway Plaisance. More enduring than the White City itself was what it represented—the emergent industrial might of the United States with its inventions, manufactured goods, and growing consumer culture.

> **REVIEW**   How did municipal governments respond to the challenges of urban expansion?

Conclusion: Who Built the Cities?

As much as the great industrialists and financiers, as much as eminent engineers like John and Washington Roebling, common workers, most of them immigrants, built the nation's cities. The unprecedented growth of urban, industrial America resulted from the labor of millions of men, women, and children who toiled in workshops and factories, in sweatshops and mines, on railroads and construction sites across America.

America's cities in the late nineteenth century teemed with life. Immigrants and blue bloods, poor laborers and millionaires, middle-class managers and corporate moguls, secretaries, salesgirls, sweatshop laborers, and society matrons lived in the cities and contributed to their growth. Townhouses, tenements, and new apartment buildings jostled for space with skyscrapers and great department stores, while parks, ball fields, amusement arcades, and public libraries provided the city masses with recreation and entertainment.

Municipal governments, straining to build the new cities, experienced the rough-and-tumble of machine politics as bosses and their constituents looked to profit from city growth. Reformers deplored the graft and corruption that accompanied the rise of the cities. But they were rarely able to oust the party bosses for long because they failed to understand the services the political machines provided for their largely immigrant and poor constituents as well as the ties between the politicians and wealthy businessmen who sought to benefit from franchises and contracts.

For America's workers, urban industrialism along with the rise of big business and corporate consolidation drastically changed the workplace. Industrialists replaced skilled workers with new machinery that could be operated by cheaper, unskilled labor. And during hard times employers did not hesitate to cut workers' already meager wages. As the Great Railroad Strike of 1877 demonstrated, when labor united, it could bring the nation to attention. Organization held out the best hope for the workers—first the Knights of Labor and later the American Federation of Labor—won converts among the nation's working class.

The rise of urban industrialism challenged the American promise, which for decades had been dominated by Jeffersonian agrarian ideals. Could such a promise exist in the changing world of cities, tenements, immigrants, and huge corporations? In the great depression that came in the 1890s, mounting anger and frustration would lead workers and farmers to join forces and create a grassroots movement to fight for change under the banner of a new People's Party.

Suggestions for Further Reading

Sven Beckert, *The Monied Metropolis: New York City and the Consolidation of the American Bourgeoisie, 1850–1896* (2001). An analysis of New York's ascendance as the nation's leading center of manufacturing and trade as the result of the determined maneuvering of the city's economic elites.

William Cronin, *Nature's Metropolis: Chicago and the Great West* (1991). A history tying nineteenth-century Chicago to the West and to global patterns of urban development.

Allan Dawley, *Struggles for Justice: Social Responsibility and the Liberal State* (1991). A historical synthesis that provides a lively and comprehensive look at the forces that shaped modern America.

David Montgomery, *The Fall of the House of Labor: The Workplace, the State, and American Labor Activism, 1865–1925* (1987). A masterful history of the American workplace and how workers mobilized to fight for their interests.

Roy Rosenzweig, *Eight Hours for What We Will: Workers and Leisure in an Industrial City, 1870–1920* (1983). A case study of American working-class recreation in Worcester, Massachusetts.

▶ FOR MORE BOOKS ABOUT TOPICS IN THIS CHAPTER, see the Online Bibliography at bedfordstmartins.com/roarkcompact.

▶ FOR ADDITIONAL FIRSTHAND ACCOUNTS OF THIS PERIOD, see Chapter 19 in Michael Johnson, ed., *Reading the American Past,* Third Edition.

▶ FOR WEB SITES AND DOCUMENTS RELATED TO TOPICS AND PLACES IN THIS CHAPTER, see "HistoryLinks," "DocLinks," and "PlaceLinks" at bedfordstmartins.com/roarkcompact.

REVIEWING THE CHAPTER

Follow these steps to review and strengthen your understanding of the chapter.

STEP 1: *Study the* **Key Terms** *and* **Timeline** *to identify the significance of each item listed.*

STEP 2: *Answer the* **Review Questions**, *drawing on key terms and dates to support your answers.*

STEP 3: *Drawing on the Key Terms, Timeline, and Review Questions, answer the broader* **Making Connections** *questions.*

KEY TERMS

Who

John Roebling (p. 477)
Henry Cabot Lodge (p. 483)
Grover Cleveland (p. 483)
Jacob Riis (p. 484)
the Vanderbilts (p. 484)
Rutherford B. Hayes (p. 489)
Terence V. Powderly (p. 490)
Samuel Gompers (p. 491)
Albert Parsons (p. 491)
August Spies (p. 491)
John "Blackjack" Bonfield (p. 492)
John Peter Altgeld (p. 492)
Louis Sullivan (p. 495)

Frederick Law Olmsted (p. 495)
William Marcy "Boss" Tweed (p. 496)
Thomas Nast (p. 497)
Hazen S. Pingree (p. 497)
Lincoln Steffens (p. 497)

What

global migration (p. 479)
industrial core (p. 479)
rural periphery (p. 480)
Lower East Side (p. 482)
Angel Island (p. 483)
Ellis Island (p. 483)
Great Railroad Strike of 1877 (p. 488)

Workingman's Party (p. 489)
Knights of Labor (p. 490)
American Federation of Labor (AFL) (p. 491)
May Day rally (p. 491)
Haymarket bombing (p. 492)
Coney Island (p. 494)
Chicago's Great Fire of 1871 (p. 494)
Central Park (p. 495)
Tammany Hall (p. 496)
bossism (p. 496)
World's Columbian Exposition (p. 500)
White City (p. 500)

TIMELINE

1869 • Knights of Labor founded.
• Cincinnati mounts first paid baseball team, the Red Stockings.

1871 • Boss Tweed's rule in New York ends.
• Chicago's Great Fire.

1873 • Panic on Wall Street touches off depression.
• San Francisco's cable car system opens.

1877 • Great Railroad Strike.

1878 • Knights of Labor organizes workers.

1880s • Immigration from southern and eastern Europe rises.

1882 • Chinese Exclusion Act.

1883 • Brooklyn Bridge opens.

REVIEW QUESTIONS

1. Why did American cities experience explosive growth in the late nineteenth century? (pp. 478–85)

2. How did business expansion and consolidation change workers' occupations in the late nineteenth century? (pp. 485–88)

3. Why did the fortunes of the Knights of Labor rise in the late 1870s and decline in the 1890s? (pp. 488–92)

4. How did urban industrialism shape the world of leisure? (pp. 493–94)

5. How did municipal governments respond to the challenges of urban expansion? (pp. 494–500)

MAKING CONNECTIONS

1. Americans expressed both wonder and concern at the nation's mushrooming cities. Why did cities provoke such divergent responses? In your answer, discuss the dramatic demographic, environmental, and political developments associated with urbanization.

2. Why did patterns of immigration to the United States in the late nineteenth century change? How did Americans respond to new immigrant populations? In your answer, consider how industrial capitalism, nationally and globally, contributed to these developments.

3. How did urban industrialization affect Americans' lives outside of work? Describe the impact late-nineteenth-century economic developments had on home life and leisure. In your answer, consider how class, race, gender, and ethnicity contributed to diverse urban experiences.

4. When workers began to embrace organization in the late 1870s, what did they hope to accomplish? Were they successful? Why or why not? In your answer, discuss both general conditions and specific events that shaped these developments.

▶ FOR PRACTICE QUIZZES, A CUSTOMIZED STUDY PLAN, AND OTHER STUDY TOOLS, see the Online Study Guide at bedfordstmartins.com/roarkcompact.

1886 • American Federation of Labor (AFL) founded.
• Haymarket bombing.

1890s • African American migration from the South begins.
1890 • Jacob Riis publishes *How the Other Half Lives*.

1893 • Columbian Exposition.
• Panic on Wall Street touches off major economic depression.

1895 • Boston Public Library opens.

1896 • President Grover Cleveland vetoes immigrant literacy test.

1897 • Steeplechase amusement park opens on Coney Island.
• Nation's first subway system opens in Boston.

1900 • Ellis Island opens.

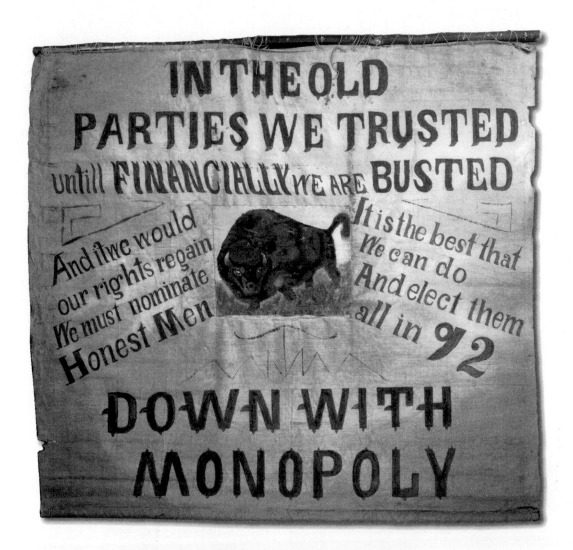

BUFFALO BANNER FROM THE 1892 POPULIST CONVENTION
This flag graphically declares the frustration with the Democratic and Republican parties that led angry Americans, particularly farmers, to gather in St. Louis in 1892 to create a new People's Party. Featuring the buffalo (American bison) as a symbol, the flag urged the election of "honest men" and proclaimed as its motto "Down with Monopoly." The buffalo was perhaps a poor choice as a mascot, for just as the great herds on the western plains had been decimated during the 1880s, the People's (or Populist) Party would not survive the '90s.

Nebraska State Historical Society.

20

Dissent, Depression, and War

1890–1900

S T. LOUIS IN FEBRUARY 1892 played host to one of the most striking political gatherings of the century. Thousands of farmers, laborers, and common people flocked to Missouri to attend a meeting, in the words of one reporter, "different from any other political meeting ever witnessed in St. Louis." The cigar-smoking politicians who generally worked the convention circuit were nowhere to be found. In their place "mostly gray-haired, sunburned and roughly clothed men" assembled under a banner that proclaimed, "We do not ask for sympathy or pity. We ask for justice."

Exposition Music Hall presented a colorful spectacle. "The banners of the different states rose above the delegates throughout the hall, fluttering like the flags over an army encamped," wrote one reporter. The fiery orator Ignatius Donnelly attacked the money kings of Wall Street. Mary Elizabeth Lease, a veteran campaigner from Kansas known for exhorting farmers to "raise less corn and more hell," added her powerful voice to the cause. Terence V. Powderly, head of the Knights of Labor, called on workers to join hands with farmers against the "nonproducing classes." And Frances Willard of the Woman's Christian Temperance Union argued against liquor and for woman **suffrage**. Between speeches the crowd sang labor songs like "Hurrah for the Toiler" and "All Hail the Power of Laboring Men."

In the course of the next few days, delegates hammered out a series of demands, breathtaking in their scope. They tackled the tough questions of the day—the regulation of business, the need for banking and currency reform, the right of labor to organize and bargain collectively, and the role of the federal government in regulating business, curbing **monopoly**, and guaranteeing **democracy**. The convention ended its work amid a chorus of cheers. According to one eyewitness,

> Hats, paper, handkerchiefs, etc., were thrown into the air; wraps, umbrellas and parasols waved; cheer after cheer thundered and reverberated through the vast hall reaching the outside of the building where thousands who had been waiting the outcome joined in the applause till for blocks in every direction the exultation made the din indescribable.

What was all the shouting about? People were building a new political party, officially named the People's Party. Dissatisfied with the Democrats and Republicans, a broad coalition of groups came together in St. Louis to fight for change. They determined to reconvene in Omaha in July to nominate candidates for the upcoming presidential election.

People's Party 1892 Convention Ribbon
The People's Party standard-bearer, General James B. Weaver, and his running mate are pictured on a ribbon promising "homes for the toilers" and "equal rights to all, special privileges to none." Populist issues are clearly proclaimed—"money, land, and transportation." The Populists' hope that these economic issues would replace sectional loyalties is evident in the symbolism of the blue Union and gray Confederate hands shaking.
Collection of Janice L. and David J. Frent.

The St. Louis gathering marked a milestone in one of the most turbulent decades in U.S. history. Unrest, agitation, agrarian revolt, labor strikes, a severe financial panic and depression, and a war of expansion shook the 1890s. While the two major political parties continued to do business as usual, Americans flocked to organizations like the Farmers' Alliance,

the American Federation of Labor, and the Woman's Christian Temperance Union, and they worked together to create the political alliance that gave rise to the People's (or **Populist**) Party. In a decade of unrest and uncertainty, the People's Party challenged **laissez-faire** economics by insisting that the federal government play a more active role to ensure greater economic equity in industrial America. This challenge to the status quo culminated in 1896 in one of the most hotly contested presidential elections in the nation's history. At the close of the tumultuous decade, the Spanish-American War helped to bring the country together as Americans rallied to support the troops. But disagreement over American **imperialism** and expansion raised questions about the nation's role on the world stage as the United States stood poised to enter the twentieth century.

Nebraska Farm Family
A Nebraska farm family poses in front of their sod house. Their shriveled corn testifies to the drought conditions they faced. Drought and falling crop prices devastated farmers in the 1880s. Midwestern farmers lost their land to bank foreclosure when they could not make mortgage payments. By 1894 nearly half the farms in Kansas had been foreclosed. Many farmers retreated from the plains in covered wagons carrying the slogan "In God we Trusted, In Kansas we Busted." Growing discontent among farmers in the Midwest and South led to the growth of the Farmers' Alliance in the 1880s and the People's Party in the 1890s.
Nebraska State Historical Society.

The Farmers' Revolt

Farmers counted themselves among the most disaffected Americans, and hard times in the 1880s created a groundswell of agrarian revolt. Farmers in all regions of the country saw themselves as victims of policies such as the **gold standard** and the protective tariff that worked to the advantage of big business. Across the United States, angry farmers raised a chorus of protest and in the process created new political alliances.

The Farmers' Alliance

Farmers faced hard times by the 1890s. Farm prices had fallen decade after decade. Wheat that sold for a dollar a bushel in 1870 dropped to sixty cents in the 1890s. Cotton plummeted from fifteen cents to five cents a pound. Corn started at forty-five cents and fell to thirty cents a bushel. At the same time, consumer prices soared, leaving farmers' income less than their expenditures. By 1894, in Kansas alone almost half the farms had fallen into the hands of the banks because poor farmers could not afford to pay their mortgages.

In the West, farmers rankled under a system that allowed railroads to charge them exorbitant freight rates while granting rebates to large ship-

The First Farmers' Alliance Flag
In 1878 a "Grand State Farmers' Alliance" formed in Texas as a self-help organization. Growing out of a meeting in Lampasas County a year earlier, the group was part of a spontaneous Farmers' Alliance movement that spread rapidly during the 1880s. By 1900 the Alliance boasted over 3 million members in the South alone. This flag commemorates the organization's founding and spells out what the Alliance stood for—"free trade," "The most good for the most people," and "Wisdom, Justice, & Moderation." The last claim many would view skeptically, seeing the Alliance not as a moderate group but as a force for sweeping change.
Torreyson Library, University of Central Arkansas.

pers (see chapter 17). Also, the railroads' policy of charging higher rates for short hauls meant that large grain elevator companies could ship their wheat from Chicago to New York for less money than it cost a Dakota farmer to send his crop to nearby Minneapolis. In the South, lack of currency and credit drove farmers to the stopgap credit system of the crop lien: In order to pay for seed and supplies, farmers pledged their crops to local creditors (furnishing merchants). At the heart of the problem stood a banking system dominated by eastern commercial banks committed to the gold standard, a railroad rate system capricious and unfair, and rampant speculation that drove up the price of land.

Farm protest was not new. In the 1870s, farmers supported the Grange and the Greenback Labor Party. And as the farmers' situation grew more desperate, the 1880s saw farmers organize into regional alliances. The Farmers' Alliance movement began when a group of farmers gathered at a Lampasas County farm in Texas and banded together to fight "landsharks and horse thieves." During the 1880s the movement spread rapidly. In **frontier** farmhouses in Texas, in log cabins in backwoods Arkansas, in the rural

parishes of Louisiana, separate groups of farmers formed similar alliances for self-help.

As the movement grew, farmers' groups consolidated into two regional alliances: The Northwestern Farmers' Alliance was active in Kansas, Nebraska, and other midwestern Granger states. The more radical Southern Farmers' Alliance, which got its start in Texas, soon spread to Georgia, Louisiana, and Arkansas. By 1890, the Southern Alliance counted more than three million members.

Determined to reach black farmers as well as whites, the Southern Alliance worked with the Colored Farmers' Alliance, an African American group founded in Texas in the 1880s. By 1891, the Southern Alliance claimed a membership of 1.2 million. Although the Colored Farmers' Alliance did not always agree with the Southern Alliance, blacks and whites attempted to make common cause. As Georgia's Tom Watson, a Southern Alliance stalwart, pointed out, "The colored tenant is in the same boat as the white tenant,…and…the accident of color can make no difference in the interests of farmers, croppers, and laborers."

At the heart of the Alliance movement stood a series of farmers' cooperatives. By "bulking" their cotton—that is, selling it together—farmers could negotiate a better price. And by setting up trade stores and exchanges, they sought to escape the grasp of the merchant/creditor. Through the cooperatives, the Farmers' Alliance promised to change the way farmers lived. "We are going to get out of debt and be free and independent people once more," exulted one Georgia farmer. But the Alliance failed in its attempt to replace the southern furnishing merchant with cooperative stores. Opposition by merchants, bankers, wholesalers, and manufacturers made it impossible for the cooperatives to get credit. Farmers soon realized that the cooperatives stood little chance of working unless fundamental changes were made in the money and credit system of the United States.

As the cooperative movement died, the Farmers' Alliance moved toward direct political action. Texas farmers drafted a set of demands in 1886 and pressured political candidates to endorse them. In 1890 the Southern Alliance called for railroad regulation, laws against land speculation, and currency and credit reform. Confounded by the failure of the Democrats and Republicans to break with commercial interests and support the farmer, Alliance leaders moved, often reluctantly, toward the formation of a third party.

The Populist Movement

In the earliest days of the Alliance movement, C. W. Macune, a leader in the Southern Alliance, had insisted, "The Alliance is a strictly white man's nonpolitical, secret business association." But by 1892, it was none of those things. Although some white southern leaders, like Macune, made it clear that they would never threaten the unity of the white vote in the South by leaving the Democratic Party, advocates of a third party carried the day at the convention of laborers, farmers, and common folk in St. Louis in 1892. There, the Farmers' Alliance gave birth to the People's Party and launched the Populist movement.

The Populists mounted a critique of industrial society and a call for action. Convinced that the money and banking systems worked to the advantage of the wealthy few, they demanded economic democracy. To help farmers get the credit they needed at reasonable rates, southern farmers hit on the ingenious idea of a subtreasury—a plan that would allow farmers to store nonperishable crops in government storehouses until market prices rose. At the same time, borrowing against their crops, farmers would receive commodity credit from the federal government to enable them to buy needed supplies and seed for the coming year. In the South the subtreasury promised to eliminate the crop lien system once and for all. Although the idea would be enacted piecemeal in **progressive** and **New Deal** legislation in the twentieth century, **conservatives** in the 1890s dismissed it as farfetched and communistic.

For the western farmer, the Populists promised land reform, championing a plan that would reclaim excessive lands granted to railroads or sold to foreign investors. The Populists' boldest proposal called for government ownership of the railroads and telegraph system to put an end to discriminatory rates. With the powerful railroads dominating politics and effectively nullifying the Interstate Commerce Act of 1887, Populists did not shrink from advocating what their opponents called state **socialism**.

Currency was the third major focus of the Populist movement. Farmers in all sections rallied to the cry for cheaper currency, endorsing platform planks calling for **free silver** and greenbacks—attempts to increase the nation's tight money supply and thus make credit easier to obtain. Because they shared common cause with labor against corporate interests, Populists supported the eight-hour workday and an end to contract labor. To empower the common people, the Populist platform called for the direct election of senators and electoral reforms including the secret ballot and the right to initiate legislation, to recall elected officials, and to submit issues to the people by means of a referendum. More than just a response to hard times, Populism presented an alternative vision of American economic democracy. (See "Documenting the American Promise," page 510.)

> **REVIEW**   Why did American farmers organize alliances in the late nineteenth century?

The Labor Wars

While farmers united to fight for change, industrial laborers fought their own battles in a series of bloody strikes so fiercely waged on both sides that historians have called them the "labor wars." Coal miners struck to fight the use of convict labor in the mines of eastern Tennessee. Miners in Coeur d'Alene, Idaho, battled the bosses and founded the militant Western Federation of Miners (WFM). Railroad switchmen went on strike in Buffalo, New York, and a general strike closed down the port of New Orleans. Industrial workers felt increasingly threatened and in the 1890s made their stand. At issue was the right of labor to organize and speak through unions to bargain collectively and fight for better working conditions, higher wages, shorter hours, and greater worker control in the face of increased mechanization.

Three major conflicts of the period, the lockout of steelworkers in Homestead, Pennsylvania, in 1892, the miners' strike in Cripple Creek, Colorado, in 1894, and the Pullman strike in Illinois that same year raised fundamental questions about the rights of labor and the sanctity of private property.

The Homestead Lockout

In 1892, steelworkers in Pennsylvania squared off against Andrew Carnegie in a decisive struggle over the right to organize in the Homestead steel mills. At first glance it seemed ironic that Carnegie became the adversary in the workers' fight for the right to unionize. Andrew Carnegie was unusual among industrialists as a self-styled friend of labor. In 1886 he had written, "The right of the workingmen to combine and to form trades unions is no less sacred than the right of the manufacturer to enter into associations and conferences with his fellows." Yet as much as he cherished his **liberal** beliefs, Carnegie cherished his profits more. By the 1890s, Carnegie had beat out his competitors, and the only thing standing in the way of his control of the industry was the Amalgamated Association of Iron and Steel Workers, one of the largest and richest of the craft unions that made up the American Federation of Labor (AFL).

In 1892, when the Amalgamated attempted to renew its contract at Carnegie's Homestead mill, its leaders were told that since "the vast majority of our employees are Non union, the Firm has decided that the minority must give place to the majority." While it was true that only 800 skilled workers belonged to the elite Amalgamated, the union had long enjoyed the support of the plant's 3,000 nonunion workers. Never before had the Amalgamated been denied a contract.

Carnegie preferred not to be directly involved in the union busting that lay on the horizon, so that spring he sailed to Scotland and left Henry Clay Frick, the toughest antilabor man in the industry, in charge of the Homestead plant. By summer, a strike looked inevitable. Frick prepared by erecting a fifteen-foot fence around the plant and topping it with barbed wire. Workers aptly dubbed it "Fort Frick." To defend his fort, Frick hired 316 mercenaries from the Pinkerton Detective Agency at the rate of $5 per day, more than double the wage of the average Homestead worker.

The Pinkerton National Detective Agency, founded before the Civil War, came into its own in the 1880s as businessmen like Frick used Pinkerton agents as a private security force. They were a motley crew, recruited from all levels of society, from urban thugs to college boys. The "Pinks" earned the hatred of workers by protecting strikebreakers and acting as company spies.

On June 28, Frick locked the workers out of the mills. Hugh O'Donnell, the young Irishman who led the union, vowed to prevent strikebreakers from entering the plant. On July 6 at four in the morning, a lookout spotted two barges moving up the Monongahela River in the fog. Frick was attempting to smuggle his Pin-

Homestead Workers Attack the Pinkertons

The nation's attention was riveted on labor strife at Homestead in the summer of 1892. *Frank Leslie's Illustrated Weekly* ran a cover story on the violence that Pinkerton agents faced from a crowd of men, women, and children armed with clubs, guns, and ax handles. The workers, who had been locked out by Henry Clay Frick, were enraged that Frick had hired the Pinkertons to bring in strikebreakers. In a standoff with workers, the Pinkertons fired into the crowd, killing three men and wounding scores. A truce was negotiated, but when the Pinkertons came ashore, the crowd could not contain its rage and viciously attacked the hated "Pinks." The illustration shows a boy with a gun in the foreground. Although the mob was armed, none of the Pinkertons were shot as they ran the gantlet. Almost all, however, were beaten. How does the cover illustration portray the crowd? Can you tell whose side the magazine was on?

The New-York Society Library.

kertons into Homestead. Workers sounded the alarm, and within minutes a crowd of more than a thousand, hastily armed with rifles, hoes, and fence posts, rushed to the riverbank to meet the enemy. When the Pinkertons attempted to come ashore, gunfire broke out, and more than a dozen Pinkertons and some thirty strikers fell,

Voices of Protest

Populists spoke with passion and fire, documenting the plight of farmers, workers, and the nation's dispossessed. Intending to educate as well as to agitate, Populist speakers larded their speeches with statistics, but the speeches were never dull. The sense of a new day dawning when the people would rule brought apocalyptic vision and religious fervor to their rhetoric.

DOCUMENT 1
Mary Elizabeth Lease,
Address to the WCTU, 1890

Populist orator Mary Elizabeth Lease, born in Pennsylvania in 1850, moved to Kansas in 1868, where she became a schoolteacher, studied law, and gained admittance to the bar. Lease spent ten years trying to make a living farming, then gave up and moved with her husband, a pharmacist, to Wichita in 1883. She lent her voice to many causes, including temperance, and spoke in support of the Knights of Labor and the Farmers' Alliance. She earned her greatest fame in the 1890s when she spoke in support of Populist causes. Her charismatic speaking style led Kansas editor William Allen White to observe, "she could recite the multiplication table and set a crowd hooting and harrahing at her will." In a speech given before the WCTU in 1890, Lease explained why women supported the Farmers' Alliance.

...You wonder, perhaps, at the zeal and enthusiasm of the Western woman in this reform movement. Let me tell you why they are interested. Turn to your school-maps and books of a quarter of a century ago, and you will find that what is now a teeming and fruitful West was then known as the Treeless Plain, the Great American Desert. To this sterile and remote region, infested by savage beasts and still more savage men, the women of the New England states, the women of the cultured East, came with husbands, sons and brothers to help them build up a home upon the broad and vernal prairies of the West. We came with roses of health on our cheek, the light of hope in our eyes, the fire of youth and hope burning in our hearts.... We endured hardships, dangers and privations; hours of loneliness, fear and sorrow; our little babes were born upon these wide, unsheltered prairies; and there, upon the sweeping prairies beneath the cedar trees our hands have planted to mark the sacred place, our little ones lie buried. We toiled in the cabin and in the field; we planted trees and orchards; we helped our loved ones to make the prairie blossom as the rose. The neat cottage took the place of the sod shanty, the log-cabin and the humble dug-out.

Yet, after all our years of toil and privation, dangers and hardships upon the Western frontier, monopoly is taking our homes from us by the infamous system of mortgage foreclosure, the most infamous that has ever disgraced the statutes of a civilized nation. It takes from us at the rate of five hundred a month the homes that represent the best years of our life, our toil, our hopes, our happiness. How did it happen? The government, at the bid of Wall Street, repudiated its contracts with the people; the circulating medium was contracted...from $54 per capita to less than $8 per capita; or,...as grand Senator [William Morris] Stewart [of Nevada] put it, "For twenty years the market value of the dollar has gone up and the market value of labor has gone down, till to-day the American laborer, in bitterness and wrath, asks which is the worst—the black slavery that has gone or the white slavery that has come?"

Do you wonder the women are joining the [Farmers'] Alliance? I wonder if there is a woman in all the broad land who can afford to stay out of the Alliance....

SOURCE: Joan M. Jensen, *With These Hands: Women Working on the Land* (New York: McGraw-Hill, 1981), 154–60.

DOCUMENT 2
Ignatius Donnelley,
Address to the People's
Party Convention, 1892

An Irish immigrant, Ignatius Donnelley practiced law in Philadelphia before moving to St. Paul in Minnesota Territory in 1856. By turns a liberal Republican and a member of the Greenback Party, Donnelley became a leader in the midwest Populist movement in the 1890s. His hellfire rhetoric earned him the spot as keynote speaker at the Populist convention in St. Louis in 1892, where he delivered a speech (excerpted below), which later became the preamble to the platform of the People's Party.

We meet in the midst of a nation brought to the verge of moral, political, and material ruin. Corruption dominates the ballot-box, the legislatures, the Congress, and touches even the ermine of the bench. The people are demoralized; most of the States have been compelled to isolate the voters at the polling-places to prevent universal intimidation or bribery. The newspapers are largely subsidized or muzzled; public opinion silenced; business prostrated; our homes covered with mortgages; labor impoverished; and the land concentrating in the hands of the capitalists. The urban workmen are denied the right of organization for self-protection; imported pauperized labor beats down their wages; a hireling standing army, unrecognized by our laws, is established to shoot them down, and they are rapidly degenerating into European conditions. The fruits of the toil of millions are boldly stolen to build up colossal fortunes for a few, unprecedented in the history of mankind; and the possessors of these, in turn, despise the republic and endanger liberty. From the same prolific womb of governmental injustice we breed the two great classes—tramps and millionaires....

SOURCE: Norman Pollack, ed., *The Populist Mind* (Indianapolis: Bobbs-Merrill, 1967), 59–60.

DOCUMENT 3
Lorenzo Lewelling,
Inaugural Address, 1893

By turns a schoolteacher, newspaper reporter, and farmer, Lorenzo Lewelling moved to Wichita, Kansas, in 1887 and *soon became active in the Farmers' Alliance and later the Populist Party. Elected governor on the People's Party ticket in 1893, he used his inaugural address to attack social Darwinism and define a new role for government as the champion of the people.*

The survival of the fittest is the government of brutes and reptiles, and such philosophy must give place to a government which recognizes human brotherhood. It is the province of government to protect the weak, but the government of to-day is resolved into a struggle of the masses with the classes for supremacy and bread, until business, home, and personal integrity are trembling in the face of possible want in the family. Feed a tiger regularly and you tame and make him harmless, but hunger makes tigers of men. If it be true that the poor have no right to the property of the rich let it also be declared that the rich have no right to the property of the poor....

The problem of to-day is how to make the State subservient to the individual, rather than to become his master.... What is the State to him who toils, if labor is denied him and his children cry for bread? What is the State to the farmer, who wearily drags himself from dawn till dark to meet the stern necessities of the mortgage on the farm? What is the State to him if it sanctions usury and other legal forms by which his home is destroyed and his innocent ones become a prey to the fiends who lurk in the shadow of civilization? What is the State to the business man, early grown gray, broken in health and spirit by successive failures; anxiety like a boding owl his constant companion by day and the disturber of his dreams by night? How is life to be sustained, how is liberty to be pursued under such adverse conditions as the State permits if it does not sanction? Is the State powerless against these conditions?

This is the generation which has come to the rescue. Those in distress who cry out from the darkness shall not be heard in vain. Conscience is in the saddle. We have leaped the bloody chasm and entered a contest for the protection of home, humanity, and the dignity of labor....

SOURCE: Norman Pollock, ed., *The Populist Mind* (Indianapolis: Bobbs-Merrill, 1967), 51–54.

QUESTIONS FOR ANALYSIS AND DEBATE

1. According to Mary Elizabeth Lease, what accounts for the high rate of foreclosures on Kansas farms?

2. When Ignatius Donnelley refers to "a hireling army, unrecognized by our laws" in his 1892 keynote speech at the St. Louis convention of the People's Party, what current event is he referencing?

3. Kansas governor Lorenzo Lewelling's inaugural address in 1893 states, "If it be true that the poor have no right to the property of the rich let it also be declared that the rich have no right to the property of the poor." What does he mean by the "property of the poor"? What does he want the state to do?

killed or wounded. The Pinkertons retreated to the barges.

For twelve hours, the workers (joined by their family members) threw everything they had at the barges. Finally, the Pinkertons hoisted a white flag and arranged with O'Donnell to surrender. With three workers dead and scores wounded, the crowd, numbering perhaps 10,000, was in no mood for conciliation. As the hated "Pinks" came up the hill, they were forced to run a gantlet of screaming, cursing men, women, and children. When a young guard dropped to his knees, weeping for mercy, a woman used her umbrella to poke out his eye. One Pinkerton had been killed in the siege on the barges. In the grim rout that followed their surrender, not one avoided injury.

The "battle of Fort Frick" ended in a dubious victory for the workers. They took control of the plant and elected a council to run the community. At first, public opinion favored their cause. Newspapers urged Frick to negotiate or submit to arbitration. A congressman castigated Carnegie for "skulking in his castle in Scotland," and the Populists condemned the use of "hireling armies."

But the action of the Homestead workers struck at the heart of the capitalist system, pitting the workers' right to their jobs against the rights of private property. Four days after the confrontation, Pennsylvania's governor, who sympathized with the workers, nonetheless yielded to pressure from Frick and ordered 8,000 National Guard troops into Homestead to protect Carnegie's mills. The strikers, thinking they had nothing to fear from the militia, welcomed the troops with a brass band. But they soon understood the reality. The troops' 95-day occupation not only protected Carnegie's property but also enabled Frick to reopen the mills using strikebreakers. "We have been deceived," one worker bitterly complained. "We have stood idly by and let the town be occupied by soldiers who come here, not as our protectors, but as the protectors of non-union men.... If we undertake to resist the seizure of our jobs, we will be shot down like dogs."

Then, in a misguided effort to ignite a general uprising, Alexander Berkman, a Russian immigrant and **anarchist**, attempted to assassinate Frick. Berkman bungled his attempt. Shot twice and stabbed with a dagger, Frick nevertheless survived. After the assassination attempt, public opinion turned against the workers. Berkman was quickly tried and sentenced to prison. Although the Amalgamated and the AFL denounced his action, the incident linked anarchism and unionism, already associated in the public mind as a result of the Haymarket bombing in 1886 (see chapter 19). Hugh O'Donnell later wrote "the bullet from Berkman's pistol, failing in its foul intent, went straight through the heart of the Homestead strike."

In the end, the workers capitulated after four and a half months. The Homestead mill reopened in November and the men returned to work, except for the union leaders, now blacklisted in every steel mill in the country. With the owners firmly in charge, the company slashed wages, reinstated the twelve-hour day, and eliminated five hundred jobs.

In the drama of events at Homestead, the significance of what occurred often remained obscured: The workers at Homestead had been taught a lesson. They would never again, in the words of the National Guard commander, "believe the works are their's [sic] quite as much as Carnegie's." Another forty-five years would pass before steelworkers, unskilled as well as skilled, successfully unionized. In the meantime, Carnegie's production tripled, even in the midst of a depression. "Ashamed to tell you profits these days," Carnegie wrote a friend in 1899. And no wonder: Carnegie's profits had grown from $4 million in 1892 to $40 million in 1900.

The Cripple Creek Miners' Strike of 1894

Less than a year after the Homestead lockout, a stock market crash on Wall Street in the spring of 1893 touched off a bitter economic depression. In the West, silver mines fell on hard times. Looking for work, many miners left for the goldfields of Cripple Creek, Colorado, where miners enjoyed relatively high wages—$3 a day. When conservative mine owners moved to lengthen the workday from eight to ten hours, the newly formed Western Federation of Miners (WFM) vowed to hold the line. The mine owners divided. Some quickly settled with the WFM. Others continued to stand against the union, provoking a strike in February 1894.

The striking miners received help from many quarters. Working miners supported the strikers, and local businesses and grocers provided credit. And, although the mine owners controlled the county sheriff and used him as their tool, many local officials, including the governor, sympathized with the miners. When the sheriff appealed to Governor Davis H. Waite to send troops to put down the strike, Waite, a Populist elected in 1892, refused to use the power of the state against the peaceful strikers. He asked the strikers to lay down their arms and demanded that the mine owners disperse their hired deputies. The miners agreed to arbitration and selected Waite as their sole arbitrator. By May, the recalcitrant mine owners capitulated, and the union won an eight-hour day.

A decade later in 1904, mine owners, this time with support from state troops, took back control of the mines, defeating the WFM and blacklisting all its members. In retrospect, the Cripple Creek miner's strike of 1894 proved the exception to the rule of state intervention on the side of private property, a pattern that had begun with the Great Railway Strike of 1877 and continued in Homestead and across the country in Pullman, Illinois.

Eugene V. Debs and the Pullman Strike

The economic depression swelled the ranks of the unemployed to 3 million by 1894, almost half of the working population. "A fearful crisis is upon us," wrote a labor publication. "Countless thousands of our fellow men are unemployed; men, women and children are suffering the pangs of hunger." Nowhere were workers more demoralized than in the model town of Pullman on the outskirts of Chicago.

In the wake of the Great Railroad Strike of 1877 George M. Pullman, the builder of Pullman railroad cars, had moved his plant and workers away from the "snares of the great city." In 1880 he purchased forty-three hundred acres nine miles south of Chicago on the shores of Lake Calumet and built a model town. He intended the company town to be orderly, clean, and with the appearance of luxury, like the Pullman Palace cars that made his fortune. The town of Pullman boasted parks, fountains, playgrounds, an auditorium, a library, a hotel, shops, and markets along with eighteen hundred units of housing. Noticeably absent was a saloon.

The housing in Pullman was clearly superior to that in neighboring areas, but workers paid a high price to live in the model town. George M. Pullman expected a 6 percent return on his investment. As a result, Pullman's rents ran 10 to 20 percent higher than housing costs in nearby communities. And a family in Pullman could never own its own home. George Pullman refused to "sell an acre under any circumstances." As long as he controlled the town absolutely, he held the powerful whip of eviction over his employees and could quickly get rid of "troublemakers." Although observers at first praised the beauty and orderliness of the town, critics by the 1890s compared Pullman's model town to a "gilded cage" for workers.

The depression brought hard times to Pullman. Workers saw their wages slashed five times between May and December 1893, with cuts totaling at least 28 percent. At the same time, Pullman refused to lower the rents in his model town, insisting that "the renting of the dwellings and the employment of workmen at Pullman are in no way tied together." When workers went to the bank to cash their paychecks, they found the rent had been taken out. One worker discovered only forty-seven cents in his pay envelope for two weeks' work. When the bank teller asked him whether he wanted to apply it to his back rent, he retorted, "If Mr. Pullman needs that forty-seven cents worse than I do, let him have it." At the same time Pullman continued to pay his stockholders an 8 percent dividend, and the company accumulated a $25 million surplus.

At the heart of the labor problems at Pullman lay not only economic inequity but also the company's attempt to control the work process, substituting piecework for day wages and undermining skilled craftsworkers. The Pullman workers rebelled. During the spring of 1894, Pullman's desperate workers, seeking help, flocked to the ranks of the American Railway Union (ARU), led by the charismatic Eugene V. Debs. The ARU, unlike the skilled craft unions of the AFL, pledged to organize all railway workers—from engineers to engine wipers.

George Pullman responded to union organization at his plant by firing three of the union's leaders the day after they led a delegation to protest wage cuts. Angry men and women walked off the job in disgust. What began as a spontaneous protest in May 1894 quickly blossomed into a strike that involved more than 90 percent of Pullman's thirty-three hundred workers. "We do not know what the outcome will be, and in fact we do not much care," one worker confessed. "We do know that we are working for less wages than will maintain ourselves and families in the necessaries of life, and on that proposition we refuse to work any longer." Pullman countered by shutting down the plant.

In June, the Pullman strikers appealed to the ARU to come to their aid. Debs hesitated to commit his fledgling union to a major strike in the midst of a depression. He pleaded with the workers to find another solution. When George Pullman adamantly refused arbitration, the ARU membership voted to boycott all Pullman cars. Beginning on June 29, switchmen across the United States refused to handle any train that carried Pullman cars.

The conflict escalated quickly. The General Managers Association (GMA), an organization of managers from twenty-four different railroads, acted in concert to quash the boycott. Determined to kill the ARU, they recruited strikebreakers and fired all the protesting switchmen. Their tactics set off a chain reaction. Entire train crews walked off the job in a show of solidarity with the Pullman workers. In a matter of days the boycott/strike spread to more than fifteen railroads and affected twenty-seven states and territories. By July 2, rail lines from New York to California lay paralyzed. Even the GMA was forced to concede that the railroads had been "fought to a standstill."

The boycott remained surprisingly peaceful. Mobs stopped trains carrying Pullman cars and forced train crews to uncouple the cars and leave them on the sidings. In contrast to the Great Railroad Strike of 1877, no major riots broke out, and no serious property damage occurred. Debs, in a whirlwind of activity, fired off telegrams to all parts of the country advising his followers to avoid violence and respect law and order. But the nation's newspapers, fed press releases by the GMA, distorted the issues and misrepresented the strike. Across the country, papers ran headlines like "Wild Riot in Chicago" and "Mob Is in Control."

In Washington, Attorney General Richard B. Olney, a lawyer with strong ties to the railroads, determined to put down the strike. In his way stood the governor of Illinois, John Peter Altgeld, who, observing that the boycott remained peaceful, refused to call out troops. To get around Altgeld, Olney convinced President Grover Cleveland that federal troops had to intervene to protect the mails. To further cripple the boycott, two conservative Chicago judges issued an injunction so sweeping that it prohibited Debs

from speaking in public. By issuing the injunction, the court made the boycott a crime punishable by jail sentence for contempt of court, a civil process that did not require trial by jury. Even the conservative *Chicago Tribune* judged the injunction "a menace to liberty...a weapon ever ready for the capitalist." Furious, Debs risked jail by refusing to honor it.

Olney's strategy worked. With the strikers violating a federal injunction and with the mails in jeopardy (the GMA made sure that Pullman cars were put on every mail train), Cleveland called out the army. On July 5, nearly 8,000 troops marched into Chicago. Violence immediately erupted. In one day, troops killed 25 workers and wounded more than 60. In the face of bullets and bayonets, the strikers held firm. "Troops cannot move trains," Debs reminded his followers, a fact that was borne out as the railroads remained paralyzed despite the military intervention. But if the army could not put down the boycott, the injunction could and did. Debs was arrested and imprisoned for contempt of court. With its leader in jail, its headquarters raided and ransacked, and its members demoralized, the ARU was defeated along with the boycott. Pullman reopened his factory, hiring new workers to replace many of the strikers and leaving 1,600 workers without jobs.

In the aftermath of the strike, a special commission investigated the events at Pullman, taking testimony from 107 witnesses, from the lowliest workers to George M. Pullman himself. Stubborn and self-righteous, Pullman spoke for the business orthodoxy of his era, steadfastly affirming the right of business to safeguard its interests through confederacies like the GMA and at the same time denying labor's right to organize. "If we were to receive these men as representatives of the union," he stated, "they could probably force us to pay any wages which they saw fit."

From his jail cell, Eugene Debs reviewed the events of the Pullman strike. With the courts and the government ready to side with industrialists in the interest of defending private property, Debs realized that labor had little recourse. Strikes seemed futile and unions remained helpless; workers would have to take control of the state itself. Debs went into jail a trade unionist and came out six months later a socialist. At first he turned to the Populist Party, but after its demise he formed the Socialist Party in 1900 and ran for president on its ticket five times. Debs's dissatisfaction with the status quo was shared by

National Guard Occupying Pullman, Illinois
After President Grover Cleveland called out the troops to put down the Pullman strike in 1894, the National Guard occupied the town of Pullman to protect George M. Pullman's property. Here the guard rings the Arcade building, the town shopping center, while curious men and women look on. The intervention of troops in Homestead and Pullman enabled the owners to bring in strikebreakers and defeat the unions. In Cripple Creek, Colorado, where a Populist governor used militia only to maintain the peace and not against the strikers, striking miners won the day in 1894.
Chicago Historical Society.

another group even more alienated from the political process—women.

> **REVIEW** Why did the strikes of the 1890s fail to produce permanent gains for workers?

Women's Activism

"Do everything," Frances Willard urged her followers in 1881. The new president of the Woman's Christian Temperance Union (WCTU) meant what she said. The WCTU followed a trajectory that was common for women in the late nineteenth century. As women organized to deal with issues that touched their homes and families, they moved into politics, lending new urgency to the cause of woman suffrage. Urban industrialism

dislocated women's lives no less than men's. Like men, women sought political change and organized to promote issues central to their lives, from temperance and suffrage to antilynching (see chapter 17).

Frances Willard and the Woman's Christian Temperance Union

Frances Willard, the visionary leader of the WCTU, spoke for a group left almost entirely out of the U.S. electoral process—women. In 1890, only one state, Wyoming, allowed women to vote in national elections. But lack of the **franchise** did not mean that women were apolitical. The WCTU demonstrated the breadth of women's political activity in the late nineteenth century.

Women supported the **temperance movement** because they felt particularly vulnerable to the effects of drunkenness. Dependent on men's wages, women and children suffered when money went for drink. The drunken, abusive husband epitomized the evils of a nation in which women remained second-class citizens. Composed entirely of women, the WCTU viewed all women's interests as essentially the same—crossing class, ethnic, and racial lines—and therefore did not hesitate to use the singular *woman* to emphasize gender solidarity. Although mostly white and middle class, WCTU members resolved to speak for their entire sex.

When Frances Willard became president in 1879, she radically changed the direction of the organization. Moving away from a religious approach, the WCTU began to view alcoholism as a disease rather than a sin, and poverty as a cause rather than a result of drink. Accordingly, social action replaced prayer as women's answer to the threat of drunkenness. By the 1890s the WCTU worked to establish women's reformatories, promoted the hiring of female police officers, and sponsored day nurseries, industrial training schools for women, missions for the homeless, medical dispensaries, and lodging houses for the poor. At the same time, the WCTU became involved in labor issues, joining with the Knights of Labor to press for better working conditions for women workers. Describing workers in a textile mill, a WCTU member wrote, "It is dreadful to see these girls, stripped almost to the skin … and running like racehorses from the beginning to the end of the day." "The hard slavish work," she concluded, "is drawing the girls into the saloon."

Willard capitalized on the **cult of domesticity** as a shrewd political tactic to move women into public life and gain power to ameliorate social problems. Using "home protection" as her watchword, she argued as early as 1884 that women needed the vote to protect home and family. By the 1890s, the WCTU's grassroots network of local unions had spread to all but the most isolated rural areas of the country. Strong and rich, with over 150,000 dues-paying members, the WCTU was a formidable group.

Willard worked to create a broad reform coalition in the 1890s, embracing the Knights of Labor, the People's Party, and the Prohibition Party. Until her death in 1898, she led, if not a women's rights movement, then the first organized mass movement of women united around a women's issue. By 1900, thanks largely to the WCTU, women could claim a generation of experience in political action—speaking, lobbying, organizing, drafting legislation, and running private charitable institutions. As Willard observed, "All this work has tended more toward the liberation of women than it has toward the extinction of the saloon."

Elizabeth Cady Stanton, Susan B. Anthony, and the Movement for Woman Suffrage

Unlike the WCTU, the organized movement for woman suffrage remained small and relatively weak in the late nineteenth century. The women's rights movement, begun by Elizabeth Cady Stanton at Seneca Falls in 1848 (see chapter 12), split in 1867 over whether the Fourteenth and Fifteenth Amendments, which granted voting rights to African American men, should have extended the vote to women as well. Stanton and her ally, Susan B. Anthony, launched the National Woman Suffrage Association (NWSA) in 1869, demanding the vote for women (see chapter 17). A more conservative group, the American Woman Suffrage Association (AWSA), formed the same year. Composed of men as well as women, the AWSA believed that women should vote in local but not national elections.

By 1890 the split had healed and the newly united National American Woman Suffrage Association (NAWSA) launched campaigns on the state level to gain the vote for women. Twenty years had made a great change. Woman suffrage, though not yet generally supported, was no longer considered a crackpot idea. Thanks to the WCTU's support of the "home protection ballot," suffrage had become accepted as a means to an end even when it was not embraced as woman's natural right.

Stanton and Anthony, both in their seventies, were coming to the end of their public careers. Since the days of the Seneca Falls Woman's Rights Convention they had worked for reforms for their sex, including property rights, custody rights, and the right to education and gainful employment. But the prize of woman suffrage still eluded them. Suffragists won victories in Colorado in 1893 and Idaho in 1896. One more state joined the suffrage column in 1896 when Utah entered the Union. But women suffered a bitter defeat in a California referendum on woman suffrage that same year. Never losing faith, Susan B. Anthony remarked in her last public

Campaigning for Woman Suffrage

In 1896 women voted in only four states—Wyoming, Colorado, Idaho, and Utah. The West led the way in the campaign for woman suffrage, partially because of demographics, as in the case of Wyoming, where only 16 votes were needed in the state's tiny legislature to obtain passage of the vote for women. This poster calls on Nebraska to join the suffrage column while the flag illustrates the number of states where women voted.

Poster: Nebraska State Historical Society; flag: Smithsonian Institution, Washington, D.C.

appearance in 1906, "Failure is impossible." Although it would take another two decades for all women to gain the vote with the ratification of the Nineteenth Amendment in 1920, the unification of the two woman suffrage groups in 1890 signaled a new era in women's fight for the vote, just as Frances Willard's place on the platform in 1892 at the founding of the People's Party in St. Louis symbolized women's growing role in politics and reform.

> **REVIEW** How did women's temperance activism contribute to the cause of woman suffrage?

Depression Politics

The depression that began in the spring of 1893 and lasted for more than four years put nearly half of the labor force out of work, a higher percentage than during the Great Depression of the 1930s. The country swarmed with people looking for jobs and begging for food. The human cost of the depression was staggering. "I Take my pen in hand to let you know that we are Starving to death," a Kansas farm woman wrote to the governor in 1894. "Last cent gone," wrote a young widow in her diary. "Children went to work without their breakfasts." The burden of feeding and sheltering the unemployed and their families fell to private charity, city government, and some of the stronger trade unions. Following the harsh dictates of **social Darwinism** and laissez-faire, the majority of America's elected officials believed that it was inappropriate for the government to intervene. But the scope of the depression made it impossible for local agencies to supply sufficient relief, and increasingly Americans called on the federal government to take action. Armies of the unemployed marched on Washington to demand relief, and the Populist Party experienced a surge of support as the election of 1896 approached.

Coxey's Army

Masses of unemployed Americans marched to Washington, D.C., in the spring of 1894 to call attention to their plight and to urge Congress to

Coxey's Army

This contingent of Coxey's army on the way to Washington, D.C., is led by Carl Browne, Coxey's principal aide, on horseback. A "petition in boots," Coxey's followers were well dressed—notice the men in white shirts, vests, neckties, and bowler hats in the foreground. The marchers insisted on their right to petition Congress for relief. Their action stirred the fears of many conservative Americans, who predicted an uprising of the unemployed. Most members of Congress wished to see the marchers halted, but Populist senator William V. Allen of Nebraska argued that their grievances should be heard by a congressional committee. Instead, Coxey was arrested and jailed when he reached Washington, D.C., for "walking on the grass."

Library of Congress.

enact a public works program to end unemployment. From as far away as Seattle, San Francisco, Los Angeles, and Denver, hundreds joined the march. Jacob S. Coxey of Massilon, Ohio, led the most publicized contingent. Convinced that men could be put to work building badly needed roads for the nation, Coxey proposed a scheme to finance public works through non-interest-bearing bonds. "What I am after," he maintained, "is to try to put this country in a condition so that no man who wants work shall be obliged to remain idle."

Starting out from Ohio with one hundred men, Coxey's "army," as it was dubbed by journalists, swelled as it marched east through the spring snows of the Alleghenies. In Pennsylvania, Coxey recruited several hundred from the ranks of those left unemployed by the Homestead lockout. Called by Coxey the Commonweal of Christ, the army advanced to the tune of "Marching through Georgia":

> We are not tramps nor vagabonds,
>   that's shirking honest toil,

> But miners, clerks, skilled artisans,
>   and tillers of the soil
> Now forced to beg our brother worms
>   to give us leave to toil,
> While we are marching with Coxey.
> Hurrah! hurrah! for the unemployed's appeal
> Hurrah! hurrah! for the marching commonweal!

On May 1, Coxey's army arrived in Washington. When Coxey defiantly marched his men onto the Capitol grounds, police set upon the demonstrators with nightsticks, cracking skulls and arresting Coxey and his lieutenants.

Mass demonstrations of the unemployed served only to frighten comfortable Americans, who saw the specter of insurrection and rebellion everywhere in 1894. Those who had trembled for the safety of the Republic heaved a sigh of relief after Coxey's arrest, hoping that it would halt the march on Washington. But other armies of the unemployed, totaling possibly as many as 5,000 people, were still on their way. Too poor to pay for railway tickets, they rode the rails as "freeloaders." The more daring contingents commandeered entire trains, stirring fears of revolution. Journalists who covered the march did little to quiet the nation's fears. To boost newspaper sales, they gave to the episode a tone of urgency and heightened the sense of a nation imperiled.

By August, the leaderless, tattered armies dissolved. Although the "On to Washington" movement proved ineffective in forcing federal relief legislation, Coxey's army dramatized the plight of the unemployed and acted, in the words of one participant, as a "living, moving object lesson." Like the Populists, Coxey's army called into question the underlying values of the new industrial order and demonstrated how ordinary citizens turned to means outside the regular party system to influence politics in the 1890s.

The People's Party and the Election of 1896

Even before the depression of 1893 gave added impetus to their cause, the Populists had railed against the status quo. "We meet in the midst of a nation brought to the verge of moral, political, and material ruin," Ignatius Donnelly had declared in his keynote address at the creation of the People's Party in St. Louis in 1892.

> Corruption dominates the ballot-box, the legislatures, the Congress, and touches even the ermine of the bench....The fruits of the toil of millions are boldly stolen to build up colossal fortunes for a few....From the same prolific womb of governmental injustice we breed the two great classes—tramps and millionaires.

The fiery rhetoric frightened many who saw in the People's Party a call not to reform but to revolution. Throughout the country, the press denounced the Populists as "cranks, lunatics, and idiots." When one righteous editor dismissed them as "calamity howlers," Populist governor Lorenzo Lewelling of Kansas shot back, "If that is so I want to continue to howl until those conditions are improved."

The People's Party captured more than a million votes in the presidential election of 1892, a respectable showing for a new party. The Populists might have done better, but on the eve of the convention they lost their standard-bearer when Leonidis L. Polk, president of the Southern

Mary Elizabeth Lease
This photograph of Lease, taken in 1895 at the height of her political activities in Kansas, shows a well-dressed, mild-eyed woman—belying her reputation as a hell-raiser who supposedly exorted Kansas farmers to "raise less corn and more hell." Lease brought her considerable oratorical skills to the causes of temperance, suffrage, and the Populist Party. Her admirers styled her "The People's Joan of Arc." But in the eyes of her detractors, who attacked not only her speeches but the propriety of a woman who dared a career as public speaker, she appeared "a lantern-jawed, google-eyed nightmare" and "a petticoated smut-mill."
Kansas State Historical Society.

Farmers' Alliance, died suddenly. Scrambling to find a replacement, the convention nominated General James B. Weaver of Iowa, a former Union general who had run for president on the Greenback Labor ticket in 1880. Many southern Populists could not bring themselves to vote for a Yankee general and stayed away from the polls.

Increasingly, sectional and racial animosities threatened party unity. More than their alliance with the Yankee North, it was the Populists' willingness to form common cause with black farmers that made them anathema in the white South. Tom Watson of Georgia had tackled the "Negro question" head-on in 1892. Realizing that race prejudice obscured the common economic interests of black and white farmers, Watson openly courted African Americans, appearing on platforms with black speakers and promising "to wipe out the color line."

As the 1896 presidential election approached, the depression intensified cries for reform not only from the Populists but also throughout the electorate. Depression worsened the tight money problem caused by the deflationary pressures of the gold standard. Once again, proponents of free silver (the unlimited coinage of silver in addition to gold) stirred rebellion in the ranks of both the Democratic and the Republican parties. When the Republicans nominated Ohio governor William McKinley on a platform pledging the preservation of the gold standard, western advocates of free silver representing miners and farmers walked out of the convention. Open rebellion also split the Democratic Party as vast segments in the West and South repudiated President Grover Cleveland because of his support for gold. In South Carolina, Benjamin Tillman won his race for Congress by promising, "Send me to Washington

and I'll stick my pitchfork into [Cleveland's] old ribs!"

The spirit of revolt animated the Democratic National Convention in Chicago in the summer of 1896. "Pitchfork Ben" Tillman set the tone by attacking the party's president, denouncing the Cleveland administration as "undemocratic and tyrannical." But the man of the hour was William Jennings Bryan of Nebraska, the thirty-six-year-old "boy orator from the Platte," who whipped the convention into a frenzy with his passionate call for free silver. In his keynote address, Bryan masterfully cataloged the grievances of farmers and laborers, closing his dramatic speech with a ringing exhortation: "Do not crucify mankind upon a cross of gold." Pandemonium broke loose as delegates stampeded to nominate Bryan, the youngest candidate ever to run for the presidency.

The juggernaut of free silver rolled out of Chicago and on to St. Louis, where the People's Party met a week after the Democrats adjourned. Smelling victory, many western Populists urged the party to ally with the Democrats and endorse Bryan. A major obstacle in the path of fusion, however, was Bryan's running mate, Arthur M. Sewall. A Maine railway director and bank president, Sewall had been placed on the ticket to appease conservative Democrats. An easterner, a banker, and a railroad director, Sewall embodied everything the Populists opposed.

Populism's regional constituencies remained as divided on tactics as they were uniform in their call for change. Western Populists, including a strong coalition of farmers and miners in states like Idaho and Colorado, championed free silver as a way to put the ailing Rocky Mountain silver industry back on its feet and restore prosperity to the region. In these largely Republican states, Populists had joined forces with Democrats in previous elections and saw no problem with becoming "Popocrats" once Bryan led the Democratic ticket on a free-silver platform. Similarly

Gold Elephant Campaign Button and Silver Ribbon from St. Louis, 1896

Mechanical elephant badges that opened to show portraits of William McKinley and his running mate, Garret Hobart, were popular campaign novelties in the election of 1896. The elephant, the mascot of the Republican Party, is gilded to indicate the party's support of the gold standard. In contrast, the delegate ribbon from the St. Louis National Silver Convention in 1896 features a silver eagle testifying to the power of free silver as a campaign issue. Democrats nominated William Jennings Bryan on a free-silver platform, and Populists meeting in St. Louis put him on their ticket as well.

Pin: Collection of Janice L. and David J. Frent; ribbon: Nebraska State Historical Society.

in the Midwest, a Republican stronghold, Populists who had used fusion with the Democrats as a tactic to win elections had little trouble backing Bryan. But in the South, where Democrats had resorted to fraud and violence to steal elections from the Populists in 1892 and 1894, support for a Democratic ticket proved especially hard to swallow. Diehard southern Populists wanted no part of fusion.

All of these tactical differences emerged as Populists met in St. Louis in 1896 to nominate a candidate for president. To show that they remained true to their principles, delegates first voted to support all the planks of the 1892 platform, added to it a call for public works projects for the unemployed, and only narrowly defeated a plank for woman suffrage. To deal with the problem of fusion, the convention selected the vice presidential candidate first. The nomination of Tom Watson undercut opposition to Bryan's candidacy. And, although Bryan quickly wired to protest that he would not drop Sewall as his running mate, mysteriously, his message never reached the convention floor. Fusion triumphed. Watson's vice presidential nomination paved the way for the selection of Bryan by a lopsided vote. The Populists did not know it, but their cheers for Bryan signaled not a chorus of victory but the death knell of the People's Party.

Few contests in the nation's history have been as fiercely fought and as full of emotion as the presidential election of 1896. On one side stood Republican William McKinley, backed by the wealthy industrialist and party boss Mark Hanna. Hanna played on the business community's fears of Populism to raise more than $4 million for the Republican war chest, double the amount of any previous campaign. On the other side, William Jennings Bryan, with few assets beyond his silver tongue, struggled to make up in energy and eloquence what his party lacked in campaign funds. He set a new style for presidential campaigning, crisscrossing the country in a whirlwind tour, traveling more than eighteen thousand miles and delivering more than six hundred speeches in three months. According to his own reckoning, he visited twenty-seven states and spoke to more than five million Americans.

As election day approached, the silver states of the Rocky Mountains lined up solidly for Bryan. The Northeast stood solidly for McKinley. Much of the South, with the exception of the border states, abandoned the Populists and returned to the Democratic fold, leaving Tom Watson to lament that "[Populists] play Jonah while [Democrats] play the whale." The Midwest hung in the balance. Bryan intensified his campaign in Illinois, Michigan, Ohio, and Indiana. But midwestern farmers proved less receptive than western voters to the blandishments of free silver.

On election day, four out of every five voters went to the polls in an unprecedented turnout. In the critical midwestern states, as many as 95 percent of the eligible voters cast their ballots. In the end, the election outcome hinged on from 100 to 1,000 votes in several key states, including Wisconsin, Iowa, and Minnesota. Although McKinley won twenty-three states to Bryan's twenty-two, the electoral vote showed a lopsided 271 to 176 in McKinley's favor (Map 20.1).

The biggest losers in 1896 turned out to be the Populists. On the national level, they polled fewer than 300,000 votes, over a million fewer than in 1894. In the clamor to support Bryan, Populists in the South drifted back to the Democratic Party. The People's Party was crushed, and with it died the agrarian revolt.

But if Populism proved unsuccessful at the polls, it nevertheless set the domestic political agenda for the United States in the next decades, highlighting issues such as banking and currency reform, electoral reforms, and an enlarged

MAP 20.1   The Election of 1896

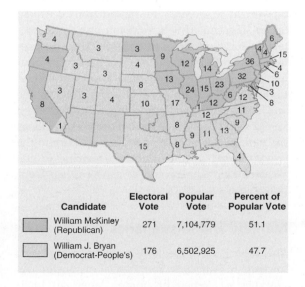

Candidate	Electoral Vote	Popular Vote	Percent of Popular Vote
William McKinley (Republican)	271	7,104,779	51.1
William J. Bryan (Democrat-People's)	176	6,502,925	47.7

role for the federal government in the economy. Meanwhile, as the decade ended, the bugle call to arms turned America's attention to foreign affairs and effectively drowned out the trumpet of reform. The struggle for social justice gave way to a war for empire as the United States asserted its power on the world stage.

> **REVIEW**   Why was the People's Party unable to translate national support into victory in the 1896 election?

The United States and the World

Throughout much of the last half of the nineteenth century, U.S. interest in foreign policy took a backseat to domestic developments. Intent on its own continental expansion, the United States stood aloof while Great Britain, France, Germany, Spain, Belgium, and the increasingly powerful Japan competed for empires in Asia, Africa, Latin America, and the Pacific. Between 1870 and 1900, European nations **colonized** more than 20 percent of the world's landmass and 10 percent of the world's population.

At the turn of the twentieth century, American foreign policy consisted of two currents—**isolationism** and expansionism. Although the determination to remain aloof from European politics had been a hallmark of U.S. foreign policy since the nation's founding, Americans simultaneously believed in **manifest destiny**—the "obvious" right to expand the nation from ocean to ocean. The United States's determination to protect its sphere of influence in the Western Hemisphere at the same time it expanded its trading in Asia moved the nation away from isolationism and toward a more active role on the world stage. The push for commercial expansion joined with a sense of Christian mission to refocus the nation's attention abroad and led both to the strengthening of the **Monroe Doctrine** in the Western Hemisphere and to a new Open Door policy in Asia.

Markets and Missionaries

The depression of the 1890s provided a powerful impetus to American commercial expansion. As markets weakened at home, American businesses looked abroad for profits. Although not all U.S. business leaders thought it advantageous to undertake adventures abroad, the logic of acquiring new markets to absorb the nation's growing capacity for production proved convincing to many. As the depression deepened, one diplomat warned that Americans "must turn [their] eyes abroad, or they will soon look inward upon discontent."

Exports constituted a small but significant percentage of the profits of American business in the 1890s. And where American interests led, businessmen expected the government's power and influence to follow to protect their investments. America's foreign policy often appeared little more than a sidelight to business development. In Hawaii (first called the Sandwich Islands), American sugar interests fomented a rebellion in 1893, toppling the increasingly anti-American Queen Liliuokalani. They pushed Congress to annex the islands, which would allow planters to avoid the high McKinley tariff on sugar. When President Cleveland learned that Hawaiians opposed annexation, he withdrew the proposal from Congress. But expansionists still coveted the islands and continued to look for an excuse to push through annexation.

However compelling the economic arguments about overseas markets proved, business interests alone did not account for the new expansionism that seized the nation during the 1890s. As naval strategist Alfred Thayer Mahan confessed, "Even when material interests are the original exciting cause, it is the sentiment to which they give rise, the moral tone which emotion takes that constitutes the greater force." Much of that moral tone was set by American missionaries intent on spreading the gospel of Christianity to the "heathen." No area on the globe constituted a greater challenge than China. In 1858, the Tientsin treaty admitted foreign missionaries. Roman Catholics from France and Protestants from Britain, Germany, and the United States rushed to China.

Increased missionary activity and Western enterprise touched off a series of antiforeign outbreaks in China culminating in the Boxer uprising of 1900. Although for the most part Christian missionaries proved unsuccessful, converting only 100,000 in a population of 400 million, the Chinese nevertheless resented the interference of missionaries in village life and the preference and protection they afforded their Christian converts. Opposition to foreign missionaries took the form of antiforeign secret societies, most notably the Boxers, whose Chinese name translated to "Righteous Harmonious Fist." No simple boxing club, in 1899 the Boxers began to terrorize Chinese Christians and missionaries in northwestern Shandong Province. Men and women were hacked to death with swords, burned alive in their houses, and dragged by howling mobs to their execution. With the tacit support of China's Dowager Empress, the Boxers became bolder. Under the slogan "Uphold the Ch'ing Dynasty, Exterminate the Foreigners," they marched on the cities. Their rampage eventually led to the massacre of some 30,000 Chinese converts and 250 foreign nuns, priests, and missionaries along with their families.

As the Boxers spread terror throughout northern China, some 800 Americans and Europeans sought refuge in the foreign legation buildings in Beijing (then called Peking). Along with missionaries from the countryside came thousands of their Chinese converts, fleeing the Boxers. Unable to escape and cut off from outside aid and communication, the Americans and Europeans in Beijing mounted a defense to face the Boxer onslaught and held up under siege for two months. American missionary Luella Miner wrote sadly, "We are isolated here as if we were on a desert island.... Are our Christians everywhere being slaughtered?"

Americans back home who learned of the fate of their countrymen and women at the hands of the Chinese showed little toleration for the cautious diplomatic approach favored by Secretary of State John Hay. In August 1900, 2,500 U.S. troops joined an international force sent to rescue the foreigners besieged in Beijing. After routing the Boxers, the troops looted the Forbidden City, home of the imperial court, forcing the Dowager Empress to flee disguised as a peasant. In 1901 the European powers imposed the humiliating Boxer Protocol, giving them the right to maintain military forces in the Chinese capital and requiring the Chinese government to pay an indemnity of $333 million for the loss of life and property resulting from the Boxer uprising.

In the aftermath of the uprising, missionaries voiced no concern at the paradox of bringing Christianity to China at gunpoint. "It is worth any cost in money, worth any cost in bloodshed," argued one bishop, "if we can make millions of Chinese true and intelligent Christians." Merchants and missionaries alike shared such moralistic reasoning. Indeed, they worked hand in hand; trade and Christianity marched into Asia together. "Missionaries," admitted the American clergyman Charles Denby, "are the pioneers of trade and commerce.... The missionary, inspired by holy zeal, goes everywhere and by degrees foreign commerce and trade follow."

The Monroe Doctrine and the Open Door Policy

The emergence of the United States as a world power pitted the nation against the colonial powers, particularly Germany and Japan, which posed a threat to the twin pillars of America's expansionist foreign policy—one dating back to President James Monroe in the 1820s, the other formalized in 1900 under President William McKinley. The first, the Monroe Doctrine, came to be interpreted as establishing the Western Hemisphere as an American "sphere of influence" and warned European powers to stay away or risk war. The second, the Open Door, dealt with maintaining market access to China.

American diplomacy actively worked to buttress the Monroe Doctrine, with its assertion of American hegemony (domination) in the Western Hemisphere. In the 1880s, Republican secretary of state James G. Blaine promoted hemispheric peace and trade through Pan-American cooperation but at the same time used American troops to intervene in Latin American border disputes. In 1895, Americans risked war with Great Britain to enforce the Monroe Doctrine when a conflict developed between Venezuela and British Guiana. President Cleveland asserted the U.S. prerogative to step in and mediate, reducing Venezuela to the role of mere onlooker in its own affairs. At first, Britain refused to accept U.S. mediation and conflict seemed imminent. "Let the fight come if it must," wrote rising Republican neophyte Theodore Roosevelt. Seeing an opportunity to extend manifest destiny to the north, Roosevelt vowed "we [will] take Canada." But the British, who feared the possibility of war in Europe and as a consequence wished to avoid conflict in Latin America, accepted the terms of U.S. mediation.

In Central America, American business triumphed in a bloodless takeover that saw French and British interests routed by behemoths like the United Fruit Company of Boston. United Fruit virtually dominated the Central American nations of Costa Rica and Guatemala, while an importer from New Orleans turned Honduras into a "banana republic" (a country run by U.S. business interests). Thus, by 1895, the Venezuelan crisis

The Open Door

The trade advantage gained by the United States through the Open Door policy, enunciated by Secretary of State John Hay in 1900, is portrayed graphically in this political cartoon. Uncle Sam stands prominently in the "open door" while representatives of the other great powers seek admittance to the "Flowery Kingdom" of China. Great Britain is symbolized by the stocky figure of John Bull; czarist Russia is portrayed by the bearded figure with the hat sporting the imperial double eagle. Other imperialist powers variously represented have yielded to Uncle Sam, who holds the golden key of "American Diplomacy" while the Chinese beam with pleasure. In fact, the Open Door policy promised equal access for all powers to the China trade, not U.S. preeminence as the cartoon implies.

Culver Pictures.

FOR MORE HELP ANALYZING THIS IMAGE, see the visual activity for this chapter in the Online Study Guide at bedfordstmartins.com/roarkcompact.

The Samoan Islands, 1889

signaled the extent to which the United States, through business as well as diplomacy, had successfully achieved hegemony in Latin America and the Caribbean, forcing even the British to concur with the secretary of state that "the infinite resources [of the United States] combined with its isolated position render it master of the situation and practically invulnerable as against any or all other powers."

At the same time that American foreign policy warned European powers to stay out of the Western Hemisphere, the United States competed with the colonial powers for trade in the Eastern Hemisphere. As American interests in China grew, the United States became more aggressive in defending its presence in Asia and the Pacific. The United States risked war with Germany in 1889 to guarantee the U.S. navy access to a port for refueling on the way to Asia. The United States held treaty rights to the harbor at Pago

Pago in the Samoan Islands. Germany, seeking dominance over the islands, challenged the United States by sending warships to the region. But before fighting broke out, a great typhoon destroyed the German and American ships. Acceding to the will of nature, the potential combatants later divided the islands amicably in the 1899 Treaty of Berlin.

The biggest prize in Asia remained the China market. In the 1890s, China, weakened by years of warfare, was beginning to be partitioned into spheres of influence by England, Japan, Germany, France, and Russia. Concerned about the integrity of China and no less about American trade, Secretary of State John Hay in 1899–1900 hastily wrote a series of notes calling for an "open door" policy that would ensure trade access to all and maintain Chinese sovereignty. Hay skillfully managed to maneuver the major powers into doing his bidding and boldly announced in 1900 the Open Door as international policy. The United States, by insisting on an Open Door policy, managed to secure access to Chinese markets, expanding its economic power while avoiding the problems of maintaining a far-flung colonial empire on the Asian mainland. But as the Spanish-American War demonstrated,

Americans found it hard to resist the temptations of empire.

REVIEW   Why did the United States largely abandon its isolationist foreign policy in the 1890s?

War and Empire

The Spanish-American War began as a humanitarian effort to free Cuba from Spain's colonial grasp and ended with the United States itself becoming a colonial power and fighting a dirty **guerrilla war** with Filipino nationalists, who, like the Cubans, sought independence. Yet behind the contradiction stood the twin pillars of American foreign policy: The Monroe Doctrine made Spain's presence in Cuba unacceptable, and U.S. determination to keep open the door to Asia made the Philippines attractive as a stepping-stone to China.

"A Splendid Little War"

Looking back on the Spanish-American War of 1898, Secretary of State John Hay judged it "a splendid little war; begun with the highest motives, carried on with magnificent intelligence and spirit, favored by that fortune which loves the brave." At the close of a decade marred by bitter depression, social unrest, and political upheaval, the war offered Americans a chance to wave the flag and march in unison. War fever proved as infectious as the tune of a John Philip Sousa march. Few argued the merits of the conflict until it was over and the time came to divide the spoils.

The war began with moral outrage over the treatment of Cuban revolutionaries, who had launched a fight for independence against the Spanish colonial regime in 1895. In an attempt to isolate the guerrillas, Spanish general Valeriano Weyler herded Cubans into crowded and unsanitary concentration camps, where thousands died of hunger, disease, and exposure. Starvation soon spread to the cities. Tens of thousands of Cubans died, and countless others were left without food, clothing, or shelter. By 1898, fully a quarter of the island's population had perished in the Cuban revolution.

As the Cuban rebellion dragged on, pressure for American intervention mounted. American newspapers fueled public outrage at Spain. A fierce circulation war raged in New York City between William Randolph Hearst's *Journal* and Joseph Pulitzer's *World*. Newspapers fed the American people a daily diet of "Butcher" Weyler and Spanish atrocities. Hearst sent artist Frederic Remington to document the horror, and when Remington wired home, "There is no trouble here. There will be no war," Hearst shot back, "You furnish the pictures and I'll furnish the war."

American interests in Cuba were, in the words of the U.S. minister to Spain, more than "merely theoretical or sentimental." American business had more than $50 million invested in Cuban sugar, and American trade with Cuba, a brisk $100 million a year before the rebellion, had dropped to near zero. Nevertheless, the business community balked, wary of a war with Spain. When industrialist Mark Hanna, the Republican kingmaker and senator from Ohio, urged restraint, a hotheaded Theodore Roosevelt exploded, "We will have this war for the freedom of Cuba, Senator Hanna, in spite of the timidity of commercial interests."

To expansionists like Roosevelt, more than Cuban independence was at stake. War with Spain opened up the prospect of expansion into Asia as well, since Spain controlled not only Cuba and Puerto Rico but also Guam and the Philippine Islands. Appointed assistant secretary of the navy in April 1897, Roosevelt worked for preparedness whenever his boss's back was turned. During the hot summer while the navy secretary vacationed, Roosevelt took the helm in his absence and audaciously ordered the U.S. fleet to Manila in the Philippines. In the event of conflict with Spain, Roosevelt put the navy in a position to capture the islands and gain an entry point to China.

President McKinley slowly moved toward intervention. In a show of American force, he dispatched the battleship *Maine* to Cuba. On the night of February 15, 1898, a mysterious explosion destroyed the *Maine*, killing 267 crew members. The source of the explosion remained unclear, but inflammatory stories in the press enraged Americans, who immediately blamed the Spanish government. Rallying to the cry "Remember the *Maine*," Congress declared war on Spain in April. In a surge of patriotism, more than 235,000 men enlisted. War brought with it a unity of purpose and national harmony that ended a decade of political dissent and strife. "In April, everywhere over this good fair land, flags were flying," wrote the Kansas editor William

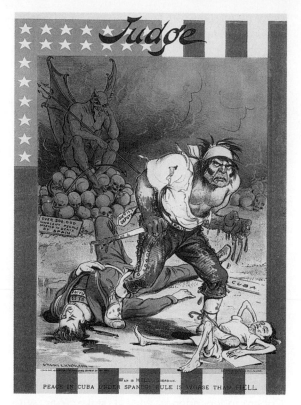

Yellow Journalism

Most cartoonists followed the lead of Hearst and Pulitzer in promoting war with Spain. Cartoonist Grant Hamilton drew this cartoon for *Judge* magazine in March 1898. It shows a brutish Spain (the "Devil's Deputy") with bloody hands trampling on a sailor from the *Maine*. Cuba is prostrate, and skulls represent civilians "starved to death" by Spain. Such vicious representations of Spain became common in the American press in the weeks leading up to the Spanish-American War. What does the cartoon say about American attitudes toward race?

Collection of the New-York Historical Society.

Allen White. "At the stations, crowds gathered to hurrah for the soldiers, and to throw hats into the air, and to unfurl flags."

Soon they had something to cheer about. Five days after McKinley signed the war resolution, a U.S. navy squadron commanded by Admiral George Dewey destroyed the Spanish fleet in Manila Bay (Map 20.2). Dewey's stunning victory caught the United States by surprise. Although naval strategists including Theodore Roosevelt had been orchestrating the move for some time, few Americans had ever heard of the Philippines. Even McKinley confessed that he could not immediately locate the archipelago on the map. He nevertheless recog-

nized the strategic importance of the Philippines and dispatched U.S. troops to secure the islands.

The war in Cuba ended almost as quickly as it began. The first troops landed on June 22, and after a handful of battles the Spanish surrendered on July 17. The war lasted just long enough to elevate Theodore Roosevelt to the status of bona fide war hero. Roosevelt resigned his navy post and formed the Rough Riders, a regiment composed about equally of Ivy League polo players and cowboys Roosevelt knew from his stint as a cattle rancher in the Dakotas. When the Rough Riders shipped out to Cuba, journalists fought for a berth with the colorful regiment. Roosevelt's charge up Kettle Hill and his role in the decisive battle of San Juan Hill made front-page news. Overnight, Roosevelt became the most famous man in America. By the time he sailed home from Cuba, a coalition of independent Republicans was already plotting his political future.

The Debate over American Imperialism

After a few brief campaigns in Cuba and Puerto Rico brought the Spanish-American War to an end, the American people woke up in possession of an empire that stretched halfway around the globe. As part of the spoils of war, the United States acquired Cuba, Puerto Rico, Guam, and the Philippines. Yielding to pressure from American sugar growers, McKinley expanded the empire farther, annexing Hawaii in July 1898.

Cuba, freed from Spanish rule, failed to gain full autonomy. Contemptuous of the Cubans, whom General William Shafter declared "no more fit for self-government than gun-powder is for hell," the U.S. government dictated a Cuban constitution. It included the so-called Platt Amendment—a series of provisions that granted the United States the right to intervene to protect Cuba's "independence" as well as the power to oversee Cuban debt so that European creditors could not find an excuse for intervention. For good measure, the United States gave itself a ninety-nine-year lease on a naval base at Guantánamo. In return, McKinley promised to implement an extensive sanitation program to clean up the island, making it more attractive to American investors.

The formal Treaty of Paris ending the war with Spain ceded the Philippines to the United

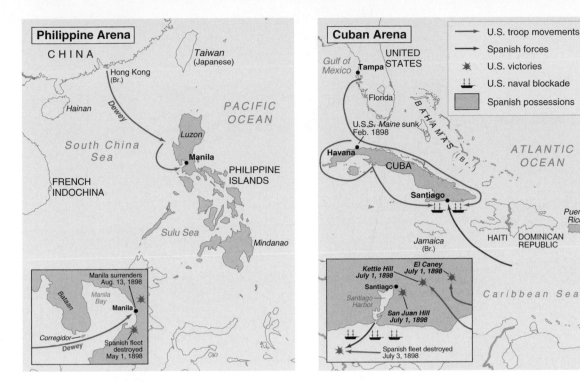

MAP 20.2 The Spanish-American War, 1898

The Spanish-American War was fought in two theaters, the Philippine Islands and Cuba. Five days after President William McKinley called for a declaration of war, Admiral George Dewey captured Manila without the loss of a single American sailor. The war lasted only eight months. Troops landed in Cuba in mid-June and by mid-July had taken Santiago and Havana and destroyed the Spanish fleet.

READING THE MAP: Which countries held imperial control over countries and territories immediately surrounding the Philippine Islands and Cuba? Which imperial power provided the launching point for the U.S. fleet before Dewey captured Manila?

CONNECTIONS: What role did American newspapers play in the start of the war? How did the results of the war with Spain serve American aims in both Asia and the Western Hemisphere?

FOR MORE HELP ANALYZING THIS MAP, see the map activity for this chapter in the Online Study Guide at bedfordstmartins.com/roarkcompact.

States along with Spain's former colonies in Puerto Rico and Guam (Map 20.3). Empire did not come cheap. When Spain balked, the United States agreed to pay an indemnity of $20 million for the islands. Nor was the cost measured in money alone. Filipino revolutionaries under Emilio Aguinaldo, who had greeted U.S. troops as liberators, bitterly fought the new masters. It would take seven years and 4,000 American dead—almost ten times the number killed in Cuba—not to mention an estimated 20,000 Filipino casualties, to defeat Aguinaldo and secure American control of the Philippines, America's coveted stepping-stone to China.

At home, a vocal minority, mostly Democrats and former Populists, resisted the country's foray into empire, judging it unwise, immoral, and unconstitutional. William Jennings Bryan, who enlisted in the army but never saw action, came to the conclusion that American expansionism only distracted the nation from problems at home. What did imperialism offer the ordinary American, Bryan asked, except "heavier taxes, Asiatic emigration and an opportunity to furnish more sons for the army."

The anti-imperialists were soon drowned out by cries for empire. The moral tone of the age, set by social Darwinism with its emphasis on survival of the fittest and Anglo-Saxon racial superiority, proved ideally suited to imperialism. Congregational minister Josiah Strong revealed the mixture of racism and missionary zeal that fueled American adventurism abroad when he

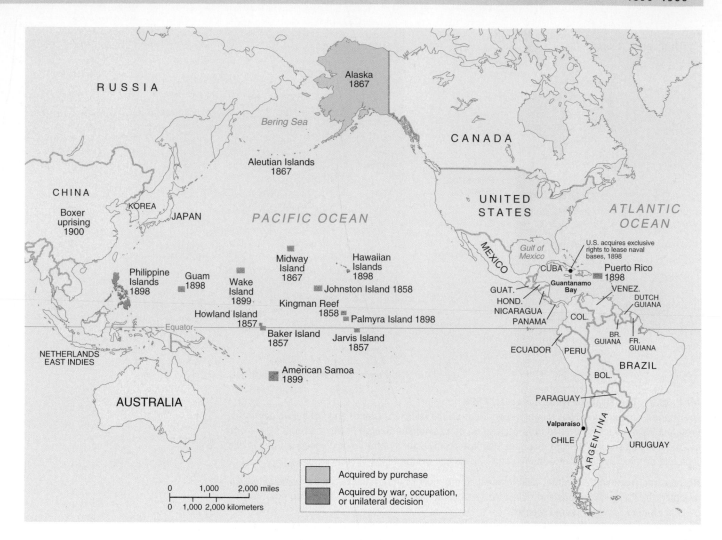

MAP 20.3 U.S. Territorial Expansion through 1900
The United States extended its interests abroad with a series of territorial acquisitions. Although Cuba was granted independence, the Platt Amendment kept the new nation firmly under U.S. control. In the wake of the Spanish-American War, the United States woke up to find that it held an empire extending halfway around the globe.

remarked, "It seems to me that God, with infinite wisdom and skill, is training the Anglo Saxon race for an hour sure to come in the world's future." The *Washington Post* trumpeted, "The taste of empire is in the mouth of the people," thrilled at the prospect of "an imperial policy, the Republic renascent, taking her place with the armed nations."

REVIEW Why did the United States declare war on Spain in 1898?

Conclusion: Rallying around the Flag

A decade of domestic strife ended amid the blare of martial music and the waving of flags. The Spanish-American War drowned out the calls for social reform that had fueled the Populist politics of the 1890s. During that decade, angry farmers facing hard times looked to the Farmers' Alliance to fight for their vision of economic democracy, workers staged bloody battles across the country to assert their rights, and women attacked drunkenness and the conditions that fostered it and mounted a suffrage movement to secure their basic political rights. In St. Louis in 1892, disaffected groups came together to form a new People's Party to fight for change.

The bitter depression that began in 1893 led to increased labor strife. The Pullman boycott brutally dramatized the power of property and the conservatism of the laissez-faire state. Even the miners' victory in Cripple Creek, Colorado, in 1894 proved short-lived. But workers' willingness to confront capitalism on the streets of Chicago, Homestead, Cripple Creek, and a host of other sites across America eloquently testified to labor's growing determination, unity, and strength.

As the depression deepened, the sight of Coxey's army of unemployed marching on Washington to demand federal intervention in the economy signaled a growing shift in the public mind against the stand-pat politics of laissez-faire. The call for the government to take action to better the lives of workers, farmers, and the dispossessed manifested itself in the fiercely fought presidential campaign of William Jennings Bryan in 1896. With the outbreak of the Spanish-American War in 1898, the decade ended on a harmonious note with patriotic Americans rallying around the flag and cheering America's foray into empire. The United States took its place on the world stage, buttressing its hemispheric domination with the Monroe Doctrine and employing the Open Door policy, which promised access to the riches of China. But even though Americans basked in patriotism and contemplated empire, old grievances had not been laid to rest. The People's Party had been beaten, but the Populists' call for greater government involvement in the economy, expanded opportunities for direct democracy, and a more equitable balance of profits and power between the people and the big corporations sounded the themes that would be taken up by a new gener-

ation of progressive reformers in the first decades of the twentieth century.

Suggestions for Further Reading

Alan Dawley, *Struggles for Justice: Social Responsibility and the Liberal State* (1991). A good overview of politics at the turn of the century.

Steven Hahn, *A Nation under Our Feet: Black Political Struggles in the Rural South from Slavery to the Great Migration* (2003). A masterful study of black political activism that looks in detail at black alliances with the Readjusters and the Populists.

Kristin Hoganson, *Fighting for American Manhood: How Gender Politics Provoked the Spanish-American and Philippine-American Wars* (1998). An intriguing look at how gender issues influenced political leaders and foreign policy.

Matthew Frye Jacobson, *Barbarian Virtues: The United States Encounters Foreign Peoples at Home and Abroad, 1876–1917* (2000). An examination of the relationship between immigration at home and empire building abroad.

Elizabeth Jameson, *All That Glitters: Class, Conflict, and Community in Cripple Creek* (1998). A rich history of Cripple Creek and its two strikes, the success of the miners in 1894, and the union's defeat in 1904.

Ivan Musicant, *Empire by Default: The Spanish American War and the Dawn of the American Century* (1998). A colorful history of the war and its significance to America's position in the world.

▶ **For more books about topics in this chapter,** see the Online Bibliography at bedfordstmartins.com/roarkcompact.

▶ **For additional firsthand accounts of this period,** see Chapter 20 in Michael Johnson, ed., *Reading the American Past,* Third Edition.

▶ **For Web sites and documents related to topics and places in this chapter,** see "HistoryLinks," "DocLinks," and "PlaceLinks" at bedfordstmartins.com/roarkcompact.

REVIEWING THE CHAPTER

Follow these steps to review and strengthen your understanding of the chapter.

STEP 1: *Study the* **Key Terms** *and* **Timeline** *to identify the significance of each item listed.*

STEP 2: *Answer the* **Review Questions**, *drawing on key terms and dates to support your answers.*

STEP 3: *Drawing on the Key Terms, Timeline, and Review Questions, answer the broader* **Making Connections** *questions.*

KEY TERMS

Who

Ignatius Donnelly (pp. 505, 519)
Mary Elizabeth Lease (p. 505)
Frances Willard (pp. 505, 515)
Andrew Carnegie (p. 508)
Henry Clay Frick (p. 509)
Alexander Berkman (p. 512)
Davis H. Waite (p. 513)
George M. Pullman (p. 513)
Eugene V. Debs (p. 513)
Grover Cleveland (p. 514)
Elizabeth Cady Stanton (p. 516)
Susan B. Anthony (p. 516)
Jacob S. Coxey (p. 518)
James B. Weaver (p. 519)
Tom Watson (p. 519)
William McKinley (p. 520)
William Jennings Bryan (p. 520)
Mark Hanna (p. 521)
John Hay (p. 523)
Valeriano Weyler (p. 525)
William Randolph Hearst (p. 525)
Joseph Pulitzer (p. 525)
Theodore Roosevelt (p. 525)

George Dewey (p. 526)
Emilio Aguinaldo (p. 527)

What

People's Party (Populist Party) (pp. 506, 508)
agrarian revolt (p. 506)
crop lien (p. 507)
Farmers' Alliance (p. 507)
Colored Farmers' Alliance (p. 507)
subtreasury (p. 508)
Western Federation of Miners (p. 508)
Homestead lockout (p. 508)
Amalgamated Association of Iron and Steel Workers (p. 509)
Pinkerton National Detective Agency (p. 509)
stock market crash of 1893 (p. 512)
Cripple Creek miners' strike of 1894 (p. 512)
Pullman strike (p. 513)
American Railway Union (p. 513)
General Managers Association (p. 514)

Woman's Christian Temperance Union (p. 515)
National American Woman Suffrage Association (p. 516)
"home protection ballot" (p. 516)
Coxey's "army" (p. 518)
gold standard (p. 520)
free silver (p. 520)
expansionism (p. 522)
manifest destiny (p. 522)
Monroe Doctrine (p. 522)
Boxer uprising (p. 522)
Venezuelan crisis (p. 523)
Samoan Islands (p. 524)
1899 Treaty of Berlin (p. 524)
Open Door policy (p. 524)
Spanish-American War (p. 525)
the *Maine* (p. 525)
Rough Riders (p. 526)
battle of San Juan Hill (p. 526)
imperialism (p. 526)
annexation of Hawaii (p. 526)
Platt Amendment (p. 526)
Treaty of Paris (p. 526)

TIMELINE

◀ **1884** • Woman's Christian Temperance Union calls for woman suffrage.

1889 • Typhoon averts hostilities between German and U.S. ships in Samoan Islands.

1890 • National American Woman Suffrage Association (NAWSA) formed.

WOMEN VOTE
FOR
PRESIDENT
Wyoming, Colorado, Utah and Idaho
WHY NOT
NEBRASKA?

• Wyoming enters Union with woman suffrage.
• Southern Farmers' Alliance numbers 3 million members.

1892 • People's Party (Populist Party) founded.
• Homestead lockout.
• Pennsylvania National Guard takes over Homestead mills.
• Anarchist Alexander Berkman attempts to assassinate Henry Clay Frick.
• People's Party wins more than 1 million votes in presidential election.

1893 • Panic on Wall Street touches off severe economic depression.
• President Grover Cleveland nixes attempt to annex Hawaii.

1894 • Miners strike in Cripple Creek, Colorado.
• Coxey's "army" marches to Washington, D.C.
• Federal troops and court injunction crush Pullman strike.
• Union leader Eugene V. Debs jailed.

REVIEW QUESTIONS

1. Why did American farmers organize alliances in the late nineteenth century? (pp. 506–08)

2. Why did the strikes of the 1890s fail to produce permanent gains for workers? (pp. 508–15)

3. How did women's temperance activism contribute to the cause of woman suffrage? (pp. 515–17)

4. Why was the People's Party unable to translate national support into victory in the 1896 election? (pp. 517–22)

5. Why did the United States largely abandon its isolationist foreign policy in the 1890s? (pp. 522–25)

6. Why did the United States declare war on Spain in 1898? (pp. 525–28)

MAKING CONNECTIONS

1. In the late nineteenth century Americans clashed over the disparity of power brought about by industrial capitalism. Why did many working Americans look to the government to help advance their vision of economic justice? In your answer, discuss specific reforms working-class Americans pursued and the strategies they employed.

2. In the 1890s, workers mounted labor protests and strikes. What circumstances gave rise to these actions? How did they differ from earlier strikes, like the Great Railroad Strike of 1877? In your answer, discuss specific actions, being sure to consider how local and national circumstances contributed to their ultimate resolution.

3. How did women's activism in the late nineteenth century help advance the cause of woman suffrage? How did women activists in the late nineteenth century differ from their predecessors? In your answer, discuss specific gains made in the late nineteenth century as well as shifts in reformers' strategies.

4. The late nineteenth century was a watershed in American foreign policy. Why did the United States strengthen its presence in the Americas and beyond in the 1890s? How did these actions reinforce or revise earlier national foreign policy? In your answer, discuss how private and national interests shaped these actions.

▶ **FOR PRACTICE QUIZZES, A CUSTOMIZED STUDY PLAN, AND OTHER STUDY TOOLS,** see the Online Study Guide at bedfordstmartins.com/roarkcompact.

1895 • President Grover Cleveland defends Monroe Doctrine in border dispute between British Guiana and Venezuela.

    1896 • Democrats and Populists support William Jennings Bryan for president.
          • Republican William McKinley elected president.

        1898 • U.S. battleship *Maine* explodes in Havana harbor.
             • Congress declares war on Spain.
             • Admiral George Dewey destroys Spanish fleet in Manila Bay, the Philippines.
             • U.S. troops defeat Spanish forces in Cuba.
             • Treaty of Paris.
             • United States annexes Hawaii.
             • Congress passes Platt Amendment.

           1899 • Treaty of Berlin.

      1899–1900 • Secretary of State John Hay enunciates Open Door policy in China.
             • Boxer uprising in China.

                1901 • Boxer Protocol imposed on Chinese government.

PROGRESSIVE PARTY CAMPAIGN SOUVENIR

This colorful cotton bandana, a campaign novelty from the 1912 presidential race, celebrates the Progressive Party and its candidate Theodore Roosevelt. The progressive reform movement grew out of the crises of the 1890s to emerge full-blown in the first decades of the twentieth century. Progressives challenged laissez-faire liberalism and argued for government action to counter the power of big business and ensure greater social justice. Theodore Roosevelt, whose presidency set the tone for the era, became so closely associated with progressivism that when he failed to win the Republican nomination in 1912, his followers formed a new Progressive Party proclaiming, as the bandana notes, "We Want Our Teddy Back." Accepting the nomination, Roosevelt announced that he felt "as fit as a bull moose," giving the new party a mascot. But progressivism was more than one man or one party. A movement that ran from the grass roots to the White House, it included not only members of the short-lived Progressive Party but also Democrats and Republicans whose belief in government activism would reshape the liberal state of the twentieth century.

Collection of Janice L. and David J. Frent.

Progressivism from the Grass Roots to the White House

1890–1916

I N THE SUMMER OF 1889, a young woman leased the upper floor of a dilapidated mansion on Chicago's West Side in the heart of a burgeoning immigrant population. Watching the preparations, neighbors scratched their heads, wondering why the well-dressed woman, who surely could afford a better house in a better neighborhood, chose to live on South Halsted Street. Yet the house built by Charles Hull precisely suited the needs of Jane Addams.

For Addams, personal action marked the first step in the search for solutions to the social problems fostered by urban industrialism. Her object was twofold: She wanted to help her immigrant neighbors, and she wanted to offer an opportunity for educated women like herself to find meaningful work. As she later wrote in her autobiography, *Twenty Years at Hull-House* (1910), "I gradually became convinced that it would be a good thing to rent a house in a part of the city where many primitive and actual needs are found, in which young women who had been given over too exclusively to study might restore a balance of activity along traditional lines and learn of life from life itself." Addams's emphasis on the reciprocal relationship between the social classes made Hull House different from other philanthropic enterprises. She wished to do things with, not just for, Chicago's poor.

In the next decade, Hull House expanded from one rented floor in the old brick mansion to some thirteen buildings housing a remarkable variety of activities. Addams converted the bathrooms in the basement into public baths, opened a coffee shop and restaurant to sell take-out food to working women too tired to cook after their long shifts, and sponsored a nursery and kindergarten for neighborhood children. Hull House offered classes, lectures, art exhibits, musical instruction, and college extension courses. It boasted a gymnasium, a theater, a manual training workshop, a labor museum, and the first public playground in Chicago.

But Hull House was more than a group of buildings. From the first, it attracted an extraordinary set of reformers. Some stayed for decades, as did Julia Lathrop before she went to Washington, D.C., in 1912 to head the Children's Bureau. Others, like Gerard Swope, who later became president of the General Electric Company, came for only a short time. Hull House residents pioneered the scientific investigation of urban ills. Armed with statistics, they launched

Jane Addams

Jane Addams was twenty-nine years old when she founded Hull House on South Halsted Street in Chicago. She and her college roommate, Ellen Gates Starr, established America's premier social settlement. Her desire to live among the poor and her insistence that settlement house work benefited educated women like herself as well as her immigrant neighbors separated her from the charity workers who had come before her and marked the distance from philanthropy to progressive reform.

Jane Addams Memorial Collection, Special Collection, University Library, University of Illinois at Chicago.

campaigns to improve housing, end child labor, fund playgrounds, mediate between labor and management, and lobby for laws to protect workers.

Addams quickly learned that it was impossible to deal with urban problems without becoming involved in political action. Her determination to clean up the garbage on Halsted Street led her into politics. Piles of decaying garbage overflowed the street's wooden trash bins, breeding flies and disease. Investigation revealed that the local ward boss awarded the contract to pick up the trash as a political plum to one of his henchmen who felt under no obligation to provide adequate service. To end the graft, Addams got herself appointed garbage inspector. Out on the streets at six in the morning, she rode atop the garbage wagon to make sure it made its rounds. Addams mounted several unsuccessful political campaigns to oust the corrupt ward boss but eventually realized that bossism was a symptom and not the cause of urban blight. Recognizing that bosses stayed in power by providing jobs and services to their constituents, she moved instead to sponsor legislation to help her neighbors. Eventually her struggle to aid the urban poor led her not only to city hall but on to the state capitol and to Washington, D.C.

Under Jane Addams's leadership, Hull House became a "spearhead for reform," part of a broader movement that contemporaries called **progressivism**. The transition from personal action to political activism that Addams personified became one of the hallmarks of this reform period, which lasted from the 1890s to World War I.

By the 1890s it had become clear to many Americans that the **laissez-faire** approach of government toward business no longer worked. The classical **liberalism** of the nation's Founders, with its emphasis on opposition to the tyranny of centralized government, had not reckoned on the enormous private wealth and power of the Gilded Age's business giants. As the gap between rich and poor widened in the 1890s, issues of social justice challenged traditional notions of laissez-faire liberalism. The violence and militancy of the 1890s—labor strikes, farmers' revolt, **suffrage** rallies—eloquently testified to the growing polarities in society. Yet a laissez-faire state only exacerbated the inequalities of class, race, and gender. A generation of progressive reformers demanded government intervention to guarantee a more equitable society. The willingness to use the government to promote change and to counterbalance the power of private interests redefined liberalism in the twentieth century.

Faith in activism in both the political and the private realms formed a common thread that united an otherwise diverse group of progressive reformers. A sense of Christian mission inspired some. Others, fearing social upheaval, sought to remove some of the worst evils of urban industrialism—tenements, child labor, and harsh working conditions. Progressives shared a growing concern about the power of wealthy individuals and corporations and a strong dislike of the **trusts**. But often they feared the immigrant poor and sought to control and Americanize them. Along with moral fervor, a belief in technical expertise and scientific management infused progressivism and made the cult of efficiency part and parcel of the movement. All of these elements—uplift and efficiency, social justice and social control—came together in the Progressive Era and characterized the progressive movement both at the grassroots level in the cities and states and in the presidencies of Theodore Roosevelt and Woodrow Wilson.

Grassroots Progressivism

Much of progressive reform began at the grassroots level and percolated upward into local, state, and eventually national politics as reformers attacked the social problems fostered by urban industrialism. While reform flourished in many different settings across the country, urban problems inspired the progressives' greatest efforts. In their zeal to "civilize the city," reformers founded settlement houses, professed a new Christian **social gospel**, and campaigned against vice and crime in the name of "social purity." Allying with the working class, they sought to better the lot of sweatshop garment workers and to end child labor. Their reform efforts often began on the local level but ended up being debated in state legislatures and in the U.S. Congress.

Civilizing the City

Progressives attacked the problems of the city on many fronts. The settlement house movement attempted to bridge the distance between the classes. The social gospel called for the churches to play a new role in social reformation. And the **social purity movement** campaigned to clean up vice, particularly prostitution.

The settlement house movement that began in England came to the United States in 1886 with the opening of the University Settlement House in New York City. The needs of poor urban neighborhoods provided the impetus for these social settlements. In 1893, Lillian Wald, a nurse attending medical school in New York, went to care for a woman living in a dilapidated tenement. The experience led Wald to leave medical school and recruit several other nurses to move to New York City's Lower East Side "to live in the neighborhood as nurses, identify ourselves with it socially, and…contribute to it our citizenship." Expanded in 1895, the Henry Street settlement pioneered public health nursing. Although Wald herself was Jewish, she insisted that the Henry Street settlement remain independent of religious ties, making it different from the avowedly religious English settlements.

Women, particularly college-educated women like Jane Addams and Lillian Wald, formed the backbone of the settlement house movement. Eager to use their knowledge, they often found themselves blocked from medicine, law, and the clergy (fewer than 1,500 women practiced law in 1900, and women constituted only 6 percent of the medical profession). Settlement houses gave college-educated women a place to put their talents to work in the service of society. Largely due to women's efforts, settlements like Hull House grew in number from six in 1891 to more than four hundred in 1911. In the process, settlement house women created a new profession—social work.

Churches confronted urban social problems by enunciating a new social gospel, one that saw its mission not simply to reform individuals but to reform society. The social gospel offered a powerful corrective to the **gospel of wealth**, with its belief that riches somehow signaled divine favor. Washington Gladden, a prominent social gospel minister, challenged that view when he urged Congregationalists to turn down a gift from John D. Rockefeller, arguing that it was "tainted money." In place of the gospel of wealth, progressive clergy exhorted their congregations to put Christ's teachings to work in their daily lives. For Walter Rauschenbusch, a Baptist minister working in New York's tough Hell's Kitchen neighborhood, the social gospel grew out of the depression of the 1890s, which left thousands of people unemployed. "They wore down our threshold and they wore away our hearts," he later wrote. "One could hear human virtue cracking and crumbling all around." In *Christianity and the Social Crisis* (1907), Rauschenbusch called for the church to play a new role in promoting social justice, and many congregations across the country heeded the call.

Ministers also played an active role in the social purity movement, the campaign to attack vice. To end the "social evil," as reformers euphemistically called prostitution, the social purity movement brought together ministers who wished to stamp out sin, doctors concerned about the spread of venereal disease, and women reformers determined to fight the double standard that made it acceptable for men to engage in premarital and extramarital sex but punished women who strayed. Together, they waged campaigns to close red-light districts in cities across the country and lobbied for the Mann Act, passed in 1910, which made it illegal to transport women across state lines for "immoral purposes." On the state level, they struck at venereal disease by securing legislation to require a blood test for syphilis before marriage.

Attacks on alcohol went hand in hand with the push for social purity. The **temperance** campaign launched by the Woman's Christian Temperance Union (WCTU) heated up in the early twentieth century. The Anti-Saloon League, formed in 1895 under the leadership of **Protestant** clergy, campaigned for an end to the sale of liquor. Reformers pointed to links between drinking, prostitution, wife and child abuse, unemployment, and industrial accidents. The powerful liquor lobby fought back, spending liberally in election campaigns, fueling the charge that liquor corrupted the political process.

An element of **nativism** (dislike of foreigners) ran through the movement for prohibition, as it did in a number of progressive reforms. The Irish, the Italians, and the Germans were among the groups stigmatized by temperance reformers for their drinking. Progressives often failed to see the important role the tavern played in many ethnic communities. Unlike the American saloon, an almost exclusively male domain, the tavern often provided a family retreat. German Americans of all ages socialized at beer gardens after church on Sunday. Even though most workers toiled six days a week and had only Sunday for recreation and relaxation, some progressives campaigned on the local level to enforce the Sunday closing of taverns. To deny the working class access to alcohol, these progressives pushed for state legislation to outlaw the sale of liquor; by 1912, seven states were "dry."

Progressives' efforts to civilize the city demonstrated their willingness to take action, their belief that environment, not heredity alone, determined human behavior, and their optimism that conditions could be corrected through government action without radically altering America's economy or institutions. All of these attitudes characterized the progressive movement.

Progressives and the Working Class

Day-to-day contact with their neighbors made settlement house workers particularly sympathetic to labor unions. When Mary Kenney O'Sullivan complained that her bookbinders' union met in a dirty, noisy saloon, Jane Addams invited the union to meet at Hull House. And during the Pullman strike in 1894, Hull House residents organized strike relief. "Hull-House has been so unionized," grumbled one Chicago businessman, "that it has lost its usefulness and become a detriment and harm to the community."

But to the working class, the support of middle-class reformers marked a significant gain.

Attempts to forge a cross-class alliance became institutionalized in 1903 with the creation of the Women's Trade Union League (WTUL). The WTUL brought together women workers and middle-class "allies." Its goal was to organize working women into unions under the auspices of the American Federation of Labor (AFL). However, the AFL paid little more than lip service to unionizing women. As one working woman confided, "The men think that the girls should not get as good work as the men and should not make half as much money as a man."

The WTUL's most notable success came in 1909 in the "uprising of twenty thousand." In November, hundreds of women employees of the Triangle Shirtwaist Company in New York City went on strike to protest low wages, dangerous and demeaning working conditions, and management's refusal to recognize their union, the International Ladies' Garment Workers Union (ILGWU). In support of the walkout, the ILGWU called for a general strike of all garment workers. An estimated 20,000 workers, most of them teenage girls and many of them Jewish and Italian immigrants, stayed out on strike, picketing through the winter. By the time the strike ended in February 1910, the workers had won important demands in many shops. The solidarity shown by the women workers proved to be the strike's greatest achievement. As Clara Lemlich, one of the strike's leaders, exclaimed, "They used to say that you couldn't even organize women. They wouldn't come to union meetings. They were 'temporary' workers. Well we showed them!"

The WTUL made enormous contributions to the strike. It provided volunteers for the picket lines, posted more than $29,000 in bail, protested police brutality, organized a parade of 10,000 strikers, took part in the arbitration conference, appealed for funds, and generated publicity for the strike. Under the leadership of the WTUL, women from every class of society, from J. P. Morgan's daughter Anne to **socialists** on New York's Lower East Side, joined the strikers in a dramatic demonstration of cross-class alliance.

Despite its demonstration of solidarity, the strike failed to change the dangerous conditions faced by women workers. In March 1911, a little over a year after the strike ended, fire alarms sounded at the Triangle Shirtwaist factory. The building, full of lint and combustible cloth,

14. Viewing the unfortunates at the M

Triangle Fire Morgue

After the Triangle fire on March 26, 1911, New York City set up a makeshift morgue at the end of Manhattan's Charities Pier. There the remains of more than a hundred young women and two dozen young men were laid out in coffins for their friends and relatives to identify. Victims who had jumped to their deaths from the ninth-floor windows or leaped down the elevator shaft could be easily recognized. Those trapped in the building were burned beyond recognition. A ring, a charred shoe, a melted hair comb often provided the only clues to the identity of a sister, a daughter, or a sweetheart. In the *New York Evening Journal* (right), a survivor recounted the horror inside when the girls discovered that one of the two doors leading out of the building was locked, barring their escape. In the trial that followed the fire, the owners of the Triangle Shirtwaist Company avoided penalty when their skillful lawyer challenged the credibility of witnesses like the woman in the news story, who testified that one door had been locked to keep girls from pilfering.

UNITE Archives, Kheel Center, Cornell University, Ithaca, NY 14853-3901.

burned to rubble in half an hour. A WTUL member described the scene below on the street: "Two young girls whom I knew to be working in the vicinity came rushing toward me, tears were running from their eyes and they were white and shaking as they caught me by the arm. 'Oh,' shrieked one of them, 'they are jumping. Jumping from ten stories up! They are going through the air like bundles of clothes.'"

The terrified Triangle workers had little choice but to jump. Flames blocked one exit, and the other door had been locked to prevent workers from pilfering. The flimsy, rusted fire escape collapsed under the weight of fleeing workers, killing dozens. Trapped, 54 workers jumped from the ninth-floor windows, only to smash to their deaths on the sidewalk. Of 500 workers, 146 died and scores of others were injured. The owners of the Triangle firm went to trial for negligence, but they avoided conviction when authorities determined that the fire had been started by a careless smoker.

The Triangle fire tested severely the bonds of the cross-class alliance. WTUL leaders experienced a growing sense of futility. It seemed not enough to organize and to strike. Increasingly, the WTUL turned its efforts to lobbying for protective legislation—laws that would limit hours and regulate working conditions for women workers.

Advocates of protective legislation won a major victory in 1908 when the U.S. Supreme

Court, in *Muller v. Oregon*, reversed its previous rulings and upheld an Oregon law that limited to ten the hours women could work in a day. A mass of sociological evidence put together by Florence Kelley of the National Consumers' League and Josephine Goldmark of the WTUL demonstrated the ill effects of long hours on the health and safety of women. The data convinced the Court that long hours endangered women and therefore the entire race. The Court's ruling set a precedent, but one that separated the well-being of women workers from that of men by arguing that women's reproductive role justified special treatment. Later generations of women fighting for equality would question the effectiveness of this strategy and argue that it ultimately closed good jobs to women. The WTUL, however, greeted protective legislation as a first step in the attempt to ensure the safety of all workers.

The National Consumers' League (NCL), like the WTUL, fostered cross-class alliance. When Florence Kelley took over the leadership of the NCL in 1899, she urged middle-class women to boycott stores and exert pressure for decent wages and working conditions for women employees, primarily saleswomen. Like the WTUL, the National Consumers' League turned increasingly to protective legislation. Frustrated by the reluctance of the private sector to respond to the need for reform, progressives turned to government at all levels. Critics would later charge that the progressives assumed too easily that government regulation could best solve social problems.

> **REVIEW** Why did cities become one of the primary sites for progressive reform?

Progressivism: Theory and Practice

Progressive reformers developed a theoretical basis for their activist approach by countering **social Darwinism** with a dynamic new **reform Darwinism**. And their enthusiasm for speed and productivity inspired **scientific management** and a new cult of efficiency. These varied strands of progressive theory found practical application in state and local politics, where reformers challenged traditional laissez-faire government.

Reform Darwinism and Social Engineering

The active, interventionist approach of the progressives directly challenged social Darwinism, with its insistence that the world operated on the principle of survival of the fittest and that human beings stood powerless in the face of the law of natural selection. Without abandoning the evolutionary framework of Darwinism, a new group of sociologists argued that evolution could be advanced more rapidly if men and women used their intellects to alter the environment. Dubbed "reform Darwinism," the new sociological theory condemned laissez-faire, insisting that the liberal state should play a more active role in solving social problems.

Efficiency and *expertise* became watchwords in the progressive vocabulary. The journalist and critic Walter Lippmann in *Drift and Mastery* (1914) called for skilled "technocrats" to use scientific techniques to control social change, substituting social engineering for aimless drift. Progressive reformers' emphasis on expertise inevitably fostered a kind of elitism.

At its extreme, the application of expertise and social engineering took the form of scientific management, which by elevating productivity and efficiency alienated the working class. Frederick Winslow Taylor pioneered "systematized shop management." After dropping out of Harvard, Taylor went to work as a machinist at Midvale Steel in Philadelphia in the 1880s. He carefully timed workers with his stopwatch and attempted to break down their work into its simplest components, one repetitive action after another, on the theory that productivity would increase if tasks were reduced to their simplest parts. Labor hated the monotony of systematized shop management and argued that it pushed workers to produce more in less time and for less pay. But advocates of "Taylorism" applauded the increased productivity and efficiency of Taylor's system.

Progressive Government: City and State

The politicians who became premier progressives were generally the followers, not the leaders, in a movement already well advanced at the grassroots level. Yet they left their stamp on the movement. Tom Johnson made Cleveland, Ohio, a model of progressive reform; Robert La Follette

Tom Johnson

Tom Johnson, the reform mayor of Cleveland, Ohio, from 1901 to 1909, is shown here campaigning in Cleveland's Wade Park in 1908. For more than seven years, Mayor Johnson fought for a three-cent streetcar fare, winning the support of the working class and angering the business interests who ran the city's streetcars. To get this low fare, Johnson finally instituted municipal ownership of the transit system. The three-cent token was a campaign novelty distributed during Johnson's bid for reelection in 1907.

The Western Reserve Historical Society, Cleveland, Ohio.

turned Wisconsin into a laboratory for progressivism; and Hiram Johnson ended the domination of the Southern Pacific Railroad in California politics.

Progressivism burst forth at every level of government in 1900, but nowhere more forcefully than in Cleveland, with the election of Thomas Lofton Johnson mayor. A self-made millionaire by age forty, Johnson pledged during the campaign to reduce the streetcar fare from five cents to three. During his tenure as mayor, Johnson fought for fair taxation even as he called for greater **democracy** through the use of the initiative, referendum, and recall—devices that allowed voters to have a direct say in legislative and judicial matters. He successfully championed municipal ownership of street railways and public utilities, a tactic that progressives called "gas and water socialism." After a seven-year battle, the city bought the streetcar system and instituted the three-cent fare. Under Johnson's administration, Cleveland became, in the words of journalist Lincoln Steffens, the "best governed city in America."

In Wisconsin, Robert M. La Follette, who had supported William McKinley, converted to the progressive cause early in the 1900s. An astute politician, La Follette capitalized on the grass-roots movement for reform to launch his long political career, first as governor (1901–1905) and later as a U.S. senator (1906–1925). A graduate of the University of Wisconsin, La Follette brought scientists and professors into his administration and used the university, not far from the state-house, as a resource in drafting legislation. As governor he lowered railroad rates, raised railroad taxes, improved education, preached conservation, established factory regulation and workers' compensation, instituted the first direct primary in the country, and inaugurated the first state income tax. Under his leadership, Wisconsin earned the title "laboratory of democracy."

A fiery orator, "Fighting Bob" La Follette united his supporters around issues that transcended party loyalties. This emphasis on reform characterized progressivism, which attracted followers from both major parties. Democrats like Tom Johnson and Republicans like Robert La Follette could lay equal claim to the label "progressive."

West of the Rockies, progressivism arrived somewhat later and found a champion in Hiram Johnson of California, who served as governor from 1911 to 1917 and U.S. senator from 1917 to 1945. Since the 1870s, California politics had been dominated by the Southern Pacific Railroad. Johnson ran for governor in 1910 on the promise to "kick the Southern Pacific out of politics." With the support of the reform wing of the Republican Party, he handily won. As governor he introduced the direct primary; supported the initiative, referendum, and recall; strengthened the state's railroad commission; supported conservation; and signed an employer's liability law. He boasted that by regulating the Southern Pacific Railroad he had saved shippers more than $2 million.

REVIEW How did progressives justify their demand for more activist government?

Progressivism Finds a President: Theodore Roosevelt

On September 6, 1901, President William McKinley was shot and killed by Leon Czolgosz, an **anarchist**, while attending the Pan-American Exposition in Buffalo, New York. When news of his assassination reached his friend and political mentor Mark Hanna, Hanna is said to have growled, "Now that damned cowboy is president." He was speaking of Vice President Theodore Roosevelt, the colorful hero of San Juan Hill, who had indeed punched cattle in the Dakotas in the 1880s.

At age forty-two, Roosevelt became the youngest man ever to move into the White House. A patrician by birth and an activist by temperament, Roosevelt brought to the job enormous talent and energy. As president he would use that energy to strengthen the power of the federal government, putting business on notice that it could no longer count on laissez-faire to give it free rein.

The Square Deal

The "absolutely vital question" facing the country, Roosevelt wrote to a friend in 1901, was "whether or not the government has the power to control the trusts." The Sherman Antitrust Act of 1890 had been badly weakened by a conservative Supreme Court. To determine if the law had any teeth left, Roosevelt, in one of his first acts as president, ordered his attorney general to begin a secret antitrust investigation of the Northern Securities Company. He chose a good target. Northern Securities monopolized railroad

Theodore Roosevelt
Described aptly by a contemporary observer as "a steam engine in trousers," Theodore Roosevelt at forty-two was the youngest president to occupy the White House. He brought to the office energy, intellect, and activism in equal measure. Roosevelt boasted that he used the presidency as a "bully pulpit"—a forum from which he advocated reforms ranging from trust-busting to conservation.
Library of Congress.

traffic in the Northwest and to many small investors and farmers symbolized corporate high-handedness.

Five months later, in February 1902, Wall Street rocked with the news that the government had filed an antitrust suit against Northern Securities. As one newspaper editor sarcastically observed, "Wall Street is paralyzed at the thought that a President of the United States would sink so low as to try to enforce the law." Roosevelt's thunderbolt put Wall Street on notice that the new president expected to be treated as an equal and was willing to use government as a weapon to curb business excesses. Perhaps sensing the new mood, the Supreme Court, in a significant turnaround, upheld the Sherman Act and called for the dissolution of Northern Securities in 1904.

"Hurrah for Teddy the Trustbuster," cheered the papers. Roosevelt went on to use the Sherman Act against forty-three trusts, including such giants as American Tobacco, Du Pont, and Standard Oil. Always the moralist, he insisted on a "rule of reason." He would punish "bad" trusts (those that broke the law) and leave "good" ones alone. In practice, he preferred regulation to antitrust suits. In 1903, he pressured Congress to pass the Elkins Act, outlawing railroad rebates (money returned to a shipper to guarantee repeat business). And he created the new cabinet-level Department of Commerce and Labor with a subsidiary Bureau of Corporations to act as a corporate watchdog.

In his handling of the anthracite coal strike in 1902, Roosevelt again demonstrated his willingness to assert the moral and political authority of the presidency, this time to mediate between labor and management. In May, 147,000 coal miners in Pennsylvania went on strike. The United Mine Workers (UMW) demanded a reduction in the workday from twelve to ten hours, an equitable system of weighing each miner's output, and a 10 percent wage increase, along with recognition of the union.

When asked about the appalling conditions in the mines that led to the strike, George Baer, the mine operators' spokesman, scoffed, "The miners don't suffer, why they can't even speak English." Buttressed by social Darwinism, Baer observed that "God in his infinite wisdom" had placed "the rights and interests of the laboring man" in the hands of the capitalists, not "the labor agitators." His Olympian confidence rested on the fact that six eastern railroads owned over 70 percent of the anthracite mines.

With the power of the railroads behind them, Baer and the mine owners refused to budge.

The strike dragged on through the summer and into the fall. Hoarding and profiteering drove the price of coal from $2.50 to $6.00 a ton. Coal heated nearly every house, school, and hospital in the Northeast, and as winter approached, coal shortages touched off near riots in the nation's big cities. In the face of mounting tension, Roosevelt did what no president had ever done. He stepped in to mediate, issuing a personal invitation to representatives from both sides to meet in Washington in October. At the meeting, Baer and the mine owners refused to talk with the union representatives. Angered by the "wooden-headed obstinacy and stupidity" of management, Roosevelt threatened to seize the mines and run them with federal troops. The specter of federal troops being used to operate the mines quickly brought management around. At the prompting of J. P. Morgan, the mine owners agreed to arbitration. In the end, the miners won a reduction in hours and a wage increase, but the owners succeeded in preventing formal recognition of the UMW.

Taken together, Roosevelt's actions in the Northern Securities case and in the anthracite coal strike marked a dramatic departure from the presidential passivity of his predecessors in the Gilded Age. Roosevelt demonstrated conclusively that government intended to act as a force independent of big business. Pleased with his role in the anthracite strike, he announced that all he had tried to do was give labor and capital a "square deal."

The phrase "Square Deal" became his slogan in the 1904 election campaign. To win the presidency in his own right, Roosevelt wrested control of the Republican Party from party boss Mark Hanna. In the presidential election of 1904, he swept into office with the largest popular majority—57.9 percent—any candidate had polled to that time.

Roosevelt the Reformer

"Tomorrow I shall come into my office in my own right," Roosevelt is said to have remarked on the eve of his election. "Then watch out for me!" Roosevelt's stunning victory gave him a mandate for reform. He would need all the popularity and political savvy he could muster, however, to guide his reform measures through Congress. The Senate remained controlled by a staunchly **conservative** Republican "old guard," with many senators on the payrolls of the corporations Roosevelt sought to curb. Roosevelt's pet project remained railroad regulation. The Elkins Act prohibiting rebates had not worked. No one could stop big shippers like Standard Oil from wringing concessions from the railroads. Roosevelt determined that the only solution lay in giving the Interstate Commerce Commission (ICC) real power to set rates and prevent discriminatory practices. But the right to determine the price of goods or services was an age-old prerogative of private enterprise, and one that business had no intention of yielding to government.

To ensure passage of the Hepburn Act, which would increase the power of the ICC, Roosevelt worked skillfully behind the scenes. In its final form, the Hepburn Act, passed in May 1906, gave the ICC power to set rates subject to court review. Committed progressives like La Follette judged the law a defeat for reform. Die-hard conservatives branded it a "piece of populism." Both sides exaggerated. The law left the courts too much power and failed to provide adequate means for the ICC to determine rates, but its passage proved a landmark in federal control of private industry. For the first time, a government commission had the power to investigate private business records and to set rates.

Passage of the Hepburn Act marked the high point of Roosevelt's presidency. In a serious political blunder, Roosevelt had announced on the eve of his election in 1904 that he would not run again. By 1906, he had become a "lame duck" at the very moment he enjoyed his greatest public popularity.

Always an apt reader of the public temper, Roosevelt witnessed a growing appetite for reform fed by the revelations of corporate and political wrongdoing and social injustice that filled the papers and boosted the sales of popular periodicals. (See "The Promise of Technology," page 544.) Roosevelt, who wielded publicity like a weapon in his pursuit of reform, counted many of the new investigative journalists, including Jacob Riis, among his friends. But he warned them against going too far, citing the allegorical character in *Pilgrim's Progress* who was so busy raking muck that he took no notice of higher things. Roosevelt's criticism gave the American vocabulary a new word, *muckraker*, which journalists soon appropriated as a title of honor.

Muckraking, as Roosevelt well knew, provided enormous help in securing progressive legislation. In the spring of 1906, publicity generated by the muckrakers about poisons in patent medicines goaded the Senate, with Roosevelt's backing, into passing a pure food and drug bill. Opponents in the House of Representatives hoped to keep the legislation locked up in committee. There it would have died, were it not for publication of Upton Sinclair's novel *The Jungle* (1906), with its sensational account of filthy conditions in meatpacking plants. A massive public outcry led to the passage of a Pure Food and Drug Act and a Meat Inspection Act.

In the waning years of his administration, Roosevelt allied with the more progressive elements of the Republican Party. In speech after speech, he attacked "malefactors of great wealth." Styling himself a "radical," he claimed credit for leading the "ultra conservative" party of McKinley to a position of "progressive conservatism and conservative radicalism."

When an economic panic developed in the fall of 1907, business interests quickly blamed the president. The panic of 1907 proved severe but short. Once again J. P. Morgan stepped in to avert disaster, this time switching funds from

The Jungle

Novelist Upton Sinclair, a lifelong socialist, wrote *The Jungle* to expose the evils of capitalism. But readers were more horrified by the unsanitary conditions he described in the meatpacking industry, where the novel's hapless hero sees rats, filth, and diseased animals processed into meat products. It was rumored that after reading the book, President Theodore Roosevelt could no longer stomach sausage for breakfast. The president immediately ordered a thorough study of conditions in the meatpacking industry. The public outcry surrounding *The Jungle* contributed to the enactment of pure food and drug legislation and a federal meat inspection law. Sinclair ruefully remarked, "I aimed at the public's heart, but I hit them in the stomach."

By permission of the Houghton Library, Harvard University.

one bank to another to prop up weak institutions. For his services, he claimed the Tennessee Coal and Iron Company, an independent steel business that had long been coveted by his U.S. Steel Corporation. Morgan dispatched his lieutenants to Washington, where they told Roosevelt that the sale of the company would aid the economy "but little benefit" U.S. Steel. Willing to take the word of a gentleman, Roosevelt tacitly agreed not to institute antitrust proceedings against U.S. Steel. Roosevelt later learned that Morgan had been less than candid. The episode would give rise to the charge that Roosevelt acted as a tool of the Morgan interests.

Convinced that regulation and not trust-busting offered the best way to deal with big business, Roosevelt never acknowledged that his regulatory policies fostered an alliance between business and government that today is called corporate liberalism. Despite his harsh attacks on "malefactors of great wealth," Roosevelt's actions in the panic of 1907 demonstrated his indebtedness to Morgan, who still functioned as the national bank and would continue to do so until passage of the Federal Reserve Act six years later.

Roosevelt and Conservation

In at least one area, Roosevelt proved well ahead of his time. Robert La Follette, who thought Roosevelt a lukewarm progressive and found much to criticize in his presidency, hailed as Roosevelt's "greatest work" his efforts in the conservation of natural resources. When Roosevelt took office, some 45 million acres of land remained as government reserves. He more than tripled that number to 150 million acres, buying land and creating national parks and wildlife preserves by executive order. To conserve natural resources, he fought western cattle barons, lumber kings, mining interests, and powerful leaders in Congress, including Speaker of the House Joseph Cannon, who was determined to spend "not one cent for scenery."

As the first president to have lived and worked in the West—as a rancher in the Dakotas—Roosevelt came to the White House convinced of the need for better management of the nation's rivers and forests. During the 1890s, concern for the wanton exploitation of natural resources led Congress to pass legislation giving the president the power to "reserve" forest land from commercial development by executive proclamation. During his presidency, Roosevelt did not hesitate to wield that power. Roosevelt, along with his chief forester, Gifford Pinchot, preached conservation—the efficient use of natural resources. Willing to permit grazing, lumbering, and the development of hydroelectric power, conservationists fought private interests only when they felt business acted irresponsibly or threatened to monopolize water and electric power.

Roosevelt's conservation policies drew criticism from many quarters. Progressives criticized the Newlands Reclamation Act of 1902, arguing that the legislation encouraged the growth of large-scale farming at the expense of small farmers. The law established a Reclamation Bureau within the Department of the Interior and provided federal funding for irrigation projects. The growing involvement of the federal government in the management of water resources, a critical issue in the West, marked another victory for the policy of federal intervention that characterized progressivism and marked the end of laissez-faire liberalism.

Preservationists like John Muir, founder of the Sierra Club, believed the wilderness needed to be protected from all commercial exploitation. Muir soon clashed with Roosevelt. After a devastating earthquake in 1906, San Francisco sought federal approval for a project to supply fresh water and electric power to the city. The plan called for building a dam that would flood the spectacular Hetch Hetchy Valley in Yosemite National Park. Muir, who had played a central role in establishing Yosemite as a national park, fiercely opposed Roosevelt and Pinchot, who saw the Hetch Hetchy project as a progressive victory because it placed control of the water supply in the hands of the municipal government and not private developers. After a protracted publicity battle, Roosevelt and the conservationists prevailed.

In 1907, Congress put the brakes on Roosevelt's conservation program by passing a law limiting his power to create forest reserves in six western states. In the days leading up to the law's enactment, Roosevelt feverishly created twenty-one new reserves and enlarged eleven more. And when Congress denied Pinchot the right to withdraw hydroelectric power sites from private use, he managed to save 2,500 by designating them "ranger stations." Firm in his commitment to conservation, Roosevelt proved

Flash Photography and the Birth of Photojournalism

The camera was not new at the turn of the twentieth century. As early as the 1840s, Americans had eagerly imported the technology developed by Frenchman L. J. M. Daguerre to make portraits known as daguerreotypes. By the 1880s, the invention of dry plates had simplified photography, and by the 1890s, Americans could purchase a Kodak camera marketed by George Eastman. But for Jacob Riis, who wished to document the horrors of tenement life, photography was useless because it required daylight or careful studio lighting. Riis, a progressive reformer and journalist who covered the police beat for the *New York Tribune,* never thought of buying a camera. He could only rudely sketch the dim hovels, the criminal nightlife, and the windowless tenement rooms of New York. Then came the breakthrough. "One morning scanning my newspaper at the breakfast table," he wrote, "I put it down with an outcry.... There it was, the thing I had been looking for all these years.... A way had been discovered...to take pictures by flashlight. The darkest corner might be photographed that way."

The new technology involved a pistol lamp that fired magnesium cartridges to provide light for instantaneous photography. Armed with the new flash pistols, Riis and a band of amateur photographers soon set out to shine light in the dark corners of New York. "Our party carried terror wherever it went," Riis later recounted. "The spectacle of strange men invading a house in the mid-night hours armed with [flash] pistols which they shot off recklessly was hardly reassuring...and it was not to be wondered at if the tenants bolted through the windows and down fire-escapes."

Unhappy with the photographers he hired to follow him on his nighttime forays into the slums, Riis determined to try his own hand at taking pictures and laid out $25 for his first photographic equipment in 1888. It consisted of a four-by-five-inch wooden box camera, glass plates, a tripod, a safety lantern, flash pistols, developing trays, and a printing frame. He soon replaced the pistols with a newer flash technology developed in 1887 that used magnesium powder blown through an alcohol flame. Riis carried a frying pan in which to ignite the powder, observing, "It seemed more homelike."

Flash photography was dangerous. The pistol lamp cartridges contained highly explosive chemicals that could seriously burn the photographer. The newer technology employing magnesium powder also proved risky. Riis once blew the flash into his own eyes, and only his glasses saved him from being blinded. Nor was Riis the only one in peril. When he photographed the residents of a tenement on "Blind Man's Alley," he set the place on fire when he ignited the flash. He later claimed the tenement, nicknamed the "Dirty Spoon," was so filthy it wouldn't burn. He was able to douse the flames without his blind subjects ever realizing their danger.

Riis turned his photographs into slides that he used to illustrate his lectures on tenement life. They helped spread his message, but not until *Scribner's* magazine printed his story entitled "How the Other Half Lives" in December 1889 did he begin to develop a mass audience. The article, illustrated with line drawings of Riis's photographs, became the basis for his best-selling book of the same title published in 1890.

---

willing to stretch the law when it served his ends. Today, the six national parks, sixteen national monuments, and fifty-one wildlife refuges that he created stand witness to his substantial accomplishments as a conservationist (Map 21.1).

Roosevelt the Diplomat

Roosevelt's activism extended to his foreign policy, where he worked to buttress the nation's newly won place among world leaders. A fierce proponent of America's interests abroad, he

Jacob Riis and Baxter Court

Jacob Riis (to the right), a Danish immigrant who knew the squalor of New York's lodging houses and slums from his early days in the city, vigorously campaigned for tenement reform. He warned slumlords (some of them prominent New Yorkers) that their greed bred crime and disease and might provoke class warfare. Flash photography enabled Riis to expose the dark alleys and tenements of New York. He took his camera (much like the one pictured in the inset) into Baxter Street Court, then recorded these observations: "I counted the other day the little ones, up to ten years old in a...tenement that for a yard has a...space in the center with sides fourteen or fifteen feet long, just enough for a row of ill-smelling [water] closets...and a hydrant.... There was about as much light in the 'yard' as in the average cellar....I counted one hundred twenty eight [children] in forty families."

How the Other Half Lives made photographic history. It contained, along with Riis's text and the line drawings that had appeared in *Scribner's*, seventeen halftone prints of Riis's photographs. Riis's text and pictures shined the light on New York's darkest corners—vagrants in filthy lodging houses; "street arabs," homeless boys who lived by their wits on the streets; the saloons and dives of lower New York; evil-smelling tenement yards, stifling sweatshops. For the first time, unposed action pictures taken with a flash documented social conditions. Riis's pioneering photojournalism shocked the nation and led not only to tenement reform but also to the development of city playgrounds, neighborhood parks, and child labor laws.

believed that Congress was inept in foreign affairs, and he relied on executive power to effect a vigorous foreign policy, sometimes stretching the powers of the presidency beyond legal limits. A man who relished military discipline and viewed life as a constant conflict for supremacy, Roosevelt believed that "civilized nations" should police the world and hold "backward" countries in line. In his relations with the European powers, he relied on military strength and diplomacy, a combination he aptly described with the aphorism "Speak softly but carry a big stick."

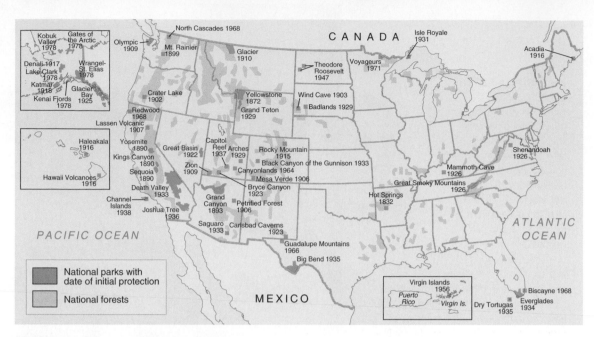

MAP 21.1   National Parks and Forests
The national park system in the West began with Yellowstone in 1872. Grand Canyon, Yosemite, Kings Canyon, and Sequoia followed in the 1890s. During his presidency, Theodore Roosevelt added six parks—Crater Lake, Wind Cave, Petrified Forest, Lassen Volcanic, Mesa Verde, and Zion.

READING THE MAP: Collectively, do national parks or national forests contain larger tracts of land? According to the map, how many national parks were created before 1910? How many were created after 1910?

CONNECTIONS: How do conservation and preservation differ? Why did Theodore Roosevelt believe conservation was important? What principle guided the national land use policy of the Roosevelt administration?

FOR MORE HELP ANALYZING THIS MAP, see the map activity for this chapter in the Online Study Guide at **bedfordstmartins.com/roarkcompact**.

In the Caribbean, Roosevelt jealously guarded the U.S. sphere of influence defined in the **Monroe Doctrine**. In 1902, he risked war to keep Germany from intervening in Venezuela when that country's dictator borrowed money in Europe and could not repay it. Roosevelt issued an ultimatum to the German kaiser, warning him not to intervene in Venezuela to secure payment of the debt. Roosevelt's message was blunt—stay out of Latin America or face war with the United States. Both sides eventually backed down and agreed to arbitration.

Roosevelt's proprietary attitude toward the Western Hemisphere became evident in the case of the Panama Canal. A firm advocate of naval power and an astute naval strategist, Roosevelt had long been a supporter of a canal linking the Caribbean and the Pacific. By enabling ships to move quickly from the Atlantic to the Pacific, a canal could effectively double the navy's power.

Having decided on a route across the Panamanian isthmus (a narrow strip of land connecting North and South America), then a part of Colombia, Roosevelt in 1902 offered the Colombian government a one-time sum of $10 million and an annual rent of $250,000. When the government in Bogotá refused to accept the offer, Roosevelt became incensed at what he called the "homicidal corruptionists" in Colombia for trying to "blackmail" the United States. At the prompting of a group of New York investors, the Panamanians staged an uprising in 1903 and with unseemly haste the U.S. government recognized the new government within twenty-four hours. The Panamanians promptly accepted the $10 million, and the building got under way (Map 21.2). The canal would take eleven years and $375 million to complete; it opened in 1914.

In the wake of the Panama affair, the confrontation with Germany over Venezuela, and yet another default on a European debt, this time in the Dominican Republic, Roosevelt announced in 1904 what became known as the Roosevelt Corollary to the Monroe Doctrine. Couched in the moral rhetoric typical of Roosevelt, the corollary declared the United States would not intervene in Latin America as long as nations there conducted their affairs with "decency." But the United States would step in if any Latin American nation proved guilty of "brutal wrongdoing." The Roosevelt Corollary in effect made the United States the policeman of the Western Hemisphere and served notice to the European powers to keep out. To ensure the pay-ment of debts, Roosevelt immedi-ately put the corollary into prac-tice by intervening in Costa Rica and by taking over the custom-house in the Dominican Republic to ensure the repayment of European debt.

In Asia, Roosevelt inherited the Open Door policy initiated by Secretary of State John Hay in 1899, designed to ensure U.S. commercial entry into China. As Britain, France, Russia, Japan, and Germany raced to secure Chinese

The Roosevelt Corollary in Action

Theodore Roosevelt and the Big Stick

In this political cartoon from 1904, President Theodore Roosevelt, dressed in his Rough Rider uniform and carrying his "big stick," turns the Caribbean into a Yankee pond. The Roosevelt Corollary to the Monroe Doctrine did exactly that.

Granger Collection.

FOR MORE HELP ANALYZING THIS IMAGE, see the visual activity for this chapter in the Online Study Guide at **bedfordstmartins.com/roarkcompact**.

THE BIG STICK IN THE CARIBBEAN SEA

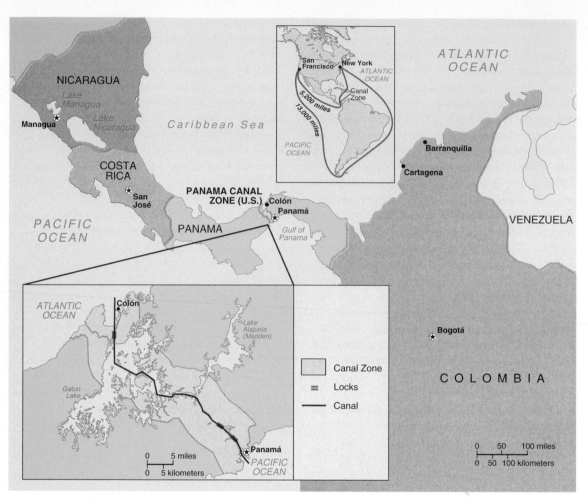

MAP 21.2 The Panama Canal, 1914
The Panama Canal, completed in 1914, bisected the isthmus in a series of massive locks and dams. As Theodore Roosevelt had planned, the canal greatly strengthened the navy by allowing ships to move from the Atlantic to the Pacific in a matter of days.

trade and territory, Roosevelt was tempted to use force to enter the fray and gain economic or possibly territorial concessions. As a result of victory in the Spanish-American War, the United States already enjoyed a foothold in the region by virtue of its control of the Philippines. Realizing that Americans would not support an aggressive Asian policy, Roosevelt sensibly held back.

In his relations with Europe, Roosevelt sought to establish the United States, fresh from its victory over Spain, as a rising force in world affairs. When tensions flared between France and Germany in Morocco in 1905, Roosevelt mediated at a conference in Algeciras, Spain, where he worked to maintain a balance of power that

helped neutralize German ambitions. His skillful mediation gained him a reputation as an astute player on the world stage and demonstrated the nation's new presence in world affairs.

Roosevelt earned the Nobel Peace Prize in 1906 for his role in negotiating an end to the Russo-Japanese War, which had broken out when the Japanese invaded Chinese Manchuria, threatening Russia's sphere of influence in the area. Once again, Roosevelt sought to maintain a balance of power, in this case working to curb Japanese expansionism. Roosevelt admired the Japanese, judging them "the most dashing fighters in the world," but he did not want Japan to become too strong in Asia. He presided over the peace conference at Portsmouth, New Hampshire, where he was able to prevent Japan from dominating Manchuria. He had no qualms, however, about initiating the Taft-Katsura agreement that granted Japan control of the sovereign nation of Korea in exchange for a pledge that Japan would not threaten the Philippines.

When good relations with Japan were jeopardized by discriminatory legislation in California calling for segregated public schools for "Orientals," Roosevelt smoothed over the incident and negotiated a "Gentleman's Agreement" in 1907 that allowed the Japanese to save face by voluntarily restricting immigration to the United States. To demonstrate America's naval power and counter Japan's growing bellicosity, Roosevelt dispatched the Great White Fleet, sixteen of the navy's most up-to-date battleships, on a "goodwill mission" around the world. U.S. relations with Japan improved, and in the 1908 Root-Takahira agreement the two nations pledged to maintain the Open Door and support the status quo in the Pacific. Roosevelt's show of American force constituted a classic example of his dictum "Speak softly but carry a big stick." Political cartoonists delighted in caricaturing the president wielding a cudgel in foreign affairs, and the American public relished the image.

> **REVIEW** How did Roosevelt's policies advance progressive reform?

Progressivism Stalled

Roosevelt retired from the presidency in 1909 at age fifty and removed himself from the political scene by going on safari in Africa. He turned the White House over to his handpicked successor, William Howard Taft, a lawyer who had served as governor general of the Philippines. In the presidential election of 1908, Taft soundly defeated the perennial Democratic candidate, William Jennings Bryan. But Taft's popular majority amounted to only half of Roosevelt's record win in 1904.

Any man would have found it difficult to follow in Roosevelt's footsteps, but Taft proved hopelessly ill suited to the task. A genial man with a talent for law, Taft had no experience in elective

office, no feel for politics, and no nerve for controversy. Taft's presidency was marked by a progressive stalemate, a bitter break with Roosevelt, and a schism in the Republican Party.

The Troubled Presidency of William Howard Taft

Once in office, Taft proved a perfect tool in the hands of Republicans who yearned for a return to the days of a less active executive. A lawyer by training and instinct, Taft believed that it was up to the courts, not the president, to arbitrate social issues. Roosevelt had carried presidential power to a new level, often flouting the separation of powers. Taft the legalist found it difficult to condone Roosevelt's actions. Wary of the progressive insurgents in Congress, Taft relied increasingly on conservatives in the Republican Party. As a progressive senator lamented, "Taft is a ponderous and amiable man completely surrounded by men who know exactly what they want."

Taft's troubles began on the eve of his inaugural when he called a special session of Congress to deal with the tariff. Roosevelt had been too politically astute to tackle the troublesome tariff issue, even though he knew that rates needed to be lowered. Taft blundered into the fray. The House of Representatives passed a modest downward revision and, to make up for lost revenue, imposed a small inheritance tax. Led by Senator Nelson Aldrich of Rhode Island, the conservative Senate struck down the tax and added more than eight hundred crippling amendments to the tariff. The Payne-Aldrich bill that emerged actually raised the tariff, benefiting big business and the trusts at the expense of consumers. As if paralyzed, Taft neither fought for changes nor vetoed the measure. On a tour of the Midwest in 1909, he was greeted with jeers when he claimed, "I think the Payne bill is the best bill that the Republican Party ever passed." In the eyes of a growing number of Americans, his praise of the tariff made him either a fool or a liar.

Taft's legalism soon got him into hot water in the area of conservation. He undid Roosevelt's work to preserve hydroelectric power sites when he learned that they had been improperly designated as ranger stations. And when Gifford Pinchot publicly denounced Taft's secretary of the interior as a tool of western land-grabbers, Taft fired Pinchot, touching off a storm of controversy that damaged Taft and alienated Roosevelt.

When Roosevelt returned to the United States in June 1910, he received a hero's welcome and attracted a stream of visitors and reporters seeking his advice and opinions. Hurt, Taft kept his distance. By late summer, Roosevelt had taken sides with the progressive insurgents in his party. "Taft is utterly hopeless as a leader," Roosevelt confided to his son as he set out on a speaking tour of the West. Reading the mood of the country, Roosevelt began to sound more and more like a candidate.

With the Republican Party divided, the Democrats swept the congressional elections of 1910. Branding the Payne-Aldrich tariff "the mother of trusts," they captured a majority in the House of Representatives and won several key governorships. The revitalized Democratic Party could look to new leaders, among them the progressive governor of New Jersey, Woodrow Wilson.

The new Democratic majority in the House, working with progressive Republicans in the Senate, achieved a number of key reforms, including legislation to regulate mine and railroad safety, to create a Children's Bureau in the Department of Labor, and to establish an eight-hour day for federal workers. Two significant constitutional amendments—the Sixteenth Amendment, which provided for a modest graduated income tax, and the Seventeenth Amendment, which called for the direct election of senators (formerly chosen by state legislatures)—went to the states, where they would win ratification in 1913. While Congress rode the high tide of progressive reform, Taft sat on the sidelines.

In foreign policy, too, Taft had a difficult time following in Roosevelt's footsteps. His policy of "dollar diplomacy" championed commercial goals rather than the strategic aims Roosevelt had pursued. Taft naively assumed he could substitute "dollars for bullets." In the Caribbean, he provoked anti-American feeling by attempting to force commercial treaties on Nicaragua and Honduras and by dispatching the U.S. marines to Nicaragua and the Dominican Republic in 1912 pursuant to the Roosevelt Corollary. In Asia, he openly avowed his intent to promote in China "active intervention to secure for…our capitalists opportunity for profitable investment." Lacking Roosevelt's understanding of power politics, Taft never recognized that an aggressive commercial policy could not exist without the willingness to use military might to back it up. When revolution broke out in Mexico in 1911, Taft faced the limits of dollar diplomacy. Under pressure to protect American investment, which amounted to more than $4 billion, he mobilized troops along the border. But in the end, with no popular support for a war with Mexico, he had to fall back on diplomatic pressure to salvage American interests.

Taft hoped to encourage world peace through the use of a world court and arbitration. He unsuccessfully sponsored a series of arbitration treaties that Roosevelt, who prized national honor more than international law, vehemently opposed as weak and cowardly. By 1910, Roosevelt had become a vocal critic of Taft's foreign policy, which he dismissed as "maudlin folly."

The final breach between Taft and Roosevelt came in 1911, when Taft's attorney general filed an antitrust suit against U.S. Steel. In its brief against the corporation, the government cited Roosevelt's agreement with the Morgan interests in the 1907 acquisition of Tennessee Coal and Iron. The incident greatly embarrassed Roosevelt. Thoroughly enraged, he lambasted Taft's "archaic" antitrust policy and hinted that he might be persuaded to run for president again.

Progressive Insurgency and the Election of 1912

In February 1912, Roosevelt challenged Taft for the Republican nomination, announcing, "My hat is in the ring." But for all his popularity, Roosevelt no longer controlled the party machinery. Taft, with uncharacteristic strength, refused to step aside. As he bitterly told a journalist, "Even a rat in a corner will fight." Roosevelt took advantage of newly passed primary election laws and ran in thirteen states, winning 278 delegates to Taft's 48. But at the Chicago convention, Taft's bosses refused to seat the Roosevelt delegates. Fistfights broke out on the convention floor as Taft won nomination on the first ballot. Crying robbery, Roosevelt's supporters bolted the party.

Seven weeks later, in the same Chicago auditorium, a hastily organized Progressive Party met to nominate Roosevelt. Amid a thunder of applause, Jane Addams seconded Roosevelt's

Taft's "Dollar Diplomacy"

U.S. intervention
- Nicaragua
- Honduras
- Dominican Republic

nomination. Full of reforming zeal, the delegates chose Roosevelt and Hiram Johnson to head the new party and approved the most ambitious platform since the Populists'. Planks called for woman suffrage, presidential primaries, conservation of natural resources, an end to child labor, minimum wages for women, workers' compensation, social security, and a federal income tax.

Roosevelt arrived in Chicago to accept the nomination and announced that he felt "as strong as a bull moose," giving the new party a nickname and a mascot. But for all the excitement and the cheering, the new Progressive Party was doomed, and the candidate knew it. The people may have supported the party, but the politicians, even progressives like La Follette,

stayed within the Republican fold. "I am under no illusion about it," Roosevelt confessed to a friend. "It is a forlorn hope." But he had gone too far to turn back. He led the Bull Moose Party into the fray, exhorting his followers in ringing biblical tones, "We shall not falter, we stand at Armageddon and do battle for the Lord."

The Democrats, delighted at the split in the Republican ranks, smelled victory. Their convention turned into a bitter fight for the nomination. After forty-six ballots, Woodrow Wilson became the party's nominee. Wilson's career in politics was nothing short of meteoric. Elected governor of New Jersey in 1910, after only eighteen months in office the former professor of political science and president of Princeton University found himself running for president of the United States.

Voters in 1912 could choose among three candidates who claimed to be progressives. That the term *progressive* could stretch to cover the three underscored major disagreements in progressive thinking about the relation between business and government. Taft, in spite of his trustbusting, was generally viewed as the candidate of the old guard. The real contest for the presidency was between Roosevelt and Wilson and the two political philosophies summed up in their respective campaign slogans: "The New Nationalism" and "The New Freedom."

The New Nationalism expressed Roosevelt's belief in federal planning and regulation. He accepted the inevitability of big business but demanded that government act as "a steward of the people" to regulate the giant corporations. Roosevelt called for an increase in the power of the federal government, a decrease in the power of the courts, and an active role for the president. He hoped to use an active federal government to promote social justice and democracy, replacing

Novelty Postcards of the Election of 1912
These postcards picture the mascot of each party with a moving spring for a tail—the Democrats' donkey, the Progressives' bull moose, and the Republicans' elephant. The hat shown with Roosevelt comes from his phrase "My hat is in the ring," signifying his challenge to incumbent William Howard Taft. Taft's Grand Old Party (GOP) elephant is shown with a steamroller. Many critics charged that Taft won the Republican nomination from Roosevelt in 1912 by steamrolling the party's convention. The caption asks "Has He Got Enough Steam?" In a more obscure reference, Woodrow Wilson is pictured with "The New Jersey Mosquito," and the caption asks "Will He Get Stung?"
Collection of Janice L. and David J. Frent.

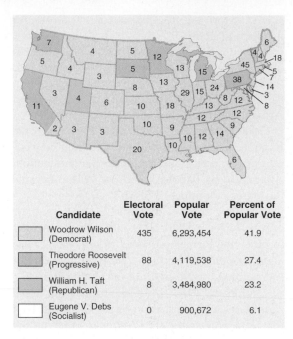

Candidate	Electoral Vote	Popular Vote	Percent of Popular Vote
Woodrow Wilson (Democrat)	435	6,293,454	41.9
Theodore Roosevelt (Progressive)	88	4,119,538	27.4
William H. Taft (Republican)	8	3,484,980	23.2
Eugene V. Debs (Socialist)	0	900,672	6.1

MAP 21.3   The Election of 1912

the laissez-faire policies of the old liberal state with a new form of liberalism.

Wilson, schooled in the Democratic principles of limited government and **states' rights**, set a markedly different course with his New Freedom. Wilson promised to use antitrust legislation to get rid of big corporations and to give small businesses and farmers better opportunities in the marketplace.

Wilson and Roosevelt fought it out, and the energy and enthusiasm of the Bull Moosers made the race seem closer than it really was. In the end, the Republican vote split while the Democrats remained united. No candidate claimed a majority in the race. Wilson captured a bare 42 percent of the popular vote. Roosevelt and his Bull Moose Party won 27 percent of the vote, an unprecedented tally for a new party. Taft came in third with 23 percent. The Socialist Party, led by Eugene V. Debs, captured 6 percent. But in the electoral college, Wilson won a decisive 435, with 88 going to Roosevelt and only 8 to Taft (Map 21.3). The Bull Moose Party essentially collapsed after Roosevelt's defeat. It had always been, in the words of one astute observer, "a house divided against itself and already mortgaged."

REVIEW   Why did Roosevelt become the presidential nominee of the Progressive Party in 1912?

Woodrow Wilson and Progressivism at High Tide

Born in Virginia and raised in Georgia, Woodrow Wilson became the first southerner to be elected president since 1844 and only the second Democrat to occupy the White House since Reconstruction. Democrats who anticipated a wild celebration when Wilson took office had their hopes dashed. The son of a Presbyterian minister, Wilson was a teetotaler more given to scripture than to celebration. He called instead for a day of prayer.

This lean, ascetic man was, as one biographer conceded, a man whose "political convictions were never as fixed as his ambition." Although he owed his governorship to the Democratic machine, he quickly turned his back on the bosses and put New Jersey in the vanguard of progressivism. A year into his term, Wilson had his eye on the presidency. Always able to equivocate, Wilson proved rarely able to compromise. He brought to the White House a gift for oratory, a stern will, and a set of fixed beliefs. His tendency to turn differences of opinion into personal hatreds would impair his leadership and damage his presidency. Fortunately for Wilson, he came to power with a Democratic Congress eager to do his bidding.

Although he opposed big government in his campaign, Wilson was prepared to work on the base built by Roosevelt to strengthen presidential power, exerting leadership and working through his party in Congress to accomplish the Democratic agenda. Before he was finished, Wilson presided over progressivism at high tide and lent his support not only to the platform of the Democratic Party but to many of the Progressive Party's social reforms as well.

Wilson's Reforms: Tariff, Banking, and the Trusts

In March 1913, Wilson became the first president since John Adams to go to Capitol Hill and speak directly to Congress, calling for tariff reform. "The object of the tariff," Wilson told Congress, "must be effective competition." Eager to topple the high tariff, the Democratic House of Representatives hastily passed the Underwood tariff, which lowered rates by 15 percent. To compensate for lost revenue, the House approved a moderate federal income tax, made possible by ratification of the Sixteenth Amendment a month earlier. In the Senate, lobbyists for industries quietly went to work to get the tariff raised, but Wilson rallied public opinion by attacking the "industrious and insidious lobby." In the harsh glare of publicity, the Senate passed the Underwood tariff, which earned praise as "the most honest tariff since the Civil War."

Wilson next turned his attention to banking. The panic of 1907 dramatically testified to the failure of the banking system. That year, Roosevelt, like President Grover Cleveland before him, had to turn to J. P. Morgan to avoid economic catastrophe. But by the time Wilson came to office, Morgan's legendary power had come under close scrutiny. In 1913, a Senate committee investigated the "money trust," calling J. P. Morgan himself to testify. The committee uncovered an alarming concentration of banking power. J. P. Morgan and Company and its affiliates held 341 directorships in 112 corporations, controlling assets of more than $22 billion. The sensational findings created a mandate for banking reform.

The Federal Reserve Act of 1913 marked the most significant piece of domestic legislation of Wilson's presidency. It established a national banking system composed of twelve regional banks, privately controlled but regulated and supervised by a Federal Reserve Board appointed by the president. It gave the United States its first efficient banking and currency system and, at the same time, provided for a greater degree of government control over banking. The new system made currency more elastic and credit adequate for the needs of business and agriculture. It did not, however, attempt to take control of the boom and bust cycles in the U.S. economy, which would produce the Great Depression of the 1930s.

Wilson, flushed with success, tackled the trust issue next. When Congress reconvened in January 1914, he supported the introduction of the Clayton Antitrust Act to outlaw "unfair competition"—practices such as price discrimination and interlocking directorates (directors from one corporation sitting on the board of another). By spelling out unfair practices, Wilson hoped to guide business activity back to healthy competition without resorting to regulation.

In the midst of the fight for the Clayton Act, Wilson changed course and threw his support behind the creation of the Federal Trade Commission (FTC), precisely the kind of federal regulatory agency that Roosevelt had advocated in his New Nationalism platform. The FTC, cre-

ated in 1914, had not only wide investigatory powers but the authority to prosecute corporations for "unfair trade practices" and to enforce its judgments by issuing "cease and desist" orders. Despite his campaign promises, Wilson's antitrust program worked to regulate rather than to break up big business.

By the fall of 1914, Wilson had exhausted the stock of ideas that made up the New Freedom. He alarmed progressives by declaring that the progressive movement had fulfilled its mission and that the country needed "a time of healing." Disgruntled progressives also disapproved of Wilson's conservative appointments. Having fought provisions in the Federal Reserve Act that would give bankers control, Wilson promptly named a banker as the first chief of the Federal Reserve Board. Appointments to the new FTC also went to conservative businessmen. The progressive penchant for expertise helps explain Wilson's choices. Believing that experts in the field could best understand the complex issues at stake, Wilson appointed bankers to oversee the banks and businessmen to regulate business.

Wilson, Reluctant Progressive

Progressives watched in dismay as Wilson repeatedly obstructed or obstinately refused to endorse further progressive reforms. He failed to support labor's demand for an end to court injunctions against labor unions. He twice threatened to veto legislation providing for farm credits on nonperishable crops. He refused to support child labor legislation or woman suffrage. Wilson used the rhetoric of the New Freedom to justify his actions, claiming that his administration would condone "special privileges to none." But in fact his stance often reflected the interests of his small-business constituency.

In the face of Wilson's obstinacy, reform might have ended in 1913 had not politics intruded. In the congressional elections of 1914, the Republican Party, no longer split by Roosevelt's Bull Moose faction, won substantial gains. Democratic strategists, with their eyes on the 1916 presidential race, recognized that Wilson needed to pick up support in the Midwest and the West by capturing votes from former Bull Moose progressives.

Wilson responded belatedly by lending his support to reform in the months leading up to the election of 1916. In a sharp about-face, he cultivated union labor, farmers, and social reformers. To please labor, he appointed progressive Louis

Breaker Boys

Child labor in America's mines and mills was common at the turn of the twentieth century, despite state laws that tried to restrict it. Here "breaker boys," some as young as seven years old, pick over coal in a Pennsylvania mine. Their unsmiling faces bear testimony to the difficulty and danger of their work. A committee investigating child labor found more than 10,000 children illegally employed in the Pennsylvania coalfields. In 1916, progressives worked hard to enact the Keating-Owen act prohibiting child labor. Two years later, the Supreme Court struck down the law, ruling that Congress could not regulate manufacturing within states. Brown Brothers.

Democrats had "opened their hearts to the demands of social justice" and had "come very near to carrying out the platform of the Progressive Party." Wilson's shift toward reform, along with his claim that he had kept the United States out of the war in Europe (see chapter 22), helped him win reelection in 1916.

> **REVIEW** How and why did Wilson's reform program evolve during his first term?

The Limits of Progressive Reform

While progressivism called for a more active role for the liberal state, at heart it was a movement that sought reforms designed to preserve American institutions and stem the tide of more radical change. Its basic conservatism can be seen by comparing it to more radical movements of the era—socialism, radical labor, and birth control—and by looking at the groups progressive reform left behind, including women and African Americans.

Radical Alternatives

The year 1900 marked the birth of the Social Democratic Party in America, later called simply the Socialist Party. Like the progressives, the socialists were middle class and native-born. They had broken with the older, more militant Socialist Labor Party precisely because of its dogmatic approach and immigrant constituency. The new group of socialists proved eager to appeal to a broad mass of disaffected Americans.

The Socialist Party chose as its standard-bearer Eugene V. Debs, whose experience in the Pullman strike of 1894 convinced him that "there is no hope for the toiling masses of my countrymen, except by the pathways mapped out by Socialism." Debs's brand of socialism advocated cooperation over competition and urged men and women to liberate themselves from "the barbarism of private ownership and wage slavery." Roosevelt labeled Debs a "mere inciter to murder and preacher of applied anarchy." Debs, for his part, pointed to the conservatism that underlay Roosevelt's rhetoric. In the 1912 election, Debs

Brandeis to the Supreme Court. To woo farmers, he threw his support behind legislation to obtain rural credits. And he won praise from labor by supporting workers' compensation and the Keating-Owen child labor law (1916), which outlawed the regular employment of children younger than sixteen. When a railroad strike threatened in the months before the election, Wilson practically ordered Congress to establish an eight-hour day on the railroads. He had moved a long way from his position in 1912 to embrace many of the social reforms championed by Theodore Roosevelt. As Wilson boasted, the indicted both old parties as "Tweedledee and Tweedledum," each dedicated to the preservation of capitalism and the continuation of the wage system. The Socialist Party alone, he argued, was the "revolutionary party of the working class." Debs would run for president five times, in every election (except 1916) from 1900 to 1920. His best showing came in 1912, when he polled 6 percent of the popular vote, capturing almost a million votes.

Farther to the left of the socialists stood the Industrial Workers of the World (IWW), nicknamed the Wobblies. In 1905, Debs, along with Western Federation of Miners leader William Dudley "Big Bill" Haywood, created the IWW, "one big union" dedicated to organizing the most destitute segment of the workforce, the unskilled workers disdained by Samuel Gompers's AFL—western miners, migrant farmworkers, lumbermen, and immigrant textile workers. Haywood, a craggy-faced miner with one eye (he had lost the other in a childhood accident), was a charismatic leader and a proletarian intellectual. Seeing workers on the lowest rung of the social ladder as the victims of violent repression, the IWW unhesitatingly advocated direct action, sabotage, and the general strike—tactics designed to trigger a workers' uprising. The IWW never had more than 10,000 members at any one time, although possibly as many as 100,000 workers belonged to the union at one time or another in the early twentieth century. Nevertheless, the IWW's influence on the country extended far beyond its numbers.

In contrast to political radicals like Debs and Haywood, Margaret Sanger promoted birth control as a movement for social change. Sanger, a nurse who had worked among the poor on New York's Lower East Side, coined the term *birth control* in 1915 and launched a movement with broad social implications. Sanger and her followers saw birth control not only as a sexual and medical reform but also as a means to alter social and political power relationships and to alleviate human misery.

Convinced that women needed to be able to control their pregnancies but unsure of the best methods to do so, Sanger traveled to Europe in 1913 to learn more about contraceptive techniques. On her return, she promoted birth control in her militant **feminist** journal, *The Woman Rebel*. Social purity laws passed in the 1870s made it illegal to distribute either information on birth control or contraceptive devices, classing both as "obscene." The post office confiscated Sanger's magazine and brought charges against her. Facing arrest, she fled to Europe only to return in 1916 something of a national celebrity. In her absence, birth control had become linked with free speech and had been taken up as a liberal cause. Under public pressure, the government dropped the charges against Sanger, who undertook a nationwide tour to publicize the birth control cause.

Sanger then turned to direct action, opening the nation's first birth control clinic in the Brownsville section of Brooklyn in October 1916. Located in the heart of a Jewish and Italian immigrant neighborhood, the clinic attracted 464 clients in the nine days it remained open. On the tenth day, police shut down the clinic and threw Sanger in jail. By then she had become a national figure, and the cause she championed had gained legitimacy, if not legality. After World War I, the birth control movement would become much less radical as Sanger turned to medical doctors for support and mouthed the racist theories of the eugenics movement. But in its infancy, the movement Sanger led was part of a radical vision for reforming the world that made common cause with the socialists and the IWW in challenging the limits of progressive reform.

Progressivism for White Men Only

The day before President Woodrow Wilson's inauguration in March 1913, the largest mass march to date in the nation's history took place as more than five thousand demonstrators took to the streets in Washington to demand the vote for women. A rowdy crowd on hand to celebrate the Democrats' triumph heckled the marchers, as did the police. "If my wife were where you are," a burly cop told one suffragist, "I'd break her head." But for all the marching, Wilson, who didn't believe that a "lady" should vote, pointedly ignored woman suffrage in his inaugural address the next day.

The march served as a reminder that the political gains of progressivism were not spread equally in the population. As the twentieth century dawned, women still could not vote in most states. Increasingly, however, woman suffrage had become an international movement. In

Great Britain, Emmeline Pankhurst and her daughters Cristabel and Sylvia promoted a new, militant suffragism. They seized the spotlight in a series of marches, mass meetings, and acts of civil disobedience, which sometimes escalated into riots, violence, and arson.

Alice Paul, a Quaker social worker who had visited England and participated in suffrage activism there, returned to the United States in 1910 in time to plan the mass march on the eve of Wilson's inauguration and to lobby for a federal amendment to give women the vote. Paul's dramatic tactics alienated many in the National American Woman Suffrage Association (NAWSA). In 1916, Paul founded the militant National Woman's Party (NWP), which became the radical voice of the suffrage movement, advocating direct action such as mass marches and civil disobedience.

The NAWSA, spurred by the actions of Paul and her followers, gained new direction after Carrie Chapman Catt became president in 1915.

Margaret Sanger's Brownsville Birth Control Clinic

Margaret Sanger opened the first birth control clinic in the United States in the Brownsville section of Brooklyn in 1916. During the nine days it operated before police shut it down, more than four hundred women visited the clinic. Here they are shown waiting patiently in line with their baby carriages. Sanger published her flyers in English, Yiddish, and Italian, and her clinic attracted immigrant women, proving that Italian Catholics and Russian Jews wanted birth control information as much as their middle- and upper-class Protestant counterparts did. What does the picture say about which women sought birth control, married or single women?

Sophia Smith Collection, Smith College.

Catt revitalized the organization with a carefully crafted "winning plan" designed to achieve suffrage in six years. While Paul and her NWP held a six-month vigil outside the White House—holding banners that read "Mr. Wilson, What Will You Do for Woman Suffrage?"—Catt led a centrally directed effort that worked on several levels. Catt's strategy was to "keep so much 'suffrage noise' going all over the country that neither the enemy [n]or friends will discover where the real battle is." Catt's "winning plan" worked effectively, taking only four years instead of the six Catt had predicted to ratify a constitutional amendment for woman suffrage.

Women weren't the only group left out in progressive reform. Progressivism, as it was practiced in the West and South, was tainted with racism and sought to limit the rights of African and Asian Americans. Anti-Asian bigotry in the West led to a renewal of the Chinese Exclusion Act in 1902. At first, California governor Hiram Johnson stood against the strong anti-Asian prejudice of his state; then in 1913 he caved in to near unanimous pressure and signed the Alien Land Law, which barred Japanese immigrants from purchasing land in California. The law was largely symbolic—ineffectual in practice because Japanese children born in the United States were U.S. citizens and property could be purchased in their names.

South of the Mason-Dixon line, the progressives' racism targeted African Americans. Progressives preached the disfranchisement of black voters as a "reform." During the bitter electoral fights that had pitted Populists against Democrats in the 1890s, the party of white supremacy held its power by votes purchased or coerced from African Americans. Southern progressives proposed to "reform" the electoral system by eliminating black voters. Beginning in 1890 with Mississippi, southern states curtailed the African American vote through devices such as poll taxes (fees required for voting) and literacy tests. The racist intent of southern voting legislation became especially clear after 1900 when states resorted to the grandfather clause, a legal provision that allowed men who failed a literacy test to vote if their grandfathers had cast a ballot. Grandfathering permitted southern white men to vote while excluding nearly all blacks.

The Progressive Era also witnessed the rise of **Jim Crow** laws to segregate public facilities (Jim Crow was the name of a character in a popular minstrel song). The new railroads precipitated segregation in the South where it had rarely existed before, at least on paper. Blacks traveling by train found themselves restricted to Jim Crow coaches even when they paid the first-class fare. Soon separate waiting rooms, separate bathrooms, and separate dining facilities for blacks sprang up across the South. In courtrooms in Mississippi, blacks were even required to swear on a separate Bible.

In the face of this growing repression, Booker T. Washington, the preeminent black leader of the day, urged caution and restraint. A former slave, Washington had opened the Tuskegee Institute in Alabama in 1881 to teach vocational skills to African Americans. He emphasized education and economic progress for his race and urged African Americans to put aside issues of political and social equality. In an 1895 speech in Atlanta, which came to be known as the "Atlanta Compromise," he stated, "In all things that are purely social we can be as separate as the fingers, yet one as the hand in all things essential to mutual progress." Washington's accommodationist policy appealed to whites and elevated "the wizard of Tuskegee" to the role of national spokesman for African Americans.

The year after Washington proclaimed the Atlanta Compromise, the Supreme Court upheld the legality of racial segregation, affirming in *Plessy v. Ferguson* (1896) the constitutionality of the doctrine of "separate but equal." Blacks could be segregated in separate schools, restrooms, and other facilities, as long as the facilities were "equal" to those provided for whites. In actuality, facilities for blacks rarely proved equal. In the North, where racism of a different sort led to a clamor for legislation to restrict immigration, support for African American equality found few advocates. And with anti-Asian bigotry strong in the West, the doctrine of "white supremacy" found increasing support in all sections of the country.

When Theodore Roosevelt invited Booker T. Washington to dine at the White House in 1901, a storm of racist criticism erupted. One southern editor fumed that the White House "had been painted black." But Roosevelt summoned Washington to talk politics and patronage, not African American rights. His racial prejudice became obvious in the Brownsville incident in 1906, when he dishonorably discharged three companies of black soldiers because he suspected (although there was no proof) that they were shielding the murderer of a white saloon-keeper killed in a shoot-out in the Texas town.

EQUALITY

DINNER GIVEN AT THE WHITE HOUSE BY PRESIDENT ROOSEVELT TO BOOKER T. WASHINGTON, OCTOBER 17th, 1901

Booker T. Washington and Theodore Roosevelt Dine at the White House
When Theodore Roosevelt invited Booker T. Washington to the White House in 1901, he stirred up a hornet's nest of controversy that continued into the election of 1904. This Republican campaign piece gives the meeting a positive slant, showing Roosevelt and Washington sitting under a portrait of Abraham Lincoln, a symbol of the party's historic commitment to African Americans. Can you tell from this illustration that Washington is African American? Democrats portrayed the meeting in a very different light; their campaign buttons pictured Washington with darker skin and implied that Roosevelt favored "race mingling."
Collection of Janice L. and David J. Frent.

Woodrow Wilson brought to the White House southern attitudes toward race and racial segregation. At the prompting of his wife, he instituted segregation in the federal workforce, especially the post office, and approved segregated drinking fountains and restrooms in the nation's capital. When critics attacked the policy, Wilson insisted that segregation was "in the interest of the Negro."

Faced with intolerance and open persecution, educated blacks in the North rebelled against the conservative leadership of Booker T. Washington. In *The Souls of Black Folk* (1903), Harvard graduate

W. E. B. Du Bois attacked the "Tuskegee Machine," comparing Booker T. Washington to a political boss who used his influence to silence his critics and reward his followers. Du Bois founded the Niagara movement in 1905, calling for universal male suffrage, civil rights, and leadership by a black intellectual elite. In 1909, the Niagara movement helped found the National Association for the Advancement of Colored People (NAACP), a coalition of blacks and whites that sought legal and political rights for African Americans through the courts. Like many progressive reform coalitions, the NAACP attracted a diverse group—

social workers, socialists, and black intellectuals. In the decades that followed, the NAACP came to represent the future for African Americans, while Booker T. Washington, who died in 1915, represented the past.

> **REVIEW** How did race and gender shape the limits of progressive reform?

Conclusion: The Transformation of the Liberal State

Progressivism was never a radical movement. Its goal remained to reform the existing system—by government intervention if necessary, but without uprooting any of the traditional American political, economic, or social institutions. As Theodore Roosevelt, the bellwether of the movement, insisted, "The only true conservative is the man who resolutely sets his face toward the future." Roosevelt was such a man, and progressivism was such a movement. But although progressivism was never radical, neither was it the laissez-faire liberalism of the previous century. Progressives' willingness to use the power of government to regulate business and achieve a measure of social justice redefined liberalism in the twentieth century, tying it to the expanded power of the state.

Progressivism contained many paradoxes. A diverse coalition of individuals and interests, the progressive movement began at the grass roots but left as its legacy a stronger presidency and unprecedented federal involvement in the economy and social welfare. A movement that believed in social justice, progressivism often promoted social control. And while progressives called for greater democracy, they fostered elitism with their worship of experts and efficiency.

But whatever its inconsistencies and limitations, progressivism took action to deal with the problems posed by urban industrialism. Progressivism saw grassroots activists address social problems on the local and state levels and search for national solutions as well. By increasing the power of the presidency and expanding

the power of the state, progressives worked to bring about greater social justice and to achieve a better balance between government and business. Jane Addams and Theodore Roosevelt could lay equal claim to the movement that redefined liberalism and launched the liberal state of the twentieth century. War on a global scale would provide progressivism with yet another challenge even before it had completed its ambitious agenda.

Suggestions for Further Reading

James Chace, *1912: Wilson, Roosevelt, Taft and Debs— The Election That Changed the Country* (2004). A lively account of the 1912 contest.

Alan Dawley, *Changing the World: American Progressives in War and Revolution* (2003). A skillful interweaving of foreign policy and domestic issues that demonstrates how progressivism developed in its international context.

Gary Gerstle, *American Crucible: Race and Nation in the Twentieth Century* (2002). An account detailing how progressives like Theodore Roosevelt established a prototype of racial nationalism that influenced social, diplomatic, and economic policies.

Michael McGerr, *A Fierce Discontent: The Rise and Fall of the Progressive Movement in America, 1870–1920* (2003). A vivid portrait of how middle-class progressives set out to remake America in their own image.

Daniel T. Rodgers, *Atlantic Crossings: Social Politics in a Progressive Age* (1998). A prize-winning study of the international intellectual and political currents that shaped the Progressive Era.

Kathryn Kish Sklar, *Florence Kelley and the Nation's Work: The Rise of Women's Political Culture, 1830– 1900* (1995). A study of Kelley's life, demonstrating women's role in progressive reform.

▶ **For more books about topics in this chapter,** see the Online Bibliography at **bedfordstmartins.com/roarkcompact.**

▶ **For additional firsthand accounts of this period,** see Chapter 21 in Michael Johnson, ed., *Reading the American Past,* Third Edition.

▶ **For Web sites and documents related to topics and places in this chapter,** see "HistoryLinks," "DocLinks," and "PlaceLinks" at **bedfordstmartins.com/roarkcompact.**

REVIEWING THE CHAPTER

Follow these steps to review and strengthen your understanding of the chapter.

STEP 1: *Study the* **Key Terms** *and* **Timeline** *to identify the significance of each item listed.*

STEP 2: *Answer the* **Review Questions***, drawing on key terms and dates to support your answers.*

STEP 3: *Drawing on the Key Terms, Timeline, and Review Questions, answer the broader* **Making Connections** *questions.*

KEY TERMS

Who

Jane Addams (p. 533)
Lillian Wald (p. 535)
Florence Kelley (p. 538)
Frederick Winslow Taylor (p. 538)
Tom Johnson (p. 538)
Robert M. La Follette (p. 539)
Hiram Johnson (p. 540)
William McKinley (p. 540)
Leon Czolgosz (p. 540)
Theodore Roosevelt (p. 540)
Upton Sinclair (p. 542)
Gifford Pinchot (p. 543)
John Muir (p. 543)
William Howard Taft (p. 549)
Woodrow Wilson (p. 552)
Eugene V. Debs (p. 554)
William Dudley "Big Bill"
    Haywood (p. 555)
Margaret Sanger (p. 555)
Alice Paul (p. 556)
Carrie Chapman Catt (p. 556)
Booker T. Washington (p. 557)
W. E. B. Du Bois (p. 558)

What

settlement house movement (p. 535)
social gospel (p. 535)
social purity movement (p. 535)
Women's Trade Union League (WTUL)
    (p. 536)
Triangle fire (p. 536)
Muller v. Oregon (p. 538)
National Consumers' League (p. 538)
reform Darwinism (p. 538)
Elkins Act (p. 541)
"Square Deal" (p. 541)
Interstate Commerce Commission
    (p. 542)
Hepburn Act (p. 542)
The Jungle (p. 542)
Pure Food and Drug Act and Meat
    Inspection Act (p. 542)
panic of 1907 (p. 542)
Newlands Reclamation Act (p. 543)
Panama Canal (p. 546)
Roosevelt Corollary (p. 547)
Root-Takahira agreement (p. 549)
Payne-Aldrich bill (p. 549)

Sixteenth Amendment (p. 550)
Seventeenth Amendment (p. 550)
dollar diplomacy (p. 550)
Progressive Party (Bull Moose Party)
    (p. 551)
"The New Nationalism" (p. 551)
"The New Freedom" (p. 551)
Underwood tariff (p. 552)
Federal Reserve Act of 1913 (p. 553)
Clayton Antitrust Act (p. 553)
Federal Trade Commission (FTC)
    (p. 553)
Keating-Owen child labor law (p. 554)
Socialist Party (p. 554)
Industrial Workers of the World
    (Wobblies) (p. 555)
National Woman's Party (p. 556)
Atlanta Compromise (p. 557)
Plessy v. Ferguson (p. 557)
National Association for the
    Advancement of Colored People
    (NAACP) (p. 558)

TIMELINE

1889 • Jane Addams opens Hull House.

1895 • Booker T. Washington enunciates "Atlanta Compromise."

1896 • *Plessy v. Ferguson.*

1900 • Socialist Party founded.

1901 • McKinley assassinated; Theodore Roosevelt becomes president.

1902 • Antitrust lawsuit filed against Northern Securities Company.
• Roosevelt mediates anthracite coal strike.
• Newlands Reclamation Act.

1903 • Women's Trade Union League (WTUL) founded.
• United States begins construction of Panama Canal.
• Elkins Act passed, outlawing railroad rebates.

1904 • Roosevelt Corollary to Monroe Doctrine.

1905 • Industrial Workers of the World founded.
• W. E. B. Du Bois founds Niagara movement.
• Roosevelt mediates at Algeciras conference.

1906 • Pure Food and Drug Act and
        Meat Inspection Act.
• Hepburn Act.

REVIEW QUESTIONS

1. Why did cities become one of the primary sites for progressive reform? (pp. 535–38)

2. How did progressives justify their demand for more activist government? (pp. 538–40)

3. How did Roosevelt's policies advance progressive reform? (pp. 540–49)

4. Why did Roosevelt become the presidential nominee of the Progressive Party in 1912? (pp. 549–52)

5. How and why did Wilson's reform program evolve during his first term? (pp. 552–54)

6. How did race and gender shape the limits of progressive reform? (pp. 554–59)

MAKING CONNECTIONS

1. Diverse approaches to reform came under the umbrella of progressivism. Discuss the work of three progressive reformers working at the grassroots or local government level. What do your examples reveal about progressivism? What characteristics connected their reform efforts? What separated them?

2. Opponents on the campaign stump, Theodore Roosevelt and Woodrow Wilson shared a commitment to domestic reform. Compare their legislative programs, including the evolution of their policies over time and their ability to respond to shifting political circumstances. What do their policies reveal about their understandings of the roles of the executive and the federal government?

3. During the Gilded Age, industrial capitalism had concentrated power in the hands of corporations. Americans searched for ways to shift the balance, including strikes, antitrust actions, and regulation. How did Theodore Roosevelt attempt to respond to this problem? How did his approach differ from earlier efforts? Was it effective?

4. What contemporary movements lay beyond the limits of progressive reform? Why did progressive reform coincide with the restriction of minority rights? In your answer, discuss how radical movements provide insights into the character of progressivism itself.

▶ For practice quizzes, a customized study plan, and other study tools, see the Online Study Guide at bedfordstmartins.com/roarkcompact.

1907 • Panic on Wall Street.
      • Roosevelt signs "Gentleman's Agreement" with Japan restricting immigration.

1908 • *Muller v. Oregon.*
        • Republican William Howard Taft elected president.

1909 • Garment workers' strike in New York City.
        • National Association for the Advancement of Colored People (NAACP) formed.

1910 • Hiram Johnson elected governor of California.

1911 • Triangle fire in New York City.
        • Taft launches antitrust suit against U.S. Steel.

1912 • Roosevelt runs for president on Progressive Party ticket.
        • Democrat Woodrow Wilson elected president.

1913 • Suffragists march in Washington, D.C.
        • Federal Reserve Act.

1914 • Wilson signs legislation establishing Federal Trade Commission (FTC).
        • Clayton Antitrust Act.

1916 • Alice Paul launches National Woman's Party.
        • Margaret Sanger opens first U.S. birth control clinic.
        • Keating-Owen child labor law.

1918 • Supreme Court declares Keating-Owen unconstitutional.

GAS MASK

Prior to World War I, the use of poison gas
was considered uncivilized, but desperate
fighting eroded old moral boundaries. On April
22, 1915, the Germans used poison gas for the first
time in battle, and after that soldiers faced death from chemical weapons as well as from artillery, rifles, mortars, machine guns, hand
grenades, tanks, airplanes, bayonets, and flamethrowers. The Allies condemned the German innovation
as diabolic but quickly developed research programs of their own. Poison gas caused large numbers of
casualties early on; then improved gas masks brought a sharp decline in deaths from gas. Despite the
crude appearance of this gas mask, filter respirators (using charcoal or antidote chemicals) proved highly
effective. Some 50,300 American soldiers were killed in action during the war, but fewer than 1,500 died
from gas. Many of those who were gassed and survived, however, were disabled and likely to die young.

Collection of Colonel Stuart S. Corning Jr. / Picture Research Consultants & Archives.

World War I: The Progressive Crusade at Home and Abroad

1914–1920

WHEN THE UNITED STATES entered World War I against Germany and its allies in 1917, it had neither a grand army nor a commander to lead one. But President Woodrow Wilson quickly tapped Major General John "Black Jack" Pershing, a ramrod-straight West Point graduate, to command the American Expeditionary Force (AEF) on the battlefields of France. Pershing had much to recommend him: He fought Apaches in the West in the 1880s, led a company of African American soldiers up San Juan Hill in Cuba in 1898 (hence his nickname "Black Jack"), overcame fierce resistance in the Philippine jungles in the first decade of the twentieth century, and headed Wilson's Punitive Expedition into Mexico in 1916 and 1917 in pursuit of the revolutionary bandit Pancho Villa. Pershing's courage and resilience had been severely tested in 1915 when he suffered the irretrievable loss of his wife and three daughters in a fire at their home in San Francisco.

On June 13, 1917, Pershing and his officer corps arrived in war-weary France, where huge crowds shouted "Vive l'Amérique!" and greeted the Americans as saviors. But Pershing knew that it would be months before America's disorganized war effort succeeded in supplying a steady stream of "doughboys," as American troops would be called. Pershing, who was responsible for organizing, training, and supplying this inexperienced force that eventually numbered more than 2 million, put his own stamp on the AEF. "The standards for the American Army will be those of West Point," he announced. "The upright bearing, attention to detail, uncomplaining obedience to instruction required of the cadet will be required of every officer and soldier of our armies in France." Hard and relentless, Pershing more than once chewed out an exhausted soldier for having mud on his boots and his collar unbuttoned.

Pershing found himself waging two wars, one against the Germans and the other against America's allies, as he constantly rebuffed French and British efforts to use his soldiers in their badly depleted front lines. Having seen too much of Europe's trench warfare, where enemies dug in, pounded one another with artillery, and squandered thousands of lives in hopeless assaults, Pershing insisted on keeping American soldiers under his own command. He believed that the Americans could break the impasse by relying on the rifle and rapid movement tactics taught at West Point to create "open warfare," an American

Pershing Button

Steely-eyed and determined, General John J. Pershing, surrounded by the flags of the Allied nations, stares at the viewer. The words circling the button declare that the Allies fight in the "cause of liberty," echoing President Woodrow Wilson's insistence that American democratic ideals were universal and could be achieved internationally through U.S. participation in the war.

Collection of Janice L. and David J. Frent.

style of warfare. But as a disgusted British journalist observed, "After eight months…you haven't really fired a damned shot!"

By the summer of 1918, when the Allied armies began preparing a massive attack against the Germans, Ferdinand Foch, head of the French army, rushed to Pershing's headquarters to "insist" once again that American troops merge with his decimated divisions. Pershing responded: "Marshal Foch, you may insist all you please, but…our army will fight…only as an independent American Army." Foch stormed out, and Pershing readied his army to strike at the German forces dug in at Saint-Mihiel and to begin what he was certain would be a victory march to Berlin. Assembling his officers, Pershing praised them for what they were about to do— break the stalemate of trench warfare. But American troops met a storm of machine-gun and artillery fire, and it took forty days and 100,000 casualties for the Americans to reach the German border, something Pershing had thought his soldiers could do in a few days. Nevertheless, fresh American troops helped destroy the German will to continue the war. In November 1918, Berlin asked for an immediate armistice, and the "Great War," as participants called the conflict, ended.

Pershing's stubborn effort to protect the autonomy of his army was only part of America's tortuous struggle to identify its interests in World War I and to maintain its national independence. When Wilson entered the White House, he believed that war was an affliction that modern diplomacy would eventually eradicate. He proclaimed America's absolute neutrality when war

erupted in Europe in 1914. By standing apart, Wilson explained, America could offer "impartial mediation" and broker a healing peace. But trade and principle soon entangled the United States in Europe's troubles. When the nation was finally drawn into the war in 1917, Wilson sought to maintain America's grand purpose, hoping that America's participation would uplift both the United States and the entire world.

At home, the war helped reformers finally achieve their goals of national prohibition and woman **suffrage**, but war also promoted a vicious attack on Americans' civil liberties. Hyperpatriotism meant intolerance, repression, and vigilante violence. Overseas, Pershing's troops helped win the war in 1918, and in 1919 Wilson sailed for Europe to secure a just peace. Unable to dictate a settlement to the victors, Wilson accepted disappointing compromises. Upon his return to the United States he met a crushing defeat that marked the end of Wilsonian internationalism. Crackdowns on dissenters, immigrants, racial and ethnic minorities, and unions signaled the end of the **Progressive** Era at home.

Woodrow Wilson and the World

Shortly after winning election to the presidency in 1912, Woodrow Wilson confided to a friend: "It would be an irony of fate if my administration had to deal with foreign affairs." Indeed, Wilson had based his life and career on domestic concerns, seldom venturing far from home and traveling abroad only on brief vacations. As president of Princeton University and then governor of New Jersey, he had remained rooted in local affairs. In his campaign for the presidency, Wilson spoke passionately about domestic reform but hardly mentioned foreign affairs.

But Wilson could not avoid the world and the rising tide of militarism, **nationalism**, and violence that beat against American shores. America's own economic needs also compelled the nation outward. Moreover, Wilson was drawn abroad by his own progressive political principles. He believed that the United States had a moral duty to champion national self-determination, peaceful free trade, and political **democracy**. "We have no selfish ends to serve," he proclaimed. "We desire no conquest, no dominion.…We are but one of the champions of the rights of mankind." Yet as president, Wilson revealed he was as ready as any American president to apply military solutions to problems of foreign policy.

Taming the Americas

When he took office, Wilson sought to distinguish his foreign policy from that of his Republican predecessors. To Wilson, Theodore Roosevelt's "big stick" and William Howard Taft's "dollar diplomacy" appeared a crude flexing of military and economic muscle. To signal a new direction, Wilson appointed William Jennings Bryan as secretary of state. A pacifist, Bryan immediately turned his attention to making agreements with thirty nations for the peaceful settlement of disputes.

But Wilson and Bryan, like Roosevelt and Taft, also believed that the **Monroe Doctrine** gave the United States special rights and responsibilities in the Western Hemisphere. Issued in 1823 to warn Europeans not to attempt to **colonize** the New World again, the doctrine had become a cloak for American domination. Wilson thus authorized U.S. military intervention in Nicaragua, Haiti, and the Dominican Republic, which allowed American banks and corporations to take financial control. All the while, Wilson believed that American actions were promoting order and democracy. "I am going to teach the South American Republics to elect good men!" he declared. He did not mention protecting the Panama Canal and American investments (Map 22.1).

Wilson's most serious involvement in Latin America came in Mexico. When General Victoriano Huerta seized power by violent means, Wilson refused to recognize Huerta as the new Mexican president, declaring that he would not support a "government of butchers." In April 1914, Wilson sent 800 marines to seize

MAP 22.1   U.S. Involvement in Latin America and the Caribbean, 1895–1941
Victory against Spain in 1898 made Puerto Rico an American possession and Cuba a protectorate. The United States also gained control over the Panama Canal. The nation proved quick to protect expanding economic interests with military force by propping up friendly, though not necessarily democratic, governments.

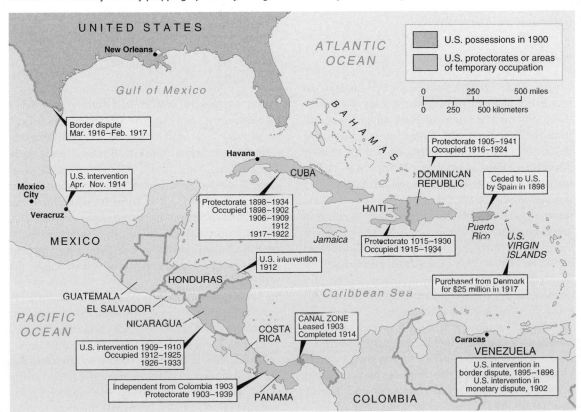

the port of Veracruz to prevent the unloading of a large shipment of arms for Huerta, who was by then involved in a civil war of his own. Huerta fled to Spain, and the United States welcomed a more compliant government.

Wilson was not able to subdue Mexico that easily, however. A rebellion erupted among desperately poor farmers who believed that the new government, aided by American business interests, had betrayed the revolution's promise to help the common people. In January 1916, the rebel army, commanded by Francisco "Pancho" Villa, seized a train carrying gold to Texas from an American-owned mine in Mexico and killed the seventeen American engineers aboard. Another band of Villa's men crossed the border on March 9 for a predawn raid on Columbus, New Mexico, that cost several more lives and left the town in flames. Wilson promptly dispatched 12,000 troops, led by General John J. Pershing. The wily Villa avoided capture, and in January 1917 Wilson recalled Pershing so that he might prepare the army for the possibility of fighting in the Great War.

U.S. Intervention in Mexico, 1916–1917

The European Crisis

Before 1914, Europe had enjoyed decades of peace, but just beneath the surface lay the potentially destructive forces of nationalism and **imperialism**. The consolidation of the German and Italian states into unified nations and the similar ambition of Russia to create a "Pan-Slavic" union initiated new rivalries throughout Europe. As the conviction spread that colonial possessions were a mark of national greatness, competition expanded onto the world stage. Most ominously, Germany's efforts under Kaiser Wilhelm II to challenge Great Britain's world supremacy by creating industrial muscle at home, an empire abroad, and a mighty navy threatened the balance of power and thus the peace.

European nations sought to avoid an explosion with a complex web of military and diplomatic alliances. By 1914, Germany, Austria-Hungary, and Italy (the Triple Alliance) stood opposed to Great Britain, France, and Russia (the Triple Entente, also known as "the Allies").

But in their effort to prevent war through a balance of power, Europeans had actually magnified the possibility of large-scale conflict by creating trip wires along the boundaries of two heavily armed power blocs (Map 22.2). Treaties, some of them secret, obligated members of the alliances to come to the aid of another member if attacked.

The fatal sequence began on June 28, 1914, in the Bosnian city of Sarajevo, when a Bosnian Serb terrorist assassinated Archduke Franz Ferdinand, heir to the Austro-Hungarian throne. The next day, Austria declared war on Serbia, holding it accountable for the killing. The elaborate **alliance system** meant that the war could not remain local. Russia announced that it would back the Serbs. Compelled to support Austria-Hungary, Germany on August 6 declared war on Russia and on France. In response, Great Britain, upholding its pact with France, declared war on Germany. Within weeks, Europe was engulfed in war. The conflict became a world war when Japan, seeing an opportunity to rid itself of European competition in China, joined the cause against Germany.

The evenly matched alliances would fight a long and bloody war lasting more than four years, at a cost of 8.5 million soldiers' lives—an entire generation of young men. A war that started with a solitary murder proved impossible to stop.

The Ordeal of American Neutrality

Woodrow Wilson announced that the war was a European matter, that the United States would remain neutral and continue normal relations with the warring nations. America had traditionally insisted that "free ships made free goods"—that neutral nations were entitled to trade freely with all nations at war. But more was involved than lofty principle. In the year before Europe went to war, the American economy had slipped into a recession that wartime disruption of European trade could drastically worsen.

Although Wilson proclaimed neutrality, his sympathies, like those of many Americans, lay with Great Britain and France. Americans shared with the English a language, a culture, and a commitment to **liberty**. Germany, in contrast, was a monarchy with strong militaristic traditions. The British portrayed the German ruler, Kaiser Wilhelm II, as personally responsible for the war's atrocities, and before long American newspapers were labeling him "the Mad Dog of Europe" and "the Beast of Berlin." Still, Wilson insisted on neutrality, in part because he feared the conflict's effects on the United States as a nation of immigrants, millions of whom had only recently come from countries now at war. As he told the German ambassador, "We definitely have to be neutral, since otherwise our mixed populations would wage war on each other."

Britain's powerful fleet controlled the seas and quickly set up an economic blockade of Germany. The United States vigorously protested, but Britain refused to give up its naval advantage. The blockade actually had little economic impact on the United States. Between 1914 and the spring of 1917, while trade with Germany evaporated, war-related exports to Britain—food, clothing, steel, and munitions—escalated by some 400 percent, enough to pull the American economy out of its prewar slump. Although the British blockade bruised American feelings and clearly violated American neutrality, the Wilson administration gradually and reluctantly acquiesced, thus beginning the fateful process of alienation from Germany.

Germany retaliated with a submarine blockade of British ports. This terrifying new form of combat by *Unterseebooten*, or U-boats, threatened traditional rules of war. Unlike surface warships that could harmlessly stop freighters and prevent them from entering a war zone, submarines relied on surprising and sinking their quarry. And once they sank a ship, the tiny U-boats could not possibly pick up survivors. Britain portrayed the submarine as an outlaw weapon that violated notions of "civilized" warfare. Nevertheless, in February 1915, Germany announced that it intended to sink on sight enemy ships en route to the British Isles. On May 7, 1915, a German U-boat torpedoed the British passenger liner *Lusitania*, killing 1,198 passengers, 128 of them U.S. citizens.

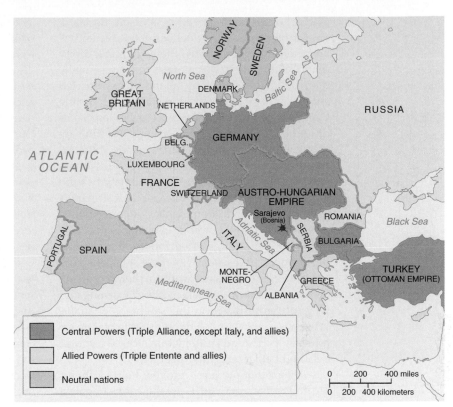

MAP 22.2 European Alliances after the Outbreak of World War I
With Germany and the Austro-Hungarian empire wedged between their Entente rivals, and all parties fully armed, Europe was poised for war when Archduke Franz Ferdinand of Austria was assassinated in Sarajevo in July 1914.

Sinking of the *Lusitania*, 1915

Front pages of American newspapers featured drawings of drowning women and children, and some demanded war. Others, however, pointed out that the *Lusitania* carried millions of rounds of ammunition and so was a legitimate target. Secretary of State Bryan resisted the hysteria and declared that a ship carrying war materiel "should not rely on passengers to protect her from attack—it would be like putting women and children in front of an army." He counseled Wilson to warn American citizens that they traveled on ships of belligerent countries at their own risk.

Wilson sought a middle course that would retain his commitment to peace and neutrality without condoning German attacks on passenger ships. Any further destruction of ships, Wilson declared, would be regarded as "deliberately unfriendly" and might lead the United States to break diplomatic relations with Germany. Wilson essentially demanded that Germany abandon unrestricted submarine warfare. Bryan resigned, predicting that the president had placed the United States on a collision course with Germany. Wilson's replacement for Bryan, Robert Lansing, was far from neutral. He announced that "the German Government is utterly hostile to all nations with democratic institutions." Because of Germany's "ambition for world dominance," it "must not be permitted to win this war or even to break even."

After Germany apologized for the civilian deaths on the *Lusitania,* however, tensions subsided. In 1916, Germany went further, promising no more submarine attacks without warning and without provisions for the safety of civilians. Wilson's supporters celebrated the success of his middle-of-the-road strategy that steered a course between belligerence and pacificism.

Wilson's diplomacy proved helpful in his bid for reelection in 1916. In the contest against Republican Charles Evans Hughes, the Democratic Party ran Wilson under the slogan "He kept us out of war." Wilson felt uneasy with the claim, recognizing that any "little German lieutenant can push us into the war at any time by some calculated outrage." But Wilson's case for neutrality appealed to the majority in favor of peace. Wilson won, but only by the razor-thin margins of 600,000 popular and 23 electoral votes.

The United States Enters the War

Step by step, the United States backed away from "absolute neutrality" and grew more forthrightly pro-Allies (that is, pro–Triple Entente). The consequence of protesting the German blockade of Great Britain but accepting the British blockade of Germany was that by 1916 the United States was supplying the Allies with 40 percent of their war materiel. When France and Britain ran short of money to pay for American goods and asked for loans, Wilson argued that "Loans by American bankers to any foreign government which is at war are inconsistent with the true spirit of neutrality." But rather than jeopardize America's wartime prosperity, Wilson relaxed his objections, and billions of dollars in loans kept American goods flowing to Britain and France.

In January 1917, Germany decided that it could no longer afford to allow neutral shipping to reach Great Britain while the enemy blockade gradually starved Germany. It announced that it would resume unrestricted submarine warfare and sink without warning any ship, enemy and neutral, found in the waters off Great Britain. Germany understood that the decision would probably bring the United States into the war but gambled that the submarines would strangle the British economy and allow German armies to win a military victory in France before American troops arrived in Europe.

Wilson continued to hope for a negotiated peace and only broke off diplomatic relations with Germany. Then on February 25, 1917, British authorities informed Wilson of a secret telegram sent by the German foreign secretary, Arthur Zimmermann, to the German minister in Mexico. It promised that in the event of war between Germany and the United States, Germany would see that Mexico regained its "lost provinces" of Texas, New Mexico, and Arizona if Mexico would declare war against the United States. Wilson angrily responded to the Zimmermann telegram by asking Congress to approve a policy of "armed neutrality" that would allow merchant ships to fight back against any attackers. Germany's overture to Mexico convinced Wilson that the war was, indeed, a defense of democracy against German aggression.

In March, German submarines sank five American vessels off Britain, killing 66 Americans. On April 2 the president asked Congress to issue a declaration of war. He accused Germany of "warfare against all mankind." Still, he called for a "war without hate" and insisted that the destruction of Germany was not the goal of the United States. Rather, America fought to "vindicate the principles of peace and justice"; he promised a world made "safe for democracy." On April 6, 1917, by majorities of 373 to 50 in the House and 82 to 6 in the Senate, Congress voted to declare war.

Wilson feared what war would do at home. He said despairingly, "Once lead this people into war, and they'll forget there ever was such a thing as tolerance. To fight you must be brutal and ruthless, and the spirit of ruthless brutality will infect Congress, the courts, the policeman on the beat, the man in the street."

REVIEW Why did President Wilson authorize repeated military interventions in the Americas?

"Over There"

American soldiers sailed for France with song-writer George M. Cohan's rousing "Over There" ringing in their ears:

> Over there, over there
> Send the word, send the word over there,
> That the Yanks are coming, the Yanks are coming
> The drums rum-tumming ev'rywhere.

Two million American troops eventually reached Europe, by far the largest military venture the United States had ever undertaken on foreign soil. Filled with a sense of democratic mission and trained to be morally upright as well as fiercely effective, some doughboys found the adventure exhilarating and maintained their idealism to the end. The majority, however, saw little that was gallant in rats, lice, and poison gas, and—despite the progressives' hopes—little to elevate the human soul in a landscape of utter destruction and death.

The Call to Arms

When America entered the war, Britain and France were nearly exhausted after almost three years of conflict. Hundreds of thousands of soldiers had perished; morale and food supplies were dangerously low. Another Allied power, Russia, was in turmoil. In March 1917, a revolution had forced Czar Nicholas II to abdicate, and eight months later in a separate peace with Germany the Bolshevik revolutionary government removed Russia from the war. On May 18, 1917, to meet the demand for fighting men, Wilson signed a sweeping Selective Service Act, authorizing a **draft** of all young men into the armed forces. **Conscription** soon transformed a tiny volunteer armed force of 80,000 men into a vast army and navy. Draft boards eventually inducted 2.8 million men into the armed services, in addition to the 2 million who volunteered.

Progressives in the government were determined that the training camps that transformed raw recruits into fighting men would have the highest moral and civic purposes. Secretary of War Newton D. Baker created a Commission on Training Camp Activities staffed by YMCA workers and veterans of the settlement house and playground movements. The army asked soldiers to stop thinking about sex, explaining that a "man who is thinking below the belt is not efficient." Instead, military training included games, singing, and college extension courses. The Military Draft Act of 1917 prohibited prostitution and alcohol near training camps. Wilson's choice to command the American Expeditionary Force (AEF), "Black Jack" Pershing, described by one observer as "lean, clean, keen," gave progressives perfect confidence.

The War in France

At the front, the AEF discovered a desperate situation. The war had degenerated into a stalemate of armies dug defensively into hundreds of miles of trenches across France. Huddling in the mud among the corpses and rats, soldiers were separated from the enemy by only a few hundred yards of "no-man's-land." When ordered "over the top," troops raced desperately toward the enemy's trenches, only to be entangled in barbed wire, enveloped in poison gas, and mowed down by machine guns. The three-day battle of the Somme in 1916 cost the French and British forces 600,000 dead and wounded and the Germans 500,000. The deadliest battle of the war allowed the Allies to advance their trenches only a few meaningless miles across devastated land.

Still, American troops saw almost no combat in 1917. Instead, they continued to train and used much of their free time to explore places that most of them otherwise could never have hoped to see. True to the crusader image, American officials allowed only uplifting tourism. Paris temptations were off-limits, and French premier Georges Clemenceau's offer to supply American troops with licensed prostitutes was declined with the half-serious remark that if Wilson found out he would stop the war.

The sightseeing ended abruptly in March 1918. The Brest-Litovsk treaty signed that month by Germany and the Bolsheviks officially took Russia out of the war, and the Germans launched a massive offensive aimed at French ports on the Atlantic. After six thousand cannons unleashed the heaviest barrage in history, a million German soldiers smashed a hole in the Allied lines at a cost of 250,000 casualties on each side. Pershing, who believed the right moment for U.S. action had finally come, visited Foch to ask for the "great honor" of becoming "engaged in the greatest battle in history." Foch agreed to Pershing's terms of a separate American command and in May assigned the Americans to the central sector.

Life in the Trenches

U.S. soldiers in a rat-infested trench tensely look out for danger or slump in exhausted sleep. They offer a glimpse of the reality of the Great War, minus the noise, stench, and danger. This trench is dry for the moment, but with the rains came mud so deep that wounded men drowned in it. By the time American doughboys arrived in Europe, hostile troops had faced one another for more than three years, burrowed into a double line of trenches, protected by barbed wire, machine-gun nests, and mortars, backed by heavy artillery. Trenches with millions of combatants stretched from French ports on the English Channel all the way to Switzerland. Nothing could make living in such holes anything better than miserable, but a decent shave with a Gillette safety razor, a pair of dry boots, and a set of checkers offered doughboys temporary relief. Inevitably, however, whistles would blow, ending the boredom, fatigue, and discomfort of trench life and sending young men "over the top," rushing toward enemy lines.

FOR MORE HELP ANALYZING THIS IMAGE, see the visual activity for this chapter in the Online Study Guide at bedfordstmartins.com/roarkcompact.

Photo: Imperial War Museum; shaving kit and boots: Collection of Colonel Stuart S. Corning Jr. / Picture Research Consultants, Inc.

Once committed, the Americans remained true to their way of war. In May and June, at Cantigny and then at Château-Thierry, the eager but green Americans checked the German advance with a series of dashing assaults (Map 22.3). Then they headed toward the forest stronghold of Belleau Wood, moving against streams of retreating Allied soldiers who cried defeat: "La guerre est finie!" (The war is over!). A French officer commanded American sol-

diers to retreat with them, but the American commander replied sharply, "Retreat, hell. We just got here." After charging through a wheat field against withering machine-gun fire, the marines plunged into hand-to-hand combat. Victory came hard, but a German report praised the enemy's spirit, noting that "the Americans' nerves are not yet worn out." Indeed, it was German morale that was on the verge of cracking.

MAP 22.3   The American Expeditionary Force, 1918

In the last year of the war, the AEF joined the French army on the western front to counterattack the final German offensive and pursue the retreating enemy until surrender.

READING THE MAP: Across which rivers did the Germans advance in 1918? Where did the armistice line of November 11, 1918, lie in relation to the stabilized front of 1915–1917? Through which countries did the armistice line run?

CONNECTIONS: What events paved the way for the American Expeditionary Force to join the combat in 1918? What characteristic(s) differentiated American troops from other Allied forces and helped them achieve victory?

FOR MORE HELP ANALYZING THIS MAP, see the map activity for this chapter in the Online Study Guide at bedfordstmartins.com/roarkcompact.

In the summer of 1918, the Allies launched a massive counteroffensive that would end the war. A quarter of a million American troops joined in the rout of German forces along the Marne River. In September, more than a million Americans took part in the assault that threw the Germans back from positions along the Meuse River. In November, a revolt against the German government sent Kaiser Wilhelm II fleeing to Holland. On November 11, 1918, a delegation from the newly established German republic met with the French high command to sign an armistice that brought the fighting to an end.

The adventure of the AEF was brief, bloody, and victorious. When Germany resumed unrestricted U-boat warfare in 1917, it was gambling that it could defeat Britain and France before the Americans could raise and train an army and ship it to France. The German military had miscalculated. Of the 2 million American troops in Europe, 1.3 million saw at least some action. By the end, 112,000 AEF soldiers perished from wounds and disease. Another 230,000 Americans suffered casualties but survived, many of them with permanent physical and psychological disabilities. Only the Civil War, which lasted much longer, had been more costly in American lives. European nations, however, suffered much greater losses: 2.2 million Germans, 1.9 million

Russians, 1.4 million French, and 900,000 Britons. Where they had fought, the landscape was as blasted and barren as the moon.

> **REVIEW**   How did the American Expeditionary Force contribute to the defeat of Germany?

The Crusade for Democracy at Home

Many progressives hoped that war would improve the quality of American life as well as free Europe from its bondage to tyranny and militarism. Progressives enthusiastically channeled industrial and agricultural production into the war effort. Labor shortages caused by workers entering the military provided new opportunities for women in the booming wartime economy. With labor at a premium, unionized workers gained higher pay and shorter hours. To instill loyalty in Americans whose ancestry was rooted in the belligerent nations, Wilson launched a campaign to foster patriotism. The campaign included the creation of a government agency to promote official propaganda, indoctrination in the schools, and parades, rallies, and films. But boosting patriotism led to suppressing dissent. When the government launched a harsh assault on civil liberties, mobs gained license to attack those whom they considered disloyal. The progressive ideals of rational progress and free expression took a beating as the nation undertook its crusade for democracy.

The Progressive Stake in the War

The idea of the war as an agent of social improvement fanned the old zeal of the progressive movement. The Wilson administration realized that Washington would have to assert greater control to mobilize the nation's human and physical resources. The nation's capital soon

bristled with hastily created agencies charged with managing the war effort. Bernard Baruch headed the War Industries Board (WIB), created to stimulate and direct industrial production. At once a wealthy southern gentleman, a Jewish Wall Street stockbroker, and a reform Democrat, Baruch brought industrial management and labor together into a team that produced everything from boots to bullets and made American troops the best-equipped soldiers in the world.

Herbert Hoover, a self-made millionaire engineer, headed the Food Administration. He led remarkably successful "Hooverizing" campaigns for "meatless" Mondays and "wheatless" Wednesdays and other ways of conserving resources. Guaranteed high prices, the American heartland not only supplied the needs of U.S. citizens and armed forces but also became the breadbasket of America's allies. Even Wilson's family did its part with a White House "victory garden" and sheep put to graze on the White House lawn when the gardeners took war-related work.

Other wartime agencies abounded: The Railroad Administration directed railroad traffic, the Fuel Administration coordinated the coal industry and other fuel suppliers, the Shipping Board organized the merchant marine, and the National War Labor Policies Board resolved labor disputes. Their successes gave progressives reason to believe that the war promoted harmony between business and labor and progressive reform in general. Some progressives, however, stubbornly refused to accept the argument that war and reform marched together. Wisconsin senator Robert La Follette attacked the war unrelentingly, claiming that Wilson's promises of peace and democracy were a case of "the blind leading the blind," at home and abroad.

Industrial leaders found that wartime agencies helped corporate profits triple. Some working people also had cause to celebrate. Mobilization meant high prices for farmers and plentiful jobs in the new war industries (Figure 22.1). Because increased industrial production required peaceful labor relations, the National War Labor Policies Board enacted the eighthour day, a living minimum wage, and **collective bargaining** rights in some

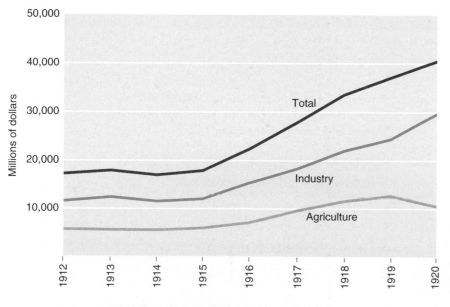

Agriculture: cash receipts.
Industry: includes mining, electric power, manufacturing, construction, and communications.

FIGURE 22.1   Industrial Wages, 1912–1920
With help from unions and progressive reformers, wage workers gradually improved their economic condition. The entry of millions of young men into the armed forces caused labor shortages and led to a rapid surge in wages.

industries. Wages rose sharply during the war (as did prices), and the American Federation of Labor (AFL) saw its membership soar from 2.7 million to more than 5 million.

The war also provided a huge boost to the stalled moral crusade to ban alcohol. By 1917, prohibitionists had convinced nineteen states to go dry. Liquor's opponents argued that banning alcohol would make the cause of democracy powerful and pure. At the same time, shutting down the distilleries would save millions of bushels of grain that could feed the United States and its allies. "Shall the many have food or the few drink?" the drys asked. Prohibitionists added a patriotic twist by arguing that closing breweries with German names like Schlitz, Pabst, and Anheuser-Busch would deal a blow to the German cause. In December 1917, Congress passed the Eighteenth Amendment, which banned the manufacture, transportation, and sale of alcohol. After swift ratification by the states, the amendment went into effect on January 1, 1920.

Women, War, and the Battle for Suffrage

Women had made real strides during the Progressive Era, but war presented new opportunities. More than 25,000 women served in France. About half were nurses; the others drove ambulances, ran canteens for the Red Cross and YMCA, worked with French civilians in devastated areas, and acted as war correspondents. Like men, women struggled against disillusionment and depression. One woman explained: "Over in America, we thought we knew something about the war...but when you get here the difference is [like the one between] studying the laws of electricity and being struck by lightning."

At home, long-standing barriers against hiring women fell when millions of working men became soldiers and few new immigrant workers crossed the Atlantic. The new Women's Bureau of the Department of Labor, along with the Women's Trade Union League (WTUL), helped open jobs to women. Tens of thousands of women found work with the railroads and in defense plants as welders, metalworkers, and heavy machine operators, jobs traditionally reserved for men. Between 1910 and 1920, the number of women clerks

doubled. Before the war ended, more than a million women found work in war industries. "This is the women's age," exaggerated Margaret Dreier Robins, president of the WTUL. "At last...women are coming into the labor and festival of life on equal terms with men."

The most dramatic advance for women came in the political arena. Since the Seneca Falls convention of 1848, where women voiced their first formal demand for the ballot, the struggle for woman suffrage had inched forward. Adopting a state-by-state approach, suffragists had achieved some success, but by 1910 only four small western states had adopted woman suffrage (Map 22.4). Elsewhere, voting rights for women met strong hostility and defeat. After 1910, suffrage leaders added a federal campaign to amend the Constitution to the traditional state-by-state strategy for suffrage.

The radical wing of the suffragists, led by the indomitable Alice Paul, picketed the White House, where they unfurled banners that proclaimed: "America Is Not a Democracy. Twenty Million Women Are Denied the Right to Vote." They chained themselves to fences and went to jail, where many engaged in hunger strikes. "They seem bent on making their cause as obnoxious as possible," Woodrow Wilson declared. His wife,

MAP 22.4 Women's Voting Rights before the Nineteenth Amendment
The long campaign for women's voting rights reversed the pioneer epic that moved from east to west. From its first successes in the new democratic West, suffrage rolled eastward toward the entrenched, male-dominated public life of the Northeast and South.

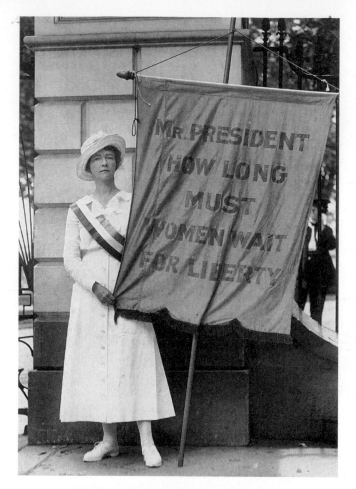

Picketing the White House for the Vote
Mrs. William L. Colt pickets Woodrow Wilson's home to demand women's right to vote. Because of such direct pressure and in recognition of women's service in the defense industry at home and in France as nurses and Red Cross workers, Wilson finally pledged support for the suffrage amendment. A gentleman from the old school, he believed women could tame men's aggressive tendencies, and he hoped that women's moderating influence would help make the Great War the war to end all wars.
© Bettmann / Corbis.

Edith, detested the idea of "masculinized" voting women. But membership in the mainstream organization, the National American Woman Suffrage Association, led by Carrie Chapman Catt, soared to some 2 million members. NAWSA even accepted African American women into its ranks, although not on an equal basis. Seeing the handwriting on the wall, the Republican and Progressive parties endorsed woman suffrage in 1916.

In 1918, Wilson gave his support to suffrage, calling the amendment "vital to the winning of the war." He conceded that it would be wrong not to reward the "partnership of suffering and sacrifice" with a "partnership of privilege and right." By linking their cause to the wartime emphasis on national unity, the advocates of woman suffrage finally triumphed. In 1919, Congress passed the Nineteenth Amendment, granting women the vote, and by August 1920, the states had ratified it. As Carrie Chapman Catt later recalled, "to get that word, male, out of the Constitution, cost the women of the country fifty-two years of campaigning." But rather than woman suffrage being the end of the long road to women's full equality, as some suffragists contended, it proved to be only the beginning.

Rally around the Flag, or Else

When Congress committed the nation to war, most peace advocates rallied around the flag. The Carnegie Endowment for International Peace adopted new stationery with the heading "Peace through Victory" and issued a resolution saying that "the most effectual means of promoting peace is to prosecute the war against the Imperial German Government."

Only a handful of reformers resisted the tide of patriotism. The Women's Peace Party that emerged in 1915 and its foreign affiliates in the Women's International League for Peace and Freedom (WILPF) led the struggle to persuade governments to negotiate peace and spare dissenters from harsh punishment. After America entered the conflict, advocates for peace were routinely labeled cowards and traitors, their efforts crushed by the steamroller of conformity.

To suppress criticism of the war, Wilson stirred up patriotic fervor. In 1917, the president created the Committee on Public Information (CPI) under the direction of George Creel, who became the nation's cheerleader for war. He sent "Four-Minute Men," a squad of 75,000 volunteers, around the country to give brief pep talks that celebrated successes on the battlefields and in the factories. Posters, pamphlets, and cartoons depicted brave American soldiers and sailors defending freedom and democracy against the evil "Hun," the derogatory nickname applied to German soldiers.

America rallied around Creel's campaign. The film industry cranked out reels of melodrama about battle-line and home-front heroes and taught audiences to hiss at the German kaiser. A musical, *The Kaiser: The Beast of Berlin*, opened on Broadway in 1918. Colleges and universities generated war propaganda in the guise of scholarship. When Professor James McKeen Cattell of Columbia University urged that America seek peace with Germany short of victory, university president Nicholas Murray Butler fired him on the grounds that "what had been folly is now treason."

A firestorm of anti-German passion erupted. Across the nation, "100% American" campaigns enlisted ordinary people to sniff out disloyalty. German, the most widely taught foreign language in 1914, practically disappeared from the nation's schools. Targeting German-born Americans, *The Saturday Evening Post* declared that it was time to rid the country of "the scum of the melting pot." The rabid attempt to punish Germans reached its extreme with the lynching of Robert Prager, a baker in Collinsville, Illinois. In the eyes of the mob, it was enough that Prager was German-born and had **socialist** leanings, even though he had not opposed American participation in the war. Persuaded by the defense lawyer who praised what he called a "patriotic murder," the jury at the trial of the killers took only twenty-five minutes to acquit.

As hysteria increased, the campaign reached absurd levels. In Montana, a school board barred a history text that had good things to say about medieval Germany. Menus across the nation changed German toast to French toast and sauerkraut to liberty cabbage. In Milwaukee, vigilantes mounted a machine gun outside the Pabst Theater to prevent the staging of Schiller's *Wilhelm Tell*, a powerful protest against tyranny. One vigilant citizen claimed to see a periscope in the Great Lakes, and the fiancée of one of the war's leading critics, caught dancing on the dunes of Cape Cod, was held on suspicion of signaling to German submarines.

The Wilson administration's zeal in suppressing dissent contrasted sharply with its war aims of defending democracy. In the name of self-defense, the Espionage Act (June 1917), the Trading with the Enemy Act (October 1917), and the Sedition Act (May 1918) gave the government sweeping powers to punish any opinion or activity it considered "disloyal, profane, scur-

rilous, or abusive." When Postmaster General Albert Burleson blocked mailing privileges for publications he considered disloyal, dozens of dissenting journals were forced to close down. Of the fifteen hundred individuals eventually charged with sedition, all but a dozen had merely spoken words the government found objectionable. One of them was Eugene V. Debs, the leader of the Socialist Party, who was convicted under the Espionage Act for speeches condemning the war as a capitalist plot and sent to the Atlanta penitentiary.

The president hoped that national commitment to the war would subdue partisan politics, but his Republican rivals used the war as a weapon against the Democrats. The trick was to oppose Wilson's conduct of the war but not the war itself. Republicans outshouted Wilson on the nation's need to mobilize for war but then complained that Wilson's War Industries Board was a tyrannical agency that crushed free enterprise. Such attacks appealed to widely diverse business, labor, and patriotic groups. As the war progressed, Republicans gathered power against the Democrats who had narrowly reelected Wilson in 1916.

In 1918, Republicans gained a narrow majority in both House and Senate. The end of Democratic control of Congress not only halted further domestic reform but also meant that the United States would advance toward military victory in Europe with political power divided between a Democratic president and a Republican Congress likely to challenge Wilson's plans for international cooperation.

REVIEW   How did progressive ideals fare during wartime?

A Compromised Peace

Wilson decided to reaffirm his noble war ideals by announcing his peace aims before the end of hostilities. He hoped the victorious Allies would adopt his plan for international democracy, but he was sorely disappointed. The leaders of England, France, and Italy (which joined the Allies in 1915 in hopes of postwar gains) understood that Wilson's principles jeopardized their own postwar plans for the acquisition of enemy territory, new colonial empires, and reparations. Wilson also faced strong opposition at home from those who feared that his enthusiasm for international cooperation would undermine American sovereignty.

Wilson's Fourteen Points

On January 8, 1918, President Wilson revealed to Congress his vision of a generous peace. Wilson's Fourteen Points provided a blueprint for a new democratic world order. The first five points affirmed basic liberal ideals: "open covenants of peace, openly arrived at," that is, an end to secret treaties; freedom of the seas; removal of economic barriers to free trade; reduction of weapons of war; and recognition of the rights of colonized peoples. The next eight points supported the right to self-determination of European peoples who had been dominated by Germany or its allies. Wilson's fourteenth point called for a "general association of nations"—a League of Nations—to provide "mutual guarantees of political independence and territorial integrity to great and small states alike." The insistence on a League of Nations reflected Wilson's lifelong dream of a "parliament of man." Only such an organization, he believed, could justify the war and secure a lasting peace.

Citizens of the United States and of every Allied country greeted the Fourteen Points enthusiastically. Wilson felt confident that he could prevail against undemocratic forces at the peace table. During the final year of the war, he pressured the Allies to accept the Fourteen Points as the basis of the settlement. If necessary, Wilson was willing to speak over the heads of government leaders directly to the people and thus expand his role as spokesman for Americans to the champion of all the world's people. The Allies had won the war; Wilson would win the peace.

The Paris Peace Conference

From January 18 to June 28, 1919, the eyes of the world focused on Paris. There, powerful men wrestled with difficult problems. Although no other American president had ever gone to Europe while in office, Wilson decided to head the U.S. delegation. He believed he owed it to the American soldiers. "It is now my duty," he announced, "to play my full part in making

good what they gave their life's blood to obtain." A dubious British diplomat retorted that Wilson was drawn to Paris "as a debutante is entranced by the prospect of her first ball." The decision to leave the country at a time when his political opponents challenged his leadership was risky enough, but his stubborn refusal to include prominent Republicans in the delegation proved foolhardy and eventually cost him his dream of a new world order with America at its center.

Huge crowds cheered the American president's motorcade on its way to Paris. After four terrible years of war, Europeans looked on Wilson as someone who would create a safer, more decent world. When the conference convened at Louis XIV's magnificent palace at Versailles, however, Wilson encountered a different reception. Representing the Allies were the decidedly unidealistic David Lloyd George of Britain, Georges Clemenceau of France, and Vittorio Orlando of Italy. To the Allied leaders, Wilson appeared a naive and impractical moralist. His desire to gather former enemies within a new international democratic order showed how little he understood hard European realities. The French premier claimed that Wilson "believed you could do everything by formulas" and "empty theory." Disparaging the Fourteen Points, he added, "God himself was content with ten commandments."

The Allies wanted to fasten blame for the war on Germany, totally disarm it, and make it pay so dearly that it would never threaten its neighbors again. The French demanded retribution in the form of territory containing Germany's richest mineral resources. The British made it clear that they were not about to give up the powerful weapon of naval blockade for the vague principle of the freedom of the seas.

The Allies forced Wilson to make drastic compromises. In return for France moderating its territorial claims, he agreed to support Article 231 of the peace treaty, assigning war guilt to Germany. Though saved from permanently losing Rhineland territory to the French, Germany was outraged at being singled out as the instigator of the war and saddled with more than $33 billion in damages. Many Germans felt that their nation had been betrayed. After agreeing to an armistice on the belief that peace terms would be based on Wilson's generous Fourteen Points, they faced hardship and humiliation instead.

Wilson had better success in establishing the principle of self-determination. But from the beginning, Secretary of State Robert Lansing knew that Wilson's "phrase is simply loaded with dynamite." Lansing wondered, "What unit has he in mind? Does he mean a race, a territorial area, or a community?" Lansing suspected that the notion of self-determination "will raise hopes which can never be realized. It will, I fear, cost thousands of lives. In the end it is bound to be discredited, to be called the dream of an idealist who failed to realize the danger until it was too late."

Yet on the basis of self-determination, the conference redrew the map of Europe and parts of the rest of the world. Portions of the Austro-Hungarian empire were ceded to Italy, Poland, and Romania, and the remainder was reassembled into Austria, Hungary, Czechoslovakia, and Yugoslavia—independent republics with boundaries determined according to concentrations of ethnic groups. More arbitrarily, the Ottoman empire was carved up into small mandates (including Palestine) run by local leaders but under the control of France and Great Britain. The conference reserved the mandate system for those regions it deemed insufficiently "civilized" to have full independence. Thus, the reconstructed nations—each beset with ethnic and nationalist rivalries—faced the challenge of making a new democratic government work (Map 22.5). Many of today's bitterest disputes—in the Balkans and Iraq, between Greece and Turkey, between Arabs and Jews—have roots in the decisions made in Paris in 1919.

Wilson hoped that self-determination would also dictate the fate of Germany's colonies in Asia and Africa. But the Allies who had taken over the colonies during the war only allowed the League of Nations a mandate to administer them. Technically, the mandate system rejected imperialism, but in reality it only avoided outright imperialism while still allowing Europeans to maintain control. While denying Germany its colonies, the Allies retained their own colonial empires.

The cause of democratic equality suffered another setback when the peace conference rejected Japan's call for a principle of racial equality. Wilson's belief in the superiority of whites, as well as his apprehension about how white Americans would respond to such a declaration, led him to oppose the clause. To soothe hurt feelings, Wilson agreed to grant Japan a

Leaders of the Paris Peace Conference
The three leaders in charge of putting the world back together after the Great War—from left to right, David Lloyd George, prime minister of Great Britain; Georges Clemenceau, premier of France; and U.S. president Woodrow Wilson—amiably and confidently stride toward the peace conference at the palace of Versailles. Clemenceau is caught offering animated instruction to Wilson, whom he considered naively idealistic. Indeed, in an unguarded moment, Clemenceau expressed his contempt for the entire United States as a country that was unique in having passed directly from barbarism to decadence without an intervening period of civilization. Walking silently alongside, Lloyd George maintains the poker face that helped keep his views carefully guarded throughout the conference.
Gamma Liaison.

mandate over the Shantung Peninsula in northern China, which had formerly been controlled by Germany. The gesture mollified Japan's moderate leaders, but the military faction preparing to take over the country used bitterness toward racist Western colonialism to build support for expanding Japanese power throughout Asia.

Closest to Wilson's heart was finding a new way of managing international relations. In

MAP 22.5 Europe after World War I
The post–World War I settlement redrew boundaries to create new nations based on ethnic groupings. This outcome left within defeated Germany and Russia bitter peoples who resolved to recover territory that the new arrangements took from their homelands.

Wilson's view, war had finally discredited the old strategy of balance of power. Instead, he proposed a League of Nations that would provide **collective security** and order. The league would establish rules of international conduct and resolve conflicts between nations through rational and peaceful means. When the Allies agreed to the league, Wilson was overjoyed. He believed that the league would rectify the errors his colleagues had forced on him in Paris. The league would solidify and extend the noble work he had begun.

To many Europeans and Americans, the Versailles treaty came as a bitter disappointment. Wilson's admirers were shocked that the president dealt in compromise like any other politician. But without Wilson's presence, the treaty that was signed on June 28, 1919, surely would have been more vindictive. Wilson returned home in July 1919 consoled that, despite his frustrations, he had gained what he most wanted—a League of Nations. In Wilson's judgment, "We have completed in the least time possible the greatest work that four men have ever done."

The Fight for the Treaty

The tumultuous reception Wilson received when he arrived home persuaded him, probably correctly, that the American people supported the treaty. When the president submitted the treaty to the Senate in July 1919, he warned that failure to ratify it would "break the heart of the world." By then, however, criticism of the treaty was mounting, especially from Americans convinced that their countries of ethnic origin had not been given fair treatment. Irish Americans, Italian Americans, and German Americans launched especially sharp attacks. Others worried that the president's concessions at Versailles had jeopardized the treaty's capacity to provide a generous plan for rebuilding Europe and to guarantee world peace.

Some of the most potent critics were found in the Senate. Bolstered by a slight Republican majority in Congress, a group of Republican "irreconcilables," which included such powerful **isolationist** senators as Hiram Johnson of California and William Borah of Idaho, condemned the treaty for entangling the United States in world affairs. A larger group of Republicans did not object to American participation in world politics but feared that membership in the League of Nations would jeopardize the nation's independence. No Republican, in any case, was eager to hand Wilson and the Democrats a foreign policy victory with the 1920 presidential election little more than a year away.

At the center of Republican opposition was Wilson's archenemy, Senator Henry Cabot Lodge of Massachusetts. Lodge's hostility was in part personal. "I never thought I could hate a man as much as I hate Wilson," he once admitted. But Lodge also raised cogent objections to the treaty and the league. Lodge was no isolationist, but he thought that much of the Fourteen Points was a "general bleat about virtue being better than vice." Lodge expected the United States's economic and military power to propel the nation into a major role in world affairs. But he insisted that membership in the League of Nations, which would require collective action to maintain peace, threatened the nation's freedom of choice in foreign relations.

Lodge used his position as chairman of the Senate Foreign Relations Committee to air every sort of complaint. Out of the committee hearings came several amendments, or "reservations," that sought to limit the consequences of American membership in the league. For example, several reservations required approval of both House and Senate before the United States could participate in league-sponsored economic sanctions or military action.

It gradually became clear that ratification of the treaty depended on acceptance of the Lodge reservations. Democratic senators, who overwhelmingly supported the treaty, urged Wilson to accept Lodge's terms, arguing that they left the essentials of the treaty intact. Wilson, however, insisted that the reservations cut "the very heart out of the treaty." He expressed personal hatred as well. "Lodge reservations?" he thundered. "Never! I'll never consent to adopt any policy with which that impossible name is so prominently identified."

Wilson decided to take his case directly to the people. On September 3, 1919, he set out by train on the most ambitious speaking tour ever undertaken by a president. He enjoyed some early success, but on September 25 in Pueblo, Colorado, Wilson collapsed and had to return to Washington. There he suffered a massive stroke that partially paralyzed him. From his bedroom,

Wilson sent messages instructing Democrats in the Senate to hold firm against any and all reservations. If the Senate approved the treaty with reservations, he said, he would not sign it. In the end, Wilson commanded enough loyalty to ensure a vote against the Lodge reservations. But when the treaty without reservations came before the Senate in March 1920, the combined opposition of the Republican irreconcilables and Republican reservationists left Wilson six votes short of the two-thirds majority needed for passage.

The nations of Europe organized the League of Nations at Geneva, Switzerland, but the United States never became a member. Whether American membership could have prevented the world war that began in Europe in 1939 is highly unlikely, but America's failure to join certainly weakened the league from the start. In refusing to accept relatively minor compromises with Senate moderates, Wilson lost his treaty and American membership in the league. Woodrow Wilson and Henry Cabot Lodge both died in 1924, never seeing international order or security, never knowing the whirlwind of resentment and violence that would eventually follow the Great War's failure to make the world safe for democracy.

REVIEW   Why did the Senate fail to ratify the Treaty of Versailles?

Democracy at Risk

The defeat of Wilson's idealistic plan for international democracy proved the crowning blow to progressives who had hoped that the war could further reform at home. When the war ended, Americans wanted to demobilize swiftly. In the process, servicemen, defense workers, and farmers lost their war-related jobs. The volatile combination—of unemployed veterans returning home, a stalled economy, and leftover wartime patriotism looking for a new cause—threatened to explode. Wartime anti-German passion was quickly followed by antiradicalism, a fevered campaign that ensnared unionists, socialists, dissenters, and African Americans and Mexicans who had committed no offense but to seek to escape rural poverty.

"The Warrior's Return"
About 16,000 Native Americans served in the U.S. armed forces during World War I. This magazine cover offers a romanticized reconstruction of one homecoming. The young soldier, still in uniform and presumably fresh from France, rides his pony to the tepee of his parents, who proudly welcome their brave warrior. The tepee is decorated with a star, a national symbol that families with sons in the military displayed on their homes. The painting sought to demonstrate that even Americans on the margins of national life were sufficiently assimilated and loyal to join the national sacrifice to defeat the enemy.
Picture Research Consultants & Archives.

Economic Hardship and Labor Upheaval

Americans greeted peace with a demand that the United States return to a peacetime economy. The government abruptly abandoned its wartime controls on the economy and canceled war contracts worth millions of dollars. In a matter of months, more than three million soldiers were mustered out of the military with only $60 and a one-way ticket home. When war production ceased and veterans flooded the job market, unemployment rose sharply. At the same time, consumers went on a postwar spending spree that drove inflation skyward. In 1919, prices rose 75 percent over prewar levels, and in 1920, prices rose another 28 percent.

Most of the gains workers had made during the war evaporated. Freed from wartime control, business turned against the eight-hour day and attacked labor unions. Workers fought back. The year 1919 witnessed nearly 3,600 strikes involving 4 million workers. The most spectacular strike occurred in February 1919 in Seattle, where shipyard workers had been put out of work by demobilization. When a coalition of the radical International Workers of the World (IWW) and the moderate American Federation of Labor (AFL) called a general strike, the largest work stoppage in American history shut down the city. Newspapers across the nation claimed that the walkout was "a Bolshevik effort to start a revolution." The suppression of the strike by Seattle officials cost the AFL many of its wartime gains and contributed to the destruction of the IWW soon afterward.

A strike by Boston policemen in the fall of 1919 underscored postwar hostility toward labor militancy. Though paid less than pick-and-shovel laborers, the police won little sympathy. Once the officers stopped walking their beats, looters sacked the city. After two days of near anarchy, Massachusetts governor Calvin Coolidge called in the National Guard to restore order. The public, yearning for peace and security in the wake of war, welcomed Coolidge's anti-union assurance that "there is no right to strike against the public safety by anybody, anywhere, any time."

Labor strife climaxed in the grim steel strike of 1919. Faced with the steel industry's plan to revert to seven-day weeks, twelve-hour days, and weekly wages of about $20, the AFL tried to unionize steelworkers. When U.S. Steel and Bethlehem Steel refused to negotiate, Samuel Gompers, head of the AFL, called for a strike. In response, 350,000 workers in fifteen states walked out in September 1919. The steel industry hired 30,000 strikebreakers (many of them African Americans) and convinced the public that the strikers were radicals bent on subverting the Republic. State and federal troops protected scabs who crossed picket lines. In January 1920, after eighteen striking workers had been killed, the strike collapsed. That devastating defeat initiated a sharp decline in the fortunes of the labor movement, a trend that would continue for almost twenty years.

The Red Scare

Suppression of labor strikes was one response to the widespread fear of internal subversion that swept the nation in 1919. The "Red scare" (*red*

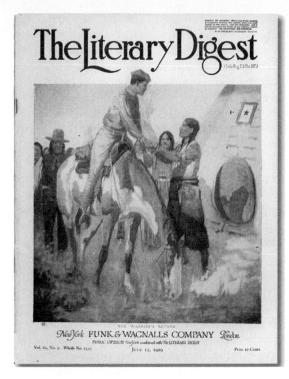

"The Warrior's Return"
About 16,000 Native Americans served in the U.S. armed forces during World War I. This magazine cover offers a romanticized reconstruction of one homecoming. The young soldier, still in uniform and presumably fresh from France, rides his pony to the tepee of his parents, who proudly welcome their brave warrior. The tepee is decorated with a star, a national symbol that families with sons in the military displayed on their homes. The painting sought to demonstrate that even Americans on the margins of national life were sufficiently assimilated and loyal to join the national sacrifice to defeat the enemy.
Picture Research Consultants & Archives.

Economic Hardship and Labor Upheaval

Americans greeted peace with a demand that the United States return to a peacetime economy. The government abruptly abandoned its wartime controls on the economy and canceled war contracts worth millions of dollars. In a matter of months, more than three million soldiers were mustered out of the military with only $60 and a one-way ticket home. When war production ceased and veterans flooded the job market, unemployment rose sharply. At the same time, consumers went on a postwar spending spree that drove inflation skyward. In 1919, prices rose 75 percent over prewar levels, and in 1920, prices rose another 28 percent.

Most of the gains workers had made during the war evaporated. Freed from wartime control, business turned against the eight-hour day and attacked labor unions. Workers fought back. The year 1919 witnessed nearly 3,600 strikes involving 4 million workers. The most spectacular strike occurred in February 1919 in Seattle, where shipyard workers had been put out of work by demobilization. When a coalition of the radical International Workers of the World (IWW) and the moderate American Federation of Labor (AFL) called a general strike, the largest work stoppage in American history shut down the city. Newspapers across the nation claimed that the walkout was "a Bolshevik effort to start a revolution." The suppression of the strike by Seattle officials cost the AFL many of its wartime gains and contributed to the destruction of the IWW soon afterward.

A strike by Boston policemen in the fall of 1919 underscored postwar hostility toward labor militancy. Though paid less than pick-and-shovel laborers, the police won little sympathy. Once the officers stopped walking their beats, looters sacked the city. After two days of near anarchy, Massachusetts governor Calvin Coolidge called in the National Guard to restore order. The public, yearning for peace and security in the wake of war, welcomed Coolidge's anti-union assurance that "there is no right to strike against the public safety by anybody, anywhere, any time."

Labor strife climaxed in the grim steel strike of 1919. Faced with the steel industry's plan to revert to seven-day weeks, twelve-hour days, and weekly wages of about $20, the AFL tried to unionize steelworkers. When U.S. Steel and Bethlehem Steel refused to negotiate, Samuel Gompers, head of the AFL, called for a strike. In response, 350,000 workers in fifteen states walked out in September 1919. The steel industry hired 30,000 strikebreakers (many of them African Americans) and convinced the public that the strikers were radicals bent on subverting the Republic. State and federal troops protected scabs who crossed picket lines. In January 1920, after eighteen striking workers had been killed, the strike collapsed. That devastating defeat initiated a sharp decline in the fortunes of the labor movement, a trend that would continue for almost twenty years.

The Red Scare

Suppression of labor strikes was one response to the widespread fear of internal subversion that swept the nation in 1919. The "Red scare" (*red* affairs. A larger group of Republicans did not object to American participation in world politics but feared that membership in the League of Nations would jeopardize the nation's independence. No Republican, in any case, was eager to hand Wilson and the Democrats a foreign policy victory with the 1920 presidential election little more than a year away.

At the center of Republican opposition was Wilson's archenemy, Senator Henry Cabot Lodge of Massachusetts. Lodge's hostility was in part personal. "I never thought I could hate a man as much as I hate Wilson," he once admitted. But Lodge also raised cogent objections to the treaty and the league. Lodge was no isolationist, but he thought that much of the Fourteen Points was a "general bleat about virtue being better than vice." Lodge expected the United States's economic and military power to propel the nation into a major role in world affairs. But he insisted that membership in the League of Nations, which would require collective action to maintain peace, threatened the nation's freedom of choice in foreign relations.

Lodge used his position as chairman of the Senate Foreign Relations Committee to air every sort of complaint. Out of the committee hearings came several amendments, or "reservations," that sought to limit the consequences of American membership in the league. For example, several reservations required approval of both House and Senate before the United States could participate in league-sponsored economic sanctions or military action.

It gradually became clear that ratification of the treaty depended on acceptance of the Lodge reservations. Democratic senators, who overwhelmingly supported the treaty, urged Wilson to accept Lodge's terms, arguing that they left the essentials of the treaty intact. Wilson, however, insisted that the reservations cut "the very heart out of the treaty." He expressed personal hatred as well. "Lodge reservations?" he thundered. "Never! I'll never consent to adopt any policy with which that impossible name is so prominently identified."

Wilson decided to take his case directly to the people. On September 3, 1919, he set out by train on the most ambitious speaking tour ever undertaken by a president. He enjoyed some early success, but on September 25 in Pueblo, Colorado, Wilson collapsed and had to return to Washington. There he suffered a massive stroke that partially paralyzed him. From his bedroom,

Wilson sent messages instructing Democrats in the Senate to hold firm against any and all reservations. If the Senate approved the treaty with reservations, he said, he would not sign it. In the end, Wilson commanded enough loyalty to ensure a vote against the Lodge reservations. But when the treaty without reservations came before the Senate in March 1920, the combined opposition of the Republican irreconcilables and Republican reservationists left Wilson six votes short of the two-thirds majority needed for passage.

The nations of Europe organized the League of Nations at Geneva, Switzerland, but the United States never became a member. Whether American membership could have prevented the world war that began in Europe in 1939 is highly unlikely, but America's failure to join certainly weakened the league from the start. In refusing to accept relatively minor compromises with Senate moderates, Wilson lost his treaty and American membership in the league. Woodrow Wilson and Henry Cabot Lodge both died in 1924, never seeing international order or security, never knowing the whirlwind of resentment and violence that would eventually follow the Great War's failure to make the world safe for democracy.

REVIEW Why did the Senate fail to ratify the Treaty of Versailles?

Democracy at Risk

The defeat of Wilson's idealistic plan for international democracy proved the crowning blow to progressives who had hoped that the war could further reform at home. When the war ended, Americans wanted to demobilize swiftly. In the process, servicemen, defense workers, and farmers lost their war-related jobs. The volatile combination—of unemployed veterans returning home, a stalled economy, and leftover wartime patriotism looking for a new cause—threatened to explode. Wartime anti-German passion was quickly followed by antiradicalism, a fevered campaign that ensnared unionists, socialists, dissenters, and African Americans and Mexicans who had committed no offense but to seek to escape rural poverty.

refers to the color of the Bolshevik flag), which far outstripped the assault on civil liberties during the war, had homegrown causes: the postwar recession, labor unrest, and the difficulties of reintegrating millions of returning veterans. But unsettling events abroad also added to Americans' anxieties. Russian bolshevism became even more menacing in March 1919 when the new Soviet leaders created the Comintern, a worldwide association of **Communist** leaders intent on fomenting revolution in capitalist countries. (See "Beyond America's Borders," page 582.) A Communist revolution in the United States was extremely unlikely, but edgy Americans faced with a flurry of terrorist acts, most notably thirty-eight bombs mailed to prominent individuals, believed otherwise. Fear, anger, and uncertainty led swiftly to a hunt for terrorists, led by Attorney General A. Mitchell Palmer. Targeting men and women who harbored what Palmer considered ideas that could lead to violence, even though they may not have done anything illegal, the Justice Department sought to purge the supposed enemies of America.

In January 1920, Palmer ordered a series of raids that netted 6,000 alleged subversives. Finding no revolutionary conspiracies, Palmer nevertheless ordered 500 noncitizen suspects deported. His action came in the wake of a campaign against the most notorious radical alien, Russian-born Emma Goldman. Before the war, Goldman's passionate support of labor strikes, women's rights, and birth control had made her a symbol of radicalism. Finally, after a stay in prison for attacking military conscription, she was ordered deported by J. Edgar Hoover, the eager director of the Justice Department's Radical Division. In December 1919, Goldman and 250 others boarded a ship for exile in Russia.

The effort to rid the country of alien radicals was matched by efforts to crush troublesome citizens. Law enforcement officials and vigilante groups joined hands against the so-called Reds. In Centralia, Washington, when a menacing crowd gathered in front of the IWW hall, nervous members opened fire, killing three people. Three IWW members were arrested and later convicted of murder, but another, an ex-soldier, was carried off by a mob who castrated him and then, after hanging him from a bridge, riddled his body with bullets. His death was officially ruled a suicide.

Public institutions joined the attack on civil liberties. Local libraries removed dissenting books. Schools fired unorthodox teachers. Police shut down radical newspapers. State legislatures refused to seat elected representatives who professed socialist ideas, and in 1919, Congress removed its lone socialist representative, Victor Berger, on the grounds that he was a threat to national safety.

That same year, the Supreme Court provided a formula for restricting free speech. In upholding the conviction of socialist Charles Schenck for publishing a pamphlet urging resistance to the draft during wartime (*Schenck v. United States*), the Court established a "clear and present danger" test. Such utterances as Schenck's during a time of national peril, Justice Oliver Wendell Holmes wrote, were equivalent to shouting "Fire!" in a crowded theater. But Schenck's pamphlet had little power to provoke a public firmly opposed to its message.

In time, the Red scare lost credibility, especially after Attorney General Palmer warned that radicals were planning to celebrate the Bolshevik Revolution with a nationwide wave of violence. Officials called out state militia, fortified public buildings and churches, mobilized bomb squads, even placed machine-gun nests at major city intersections. When May 1 came and went without a single disturbance, the public mood turned from fear to scorn. The Red scare collapsed in its excesses.

The Great Migrations of African Americans and Mexicans

Before the Red scare lost steam, the government raised alarms about the loyalty of African Americans. A Justice Department investigation concluded that Reds were fomenting racial unrest among blacks. While the report was wrong about Bolshevik influence, it was correct in noticing a new stirring among African Americans, an assertiveness borne of participation in the war effort and in a massive migration out of the South.

In 1900, nine of every ten blacks still lived in the South, where poverty, disfranchisement, segregation, and violence dominated their lives. Thirty-five years after **emancipation**, African Americans had made little progress toward full citizenship. And whites remained committed to keeping blacks down. "If we own a good farm or horse, or cow, or bird-dog, or yoke of oxen," a black sharecropper in Mississippi observed in 1913, "we are harassed until we are

Bolshevism

One month before Woodrow Wilson asked Congress for a declaration of war against Germany, revolutionary forces in Russia overthrew Czar Nicholas II and installed a democratic government. The March 1917 revolution removed the last despot among the Allies fighting Germany and bolstered Wilson's confidence that the war really was a clear-cut fight between "democracy and autocracy." The American president embraced the revolution, declaring Russia "a fit partner for a league of honour."

In November 1917, Russia experienced a second revolution. Marxist radicals calling themselves Bolsheviks seized control and made their leader, Vladimir Ilyich Lenin, ruler of Russia. Lenin scoffed at the idea that the Allies were fighting for democracy and insisted that greedy capitalists were waging war for international dominance. In March 1918, he shocked Wilson and the Allies by signing a separate peace with Germany and withdrawing Russia from the war. Still locked in the desperate struggle with Germany, the Allies cried betrayal and feared that vast numbers of German soldiers who had been fighting the Russian army on the eastern front would turn to confront exhausted Allied troops on the western front.

Prodded by British leader Winston Churchill, who declared that "the Bolshevik infant should be strangled in its cradle," Britain and France urged the United States to join them in sending troops to Russia in support of Russian democrats opposing the new revolutionary regime. Wilson hesitated before committing American troops to a civil war in Russia. He told his trusted adviser Colonel House, "I've been sweating blood over the question of what is right and feasible to do in Russia." Several prominent Americans spoke out against American intervention. Senator William Borah of Idaho declared: "The Russian people have the same right to establish a Socialist state as we have to establish a republic." But Wilson concluded that the Bolsheviks were a dictatorial party that had come to power through a violent coup that denied Russians political choice, and he figured that if anti-Bolshevik forces were successful, Russia might reenter the war on the Allied side, against Germany. Thus by September 1918, on the pretext of helping 60,000 trapped Czechoslovakians return to the western front to fight the Germans, Wilson had ordered 14,000 American troops to Russia to join British and French forces there.

After the Allies defeated Germany in November 1918, they could no longer rationalize the continued presence of Western troops in Russia as part of the war with Germany. It became clear that the American, British, and French troops were fighting to overthrow Lenin and annul the Bolshevik Revolution. But the Bolsheviks (by now calling themselves Communists) prevailed, and American troops withdrew from Russia in June 1919, after the loss of more than 200 American lives.

The Bolshevik regime dedicated itself not only to ending capitalism in Russia (known as the Soviet Union after 1922) but also to overthrowing capitalist and imperialist regimes everywhere. Clearly, Lenin's imagined future was at odds with Wilson's proposed liberal new world order. Wilson withheld U.S. diplomatic recognition of the Soviet Union (a policy that persisted until 1934) and joined the Allies in an economic boycott to bring down the Bolshevik government. Unbowed, Lenin promised that his party would "incite rebellion among all the peoples now oppressed," and revolutionary agitation became central to Soviet foreign policy. Communist revolutions erupted in Bavaria and Hungary. Though short-lived, the Communist regimes there sent shock waves throughout the West. In 1919, moreover, a Russian official bragged that monies being sent to Europe to foment Bolshevik rebellion were "nothing compared to the funds transmitted to New York for the purpose of spreading bolshevism in the United States." American attention shifted from revolutionaries in Europe to revolutionaries at home. The Red scare was on.

Having failed to make the world "safe for democracy," the Wilson administration set out to make democracy safe in America. Attorney General A. Mitchell Palmer perceived a "blaze of Revolution sweeping over every American institution of law and order ... licking the altars of churches ... crawling into the sacred corners of American homes." The U.S. government launched an all-out attack on the Communist ("Red") menace. Rather than looking on the Bolshevik success as monstrous, a few Americans saw Russia as the world's best hope, especially after the Versailles treaty shattered Wilson's grand plans for the peace. Some traveled to Russia and wrote rapturously about the society that promised economic and social justice and the end of the exploitation of workers by capitalist bosses. The vast majority of Americans, however, were no more drawn to communism than to czarism. In 1919, disgruntled socialists founded the American Communist Party, but the party attracted only a handful of members, who spent most of their time arguing the fine points of doctrine, not manufacturing bombs.

But a few radicals did resort to bombs and in 1919, one observer warned that "Bolshevism means chaos, wholesale murder, the complete destruction of civilization." Even mild dissenters faced bullying and threats. Workers seeking better wages and conditions, women and African Americans demanding equal rights, and anyone else pushing for change found the government hurling the epithet "Red" at critics of the status quo. Beatings, jailings, and deportation often followed. After the sailing of the "Soviet Ark," which deported Emma Goldman and other radicals on December 21, 1919, the hysteria subsided.

The Bolshevik Revolution in Russia had endless consequences. In the Soviet Union it initiated a brutal reign of terror that lasted more than seven decades. In international politics it set up a polarity that lasted nearly as long. In a very

Attorney General A. Mitchell Palmer
On January 2, 1920, Attorney General A. Mitchell Palmer ordered hundreds of federal agents to 33 American cities to smash the alleged Bolshevik conspiracy. Led by J. Edgar Hoover, the agents arrested more than 6,000 individuals on charges of plotting to overthrow the government. Palmer revealed much more about himself than about those arrested when he said, "Out of the sly and crafty eyes of many of them leap cupidity, cruelty, insanity, and crime; from their lopsided faces, sloping brows, and misshapen features may be recognized the unmistakable criminal type."
Library of Congress.

real sense, the cold war, which set the United States and the Soviet Union at each other's throats after World War II, began in 1917. America's abortive military intervention against the Bolshevik regime and the Bolsheviks' call for worldwide revolution convulsed relations from the very beginning. In the United States, the rabid anti-radicalism of the Red scare did significant damage to traditional American values. Commitment to

the protection of dissent succumbed to irrational anticommunism. Even mild reform became tarred with the brush of bolshevism. Although the Red scare quickly withered, the habit of crushing dissent in the name of security would live on. Years later, when Americans' anxiety mounted and confidence waned once again, witch hunts against radicalism would again undermine American democracy.

If You are a Stranger in the City

If you want a job   If you want a place to live
If you are having trouble with your employer
If you want information or advice of any kind
CALL UPON

The CHICAGO LEAGUE ON URBAN
CONDITIONS AMONG NEGROES
3719 South State Street
Telephone Douglas 9098   T. ARNOLD HILL, Executive Secretary

No charges—no fees. We want to help YOU

SELF-HELP

1. Do not loaf. Get a job at once.
2. Do not live in crowded rooms.
   Others can be obtained.
3. Do not carry on loud conversations
   in street cars and public places.
4. Do not keep your children out of
   school.
5. Do not send for your family until
   you get a job.
6. Do not think you can hold your
   job unless you are industrious,
   sober, efficient and prompt.

Cleanliness and fresh air are
necessary for good health. In
case of sickness send immediately for a good physician.
Become an active member in
some church as soon as you
reach the city.

Issued by

African Americans Migrate North

In 1912, the members of this southern family arrived in their new home in an unnamed northern
city. Wearing their Sunday best, they carried the
rest of what they owned in two suitcases. Several
factors combined to prompt the massive African
American migration out of the South. To the
burden of racism was added the steady erosion of opportunities to make a living. In the 1920s, many rural blacks lost work
when boll weevils devoured the cotton crop. Then mechanization and government programs to support crop prices by reducing
acreage drove many more people off the land. In Chicago, the young Urban League sought to ease the transition of southern
blacks to life in the North. As the card suggests, new arrivals—mostly rural, agricultural people—faced a raft of difficulties, including finding work in factories, locating places to live in a confusing, congested city, and getting along with their northern
employers. Other Urban League cards advised hard work, sobriety, cleanliness, finding a church, getting children into school,
and speaking softly in public places.

Photograph: Photographs and Prints Division, Schomburg Center for Research in Black Culture, New York Public Library, Astor, Lenox and Tilden
Foundations; card: Special Collections, The University Library, University of Illinois at Chicago.

bound to sell, give away, or run away, before we can have any peace in our lives."

The First World War provided African Americans with the opportunity to escape the South's cotton fields and kitchens. When the war caused acute labor shortages in northern industries, industrialists turned to black labor. Black men found work in steel mills, shipyards, munitions plants, railroad yards, and mines. From 1915 to 1920, a half million blacks (approximately 10 percent of the South's black population) boarded trains bound for Philadelphia, Detroit, Cleveland, Chicago, St. Louis, and other industrial cities.

Thousands of migrants wrote home to tell family and friends about their experiences in the North. One man announced proudly that he had recently been promoted to "first assistant to the head carpenter." He added, "I should have been here twenty years ago. I just begin to feel like a man.... My children are going to the same school with the whites and I don't have to [h]umble to no one. I have registered—will vote the next election and there ain't any 'yes sir'—it's all yes and no and Sam and Bill."

But the North was not the promised land. Black men stood on the lowest rungs of the labor ladder. Jobs of any kind proved scarce for black women. Limited by both race and sex, most worked as domestic servants as they did in the South. The existing black middle classes sometimes shunned the less educated, less sophisticated rural Southerners crowding into northern cities. Savage race riots ripped through two dozen northern cities. The worst occurred in July 1917 when a mob of whites invaded a section of East St. Louis, Illinois, crowded with blacks who had been recruited to help break a strike. The mob murdered at least 39 people and left most of the black district in flames. In 1918, the nation witnessed 96 lynchings of blacks, some of them returning war veterans still in uniform.

Still, most migrants to the North stayed and encouraged friends and family to follow. By 1940, more than one million blacks had left the South, profoundly changing their own lives and the course of the nation's history. Black enclaves, "cities within cities," such as Harlem in New York and the South Side of Chicago, emerged in the North. These assertive communities provided a foundation for black protest and political organization in the years ahead.

At nearly the same moment that black Americans streamed into northern cities, another migration was under way in the American Southwest. Between 1910 and 1920, the Mexican-born population in the United States soared from 222,000 to 478,000. Mexican immigration resulted from developments on both sides of the border. In Mexico, poverty and revolutionary violence helped turn the trickle of migration into a flood. North of the border, the Chinese Exclusion Act of 1882 and then the disruption of World War I cut off the supply of cheap foreign labor and caused western employers in the expanding rail, mining, construction, and agricultural industries to look south to Mexico for workers.

As a result of Americans' racial stereotyping of Mexicans—a U.S. government economist described them as "docile, patient, usually orderly in camp, fairly intelligent under competent supervision, obedient and cheap"—Mexicans were considered excellent prospects for manual labor but not for citizenship. In 1917, when anti-immigration advocates convinced Congress to do something about foreigners coming into the United States, the restrictive legislation bowed to southwestern industry and exempted Mexicans. By 1920, ethnic Mexicans made up some three-fourths of California's farm laborers. They were also crucial to the Texas economy, comprising 75 percent of laborers in the cotton fields and in construction.

Like immigrants from Europe and black migrants from the South, Mexicans in the American Southwest dreamed of a better life. And like the others, they found both opportunity and disappointment. Wages were better than in Mexico, but life in the fields, mines, and factories was hard, and living conditions—in box cars or labor camps or urban barrios—often were dismal. Signs warning "No Mexicans Allowed" increased rather than declined. Mexicanas nurtured families, but many women also worked for wages. Thousands of women picked cotton, sometimes dragging hundred-pound cotton sacks with a baby perched on top. Among Mexican Americans, some of whom had lived in the Southwest for a century or more, *los recien llegados* (the recent arrivals) encountered mixed reactions. One Mexican American expressed the ambivalence: "We are all Mexicans anyway because the *gueros* [Anglos] treat us all alike," he declared, but he also called for immigration quotas because the recent arrivals drove down wages and incited white prejudice that affected all ethnic Mexicans.

Mexican Women Arriving in El Paso, 1911
These new arrivals, carrying bundles and wearing traditional shawls, try to get their bearings on arriving in El Paso, Texas—the Ellis Island for Mexican immigrants. Perhaps they are looking for a family member who preceded them, or perhaps they are alone and calculating their next step. In any case, these women were part of the first modern wave of Mexican immigration to the United States. Women like them found work in the cotton and sugar-beet fields, canneries, and restaurants of the Southwest, and at home taking in sewing, laundry, and boarders. Whatever their work, their journey across the border proved life changing.
Courtesy of the Rio Grande Historical Collections, New Mexico State University Library, Las Cruces, New Mexico.

Despite friction, large-scale immigration into the Southwest meant a resurgence of the Mexican cultural presence, which became the basis for greater solidarity and political action for the ethnic Mexican population. Shortly after World War I, Mexican Americans began organizing, a development that culminated with the formation of the League of United Latin American Citizens (LULAC) in Texas in 1929.

Postwar Politics and the Election of 1920

Two thousand miles away in Washington, D.C., President Woodrow Wilson, bedridden and par-

alyzed, stubbornly ignored the mountain of domestic troubles—labor strikes, the Red scare, race riots, immigration backlash—and insisted that the 1920 election would be a "solemn referendum" on the League of Nations. Dutifully, the Democratic nominees for president, James M. Cox of Ohio, and for vice president, Franklin Delano Roosevelt of New York, campaigned on Wilson's international ideals. The Republican Party chose a very different sort of candidate: handsome, gregarious Warren Gamaliel Harding, senator from Ohio. Harding's rise in Ohio politics was a tribute to his amiability, not his mastery of the issues.

Harding found the winning formula when he declared that "America's present need is not heroics, but healing; not nostrums [questionable remedies] but normalcy." But what was "normalcy"? Harding explained: "By 'normalcy' I don't mean the old order but a regular steady order of things. I mean normal procedure, the natural way, without excess." Eager to put wartime crusades and postwar strife behind them, voters responded by giving Harding the largest presidential victory ever: 60.5 percent of the popular vote and 76 percent of the electoral vote (Map 22.6). Once in office, the Hardings threw open the White House gates, which had been closed since the declaration of war in 1917. Their welcome brought throngs of visitors and lifted the

MAP 22.6   The Election of 1920

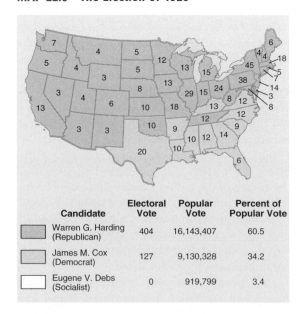

Candidate	Electoral Vote	Popular Vote	Percent of Popular Vote
Warren G. Harding (Republican)	404	16,143,407	60.5
James M. Cox (Democrat)	127	9,130,328	34.2
Eugene V. Debs (Socialist)	0	919,799	3.4

national pall, signaling a new era of easygoing good cheer.

REVIEW   How did the Red scare contribute to the erosion of civil liberties after the war?

Conclusion: Troubled Crusade

America's experience in World War I was exceptional. For much of the world, the Great War produced great destruction, acres of blackened fields, ruined factories, and millions of casualties. But in the United States, war and prosperity marched hand in hand. America emerged from the war with the strongest economy in the world and a position of international preeminence.

Still, the nation paid a heavy price both at home and abroad. American soldiers and sailors encountered unprecedented horrors—submarines, poison gas, machine guns—and more than 100,000 died. Rather than redeeming their sacrifice, however, as Wilson promised, the peace that followed the armistice tarnished it. At home, rather than permanently improving working conditions, advancing public health, and spreading educational opportunity, as progressives had hoped, the war threatened to undermine the achievements of the previous two decades. Moreover, rather than promoting American democracy, the war bred fear, intolerance, and repression that led to a crackdown on dissent and a demand for conformity. Reformers could count only woman suffrage as a permanent victory.

Woodrow Wilson had promised more than anyone could deliver. Progressive hopes of extending democracy and **liberal** reform nationally and internationally were dashed. In 1920, a bruised and disillusioned society stumbled into a new decade. The era coming to an end had called on Americans to crusade and sacrifice. Now whoever could promise them peace, prosperity, and a good time would have the best chance to win their hearts.

Suggestions for Further Reading

Thomas Fleming, *The Illusion of Victory: America in World War I* (2003). A lively and critical account of Wilson's wartime presidential leadership.

Maurine Weiner Greenwald, *Women, War, and Work: The Impact of World War I on Women Workers in the United States* (1980). A thorough analysis of the war's impact on women's working lives.

Margaret Olwen Macmillan, *Paris 1919: Six Months That Changed the World* (2002). An eloquent consideration of the Versailles treaty and its global consequences.

Gene Smith, *Until the Last Trumpet Sounds: The Life of General of the Armies John J. Pershing* (1998). A fine biography of the commander of the American Expeditionary Force in Europe.

Joe William Trotter Jr., ed., *The Great Migration in Historical Perspective* (1991). A collection of essays that carefully considers the complex consequences of black migration from the South.

Robert H. Zieger, *America's Great War: World War I and the American Experience* (2000). A comprehensive and accessible survey of Americans' responses to the war in Europe.

▶ FOR MORE BOOKS ABOUT TOPICS IN THIS CHAPTER, see the Online Bibliography at bedfordstmartins.com/roarkcompact.

▶ FOR ADDITIONAL FIRSTHAND ACCOUNTS OF THIS PERIOD, see Chapter 22 in Michael Johnson, ed., *Reading the American Past*, Third Edition.

▶ FOR WEB SITES AND DOCUMENTS RELATED TO TOPICS AND PLACES IN THIS CHAPTER, see "HistoryLinks," "DocLinks," and "PlaceLinks" at bedfordstmartins.com/roarkcompact.

REVIEWING THE CHAPTER

Follow these steps to review and strengthen your understanding of the chapter.

STEP 1: *Study the **Key Terms** and **Timeline** to identify the significance of each item listed.*

STEP 2: *Answer the **Review Questions**, drawing on key terms and dates to support your answers.*

STEP 3: *Drawing on the Key Terms, Timeline, and Review Questions, answer the broader **Making Connections** questions.*

KEY TERMS

Who

John "Black Jack" Pershing (p. 563)
Ferdinand Foch (p. 564)
Woodrow Wilson (p. 564)
William Jennings Bryan (p. 565)
Victoriano Huerta (p. 565)
Francisco "Pancho" Villa (p. 566)
Wilhelm II (p. 566)
Archduke Franz Ferdinand (p. 566)
Robert Lansing (p. 568)
Nicholas II (p. 569)
Alice Paul (p. 573)
Carrie Chapman Catt (p. 574)
George Creel (p. 574)
David Lloyd George (p. 576)
Georges Clemenceau (p. 576)
Vittorio Orlando (p. 576)
Henry Cabot Lodge (p. 579)
Calvin Coolidge (p. 580)
A. Mitchell Palmer (p. 581)
Emma Goldman (p. 581)

James M. Cox (p. 586)
Warren G. Harding (p. 586)

What

American Expeditionary Force
     (pp. 563, 569)
Triple Alliance (p. 566)
Triple Entente ("the Allies") (p. 566)
economic blockade (p. 567)
U-boats (p. 567)
Lusitania (p. 567)
Zimmermann telegram (p. 568)
Selective Service Act (p. 569)
Brest-Litovsk treaty (p. 569)
War Industries Board (p. 572)
Food Administration (p. 572)
prohibition (p. 573)
Eighteenth Amendment (p. 573)
Women's Trade Union League (p. 573)
National American Woman Suffrage
     Association (p. 574)

Nineteenth Amendment (p. 574)
Women's Peace Party (p. 574)
Committee on Public Information
     (p. 574)
Sedition Act (p. 575)
Wilson's Fourteen Points (p. 576)
League of Nations (p. 576)
Paris peace conference (p. 576)
mandate system (p. 577)
Treaty of Versailles (p. 578)
Seattle general strike of 1919 (p. 580)
Boston police strike of 1919 (p. 580)
steel strike of 1919 (p. 580)
Red scare (p. 580)
Comintern (p. 581)
Schenck v. United States (p. 581)
great migrations (p. 581)
East St. Louis race riot (p. 585)
League of United Latin American
     Citizens (p. 586)

TIMELINE

1914 • **April.** U.S. marines occupy Veracruz, Mexico.
- **June 28.** Assassination of Archduke Franz Ferdinand.
- **July 28.** Austria declares war on Serbia.
- **August 6.** Germany declares war on Russia and France; Great Britain declares war on Germany.

    1915 • *Lusitania* is sunk.
- Women's Peace Party formed.
- Italy joins the Allies.

        1916 • General Pershing pursues Pancho Villa.
- Wilson reelected.

           1917 • Zimmermann telegram intercepted.
- **April 6.** United States declares war on Germany.
- Committee on Public Information created.
- Selective Service Act.
- Espionage Act.
- East St. Louis, Illinois, race riot.
- Russia arranges separate peace with Germany.

REVIEW QUESTIONS

1. Why did President Wilson authorize repeated military interventions in the Americas? (pp. 564–68)

2. How did the American Expeditionary Force contribute to the defeat of Germany? (pp. 569–71)

3. How did progressive ideals fare during wartime? (pp. 571–75)

4. Why did the Senate fail to ratify the Treaty of Versailles? (pp. 575–79)

5. How did the Red scare contribute to the erosion of civil liberties after the war? (pp. 579–87)

MAKING CONNECTIONS

1. Why did the United States at first resist intervening in World War I? Why did it later retreat from this policy and send troops? In your answer, discuss whether these decisions revised or reinforced earlier U.S. foreign policy.

2. Some reformers were optimistic that World War I would advance progressive ideals at home. Discuss specific wartime domestic developments that displayed progressivism's influence. How did war contribute to these developments? Did they endure in peacetime? Why or why not?

3. A conservative reaction in American politics followed peace, most vividly in the labor upheaval and Red scare that swept the nation. What factors drove these developments? How did they shape the postwar political spectrum?

4. During World War I, the nation witnessed important demographic changes. What drove African American and Mexican migration north? How did the war facilitate these changes? In your answer, explain the significance of these developments to the migrants and the nation.

▶ **For practice quizzes, a customized study plan, and other study tools,** see the Online Study Guide at **bedfordstmartins.com/roarkcompact.**

1918 • **January 8.** President Wilson gives Fourteen Points speech.
• **May–June.** U.S. marines see first major combat at Cantigny and Château-Thierry.
• **November 11.** Armistice signed ending World War I.

   1919 • **January.** Paris peace conference begins.
   • **June.** Treaty of Versailles signed.
   • **September.** Wilson undertakes speaking tour.
   • Wave of labor strikes.

      1920 • **January 1.** Prohibition begins.
      • Palmer raids.
      • Senate votes against ratification of Treaty of Versailles.
      • **August 18.** Nineteenth Amendment ratified.
      • **November.** Republican Warren G. Harding elected president.

MODEL T FORD

Nothing symbolized the 1920s more than automobiles. Americans drove millions of them—Briscoes, Dodges, Lexingtons, Cadillacs, Maxwells, and especially Model T Fords. When Henry Ford introduced the Model T in 1908, Americans thought of automobiles as toys of the rich, far too costly for average people. By the 1920s, millions of Americans owned Fords, and their lives were never the same. Oklahoma humorist Will Rogers claimed that Henry Ford "changed the habits of more people than Caesar, Mussolini, Charlie Chaplin, Clara Bow, Xerxes, Amos 'n Andy, and Bernard Shaw." One of novelist Booth Tarkington's characters expressed some reservation about automobiles: "With all their speed forward, they may be a step backward in civilization." But most Americans loved their automobiles and sped away into the future.

National Museum of American History, Smithsonian Institution, Behring Center.

23

From New Era to Great Depression

1920–1932

AMERICANS IN THE 1920s cheered Henry Ford as an authentic American hero. When the decade began, he had already produced 6,000,000 automobiles; by 1927, the figure reached 15,000,000. In 1920, one car rolled off the Ford assembly line every minute; in 1925, one appeared every ten seconds. In 1920, a Ford car cost $845; in 1928, the price was less than $300, within range of most of the country's skilled workingmen. Henry Ford put America on wheels, and in the eyes of most Americans he was an honest man who made an honest car: basic, inexpensive, and reliable. He became the greatest example of free enterprise's promise and achievement. But like the age in which he lived, Henry Ford was many-sided, more complex and contradictory than this simple image suggests.

Born in 1863 on a farm in Dearborn, Michigan, Ford hated the drudgery of farmwork and loved tinkering with machines. At sixteen, he fled rural life for Detroit, where he became a journeyman machinist and experimented with internal combustion engines. In 1893, he put together one of the first successful gasoline-driven carriages in the United States. His ambition, he said, was to "make something in quantity." The product he chose reflected American restlessness, the desire to be on the move. "Everybody wants to be someplace he ain't," Ford declared. "As soon as he gets there he wants to go right back." In 1903, with $28,000 from a few backers, Ford gathered twelve workers in a 250-by-50-foot shed and created the Ford Motor Company.

Ford's early cars were custom-made one at a time. By 1914, his cars were being built along a continuously moving assembly line; workers bolted on parts brought to them by cranes and conveyor belts. Ford made only one kind of car, the Model T, which became synonymous with mass production. A boxlike black vehicle, it was cheap, easy to drive, and simple to repair. The Model T dominated the market. Throughout the rapid expansion of the automotive industry, the Ford Motor Company remained the industry leader, peaking in 1925 when it outsold all its rivals combined (Map 23.1).

Nobody entertained grander or more contradictory visions of the new America he had helped to create than Henry Ford himself. When he began his rise, **progressive** critics condemned the industrial giants of the nineteenth century as "robber barons" who lived in luxury while reducing their workers to wage slaves. Ford, however, identified with the common folk and saw himself as the benefactor of Americans yearning to be free and mobile.

Ford's automobile plants made him a billionaire, but their highly regimented assembly lines reduced Ford workers to near robots. On the cutting

Henry and Edsel
In this 1924 photograph, Henry Ford looks fondly at his first car while his son, Edsel, stands next to the ten millionth Model T. Edsel, the Fords' only child, remained unspoiled by his father's enormous wealth. Forsaking college, he entered the family business out of high school. Serious, disciplined, and an acute observer, Edsel Ford realized by the mid-1920s that General Motors's more advanced Chevrolet was about to surpass the Model T. Henry Ford stubbornly refused to change his automobile, insisting that the "Model T is the most perfect car in the world." Under Edsel's leadership, however, the Ford Motor Company moved beyond the plain, boxy, black, and fabulously successful Model T.
Henry Ford Museum and Greenfield Village.

others condemned postwar society for its vulgar materialism. A great outpouring of artistic talent led, ironically, to incessant critiques of America's artistic barrenness. The Ku Klux Klan and other champions of an idealized older America resorted to violence as well as words when they chastised the era's "new women," "new Negroes," and surging immigrant populations.

The public, disillusioned with the outcome of World War I, turned from the Christian moralism and idealism of the Progressive Era. In the twenties, Ford and businessmen like him replaced political reformers such as Theodore Roosevelt and Woodrow Wilson as the models of progress. The U.S. Chamber of Commerce crowed, "The American businessman is the most influential person in the nation." Social justice gave way to individual advancement. At the center of it all, President Calvin Coolidge spoke in praise of those in power when he declared, "The business of America is business." The fortunes of the era rose, then crashed, according to the values and practices of the business community.

The New Era

The rejection of progressives' pleas for government intervention and regulation in favor of the revival of free-enterprise individualism helped make the 1920s a time of contradiction and ambivalence. Once Woodrow Wilson left the White House, energy flowed away from civic reform and toward private economic endeavor. The rise of a freewheeling economy and a heightened sense of individualism caused Secretary of Commerce Herbert Hoover to declare that America had entered a "New Era," one of many labels used to describe the complex 1920s. Some terms focus on the decade's high-spirited energy and cultural changes: Roaring Twenties, Jazz Age, Flaming Youth, Age of the Flapper. Others echo the rising importance of money—Dollar Decade, Golden Twenties, Prosperity Decade— or reflect the sinister side of gangster profiteering—Lawless Decade. Still others emphasize the lonely confusion of a Lost Generation and the stress and anxiety of the Aspirin Age.

America in the twenties was many things, but there was no getting around the truth of Calvin Coolidge's insight: The business of America was business. Politicians and diplomats proclaimed business the heart of American civi-

edge of modern technology, Ford nevertheless remained nostalgic about rural values. He sought to revive the past in Greenfield Village, a museum outside Detroit, where he relocated buildings from a bygone era, including his parents' farmhouse. His museum contrasted sharply with the roaring Ford plant farther along the Detroit River at River Rouge. The African American and immigrant workers who worked there found no place in Greenfield Village. Yet all would be well, Ford insisted, if Americans remained true to their agrarian past and somehow managed to be modern and scientific at the same time.

Tension between traditional values and modern conditions lay at the heart of the conflicted 1920s. For the first time, more Americans lived in urban than in rural areas, yet Americans remained nostalgic about farms and small towns. Although the nation generally prospered, the new wealth widened the gap between rich and poor. While millions admired urban America's sophisticated new style and consumer products,

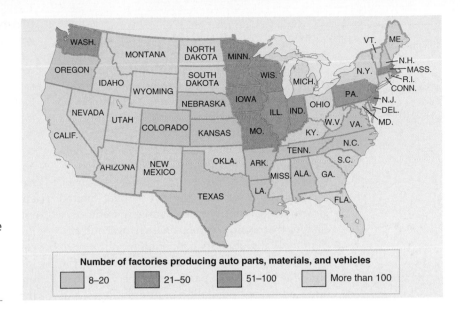

MAP 23.1 Auto Manufacturing
By the mid-1920s, the massive coal and steel industries of the Midwest had made that region the center of the new automobile industry. A major road-building program by the federal government carried the thousands of new cars produced each day to every corner of the country.

Number of factories producing auto parts, materials, and vehicles

8–20	21–50	51–100	More than 100

lization. Average men and women bought into the idea that business and its wonderful products were what made America great, as they snatched up the unprecedented flood of new consumer items American factories sent forth.

A Business Government

Republicans controlled the White House from 1921 to 1933. The first of the three Republican presidents was Warren Gamaliel Harding, the Ohio senator who in his 1920 campaign called for a "return to normalcy," by which he meant the end of public crusades and a return to private pursuits. Harding, who had few qualifications for the presidency, appointed to his cabinet a few men of real stature. Herbert Hoover, the self-made millionaire and former head of the wartime Food Administration, became secretary of commerce and, according to one wag who testified to Hoover's ambition and energy, assistant secretary of everything else. But wealth also counted. Most significantly, Harding appointed Andrew Mellon, one of the richest men in America, secretary of the treasury. And friendship counted, too. Harding handed out jobs to his old "Ohio gang" for whom friendship was their only qualification.

When Harding was elected in 1920 in a landslide over Democratic opponent James Cox (see chapter 22, Map 22.6), the unemployment rate hit 20 percent, the highest ever up to that point. Farmers fared the worst, as their bankruptcy rate increased tenfold. Harding pushed measures to aid American enterprise and regain national prosperity—high tariffs to protect American businesses (the Fordney-McCumber tariff in 1922 raised duties to unprecedented heights), price supports for agriculture, and the dismantling of wartime government control over industry in favor of unregulated private business. "Never before, here or anywhere else," the U.S. Chamber of Commerce said proudly, "has a government been so completely fused with business."

Harding's policies to boost American enterprise made him very popular, but ultimately his small-town congeniality and trusting ways did him in. Some of his friends in the "Ohio gang" were up to their necks in lawbreaking. Three of Harding's appointees would go to jail and others would be indicted. Interior Secretary Albert Fall was convicted of accepting bribes of more than $400,000 for leasing oil reserves on public land in Teapot Dome, Wyoming, and "Teapot Dome" became a synonym for political corruption.

Baffled about how to deal with "my God-damned friends," Harding in the summer of 1923 set off on a trip to Alaska to escape his troubles. But the president found no rest and his health declined. On August 2, 1923, a shocked nation learned of the fifty-eight-year-old Harding's sudden death from a heart attack.

Vice President Calvin Coolidge, a spare, solemn man steeped in old-fashioned Yankee morality, became president. Coolidge once expressed his belief that "the man who builds a factory builds a temple, the man who works there worships there." Reverence for free enterprise meant that Coolidge continued and extended Harding's policies of promoting business and limiting government. With Coolidge's approval, Secretary of the Treasury Andrew Mellon reduced the government's control over the economy. Tax cuts for corporations and wealthy individuals sliced government tax revenue by about half. New rules for the Federal Trade Commission severely limited its power to regulate business. Secretary of Commerce Herbert Hoover limited government authority by encouraging trade associations that would keep business honest and efficient through voluntary cooperation.

Coolidge found a staunch ally in the Supreme Court. For many years the Court had opposed federal regulation of hours, wages, and working conditions on the grounds that such legislation was the proper concern of the states. With Coolidge, the Court also found ways to curtail a state's ability to regulate business. It ruled against **closed shops**—businesses where only union members could be employed—while confirming the right of owners to form exclusive trade associations. In 1923, the Court declared unconstitutional the District of Columbia's minimum-wage law for women, asserting that the law interfered with the freedom of employer and employee to make labor contracts. On a broad front, the Court and the president attacked government intrusion in the free market, even when the prohibition of government regulation threatened the welfare of workers.

The election of 1924 confirmed the defeat of the progressive principle that the state should take a leading role in ensuring the general welfare. To oppose Coolidge, the Democrats nominated John W. Davis, a corporate lawyer whose conservative views differed little from Republican principles. Only the Progressive Party and its presidential nominee, Senator Robert La Follette of Wisconsin, offered a genuine alternative. When La Follette championed labor unions, regulation of business, and protection of civil liberties, Republicans coined the slogan "Coolidge or Chaos." By 1924, most Americans had turned their backs on what they considered labor radicalism and reckless reform, and Coolidge captured more votes than his two opponents put together. The election proved that Coolidge was right when he declared, "This is a business country, and it wants a business government." What was true of the government's relationship to business at home was also true abroad.

Promoting Prosperity and Peace Abroad

After orchestrating the Senate's successful effort to block American membership in the League of Nations, Henry Cabot Lodge boasted, "We have torn Wilsonism up by the roots." But repudiation of Wilsonian internationalism and rejection of **collective security** through the League of Nations did not mean that the United States retreated into **isolationism**. The United States emerged from World War I with its economy intact and enjoyed a decade of stunning growth. Economic involvement in the world and the continuing chaos in Europe made withdrawal impossible. Corporate chieftain Owen Young observed: "Whether the United States will sit in the court of great economic movements throughout the world is not a question which the Senate, or even all of our people combined can decide. We are there…inescapably there." New York replaced London as the center of world finance, and the United States became the world's chief creditor. American banks poured billions into war-torn Europe's economic recovery. Europe not only absorbed American loans and products but encountered a flood of American popular culture in the form of fashion, style, and Hollywood motion pictures.

One of the Republicans' most ambitious foreign policy initiatives was the Washington Disarmament Conference that convened to establish a global balance of naval power. Secretary of State Charles Evans Hughes shaped the Five-Power Naval Treaty of 1922 committing Britain, France, Japan, Italy, and the United States to a proportional reduction of naval forces. The treaty led to the scrapping of more than two million tons of warships, by far the world's greatest success in disarmament. Americans celebrated President Harding for safeguarding the peace while remaining outside the League of Nations. By fostering international peace, he also helped make the world a safer place for American trade.

A second major effort on behalf of world peace came in 1928 when American secretary of state Frank Kellogg joined French foreign minister Aristide Briand to produce the Kellogg-Briand pact. Nearly fifty nations signed the solemn pledge to renounce war and settle international disputes peacefully. The nation's signature affirmed its commitment to peace rather than to Wilson's foolish notion of a progressive, uplifting war.

But Republican administrations preferred private sector diplomacy to state action. With the

Colorado Filling Station and Gas Pump
Gulf Oil Company gave away the first free road map in 1914. By 1929, when Conoco (Continental Oil Company) produced this lavish map with Colorado's spectacular mountains looming in the background, nearly every oil company was supplying road maps as part of its campaign to attract the booming tourist trade. This appealing drive-through station is a far cry from the first retail outlets for gas—blacksmith and hardware stores, the same places individuals bought kerosene to burn in lamps. Because motorists did not trust what they could not see, companies in the 1910s introduced glass-cylinder, gravity-flow pumps.
Courtesy, Colorado Historical Society.

FOR MORE HELP ANALYZING THIS IMAGE, see the visual activity for this chapter in the Online Study Guide at
bedfordstmartins.com/roarkcompact.

blessing of the White House, a team of American financiers led by the Chicago banker Charles Dawes swung into action when Germany suspended its war reparation payments in 1923. Impoverished, Germany was staggering under the massive bill of $33 billion presented by the victorious Allies in the Versailles treaty. When Germany failed to meet its annual payment, France occupied Germany's industrial Ruhr Valley. In 1924, American corporate leaders produced the Dawes Plan, which halved Germany's annual reparation payments, initiated fresh American loans to Germany, caused the French to retreat from the Ruhr, and got money flowing again in Germany's financial markets. Although the United States failed to join the league, it continued to exercise significant economic and diplomatic influence abroad. These Republican successes overseas helped to fuel prosperity at home.

Automobiles, Mass Production, and Assembly-Line Progress

The automobile industry emerged as the largest single manufacturing industry in the nation. Henry Ford shrewdly located his company in Detroit. Key materials for the automobile were manufactured in nearby states, making their transport convenient. Keystone of the American economy, the automobile industry not only employed hundreds of thousands of workers directly but also brought whole industries into being—filling

Detroit and the Automobile Industry in the 1920s

stations, garages, fast-food restaurants, and "guest cottages" (motels). The need for tires, glass, steel, highways, oil, and refined gasoline for automobiles provided millions of related jobs. By 1929, one American in four found employment directly or indirectly in the automobile industry. "Give us our daily bread" was no longer addressed to the Almighty, one commentator quipped, but to Detroit.

Automobiles altered the face of America. Cars changed where people lived, what work they did, how they spent their leisure, even how they thought. Hundreds of small towns decayed because the automobile enabled rural people to bypass them in favor of more distant cities and towns. The one-room schoolhouse and the crossroads church began to vanish from the landscape. Urban streetcars began to disappear as workers moved from the cities to the suburbs and commuted to work along crowded highways. Nothing shaped modern America more than the automobile. And efficient mass production made the automobile revolution possible.

Mass production by the assembly-line technique had become standard in almost every factory, from automobiles to meatpacking to cigarettes. To improve efficiency, corporations reduced assembly-line work to the simplest, most repetitive tasks. They also established specialized divisions—procurement, production, marketing, and employee relations—each with its own team of professionally trained managers. Changes on the assembly line and in management, along with technological advances, significantly boosted overall efficiency. Between 1922 and 1929, productivity in manufacturing increased 32 percent. Average wages, however, increased only 8 percent. As assembly lines became standard, laborers lost many of the skills in which they had once taken pride, but corporations reaped great profits from these changes.

Industries also developed programs for workers that came to be called **welfare capitalism**. Some businesses improved safety and sanitation inside factories and instituted paid vacations and pension plans. Welfare capitalism purposely encouraged loyalty to the company and discouraged traditional labor unions. Not wanting to relive the chaotic strikes of 1919, industrialists sought to eliminate reasons for

workers to join unions. One labor organizer in the steel industry bemoaned the success of welfare capitalism. "So many workmen here had been lulled to sleep by the company union, the welfare plans, the social organizations fostered by the employer," he declared, "that they had come to look upon the employer as their protector, and had believed vigorous trade union organization unnecessary for their welfare."

Consumer Culture

Mass production fueled corporate profits and national economic prosperity. Despite a brief postwar recession, the economy grew spectacularly during the 1920s. Per capita income increased by a third, the cost of living stayed the same, and unemployment remained low. But the rewards of the economic boom were not evenly distributed. Americans who labored with their hands inched ahead, while white-collar Americans enjoyed significantly more spending money and more leisure time to spend it. Mass production of a broad range of new products—automobiles, radios, refrigerators, electric irons, washing machines—produced a consumer-goods revolution. (See "The Promise of Technology," page 598.)

In this new era of abundance, more people than ever conceived of the American dream in terms of the things they could acquire. How the business boom and business values of the 1920s affected average Americans is revealed in the classic *Middletown* (1929), an analysis of the lives of the inhabitants of Muncie, Indiana. Muncie was, above all, "a culture in which everything hinges on money." Moreover, faced with technological and organizational change beyond their comprehension, many citizens had lost confidence in their ability to play an effective role in civic affairs. Instead, they deferred to the supposed expertise of leaders in politics and economics.

The pied piper of these disturbing changes, according to *Middletown*, was the rapidly expanding business of advertising, which stimulated the desire for new products and hammered away at the traditional values of thrift and saving. Newspapers, magazines, radios, and billboards told Americans what they had to have in order to be popular, secure, and successful. Advertising linked material goods to the fulfillment of every spiritual and emotional need. Americans increasingly defined and measured their social status, and indeed their personal worth, on the yardstick of material possessions. Happiness itself rode on owning a car and choosing the right cigarettes and toothpaste.

By the 1920s, the United States had achieved the physical capacity to satisfy Americans' material wants. The economic problem shifted from production to consumption: Who would buy the goods flying off American assembly lines? One solution was to expand America's markets in foreign countries, and government and business joined in that effort. Another solution to the problem of consumption was to expand the market at home.

Henry Ford realized early on that "mass production requires mass consumption." Understanding that automobile workers not only produced cars but would buy them if they made enough money, Ford in 1914 raised wages in his factories to $5 a day, more than twice the going rate. High wages made for workers who were more loyal and more exploitable, and high wages returned as profits when workers bought Fords.

Not all industrialists were as far-seeing as Ford. Because the wages of many workers barely edged upward, many people's incomes were too puny to satisfy the growing desire for consumer goods. Business supplied the solution: Americans could realize their dreams through credit. Installment buying—a little money down, a payment each month—allowed people to purchase expensive items they could not otherwise afford or purchase items before saving the necessary money. As one newspaper announced, "The first responsibility of an American to his country is no longer that of a citizen, but of a consumer." During the 1920s, America's motto became spend, not save, and replace, rather than make do. American culture had shifted.

> **REVIEW** How did the spread of the automobile transform the United States?

The Roaring Twenties

By the beginning of the decade, psychoanalyst Sigmund Freud had become a household name. Most Americans knew little of the complexity of his pioneering work in the psychology of the unconscious because they learned about his therapies in popular magazines. Still, people realized that Freud offered a way of looking at the world that was as radically different and important to the twentieth century as Charles Darwin's theory of evolution had been to the century before. In the twenties, much to Freud's disgust, the American media turned his therapeutic wisdom about the sexual origins of behavior on its head. If it is wrong to deny that we are sexual beings, some reasoned, then the key to health and fulfillment must lie in following impulse freely. Those who doubted this reasoning were simply "repressed."

The new ethic of personal freedom excited a significant number of Americans to seek pleasure without guilt in a whirl of activity that earned the decade the name "Roaring Twenties." Prohibition made lawbreakers of millions of otherwise decent folks. Flappers and "new women" challenged traditional gender boundaries. Other Americans enjoyed the "Roaring Twenties" at a safe distance through the words and images of vastly expanded mass communication. Motion pictures, radio, and magazines marketed celebrities. In the freedom of America's big cities, particularly New York, a burst of creativity produced a "New Negro," who confounded and disturbed white Americans. A "lost generation" of writers, profoundly disillusioned with mainstream America's cultural direction, fled the country.

Prohibition

Republicans generally sought to curb the powers of government and liberate private initiative, but the twenties witnessed a great exception to this rule when the federal government implemented one of the last reforms of the Progressive Era: the Eighteenth Amendment, which banned the manufacture and sale of alcohol and took effect in January 1920 (see chapter 22, page 573). Drying up the rivers of liquor that Americans consumed, supporters of prohibition declared, would boost production, eliminate crime, and lift the nation's morality. Women particularly supported prohibition because heavy drinking was closely associated with domestic violence and poverty. Charged with enforcing prohibition, the Treasury Department put more than 3,000 agents in the field, and in 1925 alone, they smashed more than 172,000 illegal stills.

Treasury agents faced a staggering task. In 1929, an agent in Indiana reported, "Conditions in most important cities very bad. Lax and corrupt public officials great handicap...prevalence of drinking among minor boys and the... middle or better class of adults." The "speakeasy," a place where men (and, increasingly,

Better Living through Electricity

In the 1920s, after forty years of technical development, prophecies that electricity would be a bearer of leisure and culture seemed about to come true. Thomas Edison, America's greatest inventor of electric marvels, cheerfully predicted that electrified homes would free women from household drudgery. Warming to his subject, Edison suggested that some women might then be able to develop their minds as highly as men. Perpetual light might eliminate the need for sleep. Perhaps, he concluded, someone might even invent electrical means for communicating with the dead.

Edison's hard-driving protégé Samuel Insull led in expanding electricity from commercial to domestic use. Insull's Chicago-based Commonwealth Edison Company, with General Electric and Westinghouse close behind, provided the power to increase the number of homes with electricity from 14 percent in 1910 to 70 percent in 1930. Now the lights that had shown exclusively on the privileged could also shine on average Americans and their aspirations— as long as they lived in the cities.

A barrage of advertising— General Electric alone raised its annual budget from $2 million to $12 million between 1922 and 1930— fanned Americans' expectations of a better life. Without sooty gaslights, their houses would be easier to maintain, and electric vacuum cleaners would lessen whatever toil was still necessary. Electric refrigerators would keep a wide array of food available for elegant entertaining, electric washers and irons would facilitate high fashion, and radios would bring knowledge and music into comfortable, airconditioned homes. One General Electric ad cheerily announced that, nowadays, "nobody works but ol' man river." Chiding foolish backwardness, other ads insisted that "any woman who turns the wringer [on a hand-operated clothes washer]…who cooks in a hot stuffy kitchen is doing work which electricity will do for a few cents per day." Rather than struggling with wringers and scrub boards, women could relax and listen to the radio "soap operas" sponsored by the makers of the laundry detergents foaming in their automatic washers.

Yet, despite $555 million in utility revenues by 1928, the promise of an idyllic electric future was hard to keep. Because electric companies saw little profit in running lines into sparsely settled rural areas, country folk lacked access. And the urban poor could not afford to buy into the fully wired paradise. Most city homes, for example, stayed with iceboxes until the late 1930s because they were considerably cheaper to buy and use than electric refrigerators. Freezers were so much more expensive that, although the advantages of frozen food were known in the 1920s, their use was limited to hotels and ocean liners until the late 1940s. Television, another invention of the 1920s, remained undeveloped for lack of financial support, and air conditioning was rarely used because the very people in the hottest parts of the country who needed it most were least able to afford it.

To the extent that electric appliances found a place in American homes, they did not bear out utopian dreams of leisure. The gleaming new devices fostered expectations of higher standards of cleanliness that housewives could meet only by operating their appliances early and often. In some affluent homes, the burden was lightened by servants who used the appliances. But the number of domestic servants was declining because the booming 1920s economy offered better-paying work in offices and factories—including those that manufactured electric appliances.

women) drank publicly, became a common feature of the urban landscape. Otherwise upright people discovered the thrill of breaking the law. One dealer, trading on common knowledge that whiskey still flowed in the White House, distributed cards advertising himself as the "President's Bootlegger."

Eventually, serious criminals took over the liquor trade. Alphonse "Al" Capone became the era's most notorious gang lord by establishing in Chicago a bootlegging empire that reputedly grossed more than $60 million in a single year. During the first four years of prohibition, Chicago witnessed over 200 gang-related killings as rival

Electricity boosters, however, remained unfazed until the end of the decade.

The gap between technology's promises and real life was magnified by the 1929 stock market crash and ensuing depression, which shattered many consumer dreams. While the means to pay for electricity dwindled, the collapse of Insull's electric empire revealed a tangle of fraud and corruption. Insull was indicted and vilified as the bearer of technology's false hopes. Ironically, in the face of such woes, one of the most popular electric inventions, the radio, provided old-fashioned reassurance. In the 1930s, families that had been lured from their traditional closeness around the hearth by central heating and electric light in every room huddled around technology's electronic hearth—the radio—to hear President Franklin Roosevelt pledge protection of their homes and basic values in his fireside chats (see chapter 24). Once prosperity returned, they were assured, the promise of a bright electric future would be renewed.

Hard times eventually eased, and sales of new appliances soared again. But surveys showed that the hours people spent taking care of their households remained essentially the same as before the advent of electricity. Only in the boom years after World War II would electricity begin to deliver on its promise.

Westinghouse

Advertisements like this one from a 1931 issue of *The Saturday Evening Post* often presented the promise of electricity in terms of its almost magical powers. The illustrator, Rockwell Kent, makes the generating plant in the background puny in comparison with the superhuman reflector of lightning and the fireball next to her. As a result, the "completely balanced" electric refrigerator seems a marvel created out of nature by divine genius. Still, scientists and managers at the corporate giant Westinghouse gladly accepted credit.

Picture Research Consultants & Archives.

mobs struggled for control of the lucrative liquor trade. The most notorious event came on St. Valentine's Day, 1929, when Capone's Italian-dominated mob machine-gunned seven members of a rival Irish gang. Federal authorities finally sent Capone to prison for income tax evasion, but by then he had become a hero to some immigrant youth eager to escape poor ethnic ghettos as Capone had done. Capone was a gangster, but he was also a resourceful entrepreneur and successful businessman.

Gang-war slayings prompted demands for the repeal of the Eighteenth Amendment. In 1931, a panel of distinguished experts reported that prohibition, which supporters had defended as "a great social and economic experiment," had failed. The social and political costs of prohibition outweighed the benefits. Prohibition caused ordinary citizens to disrespect the law, corrupted the police, and demoralized the judiciary. In 1933, after thirteen years, the nation ended prohibition.

The New Woman

Of all the changes in American life in the 1920s, none sparked more heated debate than the alternatives offered to the traditional roles of women.

Lucky Strike

Cigarette smoking promised instant maturity, sophistication, and worldlinesss—and, as revealed in this 1929 advertisement for the popular brand Lucky Strike, a svelte figure. Any woman seeking to remain attractive by avoiding matronly extra pounds could simply reach for her Luckies. In the 1920s, Americans smoked billions of cigarettes each year, and ads assured them that they could puff each Lucky and feel confident about its purity because "It's toasted." How did smokers know that they ran no health risk? Because precisely 20,679 physicians said so! How has cigarette advertising changed? How has it remained the same?

Gaslight Advertising Archives.

Increasing numbers of women worked and went to college, defying older gender hierarchies and norms. Even mainstream magazines like *The Saturday Evening Post* began publishing stories about young, college-educated women who drank gin cocktails, smoked cigarettes, wore skimpy dresses and dangly necklaces, daringly rolled their stockings at the knee, and enjoyed sex. Before the Great War, the "new woman" dwelt in New York City's bohemian Greenwich Village, but afterward the mass media brought her into middle-class America's living rooms.

Politically, women entered uncharted territory when the Nineteenth Amendment, ratified in 1920, granted them the vote. **Feminists** expected women to reshape the political landscape. Women began pressuring Congress to pass laws that especially concerned women, including measures to protect women in factories and grant federal aid to schools. Black women lobbied particularly for federal courts to assume jurisdiction over the crime of lynching. But women's only significant legislative success came in 1921 when Congress enacted the Sheppard-Towner Act, which extended federal assistance to states seeking to reduce shockingly high infant mortality rates. Rather than the beginning of women's political success, the act marked the high tide of women's influence in the 1920s.

A number of factors helped to thwart women's political influence. Male domination of both political parties, the rarity of female candidates, and lack of experience in voting, especially among recent immigrants, kept many women away from the polls. In the South, poll taxes, literacy tests, and outright terrorism continued to decimate the vote of African Americans, men and women alike.

Most important, rather than forming a solid voting bloc, feminists divided. Some argued for women's right to special protection; others demanded equal protection. The radical National Woman's Party fought for an Equal Rights Amendment that stated flatly: "Men and women shall have equal rights throughout the United States...." The more moderate League of Women Voters feared that the amendment's wording threatened state laws that provided women special protection, such as barring women from night work. Put before Congress in 1923, the Equal Rights Amendment went down to defeat, and radical women were forced to act within a network of private agencies and reform associations to advance the causes of birth control, legal equality for minorities, and the end of child labor.

Economically, more women worked for pay—approximately one in four by 1930—but they clustered in "women's jobs." The proportion of women working in manufacturing fell, while the number of women working as secretaries, stenographers, and typists skyrocketed. Women almost monopolized the occupations of librarian, nurse, elementary school teacher, and telephone operator. Women also represented 40 percent of salesclerks by 1930. More female white-collar workers meant fewer women were interested in protective legislation for women; "new women" wanted salaries and opportunities equal to men's.

Increased earnings gave working women more buying power and a special relationship with the new **consumer culture**. A stereotype soon emerged of the flapper, so called because of the short-lived fad of wearing unbuckled galoshes. The flapper had short "bobbed" hair and wore lipstick and rouge. She spent freely on the latest styles—dresses with short skirts and drop waists, bare arms, and no petticoats—and she danced all night to wild jazz.

The new woman both reflected and propelled the modern birth control movement. Margaret Sanger, the crusading pioneer for contraception during the Progressive Era, restated her principal conviction in 1920: "No woman can call herself free until she can choose consciously whether she will or will not be a mother." By shifting strategy in the twenties, Sanger courted the conservative American Medical Association, linked birth control with the eugenics movement, which advocated limiting reproduction among "undesirable" groups, and thus made contraception a respectable subject for discussion.

Flapper style and values spread from coast to coast through films, novels, magazines, and advertisements. New women challenged American convictions about **separate spheres** for women and men, the double standard of sexual conduct, and Victorian ideas of proper female appearance and behavior. While only a minority of American women in the 1920s became flappers, all women, even those who remained at home, felt the great changes of the era.

The New Negro

The 1920s witnessed the emergence not only of a "new woman" but of a "New Negro." Both new identities riled conservatives and reactionaries. African Americans who challenged the caste system that confined dark-skinned Americans to

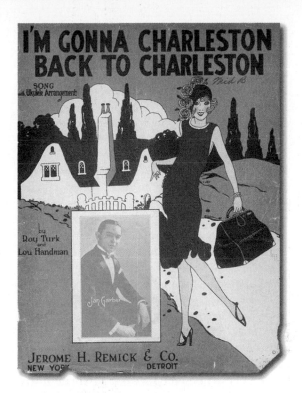

Charleston Flapper
The sheet music for this popular 1920s tune portrays the kind of postadolescent girl who was making respectable families frantic. Flappers scandalized their middle-class parents by ripping up the old moral codes. This saucy young woman wears the latest fashion and clearly suffers from what one critic called "the intoxication of rouge." She's kicking up her high heels in anticipation of doing the Charleston, one of those modern dances the *Catholic Telegraph* of Cincinnati denounced: "The music is sensuous, the embracing of partners—the female only half dressed—is absolutely indecent; and the motions—they are such as may not be described, with any respect for propriety, in a family newspaper."
Picture Research Consultants & Archives.

the lowest levels of society confronted whites who insisted that race relations would not change. Cheers for black soldiers quickly faded after their return from the First World War, and African Americans soon faced grim days of economic hardship and race riots (see chapter 22).

During the 1920s, the prominent African American intellectual W. E. B. Du Bois and the National Association for the Advancement of Colored People (NAACP) aggressively pursued the passage of a federal antilynching law to counter mob violence against blacks in the South. Many poor blacks, however, disillusioned with mainstream politics, turned for new leadership to a Jamaican-born visionary named Marcus Garvey.

Garvey urged African Americans to rediscover the heritage of Africa, take pride in their own culture and achievements, and maintain racial purity by avoiding **miscegenation**. In 1917, Garvey launched the Universal Negro Improvement Association (UNIA) to help African Americans gain economic and political independence entirely outside white society. In 1919, the UNIA created its own shipping company, the Black Star Line, to support a "Back to Africa" movement among black Americans. In 1927, the federal government pinned charges of illegal practices on Garvey and deported him to Jamaica. Nevertheless, the issues Garvey raised about racial pride, black identity, and the search for equality persisted, and his legacy remains at the center of **black nationalist** thought.

Still, most African Americans maintained hope in the American promise. In New York City, hope and talent came together. In Harlem in uptown Manhattan, an extraordinary mix of black artists, sculptors, novelists, musicians, and poets deliberately set out to create a distinctive African American culture that drew on their identities as Americans and Africans. As scholar Alain Locke put it in 1925, they introduced to the world a "New Negro," who rose from the ashes of slavery and segregation to proclaim African Americans' creative genius. The emergence of the New Negro came to be known as the Harlem Renaissance. Building on the independence and pride displayed by black soldiers during the war, black artists sought to defeat the fresh onslaught of racial discrimination and violence with poems, paintings, and plays. "We younger Negro artists…intend to express our individual dark-skinned selves without fear or shame," Langston Hughes, a determined young black poet, said of the Harlem Renaissance. "If white people are pleased, we are glad. If they are not, it doesn't matter. We know we are beautiful. And ugly, too."

The Harlem Renaissance produced dazzling talent. Black writer James Weldon Johnson, who in 1903 had written the Negro national anthem, "Lift Every Voice," wrote "God's Trombones" (1927), in which he expressed the wisdom and beauty of black folktales from the South. The poetry of Langston Hughes, Claude McKay, and Countee Cullen celebrated the vitality of life in Harlem. Zora Neale Hurston's novel *Their Eyes Were Watching God* (1937) explored the complex passions of black people in a southern commu-

nity. Black painters, led by Aaron Douglas, linked African art, which had recently inspired European modernist artists, to the concept of the New Negro. In bold, colorful scenes, Douglas combined biblical and African myths in ways that expressed a powerful cultural heritage for African Americans.

Despite such vibrancy, Harlem for most whites remained a separate black ghetto known only for its lively nightlife. Fashionable whites crowded into Harlem's nightclubs where, whites believed, they could hear "real" jazz, a relatively new musical form, in its "natural" surroundings. The vigor and optimism of the Harlem Renaissance left a powerful legacy for black Americans, but the creative burst did little in the short run to dissolve the prejudice of a white society.

Mass Culture

By the late 1920s, jazz had captured the nation. Americans who clung to symphonic music called jazz "jungle music," but jazz giants such as Louis Armstrong, Jelly Roll Morton, and Duke Ellington, accompanied by singers such as Ma Rainey, Bessie Smith, and Ethel Waters, entertained huge audiences. Jazz was only one of the entertainment choices of Americans, however. In the twenties, popular culture, like consumer goods, was mass-produced and mass-consumed. Since politics was undemanding and uninteresting, Americans looked elsewhere for excitement. The proliferation of movies, radios, music, and sports meant that they found plenty to do, and in doing the same things, they helped create a national culture.

Nothing offered such escapist delights as the movies. Admission was cheap, and in the dark, Americans of all classes could savor the same ideal of the good life. Blacks and whites, however, still entered theaters through separate entrances and sat separately. Hollywood, California, discovered the successful formula of combining opulence, sex, and adventure. By 1929, Hollywood was drawing more than 80 million people to the movies in a single week, as many as lived in the entire country. Rudolph Valentino, described as "catnip to women," and Clara Bow, the "It Girl" (everyone knew what *it* was), became household names. "America's Sweetheart," Mary Pickford, and her real-life husband, Douglas Fairbanks, offered more wholesome adventure. Most loved of all was the comic Charlie Chaplin, whose famous character, the wistful Little Tramp, showed an endearing inability to cope with the rules and complexities of modern life.

Heroes and Heroines

Two kinds of women look up adoringly at two kinds of 1920s heroes. A wholesome image is seen to the left on this 1927 cover of *People Popular Monthly* magazine. The healthy outdoor girl, smartly turned out in her raccoon coat and pennant, flatters a naive college football hero but remains in control. At the right, the pale, sensitive Vilma Banky kneels imploringly before the hypnotic gaze of the movies' greatest heart-throb, Rudolph Valentino. The 1926 movie poster titillates with ambivalence: Is the pale heroine beseeching her kidnapper to release her? Or is she swooning with desire as the sheik begins to disrobe?

Magazine: Picture Research Consultants & Archives; poster: Billy Rose Theatre Collection, The New York Public Library at Lincoln Center.

Americans also found heroes in sports. Baseball, professionalized since 1869 and segregated into white and black leagues, solidified its place as the national pastime in the 1920s. It remained essentially a game played by and for the working class, an outlet for raw energy with a tinge of rebelliousness. In George Herman "Babe" Ruth, baseball had the most cherished free spirit of the time. Ruth mixed his record-setting home runs with rowdy escapades, satisfying the view that sports offered a way to break out of the ordinariness of everyday life.

The public also fell in love with a young boxer from the grim mining districts of Colorado. As a teenager, Jack Dempsey had made his living hanging around saloons betting he could beat anyone in the house. When he took the heavyweight crown just after World War I, he was revered as the people's champ, an American equalizer who was a stand-in for the average American who felt increasingly confined by bureaucracy and machine-made culture.

Football, essentially a college sport, held greater sway with the upper classes. The most famous coach, Knute Rockne of Notre Dame, celebrated football for its life lessons of hard work and teamwork. Let the professors make learning as interesting and significant as football, Rockne advised, and the problem of getting youth to learn would disappear. But in keeping with the times, football moved toward a more commercial spectacle. Harold "Red" Grange, the "Galloping

Ghost," led the way by going from stardom at the University of Illinois to the Chicago Bears in the new professional football league.

The decade's hero worship reached its zenith in the celebration of Charles Lindbergh, a young pilot who set out on May 20, 1927, from Long Island in his plane, *The Spirit of St. Louis*, to be-come the first person to fly nonstop across the Atlantic. Newspapers tagged Lindbergh the "Lone Eagle"—the perfect hero for an age that celebrated individual accomplishment. "Charles Lindbergh," one journalist proclaimed, "is the stuff out of which have been made the pioneers that opened up the wilderness. His are the qualities which we, as a people, must nourish." Lindbergh realized, however, that technical and organizational complexity was fast reducing chances for solitary achievement. Consequently, he entitled his book about the flight *We* (1927) to include the machine that made it all possible.

Another machine—the radio—became important to mass culture in the 1920s. The nation's first licensed radio station, KDKA in Pittsburgh, began broadcasting in 1920, and soon American airwaves buzzed with news, sermons, soap operas, sports, comedy, and music. Americans on the West Coast laughed at the latest jokes from New York. Because they could now reach prospective customers in their own homes, advertisers bankrolled radio's rapid growth. Between 1922 and 1929, the number of radio stations in the United States increased from 30 to 606. In those seven short years, homes with radios jumped from 60,000 to a staggering 10,250,000.

Radio added to the spread of popular music, especially jazz. Jazz—with its energy and freedom—provided the soundtrack for a new, distinct social class of youth. As the traditional bonds of community, religion, and family loosened, the young felt less pressure to imitate their elders and more freedom to develop their own culture. An increasing number of college students helped the "rah-rah" style of college life become a fad promoted in movies, songs, and advertisements. The collegiate set was the vanguard of the decade's "flaming youth."

The Lost Generation

Some writers and artists felt alienated from America's mass-culture society, which they found shallow, anti-intellectual, and materialistic. Adoration of silly movie stars disgusted them. Moreover, they believed that business culture blighted American life. To their minds, Henry Ford made a poor hero. Young, white, and mostly college educated, these expatriates, as they came to be called, felt embittered by the war and renounced the progressives who had promoted it as a crusade. For them, Europe—not Hollywood or Harlem—seemed the place to seek their renaissance.

The American-born writer Gertrude Stein, long established in Paris, remarked famously as the young exiles gathered around her, "They are the lost generation." Most of the expatriates, however, believed to the contrary that they had finally found themselves. Far from the complications of home, the expatriates helped launch the most creative period in American art and literature in the twentieth century. The novelist whose spare, clean style best exemplified the expatriate efforts to make art mirror basic reality was Ernest Hemingway. Hemingway's experience in the war convinced him that the world in which he was raised, with its Christian moralism and belief in progress, was bankrupt. Admirers found the terse language and hard lessons of his novel *The Sun Also Rises* (1926) to be perfect expressions of a world stripped of illusions.

Many writers who remained in America were exiles in spirit. Before the war, intellectuals had eagerly joined progressive reform movements. Afterward, they were more likely to act as lonely critics of American cultural vulgarity. With prose dripping with scorn for conventional values, novelist Sinclair Lewis in *Main Street* (1920) and *Babbitt* (1922) satirized his native Midwest as a cultural wasteland. Humorists like James Thurber created outlandish characters to poke fun at American stupidity and inhibitions. And southern writers, led by William Faulkner, explored the South's grim class and race heritage. Worries about alienation surfaced as well. Although he gained fame and wealth as chronicler of flaming youth, F. Scott Fitzgerald spoke sadly in *This* *Side of Paradise* (1920) of a disillusioned generation "grown up to find all Gods dead, all wars fought, all faiths in man shaken."

REVIEW How did the new freedoms of the 1920s challenge older conceptions of gender and race?

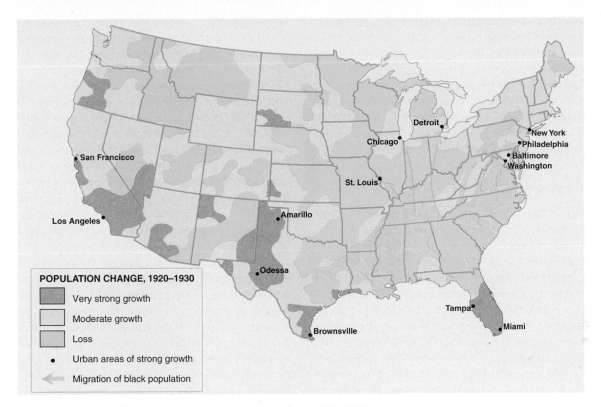

POPULATION CHANGE, 1920–1930

- Very strong growth
- Moderate growth
- Loss
- • Urban areas of strong growth
- ← Migration of black population

MAP 23.2 The Shift from Rural to Urban Population, 1920–1930
The movement of whites and Hispanics toward urban and agricultural opportunity made Florida, the West, and the Southwest the regions of fastest population growth. In contrast, large numbers of blacks left the rural South to find a better life in the North. Because almost all migrating blacks went from the countryside to cities in distant parts of the nation, while white and Hispanic migrants tended to move shorter distances toward familiar places, the population shift brought more drastic overall change to blacks than to whites and Hispanics.

READING THE MAP: Which states held the areas of strongest growth? To which cities did southern blacks predominantly migrate?
CONNECTIONS: What conditions in the countryside made the migration to urban areas appealing to many rural Americans? In what social and cultural ways did rural America view itself as different from urban America?

FOR MORE HELP ANALYZING THIS MAP, see the map activity for this chapter in the Online Study Guide at bedfordstmartins.com/roarkcompact.

Resistance to Change

Large areas of the country did not share in the wealth of the 1920s and had little confidence that they would anytime soon. By the end of the decade, 40 percent of the nation's farmers were landless, and 90 percent of rural homes had no indoor plumbing, gas, or electricity. Rural America's wariness and distrust of urban America turned to despair in 1920s when the census reported that the majority of the population had shifted from the country to the city (Map 23.2). Urban domination over the nation's political and cultural life and sharply rising economic disparity drove rural Americans in often ugly, reactionary directions.

Cities seemed to stand for everything rural areas stood against. Rural America imagined itself as solidly Anglo-Saxon (despite the presence of millions of African Americans in the South and Mexican Americans, Native Americans, and Asian Americans in the West), and the cities seemed to be filled with undesirable immigrants. Rural America was the home of old-time Protestant religion, and the cities teamed with Catholics, Jews, liberal **Protestants**, and atheists. Rural America championed old-fashioned moral standards—abstinence and self-denial—while the cities spawned every imaginable vice. Once the "backbone of the republic," rural Americans had become poor country cousins. In the 1920s, frustrated rural people sought to recapture their country by helping to push through prohibition, dam the flow of immigrants, revive the Ku Klux Klan, defend the Bible as literal truth, and defeat an urban Roman Catholic for president.

Rejecting the Undesirables

Before the war, when about a million immigrants arrived each year, some Americans warned that unassimilable foreigners were smothering the nation. War against Germany and its allies expanded **nativist** and antiradical sentiment. After the war, large-scale immigration resumed (another 800,000 immigrants arrived in 1921) at a moment when industrialists no longer needed new factory laborers. African American and Mexican migration had relieved labor shortages. Moreover, union leaders feared that millions of poor immigrants would undercut their efforts to organize American workers. Rural America's God-fearing Protestants were particularly alarmed that most of the immigrants were Catholic, Jewish, or atheist. In 1921, Congress responded by severely restricting immigration.

In 1924, Congress very nearly slammed the door shut. The Johnson-Reid Act limited the number of immigrants to no more than 161,000 a year and gave each European nation a quota based on 2 percent of the number of people from that country in America in 1890. The act revealed the fear and bigotry that fueled anti-immigration legislation. While it cut immigration by more than 80 percent, it squeezed some nationalities far more than others. Backers of Johnson-Reid openly declared that America had become the "garbage can and the dumping ground of the world," and they manipulated quotas to ensure entry only to "good" immigrants. By basing quotas on the 1890 census, in which western Europeans predominated, the law effectively reversed the trend toward immigration from southern and eastern Europe, which by 1914 had amounted to 75 percent of the yearly total. For example, the Johnson-Reid Act allowed Great Britain 62,458 entries, but Russia could send only 1,992.

The 1924 law reaffirmed the 1880s legislation barring Chinese immigrants and added Japanese and other Asians to the list of the excluded. But it left open immigration from the Western Hemisphere, and during the 1920s, some 500,000 Mexicans crossed the border. Farm interests preserved Mexican immigration because of Mexicans' value in southwestern agriculture.

Rural Americans, who had most likely never laid eyes on a Polish packing-house worker, a Slovak coal miner, an Armenian sewing-machine operator, or a Chinese laundry worker strongly supported the 1924 law, as did industrialists and labor leaders. The immigration restriction laws of the 1920s provided the basic framework for immigration policy until the 1960s. They marked the end of an era, the denial of the Statue of Liberty's open-arms welcome to Europe's "huddled masses yearning to breathe free."

Antiforeign hysteria climaxed in the trial of two **anarchist** immigrants from Italy, Nicola Sacco and Bartolomeo Vanzetti. Arrested in 1920 for robbery and murder in South Braintree, Massachusetts, the men were sentenced to death by a judge who openly referred to them as "anarchist bastards." In response to doubts about the fairness of the verdict, the governor of Massachusetts named a blue-ribbon review committee that found the trial judge guilty of a "grave breach of official decorum" but refused to recommend a motion for retrial. When Massachusetts executed Sacco and Vanzetti on August 23, 1927, 50,000 mourners followed the caskets in the rain, convinced that the men had died because they were immigrants and radicals, not because they were murderers.

The Rebirth of the Ku Klux Klan

The nation's sour, antiforeign mood struck a responsive chord in members of the Ku Klux Klan. The Klan first appeared in the South during Reconstruction to thwart black freedom and expired with the reestablishment of white supremacy. The Klan was reborn at Stone Mountain, Georgia, early in the twentieth century. When it extended its targets beyond black Americans, the new Klan rapidly spread beyond the South. Under a banner proclaiming "100 percent Americanism," the Klan promised to defend family, morality, and traditional American values against the threats posed by blacks, immigrants, radicals, feminists, Catholics, and Jews.

Building on the frustrations of rural America, the Klan attracted some 3 to 4 million members—women as well as men. By the mid-1920s, the Klan had spread throughout the nation, almost controlling Indiana and influencing politics in Illinois, California, Oregon, Texas, Louisiana, Oklahoma, and Kansas. The Klan's

WKKK Badge
Some half a million women were members of Women of the Ku Klux Klan (WKKK). Young girls could join the female youth auxiliary, the Tri-K for Girls. Klanswomen fit perfectly within the organization because it proclaimed itself the defender of the traditional virtues of pure womanhood and decent homes. This badge from Harrisburg, Pennsylvania, advertises the local WKKK's support for a home for needy and orphan children. Klanswomen also joined in boycotts of businesses owned by Jews and others whom they did not consider "100% American."
Collection of Janice L. and David J. Frent.

secrecy, uniforms, and rituals helped counter a sense of insignificance among people outside the new world of cities and corporations. At the same time, the Klan enabled its hooded members to beat and intimidate their victims anonymously with little fear of consequences. The Klan offered a certain counterfeit dignity for old-stock, Protestant, white Americans who felt passed over.

Eventually, social changes, along with lawless excess, brought the Klan down. Immigration restrictions eased the worry about invading foreigners, and sensational wrongdoing by Klan leaders cost it the support of traditional moralists. Grand Dragon David Stephenson of Indiana, for example, went to jail for the kidnap and rape of a woman who subsequently committed suicide. Yet the social grievances, economic problems, and religious anxieties of the countryside and small towns remained, ready to be ignited.

The Scopes Trial

In 1925 in a steamy Tennessee courtroom, old-time religion and the new spirit of science went head to head. The confrontation occurred after several southern states passed legislation against the teaching of Charles Darwin's theory of evolution in the public schools. **Fundamentalist** Protestants insisted that the Bible's creation story be taught as

the literal truth. In answer to a clamor from scientists and civil liberties organizations for a challenge to the law, John Scopes, a young biology teacher in Dayton, Tennessee, offered to test his state's ban on teaching evolution. When Scopes came to trial in the summer of 1925, Clarence Darrow, a brilliant defense lawyer from Chicago, volunteered to defend him. Darrow, an avowed agnostic, took on the prosecution's William Jennings Bryan, three-time Democratic nominee for president, symbol of rural America, and fervent fundamentalist, who was eager to defeat the proposition that humans had evolved from apes.

The Scopes trial quickly degenerated into a media circus. The first trial to be covered live on radio, it attracted an avid nationwide audience. Most of the reporters from big-city papers were hostile to Bryan, none more so than the cynical H. L. Mencken, who painted Bryan as a sort of Darwinian missing link ("a sweating anthropoid," a "gaping primate"). When, under relentless questioning by Darrow, Bryan declared on the witness stand that he did indeed believe the world was created in six days and that Jonah had lived in the belly of a whale, his humiliation in the eyes of most urban observers was complete. Nevertheless, the Tennessee court upheld the law and punished Scopes with a $100 fine. Although fundamentalism won the battle, it lost the war. Mencken had the last word in a merciless obituary for Bryan, who died just a week after the trial ended. Portraying the "monkey trial" as a battle between the country and the city, Mencken flayed Bryan as a "charlatan, a mountebank, a zany without shame or dignity," motivated solely by "hatred of the city men who had laughed at him for so long."

As Mencken's acid prose indicated, Bryan's humiliation was not purely a victory of reason and science. It also revealed the disdain urban people felt for country people and the values they clung to. The Ku Klux Klan revival and the Scopes trial dramatized and inflamed divisions between city and country, intellectuals and the unlettered, the privileged and the poor, the scoffers and the faithful.

Al Smith and the Election of 1928

The presidential election of 1928 brought many of the developments of the 1920s—prohibition, immigration, religion, and the clash of rural and urban values—into sharp focus. Republicans emphasized the economic success of their party's pro-business government. But because

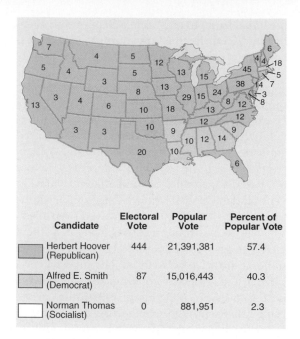

Candidate	Electoral Vote	Popular Vote	Percent of Popular Vote
Herbert Hoover (Republican)	444	21,391,381	57.4
Alfred E. Smith (Democrat)	87	15,016,443	40.3
Norman Thomas (Socialist)	0	881,951	2.3

MAP 23.3   The Election of 1928

both parties generally agreed that the American economy was basically sound, the campaign turned on social issues that divided Americans. Tired of the limelight, Calvin Coolidge chose not to seek reelection, and the Republicans turned to Herbert Hoover, the energetic secretary of commerce and the leading public symbol of 1920s prosperity.

The Democrats nominated four-time governor of New York, Alfred E. Smith. A New Yorker, Smith adopted "The Sidewalks of New York" as a campaign theme song and seemed to represent all that rural Americans feared and resented. A child of immigrants, Smith got his start in politics with the help of Tammany Hall, New York City's Irish-dominated political machine, the epitome of big-city corruption in many minds. He believed that immigration quotas were wrong, and he spoke out against restriction. He signed New York State's anti-Klan bill and condemned the decade's growing intolerance. Smith also opposed prohibition, believing that it was a nativist attack on immigrant customs. When Smith supposedly asked reporters in 1922, "Wouldn't you like to have your foot on the rail and blow the foam off some suds?" prohibition forces dubbed him "Alcohol Al."

Smith's greatest vulnerability in the heartland, however, was his religion. He was the first Catholic to run for president. A Methodist bishop in Virginia denounced Roman Catholicism as

"the Mother of ignorance, superstition, intolerance and sin" and begged Protestants not to vote for a candidate who represented "the kind of dirty people that you find today on the sidewalks of New York."

Hoover, who neatly combined the images of morality, efficiency, service, and prosperity, won the election by a landslide (Map 23.3). He received 58 percent of the vote and gained 444 electoral votes to Smith's 87. The Republicans' most notable success came in the previously solid Democratic South, where Smith's religion, views on prohibition, and big-city persona allowed them to take four states. Smith carried the Lower South, where the Democratic Party's identification with white supremacy prevailed. The Republican victory was marred only by the party's reduced support in the cities and among discontented farmers. The nation's largest cities voted Democratic in a striking reversal of 1924, indicating the rising strength of ethnic minorities, including Smith's fellow Catholics.

> **REVIEW**   Why did the relationship between urban and rural America deteriorate in the 1920s?

The Great Crash

At his inauguration in 1929, Herbert Hoover told the American people, "given a chance to go forward with the policies of the last eight years, we shall soon with the help of God be in sight of the day when poverty will be banished from this nation." Those words came back to haunt Hoover, for in eight short months the Roaring Twenties came to a crashing halt. The prosperity Hoover touted collapsed with the stock market, and the nation ended nearly three decades of barely interrupted economic growth and fell into the most serious economic depression of all time. Hoover and his reputation were among the first casualties, along with the reverence for business that had been the hallmark of the New Era.

Herbert Hoover: The Great Engineer

When Herbert Hoover became president in 1929, he seemed the perfect choice to lead a prosperous business nation. He personified America's rags-to-riches ideal, having risen from poor Iowa orphan to one of the world's most successful mining engineers by the time he was thirty. His success in managing efforts to feed civilian victims of the fighting during World War I won him acclaim as the "Great Humanitarian" and led Woodrow Wilson to name him head of the Food Administration once the United States entered the war. Hoover's reputation soared even higher as secretary of commerce in the Harding and Coolidge administrations.

Hoover was no old-fashioned pro-business advocate like most of the men who gathered in Washington during the 1920s. He belonged to the progressive wing of his party, and as early as 1909 he declared, "The time when the employer could ride roughshod over his labor is disappearing with the doctrine of '**laissez-faire**' on which it is founded." He urged a limited business-government partnership that would actively manage the sweeping changes Americans experienced. When Hoover entered the White House, he brought a reform agenda: "We want to see a nation built of home owners and farm owners. We want to see their savings protected. We want to see them in steady jobs. We want to see more and more of them insured against death and accident, unemployment and old age. We want them all secure."

But Hoover also had ideological and political liabilities. Principles that appeared strengths in the prosperous 1920s—individual self-reliance, industrial self-management, and a limited federal government—became straitjackets when economic catastrophe struck. Moreover, Hoover had never held an elected public office, had a poor political touch, and was too thin-skinned to be an effective politician. Even so, most Americans considered him "a sort of superman" able to solve any problem. Prophetically, he confided to a friend his fear that "If some unprecedented calamity should come upon the nation…I would be sacrificed to the unreasoning disappointment of a people who expected too much." The distorted national economy set the stage for the calamity Hoover so feared.

The Distorted Economy

In the spring of 1929, the United States enjoyed a fragile prosperity. Although America had become the world's leading economy, it had done little to help rebuild Europe's shattered economy after the First World War. Instead, the Republican administrations demanded that European nations repay their war loans. To boost American business, the United States enacted tariffs that prevented other nations from selling their goods to Americans. Foreign nations thus had less money to buy American goods, which were pouring out

in record abundance. American banks propped up the nation's export trade by extending credit to foreign customers, and debt piled onto debt in an absurd pyramid.

The domestic economy was also in trouble. Wealth was badly distributed. Farmers continued to suffer from low prices; the average income of families working the land amounted to only $240 per year. Industrial workers, though enjoying a slight rise in wages during the decade, failed to keep up with productivity and corporate profits. Overall, nearly two-thirds of all American families lived on less than the $2,000 per year that economists estimated would "supply only basic necessities." The top 1 percent received 15 percent of the nation's income, an amount equal to that received by the bottom 42 percent of the population. The Coolidge administration worsened the deepening inequality by cutting taxes on the wealthy.

By 1929, the inequality of wealth produced a serious problem in consumption. The rich, brilliantly portrayed in F. Scott Fitzgerald's *The Great Gatsby* (1925), gilded the era with their lavish spending; but they could absorb only a tiny fraction of the nation's output. Ordinary folk, on whom the system ultimately depended, were unable to take up the slack. For a time, the new device of installment buying—buying on credit—kept consumer demand up; by the end of the decade, four out of five cars and two out of three radios were bought on credit. Personal indebtedness rose to an all-time high that could not be sustained.

Signs of economic trouble began to appear at mid-decade. New construction slowed down. Automobile sales faltered. With nearly 30 million cars on the road, demand had been met, and companies began cutting back production and laying off workers. Banks followed suit. Between 1921 and 1928, as investment and loan opportunities faded, 5,000 banks failed. Still, the boom seemed to roar on, muffling the sounds of economic distress just beneath the surface.

The Crash of 1929

Even as the economy faltered, America's faith in it remained unshaken. Hoping for even bigger slices of the economic pie, Americans speculated wildly in the stock market on Wall Street. Between 1924 and 1929, the values of stocks listed on the New York Stock Exchange increased by more than 400 percent. Buying stocks on margin—that is, putting up only part of the money at the time of purchase—grew rampant. Many people got rich this way, but those who bought on credit could finance their loans only if their stock increased in value. Speculators could not imagine that the market might fall and they would be forced to meet their margin loans with cash they did not have.

Finally, in the autumn of 1929, the market hesitated. Sniffing danger, investors nervously began to sell their overvalued stock. The dip quickly became a panic on October 24, the day that came to be known as Black Thursday. Brokers jammed the stock exchange desperately trying to unload shares. But more panic selling came on Black Tuesday, October 29, the day the market suffered a greater fall than ever before. In the next six months, the stock market lost six-sevenths of its total value.

It was once thought that the crash alone caused the Great Depression. It did not. In 1929, the national and international economies were already riddled with severe problems. But the dramatic losses in the stock market crash and the fear of risking what was left acted as a great brake on economic activity. The collapse on Wall Street shattered the New Era's aggressive confidence that America would enjoy perpetually expanding prosperity.

Hoover and the Limits of Individualism

At first, Americans expressed relief that Herbert Hoover resided in the White House when the bubble broke. Hoover believed that "we should use the powers of government to cushion the situation" by preventing future financial panics and mitigating the hardships of farmers and the unemployed. Hoover was no do-nothing president, but there were limits to his activism.

In November 1929, to keep the stock market collapse from ravaging the entire economy, Hoover called a White House conference of business and labor leaders and urged them to join in a voluntary plan for recovery: Businesses would maintain production and keep their workers on the job; labor would accept existing wages, hours, and conditions. Within a few months, however, the bargain fell apart. As demand for their products declined, industrialists cut production, sliced wages, and laid off workers. Poorly paid or unemployed workers could not buy much, and their decreased spending led to further cuts in production and further loss of jobs. Thus began the terrible spiral of economic decline.

To deal with the problems of rural America, Hoover got Congress to pass the Agricultural Marketing Act in 1929. The act created the Farm Board, which used its budget of $500 million to buy up agricultural surpluses and thus, it was hoped, raise prices. But prices declined. To help end the decline, Hoover joined conservatives in urging protective tariffs on agricultural goods, and the Hawley-Smoot tariff of 1930 established the highest rates in history. Congress also authorized $420 million for public works projects to give the unemployed jobs and create more purchasing power. In three years, the Hoover administration nearly doubled federal public works expenditures.

But with each year of Hoover's term, the economy weakened. Tariffs did not end the suffering of farmers because foreign nations retaliated with increased tariffs of their own that crippled American farmers' ability to sell abroad. In 1932, Hoover hoped to help hard-pressed industry with the Reconstruction Finance Corporation (RFC), a federal agency empowered to lend government funds to endangered banks and corporations. The theory was **trickle-down economics**: Pump money into the economy at the top, and in the long run the people at the bottom would benefit. Or as one wag put it, "feed the sparrows by feeding the horses." In the end, very little of what critics of the RFC called a "millionaires' dole" trickled down to the poor.

And the poor multiplied. Hundreds of thousands of workers lost their jobs each month. By 1932, an astounding one-quarter of the American workforce—more than 12 million people—were unemployed. There was no direct federal assistance, and state services and private charities were swamped. Cries grew louder for the federal government to give hurting people relief.

In responding, Hoover revealed the limits of his conception of government's proper role. He compared direct federal aid to the needy to the "dole" in England, which he thought destroyed the moral fiber of the chronically unemployed. In 1931, he allowed the Red Cross to distribute government-owned agricultural surpluses to the hungry. In 1932, he offered small federal loans, not gifts, to the states to help them in their relief efforts. But these concessions were no more than Band-Aids on deep wounds. Hoover's circumscribed notions of legitimate government action proved vastly inadequate to the problems of restarting the economy and ending human suffering.

REVIEW   Why did the American economy collapse in 1929?

Life in the Depression

In 1930, suffering on a massive scale set in, and despair settled over the land. Men and women hollow-eyed with hunger grew increasingly bewildered and angry in the face of cruel contradictions. They saw agricultural surpluses pile up in the countryside and knew that their children were going to bed hungry. They saw factories standing idle and knew that they and millions of others were willing to work. The gap between the American people and leaders who failed to resolve these contradictions widened as the depression deepened. By 1932, America's economic problems had created a dangerous social and political crisis.

The Human Toll

Statistics only hint at the human tragedy of the Great Depression. When Herbert Hoover took office in 1929, the American economy stood at its peak. When he left in 1933, it had reached its twentieth-century low (Figure 23.1). In 1929, national income was $88 billion. By 1933, it had declined to $40 billion. In 1929, unemployment was 3.1 percent, one and a half million workers. By 1933, unemployment stood at 25 percent, twelve and a half million workers. By 1932, more than nine thousand banks had shut their doors, and depositors had lost more than $2.5 billion. The nation's steel industry operated at only 12 percent of capacity.

Jobless, homeless victims wandered in search of work, and the tramp, or hobo, became one of the most visible figures of the decade. Riding the rails or hitchhiking, the vagabonds tended to move southward and westward, toward the sun and opportunities, they hoped, for seasonal agricultural work. Other unemployed men and women, sick or less hopeful, huddled in doorways. Scavengers haunted alleys behind restaurants and picked over garbage dumps in search of food. One writer told of an elderly woman who always took off her glasses to avoid seeing the maggots crawling over the garbage she ate. Starvation claimed its victims, but enervating malnutrition posed the greater threat. The Children's Bureau announced that one in five schoolchildren did not get enough to eat.

Rural poverty was most acute. Tenant farmers and sharecroppers, mainly in the South, came to symbolize how poverty crushed the human spirit. Eight and a half million people, three million of them black, crowded into two- and three-room cabins lacking screens or even doors, without plumbing, electricity, running water, or sanitary wells. They subsisted—just barely—on salt pork, cornmeal, molasses, beans, peas, and whatever they could hunt or fish. All the diseases of dietary and vitamin deficiencies wracked them. When

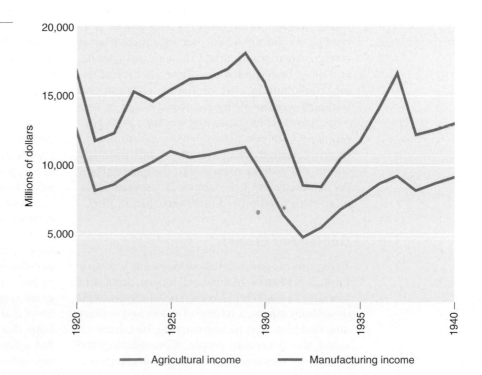

FIGURE 23.1 Manufacturing and Agricultural Income, 1920–1940
After economic collapse, recovery in the 1930s began under New Deal auspices. The sharp declines in 1937–1938, when federal spending was reduced, indicated that New Deal stimuli were still needed to restore manufacturing and agricultural income.

economist John Maynard Keynes was asked whether anything like this degradation had existed before, he replied, "Yes, it was called the Dark Ages and it lasted four hundred years."

There was no federal assistance to meet this human catastrophe, only a patchwork of strapped charities and destitute state and local agencies. For a family of four without any income, the best the city of Philadelphia could do was provide $5.50 per week. That was not enough to live on but was still comparatively generous. New York City, where the greatest number of welfare cases gathered, provided only $2.39 per week; and Detroit, devastated by the auto industry's failure, allotted sixty cents a week before the city ran out of money altogether.

The deepening crisis roused old fears and caused some Americans to look for scapegoats. Among the most thoroughly scapegoated were Mexican Americans. During the 1920s, cheap agricultural labor from Mexico flowed legally across the U.S. border, welcomed by the large farmers. In the 1930s, however, public opinion turned on the newcomers, denouncing them as dangerous aliens who took jobs from Americans. Government officials, most prominently those in Los Angeles County, targeted Mexican residents for deportation regardless of citizenship status. As many as half a million Mexicans and Mexican Americans were deported or fled to Mexico.

The depression deeply affected the American family. Young people postponed marriage; when they did marry, they produced few children. White women, who generally worked in low-paying service areas, did not lose their jobs as often as men who worked in steel, automobile, and other heavy industries. After a decade of rising consumption and conflating consumption with self-worth, idle men suffered a loss of self-respect and resented women workers. Both government and private employers discriminated against married women workers, but necessity continued to drive women into the marketplace. As a result, by 1940, some 25 percent more women were employed for wages than in 1930.

Denial and Escape

To express his optimism about economic recovery, President Hoover maintained formal dress and manners in the White House, and at dinner, with or without guests, a retinue of valets and waiters attended him. No one was starving, he calmly assured the American people. Contradicting the president's message were makeshift shantytowns,

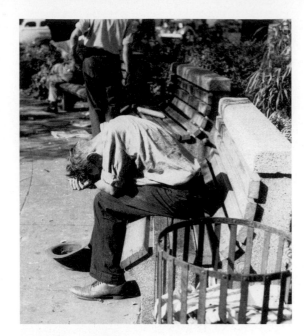

Unemployed Youth
Joblessness was frightening and humiliating. Brought up to believe that if you work hard, you get ahead, the unemployed had difficulty seeing failure to find work as anything other than personal failure. Many slipped into despair and depression. We can only imagine this young man's story. Utterly alone, sitting on a bench that might be his bed, his hat on the ground and his head in his hands, he looks emotionally battered and perhaps defeated. Whether he found work, joined the throngs of beggars and panhandlers on the streets, or cast his lot with the army of hoboes who rode the rails looking for something better is unknown.
Library of Congress.

called "Hoovervilles," that sprang up on the edges of America's cities. Newspapers used as cover by those sleeping on the streets were "Hoover blankets." An empty pocket turned inside out was a "Hoover flag," and jackrabbits caught for food were "Hoover hogs." Innumerable bitter jokes circulated about the increasingly unpopular president. One told of Hoover asking for a nickel to telephone a friend. Flipping him a dime, an aide said, "Here, call them both."

While Hoover practiced denial, other Americans sought refuge from reality at the movies. Throughout the depression, between sixty and seventy-five million people (nearly two-thirds of the nation) managed to scrape together enough change to fill the movie palaces every week. Box office hits such as *Forty-Second Street* and *Gold Diggers of 1933* capitalized on the hope that prosperity lay just around the corner. But a few filmmakers grappled with hard realities rather than escape them. *Our Daily Bread*

(1932) expressed compassion for the down-and-out, while *The Public Enemy* (1931) taught hard lessons about gangsters' ill-gotten gains. Indeed, under the new production code of 1930, designed to protect public morals, all movies had to find some way to show that crime does not pay.

Despite Hollywood's efforts to keep Americans on the right side of the law, crime increased. Away from the movie palaces, out in the countryside, the plight of people who had lost their farms to bank foreclosures led to the romantic idea that bank robbers were only getting back what banks had stolen from the poor. Woody Guthrie, the populist folk singer from Oklahoma, captured the public's tolerance for out-laws in his widely admired tribute to a murderous bank robber with a choirboy face, "The Ballad of Pretty Boy Floyd":

> Yes, as through this world I ramble,
> I see lots of funny men,
> Some will rob you with a six-gun,
> Some will rob you with a pen.
> But as through your life you'll travel,
> Wherever you may roam,
> You won't never see an outlaw drive
> A family from their home.

Working-Class Militancy

Members of the nation's working class bore the brunt of the economic collapse. In Chicago, working women received less than twenty-five cents an hour. Sawmill workers in the West got a nickel. Although slow to respond, William Green, head of the dominant American Federation of Labor, had turned militant by 1931. "I warn the people who are exploiting the workers," he shouted, "that they can drive them only so far before they will turn on them and destroy them. They are taking no account of the history of nations in which governments have been overturned. Revolutions grow out of the depths of hunger."

Like the labor leaders, the American people were slow to anger, then strong in protest. On the morning of March 7, 1932, several thousand unemployed autoworkers massed at the gates of Henry Ford's River Rouge factory in Dearborn, Michigan, to demand work. Ford sent out his private security forces, and when the workers began throwing rocks, Ford's army responded with gunfire, killing four demonstrators. An outraged public—forty thousand strong—turned out for the unemployed men's funerals.

Farmers mounted uprisings of their own. When Congress refused to guarantee farm prices that would at least equal the cost of production, several thousand farmers created the National Farmers' Holiday Association to force farmers to take a "holiday" from shipping crops to market. Farm militants also resorted to what they called "penny sales." When banks foreclosed and put farms up for auction, neighbors warned others not to bid, bought the foreclosed property for a few pennies, and returned it to the bankrupt owners. In California in 1933, when landowners cut their laborers' already substandard wages, more than 50,000 farmworkers, most of them Mexicans, went on strike. Militancy won farmers little in the way of long-term solutions, but one individual observed that "the biggest and finest crop of revolutions you ever saw is sprouting all over the country right now."

The Great Depression—the massive failure of Western capitalism—brought **socialism** back to life and propelled the **Communist Party** to its greatest size and influence in American history. Some 100,000 Americans—workers, intellectuals, college students—joined the Communist Party in the belief that only an overthrow of the capitalist system could save the victims of depression. In 1931, the party, through its National Miners Union, carried its convictions into Harlan County, Kentucky, to support a strike by brutalized coal miners. Newspapers and newsreels provided graphic portrayals of the violence unleashed by mine owners' thugs against the strikers. Eventually, the owners beat the miners down, but the Communist Party emerged from the coalfields with a reputation as the most dedicated and fearless champion of the union cause.

The left also led the fight against racism. While both major parties refused to challenge segregation in the South, the Socialist Party, led by Norman Thomas, attacked the system of sharecropping that left many African Americans in near servitude. The Communist Party also took action. When nine young black men in Scottsboro, Alabama (the "Scottsboro Boys"), were arrested on trumped-up rape charges in 1931, a team of lawyers sent by the party saved the defendants from the electric chair.

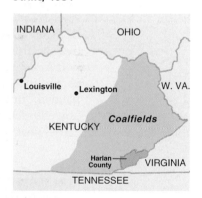

Harlan County, Kentucky, Coal Strike, 1931

"Scottsboro Boys"
Nine black youths, ranging in age from thirteen to twenty-one, stand in front of rifle-bearing National Guard troops called up by Alabama governor B. M. Miller, who feared a mob lynching after two white women accused the nine of rape in March 1931. In less than two weeks, an all-white jury heard flimsy evidence, convicted the nine of rape, and sentenced them to death. Although none was executed, all nine spent years in jail. Eventually, the state dropped charges against the youngest four and granted paroles to others. The last "Scottsboro Boy" left jail in 1950.
© Bettmann / Corbis.

Radicals on the left often sparked action, but protests by moderate workers and farmers occurred on a far greater scale. Breadlines, soup kitchens, foreclosures, unemployment, and cold despair drove patriotic men and women to question American capitalism. "I am as conservative as any man could be," a Wisconsin farmer explained, "but any economic system that has in its power to set me and my wife in the streets, at my age—what can I see but red?"

REVIEW   How did the Depression reshape American politics?

Conclusion: Dazzle and Despair

In the aftermath of World War I, America turned its back on progressive crusades and embraced conservative Republican politics, the growing influence of corporate leaders, and business values. Changes in the nation's economy—Henry Ford's automobile revolution, advertising, mass production—propelled fundamental change throughout society. Living standards rose, economic opportunity increased, and Americans threw themselves into private pleasures—gobbling up the latest household goods and fashions, attending baseball and football games and boxing matches, gathering around the radio, and going to the movies. As big cities came to dominate American life, the culture of youth and flappers became the leading edge of what one observer called a "revolution in manners and morals." At home in Harlem and abroad in Paris, American literature, art, and music flourished.

For many Americans, however, none of the glamour and vitality had much meaning. Instead of seeking thrills at speakeasies, plunging into speculation on Wall Street, or escaping abroad, the vast majority struggled just to earn a decent living. Blue-collar America did not participate fully in white-collar prosperity. Rural America was almost entirely left out of the Roaring Twenties. Country folks, deeply suspicious and profoundly discontented, championed prohibition, revived the Klan, attacked immigration, and defended old-time Protestant religion.

Just as the dazzle of the Roaring Twenties hid deep divisions in society, extravagant prosperity masked structural flaws in the economy. The crash of 1929 and the depression that followed starkly revealed the economy's crises of international trade and consumption. Hard times swept high living off the front pages of the nation's newspapers. Different images emerged: hoboes hopping freight trains, strikers confronting police, and malnourished sharecroppers staring blankly into the distance.

The depression hurt everyone, but the poor were hurt most. As farmers and workers sank into aching hardship, businessmen rallied around Herbert Hoover to proclaim that private enterprise would get the country moving again. But things fell apart, and Hoover faced increasingly more radical opposition. Membership in the Socialist and Communist parties surged, and more and more Americans contemplated desperate measures. By 1932, the depression had nearly brought the nation to its knees. America faced its greatest crisis since the Civil War, and citizens demanded new leaders who would save them from the "Hoover Depression."

Suggestions for Further Reading

William J. Barber, *From New Era to New Deal: Herbert Hoover, the Economists, and American Economic Policy, 1921–1933* (1985). A probing analysis of the responses of the Republican administrations to prosperity and depression.

Douglas Brinkley, *Wheels for the World: Henry Ford, His Company, and a Century of Progress, 1903–2003* (2003). A lively story of Henry Ford and the Ford Motor Company.

Roger Daniels, *Guarding the Golden Door: American Immigration Policy and Immigrants since 1882* (2004). A thoughtful investigation of changing American attitudes and policies toward immigration.

Nancy MacLean, *Behind the Mask of Chivalry: The Making of the Second Ku Klux Klan* (1994). A perceptive analysis of the second Klan that focuses particularly on the role of women.

Michael Parrish, *Anxious Decades: America in Prosperity and Depression, 1920–1941* (1992). An insightful survey of American life through two contrasting decades.

Studs Terkel, *Hard Times: An Oral History of the Great Depression* (1979, 1986). A powerful collection of interviews with individuals who personally experienced the depression.

▶ For more books about topics in this chapter, see the Online Bibliography at bedfordstmartins.com/roarkcompact.

▶ For additional firsthand accounts of this period, see Chapter 23 in Michael Johnson, ed., *Reading the American Past*, Third Edition.

▶ For Web sites and documents related to topics and places in this chapter, see "HistoryLinks," "DocLinks," and "PlaceLinks" at bedfordstmartins.com/roarkcompact.

REVIEWING THE CHAPTER

Follow these steps to review and strengthen your understanding of the chapter.

STEP 1: *Study the* **Key Terms** *and* **Timeline** *to identify the significance of each item listed.*

STEP 2: *Answer the* **Review Questions**, *drawing on key terms and dates to support your answers.*

STEP 3: *Drawing on the Key Terms, Timeline, and Review Questions, answer the broader* **Making Connections** *questions.*

KEY TERMS

Who

Henry Ford (p. 591)
Warren Gamaliel Harding (p. 593)
Albert Fall (p. 593)
Calvin Coolidge (p. 593)
Al Capone (p. 598)
Margaret Sanger (p. 601)
W. E. B. Du Bois (p. 601)
Marcus Garvey (p. 601)
Langston Hughes (p. 602)
James Weldon Johnson (p. 602)
Zora Neale Hurston (p. 602)
Aaron Douglas (p. 602)
Charles Lindbergh (p. 604)
Ernest Hemingway (p. 604)
F. Scott Fitzgerald (p. 604)
Nicola Sacco (p. 606)
Bartolomeo Vanzetti (p. 606)
John Scopes (p. 607)
Clarence Darrow (p. 607)
William Jennings Bryan (p. 607)
Herbert Hoover (p. 608)
Alfred E. Smith (p. 608)

Norman Thomas (p. 613)
"Scottsboro Boys" (p. 613)

What

Model T (p. 591)
New Era (p. 592)
Fordney-McCumber tariff (p. 593)
"Teapot Dome" (p. 593)
Five-Power Naval Treaty of 1922 (p. 594)
Kellogg-Briand pact (p. 594)
Dawes Plan (p. 595)
mass production (p. 596)
welfare capitalism (p. 596)
Middletown (p. 596)
installment buying (p. 597)
prohibition (p. 597)
"new woman" (p. 600)
Sheppard-Towner Act (p. 600)
National Woman's Party (p. 600)
Equal Rights Amendment (p. 600)
League of Women Voters (p. 600)
flapper (p. 601)

New Negro (p. 601)
National Association for the Advancement of Colored People (NAACP) (p. 601)
Universal Negro Improvement Association (UNIA) (p. 602)
Black Star Line (p. 602)
Harlem Renaissance (p. 602)
Lost Generation (p. 604)
Johnson-Reid Act (p. 606)
Ku Klux Klan (p. 606)
Scopes trial (p. 607)
crash of 1929 (p. 610)
Farm Board (p. 610)
Hawley-Smoot tariff (p. 610)
Reconstruction Finance Corporation (p. 610)
American Federation of Labor (p. 613)
National Farmers' Holiday Association (p. 613)
Communist Party (p. 613)
National Miners Union (p. 613)
Socialist Party (p. 613)

TIMELINE

1920 • Eighteenth Amendment goes into effect.
• Nineteenth Amendment ratified.
• Republican Warren G. Harding elected president.

    1921 • Sheppard-Towner Act.
    • Congress restricts immigration.

        1922 • Fordney-McCumber tariff.
        • Five-Power Naval Treaty.

            1923 • Equal Rights Amendment introduced in Congress.
            • Harding dies; Vice President Calvin Coolidge becomes president.

                1924 • Dawes Plan.
                • Calvin Coolidge elected president.
                • Johnson-Reid Act.

                    1925 • John Scopes convicted.
                    • *The New Negro* published.

                        1926 • *The Sun Also Rises* published.

REVIEW QUESTIONS

1. How did the spread of the automobile transform the United States? (pp. 592–97)

2. How did the new freedoms of the 1920s challenge older conceptions of gender and race? (pp. 597–604)

3. Why did the relationship between urban and rural America deteriorate in the 1920s? (pp. 605–08)

4. Why did the American economy collapse in 1929? (pp. 608–10)

5. How did the Depression reshape American politics? (pp. 611–14)

MAKING CONNECTIONS

1. In the 1920s, Americans' wariness of the concentration of power in the hands of industrial capitalists gave way to unrestrained confidence in American business. What drove this shift in popular opinion? How did it influence Republicans' approach to governance and the development of the American economy in the 1920s?

2. Americans' encounters with the wealth and increased personal freedom characteristic of the 1920s varied greatly. Discuss the impact such variation had on Americans' responses to new circumstances. Why did some embrace the era's changes, while others resisted them? Ground your answer in discussion of specific political, legal, or cultural conflicts.

3. How did shifting government policy contribute to both the boom of the 1920s and the bust of 1929? In your answer, consider the part domestic and international policy played in these developments, including matters of taxation, tariffs, and international banking.

4. The Great Depression plunged the nation into a profound crisis with staggering personal and national costs. How did Americans attempt to lessen the impact of these circumstances? In your answer, discuss and compare the responses of individual Americans and the federal government.

▶ FOR PRACTICE QUIZZES, A CUSTOMIZED STUDY PLAN, AND OTHER STUDY TOOLS, see the Online Study Guide at bedfordstmartins.com/roarkcompact.

1927 • Charles Lindbergh flies nonstop and alone across Atlantic.
• Nicola Sacco and Bartolomeo Vanzetti executed.

    1928 • Kellogg-Briand pact.
    • Republican Herbert Hoover elected president.

        1929 • St. Valentine's Day massacre.
        • Farm Board created.
        • Stock market collapses.

            1930 • Congress authorizes $420 million for public works projects.
            • Hawley-Smoot tariff.

                1931 • "Scottsboro Boys" arrested.
                • Harlan County, Kentucky, coal strike.

                    1932 • River Rouge factory demonstration.
                    • Reconstruction Finance Corporation established.
                    • National Farmers' Holiday Association formed.

**FRANKLIN ROOSEVELT'S
MICROPHONE**

President Roosevelt used this microphone to broadcast his popular fireside
chats explaining New Deal programs to
ordinary Americans. These chats traveled on
airwaves into homes throughout the nation, reassuring
listeners that Washington cared about the suffering the Great
Depression was spreading across the land. Shortly after the first chat in March 1933, a New Yorker, "a
citizen of little or no consequence" as he called himself, wrote the White House in gratitude for "the
President's broadcast. I felt that he walked into my home, sat down and in plain and forceful language
explained to me how he was tackling the job I and my fellow citizens gave him.... Such forceful, direct
and honest action commands the respect of all Americans, it is certainly deserving of it."

National Museum of American History, Smithsonian Institution, Behring Center.

The New Deal Experiment
1932–1939

IN THE DEPTHS OF THE GREAT DEPRESSION, a Pennsylvania mother with three small children appealed to the Hoover administration for help for her husband "who is a world war Veteran and saw active service in the trenches, became desperate and applied for Compensation or a pension from the Government and was turned down." With a weekly income of only $15.60, she declared, there ought to be "enough to pay all world war veterans a pension…and there by relieve a lot of suffering, and banish resentment that causes Rebellions and Bolshevism." She asked questions murmured by millions of other desperate Americans: "Oh why is it that it is always a bunch of overley rich, selfish, dumb ignorant money hogs that persist in being Senitors, legislatures, representitives? Where would they and their possessions be if it were not for the Common Soldier, the common laborer that is compelled to work for a starvation wage[?]…Right now our good old U.S.A. is sitting on a Seething Volcano."

This mother's plea echoed in the demands of tens of thousands of World War I veterans who gathered in Washington, D.C., during June and July 1932 to lobby for immediate payment of the pension (known as a "bonus"). The veterans came from every state and by nearly every means of transportation. The throng that congregated in a huge camp on the outskirts of Washington appeared "dusty, weary, and melancholy" to a Washington reporter who noted that the veterans included jobless "truck drivers and blacksmiths, steel workers and coal miners, stenographers and common laborers," in all "a fair cross section" of the nation: immigrants and natives; whites, blacks, and Indians united in economic suffering. They were all, one journalist wrote, "down at the heel."

Calling themselves Bonus Marchers or the Bonus Army, the veterans hoped their numbers, solidarity, and poverty would persuade Congress to give them the bonus they had been promised in 1924: $1 for every day they had been in uniform and a bit extra for time served overseas. Instead of cash payments, Congress decided to hand out promissory notes that veterans could not convert to cash until 1945. Bonus Marchers condemned this "tombstone bonus" that would not be paid until many of them were dead. As veterans from Utah and California emblazoned their truck, "We Done a Good Job in France, Now You Do a Good Job in America—We Need the Bonus."

The veterans had supporters in Congress but not in the White House. President Hoover opposed the payment of an expensive bonus that would require the government to go into debt. Hoover refused to meet with representatives of the Bonus Army, who, his press secretary charged, were "communists or bums." The House of Representatives, controlled by Democrats, voted to pay the promised bonus of $2.4 billion, but the Senate, dominated by Hoover's fellow Republicans, rejected the bonus. Upon hearing of their defeat in the Senate, the Bonus Marchers did not confirm Republican fears of a **Communist** mob but instead joined in singing "America" before slowly drifting back to their camp.

About 20,000 veterans remained in Washington, determined, as one of them proclaimed, "to stay here until 1945 if necessary to get our bonus."

Attack on the Bonus Marchers

Washington police, spearheaded by 500 army soldiers commanded by General Douglas MacArthur, participated in the attack on the Bonus Marchers. Soldiers lobbed tear gas grenades toward the Bonus Marchers, quickly breaking up skirmishes like the one shown here, then advanced into the veterans' camp and torched it. At the head of the mounted cavalry attacking the veterans was George S. Patton, later a famous general in World War II. MacArthur's chief aide was Dwight D. Eisenhower, who subsequently commanded the Allied assault on Nazi Germany and became president. Eisenhower recalled that he "told that dumb son-of-a-bitch [MacArthur] he had no business going down there" to destroy the Bonus Marchers' camp, in violation of Hoover's orders. Hoover, however, did not discipline MacArthur for his insubordination.

National Archives.

FOR MORE HELP ANALYZING THIS IMAGE, see the visual activity for this chapter in the Online Study Guide at bedfordstmartins.com/roarkcompact.

While the Bonus Army hunkered down in their shanties, Hoover feared the veterans would riot and spark uprisings throughout the country. He ordered General Douglas MacArthur to evict the Bonus Marchers from the city but not to invade their camp.

On July 28, MacArthur led an attack force of five tanks and 500 soldiers armed with loaded weapons and fixed bayonets through the streets of Washington. Exceeding Hoover's orders, MacArthur pushed the Bonus Marchers back into their camp, where his soldiers torched the veterans' humble dwellings. While their camp burned, the Bonus Marchers raced away. MacArthur boasted that without his victory over the veterans, "the institutions of our Government would have been severely threatened."

MacArthur's expulsion of the Bonus Army undermined public support for the beleaguered, fearful Hoover. When the Democrats' recently nominated presidential candidate, Franklin Delano Roosevelt, heard about the attack, he correctly predicted that it "will elect me." Voters rejected Hoover, who seemed unsympathetic to the suffering caused by the Great Depression. In his inaugural address in March 1933, barely seven months after the expulsion of the Bonus Army, Roosevelt proclaimed, "The only thing we have to fear is fear itself." Instead of succumbing to fear and suspicion, Roosevelt said, Americans should roll up their sleeves and find some way out of their present difficulties. Roosevelt's confidence that the government could provide help energized **New Deal** policies and his presidency, the longest in American history.

When several thousand veterans reassembled in Washington to lobby again for the bonus a few months after Roosevelt's inauguration, the president arranged for the veterans to be housed in abandoned military barracks and fed at government expense. He invited a delegation of veterans to the White House, where he chatted casually with them, explaining that he could not support the bonus because it was too expensive, although he was determined to help them and other victims of the depression. And, to the veterans' surprise and delight, Eleanor Roosevelt slogged through rain and mud to talk personally with the veterans, to express her sympathy, and to lead them in singing their favorite songs. As the veterans voluntarily left their encampment in Washington, one remarked, "Hoover sent the Army; Roosevelt sent his wife."

Unlike the Bonus Marchers, the tens of millions of other Americans suffering from the Great Depression did not flock to Washington to lobby the government. But like the Bonus Marchers, they appreciated Roosevelt's optimism and expressions of concern. Even more, they welcomed government help from Roosevelt's New Deal initiatives to provide relief for the needy, to speed economic recovery, and to reform basic economic and governmental institutions. Roosevelt's New Deal elicited bitter opposition from critics on the right and left and failed to satisfy fully its own goals of relief, recovery, and reform. But within the Democratic Party the New Deal energized a powerful political coalition that helped millions of Americans withstand the privations of the Great Depression and, in the process, made the federal government a major presence in the daily lives of most American citizens.

Franklin D. Roosevelt: A Patrician in Government

Unlike the millions of Americans in 1932 who had no work, little food, and still less hope, Franklin Roosevelt came from a wealthy and privileged background that contributed to his optimism, self-confidence, and vitality. He constantly drew upon these personal qualities in his political career to bridge the economic, social, and cultural chasm that separated him from the struggles of ordinary Americans. During the twelve years he served as president (1933–1945), many elites came to hate him as a traitor to his class, while millions more Americans, especially the hardworking poor and dispossessed, revered him because he cared about them and their problems.

The Making of a Politician

Born in 1882, Franklin Delano Roosevelt grew up on his father's leafy estate at Hyde Park on the Hudson River, north of New York City. Insulated from the privations experienced by working people, Roosevelt was steeped at home and school in high-minded doctrines of public service and Christian duty to help the poor and weak. He prepared for a career in politics, hoping to follow in the political footsteps of his fifth cousin, Theodore Roosevelt.

Unlike cousin Teddy, Franklin Roosevelt sought his political fortune in the Democratic Party. After a two-year stint in the New York legislature, he ascended to national office when Woodrow Wilson appointed him assistant secretary of the navy. In 1920, he catapulted to the second spot on the national Democratic ticket, as the vice presidential candidate of presidential nominee James M. Cox. Although the Republicans' Warren G. Harding trounced Cox in the general election (see chapter 23), Roosevelt's energetic campaigning convinced Democratic leaders that he had a bright future in national politics.

In the summer of 1921, however, his life took a painful detour. He became infected with the polio virus, which paralyzed both his legs. For the rest of his life, he could stand only with his legs encased in heavy steel braces, and he could walk a few awkward steps only by leaning on another person. Tireless physical therapy helped him regain his vitality and intense desire for high political office. But he had to recapture his political momentum mostly from a sitting position, although he studiously avoided being photographed in the wheelchair he used routinely.

After his polio attack, Roosevelt frequently visited a polio therapy facility at Warm Springs, Georgia. There, he combined the health benefits of the soothing waters with political overtures to southern Democrats, which helped make him a rare political creature: a New Yorker from the Democratic Party's urban and immigrant wing with whom whites from the Democratic Party's entrenched southern wing felt comfortable.

Roosevelt's Common Touch

In his campaign for reelection as governor of New York in 1930, Franklin Roosevelt boosted his vote total by 700,000 over his slender victory margin of 25,000 in 1928, and he became the first Democratic candidate for governor to win the vote outside New York City. Sensing that his presentation of himself as a good neighbor was responsible for much of his popularity, Roosevelt arranged to have a friendly chat outside polls in his hometown of Hyde Park with working-class voter Ruben Appel. In this photograph, Appel seems unaware that Roosevelt's standing was itself a feat of stagecraft. His legs rendered useless by polio, Roosevelt could remain upright only by using the strength he had developed in his arms and shoulders to prop himself up on his cane. Rare photos like this and a taboo against showing Roosevelt in his wheelchair kept the public from thinking of Roosevelt as a "cripple" and unfit for office, or in many cases from even realizing that he was disabled.

Franklin D. Roosevelt Library.

Roosevelt's chance to return to political office came in 1928 when he won the race for governor of New York. As governor of the nation's most populous state, Roosevelt was poised to showcase his leadership and his suitability for a presidential bid of his own. His activist policies made his governorship a dress rehearsal for his subsequent actions as president.

Governor Roosevelt believed government should intervene to protect citizens from economic hardships, rather than wait for the law of supply and demand to improve the economy. Roosevelt's sympathy for the underdog contrasted with the traditional **laissez-faire** views of many **conservatives**—both Republicans and Democrats—that the depression represented the hard hand of the market winnowing the strong from the weak. Conservatives believed government help for the needy would sap individual initiative and impede the self-correcting forces of the market by rewarding the losers in the economic struggle to survive. Roosevelt lacked a full-fledged counterargument, but he proclaimed, "To these unfortunate citizens aid must be extended by governments, not as a matter of charity but as a matter of social duty.…[No one should go] unfed, unclothed, or unsheltered." The highlight of Roosevelt's efforts to relieve the economic hardships of New Yorkers was the $20 million Temporary Emergency Relief Administration (TERA), created in 1931, which earned him the gratitude of New Yorkers and the attention of national politicians.

To his supporters, Roosevelt seemed to be a leader determined to attack the economic crisis without deviating from **democracy**—unlike **fascist** parties gaining strength in Europe—or from capitalism—unlike Communists in power in the Soviet Union. Roosevelt's ideas about precisely how to revive the economy were vague. A prominent journalist characterized Roosevelt in 1931 as "a kind of amiable boy scout…a pleasant man who, without any important qualifications for the office, would very much like to be president." But Roosevelt's conviction that government could and should do something to help Americans climb out of the economic abyss propelled him into the front ranks of the national Democratic Party.

The Election of 1932

The Democrats who convened in Chicago in July 1932 to nominate their presidential candidate knew that Hoover's unpopularity gave them a historic opportunity to recapture the White House.

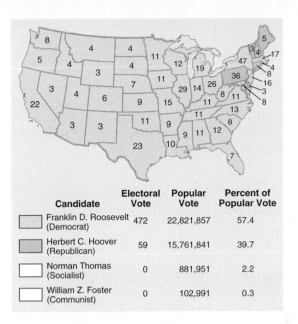

In 56 of the 72 years since Abraham Lincoln's election, the White House had been a Republican preserve. Now, Democrats might reverse generations of Republican rule if they chose the right nominee.

Opposition to Republicans and hunger for office, but little else, united Democrats. Warring factions divided Democrats by region, religion, culture, and commitment to the status quo. Southern Democrats chaired powerful committees in Congress thanks to their continual reelection in the one-party South devoted to white supremacy. This southern, native-born, white, rural, **Protestant**, conservative wing of the Democratic Party found little common ground with the northern, immigrant, urban, disproportionately Catholic, **liberal** wing. Rural and small-town drys (supporters of prohibition) clashed with urban and foreign-born wets (opponents of prohibition). Eastern-establishment Democratic dignitaries shared few goals with angry farmers and factory workers. Nonetheless, this unruly coalition of constituencies finally agreed to nominate Franklin Roosevelt as their presidential candidate.

In his acceptance speech, Roosevelt proclaimed his commitment to "the forgotten man at the bottom of the pyramid"—such as the Bonus Marchers then in Washington—and he promised "bold, persistent experimentation" to find ways to help. Highlighting his differences with Hoover and Republicans, he announced, "I pledge you, I pledge myself, to a new deal for the American people."

Few details about what Roosevelt meant by a "new deal" emerged in the presidential campaign. He declared that "the people of America want more than anything else…two things; work…with all the moral and spiritual values that go with work…and a reasonable measure of security…for themselves and for their wives and children." Voters responded in no uncertain terms.

Roosevelt won in a historic landslide (Map 24.1). He received 57 percent of popular votes and amassed an 89 percent majority in the electoral college, carrying state after state that had voted Republican for years (Map 24.2). Roosevelt's coattails also swept Democrats into control of

Candidate	Electoral Vote	Popular Vote	Percent of Popular Vote
Franklin D. Roosevelt (Democrat)	472	22,821,857	57.4
Herbert C. Hoover (Republican)	59	15,761,841	39.7
Norman Thomas (Socialist)	0	881,951	2.2
William Z. Foster (Communist)	0	102,991	0.3

MAP 24.1 The Election of 1932

Congress by large margins. Voters gave him a mandate for change.

Roosevelt's victory represented the emergence of what came to be known as the New Deal coalition. Attracting support from farmers, factory workers, immigrants, city folk, African Americans, women, and **progressive** intellectuals, Roosevelt

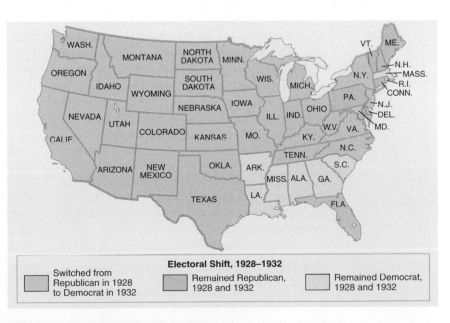

Electoral Shift, 1928–1932

Switched from Republican in 1928 to Democrat in 1932

Remained Republican, 1928 and 1932

Remained Democrat, 1928 and 1932

MAP 24.2 Electoral Shift, 1928–1932
Democratic victory in 1932 signaled the rise of a New Deal coalition within which women and minorities, many of them new voters, made the Democrats the majority party for the first time in the twentieth century.

launched a realignment of the nation's political loyalties. The New Deal coalition dominated American politics throughout Roosevelt's presidency and remained powerful long after his death in 1945. United less by ideology or support for specific policies, voters in the New Deal coalition instead expressed faith in Roosevelt's promise of a government that would, somehow, change things for the better.

REVIEW Why did Franklin D. Roosevelt win the 1932 presidential election by such a large margin?

Launching the New Deal

At noon on March 4, 1933, Americans gathered around their radios to hear the inaugural address of the newly elected president. Roosevelt began by asserting his "firm belief that the only thing we have to fear is fear itself—nameless, unreasoning, unjustified terror which paralyzes needed efforts to convert retreat into advance." Roosevelt promised "direct, vigorous action" in order "to wage war against the emergency" confronting "a stricken Nation in the midst of a stricken world." The first months of Roosevelt's administration, termed "the Hundred Days," fulfilled that promise in a whirlwind of government initiatives that launched the New Deal.

Roosevelt and his advisers had three interrelated objectives: to provide relief to the destitute, especially the one out of four Americans who were unemployed; to foster the economic recovery of farms and businesses, thereby creating jobs and reducing the need for relief; and to reform the government and economy in ways that would reduce the risk of devastating consequences in future economic slumps. The New Deal never fully achieved these goals of relief, recovery, and reform. But by aiming for them, Roosevelt's experimental programs enormously expanded government's role in the nation's economy and society.

The New Dealers

To design and implement the New Deal, Roosevelt needed ideas and people. As governor of New York, he frequently hosted private, informal conversations about social and economic policy with a small group of professors from Columbia University. Dubbed the "Brains Trust,"

these men and others continued to advise the new president about the problems faced by the nation and how to deal with them.

Hundreds of other reformers rushed to join the Roosevelt administration. Among the most important were two veterans of Roosevelt's New York governorship: Harry Hopkins and Frances Perkins. Hopkins administered New Deal relief efforts and served as one of the president's loyal confidants. Perkins, like Hopkins, embraced the **social gospel** tradition, having worked for a time in Jane Addams's Hull House in Chicago. Roosevelt tapped Perkins to serve as secretary of labor, the first woman cabinet member in American history—an indication of her expertise and of the growing strength of women in the Democratic Party.

No New Dealers were more important than the president and his wife, Eleanor. The gregarious president radiated charm and good cheer, giving the New Deal's bureaucratic regulations a benevolent human face. Eleanor Roosevelt became the New Deal's unofficial ambassador. She served as her husband's eyes and ears—and legs—as she traveled throughout the nation connecting the corridors of power in Washington to Americans of all colors and creeds in church basements, meeting halls, and front parlors.

As Roosevelt's programs swung into action, many Americans benefited directly through jobs and relief or indirectly from economic improvements. In time, the millions of beneficiaries of the New Deal became grassroots New Dealers who expressed their appreciation by voting Democratic on election day. A signal success of the New Deal was to create a durable political coalition of Democrats that would reelect Roosevelt in 1936, 1940, and 1944.

As Roosevelt and his advisers developed plans to meet the economic emergency, their watchwords were *action*, *experiment*, and *improvise*. Without a sharply defined template for how to provide relief, recovery, and reform, they moved from ideas to policies as quickly as possible, hoping to identify ways to help people and to boost the economy. But underlying New Dealers' experimentation and improvisation were four guiding ideas.

First, Roosevelt and his advisers sought capitalist solutions to the economic crisis. They believed that the depression resulted from basic imbalances in the nation's capitalist economy, imbalances they wanted to correct. They had no desire to eliminate private property or impose socialist programs, such as public ownership of productive resources. Instead, they hoped to save the capitalist economy by remedying its flaws.

Second, Roosevelt's Brains Trust persuaded him that the greatest flaw of America's capitalist economy was underconsumption, the root cause of the current economic paralysis. Underconsumption, New Dealers argued, resulted from the gigantic productive success of capitalism. Factories and farms produced more than they could sell to consumers, causing factories to lay off workers and farmers to lose money on bumper crops. Workers without wages and farmers without profits shrank consumption and choked the economy. Somehow, the balance between consumption and production needed to be restored.

Third, New Dealers believed that the immense size and economic power of American corporations needed to be counterbalanced by government and by organization among workers and small producers. New Dealers did not seek to splinter big businesses. Huge businesses had developed for good economic reasons and were here to stay. Roosevelt and his advisers hoped to counterbalance big economic institutions and their quest for profits with government programs focused on protecting individuals and the public interest.

Fourth, New Dealers felt that government must somehow

moderate the imbalance of wealth created by American capitalism. Wealth concentrated in a few hands reduced consumption by most Americans and thereby contributed to the current economic gridlock. In the long run, government needed to find a way to permit ordinary working people to share more fully in the fruits of the economy. In the short term, New Dealers sought to lend a helping hand to poor people who suffered from the maldistribution of wealth.

Banking and Finance Reform

Roosevelt wasted no time making good on his inaugural pledge for "action now." As he took the oath of office on March 4, the nation's banking system was on the brink of collapse. Since 1930 more than 5,000 banks had collapsed. Roosevelt immediately declared a four-day "bank holiday" in order to devise a plan to shore up banks and restore depositors' confidence. Working round the clock, New Dealers drafted the Emergency Banking Act, which gave the secretary of the treasury the power to decide which banks could be safely reopened and to release funds from the Reconstruction Finance Corporation (RFC) to bolster banks' assets. To secure the confidence of depositors, Congress passed the Glass-Steagall Banking Act, setting up the Federal Deposit Insurance Corporation (FDIC), which guaranteed bank

Emergency Money

When bank failures in 1933 caused prudent depositors to withdraw their money from their accounts and hide it away, the resulting scarcity of currency paralyzed businesses. Store owners, service clubs, and communities created "emergency money" to keep the wheels of local commerce turning. Leiter's Pharmacy in Pismo Beach, California, for example, used clamshells for currency; other places issued buckskin and wooden dollars. Such improvisation demonstrates the collapse of the banking system and the creative solutions of some of its victims.

National Museum of American History, Smithsonian Institution, Behring Center.

customers that the federal government would reimburse them for deposits if their banks failed.

On Sunday night, March 12, while the banks were still closed, Roosevelt broadcast the first of what became a series of "fireside chats." Speaking in a friendly, informal manner, he addressed the millions of Americans who tuned their radios to hear the president explain these first New Deal initiatives. The new banking legislation, he said, made it "safer to keep your money in a reopened bank than under the mattress." With such plain talk, Roosevelt translated complex matters into common sense. This and subsequent fireside chats forged a direct connection—via radio waves—between Roosevelt and millions of Americans. Evidence of their link to Roosevelt piled up in the White House mail room. Millions shared the views of a man from Paris, Texas, who wrote Roosevelt, "you are the one & only President that ever helped a Working Class of People.... Please help us some way I Pray to God for relief."

The banking legislation and fireside chat worked. Within a few days, most of the nation's major banks reopened, and they remained solvent as reassured depositors switched funds from their mattresses to their accounts. Some radical critics of the New Deal believed Roosevelt should have nationalized the banks and made them a cornerstone of economic planning by the federal government. Instead, these first New Deal measures propped up the private banking system with federal funds and subjected banks to federal regulation and oversight.

In his inaugural address Roosevelt criticized financiers for their greed and incompetence. To prevent the fraud, corruption, insider trading, and other abuses that had tainted Wall Street and contributed to the crash of 1929, Roosevelt pressed Congress to regulate the stock market. Legislation in 1934 created the Securities and Exchange Commission (SEC) to oversee financial markets by licensing investment dealers, monitoring all stock transactions, and requiring corporate officers to make full disclosures about their companies. Cleaned up and regulated, Wall Street slowly recovered, but the stock market stayed well below its heights of the 1920s.

Relief and Conservation Programs

Patching up the nation's financial structure provided little relief for the hungry and unemployed. A poor man from Nebraska asked Eleanor Roosevelt "if the folk who was borned here in America...are this Forgotten Man, the President had in mind, [and] if we are this Forgotten Man then we are still Forgotten." Since its founding, the federal government had never assumed responsibility for needy people, except in moments of natural disaster or emergencies such as the Civil War. Instead, churches, private charities, county and municipal governments, and occasionally states assumed the burden of poor relief, usually with meager payments. To persuade Americans that the depression necessitated unprecedented federal relief efforts, Harry Hopkins dispatched investigators throughout the nation to describe the plight of impoverished Americans. As one New Yorker reported, "We work, ten hours a day for six days. In the grime and dirt of a nation [for]…low pay [making us]…slaves—slaves of the depression!"

Hopkins's investigators galvanized support for the Federal Emergency Relief Administration (FERA), which provided $500 million to feed the hungry and create jobs. Established in May 1933, FERA supported 4 to 5 million households with $20 or $30 a month. FERA also created jobs for the unemployed on thousands of public works projects, organized by Hopkins into the Civil Works Administration (CWA), which put paychecks worth over $800 million into the hands of previously jobless workers. Earning wages between forty and sixty cents an hour, laborers renovated schools, dug sewers, and rebuilt roads and bridges.

The most popular work relief program was the Civilian Conservation Corps (CCC), established in March 1933. It offered unemployed young men a chance to earn wages while working to conserve natural resources, a long-standing interest of Roosevelt. By the end of the program in 1942, the 3 million CCC workers had checked soil erosion, tamed rivers, and planted more than 2 billion trees. Just as important, CCC, CWA, and other work relief efforts replaced the stigma of welfare with the dignity of jobs. As one woman said, "We aren't on relief anymore. My husband is working for the Government."

The New Deal also sought to harness natural resources for hydroelectric power. Continuing a project begun under Hoover, the New Deal completed the colossal Hoover Dam across the Colorado River in Nevada, providing not only electricity but also flood control and irrigation water for Arizona and southern California. In addition, building the dam provided badly needed jobs and wages for unemployed workers.

The New Deal's most ambitious and controversial natural resources development project was the Tennessee Valley Authority (TVA), created in May 1933 to build dams along the Tennessee River to supply impoverished rural communities with cheap electricity (Map 24.3). The TVA set out to demonstrate that a partnership between the federal government and local residents could overcome barriers of state governments and of private enterprises to make efficient use of abundant natural resources and break the ancient cycle of poverty. TVA never fully realized these utopian ends, but it improved the lives of millions in the region with electric power, flood protection, soil reclamation, and jobs.

New sources of hydroelectric power helped the New Deal bring the wonders of electricity to country folk, fulfilling an old progressive dream. When Roosevelt became president, 90 percent of rural Americans lacked electricity. Private electric companies refused to build transmission lines into the sparsely settled countryside when they had a profitable market in more accessible and densely populated urban areas. Beginning in 1935, the Rural Electrification Administration (REA) made low-cost loans available to local cooperatives for power plants and transmission lines to serve rural communities. Within ten years, the REA delivered electricity to nine out of ten farms, giving rural Americans access for the first time to modern conveniences that urban people had enjoyed for decades.

Agricultural Initiatives

Farmers had been mired in depression since the end of World War I. New Dealers diagnosed farmers' plight as a classic case of overproduction and underconsumption. Following age-old practices, farmers tried to compensate for low crop prices by growing more crops, hoping to boost their earnings by selling larger quantities. Instead, producing more pushed prices lower still. Farm income sank from a disastrously low $6 billion in 1929 to a catastrophically low $2 billion in 1932. The median annual income among farm families plunged to $167, barely one-tenth of the national average.

New Dealers sought to cut agricultural production, thereby raising crop prices and farmers' income. To reduce production, the Agricultural Adjustment Act (AAA) authorized the "domestic allotment plan," which paid farmers not to grow crops: Individual farmers who agreed not to plant crops on a portion of their fields (their

Sketch for a Federal Arts Program Mural
This sketch for a mural commissioned for Lenoir City, Tennessee, is typical of the Federal Arts Program's goal to memorialize significant moments of achievement in every region of the country. For rural folk, the sight of Rural Electrification Authority (REA) workers extending power lines was an exciting symbol of the New Deal. When the REA came into existence in 1935, less than 10 percent of the nation outside the cities had electricity. Ten years later the figure had risen to 90 percent, and the gulf of silence and darkness between town and country was successfully bridged.
Public Buildings Service, General Services Administration.

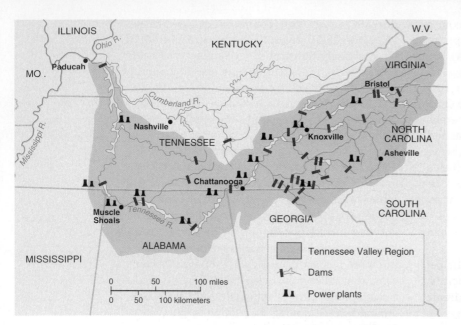

MAP 24.3   The Tennessee Valley Authority
The New Deal created the Tennessee Valley Authority to modernize a vast impoverished region with hydroelectric power dams and, at the same time, to reclaim eroded lands and preserve old folkways.

READING THE MAP: How many states were affected by the TVA? How many miles of rivers (approximately) were affected?
CONNECTIONS: What kinds of benefits—economic as well as social and cultural—did TVA programs bring to the region? How might the lives of a poor farming family in Alabama or Tennessee have changed after the mid-1930s owing to these programs?

FOR MORE HELP ANALYZING THIS MAP, see the map activity for this chapter in the Online Study Guide at bedfordstmartins.com/roarkcompact.

"allotment") would receive a government payment compensating them for the crops they did not plant. Since crops were already in the ground by the time AAA passed in May 1933, drastic measures were necessary to reduce production immediately. While millions of Americans went to bed hungry, farmers slaughtered millions of cattle, hogs, sheep, and other livestock and destroyed millions of acres of crops in order to qualify for their allotment payments.

With the formation of the Commodity Credit Corporation, the federal government allowed farmers to hold their harvested crops off the market and wait for a higher price. In the meantime, the government stored the crop and gave farmers a "commodity loan" based on a favorable price. If the market price rose above that level, the farmer could repay the loan, sell the crop, and pocket the difference. If the market price never rose above the loan level, the farmer simply took the loan as payment, and the government kept the crop. In effect, commodity loans addressed the problem of underconsumption by making the federal government a major consumer of agricultural goods and reducing farmers' vulnerability to low prices. New Dealers also sponsored the Farm Credit Act (FCA) to provide long-term credit on mortgaged farm property, allowing debt-ridden farmers to avoid foreclosures that were driving thousands off their land.

Crop allotments, commodity loans, and mortgage credit made farmers major beneficiaries of the New Deal. Crop prices rose impressively, farm income jumped 50 percent by 1936, and FCA loans financed 40 percent of farm mortgage debt by the end of the decade. These gains were distributed fairly equally among farmers in the corn, hogs, and wheat region of the Midwest. In the South's cotton belt, however, landlords controlled the distribution of New Deal agricultural benefits and shamelessly rewarded themselves while denying benefits to many sharecroppers and tenant farmers—blacks and whites—by taking the land they had worked out of production and assigning it to the allotment program. Many such tenants and sharecroppers could no longer find work, and their privation worsened.

Industrial Recovery

Unlike farmers, industrialists cut production with the onset of the depression. Between 1929 and 1933, industrial production fell more than 40 percent, to balance low demand with low supply and maintain prices. But the industrialists' strategy created major economic and social problems for Roosevelt and his advisers, since falling industrial production meant that millions of working people lost their jobs. Mass unemployment also reduced consumer demand for industrial products, contributing to a downward spiral with no end in sight. New Dealers struggled to find a way to break this cycle of unemployment and underconsumption, a way consistent with corporate profits and capitalism.

The New Deal's National Industrial Recovery Act (NIRA) opted for a government-sponsored form of industrial self-government through the National Recovery Administration (NRA), established in June 1933. The NRA encouraged industrialists in every part of the economy to agree on rules—known as codes—to define fair working conditions, to set prices, and to minimize competition. The idea behind codes was to stabilize existing industries and maintain their workforces while avoiding what both industrialists and New Dealers termed "destructive competition" that forced employers to cut both wages and jobs. Industry after industry wrote elaborate codes addressing detailed features of production, pricing, and competition. In exchange for relaxing federal antitrust regulations that prohibited such business agreements, the NRA received a promise from participating businesses that they would recognize the right of working people to organize and engage in **collective bargaining**. To encourage consumers to patronize businesses participating in NRA codes, the New Deal mounted a public relations campaign that displayed the NRA's Blue Eagle in shop windows and on billboards throughout the nation.

New Dealers hoped that NRA codes would yield businesses with a social conscience, ensuring fair treatment for workers and consumers and promotion of the general economic welfare. Instead, NRA codes tended to strengthen conventional business practices. Large corporations wrote codes that served primarily the interests of corporate profits rather than the needs of workers or the welfare of the national economy. Many business leaders criticized NRA codes as heavy-handed government regulation of private enterprise. In reality, however, compliance with NRA codes was voluntary, and government enforcement efforts were weak to nonexistent. The NRA did little to reduce unemployment, raise consumption, or relieve the depression. In effect, the NRA represented a peace offering to business leaders by Roosevelt and his advisers, conveying the message that the New Deal did not intend to wage war against profits or private enterprise. The peace offering failed, however. Most corporate leaders became active and often bitter opponents of Roosevelt and the New Deal.

> **REVIEW**   How did the New Dealers try to steer the nation toward recovery from the Great Depression?

Major Legislation of the New Deal's First Hundred Days

	Name of Act	Basic Provisions
March 9, 1933	Emergency Banking Act	Provided for reopening stable banks and authorizing RFC to supply funds
March 31, 1933	Civilian Conservation Corps Act	Provided jobs for unemployed youth
May 12, 1933	Agricultural Adjustment Act	Provided funds to pay farmers for not growing surplus crops
May 12, 1933	Federal Emergency Relief Act	Provided relief funds for the destitute
May 18, 1933	Tennessee Valley Authority Act	Set up authority for development of electric power and conservation
June 16, 1933	National Industrial Recovery Act	Specified cooperation among business, government, and labor in setting fair prices and working conditions
June 16, 1933	Glass-Steagall Banking Act	Created Federal Deposit Insurance Corporation (FDIC) to insure bank deposits

Challenges to the New Deal

The first New Deal initiatives engendered fierce criticism and political opposition. From the right, Republicans and business people charged that New Deal programs were too radical, undermining private property, economic stability, and democracy. Critics on the left faulted the New Deal for its failure to allay the human suffering caused by the depression and for its timidity in attacking corporate power and greed.

Resistance to Business Reform

New Deal programs rescued capitalism. That did not prevent business leaders from criticizing Roosevelt, even though their economic prospects improved more than those of most other Americans during the depression. Concentrated corporate power avoided reform, but business leaders still mounted stridently anti–New Deal campaigns that expressed their own resentment and fear of new regulations, taxes, and unions. By 1935, two major business organizations, the National Association of Manufacturers and the Chamber of Commerce, had become openly anti–New Deal. Their critiques were amplified by the American Liberty League, founded in 1934, which decried the New Deal for betraying basic constitutional guarantees of freedom and individualism. To them, the AAA was a "trend toward fascist control of agriculture," relief programs marked "the end of democracy," and the NRA was a plunge into the "quicksand of visionary experimentation."

Economic planners who favored rational planning in the public interest and labor leaders who sought to influence wages and working conditions by organizing unions attacked the New Deal from the left. In their view, the NRA stifled enterprise by permitting **monopolistic** practices. They pointed out that industrial trade associations twisted NRA codes to suit their aims, thwarted competition, and engaged in price gouging. Labor leaders especially resented the NRA's willingness to allow businesses to form company-controlled unions while blocking workers from organizing genuine grassroots unions to bargain for themselves.

The Supreme Court stepped into this crossfire of criticisms in May 1935 and declared that the NRA unconstitutionally conferred powers reserved to Congress on an administrative agency staffed by government appointees. The NRA codes lost the little authority they had. The failure of the NRA demonstrated the depth of many Americans' resistance to economic planning and the stubborn refusal of business leaders to yield to government regulations or reforms.

Casualties in the Countryside

The AAA weathered critical battering by champions of the old order better than the NRA. Allotment checks for keeping land fallow and crop prices high created loyalty among farmers with enough acreage to participate. As a white farmer in North Carolina declared, "I stand for the New Deal and Roosevelt... the AAA...and crop control." Agricultural processors and distrib-

utors, however, criticized the AAA. They objected that the program reduced the volume of crop production—the only source of their profits—while they paid a tax on processed crops that funded the very program that disadvantaged them. In 1936, the Supreme Court agreed with their contention that they were victims of an illegal attempt to tax one group (processors and distributors) to enrich another (farmers). Down but not out, the AAA rebounded from the Supreme Court ruling by eliminating the offending tax and funding allotment payments from general government revenues.

Protests stirred, however, among those who did not qualify for allotments. The Southern Farm Tenants Union argued passionately that the AAA enriched large farmers and impoverished small farmers who rented rather than owned their land. One black sharecropper explained why only $75 a year from New Deal agricultural subsidies trickled down to her: "De landlord is landlord, de politicians is landlord, de judge is landlord, de shurf [sheriff] is landlord, ever'body is landlord, en we [sharecroppers] ain' got nothin'!" Such testimony showed that the AAA, like the NRA, tended to help most those who least needed help. Roosevelt's political dependence on southern Democrats caused him to avoid confronting such economic and racial inequities in the South's entrenched order.

Displaced tenants often joined the army of migrant workers who straggled across rural America during the 1930s, some to flee Plains dust storms. Many migrants came from Mexico to work Texas cotton, Michigan beans, Idaho sugar beets, and California crops of all kinds. But since people willing to take agricultural jobs usually exceeded the jobs available, wages fell and native-born white migrants fought to reserve even these low-wage jobs for themselves. Hundreds of thousands of "Okie" migrants streamed out of the Dust Bowl of Oklahoma, Kansas, Texas, and Colorado, where chronic drought and harmful agricultural practices blasted crops and hopes. Parched, poor, and windblown,

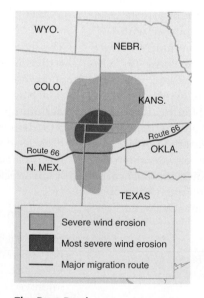

The Dust Bowl

Severe wind erosion

Most severe wind erosion

— Major migration route

Okies—like the Joad family immortalized in John Steinbeck's novel *The Grapes of Wrath* (1939)—migrated to the lush fields and orchards of California, congregating in labor camps and hoping to find work and a future. But migrant laborers seldom found steady or secure work. As one Okie said, "When they need us they call us migrants, and when we've picked their crop, we're bums and we got to get out."

Politics on the Fringes

Politically, the New Deal's staunchest opponents were in the Republican Party—organized, well-heeled, mainstream, and determined to challenge Roosevelt at every turn. But from the political fringes the New Deal also faced challenges, fueled by the hardship of the depression and the hope for a cure-all.

Socialists and Communists accused the New Deal of being the handmaiden of business elites and of rescuing capitalism from its self-inflicted crisis. Socialist author Upton Sinclair ran for governor of California in 1934 on a plan he called "End Poverty in California." Sinclair demanded that the state take ownership of idle factories and unused land and give them to cooperatives of working people, a first step toward what he envisioned as a "Cooperative Commonwealth" that would put the needs of people above profits. Sinclair lost the election, ending the most serious socialist electoral challenge to the New Deal.

Many other intellectuals and artists sought to advance the cause of more radical change by joining left-wing organizations, including the American Communist Party. At its high point in the 1930s, the party had about 30,000 members, the large majority of them immigrants. Individual Communists worked to organize labor unions, protect the civil rights of black people, and help the destitute, but the party preached the overthrow of "bourgeois democracy" and the destruction of capitalism in favor of Soviet-style communism. Party spokesmen termed the NRA a "fascist slave program" and likened Roosevelt and the New Deal to Hitler and the Nazis. Such talk attracted few followers among the nation's millions of poor and unemployed. They wanted jobs and economic security within American capitalism and democracy, not violent revolution to establish a dictatorship of the Communist Party.

More powerful radical challenges to the New Deal sprouted from homegrown roots.

Black Sharecroppers
An unintended consequence of the New Deal plan to maintain farm prices by reducing acreage in production was the eviction of tenant farmers when the land they worked was unused. Champions of the tenant farmers, most notably the Southern Farm Tenants Union, protested in vain that federal crop subsidies should be shared between owners and those who usually worked the land. Often, however, sharecroppers like these were simply cast adrift, and lobbies for farm owners thwarted any governmental challenge. Tenant farmers' sad state continued until World War II provided opportunities for displaced tenants to escape to the cities. Corbis.

Many Americans felt overlooked by New Deal programs that concentrated on finance, agriculture, and industry but did little to produce jobs or aid the poor. The merciless reality of the depression also continued to erode the security of people who still had a job but worried constantly about when they too might be pushed into the legions of the unemployed and penniless.

A Catholic priest in Detroit named Charles Coughlin spoke to, and for, many worried Americans in his weekly radio broadcasts, which reached a nationwide audience of 40 million. Father Coughlin expressed outrage at the suffering and inequities that he blamed on Communists, bankers, and "predatory capitalists" who, he claimed, were mostly Jews. In 1932, Coughlin applauded Roosevelt's election and declared, "The

New Deal is Christ's deal." But frustrated by Roosevelt's refusal to grant him influence, Coughlin turned against the New Deal and founded the National Union for Social Justice, or Union Party, to challenge Roosevelt in the 1936 presidential election. Tapping the popular appeal of anti-Semitism, Coughlin's Union Party called for an expanded money supply backed by silver so that the poor could be rescued from the "international bankers" responsible for the depression and coddled by Roosevelt.

Among those who answered Father Coughlin's call was Dr. Francis Townsend in Long Beach, California. Angry that many of his retired patients lived in misery, Townsend proposed in 1934 the creation of an Old Age Revolving Pension that would pay every American over age sixty a pension of $200 a month. In order to receive the pension, senior citizens had to agree to spend the entire amount within thirty days, thereby stimulating the economy. Townsend organized pension clubs with more than 2 million paying members and petitioned the federal government to enact his scheme. When the major political parties rebuffed his impractical plan, Townsend merged his forces with Coughlin's Union Party in time for the 1936 election.

A more formidable challenge to the New Deal came from the southern wing of the Democratic Party. Huey Long, son of a back-country Louisiana farmer, was elected governor of the state in 1928 with his slogan "Every man a king, but no one wears a crown." As governor, Long delivered on his promises to provide jobs and build roads, schools, and hospitals. Swaggering and bullying to get his way, Long delighted his supporters, who elected him to the U.S. Senate in 1932 (see "Historical Question," page 634). Senator Long introduced a sweeping "soak the rich" tax bill that would outlaw personal incomes of more than $1 million and inheritances of more than $5 million. When the Senate rejected his proposal, Long decided to run for president, mobilizing more than 5 million Americans behind his "Share Our Wealth" plan. Like Townsend's scheme, Long's program promised far more than it could deliver. Although the Share Our Wealth campaign died when Long was assassinated in 1935, his constituency and the wide appeal of a more equitable distribution of wealth persisted.

The challenges to the New Deal from Republicans as well as from more radical groups stirred Democrats to solidify their winning coalition. In the midterm congressional elections of 1934—normally a time when a seated president loses support—voters gave New Dealers a landslide victory. Democrats increased their majority in the House of Representatives and gained a two-thirds majority in the Senate.

> **REVIEW** Why did the New Deal face criticism from both ends of the political spectrum?

Toward a Welfare State

The popular mandate for the New Deal revealed by the congressional elections persuaded Roosevelt to press ahead with bold new efforts of relief, recovery, and reform. Despite the initiatives of the Hundred Days, the depression still strangled the economy. Rumbles of discontent from Father Coughlin, Huey Long, and their supporters showed that New Deal programs had fallen far short of their goals. In 1935, Roosevelt capitalized on his congressional majorities to enact major new programs that signaled the emergence of an American **welfare state**.

Taken together, these New Deal efforts stretched a safety net under the lives of ordinary Americans. Although many citizens remained unprotected, New Deal programs helped millions with jobs, relief, and government support. Knitting together the safety net was the idea that the federal government bore responsibility for the welfare of individual Americans. When individuals suffered because of economic and social forces beyond their control—as in the Great Depression—the federal government had the duty to provide them a measure of support and protection. The safety net of welfare programs tied the political loyalty of working people to the New Deal and the Democratic Party. As a North Carolina mill worker said, "Mr. Roosevelt is the only man we ever had in the White House who would understand that my boss is a sonofabitch."

Relief for the Unemployed

First and foremost, Americans still needed jobs. Since the private economy left 8 million people jobless by 1935, Roosevelt and his advisers launched a massive work relief program. With a congressional appropriation of nearly $5 billion—

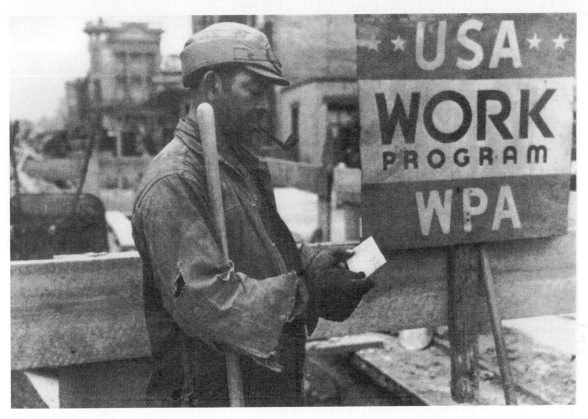

WPA Paycheck
WPA projects gave jobs and paychecks to millions of Americans who, like this man in Washington, D.C., dug ditches. Workers on New Deal public works projects also built the San Francisco–Oakland Bay Bridge, the Lincoln Tunnel in New York, and the Overseas Highway in the Florida Keys, as well as thousands of other bridges, roads, and buildings still in use today.
National Archives.

more than all government revenues in 1934—the New Deal created the Works Progress Administration (WPA) to give unemployed Americans government-funded jobs on public works projects. The WPA put millions of jobless citizens to work on roads, bridges, parks, public buildings, and more. In addition, Congress passed—over Roosevelt's veto—the bonus long-sought by the Bonus Marchers, giving veterans an average of $580, further stimulating the economy.

By 1936, WPA funds provided jobs for 7 percent of the nation's labor force. In effect, the WPA made the federal government the employer of last resort, creating useful jobs when the capitalist economy failed to do so. By the time the WPA ended in 1943—because mobilization for World War II created full employment—it had made major contributions to both relief and recovery. WPA jobs put 13 million men and women to work and gave them paychecks worth $10 billion.

About three out of four WPA jobs involved construction and renovation of the nation's physical infrastructure. In addition to work with picks, shovels, hammers, nails, bricks, and mortar, the WPA gave jobs to artists, musicians, actors, journalists, poets, and novelists. WPA projects throughout the nation displayed tangible evidence of the New Deal's commitment to public welfare.

Empowering Labor

During the Great Depression, factory workers who managed to keep their jobs worried constantly about being laid off while their wages and working hours were cut. When workers tried to organize labor unions to protect themselves, municipal and state governments usually sided with employers. Since the Gilded Age, the state and federal governments had been far more effective at busting unions than at busting **trusts**.

Huey Long: Demagogue or Champion of the Dispossessed?

From the time he was a small child, Huey Pierce Long was what one exasperated neighbor called a "pesterance." Defiant at school, artful at avoiding any disagreeable chores, ruthlessly driven to be the center of attention, Long got ahead with his intelligence and willingness to flout conventional rules. Though he spent only brief periods studying law at the University of Oklahoma and Tulane University, he cajoled a judge to convene a special bar examination, which he passed easily at the age of twenty-one. Declaring that he came out of that examination "running for office," Long rose swiftly from election as state railroad commissioner in 1918 to governor ten years later, dazzling the public with his brash style.

Louisiana's established leaders made white supremacy the cornerstone of their rule. Out of step with majority opinion on race, Long advanced his fortunes by appealing to class division—poor against rich, rural against urban, the humble against the elite—rather than white against black. He focused his reform program on a more equitable distribution of income and opportunity. At St. Martinsville, deep in swampy Cajun country, he asked, "Where are the schools that you have waited for your children to have, that have never come? Where are the roads and the highways that you sent your money to build…? Where are the institutions to care for the sick and disabled?" When Long became governor, Louisiana had only 331 miles of paved roads outside the cities. It was also the most illiterate state in the nation. In 1893, when Long was born, 45 percent of those above the age of ten could not read; by 1920, the rate of illiteracy was still 22 percent, including 38 percent of all blacks.

Long articulated the grievances and hopes of the poor people of Louisiana. He also behaved ruthlessly to achieve his goals. After overcoming an **impeachment** effort in 1929, Long moved to consolidate his power. "I used to try to get things done by saying 'please,'" he said. "That didn't work and now I'm a dynamiter. I dynamite 'em out of my path." By 1930, Long completely dominated the state. Journalists around the country routinely referred to him as the "dictator of Louisiana." He made no effort to hide his power. Once an angry opponent thrust a volume in his face and shouted, "Maybe you've heard of this book. It's the constitution of the state of Louisiana." Long shrugged and said, "I'm the constitution here now." He bullied and bribed the state legislature into a rubber-stamp body that passed a series of laws giving him the power to count ballots and thus determine the outcome of elections. Every state employee knew that his or her job depended on loyalty to "the Kingfish," as Long liked to call himself.

His grasp on Louisiana firm, Long leaped into the national limelight by winning election to the U.S. Senate in 1932, where he quickly introduced a sweeping "soak-the-rich" tax bill that would have outlawed annual personal incomes of more than $1 million and inheritances of more than $5 million. Swift rejection by the Senate triggered his long-range strategy of becoming president by mobilizing the vast numbers of low-income Americans into a Share Our Wealth protest movement. Long's plan was to mount a presidential campaign in

The New Deal dramatically reversed the federal government's stance toward unions. With legislation and political support, the New Deal encouraged an unprecedented wave of union organizing among the nation's working people. When the head of the United Mine Workers, John L. Lewis, told coal miners that "the President wants you to join a union," he exaggerated only a little. New Dealers believed unions would counterbalance the organized might of big corporations by defending working people, maintaining wages, and replacing the bloody violence that often accompanied strikes with economic peace and commercial stability.

1936 that would take enough votes from Roosevelt to tip the election to the Republican candidate. Then in 1940, after four years of Republican failure to alleviate the depression with conservative policies, Long would sweep into the presidency, the savior of a suffering people.

The electoral showdown never came, however. On September 8, 1935, Carl Austin Weiss, a young physician enraged by the dishonor Long had visited on his family by removing his father from the Louisiana bench and suggesting black ancestry, fatally shot Long in a corridor of the Louisiana State House and was immediately gunned down by Long's bodyguards. The long lines of worn and ragged people passing by Long's coffin in the capitol and the smaller number of better-dressed mourners at Weiss's funeral testified to the split in Louisiana along class lines.

Long always answered charges that he was a dictator rather than a man of the people by insisting that the polite ways of conventional democratic rules could never cure the nation's deepest ills. Only forceful means, he insisted, could finally break the hold of the privileged and extend opportunity to everyone. He could point to real achievements in Louisiana. As promised, he taxed the oil companies and utilities that had run Louisiana for decades, and he

Huey Long
The ability to adapt his captivating stump-speech style to the radio made Huey Long the one rival politician who gave Roosevelt serious concern in the mid-1930s. Here Long is shown in 1932 campaigning in Arkansas in support of Hattie Carraway's bid for election to the U.S. Senate. Stigmatized as both a woman and a populist reformer, Carraway seemed a sure loser until Long crossed the border from Louisiana on her behalf. In a mere two weeks of speaking and pressing the flesh, Long brushed aside criticism that he was an interloper and boosted Carraway to victory as part of his crusade to share the wealth.
Corbis.

funneled the revenue into programs to benefit those who had been left out. While he built monuments to his own vanity, Long also addressed many of the state's genuine social needs. At one time, Louisiana's road-building program was the biggest in the nation, and by 1935 the state had ten times more paved roads than when Long became governor. He made Louisiana State University a major institution of higher learning. He greatly expanded the state's pitiful public health facilities. For children, he provided free schoolbooks and new schools. For adults, he started night schools to combat illiteracy.

Disdainful both of Long and of those who turned to him, critics labeled Long a homegrown fascist and called him the "Messiah of the Rednecks." They compared him to Mussolini and Hitler and expressed relief that his life, and thus the damage he and the "rabble" who supported him could do, was cut short. Roosevelt recognized that the New Deal had to reach out to the "forgotten man," but Long reached farther to connect with neglected citizens. He gave Americans the only chance they ever had, for better or worse, to vote for a candidate with a broad national following who offered sweeping change comparable to that of parties on the radical right and left in other countries during the 1930s.

Violent battles on the nation's streets and docks showed the determination of militant labor leaders to organize unions that would protect jobs as well as wages. In 1934, striking workers in Toledo, Minneapolis, San Francisco, and elsewhere were beaten and shot by police and the National Guard. In Congress, labor leaders lobbied for the National Labor Relations Act (NLRA), a bill sponsored by Senator Robert Wagner of New York that authorized the federal government to intervene in labor disputes and supervise the organization of labor unions. Justly considered a "Magna Carta for labor," the Wagner Act, as it came to be called, guaranteed workers the right to organize unions, putting the might of federal law behind the appeals of labor leaders. The Wagner Act created the National Labor Relations Board (NLRB) to sponsor and oversee elections for union representation. If the majority of workers at a company voted for a union, then the union became the sole bargaining agent for the entire workplace, and the employer was required to negotiate with the elected union leaders. Roosevelt signed the Wagner Act in July 1935, providing for the first time federal support for labor organization—the most important New Deal reform of the industrial order.

The achievements that flowed from the Wagner Act and renewed labor militancy were impressive. When Roosevelt became president in 1933, union membership—almost entirely composed of skilled workers in trade unions affiliated with the American Federation of Labor (AFL)—stood at 3 million, down by half since the end of World War I. With the support of the Wagner Act, union membership expanded almost fivefold, to 14 million by the time of Roosevelt's death in 1945. By then, 30 percent of the workforce was unionized, the highest union representation in American history.

Most of the new union members were factory workers and unskilled laborers, many of them immigrants and African Americans. For decades, established AFL unions had no desire to organize factory and unskilled workers, who struggled along without unions. In 1935, under the aggressive leadership of the mine workers' John L. Lewis, and the head of the Amalgamated Clothing Workers, Sidney Hillman, a coalition of unskilled workers formed the Committee for Industrial Organization (CIO; later the Congress of Industrial Organizations). The CIO, helped by the Wagner Act, mobilized organizing drives in major industries. The exceptional courage and organizing skill of labor militants, a few of them Communists, earned the CIO the leadership role in the campaign to organize the bitterly anti-union automobile and steel industries.

The bloody struggle by the CIO-affiliated United Auto Workers (UAW) to organize workers at General Motors climaxed in January 1937 when striking workers occupied the main assembly plant in Flint, Michigan, in a "sit-down" strike that slashed the plant's production of 15,000 cars a week to a mere 150. Stymied, General Motors surrendered and agreed to make the UAW the sole bargaining agent for all the company's workers and to refrain from interfering with union activity. Having subdued the auto industry's leading producer, the UAW expanded its campaign until, after much violence, the entire industry was unionized when the Ford Motor Company capitulated to the union in 1941.

The CIO hoped to ride organizing success in auto plants to victory in the steel mills. But after unionizing the industry giant U.S. Steel, the CIO ran up against fanatic opposition from smaller steel firms. Following a police attack that killed ten strikers at Republic Steel outside Chicago in May 1937, the battered steelworkers halted their organizing campaign. In steel and other major industries, such as the stridently anti-union southern textile mills, organizing efforts stalled until after 1941, when military mobilization created labor shortages that gave workers greater bargaining power.

Social Security and Tax Reform

The single most important feature of the New Deal's emerging welfare state was Social Security. An ambitious, far-reaching, and permanent reform, Social Security was designed to provide a modest income to relieve the poverty of elderly people. Prompted by the popular but impractical panaceas of Dr. Townsend, Father Coughlin, and Huey Long, Roosevelt became the first president to advocate protection for the elderly.

The political struggle for Social Security highlighted class differences among Americans. Support for the measure came from a coalition of advocacy groups for the elderly and the poor, traditional progressives, leftists, social workers, and labor unions. Arrayed against them were economic conservatives, including the Liberty League, the National Association of Manufacturers, the Chamber of Commerce, and the American Medical Association. Enact the Social Security system, these conservatives and their representatives in the Republican Party warned, and the government will gain a whip hand over private property, destroy initiative, and reduce proud individuals to spineless loafers.

The large New Deal majority in Congress carried the day in August 1935. Yet the strong objections to federal involvement in matters traditionally left to individuals and local charities persuaded the framers of Social Security to strike an awkward balance among federal, state, and personal responsibility. The Social Security Act required that pensions for the elderly be funded not by direct government subsidies but instead by tax contributions from workers and their employers. Although this provision subtracted money from consumption—hindering economic recovery—it gave contributing workers a personal stake in the system and made it politically invulnerable. Social Security also created unemployment insurance, paid for by employers' contributions, that provided modest benefits for workers who lost their jobs. In a bow to traditional beliefs about local governments' responsibility for public assistance, Social Security also issued multi-million-dollar grants to the states to use to support dependent children (a program expanded in 1950 to provide "Aid to Families with Dependent Children"), public health services, and the blind. After a Supreme Court decision in 1937 upheld the right of Congress to require all citizens to pay for Social Security through federal taxes, the program was expanded to include benefits for dependent survivors of deceased recipients. Although the first Social Security check (for $41.30) was not issued until 1940, the system gave working people assurance that in the future, when they became too old to work, they would receive a modest income from the government. This safety net protected ordinary working people from fears of a penniless and insecure old age.

Fervent opposition to Social Security struck New Dealers as evidence that the rich had learned little from the depression. Roosevelt had long felt contempt for the moneyed elite who ignored the sufferings of the poor. He looked for a way to redistribute wealth that would weaken conservative opposition, advance the cause of social equity, and defuse political challenges from Huey Long and Father Coughlin. In June 1935, as the Social Security Act was being debated, Roosevelt delivered a message to Congress outlining comprehensive tax reform. Charging that large fortunes put "great and undesirable concentration of control in [the hands of] relatively few individuals," Roosevelt urged a graduated tax on corporations, an inheritance

tax, and an increase in maximum personal income taxes. Congress endorsed Roosevelt's basic principle by taxing those with higher incomes at a somewhat higher rate.

Neglected Americans and the New Deal

While the WPA and other work relief programs aided working people, the average unemployment rate for the 1930s stayed high—17 percent, about one of every six workers. Even many working people remained more or less untouched by New Deal benefits. Workers in industries that resisted unions received little help from the Wagner Act or the WPA. Domestic workers—almost all of them women—and agricultural workers—many of them African, Hispanic, or Asian Americans—were neither unionized nor eligible for Social Security. The patchwork of New Deal reforms erected a two-tier welfare state. In the top tier, organized workers in major industries were the greatest beneficiaries of New Deal initiatives. In the bottom tier, millions of neglected Americans—women, children, old folks, the unorganized, unskilled, uneducated, and unemployed—often fell through the New Deal safety net.

The New Deal neglected few citizens more than African Americans. About half of black Americans in cities were jobless, double the unemployment rate among whites. In the rural South, where the vast majority of African Americans lived, conditions were worse. New Deal agricultural policies like the AAA favored landowners and often resulted in black sharecroppers and tenants being pushed off land they farmed.

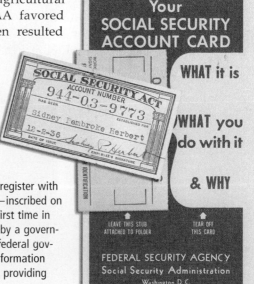

Social Security Card

The Social Security Act required each working American who participated in the system to register with the government and obtain a unique number—the "SSN" familiar to every citizen today—inscribed on an identity card, making benefits portable from one job and one state to another. For the first time in the nation's history, millions of ordinary citizens were numbered, registered, and identified by a government bureaucracy, creating a personal, individualized connection between people and the federal government. Administering the massive agency needed to collect, monitor, and regulate this information and distribute the benefits that flowed from it gave government jobs to tens of thousands, providing security for government workers as well as for Social Security beneficiaries.

Picture Research Consultants & Archives.

Disfranchisement by intimidation and legal sub-terfuge prevented southern blacks from protest-ing their plight at the ballot box. Protest risked vi-cious retaliation from local whites. Only 11 of more than 10,000 WPA supervisors in the South were black, even though African Americans com-prised about a third of the region's population. Up north, a riot in 1935 that focused on white-owned businesses in Harlem dramatized blacks'

Mary McLeod Bethune

At the urging of Eleanor Roosevelt, Mary McLeod Bethune, a southern educational and civil rights leader, became director of the National Youth Administration's Division of Negro Affairs. The first black woman to head a federal agency, Bethune used her position to promote social change. Here Bethune takes her mission to the streets to protest the discriminatory hiring prac-tices of the Peoples Drug Store chain in the nation's capital.

Moorland-Spingarn Research Center, Howard University.

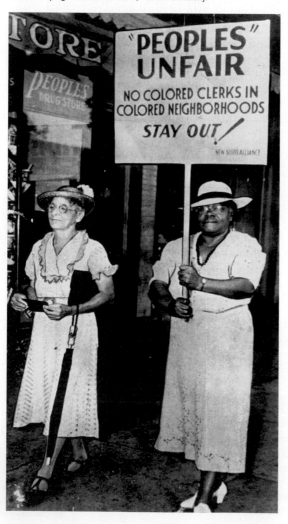

resentment and despair. Bitter critics charged that the New Deal's NRA stood for "Negro Run Around" or "Negroes Ruined Again."

Roosevelt responded to such criticisms with great caution since New Deal reforms required the political support of powerful conservative, segregationist, southern Democrats, who would be alienated by programs that aided blacks. A white Georgia relief worker expressed the com-mon view that "Any Nigger who gets over $8 a week is a spoiled Nigger, that's all." Stymied by the political clout of entrenched white racism, New Dealers still tried to attract political support from black leaders. Roosevelt's overtures to African Americans prompted northern black voters to shift in the 1934 elections from the Republican to the Democratic Party, helping elect New Deal Democrats.

Eleanor Roosevelt sponsored the appoint-ment of Mary McLeod Bethune—the energetic cofounder of the National Council on Negro Women—as head of the Division of Negro Affairs in the National Youth Administration. The highest-ranking black official in Roosevelt's administration, Bethune used her position to guide a small number of black professionals and civil rights activists to posts within New Deal agencies. Nicknamed the "Black Cabinet," these men and women comprised the first sizable representation of African Americans in white-collar posts in the federal government, and they ultimately helped about one in four African Americans get access to New Deal relief pro-grams.

Despite these gains, by 1940 African Ameri-cans still suffered severe handicaps. Most of the 13 million black workers toiled at low-paying menial jobs, unprotected by the New Deal safety net. Infant mortality was 50 percent greater than for whites, and life expectancy was twelve years shorter. Making a mockery of the "separate but equal" doctrine, segregated black schools had less money and worse facilities than white schools, and only 1 percent of black students earned college degrees. In southern states, there were no black police officers or judges and hardly any black lawyers, and vigilante violence against blacks went unpunished. To these prob-lems of black Americans, the New Deal offered few remedies.

Hispanic Americans fared no better. About a million Mexican Americans lived in the United States in the 1930s, most of them first-or second-generation immigrants who worked at stoop labor tending crops throughout the West. During the depression, field workers saw their low wages plunge lower still to about a dime an hour. To preserve scarce jobs for U.S. citizens, the federal government choked off immigration from Mexico while state and local officials prohibited employment of aliens on work relief projects and summarily deported tens of thousands of Mexican Americans, many with their American-born children. Local white administrators of many New Deal programs throughout the West discriminated against Hispanics and other people of color. A New Deal study concluded that "The Mexican is…segregated from the rest of the community as effectively as the Negro…[by] poverty and low wages."

Asian Americans had similar experiences. Asian immigrants were still excluded from U.S. citizenship and in many states were not permitted to own land. Although by 1930 more than half of Japanese Americans had been born in the United States, they were still liable to discrimination. Even college-educated Asian Americans worked in family shops, restaurants, and laundries. One young Asian American expressed frustrations felt by many others: "I am a fruitstand worker. I would much rather it were doctor or lawyer…but my aspirations [were] frustrated long ago by circumstances [and] I am only what I am, a professional carrot washer."

Native Americans—like blacks, Hispanics, and Asian Americans—suffered neglect from New Deal agencies. As a group, they remained the poorest of the poor. Since the Dawes Act of 1887, the federal government had encouraged Native Americans to assimilate, to abandon their Indian identities and adopt the cultural norms of the majority society. Under the leadership of the New Deal's commissioner of Indian affairs, John Collier, the New Deal's Indian Reorganization Act (IRA) of 1934 largely reversed that policy. Collier claimed that "the most interesting and important fact about Indians" was that they "do not expect much, often they expect nothing at all; yet they are able to be happy." Given such views, the IRA provided little economic aid to Native Americans, but it did restore their right to own land communally and to have greater control over their own affairs. The IRA brought little immediate benefit to Native Americans and remained a divisive issue for decades, but it did provide an important foundation for Indians'

Hispanic-American Alliance Banner
Between 1910 and 1940, when refugees from the Mexican revolution poured across the American border, the Hispanic-American Alliance and other organizations sought to protect Mexican Americans' rights against nativist fears and hostility. In the years between the world wars, many alliance banners like this one flew in opposition to the deportation of Mexican aliens, to an attempt in 1926 to bar Mexican Americans from city jobs in Los Angeles, and to the disproportionately high use of the death penalty against Mexicans convicted of crimes. Throughout these and other trials, the alliance steadfastly emphasized the desire of Mexican Americans to receive permanent status in the United States.
The Oakland Museum.

economic, cultural, and political resurgence a generation later.

REVIEW How did Roosevelt try to extend the social safety net in his second term?

John Collier Meets with Navajo Representatives
Commissioner of Indian Affairs John Collier receives a Navajo delegation protesting restrictions in the Indian Reorganization Act of 1934. The Navajos display a blanket made from the wool of their own sheep to protest limits on the number of sheep they could raise. Collier had crafted the act to revive Native American society by granting tribes an independent land base and many self-governing powers. However, his attempt to make the reservations economically viable through conservation measures, including restrictions on grass-devouring sheep, roused resistance by Indians who chose traditional ways of using resources. The tension between federal benevolence and Indians' views of their own ways of life remains a painful issue.
Wide World Photos, Inc.

The New Deal from Victory to Deadlock

To accelerate the sputtering economic recovery, Roosevelt shifted the emphasis of the New Deal in the mid-1930s. Instead of seeking cooperation from conservative business leaders, he decided to rely on the growing New Deal coalition to enact reforms over the strident opposition of Republicans and corporate interests.

Added to New Deal strength in farm states and big cities were some new allies on the left. Throughout Roosevelt's first term, socialists and Communists denounced the slow pace of change and accused the New Deal of failing to serve the interests of the workers who produced the nation's wealth. But in 1935 the Soviet Union, worried about the threat of fascism in Europe, instructed Communists throughout the world to join hands with non-Communist progressives in a "Popular Front" to advance the fortunes of the working class. With varying degrees of enthusiasm, many radicals switched from opposing the New Deal to supporting its relief programs and encouragement of labor unions.

Roosevelt's conservative opponents reacted to the massing of New Deal force by intensifying their opposition to the welfare state. To Roosevelt, the situation seemed part of a drama that had played out since the nation's beginning, pitting a Hamiltonian faction of wealth and privilege against the heirs of Jefferson who, like Roosevelt himself, favored a more equitable distribution of wealth and opportunity.

The Election of 1936

Roosevelt believed that the presidential election of 1936 would test his leadership and progressive ideals. The depression still had a stranglehold on the economy. Nearly 8 million remained jobless, and millions more were stuck in poverty. Conservative leaders believed that the New Deal's failure to lift the nation out of the depression indicated that Americans were ready for a change. Left-wing critics insisted that the New Deal had missed the opportunity to displace capitalism with a socialist economy and would lose votes to candidates who recommended more radical remedies.

Republicans turned to the Kansas heartland to select Governor Alfred (Alf) Landon as their presidential nominee. A moderate who had supported some New Deal measures, Landon stressed mainstream Republican proposals to achieve a balanced federal budget and to ease the perils of illness and old age with old-fashioned neighborliness instead of faceless government bureaucracies like Social Security.

Roosevelt put his faith in the growing coalition of New Deal supporters, who he believed

Faces of the Depression

New Deal agencies dispatched dozens of photographers to document the lives of Americans during the 1930s. In thousands of pictures, the photographers captured the faces of the depression. Their photographs, the sources of the portraits shown here, demonstrate that working Americans were not faceless drones but human individuals struggling to survive—whether dispossessed black sharecroppers in the South, Japanese American mothers and daughters in California produce fields, Mexican laborers in the Southwest, or mothers and children in California labor camps. As these portraits suggest, working people knew that, while the New Deal might provide welcome aid, they depended in the end on their own resourcefulness and the support of family and friends.

Library of Congress.

shared his conviction that the New Deal was the nation's liberator from a long era of privilege and wealth for a few and "economic slavery" for the rest. At the end of the campaign, Roosevelt assailed his "old enemies...business and financial monopoly, speculation, reckless banking, [and] class antagonism," and proclaimed, "Never before in all our history have these forces been so united against one candidate as they stand today. They are unanimous in their hate for me—and I welcome their hatred."

Roosevelt triumphed spectacularly. He won 60.8 percent of the popular vote, 11 million more votes than Landon, the widest presidential margin to date. He carried the electoral votes of every state except Maine and Vermont. Third parties—including the Socialists and the Communists—fell pitifully short of the support they expected and never again mounted a significant challenge to the New Deal. Congressional results were equally lopsided, with Democrats outnumbering Republicans more than three to one in both houses.

In his inaugural address, Roosevelt pledged to use his mandate to help all citizens achieve a decent standard of living. He announced, "I see one third of a nation ill-housed, ill-clad, [and] ill-nourished," and he promised to devote his second term to alleviate their wants.

Court Packing

In the afterglow of his reelection triumph, Roosevelt pondered how to remove the remaining obstacles to New Deal reforms. He decided to target the Supreme Court. Laden with conservative justices appointed by Republican presidents, the Court had invalidated eleven New Deal measures as unconstitutional interferences with free enterprise. Now, Social Security, the Wagner Act, the Securities and Exchange Commission, and other New Deal innovations were moving toward an ominous rendezvous with the justices.

Roosevelt concluded that he must do something to ensure that the Supreme Court's "horse and buggy" notions did not dismantle the New Deal. He proposed that one new justice be added for each existing judge who had already served for ten years and was over the age of seventy. In effect, the proposed law would give Roosevelt the power to pack the Court with up to six New Dealers who could outvote the elderly, conservative, Republican justices.

But the president had not reckoned with Americans' deeply rooted deference to the independent authority of the Supreme Court. More than two-thirds of Americans believed the Court should be free from political interference. Even New Deal supporters were disturbed by the "court-packing" scheme. The suggestion that individuals over seventy had diminished mental capacity also offended many elderly members of Congress. Although Roosevelt insisted that the bill was intended to improve the efficiency of an "overworked" Court, the real purpose was to make room for supporters of New Deal initiatives. A storm of public protest whipped up by conservatives prompted the heavily Democratic Senate to defeat the bill.

Although Roosevelt's court-packing plan failed, Supreme Court justices nonetheless got Roosevelt's message. After the furor abated, Chief Justice Charles Evans Hughes and fellow moderate Owen Roberts moderated their views enough to keep the Court from invalidating the Wagner Act and Social Security. Then the most conservative of the elderly justices—the "four horsemen of reaction," one New Dealer called them—retired. Roosevelt eventually named eight justices to the Court—more than any other president. His choice of liberals to fill vacancies on the Court ultimately gave safe passage to New Deal laws through the shoals of judicial review.

Reaction and Recession

Emboldened by their defeat of the court-packing plan, Republicans and southern Democrats rallied around their common conservatism to obstruct additional reforms. Arguments over whether the New Deal needed to be expanded—and, if so, how—undermined consensus among reformers and sparked antagonism between Congress and the White House. The ominous rise of belligerent regimes in Germany, Italy, Japan, and elsewhere slowed reform as some Americans began to worry more about defending the nation than changing it.

Roosevelt himself favored slowing the pace of the New Deal. He believed that existing New Deal measures had steadily boosted the economy and largely eliminated the depression crisis. In fact, the gross national product in 1937 briefly equaled the 1929 level, before drooping lower for the rest of the decade. Unemployment declined to 14 percent in 1937 but quickly spiked upward and stayed higher until 1940. Roosevelt's unwarranted optimism about the economic recovery persuaded him that additional deficit spending by the federal government was no longer necessary. Accordingly, Roosevelt moved cautiously toward a balanced budget by cutting funds for relief projects.

Roosevelt's retrenchment soon backfired. The reduction in deficit spending reversed the improving economy. Even at the high-water mark of recovery in the summer of 1937, 7 million people lacked jobs. In the next few months, national income and production slipped backward so steeply that almost two-thirds of the economic gains since 1933 were lost by June 1938.

This economic reversal hurt the New Deal politically. Conservatives argued that this recession proved New Deal measures produced only an illusion of progress. The way to weather the recession was to tax and spend less and wait for the natural laws of supply and demand to restore prosperity. Many New Dealers insisted instead that the continuing depression demanded that Roosevelt revive federal spending and redouble efforts to stimulate the economy. In 1938, Congress heeded such pleas and enacted a massive new program of federal spending.

The New Deal's ad hoc methods received support from new economic ideas advanced by the brilliant British economist John Maynard Keynes. In his influential work *The General Theory of Employment, Interest, and Money* (1936), Keynes made a sophisticated, theoretical argument in favor of practices that New Deal relief agencies had developed in a commonsense way. Keynes declared that the depression illustrated that a nation's economic activity could become stalled at a level far short of its true potential. When that happened, only government intervention could pump enough money into the system to restore prosperity.

Roosevelt never had the inclination or the time to follow his economic advisers into the thicket of **Keynesian** theory. But the recession scare of 1938 taught the president the Keynesian lesson that economic growth had to be carefully nurtured.

The Last of the New Deal Reforms

From the moment he was sworn in, Roosevelt sought to expand the powers of the presidency. He believed that the president needed more authority to meet emergencies such as the depression and to administer the sprawling federal bureaucracy. In September 1938 Congress passed the Administrative Reorganization Act, which gave Roosevelt (and future presidents) new influence over the bureaucracy. Combined with a Democratic majority in Congress, a now friendly Supreme Court, and the revival of deficit spending, the newly empowered White House seemed to be in a good position to move ahead with a revitalized New Deal.

Resistance to further reform was also on the rise, however. Conservatives argued that the New Deal had pressed government centralization too far. Even the New Deal's friends became weary of one emergency program after another. By the midpoint of Roosevelt's second term, restive members of Congress balked at new initiatives. Clearly, the New Deal was losing momentum, but enough energy remained for one last burst of reform.

In 1937, the Agriculture Department created the Farm Security Administration (FSA) to provide housing and loans to help tenant farmers become independent. But the FSA was starved for funds and ran up against the major farm organizations intent on serving their own interests. For those who owned farms, the New Deal offered renewed prosperity with a second Agricultural Adjustment Act (AAA) in 1938. To moderate price swings by regulating supply, the plan combined production quotas on five staple crops—cotton, tobacco, wheat, corn, and rice—with storage loans through its Commodity Credit Corporation. The most prosperous farmers benefited most, but the act's Federal Surplus Commodities Corporation added an element of charity by issuing food stamps so that the poor could obtain surplus food. The AAA of 1938 brought stability to American agriculture and ample food to most—but not all—tables.

Advocates for the urban poor also made modest gains after decades of neglect. New York senator Robert Wagner convinced Congress to pass the National Housing Act in 1937. By 1941, some 160,000 residences had been made available to poor people at affordable rents. The project did not come close to meeting the need for affordable housing, but for the first time the federal government took an active role in providing decent urban housing.

The last major piece of New Deal labor legislation, the Fair Labor Standards Act of June 1938, reiterated the New Deal pledge to provide workers with a decent standard of living. After lengthy haggling and compromise that revealed the waning strength of the New Deal, Congress finally agreed to intervene in the long-sacrosanct realm of worker contracts. The new law set wage and hours standards and at long last curbed the use of child labor. The minimum-wage level was modest—twenty-five cents an hour for a maximum of forty-four hours a week. And, in order to attract enough conservative votes, the act exempted merchant seamen, fishermen, domestic help, and farm laborers—relegating most women and African Americans to lower wages. Nevertheless, the Fair Labor Standards Act advanced Roosevelt's inaugural promise to improve the living standards of the poorest Americans.

The final New Deal reform effort failed to make much headway against the hidebound system of racial segregation. Although Roosevelt denounced lynching as murder, he would not jeopardize his vital base of southern political support by demanding antilynching legislation. In 1934 and 1935, Congress voted down attempts to make lynching a federal crime, and in 1938 the last antilynching bill of the decade died in a Senate filibuster. Laws to eliminate the poll tax—used to deny blacks the opportunity to vote—encountered the same overwhelming resistance. The New Deal refused to confront the injustice of racial segregation with the same vigor it brought to bear on economic hardship.

By the end of 1938, the New Deal had lost steam and encountered stiff opposition. In the congressional elections of 1938, Republicans picked up seven seats in the Senate and eighty in the House, giving them more congressional influence than they had enjoyed since 1932. New Dealers could claim unprecedented and resounding achievements since 1933, but nobody needed reminding that those achievements had not ended the depression. In his annual message to Congress in January 1939, Roosevelt signaled a halt to New Deal reforms by speaking about preserving the progress already achieved rather than extending it. He pointed to the threat posed by fascist aggressors in Europe and Asia, and he proposed defense expenditures that surpassed New Deal appropriations for relief and economic recovery.

REVIEW   How did Roosevelt attempt to insulate New Deal reforms from legal challenges?

Conclusion: Achievements and Limitations of the New Deal

The New Deal replaced the fear symbolized by Hoover's expulsion of the Bonus Army with Roosevelt's confidence, optimism, and energetic pragmatism. A growing majority of Americans agreed with Roosevelt that the federal government should help those in need, thereby strengthening the political coalition that propelled the New Deal. In the process of seeking relief for victims of the depression, recovery of the general economy, and basic reform of major economic institutions, the New Deal vastly expanded the size and influence of the federal government and changed the way the American people viewed Washington. New Dealers achieved significant victories such as Social Security, labor's right to organize, and guarantees that farm prices would be maintained through controls on production and marketing. New Deal measures marked the emergence of a welfare state, but the New Deal's limited, two-tier character left many needy Americans with little aid.

Full-scale relief, recovery, and reform eluded New Deal programs. Even though millions of Americans benefited directly from the alphabet soup of agencies and programs, both relief and recovery were limited and temporary. In 1940 the depression still plagued the economy. The most durable New Deal achievements were reforms that stabilized agriculture, encouraged the organization of labor unions, and created the safety net of Social Security and fair labor standards. Perhaps the most impressive achievement of the New Deal was what did not happen: Authoritarian governments and anti-capitalist policies were common during the 1930s outside the United States, but they were shunned by the New Deal. The greatest economic crisis the nation had ever faced did not cause Americans to abandon democracy, as happened in Germany, where Adolf Hitler seized dictatorial power. Nor did the nation turn to radical alternatives such as socialism or communism.

Republicans and other conservatives claimed that the New Deal amounted to a form of socialism that threatened democracy and capitalism. But rather than attack capitalism, Franklin Roosevelt sought to save it, and he succeeded.

That success also marked the limits of the New Deal's achievements. Like his cousin Teddy, Franklin Roosevelt understood that a strengthened national government was necessary to curb the destructive tendencies of concentrated economic power. A shift of authority toward the federal government, both Roosevelts believed, would allow capitalist enterprises to be balanced by the nation's democratic tradition. The New Deal stopped far short of challenging capitalism either by undermining private property or by imposing strict national planning.

New Dealers repeatedly described their programs as a kind of warfare against the economic adversities of the 1930s. In the next decade, with the depression only partly vanquished, the Roosevelt administration had to turn from the New Deal's war against economic crisis at home to participate in a worldwide conflagration to defeat the enemies of democracy abroad.

Suggestions for Further Reading

William H. Chafe, ed., *The Achievement of American Liberalism: The New Deal and Its Legacies* (2003). A collection of essays that examine the New Deal in historical perspective.

Lizbeth Cohen, *Making a New Deal: Industrial Workers in Chicago, 1919–1939* (1990). An insightful case study of Chicago industrial workers and New Deal policies.

Alonzo Hamby, *For the Survival of Democracy: Franklin Roosevelt and the World Crisis of the 1930s* (2004). A useful analysis of the global challenges confronted by the New Deal.

David M. Kennedy, *Freedom from Fear: The American People in Depression and War, 1929–1945* (1999). A Pulitzer Prize–winning survey of Americans during Roosevelt's administrations.

Alice Kessler-Harris, *In Pursuit of Equity: Women, Men, and the Quest for Economic Citizenship in Twentieth Century America* (2001). A revealing account of working people's struggle for economic rights.

Clyde P. Weed, *The Nemesis of Reform: The Republican Party during the New Deal* (1994). A valuable study of the New Deal's most powerful political opponents.

▶ FOR MORE BOOKS ABOUT TOPICS IN THIS CHAPTER, see the Online Study Guide at bedfordstmartins.com/roarkcompact.

▶ FOR ADDITIONAL FIRSTHAND ACCOUNTS OF THIS PERIOD, see Chapter 24 in Michael Johnson, ed., *Reading the American Past,* Third Edition.

▶ FOR WEB SITES AND DOCUMENTS RELATED TO TOPICS AND PLACES IN THIS CHAPTER, see "History Links," "DocLinks," and "PlaceLinks" at bedfordstmartins.com/roarkcompact.

REVIEWING THE CHAPTER

Follow these steps to review and strengthen your understanding of the chapter.

STEP 1: *Study the* **Key Terms** *and* **Timeline** *to identify the significance of each item listed.*

STEP 2: *Answer the* **Review Questions**, *drawing on key terms and dates to support your answers.*

STEP 3: *Drawing on the Key Terms, Timeline, and Review Questions, answer the broader* **Making Connections** *questions.*

KEY TERMS

Who

Bonus Marchers (p. 619)
Herbert Hoover (p. 619)
Douglas MacArthur (p. 620)
Franklin Delano Roosevelt (p. 621)
Harry Hopkins (p. 624)
Frances Perkins (p. 624)
Eleanor Roosevelt (p. 624)
Okies (p. 630)
Upton Sinclair (p. 631)
Charles Coughlin (p. 631)
Francis Townsend (p. 632)
Huey Long (p. 632)
Robert Wagner (p. 635)
Mary McLeod Bethune (p. 638)
John Collier (p. 639)
Alfred (Alf) Landon (p. 640)
John Maynard Keynes (p. 643)

What

Bonus Army (p. 619)
New Deal coalition (p. 623)
the Hundred Days (p. 624)
"Brains Trust" (p. 624)
Emergency Banking Act (p. 625)

Federal Deposit Insurance Corporation (FDIC) (p. 625)
fireside chats (p. 626)
Securities and Exchange Commission (SEC) (p. 626)
Federal Emergency Relief Administration (FERA) (p. 626)
Civil Works Administration (CWA) (p. 626)
Civilian Conservation Corps (CCC) (p. 626)
Tennessee Valley Authority (TVA) (p. 627)
Rural Electrification Administration (REA) (p. 627)
Agricultural Adjustment Act (AAA) (p. 627)
Commodity Credit Corporation (p. 628)
Farm Credit Act (FCA) (p. 628)
National Recovery Administration (NRA) (p. 629)
American Liberty League (p. 630)
Southern Farm Tenants Union (p. 630)
National Union for Social Justice (Union Party) (p. 632)

Works Progress Administration (WPA) (p. 633)
Wagner Act/National Labor Relations Act (NLRA) (p. 635)
Committee for Industrial Organization (CIO) (p. 636)
"sit-down" strike (p. 636)
Social Security (p. 636)
unemployment insurance (p. 637)
Division of Negro Affairs (p. 638)
"Black Cabinet" (p. 638)
Indian Reorganization Act (IRA) (p. 639)
"Popular Front" (p. 640)
Administrative Reorganization Act (p. 643)
Farm Security Administration (FSA) (p. 643)
second Agricultural Adjustment Act (AAA) (p. 643)
Commodity Credit Corporation (p. 643)
National Housing Act (p. 643)
Fair Labor Standards Act (p. 643)

TIMELINE

1932 • Bonus Army marches on Washington.

1933 • Democrat Franklin D. Roosevelt assumes presidency.
• **March–June.** Legislation of the Hundred Days establishes New Deal.
• Roosevelt closes nation's banks for four-day "holiday."
• Federal Emergency Relief Administration (FERA) established.

1934 • Securities and Exchange Commission (SEC) created.
• Upton Sinclair loses bid for governorship of California.
• Wealthy conservatives of American Liberty League oppose New Deal.
• Dr. Francis Townsend devises Old Age Revolving Pension scheme.
• Indian Reorganization Act.

REVIEW QUESTIONS

1. Why did Franklin D. Roosevelt win the 1932 presidential election by such a large margin? (pp. 621–24)

2. How did the New Dealers try to steer the nation toward recovery from the Great Depression? (pp. 624–29)

3. Why did the New Deal face criticism from both ends of the political spectrum? (pp. 629–32)

4. How did Roosevelt try to extend the social safety net in his second term? (pp. 632–39)

5. How did Roosevelt attempt to insulate New Deal reforms from legal challenges? (pp. 640–44)

MAKING CONNECTIONS

1. Franklin Roosevelt's landslide victory in 1932 changed the political landscape. How did Roosevelt build an effective interregional political coalition for the Democratic Party? How did the challenges of balancing interests within the coalition shape the policies of the New Deal? In your answer, discuss the character of the coalition and specific reforms.

2. New Dealers experimented with varied solutions to the economic disorder of the 1930s. Compare reform efforts targeting rural and industrial America. Were they effective? Why or why not? What do they reveal about how the Roosevelt administration understood the underlying causes of the Great Depression?

3. Although the New Deal enjoyed astonishing popularity, some Americans were consistently critical of Roosevelt's reforms. Why? In your answer, discuss three opponents of the New Deal, being attentive to changes over time in their opinions. Were they able to influence the New Deal? How?

4. Although the New Deal extended help to many Americans, all did not benefit equally from the era's reforms. Who remained outside the reach of New Deal assistance? Why? In your answer, consider how politics shaped the limits of reform, both in constituents' ability to demand assistance and in the federal government's response to their demands.

> ► **FOR PRACTICE QUIZZES, A CUSTOMIZED STUDY PLAN, AND OTHER STUDY TOOLS**, see the Online Study Guide at **bedfordstmartins.com/roarkcompact**.

1935 • Louisiana senator Huey Long assassinated.
• Legislation creates Works Progress Administration (WPA).
• Wagner Act.
• Committee for Industrial Organization (CIO) founded.
• Social Security Act.
• Father Charles Coughlin begins National Union for Social Justice.

       1936 • John Maynard Keynes publishes *The General Theory of Employment, Interest, and Money.*
          • Franklin Roosevelt elected to a second term by a landslide.

            1937 • CIO stages successful sit-down strike at General Motors plant in Flint, Michigan.
              • Roosevelt's court-packing legislation defeated in Senate.

         1937–1938 • Economic recession slows recovery from depression.

                  1938 • Second Agricultural Adjustment Act and Fair Labor Standards Act.
                     • Congress rejects administration's antilynching bill.
                     • Administrative Reorganization Act.

GI WEB GEAR

Millions of American GIs strapped on web belts hooked with canteens, knives, and other military gear as they went into battle. Navy medical corpsman Leo H. Scheer wore this belt when Allied forces stormed the Normandy beaches on D Day, June 6, 1944. Scheer's landing craft sank as it approached Omaha Beach, and he swam ashore wearing this web gear. Once on land, he grabbed unused bandages from the belts of dead soldiers to bind the wounds of the living. The pockets of this belt are still stuffed with the bandages Scheer collected while Americans and their allies secured the beach and launched the great western offensive against Nazi Germany.

Jackson Hill / The National D-Day Museum.

25

The United States and the Second World War

1939–1945

O N A SUN-DRENCHED FLORIDA AFTERNOON in January 1927, Paul Tibbets took his first airplane ride. Twelve-year-old Tibbets cinched on a leather helmet, clambered into the front seat of the open cockpit of a cloth-covered red, white, and blue biplane, and sailed aloft over Miami. While the barn-storming pilot sitting behind him brought the plane in low over the Hialeah race track, Tibbets pitched Baby Ruth candy bars tethered to small paper parachutes to racing fans in the grandstands below. After two more candy-bar drops over the race track, the pilot raced to the beach and swooped down to 200 feet as Tibbets tossed out the remaining candy bars and watched the bathers scramble for chocolate from heaven. After Tibbets and the pilot repeated their stunt for a week, sales of Baby Ruths soared for Tibbets's father's candy business, and Tibbets was hooked on flying.

Born in Quincy, Illinois, in 1915, Tibbets entered the University of Florida in 1933 and took flying lessons at the Gainesville airport. He continued to fly in his spare time and in 1937 decided to join the Army Air Corps to become a military pilot. Shortly after the Japanese attack on Pearl Harbor, Tibbets led a squadron of airplanes flying antisubmarine patrol against German U-boats lurking along the East Coast. When the heavily armored B-17 Flying Fortress bombers began to come off American assembly lines early in 1942, he took a squadron of the new planes from the United States to England. On August 17, 1942, he led the first American daytime bombing raid on German-occupied Europe, releasing 1,100 pounds of bombs from his B-17, nicknamed "Butcher Shop," on the railroad yards of Rouen in northern France—the first of some 700,000 tons of explosives dropped by American bombers during the air war in Europe.

After numerous raids over Europe, Tibbets was reassigned to the North African campaign, where his duties included ferrying the American commander, General Dwight D. Eisenhower, into the battle zone. After eight months of combat missions, Tibbets returned to the United States and was ordered to test the new B-29 Super Fortress being built in Wichita, Kansas. The B-29 was much bigger than the B-17 and could fly higher and faster, making it ideal for the campaign against Japan. Tibbets's mastery of the B-29 caused him to be singled out in September 1944 to command a top-secret unit training for a special mission.

The mission, officials confided to Tibbets, was to be ready to drop on Japan a bomb that was so powerful it might bring the war to an end. No such bomb yet existed, but American scientists and engineers were working then execute a dangerous, sharp, diving turn of 155 degrees that tested the limits of the aircraft but moved it beyond the range of the expected blast.

In May 1945, Tibbets took his B-29s and men to Tinian Island and trained for their secret mission by flying raids over Japanese cities and dropping ordinary bombs. The atomic bomb arrived on Tinian on July 26, just ten days after the successful test explosion in the New Mexico desert. Nicknamed "Little Boy," the bomb packed the equivalent of 40 million pounds of TNT or 200,000 of the 200-pound bombs Tibbets and other American airmen dropped on Europe.

At 2:30 a.m. on August 6, 1945, Tibbets, his crew, and their atomic payload took off in the B-29 bomber *Enola Gay* and headed for Japan. Less than seven hours later, over the city of Hiroshima, Tibbets and his men released Little Boy from the *Enola Gay*'s bomb bay. The plane bucked upward after dropping the 4.5-ton explosive, while Tibbets banked the plane sharply to the right and struggled to maintain control as the shock wave from the explosion blasted past and a purple cloud mushroomed nearly ten miles into the air. Three days later, Tibbets's men dropped a second atomic bomb on Nagasaki, and in five days Japan surrendered.

Paul Tibbets's experiences traced an arc followed by millions of his fellow Americans during World War II, from the innocence of bombarding Miami with candy bars to the deadly nuclear firestorms that rained down on Japan. Like Tibbets, Americans joined their allies to fight the Axis powers in Europe and Asia. Like his *Enola Gay* crewmen—who hailed from New York, Texas, California, New Jersey, New Mexico, Maryland, North Carolina, Pennsylvania, Michigan, and Nevada—Americans from all regions united to defeat the **fascist** aggressors. American industries mobilized to produce advanced bombers—like the ones Tibbets piloted over Europe, North Africa, and Japan—along with enough other military equipment to supply the American armed forces and their allies. At enormous cost in human life and suffering, the war brought full employment and prosperity to Americans at home, ending the depression, providing new opportunities for women, and ushering the nation into the postwar world as a triumphant economic and—on the wings of Paul Tibbets's *Enola Gay*—atomic superpower.

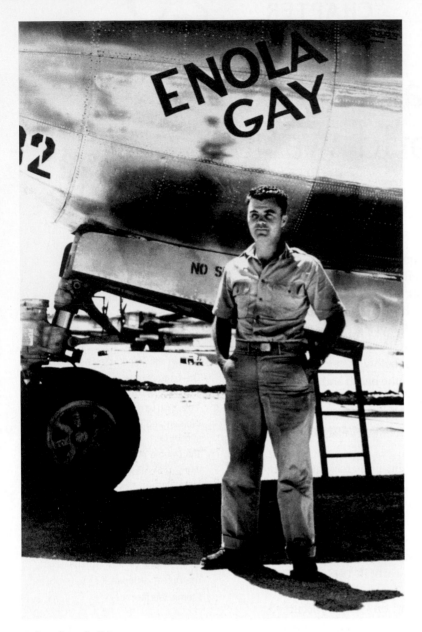

Colonel Paul Tibbets

Before taking off to drop the world's first atomic bomb on Hiroshima, Colonel Paul Tibbets posed on the tarmac next to his customized B-29 Super Fortress bomber, named *Enola Gay* in honor of his mother. A crew of eleven handpicked airmen accompanied Tibbets in the *Enola Gay* on their top-secret mission. After the war, President Harry S. Truman invited Tibbets to the White House and told him, "Don't you ever lose any sleep over the fact that you planned and carried out that mission. It was my decision. You had no choice."

© Bettmann/Corbis.

around the clock to build one. Tibbets kept this secret from his men but took them and his B-29s to Utah to develop a way to drop such a powerful weapon without getting blown up by it. Tibbets trained his pilots to fly at 31,000 feet,

Peacetime Dilemmas

The First World War left a dangerous and ultimately deadly legacy. The victors—especially Britain, France, and the United States—sought to avoid future wars at almost any cost. The defeated nations as well as those who felt humiliated by the Versailles peace settlement—particularly Germany, Italy, and Japan—aspired to reassert their power and avenge their losses by means of renewed warfare. Japan invaded the northern Chinese province of Manchuria in 1931 with ambitions to expand throughout Asia. Italy, led by the fascist Benito Mussolini since 1922, hungered for an empire in Africa. In Germany, National Socialist Adolf Hitler rose to power in 1933 in a quest to dominate Europe and the world. These aggressive, militaristic, antidemocratic regimes seemed a smaller threat to most people in the United States during the 1930s than the economic crisis at home. Shielded from external threats by the Atlantic and Pacific oceans, Americans hoped to avoid entanglement in foreign woes and to concentrate on climbing out of the nation's economic abyss.

Roosevelt and Reluctant Isolation

Like most Americans during the 1930s, Franklin Roosevelt believed that the nation's highest priority was to attack the domestic causes and consequences of the depression. But unlike most Americans, Roosevelt had long advocated an active role for the United States in international affairs. After World War I, Roosevelt embraced Woodrow Wilson's vision that the United States should take the lead in making the world "safe for democracy," and he continued to advocate American membership in the League of Nations during the **isolationist** 1920s.

The depression forced Roosevelt to retreat from his previous internationalism. He came to believe that energetic involvement in foreign affairs diverted resources and political support from domestic recovery. During his 1932 presidential campaign, he pulled back from his endorsement of the League of Nations and reversed his previous support for forgiving European war debts. Once in office, Roosevelt sought to combine domestic economic recovery with a low-profile foreign policy that encouraged free trade and disarmament.

In pursuit of international amity, Roosevelt was constrained by economic circumstances and American popular opinion. After an opinion poll demonstrated popular support for recognizing the Soviet Union—an international pariah since the Bolshevik Revolution in 1917—Roosevelt established formal diplomatic relations in 1933. But when the League of Nations condemned Japanese and German aggression, Roosevelt did not enlist the nation in the League's attempts to keep the peace because he feared jeopardizing isolationists' support for **New Deal** measures in Congress. America watched from the sidelines when Japan and Germany withdrew from the League and expanded their military forces. Roosevelt worried that the League's inability to curb German and Japanese violations of league sanctions and the Versailles settlement threatened world peace. But he reassured Americans that the nation would not "use its armed forces for the settlement of any [international] dispute anywhere."

The Good Neighbor Policy

In his 1933 inaugural address, Franklin Roosevelt announced that the United States would pursue "the policy of the good neighbor" in international relations. A few weeks later, he emphasized that this policy applied specifically to Latin America, where U.S. military forces had often intervened in local affairs. Now, Roosevelt said, the old policy of arrogant intervention would be replaced by a "helping hand" extended in a desire for friendly cooperation to create "more order in this hemisphere and less dislike." In December 1933 at the Inter-American Conference in Montevideo, Uruguay, Secretary of State Cordell Hull formalized the good-neighbor pledge that no nation had the right to intervene in the internal or external affairs of another.

The good neighbor policy did not indicate a U.S. retreat from empire in Latin America. Instead, it declared that the United States would not depend on military force to exercise its influence in the region. When Mexico nationalized American oil holdings and revolution boiled over in Nicaragua, Guatemala, and Cuba during the 1930s, Roosevelt refrained from sending in the marines to defend the interests of American corporations. While nonintervention honored the principle of national self-determination, it also permitted the rise of dictators like Anastasio Somoza in Nicaragua and Fulgencio Batista in Cuba, who exploited and terrorized their nations with private support from U.S. businesses and the hands-off policy of Roosevelt's administration.

Military nonintervention also did not prevent the United States from exerting its economic influence in Latin America. In 1934, Congress passed the Reciprocal Trade Agreements Act, which gave the president power to reduce tariffs on goods imported into the United States from nations that agreed to lower their own tariffs on U.S. exports. By 1940, twenty-two nations had agreed to reciprocal tariff reductions, helping U.S. exports to Latin America double during Roosevelt's first two terms and contributing to the New Deal's goal of boosting the domestic economy through free trade. Although the economic power of the United States continued to overshadow that of its neighbors, the nonintervention policy planted seeds of friendship and hemispheric solidarity that grew in importance while events in Europe and Asia continued to erode international peace.

The Price of Noninvolvement

In Europe, fascist governments in Italy and Germany threatened military aggression. When Hitler vigorously rebuilt Germany's military strength in open defiance of the terms of the Versailles peace treaty, Britain and France only registered verbal protests. Emboldened, Hitler plotted to avenge defeat in World War I by recapturing territories with German inhabitants, all the while accusing Jews of polluting the purity of the Aryan master race. The virulent anti-Semitism of Hitler and his Nazi Party unified non-Jewish Germans and attracted sympathizers among many other Europeans, even in France and Britain, thereby weakening support for opposing Hitler or defending Jews.

In Japan, a stridently militaristic government planned to follow the invasion of Manchuria in 1931 with conquests extending throughout Southeast Asia. The Manchurian invasion bogged down in a long and vicious war when Chinese Nationalists rallied around their leader Chiang Kai-shek to fight against the Japanese. Preparations for new conquests continued, however. Early in 1936, Japan openly violated naval limitation treaties it had agreed to and began to build a battle-ready fleet to achieve naval superiority in the Pacific.

In the United States, the hostilities in Asia and Europe reinforced isolationist sentiments. Popular disillusionment with the failure of Woodrow Wilson's idealistic goals caused many Americans to question the nation's participation in World War I. In 1933, Gerald Nye, a Republican from North Dakota, chaired a Senate committee that investigated why the United States had gone to war in 1917. The Nye committee concluded that greedy "merchants of death"—American weapons makers, bankers, and financiers—dragged the nation into the war to line their own pockets. The Nye committee persuaded many Americans that war profiteers might once again push the nation into a world war.

International tensions and the Nye committee report prompted Congress to pass a series of neutrality acts between 1935 and 1937, to avoid the circumstances that, they believed, had caused the nation to abandon its isolationism and become a combatant in World War I. The neutrality acts prohibited making loans and selling arms to nations at war and authorized the president to warn Americans about traveling on ships belonging to belligerent countries. The Neutrality Act of 1937 required warring nations to pay cash for nonmilitary goods and to transport them in their own ships. This "cash-and-carry" policy seemed to reconcile the nation's desire for both peace and foreign trade.

The desire for peace in France, Britain, and the United States led Germany, Italy, and Japan to launch offensives on the assumption that the western democracies lacked the will to oppose them. In March 1936, Nazi troops marched into the industry-rich Rhineland on Germany's western border, in blatant violation of the Treaty of Versailles. One month later, Italian armies completed their conquest of Ethiopia, projecting fascist power into Africa. In December 1937, Japanese invaders captured Nanking and celebrated their triumph in a deadly rampage of murder, rape, and plunder that killed 200,000 Chinese civilians.

In Spain, a bitter civil war broke out in 1936 when fascist rebels led by General Francisco

Spanish Civil War, 1936–1939

Nationalist, July 1936
Nationalist, October 1937
Nationalist, July 1938
Nationalist, February 1939
Republican, February 1939
→ Main Nationalist attacks
→ Main Republican attacks

Franco attacked the democratically elected Republican government. Both Germany and Italy reinforced Franco with soldiers, weapons, and aircraft, while the Soviet Union provided much less aid to the Republican Loyalists. The Spanish civil war seemed to many observers a dress rehearsal for a coming worldwide conflict, but it did not cause European democracies or the U.S. government to help the Loyalists, despite sympathizing with their cause. More than 3,000 individual Americans enlisted in the Russian-sponsored Abraham Lincoln Brigade to fight for the Loyalists. But, abandoned by western nations, Loyalists and their allies were defeated in 1939, and Franco built a fascist bulwark in southern and western Europe.

Hostilities in Europe, Africa, and Asia alarmed Roosevelt and other Americans. The president sought to persuade most Americans to moderate their isolationism and find a way to support the victims of fascist aggression. Speaking in Chicago, the heartland of isolationism, in October 1937, Roosevelt declared that the "epidemic of world lawlessness is spreading" and warned that "mere isolation or neutrality" offered no remedy for the "contagion" of war. Instead, he proposed that the United States "quarantine" aggressor nations and arrest the spread of war's contagion.

Roosevelt's speech ignited a storm of protest from isolationists. The strength of isolationist sentiment convinced Roosevelt that he needed to maneuver carefully if the United States were to help prevent fascist aggressors from conquering Europe and Asia, leaving the United States an isolated and imperiled island of **democracy**.

> **REVIEW** Why did Roosevelt try to honor the principle of isolationism as president?

The Onset of War

Between 1939 and 1941, fascist victories overseas eventually eroded American isolationism. But initially, fascist anti-Semitism and military conquests in China, Ethiopia, and Spain failed to arouse many Americans who were still mired in depression. By 1939, however, continuing German and Japanese aggression caused more and more Americans to believe that it was time for the nation to take a stand. At first, taking a stand was limited to providing material support

to the enemies of Germany and Japan, principally Britain, China, and the Soviet Union. But Japan's surprise attack on Pearl Harbor eliminated that restraint, and the nation began to mobilize for an all-out assault on foreign foes.

Nazi Aggression and War in Europe

Under the spell of isolationism, Americans passively watched Hitler's relentless campaign to dominate Europe. Hitler bullied Austria in 1938 into accepting incorporation—*Anschluss*—into the Nazi Third Reich, expanding the territory under Germany's control. Next Hitler turned his attention to the German-speaking Sudetenland, granted to Czechoslovakia by the Versailles treaty. British prime minister Neville Chamberlain went to Munich, Germany, in September 1938 and offered Hitler terms of "appeasement," as he called it, that would give the Sudetenland to Germany if Hitler agreed to leave the rest of Czechoslovakia alone. Hitler accepted Chamberlain's offer, and Chamberlain returned to Britain proclaiming that his diplomacy had achieved "peace in our time." But despite the Munich agreement, in March 1939, Hitler boldly marched the German army into Czechoslovakia and conquered it without firing a shot (Map 25.1).

In April 1939, Hitler demanded that Poland return the German territory it had been awarded after World War I. Britain and France finally recognized that appeasement had failed and that Hitler would continue his aggression unless he was defeated by military might. Both Britain and France assured Poland that they would go to war with Germany if Hitler launched an eastward offensive across the Polish border. In turn, Hitler negotiated with his bitter enemy, the Soviet premier Joseph Stalin, offering him concessions in order to prevent the Soviet Union from joining Britain and France in opposing a German attack on Poland. Despite the enduring hatred between fascist Germany and the **Communist** Soviet Union, the two powers signed the Nazi-Soviet treaty of nonaggression in August 1939, exposing Poland to an onslaught by the German Wehrmacht (army).

At dawn on September 1, 1939, Hitler unleashed the attack on Poland led by tanks and airplanes that gave lethal mechanized support to the invading infantry. The attack triggered declarations of war from France and Britain two days later, igniting a conflagration that raced around the globe, killing over 60 million people and

MAP 25.1   Axis Aggression through 1941
For different reasons, Hitler and Mussolini launched a series of surprise military strikes. Mussolini sought to re-create the Roman empire in the Mediterranean. Hitler struck to reclaim German territories occupied by France after World War I and to annex Austria. When the German dictator began his campaign to rule "inferior" peoples beyond Germany's border by attacking Poland, World War II broke out.

maiming untold millions more until it finally ended after Paul Tibbets's historic flight in August 1945. But in September 1939, Germany seemed invincible as its armies sped across Poland, causing many people to wonder if any nation could stop the Nazi war machine.

After the Nazis overran Poland, Hitler paused for a few months before launching a westward *blitzkrieg* (literally, "lightning war") attack. In April 1940, German forces smashed through Denmark and Norway. In May, Germany invaded the Netherlands, Belgium, and Luxembourg, and then France. The French believed that their

Maginot Line, a concrete fortification built after World War I and stretching from the Swiss border to the forested Ardennes region on the edge of Belgium, would halt the German attack (see Map 25.1). But the Maginot Line proved little more than a detour for Hitler's mechanized divisions, which wheeled around the fortification's northern end and raced south toward Paris.

The speed of the German attack trapped more than 300,000 British and French soldiers, who retreated to the port of Dunkirk, where an improvised armada of English vessels hurriedly ferried them to safety across the English Channel.

By mid-June 1940, France had surrendered the largest army in the world, signed an armistice that gave Germany control of the entire French coastline and nearly two-thirds of the countryside, and installed a collaborationist government at Vichy in southern France headed by Philippe Pétain. With an empire that stretched across Europe from Poland to France, Hitler seemed poised to vault the English Channel and attack Britain.

The new British prime minister, Winston Churchill, vowed that Britain, unlike France, would never accept a humiliating surrender to Hitler. "We shall fight on the seas and oceans [and]…in the air," he proclaimed, and "we shall never surrender." Churchill's defiance stiffened British resolve for a last-ditch defense against Hitler's attack, which began in mid-June 1940 with wave after wave of German bombers targeting British military installations and cities, killing tens of thousands of civilians. The undermanned and outgunned Royal Air Force, fighting as doggedly as Churchill had predicted, finally won the Battle of Britain by November, clearing German bombers from British skies and handing Hitler his first frustrating defeat. The valiant British pilots had advance knowledge of German plans made possible by British use of the new technology of radar and the ability to decipher Germany's top-secret military codes. But battered and exhausted, Britain could not hold out forever without American help, as Churchill repeatedly wrote Roosevelt in private.

From Neutrality to the Arsenal of Democracy

When the Nazi attack on Poland ignited the war in Europe, Roosevelt issued an official proclamation of American neutrality. But Roosevelt feared that if Congress did not repeal the arms embargo mandated by the Neutrality Act of 1937, France and Britain would soon succumb to the Nazi onslaught. The president's request for repeal of the arms embargo provoked isolationists to protest that the United States had no business interfering in a European conflict. After heated debate, Congress voted in November 1939 to revise the neutrality legislation and allow belligerent nations to buy arms, as well as nonmilitary supplies, on a cash-and-carry basis.

Churchill pleaded for American destroyers, aircraft, and munitions but had no money to buy them under the prevailing cash-and-carry neutrality law. In May 1940, Roosevelt asked Congress for almost $1.3 billion in defense spending to expand the navy and multiply the production of airplanes to 50,000 a year. By late summer, as the Battle of Britain raged in the skies over England, Roosevelt concocted a scheme to deliver fifty old destroyers to Britain in exchange for American access to British bases in the Western Hemisphere. Claiming the constitutional power to strengthen America's defenses by swapping destroyers for bases, Roosevelt took the first steps toward building a firm Anglo-American alliance against Hitler.

While German Luftwaffe (air force) pilots bombed Britain, Roosevelt decided to run for an unprecedented third term as president in 1940. He hoped to woo voters away from their complacent isolationism to back the nation's international interests as well as New Deal reforms. But the presidential election, which Roosevelt won handily, provided no clear mandate for American involvement in the European war. The Republican candidate, Wendell Willkie, a former Democrat who generally favored New Deal measures and Roosevelt's foreign policy, attacked Roosevelt as a warmonger. Willkie's accusations caused the president to promise voters, "Your boys are not going to be sent into any foreign wars," a pledge counterbalanced by his repeated warnings about the threats to America posed by Nazi aggression.

Empowered by the voters for another presidential term, Roosevelt maneuvered to support Britain in every way short of war. In a fireside chat shortly after Christmas 1940, he proclaimed that it was incumbent on the United States to become "the great arsenal of democracy" and send "every ounce and every ton of munitions and supplies that we can possibly spare to help the defenders who are in the front lines." In January 1941, he proposed the Lend-Lease Act, which would allow the British to obtain arms from the United States without paying cash but with the promise to reimburse the United States when the war ended. The purpose of Lend-Lease, Roosevelt proclaimed, was to defend democracy and human rights throughout the world, specifically the Four Freedoms: "freedom of speech and expression…freedom of every person to worship God in his own way…freedom from want…[and] freedom from fear." Congress passed the Lend-Lease Act in March 1941, starting a flow of support to Britain that totaled more than $50 billion during the war, far more than all federal expenditures combined since Roosevelt had become president in 1933.

Stymied in his plans for an invasion of England, Hitler turned his massive army eastward and on June 22, 1941, sprang a surprise attack on the Soviet Union, his erstwhile ally in the 1939 Nazi-Soviet nonaggression pact. Neither Roosevelt nor Churchill had any love for Joseph Stalin or communism, but they both welcomed the Soviet Union to the anti-Nazi cause. Both Western leaders understood that Hitler's attack on Russia would provide relief for the hard-pressed British. Roosevelt quickly persuaded Congress to extend Lend-Lease to the Soviet Union, beginning the shipment of millions of tons of trucks, jeeps, locomotives, and other equipment that, in all, supplied about 10 percent of Russian war materiel.

As Hitler's Wehrmacht raced across the Russian plains and Nazi U-boats tried to choke off supplies to Britain and the Soviet Union, Roosevelt met with Churchill aboard a ship near Newfoundland to cement the Anglo-American alliance. In August 1941, the two leaders issued the Atlantic Charter, pledging the two nations to freedom of the seas and free trade as well as the right of national self-determination. Roosevelt told Churchill privately that the United States would continue to serve as the arsenal of democracy and that he would be watching for some incident that might trigger public support for full-scale American entry into the war against Germany.

Japan Attacks America

Although the likelihood of war with Germany preoccupied Roosevelt, Hitler exercised a measure of restraint in directly provoking America. Japanese ambitions in Asia clashed more openly with American interests and commitments, especially in China and the Philippines. And unlike Hitler, the Japanese high command planned to attack the United States if necessary to pursue their aspirations to rule an Asian empire they termed the Greater East Asia Co-Prosperity Sphere. Appealing to widespread Asian bitterness toward white colonial powers like the British in India and Burma, the French in Indochina (now Vietnam), and the Dutch in the East Indies (now Indonesia), the Japanese campaigned to preserve "Asia for the Asians." Japan's invasion of China—which had lasted for ten years by 1941—proved that Japan's true goal was Asia for the Japanese (Map 25.2).

In 1940, Japan signaled a new phase of its **imperial** designs by entering a defensive alliance with Germany and Italy—the Tripartite Pact. By 1941, U.S. naval intelligence cracked the Japanese secret code and learned that Tokyo also planned to invade the resource-rich Dutch East Indies. To thwart these plans, in July 1941 Roosevelt announced a trade embargo that denied Japan access to oil, scrap iron, and other goods essential for its war machines. Roosevelt hoped the embargo would strengthen factions within Japan who opposed the militarists and sought to restore relations with the United States.

The American embargo played into the hands of Japanese militarists headed by General Hideki Tojo, who seized control of the government in October 1941 and persuaded other leaders, including Emperor Hirohito, that swift destruction of American naval bases in the Pacific would leave Japan free to follow its destiny. Early on the morning of December 7, 1941, 183 attack aircraft lifted off six Japanese carriers that had secretly steamed within striking range of the U.S. Pacific Fleet at Pearl Harbor on the Hawaiian island of Oahu. At about 8 o'clock, the Japanese planes streaked from the sky, bombing and torpedoing the American fleet riding serenely at anchor in the harbor and destroying hundreds of aircraft parked in neat rows on the runways of Hickam Field. The devastating surprise attack sank or disabled 18 ships, including all of the fleet's battleships, killed more than 2,400 Americans, and wounded over 1,000, almost crippling U.S. war-making capacity in the Pacific.

The Japanese scored a stunning tactical success at Pearl Harbor, but in the long run the attack proved a colossal blunder. The victory made many Japanese commanders overconfident about their military prowess. Worse for the Japanese, Americans instantly united in their de-

Bombing of Pearl Harbor, December 7, 1941

East Loch

Ford Island

U.S. Naval Air Station

Pearl Harbor

■ Sunk

□ Damaged

■ Undamaged

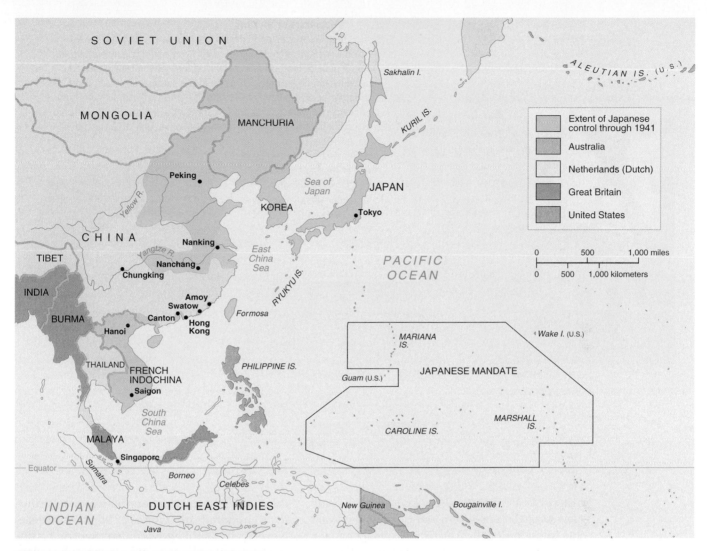

MAP 25.2 Japanese Aggression through 1941
Beginning with the invasion of Manchuria in 1931, Japan sought to force its imperialist control over most
of East Asia. Japan's aggression was driven by the need for raw materials for the country's expanding industries and by the military government's devotion to martial honor.

sire to fight and avenge the attack, which Roosevelt termed "dastardly and unprovoked,"
vowing that "this form of treachery shall never
endanger us again." On December 8, Congress
unanimously endorsed the president's call for a
declaration of war. Both Germany and Italy declared war against America on December 11,
bringing the United States into all-out war with
Axis powers in both Europe and Asia.

REVIEW How did Roosevelt attempt to balance
American isolationism with the increasingly ominous
international scene of the late 1930s?

Mobilizing for War

The time had come, Roosevelt announced, for the
prescriptions of "Dr. New Deal" to be replaced by
the stronger medicines of "Dr. Win-the-War."
Military and civilian leaders rushed to secure the
nation against possible attacks by its enemies,
causing Americans of Japanese descent to be stigmatized and sent to internment camps. Roosevelt
and his advisers lost no time enlisting millions
of Americans in the armed forces to bring the
isolationist-era military to fighting strength for a
two-front war. The war emergency also required
economic mobilization unparalleled in the nation's

Pearl Harbor Victims

Brothers Wesley and Edward Heidt from California—shown here posing in their Navy uniforms—were two of 34 pairs of brothers killed when Japanese warplanes attacked and sank the battleship *Arizona* in the surprise attack on Pearl Harbor on December 7, 1941. The life preserver and pennant from the *Arizona* were salvaged a few days after the attack. The official telegram informed the Heidt brothers' mother that they "lost their life in the service of their country," a tragic message received by hundreds of thousands of other American parents during the next four years.

U.S.S. *Arizona* Memorial, Hawaii, National Park Service/photos by Douglas Peebles.

history. As Dr. Win-the-War, Roosevelt set aside New Deal goals of reform and plunged headlong into transforming the American economy into the world's greatest military machine, thereby achieving full employment and economic recovery, goals that had eluded the New Deal.

Home-Front Security

Shortly after declaring war against the United States, Hitler dispatched German submarines to hunt American ships along the Atlantic coast from Maine to Florida, where Paul Tibbets and other American pilots tried to destroy them. But the U-boats had devastating success for about eight months, sinking hundreds of U.S. ships and threatening to disrupt the Lend-Lease lifeline to Britain and the Soviet Union.

Hulks of destroyed vessels littered Atlantic beaches, but by mid-1942 the U.S. navy had chased German submarines away from the East Coast and into the mid-Atlantic, reducing the direct threat to the nation's homeland. Within the continental United States, Americans remained sheltered by the Atlantic and Pacific oceans from

the chaos and destruction the war was bringing to hundreds of millions in Europe and Asia. Nevertheless, the government worried constantly about espionage and internal subversion. Billboards and posters warned Americans that "Loose lips sink ships" and "Enemy agents are always near; if you don't talk, they won't hear." The campaign for patriotic vigilance focused on German and Japanese foes, but Americans of Japanese descent became targets of official and popular persecution.

About 320,000 people of Japanese descent lived in the United States in 1941, two-thirds of them in Hawaii, where they largely escaped wartime persecution because they were essential and valued members of society. On the mainland, in contrast, Japanese Americans were a tiny minority—even along the West Coast, where most of them worked on farms and in small businesses—subject to frenzied wartime suspicions and persecution. Although an official military survey concluded that Japanese Americans posed no danger, popular hostility fueled a campaign to round up all mainland Japanese Americans—two-thirds of them U.S. citizens.

"A Jap's a Jap.... It makes no difference whether he is an American citizen or not," one official declared.

On February 19, 1942, Roosevelt issued Executive Order 9066, which authorized sending all Americans of Japanese descent to ten makeshift prison (or internment) camps located in remote areas of the West, euphemistically termed "relocation centers" (Map 25.3). Allowed little time to secure or sell their properties, Japanese Americans lost homes and businesses worth about $400 million and lived out the war penned in by barbed wire and armed guards. Although several thousand Japanese Americans served with distinction in the U.S. armed forces and no case of subversion by Japanese Americans was ever uncovered, the Supreme Court, in its 1944 *Korematsu* decision, upheld Executive Order 9066's blatant violation of constitutional rights as justified by "military necessity."

Building a Citizen Army

In 1940, Roosevelt encouraged Congress to pass the Selective Service Act to register men of military age who would be subject to **draft** into the armed forces if the need arose. More than 6,000 local draft boards registered over 30 million men and, when war came, rapidly inducted them into military service. In all, more than 16 million men and women served in uniform during the war, two-thirds of them draftees, mostly young men between the ages of 18 and 26. By the time the war ended, over 10 million had served in the army, nearly 4 million in the navy, 600,000 in the marines, and 240,000 in the coast guard. In addition, 350,000 women joined the Nurse's Corps and women's military units in the army, navy, and Marine Corps. Though barred from combat duty, these women worked at nearly every noncombatant assignment, eroding traditional barriers to women's military service.

The Selective Service Act prohibited discrimination "on account of race or color," and almost a million African American men and women donned uniforms, as did half a million Mexican Americans, 25,000 Native Americans, and 13,000 Chinese Americans. The racial insults and discrimination suffered by all people of color made some soldiers ask, as a Mexican American GI said on his way to the European front, "Why fight for America when you have not been treated as an American?" Only black Americans were trained in segregated camps, confined in segregated barracks, and assigned to

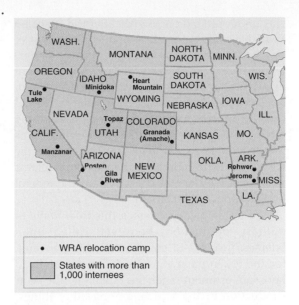

MAP 25.3   Western Relocation Authority Centers
Responding to prejudice and fear of sabotage, in 1942 President Roosevelt authorized the roundup and relocation of all Americans of Japanese descent. Taken from their homes in the cities and fertile farms of the far West, Japanese Americans were confined in desolate areas scattered as far east as the Mississippi River.

segregated units. Secretary of War Henry Stimson opposed any change in the segregation of blacks, declaring that the military effort should not serve as a "sociological laboratory." Accordingly, most black Americans were consigned to manual labor positions, and relatively few served in combat until late in 1944, when the need for military manpower in Europe intensified. Then, as General George Patton told black soldiers in a tank unit in Normandy, "I don't care what color you are, so long as you go up there and kill those Kraut sonsabitches."

Homosexuals also served in the armed forces, although in much smaller numbers than black Americans. Allowed to serve, gay Americans, like other minorities, sought to demonstrate their worth under fire. "I was superpatriotic," a gay combat veteran recalled. Another gay GI remarked, "Who in the hell is going to worry about [homosexuality]" in the midst of the life-or-death realities of war?

Conversion to a War Economy

In 1940, nearly one worker in seven was still without a job, factories operated far below their productive capacity, and the total federal budget was under $10 billion. Shortly after the attack on Pearl Harbor, Roosevelt announced the goal of converting the economy to produce "overwhelming…crushing superiority of equipment in any theater of the world war." In a rush to produce military supplies, factories were converted from producing passenger cars to assembling tanks and airplanes, and production was ramped up to record levels. By the end of the war, there were more jobs than workers, plants were operating at full capacity, and the federal budget topped $100 billion.

To organize and oversee this tidal wave of military production, Roosevelt called upon business leaders to come to Washington and, for the token payment of a dollar a year, head new government agencies such as the War Production Board, which, among other things, set production priorities and pushed for maximum output. Contracts flowed to large corporations such as General Electric, Ford, and U.S. Steel, often on a basis that guaranteed their profits. During the first half of 1942, the government issued contracts worth over $100 billion, a sum greater than the entire gross national product in 1941.

Booming wartime employment swelled union membership. To speed production, the government asked unions to pledge not to strike. Despite the relentless pace of work, union members kept their no-strike pledge, with the important exception of the United Mine Workers, who walked out of the coal mines in 1943, demanding a pay hike and earning the enmity of many Americans.

Overall, conversion to war production achieved Roosevelt's ambitious goal of "overwhelming…,crushing superiority" in military goods. At a total cost of $304 billion during the war, the nation produced an avalanche of military equipment, including 300,000 airplanes, 88,000 tanks, 7,000 ships, 3 million vehicles, as well as billions of bullets, and much more—in all more than double the combined production of Germany, Japan, and Italy. Giving tangible meaning to the term "arsenal of democracy," this outpouring of military goods supplied not only U.S. forces but also sizable portions of the military needs of the Allies.

> **REVIEW**   How did the Roosevelt administration steer the mobilization of human and industrial resources necessary for a two-front war?

Fighting Back

The United States confronted a daunting military challenge in December 1941. The attack on Pearl Harbor destroyed much of its Pacific fleet, crippling the nation's ability to defend against Japan's massive offensive throughout the southern Pacific. In the Atlantic, Hitler's U-boats sank American ships, while German armies occupied most of western Europe and relentlessly advanced eastward into the Soviet Union. Roosevelt and his military advisers believed defeating Germany took top priority. To achieve that victory required preventing Hitler from defeating America's allies, Britain and the Soviet Union. If they fell, Hitler would command all the resources of Europe in a probable assault on the United States. To fight back effectively against Germany and Japan, the United States had to coordinate military and political strategy with its allies and muster all its human and economic assets. But in 1941, nobody knew if that would be enough.

Turning the Tide in the Pacific

In the Pacific theater, Japan's leading military strategist, Admiral Isoroku Yamamoto, ordered an all-out offensive throughout the southern Pacific. He believed that if his forces did not quickly conquer and secure the territories they targeted, Japan would eventually lose the war to America's far greater resources. Swiftly, the Japanese assaulted American airfields in the Philippines and captured U.S. outposts on Guam and Wake Island. Singapore, the great British naval base in Malaya, surrendered to the Japanese in February 1942, and most of Burma had fallen by March. All that stood in the way of Japan's domination of the southern Pacific was the American stronghold in the Philippines.

The Japanese unleashed a withering assault against the Philippines in January 1942, causing the American commander General Douglas MacArthur to retreat to Australia in March and defeating American and Philippine defenders by May. The Japanese victors were responsible for the deaths of thousands of captured American and Filipino soldiers on the Bataan Death March to a concentration camp. By the summer of 1942, the Japanese war machine had conquered the oil-rich Dutch East Indies and was poised to strike Australia and New Zealand.

The Japanese had larger, faster, and more heavily armed ships than the United States, and their airplanes outperformed anything the Americans could send up against them. But a daring raid on Tokyo in April 1942 by a squadron of carrier-based B-25 bombers led by Lieutenant Colonel James Doolittle boosted American morale and demonstrated that even the Japanese imperial capital lay within reach (barely) of American might.

In the spring of 1942, U.S. forces launched a major two-pronged counteroffensive that military officials hoped would reverse the Japanese advance. Forces led by General MacArthur moved north from Australia and attacked the Japanese in the Philippines. Far more decisively, Admiral Chester W. Nimitz sailed his battle fleet west from Hawaii to retake Japanese-held islands in the mid-Pacific. On May 7–8, 1942, in the Coral Sea just north of Australia, the American fleet and carrier-based warplanes defeated a Japanese armada that was sailing around the coast of New Guinea.

Nimitz then learned from an intelligence intercept that the Japanese were massing an invasion force aimed at Midway Island, an outpost guarding the Hawaiian Islands. Nimitz maneuvered his carriers and cruisers into the Central Pacific to surprise the Japanese. In a furious battle that raged from June 3 to June 6, American naval ships and planes delivered a devastating blow to the Japanese navy. The Battle of Midway reversed the balance of naval power in the Pacific and put the Japanese at a disadvantage for the rest of the war. It turned the tide of Japanese advance in the Pacific but did little to dislodge Japan from the many places it had conquered and now stoutly defended.

The Campaign in Europe

In the dark months after Pearl Harbor, Hitler's eastern-front armies marched ever deeper into the Soviet Union while his western forces prepared to invade Britain. As in World War I, the Germans attempted to starve the British into submission by destroying their seaborne lifeline. Technological advances made German U-boats much more effective than they had been in World War I; in 1941 and 1942 they sank Allied ships faster than new ones could be built.

Until mid-1943, the outcome of the war in the Atlantic remained in perilous doubt. Then,

Japanese Pilot's Flag
Japanese pilots often carried small flags covered with admonitions to fight hard and well. This flag belonged to a pilot named Imano, whose relatives sent him aloft with inscriptions that read "Let your divine plane soar in the sky. We who are left behind pray only for your certain success in sinking an enemy ship." Notably, the inscription emphasized harming Japan's enemies rather than returning home safe and sound.
U.S. Naval Academy Museum / photo by Richard D. Bond Jr.

newly invented radar detectors and production of sufficient destroyer escorts for merchant vessels allowed the Allies to prey upon the lurking U-boats. After suffering a 75 percent casualty rate among U-boat crews, Hitler withdrew German submarines from the North Atlantic in late May 1943. Winning the battle of the Atlantic allowed the United States to continue to supply its British and Soviet allies for the duration of the war and to reduce the imminent threat of a German invasion of Britain.

The most important strategic question confronting the United States and its allies was when and where to open a second front against the Nazis. Stalin demanded that America and Britain mount an immediate and massive assault across the English Channel into western France. A cross-channel invasion would force

Hitler to divert his armies from the eastern front and relieve the pressure on the Soviet Union, which was fighting alone against the full strength of the German Wehrmacht. Churchill and Roosevelt instead delayed opening a second front, allowing the Germans and the Soviets to slug it out, weakening both the Nazis and the Communists, and making an eventual Allied attack on western France more likely to succeed. Both Churchill and Roosevelt promised Stalin that they would open a second front, but they decided to strike first in southern Europe and the Mediterranean, which Churchill termed Europe's "soft under-belly."

The plan targeted a region of long-standing British influence in the eastern Mediterranean. In October 1942, British forces at El-Alamein in Egypt halted German general Erwin Rommel's drive to capture the Suez Canal, Britain's lifeline to the oil of the Middle East and to British colonies in India and South Asia. In November, an American army under General Dwight D. Eisenhower landed far to the west, in French Morocco. Propelled by American tank units commanded by General George Patton, the Allied armies defeated the Germans in North Africa by May 1943. The North African campaign killed and captured 350,000 Axis soldiers, pushed the Germans out of Africa, made the Mediterranean safe for Allied shipping, and opened the door for an Allied invasion of Italy.

In January 1943, while the North African campaign was still under way, Roosevelt traveled to the Moroccan city of Casablanca to confer with Churchill and other Allied leaders. Stalin urged his allies to keep their promise of opening a major second front in western Europe. Roosevelt and Churchill announced that they would accept nothing less than the "unconditional surrender" of the Axis powers, ruling out peace negotiations. But Churchill and Roosevelt concluded that they needed more time to amass sufficient forces for the cross-channel invasion of France that Stalin demanded. In the meantime, they planned to capitalize on their success in North Africa and strike against Italy.

On July 10, 1943, combined American and British amphibious forces landed 160,000 troops in Sicily. The badly equipped Italian defenders quickly withdrew to the mainland. Soon afterward, Mussolini was deposed in Italy, ending the reign of Italian fascism. Quickly, the Allies invaded the mainland, and the Italian government surrendered unconditionally. The Germans responded by rushing reinforcements to Italy and seizing control of Rome, turning the Allies' Italian campaign into a series of battles to liberate Italy from German occupation.

German troops dug into strong fortifications and fought to defend every inch of Italy's rugged terrain. Only after a long, deadly, and frustrating campaign up the Italian peninsula did the Allies finally liberate Rome in June 1944. Allied forces continued to push into northern Italy against stubborn German defenses for the remainder of the war, making the Italian campaign the war's deadliest for American infantrymen. One soldier wrote that his buddies "died like butchered swine."

REVIEW   How did the United States gain advantage over the Japanese navy in the Pacific?

The Wartime Home Front

The war effort mobilized Americans as never before. Factories strained to churn out ever more bombs, bullets, tanks, ships, and airplanes, which workers rushed to assemble, leaving farms and small towns to congregate in cities. Women took jobs with wrenches and welding torches, boosting the nation's workforce and fraying traditional notions that women's place was in the home rather than on the assembly line. Despite rationing and shortages, unprecedented government expenditures for war production brought prosperity to many Americans after years of depression-era poverty. While Americans in uniform risked their lives on battlefields in Europe and Asia, where millions of civilians suffered bombing, strafing, and all-out military assaults, Americans on the mainland enjoyed complete immunity from foreign attack—in sharp contrast to their Soviet and British allies. The wartime ideology of human rights provided justification for the many sacrifices Americans were required to make in support of the military effort, as well as establishing a standard of basic human equality that became a potent weapon in the campaign for equal rights at home.

Women and Families, Guns and Butter

Millions of American women gladly left home toting a lunch pail and changed into overalls and work gloves to take their places on assembly lines in defense industries. At the start of the war, about a quarter of adult women worked outside the home, most as teachers, nurses, social workers, or domestic servants. Few women worked in factories, except for textile mills and sewing industries, because employers and male workers often discriminated against them. But wartime mobilization of the economy and the siphoning of millions of men into the armed forces left factories begging for women workers.

Government advertisements urged women to take industrial jobs by assuring them that their household chores had prepared them for work on the "Victory Line." One billboard proclaimed, "If you've sewed on buttons, or made buttonholes, on a [sewing] machine, you can learn to do spot welding on airplane parts....If you've followed recipes exactly in making cakes, you can learn to load a shell." Millions of women responded, and

by the end of the war, women working outside the home numbered eighteen million, 50 percent more than in 1939. Contributing to the war effort also paid off in wages that averaged $31 for a forty-eight-hour week, more than the typical steelworker earned in 1941. A Kentucky woman remembered her job at a munitions plant where she earned "the fabulous sum of $32 a week. To us it was an absolute miracle. Before that, we made nothing." Although men got paid an average of $54 for comparable wartime work, women accepted the pay differential and welcomed their chance to earn wages and help win the war at the same time.

The majority of married women remained at home, occupied with domestic chores and child care. But they, too, pitched in to the war effort, planting Victory Gardens of home-grown vegetables, saving tin cans and newspapers for recycling into war materials, and hoarding pennies and nickels to buy war bonds. Many families scrimped to cope with the 30 percent inflation during the war. But families supported by men and women in manufacturing industries enjoyed wages that grew twice as fast as inflation.

The wartime prosperity and abundance enjoyed by most Americans contrasted with the experiences of their hard-pressed allies. Personal consumption fell by 22 percent in Britain, and in the Soviet Union food output plummeted to just one-third of prewar levels, creating widespread hunger and even starvation.

The Double V Campaign

Fighting against Nazi Germany and its ideology of Aryan racial supremacy confronted Americans with the extensive racial prejudice in their own society. Roosevelt declared that black Americans were in the war "not only to defend America but...to establish a universal freedom under which a new basis of security and prosperity can be established for all—regardless of station, race, or creed." The *Pittsburgh Courier*, a leading black newspaper, asserted that the wartime emergency called for a "Double V" campaign seeking "victory over our enemies at home and victory over our enemies on the battlefields abroad." It was time, the *Courier* proclaimed, "to persuade, embarrass, compel and shame our government and our nation...into a more enlightened attitude."

Female Defense Worker
The war effort brought persons and activities together in unlikely ways, leading to unexpected outcomes. This photo appearing in the army magazine *Yank* sought to boost morale by presenting a defense worker as pinup girl. No one could know that the young propeller technician, nineteen-year-old Norma Jean Baker Dougherty, would later remake herself as the most glamorous of movie stars, Marilyn Monroe.
David Conover Images; © Norma Jean Enterprises, a division of 733548 Ontario Limited.

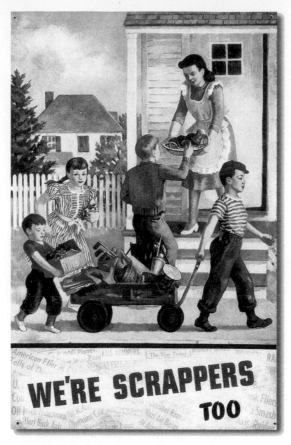

Pitching in at Home
This poster adapts the standard children's book illustration style of the period to the war effort. White and middle class all, mother and children collect old golf clubs, cocktail shakers, and trophies—which dad, away at war, will never miss—so that these symbols of the American way of life can be recycled into armaments for defense.
Chicago Historical Society.

FOR MORE HELP ANALYZING THIS IMAGE, see the visual activity for this chapter in the Online Study Guide at bedfordstmartins.com/roarkcompact.

In 1941, black organizations demanded that the federal government require companies receiving defense contracts to integrate their workforces. A. Philip Randolph, head of the Brotherhood of Sleeping Car Porters, promised that 100,000 African American marchers would descend on Washington if the president did not eliminate discrimination in defense industries. Roosevelt decided to risk offending his white allies in the South and in unions and issued Executive Order 8802 in mid-1941. It authorized a Committee on Fair Employment Practices to investigate and prevent race discrimination in employment. Civil rights champions hailed the act, and Randolph triumphantly called off the march.

Progress came slowly, however. In search of better jobs and living conditions, five and a half million black Americans migrated from the South during the war to centers of industrial production in the North and West, making a majority of African Americans city dwellers for the first time in U.S. history. Many discovered that unskilled jobs were available but unions and employers often barred blacks from skilled trades. Severe labor shortages and government fair employment pressures opened assembly-line jobs in defense plants to African American workers, causing black unemployment to drop by 80 percent during the war. Even so, by the end of the conflict black families' income still stood at half of white families' income.

Blacks' migration to defense jobs intensified racial antagonisms, which boiled over in the hot summer of 1943 when 242 race riots erupted in 47 cities. In Los Angeles, hundreds of white servicemen, claiming they were punishing draft dodgers, chased and beat young Chicano men who dressed in distinctive broad-shouldered, peg-legged zoot suits. The worst mayhem occurred in Detroit, where conflict between whites and blacks at a city park ignited a race war. In two days of violence, 25 blacks and 9 whites were killed, and scores more were injured.

Racial violence created impetus for the Double V campaign, officially supported by the National Association for the Advancement of Colored People (NAACP), which asserted black Americans' demands for the rights and privileges enjoyed by all other Americans—demands reinforced by the Allies' wartime ideology of freedom and democracy. While the NAACP focused on court challenges to segregation, a new organization founded in 1942, the Congress of Racial Equality (CORE), organized picketing and sit-ins against **Jim Crow** restaurants and theaters. The Double V campaign greatly expanded membership in the NAACP but achieved only limited success against racial discrimination during the war.

Wartime Politics and the 1944 Election

Americans rallied around the war effort in unprecedented unity. Despite the consensus on war aims, the strains and stresses of the nation's massive wartime mobilization made it difficult for Roosevelt to maintain his political coalition. Whites often resented blacks who migrated to northern cities, took jobs, and made themselves at home. Many Americans complained about government price controls and the rationing of scarce goods, while the war dragged on.

Republicans seized the opportunity to roll back New Deal reforms. A **conservative** coalition of Republicans and southern Democrats succeeded in abolishing several New Deal agencies in 1942 and 1943, including the Work Projects Administration and the Civilian Conservation Corps. But the Democratic administration fought back, and in June 1944, Congress unanimously approved the landmark GI Bill of Rights, promising to give veterans government funds for education, housing, and health care, and to provide loans to start businesses and buy homes when they returned from overseas. The GI Bill put the financial resources of the federal government behind the abstract goals of freedom and democracy for which veterans were fighting, and it empowered millions of GIs to better themselves and their families after the war.

After twelve turbulent years in the White House, Roosevelt was exhausted and gravely ill with heart disease. But he was determined to remain president until the war ended. Roosevelt's poor health made the selection of a vice presidential candidate unusually important. Roosevelt chose Senator Harry S. Truman of Missouri as his running mate. A reliable party man from a southern border state, Truman satisfied urban Democratic leaders while not worrying white southerners who were nervous about challenges to racial segregation.

The Republicans, confident of a strong conservative upsurge in the nation, nominated as their presidential candidate the governor of New York, Thomas E. Dewey, who had made his reputation as a tough crime fighter. In the 1944 presidential election, Roosevelt's failing health alarmed many observers, but his frailty was outweighed by Americans' unwillingness to change presidents in the midst of the war and by Dewey's failure to persuade most voters that the New Deal was a creeping **socialist** menace. Voters gave Roosevelt a 53.5 percent majority, his narrowest presidential victory, ensuring his continued leadership as Dr. Win-the-War.

Reaction to the Holocaust

The political cross-currents in the United States were tame in comparison with Hitler's vicious campaign to exterminate Jews. Since the 1930s, Nazis had persecuted Jews in Germany and every German-occupied territory, causing many Jews to seek asylum beyond Hitler's reach. (See "Beyond America's Borders," page 666.) America's immigration restriction laws of the 1920s allowed only a small quota of immigrants from each nation. After Hitler's Anschluss in 1938, thousands of Austrian Jews sought to immigrate to the United States, but 82 percent of Americans opposed admitting them, and they were turned away. Friends of the refugees introduced legislation in Congress in 1939 that would have granted asylum to 20,000 German refugee children, most of them Jewish. The bill was defeated, in large measure because of American anti-Semitism.

In 1942, numerous reports filtered out of German-occupied Europe that Hitler was implementing a "final solution": Jews and other "undesirables"—such as Gypsies, religious and political dissenters, and homosexuals—were being sent to concentration camps. Old people, children, and others deemed too weak to work were systematically slaughtered and cremated while the able-bodied were put to work at slave labor until they died of starvation and abuse. Most Americans, including top officials, believed the reports of the killing camps were exaggerated and refused to allow the nation to become a haven for persecuted Jews.

The nightmare of the Holocaust was all too real. When Russian troops arrived at Auschwitz in Poland in February 1945, the truth about the Nazis' Holocaust began to be known beyond the Germans who perpetrated and tolerated these atrocities and the men, women, and children who succumbed to genocide. But by then it was too late for the nine million victims—mostly Jews—of the Nazis' crimes against humanity.

The Holocaust, 1933–1945

SWEDEN
DENMARK
LITH.
East Prussia
GERMANY
POLAND
CZECHOSLOVAKIA
SWITZ. AUSTRIA HUNGARY
ITALY
YUGOSLAVIA

● Principal German concentration and extermination camp

REVIEW Why did women and minorities enter the industrial workforce in unprecedented numbers during the war?

Nazi Anti-Semitism and the Atomic Bomb

During the 1930s, Jewish physicists fled Adolf Hitler's fanatical anti-Semitic persecutions and came to the United States, where they played a leading role in the research and development of the atomic bomb. In this way, Nazi anti-Semitism contributed to making the United States the first atomic power.

One of Germany's greatest scientists, Albert Einstein, won the Nobel Prize for physics in 1921. Among other things, Einstein's work demonstrated that the nuclei of atoms of physical matter stored almost inconceivable quantities of energy. A fellow scientist praised Einstein's discoveries as "the greatest achievements in the history of human thought."

Einstein was born in Germany in 1879, grew up in Munich, and by 1914 headed the Kaiser Wilhelm Institute for Physics in Berlin. But he was a Jew, and his ideas were ridiculed by German anti-Semites. A German physicist who had won the Nobel Prize in 1905 attacked Einstein for his "Jewish nonsense" that was "hostile to the German spirit." Einstein wrote to a friend, "Anti-Semitism is strong here [in Berlin] and political reaction is violent." In 1922, anti-Semitic extremists assassinated the German foreign minister, Walter Rathenau, a Jewish chemist and friend of

Einstein. Einstein's associates warned him that he, too, was a target.

By 1921, when Einstein won the Nobel Prize, Adolf Hitler, a former corporal in the German infantry, had already organized the Nazi Party and recruited a large private army to intimidate his opponents—Jews foremost among them. Jailed in 1923 for attempting to overthrow the German government, Hitler wrote his Nazi manifesto, *Mein Kampf*, which proclaimed that Jews and Communists had betrayed Germany in the First World War and needed to be eliminated. Jews, Hitler insisted, were "a foreign people," "inferior beings," the "personification of the devil," "a race of dialectical liars," "parasites," and "eternal blood-suckers" who had the "clear aim of ruining the ...white race." Hitler's rantings attracted a huge audience in Germany, and his personal Nazi army, which numbered 400,000 by 1933, terrorized and murdered anyone who got in the way.

In January 1933, just weeks before Franklin Roosevelt's inauguration as president of the United States, Hitler became chancellor of Germany on a tidal wave of popular support for his Nazi Party. Within months, he abolished freedom of speech and assembly, outlawed all political opposition, and exercised

absolute dictatorial power. On April 7, Hitler announced the Law for the Restoration of the Professional Civil Service, which stipulated that "civil servants of non-Aryan descent must retire." A non-Aryan was defined as any person "descended from non-Aryan, especially Jewish, parents or grandparents." The law meant that scientists of Jewish descent who worked for state institutions, including universities, no longer had jobs. About 1,600 intellectuals in Germany immediately lost their livelihood and their future in Hitler's Reich. Among them were about a quarter of the physicists in Germany, including Einstein and ten other Nobel Prize winners. The Nazis' anti-Semitism laws forced many leading scientists to leave Germany. Between 1933 and 1941, Einstein and about 100 other Jewish physicists joined hundreds of Jewish intellectuals in an exodus from Nazi Germany to the safety of the United States.

The refugee physicists scrambled to find positions in American universities and research institutes that would allow them to continue their studies. The accelerating pace of research in physics during the 1930s raised the possibility that a way might exist to release the phenomenal energy bottled up in atomic nuclei, perhaps even to create a superbomb. Einstein and other scientists considered that possibility remote. But many worried that if scientists loyal to Germany discovered a way to harness nuclear energy, then Hitler would have the power to spread Nazi terror throughout the globe.

The refugee physicists asked Einstein to write a letter to

President Roosevelt explaining the military and political threats posed by the latest research in nuclear physics. In early October 1939, as Hitler's blitzkreig swept through Poland, Roosevelt received Einstein's letter and immediately grasped the central point, exclaiming, "what you are after is to see that the Nazis don't blow us up." Roosevelt quickly convened a small group of distinguished American scientists, who convinced the president to authorize an all-out effort to learn whether an atomic bomb could be built and, if so, to build it. Only weeks before the Japanese attack on Pearl Harbor, Roosevelt decided to launch the Manhattan Project, the top-secret atomic bomb program.

Leading scientists from the United States and Britain responded to the government's appeal: "No matter what you do with the rest of your life, nothing will be as important to the future of the World as your work on this Project right now." Many of the most creative, productive, and irreplaceable scientists involved in the Manhattan Project were physicists who had fled Nazi Germany. Their efforts had brought the possibility of an atomic bomb to Roosevelt's attention. Having personally experienced Nazi anti-Semitism, they understood what was at stake—an atomic bomb in the hands of Hitler or of his enemies.

In the end, Hitler's scientists failed to develop an atomic bomb, and Germany surrendered before the American bomb was ready to go. But the Manhattan Project succeeded, as Paul Tibbets proved over Hiroshima, Japan, on August 6, 1945. After the war, Leo Szilard, a leader among the refugee physicists, remarked, "If Congress knew the true history of the atomic energy project...it would create a special medal to be given to meddling foreigners for distinguished services."

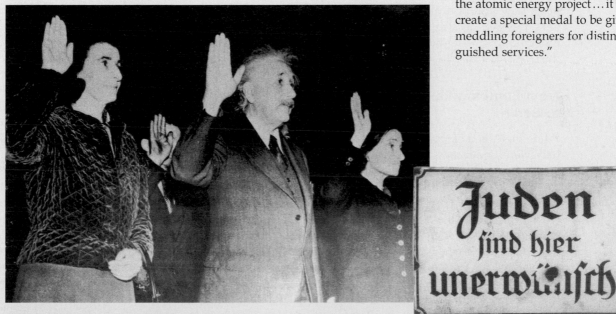

Einstein Becomes a U.S. Citizen

Nazi laws that prohibited Jewish scientists from working in universities and research institutes also excluded Jews from public places such as shops, parks, and theaters—as proclaimed by signs like the one shown here. Nazi anti-Semitism caused Albert Einstein to renounce his German citizenship, emigrate to the United States, and—in the naturalization ceremony recorded in this photo—officially become an American citizen in 1940, along with his secretary Helen Dukas and his stepdaughter Margot Einstein.

Photo: Courtesy, American Institute of Physics Emilio Segré Visual Archives; sign: Arnold Kramer / United States Holocaust Memorial Museum.

Toward Unconditional Surrender

By February 1943, Soviet defenders had finally defeated the massive German offensive against Stalingrad, turning the tide of the war in Europe. After gargantuan sacrifices in fighting that had lasted for eighteen months and killed more than 95 percent of the Russian soldiers and noncommissioned officers engaged at Stalingrad, the Red Army forced Hitler's Wehrmacht to turn back toward the west. Now the Soviets and their western allies faced the task of driving the Nazis out of eastern and western Europe and forcing them to surrender. It was long past time, Stalin proclaimed, for Britain and the United States to open a second front in France, but that offensive was postponed for more than a year after the Red Army's victory at Stalingrad. In the Pacific, the Allies had halted the expansion of the Japanese empire but now had the deadly task of dislodging Japanese defenders from the far-flung outposts they still occupied. Allied military planners devised a strategy to annihilate Axis resistance by taking advantage of America's industrial superiority.

From Bombing Raids to Berlin

While the Allied campaigns in North Africa and Italy were under way, British and American pilots flew bombing missions from England to the continent as an airborne substitute for the delayed second front on the ground. Beginning with Paul Tibbets's flight in August 1942, American pilots flew heavily armored B-17s from English airfields in daytime raids on industrial targets vital for the German war machine, especially oil refineries and ball bearing factories.

German air defenses took a fearsome toll on Allied pilots and aircraft. In 1943, two-thirds of American airmen did not survive to complete their 25-mission tour of duty. In all, 85,000 American airmen were killed in the skies over Europe. The arrival in February 1944 of America's durable and deadly P-51 Mustang fighter gave Allied bomber pilots superior protection and slowly began to sweep the Luftwaffe from the skies, allowing bombers to penetrate deep into Germany and pound civilian and military targets around the clock.

In November 1943, Churchill, Roosevelt, and Stalin met in Teheran, Iran, to plan the Allies' next step. Roosevelt conceded to Stalin that the Soviet Union would exercise de facto control of the eastern European countries that the Red Army occupied as it rolled back the still-potent German Wehrmacht. Stalin agreed to enter the war against Japan once Germany finally surrendered, in effect promising to open a second front in the Pacific theater. Roosevelt and Churchill promised that they would at last launch a massive second-front assault in northern France. Code-named Overlord, the offensive was scheduled to begin in May 1944 with the combined manpower of four million Americans massed in England along with fourteen divisions from Britain, three from Canada, and one each from Poland and France.

General Eisenhower was assigned overall command of Allied forces. German defenders, directed by General Erwin Rommel, fortified the cliffs and mined the beaches of northwestern France. But the huge deployment of Hitler's armies in the east trying to halt the Red Army's westward offensive left too few German troops to stop the millions of Allied soldiers waiting in England. More decisive, years of Allied air raids had decimated the German Luftwaffe, which could send aloft only 300 fighter planes against 12,000 Allied aircraft.

Diversionary bombing and false radio messages about armies that in fact did not exist encouraged the Germans to expect an Allied invasion where the English Channel is narrowest. The actual invasion site was 300 miles away on the beaches of Normandy (Map 25.4). After frustrating delays caused by stormy weather, Eisenhower launched the largest amphibious assault in world history on D Day, June 6, 1944. Rough seas and deadly fire from German machine guns slowed the assault, but Allied soldiers finally secured the beachhead.

Within a week, an avalanche of soldiers, tanks, and other military equipment rolled across the Normandy beaches and propelled Allied forces toward Germany. As the giant pincers of the Allied and Soviet armies closed on Germany in December 1944, Hitler ordered a counterattack to capture the Allies' essential supply port at Antwerp, Belgium. In the Battle of the Bulge (December 16, 1944–January 31, 1945), as the Allies termed it, German forces drove fifty-five miles into Allied lines before being stopped

MAP 25.4   The European Theater of World War II, 1942–1945
Russian reversal of the German offensive by breaking the sieges of Stalingrad and Leningrad, combined with
Allied landings in North Africa and Normandy, placed Germany in a closing vise of armies from all sides.

at Bastogne. More than 70,000 Allied soldiers were killed, including more Americans than in any other battle of the war. But the Nazis lost 100,000 men and hundreds of tanks, fatally depleting Hitler's reserves.

In February 1945, while Allied armies relentlessly pushed German forces backward, Churchill, Stalin, and Roosevelt met secretly at Yalta, a Russian resort town on the Black Sea, to discuss the plans for the postwar future.

Seriously ill and noticeably frail, Roosevelt managed to secure Stalin's promise to permit votes of self-determination by people in the eastern European countries occupied by the Red Army. The Allies pledged to support Chiang Kai-shek as the leader of China. The Soviet Union obtained a role in the postwar government of Korea and Manchuria in exchange for entering the war against Japan after the defeat of Germany.

The "Big Three" also agreed on the creation of a new international peacekeeping organization, the United Nations (UN). All nations would have a place in the UN's General Assembly, but the Security Council would wield decisive power, and its permanent representatives from the Allied powers—China, France, Great Britain, the Soviet Union, and the United States—would possess a veto over UN actions. American response to the creation of the UN reflected the triumph of internationalism during the nation's mobilization for war. The Senate ratified the United Nations Charter in July 1945 by a vote of 89 to 2.

While Allied armies sped toward Berlin, Allied war planes dropped more bombs after D Day than in all previous European bombing raids combined. In February 1945, Allied bombers rained a firestorm of death and destruction on

D Day Invasion

"Taxi to Hell—and Back" is what Robert Sargent called his photograph of the D Day invasion of Normandy on June 6, 1944. Amid a dense fleet of landing craft, men lucky enough to have made it through rough seas and enemy fire struggle onto the beach to open a second front in Europe. The majority of soldiers in this first wave were cut down by enemy fire from the high cliffs beyond the beach.
Library of Congress.

Berlin and Dresden, killing 60,000 civilians. By April 11, Allied armies sweeping in from the west reached the banks of the Elbe River, the agreed-upon rendezvous with the Red Army, and paused while the Soviets smashed into Berlin. In three weeks of vicious house-to-house fighting, the Red Army captured Berlin on May 2. Hitler committed suicide on April 30, and on May 7 a provisional German government surrendered unconditionally. The war in Europe was finally over, with the sacrifice of 135,576 American soldiers, nearly 250,000 British troops, and 9 million Russian combatants.

Roosevelt did not live to witness the end of the war. On April 12, while resting in Warm Springs, Georgia, the president suffered a fatal stroke. Americans grieved for the man who had led them through years of depression and world war, and they worried aloud about his successor, Vice President Harry Truman, who would have to steer the nation to victory over Japan and protect American interests in the postwar world.

The Defeat of Japan

After the punishing defeats in the Coral Sea and at Midway, Japan had to quell renewed resistance on the Asian mainland and to fend off Allied naval and air attacks. In 1943 British and American forces, along with Indian and Chinese allies, launched an offensive against Japanese outposts in southern Asia, pushing through Burma and into China, where the armies of Chiang Kai-shek continued to resist conquest. In the Pacific, Americans and their allies attacked Japanese strongholds by sea, air, and land, moving island by island toward the Japanese homeland (Map 25.5). The island-hopping campaign began in August 1942 when American marines landed on Guadalcanal in the southern Pacific. For the next six months, a savage battle raged for control of the strategic area. Finally, during the night of February 7, 1943, Japanese forces withdrew. The terrible losses on both sides indicated to the marines how costly it would be to defeat Japan.

In mid-1943, American, Australian, and New Zealand forces launched offensives in New Guinea and the Solomon Islands that gradually secured the South Pacific. In the Central Pacific, amphibious forces conquered the Gilbert and Marshall Islands, which served as forward bases for decisive air assaults on the Japanese home islands. As the Allies attacked island after island,

Japanese soldiers were ordered to refuse to surrender no matter how hopeless their plight. At Tarawa, a barren coral island of less than three square miles, three thousand Japanese defenders battled American marines for three days, killing a thousand marines and wounding two thousand until the seventeen Japanese survivors finally succumbed.

While the island-hopping campaign kept pressure on Japanese forces, the Allies invaded the Philippines in the fall of 1944. In the three-day battle of Leyte Gulf, the greatest naval encounter in world history, the American fleet crushed the Japanese armada, clearing the way for Allied victory in the Philippines. While the Philippine campaign was under way, American forces captured two crucial islands—Iwo Jima and Okinawa—from which they planned to launch an attack on the Japanese homeland. To defend Okinawa and prevent the American invaders from getting within close bombing range of their home islands, Japanese leaders ordered thousands of suicide pilots, known as *kamikaze,* to crash their bomb-laden planes into Allied ships. Like airborne torpedoes, kamikaze caused fearsome destruction. But instead of destroying the American fleet, the kamikaze demolished the last vestige of the Japanese air force. By June 1945, the Japanese were nearly defenseless on sea and in the air. Still, their leaders prepared to fight to the death for their homeland.

Atomic Warfare

In mid-July 1945, as Allied forces were preparing for the final assault on Japan, American scientists tested a secret weapon at an isolated desert site near Los Alamos, New Mexico. In 1942, Roosevelt had authorized the top-secret Manhattan Project to find a way to convert nuclear energy into a superbomb before the Germans added such a weapon to their arsenal. More than 100,000 Americans, led by scientists, engineers, and military officers at Los Alamos, worked frantically to win the fateful race for an atomic bomb. Germany surrendered two and a half months before the test on July 16, 1945, when scientists first witnessed an awesome explosion that sent a mushroom cloud of debris eight miles into the atmosphere.

A delegation of scientists and officials, troubled by the bomb's destructive force, secretly proposed that the United States give a public demonstration of the bomb's cataclysmic power,

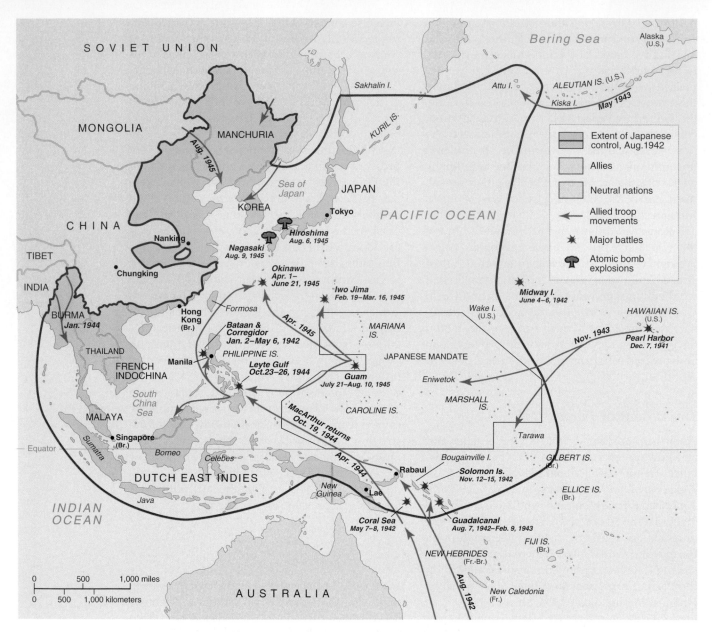

MAP 25.5 The Pacific Theater of World War II, 1941–1945
To drive the Japanese from their far-flung empire, the Allies launched two combined naval and military offensives—one to recapture the Philippines and then
attack Japanese forces in China, the other to hop from island to island in the
Central Pacific toward the Japanese mainland.

READING THE MAP: What was the extent of Japanese control up until August 1942?
Which nations in the Pacific theater sided with the Allies? Which nations remained
neutral?

CONNECTIONS: Describe the economic and military motivations behind Japan's
domination of the region. How and when did the Japanese achieve this dominance?
Judging from this map, what strategic and geographic concerns might immediately
have prompted Truman and his advisers to consider using the atomic bomb
against Japan?

FOR MORE HELP ANALYZING THIS MAP, see the map activity for this chapter in the
Online Study Guide at bedfordstmartins.com/roarkcompact.

hoping to persuade Japan's leaders to surrender. With the Japanese incapable of offensive action and blockaded by the Allied fleet, proponents of a demonstration were encouraged because Japanese emissaries were already putting out feelers about peace negotiations. But U.S. government officials quickly rejected such a demonstration: Americans had enough nuclear material for only three bombs, the demonstration bomb might fail to explode, and the Japanese might not surrender even if it did. Also, despite numerous defeats, Japan still had more than 6 million reserves at home fortified by over 5,000 kamikaze aircraft stockpiled for a last-ditch defense against the anticipated Allied assault, which U.S. military advisers estimated would cost the lives of at least 250,000 Americans.

President Truman heard about the successful bomb test when he was in Potsdam, Germany, negotiating with Stalin about postwar issues. Truman realized that the atomic bomb could hasten the end of the war with Japan, perhaps before the Russians could attack the Japanese in Korea and Manchuria, as Stalin pledged at Yalta to do. Within a few months after the defeat of Germany, Truman also recognized that the bomb gave the United States a devastating atomic **monopoly** that could be used to counter Soviet ambitions and advance American interests in the postwar world.

Truman saw no reason not to use the atomic bomb against Japan if doing so would save American lives. But first he issued an ultimatum: Japan must surrender unconditionally

Hiroshima Bombing

This rare shot taken by a news photographer in Hiroshima immediately after the atomic bomb exploded on August 6, 1945, suggests the shock and incomprehension that survivors later described as their first reaction. On August 9, another atomic bomb created similar devastation in Nagasaki.

UN photo.

or face utter ruin. When the Japanese failed to respond by the deadline, Truman ordered that a bomb be dropped on a Japanese city not already heavily damaged by American raids. On August 6, Colonel Paul Tibbets piloted the *Enola Gay* over Hiroshima and released an atomic bomb, leveling the city and incinerating 78,000 people. Three days later, after the Japanese government still refused to surrender, Tibbets-trained airmen dropped a second atomic bomb on Nagasaki, killing more than 100,000 civilians.

At last, a peace faction took control of the Japanese government, and with American assurance that the emperor could retain his throne after the Allies took over, Japan surrendered on August 14. On a troop ship departing from Europe for what would have been the final assault on Japan, an American soldier spoke for millions of others when he heard the wonderful news that the killing was over: "We are going to grow to adulthood after all."

REVIEW Why did Truman elect to use an atomic bomb against Japan in August 1945?

Conclusion: Allied Victory and America's Emergence as a Superpower

Shortly after Pearl Harbor, Hitler pronounced America "a decayed country" without "much future," a country "where everything is built on the dollar" and bound to fall apart. American mobilization for World War II disproved Hitler's arrogant prophecy, as Paul Tibbets's historic flight dramatized. At a cost of 405,399 American lives, the nation united with its allies to battle Axis aggressors in Europe and Asia and eventually to crush them into unconditional surrender. Almost all Americans believed they had won a "good war" against totalitarian evil. The Allies saved Asia and Europe from enslavement and finally halted the Nazis' genocidal campaign against Jews and others whom the Nazis considered inferior. To secure human rights and protect the world against future wars, the Roosevelt administration took the lead in creating the United Nations.

Wartime production lifted the nation out of the Great Depression. The gross national product soared to four times what it had been when Roosevelt became president in 1933. Jobs in defense industries eliminated chronic unemployment, provided wages for millions of women workers and African American migrants from southern farms, and boosted Americans' prosperity. Ahead stretched the challenge of maintaining that prosperity while reintegrating millions of uniformed men and women coming home from overseas.

By the end of the war, the United States had emerged as a global superpower. Wartime mobilization made the American economy the strongest in the world, buttressed by the military clout of the nation's nuclear monopoly. While the war left much of the world a smoldering wasteland, the American mainland enjoyed immunity from attack. The Japanese occupation of China left 50 million people without homes and millions more dead, maimed, and orphaned. The German offensive against the Soviet Union killed more than 26 million Russian soldiers and civilians. Germany and Japan lay in ruins, their economies as shattered as their military forces. The Allies killed more than 4 million Nazi soldiers and over 1.2 million Japanese combatants, as well as hundreds of thousands of civilians. But in the gruesome balance sheet of war, the Axis powers inflicted far more grief, misery, and destruction upon the global victims of their aggression than they suffered in return.

As the dominant Western nation in the postwar world, the United States asserted leadership in the reconstruction of Europe while occupying Japan and overseeing its economic and political recovery. America soon confronted new challenges in the tense aftermath of the war, as Soviets seized political control of Eastern Europe, a Communist revolution swept China, and national liberation movements emerged in the colonial empires of Britain and France. The surrender of the Axis powers ended the battles of World War II, but the forces unleashed by the war shaped the United States and the rest of the world for decades to come.

Suggestions for Further Reading

Michael Beschloss, *The Conquerors: Roosevelt, Truman, and the Destruction of Hitler's Germany* (2002). An interesting account of American wartime strategy in Europe.

John Dower, *War without Mercy: Race and Power in the Pacific War* (1986). A powerful exploration of the significance of racial attitudes among belligerents in the Pacific theater.

Max Hastings, *Armageddon: The Battle for Germany, 1944–1945* (2005). A compelling analysis of Allied attacks from both east and west that finally defeated Germany.

John W. Jeffries, *Wartime America: The World War II Home Front* (1996). An informative survey of wartime transformations of domestic life.

Wendy Ng, *Japanese American Internment during World War II* (2002). A revealing examination of U.S. government internment of Japanese Americans as wartime security risks.

Richard Rhodes, *The Making of the Atomic Bomb* (1986). A fascinating account of the intellectual, industrial, and military mobilization to build the atomic bomb.

▶ For more books about topics in this chapter, see the Online Study Guide at bedfordstmartins.com/roarkcompact.

▶ For additional firsthand accounts of this period, see Chapter 25 in Michael Johnson, ed., *Reading the American Past,* Third Edition.

▶ For Web sites and documents related to topics and places in this chapter, see "History Links," "DocLinks," and "PlaceLinks" at bedfordstmartins.com/roarkcompact.

REVIEWING THE CHAPTER

Follow these steps to review and strengthen your understanding of the chapter.

STEP 1: *Study the* **Key Terms** *and* **Timeline** *to identify the significance of each item listed.*

STEP 2: *Answer the* **Review Questions***, drawing on key terms and dates to support your answers.*

STEP 3: *Drawing on the Key Terms, Timeline, and Review Questions, answer the broader* **Making Connections** *questions.*

KEY TERMS

Who

Paul Tibbets (p. 649)
Benito Mussolini (pp. 651, 662)
Adolf Hitler (pp. 652, 653)
Chiang Kai-shek (p. 652)
Gerald Nye (p. 652)
Francisco Franco (p. 652)
Neville Chamberlain (p. 653)
Joseph Stalin (p. 653)
Philippe Pétain (p. 655)
Winston Churchill (p. 655)
Wendell Willkie (p. 655)
Hideki Tojo (p. 656)
Emperor Hirohito (p. 656)
Isoroku Yamamoto (p. 660)
Douglas MacArthur (p. 660)
James Doolittle (p. 661)
Chester W. Nimitz (p. 661)
Dwight D. Eisenhower
  (pp. 662, 668)
Erwin Rommel (pp. 662, 668)
George Patton (p. 662)
A. Philip Randolph (p. 664)

Harry S. Truman (p. 665)
Thomas E. Dewey (p. 665)

What

Enola Gay (pp. 650, 674)
Hiroshima and Nagasaki (pp. 650, 674)
good neighbor policy (p. 651)
Reciprocal Trade Agreements Act (p. 652)
Neutrality Act of 1937 (p. 652)
rape of Nanking (p. 652)
Spanish civil war (p. 653)
Anschluss (p. 653)
Third Reich (p. 653)
Munich agreement (p. 653)
Nazi-Soviet treaty of nonaggression
  (p. 653)
Maginot Line (p. 654)
Battle of Britain (p. 655)
Lend-Lease Act (p. 655)
Atlantic Charter (p. 656)
Tripartite Pact (p. 656)
Pearl Harbor (p. 656)
U-boats (pp. 658, 661)

internment camps (p. 659)
Korematsu decision (p. 659)
Selective Service Act (p. 659)
War Production Board (p. 660)
Bataan Death March (p. 660)
Battle of Midway (p. 661)
Double V campaign (p. 663)
Brotherhood of Sleeping Car Porters
  (p. 664)
Committee on Fair Employment
  Practices (p. 664)
Congress of Racial Equality (CORE)
  (p. 664)
GI Bill of Rights (p. 665)
Holocaust (p. 665)
Overlord (p. 668)
D Day (p. 668)
Yalta Conference (p. 669)
United Nations (UN) (p. 670)
battle of Leyte Gulf (p. 671)
kamikaze (p. 671)
Manhattan Project (p. 671)

TIMELINE

1935– • Congress passes neutrality acts.
1937

    1936 • Nazi Germany occupies Rhineland.
           • Mussolini conquers Ethiopia.
           • Spanish civil war begins.

        1937 • Japanese troops capture Nanking.
                • Roosevelt delivers "quarantine" speech.

            1938 • Hitler annexes Austria.
                   • Munich agreement.

                1939 • German troops occupy Czechoslovakia.
                     • Nazi-Soviet nonaggression pact.
                     • **September 1.** Germany's attack on Poland begins World War II.

                   1940 • **May–June.** British evacuation at Dunkirk.
                     • **June.** German occupation of France begins.

                    1941 • Lend-Lease Act.

                     • **June.** Germany invades Soviet Union.
                     • **August.** Atlantic Charter issued.
                     • **December 7.** Japanese attack Pearl Harbor.

REVIEW QUESTIONS

1. Why did Roosevelt try to honor the principle of isolationism as president? (pp. 651–53)

2. How did Roosevelt attempt to balance American isolationism with the increasingly ominous international scene of the late 1930s? (pp. 653–57)

3. How did the Roosevelt administration steer the mobilization of human and industrial resources necessary for a two-front war? (pp. 657–60)

4. How did the United States gain advantage over the Japanese navy in the Pacific? (pp. 660–62)

5. Why did women and minorities enter the industrial workforce in unprecedented numbers during the war? (pp. 662–65)

6. Why did Truman elect to use an atomic bomb against Japan in August 1945? (pp. 668–74)

MAKING CONNECTIONS

1. Does isolationism bolster or undermine national security and national economic interests? Discuss Roosevelt's evolving answer to this question as revealed in his administration's policies toward Europe. In your answer, consider how other constraints (such as politics, history, and ethics) affected administration policies.

2. World War II brought new prosperity to many Americans. Why did war succeed in creating the full economic recovery that the New Deal had pursued with more limited success? In your answer, discuss both the objectives of specific New Deal economic reforms and the needs of the wartime economy.

3. Japan's attack on Pearl Harbor plunged the United States into war with the Axis powers. How did the United States recover from this attack to play a decisive role in the Allies' victory? Discuss three American military or diplomatic actions and their contribution to the defeat of the Axis powers.

4. As the United States battled racist regimes abroad, the realities of discrimination at home came sharply into focus. How did minorities' contributions to the war effort as soldiers and laborers draw attention to these problems? What were the political implications of these developments? In your answer, consider both grassroots political action and federal policy.

▶ **For practice quizzes, a customized study plan, and other study tools,** see the Online Study Guide at bedfordstmartins.com/roarkcompact.

1942 • Japan captures Philippines.
• Congress of Racial Equality (CORE) founded.
• Battles of Coral Sea and Midway.
• Roosevelt authorizes Manhattan Project.
• **November.** U.S. forces invade North Africa.
• Roosevelt authorizes internment of Japanese Americans.

    1943 • Allied leaders demand unconditional surrender of Axis forces.
    • Zoot suit riots.
    • U.S. forces invade Sicily.

        1944 • **June 6.** D Day.

            1945 • Yalta Conference.
            • **April 12.** Roosevelt dies; Vice President Harry Truman becomes president.
            • **April 30.** Hitler commits suicide.
            • **May 7.** Germany surrenders.
            • **July.** United States joins United Nations.
            • **August 6.** United States drops atomic bomb on Hiroshima.
            • **August 9.** United States drops atomic bomb on Nagasaki.
            • **August 14.** Japan surrenders, ending World War II.

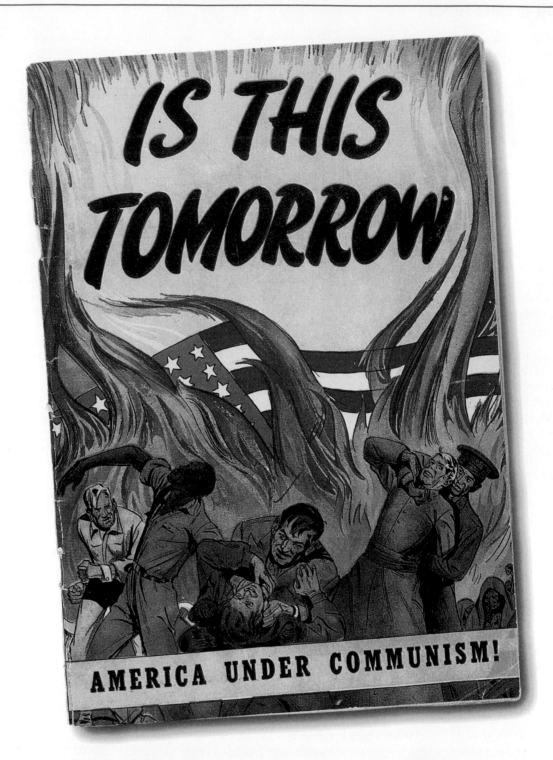

COLD WAR COMIC BOOK
Americans barely had time to celebrate the Allied victory in World War II when they perceived a new threat, posed by the Soviet Union. Fear of communism dominated much of postwar American life and politics, even invading popular culture. Four million copies of this comic book, published by a religious organization in 1947, painted a terrifying picture of what would happen to Americans if the Soviets took over the country. Such takeover stories appeared in movies, cartoons, and magazines as well as in other comic books.

Collection of Charles H. Christensen.

Cold War Politics
in the Truman Years
1945–1953

O N NOVEMBER 5, 1946, President Harry S. Truman, his wife, and his daughter boarded the train back to Washington from Independence, Missouri, where they had gone home to vote in the congressional elections. During the campaigns, Republicans had blasted Truman as incapable of dealing with economic problems and the threat of **communism**. Campaign slogans had jeered, "To Err is Truman," while the president's approval rating sank to a mere 32 percent. Many Democratic candidates had avoided mentioning his name and instead used recordings of the late Franklin Roosevelt's voice to stir voters. Playing poker with reporters on the train as the returns came in, Truman appeared unconcerned. But the results were devastating: The Republicans captured both the House and the Senate by substantial majorities, dominating Congress for the first time since 1932.

When Truman arrived in Washington at the lowest point of his presidency, only one member of his administration showed up to greet him, Undersecretary of State Dean Acheson. Acheson's gesture signaled a developing relationship of central importance to the two men and to postwar history. The fifty-three-year-old Acheson shared most of Truman's political principles, though their backgrounds differed sharply. Acheson had enjoyed an upper-class education at a private prep school, Yale University, and Harvard Law School. After clerking for Supreme Court justice Louis Brandeis, he earned a comfortable living as a corporate lawyer. In contrast, Truman, the son of a Missouri farmer, had not attended college and had failed in a business venture before entering local politics in the 1920s.

Despite his wealth and privilege, Acheson supported much of the **New Deal** and staunchly defended organized labor. He spoke out against **isolationism** in the 1930s, and in 1941 he accepted President Roosevelt's offer of a job at the State Department. Shortly after Truman became president, the supremely confident Acheson wrote privately about shortcomings in Truman's "judgment and wisdom that the limitations of his experience produce," but he also found the fledgling president "straightforward, decisive, simple, entirely honest," a man who "will learn fast and will inspire confidence." In June 1947, Acheson left the State Department, but Truman lured him back in 1949 to be secretary of state during the president's second term. Acheson appreciated Truman's willingness to make tough decisions and admiringly noted that Truman's "ego never came between him and his job." Truman cherished Acheson's abiding loyalty, calling him "my good right hand."

Truman needed all the help he could get. The "accidental president" lacked the charisma, experience, and political skills with which Roosevelt had transformed both foreign and domestic policy, won four presidential elections, and forged a Democratic Party coalition that dominated national politics. Initially criticized and abandoned by many Roosevelt loyalists, Truman faced a resurgent Republican Party as well as revolts from within his own party. Besides addressing domestic problems that the New Deal had not solved—how to sustain economic growth and avoid another depression without the war to fuel the economy—Truman had to redefine the nation's foreign policy goals in a new international context.

Dean Acheson was instrumental in forging that foreign policy. As early as 1946, Acheson became convinced that the Soviet Union posed a major threat to U.S. security. With other officials, he helped to shape a policy designed to contain and thwart Soviet power wherever it threatened to spread. By 1947, a new term had been coined to describe the intense rivalry between the superpowers—**cold war**. The **containment** policy worked in Western Europe with the enunciation of the **Truman Doctrine**, implementation of the Marshall Plan, and creation of **NATO**; but communism spread in Asia, and at home a wave of anti-Communist hysteria harmed many Americans and stifled dissent and debate about U.S. policies.

As the preeminent foreign policy official, Acheson too reaped abuse from Republicans for being "soft on communism." At the height of the anti-Communist frenzy, Acheson received so much hate mail that guards were posted at his house. Yet he kept both his job and his sense of humor. When cab drivers asked him, "Aren't you Dean Acheson?" he would reply, "Yes. Do I have to get out?"

From the Grand Alliance to Containment

With Japan's surrender in August 1945, Americans besieged the government for the return of their loved ones. Baby booties arrived at the White House with a note, "Please send my daddy home." Americans looked forward to the dismantling of the large military establishment and expected the Allies, led by the United States and working within the United Nations, to cooperate in the management of international peace. Postwar realities quickly dashed these expectations. A dangerous new threat seemed to arise as the wartime alliance forged by the

Dean Acheson
No individual had more to do with transforming America's role in the world after World War II than Dean Acheson, President Truman's closest foreign policy adviser. Acheson, shown here with Truman in 1945, criticized those who saw the cold war in black-and-white terms and communism as an evil that the United States could expel from the earth. Rather, he advocated that American leaders learn "to limit objectives, to get ourselves away from the search for the absolute, to find out what is within our powers."
Harry S. Truman Library.

United States, Great Britain, and the Soviet Union crumbled, and the United States began to develop the means to contain the spread of Soviet power around the globe.

The Cold War Begins

"The guys who came out of World War II were idealistic," reported Harold Russell, a young paratrooper who lost both hands in a training accident. "We felt the day had come when the wars were all over." Public opinion polls echoed the veterans' confidence in the promise of peace. But political leaders were less optimistic. Once the Allies had overcome a common enemy, the prewar mistrust and antagonism between the Soviet Union and the West resurfaced over their very different visions of the postwar world.

The Western Allies' delay in opening a second front in Western Europe aroused Soviet suspicions during the war. The Soviet Union made supreme wartime sacrifices, losing more than twenty million citizens and vast portions of its agricultural and industrial capacity. At the war's end, Soviet leader Joseph Stalin wanted to make Germany pay for the rebuilding of the Soviet economy and to expand Soviet influence in the world. Above all, he wanted friendly governments on the Soviet Union's borders in Eastern Europe.

In contrast, enemy fire had never touched the mainland of the United States, and its 405,000 dead amounted to just 2 percent of the Soviet loss. With a vastly expanded economy and a monopoly on atomic weapons, the United States was the most powerful nation on the planet. That sheer power, along with U.S. economic interests, policymakers' views about how the recent war might have been avoided, and a belief in the superiority of American institutions and intentions, all affected how American leaders approached the Soviet Union after the war.

Fearing a return of the depression, U.S. officials believed that a healthy economy depended on opportunities abroad. American companies needed access to raw materials, markets for their goods, and security for their investments overseas. These needs could be met best in countries with similar economic and political systems, not in those where government controls interfered with the free flow of products and dollars. As Truman put it in 1947, "The American system can survive in America only if it becomes a world system."

Yet both leaders and citizens regarded their foreign policy not as a self-interested campaign to guarantee economic interests, but as the means to preserve national security and bring freedom, **democracy**, and capitalism to the rest of the world. Laura Briggs spoke for many Americans who believed "it was our destiny to prove that we were the children of God and that our way was right for the world."

Recent history also shaped postwar foreign policy. Americans believed that Britain and France might have prevented World War II had they resisted rather than appeased Hitler's initial aggression. Navy Secretary James V. Forrestal, for example, argued against trying to "buy [the Soviets'] understanding and sympathy. We tried that once with Hitler." This "appeasement" analogy would be invoked repeatedly when the United States faced challenges to the international status quo.

The man with ultimate responsibility for U.S. policy was a keen student of history but came to the White House with little international experience. When Germany attacked the Soviet Union in 1941, then-Senator Truman expressed his hope that the two would kill each other off. As president he envisioned Soviet-American cooperation, as long as the Soviet Union conformed with U.S. plans for the postwar world and restrained its expansionist impulses. Proud of his ability to make quick decisions, Truman determined to be firm with the Soviets, knowing well that America's nuclear monopoly gave him the upper hand.

Soviet and American interests clashed first in Eastern Europe. Stalin insisted that the Allies' wartime agreements gave him a free hand in the countries defeated or liberated by the Red Army, just as the United States was unilaterally reconstructing governments in Italy and Japan. The Soviet dictator used harsh methods to install Communist governments in neighboring Poland and Bulgaria. Elsewhere, the Soviets initially tolerated non-Communist governments in Hungary and Czechoslovakia. And in the spring of 1946, Stalin responded to pressure from the West and removed troops from Iran on the Soviet Union's southwest border, allowing United States access to rich oil fields there.

Stalin considered U.S. officials hypocritical in demanding democratic elections in Eastern Europe while supporting dictatorships friendly to U.S. interests in Latin American countries. The United States clung to its sphere of influence while opposing Soviet efforts to create its own. But the Western Allies were unwilling to match tough words with military force, and their sharp protests failed to prevent the Soviet

Joseph Stalin: From Ally to Enemy
These two portrayals of the Soviet leader indicate how quickly the World War II alliance disintegrated into the cold war. On the left in a 1944 issue of the popular magazine *Look,* Stalin is photographed with adoring schoolchildren. The accompanying article depicts him as an effective leader but also as a sensitive man who wrote poetry and loved literature. Only four years later, in 1948, *Look* published Stalin's life story. The photo on the right frames his face with communism's emblem, the hammer and sickle, symbolizing the alliance of workers and peasants. The 1944 piece called Stalin a "man of trenchant speech, indomitable will and extraordinary mental capacity [and] lover of literature." The 1948 article emphasized his "rise to absolute power over millions of lives" and depicted him as a "small man with drooping shoulders [who] tyrannizes one-fifth of the world." What do these two items suggest about the role of the press in American society?
The Michael Barson Collection/Past Perfect.

Union from establishing satellite countries in most of Eastern Europe.

In 1946, the wartime Allies contended over Germany's future. American policymakers wanted to demilitarize Germany, but they also sought rapid industrial revival there to foster European economic recovery and thus America's own long-term prosperity. By contrast, the Soviet Union wanted Germany weak militarily and economically, as well as heavy reparations to help rebuild the devastated Soviet economy. Unable to settle their differences, the Allies divided Germany. The Soviet Union installed a puppet Communist government in the eastern section, and in December 1946, Britain, France, and the United States unified their occupation zones, beginning the process that established the Federal Republic of Germany—West Germany—in 1949 (Map 26.1).

The war of words escalated early in 1946. Boasting of the superiority of the Soviet system, Stalin told a Moscow audience in February that capitalism inevitably produced war. One month later, Truman traveled with Winston Churchill to Fulton, Missouri, where the former prime minister denounced Soviet suppression of the popular will in Eastern and central Europe. "From Stettin in the Baltic to Trieste in the Adriatic, an iron curtain has descended across the Continent," Churchill said. (See "Documenting the American Promise," page 684.) Although Truman did not officially endorse Churchill's **iron curtain** speech, his presence implied agreement with the idea of joint British-American action to combat Soviet aggression. Stalin regarded the speech as "a call to war against the USSR."

MAP 26.1   The Division of Europe after World War II
The "iron curtain," a term coined by Winston Churchill to refer to the Soviet grip on Eastern and central Europe, divided Europe for nearly fifty years. Communist governments controlled the countries along the Soviet Union's western border. The only exception was Finland, which remained neutral.

In February 1946, George F. Kennan, a career diplomat with experience in Eastern Europe and Moscow, wrote a comprehensive rationale for hard-line foreign policy. Downplaying the influence of Communist ideology in Soviet policy, he instead stressed the Soviets' insecurity and their need to maintain authority at home, which he believed prompted Stalin to exaggerate threats from abroad and to expand Soviet power. These circumstances, Kennan argued, made it impossible to negotiate with Stalin. Secretary of State James F. Byrnes, Undersecretary Acheson, and other key Truman advisers agreed with him.

Kennan predicted that the Soviet Union would retreat from its expansionist efforts "in the face of superior force," and he recommended that the United States respond with "unalterable counterforce"—the approach that came to be called containment. Kennan expected that containment would eventually end in "either the breakup or the gradual mellowing of Soviet power." This message reached a larger audience when Kennan's views were published in *Foreign Affairs* magazine in July 1947. His analysis marked a critical turning point in the development of the cold war, providing a compelling rationale for using U.S. power throughout the world.

Not all public figures accepted the toughening line. In September 1946, Secretary of Commerce Henry A. Wallace, Truman's predecessor as vice president, urged greater understanding of the Soviets' concerns about their nation's security, insisting that "we have no more business in the political affairs of Eastern Europe than Russia has in the political affairs of Latin America." (See "Documenting the American Promise," page 684.)

The Emerging Cold War

Although antagonism between the Soviet Union and the West stretched back to the Russian Revolution of 1917, the United States, the Soviet Union, Britain, and other powers had cooperated to win World War II. Early in 1946, however, Soviet and Western leaders publicly expressed distrust and attributed hostile motivations to each other. Within the United States, disagreement arose about how to deal with the Soviet Union.

DOCUMENT 1
Joseph Stalin Addresses a Rally in Moscow, February 9, 1946

In early 1946, Premier Joseph Stalin called on the Soviet people to support his program for economic development. Although Stalin did not address cold war issues, leaders in the West viewed his comments about communism and capitalism and his boasts about the strength of the Red Army as a threat to peace.

The [Second World] war arose as the inevitable result of the development of the world economic and political forces on the basis of monopoly capitalism....

The uneven development of the capitalist countries leads in time to sharp disturbances in their relations, and the group of countries which consider themselves inadequately provided with raw materials and export markets try usually to change this situation and to change the position in their favor by means of armed force. As a result of these factors, the capitalist world is split into two hostile camps and war follows. ... The Soviet social system has proved to be more capable of life and more stable than a non-Soviet social system....

It was the Soviet armed forces that won.... The Red Army heroically withstood all the adversities of the war, routed completely the armies of our enemies and emerged victoriously from the war. This is recognized by everybody—friend and foe.

[Stalin talks about his new Five-Year Plan.] Apart from the fact that in the very near future the rationing system will be abolished, special attention will be focused on expanding the production of goods for mass consumption, on raising the standard of life of the working people by consistent and systematic reduction of the costs of all goods, and on wide-scale construction of all kinds of scientific research institutes to enable science to develop its forces. I have no doubt that if we render the necessary assistance to our scientists they will be able not only to overtake but also in the very near future to surpass the achievements of science outside the boundaries of our country.

SOURCE: Excerpts from Joseph Stalin, *Vital Speeches of the Day*, February 9 (1946). Reprinted with permission.

DOCUMENT 2
Winston Churchill Delivers His "Iron Curtain" Speech at Westminster College in Fulton, Missouri, March 5, 1946

With Truman sitting on the podium, Winston Churchill, former prime minister of Britain, assessed Soviet actions in harsh terms. Stalin called the speech "a call to war with the Soviet Union."

The United States stands at this time at the pinnacle of world power. It is a solemn moment for the American democracy. With primacy in power is also joined an awe-inspiring accountability to the future. [Churchill then speaks of the need to support the United Nations.]

It would nevertheless be wrong and imprudent to intrust the secret knowledge or experience of the atomic bomb, which the United States, Great Britain and Canada now share, to the world organization [the United Nations], while it is still in its infancy. It would be criminal madness to cast it adrift in this still agitated and ununited world....

...I have a strong admiration and regard for the valiant Russian people and for my war-time comrade, Marshal Stalin.... We understand the Russians need to be secure on her western frontiers from all renewal of German aggression.... It is my duty, however, to place before you certain facts....

From Stettin in the Baltic to Trieste in the Adriatic, an iron curtain has descended across the Continent. Behind that line lie all the capitals of the ancient states of central and eastern Europe. Warsaw, Berlin, Prague, Vienna, Budapest, Belgrade, Bucharest and Sofia, all these famous cities and the populations around them lie in the Soviet sphere and all are subject in one form or another, not only to Soviet influence but to a very high and increasing measure of control from Moscow.... The Communist parties, which were very small in all these eastern states of Europe, have been raised to pre-eminence and power far beyond their numbers and are seeking everywhere to obtain totalitarian control. Police governments are prevailing in nearly every case....

...In a great number of countries, far from the Russian frontiers and throughout the world, Communist fifth columns are established and work in complete unity and absolute obedience to the directions they receive from the Communist center.

I do not believe that Soviet Russia desires war. What they desire is the fruits of war and the indefinite expansion of their power and doctrines....Our difficulties and dangers will not be removed by...mere waiting to see what happens; nor will they be relieved by a policy of appeasement....I am convinced that there is nothing they [the Russians] admire so much as strength, and there is nothing for which they have less respect than for military weakness.

SOURCE: Excerpts from Winston Churchill, *Vital Speeches of the Day,* March 5 (1946). Reprinted with permission.

DOCUMENT 3
Henry A. Wallace Addresses an Election Rally at Madison Square Garden, New York, September 12, 1946

Throughout 1946, Henry A. Wallace, Truman's secretary of commerce, urged the president to take a more conciliatory approach toward the Soviet Union, a position reflected in a speech Wallace gave to a rally of leftist and liberal groups in New York City. Truman believed that Wallace's words undermined his foreign policy and asked for Wallace's resignation.

We cannot rest in the assurance that we invented the atom bomb—and therefore that this agent of destruction will work best for us. He who trusts in the atom bomb will sooner or later perish by the atom bomb— or something worse....

To achieve lasting peace, we must study in detail just how the Russian character was formed— by invasions of Tartars, Mongols, Germans, Poles, Swedes, and French; by the czarist rule based on ignorance, fear and force; by the intervention of the British, French and Americans in Russian affairs from 1919 to 1921; by the geography of the huge Russian land mass situated strategically between Europe and Asia; and by the vitality derived from the rich Russian soil and the strenuous Russian climate. Add to all this the tremendous emotional power which Marxism and Leninism gives to the Russian leaders—and then we can realize that we are reckoning with a force which cannot be handled successfully by a "Get tough with Russia" policy. "Getting tough" never bought anything real and lasting—whether for schoolyard bullies or businessmen or world powers. The tougher we get, the tougher the Russians will get....

...We want cooperation. And I believe that we can get cooperation once Russia understands that our primary objective is neither saving the British Empire nor purchasing oil in the Near East with the lives of American soldiers....

On our part we should recognize that we have no more business in the political affairs of Eastern Europe than Russia has in the political affairs of Latin America, Western Europe and the United States....We have to recognize that

the Balkans are closer to Russia than to us—and that Russia cannot permit either England or the United States to dominate the politics of that area....

...Under friendly peaceful competition the Russian world and the American world will gradually become more alike. The Russians will be forced to grant more and more of the personal freedoms; and we shall become more and more absorbed with the problems of social-economic justice.

SOURCE: Excerpts from Henry A. Wallace, *Vital Speeches of the Day,* September 12 (1946). Reprinted with permission.

QUESTIONS FOR ANALYSIS AND DEBATE

1. What lessons do these three leaders draw from World War II? What do they see as the most critical steps to preventing another war?

2. What differences do these men see between the political and economic systems of the Soviet Union on the one hand and the United States and Western Europe on the other? How do their predictions about these systems differ?

3. What motives do these three men ascribe to Soviet actions? How do Churchill and Wallace differ in their proposals for the Western response to the Soviet Union?

4. Which leader do you think was most optimistic about the prospects for good relationships between Russia and the West? Which was most correct? Why?

State Department officials were furious, and Truman fired him.

The Truman Doctrine and the Marshall Plan

In 1947, the United States began to implement the doctrine of containment that would guide foreign policy for the next four decades. It was not an easy transition; Americans approved a verbal hard line but wanted to keep their soldiers and tax dollars at home. In addition to selling containment to the public, Truman had to gain the support of a Republican-controlled Congress, which included a forceful bloc, led by Ohio senator Robert A. Taft, opposed to a strong U.S. presence in Europe.

Crises in two Mediterranean countries triggered the implementation of containment. In February 1947, Britain informed the United States that its crippled economy could no longer sustain military assistance either to Greece, where the autocratic government faced a leftist uprising, or to Turkey, which was trying to resist Soviet pressures. Truman promptly sought authority to send military and economic missions, along with $400 million in aid, to the two countries. Meeting with congressional leaders, Undersecretary of State Acheson predicted that if Greece and Turkey fell, communism would soon consume three-fourths of the world. After a stunned silence, Michigan senator Arthur Vandenberg, the Republican foreign policy leader and a recent convert from isolationism, warned that to get approval Truman would have to "scare hell out of the country."

Truman did just that. Outlining what would later be called the **domino theory**, he warned that if Greece fell to the rebels, "confusion and disorder might well spread throughout the entire Middle East" and then create instability in Europe. According to what came to be called the Truman Doctrine, the United States would not only resist Soviet military power but also "support free peoples who are resisting attempted subjugation by armed minorities or by outside pressures." Congress did not formally accept the Truman Doctrine when it approved aid for Greece and Turkey. Yet the

assumption that national security depended on rescuing any anti-Communist government from internal rebels or outside pressure became the cornerstone of U.S. foreign policy until the end of the 1980s.

A much larger assistance program for Europe followed aid to Greece and Turkey. In May 1947, Dean Acheson described a war-ravaged Western Europe, with "factories destroyed, fields impoverished, transportation systems wrecked, populations scattered and on the borderline of starvation." American citizens were sending generous amounts of private aid, but Europe needed large-scale assistance. It was "a matter of national self-interest," Acheson argued, for the United States to provide aid. Only economic recovery could halt the growth of **socialist** and Communist parties in France and Italy and confine Soviet influence to Eastern Europe.

In March 1948, Congress approved the European Recovery Program—known as the Marshall Plan, after retired general George C. Marshall, who as secretary of state proposed the plan—and over the next five years the United States spent $13 billion to restore the economies of sixteen Western European nations. Marshall invited all of Europe and the Soviet Union to cooperate in a request for aid, but as administration officials expected, the Soviets objected to the American terms of free trade and financial disclosure and ordered their East European satellites likewise to reject the offer. The assistance program was good business for the United States, because the European nations spent most of the dollars to buy American products, and Europe's economic recovery created new opportunities for American capitalists.

In February 1948, while Congress debated the Marshall Plan, the Soviets staged a brutal coup against the government of Czechoslovakia and installed a Communist regime. Next, Soviet leaders threatened Western access to Berlin. The former capital of Germany lay within Soviet-controlled East Germany, but all four Allies jointly occupied Berlin, dividing it into separate administrative units. As the Western Allies moved to organize West Germany as a sepa-

Berlin Divided, 1948

rate nation, the Soviets retaliated by blocking roads and rail lines between West Germany and the Western-held sections of Berlin, cutting off food, fuel, and other essentials to two million inhabitants.

"We stay in Berlin, period," Truman vowed. Yet he wanted to avoid a confrontation with Soviet troops. So for nearly a year U.S. and British pilots airlifted 2.3 million tons of goods to sustain the West Berliners. Stalin hesitated to shoot down these cargo planes, and in 1949 he lifted the blockade. The city was then divided into East Berlin, under Soviet control, and West Berlin, which became part of West Germany. For many Americans, the Berlin airlift confirmed the wisdom of containment: When challenged, the Russians backed down, as Kennan had predicted.

Building a National Security State

During the Truman years, advocates of the new containment policy fashioned a five-pronged defense strategy: (1) development of atomic weapons, (2) strengthening traditional military power, (3) military alliances with other nations, (4) military and economic aid to friendly nations, and (5) an espionage network and secret means to subvert Communist expansion.

In September 1949, the United States lost its nuclear **monopoly** when officials confirmed that the Soviets had detonated an atomic bomb. Within months, Truman approved development of a hydrogen bomb equivalent to five hundred atomic bombs. This "super bomb" was ready by 1954, but the U.S. advantage was brief. In November 1955, the Soviets exploded their own hydrogen bomb.

From the 1950s through the 1980s, **deterrence** formed the basis of American nuclear strategy. To deter the Soviet Union from attacking, the United States strove to maintain a nuclear force more powerful than the Soviets'. Because the Russians pursued a similar policy, the superpowers became locked in an ever-escalating nuclear-weapons race. Albert Einstein, whose mathematical discoveries had laid the foundations for nuclear weapons, commented grimly on the enormous destructive force now possessed by the superpowers. The war that came after World War III, he warned, would "be fought with sticks and stones."

To implement the second component of containment strategy, the United States beefed up its conventional military power to deter Soviet threats that might not warrant nuclear retaliation. The National Security Act of 1947 streamlined defense planning by uniting the military branches under a single secretary of defense and creating the National Security Council (NSC) to advise the president. During the Berlin crisis, Congress hiked military appropriations and enacted a peacetime **draft**. Congress also granted permanent status to the women's military branches, though it limited their numbers and rank. With 1.5 million men and women in uniform in 1950, the military strength of the United States had quadrupled since the 1930s, and defense expenditures claimed one-third of the federal budget.

Collective security, the third prong of postwar military strategy, also developed during the Berlin showdown. In June 1948, the Senate approved the general principle of regional military alliances. One year later, the United States joined Canada and Western European nations in its first peacetime military alliance, the North Atlantic Treaty Organization (NATO), designed to counter a Soviet threat to Western Europe (see Map 26.1). For the first time in its history, the United States pledged to go to war if one of its allies were attacked.

The fourth element of defense strategy involved foreign assistance programs to strengthen friendly countries, such as aid to Greece and Turkey and the Marshall Plan. In addition, in 1949 Congress approved $1 billion of military aid to its NATO allies and began economic assistance to nations in other parts of the world.

The fifth element of containment improved the government's espionage capacities and ability to deter communism through covert activities. The National Security Act of 1947 created the Central Intelligence Agency (CIA) to gather information and to perform any "functions and duties related to intelligence affecting the national security" that the NSC might authorize. Eventually, CIA agents secretly helped topple legitimate foreign governments and violated the rights of U.S. citizens. In many respects, the CIA was virtually unaccountable to Congress or the public.

By 1950, the United States had abandoned age-old tenets of foreign policy. Isolationism and neutrality had given way to a peacetime military alliance and efforts to control events far beyond

Cold War Spying

"Intelligence," the gathering of information to determine the capabilities and intentions of the enemy, was as old as human warfare, but it took on new importance with the onset of the cold war. Created by the National Security Act of 1947, the Central Intelligence Agency (CIA) became one of the most important tools for obtaining Soviet secrets, deceiving the enemy about U.S. plans, countering subversive activities by Communists, and assisting local forces against leaders whom the United States wanted to oust. While much of the CIA's intelligence function took place in Washington, where analysts combed through Communist newspapers, official reports, and leaders' speeches, secret agents operating behind the iron curtain gathered information with bugs and devices such as these cameras hidden in cigarette packs. Spying soon gained a prominent place in popular culture, most notably in more than a dozen movies featuring James Bond, British agent 007, the character created by former British naval intelligence agent Ian Fleming in 1952 and first appearing on-screen in *Dr. No* in 1962.

Jack Naylor Collection.

U.S. borders. Short of war, the United States could not stop the descent of the iron curtain, but it aggressively and successfully promoted economic recovery and a military shield for the rest of Europe.

Superpower Rivalry around the Globe

Efforts to implement containment moved beyond Europe. In Africa, Asia, and the Middle East, World War II accelerated a tide of national libera-

tion movements against war-weakened **imperial** powers. By 1960, forty countries, with more than a quarter of the world's people, had won their independence. These nations came to be referred to collectively, along with Latin America, as the **third world**, a term denoting countries outside the Western (first world) and Soviet (second world) orbits that had not yet developed industrial economies. Like Woodrow Wilson during World War I, Roosevelt and Truman promoted the ideal of self-determination: The United States granted independence to the Philippines in 1946, applauded the British withdrawal from India, and encouraged France to relinquish its empire in Indochina. At the same time, both the United States and the Soviet Union cultivated in emerging nations governments that were friendly to their own interests.

Leaders of many liberation movements, impressed with the rapid economic growth of Russia, adopted socialist or Communist ideas. Although few had formal ties with the Soviet Union, American leaders saw these movements as a threatening extension of Soviet power. Seeking to hold communism at bay by fostering economic development and political stability, in 1949 the Truman administration initiated the Point IV Program, providing technical aid to developing nations. These modest amounts of aid contrasted sharply with the huge sums provided to Europe.

In Asia, civil war raged in China, where the Communists, led by Mao Zedong (Mao Tsetung), fought the official Nationalist government under Chiang Kai-shek. While the Communists gained support among the peasants for their land reforms and valiant stand against the Japanese, Chiang's corrupt and incompetent government alienated much of the population. Failing in its effort to promote negotiations, the United States provided almost $3 billion in aid to the Nationalists during the civil war. Truman and his advisers believed that further aid would be futile, given the ineptness of Chiang's government.

In October 1949, Mao established the People's Republic of China (PRC), and the Nationalists fled to the island of Taiwan. The United States refused to recognize the PRC, blocked its admission to the United Nations, and supported the Nationalist government in Taiwan. Only a massive U.S. military commitment could have stopped the Chinese Communists, but some Republicans cried that Truman and "the pro-Communists in the State Department" had "lost" China. China became a political albatross for the Democrats, who resolved never again to be vulnerable to charges of being soft on communism.

With China in turmoil, the administration reconsidered its plans for postwar Japan. Initially, the U.S. military occupation had aimed to reform the Japanese government, purge militarists from official positions, and decentralize the economy. But by 1948, U.S. policy had shifted to helping Japan rapidly reindustrialize and secure access to food, markets, and natural resources in Asia. In a short time the Japanese economy was flourishing. American soldiers remained on military bases in Japan, but the official occupation ended when the two nations signed a peace treaty and a mutual security pact in September 1951. Like West Germany, Japan now sat squarely within the American orbit.

The one area where cold war considerations did not control American policy was Palestine. In 1943, then-Senator Harry Truman spoke passionately about Nazi Germany's annihilation of Jews, asserting, "This is not a Jewish problem, it is an American problem—and we must…face it squarely and honorably." As president, he had the opportunity to make good on his words. Jews had been migrating to Palestine, their biblical homeland, since the nineteenth century, resulting in tension and hostilities between Palestinian Arabs and Jews. After World War II, as hundreds of thousands of European Jews sought refuge and creation of a national homeland in Palestine,

fighting devolved into brutal terrorism on both sides.

Truman's foreign policy experts saw American-Arab friendship as a critical barrier against Soviet influence in the Middle East and as a means to secure access to Arabian oil. Uncharacteristically defying his advisers, the president responded instead to pleas from Jewish organizations, his moral commitment to Holocaust survivors, and his interest in the American Jewish vote for the 1948 elections. When Jews in Palestine declared the state of Israel in May 1948, Truman quickly recognized the new country and made its defense the cornerstone of U.S. policy in the Middle East.

Israel, 1948

REVIEW Why did relations between the United States and the Soviet Union deteriorate after the end of World War II?

Haganah Troops Mobilize in Palestine

The Haganah originated in the 1910s as a paramilitary group to defend Jewish settlers in Palestine as they struggled with Arabs hostile to the growing presence of Zionists committed to building a Jewish state there. Because Palestine was governed by the British under a League of Nations mandate, Haganah was an illegal, underground organization, yet it gathered substantial numbers and weapons by the end of World War II. After Israel declared itself a nation in 1948, Haganah became the core of the Israel Defense Forces, Israel's main military organization. In this photo, Haganah troops are mobilizing in July 1948 to defend the new state from the armies of the surrounding nations of Syria, Jordan, Egypt, Lebanon, and Iraq. The Israelis won the war, but the consolidation of the state of Israel created 700,000 Arab refugees and an issue that would fuel turmoil in the area for decades to come.
© Bettmann / Corbis.

Truman and the Fair Deal at Home

Referring to the Civil War general who coined the phrase "War is hell," Truman said in December 1945, "Sherman was wrong. I'm telling you I find peace is hell." Challenged by crises abroad, Truman also faced shortages, strikes, inflation, and other problems attending the reconversion of the economy to peacetime production. At the same time, he tried to expand New Deal reform with his own "Fair Deal" agenda of initiatives in civil rights, housing, education, and health care. In sharp contrast to his success with Congress in foreign policy, however, Truman achieved but a modest slice of his domestic agenda.

Reconversion and the Postwar Economic Boom

Despite scarcities during World War II, most Americans had enjoyed a higher standard of living than ever before. Economic experts as well as ordinary citizens worried about sustaining that standard and providing jobs for millions of returning soldiers. Truman wasted no time unveiling his plan, asking Congress to enact a twenty-one-point program of social and economic reforms. "Not even President Roosevelt ever asked for as much at one sitting," exploded Republican leader Joseph W. Martin Jr.

Congress approved only one of Truman's key proposals—full-employment legislation—and even that was watered down. The Employment Act of 1946 invested the federal government with responsibility "to promote maximum employment, production, and purchasing power," thereby formalizing what had been implicit in Roosevelt's actions to counter the depression—government's responsibility for maintaining a healthy economy. The law created a Council of Economic Advisors to assist the president, but it authorized no new powers to translate the government's obligation into effective action.

Inflation, not unemployment, turned out to be the most severe problem in the early postwar years. In 1945 consumers had $30 billion of savings from the war years, but shortages of meat, automobiles, housing, and a host of other items persisted. Housing was so scarce that some veterans lived in basements and garages. Until industry could convert fully to civilian production and make more goods available, consumer demand would continue to drive up prices.

Labor relations were another thorn in Truman's side. Organized labor survived the war stronger than ever, its 14.5 million members making up 35 percent of the civilian workforce. Yet union members feared erosion of wartime gains. With wages frozen during the war, the rising incomes of working-class families had come from the availability of higher-paying jobs and the chance to work longer hours. The end of overtime meant a 30 percent cut in take-home pay for most workers.

Women also saw their earnings decline. Polls indicated that as many as 68 to 85 percent wanted to keep their wartime jobs, but most who remained in the workforce had to settle for relatively low-paying jobs in light industry or the service sector. Displaced from her shipyard work, Marie Schreiber took a cashier's job, lamenting, "You were back to women's wages, you know … practically in half."

Paying scant attention to the problems of women workers, unions sought to preserve wartime gains with the weapon they had set aside during the war. Five million workers struck in 1946, affecting nearly every major industry. Workers saw corporate executives profiting at their expense. Shortly before voting to strike, a former marine and the men he carpooled with calculated that a lavish party given by a company executive had cost more than they would earn in a whole year at the steel mill. "That sort of stuff made us realize, hell we had to bite the bullet … the bosses sure didn't give a damn for us."

Although most Americans approved of unions in principle, they became fed up with strikes, blamed unions for rising prices and shortages of consumer goods, and called for government restrictions on organized labor. Truman, too, was dismayed that wartime unity had crumbled, but he spread the blame around, writing to his mother in October 1945: "The Congress [is] balking, labor has gone crazy, and management isn't far from insane in selfishness." When the massive wave of strikes subsided at the end of 1946, workers had won wage increases of about 20 percent, but the loss of overtime along with rising prices left their purchasing power only slightly higher than in 1942.

By 1947, the nation had survived the strains of reconversion and avoided a postwar depression. Wartime profits enabled businesses to invest in new plants and equipment. Eventually consumers could spend their wartime savings on houses, cars, and appliances that had lain beyond their reach during the depression and war. Defense spending and the $38 billion in aid that enabled war-stricken countries to purchase American products also stimulated the economy. A soaring birthrate further sustained consumer demand. Although prosperity was far from universal, the United States entered into a remarkable economic boom that lasted through the 1960s and led to a flood of new consumer goods. (See chapter 27.)

Yet another economic boost came from the only large welfare measure passed after the New Deal. The Servicemen's Readjustment Act (the GI Bill), enacted in 1944, offered 16 million veterans job training and education; unemployment compensation while they looked for jobs; and low-interest loans to purchase homes, farms, and small businesses. By 1948, some 1.3 million veterans had bought houses with government loans. Helping 2.2 million ex-soldiers attend college, the subsidies sparked a boom in higher education. A drugstore clerk before his military service, Don Condren was able to get an engineering degree and buy his first house. "I think the GI Bill gave the whole country an upward boost economically," he said.

Black and Mexican American Protest and the Politics of Civil Rights

"I spent four years in the army to free a bunch of Frenchmen and Dutchmen," an African American corporal declared, "and I'm hanged if I'm going to let the Alabama version of the Germans kick me around when I get home." Black veterans as well as civilians resolved that the return to peace would not be a return to the racial injustices of prewar America. Their political clout had grown with the migration of two million African Americans to northern and western cities, where they could vote and their ballots could make a difference. Even in the South, the proportion of blacks who could vote inched up from 2 percent to 12 percent in the 1940s. Pursuing civil rights through the courts and Congress, the National Association for the Advancement of Colored People (NAACP) counted half a million members.

In the postwar years, individual African Americans broke through the color barrier, achieving several "firsts." Jackie Robinson integrated major league baseball when he played first base for the Brooklyn Dodgers in 1947, braving abuse from fans and players to win the Rookie of the Year Award. In 1950,

Segregation

Signs like this one in Mobile, Alabama, were a normal feature of life in the South from the late nineteenth century until the 1960s. State and local laws mandated segregation in every aspect of life, literally from the cradle to the grave. African Americans could not use white hospitals, cemeteries, schools, libraries, swimming pools, playgrounds, restrooms, or drinking fountains. They were relegated to balconies in movie theaters and kept apart from whites in all public meetings. This scene was captured by the self-trained Gordon Parks, an African American who was one of the most notable photographers of the twentieth century as well as a filmmaker, composer, and author.

© Gordon Parks.

Ralph J. Bunche received the Nobel Peace Prize for his United Nations work, and Gwendolyn Brooks was awarded the Pulitzer Prize for poetry.

Still, in most respects little had changed, especially in the South, where violence greeted African Americans' attempts to assert their rights. A mob lynched Isaac Nixon for voting in Georgia, and an all-white jury acquitted the men accused of his murder. In the South, governors, U.S. senators, other politicians, and local vigilantes routinely intimidated potential black voters with threats of economic retaliation and violence.

The cold war heightened American leaders' sensitivity to racial issues, as the United States and Soviet Union vied for the allegiance of newly independent nations with nonwhite populations. Soviet propaganda pointed to racial injustice in the United States, and African Americans themselves petitioned the United Nations to pressure the government on their behalf. Even Dean Acheson, far from a champion of racial equality, recognized how discrimination and segregation endangered "our moral leadership of the free and democratic nations of the world."

"My very stomach turned over when I learned that Negro soldiers just back from overseas were being dumped out of army trucks in Mississippi and beaten," wrote Truman, shaken by the violence and under pressure to act by civil rights leaders and **liberals**. Wrestling with the Democrats' need for northern black and liberal votes as well as white southern votes, Truman acted more boldly on civil rights than any previous president. In 1946, he created a President's Committee on Civil Rights, and in February 1948 he asked Congress to enact the committee's recommendations. The first president to address the NAACP, in June 1947, Truman asserted that all Americans should have equal rights to housing, education, employment, and the ballot.

As with much of his domestic program, the president failed to act aggressively on his bold words. Running for re-election in 1948 and pressured by civil rights activists, Truman issued an executive order to desegregate the armed services, but it lay unimplemented until the Korean War. A large gap loomed between what Truman said about civil rights and what his government accomplished, yet desegregation of the military and the administration's support of civil rights cases in the Supreme Court contributed to far-reaching changes, while his Committee on Civil Rights set an agenda for years to come. Breaking with the past, Truman used his office to set a moral agenda for the nation's longest unfulfilled promise.

Although discussion of race and civil rights usually focused on African Americans, Mexican Americans endured similar injustices. In 1929, they had formed the League of United Latin-American Citizens (LULAC) to combat discrimination and segregation in the Southwest. Like black soldiers after World War II, Mexican American veterans believed, as one of them insisted, "We had earned our credentials as American citizens. We had paid our dues.... We were not about to take any crap." Responding to difficulties Mexican Americans encountered in trying to obtain veterans' benefits, in 1948 a group in Corpus Christi, Texas, led by Dr. Héctor Peréz García, a Bronze Star combat surgeon, formed the American GI Forum. The organization took off when the wife of Felix Longoria, who had given his life in the Philippines, was refused the use of a white funeral chapel in Three Rivers, Texas, and was told that her husband would be buried in the Mexican section of the cemetery. With the help of Senator Lyndon

Johnson, they arranged for burial in Arlington National Cemetery, and the GI Forum went on to become a key national organization battling discrimination and electing sympathetic officials.

The routine segregation of children in the public schools also energized Mexican Americans. Parents filed a class action suit in Orange County, California, winning a federal court decision in 1947 that outlawed the practice of separating Mexican American and white children in the schools. In 1948, LULAC and the GI Forum won a federal court verdict that prohibited any Texas school district from segregating Mexican American students in separate schools or classes. Such projects, along with challenges to discrimination in employment and efforts for political representation, demonstrated a growing mobilization of Mexican Americans in the Southwest.

The Fair Deal Flounders

Republicans capitalized on public frustrations with economic reconversion in the 1946 congressional elections, accusing the administration of "confusion, corruption, and communism." Winning Congress for the first time in fourteen years, Republicans looked eagerly to the 1948 presidential campaign. Many had campaigned against New Deal "bureaucracy" and "radicalism" in 1946, and the Eightieth Congress weakened some reform programs and enacted tax cuts favoring higher-income groups.

Organized labor took the most severe attack when Congress passed the Taft-Hartley Act over Truman's veto in 1947. Called "Tuff-Heartless" by unions, the law reduced the power of organized labor and made it more difficult to organize workers. For example, states could now pass "right-to-work" laws, which banned the practice of requiring all workers to join a union once a majority had voted for it. Many states, especially in the South and West, rushed to enact such laws, encouraging the relocation of industry there. Taft-Hartley maintained the New Deal principle of government protection for **collective bargaining**, but it put the government more squarely between labor and management.

As the 1948 elections approached, Truman faced not only a resurgent Republican Party headed by its nominee, Thomas E. Dewey, but also two revolts within his own party. On the left, Henry A. Wallace, whose foreign policy views had cost him his cabinet seat, led a new Progressive Party. On the right, South Carolina governor J. Strom Thurmond headed the States'

Truman's Whistle-Stop Campaign

Harry Truman rallies a crowd from his campaign train at a stop in Bridgeport, Pennsylvania, in October 1948. His campaign theme song, "I'm Just Wild about Harry," was borrowed, with the words slightly changed, from the 1921 musical *Shuffle Along*. This was the last presidential election in which the pollsters predicted the wrong winner. They stopped taking polls in mid-October, after which many voters apparently changed their minds. One commentator praised the American citizenry, who "couldn't be ticketed by the polls, knew its own mind and had picked the rather unlikely but courageous figure of Truman to carry on its banner." In what ways have presidential campaigns changed since Harry Truman's time? Photo: Truman Library; sheet music: Collection of Janice L. and David J. Frent.

FOR MORE HELP ANALYZING THIS IMAGE, see the visual activity for this chapter in the Online Study Guide at bedfordstmartins.com/roarkcompact.

Rights Party—the Dixiecrats—formed by southern Democrats who had walked out of the 1948 Democratic Party convention when it passed a liberal civil rights plank.

Almost alone in believing he could win, Truman crisscrossed the country by train, answering supporters' cries of "Give 'em hell, Harry." So bleak were Truman's prospects that the confident Dewey ran a low-key campaign and, on election night, the *Chicago Daily Tribune* printed its next day's issue with the headline DEWEY DEFEATS TRUMAN. But Truman took 303 electoral votes to Dewey's 189, and his party re-

gained control of Congress (Map 26.2). His unexpected victory attested to his skills as a campaigner, broad support for his foreign policy, the enduring popularity of New Deal reform, and appreciation of the booming economy.

Truman failed to turn his victory into success for his Fair Deal agenda. Congress made modest improvements in Social Security and raised the minimum wage, but it passed only one significant reform measure. The Housing Act of 1949 authorized 350,000 units of government-constructed housing over the next fifteen years. Although it fell far short of actual need,

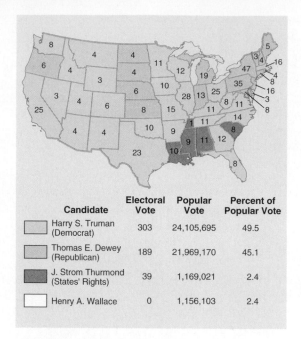

Candidate	Electoral Vote	Popular Vote	Percent of Popular Vote
Harry S. Truman (Democrat)	303	24,105,695	49.5
Thomas E. Dewey (Republican)	189	21,969,170	45.1
J. Strom Thurmond (States' Rights)	39	1,169,021	2.4
Henry A. Wallace	0	1,156,103	2.4

MAP 26.2   The Election of 1948

the legislation represented a landmark commitment by the government to address the housing needs of the poor.

With southern Democrats often joining the Republicans, Congress rejected Truman's civil rights measures and proposals for a federal health care program, aid to education, and a new agriculture program to benefit small farmers and consumers. His efforts to revise immigration policy produced the McCarran-Walter Act of 1952, ending the outright ban on immigration and citizenship for Japanese and other Asians. But the law also authorized the government to bar suspected Communists and homosexuals and maintained the discriminatory quota system established in the 1920s. Truman denounced that provision as "unworthy of our traditions and our ideals," but Congress overrode his veto. Although he blamed political opponents for defeating his Fair Deal, in fact Truman devoted much more energy to foreign policy than to his domestic proposals. Moreover, by late 1950, the Korean War embroiled Truman in controversy, diverted his attention from domestic affairs, and depleted his power as a legislative leader.

The Domestic Chill: McCarthyism

Truman's domestic program also suffered from a wave of anti-Communist hysteria that weakened liberal and left forces. Both "Red-baiting" (at-

tempts to discredit individuals or ideas by associating them with Communism) and official retaliation against leftist critics of the government had flourished during the Red scare at the end of World War I (see chapter 22). A second Red scare convulsed the nation after World War II, born of partisan political maneuvering, collapse of the Soviet-American alliance, setbacks in U.S. foreign policy, and disclosures of Soviet espionage.

Republicans who had attacked the New Deal as a plot of radicals now jumped on cold war setbacks, such as the Communist triumph in China, to accuse Democrats of fostering internal subversion. Wisconsin senator Joseph R. McCarthy avowed that "the Communists within our borders have been more responsible for the success of Communism abroad than Soviet Russia." Such charges gained some credibility when a number of ex-Communists, including Whittaker Chambers and Elizabeth Bentley, testified that they and others had provided secret documents to the Soviets. In 1950, a British physicist working on the atomic bomb project confessed that he was a spy and implicated several Americans, including Ethel and Julius Rosenberg. The Rosenbergs pleaded innocent but were convicted of conspiracy to commit espionage and electrocuted in 1953.

Records opened in the 1990s showed that the Soviet Union did receive secret documents from Americans, such as Julius Rosenberg, information that possibly hastened Soviet development of nuclear weapons to a small extent. At the peak of the hysteria, the U.S. Communist Party counted only about 20,000 members, some of them undercover FBI agents. The vast majority of individuals prosecuted in the Red scare had simply joined the Communist Party, associated with Communists, or supported radical causes. And most of those activities took place long before the cold war had made the Soviet Union an enemy. Red-hunters cared little for such distinctions, however. For more than ten years following World War II, congressional committees and a host of other official bodies ordered citizens to testify about their past and present political associations. If they refused, anti-Communists charged that silence was tantamount to confession, and these "unfriendly witnesses" lost their jobs and suffered public ostracism.

Senator McCarthy's influence was so great that **McCarthyism** became a term synonymous with the anti-Communist crusade. Attacking individuals recklessly, in 1950 McCarthy claimed to have a list of 205 "known Communists" employed in the State Department. Even though most of his charges were absurd—such as the allegation that retired general George C. Marshall belonged to a Communist conspiracy—the press covered McCarthy avidly.

Not all Republicans joined McCarthy, nor did the party have a monopoly on the politics of anticommunism. Shortly after being stung with charges of communism in the 1946 midterm elections, in March 1947 President Truman issued Executive Order 9835 requiring investigation of every federal employee. In effect, Truman's "loyalty program" violated the principles of American justice by allowing anonymous informers to make charges and placing the burden of proof on the accused. More than 2,000 civil service employees lost their jobs, and another 10,000 resigned while the program continued into the mid-1950s. "A nightmare from which there [was] no awakening" was how State Department employee Esther Brunauer described it when she and her husband, a chemist in the navy, both lost their jobs. Years later, Truman admitted that the loyalty program had been a mistake.

The administration also went directly after the Communist Party, prosecuting its leaders under the Smith Act, passed in 1940, which made it a crime to "advocate the overthrow and destruction of the Government of the United States by force and violence." Although civil libertarians argued that the guilty verdicts violated First Amendment rights to freedom of speech, press, and association, the Supreme Court ruled in 1951 (*Dennis v. United States*) that the Communist threat overrode constitutional guarantees.

The domestic cold war spread beyond the nation's capital. State and local governments investigated citizens, demanded loyalty oaths, fired individuals suspected of disloyalty, banned books from public libraries, and more. Universities dismissed professors, and public school teachers lost their jobs in New York, Los Angeles, and elsewhere. The House Un-American Activities Committee (HUAC) took on the movie industry in 1947; ten writers and directors who refused to testify went to prison and later were blacklisted from Hollywood jobs.

Because the Communist Party had helped organize unions and championed racial justice, labor and civil rights activists, too, fell prey to McCarthyism. African American activist Jack O'Dell remembered segregationists who insisted that they did not oppose equal rights for blacks. "They were against communism. But their inter-

pretation of Communist was anybody who supported the right of blacks to have civil rights." In addition, a 1950 Senate report claiming that "moral turpitude" and susceptibility to blackmail made homosexuals unfit for government jobs contributed to the persecution of gay men and lesbians who were fired from civil service jobs, drummed out of the military, and subject to surveillance and harassment at the hands of the FBI and local police forces.

McCarthyism caused untold economic and psychological harm to individuals innocent of breaking any law. Thousands of people were humiliated and discredited, hounded from their jobs, even in some cases imprisoned. The anti-Communist crusade violated fundamental constitutional rights of freedom of speech and association, stifled expression of dissenting ideas, and removed unpopular causes from public contemplation.

> **REVIEW**   Why did Truman have limited success in implementing his domestic agenda?

The Cold War Becomes Hot: Korea

The cold war erupted into a shooting war in June 1950, when troops from Communist North Korea invaded South Korea. For the first time, Americans went into battle to implement containment. Confirming the global reach of the Truman Doctrine, U.S. involvement in Korea also marked the militarization of American foreign policy. The United States, in concert with the United Nations, ultimately held the line in Korea, but at a great cost in lives, dollars, and domestic unity.

Korea and the Military Implementation of Containment

The war grew out of the artificial division of Korea after World War II. Having expelled the Japanese, who had controlled Korea since 1904, the United States and the Soviet Union created two occupation zones separated by the thirty-eighth parallel (Map 26.3). The Soviets supported the Korean Communist Party in the north, while the United States backed the Korean Democratic Party in the south. With Moscow and Washington

MAP 26.3   The Korean War, 1950–1953
Although each side had plunged deep into its enemy's territory, the war ended in 1953 with the dividing line between North and South Korea nearly where it had been before the fighting began.

READING THE MAP: How far south did the North Korean forces progress at the height of their invasion? How far north did the UN forces get? What countries border Korea? **CONNECTIONS:** What dangers did the forays of MacArthur's forces to within forty miles of the Korean-Chinese border pose? Why did Truman forbid MacArthur to approach that border? What political considerations on the home front influenced Truman's policy and military strategy regarding Korea?

FOR MORE HELP ANALYZING THIS MAP, see the map activity for this chapter in the Online Study Guide at bedfordstmartins.com/roarkcompact.

unable to agree on a unification plan, in July 1948 the United Nations sponsored elections in South Korea. The American-favored candidate, Korean nationalist Syngman Rhee, was elected president, and the United States withdrew most of its troops. In the fall of 1948, the Soviets established the

People's Republic of North Korea under Kim Il-sung and also withdrew. Although doubting that Rhee's repressive government could sustain popular support, U.S. officials appreciated his staunch anti-Communism and provided small amounts of economic and military aid to South Korea.

Skirmishes between North and South Korean troops had occurred since 1948. In June 1950, however, 90,000 North Koreans swept into South Korea. Truman's advisers immediately assumed that the Soviet Union, China, or both had instigated the attack. Revelations decades later indicated that the Russians and the Chinese had acquiesced, but with little enthusiasm.

On June 30, six days after learning of the attack, Truman decided to commit ground troops, viewing Korea as "the Greece of the Far East." Moreover, a non-Communist South Korea was a key element in U.S. plans to revive Japan economically and to make that nation the core of America's defense strategy in Asia. With the Soviet representative absent from the Security Council, the United States obtained UN sponsorship of a collective effort to repel the attack. Authorized to appoint a commander for the UN force, Truman named General Douglas MacArthur, World War II hero and head of the postwar occupation of Japan.

Sixteen nations, including many NATO allies, sent troops to Korea, but the United States furnished most of the personnel and weapons, deploying almost 1.8 million troops and dictating military strategy. By failing to ask Congress for a declaration of war, Truman violated the spirit if not the letter of the Constitution. Moreover, although Congress authorized the mobilization of troops and appropriated funds to fight the war, the president's political opponents called it "Truman's war" when the military situation worsened.

The first American soldiers rushed to Korea unprepared and ill equipped. The North Koreans took the capital of Seoul and drove deep into the south, forcing UN troops to retreat south to Pusan by September. Then General MacArthur launched a bold counteroffensive at Inchon, 180 miles behind North Korean lines. By mid-October, UN forces had pushed the North Koreans back to the thirty-eighth parallel. Now came the momentous decision of whether to invade North Korea and seek to unify Korea.

From Containment to Rollback to Containment

"Troops could not be expected…to march up to a surveyor's line and stop," remarked Dean Acheson, now secretary of state, reflecting popular and official support for transforming the military objective from containment to elimination of the enemy and unification of Korea. Thus, for the only time during the cold war, the United States tried to roll back communism. With UN approval, on September 27, 1950, Truman authorized MacArthur to cross the thirty-eighth parallel. Concerned about possible intervention by China or the Soviet Union, the president directed the general to keep UN troops away from the Korean-Chinese border. Disregarding the order, MacArthur sent UN forces to within forty miles of China, whereupon 150,000 Chinese troops crossed the Yalu River into Korea. With Chinese help, by December 1950, the North Koreans had recaptured Seoul.

Then, under the leadership of General Matthew B. Ridgway, the Eighth Army turned the tide again. During three months of grueling battle, UN forces fought their way back to the thirty-eighth parallel, whereupon Truman decided to seek a negotiated settlement. MacArthur was furious when the goal of the war reverted to containment, which to him represented defeat. Truman and his advisers, however, adamantly opposed a wider war in Asia. According to General Omar Bradley, chairman of the Joint Chiefs of Staff, MacArthur wanted to wage "the wrong war, at the wrong place, at the wrong time, with the wrong enemy."

MacArthur took his case public, in effect challenging both the president's authority over foreign policy and the principle of civilian control over the military. Fed up with MacArthur's insubordination, Truman fired him in April 1951. Many Americans, however, sided with MacArthur and castigated Truman. "Quite an explosion.…Letters of abuse by the dozens," Truman recorded in his diary.

The adulation of MacArthur reflected American frustrations with containment. Why should Americans die simply to preserve the status quo rather than destroy the enemy once and for all? Siding with MacArthur enabled Americans to hold on to their belief that the United States was all-powerful and to pin the Korean stalemate on the government's ineptitude or willingness to shelter subversives. Moreover, Truman's earlier success in "scaring the hell" out of the country over the threat of communism in Greece and Turkey came back to haunt him. If communism was so evil, why not stamp it out as MacArthur wanted? When Congress investigated MacArthur's firing, all of the top military leaders supported the president, yet Truman never recovered from the political fallout. Nor was he able to end the war. Cease-fire negotiations began in July 1951, but peace talks dragged on for two more years while 12,000 more U.S. soldiers died.

Korea, Communism, and the 1952 Election

Popular discontent with Truman's war boosted Republican candidates in the election battles of 1952. The Republicans' presidential nominee, General Dwight D. Eisenhower, had emerged from World War II with immense popularity. Reared in modest circumstances in Abilene, Kansas, Eisenhower attended West Point and rose steadily through the army ranks. As supreme commander in Europe, he won widespread acclaim for leading the Allied armies to victory over Germany. In 1950, Truman appointed Eisenhower the first supreme commander of NATO forces.

Both Republicans and Democrats had courted Eisenhower for the presidency in 1948. Although the general believed that professional soldiers should keep out of politics, he found compelling reasons to run in 1952. Eisenhower generally agreed with Democratic foreign policy, but he deplored the Democrats' propensity to solve domestic problems with costly new federal programs. He equally disliked the foreign policy views of the leading Republican presidential contender, Senator Robert A. Taft, who attacked containment and sought to cut defense spending. Eisenhower decided to run both to stop Taft and the **conservative** wing of the party and to turn the Democrats out of the White House.

Eisenhower defeated Taft for the nomination, but the old guard prevailed on the party platform. It excoriated containment as "negative, futile, and immoral" and charged the Truman administration with shielding "traitors to the Nation in high places." By choosing thirty-nine-year-old Senator Richard M. Nixon for his running mate, Eisenhower helped to appease the Republican right wing and ensured that anticommunism would be a major theme of the campaign.

Richard Milhous Nixon grew up in southern California, served in the navy, and briefly practiced law. In 1946, he entered politics, helping the Republicans recapture Congress by defeating a liberal incumbent for a seat in the House of Representatives. Nixon quickly made a name for himself as a member of HUAC and a key anti-Communist. In his 1950 bid for the Senate, he ran an effective smear campaign against the liberal congresswoman Helen Gahagan Douglas, charging her with being "pink [Communist] right down to her underwear."

The Democrats nominated Adlai E. Stevenson, the popular governor of Illinois, acceptable to both liberals and southern Democrats. He could not escape the domestic fallout from the Korean War, however, nor could he match the widespread appeal of Eisenhower, the World War II hero.

Republican campaigners harped on communism and the failure to achieve victory in Korea. Shortly before the election, Eisenhower announced dramatically, "I shall go to Korea," and voters registered their confidence in his ability to end the war. Cutting sharply into traditional Democratic territory, Eisenhower won several southern states and, overall, 55 percent of the popular vote. His coattails carried a narrow Republican majority to Congress.

An Armistice and the War's Costs

Eisenhower made good on his pledge to end the Korean War. In July 1953, the two sides reached an armistice that left Korea divided just as it had been three years earlier (see Map 26.3). The war took the lives of 36,000 Americans and wounded more than 100,000. Nick Tosques, among thousands of U.S. soldiers who were taken prisoners of war, spent two and a half years in a POW camp. "They interrogated us every day," he recalled. "You never knew when they were coming for you.... Pretty soon I was telling them anything, just to keep from getting hit." South Korea lost more than 1 million people to war-related causes, and more than 1.8 million North Koreans and Chinese were killed or wounded.

The Truman administration judged the war a success for containment, since the United States had supported its promise to help nations that were resisting communism. Both Truman and Eisenhower managed to contain what amounted to a world war—involving twenty nations altogether—within a single country.

Moreover, despite both presidents' threats to use nuclear bombs, they authorized only conventional weapons in Korea.

Korea had an enormous effect on defense policy and spending. In April 1950, two months before the war began, the National Security Council completed a top-secret report on the nation's military strength. The document, known as NSC 68, warned that the survival of the nation required a massive military buildup and the tripling of the defense budget. Truman took no immediate action on these recommendations, but the Korean War brought about nearly all of the military expansion called for in NSC 68, vastly increasing U.S. capacity to act as a global power. Using the Korean crisis to expand American clout elsewhere, Truman won congressional approval to rearm West Germany and commit troops to NATO. Military spending shot up from $14 billion in 1950 to $50 billion in 1953 and remained above $40 billion thereafter. By 1953, defense spending claimed 60 percent of the federal budget, and the size of the armed forces had tripled.

To General Matthew Ridgway, MacArthur's successor as commander of the UN forces, Korea taught the lesson that U.S. forces should never again fight a land war in Asia. Eisenhower concurred. Nevertheless, the Korean War induced the Truman administration to expand its role in Asia by increasing aid to the French, who were fighting to hang on to their colonial empire in Indochina. As U.S. marines retreated from a battle against Chinese soldiers in 1950, they sang, prophetically, "We're Harry's police force on call, / So put back your pack on, / The next step is Saigon, / Cheer up, me lads, bless 'em all."

> **REVIEW**   How did the Korean War shape American foreign policy in the 1950s?

Conclusion: The Cold War's Costs and Consequences

Dean Acheson titled his memoir about the Truman years *Present at the Creation*, aptly capturing the magnitude of change that marked the aftermath of World War II. More than any development in the postwar world, the cold war defined American politics and society for decades to come. Truman's decision to oppose communism throughout the world marked the most momentous foreign policy initiative in the nation's history. It transformed the federal government, shifting its priorities from domestic to external affairs, greatly expanding its budget, and substantially increasing the power of the president. Military spending helped transform the nation itself, as defense contracts encouraged economic and population booms in the West and Southwest. The nuclear arms race put the people of the world at risk, consumed resources that might have been used to improve living standards, and skewed the economy toward dependence on military projects. While debate persisted about who was responsible for the cold war and whether it could have been avoided, no one could doubt its impact on American society or the world.

In sharp contrast to foreign policy, the domestic policies of the postwar years reflected continuity with the past. Preoccupied with foreign policy, Truman failed to mobilize support for his initiatives in education, health, agriculture, and civil rights. Although Congress forced some limitations on labor, Truman successfully defended most New Deal reforms. The poor and minorities suffered from the inattention to domestic problems, yet the boost to industry from cold war spending and the reconstruction of Western Europe and Japan contributed to an economic boom that lifted the standard of living for a majority of Americans.

Many Americans had difficulty accepting the terms of the cold war, not accustomed to paying sustained attention to the rest of the world or to fighting wars without total defeat of the enemy. Consequently, another high cost of the cold war was the anti-Communist hysteria, which stifled debate and narrowed the range of ideas acceptable for political discussion. Partisan politics and administration warnings about the Communist menace fueled McCarthyism, but the obsession with subversion also fed on popular frustrations over the failure of containment to produce clear-cut victories. Convulsing the nation in bitter disunity, McCarthyism reflected a loss of confidence in American power. It would be a major challenge of the next administration to restore that unity and confidence.

Suggestions for Further Reading

Kai Bird and Martin J. Sherwin, *American Prometheus: The Triumph and Tragedy of J. Robert Oppenheimer* (2005). The life story of a man central to the development of the atomic bomb told within the context of World War II and cold war politics.

Alonzo L. Hamby, *Man of the People: A Life of Harry S. Truman* (1995). A thorough biography that focuses on Truman's presidency.

Brenda Gayle Plummer, *Rising Wind: Black Americans and U.S. Foreign Affairs, 1935–1960* (1996). An examination of the connections between civil rights in the United States and cold war foreign policy.

Ellen W. Schrecker, *Many Are the Crimes: McCarthyism in America* (1998). An assessment of the roots, varieties, longevity, and effects of the Red scare on individuals, politics, and culture.

William Stueck, *The Korean War: An International History* (1995). A narrative of the diplomatic and military events of the Korean War in a world context.

Jules Tygiel, *Baseball's Great Experiment: Jackie Robinson and His Legacy* (1997). An account of Robinson's life in the contexts of American baseball and civil rights struggles.

▶ **FOR MORE BOOKS ABOUT TOPICS IN THIS CHAPTER,** see the Online Study Guide at **bedfordstmartins.com/roarkcompact**.

▶ **FOR ADDITIONAL FIRSTHAND ACCOUNTS OF THIS PERIOD,** see Chapter 26 in Michael Johnson, ed., *Reading the American Past*, Third Edition.

▶ **FOR WEB SITES AND DOCUMENTS RELATED TO TOPICS AND PLACES IN THIS CHAPTER,** see "History Links," "DocLinks," and "PlaceLinks" at **bedfordstmartins.com/roarkcompact**.

REVIEWING THE CHAPTER

Follow these steps to review and strengthen your understanding of the chapter.

STEP 1: *Study the **Key Terms** and **Timeline** to identify the significance of each item listed.*

STEP 2: *Answer the **Review Questions**, drawing on key terms and dates to support your answers.*

STEP 3: *Drawing on the Key Terms, Timeline, and Review Questions, answer the broader **Making Connections** questions.*

KEY TERMS

Who

Harry S. Truman (p. 679)
Dean Acheson (p. 679)
Joseph Stalin (p. 681)
George F. Kennan (p. 683)
Henry A. Wallace (pp. 683, 692)
Robert A. Taft (p. 686)
George C. Marshall (p. 686)
Mao Zedong (p. 688)
Chiang Kai-shek (p. 688)
Jackie Robinson (p. 691)
Thomas E. Dewey (p. 692)
J. Strom Thurmond (p. 692)
Joseph R. McCarthy (p. 694)
Ethel and Julius Rosenberg (p. 694)
Syngman Rhee (p. 696)
Kim Il-sung (p. 696)
Douglas MacArthur (p. 696)

Dwight D. Eisenhower (p. 697)
Richard M. Nixon (p. 697)

What

iron curtain (p. 682)
containment (p. 683)
Truman Doctrine (p. 686)
Marshall Plan (European Recovery Program) (p. 686)
Berlin airlift (p. 687)
hydrogen bomb (p. 687)
National Security Act of 1947 (p. 687)
collective security (p. 687)
North Atlantic Treaty Organization (NATO) (p. 687)
Central Intelligence Agency (CIA) (p. 687)
national liberation movements (p. 688)

third world (p. 688)
Fair Deal (p. 690)
Employment Act of 1946 (p. 690)
Servicemen's Readjustment Act (GI Bill) (p. 691)
President's Committee on Civil Rights (p. 692)
League of United Latin-American Citizens (LULAC) (p. 692)
American GI Forum (p. 692)
Taft-Hartley Act (p. 692)
Housing Act of 1949 (p. 693)
McCarran-Walter Act of 1952 (p. 694)
McCarthyism (p. 694)
Truman's loyalty program (p. 695)
House Un-American Activities Committee (HUAC) (p. 695)
NSC 68 (p. 698)

TIMELINE

1945 • Roosevelt dies; Vice President Harry S. Truman becomes president.

    1946 • Postwar labor unrest.
        • President's Committee on Civil Rights created.
        • United States grants independence to Philippines.
        • Employment Act.
        • Republicans gain control of Congress.

        1947 • George F. Kennan's article on containment policy published.
            • National Security Act: National Security Council (NSC) and Central Intelligence Agency (CIA) created.
            • Truman asks for aid to Greece and Turkey and announces Truman Doctrine.
            • Truman establishes a loyalty and security program.

            1948 • Congress approves Marshall Plan.
                • Women become permanent part of armed services.
                • Truman orders desegregation of armed services.
                • American GI Forum founded.
                • United States recognizes state of Israel.
                • Truman elected president.

          1948–1949 • Berlin crisis and airlift.

REVIEW QUESTIONS

1. Why did relations between the United States and the Soviet Union deteriorate after the end of World War II? (pp. 680–89)

2. Why did Truman have limited success in implementing his domestic agenda? (pp. 690–95)

3. How did the Korean War shape American foreign policy in the 1950s? (pp. 695–98)

MAKING CONNECTIONS

1. Containment shaped American actions abroad for almost half a century. Why did it become the dominant feature of American foreign policy after World War II? In your answer, discuss both proponents and opponents of the policy.

2. How did returning American servicemen change postwar domestic life in the areas of labor and civil rights? In your answer, discuss how wartime experiences influenced their demands.

3. Why did anti-Communist hysteria sweep the country in the early 1950s? How did it shape domestic politics? In your answer, be sure to consider the influence of developments abroad and at home.

▶ For practice quizzes, a customized study plan, and other study tools, see the Online Study Guide at bedfordstmartins.com/roarkcompact.

1949 • Communists take over mainland China; Nationalists retreat to Taiwan.
 • North Atlantic Treaty Organization (NATO) formed.
 • Point IV technical aid program begins.
 • Soviet Union explodes atomic bomb.

 1950 • Senator Joseph McCarthy begins campaign against alleged Communists in United States.
 • Truman approves development of hydrogen bomb.
 • United States sends troops to South Korea.

 1951 • Truman relieves General Douglas MacArthur of command in Korea.
 • United States ends occupation of Japan and signs peace treaty and mutual security pact.

 1952 • Republican Dwight D. Eisenhower elected president.

 1953 • Armistice halts Korean War.

1956 CADILLAC CONVERTIBLE
The automobile reflected both corporate and family prosperity in the 1950s. This car was manufactured by General Motors, the biggest and richest corporation in the world and the first to sell a billion dollars' worth of products. Costing about $5,000, the Cadillac was GM's top-of-the-line car, one of the first purchases the McDonald brothers made when they struck it rich with their hamburger stand in California. Even the cheaper models that average Americans bought by the millions featured the gas-guzzling size and space-age style of this Cadillac. A massive interstate highway system begun in 1956 boosted automobile travel, and widespread car ownership went hand in hand with Americans' move to the suburbs and their devotion to consumption.

Ron Kimball Photography.

The Politics and Culture of Abundance

1952–1960

TRAILED BY REPORTERS, U.S. vice president Richard M. Nixon led Soviet premier Nikita Khrushchev through the American National Exhibition in Moscow in July 1959. The display of American consumer goods followed an exhibition of Soviet products in New York, part of a cultural exchange between the two superpowers that reflected a slight thaw in the **cold war**. Both Khrushchev and Nixon seized on the propaganda potential of the moment. As they made their way through the display, their verbal sparring turned into a slugfest of words and gestures that reporters dubbed the "kitchen debate."

Showing off a new color television set, Nixon said the Soviet Union "may be ahead of us…in the thrust of your rockets for…outer space," but he assured Khrushchev that the United States outstripped the Soviets in consumer goods. "Any steelworker could buy this house," Nixon boasted, as they walked through a six-room ranch-style model. Khrushchev retorted that in the Soviet Union "you are entitled to housing," whereas in the United States the poor were reduced to sleeping on the pavement.

While the two men inspected appliances in the model kitchen, Nixon declared, "These are designed to make things easier for our women." Khrushchev responded that his country did not have "the capitalist attitude toward women" and appreciated women's contributions to the economy, not their domesticity. The Soviet leader found many of the items on display interesting, he said, then added that "they are not needed in life.…They are merely gadgets." In reply, Nixon insisted, "Isn't it far better to be talking about washing machines than machines of war?" Khrushchev agreed, yet he affirmed the persistence of cold war tensions when he later blustered, "We too are giants. You want to threaten—we will answer threats with threats."

The Eisenhower administration in fact had begun with threats to the Soviet Union. Republican campaigners vowed to roll back **communism** and liberate "enslaved" peoples under Soviet rule. In practice, however, Eisenhower settled for a **containment** policy much like that of his predecessor, Harry S. Truman, though Eisenhower relied more on nuclear weapons and on secret actions by the Central Intelligence Agency (CIA). Yet, as Nixon's visit to Moscow demonstrated, Eisenhower took advantage of political changes in the Soviet Union to reduce tensions in Soviet-American relations.

Continuity with the Truman administration also characterized domestic policy. Although Eisenhower favored the business community with tax cuts and opposed strong federal efforts in health care, education, and race relations,

Eisenhower and the Politics of the "Middle Way"

Moderation was the guiding principle of Eisenhower's domestic agenda and leadership style. Favoring in 1953 a "middle way between untrammeled freedom of the individual and the demands for the welfare of the whole Nation," he pledged that his administration would "avoid government by bureaucracy as carefully as it avoids neglect of the helpless." Eisenhower generally resisted expanding the federal government's activities, but New Deal programs continued, and he signed key legislation establishing a national highway system. Nicknamed "Ike" by his friends and the public, the confident war hero remained popular throughout his presidency.

Modern Republicanism

In contrast to the Old Guard conservatives in his party who wanted to repeal much of the New Deal and preferred a unilateral approach to foreign policy, Eisenhower preached "modern Republicanism." Democratic control of Congress after the elections of 1954 further contributed to the moderate approach of the Eisenhower administration (1953–1961), whose record overall maintained the course charted by Roosevelt and Truman.

The new president attempted to distance himself from the anti-Communist fervor that had plagued the Truman administration. Yet Eisenhower refused to denounce Senator Joseph McCarthy publicly; thus, even under a Republican administration, McCarthy continued his allegations of Communists in the government, and thousands of federal employees lost their jobs. Finally, the senator destroyed himself, as Eisenhower had predicted he would. In 1954, McCarthy tightened his own noose when he went after the army. As he hurled reckless charges of communism against military personnel during weeks of televised hearings, public opinion turned against him. "Have you left no sense of decency?" demanded the army's lawyer. A Senate vote to condemn him in December 1954 marked the end of his influence, but Eisenhower's inaction had allowed the senator to spread his poison longer than he might otherwise have done.

Eisenhower sometimes echoed the **conservative** Republicans' conviction that government was best left to the states and economic decisions to private business. "If all Americans want is

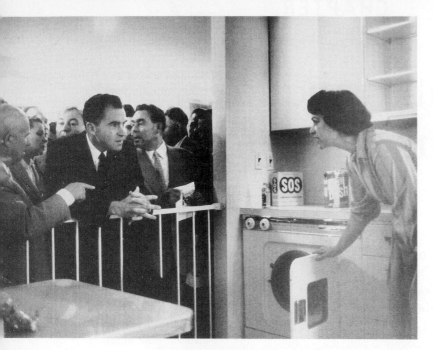

The Kitchen Debate
Soviet premier Nikita Khrushchev (left) and Vice President Richard M. Nixon (center) debate the relative merits of their nations' economies at the American National Exhibition held in Moscow in 1959. "You are a lawyer for capitalism and I am a lawyer for communism," Khrushchev told Nixon as each tried to get the best of the other.
Howard Sochurek / TimePix / Getty.

he did not propose to roll back **New Deal** programs. A majority of Americans enjoyed astounding material gains under the immensely popular president and seemed content with his "moderate Republicanism."

Cold war weapons production spurred the economy, whose vitality stimulated suburban development, contributed to the burgeoning populations and enterprise in the West and Southwest, and enabled millions of Americans to buy the products on display in Moscow. As new homes, television sets, and household appliances transformed their patterns of living, Americans took part in a dominant **consumer culture** that also celebrated marriage, family, and traditional gender roles, even as more and more married women took jobs outside their homes.

The cold war and the economic boom helped African Americans mount a strong challenge to tradition in the 1950s. Large numbers of African Americans took direct action against segregation and disfranchisement, developing the institutions, leadership, and strategies to mount a civil rights movement of unprecedented size and power.

security, they can go to prison," Eisenhower commented about social welfare in 1949. Yet, although **liberals** scorned the president's conservatism by calling him "Eisenhoover," the **welfare state** actually grew during his administration, and the federal government took on new projects.

In 1954, Eisenhower signed laws expanding Social Security and continuing the federal government's modest role in financing public housing. He enlarged the government with a new Department of Health, Education, and Welfare, naming former Women's Army Corps commander Oveta Culp Hobby to head it, the second female appointed to a cabinet post. And when the spread of polio neared epidemic proportions, Eisenhower obtained funds from Congress to distribute a vaccine, even though conservatives preferred that states assume that responsibility.

Eisenhower's greatest domestic initiative was the Interstate Highway and Defense System Act of 1956. Promoted as essential to national defense and an impetus to economic growth, the act authorized construction of a national highway system, with the federal government paying most of the costs through increased fuel and vehicle taxes. Americans benefited from greater ease of travel and improved transportation of goods, and the new highways also spurred suburban expansion and growth in the fast-food and motel industries (Map 27.1). The most substantial gains went to the trucking, construction, and automobile industries, which had lobbied hard for the law. The monumental highway project eventually exacted unforeseen costs in the form of air pollution, energy consumption, declining railroads and mass transportation in general, and decay in central cities.

In other areas, Eisenhower restrained federal activity in favor of state governments and private enterprise. His large tax cuts directed most benefits to business and the wealthy, and he stubbornly resisted a larger federal role in health care, education, and civil rights. Moreover, whereas Democrats sought to keep nuclear power in government hands, Eisenhower signed legislation authorizing the private manufacture and sale of nuclear power. Workers began building the first commercial nuclear power plant in Pennsylvania in 1954.

Termination and Relocation of Native Americans

The Eisenhower administration's efforts to restrict federal activity were consistent with a new direction in Indian policy, which reversed the

---

MAP 27.1   The Interstate Highway System, 1930 and 1970
Built with federal funds authorized in the Interstate Highway Act of 1956, superhighways soon crisscrossed the nation. Trucking, construction, gasoline, and travel were among the industries that prospered, but railroads suffered from the subsidized competition.

READING THE MAP: What regions of the United States had main highways in 1930? What regions did not? How had the situation changed by 1970?

CONNECTIONS: What impact did the growth of the interstate highway system have on migration patterns in the United States? What benefits did the new interstate highways bring to Americans and at what costs?

FOR MORE HELP ANALYZING THIS MAP, see the map activity for this chapter in the Online Study Guide at bedfordstmartins.com/roarkcompact.

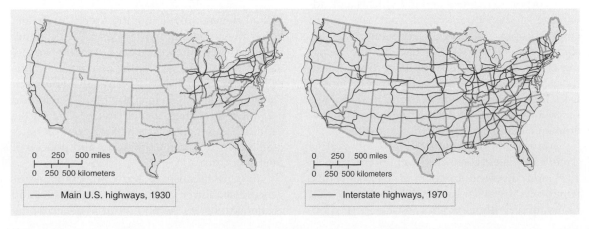

Main U.S. highways, 1930

Interstate highways, 1970

emphasis on strengthening tribal governments and preserving Indian culture established in the Indian Reorganization Act of 1934 (see chapter 24). After World War II, when some 25,000 Indians had left their homes for military service and another 40,000 for work in defense industries, policymakers began to favor assimilating Native Americans and ending their special relationships with government.

By the 1950s, the government had implemented a three-part program of compensation, termination, and relocation. In 1946, Congress established a commission to discharge outstanding claims by Native Americans for lands taken by the government. When it closed in 1978, the Indian Claims Commission had settled 285 cases with compensation exceeding $800 million. The second policy—termination—also began during the Truman administration. Believing that the Bureau of Indian Affairs should "not do anything which others can do as well or better" and "nothing for Indians which Indians can do for themselves," Truman's commissioner of Indian affairs proposed to end the trusteeship relationship between Indians and the federal government and to eliminate health and educational services to Indian tribes, initiatives that were carried out under his successor.

Beginning in 1953, Eisenhower signed bills transferring jurisdiction over tribal lands to state and local governments. The loss of federal hospitals, schools, and other special arrangements devastated Indian tribes. As had happened after passage of the Dawes Act in 1887 (see chapter 18), some corporate interests and individuals took advantage of the opportunity to purchase Indian lands cheaply. According to one Indian leader, some of his people saw termination as the "severing of ties already loose and ineffective," but to the great majority it was "like the strike of doom." Decades later the Menominees and the Klamaths secured restoration of their tribal status. The government abandoned termination in the 1960s.

Relocation, the third piece of Native American policy, began with a pilot program in 1948 and involved more than 100,000 Native Americans by 1973, although even more left reservations without federal assistance. The gov-

Selected Indian Relocations, 1950–1970

Indian reservation, 1970
← Relocations

ernment encouraged Indians to move to cities, providing one-way bus tickets and, at their destinations, relocation centers to help with housing, job training, and medical care. To make it difficult to return home, officials sent them far away from their reservations—the South Dakota Sioux to California, for example, and Alaskan Natives to Chicago. Still, about one-third of those who relocated went back to the reservation. Most who stayed in cities faced great difficulties: racism, lack of adequately paying jobs for which they had skills, poor housing in what became Indian ghettos, and the loss of their traditional culture. "I wish we had never left home," sighed one woman. "It's dirty and noisy, and people all around, crowded.... It seems like I never see the sky or trees." Her sons were headed for reform school, and her husband was out of work and drinking.

Some who overcame these obstacles applauded the program, but most urban Indians remained in or near poverty. Even many who had welcomed relocation eventually determined that they must resist "assimilation to the degree that we would lose our identity as Indian people, lose our culture and our [way] of living." Within two decades, a national pan-Indian movement emerged to do just that and demand much more for Indians. The new militancy that arose was a by-product of the urbanization of Native Americans (see chapter 28).

The 1956 Election and the Second Term

Not all citizens were living the American dream, but with the nation at peace and the economy booming, Eisenhower easily defeated Adlai Stevenson in 1956. Two years later, however, the Democrats all but wiped out the Republican Party, gaining a 64–34 majority in the Senate and a 282–135 advantage in the House. Though Ike captured voters' hearts, a majority of voters remained wedded to the programs and policies of the Democrats.

In part because of the Democratic resurgence, Eisenhower faced more serious leadership challenges in his second term. The economy plunged into a recession, and unemployment rose to 7 percent. Eisenhower fought with Congress over the budget and vetoed bills to expand housing, urban development, and public works projects. The president and Congress did reach agreement in two key areas: enacting the first, though largely symbolic, civil rights legislation in a century and establishing a new role for the government in education.

In the end, the first Republican administration after the New Deal left the size and functions of the federal government intact, though it tipped policy somewhat more in favor of corporate interests. Unparalleled prosperity graced the Eisenhower years, and inflation was kept low. The economy weathered two recessions without putting to a test the president's aversion to substantial federal intervention.

> **REVIEW** How did Eisenhower's domestic policies reflect his moderate political vision?

Liberation Rhetoric and the Practice of Containment

At his 1953 inauguration, Eisenhower warned that "forces of good and evil are massed and armed and opposed as rarely before in history." Like Truman, he saw communism as a threat to the nation's security and economic interests. Eisenhower's foreign policy differed from Truman's, however, in three areas: its rhetoric, its means, and—after Stalin's death in 1953—its movement toward accommodation with the Soviet Union.

Republican rhetoric—voiced most prominently by Secretary of State John Foster Dulles—deplored containment as "negative, futile, and immoral" because it accepted the existing Soviet sphere of control. Yet, despite promises to roll back Soviet power, the Eisenhower administration continued the containment policy, actively intervening at the margins of Communist power in Asia, the Middle East, and Latin America, but not at its core in Europe.

The "New Look" in Foreign Policy

To meet his goals of balancing the budget and cutting taxes, Eisenhower determined to control military expenditures. Moreover, he feared that massive defense spending would threaten the nation's economic strength. A state based on

warfare could destroy the very society it was intended to protect. As he declared in 1953, "Every gun that is made, every warship launched, every rocket fired signifies, in the final sense, a theft from those who hunger and are not fed, those who are cold and not clothed."

Reflecting Americans' confidence in technology and opposition to a large peacetime army, Eisenhower's defense strategy concentrated U.S. military strength in nuclear weapons along with planes and missiles to deliver them. Instead of spending huge amounts for large ground forces of its own, the United States would give friendly nations American weapons and back them up with an ominous nuclear arsenal. This was Eisenhower's "New Look" in foreign policy. Airpower and nuclear weapons provided, in Defense Secretary Charles Wilson's words, a "bigger bang for the buck." Secretary of State Dulles believed that America's willingness to "go to the brink" of war

The Nuclear Arms Race

This *Newsweek* cover showing Soviet leader Nikita Khrushchev and President Dwight D. Eisenhower balanced on the head of a nuclear missile suggests the precarious world created by the nuclear arms race. The table on which the two men sit refers to the arms limitation negotiations under way when the magazine came off the press in 1959.

with its intimidating nuclear weapons—a strategy called **brinksmanship**—would block any Soviet efforts to expand.

Nuclear weapons could not stop a Soviet nuclear attack, but, in response to one, they could inflict enormous destruction on the USSR. This certainty of "massive retaliation" was meant to deter the Soviets from launching an attack. Because the Soviet Union could respond similarly to an American first strike, this nuclear standoff became known as mutually assured destruction, or MAD. Winston Churchill called it a "mutual balance of terror." As leaders of each nation sought not just balance but nuclear superiority, they pursued an ever-escalating arms race.

Nuclear weapons were useless, however, in rolling back the **iron curtain**, because they would destroy the very peoples whom the United States promised to liberate. When a revolt against the Soviet-controlled government began in Hungary in 1956, Dulles's liberation rhetoric proved to be empty. Eisenhower was unwilling to risk U.S. soldiers and possible nuclear war, and Soviet troops soon suppressed the insurrection, killing 30,000 Hungarians.

Applying Containment to Vietnam

A major challenge to the containment policy came in Southeast Asia, where in 1945 a **nationalist** coalition called the Vietminh, led by Ho Chi Minh, had proclaimed Vietnam's independence from France. When France fought to maintain its colony, Ho fought back, and the area plunged into war (see Map 29.2 in chapter 29). Because Ho declared himself a Communist, the Truman administration quietly began to provide aid to the French.

Eisenhower viewed communism in Vietnam much as Truman had regarded it in Greece and Turkey, a view that became known as the **domino theory**. "You have a row of dominoes," Eisenhower explained, and "you knock over the first one, and what will happen to the last one is the certainty that it will go over very quickly." A Communist victory in Southeast Asia, he warned, could trigger the fall of Japan, Taiwan, and the Philippines. By 1954, the United States was contributing 75 percent of the cost of

Geneva Accords of 1954

France's war, but Eisenhower resisted a larger role. When the French asked for troops and airplanes from the United States to avert almost certain defeat at Dien Bien Phu, Eisenhower firmly said no. Conscious of U.S. losses in the Korean War, he would not commit troops to another ground war in Asia.

Dien Bien Phu fell in May 1954 and with it the French colony of Vietnam. Two months later in Geneva, France signed a truce. The Geneva accords temporarily partitioned Vietnam at the seventeenth parallel, separating the Vietminh in the north from the puppet government established by the French in the south. Within two years, the Vietnamese people were to vote in elections for a unified government. The United States promised to support free elections but did not sign the accords.

Some officials warned against U.S. involvement in Vietnam. Defense Secretary Wilson could "see nothing but grief in store for us if we remained in that area." Eisenhower and Dulles nonetheless moved to prop up the dominoes with a new alliance. In September 1954, the United States joined with Britain, France, Australia, New Zealand, Thailand, Pakistan, and the Philippines in the Southeast Asia Treaty Organization (SEATO), committed to the defense of Cambodia, Laos, and South Vietnam. Shortly thereafter the United States began to send weapons and military advisers to South Vietnam and put the CIA to work infiltrating and destabilizing North Vietnam. Fearing a Communist victory in the mandated elections, the United States supported South Vietnamese prime minister Ngo Dinh Diem's refusal to hold the vote.

Between 1955 and 1961, the United States provided $800 million to the South Vietnamese army (Army of the Republic of Vietnam). Yet the ARVN proved grossly unprepared for the **guerrilla warfare** that began in the late 1950s. With assistance from Ho Chi Minh's government in Hanoi, Vietminh rebels in the south stepped up their guerrilla attacks on the Diem government. The insurgents gained control over villages in part because the largely Buddhist peasants were outraged by the repressive regime of the Catholic, Westernized Diem. Unwilling to abandon containment, Eisenhower left his successor with the deteriorating situation and a firm commitment to defend South Vietnam.

Interventions in Latin America and the Middle East

While buttressing friendly governments in Asia, the Eisenhower administration worked to topple unfriendly ones in Latin America and the Middle East. The CIA became an important arm of foreign policy in the 1950s, as Eisenhower relied on behind-the-scenes efforts and covert activities against governments that appeared too leftist and threatened U.S. economic interests. Increasingly, the administration conducted foreign policy behind the back of Congress.

The Eisenhower administration employed clandestine activities in Guatemala, where the government was not Communist or Soviet controlled but accepted support from the local Communist Party (see Map 29.1 in chapter 29). In 1954, when the reformist president Jacobo Arbenz sought to nationalize land owned but not used by a U.S. corporation, United Fruit Company, Eisenhower authorized the CIA to carry out covert operations destabilizing Guatemala's economy and assisting a coup. A military dictatorship friendly to United Fruit replaced Arbenz's popularly elected government.

"We're going to take care of Castro just like we took care of Arbenz," promised a CIA agent when Cubans' desire for political and economic autonomy erupted in 1959. American companies had long controlled major Cuban resources—especially sugar, tobacco, and mines—and decisions made in Washington directly influenced the lives of the Cuban people. An uprising in 1959 led by Fidel Castro drove out the U.S.-supported dictator Fulgencio Batista and led the CIA to warn Eisenhower that "Communists and other extreme radicals appear to have penetrated the Castro movement." When the United States denied Castro's requests for loans, he turned to the Soviet Union. And when U.S. companies refused Castro's offer to purchase them at their assessed value, he began to nationalize their property. Many anti-Castro Cubans fled to the United States and reported his atrocities, including the execution of hundreds of Batista's supporters. Before leaving office, Eisenhower broke off diplomatic relations with Cuba and authorized the CIA to train Cuban exiles for an invasion.

In the Middle East, as in Guatemala, the CIA intervened to support an unpopular dictatorship and help American corporations (see Map 30.2 in chapter 30). In 1951, the left-leaning prime minister of Iran, Mohammed Mossadegh, had nationalized oil fields and refineries, thereby threatening Western oil interests. While accepting support from the Iranian Communist Party, Mossadegh also challenged the power of Shah Mohammad Reza Pahlavi, Iran's hereditary leader, who favored foreign oil interests and the Iranian wealthy classes.

For all of these reasons, Eisenhower authorized CIA agents to instigate a coup against Mossadegh by bribing army officers and paying Iranians to demonstrate against the government. In August 1953, army officers captured Mossadegh and reestablished the shah's power, whereupon Iran renegotiated oil concessions, giving U.S. companies a 40 percent share. Although the intervention worked in the short run, Americans in 1979 would reap the fury of Iranian opposition to the repressive government that the United States had helped to reinstall.

Elsewhere in the Middle East, the Eisenhower administration shifted from Truman's all-out support for Israel to fostering friendships with Arab nations. Hindering such efforts, however, were U.S. demands that smaller nations take the American side in the cold war, even when those nations preferred neutrality and the opportunity for assistance from both Western and Communist nations.

In 1955, Secretary of State Dulles began talks with Egypt about American support to build the Aswan Dam on the Nile River. But in 1956, Egypt's leader, Gamal Abdel Nasser, sought arms from Communist Czechoslovakia, formed a military alliance with other Arab nations, and recognized the People's Republic of China. Unwilling to tolerate such independence, Dulles called off the deal for the dam. On July 26, 1956, Nasser responded by seizing the Suez Canal, then owned by Britain and France. Thereupon, Israel, whose forces had been skirmishing with Egyptian troops along their common border since 1948, attacked Egypt, with military help from Britain and France.

The Suez Crisis, 1956

The Suez Crisis, 1956
Oct. 29th–Nov. 5th

← Israeli troop movements

0   25   50 miles
0   50 kilometers

Eisenhower opposed the intervention, recognizing that the Egyptians had claimed their own territory and that Nasser "embodie[d] the emotional demands of the people…for independence." He put economic pressure on Britain and France while calling on the United Nations to arrange a truce. The French and British soon pulled back, forcing Israel to retreat.

Although staying out of the Suez crisis, Eisenhower made clear that the United States would actively combat communism in the Middle East. In March 1957, Congress passed a joint resolution approving economic and military aid to any Middle Eastern nation "requesting assistance against armed aggression from any country controlled by international communism." The president invoked this "Eisenhower Doctrine" to send aid to Jordan in 1957 and troops to Lebanon in 1958 to counter anti-Western pressures on those governments.

The Nuclear Arms Race

While the Eisenhower administration moved against perceived Communist inroads abroad, a number of events encouraged the president to seek reduction of superpower tensions. After Stalin's death in 1953, a more moderate leadership under Nikita Khrushchev emerged. The Soviet Union signed a peace treaty with Austria and removed its troops. Like Eisenhower, who remarked privately that the arms race would lead "at worst to atomic warfare, at best to robbing every people and nation on earth of the fruits of their own toil," Khrushchev wanted to reduce defense spending and the threat of nuclear devastation. Eisenhower and Khrushchev met in Geneva in 1955 at the first summit conference since the end of World War II. Though it produced no significant agreements, the meeting symbolized what Eisenhower called "a new spirit of conciliation and cooperation." But events left Americans uneasy.

In August 1957, the Soviets test-fired their first intercontinental ballistic missile (ICBM) and two months later beat the United States into space by launching *Sputnik*, the first artificial satellite to circle the earth. After the first American satellite exploded—news headlines called it a "Flopnik"—the United States caught up, launching a successful satellite in January 1958. Nonetheless, *Sputnik* raised fears that the United States lagged behind not only in missile development and space exploration but also in science and education. Eisenhower insisted that the United States possessed nuclear superiority and tried to diminish

public panic. He established the National Aeronautics and Space Administration (NASA) in July 1958, approved a gigantic budget increase for space research and development, and signed the National Defense Education Act, providing loans and scholarships for students in math, foreign languages, and science.

Yet even nuclear superiority could not guarantee security because the Soviet Union possessed sufficient nuclear weapons to devastate the United States. Most Americans did not follow Civil Defense Administration recommendations to construct home bomb shelters, but they did realize how precarious nuclear weapons had made their lives. "Facing a Danger Unlike Any Danger That Has Ever Existed," headlined an ad placed by the Committee for a Sane Nuclear Policy, an organization founded to oppose the nuclear arms race.

Even as the superpowers competed for nuclear dominance, they continued to talk. In 1959, Khrushchev visited the United States, and Nixon went to the Soviet Union, where he engaged in the famous kitchen debate. By 1960, the two sides were within reach of a ban on nuclear testing, and Khrushchev and Eisenhower agreed to meet again in Paris in May.

To avoid jeopardizing the summit, Eisenhower canceled espionage flights over the Soviet Union, but his order came one day too late. On May 1, 1960, a Soviet missile shot down a U-2 spy plane over Soviet territory. The State Department first denied that U.S. planes had been violating Soviet air space, but the Soviets produced the pilot and photos taken on his flight. Eisenhower and Khrushchev met briefly in Paris, but the U-2 incident dashed all prospects for a nuclear arms agreement.

Eisenhower's "more bang for the buck" defense budget enormously increased the U.S. nuclear capacity, more than quadrupling the stockpile of nuclear weapons. By the time he left office in 1961, the United States had installed ICBMs in the United States and Britain and was prepared to deploy more in Italy and Turkey. The first Polaris submarine carrying nuclear missiles was launched in November 1960.

As he left office, Eisenhower warned about the growing influence of the **military-industrial complex** in American government and life. To contain the defense budget, Eisenhower had struggled against persistent pressures from defense contractors who, in tandem with the military, sought more dollars for newer, more powerful weapons systems. In his farewell address, he warned that the "conjunction of an immense

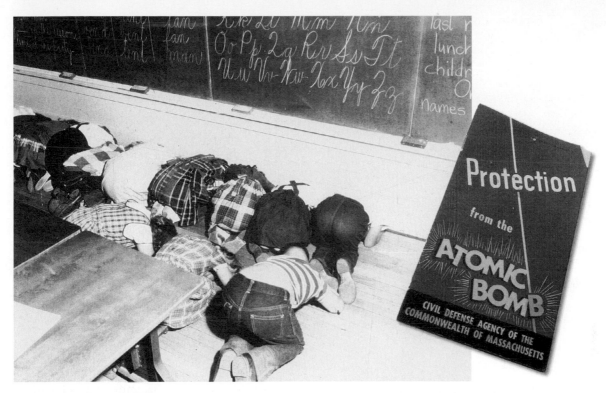

The Age of Nuclear Anxiety
Within just five years after World War II, state and local governments were educating the American people about the nuclear threat and urging them to prepare. Schools routinely held drills to prepare for possible Soviet attacks, and children directly experienced the anxiety and insecurity of the 1950s nuclear arms race. The pamphlet about how to survive an atomic attack was published by the federal government and distributed to the general public. How effective do you think the strategy pictured here would have been in the event of a nuclear attack?
Archive Photos; Lynn Historical Society.

FOR MORE HELP ANALYZING THIS IMAGE, see the visual activity for this chapter in the Online Study Guide at
bedfordstmartins.com/roarkcompact.

military establishment and a large arms indus-try…exercised a total influence…in every city, every state house, every office of the federal government." The cold war had created a warfare state.

> **REVIEW**   Where and how did Eisenhower practice containment?

New Work and Living Patterns in an Economy of Abundance

American military spending helped stimulate domestic prosperity. Economic productivity increased enormously in the 1950s (Figure 27.1), a multitude of new items came on the market, and consumption became the order of the day. Millions of Americans enjoyed new homes in the suburbs, and higher education became the norm for the middle class. Although every section of the nation enjoyed the new abundance, the West and Southwest especially boomed in production, commerce, and population.

Work itself changed: Fewer people labored on farms; service sector employment overtook manufacturing jobs; and women's employment grew. These economic shifts disadvantaged some Americans, and some forty million people—20 percent of the population—lived in poverty. Most Americans, however, enjoyed a higher standard of living, leading the economist John Kenneth Galbraith to call the United States "the affluent society."

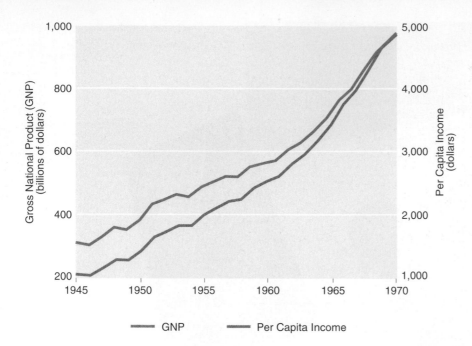

FIGURE 27.1   The Postwar Economic Boom: GNP and Per Capita Income, 1945–1970

American dominance of the worldwide market, innovative technologies that led to new industries such as computers and plastics, population growth, and increases in worker productivity all contributed to the enormous economic growth of the United States after World War II.

Technology Transforms Agriculture and Industry

Between 1940 and 1960, agricultural output mushroomed while the number of farmworkers declined by nearly one-third. Farmers achieved nearly miraculous productivity through greater crop specialization, more intensive use of fertilizers, and, above all, mechanization. Tractors, mechanical pickers, and other machines increasingly substituted for human and animal power. A single mechanical cotton picker replaced fifty people and cut the cost of harvesting a bale of cotton from $40 to $5.

The decline of family farms and the growth of large commercial farming, or **agribusiness**, were both causes and consequences of mechanization. Benefiting handsomely from federal price supports begun in the New Deal, larger farmers could afford technological improvements, whereas smaller producers lacked capital to invest in the machinery necessary to compete. Consequently, average farm size more than doubled between 1940 and 1964, and the number of farms fell by more than 40 percent.

Many small farmers who hung on constituted a core of rural poverty often overlooked in the celebration of affluence. Southern landowners replaced sharecroppers with machines, forcing them off the land. Hundreds of thousands of African Americans joined an exodus to cities, where racial discrimination and a lack of jobs for

which they could qualify mired many in urban poverty. A Mississippi woman whose family had worked on a plantation since slavery reported that most of her relatives headed for Chicago when they heard that "it was going to be machines now that harvest the crops." Worrying that "it might be worse up there," she agonized, "I'm afraid to leave and I'm afraid to stay, and whichever I do, I think it might be real bad for my boys and girls."

New technology also increased industrial production. Between 1945 and 1960, for example, the automobile industry cut in half the number of labor-hours needed to manufacture a car. Technology also transformed such industries as electronics, chemicals, and air transportation and promoted the growth of television, plastics, computers, and other newer industries. American businesses enjoyed access to cheap oil, ample markets abroad, and little foreign competition. Moreover, even with Eisenhower's conservative fiscal policies, government spending reached $80 billion annually and created new jobs.

Labor unions enjoyed their greatest success during the 1950s, and real earnings for production workers shot up 40 percent. The merger in 1955 of the American Federation of Labor (AFL) and the Congress of Industrial Organizations (CIO) improved labor's bargaining position. As one worker put it, "We saw continual improvement in wages, fringe benefits like holidays, vacation, medical plans…all sorts of things that provided more secu-

Technology Transforms Agriculture

A mechanical cotton picker was patented as early as 1850, but the abundant supply of slave labor and then sharecroppers delayed its widespread use until after World War II. In 1950, machines harvested just 5 percent of cotton in the South, but ten years later mechanization accounted for 50 percent of the crop. This kind of technological advance was both cause and effect of the movement of African Americans out of the rural South. In this photo, cotton harvesters munch their way through a North Carolina cotton field in the 1950s.

United States Department of Agriculture.

rity for people." Unlike most industrial nations, where government provided most of the benefits, the United States developed a mixed system in which company-funded programs bargained for by unions played a larger role. This system resulted in wide disparities among workers, severely disadvantaging those not represented by unions.

Union membership peaked at 27.1 percent of the labor force in 1957; then, the percentage of unionized workers began to decline. Technological advances chipped away at jobs in heavy industry, reducing the number of workers in the steel, copper, and aluminum industries by 17 percent. Moreover, the economy as a whole was shifting from production to service. Instead of making products, more workers distributed goods, performed services, kept records, provided education, or carried out government work. Unions made some headway in these fields, especially among government employees, but most service industries resisted unionization.

The growing clerical and service occupations swelled the demand for female workers. By the end of the 1950s, 35 percent of all women over age sixteen worked outside the home—twice as many as in 1940—and women held nearly one-third of all jobs. Women entered a sharply segregated workplace. The vast majority worked in clerical jobs, light manufacturing, domestic service, teaching, and nursing, and be-

cause these were female occupations, wages were relatively low. In 1960, the average full-time female worker earned just 60 percent of the average male worker's wages.

Burgeoning Suburbs and Declining Cities

Although suburbs had existed since the nineteenth century, nothing symbolized the affluent society more than their tremendous expansion in the 1950s: Eleven million of the thirteen million new homes were built in the suburbs, and by 1960, one in four Americans lived there. As Vice President Nixon boasted to Khrushchev during the kitchen debate, the suburbs were accessible to families with modest incomes. Builder William J. Levitt modified the factory assembly-line process, planning nearly identical units so that individual construction workers could move from house to house and perform the same single operation in each. In 1949, families could purchase these mass-produced houses in his 17,000-home development called Levittown, on Long Island, New York, for just under $8,000. Developments similar to Levittown, as well as more luxurious ones, quickly went up throughout the country.

The government subsidized home ownership with low-interest mortgage guarantees through the

Federal Housing Administration and the Veterans Administration and by making interest on mortgages tax deductible. The thousands of miles of interstate highway running through urban areas indirectly subsidized suburban development.

Suburban culture was not without detractors. Social critic Lewis Mumford blasted the suburbs as "a multitude of uniform, unidentifiable houses, lined up inflexibly, at uniform distances, on uniform roads, in a treeless communal wasteland, inhabited by people of the same class, the same income, the same age group." By the 1960s, suburbs came under attack for bulldozing the natural environment, creating groundwater contamination, and disrupting wildlife patterns. Moreover, the growing suburbs contributed to a more polarized society, especially along racial lines.

As white residents joined the suburban migration, blacks moved to cities in search of economic opportunity, increasing their numbers in most cities by 50 percent during the 1950s. Black migrants, however, came to cities that were already in decline, losing not only population but also commerce and industry to the suburbs or to southern

and western states. New business facilities began to ring central cities, and shoppers gradually chose suburban malls over downtown department stores. Many of the new jobs lay beyond the reach of the recent black arrivals to the inner cities.

The Rise of the Sun Belt

Americans were on the move westward as well as to the suburbs. Architect Frank Lloyd Wright quipped, "everything loose will land in Los Angeles." No regions experienced the postwar economic and population booms more intensely than the West and Southwest. After World War II, California's inhabitants more than doubled, and California overtook New York as the most populous state. Sports franchises followed fans: In 1958, the Brooklyn Dodgers moved to Los Angeles, joined by the Minneapolis Lakers three years later.

A pleasant natural environment drew new residents to the West and Southwest, but no magnet proved stronger than the promise of economic opportunity (Map 27.2). As railroads had fueled western growth in the nineteenth

MAP 27.2   The Rise of the Sun Belt, 1940–1980
The growth of defense industries, a nonunionized labor force, and the spread of air-conditioning all helped spur economic development and population growth, which made the Sun Belt the fastest-growing region of the nation between 1940 and 1980.

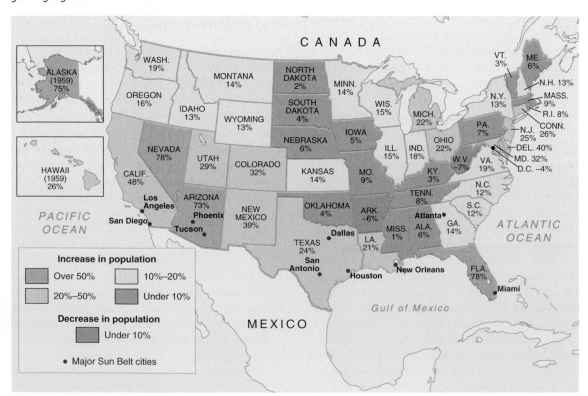

Air-Conditioning

Combining two technological advances of the late nineteenth century, refrigeration and electricity, air-conditioning developed primarily in response to the needs of industry. In 1902, Willis Haviland Carrier, a twenty-six-year-old American engineer who formulated basic theories of air-conditioning, designed the first system to control temperature and humidity and installed it in a Brooklyn printing plant. In 1915, he founded the Carrier Corporation to manufacture air-conditioning equipment.

Because fibers are sensitive to moisture, the textile industry provided an early and important market for air-conditioning. The process also helped to popularize movie theaters by making them a cool as well as an entertaining retreat during hot summer months. Room air conditioners began to appear in the 1930s. This 1950 Carrier ad promoted the clean air in homes and offices that would come with purchase of a room air conditioner. Fewer than a million homes had room air conditioners in 1950, but nearly eight million did in

1960, and more than half of all homes had some form of air-conditioning by 1975, as its status changed from a luxury to a necessity. By the end of the twentieth century, more than 80 percent of

EXCUSE MY DUST

AIR CONDITIONING · REFRIGERATION

"That's Modern Air Control!"
Ads like this one for the Carrier room air conditioner promised consumers that homes could be cool as well as clean.
Courtesy Carrier Corporation.

households had air-conditioning, and it had become standard equipment on automobiles.

Air-conditioning was a mixed blessing. On the one hand, companies no longer had to shut down and send workers home when heat and humidity became unbearable, and air quality inside businesses, homes, and cars improved. On the other hand, air conditioners consumed large amounts of energy and contributed to outdoor air pollution. Like other technologies such as television and, more recently, the Internet, air-conditioning had an isolating effect as people deserted front porches and backyards for closed-up houses and thus curtailed their interactions with neighbors. Perhaps its greatest impact on the nation was to make possible the population explosion in the Sun Belt. By facilitating the movement of commerce, industry, and tourism to the South and Southwest, air-conditioning made that region more like the rest of the nation. One historian of the South, referring disparagingly to the transformation worked by air-conditioning on that region, proclaimed that "[General Electric] has proved a more devastating invader than even General Sherman."

century, the automobile and airplane spurred the post–World War II surge. The technology of air-conditioning made possible industrial development and by 1960 cooled nearly eight million homes in the so-called **Sun Belt**, which stretched from Florida to California. (See "The Promise of Technology," above.)

So important was the defense industry to the South and West that it was later referred to as the "Gun Belt." The aerospace industry boomed in Seattle-Tacoma, Los Angeles, Tucson, and Dallas–Fort Worth, and military bases helped underwrite prosperity in cities such as San Diego and San Antonio. Although defense dollars benefited other regions, the Sun Belt captured the lion's share of cold war spending for research and production of bombers and missiles, other weapons, and satellites. By the 1960s, nearly one of every three California workers held a defense-related job.

The surging populations and industries soon raised environmental concerns. Providing sufficient water and power to cities and to agribusiness meant replacing free-flowing rivers in the West with a series of dams and reservoirs. Sprawling urban and suburban settlement without efficient public transportation contributed to blankets of smog over cities like Los Angeles. Development began to degrade the very environment that people came to enjoy.

The high-technology basis of postwar economic development drew well-educated, highly

Rounding Up Undocumented Migrants

Not all Mexican Americans who wanted to work in the United States were accommodated by the *bracero* program. In 1953, Los Angeles police arrested these men who did not have legal documents and were hiding in a freight train. Americans used the crude term "wetback" to refer to illegal immigrants because many of them swam across the Rio Grande, at the border between the United States and Mexico.

© Bettmann/Corbis.

skilled workers to the West. But the economic promise also attracted the poor. "We see opportunity all around us here.... We smell freedom here, and maybe soon we can taste it," commented a black mother in California. Between 1945 and 1960, more than one-third of the African Americans who left the South moved west, and more blacks moved to California than to any other state.

The Mexican American population also grew, especially in California and Texas. To supply California's vast agribusiness industry, the government continued the *bracero* **program** begun during World War II. Until the program ended in 1964, more than 100,000 Mexicans entered the United States each year to labor in the fields—and many of them stayed, legally or illegally. But permanent Mexican immigration was not as welcome as Mexicans' low-wage labor. The government launched a series of raids in 1954 called "Operation Wetback." Designed to ferret out and deport illegal immigrants, the operation made U.S. citizens of Mexican descent feel unwelcome and threatened them with incidents of mistaken identity.

At the same time, Mexican American citizens gained a small victory in their ongoing struggle for civil rights in *Hernandez v. Texas.* When a Texas jury convicted Pete Hernandez of murder, lawyers from the American GI Forum and the League of United Latin-American Citizens (see chapter 26) appealed on the grounds that persons of Mexican origin had been routinely excluded from jury service. In the first Mexican American civil rights case of the post–World War II era, the Supreme Court ruled unanimously that the systematic exclusion of Hispanics from juries violated the constitutional guarantee of equal protection.

Free of the discrimination faced by minorities, white Americans reaped the fullest fruits of prosperity in the West. In April 1950, when California developers advertised the opening of Lakewood, a large housing development in Los Angeles County, 30,000 people lined up to purchase tract houses for $8,000 to $10,000. Many of the new homeowners were veterans, blue-collar and lower-level white-collar workers whose defense-based jobs at McDonnell Douglas and other aerospace corporations enabled them to fulfill the American dream of the 1950s. A huge shopping mall, Lakewood Center, offered myriad products of the consumer culture. And their children had access to community colleges and

Moving into the Suburbs
In 1953, responding to an ad in a St. Louis newspaper calling for engineers to work at North American Aviation, Leo Ferguson moved his family from Alton, Illinois, to Lakewood, California. Using cash and installment payments, the Fergusons purchased a house for $10,290 and bought $6,800 worth of additional products. What does the photograph tell us about the kinds of items that fueled the consumer economy?

J. B. Eyerman/TimePix/Getty.

six state universities—all within easy reach of Lakewood.

The Democratization of Higher Education

California's system was the largest element in a spectacular transformation of higher education. Between 1940 and 1960, enrollments leaped from 1.5 million to 3.6 million; and more than 40 percent of young Americans attended college by the mid-1960s, up from 15 percent in the 1940s. More families could afford to keep their children in school longer, and the federal government subsidized the education of more than two million veterans. The cold war also sent millions of federal dollars to universities for defense-related research. Tax dollars spent on higher education more than doubled from 1950 to 1960, as state governments vastly expanded the number of public colleges and universities, and municipalities began to build two-year community colleges.

All Americans did not benefit equally from the democratization of higher education. Although the college enrollments of blacks surged from 37,000 in 1941 to 90,000 in 1961, African Americans constituted only about 5 percent of all college students, less than half their percentage of the population. In addition, the educational gap between white men and women increased. While the numbers of college women grew, they did not keep pace with those of men. In 1940, women earned 40 percent of undergraduate degrees, but as veterans flocked to college campuses, women's proportion fell to 25 percent in 1950, climbing to only 33 percent by 1960.

> **REVIEW** How did technology contribute to changes in the economy, suburbanization, and the growth of the Sun Belt?

The Culture of Abundance

With increased prosperity in the 1950s, more people married and the birthrate soared. Dominant values favored family life and traditional gender roles, consumption, and conformity. Religious observance expanded even as Americans sought satisfaction in material possessions. Television entered the homes of most Americans, helping to promote a consumer culture. Undercurrents of rebellion, especially among youth, and women's increasing employment defied some of the dominant norms but did not greatly disrupt the complacency of the 1950s.

A Consumer Culture

"If you grew up in the 1950s," journalist Robert Samuelson remembered, "you were a daily witness to the marvels of affluence…[to] a seemingly endless array of new gadgets and machines." Scorned by Khrushchev during the kitchen debate as worthless gadgets, consumer items flooded American society in the 1950s. Although the purchase and display of consumer goods had always been part of American life (see chapter 23), by the 1950s consumption had become a reigning value, vital for economic prosperity and essential to individuals' identity and status. The traditional work ethic competed with a newer norm that stressed satisfaction and joy through the purchase and use of new products.

The consumer culture rested on a firm material base. Between 1950 and 1960, both the gross national product (the value of all goods and services produced during a year) and median family income grew by 25 percent in constant dollars. Alongside a 20 percent poverty rate, economists claimed that 60 percent of Americans enjoyed middle-class incomes in 1960. By then, four of every five families owned television sets, nearly all had refrigerators, and most owned at least one car. The number of shopping centers quadrupled between 1957 and 1963.

Several forces spurred this unparalleled abundance. A population surge—from 152 million in 1950 to 180 million in 1960—expanded demand for products and boosted industries ranging from housing to baby goods. Consumer borrowing also fueled the economic boom, as people increasingly made purchases on installment plans. Diner's Club issued the first credit card in 1951. Private debt more than doubled during the decade.

Although the sheer need to support themselves and their families explained most women's employment, a desire to secure some of the new abundance pulled increasing numbers of women out of the home. In fact, married women experienced the largest increases in employment in the 1950s. As one remarked, "My Joe can't put five kids through college…and the washer had to be replaced, and Ann was ashamed to bring friends home because the living room furniture was such a mess, so I went to work." The standards for family happiness imposed by the consumer culture increasingly required a second income.

The Revival of Domesticity and Religion

Even as married women took jobs in unprecedented numbers, a dominant ideology celebrated traditional family life and conventional gender roles. Both popular culture and public figures defined the ideal family as a male breadwinner, a full-time homemaker, and three or four children in a new suburban home. The emphasis on home and family life reflected to some extent anxieties about the cold war and nuclear menace. Like Nixon in the kitchen debate, one government official saw women's role in cold war terms, charging that the Soviet Union viewed women "first as a source of manpower, second as a mother," and insisting that "the highest calling of a woman's sex is the home."

Writer and **feminist** Betty Friedan gave a name to the idealization of women's domestic roles in her book *The Feminine Mystique*, published in 1963. Friedan criticized advertisers, social scientists, educators, women's magazines, and public officials for pressuring women to seek fulfillment in serving others. According to the feminine mystique that they promulgated, biological differences dictated entirely different roles for men and women. The ideal woman kept a spotless house, raised perfect children, served her husband's career, and provided him emotional and sexual satisfaction. Not many women then directly challenged the feminine mystique, but Edith Stern, a college-educated writer, maintained that "many arguments about the joys of housewifery have been advanced, largely by those who have never had to work at it."

Although the glorification of domesticity clashed with women's increasing employment, many Americans' lives did embody the family ideal. Prosperity enabled people to marry earlier and to have more children. The American birthrate, in decline since the nineteenth century, soared between 1945 and 1965, peaking in 1957 with 4.3 million births and producing the "baby boom" generation (see appendix II, page A-29).

Along with a renewed emphasis on family life, the 1950s witnessed a surge of interest in religion. By 1960, about 63 percent of Americans belonged to churches and synagogues, up from 50 percent in 1940. Polls reported that 95 percent of all Americans believed in God. Evangelism took on new life, most notably in the nationwide crusades of Baptist minister Billy Graham, whose powerful oratory moved mass audiences to accept Christ. Congress linked religion more closely to the state by adding "under God" to the Pledge of Allegiance in 1954 and by requiring in 1955 that "In God We Trust" be printed on all currency.

Eisenhower's pastor attributed the renewed interest in religion to the prosperous economy, which "provided the leisure, the energy, and the means for a level of human and spiritual values never before reached." Religion also calmed anxieties in the nuclear age, while ministers like Graham made the cold war a holy war, labeling communism "a great sinister anti-Christian movement masterminded by Satan." Some critics questioned the depth of the religious revival, attributing it to a desire for conformity and a need for social outlets. One commentator, for example, noted that 53 percent of Americans could not name any book of the Christian Bible's New Testament.

Television Transforms Culture and Politics

Just as family life and religion offered a respite from cold war anxieties, so too did the new medium of television. In 1950, fewer than 10 percent of American homes boasted a television set, but by 1960 about 87 percent of all households owned one. On average, Americans spent more than five hours each day in front of the screen.

Viewers were especially attracted to situation comedies, which projected the family ideal and the feminine mystique into millions of homes. On TV, married women did not have jobs and they deferred to their husbands, though they often got the upper hand through subtle manipulation. In the most popular television show of the early 1950s, *I Love Lucy*, the husband-and-wife team of Lucille Ball and Desi Arnaz played the couple Lucy and Ricky Ricardo. In step with the trends, they moved from an apartment in the city to a house in suburbia. Ricky would not let Lucy get a job, and many plots depicted her zany attempts to thwart his objections.

Television began to affect politics in the 1950s. Senator McCarthy's reckless attacks on army members were televised nationwide and contributed to his downfall. Eisenhower's 1952 presidential campaign used TV ads for the first time, and by 1960, television played a key role in election campaigns. Reflecting on his narrow victory in 1960, president-elect John F. Kennedy remarked, "We wouldn't have had a prayer without that gadget."

Television transformed politics in other ways. Money played a much larger role in elections because candidates needed to pay for expensive TV spots. The ability to appeal directly to voters in their living rooms put a premium on personal attractiveness and encouraged candidates to build their own campaign organizations, relying less on political parties. The declining strength of parties and the growing power of money in elections were not new trends, but television did much to accelerate them.

The Made-for-TV Family

This scene is from the popular television sitcom *Father Knows Best*, which ran from 1954 to 1963. Along with shows such as *Ozzie and Harriet* and *Leave It to Beaver*, it idealized white family life. In these shows, no one divorced or became gravely ill, no one took drugs or seriously misbehaved, fathers held white-collar jobs, mothers did not work outside the home, and husbands and wives slept in twin beds. In what ways do today's sitcoms differ from those of the 1950s?

Culver Pictures/Picture Research Consultants.

Unlike government-financed television in Europe, American TV was paid for by private enterprise. What NBC called a "selling machine in every living room" became the major vehicle for hawking the products of the affluent society and creating a consumer culture. In the mid-1950s, advertisers spent $10 billion to push their goods on TV, and they did not hesitate to interfere with shows that might jeopardize the sale of their products. The cigarette company that sponsored the *Camel News Caravan* banned any news film clips showing "No Smoking"

signs. Television programs themselves, not just commercials, tantalized viewers with things to buy. On *Queen for a Day*, for example, the women with the most pitiful personal stories won fur coats, vacuum cleaners, and other merchandise.

In 1961, Newton Minow, chairman of the Federal Communications Commission, called television a "vast wasteland." While acknowledging some of TV's great achievements, particularly documentaries and drama, Minow depicted it as "a procession of game shows,…formula comedies about totally unbelievable families, blood and thunder, mayhem, violence, sadism, murder…and cartoons." But viewers kept tuning in. In little more than a decade, television came to dominate Americans' leisure time, influence their consumption patterns, and shape their perceptions of the nation's leadership.

Countercurrents

Pockets of dissent underlay the complacency of the 1950s. Some intellectuals took exception to the materialism and conformity of the era. In *The Lonely Crowd* (1950), sociologist David Riesman lamented a shift from the "inner-directed" to the "other-directed" individual. Sharing that distaste for the importance of "belonging," William H. Whyte Jr., in his popular book *The Organization Man* (1956), blamed the modern corporation for making employees tailor themselves to the group, thus sacrificing risk taking and independence for dull conformity. Vance Packard's 1959 best seller, *The Status Seekers*, decried "the vigorous merchandising of goods as status-symbols" and argued that "class lines…appear to be hardening."

Less direct challenges to mainstream standards appeared in the everyday behavior of young Americans. "Roll over Beethoven and tell Tchaikovsky the news!" belted out Chuck Berry in his 1956 hit record celebrating a new form of music that combined country sounds and black rhythm and blues—rock and roll. White teenagers lionized Elvis Presley, who shocked their parents with his tight pants, hip-rolling gestures, and sensuous rock-and-roll music. "Before there was Elvis…I started going crazy for 'race music,'" recalled a white man of his teenage years. "It had a beat. I loved it….That got me into trouble with my parents and the schools." His experience illustrated

African Americans' contributions to rock and roll as well as the rebellion expressed by white youths' attraction to black music.

Just as rock and roll's sexual suggestiveness violated norms of middle-class respectability, Americans' sexual behavior often departed from the family ideal of the postwar era. Two books published by Alfred Kinsey and other researchers at Indiana University—*Sexual Behavior in the Human Male* (1948) and *Sexual Behavior in the Human Female* (1953)—uncovered a surprising range of sexual conduct. Surveying more than 16,000 individuals, Kinsey found that 85 percent of the men and 50 percent of the women had had sex before marriage, half of the husbands and a quarter of the wives had engaged in adultery, and one-third of the men and one-seventh of the women reported homosexual experiences.

Although Kinsey's sampling procedures later cast doubt on his ability to generalize across the population, the books became best sellers. They also drew a firestorm of outrage, especially because Kinsey refused to make moral judgments. Evangelist Billy Graham protested "the damage this book will do to the already deteriorating morals of America," and the Rockefeller Foundation stopped funding Kinsey's work.

The most blatant revolt against conventionality came from the self-proclaimed Beat generation, a small group of literary figures based in New York City's Greenwich Village and in San Francisco. Rejecting nearly everything in mainstream culture—patriotism, consumerism, technology, conventional family life, discipline—the Beats celebrated spontaneity and absolute personal freedom, including drug consumption and freewheeling sex. In his landmark poem *Howl* (1956), Allen Ginsberg inveighed against "Robot apartments! invisible suburbs! skeleton treasuries! blind capitals! demonic industries!...monstrous bombs!" and denounced the social forces that "frightened me out of my natural ecstasy!" In 1957, Jack Kerouac, who gave the Beat generation its name, published the best-selling novel *On the Road* (1957), whose energetic, bebop-style prose narrated the impetuous cross-country travels of two young men. The Beats' rebelliousness would provide a model for a much larger movement of youthful dissidents in the 1960s.

Bold new styles in the visual arts also showed the 1950s to be more than a decade of bland conventionality. An artistic revolution that flowered in New York City, known as "action painting" or "abstract expressionism," rejected the idea that painting should represent recognizable forms. Jackson Pollock and other abstract expressionists, emphasizing spontaneity, poured, dripped, and threw paint on canvases or substituted sticks and other implements for brushes. The new form of painting so captivated and redirected the Western art world that New York replaced Paris as its center.

> **REVIEW**   Why did American consumption expand so dramatically in the 1950s, and what aspects of society and culture did it influence?

Emergence of a Civil Rights Movement

African Americans posed the most dramatic challenge to the status quo of the 1950s as they sought to overcome the political and social barriers that had replaced the literal bonds of slavery. Every southern state mandated rigid segregation in public settings ranging from hospitals and schools to drinking fountains and restrooms. Voting laws and practices in the South disfranchised the vast majority of African Americans in that region; employment discrimination kept them at the bottom of the economic ladder.

Although black protest was as old as American racism, in the 1950s a grassroots movement arose that attracted national attention and the support of white liberals. The Supreme Court delivered significant institutional reforms, but blacks themselves directed the most important changes. Ordinary African Americans in substantial numbers sought their own liberation, building a movement that would transform race relations in the United States.

African Americans Challenge the Supreme Court and the President

Several factors spurred black protest in the 1950s. Between 1940 and 1960, more than three million African Americans moved from the South into areas where they could vote and exert political pressure. The cold war raised white leaders' concern that its poor treatment of minorities handicapped the United States in competing with the Soviet Union. In the South, the very system of segregation meant that African Americans controlled certain organizational resources, such as churches and colleges, where leadership skills could be honed and a network developed.

The legal strategy of the major civil rights organization, the National Association for the Advancement of Colored People (NAACP), reached its crowning achievement with the Supreme Court decision in *Brown v. Board of Education* in 1954. *Brown* consolidated five separate suits that reflected the growing determination of black Americans to fight for their rights. Oliver Brown, a welder in Topeka, Kansas, filed suit because his eight-year-old daughter had to pass by a white school to attend a black school more than a mile away. In Virginia, sixteen-year-old Barbara Johns came home from school one day and announced, "I walked out of school this morning and carried 450 students with me." Johns called the strike to protest the wretched conditions at her black high school, and it resulted in another of the suits joined in *Brown*. The NAACP's lead lawyer, future Supreme Court justice Thurgood Marshall, urged the Court to overturn the "separate but equal" precedent established in *Plessy v. Ferguson* in 1896 (see chapter 17). A unanimous Court, headed by Chief Justice Earl Warren, declared, "Separate educational facilities are inherently unequal" and thus violated the Fourteenth Amendment.

Ultimate responsibility for enforcement of the decision lay with President Eisenhower, but he refused to endorse *Brown*. He also kept silent in 1955 when whites lynched Emmett Till, a fourteen-year-old black boy who had allegedly whistled at a white woman in Mississippi. Reflecting his own racial prejudice, his preference for limited federal intervention in the states, and a leadership style that favored consensus and gradual progress, Eisenhower kept his distance from civil rights issues. Such inaction fortified southern resistance to school desegregation and contributed to the gravest constitutional crisis since the Civil War.

The crisis came in Little Rock, Arkansas, in September 1957. Local officials dutifully prepared for the integration of Central High School, but Governor Orval Faubus sent Arkansas National Guard troops to block the enrollment of nine black students, claiming that their presence would cause public disorder. Later, after agreeing to allow the black students to enter, Faubus withdrew the National Guard, leaving the students to face an angry white mob. "During those years when we desperately needed approval from our peers," Melba Patillo Beals remembered, "we were victims of the most harsh rejection imaginable." As television cameras transmitted the ugly scene across the nation, Eisenhower was forced to send regular army troops, the first federal military intervention in the South since Reconstruction. Escorted by paratroopers, the black students stayed in school, and Eisenhower withdrew the army in November. Other southern cities avoided integration by closing public schools and using tax dollars to support private, white-only schools. Seven years after *Brown,* only 6.4 percent of southern black students attended integrated schools.

Eisenhower did order integration of public facilities in Washington, D.C., and on military bases, and he supported the first federal civil rights legislation since Reconstruction. Yet the Civil Rights Acts of 1957 and 1960 lacked effective enforcement mechanisms, leaving southern blacks still unprotected in their basic rights. Eisenhower appointed the first black professional to the White House staff, E. Frederick Morrow, but Morrow confided to his diary, "I feel ridiculous…trying to defend the administration's record on civil rights."

Montgomery and Mass Protest

From slave revolts and individual acts of defiance through the legal and lobbying efforts of the NAACP, black protest had a long tradition. What set the civil rights movement of the 1950s and 1960s apart were the masses of people involved, their willingness to confront white institutions directly, and the use of nonviolence and passive resistance to bring about change. The Congress of Racial Equality (CORE) and other groups had experimented with these tactics in the 1940s, and African Americans boycotted the segregated bus system in Baton Rouge, Louisiana, in 1953, but the first sustained protest to claim national attention began in Montgomery, Alabama, on December 1, 1955.

On that day, police arrested Rosa Parks for violating a local segregation ordinance. Riding a crowded bus home from her job as a seamstress in a department store, she refused to give up her seat so that a white man could sit down. "People always say that I didn't give up my seat because I was tired, but that isn't true," Parks recalled. "I

School Integration in Little Rock, Arkansas
The nine African American teenagers who integrated Central High School in Little Rock, Arkansas, endured nearly three weeks of threats and hateful taunts before they even got through the doors. Here Elizabeth Eckford tries to ignore angry students and adults as she approaches the entrance to the school only to be blocked by the Arkansas National Guard troops. Even after Eisenhower intervened to enable the "Little Rock Nine" to attend school, they were called names, tripped, spat upon, and otherwise harassed by some white students. When Minnijean Brown, one of the black students, could take no more, she dumped a bowl of chili on a white boy who had taunted her. After she was expelled for that, cards circulated among white students reading, "One Down...Eight to Go."
Francis Miller/TimePix/Getty.

was not tired physically...I was not old...I was forty-two. No, the only tired I was, was tired of giving in." The bus driver called the police, who promptly arrested her.

Parks had long been active in the local NAACP, headed by E. D. Nixon. They had already talked about challenging bus segregation. So had the Women's Political Council (WPC), composed of black professional women and led by Jo Ann Robinson, an English professor at Alabama State College who had been humiliated by a bus driver when she had inadvertently sat in the white section. Such local individuals and organizations, long committed to improving conditions for African Americans, laid critical foundations for the black freedom struggle throughout the South.

When word came of Parks's arrest and decision to fight the case, WPC leaders immediately mobilized teachers and students to distribute flyers calling for Montgomery blacks to stay off the buses. E. D. Nixon called a mass meeting at the Holt Street Baptist Church, where a crowd of supporters stretched for blocks outside. Those assembled founded the Montgomery Improvement Association (MIA) to organize a bus boycott. The MIA arranged volunteer car pools and marshaled more than 90 percent of the black community to sustain the year-long boycott.

Elected to head the MIA was Martin Luther King Jr., the new pastor at the Dexter Avenue Baptist Church. At only twenty-six, King had a doctorate in theology from Boston University. A captivating speaker, King spoke to mass meetings at churches throughout the boycott, inspiring blacks' courage and commitment by linking racial justice to the redeeming power of Christian love. He promised, "If you will protest courageously and yet with dignity and Christian love...historians will have to pause and say, 'There lived a great people—a black people—who injected a new meaning and dignity into the veins of civilization.'"

Montgomery blacks summoned their courage and determination in abundance. They walked miles to get to work, contributed their meager financial resources, and stood up with dignity to intimidation and police harassment. Jo Ann Robinson, a cautious driver, got seventeen traffic tickets in the space of two months. Authorities arrested several leaders, and whites firebombed King's house. Yet the movement persisted until November 1956, when the Supreme Court declared unconstitutional Alabama's laws requiring bus segregation. Blacks had demonstrated that they could sustain a lengthy protest and refuse to be intimidated.

King's face on the cover of *Time* magazine in February 1957 marked the start of his rapid rise to national and international fame. In January, black clergy from across the South had chosen King to head the Southern Christian Leadership Conference (SCLC), newly established to coordinate local protests against segregation and disfranchisement. Although dominated by ministers, the SCLC owed much of its success to Ella Baker, a seasoned activist who came from New York to set up and run its office. Meanwhile the SCLC, NAACP, and CORE developed centers in several southern cities, paving the way for a mass movement that would revolutionize the racial system of the South.

REVIEW   What were the goals and strategies of civil rights activists in the 1950s?

Conclusion: Peace and Prosperity Mask Unmet Challenges

At the American National Exhibition in Moscow in 1959, the consumer goods that Nixon proudly displayed to Khrushchev and the cold war competition that crackled through their dialogue reflected two dominant themes of the 1950s: the prosperity of the U.S. economy and the superpowers' success in keeping cold war competition within the bounds of peace. The tremendous economic growth of the 1950s, which raised the standard of living for most Americans, resulted in part from the cold war: One of every ten American jobs depended directly on defense spending.

Affluence changed the very landscape of the United States. Suburban housing developments sprang up, interstate highways began to divide cities and connect the country, farms declined in number but grew in size, and population and industry moved south and west. Daily habits and even values of ordinary people changed as the economy became more service oriented and the opportunity to buy a host of new products intensified the growth of a consumer culture.

The general prosperity and seeming conformity, however, masked a number of developments and problems that Americans would face head-on in later years: rising resistance to an unjust racial

Martin Luther King Jr. in Montgomery, Alabama
Martin Luther King Jr. preached at the First Baptist Church during the Montgomery bus boycott. First Baptist was the congregation of Ralph D. Abernathy, the man who would become King's close associate in the crusades to come. The importance of churches as inspiration for and organizing centers in the black freedom struggle was not lost on white racists, who bombed First Baptist and three other black churches in Montgomery during the boycott.
Dan Weiner, courtesy Sandra Weiner.

system, a 20 percent poverty rate, the movement of married women into the labor force, and the emergence of a self-conscious youth generation. Although the federal government's defense spending and housing, highway, and education subsidies played a large role in the economic boom, in general Eisenhower tried to curb domestic programs and let private enterprise have its way. His administration maintained the welfare state inherited from the Democrats but opposed further reforms.

In global affairs, Eisenhower exercised restraint on large issues, recognizing the limits of U.S. power. In the name of **deterrence**, he promoted development of more destructive atomic weapons, but he resisted pressures for even larger defense budgets. Still, Eisenhower took from Truman the assumption that the United States must fight communism everywhere, and when movements in Iran, Guatemala, Cuba, and Vietnam seemed too radical, too friendly to communism, or too inimical to American economic interests, he tried to undermine them, often with secret operations.

Although Eisenhower presided over eight years of peace and prosperity, his foreign policy inspired anti-Americanism, established dangerous precedents for the expansion of executive power, and forged commitments that future generations would deem unwise. As Eisenhower's successors took on the struggle against communism and grappled with the domestic challenges of race, poverty, and urban decay that he had avoided, the tranquillity and consensus of the 1950s would give way to the turbulence and conflict of the 1960s.

Suggestions for Further Reading

Taylor Branch, *Parting the Waters: America in the King Years, 1954–1963*. A dramatic narrative of Martin Luther King Jr.'s life within the context of civil rights activism.

Lizbeth Cohen, *A Consumers' Republic: The Politics of Mass Consumption in Postwar America* (2003). An exploration of how consumption and consumer movements shaped American politics, economy, and culture.

David Halberstam, *The Fifties* (1953). A history of American life that ranges across topics from politics and foreign policy to popular culture.

Joanne Meyerowitz, ed., *Not June Cleaver: Women and Gender in Postwar America* (1994). Essays on the diverse experiences and representations of women in work, public affairs, and popular culture.

James Miller, *Flowers in the Dustbin: The Rise of Rock and Roll, 1947–1977* (1999). An engaging and critical history of the music that defined a generation.

Bruce J. Shulman, *From Cotton Belt to Sunbelt: Federal Policy, Economic Development, and the Transformation of the South, 1938–1980* (1994). The classic account of the development of the Sun Belt.

▶ **FOR MORE BOOKS ABOUT TOPICS IN THIS CHAPTER,** see the Online Study Guide at bedfordstmartins.com/roarkcompact.

▶ **FOR ADDITIONAL FIRSTHAND ACCOUNTS OF THIS PERIOD,** see Chapter 27 in Michael Johnson, ed., *Reading the American Past*, Third Edition.

▶ **FOR WEB SITES AND DOCUMENTS RELATED TO TOPICS AND PLACES IN THIS CHAPTER,** see "HistoryLinks," "DocLinks," and "PlaceLinks" at bedfordstmartins.com/roarkcompact.

REVIEWING THE CHAPTER

Follow these steps to review and strengthen your understanding of the chapter.

STEP 1: *Study the* **Key Terms** *and* **Timeline** *to identify the significance of each item listed.*

STEP 2: *Answer the* **Review Questions**, *drawing on key terms and dates to support your answers.*

STEP 3: *Drawing on the Key Terms, Timeline, and Review Questions, answer the broader* **Making Connections** *questions.*

KEY TERMS

Who

Richard M. Nixon (p. 703)
Nikita Khrushchev (pp. 703, 710)
Dwight D. Eisenhower (pp. 704, 707)
John Foster Dulles (p. 707)
Ho Chi Minh (p. 708)
Ngo Dinh Diem (p. 708)
Fidel Castro (p. 709)
Mohammed Mossadegh (p. 709)
Gamal Abdel Nasser (p. 709)
William J. Levitt (p. 713)
Betty Friedan (p. 719)
Billy Graham (p. 719)
Alfred Kinsey (p. 721)
Thurgood Marshall (p. 722)
Earl Warren (p. 722)
Emmett Till (p. 722)
Rosa Parks (p. 722)
E. D. Nixon (p. 723)
Jo Ann Robinson (p. 723)
Martin Luther King Jr., (p. 723)

What

"kitchen debate" (p. 703)
Interstate Highway and Defense System Act of 1956 (p. 705)
Indian Claims Commission (p. 706)
"New Look" (p. 707)
brinksmanship (p. 708)
mutually assured destruction (MAD) (p. 708)
domino theory (p. 708)
Geneva accords (p. 708)
Southeast Asia Treaty Organization (SEATO) (p. 708)
Suez crisis (p. 709)
Eisenhower Doctrine (p. 710)
Sputnik (p. 710)
National Aeronautics and Space Administration (NASA) (p. 710)
National Defense Education Act (p. 710)
military-industrial complex (p. 710)
Levittown (p. 713)

Operation Wetback (p. 716)
Hernandez v. Texas (p. 716)
baby boom (p. 719)
Beat generation (p. 721)
National Association for the Advancement of Colored People (NAACP) (p. 722)
Brown v. Board of Education (p. 722)
Central High School, Little Rock, Arkansas (p. 722)
Civil Rights Acts of 1957 and 1960 (p. 722)
Montgomery, Alabama, Women's Political Council (WPC) (p. 723)
Montgomery bus boycott (p. 723)
Southern Christian Leadership Conference (SCLC) (p. 724)

TIMELINE

1952 • Republican Dwight D. Eisenhower elected president.
• *I Love Lucy* becomes number-one television show.

1953 • Termination of special status of American Indians and relocation of thousands off reservations.
• CIA engineers' coup against government of Iran.

1954 • CIA stages coup against government of Guatemala.
• France signs Geneva accords, withdrawing from Vietnam.
• United States organizes Southeast Asia Treaty Organization (SEATO) and begins aid to South Vietnam.
• Government launches Operation Wetback.
• Building of first commercial nuclear power plant begins.
• *Hernandez v. Texas.*
• *Brown v. Board of Education.*
• Senate condemns Senator Joseph McCarthy.

1955 • Eisenhower and Khrushchev meet in Geneva.

1955–1956 • Montgomery, Alabama, bus boycott.

REVIEW QUESTIONS

1. How did Eisenhower's domestic policies reflect his moderate political vision? (pp. 704–07)

2. Where and how did Eisenhower practice containment? (pp. 707–11)

3. How did technology contribute to changes in the economy, suburbanization, and the growth of the Sun Belt? (pp. 711–18)

4. Why did American consumption expand so dramatically in the 1950s, and what aspects of society and culture did it influence? (pp. 718–21)

5. What were the goals and strategies of civil rights activists in the 1950s? (pp. 721–24)

MAKING CONNECTIONS

1. Both President Truman and President Eisenhower perceived a grave threat in the Soviet Union and the spread of communism around the world. How did these two presidents approach foreign policy in the Cold War? In your answer, consider their similarities and differences.

2. The 1950s brought significant changes to the everyday lives of many Americans. Discuss the economic and demographic changes that contributed to the growth of suburbs and the Sun Belt. How did these trends shape the culture of abundance? In your answer, consider both Americans who participated in these trends and those who did not.

3. During the 1950s, actions by the federal government and the courts had a significant impact on African Americans, Native Americans, and Mexican Americans. Discuss how new policies and court actions came about and how law affected these groups for better and for worse.

4. Eisenhower was the first Republican president since the New Deal had transformed the federal government. How did his "modern Republicanism" address Roosevelt's legacy? How did the shape and character of government change, or not change, during Eisenhower's administration?

▶ FOR PRACTICE QUIZZES, A CUSTOMIZED STUDY PLAN, AND OTHER STUDY TOOLS, see the Online Study Guide at bedfordstmartins.com/roarkcompact.

1956
- Interstate Highway and Defense System Act.
- Eisenhower reelected by landslide to second term.
- *Howl* published.

1957
- Southern Christian Leadership Conference (SCLC) founded.
- Soviets launch *Sputnik*.
- Labor union membership peaks at 27.1 percent of labor force.
- *On the Road* published.

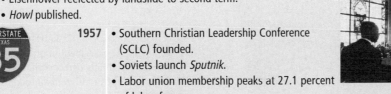

1958
- National Aeronautics and Space Administration (NASA) established.

1959
- "Kitchen debate" between Nixon and Khrushchev.

1960
- Soviets shoot down U.S. U-2 spy plane.
- 35 percent of women work outside the home.
- One-quarter of Americans live in suburbs.

"COUNTRY JOE" McDONALD'S GUITAR
Music was an omnipresent element of protest movements in the 1960s. Civil rights demonstrators sang "We Shall Overcome," antiwar rallies featured folk singers, and hippies turned on to acid rock. The guitar was the central musical instrument for each kind of music: traditional African American, folk, and rock. This wooden acoustic guitar, adorned with a peace symbol, belonged to "Country Joe" McDonald, who started his band, Country Joe and the Fish, at a draft protest in Oakland, California, in 1965. The band was one of many that originated in the San Francisco Bay area, but its popularity soon spread across the country.
The Oakland Museum of California.

28

Reform, Rebellion, and Reaction

1960–1974

O N AUGUST 31, 1962, Fannie Lou Hamer boarded a bus carrying eighteen African Americans from Ruleville, Mississippi, to the county seat in Indianola, where they intended to register to vote. Blacks comprised more than 60 percent of Sunflower County's population but only 1.2 percent of registered voters. Before young civil rights activists arrived in Ruleville to start a voter registration drive, Hamer recalled, "I didn't know that a Negro could register and vote." Her forty-five years of poverty, exploitation, and political disfranchisement typified the lives of most blacks in the rural South. The daughter of sharecroppers, Hamer began work in the cotton fields at age six, attending school in a one-room shack from December to March and only until she was twelve. She later married Perry Hamer and moved onto the plantation where he sharecropped and she worked.

At Indianola, Hamer and her companions defied a hostile, white, gun-carrying crowd and entered the county courthouse. Using a common practice to deny blacks the vote, the registrar tested Hamer on an obscure section of the state constitution, which had not been part of her schooling. She failed the test but resolved to try again. When the plantation owner ordered Hamer to withdraw her registration application or get off his land, she left the plantation. Ten days later, bullets flew into the home of friends who had taken her in. Refusing to be intimidated, she registered to vote on her third attempt, attended a civil rights leadership training conference, and began to mobilize others to vote. In 1963, she and other activists were arrested in Winona, Mississippi, and brutally beaten. Hamer went from jail to the hospital, where her sister could not recognize her battered face.

Fannie Lou Hamer's courage and determination made her a prominent figure in the civil rights movement. Such activists shook the nation's conscience, provided a protest model for other groups, and transformed national policy. Although the federal government often tried to curb civil rights activists, the two Democratic presidents of the 1960s favored using government to ameliorate social and economic problems. After John F. Kennedy was assassinated in November 1963, Lyndon B. Johnson launched the **Great Society**—a multitude of efforts to promote racial justice, education, medical care, urban development, environmental and economic health, and more. Those who struggled for racial justice lost property and sometimes their lives, but by the end of the decade, American law had caught up with the American ideal of equality.

Yet legal change did not go far enough. Strong civil rights legislation and pathbreaking Supreme Court decisions did little to mitigate the deplorable

Mississippi Freedom Democratic Party Rally
Fannie Lou Hamer (left foreground) and other activists sing at a rally outside the Democratic National Convention hall in 1964, supporting the Mississippi Freedom Democratic Party (MFDP) in its challenge to the all-white delegation sent by the regular Mississippi Democratic Party. Next to Hamer is Eleanor Holmes Norton, a civil rights lawyer, and Ella Baker (far right), who helped organize the Southern Christian Leadership Conference and later managed MFDP headquarters in Washington, D.C.
Matt Herron/Take Stock.

economic conditions of African Americans, on which Hamer and others increasingly focused after 1965. Nor were liberal politicians consistently reliable supporters, as Hamer found out in 1964 when President Johnson and his allies rebuffed black Mississippi Democrats' efforts to be represented at the Democratic National Convention. "We followed all the laws that the white people themselves made," she said, only to find that "the white man is not going to give up his power to us....We have to take for ourselves." By 1966, a minority of African American activists were demanding black power; the movement soon splintered, and white support sharply declined. A growing number of **conservatives** protested that the Great Society went too far and condemned the challenge to American values and institutions mounted by blacks, students, and others.

Although disillusioned and often frustrated, Fannie Lou Hamer remained an activist until her death in 1977, mingling with new social movements stimulated by the black freedom struggle. In 1969, she supported Mississippi Valley State College students' demands for black studies courses and a voice in campus decisions. In 1972, she attended the founding conference of the National Women's Political Caucus, established to achieve greater representation for women in government. The caucus was part of a much broader **feminist** movement that promoted a revolution in women's legal status as well as important changes in the everyday relationships between women and men.

Feminists and other groups, including ethnic minorities, environmentalists, and gays and lesbians, carried the tide of reform into the 1970s. They pushed the Republican administration of

Richard M. Nixon to sustain the **liberalism** of the 1960s with its emphasis on a strong government role in regulating the economy and guaranteeing the welfare and rights of all individuals. Despite its conservative rhetoric, the Nixon administration implemented school desegregation and **affirmative action** and adopted pathbreaking measures in environmental regulation, equality for women, and justice for Native Americans. The years between 1960 and 1974 contained the greatest efforts to reconcile America's promise with reality since the **New Deal**.

Liberalism at High Tide

At the Democratic National Convention in 1960, John F. Kennedy announced "a New Frontier" that would confront "unsolved problems of peace and war, unconquered pockets of ignorance and prejudice, unanswered questions of poverty and surplus." Four years later, Lyndon B. Johnson invoked the ideal of a "Great Society, [which] rests on abundance and liberty for all [and] demands an end to poverty and racial injustice." Acting under the liberal faith that government should use its power to solve social and economic problems, end injustice, and promote the welfare of all citizens, the Democratic administrations of the 1960s won legislation on civil rights, poverty, education, medical care, housing, consumer protection, and environmental protection.

The Unrealized Promise of Kennedy's New Frontier

John F. Kennedy grew up in privilege, the child of an Irish Catholic businessman who served in Franklin D. Roosevelt's administration and nourished political ambitions for his sons. Helped by a distinguished World War II navy record, Kennedy won election to the House of Representatives in 1946 and the Senate in 1952. His record in Congress was unremarkable, but with a powerful political machine, his family's fortune, and a dynamic appeal, Kennedy won the Democratic presidential nomination in 1960. He stunned many Democrats by choosing as his running mate Lyndon B. Johnson of Texas, who had also sought the presidency and was detested by liberals who viewed him as a typical southern conservative.

Kennedy defeated his Republican opponent, Vice President Richard M. Nixon, in an excruciatingly close election. African American voters contributed to his victory, helping to offset the 52 percent of the white vote cast for Nixon and contributing to his 120,000-vote margin overall. Lyndon Johnson helped the ticket carry most of the South, and a rise in unemployment in 1960 also favored the Democrats. Finally, Kennedy benefited from the nation's first televised presidential debates, appearing cool, confident, and handsome, beside a nervous, sweaty, and pale Nixon.

The Kennedy administration projected energy, idealism, and glamour, though in fact Kennedy was a cautious, pragmatic politician. The first president to hold live televised press conferences, Kennedy charmed the press corps and the

The Kennedy Appeal

The youth and glamour of the Kennedy administration are apparent in this photo of the president and his wife attired for his inauguration gala. The gown that Jacqueline Kennedy had designed by Oleg Cassini for the occasion bore a cockade at the waist, indicating her French ancestry and keen interest in history and culture, which were reflected in White House social events that elevated Washington's cultural scene by featuring artists, writers, scholars, and musicians throughout the Kennedy presidency. Well aware of his wife's appeal to the public, the president asked the driver of their limousine to "turn on the lights so they can see Jackie."
© Bettmann/Corbis.

people with his grace, vigor, and self-mocking wit. He kept hidden from the public serious health problems as well as affairs with several women. Journalists turned a blind eye, instead projecting warm images of an energetic, youthful president with his chic and cultured wife, Jacqueline.

At his inauguration, the forty-three-year-old Kennedy declared that a "new generation" was assuming leadership, and he called on Americans to cast off complacency and self-indulgence and serve the common good. "Ask not what your country can do for you," he implored, "ask what you can do for your country." Though Kennedy's idealism inspired many, especially the young, he failed to redeem campaign promises to expand the **welfare state**. Two central items on the Democratic agenda since the Truman administration, federal aid for education and health care for the elderly, got nowhere. Moreover, he did not assume leadership on behalf of racial justice until late in his term, when civil rights activists gave him no choice. But he did sign legislation making it illegal to pay women less than men for the same work.

Moved by the desperate conditions he observed when he campaigned in Appalachia in 1960, Kennedy helped push poverty onto the national agenda. In 1962, he read Michael Harrington's *The Other America*, which described the poverty of more than one in every five Americans "maimed in body and spirit, existing at levels beneath those necessary for human decency." By 1962, Kennedy had won support for a $2 billion urban renewal program, area redevelopment legislation that offered incentives to businesses to locate in depressed areas, and a training program for the unemployed. In the summer of 1963, Kennedy asked aides to plan a full-scale attack on poverty, and he also issued a dramatic call for a comprehensive civil rights bill, marking a turning point in his domestic agenda.

Kennedy had promised to make economic growth a key objective. "A rising tide lifts all boats" expressed Kennedy's belief that economic growth could eradicate poverty and solve most social problems as well as make the nation more competitive with the Soviet Union. Economic advisers argued that reducing taxes would infuse money into the economy and thus increase demand, boost production, and decrease unemployment. To that end, Kennedy asked Congress to pass an enormous tax cut in 1963. This use of fiscal policy to stimulate the economy even when there was no recession was called the "new economics."

Kennedy did not live to see approval of his bill. Passed in February 1964, the law contributed to the greatest economic boom since World War II. Unemployment dropped to 4.1 percent, and the gross national product shot up by 7 to 9 percent annually between 1964 and 1966. Some liberal critics of the tax cut, however, pointed out that it favored the well-off and that economic growth alone would not eliminate poverty. They argued instead for increased spending on social programs.

Kennedy's economic efforts were in their infancy when he fell victim to an assassin's bullet on November 22, 1963. That event touched Americans as had no other since the end of World War II. Within minutes of the shooting— which occurred as the Kennedy motorcade passed through Dallas, Texas, on November 22, 1963—radio and television broadcast the unfolding horror to the nation. Millions watched the return of *Air Force One* to Washington bearing the president's coffin, his widow in her bloodstained suit, and the new president, Lyndon Baines Johnson.

Stunned Americans struggled with what had happened and why. Soon after the assassination, police arrested Lee Harvey Oswald and concluded that he had fired the shots from a nearby building. Two days later, as a television audience watched Oswald being transferred from one jail to another, a local nightclub operator, Jack Ruby, killed him. Suspicions arose that Ruby murdered Oswald to cover up a conspiracy by ultraconservative Texans who hated Kennedy, or by Communists who supported Castro's Cuba. To get at the truth, President Johnson appointed a commission headed by Chief Justice Earl Warren, which concluded in September 1964 that both Oswald and Ruby had acted alone. Although several experts pointed to errors and omissions in the report, and some contested the lone-killer explanation, most scholars agreed that no conspiracy had existed.

Debate continued over how to assess Kennedy's domestic record. It had been unremarkable in his first two years, but his proposals on taxes, civil rights, and poverty in 1963 suggested an important shift. Whether Kennedy could have persuaded Congress to enact his initiatives remained in question. In the words of journalist James Reston, "What was killed was not only the president but the promise....He never reached his meridian: We saw him only as a rising sun."

Johnson Fulfills the Kennedy Promise

Lyndon Johnson assumed the presidency with a wealth of political experience. A self-made man from the Texas hill country, he had won election to the House of Representatives in 1937 and to the Senate in 1948. By 1955, he had secured the top post of Senate majority leader, which he used brilliantly to forge a Democratic consensus on the Civil Rights Acts of 1957 and 1960 and other programs.

Johnson's coarse wit, extreme vanity, and Texas accent repulsed those who preferred the sophisticated Kennedy style. Lacking his predecessor's eloquence, Johnson excelled behind the scenes, where he could entice or threaten legislators to support his objectives. The famous "Johnson treatment" became legendary. In his ability to achieve consensus around his goals, he had few peers in American history.

"I had to take the dead man's program and turn it into a martyr's cause," Johnson declared, entreating Congress to act so that "John Fitzgerald Kennedy did not live or die in vain." He won over fiscal conservatives and signed Kennedy's tax cut bill in February 1964. Still more revolutionary was passage of the Civil Rights Act of July 1964, which Kennedy had set in motion. The strongest such measure since Reconstruction, its passage required every ounce of Johnson's political skills to pry sufficient votes from Republicans to balance the "nays" of southern Democrats.

Fast on the heels of the Civil Rights Act came a response to Johnson's call for "an unconditional war on poverty." The Economic Opportunity Act of 1964 authorized ten programs under a newly created Office of Economic Opportunity, allocating $800 million for the first year (about 1 percent of the federal budget). Many provisions targeted youth, including Head Start for preschoolers, work-study grants for college students, and a Job Corps for unemployed young people. There were also loans to businesses willing to hire the long-term unemployed; aid to small farmers; and the Volunteers in Service to America (VISTA) program, which paid modest wages to volunteers working with the disadvantaged. A legal services program provided lawyers for the poor, leading to lawsuits that enforced their rights to welfare programs.

The most novel and controversial part of the law, the Community Action Program (CAP), required "maximum feasible participation" of the poor themselves in antipoverty programs. Poor people began to organize local community action programs to take control of their neighborhoods and make welfare agencies, school boards, police departments, and housing authorities more accountable to the people they served. When mayors complained that activists were challenging local governments and "fostering class struggle," Johnson backed off from pushing genuine representation for the poor. Nonetheless, CAP gave people usually excluded from government an opportunity to act on their own behalf and to develop leadership skills.

Policymaking for a Great Society

Having steered the nation through the assassination trauma and established his capacity for national leadership, Johnson projected stability and security in the midst of a booming economy. Few voters wanted to risk the dramatic change promised by his Republican opponent in the 1964 election, Arizona senator Barry M. Goldwater, who attacked the welfare state and suggested using nuclear weapons if necessary to crush **communism** in Vietnam. Although Goldwater captured five southern states, Johnson achieved a record-breaking landslide of 61 percent of the popular vote, and Democrats

The "Johnson Treatment"

Abe Fortas, a distinguished lawyer who had argued a major criminal rights case, *Gideon v. Wainwright* (1963), before the Supreme Court, was a close friend and adviser to President Lyndon Johnson. This photograph of the president and Fortas taken in July 1965 illustrates how Johnson used his body as well as his voice to bend people to his will.

Yoichi R. Okamoto/LBJ Library Collection.

won resounding majorities in the House (295–140) and Senate (68–32). Yet, as we shall see in chapter 30, Goldwater's campaign aroused considerable grassroots support, contributing to the ultimate ascendancy of conservatism in national politics.

"I want to see a whole bunch of coonskins on the wall," Johnson told his aides, using a hunting analogy to stress his ambitious legislative goals that would usher in what he called the "Great Society." In the sheer amount and breadth of new laws, Johnson succeeded mightily, persuading Congress to act on discrimination, poverty, education, medical care, housing, consumer and environmental protections, and more. Reporters called the legislation of the Eighty-ninth Congress (1965–1966) "a political miracle."

The Economic Opportunity Act of 1964 was the opening shot in the War on Poverty. Congress doubled the program's funding in 1965 and passed new initiatives to promote economic development. Targeting depressed regions that the general economic boom had bypassed, these measures—like the tax cut of 1964—sought to help the poor indirectly by stimulating economic growth and providing jobs through road building and other public works projects. In addition, the Model Cities Act authorized more than $1 billion to improve conditions in the nation's slums.

A second approach endeavored to equip the poor with the skills necessary to find jobs. The Elementary and Secondary Education Act of 1965 combatted poverty by authorizing federal funds to aid school districts. It allocated dollars based on the number of poor children whom districts educated, and it provided equipment and supplies to private and parochial schools to be used for poor children. That same year, Congress passed the Higher Education Act, vastly expanding federal assistance to colleges and universities for buildings,

A Tribute to Johnson for Medicare
George Niedermeyer, who lived in Hollywood, Florida, and received a Social Security pension, painted pieces of wood and glued them together to create this thank-you to President Johnson for establishing Medicare. He entrusted his congressional representative, Claude Pepper, known for his support for the interests of the elderly, to deliver the four-foot-tall tribute to Johnson in 1967.
LBJ Library, photo by Henry Groskinsky.

programs, scholarships, and low-interest student loans.

Other antipoverty efforts provided direct aid. A new food stamp program largely replaced surplus food distribution, giving poor people greater choice in obtaining food. Rent supplements also allowed more options, enabling some poor families to avoid public housing projects. The federal government's responsibility for health care grew even more. Trimming Truman's proposed plan for government-sponsored universal care, Johnson focused on the elderly, who constituted a large portion of the nation's poor. Congress responded with the Medicare program, providing the elderly with universal compulsory medical insurance financed largely through Social Security taxes. A separate program, Medicaid, authorized federal grants to supplement state-paid medical care for poor people.

The assumption of national responsibility for social justice also underlay key civil rights legislation. Pressured by the black freedom struggle, Johnson got Congress to pass the Voting Rights Act of 1965, which banned literacy tests like the one that stymied Fannie Lou Hamer, and authorized federal intervention to ensure access to the voting booth. Another form of discrimination fell with the Immigration and Nationality Act of 1965, which abolished fifty-year-old quotas based on national origins that were biased against immigrants from areas outside northern and western Europe. It maintained caps on the number of immigrants and for the first time limited those from the Western Hemisphere; yet the law made possible a tremendous—and unanticipated—surge of immigration near the end of the century (see chapter 31).

Great Society benefits reached well beyond victims of discrimination and the poor. Medicare covered the elderly, regardless of income. Ralph Nader and others led a growing consumer movement that won legislation to make automobiles safer and to raise standards for the food, drug, and cosmetics industries. In 1965, Johnson became the first president to send Congress a special message on the environment, obtaining measures to control water and air pollution and to preserve the natural beauty of the American landscape. The National Arts and Humanities Act of 1965 funded artists, musicians, writers, and scholars and brought their work to public audiences.

The flood of reform legislation dwindled after 1966, when the Democrats' majorities in Congress were reduced and a backlash against government programs arose. Some expressed their opposition with buttons reading "I fight poverty—I work." The Vietnam War dealt the largest blow to Johnson's ambitions, diverting his attention from domestic affairs, spawning an antiwar movement that crippled his leadership, and devouring tax dollars that might have been used for reform.

Against these odds, in 1968 Johnson pried out of Congress one more civil rights law, which banned discrimination in housing and jury service. He also signed the National Housing Act of 1968, which authorized an enormous increase in construction of low-income housing— 1.7 million units over three years—and by leaving construction and ownership in private hands, a new way of providing it. Government-guaranteed low-interest loans spurred developers to build and enabled poor people to purchase those houses.

Assessing the Great Society

Measured by statistics, the reduction in poverty in the 1960s was considerable. The number of impoverished Americans fell from over 20 percent of the population in 1959 to around 13 percent in 1968 (Figure 28.1). Those who Johnson had said "lived on the outskirts of hope" gained more control of their circumstances and a sense of their right to a fairer share of America's bounty. Assessing what turned her family of longtime welfare recipients into taxpaying workers, Rosemary Bray concluded, "What fueled our dreams and fired our belief that our lives could change for the better was the promise of the civil rights movement and the war on poverty."

Certain groups fared much better than others, however. Large numbers of the aged and male-headed families rose out of poverty, while the plight of female-headed families actually worsened. Whites escaped poverty at a faster rate than African Americans, who constituted one-third of the poor population in the 1970s.

Conservative critics charged that Great Society programs discouraged initiative by giving the poor "handouts." Liberal critics claimed that the emphasis on training and education unjustly placed the responsibility for poverty on the poor themselves rather than on an economic system that could not provide enough adequately paying jobs. Most government training

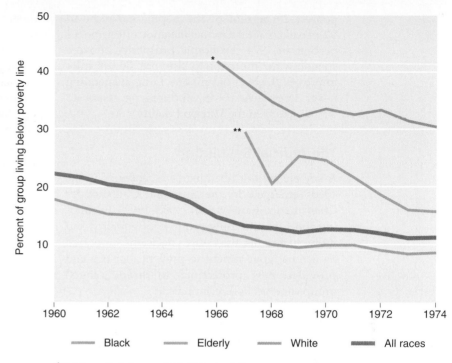

FIGURE 28.1 Poverty in the United States, 1960–1974
The short-term effects of economic growth and the Great Society's attack on poverty are seen here. Which groups experienced the sharpest decline in poverty, and what might account for the differences?

*Statistics on blacks for years 1960–1965 not available.
**Statistics on the elderly for years 1960–1966 not available.

programs prepared graduates for low-level jobs and could not guarantee employment.

Who reaped the greatest benefits from Great Society programs? Most of the funds for economically depressed areas built highways and thus helped the construction industry. Real estate developers, investors, and moderate-income families benefited most from the National Housing Act of 1968. When commercial development and high-income housing displaced the poor in slum clearance programs, blacks called urban renewal "Negro removal." Physicians' fees and hospital costs soared after enactment of Medicare and Medicaid.

Some critics argued that ending poverty required a redistribution of income—raising taxes and using those funds to create jobs, overhaul welfare systems, and rebuild slums. Great Society programs did invest more heavily in the public sector, but Johnson's efforts relied on economic growth for funding rather than new taxes on the rich or middle class. There was no significant redistribution of income, despite large increases in subsidies for food stamps, housing, medical care, and the New Deal program Aid to Families with Dependent Children (AFDC). The poorest 20 percent of the population received 5.1 percent of total national income in 1964 and 5.4 percent in 1974. Economic prosperity allowed spending for the poor to rise and significantly improved the lives of millions, but that spending never approached the amounts necessary to claim victory in the War on Poverty.

The Judicial Revolution

A key element of liberalism's ascendency in the 1960s emerged in the Supreme Court under Chief Justice Earl Warren (1953–1969). Expanding the Constitution's promise of equality and individual rights, the Court's decisions supported an activist government to prevent injustice and provided new protections to disadvantaged groups and accused criminals.

Chief Justice Warren considered *Baker v. Carr* (1963) his most important decision. The case grew out of a complaint that Tennessee electoral districts were inequitably drawn, giving sparsely populated rural districts far more representatives than densely populated urban areas. Using the Fourteenth Amendment guarantee of "equal protection of the laws," the Court in *Baker* established the principle of "one person, one vote" both for state legislatures and for the House of Representatives. Most states had to redraw electoral districts, thus making state legislatures more responsive to metropolitan interests.

The egalitarian thrust of the Warren Court also touched the criminal justice system as the justices used the Fourteenth Amendment to void a series of convictions on the grounds that the accused had been deprived of "life, liberty, or property, without due process of law." Furthermore, in decisions that transformed law enforcement practices and the treatment of individuals accused of crime, the Court declared that states as well as the federal government were subject to the Bill of Rights. For example, in *Gideon v. Wainwright* (1963), the Court ruled that when accused criminals could not afford to hire lawyers, states must provide them without charge. In 1966, in *Miranda v. Arizona*, the Court required officers to inform suspects of their rights upon arrest; and it overturned convictions based on evidence obtained by unlawful arrest, by electronic surveillance, or without a search warrant.

As Supreme Court decisions overturned judicial precedents and often moved ahead of public opinion, critics accused the justices of obstructing law enforcement and letting criminals go free. The mayor of Los Angeles, for example, equated *Miranda* with "handcuffing the police." Liberals, however, argued that these rulings promoted equal treatment in the criminal justice system: The wealthy always had access to legal counsel, and practiced criminals were well aware of their right to remain silent. The beneficiaries of the decisions were the poor and the ignorant, as well as the general population, whose right to privacy was strengthened by the stricter guidelines for admissible evidence.

The Court's decisions on prayer and Bible reading in public schools provoked even greater outrage. *Abington School District v. Schempp* (1963) ruled that a Pennsylvania law requiring Bible reading and prayer in the schools violated the First Amendment principle of separation of church and state. Later decisions ruled out official prayer in public schools even if students were not required to participate. These decisions left students free to pray on their own, but an infuriated Alabama legislator cried, "They put Negroes in the schools and now they've driven God out." The Court's supporters, however, declared that the religion cases protected the rights of non-Christians and atheists.

Two or three justices who believed that the Court was overstepping its authority often issued sharp dissents. Outside the Court, opponents worked to pass laws or constitutional amendments that would upset despised decisions, and billboards demanded, "Impeach Earl Warren." Nonetheless, the Court's major decisions withstood the test of time.

> **REVIEW**   How did the Kennedy and Johnson administrations exemplify a liberal vision of federal government?

The Second Reconstruction

As much as Supreme Court decisions, the black freedom struggle distinguished the liberalism of the 1960s from that of the New Deal. Before the Great Society reforms and, in fact, contributing to them, African Americans had mobilized a movement that struck down legal separation and discrimination in the South. The first Reconstruction reflected the power of northern Republicans in the aftermath of the Civil War, but the second Reconstruction depended heavily on the courage and determination of black people themselves. Sheyann Webb, one of the thousands of marchers in the 1965 Selma, Alabama, campaign for voting rights, recalled, "We were just people, ordinary people, and we did it."

The early black freedom struggle focused on legal rights in the South and won widespread acceptance. But when African Americans began to attack racial injustice in the rest of the country as well as the deplorable economic conditions that equal rights left untouched, a strong backlash developed as the movement itself lost cohesion.

The Flowering of the Black Freedom Struggle

The Montgomery bus boycott of 1955–1956 gave racial issues national visibility, produced a leader in Martin Luther King Jr., and demon-strated the effectiveness of mass organization. In the 1960s, protest expanded dramatically, mobilizing blacks into direct confrontation with the people and institutions that segregated and discriminated against them: retail establishments, public parks and libraries, buses and depots, voting registrars, and police forces.

Massive direct action began in February 1960, when four African American students in Greensboro, North Carolina, requested service at the whites-only Woolworth's lunch counter. Within days, hundreds of young people joined them, and others launched sit-ins in thirty-one southern cities. In April, southern student activists founded the Student Nonviolent Coordinating Committee (SNCC, pronounced "snick"). SNCC initially embraced civil disobedience and the nonviolence principles of Martin Luther King Jr.

Lunch Counter Sit-in

John Salter Jr., a professor at Tougaloo College, and students Joan Trumpauer and Anne Moody take part in a 1963 sit-in at the Woolworth's lunch counter in Jackson, Mississippi. Shortly before this photograph was taken, whites had thrown two students to the floor, and police had arrested one student. Salter was spattered with mustard and ketchup. Moody would publish a popular book in 1968 about her experiences in the black freedom struggle, *Coming of Age in Mississippi*.

State Historical Society of Wisconsin.

FOR MORE HELP ANALYZING THIS IMAGE, see the visual activity for this chapter in the Online Study Guide at bedfordstmartins.com/roarkcompact.

Students would directly confront their oppressors and stand up for their rights, but they would not respond if attacked. In the words of SNCC leader James Lawson, "nonviolence nurtures the atmosphere in which reconciliation and justice become actual possibilities."

The activists' optimism and commitment to nonviolence soon underwent severe testing. Although some cities quietly met student demands, more typically the students encountered violence. Hostile whites poured food over demonstrators, burned them with cigarettes, called them "niggers," and pelted them with rocks. Local police attacked protesters with dogs, clubs, fire hoses, and tear gas; they arrested more than 3,600 demonstrators in the year following the Greensboro sit-in.

In May 1961, the Congress of Racial Equality (CORE) organized Freedom Rides to integrate interstate transportation in the South. When a group of six whites and seven blacks got to Alabama, white hoodlums bombed their bus and beat the riders with baseball bats. After a huge mob attacked the activists in Montgomery, Attorney General Robert Kennedy dispatched federal marshals to restore order. But when Freedom Riders reached Jackson, Mississippi, they were promptly arrested, and several hundred spent part of the summer in Mississippi jails.

Encouraged by Kennedy administration officials who preferred voter registration to civil disobedience (it was more likely to benefit the Democratic Party), SNCC and other groups began a Voter Education Project in the summer of 1961. They too met violence. Whites bombed black churches, threw tenant farmers out of their homes, and beat and jailed activists like Fannie Lou Hamer. In June 1963, a white man gunned down Mississippi NAACP leader Medgar Evers in front of his house in Jackson; the murderer eluded conviction until the 1990s. Similar violence met King's 1963 campaign in Birmingham, Alabama, to integrate public facilities and open jobs to blacks. The police attacked demonstrators with dogs, cattle prods, and water hoses. Bombs exploded at King's motel and his brother's house. Four months later a bomb killed four black girls at a Birmingham Sunday school.

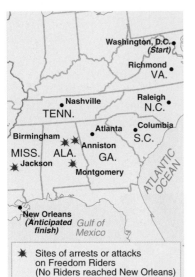

Civil Rights Freedom Rides, May 1961

Washington, D.C. (Start)
Richmond
VA.
Nashville
Raleigh
TENN.
N.C.
Birmingham
Atlanta
Columbia
MISS.
ALA.
Anniston
S.C.
Jackson
GA.
Montgomery
ATLANTIC OCEAN
New Orleans (Anticipated finish) Gulf of Mexico

✳ Sites of arrests or attacks on Freedom Riders (No Riders reached New Orleans)

The largest demonstration drew 250,000 blacks and whites to the nation's capital in August 1963, where King put his indelible stamp on the day. Speaking from the Lincoln Memorial and invoking the Bible, Negro spirituals, and patriotic anthems, King drew on all the passion and skills that made him the greatest orator of his day. "I have a dream," he repeated again and again, that "the sons of former slaves and the sons of former slave owners will be able to sit down together at the table of brotherhood." With the crowd roaring in support, he imagined the day "when all of God's children...will be able to join hands and sing...'Free at last, free at last; thank God Almighty, we are free at last.'"

Yet the euphoria of the March on Washington quickly faded as activists returned to continued violence in the South. In 1964, the Mississippi Freedom Summer Project mobilized more than a thousand northern black and white college students to conduct a voter registration drive. Resistance was fierce. By the end of the summer, only twelve hundred new voters had been allowed to register. Whites had killed several activists, beaten eighty, arrested more than a thousand, and burned thirty-five black churches. Hidden resistance came from the federal government itself, as the FBI spied on King and other leaders and expanded its activities to "expose, disrupt, misdirect, discredit, or otherwise neutralize" black protest.

Still the movement persisted. In March 1965, Alabama troopers used such fierce force to turn back a march from Selma to the state capitol in Montgomery that the incident earned the name "Bloody Sunday" and compelled President Johnson to call up the Alabama National Guard to protect the marchers. Before the Selma campaign was over, whites had killed three demonstrators. Battered and hospitalized on Bloody Sunday, John Lewis, chairman of SNCC (and later a congressman), managed to make the final march to the capitol, which he counted as one of his most meaningful experiences: "In October of that year the Voting Rights bill was passed and we all felt we'd had a part in it."

The Response in Washington

Civil rights leaders would have to wear sneakers, Lyndon Johnson said, if they were going to keep up with him. But both Kennedy and

The March on Washington
More than a quarter of a million Americans, including 50,000 whites, gathered on the Mall in the nation's capital on August 28, 1963, to pressure the government to support African Americans' civil rights. Here, Martin Luther King Jr. is about to mesmerize the crowd with his "I have a dream" speech. Afterward, Malcom X said to march organizer Bayard Rustin, "You know this dream of King's is going to be a nightmare before it's over."
Francis Miller/TimePix/Getty.

Johnson, reluctant to alienate crucial Democratic voters in the South and their representatives in Congress, acted less on their own initiative than in response to the black freedom struggle, moving only when events gave them little choice. Kennedy sent federal marshals to Montgomery to protect the Freedom Riders, dispatched troops to enable air force veteran James H. Meredith to enroll in the all-white University of Mississippi in 1962, and called up the Alabama National Guard during the Birmingham demonstrations. But, aware of the political costs of deploying federal force, he told activists pleading for more federal protection that law enforcement was a local matter.

In June 1963, Kennedy finally made good on his promise to seek strong antidiscrimination legislation. Johnson took up Kennedy's commitment with passion, assisted by a number of factors. Scenes of violence against peaceful demonstrators appalled many television viewers across the nation. The resulting public support, the "Johnson treatment," and the president's appeal

to memories of the martyred Kennedy all produced the most important civil rights law since Reconstruction.

The Civil Rights Act of 1964 guaranteed access for all Americans to public accommodations, public education, employment, and voting, thus sounding the death knell for the South's system of segregation and discrimination. The law also extended constitutional protections to Indians on reservations. Title VII of the measure banned racial and gender discrimination in every aspect of employment, including wages, hiring, and promotion; it represented a giant step toward equal employment opportunity.

Responding to black voter registration drives in the South, Johnson soon demanded a law that would remove "every remaining obstacle to the right and the opportunity to vote." In August 1965, he signed the Voting Rights Act, which empowered the federal government to intervene directly to enable African Americans to register and vote. A major transformation began in southern politics. (Map 28.1.)

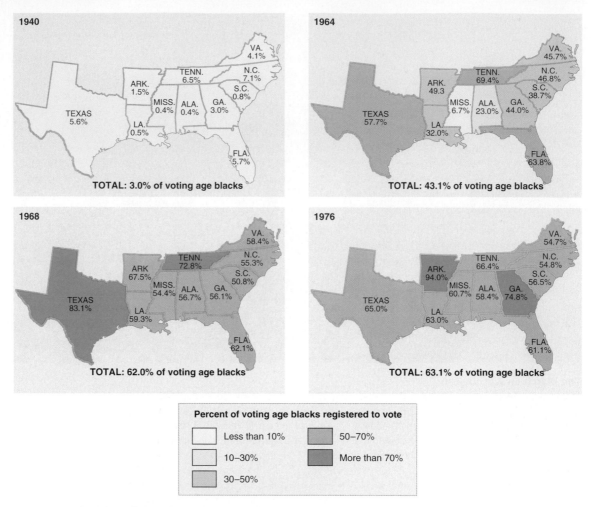

MAP 28.1   The Rise of the African American Vote, 1940–1976
Voting rates of southern blacks increased gradually in the 1940s and 1950s but shot up dramatically in the deep South after the Voting Rights Act of 1965 provided for federal agents to enforce African Americans' right to vote.

READING THE MAP: When did the biggest change in African American voter registration occur in the South? Which states had the highest and which had the lowest voter registration rates in 1968?
CONNECTIONS: What role did African American voters play in the 1960 election? What were the targets of three major voting drives in the 1960s?

FOR MORE HELP ANALYZING THIS MAP, see the map activity for this chapter in the Online Study Guide at bedfordstmartins.com/roarkcompact.

Two more measures completed Johnson's civil rights record. The Civil Rights Act of 1968 banned racial discrimination in housing and jury selection and authorized federal intervention when states failed to protect civil rights workers from violence. In addition, Johnson issued an executive order in 1965 to require employers holding government contracts (affecting about one-third of the labor force) to take affirmative action to ensure equal opportunity. Extended to cover women in 1967, the controversial affirmative action program was called "reverse discrimination" by people who incorrectly thought that it required quotas and the hiring of unqualified candidates. In fact, it required employers to counter the effects of centuries of oppression by acting forcefully to align their labor force with the available pool of qualified candidates. Most corporations came to see affirmative action as a good employment practice.

Black Nationalism and Urban Rebellions

By 1966, civil rights activism had undergone dramatic changes. Black protest had extended to the entire nation, demanding not just legal equality but also economic justice. It also no longer held nonviolence as its basic principle. None of these developments was entirely new. Some African Americans had always armed themselves in self-defense, and even in the 1950s and early 1960s many activists doubted that demonstrators' passive suffering would change the hearts of racists. Still, the black freedom struggle began to appear more threatening to the white majority.

In part the new emphases resulted from a combination of heightened activism and unrealized promise. Integration and legal equality did little to improve the material conditions of blacks, and black rage at oppressive conditions erupted in waves of urban uprisings from 1964 to 1968. The Watts district of Los Angeles in August 1965, Newark and Detroit in July 1967, and the nation's capital in April 1968 saw the most looting and destruction of property, but violence visited hundreds of cities, usually after an incident between white police and local blacks.

In the North, Malcolm X posed a powerful new challenge to the ethos of nonviolence. In 1952 he had gone to work for the Nation of Islam, which drew on the long tradition of **black nationalism** and whose adherents called themselves Black Muslims. Malcolm X attracted a large following, especially in urban ghettos, calling for black pride and autonomy, separation from the "corrupt [white] society," and self-defense against white violence. In 1964, he left the Nation of Islam, began to cultivate a wider constituency, and expressed an openness to working with whites. At a Harlem rally in February 1965, three Black Muslims shot and killed him.

The ideas espoused by Malcolm X resonated with younger activists. At a June 1966 rally in Greenwood, Mississippi, SNCC chairman Stokely Carmichael gave those principles a new name when he shouted, "We want black power." Those words quickly became the rallying cry in SNCC and CORE, and the black power movement riveted national attention in the late 1960s. A young autoworker in Detroit enthused, "I dig what Stokely Carmichael said...whites appear to be friendly by passing a few laws, but my basic situation gets worse and worse."

Carmichael called integration "a subterfuge for the maintenance of white supremacy" and re-

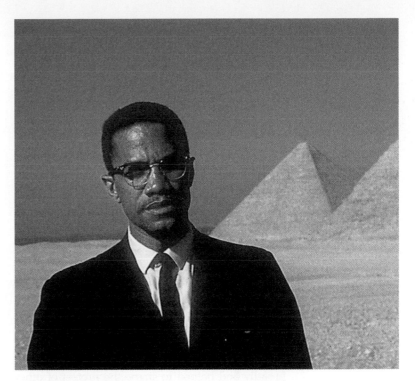

Malcolm X in Egypt
Malcolm X stands in front of the pyramids in Egypt during a trip to Africa and the Middle East in 1964. Partly as a result of meeting Muslims of all colors as well as whites who were committed to ending racism, he no longer equated whites with the devil. "The white man is not inherently evil," he concluded, "but America's racist society influences him to act evilly."
John Launois/Black Star/Stockphoto.com.

jected assimilation because it implied white superiority. African Americans were encouraged to develop independent businesses, control their own schools and communities, and form all-black political organizations. The phrase "Black is beautiful" emphasized pride in African American culture and connections to blacks around the world. According to black power advocates, nonviolence brought only more beatings and killings. After police killed an unarmed black teenager in San Francisco in 1966, Huey Newton and Bobby Seale organized the Black Panther Party for Self-Defense and armed its members for self-defense against police brutality.

The press paid considerable attention to black radicals, and the civil rights movement encountered a severe white backlash. Although the urban riots of the mid-1960s erupted spontaneously, triggered by specific incidents of police mistreatment, horrified whites blamed the riots on black power militants. By 1966, a full 85 percent of the white population thought that African Americans were pressing for too much too quickly, up from 34 percent two years earlier.

Agreeing with black power advocates on the need for "a radical reconstruction of society," Martin Luther King Jr. expanded the scope of the struggle. In 1965 he mounted a drive for better jobs, schools, and housing in Chicago and in 1968 planned a Poor People's March to Washington to seek greater antipoverty efforts. Yet he clung to nonviolence and integration. In 1968, the thirty-nine-year-old leader went to Memphis to support striking municipal garbage workers. There, on April 4, an escaped white convict murdered him.

Although they made the headlines, black power organizations failed to capture the massive support that African Americans gave King and other earlier leaders. Black militants were harassed by the FBI and jailed; some encounters left both black militants and police dead. Black nationalism's emphasis on racial pride and its critique of American institutions, however, resonated broadly and helped to shape the protest of other groups.

> **REVIEW** How did the civil rights movement change in the mid-1960s?

A Multitude of Movements

The civil rights movement's undeniable moral claims helped to make protest respectable, while its impact on public opinion and government policy encouraged other groups with grievances. Native Americans, Latinos, college students, women, and others drew on the black freedom struggle for inspiration and models of activism. These groups engaged in direct-action protests, expressed their own cultural nationalism, and challenged dominant institutions and values.

Native American Protest

Native American activism took on fresh militancy and goals in the 1960s. Contrary to their intent, the termination and relocation programs of the 1940s and 1950s stirred Indian resistance, a sense of Indian identity across tribal lines, and a determination to preserve traditional culture. In 1961, a more militant

generation of Native Americans expressed growing discontent with the government and with the older Indian leadership by forming the National Indian Youth Council (NIYC). The cry "red power" reflected the influence of black radicalism on Native Americans who rejected assimilation and sought the freedom to control their own circumstances.

Native Americans demonstrated and occupied land and public buildings, claiming rights to natural resources and territory that they had owned collectively before European settlement. For example, beginning in 1963 Northwest Indians mounted "fish-ins" to enforce century-old treaty rights. In 1969, Native American militants captured world attention when several dozen seized Alcatraz Island, an abandoned federal prison in San Francisco Bay, claiming their right of "first discovery" of this land. They remained on the island for nineteen months, using the occupation to publicize injustices against Indians, promote pan-Indian cooperation, celebrate traditional cultures, and inspire other activists.

In Minneapolis in 1968, two Chippewas, Dennis Banks and George Mitchell, founded the American Indian Movement (AIM) to attack problems in cities, where about 300,000 Indians lived. AIM sought to protect Indians from police harassment, secure antipoverty funds, and establish "survival schools" to teach Indian history and values. The new movement's appeal quickly spread beyond urban areas and filled many Indians, especially young people, with a sense of purpose. AIM members did not have "that hangdog reservation look I was used to," Lakota activist and author Mary Crow Dog wrote, and their visit to her South Dakota reservation "loosened a sort of earthquake inside me."

AIM leaders helped organize the "Trail of Broken Treaties" caravan to the nation's capitol in 1972, when some of the activists took over the Bureau of Indian Affairs to express their outrage at the bureau's policies. In 1973, a much longer siege occurred on the Lakota Sioux reservation in South Dakota, where conflicts between AIM militants and older tribal leaders led AIM to take over for seventy-two days the village of Wounded Knee, where U.S. troops had massacred more than 100 Sioux in 1890.

Although these dramatic occupations failed to achieve their specific goals, Indians won the end of relocation and termination policies; greater tribal sovereignty and control over community services; enhanced health, education, and other services; and protection of Indian religious practices. A number of laws and court decisions restored rights to ancestral lands or compensated tribes for land seized in violation of treaties. Native Americans recovered a measure of respect and pride and, in the words of President Johnson's special message on the "Forgotten American" in 1968, recognition of "the right of the First Americans to remain Indians while exercising their rights as Americans."

Latino Struggles for Justice

The fastest-growing minority group in the 1960s was Latinos, or Hispanic Americans, an extraordinarily varied population encompassing people of Mexican, Puerto Rican, and other Latin American origins. (The term *Latino* stresses their common bonds as a minority group in the United States; the less political term *Hispanic* also includes those with origins in Spain.) People of Puerto Rican and Caribbean descent flocked to East Coast cities, but more than half of the nation's Latino population—some six million Mexican Americans—lived in California, Texas, Arizona, New Mexico, and Colorado. In addition, thousands illegally crossed the two-thousand-mile border between Mexico and the United States in search of economic opportunity.

Political organization of Mexican Americans dated back to the League of United Latin-American Citizens (LULAC) in 1929, which aided newer immigrants and fought segregation and discrimination through litigation (see chapter 26). In the 1960s, however, young Mexican Americans, like African Americans and Native Americans, increasingly rejected traditional politics in favor of direct action. One symbol of this generational challenge was young activists' adoption of the term *Chicano* (from *mejicano*, the Spanish word for "Mexican").

Chicano protest drew national attention to California, where Cesar Chavez and Dolores Huerta organized a movement to improve the wretched conditions of migrant agricultural workers. As a child moving from farm to farm with his family, living in soggy tents, and exploited by labor contractors, Chavez changed schools frequently and encountered indifference and discrimination from teachers. One, he recalled, "hung a sign on me that said, 'I am a clown, I speak Spanish.'" After serving in World War II, Chavez began to organize voter registration drives among Mexican Americans and to study labor history and the ideas of Catholic reformers and India's independence leader Mahatma Gandhi.

Cesar Chavez in the Vineyards
Cesar Chavez, whose grandfather had migrated to the United States in the nineteenth century, experienced the plight of farmworkers when his family lost its business and farm in Arizona during the depression. Here he meets with grape pickers in California during the national grape boycott of 1965. The boycott's proclamation listed these aims: "just wages, humane working conditions, protection from the misuse of pesticides, and the fundamental right of collective bargaining."
Arthur Schatz/TimePix/Getty.

In contrast to Chavez, Dolores Huerta avoided the farmworkers' grinding poverty and exploitation but witnessed subtle forms of discrimination. Once a high school teacher challenged her authorship of an essay because it was so well written. After completing community college and starting a family, she met Chavez; believing that a labor union was the key to progress, they founded the United Farm Workers (UFW) in 1962. Although Chavez headed the union until his death in 1993, Huerta was indispensable to its vitality. According to another UFW leader, "Dolores was a thirty-five-year-old firebrand in 1965, and she was commanding crusty macho *campesinos* twenty years her senior." UFW strikes gained widespread support, and a national boycott of California grapes helped win a wage increase for the workers in 1970. Although the UFW struggled and lost membership, it helped politicize Mexican Americans and improved farmworkers' lives.

Chicanos mobilized elsewhere to end discrimination in employment and education, gain political power, and combat police brutality. In southwestern cities in 1968, high school students launched a wave of strikes, called "Blow Outs," to protest racism in the public schools. In Denver, Colorado, Rodolfo "Corky" Gonzales set up "freedom schools," where Chicano children studied Spanish and Mexican American history and chanted, "Chicano power." The nationalist strains of Chicano protest were evident in La Raza Unida (the United Race), a political party founded in 1970 by José Angel Gutierrez in Texas and based on cultural pride and brotherhood. With blacks and Native Americans, Chicanos continued to be overrepresented among the poor but gradually won more political offices, more effective enforcement of antidiscrimination legislation, and greater respect for their culture.

Student Rebellion, the New Left, and the Counterculture

Although materially and legally more secure than their African American, Indian, and Latino counterparts, white youth also expressed dissent, supporting the black freedom struggle and launching student protests, the antiwar movement, and the new feminist and environmental movements. Challenging establishment institutions and traditional values, young activists helped change higher education, the family, the national government, and other key institutions.

The central organization of white student protest was Students for a Democratic Society (SDS), formed in 1960 from an older **socialist**-oriented student organization. In 1962, student organizers wrote in their statement of purpose, "We are people of this generation, bred in at least modest comfort, housed now in universities, looking uncomfortably at the world we inherit." The idealistic students criticized the complacency of their elders, the remoteness of decision makers, and the powerlessness and alienation generated by a bureaucratic society. SDS aimed to mobilize a "New Left" around the goals of civil rights, peace, and universal economic security. Other forms of student activism soon followed.

The first large-scale white student protest arose at the University of California, Berkeley, in 1964, when university officials banned students from setting up tables to recruit support for various causes. Led by whites back from civil rights work in the South, the students claimed the right to freedom of expression and political action. The "free speech" movement occupied the administration building, and more than seven hundred students were arrested before the California Board of Regents overturned the new restrictions.

Hundreds of student rallies and building occupations followed on campuses across the country. Opposition to the Vietnam War activated the largest number of students. But they also demanded and won curricular reforms, more financial aid for minority and poor students, independence from paternalistic rules, and a larger voice in campus decision making.

Often overlapping the New Left and student movements was the counterculture, which drew on the ideas of the Beats of the 1950s. Cultural radicals, or "hippies," as they were called, rejected many mainstream values, such as the work ethic, materialism, rationality, order, and sexual control. Seeking personal rather than political change, they advocated "Do your own thing" and drew attention with their long hair and wildly colorful clothing. They sought to discard inhibitions and elevate their senses with illegal drugs such as marijuana and LSD.

Rock and folk music defined both the counterculture and the political left. English groups such as the Beatles and the Rolling Stones and homegrown performers such as Bob Dylan, Janis Joplin, the Jefferson Airplane, and Jerry Garcia's Grateful Dead took American youth by storm. Music during the 1960s often carried insurgent political and social messages that reflected radical youth culture. Despairing of the violence around the world and the threat of nuclear annihilation, "Eve of Destruction," a top hit of 1965, reminded young men, "You're old enough to kill but not for votin'."

The hippies faded away in the 1970s, but many elements of the counterculture—from rock music to jeans and long hair—filtered into the mainstream. More tolerant attitudes about sexual morality spawned what came to be called a "sexual revolution," with help from the birth control pill, newly available in the 1960s. Self-fulfillment became a dominant concern of many Americans, and questioning of authority became much more widespread.

A New Movement to Save the Environment

Environmentalism also contributed to a redefinition of liberalism in the 1960s and beyond. One aspect of the new environmental movement resembled the conservation movement born in the **Progressive** Era to preserve portions of nature for recreational and aesthetic purposes and conserve it for future use (see chapter 21). Especially in the West, the post–World War II explosion of economic growth and population with the resulting demand for electricity and water made such efforts seem even more critical. Environmental groups mobilized to stop construction of dams that would disrupt national parks and wilderness areas.

The new environmentalists, however, went beyond the conservationists to attack the ravaging effects of industrial development on human life and health. The polluted air and water and spread of deadly chemicals attending economic growth threatened wildlife, plants, and the delicate ecological balance that sustained human life. To the leaders of a new organization, Friends of the Earth, unlimited economic growth was "no longer healthy, but a cancer."

Biologist Rachel Carson had already drawn national attention to environmental concerns in 1962 with her best seller *Silent Spring*, which described the harmful effects of toxic chemicals like the pesticide DDT. The Sierra Club and other older conservation organizations expanded their agendas, and a host of new groups arose. Millions of Americans expressed environmental concerns on the first observation of Earth Day in April 1970. Students distributed fliers encouraging recycling, Girl Scouts removed garbage from the Potomac River, African Americans in St. Louis demonstrated the effects of poisons in lead paint, and people across the country planted trees.

Responding to these concerns, the federal government staked out a broad role in environmental regulation. Lyndon Johnson sent the first presidential message on the environment to Congress and signed laws controlling air and water pollution and preserving the American landscape. Richard Nixon's 1970 State of the Union message called "clean air, clean water, open spaces…the birthright of every American," and he created the Environmental Protection Agency

(EPA) to enforce clean air and water policies and regulate pesticides. Congress passed the Occupational Safety and Health Act (OSHA), protecting workers against workplace accidents and disease, and the Clean Air Act of 1970, setting national standards for air quality and restricting factory and automobile emissions of carbon dioxide and other pollutants. By 1990 air pollutants had decreased by one-third in major cities.

Nevertheless, the dominant value of economic growth often trumped environmental concerns, especially by the late 1970s, when antigovernment sentiment rose and the economy slumped. Corporations seeking to expand resisted restrictions. "If you're hungry and out of work, eat an environmentalist," read a union bumper sticker reflecting fears that regulations threatened jobs. Many Americans who wanted to protect the environment also valued economic expansion, personal acquisition, and convenience. Despite these conflicts, the environmental movement achieved cleaner air and water, a reduction in toxic wastes, and some preservation of endangered species and wilderness. And Americans now recognized that humans had developed the power to destroy life on earth.

> **REVIEW**   How did the black freedom struggle influence the reform movements of the 1960s and 1970s?

The New Wave of Feminism

On August 26, 1970, fifty years after women won the right to vote, tens of thousands of women across the country took to the streets—radical women in jeans and conservatively dressed suburbanites, peace activists and politicians, and a sprinkling of women of color. They carried signs reading "Sisterhood Is Powerful" and "Don't Cook Dinner—Starve a Rat Today." Some of the banners opposed the war in Vietnam, others demanded racial justice, but women's own liberation stood at the forefront.

Beginning in the 1960s, the women's movement reached high tide in the 1970s and persisted in various forms into the twenty-first century. By that time, despite a powerful countermovement, women had experienced tremendous transformations in their legal status, public opportunities, and personal and sexual relationships; and popular expectations about appropriate gender roles had shifted dramatically.

A Multifaceted Movement Emerges

Beginning in the 1940s, large demographic changes laid the preconditions for a resurgence of feminism. As ever larger numbers of women took jobs, the importance of their paid work to the economy and to their families belied the idea of women as dependent, domestic beings, awakening many, especially labor union women, to the inferior conditions of their employment. The democratization of higher education brought more women to college campuses, where their aspirations exceeded the confines of domesticity and of routine, subordinate jobs.

Policy initiatives in the early 1960s reflected both these larger transformations and the efforts of small bands of women's rights activists. In 1961, Assistant Secretary of Labor Esther Peterson persuaded Kennedy to create a President's Commission on the Status of Women (PCSW). Chaired by Eleanor Roosevelt, the commission reported its findings in October 1963, eight months after Betty Friedan attacked sex discrimination in *The Feminine Mystique* (see chapter 27). Although not challenging women's domestic roles, the commission reported widespread discrimination against women and recommended remedies. Counterparts of the PCSW sprang up in every state, filled with women eager for action.

The PCSW called attention to the age-old custom of paying women less than men for the same work. Their efforts were rewarded when Kennedy signed the Equal Pay Act in June 1963, and within a few years, women began to win pay increases and back pay worth millions of dollars, although forty-plus years later, women still had not closed the income gap.

The black freedom struggle had created a moral climate sensitive to injustice and provided precedents and strategies that feminists followed. Feminists gained the ban against sex discrimination in Title VII of the Civil Rights Act of 1964 and the extension of affirmative action to women by piggybacking onto civil rights measures. They soon grew impatient when the government failed to take these new policies seriously and moved slowly to enforce them. Deciding that they needed a "civil rights organization for women," in 1966 Betty Friedan and others founded the National Organization for Women (NOW).

Simultaneously, a more radical feminism grew among civil rights and New Left activists. In 1964, two white women in SNCC, Mary King and Casey Hayden, argued that women's actual status in the civil rights movement contradicted the ideal of equality. They contended that, like blacks, women were subject to a "caste system…forcing them to work around or outside hierarchical structures of power which may exclude them" and were also subordinated in personal relations. When most male radicals reacted with indifference or ridicule to such ideas, many women walked out of New Left organizations, and by 1967 they had created an independent women's liberation movement composed of small groups across the nation.

Women's liberation began to gain public attention, especially when dozens of women picketed the Miss America beauty pageant in 1968, protesting against being forced "to compete for male approval [and] enslaved by ludicrous 'beauty' standards." They crowned a sheep Miss America and invited women to throw away their "bras, girdles, curlers, false eyelashes, wigs," and other "objects of female torture." Women began to speak publicly about personal experiences that had always been shrouded in secrecy, such as rape and abortion. Throughout the country, women joined consciousness-raising groups where they discovered that what they had considered "personal" problems reflected an entrenched system of discrimination against and devaluation of women.

Radical feminists, who called their movement "women's liberation," differed from feminists in NOW and other more mainstream groups in several ways. NOW focused on equal treatment for women in the public sphere, while women's liberation emphasized ending women's subordination in the family and in other personal relationships. Groups like NOW wanted to integrate women into existing institutions; radical groups insisted that women's liberation required a total transformation of economic, political, and social institutions. Differences between these two strands of feminism blurred in the 1970s, as NOW and other mainstream groups embraced many of the issues raised by radicals.

Although NOW elected a black president, Aileen Hernandez, in 1970, the new feminism's leadership and constituency were predominantly white and middle class. Women of color criticized white women's organizations for their

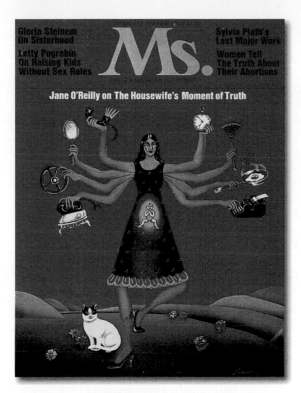

First Issue of *Ms.* Magazine

In 1972, Gloria Steinem and other journalists and writers published the premier issue of the first mass-circulation magazine for and controlled by women. *Ms.: The New Magazine for Women* ignored the recipes and fashion tips of typical women's magazines. It featured literature by women writers and articles on a broad range of feminist issues. A scholar later wrote that it was "mind-blowing. Here was, written down, what [women] had not yet admitted they felt, had always feared to say out loud, and could not believe was now before their eyes, in public, for all to read." What concerns are suggested by this cover of the first issue? What is the significance of the woman's multiple arms?

Courtesy, Lang Communications.

frequent indifference to the disproportionate poverty experienced by minority women and their vulnerability to additional layers of discrimination based on race or ethnicity. Cellestine Ware, an African American writer and a founder of New York Radical Feminists, insisted that black and white women could work together "only if the movement changes its priorities to work on issues that affect the lives of minority group women."

Yet support for feminism was exceedingly multifaceted. Most African American women worked through their own groups such as the older National Council of Negro Women and the National Black Feminist Organization, founded in 1973. Similarly, in the early 1970s American Indian women and Mexican American women founded national organizations, and Asian American women formed their own local movements. Labor union women had been fighting for workplace gender justice since the 1940s, and blue-collar women organized the National Coalition of Labor Union Women in 1974. Lesbians established collectives throughout the country as well as their own caucuses in organizations such as NOW. Women founded a host of other groups that focused on single issues such as health, abortion rights, education, and violence against women. Finally, U.S. feminists interacted with women abroad, joining a movement that crossed national boundaries. (See "Beyond America's Borders," page 748.)

Common threads underlay the great diversity of organizations, issues, and activities. Above all, feminism represented the belief that women were barred from, unequally treated in, or poorly served by the male-dominated public arena, encompassing politics, medicine, law, education, and religion. Feminists also sought equality in the private sphere, challenging traditional norms that identified women primarily as wives and mothers or sex objects, subservient to men.

Feminist Gains Spark a Countermovement

Although more an effect than a cause of women's rising employment, feminism lifted female aspirations and helped lower barriers to posts monopolized by men. Women made some inroads into skilled crafts and management positions. Between 1970 and 2000, their share of law degrees shot up from 5 percent to nearly 50 percent, and their proportion of medical degrees from less than 10 percent to more than 35 percent. Women gained political offices very slowly; yet by 2000, they constituted more than 10 percent of Congress and more than 20 percent of all state executives and legislators.

But feminists encountered frustrations along with achievements. Despite some inroads into male-dominated occupations, most women still worked in low-paying, traditionally female jobs. Employed women continued to bear primary responsibility for their homes and families, thereby working a "double day." Congress attempted to ease this burden with a comprehensive child care bill in 1971, but President Nixon vetoed it.

Despite this setback, during the 1970s women gained the most sweeping changes in

Transnational Feminisms

When American women began to protest sex discrimination in the 1960s, most were unaware that they belonged to a movement stretching back more than a century and across oceans. In 1850, Polish-born Ernestine Rose told a women's rights convention in Massachusetts, "We are not contending here for the rights of the women of New England, or of old England, but of the world." Her statement affirmed the connections among women from European countries and the United States, who wrote and visited each other and exchanged ideas and inspiration in the first international women's movement.

By the early twentieth century, women had formalized such connections. For example, the International Alliance of Women, founded in 1904 to promote global woman **suffrage**, expanded its agenda to include equal pay and employment, peace, married women's citizenship, and more. By 1929, the Alliance claimed national organizations in fifty-one countries, including the United States and most of Europe, China, Egypt, India, Japan, Palestine, and several Latin American nations.

Alliance women struggled to create a "universal sisterhood." White Christian women from the United States and Europe dominated the organization and blithely assumed that they could speak for all women. But oppression and discrimination looked quite different to women in other parts of the world. In **colonized** countries such as India and Egypt, feminism arose alongside movements for independence from the very **imperial** nations that were home to most Alliance leaders. Egyptian feminist and nationalist Huda Sha'arawi was the only Muslim among the international leadership. She worked closely with the Alliance on many issues, but she realized the need to address the particular interests of Arab women overlooked or opposed by Euro-American feminists, and she established an Arab Feminist Union in 1945.

Global connections among women increased dramatically in 1945 with the creation of the United Nations. Its Charter affirmed "the equal rights of men and women" and "fundamental freedoms for all without distinction as to race, sex, language, or religion." Two years later, the UN established a Commission on the Status of Women, creating a forum for women from around the globe to meet and be heard; and in 1948 it adopted a Universal Declaration of Human Rights, which enumerated an extensive set of rights and explicitly rejected sex discrimination. These and other international commitments to justice for women went far beyond any rights guaranteed to women by the American legal system or by the laws of most other nations, thereby setting standards and raising expectations. The UN, for example, asserted women's right to equal pay in 1951, twelve years before the U.S. Congress did so, and the international body attacked discrimination in education a decade before Congress passed Title IX.

The UN helped launch a global feminist movement of unparalleled size and diversity when it declared 1975 the International Women's Year and sponsored a conference in Mexico City. Six thousand women came to Mexico City on their own; official delegates from 125 nations approved a World Plan of Action for Women and prompted the UN to declare 1976 to 1985 the UN Decade for Women.

In response to the call for action in individual countries, the U.S. government funded a National Women's Conference in Houston, Texas, in 1977. More than 2,000 state delegates, representing a cross section of American womanhood, attended. They adopted a National Plan of Action, not only supporting ratification of the ERA and reproductive freedom but also addressing the needs of specific groups of women, including the elderly, lesbians, racial minorities, rural women, and homemakers. For the first time, the U.S. women's movement had a comprehensive national agenda setting goals for decades to come.

The three themes of the UN Decade for Women—equality, development, peace—reflected an effort to address the enormously diverse needs of women throughout the world. Feminists from Western nations who focused on equal rights met criticism from women who represented impoverished **third world**

International Women's Year Tribune

A majority of delegates at the UN International Women's Year Conference in Mexico City in July 1975 were women, but men provided the leadership, and delegates frequently took positions mandated by their government but not necessarily reflecting the interests of women. In contrast, nongovernmental organizations associated with the UN sponsored a Tribune on the other side of the city, where 6,000 women attended workshops that they or their organizations designed. There participants expressed the conflicting priorities of Western women and women from developing countries, and they argued over whether such issues as apartheid in South Africa or self-government for Palestinians were women's issues. Despite these disagreements, most women left Mexico City enlightened and energized.
© Bettye Lane.

countries and insisted that women's issues must include economic development and anticolonialism. Ever larger UN-sponsored meetings followed Mexico City—Copenhagen in 1980, Nairobi in 1985, and Beijing in 1995, where 20,000 women gathered. These global exchanges taught American feminists that to participate in a truly international movement they would have to revise their Western-centered perspective on women's needs.

American feminists also learned that theirs was not always the most advanced nation when it came to women's welfare and status. Most industrialized countries provided paid maternity leave and public child care. By 2000, women had headed governments in more than 30 countries, including India, Israel, and England. Many nations, such as Argentina, Egypt, India, and the European Union, had some form of affirmative action to increase the numbers of women in government. And while American women held 13.8 percent of the seats in the House of Representatives, women constituted 20 percent of the lower house in South Korea, 30 percent in Germany, and more than 35 percent in Norway, Denmark, and Sweden.

Despite enormous differences among women around the world, internationally minded feminists continued to seek common ground. For, as Gertrude Mongella, secretary general of the Beijing conference, insisted in 1995, "A revolution has begun and there is no going back.... This revolution is too just, too important, and too long overdue."

laws and policies since they had won the right to vote in 1920. In 1972, Congress passed an Equal Rights Amendment to the Constitution (ERA) that would outlaw differential treatment of men and women under all state and federal laws. Although public opinion polls registered support for most feminist goals, by the mid-1970s a strong countermovement focused on preventing ratification of the ERA arose. Phyllis Schlafly, a conservative activist in the Republican Party, mobilized a host of women at the grassroots level who believed that traditional gender roles were God-given and feared that feminism would devalue their own roles as wives and mothers. These women, marching on state capitols, persuaded some male legislators to block ratification. When the time limit ran out in 1982, only thirty-five states had ratified the amendment, three short of the necessary three-fourths majority. (See "Historical Question" in chapter 30, page 796, and Map 30.3.)

Feminists also pressured state legislatures to end restrictions on abortion. "Without the full capacity to limit her own reproduction," abortion rights activist Lucinda Cisler insisted, "a woman's other 'freedoms' are tantalizing mockeries that cannot be exercised." In 1973, the Supreme Court issued the landmark *Roe v. Wade* decision, ruling that the Constitution protects the right to abortion, which states cannot prohibit in the early stages of pregnancy.

This decision spurred even more intense opposition than the ERA. Many Americans believed that human life begins with conception and equated abortion with murder. The Catholic Church and other religious organizations provided institutional support for their protest; conservative politicians and their supporters constituted another segment of the right-to-life movement. Like ERA opponents with whom they often overlapped, the right-to-life movement mobilized thousands of women who believed that abortion disparaged motherhood and that feminism threatened their traditional roles.

Despite some resistance, feminists won other lasting gains. Title IX of the Education Amendments Act of 1972 banned sex discrimination in all aspects of education, such as admissions, athletics, and faculty hiring. Congress also outlawed sex discrimination in credit in 1974, opened U.S. military academies to women in 1976, and prohibited discrimination against pregnant workers in 1978. Moreover, the Supreme Court struck down laws that treated men and women differently in Social Security, welfare and military benefits, and workers' compensation. At the state and local levels, radical feminists won laws forcing police departments and the legal system to treat rape victims more justly and humanely. Activists set up shelters for battered women and won laws ensuring greater protection for victims of domestic violence and more effective prosecution of abusers.

> **REVIEW**   Why did a strong countermovement emerge to oppose feminist reform?

Liberal Reform in the Nixon Administration

Feminism was not the only movement to arouse strong antagonism. Opposition to civil rights measures, Great Society reforms, and protest groups—along with frustrations surrounding the war in Vietnam (see chapter 29)—delivered the White House to Republican Richard M. Nixon in 1968. As presidential candidate, Nixon attacked the Great Society for "pouring billions of dollars into programs that have failed," and he promised to represent the "forgotten Americans, the non-shouters, the non-demonstrators."

Yet, despite Nixon's desire to attract southern whites and other Democrats disaffected by Johnson's reforms, liberal policies persisted into the early 1970s. The Nixon administration either promoted or accepted substantially greater federal assistance to the poor; new protections for African Americans, Native Americans, women, and other groups; major environmental regulations; and financial policies deviating sharply from traditional Republican economics.

Extending the Welfare State and Regulating the Economy

A number of factors shaped the liberal policies of the Nixon administration. The Democrats continued to control Congress; and Nixon wanted to preserve support from moderates in his party and increase Republican ranks by attracting some traditional Democrats. He could not entirely ignore grassroots movements, and several of his advisers were sympathetic to particular concerns. Serious economic problems also compelled new approaches, and although Nixon's real passion lay in foreign policy, he knew that history's approving gaze would depend in part on how he handled problems at home.

Under Nixon, government assistance programs actually grew. Congress resisted his attempts to eliminate the Office of Economic Opportunity. Social Security benefits—now required to rise with the cost of living—increased; subsidies for low-income housing tripled; and a new billion-dollar program provided Pell grants for low-income students to attend college. In response to growing public concern about undernourishment, Nixon supported a huge expansion of the food stamp program, which benefited 12.5 million recipients. Noting the disparity between Nixon's political speeches and his actual practice as president, his speechwriter, the archconservative Pat Buchanan, grumbled, "Vigorously did we inveigh against the Great Society, enthusiastically did we fund it."

Nixon also acted contrary to his antigovernment rhetoric when economic crises and energy shortages induced him to increase the federal government's power in the marketplace. Throughout the post–World War II economic boom, the nation's abundant oil deposits and access to cheap Middle Eastern oil had encouraged the building of large cars and glass-enclosed skyscrapers with no concern for fuel efficiency. By the 1970s the United States, with just 6 percent of the world's population, consumed one-third of its fuel resources.

In the fall of 1973, the United States faced its first energy crisis. Arab nations, furious at the nation's support of Israel during the Yom Kippur War (see chapter 29), had cut off oil shipments to the United States. As oil supplies fell in the winter of 1973–74, long lines formed at gas stations, where prices had nearly doubled, and many homes were cold. In response, Nixon authorized temporary emergency measures allocating petroleum and establishing a national 55-mile-per-hour speed limit to save gasoline.

Soaring energy prices contributed to severe economic problems. By 1970, both inflation and unemployment had surpassed 6 percent. This unprecedented combination of a stagnant economy and inflation was dubbed "stagflation." Domestic troubles were compounded by the decline of American dominance in the international economy. Fully recovered from World War II, the economies of Japan and Western Europe grew faster than the U.S. economy in the 1970s. Foreign cars, electronic equipment, and other products competed favorably with American goods throughout the world. In 1971, for the first time in decades, the United States imported more than it exported. Because the amount of dollars in foreign hands exceeded U.S. gold reserves, the nation could no longer back up its currency with gold.

With an eye to the 1972 election, Nixon abandoned the convertibility of dollars into gold and devalued the dollar to increase exports by making American goods cheaper in foreign markets. He also imposed a 10 percent surcharge on most imports and froze wages and prices, thus enabling the government to stimulate the economy without fueling inflation. In the short run, these policies worked and Nixon was resoundingly reelected in 1972. Yet by 1974 unemployment crept back up and inflation soared, leaving to Nixon's successor the most severe economic crisis since the depression of the 1930s.

More permanently, Nixon expanded the government's regulatory role with a host of environmental protection measures. In addition to establishing the Environmental Protection Agency, he signed strong clean-air legislation and measures to regulate noise pollution, oil spill cleanup, and the dumping of pesticides into the oceans. Environmentalists claimed that Nixon failed to do enough, pointing particularly to his veto—for budgetary reasons—of the Clean Water Act of 1972, which Congress overrode. Yet Nixon's environmental initiatives surpassed those of previous administrations.

Responding to Demands for Social Justice

To woo white southerners and northern workers away from the Democratic Party, Nixon's 1968 campaign had exploited antipathy to black protest and new civil rights policies, but his administration had to answer to the courts and to Congress. In 1968, fourteen years after the *Brown* decision (see chapter 27), school desegregation had barely touched the South: Two-thirds of African American children did not have a single white schoolmate. Like Eisenhower, Nixon was reluctant to use federal power to compel integration, but the Supreme Court overruled administration efforts to delay court-ordered desegregation and compelled it to enforce the law. By the time Nixon left office, fewer than one in ten southern black children attended totally segregated schools.

Nixon also began to implement affirmative action among federal contractors and unions and awarded more government contracts and loans to minority businesses. Congress took the initiative in other areas. In 1970, it extended the Voting Rights Act of 1965 by five years, and in 1972 it strengthened the Civil Rights Act of 1964 by enlarging the powers of the law's enforcement agency, the Equal Employment Opportunity Commission, and authorizing the commission to initiate lawsuits against employers suspected of discrimination.

While women as well as minority groups benefited from the implementation of affirmative action and the strengthened EEOC, several measures of the Nixon administration specifically attacked sex discrimination. The president privately expressed patronizing attitudes about women, who he thought were more "erratic" and "emotional" than men. "Thank God we don't have any in the Cabinet," he told aides. Yet again he confronted a growing popular movement and listened to more open-minded advisers and Republican feminists. Nixon vetoed a child care bill and publicly opposed abortion, but he signed the pathbreaking Title IX and allowed his Labor Department to push affirmative action.

President Nixon gave more public support for justice to Native Americans than to any other protest group. While not giving in to radical demands, the administration dealt cautiously with extreme protests, such as the occupation of the Bureau of Indian Affairs and Wounded Knee. He signed measures recognizing claims of Alaskan and New Mexican Indians and restoring tribal status to the Menominee, whose status had been terminated in 1961. He also set in motion legislation restoring additional tribal lands and granting Indians more control over their schools and other service institutions.

> **REVIEW**   Why and how did Republican president Richard Nixon expand the liberal reforms of previous administrations?

Conclusion: Achievements and Limitations of Liberalism

Senate majority leader Mike Mansfield was not alone in concluding that Lyndon Johnson "has done more than FDR ever did, or ever thought of

doing." Yet opposition to Johnson's leadership grew so strong by 1968 that he abandoned hopes for reelection. As his liberal vision lay in ruins, he asked, "How was it possible that all these people could be so ungrateful to me after I have given them so much?"

Fannie Lou Hamer could have provided a number of reasons. Support from the federal government was minimal when her efforts and those of others to help southern blacks obtain their rights met with violence. Moreover, her efforts to use Johnson's antipoverty programs to help poor blacks in Mississippi reflected some of the shortcomings of the War on Poverty. Inadequately planned and funded, many antipoverty programs significantly benefited industry and the nonpoor. Because Johnson refused to ask for sacrifices from prosperous Americans, the Great Society never commanded the resources necessary for victory over poverty.

Black aspirations exceeded white Americans' commitment to genuine equality. When the civil rights movement moved to attack the subtle racism existing throughout the nation and sought equality in fact as well as in law, it faced a powerful backlash. By the end of the 1960s, the revolution in the legal status of African Americans was complete, but the black freedom struggle had lost much of its momentum, and African Americans remained, with Native Americans and Chicanos, at the bottom of the economic ladder.

Critics of Johnson's Great Society overlooked its more successful and lasting elements. Medicare and Medicaid provided access to health care for the elderly and the poor and contributed to a sharp decline in poverty among aged Americans. Federal aid for education and housing became permanent elements of national policy. Moreover, Richard Nixon's otherwise conservative administration implemented school desegregation in the South and affirmative action, expanded government assistance to the disadvantaged, initiated substantial environmental regulations, and secured new rights for Native Americans and women. Women especially benefited from the decline of discrimination, and significant numbers of African Americans and other minority groups began to enter the middle class.

Yet the perceived shortcomings of government programs contributed to social turmoil and fueled the resurgence of conservative politics. Young radicals launched direct confrontations with the government and universities that, together with racial conflict, escalated into political discord and social disorder. The war in Vietnam polarized American society as much as did racial issues or the behavior of young people, and Johnson's and Nixon's conduct of the war devoured resources that might have been used for social reform and undermined faith in presidential leadership.

Suggestions for Further Reading

Terry H. Anderson, *The Movement and the Sixties* (1995). A detailed look at student protest throughout the country.

Robert Dallek, *Flawed Giant: Lyndon B. Johnson, 1960–1973* (1998). A monumental study of the often larger-than-life president.

Sara Evans, *Personal Liberation: The Roots of Women's Liberation in the Civil Rights Movement and the New Left* (1978). An engaging explanation of how the radical wing of 1960s feminism arose.

Maurice Isserman and Michael Kazin, *America Divided: The Civil War of the 1960s* (2000). A highly readable account covering all aspects of the 1960s.

Charles Payne, *I've Got the Light of Freedom: The Organizing Tradition and the Mississippi Freedom Struggle* (1995). A close look at how ordinary people participated in and led the black freedom struggle.

Peter Chaat Smith and Robert Allen Warrior, *Like a Hurricane: The Indian Movement from Alcatraz to Wounded Knee* (1996). A detailed and often gripping account of Native American protests.

▶ FOR MORE BOOKS ABOUT TOPICS IN THIS CHAPTER, see the Online Study Guide at bedfordstmartins.com/roarkcompact.

▶ FOR ADDITIONAL FIRSTHAND ACCOUNTS OF THIS PERIOD, see Chapter 28 in Michael Johnson, ed., *Reading the American Past*, Third Edition.

▶ FOR WEB SITES AND DOCUMENTS RELATED TO TOPICS AND PLACES IN THIS CHAPTER, see "History Links," "DocLinks," and "PlaceLinks" at bedfordstmartins.com/roarkcompact.

REVIEWING THE CHAPTER

Follow these steps to review and strengthen your understanding of the chapter.

STEP 1: *Study the **Key Terms** and **Timeline** to identify the significance of each item listed.*

STEP 2: *Answer the **Review Questions**, drawing on key terms and dates to support your answers.*

STEP 3: *Drawing on the Key Terms, Timeline, and Review Questions, answer the broader **Making Connections** questions.*

KEY TERMS

Who

Fannie Lou Hamer (p. 729)
John F. Kennedy (p. 731)
Lee Harvey Oswald (p. 732)
Lyndon B. Johnson (p. 733)
Barry M. Goldwater (p. 733)
Earl Warren (p. 736)
Medgar Evers (p. 738)
Malcolm X (p. 741)
Stokely Carmichael (p. 741)
Cesar Chavez (p. 743)
Dolores Huerta (p. 743)
Rachel Carson (p. 745)
Betty Friedan (p. 746)
Phyllis Schlafly (p. 750)
Richard M. Nixon (p. 750)

What

Great Society (pp. 729, 734)
Economic Opportunity Act of 1964 (p. 733)

Elementary and Secondary Education Act of 1965 (p. 734)
Medicare (p. 734)
Medicaid (p. 734)
Voting Rights Act of 1965 (p. 734)
Immigration and Nationality Act of 1965 (p. 734)
Baker v. Carr (p. 736)
Gideon v. Wainright (p. 736)
Miranda v. Arizona (p. 736)
Abington School District v. Schempp (p. 736)
Student Nonviolent Coordinating Committee (SNCC) (p. 737)
Congress of Racial Equality (CORE) (p. 738)
Freedom Rides (p. 738)
Voter Education Project (p. 738)
March on Washington (p. 738)
Mississippi Freedom Summer Project (p. 738)
Selma march (p. 738)
Civil Rights Act of 1964 (p. 739)
Voting Rights Act (p. 739)
Civil Rights Act of 1968 (p. 740)

Black Panther Party for Self-Defense (p. 741)
American Indian Movement (AIM) (p. 742)
United Farm Workers (UFW) (p. 743)
La Raza Unida (p. 744)
Students for a Democratic Society (SDS) (p. 744)
Environmental Protection Agency (EPA) (p. 745)
Occupational Safety and Health Act (OSHA) (p. 745)
Clean Air Act of 1970 (p. 745)
President's Commission on the Status of Women (PCSW) (p. 746)
Equal Pay Act (p. 746)
National Organization for Women (NOW) (p. 746)
Equal Rights Amendment to the Constitution (ERA) (p. 750)
Roe v. Wade (p. 750)
Title IX (p. 750)

TIMELINE

1960 • Lunch-counter sit-ins.
• Democrat John F. Kennedy elected president.
• Student Nonviolent Coordinating Committee (SNCC) established.
• Students for a Democratic Society (SDS) founded.

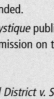

    1961 • Congress of Racial Equality (CORE) sponsors Freedom Rides.

        1962 • United Farm Workers (UFW) founded.

            1963 • *The Feminine Mystique* published.
• President's Commission on the Status of Women issues report.
• Equal Pay Act.
• *Baker v. Carr.*
• *Abington School District v. Schempp.*
• March on Washington.
• President Kennedy assassinated; Lyndon B. Johnson becomes president.

                1964 • Civil Rights Act of 1964.
• Economic Opportunity Act.
• Tax cuts enacted.

                    1965 • Selma-to-Montgomery march.
• Voting Rights Act.

                  1965–1966 • Congress passes most of Johnson's Great Society domestic programs.

REVIEW QUESTIONS

1. How did the Kennedy and Johnson administrations exemplify a liberal vision of federal government? (pp. 731–36)

2. How did the civil rights movement change in the mid-1960s? (pp. 736–42)

3. How did the black freedom struggle influence the reform movements of the 1960s and 1970s? (pp. 742–45)

4. Why did a strong countermovement emerge to oppose feminist reform? (pp. 745–50)

5. Why and how did Republican president Richard Nixon expand the liberal reforms of previous administrations? (pp. 750–52)

MAKING CONNECTIONS

1. Both Franklin Roosevelt's New Deal and Lyndon Johnson's Great Society attacked poverty. How was Johnson's approach different from Roosevelt's? Which was more successful, and what contributed to the relative successes and failures of each approach?

2. During the 1960s, African Americans made substantial gains in asserting their freedoms and rights. Discuss how the civil rights movement produced significant social change. Were there limits to its success? What part did government play in this process?

3. Women participated in various ways in the feminism that emerged in the 1960s. How can we explain the rise of this movement? What assumptions and goals were held in common in this diverse movement?

4. Most of the reform movements of the 1960s sought equality as one of their key priorities, but significant differences existed among Americans in general about what equality meant. Should equality be limited to equal treatment under the law, or should it extend to economic welfare, education, sexual relations, and other aspects of life? Examining two reform movements, discuss how different ideas of equality contributed to the accomplishments and disappointments of each movement.

▶ **For practice quizzes, a customized study plan, and other study tools,** see the Online Study Guide at **bedfordstmartins.com/roarkcompact**.

1966 • Black Panther Party founded.
• *Miranda v. Arizona.*
• National Organization for Women (NOW) founded.

   1967 • Detroit riots.

      1968 • Martin Luther King Jr. assassinated.
           • American Indian Movement (AIM) founded.
           • Republican Richard M. Nixon elected president.

         1970 • First Earth Day demonstrations.
             • Occupational Safety and Health Act.
             • Environmental Protection Agency established.
             • Clean Air Act.

           1971 • Nixon's New Economic Policy introduced.

             1972 • Title IX of Education Amendments enacted.
               • Congress passes Equal Rights Amendment, sends it to states for ratification.
               • American Indians' "Trail of Broken Treaties" caravan to Washington, D.C.

               1973 • AIM members occupy Wounded Knee.
                  • *Roe v. Wade.*

FATIGUE HAT WITH BUTTONS

The button on this fatigue hat belonging
to a veteran who served two tours of duty
demonstrates veterans' response to the many Americans who just wanted to forget the war that the United States
failed to win. Because their war was so different from other American wars, Viet-
nam veterans often returned home to hostility or indifference. The POW-MIA pin refers to prisoners of war and those
missing in action. This man was unusual in serving two tours of duty in Vietnam; most soldiers served only one year.
Why might he have gone back for a second tour? How might his experiences have differed in the two periods separated by five years?

Vietnam and the Limits of Power

1961–1975

A S CHARLES ANDERSON'S PLANE prepared to land, the pilot announced, "Gentlemen, we'll be touching down in Da Nang, Vietnam, in about ten minutes....On behalf of the entire crew and staff, I'd like to say we've enjoyed having you with us...and we hope to see all of you again next year on your way home. Goodbye and good luck." Like most soldiers after 1966, Anderson went to war on a commercial jetliner, complete with stewardesses (as they were called then) in miniskirts.

Military personnel's traveling to battle like business executives or tourists only hints at how different the Vietnam War was from America's previous wars. Marine infantry officer Philip Caputo landed at Da Nang in March 1965 confident, as were many soldiers in previous wars, that the enemy "would be quickly beaten and that we were doing something altogether noble and good." But in just a few months, "what had begun as an adventurous expedition had turned into an exhausting, indecisive war of attrition in which we fought for no other cause than our own survival."

Another soldier discovered even more quickly that "something was wrong." Wondering why the bus taking him from the air base to the compound had wire mesh over the windows, he was told, "The gooks will throw grenades through the windows." One American reported on the "changes coming over guys on our side—decent fellows, who wouldn't dream of calling an Oriental a 'gook' back home," reported one American. The problem was that "they couldn't tell who was their friend and who wasn't. Day after day, out on patrol we'd come to...a shabby village, and the elders would welcome us and the children come running with smiles on their faces, waiting for the candy we'd give them. But...just as we were leaving the village behind, the enemy would open up on us, and there was bitterness among us that the villagers hadn't given us warning."

Americans' horrifying and bewildering experiences in Vietnam grew out of **cold war** commitments made in the 1940s and 1950s by Presidents Harry S. Truman and Dwight D. Eisenhower. John F. Kennedy wholeheartedly took on those commitments, promising more flexible and vigorous efforts to thwart **communism**. The most memorable words of his 1961 inauguration declared that the United States would "pay any price, bear any burden, meet any hardship, support any friend, oppose any foe to assure the survival and the success of liberty."

Vietnam became the foremost test of Kennedy's pledge. He sent increasing amounts of American arms and personnel to sustain the South Vietnamese

Fighting the Climate and Geography
Steamy tropical conditions and inhospitable terrain were among the nonhuman enemies U.S. troops faced in Vietnam. Soldiers like this one making his way under fire through a rice paddy in 1966 were soaked for weeks on end. Veteran Philip Caputo wrote about "being pounded numb by ceaseless rain" during the monsoon; "at night we squatted in muddy holes, picked off the leeches that sucked on our veins."

Henri Gilles Huet/World Wide Photos, Inc.

government, and Lyndon B. Johnson dramatically escalated that commitment. By 1965, the civil war in Vietnam had become America's war, with 543,000 military personnel serving there at peak strength in 1968 and more than 2 million total throughout the war's duration. Yet this massive intervention not only failed to defeat North Vietnam but also created intense discord at home. It cost President Johnson another term in office and contributed to the political demise of his Republican successor, Richard M. Nixon. Some Americans lauded the government's goal in Vietnam and decried only its failure to pursue it effectively. Others believed that preserving a non-Communist South Vietnam was neither in the best interests of the United States nor within its capacity or moral right to achieve.

But none could deny the war's enormous costs. "The promises of the Great Society have been shot down on the battlefield of Vietnam," said Martin Luther King Jr. In addition to derailing domestic reform, the war exacted a heavy toll in American lives and dollars, kindled inter-

nal conflict, and led to the violation of protesters' rights, leaving a deep and lasting mark on the nation.

Even as the United States fought communism in Vietnam and, on a much smaller scale, in other **third world** countries, American leaders moved to ease cold war tensions with the major Communist powers. The United States and the Soviet Union cooperated during the 1960s to limit nuclear testing and the spread of nuclear weapons; then in 1972, they agreed for the first time to restrict the development of new nuclear weapons. In addition, Nixon's historic visit to China in 1972 marked abandonment of the policy of isolating China and paved the way for normal diplomatic relations by the end of the 1970s.

New Frontiers in Foreign Policy

John F. Kennedy moved quickly to fulfill his promise to pursue **containment** more aggressively and with more flexible means, working to expand the nation's ability to wage nuclear, conventional, or **guerrilla warfare**. To ensure U.S. superiority over the Soviet Union in every domain, Kennedy accelerated the nation's space exploration program and increased attention to the third world. To halt the spread of nuclear weapons, he took the United States to the brink of nuclear war during the 1962 Cuban missile crisis. Less dramatically but no less tenaciously, Kennedy sent increasing amounts of American arms and personnel to save the government of South Vietnam from Communist insurgents.

Meeting the "Hour of Maximum Danger"

Kennedy and other Democrats criticized the Eisenhower administration for relying too heavily on nuclear weapons. They wanted to build up conventional ground forces as well, to provide a **flexible response** to Communist expansion. They also charged that limits on defense spending had allowed the United States to fall behind even in nuclear capability. In January 1961, Kennedy warned that the nation faced a grave peril: "Each day the crises multiply....Each day we draw nearer the hour of maximum danger."

Although the president exaggerated the actual threat to national security, several developments in 1961 heightened the sense of crisis and provided rationalization for a military buildup. Shortly before Kennedy's inauguration, Soviet premier Nikita Khrushchev had publicly encouraged "wars of national liberation," thereby aligning the Soviet Union with independence movements in the third world. Khrushchev's statement reflected in part the Soviet competition with China for the allegiance of emerging nations, but U.S. officials saw in his words a threat to the status quo of containment.

Nowhere was the perceived threat closer to home than in Cuba, just ninety miles from Florida. Fidel Castro's revolution had already moved Cuba into the Soviet orbit; and under Eisenhower, the CIA had been planning an invasion by anti-Castro exiles. Kennedy ordered the invasion to proceed even though his military advisers gave it only a fair chance of success. To do otherwise, the president believed, would create an appearance of weakness.

On April 17, 1961, about 1,300 anti-Castro exiles trained and armed by the CIA landed at the Bay of Pigs on the south shore of Cuba (Map 29.1). Contrary to U.S. expectations, no popular uprising materialized to support the anti-Castro brigade. Kennedy refused to supply direct military support, and the invaders quickly fell to

---

MAP 29.1 U.S. Involvement in Latin America and the Caribbean, 1954–1994
During the cold war, the United States frequently intervened in Central American and Caribbean countries to suppress Communist or leftist movements.

READING THE MAP: How many and which Latin American countries did the United States directly invade? What was the extent of U.S. indirect involvement in other upheavals in the region?
CONNECTIONS: What role did geographic proximity play in U.S. policy toward the region? What was the significance of the Cuban missile crisis for U.S. foreign policy? Did the political party of the intervening administration make a difference? Why or why not?

FOR MORE HELP ANALYZING THIS MAP, see the map activity for this chapter in the Online Study Guide at bedfordstmartins.com/roarkcompact.

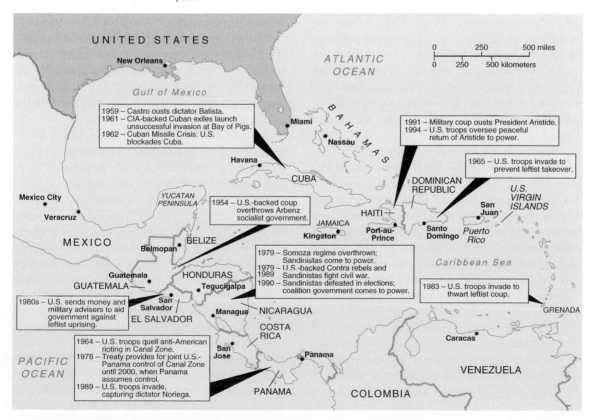

Castro's forces. The disaster humiliated Kennedy and the United States, posing a stark contrast to Kennedy's inaugural promise of a new, more effective foreign policy. The attempted armed interference in another nation evoked memories of **Yankee imperialism** among Latin Americans, aligned Cuba even more closely with the Soviet Union, and helped Castro consolidate his power.

Days before the Bay of Pigs invasion, the Soviet Union delivered a psychological blow when its astronaut became the first human to orbit the earth. In May 1961, Kennedy called for a huge new commitment to the space race in order to "win the battle that is now going on around the world between freedom and tyranny." Congress authorized the Apollo program and boosted appropriations for space exploration. In 1962, John H. Glenn orbited the earth. Then in 1969, the United States surpassed the Soviet Union when Americans became the first humans to set foot on the moon.

Kennedy hoped to show Khrushchev "that we can be as tough as he is," but when the two met in June 1961, in Vienna, Austria, Khrushchev was belligerent and shook the president's confidence. The stunned president reported privately, "He just beat [the] hell out of me.…If he thinks I'm inexperienced and have no guts…we won't get anywhere with him." Khrushchev demanded an agreement recognizing the existence of two Germanys. Otherwise, he warned, the Soviets would sign a separate treaty with East Germany, a move that would threaten America's occupation rights in and access to West Berlin, which lay some one hundred miles within East Germany.

The massive exodus of East Germans into West Berlin caused the Communists major embarrassment. To stop this flow of escapees from behind the **iron curtain**, in August 1961 East Germany erected a wall between East and West Berlin, shocking the world. With the Berlin Wall stemming the tide of migration, Khrushchev backed off from his threats. But not until 1972 did the superpowers recognize East and West Germany as separate nations and guarantee Western access to West Berlin.

Kennedy used the Berlin crisis to add $3.2 billion to the defense budget and 300,000 troops to the military. By providing for a "flexible response" strategy, this buildup of conventional forces met his demand for "a wider choice than humiliation or all-out nuclear action."

New Approaches to the Third World

Complementing Kennedy's hard-line policy toward the Soviet Union were fresh approaches to the **nationalist** movements that had convulsed the world since the end of World War II. In 1960 alone, seventeen African nations gained their independence. Much more than his predecessors, the president publicly supported third world aspirations, believing that the United States could win over developing nations by helping to fulfill hopes for autonomy and **democracy**.

To that end, Kennedy created the Alliance for Progress, promising $20 billion in aid for Latin America over the next decade. Like the Marshall Plan, the Alliance for Progress was designed to thwart communism and hold nations within the American sphere by fostering economic development. Likewise, the new Agency for International Development (AID) emphasized economic over military aid in foreign assistance programs.

In 1961, Kennedy launched his most dramatic third world initiative: the Peace Corps. The program attracted idealistic volunteers, such as one who felt uncomfortable at having been "born between clean sheets when others were issued into the dust with a birthright of hunger." After studying a country's language and culture, Peace Corps volunteers went to work directly with its people, opening schools, providing basic health care, and assisting with agriculture, nutrition, and small economic enterprises. By the mid-1970s, more than 60,000 volunteers had served two-year stints in Latin America, Africa, and Asia.

Nevertheless, Kennedy's foreign aid initiatives fell far short of their objectives. Though generally welcomed, Peace Corps projects numbered too few to make a dent in the poverty and suffering in third world countries. By 1969, the United States had provided only half of the $20 billion promised to the Alliance for Progress, much of which went to military projects or into the pockets of corrupt ruling elites. In addition, a soaring birthrate in Latin America counteracted economic gains, and these nations increasingly bore heavy foreign debt.

Kennedy also used direct military means to bring political stability to the third world, rapidly expanding the "special forces" corps that had been established under Eisenhower to aid groups sympathetic to the United States and fighting against Communist-leaning national

Peace Corps Volunteers in Bolivia

The majority of Peace Corps volunteers worked on educational projects in developing countries. Others helped increase food production, build public works, and curb diseases, as did these volunteers, Rita Helmkamp and Ed Dennison, vaccinating a young Bolivian girl. President John F. Kennedy saw the Peace Corps volunteers, with their dedication to freedom, "overcoming the efforts of Mr. Khrushchev's missionaries who are dedicated to undermining that freedom." In the course of their missions, however, some volunteers came to question the single-minded focus of U.S. policy on anticommunism.

David S. Boyer © National Geographic Society.

liberation movements. These counterinsurgency forces, including the Army Green Berets and the Navy SEALs, constituted elite military corps trained to wage guerrilla warfare and equipped with the latest technology. They got their first test in Vietnam.

The Arms Race and the Nuclear Brink

The final piece of Kennedy's defense strategy was to strengthen American nuclear dominance. The president increased the number of U.S. nuclear weapons based in Europe from 2,500 to 7,200 and multiplied fivefold the supply of intercontinental ballistic missiles (ICBMs). Concerned that this buildup would enable the United States to launch a first strike and wipe out Soviet missile sites before they could respond, the Kremlin stepped up its own ICBM program. Thus began the most intense arms race in history.

The superpowers came perilously close to using their weapons of terror in 1962, when Khrushchev decided to install nuclear missiles in Cuba. On October 16, the CIA showed Kennedy aerial photographs of launching sites under construction there. Considering this an intolerable threat to the United States, the president met daily in secret with a small group of advisers to manage the ensuing thirteen-day Cuban missile crisis. On October 22, he announced to a television audience that the military was on full alert and that the navy would turn back any Soviet vessel suspected of carrying offensive missiles to Cuba. (Only later did the United States find out that offensive missiles were already there.) Kennedy warned Khrushchev that any attack launched from Cuba would trigger a full nuclear assault against the Soviet Union.

Cuban Missile Crisis, 1962

Projecting the appearance of toughness was paramount to Kennedy. Although the missiles did not "alter the strategic balance in fact," according to one of his aides, "that balance would have been substantially altered in appearance; and in matters of national will and world leadership such appearances contribute to reality." But if Kennedy was willing to risk nuclear war for appearances, he also exercised caution. He refused advice from the military to bomb the missile sites and instead undertook negotiations. On October 24, Russian ships carrying nuclear warheads toward Cuba suddenly turned back. When one ship crossed the blockade line, Kennedy matched Khrushchev's restraint, ordering the navy to follow rather than attempt to stop it.

While Americans experienced the cold war's most fearful days, Kennedy and Khrushchev negotiated an agreement. Ultimately, the Soviets removed the missiles and pledged not to introduce new offensive weapons into Cuba. The United

States promised not to invade the island. Secretly, Kennedy also agreed to remove U.S. missiles based in Turkey and aimed at the Soviet Union. The Cuban crisis led to Khrushchev's fall from power two years later, and Kennedy emerged triumphant. The image of an inexperienced president fumbling the Bay of Pigs invasion gave way to that of a brilliant leader combining firmness with restraint, bearing the United States through its "hour of maximum danger."

Having proved his toughness, Kennedy worked with Khrushchev to prevent future confrontations by installing a special "hot line" to speed top-level communication at critical moments. In a major speech at American University in June 1963, Kennedy called for a reexamination of cold war assumptions. Acknowledging the superpowers' immense differences, Kennedy stressed what they had in common: "We all breathe the same air. We all cherish our children's future and we are all mortal." Kennedy also called for an end to "a vicious cycle" in which "new weapons beget counterweapons." In August 1963, the United States, the Soviet Union, and Great Britain signed a limited test ban treaty, reducing the threat of radioactive fallout from nuclear testing and raising hopes for further superpower accord.

A Growing War in Vietnam

In his speech at American University Kennedy criticized the idea of "a Pax Americana enforced on the world by American weapons of war," but he increased the flow of those weapons into South Vietnam. He was determined to project an image of strength, and he well remembered the political blows to the Democratic Party when China was "lost" to communism in 1949. Holding firm in Vietnam would show the Soviets that sponsoring wars of national liberation would be "costly, dangerous, and doomed to failure."

Two major obstacles, however, stood in the way of this objective. First, the South Vietnamese insurgents—called Vietcong, short for Vietnam Cong-san ("Vietnamese Communists")—were an indigenous force whose initiative came from within, not from the Soviet Union or China. Because the Saigon government refused to hold the elections promised in the Geneva accords, the rebels saw no choice but to take up arms. Increasingly, Ho Chi Minh's Communist government in North Vietnam supplied them with weapons and soldiers.

The second problem lay in the South Vietnamese government and army (the Army of the Republic of Vietnam, or ARVN), which refused to satisfy the demands of the insurgents and could not defeat them militarily. Ngo Dinh Diem, South Vietnamese premier from 1954 to 1963, chose self-serving military leaders for their personal loyalty not their effectiveness. The government's corruption and repression of opponents alienated many South Vietnamese, not just the Communists.

North Vietnam intervened, making matters worse. In 1960, the Hanoi government established the National Liberation Front (NLF), composed of South Vietnamese rebels but directed by the northern army. In addition, Hanoi constructed a network of infiltration routes (called the "Ho Chi Minh Trail") in neighboring Laos and Cambodia, through which it sent people and supplies to help liberate the south (Map 29.2). Violence escalated between 1960 and 1963, bringing the Saigon government close to collapse.

When Kennedy took office, more than $1 billion of aid and seven hundred U.S. military advisers had failed to stabilize South Vietnam. He resisted pressure from some advisers for an all-out effort, but he increased the American commitment. At the same time he worried that each step was "like taking a drink.... The effect wears off, and you have to take another." By spring 1963, military aid doubled, and the nine thousand Americans serving in Vietnam as military advisers occasionally participated in actual combat. Although the United States extracted new promises of reform from Diem, the South Vietnamese government never made good on them.

American officials assumed that the military's superior technology and sheer power could win. Yet advanced weapons were ill suited to the guerrilla warfare practiced by the enemy, whose surprise attacks were designed to weaken support for the South Vietnamese government. In addition, U.S. weapons and strategy harmed the very people they were intended to save. Thousands of peasants were uprooted and resettled in "strategic hamlets," while those left in the countryside fell victim to bombs—containing the highly flammable substance napalm—dropped by the U.S.-backed ARVN to quell the Vietcong. In January 1962, U.S. planes began to spray herbicides to destroy the Vietcong's jungle hideouts and food supply.

In a coup launched on November 2, 1963, South Vietnamese military leaders brutally executed Premier Diem and his brother who headed the secret police. Kennedy expressed shock but indicated no change in policy. In a speech to be given on the day he was assassinated, he called

---

MAP 29.2   The Vietnam War, 1964–1975
The United States sent more than two million soldiers to Vietnam and spent more than $150 billion on the longest war in American history, but it was unable to prevent the unification of Vietnam under a Communist government.

U. S. and South Vietnamese troop movements

Major North Vietnamese supply routes into South Vietnam

Important battles or actions

Americans to their responsibilities as "the watchmen on the walls of world freedom." Referring specifically to Southeast Asia, his undelivered speech warned, "We dare not weary of the task." At his death, 16,000 Americans had served in Vietnam and 100 had died there.

> **REVIEW**   Why did Kennedy believe engagement in Vietnam was crucial to his foreign policy?

Lyndon Johnson's War against Communism

The cold war assumptions that dominated most of Kennedy's foreign policy persisted under his successor. Retaining Kennedy's key advisers, Lyndon Johnson continued the massive buildup of nuclear weapons and conventional and counterinsurgency forces. In 1965, when the South Vietnamese government approached collapse, Johnson made the fateful decisions to order U.S. troops into combat and initiate sustained bombing of the north. That same year, Johnson sent U.S. marines to the Dominican Republic to crush a leftist rebellion.

An All-Out Commitment in Vietnam

Having sent more military advisers, weapons, and economic aid to South Vietnam during his first year as president, in August 1964 Lyndon Johnson seized an opportunity to increase the pressure on North Vietnam. During their routine espionage in the Gulf of Tonkin off the coast of North Vietnam, two U.S. destroyers reported that North Vietnamese gunboats had fired on them on August 2 and 4 (see Map 29.2). Johnson quickly ordered air strikes on North Vietnamese torpedo bases and oil storage facilities, and he sought authority from Congress to take "all necessary measures to repel any armed attacks against the forces of the United States and to prevent further aggression." His portrayal of the situation covered up the uncertainty about whether the second attack had even occurred and the provocative U.S. actions of staging covert raids and operating close to the North Vietnamese coast. Congress supported Johnson's plan with the Gulf of Tonkin Resolution on August 7, 1964; just two senators voted no.

U.S. Involvement in Vietnam

1954 **May.** French colonial presence ends with Vietnamese victory at Dien Bien Phu.

July. Geneva accords establish temporary division of North and South Vietnam at the seventeenth parallel and provide for free elections.

September. United States joins with European, East Asian, and other nations to form the Southeast Asia Treaty Organization (SEATO).

Eisenhower administration begins to send weapons and military advisers to South Vietnam to bolster Diem government.

1955–1961 United States sends $8 million in aid to South Vietnamese army (ARVN) to support its struggle with North Vietnamese government.

1961–1963 Under Kennedy administration, military aid to South Vietnam doubles, and number of military advisers reaches 9,000.

1963 South Vietnamese military overthrows Diem's government.

1964 President Johnson uses Gulf of Tonkin incident to escalate the war.

1965 Johnson administration initiates Operation Rolling Thunder, intensifies bombing of North Vietnam.

1965–1967 Number of U.S. troops in Vietnam increases, reaching 543,000 in 1968, but U.S. and ARVN forces make only limited progress against the guerrilla forces, resulting in a stalemate.

1968 **January 30.** Tet Offensive causes widespread destruction and heavy casualties.

March 31. Johnson announces reduction in bombing of North Vietnam, plans for peace talks, and his decision not to run for another presidential term.

1969 Nixon administration initiates secret bombing of Cambodia, increases bombing of the North while reducing U.S. troops in the South, and pursues peace talks.

1970 Nixon orders joint U.S.- ARVN invasion of Cambodia.

1970–1971 U.S. troops in Vietnam decrease from 334,600 to 140,000.

1972 With peace talks stalled in December, Nixon administration orders the most devastating bombing of North Vietnam that would occur throughout the conflict.

1973 On January 27, the United States, North Vietnam, and South Vietnam sign formal accord in Paris marking end of U.S. involvement.

1975 North Vietnam launches a new offensive in South Vietnam, defeating ARVN. Vietcong troops occupy Saigon and rename it Ho Chi Minh City.

Johnson's tough stance only two months before the 1964 elections helped counter the charges made by his opponent, Arizona senator Barry Goldwater, that he was "soft on communism." Yet the president also presented himself as the peace candidate. When Goldwater proposed massive bombing of North Vietnam, Johnson as-

sured Americans that "we are not going to send American boys nine or ten thousand miles away from home to do what Asian boys ought to be doing for themselves."

Soon after winning reelection, however, Johnson did widen the war. He rejected peace overtures from North Vietnam, which insisted on American withdrawal and a coalition government in South Vietnam as steps toward ultimate unification of the country. Instead, in February 1965, he began Operation Rolling Thunder, a strategy of gradually intensified bombing of North Vietnam. Less than a month later, Johnson ordered the first U.S. combat troops to South Vietnam, and in July he shifted U.S. troops from defensive to offensive operations, dispatching 50,000 more soldiers. Those decisions, whose import was downplayed for Congress and the public, marked a critical turning point. Now it was genuinely America's war.

Preventing Another Castro in Latin America

Closer to home, Johnson faced perpetual problems in Latin America despite the efforts of the Alliance for Progress. Thirteen times during the 1960s, military coups toppled Latin American governments, and local insurgencies grew apace. The administration's response varied from case to case but centered on the determination to prevent any more Castro-type revolutions.

In 1964, riots erupted in the Panama Canal Zone, which the United States had seized and made a U.S. territory early in the century. Instigated by Panamanians who viewed the United States as a colonial power, the riots left four U.S. soldiers and more than twenty Panamanians dead. Johnson sent troops to quell the disturbance, but he also initiated negotiations that eventually led to the transfer of the canal to Panamanian authority in 2000.

Elsewhere, Johnson's Latin American policy generated new cries of "Yankee imperialism." In 1961, voters in the Dominican Republic ousted a long-standing dictator and elected a constitutional government headed by Juan Bosch, who was overthrown by a military coup two years later. In 1965, when Bosch supporters launched an uprising against the military government, Johnson sent more than 20,000 soldiers to take control of the island. A truce was arranged, and in 1966 Dominicans voted in a constitutional government.

This first outright show of Yankee force in Latin America in four decades damaged the administration at home and abroad. Although it had justified intervention on the grounds that Communists were among the rebels, it quickly became clear that they had played no significant role, and U.S. intervention kept the reform-oriented Boschists from returning to power. Moreover, the president had not consulted the Dominicans or the Organization of American States (OAS), to which the United States had pledged to respect national sovereignty in Latin America. Once the troops had landed in the Dominican Republic, Johnson asked for approval from the OAS, but Mexico, Chile, Venezuela, and other nations refused to grant it.

The Americanized War

The military success in the Dominican Republic no doubt encouraged the president to press on in Vietnam. During Operation Rolling Thunder from 1965 to early 1968, the United States gradually escalated attacks against the North Vietnamese and their Vietcong allies, endeavoring to break their will while avoiding provoking intervention by the Chinese, as they had done in Korea. Johnson himself scrutinized military plans, boasting, "They can't even bomb an outhouse without my approval."

Over the course of the war, U.S. pilots dropped 3.2 million tons of explosives, more than the United States had launched in all of World War II. Claiming monthly death tolls of more than 2,000 North Vietnamese, the intensive bombing nonetheless failed to dampen the Hanoi government's commitment. (See "Historical Question," page 766.) In the South, the United States rained down more than twice the tonnage of bombs dropped on North Vietnam.

General William Westmoreland's strategy of attrition was designed to search out and kill the Vietcong and North Vietnamese regular army. Because there was no battlefront as in previous wars, officials calculated progress not in territory seized but in "body counts" and "kill ratios"—the number of enemies killed relative to the cost in American and ARVN lives. According to U.S. army officer Colin Powell, who served two tours in Vietnam, "The Army desperately needed something to measure. What military objectives could we claim in this week's report? A hill? A valley? A hamlet? Rarely. Consequently, bodies became the mea-

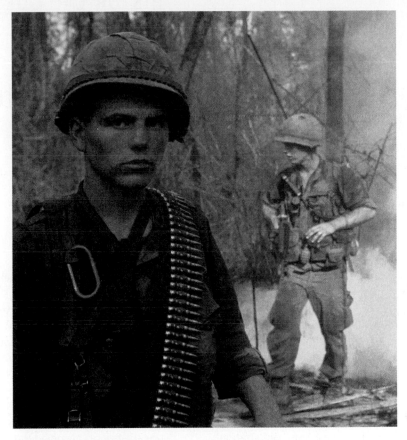

Vietnam: The War of the Young
The faces of these soldiers in the jungle near Hue in 1968 reflect the youth of the soldiers who fought the Vietnam War. Their average age was nineteen. When one young marine received his supplies, he wondered, "What did I need with shaving equipment? I was only seventeen. I didn't have hair under my arms, let alone my face." The youth of the soldiers intensified the emotional trauma felt by the military nurses who cared for them. One nurse remembered a dying soldier "in so much pain and so scared, asking for his mom." Another sobbed over a snapshot that fell out of a dying soldier's pocket: "It is a picture of the soldier and his girl—dressed for a prom."
Kyoichi Savada/Corbis.

sure." In this situation, American soldiers did not always distinguish between military combatants and civilians; according to Lieutenant Philip Caputo, the operating rule was "if it's dead and Vietnamese, it's VC [Vietcong]."

Teenagers fought the Vietnam War, in contrast to World War II, when the average soldier was twenty-six years old. Until the voting age dropped to eighteen in 1971, most soldiers, whose average age was nineteen, could not even vote for the officials who sent them to war. Men

Why Couldn't the United States Bomb Its Way to Victory in Vietnam?

World War II demonstrated the critical importance of airpower in modern war. According to the official U.S. study of strategic bombing during World War II, "No nation can long survive the free exploitation of air weapons over its homeland." In the Vietnam War, U.S. planes delivered even more explosives than they had in World War II. Why, then, did strategic bombing not bring victory in Vietnam?

"Our airpower did not fail us; it was the decision makers," asserted Admiral U. S. Grant Sharp, World War II veteran and commander in chief of the Pacific Command during the Vietnam War. Military officials welcomed President Johnson's order to begin bombing North Vietnam in February 1965 as a means to destroy the North's capacity and will to support the Communist insurgents in South Vietnam. But they chafed at Johnson's strategy of gradual escalation and the restrictions he imposed on Operation Rolling Thunder, the three-and-a-half-year bombing campaign. Military officials believed that the United States should have begun Operation Rolling Thunder with all-out massive bombing and continued until the devastation brought North Vietnam to its knees. Instead, they charged, civilian decision makers compelled the military to fight with

one hand tied behind its back. Their arguments echoed General Douglas MacArthur's criticism of Truman's policy during the Korean War—though these officials did not repeat MacArthur's insubordination.

Unlike military officials, who could single-mindedly focus on defeating the enemy, the president needed to balance military objectives against political considerations, and he found compelling reasons to limit the application of airpower. Recalling the Korean War, Johnson noted that "China is there on the [North Vietnamese] border with 700 million men," and he studiously avoided action that might provoke intervention by the Chinese, who now possessed nuclear weapons. Johnson's strategy also aimed to keep the Soviet Union out of the war, to avoid inflaming antiwar sentiment at home, and to avert international criticism of the United States.

Consequently, the president would not permit bombing of areas where high civilian casualties might result and areas near the Chinese border. He banned strikes on airfields and missile sites that were under construction and thus likely to contain Chinese or Soviet advisers, and he refused to mine North Vietnam's harbors, through which Soviet ships imported goods to North Vietnam. But Johnson did escalate the pres-

sure, increasing the intensity of the bombing fourfold by 1968. In all, Operation Rolling Thunder rained 643,000 tons of bombs on North Vietnam between 1965 and 1968.

Military leaders agreed with Johnson's desire to spare civilians. The Joint Chiefs of Staff never proposed, for example, strikes against a system of dikes and dams that could have disrupted food production and flooded Hanoi under twenty feet of water. Rather, they focused on destroying North Vietnam's industry and transportation system. Noncombatant casualties in North Vietnam contrasted sharply with those in World War II, when Anglo-American bombing of Dresden, Germany, alone took more than 35,000 civilian lives and the fire-bombing of Japan caused 330,000 civilian deaths. In three and a half years, Operation Rolling Thunder's bombing claimed an estimated 52,000 civilian lives.

The relatively low level of economic development in North Vietnam and the North Vietnamese government's ability to mobilize its citizens counteracted the military superiority of the United States. Sheer man-, woman-, and child-power compensated for the demolition of transportation sources, industry sites, and electric power plants. When bombs struck a rail line, civilians rushed with bicycles to unload a train's cargo, carry it beyond the break, and load it onto a second train. Three hundred thousand full-time workers and 200,000 farmers labored in their spare time to keep the Ho Chi Minh Trail usable in spite of heavy bombing. When bridges were destroyed, the North Vietnamese resorted to ferries and pontoons made from bamboo, and they rebuilt bridges slightly underwater to make

The B-52 Bomber
After 1965, B-52 bombers constantly filled the skies over Vietnam, and at times over Laos and Cambodia. Designed originally to deliver nuclear bombs, a single B-52 carried thirty tons of explosives. A mission of six planes could destroy an area one-half mile wide by three miles long. The B-52 flew too high to be heard on the ground, but its bombs hit with such force that they could kill people in underground shelters.
Co Rentmeester, *Life* magazine/TimePix/Getty.

them harder to detect from the air. They dispersed oil storage facilities and production centers throughout the countryside, and when bombs knocked out electric power plants, the Vietnamese turned to more than two thousand portable generators and used oil lamps and candles in their homes.

North Vietnam's military needs were relatively small, and officials found ample means to meet them. In 1967, North Vietnam had only about 55,000 soldiers in South Vietnam, and because they waged a guerrilla war with only sporadic fighting, the insurgents in the South did not require huge amounts of supplies.

Even after Communist forces in the South increased, the total nonfood needs of these soldiers were estimated at just one-fifth of what a single U.S. division required. What U.S. bombs destroyed, the North Vietnamese replaced with Chinese and Soviet imports. China provided 600,000 tons of rice in 1967 alone, and it supplied small arms and ammunition, vehicles, and other goods throughout the war. Competing with China for influence in North Vietnam and favor in the third world, the Soviets contributed tanks, fighter planes, surface-to-air missiles, and other sophisticated weapons. An estimated $2 billion of foreign aid

substantially curtailed the effect of Operation Rolling Thunder, and the Soviet-installed modern defense systems made the bombing more difficult and dangerous for U.S. pilots.

In July 1969, Seventh Air Force commander General William W. Momyer commented on Operation Rolling Thunder to the retiring air force chief of staff: "We had the force, skill, and intelligence, but our civilian betters wouldn't turn us loose." Johnson refused to turn the military loose because in addition to the goal he shared with the military—breaking Hanoi's ability to support insurgency in the South—he also wanted to keep China and the Soviet Union (and nuclear weapons) out of the war and to contain domestic and international criticism of U.S. policy. Whether a more devastating air war would have provoked Chinese or Soviet intervention can never be known.

Nor can we know whether all-out bombing of the North could have guaranteed an independent non-Communist government in the South. We do know that Johnson's military advisers imposed their own restraints, never recommending the wholesale attacks on civilians that took place in World War II. Short of decimating the civilian population, it is questionable whether more intense bombing could have completely halted North Vietnamese support for the Vietcong, given the nature of the North Vietnam economy, the determination and ingenuity of North Vietnam's people, and the plentiful assistance from China and the Soviet Union. Whether the strategic bombing that worked so well in a world war against major industrial powers could be effective in a third world guerrilla war remained in doubt after the Vietnam War.

of all classes had fought World War II, but Vietnam was the war of the poor and working class, who constituted about 80 percent of the troops. More privileged youth avoided the **draft** by using college deferments or family connections to get into the National Guard. Sent from Plainville, Kansas, to Vietnam in 1965, Mike Clodfelter could not recall "a single middle-class son of the town's businessmen, lawyers, doctors, or ranchers from my high school graduating class who experienced the Armageddon of our generation."

Because the United States did not undergo full mobilization for Vietnam, officials did not seek women's sacrifices for the war effort. Still, between 7,500 and 10,000 women served in Vietnam, the vast majority of them nurses. Although women were not allowed to carry weapons, they did come under enemy fire, and eight lost their lives. Many more struggled with their helplessness in the face of the dead and maimed bodies they tended. "When you finally saved a life," said Peggy DuVall, "you wondered what kind of life you had saved."

Early in the war, African Americans constituted 31 percent of combat troops, often choosing the military over the meager opportunities in the civilian economy. Special forces ranger Arthur E. Woodley Jr. recalled, "I was just what my country needed. A black patriot.... The only way I could possibly make it out of the ghetto was to be the best soldier I possibly could." Death rates among black soldiers were disproportionately high until 1966, when the military adjusted personnel assignments to achieve a better racial balance.

Troops faced extremely difficult conditions. Soldiers fought in thick jungles and swamps filled with leeches, in oppressive heat, rain, and humidity. Lieutenant Caputo remembered "weeks of expectant waiting and, at random intervals, conducting vicious manhunts through jungles and swamps where snipers harassed us constantly and booby traps cut us down one by one." Soldiers in previous wars had served "for the duration," but Vietnam warriors had one-year tours of duty. A commander called it "the worst personnel policy in history," because men had less incentive to fight near the end of their tour, wanting merely to stay alive and whole. The U.S. military inflicted great losses on the enemy, yet the war remained a stalemate. As infantryman Tim O'Brien reported, "We slay one of them, hit a mine, kill another, hit another mine.... And each piece of ground left behind is his [the enemy's] from the moment we are gone on our next hunt."

The South Vietnamese government itself was an obstacle to victory, even though in 1965 it settled into a period of stability led by Air Marshal Nguyen Cao Ky and General Nguyen Van Thieu. Graft and corruption continued to flourish, and Ky and Thieu failed to rally popular support. In the intensified fighting and inability to distinguish friend from foe, ARVN and American troops killed and wounded thousands of South Vietnamese civilians and destroyed their villages. By 1968, five million people, nearly 30 percent of the population, had become refugees. Huge infusions of American dollars and goods to the South Vietnamese government produced prostitution and rampant inflation, hurt local industries, and increased dependence on foreign aid.

> **REVIEW**   How did American troops serving in Vietnam differ from those who served in World War II, and how were their experiences different?

A Nation Polarized

Soon President Johnson was fighting a war on two fronts. Domestic opposition to the war in Southeast Asia grew significantly after 1965 as daily television broadcasts of the carnage of Vietnam made it the first "living-room war." Torn between his domestic critics and the military's clamor for more troops, in March 1968 Johnson announced restrictions on the bombing, a new effort at negotiations, and his decision not to pursue reelection. Throughout 1968, demonstrations, violence, and assassinations convulsed the nation. Vietnam took center stage in the election, and voters narrowly favored the Republican candidate, former vice president Richard Nixon, who promised to achieve "peace with honor."

The Widening War at Home

Johnson's authorization of Operation Rolling Thunder sparked a mass movement against the war. In April 1965, Students for a Democratic

Society (SDS) recruited 20,000 people for a demonstration in Washington, D.C., and SDS chapters sprang up on more than 300 college campuses. Thousands of young people joined campus protests against Reserve Officers Training Corps (ROTC) programs, CIA recruiters, manufacturers of war materials, and university research for the Department of Defense. Martin Luther King Jr. joined the antiwar movement and in 1967 rebuked the U.S. government as "the greatest purveyor of violence in the world today," calling opposition to the war "the privilege and burden of all of us who deem ourselves bound by allegiances and loyalties which are broader and deeper than nationalism." A new draft policy in 1967 ended deferments for postgraduate education and upped male students' stake in ending the war. In the spring of 1968, as many as one million college and high school students participated in a nationwide strike.

Antiwar sentiment also entered society's mainstream. The *New York Times* began questioning administration policy in 1965, and by 1968 media critics included the *Wall Street Journal, Life* magazine, and popular TV journalist Walter Cronkite. Clergy, businesspeople, scientists, and physicians formed their own groups to pressure Johnson to stop the bombing and start negotiations. Increasing numbers of prominent Democratic senators, including J. William Fulbright, George McGovern, and majority leader Mike Mansfield, urged Johnson to substitute negotiation for force.

Opposition to the war took diverse forms: letter-writing campaigns to officials, teach-ins on college campuses, mass marches, student strikes, withholding of federal taxes, draft card burnings, and civil disobedience against military centers and producers of war materials. Although the peace movement never claimed a majority of the population, it focused media attention on the war and severely limited the administration's options. The twenty-year-old cold war consensus had broken down.

Many would not fight in the war. The World Boxing Association stripped Muhammad Ali of his world heavyweight title when he refused to serve in what he called a "white man's war." More than 170,000 men who opposed the war on moral or religious grounds gained conscientious objector status and performed nonmilitary duties at home or in Vietnam. About 60,000 fled the country to escape the draft, and more than

Chemical Weapons
The U.S. military began to employ the tear gas CS (o-chlorobenzylidenemalononitrile) in grenades in Vietnam in 1964 and was discharging more than two million pounds of CS a year by 1969. It was used in operations such as the one shown here. The marine has just thrown a CS gas grenade into a tunnel to flush out the enemy and make the tunnel unusable for several months. Military planes also dropped or sprayed CS from the air to rid large areas of land of enemy forces. CS is usually not lethal but has incapacitating effects. Nonetheless, its use evoked criticism at home and from abroad. The *New York Times* noted that "no other country has employed such a weapon in recent warfare." The Political Committee of the UN General Assembly maintained that generally recognized rules of warfare prohibited the use of any chemical agents.
James H. Pickerell/Stock Connection; Ordinance Museum/Aberdeen Proving Grounds.

200,000 were accused of failing to register or other draft offenses.

Opponents of the war held far from unanimous views. Some wanted total withdrawal, insisting that their country had no right to interfere in another country and stressing the suffering of the Vietnamese people. A larger segment of antiwar sentiment reflected practical considerations—the belief that the war could not be won at a bearable cost. Not demanding withdrawal, those activists wanted Johnson to stop bombing North Vietnam and seek negotiations.

Working-class people were no more antiwar than other groups, but they recognized the class

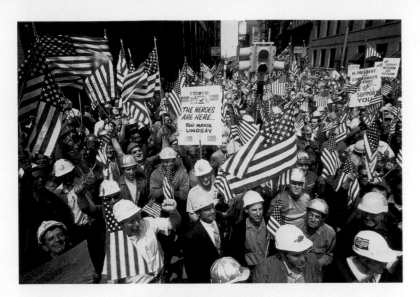

Pro-War Demonstrators
Advocates as well as opponents of the war in Vietnam took to the streets, as these New Yorkers did in support of the U.S. invasion of Cambodia in May 1970. Construction workers—called "hard hats"—and other union members marched with American flags and posters championing President Nixon's policies and blasting New York mayor John Lindsay for his antiwar position. Following the demonstration, sympathetic union leaders presented Nixon with an honorary hard hat.
Paul Fusco/Magnum Photos, Inc.

For more help analyzing this image, see the visual activity for this chapter in the Online Study Guide at **bedfordstmartins.com/roarkcompact.**

dimensions of the war and the public opposition to it. A firefighter whose son had died in Vietnam said bitterly, "It's people like us who give up our sons for the country. The business-people, they run the country and make money from it. The college types...go to Washington and tell the government what to do....But their sons don't end up in the swamps over there, in Vietnam."

The antiwar movement outraged millions of Americans who supported the war. Some members of the generation who had fought against Hitler could not understand younger men's refusal to support their government. They expressed their anger with bumper stickers that read "America: Love it or Leave it."

President Johnson tried a number of means to silence critics. He misled the public with optimistic statements about the war's progress. To avoid focusing attention on the war's costs, he eschewed price and wage controls to control inflation and delayed asking for a tax increase to pay for the war. Congress passed a 10 percent income-tax surcharge in June 1968, after Johnson promised to cut domestic spending. Great Society programs suffered, but the surcharge failed to reverse the inflationary surge. Johnson agonized over casualties, but he sought to discredit war critics by labeling them "nervous Nellies" or Communists and ordered the CIA to spy on peace advocates. Without the president's specific authorization, the FBI infiltrated the peace movement, disrupted its work, and spread false information about activists. Even the resort to illegal measures failed to subdue the opposition.

1968: Year of Upheaval

American society became increasingly polarized. On one side were the so-called **hawks**, who charged that the United States was fighting with one hand tied behind its back and called for intensification of the war. The **doves** wanted de-escalation or withdrawal. Most people were torn between weariness with the war and worry about abandoning the American commitment. As one woman said to a pollster, "I want to get out but I don't want to give up."

Grave doubts penetrated the administration itself in 1967. Secretary of Defense Robert McNamara, a principal architect of U.S. involvement, now believed that the North Vietnamese "won't quit no matter how much bombing we do." And he feared for the image of the United States, "the world's greatest superpower killing or seriously injuring 1,000 noncombatants a week, while trying to pound a tiny, backward nation into submission on an issue whose merits are hotly disputed." McNamara kept those views to himself until thirty years later, but in early 1968 he left the administration.

The critical turning point came with the Tet Offensive, which began on January 30, 1968. Just a few weeks after General Westmoreland had reported that "the enemy has been...compelled to disperse," the North Vietnamese and Vietcong attacked key cities and every major American base in South Vietnam. This was the biggest surprise of the war, and not simply because both sides had customarily observed a truce during the Vietnamese New Year holiday (called Tet). The offensive displayed the Communists' vitality and refusal to be intimidated by the presence of half a million American soldiers. Militarily, the enemy suffered a defeat, losing more than 30,000 men, ten times as many as ARVN and U.S. forces. Psychologically, however, Tet was devastating to the United States.

The Tet Offensive underscored the credibility gap between official statements and the war's actual progress. TV anchorman Walter Cronkite wondered, "What the hell is going on? I thought we were winning the war." The attacks created a million more South Vietnamese refugees as well as widespread destruction. Explaining how he had defended a village, a U.S. army official said, "We had to destroy the town to save it." The statement epitomized for more and more Americans the brutality and senselessness of the war.

In the aftermath of Tet, Johnson considered a request from Westmoreland for 200,000 more troops. He conferred with advisers in the Defense Department and an unofficial group of foreign policy experts who had been key architects of cold war policies for two decades. Dean Acheson, Truman's secretary of state, summarized their conclusion: "We can no longer do the job we set out to do in the time we have left and we must begin to take steps to disengage."

On March 31, 1968, Lyndon Johnson announced in a televised speech that the United States would reduce its bombing of North Vietnam and that he was prepared to begin peace talks. Then he made the stunning declaration that he would not run for reelection. The gradual escalation of the war was over, and military strategy shifted. The goal remained a non-Communist South Vietnam, but the United States would rely more heavily on the South Vietnamese ("Vietnamization") to achieve it.

Negotiations began in Paris in May 1968. But the United States would not agree to recognition of the Hanoi government's National Liberation Front, to a coalition government, or to American withdrawal. The North Vietnamese would agree to nothing less. Although the talks continued, so did the fighting.

Meanwhile, violence escalated at home. Some two hundred protests on college campuses occurred in the spring of 1968. In the bloodiest action, students occupied buildings at Columbia University in New York City, with demands related to the university's war-related research and to its treatment of African Americans. When negotiations failed, university officials called in the city police, who cleared the buildings, injuring

scores of demonstrators and arresting more than seven hundred. An ensuing student strike prematurely ended the academic year.

In June, two months after the murder of Martin Luther King Jr. and the ensuing riots, another assassination shook the nation. Senator Robert F. Kennedy, campaigning for the Democratic Party's nomination for president, was shot by a Palestinian Arab refugee who was outraged by Kennedy's support for Israel.

In August, protesters battled the police in Chicago, where the Democratic Party had convened to nominate its presidential ticket. Several thousand demonstrators came to the city, some to support the peace candidate Senator Eugene

Protest in Chicago
The worst violence surrounding the 1968 Democratic National Convention in Chicago came on August 28 when protesters decided to assemble in Grant Park and march to the convention site. Mayor Daley refused them a parade permit and dispatched the police and the Illinois National Guard to the park to keep them from marching. As protesters listened to speeches in the park, a group of young men tore down the American flag and replaced it with a red T-shirt, prompting the police to go after the demonstrators with their clubs. Later that night when activists tried to march to the convention, the police struck out widely and wildly, bloodying and teargassing many people who were not connected to the radicals.
Jeffrey Blankfort/Jeroboam.

McCarthy, others to act more aggressively. Many of the latter had been mobilized by the Youth International Party (Yippies), a splinter group of SDS. Its leaders, Abbie Hoffman and Jerry Rubin, urged protesters to demonstrate their hatred of the establishment by provoking the police.

Chicago's Mayor Richard J. Daley issued a ban on rallies and marches, ordered a curfew, and mobilized thousands of police. On August 25, demonstrators responded to police orders to disperse with insults and jeers, whereupon police attacked protesters with tear gas and clubs. Street battles continued for three days, culminating in a police riot on the night of August 28. Taunted by the crowd, the police used mace and nightsticks, clubbing not only those who had come to provoke violence but also reporters, peaceful demonstrators, and convention delegates.

The bloodshed in Chicago had little effect on the outcome of either major party's convention. Vice President Hubert H. Humphrey trounced peace candidate Eugene McCarthy by nearly three to one for the Democratic nomination. The Republican convention nominated former vice president Richard Nixon on the first ballot. For his running mate, Nixon chose Maryland governor Spiro T. Agnew, hoping to gather southern support.

A strong third party also entered the electoral scene. Former Alabama governor George C. Wallace, a staunch segregationist, ran on the ticket of the American Independent Party. Wallace appealed to Americans nationwide who believed that civil rights and antipoverty programs benefited the undeserving at their expense and who were outraged by assaults on traditional values by students and others. Nixon guardedly played on resentments that fueled the Wallace campaign, appealing to "the forgotten Americans, the non-shouters, the non-demonstrators."

The two major-party candidates differed little on the central issue of Vietnam. Nixon promised to "bring an honorable end" to the war but did not indicate how he would do it. Humphrey had strong reservations about U.S. policy in Vietnam, yet as vice president he wanted to avoid a break with Johnson. Johnson boosted Humphrey's campaign when he announced a halt to the bombing of North Vietnam, but it was not enough. With nearly ten million votes (13 percent of the total), the American Independent Party produced the strongest third-party finish since 1924. Nixon edged out Humphrey by just half a million popular votes, but garnered 301 electoral college votes to Humphrey's 191 and Wallace's 46. The Democrats lost a few seats in Congress but kept control of both houses.

The 1968 elections revealed deep cracks in the coalition that had kept the Democrats in power for most of the previous thirty years. Johnson's policies on race shattered a century of Democratic Party dominance in the South. Elsewhere, large numbers of blue-collar workers broke union ranks to vote for Wallace or Nixon, along with other groups associating the Democrats with racial turmoil, poverty programs, inflation, and America's impotence in Vietnam. These resentments would soon be mobilized into a resurging right in American politics (see chapter 30).

REVIEW   How did the Vietnam War shape the election of 1968?

Nixon, Détente, and the Search for Peace in Vietnam

Nixon assumed the presidency with ambitious foreign policy goals, hoping to make his mark on history by applying his broad understanding of international relations to a changing world. Diverging from Republican orthodoxy, his dramatic overtures to the Soviet Union and China reduced decades-old hostilities. Yet anticommunism remained central to American policy. In Latin America, Africa, and the Middle East, Nixon backed repressive regimes when the alternative suggested victories for the left. He aggressively pursued the war in Vietnam, expanding the conflict into Cambodia and Laos and ferociously bombing North Vietnam, but he was forced to settle for a peace without victory.

Moving toward Détente with the Soviet Union and China

In Nixon's view, the "rigid and bipolar world of the 1940s and 1950s" was giving way to "the fluidity of a new era of multi-lateral diplomacy." Working with Henry A. Kissinger, his national security assistant and key foreign policy adviser,

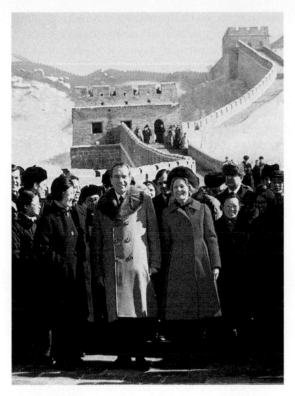

Nixon in China

"This was the week that changed the world," proclaimed President Richard M. Nixon in February 1972, emphasizing the stunning turnaround in relations with America's former enemy, the People's Republic of China. Nixon's trip was meticulously planned to dramatize the event on television and, aside from criticism from some conservatives, won overwhelming support from Americans. The Great Wall of China forms the setting for this photograph of Nixon and his wife Pat.

Nixon Presidential Materials Project, National Archives and Record Administration.

Nixon exploited the deterioration in Soviet-Chinese relations that had begun in the early 1960s. The two men believed that if these two nations checked each other's power, their threat to the United States would lessen; thus, according to Nixon, Soviet-Chinese hostility "served our purpose best if we maintained closer relations with each side than they did with each other."

Following two years of secret negotiations, in February 1972, Nixon became the nation's first president to set foot on Chinese soil—an astonishing act by a man who had climbed the political ladder as a fervent anti-Communist. Recognizing that his anti-Communist credentials were what enabled him to conduct this shift in U.S.-Chinese relations with no significant

domestic repercussions, Nixon remarked to Chinese leader Mao Zedong, "Those on the right can do what those on the left only talk about." Although the act was largely symbolic, cultural and scientific exchanges followed, and American manufacturers began to find markets in China— small steps in the process of **globalization** that would take giant strides in the 1990s (see chapter 31).

As Nixon and Kissinger hoped, the warming of U.S.-Chinese relations increased Soviet responsiveness to their strategy of **détente**, their term for easing conflict with the Soviet Union. Détente meant not abandoning containment but instead focusing on issues of common concern, such as arms control and trade. Containment would be achieved not only by military threat but also by ensuring that Soviet and Chinese stakes in a stable international order would restrain Soviet and Chinese leaders from precipitating crises. Nixon's goal was "a stronger healthy United States, Europe, Soviet Union, China, Japan, each balancing the other."

In May 1972, three months after his trip to China, Nixon visited Moscow, signing several agreements on trade and cooperation in science and space. Most significantly, Soviet and U.S. leaders concluded arms limitation treaties that had grown out of the Strategic Arms Limitation Talks (SALT) begun in 1969. Both sides agreed to limit antiballistic missile systems (ABMs) to two each. Giving up pursuit of a defense against nuclear weapons was a move of crucial importance, because it prevented either nation from building so secure an ABM defense against a nuclear attack that it would risk a first strike.

Gerald Ford, who became president when Nixon resigned in 1974 (see chapter 30), failed to sustain détente. The secrecy of the Nixon-Kissinger initiatives had alienated legislators, and some Democrats charged that détente ignored Soviet violations of human rights. Members of both parties worried that Soviet strength was overtaking that of the United States. In response, Congress derailed trade agreements with the Soviet Union, refusing economic favors unless the Soviets stopped their harsh treatment of internal dissidents and Jews.

Nonetheless, U.S., Soviet, and European leaders signed a historic agreement in 1975 in Helsinki, Finland, formally recognizing the post–World War II boundaries in Europe. The Helsinki accords outraged American **conservatives** because the accords accepted Soviet domination over countries in Eastern Europe—a condition that had triggered the cold war thirty years earlier.

Shoring Up Anticommunism in the Third World

Nixon promised in 1973, "The time has passed when America will make every other nation's conflict our own ... or presume to tell the people of other nations how to manage their own affairs." Yet in Vietnam and elsewhere Nixon and Kissinger continued to equate Marxism with a threat to U.S. interests and actively resisted social revolutions that might lead to communism.

Consequently, the Nixon administration helped to overthrow Salvador Allende, a self-proclaimed Marxist who was elected president of Chile in 1970. Since 1964, the Central Intelligence Agency (CIA) and U.S. corporations concerned about nationalization of their Chilean properties had assisted Allende's opponents. When Allende became president, Nixon ordered the CIA director to make the Chilean economy "scream" and thus destabilize his government. In 1973, with the help of the CIA, the Chilean military engineered a coup, killed Allende, and established a brutal dictatorship under General Augusto Pinochet.

In other parts of the world, too, the Nixon administration stood by repressive regimes, even those white minority governments that tyrannized blacks in southern Africa. The National Security Council assumed that the "whites are here to stay.... There is no hope for the blacks to gain the political rights they seek through violence, which will lead only to chaos and increased opportunities for Communists." In the Middle East, the United States sent secret, massive arms shipments to support

the shah of Iran's harsh regime, because Iran had enormous petroleum reserves and seemed a stable anti-Communist ally.

Like his predecessors, Nixon pursued a delicate balance between defending Israel's security and seeking the goodwill of Arab nations strategically and economically important to the United States. Conflict between Israel and the Arab nations had escalated into the Six-Day War in 1967, when Egypt massed troops on Israel's border and Israel launched a preemptive strike. Although Syria and Jordan joined the war on Egypt's side, Israel won a stunning victory, seizing territory that amounted to twice its original size. Israeli forces took control of the Sinai Peninsula and Gaza Strip from Egypt, the Golan Heights from Syria, and the West Bank from Jordan, which included the Arab sector of Jerusalem, a city sacred to Jews, Christians, and Muslims alike.

That decisive victory did not quell Middle Eastern turmoil. In October 1973, on the Jewish holiday Yom Kippur, Egypt and Syria surprised Israel with a full-scale attack. When the Nixon administration sided with Israel in the Yom Kippur War, Arab nations retaliated with an oil embargo that created severe shortages in the United States. After Israel repulsed the attack, Kissinger attempted to mediate between Israel and Arab nations, efforts that continued for the next three decades with only limited success. The Arab countries refused to recognize Israel's right to exist; Israel began to settle its citizens in territories occupied during the Six-Day War, and no solution could be found for the Palestinian refugees who had been displaced by the creation of Israel in the late 1940s. The simmering conflict contributed to anti-American sentiment among Arabs who viewed the United States as Israel's supporter.

Vietnam Becomes Nixon's War

"I'm not going to end up like LBJ, holed up in the White House afraid to show my face on the street," the new president asserted. "I'm going to stop that war. Fast." Nixon gradually withdrew U.S. ground troops,

Chile

[map of South America]

PACIFIC OCEAN

ATLANTIC OCEAN

GUYANA
SURINAME
FRENCH GUIANA
VENEZUELA
COLOMBIA
ECUADOR
PERU
BRAZIL
BOLIVIA
PARAGUAY
★ Santiago
CHILE
ARGENTINA
URUGUAY

0   250 500 miles
0   500 kilometers

Israeli Territorial Gains in the Six-Day War, 1967

LEBANON
Beirut
Damascus
Mediterranean Sea
Golan Heights
SYRIA
Tel Aviv
West Bank
Amman
Jerusalem
Gaza Strip
ISRAEL
Sinai
JORDAN
Gulf of Suez
EGYPT

☐ Israel before 1967
■ Land held by Israel since 1967
☐ Land held by Israel in 1967, returned to Egypt, 1973–1981

but he was no more willing than Eisenhower, Kennedy, or Johnson to allow South Vietnam to fall to the Communists. To Nixon and Kissinger, that goal was tied to the larger objective of maintaining American credibility. Regardless of the wisdom of the initial intervention, Kissinger asserted, "the commitment of 500,000 Americans has settled the importance of Vietnam. For what is involved now is confidence in American promises."

From 1969 to 1972, Nixon and Kissinger pursued a four-pronged approach. First, they tried to strengthen the South Vietnamese military and government. Second, to disarm the antiwar movement at home, Nixon gradually replaced U.S. forces with South Vietnamese soldiers and American technology and bombs. Third, Nixon and Kissinger negotiated with both North Vietnam and the Soviet Union. Fourth, the military applied enormous intensive bombing to persuade Hanoi to accept American terms at the bargaining table.

As part of the Vietnamization of the war, ARVN forces grew to over one million, and the South Vietnamese air force became the fourth largest in the world. U.S. advisers and funds also promoted land reform, village elections, and the building of schools, hospitals, and transportation facilities. Meanwhile, U.S. forces withdrew, decreasing from 543,000 in 1968 to 140,000 by the end of 1971. Despite reduced draft calls and casualties (from nearly 800 deaths a month in 1969 to 352 in 1970), more than 20,000 Americans perished in Vietnam during the last four years of the war.

In the spring of 1969, Nixon began a ferocious air war in Cambodia, carefully hiding it from Congress and the public for more than a year. Seeking to knock out North Vietnamese sanctuaries in Cambodia, the campaign dropped more than 100,000 tons of bombs but succeeded only in sending the North Vietnamese to other hiding places. To support a new, pro-Western Cambodian government installed through a military coup in 1970 and "to show the enemy that we were still serious about our commitment in Vietnam," in April 1970 Nixon ordered a joint U.S.-ARVN invasion of Cambodia.

U.S. Invasion of Cambodia, 1970

THAILAND
LAOS
CAMBODIA
Phnom Penh
SOUTH VIETNAM
Saigon

⟵ U.S. invasion of Cambodia

That order made Vietnam "Nixon's war" and provoked outrage at home. Nixon made a belligerent speech defending his move and emphasizing the importance of U.S. credibility: "If when the chips are down, the world's most powerful nation acts like a pitiful helpless giant, the forces of totalitarianism and anarchy will threaten free nations" everywhere. In response, more than 100,000 people protested in Washington, and students boycotted classes on hundreds of campuses. At Kent State University in Ohio, National Guard troops were dispatched after protesting students burned an old ROTC building. Then, at a peaceful rally there on May 4, 1970, nervous troops fired at students throwing rocks, killing four and wounding ten others. "They're starting to treat their own children like they treat us," commented a black woman in Harlem. In a confrontation at Jackson State College in Mississippi on May 14, police shot into a dormitory, killing two black students. In August, police used tear gas and clubs against Chicano antiwar protesters in Los Angeles.

In 1971, Vietnam veterans themselves became a visible part of the peace movement, the first men in U.S. history to protest a war in which they had fought. Veterans held a public investigation of "war crimes" in Vietnam, rallied in front of the Capitol, and cast away their war medals. In May 1971, veterans numbered among the 40,000 protesters who engaged in civil disobedience in an effort to shut down Washington. Officials made more than 12,000 arrests, which courts later ruled violations of protesters' rights.

After the spring of 1971 there were fewer massive demonstrations, but protest continued. Public attention focused on the court-martial of Lieutenant William Calley, which began in November 1970 and resulted in his conviction. During the trial, Americans learned that Calley's company had massacred more than 400 civilians in the hamlet of My Lai in March 1968. Among those murdered were children and women, an atrocity that the military had covered up for more than a year.

Administration policy suffered another blow in June 1971 with publication of the *Pentagon Papers*, a secret government study critical of U.S. policy in

Vietnam. Daniel Ellsberg, who had worked on the study and whose attempts to persuade officials of the war's futility met frustration, gave copies of the papers to the *New York Times*. After the Supreme Court overrode administration efforts to suppress publication as a violation of freedom of the press, their circulation heightened disillusionment with the war by casting doubts on the government's credibility. More than 60 percent of Americans polled in 1971 considered it a mistake to have sent American troops to Vietnam; 58 percent believed the war to be immoral.

Military morale sank in the last years of the war. Having been exposed to the antiwar movement at home, many of the remaining soldiers had less faith in the war than their predecessors had. Racial tensions among soldiers mounted, and many soldiers sought escape in illegal drugs. In a 1971 report, "The Collapse of the Armed Forces," a retired Marine Corps colonel described the lack of discipline: "Our army that now remains in Vietnam [is] near mutinous."

My Lai Massacre

When U.S. forces attacked My Lai in March 1968, they believed that the village was a Vietcong stronghold and expected a fierce fight. Even though they encountered no enemy forces, the men of Charlie Company systematically killed all the inhabitants, most of them old men, women, and children. Estimates put the death toll at more than 400 villagers. Twelve officers and enlisted men were charged with murder or assault to commit murder, but only one, First Lieutenant William Calley, was convicted. Though convicted of premeditated murder, Calley was paroled after serving less than four years in prison. This photograph of murdered villagers was taken by an army photographer.

Ron Haeberle/TimePix/Getty.

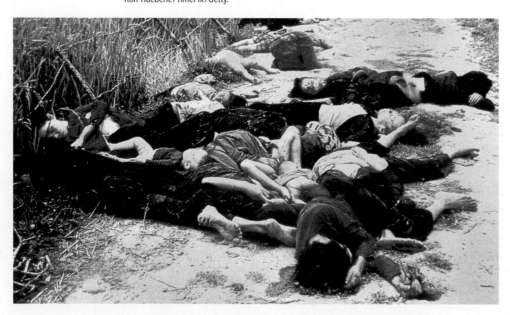

The Peace Accords and the Legacy of Defeat

Nixon and Kissinger continued to believe that intensive firepower could bring the North Vietnamese to their knees, and they combined that force with negotiation. In March 1972, responding to a strong North Vietnamese offensive, the United States resumed sustained bombing of the North, mined Haiphong and other harbors for the first time, and announced a naval blockade. With peace talks stalled, in December Nixon ordered the most devastating bombing of North Vietnam yet.

The intense bombing, called "jugular diplomacy" by Kissinger, was costly to both sides, but it brought renewed negotiations. On January 27, 1973, representatives of the United States, North Vietnam, the South Vietnamese government, and the Vietcong (now called the People's Revolutionary Government) signed a formal accord in Paris. The agreement required removal of all U.S. troops and military advisers but allowed North Vietnamese forces to remain. Both sides agreed to return prisoners of war. Nixon called the agreement "peace with honor," but it in fact allowed only a face-saving withdrawal for the United States.

Fighting resumed immediately among the Vietnamese. Nixon's efforts to support the South Vietnamese government, and indeed his ability to govern at all, were increasingly eroded by what came to be known as the Watergate scandals (discussed in chapter 30). In 1975, North Vietnam launched a new offensive and on May 1 occupied Saigon and renamed it Ho Chi Minh City to honor the Communist leader. Americans hastily evacuated along with 150,000 of their South Vietnamese allies.

During the four years it took Nixon to end the war, he expanded the conflict into Cambodia and Laos and launched massive bombing campaigns. Although increasing numbers of legislators criticized the war, Congress never denied the funds to fight it and never rescinded the Gulf of Tonkin Resolution. Only after the peace accords did the legislative branch stiffen its constitutional authority over the making of war, passing the War Powers Act in November 1973. The law required the president to report to Congress within forty-eight hours of deploying military forces abroad. If Congress failed to endorse the president's action within sixty days, the troops would have to be withdrawn.

The dire predictions of four presidents that a Communist victory in South Vietnam would set the dominoes cascading did not materialize. Although Vietnam, Laos, and Cambodia all fell within the Communist camp in the spring of 1975, Thailand, Burma, Malaysia, and the rest of Southeast Asia did not. When China and Vietnam reverted to their historically hostile relationship, the myth of a monolithic Communist power overrunning Asia evaporated.

"We would not return to cheering crowds, parades, and the pealing of great cathedral bells," wrote Philip Caputo. The failure of the United States to win the Vietnam War, lack of strong support for the war at home, and its character as a guerrilla war denied veterans the traditional homecoming of returning warriors. Veterans themselves expressed two kinds of reactions to the defeat. Many believed in the war's purposes and felt betrayed by the government for not letting them and their now-dead comrades win it. Others blamed the government for sacrificing the nation's youth in an immoral or useless war, expressing their sense of the war's futility in the way they referred to a comrade's death: He was "wasted." Sometimes identifying with the Vietnamese more than with their white comrades, veterans belonging to minority groups had more reason to doubt the nobility of their purpose. A Native American soldier assigned to resettle Vietnamese civilians found it to be "just like when they moved us to the rez [reservation]. We shouldn't have done that."

Because the Vietnam War was a civil, guerrilla war, combat was especially brutal (Table 29.1). The terrors of conventional warfare were multiplied, and so were the motivations to commit atrocities. The massacre at My Lai was only the most publicized war crime. To demonstrate the immorality of the war, peace advocates stressed the atrocities, contributing to a distorted

TABLE 29.1	VIETNAM WAR CASUALTIES	
United States		
Killed in action		47,382
Wounded		153,303
Died, noncombat		1,811
Missing, captured		10,753
South Vietnam		
Killed in action		110,357
Military wounded		499,026
Civilians killed		415,000
Civilians wounded		913,000
Communist Regulars and Guerrillas		
Killed in action		666,000

Source: U.S. Department of Defense.

image of the Vietnam War veteran as dehumanized and violent.

Most veterans came home to public neglect, while some faced harassment from antiwar activists who did not distinguish the war from the warriors. A veteran remembered the "feelings of rejection and scorn that a bunch of depressed and confused young men experienced when they returned home from doing what their country told them to do." Government benefits were less generous to Vietnam War veterans than they had been to those of the past two wars. Yet two-thirds of Vietnam veterans said that they would serve again, and most veterans readjusted well to civilian life.

Nonetheless, some suffered long after the war ended. The Veterans Administration (VA) estimated that nearly one-sixth of the three million veterans suffered from post-traumatic stress disorder, with its symptoms of fear, recurring nightmares, feelings of guilt and shame, violence, drug and alcohol abuse, and suicidal tendencies. Thirty years after performing army intelligence work in Saigon, Doris Allen "still hit the floor sometimes when I hear loud bangs." In the late 1970s, many of those who had served in Vietnam began to produce deformed children and fell ill themselves with cancer, severe skin disorders, and other ailments. Veterans claimed a link between these illnesses and Agent Orange, an herbicide that contained the deadly poison dioxin, which the military had sprayed by the millions of gallons over Vietnam, but not until 1991 did Congress provide assistance to veterans with diseases linked to the poison.

By then the climate had shifted. The war began to enter the realm of popular culture with novels, TV shows, and hit movies depicting a broad range of military experience—from soldiers reduced to brutality to men and women serving with courage and integrity. The incorporation of the Vietnam War into the collective experience was symbolized most dramatically in the Vietnam Veterans Memorial unveiled in Washington, D.C., in November 1982. In an article describing the memorial's dedication, a Vietnam combat veteran spoke to and for his former comrades: "Welcome home. The war is over."

> **REVIEW** How did Nixon try to bring American involvement in Vietnam to a close?

Conclusion: An Unwinnable War

Vietnam was America's longest war. The United States spent $150 billion and sent 2.6 million young men and women to Vietnam. Of those, 58,000 never returned, and 150,000 suffered serious injury. The war shattered consensus at home, increased presidential power at the expense of congressional authority and public accountability, and contributed to the downfall of two presidents.

Even as Nixon and Kissinger took steps to ease cold war tensions with the major Communist powers, the Soviet Union and China (who were also the main suppliers of the North Vietnamese), they also acted vigorously throughout the third world to install or prop up anticommunist governments. They embraced their predecessors' commitment to South Vietnam, because they believed that to do otherwise would threaten American credibility and make the United States appear weak. Defeat in Vietnam did not make the United States the "pitiful helpless giant" predicted by Nixon, but it did mark the relative decline of U.S. power and the impossibility of containment on a global scale.

One of the constraints on U.S. power was the tenacity of revolutionary movements determined to achieve national independence. Marine lieutenant Philip Caputo recalled the surprise at discovering "that the men we had scorned as peasant guerrillas were, in fact, a lethal, determined enemy." Overestimating the effectiveness of American technological superiority, U.S. officials badly underestimated the sacrifices that the enemy was willing to make and failed to realize how easily the United States could be perceived as a colonial intruder.

A second constraint on Eisenhower, Kennedy, Johnson, and Nixon was their resolve to avoid a major confrontation with the Soviet Union or China. For Johnson, who conducted the largest escalation of the war, caution was especially critical so as not to provoke direct intervention by the Communist superpowers. After China exploded its first atomic bomb in 1964, the potential heightened for the Vietnam conflict to escalate into worldwide disaster.

Third, in Vietnam the United States sought to prop up an extremely weak ally. The South Vietnamese government never won popular support, and the intense devastation the war brought to civilians only made things worse. Short of taking over the South Vietnamese government and military, the United States could do little to strengthen South Vietnam's ability to resist communism.

Finally, domestic opposition to the war, which by 1968 included significant portions of mainstream America, constrained the options of Johnson and Nixon. As the war dragged on, with increasing American casualties and growing evidence of the damage being inflicted on innocent Vietnamese, more and more civilians wearied of the conflict. Even some who had fought the war joined the movement, including Philip Caputo, who sent his campaign ribbons and a bitter letter of protest to the White House. In 1973, Nixon and Kissinger bowed to the resolution of the enemy and the limitations of U.S. power. As the war wound down, passions surrounding it contributed to a rising conservative movement that would substantially alter the post–World War II political order.

Suggestions for Further Reading

Philip Caputo, *A Rumor of War* (1977). A gripping narrative of an infantry officer's experiences in Vietnam in 1965 and 1966.

Charles DeBenedetti, with Charles Chatfield, *An American Ordeal: The Antiwar Movement in the Vietnam Era* (1990). A comprehensive account of antiwar protest.

Aleksandr Fursenko and Timothy J. Naftali, *One Hell of a Gamble: The Secret History of the Cuban Missile Crisis* (1998). A history of the Cuban missile crisis jointly authored by a U.S. and a Soviet historian.

Elizabeth Cobbs Hoffman, *All You Need Is Love: The Peace Corps and the Spirit of the 1960s* (1998). An engaging account of the policy behind the Peace Corps, its impact, and the experiences of volunteers.

A. J. Langguth, *Our Vietnam/Nuoc Viet Ta: A History of the War, 1954–1975* (2000). A compelling narrative of the entire war by a former journalist.

Walter A. McDougall, *The Heavens and the Earth: A Political History of the Space Age* (1985; reprint, 1997). A Pulitzer Prize–winning history of the space race.

▶ **For more books about topics in this chapter,** see the Online Study Guide at bedfordstmartins.com/roarkcompact.

▶ **For additional firsthand accounts of this period,** see Chapter 29 in Michael Johnson, ed., *Reading the American Past,* Third Edition.

▶ **For Web sites and documents related to topics and places in this chapter,** see "HistoryLinks," "DocLinks," and "PlaceLinks" at bedfordstmartins.com/roarkcompact.

REVIEWING THE CHAPTER

Follow these steps to review and strengthen your understanding of the chapter.

STEP 1: *Study the **Key Terms** and **Timeline** to identify the significance of each item listed.*

STEP 2: *Answer the **Review Questions** drawing on key terms and dates to support your answers.*

STEP 3: *Drawing on the Key Terms, Timeline, and Review Questions, answer the broader **Making Connections** questions.*

KEY TERMS

Who

John F. Kennedy (p. 758)
Nikita Khrushchev (p. 759)
Fidel Castro (p. 759)
Ho Chi Minh (p. 762)
Ngo Dinh Diem (p. 762)
Lyndon B. Johnson (p. 763)
William Westmoreland (p. 765)
Robert McNamara (p. 770)
Martin Luther King Jr. (p. 771)
Robert F. Kennedy (p. 771)
Eugene McCarthy (p. 771)
Hubert H. Humphrey (p. 772)
George C. Wallace (p. 772)
Richard M. Nixon (p. 772)
Henry A. Kissinger (p. 772)
Mao Zedong (p. 773)
Gerald Ford (p. 773)

Salvador Allende (p. 774)
Augusto Pinochet (p. 774)

What

Bay of Pigs (p. 759)
Apollo program (p. 760)
Berlin Wall (p. 760)
Alliance for Progress (p. 760)
Agency for International Development (AID) (p. 760)
Peace Corps (p. 760)
Cuban missile crisis (p. 761)
Vietcong (p. 762)
Army of the Republic of Vietnam (ARVN) (p. 762)
National Liberation Front (NLF) (p. 762)
"Ho Chi Minh Trail" (p. 762)
Gulf of Tonkin Resolution (p. 763)

Operation Rolling Thunder (p. 764)
Students for a Democratic Society (SDS) (p. 768)
Tet Offensive (p. 770)
Youth International Party (Yippies) (p. 772)
American Independent Party (p. 772)
Strategic Arms Limitation Talks (SALT) (p. 773)
Helsinki accords (p. 773)
Six-Day War (p. 774)
Yom Kippur War (p. 774)
Kent State (p. 775)
Jackson State (p. 775)
My Lai (p. 775)
Pentagon Papers (p. 775)
War Powers Act (p. 777)
Agent Orange (p. 777)

TIMELINE

1961 • Bay of Pigs invasion.
• Berlin Wall erected.
• Military aid to South Vietnam increases.
• Alliance for Progress established.
• Peace Corps created.

    1962 • Cuban missile crisis.

        1963 • Limited nuclear test ban treaty signed.

            1964 • Anti-American rioting in Panama Canal Zone.
• Gulf of Tonkin Resolution.

                1965 • First major demonstration against Vietnam War.
• Operation Rolling Thunder begins.
• Johnson increases U.S. troops in Vietnam.
• U.S. troops invade Dominican Republic.

                    1968 • Hundreds of thousands of Americans demonstrate against Vietnam War.
• Tet Offensive.
• Johnson decides not to seek second term.
• Police and protesters clash near Democratic convention.
• Republican Richard Nixon elected president.

REVIEW QUESTIONS

1. Why did Kennedy believe engagement in Vietnam was crucial to his foreign policy? (pp. 758–63)

2. How did American troops serving in Vietnam differ from those who served in World War II, and how were their experiences different? (pp. 763–68)

3. How did the Vietnam War shape the election of 1968? (pp. 768–72)

4. How did Nixon try to bring American involvement in Vietnam to a close? (pp. 772–78)

MAKING CONNECTIONS

1. Cuba featured prominently in the most dramatic foreign policy actions of Kennedy's administration. Citing specific events, discuss why Cuba was an area of great concern to the administration. How did Cuba figure into Kennedy's cold war policies? Were his actions in regard to Cuba effective?

2. Explain the Gulf of Tonkin incident and its significance to American foreign policy. How did President Lyndon Johnson respond to the incident? What considerations, domestic and international, contributed to his course of action?

3. The United States' engagement in Vietnam divided the nation. Discuss the range of American responses to the war. How did they change over time? How did domestic political concerns shape response to the war? How did the war shape domestic politics in the 1960s and early 1970s?

4. What was détente, and how did it affect the United States' cold war foreign policy? What were its achievements and limitations? In your answer, discuss how Nixon's approach to communism built on, and departed from, the previous two administrations' approaches.

▶ FOR PRACTICE QUIZZES, A CUSTOMIZED STUDY PLAN, AND OTHER STUDY TOOLS, see the Online Study Guide at bedfordstmartins.com/roarkcompact.

1969 • American astronauts land on the moon.
• Nixon orders secret bombing of Cambodia.

    1970 • Nixon orders invasion of Cambodia.
       • Students killed during protests at Kent State and Jackson State.

        1971 • *New York Times* publishes *Pentagon Papers.*

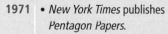

           1972 • Nixon becomes first U.S. president to visit China.
             • Nixon visits Moscow to sign arms limitation treaties with Soviets.

               1973 • Paris peace accords.
                 • War Powers Act.
                 • CIA-backed military coup in Chile.
                 • Arab oil embargo.

                    1975 • North Vietnam takes over South Vietnam, ending the war.
                      • Helsinki accords.

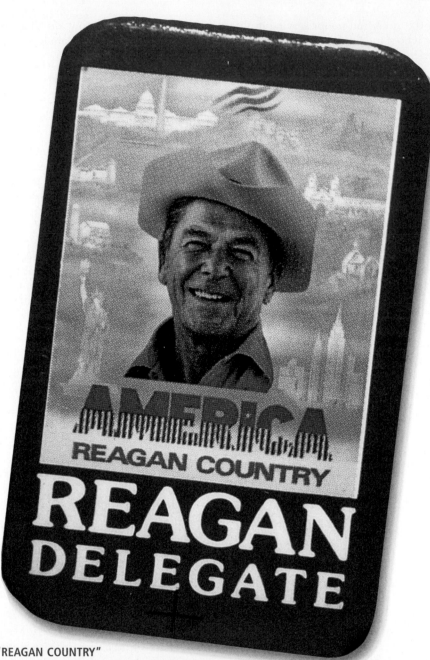

MAKING AMERICA "REAGAN COUNTRY"

This delegate badge from the 1980 Republican National Convention played on themes that would characterize Ronald Reagan's presidential campaigns and the politics and policies of the 1980s. Just as the badge appealed to patriotic sentiments with the flag, the Statue of Liberty, and the space program, Reagan encouraged Americans to take pride in their nation and celebrate its achievements instead of focusing on its shortcomings. His image as a cowboy brought to mind some of the movies he had acted in and his favorite recreation—working on his ranch in California—as well as the independence and rugged individualism of the West, where he had made his home since the 1940s. The West produced a key element in the surge of conservatism that ensured Reagan's victory in 1980, shaped his administration's antigovernment, anti-Communist agenda, and helped reverse the liberal direction that national politics had taken in the 1960s.

National Museum of American History, Smithsonian Institution, Behring Center.

America Moves to the Right

1969–1989

PHYLLIS SCHLAFLY CONSIDERED THE DAY that **conservative** Republican Barry Goldwater spoke to the National Federation of Republican Women in 1963 "one of the most exciting days of my life." Like Goldwater, she opposed the moderate Republicanism of the Eisenhower administration and current party leadership. Both Schlafly and Goldwater wanted the United States to go beyond merely containing **communism** and to eliminate that threat entirely. They also wanted to cut back the government in Washington, especially its role in providing social welfare and enforcing civil rights. Disappointed by Goldwater's loss to Lyndon Johnson in 1964, Schlafly nevertheless took heart in the conservatives' ability to engineer his nomination. She capitalized on the policy innovations and turmoil of the 1960s, adding new issues to the conservative agenda and helping to build a grassroots movement on the right that would redefine the Republican Party and American politics into the twenty-first century.

Although Schlafly was politically active and a prolific writer on behalf of conservatism, she stressed her devotion to the home. As a woman married to an attorney whose anticommunism and antigovernment passions equaled hers and the mother of six children, Schlafly claimed, "I don't think there's anything as much fun as taking care of a baby." She asserted she would "rather scrub bathroom floors" than write political articles. Yet while insisting that caring for home and family was women's most important career, Schlafly spent much of her time in politics—writing, speaking, testifying before legislative committees, and losing two bids for Congress in her heavily Democratic district in Illinois. Her book, *A Choice Not an Echo*, which she self-published in 1964, excoriated the control of the Republican Party by a **liberal** elite eastern establishment, pushed Barry Goldwater as "the obvious choice" for president, and sold over a million copies. Beginning in 1967, she also published *The Phyllis Schlafly Report*, a monthly newsletter dealing with current political issues. Throughout the 1950s and 1960s, Schlafly focused on the need for stronger efforts to combat communism at home and abroad, a more powerful military, and a less active government in domestic affairs—all traditional conservative goals.

In the 1970s, Schlafly began to address new issues, including **feminism** and the Equal Rights Amendment, abortion, gay rights, busing for racial integration, and religion in the schools. Her positions resonated with many Americans fed up with the expansion of government and the challenges to authority and tradition that seemed to define the 1960s. Moreover, the votes

The Phyllis Schlafly Report

VOL. 5, NO. 10, SECTION 2   Box 618, ALTON, ILLINOIS 62002   MAY, 1972

The Fraud Called The Equal Rights Amendment

If there ever was an example of how a tiny minority can cram its views down the throats of the majority, it is the Equal Rights Amendment, called ERA. A noisy claque of women's lib agitators rammed ERA through Congress, intimidating the men into voting for it so they would not be labeled "anti-woman."

The ERA passed Congress with big majorities on March 22, 1972 and was sent to the states for ratification. When it is ratified by 38 states, it will become the law of the land. Within two hours of Senate passage, Hawaii ratified it. New Hampshire and Nebraska, both anxious to be second, rushed their approval the next day. Then in steady succession came Iowa, Idaho, Delaware, Kansas, Texas, Maryland, Tennessee, Alaska, Rhode Island, and New Jersey. As this goes to press, 13 states have ratified it and others are on the verge of doing so.

Three states have rejected it: Oklahoma, Vermont and Connecticut.

What is ERA? The Amendment reads: "Equality of rights under the law shall not be denied or abridged by the United States or by any state on account of sex."

Does that sound good? Don't kid yourself. This innocuous-sounding amendment will take away far more important rights than it will ever give. This was made abundantly clear by the debate in Congress. Senator Sam Ervin (D., N.C.) called it "the most drastic measure in Senate history." He proved this by putting into the *Congressional Record* an article from the *Yale Law Journal* of April 1971.

The importance of this *Yale Law Journal* article is that both the proponents and the opponents of ERA agree that it is an accurate analysis of the consequences of ERA. Congresswoman Martha Griffiths, a leading proponent of ERA, sent a copy of this article to every member of Congress, stating that "It will understand the purposes and effect Rights Amendment.... The arti ERA will work in

the most important of all women's rights.

"In all states husbands are primarily liable for the support of their wives and children.... The child support sections of the criminal nonsupport laws ... could not be sustained where only the male is liable for support." (YLJ, pp. 944-945)

"The Equal Rights Amendment would bar a state from imposing greater liability for support on a husband than on a wife merely because of his sex." (YLJ, p. 945)

"Like the duty of support during marriage and the obligation to pay alimony in the case of separation or divorce, nonsupport would have to be eliminated as a ground for divorce against husbands only...." (YLJ, p. 951)

"The Equal Rights Amendment would not require that alimony be abolished but only that it be available equally to husbands and wives." (YLJ, p. 952)

2. ERA will wipe out the laws which protect only women against sex crimes such as rape.

"Courts faced with criminal laws which do not apply equally to men and women would be likely to invalidate the laws rather than extending or rewriting them to apply to women and men alike." (YLJ, p. 966)

"Seduction laws, statutory rape laws, laws prohibiting obscene language in the presence of women, prostitution and 'manifest danger' laws ... The Equal Rights Amendment would not permit such laws, which base their sex discriminatory classification on social stereotypes." (YLJ, p. 954)

"The statutory rape laws, which punish men for having sexual intercourse with any woman under an age specified by law ... suffer from a under the Equal Rights Amendmen

"To

The Phyllis Schlafly Report

Phyllis Schlafly's monthly newsletter for members of her conservative Eagle Forum began in 1967 with articles attacking federal social programs and calling for stronger measures and weapons to fight the cold war against communism. When Congress passed the Equal Rights Amendment in 1972, the *Report* began to add antifeminism and other concerns of the New Right to its agenda, including opposition to abortion rights, to sex education in the schools, and to protections for gays and lesbians. Schlafly's attacks on feminism appealed to many people; subscribers to her newsletter numbered more than 35,000 in the mid-1970s. The feminist leader Betty Friedan told Schlafly, "I consider you a traitor to your sex. I consider you an Aunt Tom." Courtesy of Phyllis Schlafly.

---

of those Americans began to reshape American politics—in Richard Nixon's victories in the presidential elections of 1968 and 1972; in the presidency of Jimmy Carter, whose policies stood substantially to the right of the Democratic administrations of the 1960s; and in conservative Ronald Reagan's capture of the Republican Party, the presidency, and the political agenda in 1980.

Although Richard Nixon did not embrace the entire conservative agenda, he sought to make the Republicans the dominant party by ap-

pealing to disaffected blue-collar and southern white Democrats. Nixon resigned the presidency in disgrace in 1974, and his Republican successor, Gerald Ford, occupied the Oval Office for little more than two years; but the shift of the political spectrum to the right continued even when the Democrats captured the White House in 1976. Antigovernment sentiment grew out of the deceptions of the Johnson administration, Nixon's abuse of presidential powers, and the inability of Presidents Ford and Carter to resolve domestic and foreign crises. As Americans saw surging unemployment and inflation decimate their incomes, many lost confidence in government and claimed that their taxes were too high.

In 1980, Phyllis Schlafly saw her call for "a choice, not an echo" realized when Ronald Reagan won the presidency. Cutting taxes and government regulations, attacking social programs, expanding the nation's military capacity, and putting pressure on the Soviet Union and communism in the **third world**, Reagan addressed the hopes of traditional conservatives. Like Schlafly, he also championed the concerns of the **New Right**, opposing abortion and sexual permissiveness and supporting a larger role for religion in public life. Reagan's goals encountered resistance from feminists, civil rights groups, environmentalists, and others who fought to keep what they had won in the 1960s. His administration failed to enact the entire conservative agenda, enormously increased the national debt, and engaged in illegal activities to thwart communism in Latin America. Nevertheless, Reagan's popularity helped send his vice president, George H. W. Bush, to the White House at the end of his second term. And Reagan's determined optimism and spirited leadership contributed to a revival in national pride and confidence.

Nixon and the Rise of Postwar Conservatism

As we saw in chapter 28, Nixon acquiesced in the continuation of most **Great Society** programs and even approved pathbreaking new measures concerning the environment and minority and women's rights. Yet his public rhetoric and certain of his actions signaled the country's rightward move in both politics and sentiment. During Nixon's presidency, a new strand of conservatism joined the older movement that focused on anticommunism, a strong national defense, and a limited role for the federal government in domestic affairs. New conservatives, whom Phyllis Schlafly helped mobilize, wanted to restore what they considered traditional moral values by increasing the presence of Christianity in public life and opposing feminism, abortion, homosexuality, and other challenges to older sexual morals.

Emergence of a Grassroots Movement

Although Lyndon Johnson's landslide victory over Barry Goldwater in 1964 seemed to signify liberalism triumphant, the election results actually concealed a rising conservative movement. Defining his purpose as "enlarging freedom at home and safeguarding it from the forces of tyranny abroad," Goldwater, an Arizona senator, echoed the ideas of conservative intellectuals who argued that government intrusions into economic life hindered prosperity, stifled personal responsibility, and interfered with individuals' rights to determine their own values. Conservatives assailed big government in domestic affairs but demanded a strong military to eradicate "Godless communism."

A growing grassroots movement, vigorous especially in the South and West and including middle-class suburban women and men, members of the rabidly anti-Communist John Birch Society, and college students in the new Young Americans for Freedom, had enabled Goldwater to win the nomination. They did not give up when he lost the election. Margaret Minek, a community organizer for Goldwater, insisted, "We have a ... flame ... burning and the energy it gives off needs to be utilized." Newly energized conservatives like Minek in California contributed to Ronald Reagan's defeat of the incumbent liberal governor, Edmund Brown, in 1966, another sign of the rising strength of the right. Reagan linked Brown with the Watts riot and student disruptions at the University of California at Berkeley, exploiting popular fears about rising taxes, student challenges to authority, and black demands for

justice. He claimed in one campaign speech that "if an individual wants to discriminate against Negroes or others in selling or renting his house he has a right to do so."

Grassroots conservatism was not limited to the West and South, but a number of **Sun Belt** characteristics made it especially strong in places such as Orange County, California; Dallas, Texas; Scottsdale, Arizona; and Jefferson Parish, Louisiana. Areas that hosted strong conservative movements contained relatively homogeneous, skilled, and affluent populations as well as military bases and defense production facilities. The West harbored a long-standing tradition of **Protestant** morality, individualism, and opposition to interference by a remote federal government. That tradition continued with the emergence of the New Right, even though it was hardly consistent with the Sun Belt's economic dependence on military and defense spending.

The South shared the West's antipathy to the federal government, but there hostility to racial change was much more central to its new conservatism. After signing the Civil Rights Act of 1964, President Lyndon Johnson remarked to a friend, "I think we just delivered the South to the Republican Party." Indeed, Barry Goldwater carried five southern states in 1964.

Grassroots movements emerged around a number of issues that conservatives believed marked the "moral decline" of their nation. For example, in 1968, Eleanor Howe mobilized her neighbors to eliminate sex education from the schools in Anaheim, California, when she examined the curriculum and found that "nothing depicted my values.... It wasn't so much the information. It was the shift in values." In 1970, Alice Moore launched a campaign in Charleston, West Virginia, against a sex education curriculum that she found anti-American and anti-Christian and based on an "atheistic and relativistic view of morality." The Warren Court's decisions on such issues as school prayer, obscenity, and birth control also galvanized conservatives to restore "traditional values" to the nation.

Nixon Courts the Right

In the 1968 campaign, Nixon had exploited hostility to black protest and new civil rights policies. As president, he used this "southern strategy" to make further inroads into traditional Democratic strongholds in the 1972 election, hoping to win northern as well as southern votes.

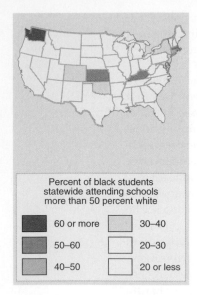

Percent of black students statewide attending schools more than 50 percent white

60 or more	30–40
50–60	20–30
40–50	20 or less

Integration of Public Schools, 1968

The Nixon administration reluctantly enforced court orders to achieve high degrees of integration in southern schools, but it resisted efforts to deal with segregation outside the South. In northern and western cities where residential patterns had resulted in de facto segregation, half of all African American children attended nearly all-black schools. After courts began to order the transfer of students between schools in white and black neighborhoods to achieve desegregation, busing became "political dynamite," according to a Gallup poll. "We've had all we can take of judicial interference with local schools," Phyllis Schlafly railed in 1972.

Although children had been riding buses to school for decades, busing for racial integration provoked outrage. Violence erupted in Boston in 1974 when black students began to attend the formerly all-white South Boston High School. White students boycotted classes, and angry whites threw rocks at black students disembarking from buses. The whites most affected came

from working-class families who remained in cities abandoned by the more affluent and whose children often rode buses to predominantly black, overcrowded schools with deficient facilities. Schlafly pointed out, "None of the justices who ordered busing ever sent their children to inner-city schools or allowed them to be the victims of forced busing." African Americans themselves were conflicted about the benefits of sending their children on long rides to schools where teachers might not welcome or respect them. Nixon failed to persuade Congress to end court-ordered busing, but after he had appointed four new justices, the Supreme Court moved in his direction in 1974, imposing strict limits on the use of busing to achieve racial balance (*Milliken v. Bradley*).

Nixon's judicial appointments also reflected the southern strategy. He believed that the Supreme Court under Chief Justice Earl Warren had been "unprecedentedly politically active… using their interpretation of the law to remake American society according to their own social, political, and ideological precepts." When Warren resigned in June 1969, Nixon replaced him with Warren E. Burger, a federal appeals court judge who was seen as a **strict constructionist**—someone inclined to interpret the Constitution nar-

School Busing
Controversy over busing as a means to integrate public schools erupted in Boston when the school year started in autumn 1974. Opposition was especially high in white ethnic neighborhoods like South Boston. Residents there resented liberal judges from the suburbs assigning them the burden of integration. Clashes between blacks and whites in South Boston, such as this one in February 1975 outside Boston's Hyde Park High School, prompted authorities to dispatch police to protect black students.
AP/Wide World.

rowly and to limit government intervention on behalf of individual rights.

Unions and civil rights groups, however, mounted strong campaigns against Nixon's next two nominees, conservative southern judges, and the Senate forced him to settle on more moderate candidates. The Burger Court proved more sympathetic than the Warren Court to the president's agenda, restricting somewhat the protections of individual rights established by the previous Court. For example, the Court limited the range of **affirmative action** in *Regents of the University of California v. Bakke* (1978). Yet that decision did allow affirmative action programs to attack the results of past discrimination as long as strict quotas or racial classifications were not involved. (The Court reaffirmed this position in 2003.) In *Bakke* and other cases, the Burger Court continued to uphold liberal programs of the 1960s.

Nixon's southern strategy and other repercussions of the civil rights revolution of the 1960s ended the Democratic hold on the "solid South." In 1964, Senator Strom Thurmond of South Carolina, who had headed the Dixiecrat challenge to Truman in 1948, changed his party affiliation to Republican. North Carolina senator Jesse Helms followed suit in 1971, and aspirants for office throughout the South began to realize that the future for Democratic candidates had darkened there. By 2005, Republicans held the majority of southern seats in both houses of Congress and governorships in seven southern states.

In addition to capitalizing on racial issues, Nixon aligned himself with those fearful about women's changing roles and new demands. In 1971, he vetoed a bill providing federal funds for day care centers with a message that combined the old and new conservatism. Parents should purchase child care services "in the private, open market," he insisted, not through government programs. He played to concerns of social conservatives by warning about the "family-weakening implications" of the measure. In response to the movement to liberalize abortion laws, Nixon sided with "defenders of the right to life of the unborn." He did not comment publicly on *Roe v. Wade* (1973), but his earlier stance against abortion anticipated the Republican Party's eventual embrace of this as a key issue for the New Right.

REVIEW   How did Nixon's policies reflect the increasing influence of conservatives on the Republican Party?

Constitutional Crisis and Restoration

Nixon's ability to attract Democrats resulted in a resounding victory in the 1972 election. Two years later, however, the so-called Watergate scandals caused him to abandon his office. Nixon's abuse of power and efforts to cover up crimes committed by subordinates betrayed the public trust and forced the first presidential resignation in history. His handpicked successor, Gerald Ford, helped to restore confidence in the presidency, but the aftermath of Watergate and severe economic problems returned the White House to the Democrats in 1976. Nonetheless, so robust was the conservative tide that it not only survived the temporary setback when Nixon resigned the presidency but also quickly challenged the Democratic administration that followed.

The Election of 1972

Nixon's spectacular foreign policy initiatives, **détente** with the Soviet Union, and the opening of relations with China (see chapter 29), heightened his prospects for reelection in 1972. Although the war in Vietnam continued, antiwar protests diminished with the decrease in American ground forces and casualties. Nixon's New Economic Policy had temporarily checked inflation and unemployment, and his attacks on busing and antiwar protesters had appealed to the right, positioning him favorably for the 1972 election.

A large field of contenders vied for the Democratic nomination, including New York representative Shirley Chisholm, the first African American politician to make a serious bid for the presidency. On the right, Governor George Wallace of Alabama captured a series of southern primaries as well as those in Michigan and Maryland, but his campaign was cut short when a shot fired by a deranged man left him paralyzed below the waist. South Dakota senator George S. McGovern came to the Democratic convention as the clear leader, and the composition of the convention delegates made his position even stronger.

After the bitter 1968 convention, the Democrats had reformed their rules, requiring delegations to represent the proportions of minorities, women, and youth in their states. These newcomers displaced many regular Democrats—officeholders, labor leaders, and representatives of traditional ethnic groups. One party regular, referring to the considerable numbers of young people and women among these newcomers who were to the left of party regulars, remarked that there was "too much hair, and not enough cigars at this convention." Though easily nominated, McGovern struggled against Nixon from the outset. Republicans portrayed him as a left extremist; and his support for busing, immediate withdrawal from Vietnam, and deep cuts in the Pentagon's budget alienated conservative Democrats.

Nixon gained 60.7 percent of the popular vote, carrying every state except Massachusetts in a landslide victory second only to Johnson's in 1964. Although the Democrats maintained control of Congress, Nixon won majorities among traditional Democrats—southerners, Catholics, urbanites, and blue-collar workers. The president, however, had little time to savor his triumph, when revelations began to emerge about crimes committed to ensure the victory.

Watergate

During the early morning hours of June 17, 1972, five men working for Nixon's reelection campaign crept into Democratic Party headquarters in the Watergate complex in Washington. Intending to repair a bugging device installed in an earlier break-in, they were discovered and arrested on the scene. In trying to cover up the connection between those arrested and administration officials, Nixon and his aides set in motion the most serious constitutional crisis since the Civil War. Reporters dubbed it "Watergate."

Over the next two years, Americans learned that Nixon and his associates had engaged in other abuses, such as accepting illegal campaign contributions, using dirty tricks to sabotage Democratic candidates, and unlawfully attempting to silence critics of the Vietnam War. Nixon was not the first president to lie to the public or to misuse power. Every president since Franklin D. Roosevelt had enlarged the powers of the presidency, justifying his actions as necessary to protect national security. This expansion of executive powers, often called the "imperial presidency," weakened the traditional **checks and balances** on the executive branch and opened the door to abuses.

Upon the arrest of the Watergate burglars, Nixon secretly plotted to conceal links between the burglars and the White House while publicly denying any connection to the break-in. In April 1973, after investigations by a grand jury and the Senate suggested that White House aides had been involved, Nixon accepted official responsibility for Watergate but denied any knowledge of the break-in or of a cover-up. He also announced the resignations of three White House aides and Attorney General Richard Kleindienst. In May, he authorized the appointment of an independent special prosecutor, Archibald Cox, to conduct an investigation.

Meanwhile, sensational revelations exploded in the Senate investigating committee, headed by Democrat Samuel J. Ervin of North Carolina. White House counsel John Dean described projects to harass "enemies" through tax audits and other illegal means and implicated the president in efforts to cover up the Watergate burglary. The most damaging blow struck when a White House aide disclosed that all conversations in the Oval Office were taped. Both Cox and the Ervin committee immediately asked for tapes related to Watergate. When Nixon refused, citing executive privilege and separation of powers, Cox and Ervin took their case to court.

The Gap in the Watergate Tapes

Franklin Roosevelt installed the first recording apparatus in the White House under his desk in 1940, but neither he, Truman, nor Eisenhower recorded conversations extensively. John F. Kennedy was the first president to put in a complete taping network; and Richard Nixon was the first to use a voice-activated system, which taped about 2,800 hours of conversations in which most participants did not know they were being recorded. When Nixon was compelled to turn over the tapes during the Watergate investigation, an 18½-minute gap was discovered in a conversation between Nixon and his chief of staff, H. R. Haldeman, just three days after the Watergate break-in. Nixon's secretary Rose Mary Woods said that her foot must have slipped on the controls while she was transcribing the tape, using the transcription machine pictured here; but others, noting that the 18 minutes contained several separate erasings, suggested that the clumsiness of the deed linked it to Nixon.

Nixon Presidential Materials Project, National Archives and Records Administration.

Additional disclosures exposed Nixon's misuse of federal funds and tax evasion. In August 1973, Vice President Spiro Agnew was compelled to resign after an investigation revealed that he had taken bribes while governor of Maryland. Although Nixon's choice of House minority leader Gerald Ford of Michigan to succeed Agnew won widespread approval, Agnew's resignation further tarnished the administration.

On October 19, 1973, Nixon ordered special prosecutor Cox to stop trying to obtain the Oval Office tapes. When Cox refused, Nixon directed Attorney General Elliot Richardson to fire Cox. Richardson instead resigned, as did the next man in line at the Justice Department. Finally, the solicitor general, Robert Bork, agreed to carry out the president's order. The press called the series of dismissals and resignations the "Saturday night massacre." Soon 250,000 telegrams condemning Nixon's action flooded the White House, and his popular support plummeted to 27 percent.

In February 1974, the House of Representatives voted to begin an **impeachment** investigation. In April, Nixon began to release edited transcripts of the tapes. As the public read passages sprinkled with "expletive deleted," the House Republican leader Hugh Scott of Pennsylvania abandoned his support of the president, calling the transcripts a "deplorable, shabby, disgusting, and immoral performance by all." The transcripts included Nixon's orders to John Mitchell, his former attorney general and head of his reelection committee, and Dean in March 1973: "I don't give a shit what happens. I want you all to stonewall it, let them plead the Fifth Amendment, cover up or anything else, if it'll save it—save the plan."

In July 1974, the House Judiciary Committee began debate over specific charges for impeachment: (1) obstruction of justice, (2) abuse of power, (3) contempt of Congress, (4) unconstitutional waging of war by the secret bombing of Cambodia, and (5) tax evasion and the selling of political favors. The last two counts failed to get a majority, but the committee voted to take the first three to the House, where a vote of impeachment seemed certain. Ordered by a unanimous Supreme Court to hand over the remaining tapes, Nixon released transcripts on August 5 that contained his conversations with aides about how to use the CIA to hinder the FBI's investigation of the burglary. This was sufficient evidence to seal his fate.

Nixon announced his resignation to a national television audience on August 8, 1974.

Acknowledging some incorrect judgments, he insisted that he had always tried to do what was best for the nation. The next morning, Nixon ended a rambling, emotional farewell to his staff with some advice: "Always give your best, never get discouraged, never get petty; always remember, others may hate you, but those who hate you don't win unless you hate them, and then you destroy yourself." Had he practiced that advice, he might have saved his presidency.

The Ford Presidency

Gerald R. Ford, who had represented Michigan in the House of Representatives since 1948, had built a reputation as a conservative party loyalist. Not a brilliant thinker, he was known for his integrity, humility, and dedication to public office. "I'm a Ford, not a Lincoln," he acknowledged. Most of official Washington and the American public looked favorably on his succession as president.

Upon taking office, Ford announced, "Our long nightmare is over," but he shocked many Americans one month later when he granted Nixon a pardon "for all offenses against the United States which he … has committed or may have committed or taken part in" during his presidency. It was the most generous presidential pardon ever issued, saving Nixon from nearly certain indictment and trial. Thirty of his associates ultimately were convicted or pleaded guilty. The pardon provoked a tremendous outcry from Congress and the public, and Democrats made impressive gains in the November congressional elections.

Congress moved to guard against the types of abuses revealed in the Watergate investigations. The Federal Election Campaign Act of 1974, for example, established public financing of presidential campaigns to help prevent the selling of political favors, but it failed to stop the ever-larger campaign donations that candidates found ways to solicit from interest groups, corporations, labor unions, and wealthy individuals. In 1978, Congress passed an independent counsel law establishing a nonpartisan procedure for the appointment of special prosecutors. The law was used to investigate possibly criminal actions by Presidents Reagan and Clinton (see chapter 31) as well as several lesser officials before it expired in 1998.

Special investigating committees in Congress discovered a host of illegal FBI and CIA activities stretching back to the 1950s and including harassment of political dissenters and plots to assassinate Fidel Castro and other foreign leaders. In response to these revelations, President Ford established new controls on covert operations, and Congress created permanent committees to oversee the intelligence agencies. Yet these measures did little to diminish the public cynicism and lack of trust in government that had been developing since the Johnson years.

Disillusionment with government grew as the Ford administration seemed unable to deal with serious economic problems: a low rate of growth, high unemployment, a foreign trade deficit, and soaring energy prices tied to dependence on oil from abroad. Ford carried these burdens into the election campaign of 1976, and he also had to fight down a major challenge from the Republican right. California governor Ronald Reagan came close to capturing the nomination.

The Democrats nominated James Earl "Jimmy" Carter Jr., former state senator and governor of Georgia. A graduate of the U.S. Naval Academy, Carter spent seven years in the navy before returning to Plains, Georgia, to run the family peanut farming business. Carefully prepared on policy issues, the soft-spoken Georgian stressed his deep religious commitment and distance from the suspect national government.

Although he selected liberal senator Walter F. Mondale of Minnesota as his running mate and accepted a platform compatible with traditional Democratic principles, Carter's nomination nonetheless marked a decided rightward turn in the party.

After the revelations of corruption in the Nixon administration, Carter, a candidate who carried his own bags, lived modestly, and taught a Bible class at his Baptist church, had considerable appeal. He also benefited from the country's economic problems and his ability to capture the traditional Democratic coalition of blacks, southerners, organized labor, and ethnic groups. Yet, although Democrats retained substantial margins in Congress, Carter received just 50 percent of the popular vote to Ford's 48 percent (Map 30.1).

> **REVIEW**   Why did Richard Nixon resign the presidency in August 1974?

The "Outsider" Presidency of Jimmy Carter

Carter promised a government that was "competent" as well as "honest, decent, open, fair, and compassionate." He also warned Americans that "we can neither answer all questions nor solve all problems." His personal honesty and decency helped to revive trust in the presidency but did not inspire confidence in his own ability to lead the nation through domestic and foreign crises. Energy shortages and stagflation (see chapter 28) became even worse, Soviet-American relations deteriorated, and instability mounted in the Middle East.

Retreat from Liberalism

Jimmy Carter vowed "to help the poor and aged, to improve education, and to provide jobs" but at the same time "not to waste money." When his desires to help and to limit spending conflicted, Carter's commitment to reform took second place. Increasing numbers of Americans unhappy about their tax dollars being used to benefit the disadvantaged while stagflation eroded their own material status welcomed Carter's approach. Liberal Democrats pushing for major welfare reform and a national health insurance program were frustrated with his fiscal stringency and

MAP 30.1   The Election of 1976

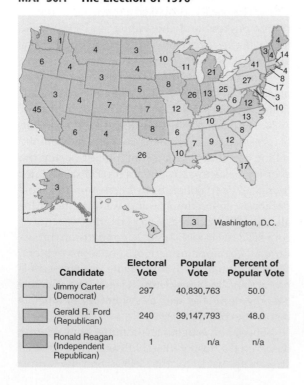

Candidate	Electoral Vote	Popular Vote	Percent of Popular Vote
Jimmy Carter (Democrat)	297	40,830,763	50.0
Gerald R. Ford (Republican)	240	39,147,793	48.0
Ronald Reagan (Independent Republican)	1	n/a	n/a

accused him of deserting the Democratic reform tradition that stretched back to Franklin D. Roosevelt.

Although Carter's outsider status helped him win the presidency, it left him without strong ties to party leaders and hampered his ability to lead. Legislators complained of inadequate consultation and Carter's tendency to flood them with a mass of unprioritized proposals. Yet even a president without those liabilities might not have done much better than Carter. Congress itself had diminished the ability of party leaders to deliver a united front. Responding to highly publicized scandals that touched congressional leaders in the 1960s, it reduced the power of committee chairs and decentralized the decision-making process.

The Carter administration failed to resolve the economic problems that had plagued the Nixon and Ford administrations—unemployment, inflation, and sluggish growth. New tax cuts and increased federal spending on public service jobs helped to lower unemployment temporarily. But in 1978, rising inflation impelled Carter to curtail federal spending and prompted the Federal Reserve Board to increase interest rates and tighten the money supply. These policies not only failed to halt inflation, which surpassed 13 percent in 1980, but also contributed to rising unemployment, reversing gains made in Carter's first two years.

Carter further attempted to ease economic woes by addressing the nation's enormous consumption of energy and its dependence on Middle Eastern oil, which contributed to gasoline shortages. "We are struggling with a profound transition from a time of abundance to a time of growing scarcity in energy," Carter noted in 1979. He created a Department of Energy and fought for a comprehensive program, but his efforts fell short. Congress did pass legislation to penalize gas-guzzling automobiles and provide other incentives to conserve energy, but these failed to decrease American dependence on foreign oil. At the end of the century, the United States consumed more than 25 percent of global oil production.

Corporations and wealthy individuals reaped some benefits during the Carter administration, including a sharp cut in the capital gains tax. When Chrysler, the tenth largest U.S. corporation, approached bankruptcy in 1979, Congress bailed it out with $1.5 billion worth of loan guarantees. In addition, Carter gave greater rein to free enterprise by gaining passage of measures deregulating the airline, banking, trucking, and railroad industries.

Carter Promotes Human Rights

Campaigning in 1976, Jimmy Carter charged his predecessors' foreign policy with violating the nation's principles of freedom and human dignity. "We're ashamed of what our government is as we deal with other nations around the world," he said. The cynical support of dictators, secret diplomacy, interference in the internal affairs of other countries, and excessive reliance on military solutions—Carter promised to reverse them all.

Human rights formed the cornerstone of his approach. Administration officials chastised governments that denied their citizens basic political and civil rights, and they applied economic pressure, denying aid or trading privileges to such nations as Argentina, Chile, El Salvador, and South Africa. Yet Carter also sacrificed human rights ideals to strategic and security considerations. He invoked no sanctions against repressive governments in Iran, South Korea, and the Philippines, for example, and he established formal diplomatic relations with the People's Republic of China in 1979, even though the Chinese government blatantly refused to grant **democratic** rights to its people.

Nicaragua provided another test for Carter's human rights principles when a popular movement overthrew an oppressive dictatorship. U.S. officials were uneasy about the leftist Sandinistas, who led the rebellion and had ties to Cuba, but once they assumed power in 1979, Carter recognized the new government and sent economic aid. In doing this, he signaled that the way in which a government treated its citizens was as important as how anti-Communist and friendly to American interests it was.

Applying moral principles to relations with Panama, Carter sped up negotiations over control of the Panama Canal and in 1977 obtained a treaty providing for joint control of the canal until 2000, when Panama would take over. Supporters viewed the treaty as recompense for the blatant use of U.S. power to obtain the canal in 1903. Angry opponents insisted on retaining the vital waterway. "We bought it, we paid for it, it's ours," claimed Ronald Reagan during the presidential primaries of 1976. It took a massive effort by the administration to get Senate ratification of the treaty.

Seeking to use his moral authority to promote peace in the Middle East, Carter seized on the courage of Egyptian president Anwar Sadat, the first Arab leader to risk his political career by talking directly with Israeli officials. Carter invited Sadat and Israeli prime minister Menachem Begin to the presidential retreat at

Camp David, Maryland, and spent thirteen days there mediating between the two. These talks led to an agreement—the Camp David accords—that Begin and Sadat signed at the White House in March 1979: Egypt became the first Arab state to recognize Israel, and Israel agreed to gradual withdrawal from the Sinai Peninsula, which it had seized in the 1967 war (Map 30.2). Although the issues of Palestinian self-determination in other Israeli-occupied territories and the plight of Palestinian refugees remained unresolved, the first meaningful steps toward peace in the Middle East had been taken.

MAP 30.2   The Middle East, 1948–1989

Determination to preserve access to the rich oil reserves of the Middle East and commitment to the security of Israel were the fundamental—and often conflicting—principles of U.S. foreign policy in that region.

READING THE MAP: Where did the United States become involved diplomatically or militarily in the Middle East between 1948 and 1989? Which countries are members of OPEC?

CONNECTIONS: What role did U.S. foreign policy regarding the Middle East and events in Israel play in provoking the 1973 Arab oil embargo against the United States? What precipitated the taking of U.S. hostages in Iran in 1979? Was U.S. intervention in the country a factor? If so, why?

FOR MORE HELP ANALYZING THIS MAP, see the map activity for this chapter in the Online Study Guide at **bedfordstmartins.com/roarkcompact**.

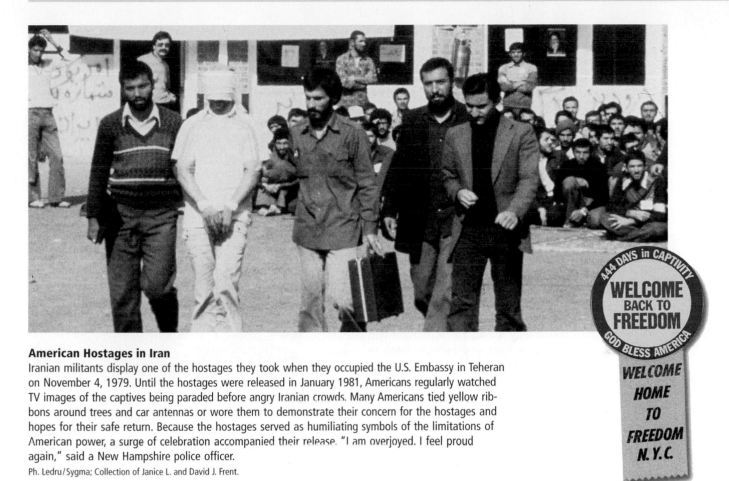

444 DAYS in CAPTIVITY
WELCOME BACK TO FREEDOM
GOD BLESS AMERICA

WELCOME HOME TO FREEDOM N.Y.C.

American Hostages in Iran

Iranian militants display one of the hostages they took when they occupied the U.S. Embassy in Teheran on November 4, 1979. Until the hostages were released in January 1981, Americans regularly watched TV images of the captives being paraded before angry Iranian crowds. Many Americans tied yellow ribbons around trees and car antennas or wore them to demonstrate their concern for the hostages and hopes for their safe return. Because the hostages served as humiliating symbols of the limitations of American power, a surge of celebration accompanied their release. "I am overjoyed. I feel proud again," said a New Hampshire police officer.

Ph. Ledru/Sygma; Collection of Janice L. and David J. Frent.

The Cold War Intensifies

Consistent with his human rights approach, Carter preferred to pursue national security through nonmilitary means and initially sought accommodation with the Soviet Union. But in 1979, he abandoned efforts to obtain Senate ratification of a new strategic arms limitation treaty and began development of an enormous new missile system and intermediate-range missiles to be deployed in Western Europe.

Carter's decision for the military buildup came in 1979 when the Soviet Union invaded Afghanistan, whose recently installed Communist government was threatened by Muslim opposition (see Map 30.2). Insisting that the Soviet aggression "could pose the greatest threat to peace since the Second World War," Carter also imposed economic sanctions on the Soviet Union, barred U.S. participation in the 1980 Olympic Games in Moscow, and obtained legislation requiring all nineteen-year-old men to register for the **draft**.

The president claimed that Soviet actions jeopardized oil supplies from the Middle East and announced his own "Carter Doctrine," threatening the use of any means necessary to prevent an outside force from gaining control of the Persian Gulf. His human rights policy fell by the wayside as the United States stepped up aid to Afghanistan's neighbor, Pakistan, then under a military dictatorship. Finally, Carter called for hefty increases in defense spending over the next five years.

Events in Iran encouraged this reversion to a hard-line, militaristic approach. All the U.S. arms and aid had not enabled the shah to quash Iranian dissidents who still resented the CIA's role in the overthrow of the Mossadegh government in 1953 (see chapter 27), condemned the shah's savage attempts to silence opposition, and detested his adoption of Western culture and values. In 1979, a revolution forced the shah out of Iran and gave Shiite Islamic **fundamentalists** control of the government. These forces were intensely hostile to the United States, which they blamed for supporting the shah's brutalities and undermining their country's religious foundations.

When Carter permitted the shah to enter the United States for medical treatment, anti-American demonstrations escalated in Teheran. On November 4, 1979, a crowd broke into the U.S. Embassy and seized more than 60 Americans, demanding that the shah be returned to Iran for trial. Carter froze Iranian assets in U.S. banks and placed an embargo on Iranian oil. In April 1980, he sent a small military operation into Iran, but the rescue mission failed and the hostages remained prisoners until January 1981.

The distrastous rescue attempt fed Americans' feelings of impotence and increased support for a more militaristic foreign policy. Opposition to Soviet-American détente, combined with the Soviet invasion of Afghanistan, nullified the thaw in relations that Nixon and Kissinger had begun. The American hostages in Iran filled the news during the 1980 presidential campaign and contributed to Carter's defeat. Iran freed the hostages on the day he left office, but relations with the United States remained tense.

> **REVIEW**   How did Carter balance commitment to human rights and anticommunism in his foreign policy?

Ronald Reagan and the Conservative Ascendancy

Ronald Reagan's election in 1980 marked the most important turning point in politics since Franklin D. Roosevelt won the presidency in 1932. Eisenhower and Nixon were middle-of-the-road Republicans, but Reagan's victory established conservatism's dominance in the Republican Party. Since the 1930s, the Democrats had defined the major issues; in the 1980s, the Republicans assumed that initiative, while the Democrats searched for voter support by moving toward the right. On the domestic front, the Reagan administration embraced the conservative Christian values of the New Right, but it left its most important mark on the economy: victory over inflation, deregulation of industry, a moratorium on social spending, enormous tax cuts, and a staggering budget deficit. Economic expansion brought great wealth to some, but the percentage of poor Americans increased, and income distribution became more unequal.

Ronald Reagan Nominated for President
Nancy and Ronald Reagan respond to cheers at the Republican National Convention where he was nominated for president in the summer of 1980. Reagan became one of the most popular presidents of the twentieth century, though his wife did not always share his high ratings from the American people.
Lester Sloan/Woodfin Camp & Associates.

Appealing to the New Right and Beyond

The oldest candidate ever nominated for the presidency, Ronald Reagan was born in Tampico, Illinois, in 1911. After attending a small religious college, he worked as a sportscaster before becoming a movie actor. He initially shared the politics of his staunchly Democratic father but moved to the right in the 1940s and 1950s and campaigned for Goldwater in 1964. Reagan's political career took off when he was elected governor of California in 1966.

Although Reagan chose the moderate Republican George H. W. Bush as his running mate, centrist Republicans balked at his nomination and at the party platform, which reflected the concerns of the party's dominant right wing. For example, after Phyllis Schlafly persuaded the party to reverse its forty-year support for the Equal Rights Amendment, moderate and liberal Republican women protested outside the convention hall. (See "Historical Question," page 796). Some of them found a more acceptable candidate in Illinois representative John B. Anderson, who deserted his party to run as an independent.

Reagan's campaign capitalized on the economic recession and the country's declining international stature, symbolized by the Americans held hostage in Iran. Repeatedly Reagan asked voters, "Are you better off now than you were four years ago?" He promised to "take government off the backs of the people" and to restore Americans' morale and other nations' respect. A narrow majority of voters, 51 percent, responded to Reagan's upbeat message. Carter won 41 percent of the vote, and 7 percent went to Anderson. The Republicans won control of the Senate for the first time since the 1950s.

While the economy and Iran sealed Reagan's victory, he also benefited from the burgeoning grassroots conservatism. An extraordinarily adept politician, Reagan appealed to a wide spectrum of groups and sentiments: free-market advocates, militant anti-Communists, fundamentalist Christians, southerners, and white working-class Democrats disenchanted with the Great Society and suffering from high inflation and unemployment rates.

A critical portion of Reagan's support came from religious conservatives, predominately Protestants, who constituted a relatively new phenomenon in politics known as the New Right or New Christian Right. During the 1970s, **evangelical** and fundamentalist Christianity claimed thousands of new adherents, making adept use of sophisticated mass-mailing techniques and the "electronic ministry." Evangelical ministers such as Jim Bakker and Pat Robertson preached to huge television audiences, attacking feminism, abortion, and homosexuality, and calling for restoration of old-fashioned "family values." They wanted prayer back in, and sex education out of, the schools.

Conservatives created a raft of political organizations, such as the Moral Majority, founded by minister Jerry Falwell in 1979 to fight "left-wing, social-welfare bills...pornography, homosexuality, the advocacy of immorality in school textbooks." The Christian Coalition, created by Pat Robertson in 1989,

claimed 1.6 million members and control of the Republican Party in more than a dozen states. The instruments of more traditional conservatives, who advocated limited government at home and militant anticommunism abroad, likewise flourished. These included publications such as the *National Review,* edited by William F. Buckley Jr., and think tanks such as the American Enterprise Institute, which supported experts who developed new policy approaches. The monthly *Phyllis Schlafly Report* merged the sentiments of the old and new right, which were also manifest in its publisher's organization, Eagle Forum.

Reagan embraced the full spectrum of conservatism, avowing agreement on abortion, school prayer, and other New Right issues. Yet his major achievements lay in areas most important to the older right—strengthening the nation's anti-Communist posture and reducing taxes and government restraints on free enterprise. "In the present crisis," Reagan argued, "government is not the solution to our problem, government is the problem."

Reagan's admirers stretched far beyond conservatives. The extraordinarily popular president was liked even by Americans who opposed his policies and even when he made glaring mistakes. He made so many misstatements that aides tried to keep him away from reporters, and they carefully scripted the former actor's public appearances. Reagan's confidence and easygoing humor were a large part of his appeal. Ignoring the darker moments of the American past, he presented a version of history that Americans could feel good about. He also gained public sympathy after being shot by a would-be assassin in March 1981. Just before surgery to remove the bullet, Reagan joked to physicians, "I hope you're Republicans." His great popularity even withstood serious charges of executive branch misconduct in his second term.

Unleashing Free Enterprise

Reagan's first domestic objective was a massive tax cut. Although tax reduction in the face of a large budget deficit contradicted traditional Republican economic doctrine, Reagan relied on a new theory called **supply-side economics**, which held that cutting taxes would actually increase revenue. Supply-siders insisted that lower taxes would enable businesses to expand, encourage individuals to work harder because they could keep more of their earnings, and increase the

Why Did the ERA Fail?

The proposed Equal Rights Amendment to the U.S. Constitution guaranteed simply that women and men would be treated equally under the law: "Equality of rights under the law shall not be denied or abridged by the United States or by any State on account of sex." Two more short sections provided that Congress would have enforcement powers and that the ERA would take effect two years after ratification. By the 1970s it had become the symbol of the late-twentieth-century women's movement.

Members of a small militant feminist organization, the National Woman's Party, first proposed an equal rights amendment to the Constitution in 1923, but it won little support either in Congress or among the public before the resurgence of feminism in the mid-1960s. In 1968, the National Organization for Women made it a key objective and, armed with support from traditional women's organizations and liberal groups, began to pressure Congress. The pressure took many forms, including civil disobedience. In early 1970, for example, NOW members disrupted a Senate subcommittee hearing on extending the vote to eighteen-year-olds, demanding Senate hearings on the ERA. Feminists and their allies, including women in both political parties, lobbied Congress and flooded some congressional offices with 1,500 letters a month.

Despite opposition in committee hearings, both houses of Congress passed the amendment by overwhelming margins, 354 to 23 in the House and 84 to 8 in the Senate. Within three hours of Senate passage in March 1972, Hawaii rushed to become the first state to ratify. By the end of 1972, 23 states had done so. Public opinion heavily favored ratification, peaking at 74 percent in favor in 1974 and never falling below 52 percent, while the opposition never surpassed 31 percent. Yet even after Congress extended the time period for ratification until 1982, the ERA failed. The Constitution requires approval of amendments by three-fourths of the states, and only 35 states ratified, three short of the minimum needed (see Map 30.3). Why did a measure with so much congressional and popular support fail?

The ERA encountered well-organized and passionate opposition linked to the growing conservative forces in the 1970s. Opponents ranged from religious organizations, such as the National Council of Catholic Women, to local groups such as HOTDOGS (Humanitarians Opposed to the Degradation of Our Girls), sponsored by the John Birch Society in Utah. Leading the resistance was Phyllis Schlafly.

Conservatives' opposition to the ERA reflected in part their distaste for big government and their demand for a strong defense system to counter communism. Schlafly predicted that the amendment would transfer power from state legislatures and even from families to the federal government. The ERA would put women in foxholes alongside men, she warned, weakening the military and making the nation more vulnerable to communism. To these arguments, the New Right added claims that the ERA would destroy the American family.

ERA opponents raised fears about the amendment by suggesting extravagant ways in which courts might interpret it. Senator Samuel J. Ervin Jr., nationally known for his chairing of the Watergate hearings, claimed that the ERA would eliminate laws against rape, require male and female prisoners to be housed together, and deprive women of alimony and child support. Others claimed that it would legalize homosexual marriage. Overall, the anti-ERA forces emphasized sex differences. By destroying the distinct sex roles on which the family was based, Erwin claimed, ERA would destroy the family and produce "increased rates of alcoholism, suicide, and possible sexual deviation."

Anti-ERA arguments spoke to many women's religious beliefs and understandings of their own self-interest. In contrast to feminists who viewed traditional sex roles as constructed by society, anti-ERA men and women believed that they were God-given. Evangelical minister and politician Jerry Falwell declared the ERA "a definite violation of holy Scripture [and its] mandate that 'the husband is the head of the wife.'" Many ERA opponents were full-time housewives who had no stake in equal treatment in the marketplace and who feared that the amendment would eliminate the duty of men to support their families. Women in both camps recognized the precariousness of economic security; but while feminists wanted to render women self-sustaining, antifeminists wanted men to bear responsibility for their support.

Phyllis Schlafly and other conservative leaders skillfully mobilized women who saw their traditional roles threatened. In October 1972, she established a national movement, STOP (Stop Taking Our Privileges) ERA, so highly organized that it could respond immediately when action was necessary. Thus when a state legislature began to consider ratification, STOP ERA women deluged legislators with letters and lobbied them personally in state capitals. In Illinois, they gave lawmakers apple pies with notes attached that read: "My heart and my hand went into this dough / For the sake of the family please vote 'no.'" Opponents also brought baby girls to the legislature wearing signs that pleaded, "Please don't draft me." Another opposition group, Happiness of Womanhood (HOW), presented California legislators with mice bearing the message, "Do you want to be a man or a mouse?"

ERA opponents had an easier task than supporters, because the framers of the Constitution had stacked the odds against revision. All opponents had to do was to convince a minority of legislators in a minority of states to preserve the status quo. Supporters, by contrast, had to persuade a majority of lawmakers in three-quarters of the states that the need to guarantee women equal rights was urgent and could not be accomplished without a constitutional amendment. In ad-

Phyllis Schlafly
The most prominent antifeminist, Phyllis Schlafly is shown in her home in Alton, Illinois, in 1987. Despite time-consuming and energetic political activities that took her all over the country, she insisted on calling herself a housewife. She poses with a pillow that signals her domesticity and political aim.
© Bettmann / Corbis.

dition, ERA forces had concentrated on winning Congress and were not prepared for the state campaigns. The intensity of the opposition took them by surprise.

Feminists had to overcome the tendency of men to trivialize women's rights. For example, when the House initially passed the ERA in 1970, the *New York Times* printed a critical editorial under the title "The Henpecked House." The conservative columnist James J. Kilpatrick called the ERA "the contrivance of a gang of professional harpies" that congressmen had voted for simply to "get these furies off their backs." The very gains feminists made in the 1960s and 1970s also worked against approval of the ERA. Congress had already banned sex discrimination in employment, education, credit, and other areas; and the Supreme Court had struck down several state and federal laws that treated men and women differently. Even though the Court did not ban all distinctions based on sex, its decisions made it harder for ERA advocates to demonstrate the urgency of constitutional revision.

So why did the ERA fail? It failed because a handful of men in a handful of state legislatures voted against it. The shift of only a few votes in states such as Illinois and

North Carolina would have meant ratification. Phyllis Schlafly's forces played a key role in the defeat, because men could vote "no" and take cover behind the many women who opposed it. And those women proved willing to commit time, energy, and money to block ratification because conservative leaders convinced them that the ERA threatened their very way of life.

Feminists did not leave the ERA battle empty-handed, however. The National Organization for Women grew enormously during the struggle for ratification. Thousands of women were mobilized across the political spectrum and participated in the political arena for the first time. Fourteen states passed their own equal rights amendments after 1970. And feminists continued to struggle in the legislative and judicial arenas for the expansion of women's rights, struggles that continue to bear fruit in the twenty-first century.

production of goods and services—the supply—which in turn would boost demand. To allay worries about the budget deficit, Reagan promised to cut federal expenditures.

In the summer of 1981, Congress passed the Economic Recovery Tax Act, the largest tax reduction in U.S. history. Tax rates of lowest-income individuals fell from 14 to 11 percent, while those of individuals with the highest incomes dropped from 70 to 50 percent. The law gave corporations tax breaks and cut taxes on capital gains, gifts, and inheritances. A second measure, the Tax Reform Act of 1986, reduced tax rates even more, lowering the maximum rate on individual income to 28 percent and on business income to 35 percent. With these cuts affluent Americans saved far more on their tax bills than did average taxpayers, and the distribution of wealth tipped farther in favor of the rich.

"Hack, chop, crunch!" were *Time* magazine's words for the administration's efforts to free private enterprise from government restraints. Carter had confined deregulation to particular industries, such as air transportation and banking, while increasing regulation in health, safety, and environmental protection. The Reagan administration, by contrast, pursued across-the-board deregulation. It declined to limit **monopoly** by enforcing the Sherman Antitrust Act (see chapter 17) against an unprecedented number of business mergers and takeovers. Reagan also loosened regulations protecting employee health and safety; and he weakened organized labor when he fired thirteen thousand members of the Professional Air Traffic Controllers Organization (PATCO) who struck in 1981. Blaming environmental laws for the nation's sluggish economy, Reagan targeted them too for deregulation, but popular support for environmental protection blocked the complete realization of Reagan's goals.

Deregulation of the banking industry, begun under Carter with bipartisan support, created a crisis in the savings and loan industry. Some of the newly deregulated savings and loan institutions (S&Ls) extended enormous loans to real estate developers and invested in other high-yield but risky ventures. S&L owners reaped lavish profits, and their depositors enjoyed high interest rates. But then real estate values began to plunge, and hundreds of S&Ls went bankrupt. After Congress voted to bail out the S&L industry in 1989, the burden of the largest financial scandal in U.S. history, estimated at more than $100 billion, fell on American taxpayers.

The S&L crisis deepened the federal deficit, which soared despite Reagan's pledge to pare federal spending. When the administration cut funds for food stamps, job training, aid to low-income students, and other social welfare programs, hundreds of thousands of people lost benefits. Increases in defense spending, however, far exceeded the budget cuts, and the deficit continued to climb: from $74 billion in 1981 to a high of $220 billion in 1986. Under Reagan, the nation's debt tripled to $2.3 trillion, and interest on the debt consumed one-seventh of all federal expenditures.

It took the severest recession since the 1930s to squeeze inflation out of the U.S. economy. Beginning in 1981, unemployment rose sharply, approaching 11 percent late in 1982, and record numbers of banks and businesses closed. The threat of unemployment further undermined organized labor, forcing unions to make concessions that management insisted were necessary for industry's survival. In 1983 the economy recovered and entered a period of unprecedented growth.

The economic upswing and Reagan's own popularity posed a formidable challenge in the 1984 elections for the Democrats, who nominated Carter's vice president, Walter F. Mondale. His precedent-breaking move in choosing as his running mate New York representative Geraldine A. Ferraro failed to save the Democrats from a humiliating defeat. Reagan charged his opponents with concentrating on America's failures while he emphasized success and possibility. Democrats, he claimed, "see an America where every day is April 15th [the due date for income tax returns]…we see an America where every day is the Fourth of July."

Voters responded to the president's sunny vision and the economic comeback, giving him a landslide with 59 percent of the popular vote and a 523-to-13 victory in the electoral college. Winning only the state of Minnesota, the Democrats pondered how to stem the exodus of longtime loyalists—particularly southern white males—to the Republican Party. Stung by Republican charges that the Democratic Party was captive to "special interests" such as labor, women, and minorities, some Democratic leaders urged a further party shift toward the right.

Winners and Losers in a Flourishing Economy

After the economy took off, some Americans won great fortunes as popular culture celebrated making money and displaying wealth. Books by business wizards topped best-seller lists, the press described lavish parties costing millions of dollars, and popular magazines featured articles such as "They're like Us, except They're Rich." College students listed making money as their primary ambition.

Participating conspicuously in the new affluence were members of the baby boom generation known popularly as "yuppies," short for "young urban professionals." These mostly white, well-educated young men and women lived in urban condominiums and pursued fast-track careers; they consumed lavishly—fancy cars, expensive vacations, and electronic gadgets. Though definitely a minority, they established consumption standards that many tried to emulate.

Many of the newly wealthy got rich from moving assets around rather than from producing goods. Notable exceptions included Steven Jobs, who invented the Apple computer in his garage, and Liz Claiborne, who turned a $250,000 investment into a billion-dollar fashion enterprise. But many others made money by manipulating debt and restructuring corporations through mergers and takeovers. "To say these guys are entrepreneurs is like saying Jesse James was an entrepreneur," opined Texas businessman Ross Perot, who defined entrepreneurship as making things, not money. Most financial wizards operated within the law, but occasionally greed led to criminal convictions. Michael Milken took home well over $50 million a year by issuing junk bonds, so called because they offered high risk and high yield. He and others landed in jail for using insider information to maximize their financial manipulations.

Other economic problems remained. The steel, automobile, and electronics industries were surpassed by those of Germany and Japan; Americans bought more Volkswagens and Hondas and fewer Fords and Chevrolets. With Americans purchasing more foreign-made goods than domestic producers were able to sell abroad, the nation's trade deficit (the difference between imports and exports) soared.

International competition forced the collapse of some older companies. Others moved factories and jobs abroad to be closer to foreign markets or to benefit from the low wages in such countries as Mexico and Korea. Service industries expanded during this process of **de-industrialization** and created new jobs at home, but these jobs paid substantially lower wages. When David Ramos was laid off in 1982 from his $12.75-an-hour job in a steel plant, his wages fell to $5 an hour as a security guard, forcing his family to rely on food stamps. The number of full-time workers earning wages below the poverty level ($12,195 for a family of four in 1990) rose from 12 to 18 percent of all workers in the 1980s.

The weakening of organized labor combined with the decline in manufacturing to erode the position of blue-collar workers. Chicago steelworker Ike Mazo, who contemplated the $6-an-hour jobs available to him, fumed: "It's an attack on the living standards of workers." Increasingly, a second income was needed to stave off economic decline. By 1990, nearly 60 percent of married women with young children worked outside the home. Yet even with two incomes, fewer young families could purchase their first home or provide a good life for their children. "I worry about their future every day," Mazo's wife confessed. "Will we be able to put them through college?…Will they be out in the workforce working for four dollars an hour?" The average $10,000 disparity between men's and women's annual earnings made things even harder for the nearly 20 percent of families headed by women.

In keeping with conservative philosophy, Reagan insisted that a booming economy would benefit everyone and avoided substantial government efforts to reverse this growing income inequality, which his tax policies encouraged. Average personal income did rise during his tenure, but the trend toward greater economic inequality that had begun in the 1970s intensified in the 1980s. The rich got richer, a portion of the middle class did well, and the poor got poorer. Personal income shot up sharply for the wealthiest 20 percent of Americans while it fell for the poorest by 9.8 percent between 1979 and 1987 (Figure 30.1).

Poverty statistics, too, revealed a reversal of the trend toward greater equality. Between 1980 and 1988, poor people increased from 11.7 to 13.5 percent of the total U.S. population—the highest poverty rate in the industrialized world. Social Security and Medicare helped keep the poverty rate among the elderly relatively low. Less fortunate were other groups that the economic boom had bypassed: racial minorities, female-headed families, and children. One child in every five lived in poverty.

FIGURE 30.1   The Growth of Inequality: Changes in Family Income, 1969–1998
For three decades after World War II, income increased for all groups on the economic ladder. After 1979, the income of the poorest families declined while the income of the richest 20 percent of the population grew substantially.
Copyright © 1989 by the New York Times Co. Reprinted by permission.

Even while the economy boomed, affluent urbanites walked past men and women sleeping in subway stations, on grates over steam vents, and on park benches. Experts debated the total number of homeless Americans—estimates ranged from 350,000 upward—but no one doubted that homelessness had increased. Those without homes included the victims of long-term unemployment, erosion of welfare benefits, and slum clearance as well as individuals suffering from mental illness, drug abuse, and alcoholism.

REVIEW   Why did economic inequality increase during Reagan's administration?

Continuing Struggles over Rights and the Environment

The rise of conservatism threw social movements on the defensive. The Reagan administration, often supported by the increasingly conservative federal courts, moved away from the national commitment to equal opportunity undertaken in the 1960s. Feminists and minority groups fought to defend protections they had recently won, and they achieved some limited gains. A newer movement advocating rights for gay men and lesbians gained visibility and edged attitudes toward greater tolerance for homosexuality. Environmentalists, too, clashed with the Reagan administration as they sought to maintain regulations enacted in the 1970s and as the world faced new threats to human life.

The Conservative Shift in the Federal Courts

Since the 1950s, liberals had counted on the federal judiciary as a powerful ally in their struggles for civil rights and social justice. But in the 1980s, they saw their allies slipping away as more and more conservative justices populated the Supreme Court and lower federal courts. Given the opportunity to appoint half of the 761 federal court judges and three new Supreme Court justices, President Reagan carefully selected conservative candidates. With these appointments, the tide began to turn in favor of strict construction—the literal interpretation of the Constitution that narrowly adheres to the words of its authors, thereby limiting judicial power to protect individual rights.

The Supreme Court did not execute an abrupt about-face: It upheld important affirmative action and antidiscrimination policies and ruled that sexual harassment in the workplace constituted sex discrimination. And, in one key case, Congress stepped in to defend antidiscrimination policy. In 1984, the Justice Department persuaded the Supreme Court to severely weaken Title IX of the Education Amendments Act of 1972, a key law promoting equal opportunity in education. *Grove City v. Bell* (1984) allowed the Justice Department to abandon dozens of civil rights cases against schools and colleges, but it also galvanized a coalition of civil rights organizations and groups representing women, the aged, the disabled, and their allies. In 1988, Congress passed the Civil Rights Restoration Act, which reversed the administration's victory in *Grove City* and banned any organization that practiced discrimination on the basis of race, color, national origin, sex, disability, or age from receiving government funds.

Nonetheless, Reagan's Supreme Court appointees tipped the balance to the right. Sandra Day O'Connor was a moderate conservative, but the appointments of Antonin Scalia and Anthony M. Kennedy gave strict constructionists a slim majority. The full impact of these appointments continued after Reagan left office. Finding constitutional limits to the power of the federal government, the Court allowed states to impose restrictions that weakened access to abortion for

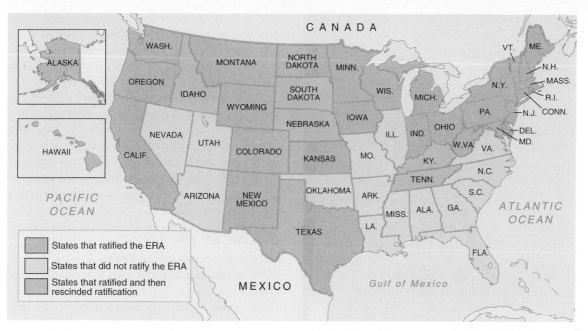

MAP 30.3 The Fight for the Equal Rights Amendment
Many states that failed to ratify the Equal Rights Amendment had previously refused to ratify the woman suffrage amendment (or ratified it decades later, as did North Carolina in 1971).

poor and uneducated women, reduced protections against employment discrimination, and whittled away at legal safeguards against the death penalty.

Feminism on the Defensive

One of the signal achievements of the New Right was capturing the Republican Party's position on women's rights. For the first time in its history, the Republican Party took an explicitly antifeminist tone, opposing both the Equal Rights Amendment and a woman's right to abortion, key goals of women's rights activists. When the time limit for ratification of the ERA ran out in 1982 (Map 30.3), Phyllis Schlafly could claim victory on the issue that first galvanized her antifeminist campaign. (See chapter 28 and "Historical Question," page 796.)

Cast on the defensive, feminists began to focus more on women's economic and family problems; and they found some common ground with the Reagan administration. The Child Support Enforcement Amendments Act helped single and divorced mothers to collect court-ordered child support payments from absent parents. The Retirement Equity Act of 1984 benefited divorced and older women by strengthening their claims to their husbands'

pensions and enabling women to qualify more easily for private retirement pensions.

The Reagan administration had its own concerns about women, specifically about the **gender gap**—women's tendency to vote for liberal and Democratic candidates in larger numbers than men did. (Party leaders welcomed the opposite element of that trend: white men's movement into Republican ranks.) Reagan appointed three women to cabinet posts and, in 1981, selected the first woman, Sandra Day O'Connor, for the Supreme Court. But these actions accompanied a general decline in the number of women and minorities in high-level government positions. And with higher poverty rates than men, women suffered most from Reagan's cuts in social programs.

Although court decisions placed restrictions on women's ability to obtain abortions, feminists fought successfully to retain the basic principles of *Roe v. Wade*. However, they hit a stone wall in efforts to improve day care services and promote pay equity—equal pay for traditionally female jobs that were comparable in worth to jobs performed primarily by men. The women's movement pursued locally what it failed to achieve at the federal level. The pay equity movement took hold in several states, and many states strengthened their laws against rape. States also increased

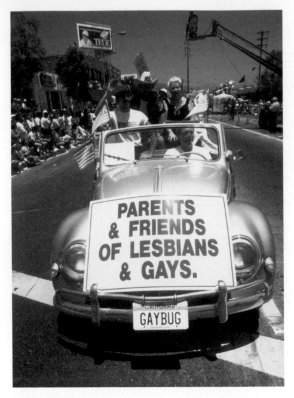

Gay Pride Parades

In June 1970, gays and lesbians marched in New York City to commemorate the first anniversary of the Stonewall riot. Since then, gay pride parades have taken place throughout the United States and in other countries every year in June. A history professor, Robert Dawidoff, pointed out that the parades were not about "flaunting private things in public," as some people charged, but a way for gay men and lesbians to express "pride in our history…in having survived the thousand petty harassments and reminders of a special status we neither seek nor merit." Increasingly, friends, supporters, and families of homosexuals participate in the parades, as these family members do in a Los Angeles parade.
© Bettmann/Corbis.

It grew out of the social upheaval of the 1960s and was sparked by the Stonewall riot of 1969, when gay men and lesbians fought back against a police raid on the Stonewall Inn, a gay bar in New York City's Greenwich Village.

Lesbians and gay men began to organize across the nation in the 1970s, demonstrating and lobbying for an end to discrimination and affirmation of their own decisions about whom to love. One result of their efforts came in 1973 when the American Psychiatric Association ended its categorization of homosexuality as a mental disease. Although the Supreme Court upheld the right of states to enforce laws against sodomy until 2003, most states had taken such laws off the books by the 1980s.

The gay and lesbian rights movement helped closeted homosexuals experience the relief of "coming out." Their visibility increased awareness, if not always acceptance, of homosexuality among the larger population. Activists organized gay rights marches throughout the country and began to win some local protections against discrimination. Beginning with the election of Elaine Noble to the Massachusetts legislature in 1974, several openly gay politicians won offices from mayor to member of Congress; and the Democrats began to include gay rights in their party platforms.

Because initially male homosexuals were disproportionately afflicted, the acquired immune deficiency syndrome (AIDS) epidemic, which researchers identified in 1981, further mobilized the gay and lesbian rights movement in the 1980s. As the disease swept through communities of gay men in New York, San Francisco, and elsewhere, gay men and lesbians organized to promote public funding for AIDS education, prevention, and treatment.

Popular attitudes about homosexuality moved toward greater tolerance but remained complex. By the end of the century, 84 percent of respondents to public opinion polls supported equal job opportunities for gays and lesbians, but 59 percent thought homosexuality was morally wrong. These diverse attitudes led to uneven changes in policies. Dozens of cities banned job discrimination against ho-

funding for domestic violence programs and stepped up efforts to protect victims and prosecute abusers.

The Gay and Lesbian Rights Movement

Influenced by minority struggles, the New Left, the counterculture, and feminism, gay men and lesbians began to claim equal rights and to express pride in their sexual identities. Although an organization for homosexual rights had existed as early as 1924, not until the 1980s did a national mass movement emerge.

Antidiscrimination Laws for Gays and Lesbians, 2000

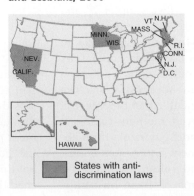

States with antidiscrimination laws

mosexuals, and beginning with Wisconsin in 1982, eleven states made sexual orientation a protected category under civil rights laws. Local governments and many large corporations began to offer health insurance and other benefits to domestic partners. In 2000, the Vermont legislature created for same-sex couples a category called "civil unions," which entitled them to rights available to married couples in areas such as inheritance, taxes, and medical decisions. Yet a strong countermovement challenged the drive for recognition of gay marriage. The Christian Right targeted gays and lesbians as symbols of national immorality and succeeded in overturning some homosexual rights measures, which lagged far behind civil rights guarantees granted to minorities and women.

Conflicts over Environmental Protections

While feminists and the gay and lesbian rights movement battled the "family values" wing of conservatism, environmentalists struggled against conservatives hostile to federal regulations on free enterprise. During the Carter administration, environmentalists won new protections. Warning of radiation leakage, potential accidents, and the hazards of nuclear wastes, environmentalists targeted nuclear power plants, which by 1977 produced about 11 percent of the country's electricity. In 1976, hundreds of members of the Clamshell Alliance went to jail for attempting to block construction of a nuclear plant in Seabrook, New Hampshire. Groups such as Abalone Alliance in California and SHAD (Sound and Hudson against Atomic Development) on Long Island, New York, sprang up across the United States to demand an environment safe from nuclear radiation and waste.

Environmentalists were also aided by disasters that brought national attention to the costs of unregulated economic development. In 1978, residents at Love Canal in Niagara Falls, New York, discovered that their homes sat atop highly toxic waste products from a nearby chemical company and fought to get officials to recognize the danger. Galvanized by the revelation, Love Canal resident Lois Gibbs explained, "I never thought of myself as an activist or organizer. I was a housewife, a mother, but all of a sudden it was my family, my children, and my neighbors."

The perils of nuclear energy claimed national attention in March 1979, when an accident occurred at the Three Mile Island nuclear facility near Harrisburg, Pennsylvania, where technicians worked for days to prevent a meltdown of the reactor core. Popular opposition and the great expense of building nuclear power plants stalled further development of the industry. The explosion of a nuclear reactor and the spread of deadly radiation in Chernobyl, Ukraine, in 1986 further solidified antinuclear concerns as part of the environmental movement.

The Carter administration addressed some environmental concerns. During the gasoline shortage brought on by the Iranian revolution in 1979, Carter won legislation to conserve energy and to provide incentives for the development of environmentally friendly alternative fuels, such as solar energy. He

---

Controversy over the Environment
Secretary of the Interior James Watt joined the Reagan cabinet committed to dismantling much of the environmental regulation of the previous two decades. His efforts drew considerable opposition, and he failed to turn back the clock substantially. In 1983, President Reagan appointed a more moderate replacement. What exactly does this *Newsweek* cover suggest that Watt wants to do to the environment?

FOR MORE HELP ANALYZING THIS IMAGE, see the visual activity for this chapter in the Online Study Guide at bedfordstmartins.com/roarkcompact.

Illustration by Wilson McLean. Reprinted with permission of the artist and *Newsweek* magazine.

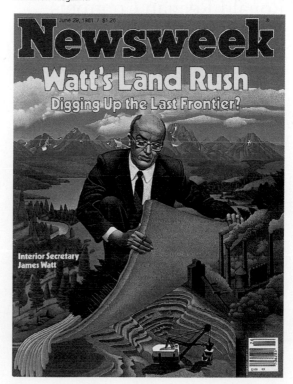

also responded to the Love Canal disaster by sponsoring legislation in 1980 to create the so-called Superfund, $1.6 billion for cleanup of hazardous wastes left by the chemical industry. In addition, Carter signed laws to improve clean air and water programs; to preserve vast areas of Alaska from commercial exploitation; and to control strip mining, which left destructive scars on the land.

Although Ronald Reagan loved the outdoors and his remote ranch in southern California, in contrast to Carter he blamed environmental laws for the nation's sluggish economic growth and targeted them for deregulation. His first secretary of the interior, James Watt, declared, "We will mine more, drill more, cut more timber," and he released federal lands to private exploitation, while the head of the Environmental Protection Agency eased enforcement of air and water pollution measures. The resulting popular outcry led to the resignation of several environmental officials and the failure of other deregulatory goals, indicating that the concerns and values of the environmental movement had to some extent become part of the public consciousness.

> **REVIEW**   What gains and setbacks did feminists, gay and lesbian rights activists, and environmentalists experience during the Reagan years?

Ronald Reagan Confronts an "Evil Empire"

Running for president in 1980, Ronald Reagan had capitalized on the Soviet invasion of Afghanistan and the Iranian hostage crisis, accusing Carter of weakening the military and losing the confidence of the nation's allies and its enemies' respect. As president, he accelerated the arms buildup begun by Carter and harshly censured the Soviet Union, calling it "an evil empire." Yet despite the new aggressiveness—or, as some argued, because of it—Reagan presided over the most impressive thaw in superpower conflict since the **cold war** had begun. On the periphery of the cold war, however, Reagan practiced militant anticommunism, authorizing aid to antileftist movements in Asia, Africa, and Central America and dispatching troops to the Middle East and the Caribbean. When Congress blocked Reagan's efforts to assist opponents of the leftist government in Nicaragua, administration officials resorted to secret and illegal means to effect their agenda.

Militarization and Interventions Abroad

Reagan expanded the military with new bombers and missiles, an enhanced nuclear force in Europe, a larger navy, and a rapid-deployment force. Despite the growing budget deficit, Congress approved most of these programs, and military expenditures shot up by one-third in the first half of the 1980s. Throughout Reagan's presidency, defense spending averaged $216 billion a year, up from $158 billion in the Carter years and higher even than in the Vietnam era.

Justifying the military buildup as a means to negotiate with the Soviets from a position of strength, Reagan provoked an outburst of pleas to halt the arms race. A rally demanding a freeze on additional nuclear weapons drew 700,000 people in New York City in 1982. Hundreds of thousands demonstrated across Europe, stimulated by fears of new U.S. missiles scheduled for deployment in **North Atlantic Treaty Organization (NATO)** countries in 1983.

Reagan startled many of his own advisers in March 1983 by announcing plans for research on the Strategic Defense Initiative (SDI). Immediately dubbed "Star Wars" by critics who doubted its feasibility, the project would deploy lasers in space to destroy enemy missiles before they could reach their targets. Reagan conceded that SDI could appear as "an aggressive policy" allowing the United States to strike first and not fear retaliation. The Soviets reacted angrily because SDI development violated the 1972 ABM treaty and would require the Soviets to invest huge sums in their own Star Wars technology.

The U.S. military buildup failed to guarantee American security. Although Iran released the American hostages, terrorism continued to threaten the United States. In October 1983, an Islamic extremist drove a bomb-filled truck into a U.S. barracks in Lebanon, killing 241 marines (see Map 30.2). The attack prompted Reagan to pull from Lebanon the U.S. troops sent there as part of a peacekeeping mission to monitor the withdrawal of Israeli and Palestinian Liberation Organization forces. Faced with other incidents of murder, kidnapping, and hijacking by various Middle Eastern extremist groups, Reagan refused to negotiate, insisting that to bargain with terrorists would only encourage more assaults.

The Reagan administration sought to contain leftist movements close to home and across the globe. In October 1983, U.S. troops invaded Grenada, a small island nation in the Caribbean that had succumbed to a left-wing, Marxist coup. In Asia, the United States moved more quietly, aiding the Afghan rebels' war against Afghanistan's Soviet-backed government. In the African nation of Angola, the United States armed rebel forces against the Soviet- and Cuban-backed government. Reagan also sided with the South African government that was brutally suppressing black protest against apartheid, forcing Congress to override his veto in order to impose economic sanctions against South Africa.

Administration officials were most fearful of left-wing movements in Central America that Reagan claimed could "destabilize the entire region from the Panama Canal to Mexico." When a leftist uprising occurred in 1981 in El Salvador, the United States sent money and military advisers to prop up the government even though it had committed murderous human rights violations. In neighboring Nicaragua, where Reagan aimed to unseat the left-wing Sandinistas, the administration aided the Contras (literally, "opposers"), a coalition of armed opposition to the Sandinistas. Fearing another Vietnam, many Americans opposed aligning the United States with reactionary forces not supported by the majority of Nicaraguans; and Congress repeatedly instructed the president to stop aid to the Contras or limit it to nonmilitary purposes.

El Salvador and Nicaragua

Deliberately violating congressional will, the administration secretly provided weapons and training to the Contras. Through legal and illegal means, the Reagan administration sustained the Contras and helped wreck the Nicaraguan economy, thereby undermining support for the Sandinista government. After nine years of civil war, Nicaragua's president, Daniel Ortega, agreed to a political settlement, and when he was defeated by a coalition of all the opposition groups, he stepped aside.

The Iran-Contra Scandal

Secret aid to the Contras was part of a larger project that came to be known as the Iran-Contra scandal. It began in 1985, when heads of the National Security Council, NSC aide marine lieutenant colonel Oliver North, and CIA director William Casey arranged to sell arms to Iran, then at war with neighboring Iraq. In exchange, Iranians were to pressure Muslim terrorists to release seven American hostages being held in Lebanon (see Map 30.2). Funds from the arms sales were then channeled through Swiss bank accounts to aid the Nicaraguan Contras. Over the objections of his secretaries of state and defense, Reagan approved the arms sales, but the three subsequently denied knowing that the proceeds were diverted to the Contras.

When news of the affair surfaced in November 1986, the Reagan administration faced serious charges. The president had allowed his aides to bargain with terrorists and violate U.S. neutrality in the Iran-Iraq War. Even worse, the administration had defied Congress's express ban on military aid for the Contras. Brought to trial by an independent prosecutor appointed by Reagan, seven individuals pleaded guilty or were convicted of lying to Congress and destroying evidence. North's felony conviction was later overturned on a technicality, and President George H. W. Bush pardoned the other six officials in December 1992. The independent prosecutor's final report found no evidence that Reagan had broken the law; but it concluded that both Reagan and Vice President Bush had known about the diversion of funds to the Contras and that Reagan had "knowingly participated or at least acquiesced" in covering up the scandal—the most serious case of executive branch misconduct since Watergate.

A Thaw in Soviet-American Relations

A momentous reduction in cold war tensions soon overshadowed the Iran-Contra scandal. The new Soviet-American accord depended both on Reagan's flexibility and on an innovative Soviet head of state who recognized that his country's domestic problems demanded an easing of cold war antagonism. Mikhail Gorbachev assumed power in 1985 determined to revitalize an inefficient Soviet economy incapable of delivering basic consumer goods. Hoping to stimulate production and streamline distribution, Gorbachev introduced some elements of free enterprise and proclaimed a new era of *glasnost* (greater freedom of expression), eventually allowing new political parties, contested elections, and challenges to Communist rule.

Concerns about immense defense budgets moved both Reagan and Gorbachev to the negotiating table. Enormous military expenditures stood between the Soviet premier and his goal of economic revival. With growing popular support for arms reductions, Reagan made disarmament a major goal in his last years in office and readily responded when Gorbachev took the initiative. A positive personal chemistry developed between them, and they met four times between 1985 and 1988. By December 1987, the superpowers had completed an intermediate-range nuclear forces (INF) agreement, eliminating all short- and medium-range missiles from Europe and providing for on-site inspection for the first time.

In 1988, Gorbachev further reduced tensions by announcing a gradual withdrawal from Afghanistan, which had become the Soviet equivalent of America's Vietnam. In Africa, the Soviet Union, United States, and Cuba agreed on a political settlement for the civil war in Angola. And in the Middle East, both superpowers supported a cease-fire and peace talks in the eight-year war between Iran and Iraq.

REVIEW   How did anticommunism shape Reagan's foreign policy?

Conclusion: Reversing the Course of Government

"Ours was the first revolution in the history of mankind that truly reversed the course of government," boasted Ronald Reagan in his farewell address in 1989. The word *revolution* exaggerated the change, but his administration did mark the slowdown or reversal of expanding federal budgets, programs, and regulations that had taken off in the 1930s. Although he did not deliver on the social or moral issues dear to the heart of the New Right, to Phyllis Schlafly, Reagan represented the "choice not an echo" that she had called for in 1964, as he used his skills as "the Great Communicator" to cultivate antigovernment sentiment and undo the liberal assumptions of the **New Deal**.

Distrust of the federal government grew along with the backlash against the reforms of the 1960s and the conduct of the Vietnam War. Watergate and other misdeeds of the Nixon administration further disillusioned Americans. Presidents Ford and Carter restored morality to the White House, but neither could solve the gravest economic problems since the Great Depression—a low rate of economic growth, stagflation, and an increasing trade deficit. Even the Democrat Carter gave higher priority to fiscal austerity than to social reform, and he began the government's retreat from regulation of key industries.

A new conservative movement helped Reagan win the presidency and flourished during his administration. Reagan's tax cuts, combined with hefty increases in defense spending, created a federal deficit crisis that justified cuts in social welfare spending and made new federal

Nuclear Freeze Campaign
Sixteen-year-old Justin Martino made this mask to wear in a march on the Pentagon in 1985 supporting disarmament and world peace. Martino wanted to symbolize his belief that "the arms race has no end except the end of life," and he later contributed the mask to the Smithsonian Museum of American History. The worldwide demonstrations for nuclear disarmament achieved limited success when the United States and Soviet Union signed arms limitation agreements in 1987.
Smithsonian Institution, Washington, D.C.

initiatives unthinkable. Many Americans continued to support specific federal programs, especially those that like Social Security and Medicare reached beyond the poor; but public sentiment about the government in general had taken a U-turn from the Roosevelt era. Instead of seeing the government as a helpful and problem-solving institution, many believed it was not only ineffective at solving national problems but often made things worse. As Reagan appointed new Supreme Court justices, the Court also retreated from its earlier liberalism, in which it had upheld the government's authority to protect individual rights and regulate the economy.

With the economic recovery that set in after 1982 and his optimistic rhetoric, Ronald Reagan lifted the confidence of Americans about their nation and its promise, confidence that had eroded with the economic and foreign policy blows of the 1970s. Beginning his presidency with harsh rhetoric against the Soviet Union and a huge military buildup, Reagan helped move the two superpowers to the highest level of cooperation since the cold war began. Although that accord was not welcome to strong anti-Communist conservatives like Phyllis Schlafly, it signaled developments that would transform American-Soviet relations—and the world—in the next decade.

Suggestions for Further Reading

Douglas Little, *American Orientalism: The United States and the Middle East since 1945* (2002). An excellent overview of American relations with this troubled region.

J. Anthony Lukas, *Common Ground: A Turbulent Decade in the Lives of Three American Families* (1986). A riveting account of race relations in Boston, culminating with the school busing crisis.

Donald G. Mathews and Jane Sherron De Hart, *Sex, Gender, and the Politics of ERA* (1990). An exploration of the experiences and emotions of feminists and antifeminists in the ERA ratification struggle.

Lisa McGirr, *Suburban Warriors: The Origins of the New American Right* (2001). A fascinating account of the complex forces behind the rise of conservatism in Orange County, California.

Jules Tygiel, *Ronald Reagan and the Triumph of American Conservatism* (2005). A concise, well-paced account of the rise and accomplishments of Reagan and conservatism.

Tom Wicker, *One of Us: Richard Nixon and the American Dream* (1991). A very readable biography by a journalist who covered Nixon.

▶ FOR MORE BOOKS ABOUT TOPICS IN THIS CHAPTER, see the Online Study Guide at bedfordstmartins.com/roarkcompact.

▶ FOR ADDITIONAL FIRSTHAND ACCOUNTS OF THIS PERIOD, see Chapter 30 in Michael Johnson, ed., *Reading the American Past*, Third Edition.

▶ FOR WEB SITES AND DOCUMENTS RELATED TO TOPICS AND PLACES IN THIS CHAPTER, see "HistoryLinks," "DocLinks," and "PlaceLinks" at bedfordstmartins.com/roarkcompact.

REVIEWING THE CHAPTER

Follow these steps to review and strengthen your understanding of the chapter.

STEP 1: *Study the **Key Terms** and **Timeline** to identify the significance of each item listed.*

STEP 2: *Answer the **Review Questions**, drawing on key terms and dates to support your answers.*

STEP 3: *Drawing on the Key Terms, Timeline, and Review Questions, answer the broader **Making Connections** questions.*

KEY TERMS

Who

Phyllis Schlafly (p. 783)
Barry Goldwater (p. 783)
Richard Nixon (pp. 784, 787)
Warren E. Burger (p. 786)
Shirley Chisholm (p. 787)
George S. McGovern (p. 787)
Archibald Cox (p. 788)
Samuel J. Ervin (p. 788)
Spiro Agnew (p. 789)
Gerald R. Ford (p. 789)
James Earl "Jimmy" Carter Jr. (p. 790)
Walter F. Mondale (p. 790)
Ronald Reagan (p. 794)
George H. W. Bush (p. 794)
John B. Anderson (p. 795)
Geraldine A. Ferraro (p. 798)
Sandra Day O'Connor (p. 800)
Oliver North (p. 805)

What

South Boston High School (p. 786)
Milliken v. Bradley (p. 786)
Regents of the University of California v. Bakke (p. 787)
Roe v. Wade (p. 787)
Watergate (p. 788)
"Saturday night massacre" (p. 789)
Federal Election Campaign Act of 1974 (p. 789)
Sandinistas (p. 791)
Camp David accords (p. 792)
Carter Doctrine (p. 793)
New Christian Right (p. 795)
supply-side economics (p. 795)
Economic Recovery Tax Act (p. 798)
S&L crisis (p. 798)
Grove City v. Bell (p. 800)
Equal Rights Amendment (p. 801)

Child Support Enforcement Amendments Act (p. 801)
Retirement Equity Act of 1984 (p. 801)
Stonewall riot (p. 802)
acquired immune deficiency syndrome (AIDS) (p. 802)
Love Canal (p. 803)
Three Mile Island (p. 803)
Superfund (p. 804)
Strategic Defense Initiative (SDI) (p. 804)
Iran-Contra scandal (p. 805)
glasnost (p. 806)
intermediate-range nuclear forces (INF) agreement (p. 806)

TIMELINE

◄ **1966** • Republican Ronald Reagan elected governor of California.

1968 • Republican Richard Nixon elected president.

1969 • Warren E. Burger appointed chief justice of U.S. Supreme Court.
• Stonewall riot in New York City.

1971 • Nixon vetoes comprehensive child care bill.

1972 • Nixon campaign aides arrested at Watergate complex.

1974 • Nixon resigns; Gerald Ford becomes president.
• Ford pardons Nixon of any crimes he may have committed while president.
• *Milliken v. Bradley.*

1976 • Democrat Jimmy Carter elected president.

1977 • United States signs Panama Canal treaty.

1978 • Camp David accords.
• *Unversity of California v. Bakke.*

1978–1980 • Congress deregulates airlines, banking, trucking, and railroad industries.

REVIEW QUESTIONS

1. How did Nixon's policies reflect the increasing influence of conservatives on the Republican Party? (pp. 784–87)

2. Why did Richard Nixon resign the presidency in August 1974? (pp. 787–90)

3. How did Carter balance commitment to human rights and anticommunism in his foreign policy? (pp. 790–94)

4. Why did economic inequality increase during Reagan's administration? (pp. 794–800)

5. What gains and setbacks did feminists, gay and lesbian rights activists, and environmentalists experience during the Reagan years? (pp. 800–04)

6. How did anticommunism shape Reagan's foreign policy? (pp. 804–06)

MAKING CONNECTIONS

1. What was Watergate's legacy for American politics in the following decade? In your answer, explain what led to Nixon's resignation. How did Congress try to prevent such abuses of power in the future?

2. Both ends of the American political spectrum changed significantly in the 1970s and 1980s. Describe these changes, and discuss how they shaped contemporary American politics. In your answer, be sure to cite specific political developments.

3. Recent experiences in Vietnam hung over the foreign policy decisions of presidents Carter and Reagan. How did each president try to reconcile the lessons of that conflict and the ongoing cold war? In your answer, be sure to discuss the legacy of the Vietnam War on the United States of the 1970s and 1980s.

4. American regional politics shifted in significant ways during the 1970s and 1980s. Why was grassroots conservatism particularly strong in the Sun Belt? What was its relationship to the civil rights and equal opportunity developments of the 1960s?

▶ **FOR PRACTICE QUIZZES, A CUSTOMIZED STUDY PLAN, AND OTHER STUDY TOOLS,** see the Online Study Guide at bedfordstmartins.com/roarkcompact.

1979 • Carter establishes formal diplomatic relations with China.
• Soviet Union invades Afghanistan.
• Hostage crisis in Iran begins.
• Moral Majority founded.

1980 • Congress passes Superfund legislation.
• Republican Ronald Reagan elected president.

1981 • Researchers identify AIDS virus.
• Economic Recovery Tax Act.

1982 • Large demonstrations against nuclear weapons.

1983 • Terrorist bomb kills 241 U.S. marines in Beirut, Lebanon.
• Reagan announces plans for Strategic Defense Initiative ("Star Wars").

1986 • Iran-Contra scandal.

1987 • INF agreement signed.

1988 • Civil Rights Restoration Act.

A SHRINKING WORLD

The cellular telephone is one of the new technologies contributing to the intensifying of globalization that occurred with the end of the cold war in 1990. Connecting users to conventional telephone networks through microwave radio frequencies, wireless phones began to be used in Tokyo in 1979, and the first American system began in 1983. By the end of the century, hundreds of millions of people used cell phones around the world, not only to call friends and business associates but also to connect to the Internet and send and receive e-mail. Cellular systems have improved communication for people in countries that lack a good wire-based telephone system, facilitating commerce as well as connecting far-flung family members and other individuals. By 2003, cell phones comprised 43 percent of all phones in the United States; in European and other countries, cell phones outnumbered traditional phones. Terrorists who struck the World Trade Center towers and the Pentagon on September 11, 2001, used mobile devices to coordinate the attacks, and many victims of the terror spoke their last words to loved ones over cell phones. Wireless phones decorated with the American flag became popular expressions of patriotism in the aftermath of the attacks.

Kit Hinricks / Pentagon Design.

The End of the Cold War and the Challenges of Globalization

Since 1989

O N APRIL 22, 1988, Ronald Reagan's national security adviser, army general Colin L. Powell, contemplated in his Moscow hotel room the plans that Premier Mikhail Gorbachev had just announced, which would dramatically alter the Soviet Union's government and economy. "Lying there in bed," Powell recalled, "I realized that one phase of my life had ended, and another was about to begin. Up until now, as a soldier, my mission had been to confront, contain, and if necessary, combat communism. Now I had to think about a world without a Cold War." For the next sixteen years, Powell would have a central place in redefining his country's role in a world transformed.

Colin Powell was born in Harlem in 1937 and grew up in the Bronx, the son of parents who had immigrated from Jamaica in 1920. His father headed the shipping department in a garment factory, where his mother worked as a seamstress. After attending public schools, Powell enrolled in City College of New York, where he joined the army's Reserve Officers Training Corps program (ROTC), the defining experience of his college years. "The discipline, the structure, the camaraderie, the sense of belonging," he said, "were what I craved." Commissioned as a lieutenant when he graduated in 1958, Powell began a lifelong career in military and public service, rising to the highest rank of four-star general. He chose to stay in the army primarily because "I loved what I was doing." But he also recognized that "for a black, no other avenue in American society offered so much opportunity."

Powell's two tours of duty in Vietnam taught him that "you do not squander courage and lives without clear purpose, without the country's backing, and without full commitment." In his subsequent capacities as national security adviser to Ronald Reagan, chairman of the Joint Chiefs of Staff in the George H. W. Bush and William Jefferson Clinton administrations, and secretary of state under George W. Bush, Powell endeavored to keep his country out of "halfhearted warfare for half-baked reasons that the American people could not understand or support."

Powell's sense that Gorbachev's reforms would bring about the end of the **cold war** became reality more quickly than anyone anticipated. Eastern Europe broke free from **Communist** control in 1989, and the Soviet Union disintegrated in 1991. As the lone superpower, throughout the 1990s the United

Secretary of State Colin Powell
Among the many characteristics that helped Colin Powell rise through the ranks of the army and serve in four presidential administrations were his loyalty and discretion. The decision by George W. Bush to invade Iraq in March 2003 ran counter to his secretary of state's commitment to acting through the international community and sacrificing American lives only when a vital interest was at stake and a plan for ending the intervention had been established. Although Powell's position lost out to the more hawkish Vice President Dick Cheney and Secretary of Defense Donald Rumsfeld, Powell stayed in his job until 2005 and defended administration policy. In this photo taken in the White House in February 2003, he listens to Rumsfeld; National Security Adviser Condoleezza Rice stands behind them.
Charles Ommanney/Contact Press Images for Newsweek.

States deployed both military and diplomatic power during episodes of instability in Latin America, the Middle East, eastern Europe, and Asia, almost always in concert with the major nations of Europe and Asia. In 1991, in its first full-fledged war since Vietnam, the United States led a United Nations–authorized force of twenty-eight nations to repel Iraq's invasion of Kuwait.

During a temporary retirement from public service in the 1990s, Powell remarked that "neither of the two major parties fits me comfortably." Many Americans seemed to agree: They turned Republican George H. W. Bush out of office in 1992 but elected Republican Congresses during Democrat Bill Clinton's administration; when Republican George W. Bush (son of George H. W. Bush) entered the White House in 2001, he faced a nearly evenly divided Congress. Between 1989 and 2000, domestic policies reflected a slight retreat from the **conservatism** of the Reagan years: The Bush administration approved tighter environmental protections and new rights for people with disabilities, and Clinton signed measures strengthening gun control and aiding low wage earners. But the pendulum swung back in the early years of the second Bush presidency.

All three presidents shared a commitment to hastening the globalizing processes that were linking nations together in an increasingly connected economy. As capital, products, and people crossed national boundaries at greater speed, the United States experienced a surge of immigration rivaling that of a century earlier, which had brought Powell's parents to the United States. Powell cheered **globalization**, predicting that the world would become "defined by trade relations, by the flow of information, capital, technology, and goods, rather than by armies glaring at each other across borders."

He was not so naive as to anticipate a world "without war or conflict," recognizing challenges such as nuclear proliferation, **nationalist** passions in areas of former Soviet dominance, civil wars in Africa, and Islamic **fundamentalism**. But he shared other Americans' shock when in September 2001 deadly terrorist attacks on New York City, the nation's economic center, and on Washington, D.C., its political and military core, exposed American vulnerability to new and horrifying threats. The administration's response to terrorism overwhelmed Secretary of State Powell's commitments to internationalism, multilateralism, and military restraint, as George W. Bush began a second war against Iraq, implementing a radical shift in U.S. foreign policy based on preemptive attacks against presumed threats and going it alone if necessary.

Domestic Stalemate and Global Upheaval: The Presidency of George H. W. Bush

Vice President George H. W. Bush announced his bid for the presidency in the 1988 election, declaring, "We don't need radical new directions." Generally satisfied with the agenda set by Ronald Reagan and facing a Democratic-controlled Congress, Bush proposed few domestic initiatives. His dispatch of troops to oust the corrupt dictator of Panama represented a much longer continuity, following a century of American intervention in Latin America. Yet, as the most dramatic changes since the 1940s swept through the world, his government confronted situations that did not fit the simpler free-world versus communism framework that had guided foreign policy since World War II. Most Americans approved of Bush's handling of two challenges to American foreign policy and military capacity: disintegration of the Soviet Union and its hold over Eastern Europe and Iraq's invasion of neighboring Kuwait. But voters' concern over a sluggish economy and other domestic problems limited Bush to one term in the White House.

Gridlock in Government

The son of a wealthy New England senator, George Herbert Walker Bush fought in World War II, earned a Yale degree, and then settled in Texas to make his own way in the oil industry and politics. He served in Congress during the 1960s and headed the CIA during the Nixon-Ford years. When Ronald Reagan achieved a commanding lead in the 1980 primaries, Bush put his own presidential ambitions on hold, adjusted his more moderate policy positions to fit Reagan's conservative agenda, and accepted second place on the Republican ticket. At the end of Reagan's second term, Republicans rewarded him with their presidential nomination.

Several candidates competed for the Democratic nomination. Reverend Jesse Jackson, whose Rainbow Coalition campaign centered on the needs of minorities, women, working-class families, and the poor, made an impressive bid, winning several primaries and 7 million votes. But a more centrist candidate, Michael Dukakis,

governor of Massachusetts, won the nomination. On election day, half the eligible voters stayed home, indicating their disgust with the negative campaigning or their satisfaction with the Republican record on peace and prosperity. Divided government would remain, however: 54 percent of the voters chose Bush, but the Democrats gained seats in the House and Senate.

Although President Bush saw himself primarily as guardian and beneficiary of the Reagan legacy, he promised "a kinder, gentler nation" and was more inclined than Reagan to approve government activity in the private sphere. For example, he signed the Clean Air Act of 1990, the strongest, most comprehensive environmental law in history. He also signed the Americans with Disabilities Act (1991), which banned job discrimination against the disabled and required that private businesses, public accommodations, and transportation be made handicapped-accessible. Cynthia Jones, publisher of a magazine on disability politics, recalling a breeze that swept the White House lawn at the signing, said, "It was kind of like a new breath of air was sweeping across America.... People knew they had rights. That was wonderful."

Yet Bush needed to satisfy party conservatives. His most famous campaign pledge was "Read my lips: No new taxes," and he opposed most proposals requiring additional federal funds. "If you're looking for George Bush's domestic program, and many people are, this is it: the veto pen," charged Democratic House majority leader Richard Gephardt. Bush vetoed thirty-six bills, including those that would have lifted abortion restrictions, extended unemployment benefits, raised taxes, mandated family and medical leave for workers, and reformed campaign financing. Press reports increasingly used the words *stalemate, gridlock,* and *divided government.*

Continuing a trend begun during the Reagan years, states tried to compensate for this paralysis, becoming more innovative than Washington. "Our federal politics are gridlocked, and governors have become the ones who have to have the courage to put their necks out," said a spokesperson for governors. States passed bills to block corporate takeovers, establish parental leave policies, require equal pay for jobs of equal worth, improve food labeling, and protect the environment. Beginning in the 1980s, a few states began to pass measures guaranteeing gay and lesbian rights. In the 1990s, dozens of cities passed ordinances requiring businesses receiving tax abatements or other city benefits to pay wages well above the federal minimum wage. And in 1999, California passed a gun control bill with much tougher restrictions on assault weapons than reformers had been able to get through Congress.

A huge **federal budget deficit** inherited from the Reagan administration impelled the president in 1990 to abandon his "no new taxes" pledge and agree to modest tax increases for high-income Americans and higher levies on gasoline, cigarettes, alcohol, and luxury items. The new taxes affected only slightly the massive tax reductions of the early 1980s, leaving intact a key element of Reagan's legacy. Moreover, new revenues and controls on spending failed to curb the deficit, boosted by rising costs in Social Security and Medicare-Medicaid as well as by spending on unforeseen emergencies of war and natural disasters.

Bush also continued Reagan's efforts to create a more conservative Supreme Court. His first nominee, federal appeals judge David Souter, won easy confirmation by the Senate. But in 1991, when the only African American on the Court, Justice Thurgood Marshall, retired, Bush set off a national controversy. He nominated Clarence Thomas, a conservative black appeals judge, who had opposed **affirmative action** as head of the Equal Employment Opportunity Commission (EEOC) under Reagan. Charging that Thomas would not protect minority rights, the National Association for the Advancement of Colored People (NAACP) and other **liberal** organizations fought the nomination. Then Anita Hill, a law professor and former EEOC employee, shook the confirmation process by accusing Thomas of sexual harassment.

Before the Senate Judiciary Committee, Thomas angrily denied the alleged incidents. Hill's testimony failed to sway the Senate, which voted narrowly to confirm him. The hearings angered many women, who expressed outrage at the shabby treatment that Hill received from senators seeking to discredit her. **Feminists** complained that men "still don't get it" and redoubled their efforts to get more women into office. But Thomas's confirmation solidified the Supreme Court's shift to the right.

Going to War in Central America and the Persian Gulf

President Bush won greater support for his actions abroad, and he twice sent U.S. soldiers into battle. Nearly every cold war president before

him had dispatched aid or troops to Central America and the Caribbean in the name of suppressing communism; but Bush intervened in Panama for different reasons. The United States had tolerated Panamanian dictator Manuel Noriega when he served as a CIA informer about Communist activities in the 1980s. But in 1989, after Noriega was indicted for drug trafficking by a grand jury in Miami, Florida, and after his troops killed an American marine, President Bush ordered 25,000 military personnel into Panama. In an invasion labeled "Operation Just Cause," U.S. forces quickly overcame Noriega's troops and captured him. Chairman of the Joint Chiefs of Staff Colin Powell noted that "our euphoria over our victory in Just Cause was not universal": Both the UN and the Organization of American States censured the unilateral action by the United States.

If the invasion of Panama fit within the century-old tradition of **Yankee imperialism**, Bush's second military engagement represented both continuity and a decided break with the past. In August 1990, the Iraqi dictator Saddam Hussein sent troops into the small, oil-rich country of Kuwait to the south (Map 31.1). Within days the invasion neared the Saudi Arabian border, threatening the world's largest oil reserves. President Bush reacted quickly, ordering a massive mobilization of American forces and assembling an international coalition to stand up to Iraq. He invoked principles of national self-determination and international law, but longstanding interests in Middle Eastern oil also drove the U.S. response. As the largest importer of oil, the United States consumed one-fourth of the world supply.

Reflecting the easing of superpower tensions, the Soviet Union joined the United States in condemning Hussein and cut off arms shipments to Iraq. The UN declared an embargo on Iraqi oil and authorized the use of force if Iraq did not withdraw from Kuwait by January 15, 1991. By early January, the United States had deployed 400,000 soldiers to Saudi Arabia, joined by 265,000 troops from some two dozen nations, including Egypt, Syria, and several other Arab states. "The community of nations has resolutely gathered to condemn and repel lawless aggression," Bush announced. "With few exceptions, the world now stands as one."

With Iraqi forces still in Kuwait, in January 1991 Bush asked Congress to approve war. Considerable sentiment favored waiting to see if the embargo and other means would force

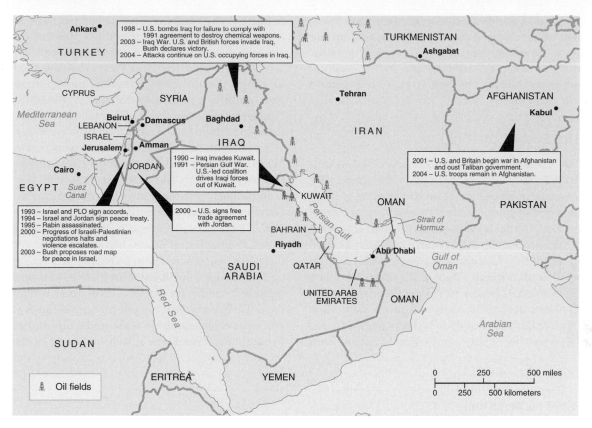

MAP 31.1 Events in the Middle East, 1989–2004

During the Persian Gulf War of 1991, Egypt, Syria, and other Middle Eastern nations joined the coalition against Iraq, and the 22-member Arab League supported the war as a means to liberate Kuwait. After September 11, 2001, the Arab League approved of U.S. military operations in Afghanistan because the attacks "were an attack on the common values of the world, not just on the United States." Yet, except for the countries where the United States had military bases—Bahrain, Kuwait, Qatar, and Saudi Arabia—no Arab country supported the American invasion and occupation of Iraq in 2003. Arab hostility to the United States also reflected the deterioration of Israeli-Palestinian relations from 2000 to 2004, as Arabs charged that the United States allowed Israel to deny Palestinians land and liberty.

Hussein to back down, a position quietly urged within the administration by Colin Powell. Linking the crisis to the failure of U.S. energy conservation, Democratic senator Edward M. Kennedy insisted, "Not a single American life should be sacrificed in a war for the price of oil." Congress debated for three days and then authorized war by margins of five votes in the Senate and sixty-seven in the House. On January 17, 1991, the U.S.-led coalition launched Operation Desert Storm, a forty-day air war against Iraq, bombing military targets, power plants, oil refineries, and transportation networks. Having severely crippled Iraq, the coalition stormed into Kuwait with massive ground forces on February 23, and within one hundred hours Hussein announced that he would withdraw from Kuwait (see Map 31.1).

"By God, we've kicked the Vietnam syndrome once and for all," President Bush exulted on March 1. Most Americans found no moral ambiguity in the Persian Gulf War and took pride in the display of military competence. In contrast to the loss of 50,000 American lives in Vietnam, 270 U.S. servicemen and women perished in Desert Storm. The United States stood at the apex of global leadership, steering a coalition in which Arab nations fought beside their former colonial rulers.

Yet victory did not bring stability to the Middle East. Israel, which had endured Iraqi missile attacks, was more secure, but the Israeli-Palestinian conflict remained intractable. Despite military losses, Saddam Hussein remained in power and turned his war machine on Iraqi Kurds and Shiite Muslims whom the United

States had encouraged to rebel. Hussein continued to develop chemical, biological, and nuclear weapons, while Iraqi citizens suffered malnutrition, disease, and death caused by the continuing embargo and the destruction of the nation's infrastructure.

The End of the Cold War

The forces of change that Gorbachev had encouraged in the Communist world (see chapter 30) swept through Eastern Europe in 1989, where popular uprisings demanded an end to state repression, official corruption, and economic bureaucracies unable to deliver an acceptable standard of living. Communist governments toppled like dominoes (Map 31.2). East Germany opened its border with West Germany, and in November 1989, ecstatic Germans danced on the Berlin Wall, which had separated East and West since 1961, using whatever was at hand

to demolish that dominant symbol of the cold war. An amazed East Berliner crossed over the line exclaiming, "They just let us go. I can't believe it."

Unification of East and West Germany sped to completion in 1990. By 2000, three former **iron curtain** countries—the Czech Republic, Hungary, and Poland—had joined NATO, and more were in line to become members. Although U.S. military forces remained in Europe as part of **NATO**, the commanding role of the United States had been eclipsed. The same was true of its economic clout: Western Europe, including unified Germany, formed a common economic market in 1992. The destiny of Europe, to which the United States and the Soviet Union had held the key for forty-five years, now lay in European hands.

Inspired by the liberation of Eastern Europe, republics within the Soviet Union soon sought their own independence, while Moscow's efforts at economic change brought widespread destitution. In December 1991 Boris Yeltsin, president of the

Fall of the Berlin Wall

After 1961, the Berlin Wall stood as the prime symbol of the cold war and the iron grip of communism over Eastern Europe and the Soviet Union. More than four hundred easterners were killed trying to flee. After Communist authorities opened the wall on November 9, 1989, permitting free travel between East and West Germany, Berliners from both sides gathered at the wall to celebrate.
Eric Bouvet/Gamma Press Images.

For more help analyzing this image, see the visual activity for this chapter in the Online Study Guide at **bedfordstmartins.com/roarkcompact**.

MAP 31.2   Events in Eastern Europe, 1989–2002

The overthrow of Communist governments throughout eastern and central Europe and the splintering of the Soviet Union into more than a dozen separate nations were the most momentous changes in world history since World War II.

READING THE MAP: Which country was the first to overthrow its Communist government? Which was the last? In which nations did elections usher in a change in government?

CONNECTIONS: What problems did Mikhail Gorbachev try to solve, and how did he try to solve them? What policy launched by Ronald Reagan contributed to Soviet dilemmas? Did it create any problems in the United States?

FOR MORE HELP ANALYZING THIS MAP, see the map activity for this chapter in the Online Study Guide at bedfordstmartins.com/roarkcompact.

Russian Republic, announced that Russia and eleven other republics had formed a new entity, the Commonwealth of Independent States (CIS), and other former Soviet states declared independence. With nothing left to govern, Gorbachev resigned. The Soviet Union had dissolved, and with it the cold war tensions that had defined American foreign policy for decades.

China and North Korea resisted the liberalizing tides sweeping the world. In 1989, Chinese soldiers killed hundreds of pro-**democracy** demonstrators in Tiananmen Square in Beijing, and the Communist government cracked down on advocates of reform, arresting some 10,000 cit-

izens. North Korea remained under a Communist dictatorship that threatened to develop nuclear weapons and to deliver materials that could help other nations achieve a nuclear capacity.

"The post–cold war world is decidedly not postnuclear," declared one U.S. official. In 1990, the United States and Soviet Union had signed a strategic arms reduction treaty (START) that cut about 30 percent of each superpower's nuclear arsenal. And, in 1996, the UN General Assembly overwhelmingly approved a total nuclear test ban treaty. Yet India and Pakistan, hostile neighbors, refused to sign and both exploded atomic devices in 1998, increasing the nuclear risk in

South Asia. Moreover, in a highly partisan vote, the Republican-controlled Senate defeated U.S. ratification of the treaty in October 1999, halting a decade of progress on nuclear weapons control.

The 1992 Election

Despite ongoing instability in the Middle East, in March 1991 Bush's chances for reelection in 1992 looked golden. The Gulf War victory catapulted his approval rating to 88 percent, causing the most prominent Democrats to opt out of the presidential race. But that did not deter William Jefferson "Bill" Clinton, who at age forty-five had served as governor of Arkansas for twelve years. Like Jimmy Carter in 1976 and Michael Dukakis in 1988, Clinton and his running mate, Tennessee senator Albert Gore Jr., presented themselves as "New Democrats." Both belonged to the Democratic Leadership Council, which Clinton had helped found in 1985 to rid the party of its liberal image.

In an approach reminiscent of Richard Nixon's appeal to the "silent majority" in 1968, Clinton promised to work for the "forgotten middle class," who "do the work, pay the taxes, raise the kids, and play by the rules." Disavowing the "tax and spend" label that Republicans pinned on his party, he promised a tax cut for the middle class and pledged to reinvigorate government and the economy. Moreover, "We're going to put an end to welfare as we know it," Clinton claimed.

With no new crises to display his talents in foreign policy, Bush was vulnerable to voters' concerns about the ailing economy and to the Clinton campaign's emphasis on bread-and-butter issues. As foreign competition drove businesses to trim budgets, victims of corporate downsizing worried about finding new jobs while other workers worried about keeping theirs. Unemployment edged over 7 percent in 1992.

The popularity of a third candidate, self-made Texas billionaire H. Ross Perot, revealed Americans' frustrations with government and the major parties. Although Perot gave no press conferences, he had plenty of money, used television extensively, and attracted a sizable grassroots movement with his down-to-earth personality and appeals to voters' disgust with Washington. Perot's candidacy hurt the president more than it hurt Clinton, and it established the federal budget deficit as a key campaign issue.

Fifty-five percent of those eligible showed up at the polls, just barely reversing the thirty-year decline in voter turnout. Americans gave Clinton 43 percent of their votes, Bush 38 percent, and Perot 19 percent—the strongest third-party finish since Theodore Roosevelt's Progressive Party candidacy in 1912. By casting two-thirds of their votes against Bush, voters suggested a mandate for change but not the direction that change should take.

REVIEW Why did George H. W. Bush lose the presidency in 1992?

The Clinton Administration's Search for the Middle Ground

The president who asserted "The era of big government is over" was not Ronald Reagan but Bill Clinton, reflecting the Democratic Party's move to the right that had begun with Jimmy Carter in the 1970s. Clinton did not completely abandon liberal principles. He signed important measures benefiting the working poor, delivered incremental reforms to feminists, environmentalists, and other groups, and spoke out in favor of affirmative action and gay rights. Yet his administration attended more to the concerns of middle-class Americans than to the needs of the poor, and it restrained federal programs and appropriations for the disadvantaged.

Clinton's eight-year presidency ended with a budget surplus and the longest economic boom in history. Although various factors generated the prosperity, many Americans identified Clinton with the buoyant economy, elected him to a second term, and continued to support him even when his reckless sexual behavior resulted in **impeachment**. The Senate did not find sufficient cause to remove him from office, but the scandal crippled Clinton's leadership in his last years in office.

Clinton's Promise of Change

Clinton moved cautiously to restore confidence in government as a force for good, reversing some Reagan and Bush policies. In 1993 he eased restrictions on abortion and signed several bills that Republicans had previously blocked, including gun control legislation and the Family and

Medical Leave Act, which entitled workers in larger companies to unpaid leave for childbirth, adoption, and family medical emergencies. The Violence against Women Act of 1994 authorized $1.6 billion and new remedies for combating sexual assault and domestic violence. Clinton won stricter air pollution controls and greater protection for wilderness areas and national forests and parks. Other liberal measures of the Clinton administration included an increase of the minimum wage, expansion of aid to low- and moderate-income college students, and creation of AmeriCorps, a program enabling students to pay for their education with community service.

Most significantly, Clinton pushed through a substantial increase in the Earned Income Tax Credit (EITC) for low wage earners, a program begun in 1975. EITC gave tax cuts to people who worked full-time at meager wages or, if they paid no taxes, a subsidy to lift their family income above the poverty line. By 2003, some 15 million low-income families were benefiting from EITC, almost one-half of them minorities. One expert called it "the largest antipoverty program since the Great Society."

Even before Clinton took office, the economy had begun to rebound, and the boom that followed helped boost his popularity through the 1990s. Economic expansion, along with budget cuts, tax increases, and declining unemployment, produced in 1998 the first surplus since 1969. Despite the biggest tax cut since 1981—a 1997 law reducing levies on estates and capital gains and providing tax credits for families with children and for higher education—the surplus grew. The seemingly inexorable growth of government debt had turned around.

Clinton stumbled badly, however, in his efforts to provide universal health insurance and curb skyrocketing medical costs. Under the direction of First Lady Hillary Rodham Clinton, the administration bill presented an ambitious, complicated plan that much of the health care industry charged would mean higher taxes and government interference in health care decisions. Although the bill failed, Congress enacted piecemeal reform enabling workers who changed jobs to retain health insurance and underwriting health care for 5 million uninsured children. Health care became an even more critical issue in the twenty-first century, as the number of uninsured Americans reached 45 million in 2004.

Along with promoting a more active federal government, Clinton used his appointing

Clinton Greets AmeriCorps Volunteers
One of President Bill Clinton's first domestic initiatives was the creation of AmeriCorps in September 1993. Based on earlier national service programs such as the Civilian Conservation Corps of the New Deal and the VISTA program of the Great Society, AmeriCorps engaged citizens, especially youth, in full-time projects aimed at the improvement of education, public safety, health, and the environment. Here Clinton greets young volunteers in September 1994, as Hillary Clinton looks on. The photo captures some of Clinton's remarkable ability to connect with citizens and make them feel that he cared about them.
© Larry Downing/Reuters/Corbis.

powers to change its face to one that "looked like America," building on the gradual progress women and minorities had made during the previous decades. In the executive branch, he appointed the most diverse group of department heads ever assembled. Of twenty-three key appointments, six were women, three African American, and two Latino. Secretary of Commerce Norman Y. Mineta became the first Asian American to hold a cabinet seat. Janet Reno became the first female attorney general and Madeleine K. Albright the first female secretary of state. Clinton's judicial appointments had a similar cast. Of his first 129 appointments to federal courts, nearly one-third were women, 31 were black, and 11 were Hispanic. In 1993, he named the second woman to the Supreme Court, feminist Ruth Bader Ginsburg, who had orchestrated the strategy that won key women's rights rulings from the Supreme Court before she became an appeals court judge in 1980.

The Clinton Administration Moves Right

While parts of Clinton's agenda fell within the liberal tradition, his presidency overall moved the party to the right. The $4.4 trillion deficit he inherited precluded significant federal spending, and the 1994 elections swept away the Democratic majorities in both houses of Congress, encouraging Clinton to embrace more strongly Republican issues such as reforming welfare and downsizing government.

A considerably more extreme antigovernment sentiment developed far from Washington in grassroots armed militias. Their stance celebrated white Christian supremacy and reflected conservatives' hostility to—for example—taxes and the United Nations. Claiming the need to defend themselves from government tyranny, they stockpiled weapons and anticipated government repression. Their ranks grew with passage of gun control legislation and after government agents stormed the headquarters of an armed religious cult in Waco, Texas, in April 1993, resulting in more than 80 deaths. On the second anniversary of that event, a bomb leveled a federal building in Oklahoma City, taking 169 lives. Authorities quickly arrested two militia members, who were tried and convicted in 1997.

Clinton bowed to conservative views on homosexual rights, backing away from a campaign promise to lift the ban on gays in the military. Instead, in 1993 he announced the "don't ask, don't tell" policy, forbidding officials from asking military personnel about their sexuality but allowing dismissal of men and women who said they were gay or engaged in homosexual behavior. There followed a 67 percent jump in discharges of homosexuals, one of whom was army Arabic linguist Cathleen Glover. "The military preaches integrity, integrity, integrity," she said, "but asks you to lie to everyone around you." In 1996, Clinton also signed the Defense of Marriage Act, prohibiting the federal government from recognizing state-licensed marriages between same-sex couples.

Clinton's efforts to cast himself as a centrist were apparent in his handling of the **New Deal** program Aid to Families with Dependent Children (AFDC), which most people called welfare. Public sentiment about poverty had been shifting since the 1960s. Instead of blaming poverty on lack of adequate jobs or other external circumstances, more people blamed the poor themselves and government welfare programs believed to trap the poor in cycles of dependency. Nearly everyone considered work better than welfare but disagreed about whether the economy could provide sufficient jobs at decent wages and how much job training, child care, and government assistance poor people needed in the transition from welfare to work.

By vetoing two measures on welfare reform, Clinton forced a less punitive bill, which he signed as the 1996 election approached. The Personal Responsibility and Work Opportunity Reconciliation Act abolished ADFC and with it the nation's fifty-year-old pledge to provide a minimum level of subsistence for all its children. The law provided grants to the states; but it limited welfare payments to two years, regardless of whether the recipient could find a job, and it set a lifetime limit of aid at five years.

A "moment of shame," cried Marian Wright Edelman, president of the Children's Defense Fund, when Clinton signed the bill. State and local officials across the country scrambled to understand the law and how to implement it. By 2003, welfare rolls had been cut by 60 percent, but that did not mean that all former welfare recipients had become self-supporting. Forty percent of former welfare mothers were not working regularly after being cut from the rolls, and those with jobs earned on average only about $12,000 a year.

Clinton's signature on the new law denied Republicans a partisan issue in the 1996 election campaign. The president ran as a moderate who would save the country from extremist Republicans, while the Republican Party also moved to the center, passing over a field of conservatives to nominate Kansan Robert Dole, a World War II hero and former Senate majority leader. Clinton won 50 percent of the votes; 41 percent went to Dole and 9 percent to third-party candidate Perot. The largest **gender gap** to date appeared in the election: Women gave 54 percent of their votes to Clinton and 38 percent to Dole, while men split their votes nearly evenly. Although Clinton won reelection with room to spare, voters sent a Republican majority back to Congress.

Impeaching the President

Clinton's genial and articulate style, his ability to capture the middle ground of the electorate, and the nation's economic resurgence enabled the self-proclaimed "comeback kid" to survive scandals and an impeachment trial in 1998. Early in his presidency, charges of illegalities related to firings of White House staff, political use of FBI records, and "Whitewater"—the nickname for the Clintons' real estate dealings in Arkansas—led to an official investigation by an independent prosecutor. The president also faced a sexual harassment lawsuit filed in 1994 by a state employee who claimed that Clinton had made unwanted sexual advances while governor. A federal court threw out her suit in 1998, but Clinton's sexual recklessness continued to threaten his presidency.

In January 1998 Kenneth Starr, independent prosecutor for Whitewater, began to investigate the charge that Clinton had had sexual relations with a twenty-one-year-old White House intern, Monica Lewinsky, and then lied about it to a federal grand jury. Clinton first vehemently denied the charge but subsequently bowed to the mounting evidence against him. Starr took his case for impeachment to the House of Representatives, which in December 1998 voted, mostly along party lines, to impeach the president on two counts: perjury and obstruction of justice. Clinton became the second president—after Andrew Johnson, in 1868—to be impeached by the House and tried by the Senate.

Most Americans condemned the president's behavior yet continued to approve his presidency and to oppose impeachment. Some saw Starr as a fanatic invading individuals' privacy; most people separated what they considered the president's private actions from his public duties. One man said, "Let him get a divorce from his wife. Don't take him out of office and disrupt the country." Those favoring impeachment insisted that the president must set a high moral standard for the nation and that lying to a grand jury, even over a private matter, was a serious offense.

The Senate trial was less partisan. A number of senators found Clinton guilty of perjury and obstruction of justice but did not believe that those actions constituted the high crimes and misdemeanors required by the Constitution for removal from office. With a two-thirds majority needed for that result, the Senate voted 45 to 55 on the perjury count and 50 to 50 on the obstruction of justice count. A majority, including some Republicans, seemed to agree with a Clinton advocate that the president's behavior, while "indefensible, outrageous, unforgivable, shameless," did not warrant his removal from office.

The investigation that triggered events leading up to impeachment ended in 2000 when the independent counsel reported insufficient evidence of illegalities related to the Whitewater land deals. The probe had cost almost $60 million of federal funds. In the face of widespread dissatisfaction with Whitewater and other investigations by special prosecutors, Congress let the independent counsel act expire in 1998.

The Booming Economy of the 1990s

Clinton's ability to weather the impeachment crisis owed much to the prosperous economy, which in 1991 began the longest period of expansion in U.S. history. During the 1990s, the gross domestic product grew by more than one-third, thirteen million new jobs were created, unemployment reached its lowest point in twenty-five years, inflation remained in check, and the stock market soared. Clinton eagerly took credit for the thriving economy, and his policies did contribute to the boom. He made deficit reduction a priority, and in exchange the Federal Reserve Board and bond market traders lowered interest rates, which in turn encouraged economic expansion by making money easier to borrow. Businesses also prospered because they had squeezed down their costs through restructuring and laying off workers. Economic problems in Europe and Asia helped American firms become more competitive in the international market. And the computer revolution and the application of information technology tremendously boosted productivity.

People at all income levels benefited from the economic boom, but it had uneven effects—in contrast to the economic expansion of the 1950s and 1960s. Gaps between rich and poor and between the rich and the middle class that had been growing since the 1970s failed to narrow. This persistence of inequality in a rising economy was linked in part to the growing use of information technology, which increased demand for highly skilled workers while the movement of manufacturing jobs abroad lessened opportunities and wages for the less skilled. In addition, deregulation and the continuing decline of unions hurt lower-skilled workers, and the national minimum wage failed to keep up with inflation.

Although more minorities than ever attained middle-class status, in general people of color remained lowest on the economic ladder. When the median income for white families surpassed $45,000 in 2003, it stood at $30,000 and

$33,000 for African American and Hispanic American households, respectively. Median family income for Asian Americans exceeded that of whites, but only because Asian families had more wage earners. In 2003, poverty afflicted about 30 percent of blacks and Latinos and 25 percent of American Indians, in contrast to a white rate of 10 percent.

> **REVIEW**   What policies of the Clinton administration reflected President Clinton's effort to move his party to the right?

The United States in a Globalizing World

America's economic success in the 1990s was linked to its dominance in the world economy. From that position, President Clinton tried to shape the tremendous transformations occurring in a process that came to be called globalization—the growing integration and interdependence of national citizens and economies. His administration lowered a number of barriers to trade across national borders, despite stiff opposition from critics who emphasized the economic deprivation and environmental devastation that often resulted.

In contrast to Clinton's clear vision about the U.S. role in the global economy, the thinking of Clinton and his advisers about the use of military and diplomatic power seemed less certain. The president took military action in Somalia, Haiti, the Middle East, and eastern Europe, and he pushed hard to ease the conflict between Israel and the Palestinians. Yet no new global strategy emerged to replace the **containment** of communism as the decisive factor in the exercise of American power abroad.

Defining America's Place in a New World Order

In 1991, President George H. W. Bush declared a "new world order" emerging from the ashes of the cold war. As the sole superpower, the United States was determined to lead the nations of the world and serve as a model of freedom and democracy. Yet policymakers struggled to define

guiding principles for the nation's use of military and diplomatic power in a post–cold war world of some 190 nations. Combatting Saddam Hussein's naked aggression and threat to vital oil reserves seemed the obvious course to Bush and his advisers in 1991. Determining the appropriate action in other areas of instability, however, proved much more difficult, and the United States under Clinton applied its force inconsistently throughout the 1990s.

Africa offers a case in point. Civil wars, famine, and extreme human suffering there rarely evoked a strong American response. In 1991, President Bush ended economic sanctions against South Africa as it began to recognize the rights of its black majority. In 1992, guided largely by humanitarian concern, Bush attached U.S. forces to a UN operation in the small northern African country of Somalia, where famine and civil war raged. In 1993, President Clinton allowed the humanitarian mission in Somalia to turn into "nation building"—an effort to establish a stable government—and 18 U.S. soldiers were killed. The outcry at home suggested that most Americans were unwilling to sacrifice lives when no vital economic or political interest seemed threatened. Indeed, both the United States and the United Nations stood by in 1994 when more than a half million people were massacred in a brutal civil war in the central African nation of Rwanda.

As always, the United States was more inclined to use force nearer its borders, but in the case of the Caribbean country of Haiti it gained international support for intervention. In 1991, after a military coup overthrew Jean-Bertrand Aristide, the democratically elected president of Haiti, thousands of Haitians tried to escape political violence and poverty, many on flimsy boats heading for Florida. Clinton got the United Nations to impose economic sanctions on Haiti and to authorize intervention by U.S. troops. In September 1994, hours before 20,000 troops were to invade Haiti, the military leaders promised to step down. U.S. forces peacefully landed and began disarming Haitian soldiers, and Aristide was restored to power. Initially a huge success, U.S. policy continued to be tested as Haiti faced grave economic challenges and a new rebellion in 2004.

In eastern Europe, the collapse of communism ignited the most severe crisis on the continent since the 1940s. During the cold war, the Communist government of Yugoslavia, a federation of six republics, had held ethnic tensions in check, and many Muslims, Croats, and Serbs had grown accustomed to living and working together. After the Communists were swept out in 1989, Yugoslavia splintered into separate states and fell into civil war as ruthless leaders exploited ethnic differences to bolster their power.

The Serbs' aggression against the Bosnian Muslims in particular horrified much of the world, but both European and U.S. leaders hesitated to use military force. As reports of terror, rape, and torture in Bosnia increased, American leaders worried about the image of the world's strongest nation unwilling to use its power to stop the violence. In November 1995, the United States brought the leaders of Serbia, Croatia, and Bosnia to Dayton, Ohio, where they hammered out a peace treaty. President Clinton then agreed to send 20,000 American troops to Bosnia as part of a NATO peacekeeping mission.

In 1998, new fighting broke out in the southern Serbian province of Kosovo, where ethnic Albanians, who constituted 90 percent of the population, were making a bid for independence. The Serbian army brutally retaliated, driving out one-third of Kosovo's 1.8 million Albanian Muslims. In 1999, NATO launched a U.S.-led bombing attack on Serbian military and government targets that, after three months, forced Serbian president Slobodan Milosevic to agree to a peace settlement. Serbians voted Milosevic out of office in October 2000, and he was brought before an international tribunal in 2002 to be tried for genocide.

Elsewhere Clinton remained willing to deploy American power when he could send missiles rather than soldiers, and he also was prepared to act without international support or UN sanction. In August 1998, bombs exploded in U.S. embassies in Kenya and Tanzania, killing 12 Americans and more than 250 Africans. Clinton retaliated with missile attacks on terrorist training camps in Afghanistan and facilities in Sudan controlled by Osama bin Laden, a Saudi-born millionaire who financed the Islamic-extremist terrorist network linked to the embassy attacks.

Breakup of Yugoslavia

Clinton also launched air strikes in December 1998 against Iraqi military installations. At the end of the Gulf War in 1991, Saddam Hussein had agreed to eliminate Iraq's chemical, germ, and nuclear weapons and to allow UN inspections. But he resisted full compliance with the agreement, prompting the U.S. attacks. Whereas Bush had acted in the Gulf War with the support of an international force that included Arab states, Clinton acted unilaterally and in the face of Arab opposition. As the lone superpower after the cold war ended, the United States saw less need to rally international support and cooperation.

Elsewhere in the Middle East, Clinton used diplomatic rather than military power, continuing the decades-long efforts to ameliorate the Israeli-Palestinian conflict. In 1993, for the first time, Yasir Arafat, head of the Palestine Liberation Organization (PLO), and Yitzhak Rabin, Israeli prime minister, recognized the existence of each other's state and agreed to Israeli withdrawal from and Palestinian self-government in the Gaza Strip and Jericho. Less than a year later, in July 1994, Clinton presided over another turning point as Rabin and King Hussein of Jordan signed a declaration of peace. Yet obdurate issues remained to be settled: control of Jerusalem, with sites sacred to Christians, Jews, and Muslims alike; the fate of Palestinian refugees; and the more than 200,000 Israeli settlers living in the West Bank, the land seized by Israel in 1967, where 3 million Palestinians were determined to establish their own state. Negotiations between the PLO and Israel broke down in 2000, and violence between Israelis and Palestinians consumed the area, strengthening anti-American sentiment among Arabs, who saw the United States as Israel's ally.

Events in Israel since 1989

1993 – Israel and PLO sign accords.
1994 – Israel and Jordan sign peace treaty.
1995 – Rabin assassinated.
2000 – Progress of Israeli-Palestinian negotiations halts and violence escalates.
2003 – Bush proposes road map for peace in Israel.
2005 – Israel withdraws from Gaza.

Debates over Globalization

Although the Clinton administration sometimes seemed uncertain about the use of military force, it moved energetically on the economic side to speed up the growth of a "global marketplace." The process of globalization had begun in the fifteenth century, when Europeans began to trade with and populate other parts of the world. Between the U.S. Civil War and World War I, products, capital, and labor crossed national boundaries in ever larger numbers. In that era, globalization was based on **imperialism**, as Western nations took direct control of foreign territories, extracted their natural resources, and restricted manufacturing. Late-twentieth-century globalization, in contrast, advanced among sovereign nations and involved the industrialization of less developed areas, such as Korea and China. Other distinguishing marks of the more recent globalization were its scope and intensity: The Internet, cell phones, and other new communications technology connected nations, corporations, and individuals—nearly the entire planet—at much greater speed and much less cost than at any previous time.

As Clinton worked to diminish impediments to the free flow of products and capital across national borders, debates about globalization raged. Which trade barriers should be eliminated and under what conditions? In a world economy characterized by **laissez-faire** capitalism, who would protect workers' health and security, human rights, and the environment? In November 1999, tens of thousands of activists dramatized the debate when they assembled in Seattle, Washington, to protest at a meeting of the World Trade Organization (WTO). The WTO had been established in 1994 to liberalize trading policies and practices and mediate economic disputes among some 135 member nations. Activists charged this international economic body with promoting a global economy that undercut standards and wages for workers, destroyed the environment, and devastated poorer, developing nations.

Tico Almeida, a new college graduate, was thrilled in Seattle to hear "workers and unions from rich and poor countries alike stand together and say, 'We want rules for workers' rights to be integrated into the global economy.'" At the WTO demonstrations and elsewhere, U.S. labor unions emphasized the flight of factory jobs to developing nations as corporate executives sought cheaper labor to lower production costs. (See "Beyond America's Borders," page 826.) For example, General Motors produced its Pontiac Le Mans in South Korea with parts manufactured in Japan, Germany, Taiwan, Singapore, Britain, Ireland, and Barbados. Critics linked globalization to the weakening of unions, the erosion of the social safety net provided for workers since the 1930s, and the growing gap between rich and poor in the United States. Demanding "fair trade" rather than simply free trade, they wanted trade treaties requiring other countries to enforce decent wage and labor standards. Environmentalists similarly wanted coun-

Protests against the WTO

Environmentalists and animal protection advocates were among the varied groups demonstrating against the World Trade Organization when it attempted to meet in Seattle, Washington, in November 1999. These activists dressed as sea turtles to protest WTO agreements permitting economic actions that they believed threatened the survival of the animals.

Wide World Photos, Inc.

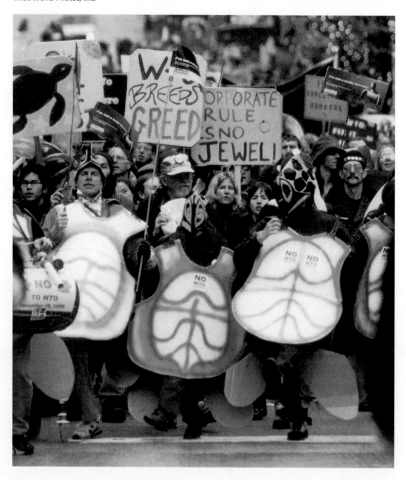

tries seeking increased commerce with the United States to adopt measures that would eliminate or reduce pollution and prevent the destruction of endangered species.

Globalization controversies often centered on relationships between the United States, which dominated the world's industrial core, and the developing nations on the periphery, whose cheap labor and lax environmental standards attracted investment. United Students Against Sweatshops, for example, attacked the international conglomerate Nike, which paid Chinese workers $1.50 per pair to produce shoes selling for more than $100 in the United States. Yet many leaders of developing nations actively sought foreign investment, insisting that wages deemed pitiful by Americans offered people in poor nations a much better living than they could otherwise obtain. At the same time developing countries often pointed to the hypocrisy of the United States in advocating free trade in industry while heavily subsidizing its own agricultural sector. "When countries like America, Britain and France subsidize their farmers," complained John Nagenda, a grower in Uganda, "we get hurt."

The demonstrations in Seattle, and protests that followed in Washington, D.C., and in other parts of the world, targeted international financial institutions such as the WTO and the International Monetary Fund (IMF). Protesters charged that the WTO and IMF forced devastating regulations on developing nations, which had little voice in trade policy decisions. For example, the IMF often required poor nations to privatize state industries, deregulate their economies, and cut social welfare spending in order to obtain loans. While globalization's cheerleaders argued that in the long run everyone would benefit, critics focused on the short-term victims. "International trade and global financial markets are very good at generating wealth," conceded American businessman George Soros, "but they cannot take care of other social needs, such as the preservation of peace, alleviation of poverty, protection of the environment, labor conditions, or human rights."

As the debates continued, Clinton sought new measures to ease restrictions on international commerce, building on steps taken by Presidents Reagan and Bush. In November 1993, Clinton won congressional approval of the North American Free Trade Agreement (NAFTA). It eliminated all tariffs and trade barriers among the United States, Canada, and Mexico, making the NAFTA trio second only to the European Union, the largest trading bloc in the world. In 1994, the Senate ratified the General Agreement on Tariffs and Trade (GATT), establishing the WTO to enforce substantial tariff reductions, the elimination of import quotas, and other provisions of the GATT treaty. And in 2005, Clinton's successor, George W. Bush, got Congress to lower more trade barriers with passage of the Central American Free Trade Agreement (CAFTA).

Critics of globalization enjoyed a few successes. In 2000, President Clinton signed an executive order requiring an environmental impact review before the signing of any trade agreement. Beyond the United States, officials from the World Bank and IMF along with representatives from wealthy economies promised in 2000 to provide poor nations more debt relief and a greater voice in decisions about loans and grants. According to World Bank president James D. Wolfensohn, "Our challenge is to make globalization an instrument of opportunity and inclusion—not fear."

The Internationalization of the United States

Globalization was typically associated with the expansion of American enterprise and culture to other countries, yet the United States experienced within its own borders the dynamic forces of globalization. Already in the 1980s, Japanese, European, and Middle Eastern investors had purchased American stocks and bonds, real estate, and corporations such as Firestone, Brooks Brothers, and 20th Century Fox. Local communities welcomed foreign capital, and states competed to recruit foreign automakers to establish plants within their boundaries. American non-union workers began to produce Hondas in Marysville, Ohio, and BMWs in Spartanburg, South Carolina. By 2002, the paychecks of nearly 4 million American workers came from European-owned companies.

Globalization was transforming not just the economy but American society as well, as the United States experienced a tremendous surge of immigration in the late twentieth century. (See appendix II, page A-30.) By 2006, more than one in every ten Americans was foreign-born. The 20 million who arrived between 1980 and 2005 surpassed the previous peak immigration of the

Jobs in a Globalizing Era

In November 2001, Paul Sufronko, a supervisor at Rocky Shoes and Boots in the small town of Nelsonville, Ohio, handed out final paychecks to the company's last sixty-seven employees in the United States, ending a process of outsourcing jobs that had begun in the 1980s. Before his own job ended, Sufronko traveled to Rocky plants in Puerto Rico and the Dominican Republic to complete the transfer of production and to train a local worker to do his job. Asked about his job loss, the thirty-six-year-old said, "I had other plans. Things just didn't work out."

Many Americans did not take the loss of their jobs to foreign workers so philosophically. One, a son of Mexican American sharecroppers, who had been laid off when Chrysler shut down Jeep production in Kenosha, Wisconsin, in 1988, mourned the loss of "pride in being an autoworker." One of his coworkers believed that "corporations are looking for a disposable workforce.... No commitment to community; no commitment to country."

In 1960, American workers made 96 percent of all shoes bought in the United States; by 2000, nearly all shoes came from abroad. The globalizing process was not a new experience for Julio Lopez, a temporary beneficiary of Rocky's outsourcing of labor. Born in Puerto Rico, he first worked in a New York toy factory, until it moved its operations overseas. Returning to Puerto Rico, he spent twenty-three years making shoes for another company until it sought cheaper labor elsewhere. In

2001, he found work at Rocky's Puerto Rico plant at the minimum wage of $5.15 an hour, less than half of what Nelsonville workers had earned. Lopez hoped that the factory would stay in Puerto Rico for eight more years. "Then I will be 62, and I can retire." His hopes were not unusual, and his concerns were not unfounded. Lillian Chaparro, the plant manager, spoke about the perpetual motion of jobs: "It's like a chain, you know? The jobs leave the U.S. They come here. Then they go to the Dominican, to China. That's why I push people—we have to be able to compete."

The athletic shoe manufacturer Nike was one of the first companies to exploit the advantages of production abroad, turning to Japan in the 1960s. When labor costs there began to rise, Nike shifted production first to South Korea. When Korean workers demanded better wages and working conditions, Nike moved production to China, Indonesia, and Thailand. Local contractors in Indonesia paid workers as little as fifteen cents an hour as they churned out 70 million pairs of shoes in 1996.

Charles Seitz, who lost his job at Eastman Kodak in Rochester, New York, when the company moved some operations to China and Mexico, was not entirely wrong when he said, "There's nothing made here anymore." In the 1950s, one-third of all American workers were employed in manufacturing; by the twenty-first century just 10 percent produced goods. Of course,

not all the job losses resulted from the transfer of work overseas. At Kodak, for example, a machine took the place of fourteen workers who previously had mixed film-making ingredients. In the 1980s and 1990s, American corporations sought intensely to increase production so that they could downsize their workforces. Moreover, some companies built plants abroad in order to be close to burgeoning markets there, as foreign automakers had done when they began operations in the United States. Because so many companies contracted out production to foreign companies rather than employing foreign workers directly, the number of U.S. jobs lost through outsourcing is difficult to calculate.

The outsourcing of work did not end with manufacturing jobs. By 2003, corporations were relying on workers abroad, especially in India, for a wide range of service and professional work. For example, 1,700 engineers and scientists conducted research for General Electric in Bangalore, India, which became the South Asian equivalent of California's Silicon Valley. Avis employed East Indians to manage its online car rentals. Technology experts in Bangalore provided telephone help for customers flummoxed by their Dell computers. And American schoolchildren received online tutoring from teachers in Cochin, India.

A research firm executive pointed to the power of technology to overcome distance and noted, "You can get crackerjack Java programmers in India right out of college for $5,000 a year versus $60,000." Some critics worried about not only the immediate loss of jobs at home but also the long-term

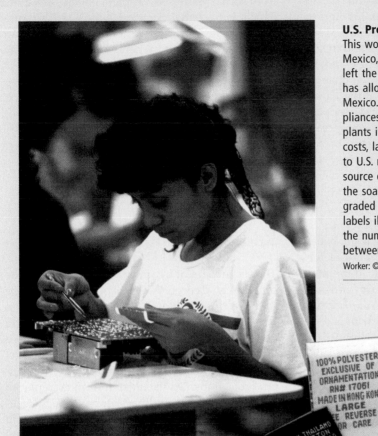

U.S. Products Made Abroad

This woman working at a maquiladora (assembly plant) in Tijuana, Mexico, is part of one process by which manufacturing jobs have left the United States. Since the 1960s, the Mexican government has allowed foreign-owned companies to establish operations in Mexico. In the 1980s and 1990s, U.S. manufacturers of home appliances, electronics, automobiles, and other products built 3,500 plants in Mexico near the U.S. border to capitalize on low labor costs, lax environmental protection measures, and close proximity to U.S. markets. For Mexico, the program proved an important source of employment for nearly one million workers by 2002, but the soaring population and dumping of hazardous wastes degraded the environment in the borderland area. The manufacturing labels illustrate the global dispersal of garment manufacturing as the number of apparel jobs in the United States was cut in half between 1994 and 2003.

Worker: © Annie Griffiths Belt/Corbis; labels: Picture Research Consultants & Archives.

consequences for the American economy. "If we continue losing these jobs," argued a computer software executive, "our schools will stop producing the computer engineers and programmers we need for the future."

The flight of jobs has not been entirely one-way. Seeking to move production closer to its market, in 1982 Honda became the first Japanese company to manufacture cars in the United States, hiring more than 150,000 American workers by 2003. Other automakers followed. In all, about 5 percent of all American workers in 2003 received their pay-checks from foreign companies operating in the United States.

The vast majority of jobs, however, moved in the opposite direction. In 2003, one of the most distinctive American products rolled off a U.S. production line for the last time. The blue jeans company founded in 1853 by Levi Strauss closed its last plants in the United States, contracting out its work to suppliers in fifty other countries from Latin America to Asia. The company's president refused to see any significance in the move. "Consumers are used to buying products from all over the world," he said. "The issue is not where they're made." But Clara Flores, who had sewn hems for twenty-four years in San Antonio, Texas, wondered, "Where are we ever going to find something like this?" Marivel Gutierez, a side-seam operator, acknowledged that workers in Mexico and elsewhere would benefit, suggesting the globalization of the American dream. "But what happens to our American dream?" Workers like these stood as stark reminders that as the benefits of the free flow of economic enterprise across national borders reached many, globalization left multitudes of victims in its wake.

first two decades in the twentieth century and exhibited a striking difference in country of origin. Eighty-five percent of the earlier immigrants had come from Europe; by the 1980s, almost half of the new arrivals were Asians, and nearly 40 percent came from Latin America and the Caribbean. Consequently, immigration changed the racial and ethnic composition of the nation. By 2002, the Asian and Pacific Islander population had grown to 13 million, and the number of Latinos increased to nearly 39 million, becoming—at 13 percent—the largest minority group in the nation.

The racial composition of the new immigration revived the century-old wariness of the native-born toward recent arrivals. Pressure for more restrictive policies stemmed from beliefs (generally unfounded) that immigrants took jobs from the native-born and fears that immigrants would erode the dominant culture and language. Americans expressed particular hostility to the millions of immigrants who entered the country illegally, even though the economy depended on their cheap labor. The Immigration Reform and Control Act of 1986, which penalized employers who hired undocumented aliens but also granted amnesty to some two million illegal immigrants who had been in the country before 1982, did little to stem the tide.

The new immigration was again making America an international, interracial society. Sushi bars and Thai restaurants appeared in midwestern cities, cable TV companies added Spanish-language stations, and a truly international sport—soccer—soared in popularity. Mixed marriages also displayed the growing fusion of cultures, recognized by the Census Bureau in 2000 when it let Americans check more than one racial category on their forms. Demographers predicted that by 2050 the American population would be just over 50 percent white, 16 percent black, 24 percent Hispanic, and 9 percent Asian.

Like their predecessors a hundred years earlier, the majority of post-1965 immigrants were unskilled and poor. They took the lowest-paying jobs, providing farm and yard work, child and elder care, and cleaning services. Yet a significant number were highly skilled workers, sought after by burgeoning high-tech industries. For example, in 1999 about one-third of the scientists and engineers who worked in California's Silicon Valley had been born abroad. A majority of the thirty-one employees of UroGenesys, Inc.,

a California biotech company, were immigrants from such countries as Vietnam, Poland, Lebanon, China, India, Israel, Scotland, and Peru. The company's owner boasted, "I cannot think of another country in the world where you could so easily put such a team together."

> **REVIEW** Who criticized free trade agreements and why?

President George W. Bush: Conservatism at Home and Radical Initiatives Abroad

The second son of a former president to gain the presidency, George W. Bush pushed an agenda that was closer to Ronald Reagan's than it was to his father's, George H. W. Bush. The younger Bush got Congress to pass tax cuts that favored the wealthy and helped send the federal budget into a huge deficit, and he reduced environmental protections. As Islamist terrorism replaced communism as the primary threat to U.S. security, the Bush administration launched a war in Afghanistan in 2001 and expanded the federal government's powers to investigate and detain individuals. In distinct contrast to his father's multilateral and cautious approach in foreign policy, George W. Bush adopted a policy of unilateralism and preemption by going to war against Iraq in 2003.

The Disputed Election of 2000

Even though Clinton's presidency ended with a flourishing economy, Albert Gore, his vice president, failed to retain the White House for the Democrats in the election of 2000. Gore's choice of running mate, Connecticut senator Joseph Lieberman, the first Jew to run on a major party ticket, was popular, and polls indicated that a majority of Americans agreed with the Democratic nominees on most issues. Yet many voters found Gore stiff and too willing to change his positions for political advantage; he was further burdened with the taint of Clinton administration scandals.

George W. Bush emerged as the Republican nominee from a series of bountifully funded, hard-fought primaries. The oldest son of former president George H. W. Bush, he had attended Yale and Harvard, worked in the oil industry, and served as governor of Texas since 1994. Inexperienced in national and international affairs, Bush chose for his running mate a seasoned official, Richard B. Cheney, who had served in the Nixon, Ford, and first Bush administrations.

Both candidates ran cautious campaigns, accommodating their positions to what polls indicated voters wanted. Bush's strategy mirrored Clinton's in 1992. Calling himself a "compassionate conservative," Bush separated himself from the extreme right wing of his party and tried to co-opt Democratic issues such as education. Like Republicans before him, he promised a substantial cut in taxes and federal spending.

Many observers predicted that the amazingly strong economy would give Gore the edge, and he did surpass Bush by more than a half million votes. Once the polls closed, however, it became clear that Florida's 25 electoral college votes would decide the presidency. Bush's margin was so tiny in Florida, where his brother served as governor, that it prompted an automatic recount of the votes, which eventually gave Bush an edge of 537 votes.

Meanwhile, the Democrats asked 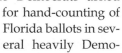 for hand-counting of Florida ballots in several heavily Democratic counties where machine errors may have left hundreds of votes unrecorded. The Republicans, in turn, went to court to try to stop the hand-counts. The outcome of the 2000 election hung in the balance for more than a month as cases went all the way up to the Supreme Court. Finally, a bitterly divided Supreme Court ruled 5 to 4 against further recounts, and Gore conceded the presidency to Bush on December 13, 2000. For the first time since 1888, a president who failed to win the popular vote took office (Map 31.3). Despite the lack of a popular mandate, the Bush administration set out to make dramatic policy changes.

The Domestic Policies of a "Compassionate Conservative"

As was the case with his predecessor, Bush's appointments brought significant diversity to the executive branch. He chose African Americans Colin

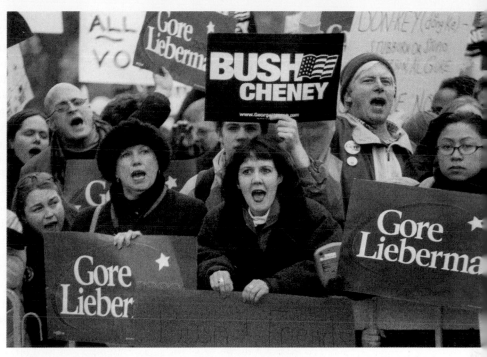

The Disputed Election
While attorneys representing presidential candidates George W. Bush and Al Gore pursued lawsuits over the counting of ballots that would determine who won Florida's 25 electoral college votes, partisan supporters took to the streets. Here backers of both sides rally outside the Supreme Court in Washington, D.C., on Monday, December 11, 2000, a day before the Court issued its five-to-four ruling that ended the hand-recounts of ballots and consequently secured the presidency for Bush. Critics charging that the five justices who voted to stop the recounts had applied partisanship rather than objectivity to the case pointed out that the decision went against those justices' custom of preferring state over federal authority.
Wide World Photos, Inc.

Powell for secretary of state and Condoleezza Rice first as national security adviser and subsequently secretary of state. Five of Bush's top-level appointees were women, including secretary of labor Elaine L. Chao, the first Asian American woman to serve in the cabinet; and he named Latino Alberto R. Gonzales attorney general.

Bush moved quickly on his domestic agenda. Although he had campaigned as a "compassionate conservative," his policies were more conservative and more compassionate toward the rich than toward average Americans. In 2001 he signed a tax-cut measure reducing taxes over the following ten years by $1.35 trillion. A 2003 bill slashed another $320 billion. The laws reduced income taxes, phased out estate taxes, cut rates on capital gains and dividends, provided benefits for married couples and families with children, offered deductions for college expenses, and gave immediate relief to all taxpayers through rebates of up to $300 each. House Majority Leader Dick Armey of Texas crowed over the bill: "The party

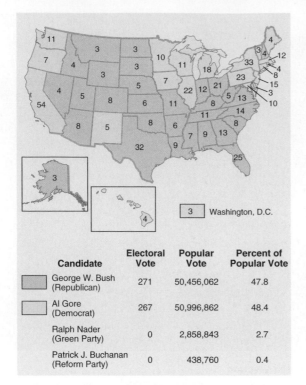

Candidate	Electoral Vote	Popular Vote	Percent of Popular Vote
George W. Bush (Republican)	271	50,456,062	47.8
Al Gore (Democrat)	267	50,996,862	48.4
Ralph Nader (Green Party)	0	2,858,843	2.7
Patrick J. Buchanan (Reform Party)	0	438,760	0.4

MAP 31.3   The Election of 2000

is over.... We're no longer going to get stoned on other people's money."

The administration insisted that the tax cuts would promote economic growth and jolt the economy out of a recession that had begun in 2001. Opponents stressed that the tax cuts favored the rich, and they pointed to a mushrooming federal deficit—the highest in U.S. history—that surpassed $400 billion in 2004. Senator Joseph Lieberman charged that Bush's tax cuts were "giving the most to those who need it least, piling more debt on the backs of our children and robbing Social Security and Medicare to pay for it."

As Clinton had done, Bush altered environmental policy by issuing regulations that did not require congressional approval. But whereas Clinton had imposed greater controls, Bush weakened environmental protection to benefit his larger goals of reducing government regulation, promoting economic growth, and increasing energy production. The Senate blocked Bush's efforts to allow drilling for oil in the Arctic National Wildlife Refuge, but elsewhere the administration opened millions of wilderness acres of public land to the mining, oil, and timber industries. Bush imposed new restrictions on diesel pollutants and relaxed environ-

mental requirements under the Clean Air and Clean Water acts. To worldwide dismay, the administration withdrew from the Kyoto Protocol on global warming, signed in 1997 by 178 nations to reduce greenhouse gas emissions.

While environmentalists pushed for measures to limit American energy consumption, the administration called for more rapid development of energy resources. During his second term, as gasoline prices reached all-time highs in 2005, Bush signed the Energy Policy Act, a compromise bill providing $14 billion of subsidies to producers of oil, coal, nuclear power, and alternative sources of energy. After hurricanes Katrina and Rita ravaged oil and natural gas production in the Gulf of Mexico in 2005, Bush asked Americans to conserve energy but proposed no new regulations.

In contrast to the partisan conflict that attended tax and environmental policy, Bush mobilized bipartisan support behind his "No Child Left Behind" Act of 2002, which marked the greatest change in federal education policy since the 1960s. Promising to end, in Bush's words, "the story of children being just shuffled through the system," the law required every school to meet annual testing standards, provided penalties for failing schools, and allowed parents to transfer their children out of them. It also authorized a 20 percent increase in federal aid aimed primarily at the poorest districts, prompting Senator Paul Wellstone of Minnesota, one of the few critics of the education bill, to ask, "How can you reach the goal of leaving no child behind on a tin cup budget?" This query anticipated problems that states would face in implementing the legislation, because only 7 percent of their education budgets came from the federal government. By 2004, most states were straining to meet the demands of the new education standards as they struggled with severe budget crises.

The Bush administration's second major effort to co-opt Democratic Party issues constituted what the president hailed as "the greatest advance in health care coverage for America's seniors" since the start of Medicare in 1965. In December 2003, the president signed a bill authorizing for the first time prescription drug benefits for the elderly and at the same time expanding the role of private insurers in the Medicare system. Most Democrats opposed the legislation. They charged that it left big gaps in coverage, subsidized private insurers with federal funds to compete with Medicare, banned imports of low-priced drugs from abroad, and prohibited the government from negotiating with drug companies to reduce prices. Legislators of both parties worried about the cost of the new drug benefit, estimated to surpass $500 billion after it took effect in 2006.

The Globalization of Terrorism

Immigrants and citizens from ninety nations shared the fate of more than 2,000 Americans killed on the morning of September 11, 2001, when U.S. civilian airplanes crashed into the twin towers of the World Trade Center in lower Manhattan and the Pentagon in Washington, D.C. In the most deadly attack ever launched on American soil, nineteen members of Osama bin Laden's Al Qaeda international terrorist organization had hijacked four planes and flown three of them into the buildings; the fourth crashed in a field in Pennsylvania. The nation, indeed the world, was stunned.

Organized from Osama bin Laden's sanctuaries in Afghanistan, where the radical Muslim Taliban government had taken control, the attacks related to globalization in several ways. Islamic extremists were enraged by the spread of Western goods, culture, and values into the Muslim world as well as by the 1991 Gulf War against Iraq and the stationing of American troops in Saudi Arabia, bin Laden's homeland. Acting on a distorted interpretation of one of the world's great religions, bin Laden sought to rid the Middle East of Western influence and install puritanical Muslim control. The technological advances and increased mobility accompanying globalization facilitated bin Laden's worldwide coordination of his Al Qaeda network and aided the hijackers' activities.

In the wake of the September 11 attacks, President Bush sought a global alliance against terrorism and won at least verbal support from most governments. On October 11, the United States and Britain began bombing Afghanistan, and American special forces aided the Northern Alliance, the Taliban government's main opposition. By December the Taliban were routed, but bin Laden had not been captured, and numerous Al Qaeda forces had escaped or remained in hiding throughout the world. Although 18,000 U.S.

Afghanistan

troops remained in Afghanistan four years later, economic stability and physical security for its people remained out of reach.

At home, the balance between **liberty** and security tilted. Throughout the country, anti-immigrant sentiment revived, and anyone appearing to be Middle Eastern or practicing Islam was likely to arouse suspicion. Authorities arrested more than a thousand Arabs and Muslims, and an internal study by the Justice Department later reported that many people with no connections to terrorism spent months in jail denied their rights. "I think America overreacted...by singling out Arab-named men like myself," said Shanaz Mohammed, who was jailed for eight months for an immigration violation.

"The smoke was still coming out of the rubble in New York City when we passed the law," said C. L. Otter, Republican representative from Idaho, referring to the USA Patriot Act, which Congress approved by huge margins in October 2001. The law gave the government new powers to monitor suspected terrorists and their associates, including the ability to pry personal information about individuals from libraries, universities, and businesses, while allowing more exchange of information between criminal investigators and those investigating foreign threats. It soon provoked calls for revision from both conservatives and liberals. One hundred fifty cities and three states passed resolutions objecting to the Patriot Act. Ann Arbor councilwoman Kathleen MacKenzie explained that "as awful as we feel about September 11 and as concerned as we were about national safety, we felt that giving up [rights] was too high a price to pay." A security official countered, "If you don't violate someone's human rights some of the time, you probably aren't doing your job."

The government also sought to protect Americans from future terrorist attacks by a major reorganization of the executive branch, the biggest since 1948. In November 2002, Congress authorized a new Department of Homeland Security combining 170,000 federal employees from twenty-two agencies through which responsibilities for different aspects of domestic security had been dispersed. Chief among the duties of the new department were intelligence analysis; overseeing immigration and border security; chemical, biological, and nuclear countermeasures; and emergency preparedness and response.

Unilateralism, Preemption, and the Iraq War

The Bush administration sought collective action against the Taliban but on most other international issues adopted a go-it-alone approach, shattering a fifty-year tradition of multilateralism. In addition to withdrawing from the Kyoto Protocol on global warming, it scrapped the 1972 Antiballistic Missile Treaty in order to develop the space-based missile-defense system—SDI—first proposed by Ronald Reagan. Bush also withdrew the United States from the UN's International Criminal Court, arguing that it would make U.S. citizens vulnerable to politically motivated prosecution. And the United States rejected an agreement to enforce bans on development and possession of biological weapons—an agreement signed by all of America's European allies.

Nowhere was the new policy of unilateralism more striking than in a new war against Iraq, a war pushed by Vice President Dick Cheney and Secretary of Defense Donald H. Rumsfeld but not Secretary of State Colin Powell. In his State of the Union message in January 2002, Bush identified Iraq, Iran, and North Korea as constituting an "axis of evil." His words alarmed political leaders in both Europe and Asia, who insisted that those three nations posed entirely different challenges. Preferring to emphasize diplomacy rather than confrontation, Bush's opponents in Europe and Asia objected to America's unilateral assessment. Nonetheless, addressing West Point graduates in June, President Bush proclaimed a new policy for American security based not on containment but on preemption.

The president said, "Traditional concepts of deterrence will not work against a terrorist enemy whose avowed tactics are wanton destruction and the targeting of innocents; whose so-called soldiers seek martyrdom in death and whose most potent protection is statelessness." Because nuclear, chemical, and biological weapons enabled "even weak states and small groups [to] attain a catastrophic power to strike great nations," the United States had to "be ready for preemptive action." For a century, the United States had intervened militarily and uni-

laterally in the affairs of small nations, but it had not gone to war except to repel aggression against itself or its allies. The president's claim that the United States had the right to start a war was at odds with many Americans' understanding of their nation's ideals and distressed most of America's great-power allies.

Nonetheless, the Bush administration moved deliberately to apply the doctrine of preemption to Iraq, whose dictator Saddam Hussein had violated UN resolutions from the 1991 Gulf War requiring Iraq to destroy and stop further development of nuclear, chemical, and biological weapons. In November 2002, the United States persuaded the UN Security Council to pass a resolution requiring Iraq to disarm or face "serious consequences." When Iraq failed to comply fully with new UN inspections, the Bush administration decided on war. Claiming that Hussein had links to Al Qaeda and harbored terrorists and that Iraq possessed weapons of mass destruction, the president insisted that the threat was immediate and great enough to justify preemptive action. Despite opposition from the Arab world and most major nations—including France, Germany, China, and Russia—which preferred to give the UN inspectors more time, the United States and Britain invaded Iraq on March 19, 2003, supported by some thirty nations (see Map 31.1). This coalition included Australia, Italy, Japan, and Spain but few major powers or traditional allies. The coalition forces won an easy and decisive victory, and Bush declared the end of the war on May 1. Saddam Hussein remained at large until December 2003.

Arabs were glad to see the end of Hussein, but many did not welcome the presence of American troops in Iraq. As the publisher of a Lebanese newspaper put it, "They [Iraqis] have to choose between the night of tyranny and the night of humiliation stemming from foreign occupation." Moreover, damage from U.S. bombing and widespread looting resulting from the failure of U.S. troops to secure order and provide basic necessities left Iraqis wondering how much they had gained. "With Saddam there was tyranny, but at least you had a salary to put food on your family's table," said a young father from Hussein's hometown of Tikrit. Tha'ar Abdul Qader, who worked at a children's hospital in Baghdad, complained, "They can take our oil, but at least they should let us have electricity and water."

More than 140,000 American forces remained in Iraq, where they came under attack almost daily from remnants of the Hussein regime, religious extremists, and hundreds of foreign terrorists now entering the chaotic country. Seeking to divide Iraqis and undermine the occupation, terrorists launched deadly assaults on other targets, such as the UN mission in Baghdad, Red Cross headquarters, a major Shiite mosque in Najaf, and Iraqi citizens.

The war became an issue in the presidential election campaign of 2004, which registered voter turnout at its highest level since 1968. Massachusetts senator John Kerry, the Democratic nominee, criticized the unilateralist approach of Bush's foreign policy and the administration's conduct of the war. A slim majority of voters, however, indicated their belief that Bush would better protect American security from terrorist threats. Once again the election turned on a single state, and Ohio's electoral vote gave Bush a 286 to 252 victory in the electoral college. The President won 50.7 percent of the popular vote to Kerry's 48.3 percent and carried Republican majorities into Congress.

In June 2004, the United States had transferred sovereignty to an interim Iraqi government, and in January 2005, about 58 percent of Iraqis eligible to vote risked their safety to elect a national assembly. The daunting challenges facing the national assembly were to write a constitution, satisfy Iraq's sharply divided political blocs, and decide to what extent Islamic religious law would shape the new government. Violence escalated against government officials, Iraqi civilians, and occupation forces. Some observers spoke of **guerrilla warfare** and "quagmire," evoking comparisons with the U.S. experience in Vietnam. By early 2006, when U.S. military deaths exceeded twenty-three hundred and Iraqi civilian casualties reached tens of thousands, public opinion polls in the United States found a majority of Americans believing the Iraq war to be a mistake.

Yes, the U.S. military felled a brutal dictator, but coalition forces were not prepared for the turmoil that followed the invasion, nor did they find the weapons of mass destruction that administration officials had insisted made the war necessary. Moreover, the administration could provide no evidence of links between Iraq and Osama bin Laden. Rather, the invasion of Iraq spawned new terrorists. In the war-induced chaos, more than a thousand terrorists

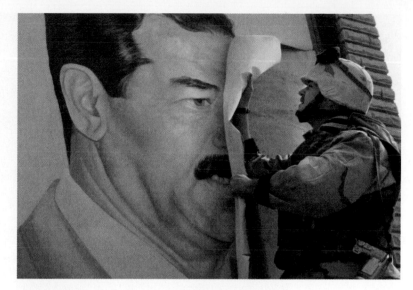

The Iraq War

"The Americans did a great thing when they got rid of that tyrant," rejoiced Hassan Naji, a Shiite Muslim who worked at a hospital in southern Iraq. He acknowledged that the occupiers' inability to provide steady electricity increased the infant death rate at his hospital, but he still insisted, "Things could even get worse here and I would still feel that way." Most Iraqis shared that initial jubilation, but the disorder and bloodshed that followed the defeat of Saddam Hussein's government threatened the Bush administration's plans to bring democracy and stability to the Middle East. In the first days of the American invasion, many Iraqis joined U.S. soldiers in removing Hussein's omnipresent image throughout the country. "We wanted to send a message that Saddam is done," reported U.S. marine major David Gurfein as he tore down a poster in the southern town of Safwan.

Chris Hondras/Getty Images.

entered Iraq—the place, according to one expert, "for fundamentalists to go ... to stick it to the West."

The war and occupation exacted a steep price in American and Iraqi lives, dollars, U.S. relations with the other great powers, and America's credibility and image in the world, especially among Arab nations. America's image was further tarnished by revelations of prisoner abuse in the Abu Graib prison in Iraq and in the Guantánamo Bay detention camp housing captives from the Afghan war. The Iraq war and occupation not only swelled the budget deficit but also diverted resources from other security-related projects, including the stabilization of Afghanistan, the elimination of bin Laden and Al Qaeda, and the

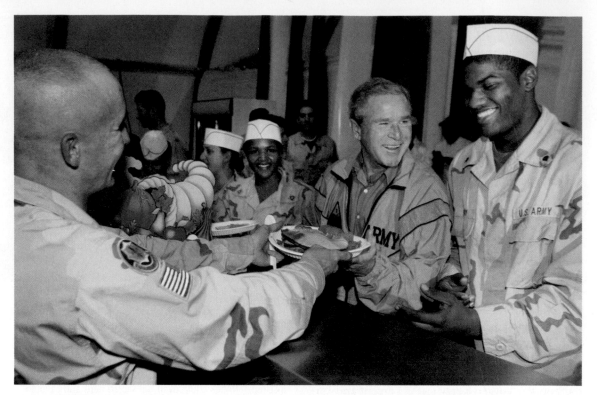

Bush Surprises the Troops
After a top-secret flight from Texas to Baghdad in November 2003, President George W. Bush stunned American GIs by showing up at their Thanksgiving dinner. The trip was designed to honor the service men and women and boost morale after unexpected turmoil, resistance, and casualties followed the initial U.S. victory over Saddam Hussein's forces in May 2003. Two years after Bush's visit, morale remained high among U.S. forces, but violence against them and among Iraqi factions persisted, causing more and more Americans to doubt the wisdom of the initial invasion, question the administration's conduct of the war, and call for a plan to withdraw U.S. troops.
Photo by Cynthia Johnson/Time Life Pictures/Getty Images.

handling of threats posed by North Korea's development of nuclear weapons. Whether the costs incurred had been in the best interests of the United States remained in question.

> **REVIEW**   Why did the United States invade Iraq in March 2003?

Conclusion: Defining the Government's Role at Home and Abroad

On March 21, 2003, some 225 years after the birth of the United States, Colin Powell referred to the unfinished nature of the American promise when he declared that the question of America's

role in the world "isn't answered yet." In fact, the end of the cold war, the rise of international terrorism, and the George W. Bush administration's radically new doctrines of preemption and unilateralism sparked new debates over the long-standing question of how the United States should act beyond its borders.

Nor had Americans set to rest questions about the role of government at home. In a population so greatly derived from people fleeing oppressive governments, Americans had debated for more than two centuries what responsibilities the government could or should shoulder and what was best left to private enterprise, families, churches, and other voluntary institutions. Far more than other democracies, the United States had taken the path of private rather than public obligation, individual rather than collective solutions. In the twentieth century, Americans had significantly enlarged the federal government's powers and responsibilities, but the last three decades of the twentieth century had seen a decline of trust in government's ability to improve people's lives, even as a poverty rate of 20 percent among children and a growing gap between rich and poor survived the economic boom of the 1990s.

The shifting of control of the government back and forth between Republicans and Democrats from 1989 to 2004 revealed a dynamic contestation over the role of the government in domestic affairs. The protections enacted for people with disabilities during the first Bush administration and Bill Clinton's incremental reforms built on a deep-rooted reform tradition that sought to realize the American promise of justice and human well-being. Those who mobilized against the ravages of globalization worked internationally for what **populists, progressives**, the New Deal reformers, and many activists of the 1960s had sought for the domestic population: protection of individual rights, curbs on laissez-faire capitalism, assistance for victims of rapid economic change, and fiscal policies that placed greater responsibility on those best able to pay for the collective good. The second Bush administration, however—with a few exceptions such as the Patriot Act—pushed the pendulum back to a more limited role for the federal government.

As it entered the twenty-first century, the United States became ever more deeply embedded in the global economy as products, information, and people crossed borders with amazing speed and frequency. While the end of the cold war brought about unanticipated cooperation between the United States and its former enemies, globalization also contributed to international instability and the threat of deadly terrorism to a nation unaccustomed to foreign attacks within its own borders. In response to those dangers, the second Bush administration began to chart a departure from the multilateral approach to foreign policy that had been built up by Republican and Democratic administrations alike since World War II. Yet as the United States became mired in reconstruction efforts in Iraq, Americans continued to debate how the nation could best maintain domestic security while still exercising its economic and military power on a rapidly changing planet.

Suggestions for Further Reading

Alan M. Dershowitz, *Supreme Injustice: How the High Court Hijacked Election 2000* (2001). A law professor's criticism of the Supreme Court's role in the 2000 election.

John F. Harris, *The Survivor: Bill Clinton in the White House* (2005). A balanced account by a White House reporter.

National Commission on Terrorist Attacks, *The 9/11 Commission Report: Final Report of the National Commission on Terrorist Attacks upon the United States* (2004). A compelling and forceful narrative of the causes and events of the tragedy.

Herbert S. Parmet, *George Bush: The Life of a Lone Star Yankee* (1997). A comprehensive biography of the first President Bush.

Joseph E. Stiglitz, *Globalization and Its Discontents* (2002). An explanation of the globalization debate by a Nobel Prize–winning economist.

Mike Tucker, *Among Warriors in Iraq: True Grit, Special Ops, and Raiding in Mosul and Fallujah*. A fast-paced account of what soldiers faced in the occupation of Iraq.

▶ **For more books about topics in this chapter**, see the Online Study Guide at bedfordstmartins.com/roarkcompact.

▶ **For additional firsthand accounts of this period**, see Chapter 31 in Michael Johnson, ed., *Reading the American Past*, Third Edition.

▶ **For Web sites and documents related to topics and places in this chapter**, see the "HistoryLinks," "DocLinks," and "PlaceLinks" at bedfordstmartins.com/roarkcompact.

REVIEWING THE CHAPTER

Follow these steps to review and strengthen your understanding of the chapter.

STEP 1: *Study the **Key Terms** and **Timeline** to identify the significance of each item listed.*

STEP 2: *Answer the **Review Questions**, drawing on key terms and dates to support your answers.*

STEP 3: *Drawing on the Key Terms, Timeline, and Review Questions, answer the broader **Making Connections** questions.*

KEY TERMS

Who

Colin L. Powell (p. 811)
George H. W. Bush (p. 813)
Jesse Jackson (p. 813)
Clarence Thomas (p. 814)
Anita Hill (p. 814)
Manuel Noriega (p. 814)
Saddam Hussein (p. 814)
William Jefferson Clinton (p. 818)
Albert Gore Jr. (pp. 818, 828)
H. Ross Perot (p. 818)
Hillary Rodham Clinton (p. 819)
Kenneth Starr (p. 821)
Monica Lewinsky (p. 821)
Osama bin Laden (pp. 823, 831)
George W. Bush (p. 828)
Richard B. Cheney (p. 829)
Donald H. Rumsfeld (p. 832)
John Kerry (p. 833)

What

Clean Air Act of 1990 (p. 813)
Americans with Disabilities Act (p. 813)
Operation Just Cause (p. 814)
Operation Desert Storm (p. 815)
Family and Medical Leave Act (p. 818)
Violence against Women Act (p. 819)
Earned Income Tax Credit (EITC) (p. 819)
Oklahoma City bombing (p. 820)
"don't ask, don't tell" policy (p. 820)
Defense of Marriage Act (p. 820)
Personal Responsibility and Work Opportunity Reconciliation Act (p. 820)
World Trade Organization (WTO) (p. 824)
International Monetary Fund (IMF) (p. 825)
North American Free Trade Agreement (NAFTA) (p. 825)

General Agreement on Tariffs and Trade (GATT) (p. 825)
Central American Free Trade Agreement (CAFTA) (p. 825)
Immigration Reform and Control Act (p. 828)
Kyoto Protocol (p. 830)
"No Child Left Behind" Act (p. 830)
Medicare reform (p. 830)
September 11 attacks (p. 831)
Al Qaeda (p. 831)
Taliban (p. 831)
USA Patriot Act (p. 831)
Department of Homeland Security (p. 831)

TIMELINE

1988 • Republican George H. W. Bush elected president.

1989 • Communism collapses in eastern Europe; Berlin Wall falls.
• United States invades Panama.

1991 • Persian Gulf War.
• Americans with Disabilities Act.

1992 • Democrat William Jefferson (Bill) Clinton elected president.

1993 • Israel and PLO sign peace accords.
• North American Free Trade Agreement (NAFTA).
• Clinton announces policy for gays in military.
• Gun control and anticrime legislation.
• Family and Medical Leave Act.

1994 • United States sends troops to Haiti.
• General Agreement on Tariffs and Trade (GATT).

1995 • Bombing of federal building in Oklahoma City.
• United States brokers peace accords for the former Yugoslavia.

1996 • Personal Responsibility and Work Opportunity Reconciliation Act.

1997 • Tax cut enacted.

REVIEW QUESTIONS

1. Why did George H. W. Bush lose the presidency in 1992? (pp. 813–18)

2. What policies of the Clinton administration reflected President Clinton's effort to move his party to the right? (pp. 818–22)

3. Who criticized free trade agreements and why? (pp. 822–28)

4. Why did the United States invade Iraq in March 2003? (pp. 828–34)

MAKING CONNECTIONS

1. How did George H. W. Bush continue the policies of his predecessor, Ronald Reagan? How did he depart from them?

2. President Bill Clinton called himself a "New Democrat." How did his policies and goals differ from those of Democrats in the past?

3. In the late twentieth century, economic globalization transformed the United States. Explain what globalization is, and describe how it affected the American economy and population in the 1990s.

4. The attacks of September 11, 2001, were unprecedented. What gave rise to the attacks? How did the nation respond?

▶ FOR PRACTICE QUIZZES, A CUSTOMIZED STUDY PLAN, AND OTHER STUDY TOOLS, see the Online Study Guide at bedfordstmartins.com/roarkcompact.

1998 • United States bombs terrorist sites in Afghanistan and Sudan.
- United States bombs Iraq.
- President Clinton impeached.

  1999 • Senate trial fails to approve articles of impeachment.
- United States, with NATO, bombs Serbia.

    2000 • Republican George W. Bush becomes president.

      2001 • **September 11.** Terrorists attack World Trade Center and the Pentagon.
- United States attacks Afghanistan, driving out its Taliban government.
- USA Patriot Act.
- $1.3 trillion tax cut.

        2002 • "No Child Left Behind" Act.
- Department of Homeland Security established.

          2003 • United States attacks Iraq, driving out the regime of Saddam Hussein.
- Major revision of Medicare enacted.

            2004 • George W. Bush reelected president.

              2006 • Polls early in year show majority of Americans believe Iraq war to be a mistake.

Documents

For additional documents see the DocLinks feature at **bedfordstmartins.com/roarkcompact**.

THE DECLARATION OF INDEPENDENCE

In Congress, July 4, 1776,

THE UNANIMOUS DECLARATION OF THE
THIRTEEN UNITED STATES OF AMERICA

When in the course of human events, it becomes necessary for one people to dissolve the political bands which have connected them with another, and to assume, among the powers of the earth, the separate and equal station to which the laws of nature and of nature's God entitle them, a decent respect to the opinions of mankind requires that they should declare the causes which impel them to the separation.

We hold these truths to be self-evident, that all men are created equal; that they are endowed by their Creator with certain unalienable rights; that among these, are life, liberty, and the pursuit of happiness. That, to secure these rights, governments are instituted among men, deriving their just powers from the consent of the governed; that, whenever any form of government becomes destructive of these ends, it is the right of the people to alter or to abolish it, and to institute a new government, laying its foundation on such principles, and organizing its powers in such form, as to them shall seem most likely to effect their safety and happiness. Prudence, indeed, will dictate that governments long established, should not be changed for light and transient causes; and, accordingly, all experience hath shown, that mankind are more disposed to suffer, while evils are sufferable, than to right themselves by abolishing the forms to which they are accustomed. But, when a long train of abuses and usurpations, pursuing invariably the same object, evinces a design to reduce them under absolute despotism, it is their right, it is their duty, to throw off such government and to provide new guards for their future security. Such has been the patient sufferance of these colonies, and such is now the necessity which constrains them to alter their former systems of government. The history of the present King of Great Britain is a history of repeated injuries and usurpations, all having, in direct object, the establishment of an absolute tyranny over these States. To prove this, let facts be submitted to a candid world:

He has refused his assent to laws the most wholesome and necessary for the public good.

He has forbidden his governors to pass laws of immediate and pressing importance, unless suspended in their operation till his assent should be obtained; and, when so suspended, he has utterly neglected to attend to them.

He has refused to pass other laws for the accommodation of large districts of people, unless those people would relinquish the right of representation in the legislature; a right inestimable to them, and formidable to tyrants only.

He has called together legislative bodies at places unusual, uncomfortable, and distant from the depository of their public records, for the sole purpose of fatiguing them into compliance with his measures.

He has dissolved representative houses repeatedly for opposing, with manly firmness, his invasions on the rights of the people.

He has refused, for a long time after such dissolutions, to cause others to be elected; whereby the legislative powers, incapable of annihilation, have returned to the people at large for their exercise; the state remaining in the mean-time exposed to all the danger of invasion from without, and convulsions within.

He has endeavoured to prevent the population of these States; for that purpose, obstructing the laws for naturalization of foreigners, refusing to pass others to encourage their migration hither, and raising the conditions of new appropriations of lands.

He has obstructed the administration of justice, by refusing his assent to laws for establishing judiciary powers.

He has made judges dependent on his will alone, for the tenure of their offices, and the amount and payment of their salaries.

He has erected a multitude of new offices, and sent hither swarms of officers to harass our people, and eat out their substance.

He has kept among us, in times of peace, standing armies, without the consent of our legislature.

He has affected to render the military independent of, and superior to, the civil power.

He has combined, with others, to subject us to a jurisdiction foreign to our Constitution, and unacknowledged by our laws; giving his assent to their acts of pretended legislation:

For quartering large bodies of armed troops among us:

For protecting them by a mock trial, from punishment, for any murders which they should commit on the inhabitants of these States:

For cutting off our trade with all parts of the world:

For imposing taxes on us without our consent:

For depriving us, in many cases, of the benefit of trial by jury:

For transporting us beyond seas to be tried for pretended offences:

For abolishing the free system of English laws in a neighbouring province, establishing therein an arbitrary government, and enlarging its boundaries, so as to render it at once an example and fit instrument for introducing the same absolute rule into these colonies:

For taking away our charters, abolishing our most valuable laws, and altering, fundamentally, the powers of our governments:

For suspending our own legislatures, and declaring themselves invested with power to legislate for us in all cases whatsoever.

He has abdicated government here, by declaring us out of his protection, and waging war against us.

He has plundered our seas, ravaged our coasts, burnt our towns, and destroyed the lives of our people.

He is, at this time, transporting large armies of foreign mercenaries to complete the works of death, desolation, and tyranny, already begun, with circumstances of cruelty and perfidy scarcely paralleled in the most barbarous ages, and totally unworthy the head of a civilized nation.

He has constrained our fellow citizens, taken captive on the high seas, to bear arms against their country, to become the executioners of their friends, and brethren, or to fall themselves by their hands.

He has excited domestic insurrections amongst us, and has endeavoured to bring on the inhabitants of our frontiers, the merciless Indian savages, whose known rule of warfare is an undistinguished destruction of all ages, sexes, and conditions.

In every stage of these oppressions, we have petitioned for redress; in the most humble terms; our repeated petitions have been answered only by repeated injury. A prince, whose character is thus marked by every act which may define a tyrant, is unfit to be the ruler of a free people.

Nor have we been wanting in attention to our British brethren. We have warned them, from time to time, of attempts made by their legislature to extend an unwarrantable jurisdiction over us. We have reminded them of the circumstances of our emigration and settlement here. We have appealed to their native justice and magnanimity, and we have conjured them, by the ties of our common kindred, to disavow these usurpations, which would inevitably interrupt our connections and correspondence. They, too, have been deaf to the voice of justice and consanguinity. We must, therefore, acquiesce in the necessity which denounces our separation, and hold them as we hold the rest of mankind, enemies in war, in peace, friends.

We, therefore, the representatives of the United States of America, in general Congress assembled, appealing to the Supreme Judge of the world for the rectitude of our intentions, do, in the name, and by authority of the good people of these colonies, solemnly publish and declare, that these united colonies are, and of right ought to be, free and independent states: that they are absolved from all allegiance to the British Crown, and that all political connection between them and the state of Great Britain is, and ought to be, totally dissolved; and that, as free and independent states, they have full power to levy war, conclude peace, contract alliances, establish commerce, and to do all other acts and things which independent states may of right do. And, for the support of this declaration, with a firm reliance on the protection of Divine Providence, we mutually pledge to each other our lives, our fortunes, and our sacred honor.

The foregoing Declaration was, by order of Congress, engrossed, and signed by the following members:

JOHN HANCOCK

New Hampshire
Josiah Bartlett
William Whipple
Matthew Thornton

Massachusetts Bay
Samuel Adams
John Adams
Robert Treat Paine
Elbridge Gerry

Rhode Island
Stephen Hopkins
William Ellery

Connecticut
Roger Sherman
Samuel Huntington
William Williams
Oliver Wolcott

New York
William Floyd
Phillip Livingston
Francis Lewis
Lewis Morris

New Jersey
Richard Stockton
John Witherspoon
Francis Hopkinson
John Hart
Abraham Clark

Pennsylvania
Robert Morris
Benjamin Rush
Benjamin Franklin
John Morton
George Clymer
James Smith
George Taylor
James Wilson
George Ross

Delaware	North Carolina	Virginia	Georgia
Caesar Rodney	William Hooper	George Wythe	Button Gwinnett
George Read	Joseph Hewes	Richard Henry Lee	Lyman Hall
Thomas M'Kean	John Penn	Thomas Jefferson	George Walton
		Benjamin Harrison	
Maryland	**South Carolina**	Thomas Nelson, Jr.	
Samuel Chase	Edward Rutledge	Francis Lightfoot Lee	
William Paca	Thomas Heyward, Jr.	Carter Braxton	
Thomas Stone	Thomas Lynch, Jr.		
Charles Carroll,	Arthur Middleton		
of Carrollton			

Resolved, That copies of the Declaration be sent to the several assemblies, conventions, and committees, or councils of safety, and to the several commanding officers of the continental troops; that it be proclaimed in each of the United States, at the head of the army.

THE CONSTITUTION OF THE UNITED STATES*

Agreed to by Philadelphia Convention, September 17, 1787. Implemented March 4, 1789.

Preamble

We the people of the United States, in order to form a more perfect union, establish justice, insure domestic tranquility, provide for the common defense, promote the general welfare, and secure the blessings of liberty to ourselves and our posterity, do ordain and establish this Constitution for the United States of America.

Article I

Section 1 All legislative powers herein granted shall be vested in a Congress of the United States, which shall consist of a Senate and a House of Representatives.

Section 2 The House of Representatives shall be composed of members chosen every second year by the people of the several States, and the electors in each State shall have the qualifications requisite for electors of the most numerous branch of the State Legislature.

No person shall be a Representative who shall not have attained to the age of twenty-five years, and been seven years a citizen of the United States, and who shall not, when elected, be an inhabitant of that State in which he shall be chosen.

Representatives and direct taxes shall be apportioned among the several States which may be included within this Union, according to their respective numbers, *which shall be determined by adding to the whole number of free persons, including those bound to service for a term of years and excluding Indians not taxed, three-fifths of all other persons.* The actual enumeration shall be made within three years after the first meeting of the Congress of the United States, and within every subsequent term of ten years, in such manner as they shall by law direct. The number of Representatives shall not exceed one for every thirty thousand, but each State shall have at least one Representative; *and until such enumeration shall be made, the State of New Hampshire shall be entitled to choose three, Massachusetts eight, Rhode Island and Providence Plantations one, Connecticut five, New York six, New Jersey four, Pennsylvania eight, Delaware one, Maryland six, Virginia ten, North Carolina five, South Carolina five, and Georgia three.*

When vacancies happen in the representation from any State, the Executive authority thereof shall issue writs of election to fill such vacancies.

The House of Representatives shall choose their Speaker and other officers; and shall have the sole power of impeachment.

Section 3 The Senate of the United States shall be composed of two Senators from each State, *chosen by the legislature thereof,* for six years; and each Senator shall have one vote.

Immediately after they shall be assembled in consequence of the first election, they shall be divided as equally as may be into three classes. The seats of the Senators of the first class shall be vacated at the expiration of the second year, of the second class at the expiration of the fourth year, and of the third class at the expiration of the sixth year, so that one-third may be chosen every second year; *and if vacancies happen by resignation or otherwise, during the recess of the legislature of any State, the Executive thereof may make temporary appointments until the next meeting of the legislature, which shall then fill such vacancies.*

---

* Passages no longer in effect are in italic type.

No person shall be a Senator who shall not have attained to the age of thirty years, and been nine years a citizen of the United States, and who shall not, when elected, be an inhabitant of that State for which he shall be chosen.

The Vice-President of the United States shall be President of the Senate, but shall have no vote, unless they be equally divided.

The Senate shall choose their other officers, and also a President *pro tempore,* in the absence of the Vice-President, or when he shall exercise the office of President of the United States.

The Senate shall have the sole power to try all impeachments. When sitting for that purpose, they shall be on oath or affirmation. When the President of the United States is tried, the Chief Justice shall preside: and no person shall be convicted without the concurrence of two-thirds of the members present.

Judgment in cases of impeachment shall not extend further than to removal from the office, and disqualification to hold and enjoy any office of honor, trust or profit under the United States: but the party convicted shall nevertheless be liable and subject to indictment, trial, judgment and punishment, according to law.

Section 4 The times, places and manner of holding elections for Senators and Representatives shall be prescribed in each State by the legislature thereof; but the Congress may at any time by law make or alter such regulations, except as to the places of choosing Senators.

The Congress shall assemble at least once in every year, and such meeting *shall be on the first Monday in December, unless they shall by law appoint a different day.*

Section 5 Each house shall be the judge of the elections, returns and qualifications of its own members, and a majority of each shall constitute a quorum to do business; but a smaller number may adjourn from day to day, and may be authorized to compel the attendance of absent members, in such manner, and under such penalties, as each house may provide.

Each house may determine the rules of its proceedings, punish its members for disorderly behavior, and with the concurrence of two-thirds, expel a member.

Each house shall keep a journal of its proceedings, and from time to time publish the same, excepting such parts as may in their judgment require secrecy; and the yeas and nays of the members of either house on any question shall, at the desire of one-fifth of those present, be entered on the journal.

Neither house, during the session of Congress, shall, without the consent of the other, adjourn for more than three days, nor to any other place than that in which the two houses shall be sitting.

Section 6 The Senators and Representatives shall receive a compensation for their services, to be ascertained by law and paid out of the treasury of the United States. They shall in all cases except treason, felony and breach of the peace, be privileged from arrest during their attendance at the session of their respective houses, and in going to and returning from the same; and for any speech or debate in either house, they shall not be questioned in any other place.

No Senator or Representative shall, during the time for which he was elected, be appointed to any civil office under the authority of the United States, which shall have been created, or the emoluments whereof shall have been increased, during such time; and no person holding any office under the United States shall be a member of either house during his continuance in office.

Section 7 All bills for raising revenue shall originate in the House of Representatives; but the Senate may propose or concur with amendments as on other bills.

Every bill which shall have passed the House of Representatives and the Senate, shall, before it become a law, be presented to the President of the United States; if he approve he shall sign it, but if not he shall return it with objections to that house in which it shall have originated, who shall enter the objections at large on their journal, and proceed to reconsider it. If after such reconsideration two-thirds of that house shall agree to pass the bill, it shall be sent, together with the objections, to the other house, by which it shall likewise be reconsidered, and, if approved by two-thirds of that house, it shall become a law. But in all such cases the votes of both houses shall be determined by yeas and nays, and the names of the persons voting for and against the bill shall be entered on the journal of each house respectively. If any bill shall not be returned by the President within ten days (Sundays excepted) after it shall have been presented to him, the same shall be a law, in like manner as if he had signed it, unless the Congress by their adjournment prevent its return, in which case it shall not be a law.

Every order, resolution, or vote to which the concurrence of the Senate and House of Representatives may be necessary (except on a question of adjournment) shall be presented to the President of the United States; and before the same shall take effect, shall be approved by him, or being disapproved by him, shall be repassed by two-thirds of the Senate and House of Representatives, according to the rules and limitations prescribed in the case of a bill.

Section 8 The Congress shall have power

To lay and collect taxes, duties, imposts, and excises, to pay the debts and provide for the common defense and general welfare of the United States;

THE CONSTITUTION OF THE UNITED STATES

but all duties, imposts and excises shall be uniform throughout the United States;

To borrow money on the credit of the United States;

To regulate commerce with foreign nations, and among the several States, and with the Indian tribes;

To establish an uniform rule of naturalization, and uniform laws on the subject of bankruptcies throughout the United States;

To coin money, regulate the value thereof, and of foreign coin, and fix the standard of weights and measures;

To provide for the punishment of counterfeiting the securities and current coin of the United States;

To establish post offices and post roads;

To promote the progress of science and useful arts by securing for limited times to authors and inventors the exclusive right to their respective writings and discoveries;

To constitute tribunals inferior to the Supreme Court;

To define and punish piracies and felonies committed on the high seas and offences against the law of nations;

To declare war, grant letters of marque and reprisal, and make rules concerning captures on land and water;

To raise and support armies, but no appropriation of money to that use shall be for a longer term than two years;

To provide and maintain a navy;

To make rules for the government and regulation of the land and naval forces;

To provide for calling forth the militia to execute the laws of the Union, suppress insurrections and repel invasions;

To provide for organizing, arming, and disciplining the militia, and for governing such part of them as may be employed in the service of the United States, reserving to the States respectively the appointment of the officers, and the authority of training the militia according to the discipline prescribed by Congress;

To exercise exclusive legislation in all cases whatsoever, over such district (not exceeding ten miles square) as may, by cession of particular States, and the acceptance of Congress, become the seat of the government of the United States, and to exercise like authority over all places purchased by the consent of the legislature of the State, in which the same shall be, for erection of forts, magazines, arsenals, dock-yards, and other needful buildings; — and

To make all laws which shall be necessary and proper for carrying into execution the foregoing powers, and all other powers vested by this Constitution in the government of the United States, or in any department or officer thereof.

Section 9 *The migration or importation of such persons as any of the States now existing shall think proper to admit shall not be prohibited by the Congress prior to the year one thousand eight hundred and eight; but a tax or duty may be imposed on such importation, not exceeding ten dollars for each person.*

The privilege of the writ of habeas corpus shall not be suspended, unless when in cases of rebellion or invasion the public safety may require it.

No bill of attainder or ex post facto law shall be passed.

No capitation, or other direct, tax shall be laid, unless in proportion to the census or enumeration herein before directed to be taken.

No tax or duty shall be laid on articles exported from any State.

No preference shall be given by any regulation of commerce or revenue to the ports of one State over those of another; nor shall vessels bound to, or from, one State be obliged to enter, clear, or pay duties in another.

No money shall be drawn from the treasury, but in consequence of appropriations made by law; and a regular statement and account of the receipts and expenditures of all public money shall be published from time to time.

No title of nobility shall be granted by the United States: and no person holding any office of profit or trust under them, shall, without the consent of the Congress, accept of any present, emolument, office, or title, of any kind whatever, from any king, prince, or foreign state.

Section 10 No State shall enter into any treaty, alliance, or confederation; grant letters of marque and reprisal; coin money; emit bills of credit; make anything but gold and silver coin a tender in payment of debts; pass any bill of attainder, ex post facto law, or law impairing the obligation of contracts, or grant any title of nobility.

No State shall, without the consent of Congress, lay any imposts or duties on imports or exports, except what may be absolutely necessary for executing its inspection laws: and the net produce of all duties and imposts, laid by any State on imports or exports, shall be for the use of the treasury of the United States; and all such laws shall be subject to the revision and control of the Congress.

No State shall, without the consent of Congress, lay any duty of tonnage, keep troops, or ships of war in time of peace, enter into any agreement or compact with another State, or with a foreign power, or engage in war, unless actually invaded, or in such imminent danger as will not admit of delay.

Article II

Section 1 The executive power shall be vested in a President of the United States of America. He shall hold his office during the term of four years, and, together with the Vice-President, chosen for the same term, be elected as follows:

Each State shall appoint, in such manner as the legislature thereof may direct, a number of electors, equal to the whole number of Senators and Representatives to which the State may be entitled in the Congress; but no Senator or Representative, or person holding an office of trust or profit under the United States, shall be appointed an elector.

The electors shall meet in their respective States, and vote by ballot for two persons, of whom one at least shall not be an inhabitant of the same State with themselves. And they shall make a list of all the persons voted for, and of the number of votes for each; which list they shall sign and certify, and transmit sealed to the seat of government of the United States, directed to the President of the Senate. The President of the Senate shall, in the presence of the Senate and House of Representatives, open all the certificates, and the votes shall then be counted. The person having the greatest number of votes shall be the President, if such number be a majority of the whole number of electors appointed; and if there be more than one who have such majority, and have an equal number of votes, then the House of Representatives shall immediately choose by ballot one of them for President; and if no person have a majority, then from the five highest on the list said house shall in like manner choose the President. But in choosing the President the votes shall be taken by States, the representation from each State having one vote; a quorum for this purpose shall consist of a member or members from two-thirds of the States, and a majority of all the States shall be necessary to a choice. In every case, after the choice of the President, the person having the greatest number of votes of the electors shall be the Vice-President. But if there should remain two or more who have equal votes, the Senate shall choose from them by ballot the Vice-President.

The Congress may determine the time of choosing the electors, and the day on which they shall give their votes; which day shall be the same throughout the United States.

No person except a natural-born citizen, *or a citizen of the United States at the time of the adoption of this Constitution,* shall be eligible to the office of President; neither shall any person be eligible to that office who shall not have attained to the age of thirty-five years, and been fourteen years a resident within the United States.

In cases of the removal of the President from office or of his death, resignation, or inability to discharge the powers and duties of the said office, the same shall devolve on the Vice-President, and the Congress may by law provide for the case of removal, death, resignation, or inability, both of the President and Vice-President, declaring what officer shall then act as President, and such officer shall act accordingly, until the disability be removed, or a President shall be elected.

The President shall, at stated times, receive for his services a compensation, which shall neither be increased nor diminished during the period for which he shall have been elected, and he shall not receive within that period any other emolument from the United States, or any of them.

Before he enter on the execution of his office, he shall take the following oath or affirmation: — "I do solemnly swear (or affirm) that I will faithfully execute the office of the President of the United States, and will to the best of my ability preserve, protect and defend the Constitution of the United States."

Section 2 The President shall be commander in chief of the army and navy of the United States, and of the militia of the several States, when called into the actual service of the United States; he may require the opinion, in writing, of the principal officer in each of the executive departments, upon any subject relating to the duties of their respective offices, and he shall have power to grant reprieves and pardons for offences against the United States, except in cases of impeachment.

He shall have power, by and with the advice and consent of the Senate, to make treaties, provided two-thirds of the Senators present concur; and he shall nominate, and by and with the advice and consent of the Senate, shall appoint ambassadors, other public ministers and consuls, judges of the Supreme Court, and all other officers of the United States, whose appointments are not herein otherwise provided for, and which shall be established by law: but Congress may by law vest the appointment of such inferior officers, as they think proper, in the President alone, in the courts of law, or in the heads of departments.

The President shall have power to fill up all vacancies that may happen during the recess of the Senate, by granting commissions which shall expire at the end of their next session.

Section 3 He shall from time to time give to the Congress information of the state of the Union, and recommend to their consideration such measures as he shall judge necessary and expedient; he may, on extraordinary occasions, convene both houses, or either of them, and in case of disagreement between them, with respect to the time of adjournment, he may adjourn them to such time as he shall think proper; he shall receive ambassadors and other public ministers; he shall take care that the laws be faithfully executed, and shall commission all the officers of the United States.

Section 4 The President, Vice-President and all civil officers of the United States shall be removed from office on impeachment for, and on conviction of, treason, bribery, or other high crimes and misdemeanors.

Article III

Section 1 The judicial power of the United States shall be vested in one Supreme Court, and in such

THE CONSTITUTION OF THE UNITED STATES

inferior courts as the Congress may from time to time ordain and establish. The judges, both of the Supreme and inferior courts, shall hold their offices during good behavior, and shall, at stated times, receive for their services a compensation which shall not be diminished during their continuance in office.

Section 2 The judicial power shall extend to all cases, in law and equity, arising under this Constitution, the laws of the United States, and treaties made, or which shall be made, under their authority; — to all cases affecting ambassadors, other public ministers and consuls; — to all cases of admiralty and maritime jurisdiction; — to controversies to which the United States shall be a party; — to controversies between two or more States; — *between a State and citizens of another State;* — between citizens of different States; — between citizens of the same State claiming lands under grants of different States, and between a State, or the citizens thereof, and foreign states, citizens or subjects.

In all cases affecting ambassadors, other public ministers and consuls, and those in which a State shall be party, the Supreme Court shall have original jurisdiction. In all the other cases before mentioned, the Supreme Court shall have appellate jurisdiction, both as to law and fact, with such exceptions, and under such regulations, as the Congress shall make.

The trial of all crimes, except in cases of impeachment, shall be by jury; and such trial shall be held in the State where said crimes shall have been committed; but when not committed within any State, the trial shall be at such place or places as the Congress may by Law have directed.

Section 3 Treason against the United States shall consist only in levying war against them, or in adhering to their enemies, giving them aid and comfort. No person shall be convicted of treason unless on the testimony of two witnesses to the same overt act, or on confession in open court.

The Congress shall have power to declare the punishment of treason, but no attainder of treason shall work corruption of blood, or forfeiture except during the life of the person attainted.

Article IV

Section 1 Full faith and credit shall be given in each State to the public acts, records, and judicial proceedings of every other State. And the Congress may by general laws prescribe the manner in which such acts, records, and proceedings shall be proved, and the effect thereof.

Section 2 The citizens of each State shall be entitled to all privileges and immunities of citizens in the several States.

A person charged in any State with treason, felony, or other crime, who shall flee from justice, and be found in another State, shall on demand of the executive authority of the State from which he fled, be delivered up, to be removed to the State having jurisdiction of the crime.

No Person held to service or labor in one State, under the laws thereof, escaping into another, shall, in consequence of any law or regulation therein, be discharged from such service or labor, but shall be delivered up on claim of the party to whom such service or labor may be due.

Section 3 New States may be admitted by the Congress into this Union; but no new State shall be formed or erected within the jurisdiction of any other State; nor any State be formed by the junction of two or more States, or parts of States, without the consent of the legislatures of the States concerned as well as of the Congress.

The Congress shall have power to dispose of and make all needful rules and regulations respecting the territory or other property belonging to the United States; and nothing in this Constitution shall be so construed as to prejudice any claims of the United States, or of any particular State.

Section 4 The United States shall guarantee to every State in this Union a republican form of government, and shall protect each of them against invasion; and on application of the legislature, or of the executive (when the legislature cannot be convened), against domestic violence.

Article V

The Congress, whenever two-thirds of both houses shall deem it necessary, shall propose amendments to this Constitution, or, on the application of the legislatures of two-thirds of the several States, shall call a convention for proposing amendments, which, in either case, shall be valid to all intents and purposes, as part of this Constitution, when ratified by the legislatures of three-fourths of the several States, or by conventions in three-fourths thereof, as the one or the other mode of ratification may be proposed by the Congress; provided *that no amendments which may be made prior to the year one thousand eight hundred and eight shall in any manner affect the first and fourth clauses in the ninth section of the first article;* and that no State, without its consent, shall be deprived of its equal suffrage in the Senate.

Article VI

All debts contracted and engagements entered into, before the adoption of this Constitution, shall be as valid against the United States under this Constitution, as under the Confederation.

This Constitution, and the laws of the United States which shall be made in pursuance thereof; and all treaties made, or which shall be made, under the authority of the United States, shall be the supreme law of the land; and the judges in every State shall be bound thereby, anything in the Constitution or laws of any State to the contrary notwithstanding.

The Senators and Representatives before mentioned, and the members of the several State legislatures, and all executive and judicial officers, both of the United States and of the several States, shall be bound by oath or affirmation to support this Constitution; but no religious test shall ever be required as a qualification to any office or public trust under the United States.

GEORGE WASHINGTON
PRESIDENT AND DEPUTY FROM VIRGINIA

Article VII

The ratification of the conventions of nine States shall be sufficient for the establishment of this Constitution between the States so ratifying the same.

Done in convention by the unanimous consent of the States present, the seventeenth day of September in the year of our Lord one thousand seven hundred and eighty-seven and of the Independence of the United States of America the twelfth. In witness whereof we have hereunto subscribed our names.

New Hampshire
John Langdon
Nicholas Gilman

Massachusetts
Nathaniel Gorham
Rufus King

Connecticut
William Samuel
  Johnson
Roger Sherman

New York
Alexander Hamilton

New Jersey
William Livingston
David Brearley
William Paterson
Jonathan Dayton

Pennsylvania
Benjamin Franklin
Thomas Mifflin
Robert Morris
George Clymer
Thomas FitzSimons
Jared Ingersoll
James Wilson
Gouverneur Morris

Delaware
George Read
Gunning Bedford, Jr.
John Dickinson
Richard Bassett
Jacob Broom

Maryland
James McHenry
Daniel of St.
  Thomas Jenifer
Daniel Carroll

Virginia
John Blair
James Madison, Jr.

North Carolina
William Blount
Richard Dobbs Spaight
Hugh Williamson

South Carolina
John Rutledge
Charles Cotesworth
  Pinckney
Charles Pinckney
Pierce Butler

Georgia
William Few
Abraham Baldwin

AMENDMENTS TO THE CONSTITUTION WITH ANNOTATIONS
(including the six unratified amendments)

IN THEIR EFFORT TO GAIN Antifederalists' support for the Constitution, Federalists frequently pointed to the inclusion of Article 5, which provides an orderly method of amending the Constitution. In contrast, the Articles of Confederation, which were universally recognized as seriously flawed, offered no means of amendment. For their part, Antifederalists argued that the amendment process was so "intricate" that one might as easily roll "sixes an hundred times in succession" as change the Constitution.

The system for amendment laid out in the Constitution requires that two-thirds of both houses of Congress agree to a proposed amendment, which must then be ratified by three-quarters of the legislatures of the states. Alternatively, an amendment may be proposed by a convention called by the legislatures of two-thirds of the states. Since 1789, members of Congress have proposed thousands of amendments. Besides the seventeen amendments added since 1789, only the six "unratified" ones included here were approved by two-thirds of both houses and sent to the states for ratification.

Among the many amendments that never made it out of Congress have been proposals to declare dueling, divorce, and interracial marriage unconstitutional as well as proposals to establish a national university, to acknowledge the sovereignty of Jesus Christ, and to prohibit any person from possessing wealth in excess of $10 million.*

---

* Richard B. Bernstein, *Amending America* (New York: Times Books, 1993), 177–81.

Among the issues facing Americans today that might lead to constitutional amendment are efforts to balance the federal budget, to limit the number of terms elected officials may serve, to limit access to or prohibit abortion, to establish English as the official language of the United States, and to prohibit flag burning. None of these proposed amendments has yet garnered enough support in Congress to be sent to the states for ratification.

Although the first ten amendments to the Constitution are commonly known as the Bill of Rights, only Amendments 1–8 actually provide guarantees of individual rights. Amendments 9 and 10 deal with the structure of power within the constitutional system. The Bill of Rights was promised to appease Antifederalists who refused to ratify the Constitution without guarantees of individual liberties and limitations to federal power. After studying more than two hundred amendments recommended by the ratifying conventions of the states, Federalist James Madison presented a list of seventeen to Congress, which used Madison's list as the foundation for the twelve amendments that were sent to the states for ratification. Ten of the twelve were adopted in 1791. The first on the list of twelve, known as the Reapportionment Amendment, was never adopted (see page A-11). The second proposed amendment was adopted in 1992 as Amendment 27 (see page A-20).

Amendment I

Congress shall make no law respecting an establishment of religion, or prohibiting the free exercise thereof; or abridging the freedom of speech, or of the press; or the right of the people peaceably to assemble, and to petition the government for a redress of grievances.

◆ ◆ ◆

The First Amendment is a potent symbol for many Americans. Most are well aware of their rights to free speech, freedom of the press, and freedom of religion and their rights to assemble and to petition, even if they cannot cite the exact words of this amendment.

The First Amendment guarantee of freedom of religion has two clauses: the "free exercise clause," which allows individuals to practice or not practice any religion, and the "establishment clause," which prevents the federal government from discriminating against or favoring any particular religion. This clause was designed to create what Thomas Jefferson referred to as "a wall of separation between church and state." In the 1960s, the Supreme Court ruled that the First Amendment prohibits prayer (see Engel v. Vitale, *online) and Bible reading in public schools.*

Although the rights to free speech and freedom of the press are established in the First Amendment, it was not until the twentieth century that the Supreme Court began to explore the full meaning of these guarantees. In 1919, the Court ruled in Schenck v. United States *(online) that the government could suppress free expression only where it could cite a "clear and present danger." In a decision that continues to raise controversies, the Court ruled in 1990, in* Texas v. Johnson, *that flag burning is a form of symbolic speech protected by the First Amendment.*

Amendment II

A well-regulated militia being necessary to the security of a free State, the right of the people to keep and bear arms shall not be infringed.

◆ ◆ ◆

Fear of a standing army under the control of a hostile government made the Second Amendment an important part of the Bill of Rights. Advocates of gun ownership claim that the amendment prevents the government from regulating firearms. Proponents of gun control argue that the amendment is designed only to protect the right of the states to maintain militia units.

In 1939, the Supreme Court ruled in United States v. Miller *that the Second Amendment did not protect the right of an individual to own a sawed-off shotgun, which it argued was not ordinary militia equipment. Since then, the Supreme Court has refused to hear Second Amendment cases, while lower courts have upheld firearms regulations. Several justices currently on the bench seem to favor a narrow interpretation of the Second Amendment, which would allow gun control legislation. The controversy over the impact of the Second Amendment on gun owners and gun control legislation will certainly continue.*

Amendment III

No soldier shall, in time of peace, be quartered in any house without the consent of the owner, nor in time of war, but in a manner to be prescribed by law.

◆ ◆ ◆

The Third Amendment was extremely important to the framers of the Constitution, but today it is nearly forgotten. American colonists were especially outraged that they were forced to quarter British troops in the years before and during the American Revolution. The philosophy of the Third Amendment has been viewed by some justices and scholars as the foundation of the modern constitutional right to privacy. One example of this can be found in Justice William O. Douglas's opinion in Griswold v. Connecticut *(online).*

Amendment IV

The right of the people to be secure in their persons, houses, papers, and effects, against unreasonable searches and seizures, shall not be violated, and no warrants shall issue but upon probable cause, supported by oath or affirmation, and particularly describing the place to be searched, and the persons or things to be seized.

◆ ◆ ◆

In the years before the Revolution, the houses, barns, stores, and warehouses of American colonists were ransacked by British authorities under "writs of assistance" or general warrants. The British, thus empowered, searched for seditious material or smuggled goods that could then be used as evidence against colonists who were charged with a crime only after the items were found.

The first part of the Fourth Amendment protects citizens from "unreasonable" searches and seizures. The Supreme Court has interpreted this protection as well as the words search *and* seizure *in different ways at different times. At one time, the Court did not recognize electronic eavesdropping as a form of search and seizure, though it does today. At times, an "unreasonable" search has been almost any search carried out without a warrant, but in the two decades before 1969, the Court sometimes sanctioned warrantless searches that it considered reasonable based on "the total atmosphere of the case."*

The second part of the Fourth Amendment defines the procedure for issuing a search warrant and states the requirement of "probable cause," which is generally viewed as evidence indicating that a suspect has committed an offense.

The Fourth Amendment has been controversial because the Court has sometimes excluded evidence that has been seized in violation of constitutional standards. The justification is that excluding such evidence deters violations of the amendment, but doing so may allow a guilty person to escape punishment.

Amendment V

No person shall be held to answer for a capital, or otherwise infamous crime, unless on a presentment or indictment of a grand jury, except in cases arising in the land or naval forces, or in the militia, when in actual service in time of war or public danger; nor shall any person be subject for the same offence to be twice put in jeopardy of life or limb; nor shall be compelled in any criminal case to be a witness against himself, nor be deprived of life, liberty, or property, without due process of law; nor shall private property be taken for public use without just compensation.

◆ ◆ ◆

The Fifth Amendment protects people against government authority in the prosecution of criminal offenses. It prohibits the state, first, from charging a person with a serious crime without a grand jury hearing to decide whether there is sufficient evidence to support the charge and, second, from charging a person with the same crime twice. The best-known aspect of

the Fifth Amendment is that it prevents a person from being "compelled...to be a witness against himself." The last clause, the "takings clause," limits the power of the government to seize property.

Although invoking the Fifth Amendment is popularly viewed as a confession of guilt, a person may be innocent yet still fear prosecution. For example, during the Red-baiting era of the late 1940s and 1950s, many people who had participated in legal activities that were associated with the Communist Party claimed the Fifth Amendment privilege rather than testify before the House Un-American Activities Committee because the mood of the times cast those activities in a negative light. Since "taking the Fifth" was viewed as an admission of guilt, those people often lost their jobs or became unemployable. (See chapter 26.) Nonetheless, the right to protect oneself against self-incrimination plays an important role in guarding against the collective power of the state.

Amendment VI

In all criminal prosecutions, the accused shall enjoy the right to a speedy and public trial, by an impartial jury of the State and district wherein the crime shall have been committed, which district shall have been previously ascertained by law, and to be informed of the nature and cause of the accusation; to be confronted with the witnesses against him; to have compulsory process for obtaining witnesses in his favor, and to have the assistance of counsel for his defence.

◆ ◆ ◆

The original Constitution put few limits on the government's power to investigate, prosecute, and punish crime. This process was of great concern to the early Americans, however, and of the twenty-eight rights specified in the first eight amendments, fifteen have to do with it. Seven rights are specified in the Sixth Amendment. These include the right to a speedy trial, a public trial, a jury trial, a notice of accusation, confrontation by opposing witnesses, testimony by favorable witnesses, and the assistance of counsel.

Although this amendment originally guaranteed these rights only in cases involving the federal government, the adoption of the Fourteenth Amendment began a process of applying the protections of the Bill of Rights to the states through court cases such as Gideon v. Wainwright *(online).*

Amendment VII

In suits at common law, where the value in controversy shall exceed twenty dollars, the right of trial by jury shall be preserved, and no fact tried by a jury shall be otherwise reexamined in any court of the United States, than according to the rules of the common law.

◆ ◆ ◆

This amendment guarantees people the same right to a trial by jury as was guaranteed by English common law in 1791. Under common law, in civil trials (those involving money damages) the role of the judge was to settle questions of law and that of the jury was to settle questions of fact. The amendment does not specify the size of the jury or its role in a trial, however. The Supreme Court has generally held that those issues be determined by English common law of 1791, which stated that a jury consists of twelve people, that a trial must be conducted before a judge who instructs the jury on the law and advises it on facts, and that a verdict must be unanimous.

Amendment VIII

Excessive bail shall not be required, nor excessive fines imposed, nor cruel and unusual punishments inflicted.

◆ ◆ ◆

The language used to guarantee the three rights in this amendment was inspired by the English Bill of Rights of 1689. The Supreme Court has not had a lot to say about "excessive fines." In recent years it has agreed that despite the provision against "excessive bail," persons who are believed to be dangerous to others can be held without bail even before they have been convicted.

Although opponents of the death penalty have not succeeded in using the Eighth Amendment to achieve the end of capital punishment, the clause regarding "cruel and unusual punishments" has been used to prohibit capital punishment in certain cases (see Furman v. Georgia, *online) and to require improved conditions in prisons.*

Amendment IX

The enumeration in the Constitution, of certain rights, shall not be construed to deny or disparage others retained by the people.

◆ ◆ ◆

Some Federalists feared that inclusion of the Bill of Rights in the Constitution would allow later generations of interpreters to claim that the people had surrendered any rights not specifically enumerated there. To guard against this, Madison added language that became the Ninth Amendment. Interest in this heretofore largely ignored amendment revived in 1965 when it was used in a concurring opinion in Griswold v. Connecticut *(online). While Justice William O. Douglas called on the Third Amendment to support the right to privacy in deciding that case, Justice Arthur Goldberg, in the concurring opinion, argued that the right to privacy regarding contraception was an unenumerated right that was protected by the Ninth Amendment.*

In 1980, the Court ruled that the right of the press to attend a public trial was protected by the Ninth Amendment. While some scholars argue that modern judges cannot identify the unenumerated rights that the framers were trying to protect, others argue that the Ninth Amendment should be read as providing a constitutional "presumption of liberty" that allows people to act in any way that does not violate the rights of others.

Amendment X

The powers not delegated to the United States by the Constitution, nor prohibited by it to the States, are reserved to the States respectively, or to the people.

◆ ◆ ◆

The Antifederalists were especially eager to see a "reserved powers clause" explicitly guaranteeing the states control over their internal affairs. Not surprisingly, the Tenth Amendment has been a frequent battleground in the struggle over states' rights and federal supremacy. Prior to the Civil War, the Democratic Republican Party and Jacksonian Democrats invoked the Tenth Amendment to prohibit the federal government from making decisions about whether people in individual states could own slaves. The Tenth Amendment was virtually suspended during Reconstruction following the Civil War. In 1883, however, the Supreme Court declared the Civil Rights Act of 1875 unconstitutional on the grounds that it violated the Tenth Amendment. Business interests also called on the amendment to block efforts at federal regulation.

The Court was inconsistent over the next several decades as it attempted to resolve the tension between the restrictions of the Tenth Amendment and the powers the Constitution granted to Congress to regulate interstate commerce and levy taxes. The Court upheld the Pure Food and Drug Act (1906), the Meat Inspection Acts (1906 and 1907), and the White Slave Traffic Act (1910), all of which affected the states, but struck down an act prohibiting interstate shipment of goods produced through child labor. Between 1934 and 1935, a number of New Deal programs created by Franklin D. Roosevelt were declared unconstitutional on the grounds that they violated the Tenth Amendment. (See chapter 24.) As Roosevelt appointees changed the composition of the Court, the Tenth Amendment was declared to have no substantive meaning. Generally, the amendment is held to protect the rights of states to regulate internal matters such as local government, education, commerce, labor, and business, as well as matters involving families such as marriage, divorce, and inheritance within the state.

Unratified Amendment

Reapportionment Amendment (proposed by Congress September 25, 1789, along with the Bill of Rights)

After the first enumeration required by the first article of the Constitution, there shall be one Representative for every thirty thousand, until the number shall amount to one hundred, after which the proportion shall be so regulated by Congress, that there shall be not less than one hundred Representatives, nor less than one Representative for every forty thousand persons, until the number of Representatives shall amount to two hundred; after which the proportion shall be so regulated by Congress, that there shall not be less than two hundred Representatives, nor more than one Representative for every fifty thousand persons.

◆ ◆ ◆

If the Reapportionment Amendment had passed and remained in effect, the House of Representatives today would have more than 5,000 members rather than 435.

Amendment XI

[Adopted 1798]

The judicial power of the United States shall not be construed to extend to any suit in law or equity, commenced or prosecuted against one of the United States by citizens of another State, or by citizens or subjects of any foreign state.

◆ ◆ ◆

In 1793, the Supreme Court ruled in favor of Alexander Chisholm, executor of the estate of a deceased South Carolina merchant. Chisholm was suing the state of Georgia because the merchant had never been paid for provisions he had supplied during the Revolution. Many regarded this Court decision as an error that violated the intent of the Constitution.

Antifederalists had long feared a federal court system with the power to overrule a state court. When the Constitution was being drafted, Federalists had assured worried Antifederalists that section 2 of Article 3, which allows federal courts to hear cases "between a State and citizens of another State," did not mean that the federal courts were authorized to hear suits against a state by citizens of another state or a foreign country. Antifederalists and many other Americans feared a powerful federal court system because they worried that it would become like the British courts of this period, which were accountable only to the monarch. Furthermore, Chisholm v. Georgia *prompted a series of suits against state governments by creditors and suppliers who had made loans during the war.*

In addition, state legislators and Congress feared that the shaky economies of the new states, as well as the country as a whole, would be destroyed, especially if loyalists who had fled to other countries sought reimbursement for land and property that had been seized. The day after the Supreme Court announced its decision, a resolution proposing the Eleventh Amendment, which overturned the decision in Chisholm v. Georgia, *was introduced in the U.S. Senate.*

Amendment XII

[Adopted 1804]

The electors shall meet in their respective States, and vote by ballot for President and Vice-President, one of whom, at least, shall not be an inhabitant of the same State with themselves; they shall name in their ballots the person voted for as President, and in distinct ballots the person voted for as Vice-President, and they shall make distinct lists of all persons voted for as President, and of all persons voted for as Vice-President, and of the number of votes for each, which lists they shall sign and certify, and transmit sealed to the seat of government of the United States, directed to the President of the Senate; — the President of the Senate shall, in the presence of the Senate and House of Representatives, open all the certificates and the votes shall then be counted; — the person having the greatest number of votes for President shall be the President, if such number be a majority of the whole number of electors appointed; and if no person have such majority, then from the persons having the highest numbers not exceeding three on the list of those voted for as President, the House of Representatives shall choose immediately, by ballot, the President. But in choosing the President, the votes shall be taken by States, the representation from each State having one vote; a quorum for this purpose shall consist of a member or members from two-thirds of the States, and a majority of all the States shall be necessary to a choice. And if the House of Representatives shall not choose a President whenever the right of choice shall devolve upon them, before *the fourth day of March* next following, then the Vice-President shall act as President, as in the case of the death or other constitutional disability of the President.

The person having the greatest number of votes as Vice-President shall be the Vice-President, if such number be a majority of the whole number of electors appointed; and if no person have a majority, then from the two highest numbers on the list the Senate shall choose the Vice-President; a quorum for the purpose shall consist of two-thirds of the whole number of Senators, and a majority of the whole number shall be necessary to a choice. But no person constitutionally ineligible to the office of President shall be eligible to that of Vice-President of the United States.

◆ ◆ ◆

The framers of the Constitution disliked political parties and assumed that none would ever form. Under the original system, electors chosen by the states would each vote for two candidates. The candidate who won the most votes would become president, while the person who won the second-highest number of votes would become vice president. Rivalries between Federalists and Antifederalists led to the formation of political parties, however, even before George Washington had left office. Though Washington was elected unanimously in 1789 and 1792, the elections of 1796 and 1800 were procedural disasters because of party maneuvering (see chapters 9 and 10). In 1796, Federalist John Adams was chosen as president, and his great rival, the Antifederalist Thomas Jefferson (whose party was called the Republican Party), became his vice president. In 1800, all the electors cast their two votes as one of two party blocs. Jefferson and his fellow Republican nominee, Aaron Burr, were tied with 73 votes each. The contest went to the House of Representatives, which finally elected Jefferson after 36 ballots. The Twelfth Amendment prevents these problems by requiring electors to vote separately for the president and vice president.

Unratified Amendment

Titles of Nobility Amendment (proposed by Congress May 1, 1810)

If any citizen of the United States shall accept, claim, receive or retain any title of nobility or honor or shall, without the consent of Congress, accept and retain any present, pension, office or emolument of any kind whatever, from any emperor, king, prince or foreign power, such person shall cease to be a citizen of the United States, and shall be incapable of holding any office of trust or profit under them or either of them.

♦♦♦

This amendment would have extended Article 1, section 9, clause 8 of the Constitution, which prevents the awarding of titles by the United States and the acceptance of such awards from foreign powers without congressional consent. Historians speculate that general nervousness about the power of the emperor Napoleon, who was at that time extending France's empire throughout Europe, may have prompted the proposal. Though it fell one vote short of ratification, Congress and the American people thought the proposal had been ratified and it was included in many nineteenth-century editions of the Constitution.

The Civil War and Reconstruction Amendments (Thirteenth, Fourteenth, and Fifteenth Amendments)

In the four months between the election of Abraham Lincoln and his inauguration, more than 200 proposed constitutional amendments were presented to Congress as part of a desperate attempt to hold the rapidly dissolving Union together. Most of these were efforts to appease the southern states by protecting the right to own slaves or by disfranchising African Americans through constitutional amendment. None were able to win the votes required from Congress to send them to the states. The relatively innocuous Corwin Amendment seemed to be the only hope for preserving the Union by amending the Constitution.

The northern victors in the Civil War tried to restructure the Constitution just as the war had restructured the nation. Yet they were often divided in their goals. Some wanted to end slavery; others hoped for social and economic equality regardless of race; others hoped that extending the power of the ballot box to former slaves would help create a new political order. The debates over the Thirteenth, Fourteenth, and Fifteenth Amendments were bitter. Few of those who fought for these changes were satisfied with the amendments themselves; fewer still were satisfied with their interpretation. Although the amendments put an end to the legal status of slavery, it took nearly a hundred years after the amendments' passage before most of the descendants of former slaves could begin to experience the economic, social, and political equality the amendments had been intended to provide.

Unratified Amendment

Corwin Amendment (proposed by Congress March 2, 1861)

No amendment shall be made to the Constitution which will authorize or give to Congress the power to abolish or interfere, within any State, with the domestic institutions thereof, including that of persons held to labor or service by the laws of said State.

♦♦♦

Following the election of Abraham Lincoln, Congress scrambled to try to prevent the secession of the slaveholding states. House member Thomas Corwin of Ohio proposed the "unamendable" amendment in the hope that by protecting slavery where it existed, Congress would keep the southern states in the Union. Lincoln indicated his support for the proposed amendment in his first inaugural address. Only Ohio and Maryland ratified the Corwin Amendment before it was forgotten.

Amendment XIII

[Adopted 1865]

Section 1 Neither slavery nor involuntary servitude, except as a punishment for crime whereof the party shall have been duly convicted, shall exist within the United States, or any place subject to their jurisdiction.

Section 2 Congress shall have power to enforce this article by appropriate legislation.

♦♦♦

Although President Lincoln had abolished slavery in the Confederacy with the Emancipation Proclamation of 1863, abolitionists wanted to rid the entire country of slavery. The Thirteenth Amendment did this in a clear and straightforward manner. In February 1865, when the proposal was approved by the House, the gallery of the House was newly opened to black Americans who had a chance at last to see their government at work. Passage of the proposal was greeted by wild cheers from the gallery as well as tears on the House floor, where congressional representatives openly embraced one another.

The problem of ratification remained, however. The Union position was that the Confederate states were part of the country of thirty-six states. Therefore, twenty-seven states were needed to ratify the amendment. When Kentucky and Delaware rejected it, backers realized that without approval from at least four former Confederate states, the amendment would fail. Lincoln's successor, President Andrew Johnson, made ratification of the Thirteenth Amendment a condition for southern states to rejoin the Union. Under those terms, all the former Confederate states except Mississippi accepted the Thirteenth Amendment, and by the end of 1865 the amendment had become part of the Constitution and slavery had been prohibited in the United States.

Amendment XIV

[Adopted 1868]

Section 1 All persons born or naturalized in the United States, and subject to the jurisdiction thereof, are citizens of the United States and of the State wherein they reside. No State shall make or enforce any law which shall abridge the privileges or immunities of citizens of the United States; nor shall any State deprive any person of life, liberty, or property, without due process of law; nor deny to any person within its jurisdiction the equal protection of the laws.

Section 2 Representatives shall be appointed among the several States according to their respective numbers, counting the whole number of persons in each State, excluding Indians not taxed. But when the right to vote at any election for the choice of Electors for President and Vice-President of the United States, Representatives in Congress, the executive and judicial officers of a State, or the members of the legislature thereof, is denied to any of the male inhabitants of such State, being twenty-one years of age and citizens of the United States, or in any way abridged, except for participation in rebellion, or other crime, the basis of representation therein shall be reduced in the proportion which the number of such male citizens shall bear to the whole number of male citizens twenty-one years of age in such State.

Section 3 No person shall be a Senator or Representative in Congress, or Elector of President and Vice-President, or hold any office, civil or military, under the United States, or under any State, who, having previously taken an oath, as a member of Congress, or as an officer of the United States, or as a member of any State legislature, or as an executive or judicial officer of any State, to support the Constitution of the United States, shall have en-gaged in insurrection or rebellion against the same, or given aid or comfort to the enemies thereof. Congress may, by a vote of two-thirds of each house, remove such disability.

Section 4 The validity of the public debt of the United States, authorized by law, including debts incurred for payment of pensions and bounties for services in suppressing insurrection or rebellion, shall not be questioned. But neither the United States nor any State shall assume or pay any debt or obligation incurred in aid of insurrection or rebellion against the United States, or any claim for the loss or emancipation of any slave; but all such debts, obligations, and claims shall be held illegal and void.

Section 5 The Congress shall have power to enforce, by appropriate legislation, the provisions of this article.

◆◆◆

Without Lincoln's leadership in the reconstruction of the nation following the Civil War, it soon became clear that the Thirteenth Amendment needed additional constitutional support. Less than a year after Lincoln's assassination, Andrew Johnson was ready to bring the former Confederate states back into the Union with few changes in their governments or politics. Anxious Republicans drafted the Fourteenth Amendment to prevent that from happening. The most important provisions of this complex amendment made all native-born or naturalized persons American citizens and prohibited states from abridging the "privileges or immunities" of citizens; depriving them of "life, liberty, or property, without due process of law"; and denying them "equal protection of the laws." In essence, it made all ex-slaves citizens and protected the rights of all citizens against violation by their own state governments.

As occurred in the case of the Thirteenth Amendment, former Confederate states were forced to ratify the amendment as a condition of representation in the House and the Senate. The intentions of the Fourteenth Amendment, and how those intentions should be enforced, have been the most debated point of constitutional history. The terms due process *and* equal protection *have been especially troublesome. Was the amendment designed to outlaw racial segregation? Or was the goal simply to prevent the leaders of the rebellious South from gaining political power?*

The framers of the Fourteenth Amendment hoped Article 2 would produce black voters who would increase the power of the Republican Party. The federal government, however, never used its power to punish states for denying blacks their right to vote. Although the Fourteenth Amendment had an immediate impact in giving black Americans citizenship, it did nothing to protect blacks from the vengeance of whites once Reconstruction ended. In the late nineteenth and early twentieth centuries, section 1 of the Fourteenth Amendment was often used to protect business inter-

ests and strike down laws protecting workers on the grounds that the rights of "persons," that is, corporations, were protected by "due process." More recently, the Fourteenth Amendment has been used to justify school desegregation and affirmative action programs, as well as to dismantle such programs.

Amendment XV

[Adopted 1870]

Section 1   The right of citizens of the United States to vote shall not be denied or abridged by the United States or by any State on account of race, color, or previous condition of servitude.

Section 2   The Congress shall have power to enforce this article by appropriate legislation.

◆ ◆ ◆

The Fifteenth Amendment was the last major piece of Reconstruction legislation. While earlier Reconstruction acts had already required black suffrage in the South, the Fifteenth Amendment extended black voting rights to the entire nation. Some Republicans felt morally obligated to do away with the double standard between North and South since many northern states had stubbornly refused to enfranchise blacks. Others believed that the freedman's ballot required the extra protection of a constitutional amendment to shield it from white counterattack. But partisan advantage also played an important role in the amendment's passage, since Republicans hoped that by giving the ballot to northern blacks, they could lessen their political vulnerability.

Many women's rights advocates had fought for the amendment. They had felt betrayed by the inclusion of the word male *in section 2 of the Fourteenth Amendment and were further angered when the proposed Fifteenth Amendment failed to prohibit denial of the right to vote on the grounds of sex as well as "race, color, or previous condition of servitude." In this amendment, for the first time, the federal government claimed the power to regulate the franchise, or vote. It was also the first time the Constitution placed limits on the power of the states to regulate access to the franchise. Although ratified in 1870, the amendment was not enforced until the twentieth century.*

The Progressive Amendments (Sixteenth–Nineteenth Amendments)

No amendments were added to the Constitution between the Civil War and the Progressive Era. America was changing, however, in fundamental ways. The rapid industrialization of the United States after the Civil War led to many social and economic problems. Hundreds of amendments were proposed, but none received enough support in Congress to be sent to the states. Some scholars believe that regional differences and rivalries were so strong during this period that it was almost impossible to gain a consensus on a constitutional amendment. During the Progressive Era, however, the Constitution was amended four times in seven years.

Amendment XVI

[Adopted 1913]

The Congress shall have power to lay and collect taxes on incomes, from whatever source derived, without apportionment among the several States, and without regard to any census or enumeration.

◆ ◆ ◆

Until passage of the Sixteenth Amendment, most of the money used to run the federal government came from customs duties and taxes on specific items, such as liquor. During the Civil War, the federal government taxed incomes as an emergency measure. Pressure to enact an income tax came from those who were concerned about the growing gap between rich and poor in the United States. The Populist Party began campaigning for a graduated income tax in 1892, and support continued to grow. By 1909, thirty-three proposed income tax amendments had been presented in Congress, but lobbying by corporate and other special interests had defeated them all. In June 1909, the growing pressure for an income tax, which had been endorsed by Presidents Roosevelt and Taft, finally pushed an amendment through the Senate. The required thirty-six states had ratified the amendment by February 1913.

Amendment XVII

[Adopted 1913]

Section 1   The Senate of the United States shall be composed of two Senators from each State, elected by the people thereof, for six years; and each Senator shall have one vote. The electors in each State shall have the qualifications requisite for electors of [voters for] the most numerous branch of the State legislatures.

Section 2   When vacancies happen in the representation of any State in the Senate, the executive authority of such State shall issue writs of election to fill such vacancies: Provided, that the Legislature of any State may empower the executive thereof to make temporary appointments until the people fill the vacancies by election as the Legislature may direct.

Section 3   This amendment shall not be so construed as to affect the election or term of any Senator chosen before it becomes valid as part of the Constitution.

◆ ◆ ◆

The framers of the Constitution saw the members of the House as the representatives of the people and the members of the Senate as the representatives of the states. Originally senators were to be chosen by the state legislators. According to reform advocates, however, the growth of private industry and transportation conglomerates during the Gilded Age had created a network of corruption in which wealth and power were exchanged for influence and votes in the Senate. Senator Nelson Aldrich, who represented Rhode Island in the late nineteenth and early twentieth centuries, for example, was known as "the senator from Standard Oil" because of his open support of special business interests.

Efforts to amend the Constitution to allow direct election of senators had begun in 1826, but since any proposal had to be approved by the Senate, reform seemed impossible. Progressives tried to gain influence in the Senate by instituting party caucuses and primary elections, which gave citizens the chance to express their choice of a senator who could then be officially elected by the state legislature. By 1910, fourteen of the country's thirty senators received popular votes through a state primary before the state legislature made its selection. Despairing of getting a proposal through the Senate, supporters of a direct-election amendment had begun in 1893 to seek a convention of representatives from two-thirds of the states to propose an amendment that could then be ratified. By 1905, thirty-one of forty-five states had endorsed such an amendment. Finally, in 1911, despite extraordinary opposition, a proposed amendment passed the Senate; by 1913, it had been ratified.

Amendment XVIII

[Adopted 1919; repealed 1933 by Amendment XXI]

Section 1   After one year from the ratification of this article the manufacture, sale, or transportation of intoxicating liquors within, the importation thereof into, or the exportation thereof from the United States and all territory subject to the jurisdiction thereof, for beverage purposes, is hereby prohibited.

Section 2   The Congress and the several States shall have concurrent power to enforce this article by appropriate legislation.

Section 3   This article shall be inoperative unless it shall have been ratified as an amendment to the Constitution by the legislatures of the several States, as provided by the Constitution, within seven years from the date of the submission thereof to the States by the Congress.

◆ ◆ ◆

The Prohibition Party, formed in 1869, began calling for a constitutional amendment to outlaw alcoholic beverages in 1872. A prohibition amendment was first proposed in the Senate in 1876 and was revived eighteen times before 1913. Between 1913 and 1919, another thirty-nine attempts were made to prohibit liquor in the United States through a constitutional amendment. Prohibition became a key element of the progressive agenda as reformers linked alcohol and drunkenness to numerous social problems, including the corruption of immigrant voters. While opponents of such an amendment

argued that it was undemocratic, supporters claimed that their efforts had widespread public support. The admission of twelve "dry" western states to the Union in the early twentieth century and the spirit of sacrifice during World War I laid the groundwork for passage and ratification of the Eighteenth Amendment in 1919. Opponents added a time limit to the amendment in the hope that they could thus block ratification, but this effort failed. (See also Amendment XXI.)

Amendment XIX

[Adopted 1920]

Section 1   The right of citizens of the United States to vote shall not be denied or abridged by the United States or by any State on account of sex.

Section 2   Congress shall have the power to enforce this article by appropriate legislation.

◆ ◆ ◆

Advocates of women's rights tried and failed to link woman suffrage to the Fourteenth and Fifteenth Amendments. Nonetheless, the effort for woman suffrage continued. Between 1878 and 1912, at least one and sometimes as many as four proposed amendments were introduced in Congress each year to grant women the right to vote. While over time women won very limited voting rights in some states, at both the state and federal levels opposition to an amendment for woman suffrage remained very strong. President Woodrow Wilson and other officials felt that the federal government should not interfere with the power of the states in this matter. Others worried that granting suffrage to women would encourage ethnic minorities to exercise their own right to vote. And many were concerned that giving women the vote would result in their abandoning traditional gender roles. In 1919, following a protracted and often bitter campaign of protest in which women went on hunger strikes and chained themselves to fences, an amendment was introduced with the backing of President Wilson. It narrowly passed the Senate (after efforts to limit the suffrage to white women failed) and was adopted in 1920 after Tennessee became the thirty-sixth state to ratify it.

Unratified Amendment

Child Labor Amendment (proposed by Congress June 2, 1924)

Section 1   The Congress shall have power to limit, regulate, and prohibit the labor of persons under eighteen years of age.

Section 2   The power of the several States is unimpaired by this article except that the operation of State laws shall be suspended to the extent necessary to give effect to legislation enacted by Congress.

◆ ◆ ◆

Throughout the late nineteenth and early twentieth centuries, alarm over the condition of child workers grew. Opponents of child labor argued that children worked in dangerous and unhealthy conditions, that they took jobs from adult workers, that they depressed wages in certain industries, and that states that allowed child labor had an economic advantage over those that did not. Defenders of child labor claimed that children provided needed income in many families, that working at a young age developed character, and that the effort to prohibit the practice constituted an invasion of family privacy.

In 1916, Congress passed a law that made it illegal to sell goods made by children through interstate commerce. The Supreme Court, however, ruled that the law violated the limits on the power of Congress to regulate interstate commerce. Congress then tried to penalize industries that used child labor by taxing such goods. This measure was also thrown out by the courts. In response, reformers set out to amend the Constitution. The proposed amendment was ratified by twenty-eight states, but by 1925, thirteen states had rejected it. Passage of the Fair Labor Standards Act in 1938, which was upheld by the Supreme Court in 1941, made the amendment irrelevant.

Amendment XX

[Adopted 1933]

Section 1 The terms of the President and Vice-President shall end at noon on the 20th day of January, and the terms of Senators and Representatives at noon on the 3rd day of January, of the years in which such terms would have ended if this article had not been ratified; and the terms of their successors shall then begin.

Section 2 The Congress shall assemble at least once in every year, and such meeting shall begin at noon on the 3rd day of January, unless they shall by law appoint a different day.

Section 3 If, at the time fixed for the beginning of the term of the President, the President-elect shall have died, the Vice-President-elect shall become President. If a President shall not have been chosen before the time fixed for the beginning of his term, or if the President-elect shall have failed to qualify, then the Vice-President-elect shall act as President until a President shall have qualified; and the Congress may by law provide for the case wherein neither a President-elect nor a Vice-President-elect shall have qualified, declaring who shall then act as President, or the manner in which one who is to act shall be selected, and such person shall act accordingly until a President or Vice-President shall have qualified.

Section 4 The Congress may by law provide for the case of the death of any of the persons from whom the House of Representatives may choose a President whenever the right of choice shall have devolved upon them, and for the case of the death of any of the persons from whom the Senate may choose a Vice-President whenever the right of choice shall have devolved upon them.

Section 5 Sections 1 and 2 shall take effect on the 15th day of October following the ratification of this article.

Section 6 This article shall be inoperative unless it shall have been ratified as an amendment to the Constitution by the Legislatures of three-fourths of the several States within seven years from the date of its submission.

♦ ♦ ♦

Until 1933, presidents took office on March 4. Since elections are held in early November and electoral votes are counted in mid-December, this meant that more than three months passed between the time a new president was elected and when he took office. Moving the inauguration to January shortened the transition period and allowed Congress to begin its term closer to the time of the president's inauguration. Although this seems like a minor change, an amendment was required because the Constitution specifies terms of office. This amendment also deals with questions of succession in the event that a president- or vice president-elect dies before assuming office. Section 3 also clarifies a method for resolving a deadlock in the electoral college.

Amendment XXI

[Adopted 1933]

Section 1 The eighteenth article of amendment to the Constitution of the United States is hereby repealed.

Section 2 The transportation or importation into any State, Territory, or Possession of the United States for delivery or use therein of intoxicating liquors, in violation of the laws thereof, is hereby prohibited.

Section 3 This article shall be inoperative unless it shall have been ratified as an amendment to the Constitution by conventions in the several States, as provided in the Constitution, within seven years from the date of the submission thereof to the States by the Congress.

♦ ♦ ♦

Widespread violation of the Volstead Act, the law enacted to enforce prohibition, made the United States a nation of lawbreakers. Prohibition caused more problems than it solved by encouraging crime, bribery, and corruption. Further, a coalition of liquor and beer manufacturers, personal liberty advocates, and constitutional scholars joined forces to challenge the amendment. By 1929, thirty proposed repeal amendments had been introduced in Congress, and the Democratic Party made repeal part of its platform in the 1932 presidential campaign. The

Twenty-first Amendment was proposed in February 1933 and ratified less than a year later. The failure of the effort to enforce prohibition through a constitutional amendment has often been cited by opponents to subsequent efforts to shape public virtue and private morality.

Amendment XXII

[Adopted 1951]

Section 1 No person shall be elected to the office of the President more than twice, and no person who has held the office of President, or acted as President, for more than two years of a term to which some other person was elected President shall be elected to the office of President more than once. But this article shall not apply to any person holding the office of President when this Article was proposed by the Congress, and shall not prevent any person who may be holding the office of President, or acting as President, during the term within which this Article becomes operative from holding the office of President or acting as President during the remainder of such term.

Section 2 This article shall be inoperative unless it shall have been ratified as an amendment to the Constitution by the legislatures of three-fourths of the several States within seven years from the date of its submission to the States by the Congress.

♦ ♦ ♦

George Washington's refusal to seek a third term of office set a precedent that stood until 1912, when former President Theodore Roosevelt sought, without success, another term as an independent candidate. Democrat Franklin Roosevelt was the only president to seek and win a fourth term, though he did so amid great controversy. Roosevelt died in April 1945, a few months after the beginning of his fourth term. In 1946, Republicans won control of the House and the Senate, and early in 1947 a proposal for an amendment to limit future presidents to two four-year terms was offered to the states for ratification. Democratic critics of the Twenty-second Amendment charged that it was a partisan posthumous jab at Roosevelt.

Since the Twenty-second Amendment was adopted, however, the only presidents who might have been able to seek a third term, had it not existed, were Republicans Dwight Eisenhower and Ronald Reagan, and Democrat Bill Clinton. Since 1826, Congress has entertained 160 proposed amendments to limit the president to one six-year term. Such amendments have been backed by fifteen presidents, including Gerald Ford and Jimmy Carter.

Amendment XXIII

[Adopted 1961]

Section 1 The District constituting the seat of Government of the United States shall appoint in such manner as the Congress may direct: A number of electors of President and Vice-President equal to the whole number of Senators and Representatives in Congress to which the District would be entitled if it were a State, but in no event more than the least populous State; they shall be in addition to those appointed by the States, but they shall be considered for the purposes of the election of President and Vice-President, to be electors appointed by a State; and they shall meet in the District and perform such duties as provided by the twelfth article of amendment.

Section 2 The Congress shall have the power to enforce this article by appropriate legislation.

♦ ♦ ♦

When Washington, D.C., was established as a federal district, no one expected that a significant number of people would make it their permanent and primary residence. A proposal to allow citizens of the district to vote in presidential elections was approved by Congress in June 1960 and was ratified on March 29, 1961.

Amendment XXIV

[Adopted 1964]

Section 1 The right of citizens of the United States to vote in any primary or other election for President or Vice-President, for electors for President or Vice-President, or for Senator or Representative in Congress, shall not be denied or abridged by the United States or any State by reason of failure to pay any poll tax or other tax.

Section 2 The Congress shall have the power to enforce this article by appropriate legislation.

♦ ♦ ♦

In the colonial and Revolutionary eras, financial independence was seen as necessary to political independence, and the poll tax was used as a requirement for voting. By the twentieth century, however, the poll tax was used mostly to bar poor people, especially southern blacks, from voting. While conservatives complained that the amendment interfered with states' rights, liberals thought that the amendment did not go far enough because it barred the poll tax only in national elections and not in state or local elections. The amendment was ratified in 1964, however, and two years later, the Supreme Court ruled that poll taxes in state and local elections also violated the equal protection clause of the Fourteenth Amendment.

Amendment XXV

[Adopted 1967]

Section 1 In case of the removal of the President from office or of his death or resignation, the Vice-President shall become President.

Section 2 Whenever there is a vacancy in the office of the Vice-President, the President shall nominate a Vice-President who shall take office upon confirmation by a majority vote of both Houses of Congress.

Section 3 Whenever the President transmits to the President pro tempore of the Senate and the Speaker of the House of Representatives his written declaration that he is unable to discharge the powers and duties of his office, and until he transmits to them a written declaration to the contrary, such powers and duties shall be discharged by the Vice-President as Acting President.

Section 4 Whenever the Vice-President and a majority of either the principal officers of the executive departments or of such other body as Congress may by law provide, transmit to the President pro tempore of the Senate and the Speaker of the House of Representatives their written declaration that the President is unable to discharge the powers and duties of his office, the Vice-President shall immediately assume the powers and duties of the office as Acting President.

Thereafter, when the President transmits to the President pro tempore of the Senate and the Speaker of the House of Representatives his written declaration that no inability exists, he shall resume the powers and duties of his office unless the Vice-President and a majority of either the principal officers of the executive department[s] or of such other body as Congress may by law provide, transmit within four days to the President pro tempore of the Senate and the Speaker of the House of Representatives their written declaration that the President is unable to discharge the powers and duties of his office. Thereupon Congress shall decide the issue, assembling within forty-eight hours for that purpose if not in session. If the Congress, within twenty-one days after receipt of the latter written declaration, or, if Congress is not in session, within twenty-one days after Congress is required to assemble, determines by two-thirds vote of both Houses that the President is unable to discharge the powers and duties of his office, the Vice-President shall continue to discharge the same as Acting President; otherwise, the President shall resume the powers and duties of his office.

♦♦♦

The framers of the Constitution established the office of vice president because someone was needed to preside over the Senate. The first president to die in office was William Henry Harrison, in 1841. Vice President John Tyler had himself sworn in as president, setting a precedent that was followed when seven later presidents died in office. The assassination of President James A. Garfield in 1881 posed a new problem, however. After he was shot, the president was incapacitated for two months before he died; he was unable to lead the country, while his vice president, Chester A. Arthur, was unable to assume leadership. Efforts to resolve questions of succession in the event of a presidential disability thus began with the death of Garfield.

In 1963, the assassination of President John F. Kennedy galvanized Congress to action. Vice President Lyndon Johnson was a chain smoker with a history of heart trouble. According to the 1947 Presidential Succession Act, the two men who stood in line to succeed him were the seventy-two-year-old Speaker of the House and the eighty-six-year-old president of the Senate. There were serious concerns that any of these men might become incapacitated while serving as chief executive. The first time the Twenty-fifth Amendment was used, however, was not in the case of presidential death or illness, but during the Watergate crisis. When Vice President Spiro T. Agnew was forced to resign following allegations of bribery and tax violations, President Richard M. Nixon appointed House Minority Leader Gerald R. Ford vice president. Ford became president following Nixon's resignation eight months later and named Nelson A. Rockefeller as his vice president. Thus, for more than two years, the two highest offices in the country were held by people who had not been elected to them.

Amendment XXVI

[Adopted 1971]

Section 1 The right of citizens of the United States, who are eighteen years of age or older, to vote shall not be denied or abridged by the United States or by any State on account of age.

Section 2 The Congress shall have power to enforce this article by appropriate legislation.

♦♦♦

Efforts to lower the voting age from twenty-one to eighteen began during World War II. Recognizing that those who were old enough to fight a war should have some say in the government policies that involved them in the war, Presidents Eisenhower, Johnson, and Nixon endorsed the idea. In 1970, the combined pressure of the antiwar movement and the demographic pressure of the baby boom generation led to a Voting Rights Act lowering the voting age in federal, state, and local elections.

In Oregon v. Mitchell (1970), the state of Oregon challenged the right of Congress to determine the age at which people could vote in state or local elections. The Supreme Court agreed with Oregon. Since the Voting Rights Act was ruled unconstitutional, the Constitution had to be amended to allow passage of a law that would lower the voting age. The amendment was ratified in a little more than three months, making it the most rapidly ratified amendment in U.S. history.

Unratified Amendment

Equal Rights Amendment (proposed by Congress March 22, 1972; seven-year deadline for ratification extended June 30, 1982)

Section 1 Equality of rights under the law shall not be denied or abridged by the United States or by any State on account of sex.

Section 2 The Congress shall have the power to enforce, by appropriate legislation, the provisions of this article.

Section 3 This amendment shall take effect two years after the date of ratification.

◆ ◆ ◆

In 1923, soon after women had won the right to vote, Alice Paul, a leading activist in the woman suffrage movement, proposed an amendment requiring equal treatment of men and women. Opponents of the proposal argued that such an amendment would invalidate laws that protected women and would make women subject to the military draft. After the 1964 Civil Rights Act was adopted, protective workplace legislation was removed anyway.

The renewal of the women's movement, as a by-product of the civil rights and antiwar movements, led to a revival of the Equal Rights Amendment (ERA) in Congress. Disagreements over language held up congressional passage of the proposed amendment, but on March 22, 1972, the Senate approved the ERA by a vote of 84 to 8, and it was sent to the states. Six states ratified the amendment within two days, and by the middle of 1973 the amendment seemed well on its way to adoption, with thirty of the needed thirty-eight states having ratified it. In the mid-1970s, however, a powerful "Stop ERA" campaign developed. The campaign portrayed the ERA as a threat to "family values" and traditional relationships between men and women. Although thirty-five states ultimately ratified the ERA, five of those state legislatures voted to rescind ratification, and the amendment was never adopted.

Unratified Amendment

D.C. Statehood Amendment (proposed by Congress August 22, 1978)

Section 1 For purposes of representation in the Congress, election of the President and Vice-President, and article V of this Constitution, the District constituting the seat of government of the United States shall be treated as though it were a State.

Section 2 The exercise of the rights and powers conferred under this article shall be by the people of the District constituting the seat of government, and as shall be provided by Congress.

Section 3 The twenty-third article of amendment to the Constitution of the United States is hereby repealed.

Section 4 This article shall be inoperative, unless it shall have been ratified as an amendment to the Constitution by the legislatures of three-fourths of the several states within seven years from the date of its submission.

◆ ◆ ◆

The 1961 ratification of the Twenty-third Amendment, giving residents of the District of Columbia

the right to vote for a president and vice president, inspired an effort to give residents of the district full voting rights. In 1966, President Lyndon Johnson appointed a mayor and city council; in 1971, D.C. residents were allowed to name a nonvoting delegate to the House; and in 1981, residents were allowed to elect the mayor and city council. Congress retained the right to overrule laws that might affect commuters, the height of federal buildings, and selection of judges and prosecutors. The district's nonvoting delegate to Congress, Walter Fauntroy, lobbied fiercely for a congressional amendment granting statehood to the district. In 1978, a proposed amendment was approved and sent to the states. A number of states quickly ratified the amendment, but, like the ERA, the D.C. Statehood Amendment ran into trouble. Opponents argued that section 2 created a separate category of "nominal" statehood. They argued that the federal district should be eliminated and that the territory should be reabsorbed into the state of Maryland. Although these theoretical arguments were strong, some scholars believe that racist attitudes toward the predominantly black population of the city was also a factor leading to the defeat of the amendment.

Amendment XXVII
[Adopted 1992]

No law, varying the compensation for the services of the Senators and Representatives, shall take effect, until an election of Representatives shall have intervened.

◆ ◆ ◆

While the Twenty-sixth Amendment was the most rapidly ratified amendment in U.S. history, the Twenty-seventh Amendment had the longest journey to ratification. First proposed by James Madison in 1789 as part of the package that included the Bill of Rights, this amendment had been ratified by only six states by 1791. In 1873, however, it was ratified by Ohio to protest a massive retroactive salary increase by the federal government. Unlike later proposed amendments, this one came with no time limit on ratification. In the early 1980s, Gregory D. Watson, a University of Texas economics major, discovered the "lost" amendment and began a single-handed campaign to get state legislators to introduce it for ratification. In 1983, it was accepted by Maine. In 1984, it passed the Colorado legislature. Ratifications trickled in slowly until May 1992, when Michigan and New Jersey became the thirty-eighth and thirty-ninth states, respectively, to ratify. This amendment prevents members of Congress from raising their own salaries without giving voters a chance to vote them out of office before they can benefit from the raises.

Facts and Figures: Government, Economy, and Demographics

PRESIDENTIAL ELECTIONS

Year	Candidates	Parties	Popular Vote	Percentage of Popular Vote	Electoral Vote	Percentage of Voter Participation
1789	**GEORGE WASHINGTON (Va.)**[*]				69	
	John Adams				34	
	Others				35	
1792	**GEORGE WASHINGTON (Va.)**				132	
	John Adams				77	
	George Clinton				50	
	Others				5	
1796	**JOHN ADAMS (Mass.)**	Federalist			71	
	Thomas Jefferson	Democratic-Republican			68	
	Thomas Pinckney	Federalist			59	
	Aaron Burr	Dem.-Rep.			30	
	Others				48	
1800	**THOMAS JEFFERSON (Va.)**	Dem.-Rep.			73	
	Aaron Burr	Dem.-Rep.			73	
	John Adams	Federalist			65	
	C. C. Pinckney	Federalist			64	
	John Jay	Federalist			1	
1804	**THOMAS JEFFERSON (Va.)**	Dem.-Rep.			162	
	C. C. Pinckney	Federalist			14	
1808	**JAMES MADISON (Va.)**	Dem.-Rep.			122	
	C. C. Pinckney	Federalist			47	
	George Clinton	Dem.-Rep.			6	
1812	**JAMES MADISON (Va.)**	Dem.-Rep.			128	
	De Witt Clinton	Federalist			89	
1816	**JAMES MONROE (Va.)**	Dem.-Rep.			183	
	Rufus King	Federalist			34	
1820	**JAMES MONROE (Va.)**	Dem.-Rep.			231	
	John Quincy Adams	Dem.-Rep.			1	
1824	**JOHN Q. ADAMS (Mass.)**	Dem.-Rep.	108,740	30.5	84	26.9
	Andrew Jackson	Dem.-Rep.	153,544	43.1	99	
	William H. Crawford	Dem.-Rep.	46,618	13.1	41	
	Henry Clay	Dem.-Rep.	47,136	13.2	37	
1828	**ANDREW JACKSON (Tenn.)**	Democratic	647,286	56.0	178	57.6
	John Quincy Adams	National Republican	508,064	44.0	83	

[*]State of residence when elected president.

Year	Candidates	Parties	Popular Vote	Percentage of Popular Vote	Electoral Vote	Percentage of Voter Participation
1832	**ANDREW JACKSON (Tenn.)**	Democratic	687,502	55.0	219	55.4
	Henry Clay	National Republican	530,189	42.4	49	
	John Floyd	Independent			11	
	William Wirt	Anti-Mason	33,108	2.6	7	
1836	**MARTIN VAN BUREN (N.Y.)**	Democratic	765,483	50.9	170	57.8
	W. H. Harrison	Whig			73	
	Hugh L. White	Whig	739,795	49.1	26	
	Daniel Webster	Whig			14	
	W. P. Mangum	Whig			11	
1840	**WILLIAM H. HARRISON (Ohio)**	Whig	1,274,624	53.1	234	80.2
	Martin Van Buren	Democratic	1,127,781	46.9	60	
	J. G. Birney	Liberty	7,069		—	
1844	**JAMES K. POLK (Tenn.)**	Democratic	1,338,464	49.6	170	78.9
	Henry Clay	Whig	1,300,097	48.1	105	
	J. G. Birney	Liberty	62,300	2.3	—	
1848	**ZACHARY TAYLOR (La.)**	Whig	1,360,967	47.4	163	72.7
	Lewis Cass	Democratic	1,222,342	42.5	127	
	Martin Van Buren	Free-Soil	291,263	10.1	—	
1852	**FRANKLIN PIERCE (N.H.)**	Democratic	1,601,117	50.9	254	69.6
	Winfield Scott	Whig	1,385,453	44.1	42	
	John P. Hale	Free-Soil	155,825	5.0	—	
1856	**JAMES BUCHANAN (Pa.)**	Democratic	1,832,995	45.3	174	78.9
	John C. Frémont	Republican	1,339,932	33.1	114	
	Millard Fillmore	American	871,731	21.6	8	
1860	**ABRAHAM LINCOLN (Ill.)**	Republican	1,865,593	39.8	180	81.2
	Stephen A. Douglas	Democratic	1,382,713	29.5	12	
	John C. Breckinridge	Democratic	848,356	18.1	72	
	John Bell	Union	592,906	12.6	39	
1864	**ABRAHAM LINCOLN (Ill.)**	Republican	2,206,938	55.0	212	73.8
	George B. McClellan	Democratic	1,803,787	45.0	21	
1868	**ULYSSES S. GRANT (Ill.)**	Republican	3,012,833	52.7	214	78.1
	Horatio Seymour	Democratic	2,703,249	47.3	80	
1872	**ULYSSES S. GRANT (Ill.)**	Republican	3,597,132	55.6	286	71.3
	Horace Greeley	Democratic; Liberal Republican	2,834,125	43.9	66	
1876	**RUTHERFORD B. HAYES (Ohio)**	Republican	4,036,572	48.0	185	81.8
	Samuel J. Tilden	Democratic	4,284,020	51.0	184	
1880	**JAMES A. GARFIELD (Ohio)**	Republican	4,454,416	48.5	214	79.4
	Winfield S. Hancock	Democratic	4,444,952	48.1	155	
1884	**GROVER CLEVELAND (N.Y.)**	Democratic	4,879,507	48.5	219	77.5
	James G. Blaine	Republican	4,850,293	48.2	182	
1888	**BENJAMIN HARRISON (Ind.)**	Republican	5,439,853	47.9	233	79.3
	Grover Cleveland	Democratic	5,540,309	48.6	168	
1892	**GROVER CLEVELAND (N.Y.)**	Democratic	5,555,426	46.1	277	74.7
	Benjamin Harrison	Republican	5,182,690	43.0	145	
	James B. Weaver	People's	1,029,846	8.5	22	
1896	**WILLIAM McKINLEY (Ohio)**	Republican	7,104,779	51.1	271	79.3
	William J. Bryan	Democratic-People's	6,502,925	47.7	176	
1900	**WILLIAM McKINLEY (Ohio)**	Republican	7,207,923	51.7	292	73.2
	William J. Bryan	Dem.-Populist	6,358,133	45.5	155	

PRESIDENTIAL ELECTIONS

Year	Candidates	Parties	Popular Vote	Percentage of Popular Vote	Electoral Vote	Percentage of Voter Participation
1904	**THEODORE ROOSEVELT (N.Y.)**	Republican	7,623,486	57.9	336	65.2
	Alton B. Parker	Democratic	5,077,911	37.6	140	
	Eugene V. Debs	Socialist	402,283	3.0	—	
1908	**WILLIAM H. TAFT (Ohio)**	Republican	7,678,908	51.6	321	65.4
	William J. Bryan	Democratic	6,409,104	43.1	162	
	Eugene V. Debs	Socialist	420,793	2.8	—	
1912	**WOODROW WILSON (N.J.)**	Democratic	6,293,454	41.9	435	58.8
	Theodore Roosevelt	Progressive	4,119,538	27.4	88	
	William H. Taft	Republican	3,484,980	23.2	8	
	Eugene V. Debs	Socialist	900,672	6.1	—	
1916	**WOODROW WILSON (N.J.)**	Democratic	9,129,606	49.4	277	61.6
	Charles E. Hughes	Republican	8,538,221	46.2	254	
	A. L. Benson	Socialist	585,113	3.2	—	
1920	**WARREN G. HARDING (Ohio)**	Republican	16,143,407	60.5	404	49.2
	James M. Cox	Democratic	9,130,328	34.2	127	
	Eugene V. Debs	Socialist	919,799	3.4	—	
1924	**CALVIN COOLIDGE (Mass.)**	Republican	15,725,016	54.0	382	48.9
	John W. Davis	Democratic	8,386,503	28.8	136	
	Robert M. La Follette	Progressive	4,822,856	16.6	13	
1928	**HERBERT HOOVER (Calif.)**	Republican	21,391,381	58.2	444	56.9
	Alfred E. Smith	Democratic	15,016,443	40.9	87	
	Norman Thomas	Socialist	267,835	0.7	—	
1932	**FRANKLIN D. ROOSEVELT (N.Y.)**	Democratic	22,809,638	57.4	472	56.9
	Herbert Hoover	Republican	15,758,901	39.7	59	
	Norman Thomas	Socialist	881,951	2.2	—	
1936	**FRANKLIN D. ROOSEVELT (N.Y.)**	Democratic	27,751,597	60.8	523	61.0
	Alfred M. Landon	Republican	16,679,583	36.5	8	
	William Lemke	Union	882,479	1.9	—	
1940	**FRANKLIN D. ROOSEVELT (N.Y.)**	Democratic	27,244,160	54.8	449	62.5
	Wendell Willkie	Republican	22,305,198	44.8	82	
1944	**FRANKLIN D. ROOSEVELT (N.Y.)**	Democratic	25,602,504	53.5	432	55.9
	Thomas E. Dewey	Republican	22,006,285	46.0	99	
1948	**HARRY S. TRUMAN (Mo.)**	Democratic	24,105,695	49.5	303	53.0
	Thomas E. Dewey	Republican	21,969,170	45.1	189	
	J. Strom Thurmond	States'-Rights Democratic	1,169,021	2.4	38	
	Henry A. Wallace	Progressive	1,156,103	2.4	—	
1952	**DWIGHT D. EISENHOWER (N.Y.)**	Republican	33,936,252	55.1	442	63.3
	Adlai Stevenson	Democratic	27,314,992	44.4	89	
1956	**DWIGHT D. EISENHOWER (N.Y.)**	Republican	35,575,420	57.6	457	60.6
	Adlai Stevenson	Democratic	26,033,066	42.1	73	
	Other	—	—		1	
1960	**JOHN F. KENNEDY (Mass.)**	Democratic	34,227,096	49.9	303	62.8
	Richard M. Nixon	Republican	34,108,546	49.6	219	
	Other	—	—		15	
1964	**LYNDON B. JOHNSON (Texas)**	Democratic	43,126,506	61.1	486	61.7
	Barry M. Goldwater	Republican	27,176,799	38.5	52	
1968	**RICHARD M. NIXON (N.Y.)**	Republican	31,770,237	43.4	301	60.9
	Hubert H. Humphrey	Democratic	31,270,533	42.7	191	
	George Wallace	American Indep.	9,906,141	13.5	46	
1972	**RICHARD M. NIXON (N.Y.)**	Republican	47,169,911	60.7	520	55.2
	George S. McGovern	Democratic	29,170,383	37.5	17	
	Other	—	—		1	

Year	Candidates	Parties	Popular Vote	Percentage of Popular Vote	Electoral Vote	Percentage of Voter Participation
1976	**JIMMY CARTER (Ga.)**	Democratic	40,828,587	50.0	297	53.5
	Gerald R. Ford	Republican	39,147,613	47.9	241	
	Other	—	1,575,459	2.1	—	
1980	**RONALD REAGAN (Calif.)**	Republican	43,901,812	50.7	489	54.0
	Jimmy Carter	Democratic	35,483,820	41.0	49	
	John B. Anderson	Independent	5,719,722	6.6	—	
	Ed Clark	Libertarian	921,188	1.1	—	
1984	**RONALD REAGAN (Calif.)**	Republican	54,455,075	59.0	525	53.1
	Walter Mondale	Democratic	37,577,185	41.0	13	
1988	**GEORGE H. W. BUSH (Texas)**	Republican	47,946,422	54.0	426	50.2
	Michael S. Dukakis	Democratic	41,016,429	46.0	112	
1992	**WILLIAM J. CLINTON (Ark.)**	Democratic	44,908,254	42.3	370	55.9
	George H. W. Bush	Republican	39,102,282	37.4	168	
	H. Ross Perot	Independent	19,721,433	18.9	—	
1996	**WILLIAM J. CLINTON (Ark.)**	Democratic	47,401,185	49.2	379	49.0
	Robert Dole	Republican	39,197,469	40.7	159	
	H. Ross Perot	Independent	8,085,294	8.4	—	
2000	**GEORGE W. BUSH (Texas)**	Republican	50,456,062	47.8	271	51.2
	Al Gore	Democratic	50,996,862	48.4	267	
	Ralph Nader	Green Party	2,858,843	2.7	—	
	Patrick J. Buchanan	—	438,760	.4	—	
2004	**GEORGE W. BUSH (Texas)**	Republican	61,872,711	50.6	286	60.3
	John F. Kerry	Democratic	58,894,584	48.1	251	
	Other	—	1,582,185	1.3	—	

PRESIDENTS, VICE PRESIDENTS, AND SECRETARIES OF STATE

The Washington Administration (1789–1797)

Vice President	John Adams	1789–1797
Secretary of State	Thomas Jefferson	1789–1793
	Edmund Randolph	1794–1795
	Timothy Pickering	1795–1797

The John Adams Administration (1797–1801)

Vice President	Thomas Jefferson	1797–1801
Secretary of State	Timothy Pickering	1797–1800
	John Marshall	1800–1801

The Jefferson Administration (1801–1809)

Vice President	Aaron Burr	1801–1805
	George Clinton	1805–1809
Secretary of State	James Madison	1801–1809

The Madison Administration (1809–1817)

Vice President	George Clinton	1809–1813
	Elbridge Gerry	1813–1817
Secretary of State	Robert Smith	1809–1811
	James Monroe	1811–1817

The Monroe Administration (1817–1825)

Vice President	Daniel Tompkins	1817–1825
Secretary of State	John Quincy Adams	1817–1825

The John Quincy Adams Administration (1825–1829)

Vice President	John C. Calhoun	1825–1829
Secretary of State	Henry Clay	1825–1829

The Jackson Administration (1829–1837)

Vice President	John C. Calhoun	1829–1833
	Martin Van Buren	1833–1837
Secretary of State	Martin Van Buren	1829–1831
	Edward Livingston	1831–1833
	Louis McLane	1833–1834
	John Forsyth	1834–1837

The Van Buren Administration (1837–1841)

Vice President	Richard M. Johnson	1837–1841
Secretary of State	John Forsyth	1837–1841

PRESIDENTS, VICE PRESIDENTS, AND SECRETARIES OF STATE

The William Harrison Administration (1841)

Vice President	John Tyler	1841
Secretary of State	Daniel Webster	1841

The Tyler Administration (1841–1845)

Vice President	None	
Secretary of State	Daniel Webster	1841–1843
	Hugh S. Legaré	1843
	Abel P. Upshur	1843–1844
	John C. Calhoun	1844–1845

The Polk Administration (1845–1849)

Vice President	George M. Dallas	1845–1849
Secretary of State	James Buchanan	1845–1849

The Taylor Administration (1849–1850)

Vice President	Millard Fillmore	1849–1850
Secretary of State	John M. Clayton	1849–1850

The Fillmore Administration (1850–1853)

Vice President	None	
Secretary of State	Daniel Webster	1850–1852
	Edward Everett	1852–1853

The Pierce Administration (1853–1857)

Vice President	William R. King	1853–1857
Secretary of State	William L. Marcy	1853–1857

The Buchanan Administration (1857–1861)

Vice President	John C. Breckinridge	1857–1861
Secretary of State	Lewis Cass	1857–1860
	Jeremiah S. Black	1860–1861

The Lincoln Administration (1861–1865)

Vice President	Hannibal Hamlin	1861–1865
	Andrew Johnson	1865
Secretary of State	William H. Seward	1861–1865

The Andrew Johnson Administration (1865–1869)

Vice President	None	
Secretary of State	William H. Seward	1865–1869

The Grant Administration (1869–1877)

Vice President	Schuyler Colfax	1869–1873
	Henry Wilson	1873–1877
Secretary of State	Elihu B. Washburne	1869
	Hamilton Fish	1869–1877

The Hayes Administration (1877–1881)

Vice President	William A. Wheeler	1877–1881
Secretary of State	William M. Evarts	1877–1881

The Garfield Administration (1881)

Vice President	Chester A. Arthur	1881
Secretary of State	James G. Blaine	1881

The Arthur Administration (1881–1885)

Vice President	None	
Secretary of State	F. T. Frelinghuysen	1881–1885

The Cleveland Administration (1885–1889)

Vice President	Thomas A. Hendricks	1885–1889
Secretary of State	Thomas F. Bayard	1885–1889

The Benjamin Harrison Administration (1889–1893)

Vice President	Levi P. Morton	1889–1893
Secretary of State	James G. Blaine	1889–1892
	John W. Foster	1892–1893

The Cleveland Administration (1893–1897)

Vice President	Adlai E. Stevenson	1893–1897
Secretary of State	Walter Q. Gresham	1893–1895
	Richard Olney	1895–1897

The McKinley Administration (1897–1901)

Vice President	Garret A. Hobart	1897–1901
	Theodore Roosevelt	1901
Secretary of State	John Sherman	1897–1898
	William R. Day	1898
	John Hay	1898–1901

The Theodore Roosevelt Administration (1901–1909)

Vice President	Charles Fairbanks	1905–1909
Secretary of State	John Hay	1901–1905
	Elihu Root	1905–1909
	Robert Bacon	1909

The Taft Administration (1909–1913)

Vice President	James S. Sherman	1909–1913
Secretary of State	Philander C. Knox	1909–1913

The Wilson Administration (1913–1921)

Vice President	Thomas R. Marshall	1913–1921
Secretary of State	William J. Bryan	1913–1915
	Robert Lansing	1915–1920
	Bainbridge Colby	1920–1921

The Harding Administration (1921–1923)

Vice President	Calvin Coolidge	1921–1923
Secretary of State	Charles E. Hughes	1921–1923

The Coolidge Administration (1923–1929)

Vice President	Charles G. Dawes	1925–1929
Secretary of State	Charles E. Hughes	1923–1925
	Frank B. Kellogg	1925–1929

The Hoover Administration (1929–1933)

Vice President	Charles Curtis	1929–1933
Secretary of State	Henry L. Stimson	1929–1933

The Franklin D. Roosevelt Administration (1933–1945)

Vice President	John Nance Garner	1933–1941
	Henry A. Wallace	1941–1945
	Harry S. Truman	1945
Secretary of State	Cordell Hull	1933–1944
	Edward R. Stettinius Jr.	1944–1945

The Truman Administration (1945–1953)

Vice President	Alben W. Barkley	1949–1953
Secretary of State	Edward R. Stettinius Jr.	1945
	James F. Byrnes	1945–1947
	George C. Marshall	1947–1949
	Dean G. Acheson	1949–1953

The Eisenhower Administration (1953–1961)

Vice President	Richard M. Nixon	1953–1961
Secretary of State	John Foster Dulles	1953–1959
	Christian A. Herter	1959–1961

The Kennedy Administration (1961–1963)

Vice President	Lyndon B. Johnson	1961–1963
Secretary of State	Dean Rusk	1961–1963

The Lyndon Johnson Administration (1963–1969)

Vice President	Hubert H. Humphrey	1965–1969
Secretary of State	Dean Rusk	1963–1969

The Nixon Administration (1969–1974)

Vice President	Spiro T. Agnew	1969–1973
	Gerald R. Ford	1973–1974
Secretary of State	William P. Rogers	1969–1973
	Henry A. Kissinger	1973–1974

The Ford Administration (1974–1977)

Vice President	Nelson A. Rockefeller	1974–1977
Secretary of State	Henry A. Kissinger	1974–1977

The Carter Administration (1977–1981)

Vice President	Walter F. Mondale	1977–1981
Secretary of State	Cyrus R. Vance	1977–1980
	Edmund Muskie	1980–1981

The Reagan Administration (1981–1989)

Vice President	George H. W. Bush	1981–1989
Secretary of State	Alexander M. Haig	1981–1982
	George P. Shultz	1982–1989

The George H. W. Bush Administration (1989–1993)

Vice President	J. Danforth Quayle	1989–1993
Secretary of State	James A. Baker III	1989–1992
	Lawrence S. Eagleburger	1992–1993

The Clinton Administration (1993–2001)

Vice President	Albert Gore	1993–2001
Secretary of State	Warren M. Christopher	1993–1997
	Madeleine K. Albright	1997–2001

The George W. Bush Administration (2001–)

Vice President	Richard Cheney	2001–
Secretary of State	Colin Powell	2001–2005
	Condoleezza Rice	2005–

SUPREME COURT JUSTICES

Name	Service	Appointed by	Name	Service	Appointed by
John Jay*	1789–1795	Washington	Lucius Q. C. Lamar	1888–1893	Cleveland
James Wilson	1789–1798	Washington	**Melville W. Fuller**	1888–1910	Cleveland
John Blair	1789–1796	Washington	David J. Brewer	1889–1910	B. Harrison
John Rutledge	1790–1791	Washington	Henry B. Brown	1890–1906	B. Harrison
William Cushing	1790–1810	Washington	George Shiras	1892–1903	B. Harrison
James Iredell	1790–1799	Washington	Howell E. Jackson	1893–1895	B. Harrison
Thomas Johnson	1791–1793	Washington	Edward D. White	1894–1910	Cleveland
William Paterson	1793–1806	Washington	Rufus W. Peckham	1896–1909	Cleveland
John Rutledge†	1795	Washington	Joseph McKenna	1898–1925	McKinley
Samuel Chase	1796–1811	Washington	Oliver W. Holmes	1902–1932	T. Roosevelt
Oliver Ellsworth	1796–1799	Washington	William R. Day	1903–1922	T. Roosevelt
Bushrod Washington	1798–1829	J. Adams	William H. Moody	1906–1910	T. Roosevelt
Alfred Moore	1799–1804	J. Adams	Horace H. Lurton	1910–1914	Taft
John Marshall	1801–1835	J. Adams	Charles E. Hughes	1910–1916	Taft
William Johnson	1804–1834	Jefferson	Willis Van Devanter	1910–1937	Taft
Henry B. Livingston	1806–1823	Jefferson	**Edward D. White**	1910–1921	Taft
Thomas Todd	1807–1826	Jefferson	Joseph R. Lamar	1911–1916	Taft
Gabriel Duval	1811–1836	Madison	Mahlon Pitney	1912–1922	Taft
Joseph Story	1811–1845	Madison	James C. McReynolds	1914–1941	Wilson
Smith Thompson	1823–1843	Monroe	Louis D. Brandeis	1916–1939	Wilson
Robert Trimble	1826–1828	J. Q. Adams	John H. Clarke	1916–1922	Wilson
John McLean	1829–1861	Jackson	**William H. Taft**	1921–1930	Harding
Henry Baldwin	1830–1844	Jackson	George Sutherland	1922–1938	Harding
James M. Wayne	1835–1867	Jackson	Pierce Butler	1923–1939	Harding
Roger B. Taney	1836–1864	Jackson	Edward T. Sanford	1923–1930	Harding
Philip P. Barbour	1836–1841	Jackson	Harlan F. Stone	1925–1941	Coolidge
John Catron	1837–1865	Van Buren	**Charles E. Hughes**	1930–1941	Hoover
John McKinley	1837–1852	Van Buren	Owen J. Roberts	1930–1945	Hoover
Peter V. Daniel	1841–1860	Van Buren	Benjamin N. Cardozo	1932–1938	Hoover
Samuel Nelson	1845–1872	Tyler	Hugo L. Black	1937–1971	F. Roosevelt
Levi Woodbury	1845–1851	Polk	Stanley F. Reed	1938–1957	F. Roosevelt
Robert C. Grier	1846–1870	Polk	Felix Frankfurter	1939–1962	F. Roosevelt
Benjamin R. Curtis	1851–1857	Fillmore	William O. Douglas	1939–1975	F. Roosevelt
John A. Campbell	1853–1861	Pierce	Frank Murphy	1940–1949	F. Roosevelt
Nathan Clifford	1858–1881	Buchanan	**Harlan F. Stone**	1941–1946	F. Roosevelt
Noah H. Swayne	1862–1881	Lincoln	James F. Byrnes	1941–1942	F. Roosevelt
Samuel F. Miller	1862–1890	Lincoln	Robert H. Jackson	1941–1954	F. Roosevelt
David Davis	1862–1877	Lincoln	Wiley B. Rutledge	1943–1949	F. Roosevelt
Stephen J. Field	1863–1897	Lincoln	Harold H. Burton	1945–1958	Truman
Salmon P. Chase	1864–1873	Lincoln	**Frederick M. Vinson**	1946–1953	Truman
William Strong	1870–1880	Grant	Tom C. Clark	1949–1967	Truman
Joseph P. Bradley	1870–1892	Grant	Sherman Minton	1949–1956	Truman
Ward Hunt	1873–1882	Grant	**Earl Warren**	1953–1969	Eisenhower
Morrison R. Waite	1874–1888	Grant	John Marshall Harlan	1955–1971	Eisenhower
John M. Harlan	1877–1911	Hayes	William J. Brennan Jr.	1956–1990	Eisenhower
William B. Woods	1880–1887	Hayes	Charles E. Whittaker	1957–1962	Eisenhower
Stanley Matthews	1881–1889	Garfield	Potter Stewart	1958–1981	Eisenhower
Horace Gray	1882–1902	Arthur	Byron R. White	1962–1993	Kennedy
Samuel Blatchford	1882–1893	Arthur	Arthur J. Goldberg	1962–1965	Kennedy
			Abe Fortas	1965–1969	L. Johnson
			Thurgood Marshall	1967–1991	L. Johnson
			Warren E. Burger	1969–1986	Nixon

*Chief Justices appear in bold type.
†Acting Chief Justice; Senate refused to confirm appointment.

Name	Service	Appointed by	Name	Service	Appointed by
Harry A. Blackmun	1970–1994	Nixon	David H. Souter	1990–	G. H. W. Bush
Lewis F. Powell Jr.	1972–1988	Nixon			
William H. Rehnquist	1972–1986	Nixon	Clarence Thomas	1991–	G. H. W. Bush
John Paul Stevens	1975–	Ford			
Sandra Day O'Connor	1981–2006	Reagan	Ruth Bader Ginsburg	1993–	Clinton
William H. Rehnquist	1986–2005	Reagan	Stephen Breyer	1994–	Clinton
			John G. Roberts Jr.	2005–	G. W. Bush
Antonin Scalia	1986–	Reagan	Samuel Anthony Alito Jr.	2006–	G. W. Bush
Anthony M. Kennedy	1988–	Reagan			

FEDERAL SPENDING AND THE ECONOMY, 1790–2002

Year	Gross National Product (in billions)	Foreign Trade (in millions) Exports	Foreign Trade (in millions) Imports	Federal Budget (in billions)	Federal Surplus/Deficit (in billions)	Federal Debt (in billions)
1790	NA	20	23	0.004	0.00015	0.076
1800	NA	71	91	0.011	0.0006	0.083
1810	NA	67	85	0.008	0.0012	0.053
1820	NA	70	74	0.018	−0.0004	0.091
1830	NA	74	71	0.015	0.100	0.049
1840	NA	132	107	0.024	−0.005	0.004
1850	NA	152	178	0.040	0.004	0.064
1860	NA	400	362	0.063	−0.01	0.065
1870	7.4	451	462	0.310	0.10	2.4
1880	11.2	853	761	0.268	0.07	2.1
1890	13.1	910	823	0.318	0.09	1.2
1900	18.7	1,499	930	0.521	0.05	1.2
1910	35.3	1,919	1,646	0.694	−0.02	1.1
1920	91.5	8,664	5,784	6.357	0.3	24.3
1930	90.4	4,013	3,500	3.320	0.7	16.3
1940	99.7	4,030	7,433	9.6	−2.7	43.0
1950	284.8	10,816	9,125	43.1	−2.2	257.4
1960	503.7	19,600	15,046	92.2	0.3	286.3
1970	977.1	42,700	40,189	195.6	−2.8	371.0
1980	2,631.7	220,600	244,871	590.9	−73.8	907.7
1990	5,832.2	393,600	495,300	1,253.2	−221.2	3,266.1
2000	9,848.0	1,070,054	1,445,438	1,788.8	236.4	5,701.9
2002	10,436.7	974,107	1,392,145	2,011.0	−157.8	6,255.4

SOURCE: *Historical Statistics of the U.S., Colonial Times to 1970* (1975), *Statistical Abstract of the U.S., 1996* (1996), *Statistical Abstract of the U.S., 1999* (1999), and *Statistical Abstract of the U.S., 2003* (2003).

POPULATION GROWTH, 1630–2000

Year	Population	Percent Increase	Year	Population	Percent Increase
1630	4,600	—	1820	9,638,453	33.1
1640	26,600	473.3	1830	12,866,020	33.5
1650	50,400	89.1	1840	17,069,453	32.7
1660	75,100	49.0	1850	23,191,876	35.9
1670	111,900	49.1	1860	31,443,321	35.6
1680	151,500	35.4	1870	39,818,449	26.6
1690	210,400	38.9	1880	50,155,783	26.0
1700	250,900	19.3	1890	62,947,714	25.5
1710	331,700	32.2	1900	75,994,575	20.7
1720	466,200	40.5	1910	91,972,266	21.0
1730	629,400	35.0	1920	105,710,620	14.9
1740	905,600	43.9	1930	122,775,046	16.1
1750	1,170,800	30.0	1940	131,669,275	7.2
1760	1,593,600	36.1	1950	150,697,361	14.5
1770	2,148,100	34.8	1960	179,323,175	19.0
1780	2,780,400	29.4	1970	203,302,031	13.4
1790	3,929,214	41.3	1980	226,542,199	11.4
1800	5,308,483	35.1	1990	248,718,302	9.8
1810	7,239,881	36.4	2000	281,422,509	13.1

SOURCE: *Historical Statistics of the U.S.* (1960), *Historical Statistics of the U.S., Colonial Times to 1970* (1975), *Statistical Abstract of the U.S., 1996* (1996), and *Statistical Abstract of the U.S., 2003* (2003).

Birthrate, 1820–2000

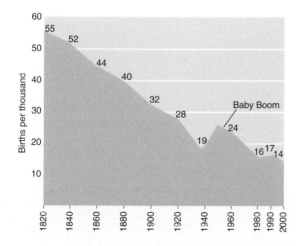

SOURCE: Data from *Historical Statistics of the U.S., Colonial Times to 1970* (1975) and *Statistical Abstract of the U.S., 2003* (2003).

Life Expectancy, 1900–2000

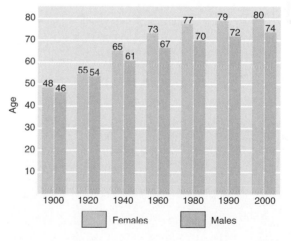

SOURCE: Data from *Historical Statistics of the U.S., Colonial Times to 1970* (1975) and *Statistical Abstract of the U.S., 2003* (2003).

Major Trends in Immigration, 1820–2000

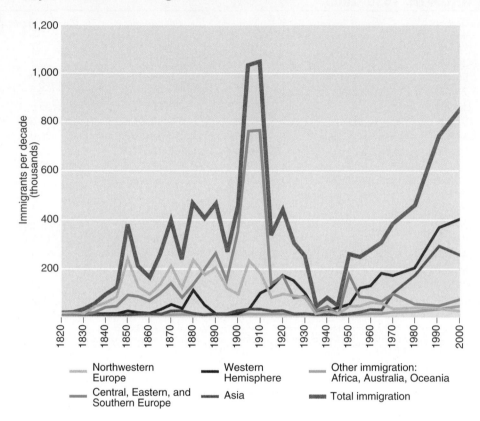

SOURCE: Data from *Historical Statistics of the U.S., Colonial Times to 1970* (1975), *Statistical Abstract of the U.S., 1999* (1999), and *Statistical Abstract of the U.S., 2003* (2003).

Research Resources in U.S. History

For help refining your research skills, finding what you need on the Web, and using it effectively, see "Online Research and Reference Aids" at bedfordstmartins.com/roarkcompact.

WHILE DOING RESEARCH IN HISTORY, you will use the library to track down primary and secondary sources and to answer questions that arise as you learn more about your topic. This appendix suggests helpful indexes, references, periodicals, and sources of primary documents. It also offers an overview of electronic resources available through the Internet. The materials listed here are not carried at all libraries, but they will give you an idea of the range of sources available. Remember, too, that librarians are an extremely helpful resource. They can direct you to useful materials throughout your research process.

Bibliographies and Indexes

American Historical Association Guide to Historical Literature. 3rd ed. New York: Oxford University Press, 1995. Offers 27,000 citations to important historical literature, arranged in forty-eight sections covering theory, international history, and regional history. An indispensable guide recently updated to include current trends in historical research.

American History and Life. Santa Barbara: ABC-Clio, 1964–. Covers publications of all sorts on U.S. and Canadian history and culture in a chronological/regional format, with abstracts and alphabetical indexes. Available in computerized format. The most complete ongoing bibliography for American history.

Freidel, Frank Burt. *Harvard Guide to American History.* Cambridge: Harvard University Press, Belknap Press, 1974. Provides citations to books and articles on American history published before 1970. The first volume is arranged topically, the second chronologically. Though it does not cover current scholarship, it is a classic and remains useful for tracing older publications.

Prucha, Francis Paul. *Handbook for Research in American History: A Guide to Bibliographies and Other Reference Works.* 2nd rev. ed. Lincoln: University of Nebraska Press, 1994. Introduces a variety of research tools, including electronic ones. A good source to consult when planning an in-depth research project.

General Overviews

Dictionary of American Biography. New York: Scribner's, 1928–1937, with supplements. Gives substantial biographies of prominent Americans in history.

Dictionary of American History. New York: Scribner's, 1976. An encyclopedia of terms, places, and concepts in U.S. history; other more specialized sets include the *Encyclopedia of North American Colonies* and the *Encyclopedia of the Confederacy.*

Encyclopedia of American Social History. New York: Scribner's, 1993. Surveys topics such as religion, class, gender, race, popular culture, regionalism, and everyday life from pre-Columbian to modern times.

Encyclopedia of the United States in the Twentieth Century. New York: Scribner's, 1996. An overview of American cultural, social, and intellectual history in articles arranged topically with useful bibliographies for further research.

Specialized Information

Black Women in America: An Historical Encyclopedia. Brooklyn: Carlson, 1993. A scholarly compilation of biographical and topical articles that constitute a definitive history of African American women.

Carruth, Gordon. *The Encyclopedia of American Facts and Dates.* 10th ed. New York: HarperCollins, 1997. Covers American history chronologically from 1986 to the present, offering information on treaties, battles, explorations, popular culture, philosophy, literature, and so on, mixing significant events with telling trivia. Tables allow for reviewing a year from a variety of angles. A thorough index helps pinpoint specific facts in time.

Cook, Chris. *Dictionary of Historical Terms.* 2nd ed. New York: Peter Bendrick, 1990. Covers a wide variety of terms—events, places, institutions, and topics—in history for all periods and places in a remarkably small package. A good place for quick identification of terms in the field.

Dictionary of Afro-American Slavery. New York: Greenwood, 1985. Surveys important people, events, and topics, with useful bibliographies; similar works include *Dictionary of the Vietnam War, Historical Dictionary of the New Deal,* and *Historical Dictionary of the Progressive Era.*

Knappman-Frost, Elizabeth. *The ABC-Clio Companion to Women's Progress in America.* Santa Barbara: ABC-Clio, 1994. Covers American women who were notable for their time as well as topics and organizations that have been significant in women's quest for equality. Each article is brief; there are a chronology and a bibliography at the back of the book.

United States Bureau of the Census. *Historical Statistics of the United States, Colonial Times to 1970.* Washington, D.C.: Government Printing Office, 1975. Offers vital statistics, economic figures, and social data for the United States. An index at the back helps locate tables by subject. For statistics since 1970, consult the annual *Statistical Abstract of the United States.*

Primary Resources

There are many routes to finding contemporary material for historical research. You may search your library catalog using the name of a prominent historical figure as an author; you may also find anthologies covering particular themes or periods in history. Consider also the following special materials for your research.

THE PRESS

American Periodical Series, 1741–1900. Ann Arbor: University Microfilms, 1946–1979. Microfilm collection of periodicals from the colonial period to 1900. An index identifies periodicals that focused on particular topics.

Herstory Microfilm Collection. Berkeley: Women's History Research Center, 1973. A microfilm collection of alternative feminist periodicals published between 1960 and 1980. Offers an interesting documentary history of the women's movement.

New York Times. New York: New York Times, 1851–. Many libraries have this newspaper on microfilm going back to its beginning in 1851. An index is available to locate specific dates and pages of news stories; it also provides detailed chronologies of events as they were reported in the news.

Readers' Guide to Periodical Literature. New York: Wilson, 1900–. This index to popular magazines started in 1900; an earlier index, *Poole's Index to Periodical Literature,* covers 1802–1906, though it does not provide such thorough indexing.

DIARIES, PAMPHLETS, BOOKS

The American Culture Series. Ann Arbor: University Microfilms, 1941–1974. A microfilm set, with a useful index, featuring books and pamphlets published between 1493 and 1875.

American Women's Diaries. New Canaan: Readex, 1984–. A collection of reproductions of women's diaries. There are different series for different regions of the country.

The March of America Facsimile Series. Ann Arbor: University Microfilms, 1966. A collection of more than ninety facsimiles of travel accounts to the New World published in English or English translation from the fifteenth through the nineteenth century.

Women in America from Colonial Times to the Twentieth Century. New York: Arno, 1974. A collection of reprints of dozens of books written by women describing women's lives and experiences in their own words.

GOVERNMENT DOCUMENTS

Congressional Record. Washington, D.C.: Government Printing Office, 1874–. Covers daily debates and proceedings of Congress. Earlier series were called *Debates and Proceedings in the Congress of the United States* and *The Congressional Globe.*

Foreign Relations of the United States. Washington, D.C.: Department of State, 1861–. A collection of documents from 1861, including diplomatic papers, correspondence, and memoranda, that provides a documentary record of U.S. foreign policy.

Public Papers of the Presidents. Washington, D.C.: Office of the Federal Register, 1957–. Includes major documents issued by the executive branch from the Hoover administration to the present.

Serial Set. Washington, D.C.: Government Printing Office, 1789–1969. A huge collection of congressional documents, available in many libraries on microfiche, with a useful index.

LOCAL HISTORY COLLECTIONS

State and county historical societies often house a wealth of historical documents; consider their resources when planning your research — you may find yourself working with material that no one else has analyzed before.

Internet Resources

The Internet has been a useful place for scholars to communicate and publish information in recent years. Electronic discussion lists, electronic journals, and primary texts are among the resources available to historians. The following sources are good places to find historical information. You can also search the Web using any of a number of search engines. However, bear in mind that there is no board of editors screening Internet sites for accuracy or usefulness. Be critical of all of your sources, particularly those found on the Internet. Note that when

INTERNET RESOURCES

this book went to press, the sites listed below were active and maintained.

The American Civil War Homepage. <http://sunsite.utk.edu/civil-war/warweb.html> A comprehensive resource bank on the American Civil War. Maintained by George Hoemann of the University of Tennessee, the site contains letters, documents, photographs, information about battles, links to other sites, and regiment rosters.

American Memory: Historical Collections for the National Digital Library Program. <http://memory.loc.gov/ammem.html> A Web site that features digitized primary source materials from the Library of Congress, among them African American pamphlets, Civil War photographs, documents from the Constitutional Convention of 1774–1790, materials on woman suffrage, and oral histories.

Douglass Archives of American Public Address. <http://douglassarchives.org> An electronic archive of American speeches and documents by a variety of people from Jane Addams to Jonathan Edwards to Theodore Roosevelt.

Historical Text Archive. <http://historicaltextarchive.com/> One of the oldest and largest Internet archives of historical documents, articles, photographs, and more. Includes sections on Native American, African American, and U.S. history, in which can be found texts of the Declaration of Independence, the Constitution of Iroquois Nations, World War II surrender documents, and a great deal more.

Index of Native American Resources on the Internet. <http://www.hanksville.org/NAresources> A vast index of Native American resources organized by category. Within the history category, links are organized under subcategories: oral history, written history, geographical areas, timelines, and photographs and photographic archives. A central place to come in the search for information on Native American history.

Internet Resources for Students of Afro-American History and Culture. <http://www.libraries.rutgers.edu/rul/rr_gateway/research_guides/history/afrores.shtml> A good place to begin research on topics in African American history. The site is indexed and linked to a wide variety of sources, including primary documents, text collections, and archival sources on African American history. Individual documents such as slave narratives and petitions, and speeches by W. E. B. Du

Bois and Martin Luther King Jr. are categorized by century.

NativeWeb. <http://www.nativeweb.org> One of the best organized and most accessible sites available on Native American issues, *NativeWeb* combines an events calendar and message board with history, statistics, a list of news sources, archives, new and updated related sites each week, and documents.

Perry-Castañeda Library Map Collection. <http://www.lib.utexas.edu/maps/> The University of Texas at Austin library has put over seven hundred United States maps on the Web along with hundreds of other maps from around the world. The collection includes both historical and contemporary maps.

Smithsonian Institution. <http://www.si.edu> Organized by subject, such as military history or Hispanic/Latino American resources, this site offers selected links to sites hosted by Smithsonian museums and organizations. Content includes graphics of museum pieces and relevant textual information, book suggestions, maps, and links.

Supreme Court Collection. <http://www.law.cornell.edu/supct/> This database can be used to search for information on various Supreme Court cases. Although the site primarily covers cases that occurred after 1990, there is information on some earlier historic cases. The justices' opinions, as originally written, are also included.

United States Holocaust Memorial Museum. <http://www.ushmm.org> This site contains information about the Holocaust Museum in Washington, D.C., in particular and the Holocaust in general, and it lists links to related sites.

Women's History Resources. <http://www.mcps.k12.md.us/curriculum/socialstd/Women_Bookmarks.html> An extensive listing of women's history sources available on the Internet. The site indexes resources on subjects as diverse as woman suffrage, women in the workplace, and celebrated women writers. Some of the links are to equally vast indexes, providing an overwhelming wealth of information.

WWW-VL History Index. <http://www.ukans.edu/history/VL> A vast list of more than 1,700 links to sites of interest to historians, arranged by general topic and by continent and country. The United States history page includes links to online research tools as well as links arranged by topic and historical period.

Embedded Artifact Credits

p. 17 (mica hand) Ohio Historical Society; p. 20 (dolls) Photo courtesy of the Oakland Museum, California; p. 31 (caravel) National Maritime Museum, London; p. 39 (crucifix) Courtesy of the Historical Archaeology Collections of the Florida Museum of Natural History; p. 57 (pot) Valentine Museum, Cook Collection; p. 65 (pipe) Niemeyer Nederlands Tabacologisch Museum; p. 68 (stirrup) © George H. H. Huey; p. 86 (dice) Courtesy of Association for the Preservation of Virginia Antiquities; p. 91 (cradle) Wadsworth Atheneum, Hartford, Wallace Nutting Collection, Gift of J. Pierpont Morgan; p. 95 (scales) Concord Museum; p. 106 (pitcher) Pocumtuck Valley Memorial Association, Memorial Hall Museum, Deerfield, MA; p. 110 (*Poor Richard's Almanack*) Courtesy, American Antiquarian Society; p. 116 (slave's doll) The Stagville Center, Division of Archives and History, North Carolina Department of Cultural Resources; p. 117 (mirror) Concord Museum; p. 142 (stamp) Courtesy of the Trustees of the British Library; p. 144 (teapot) Peabody Essex Museum, Salem, MA; p. 152 (pistol) Concord Museum; p. 152 (musket) Private Collection, on view at the Concord Museum, Concord, MA; p. 154 (Wheatley title page) Library of Congress; p. 164 (drum) Massachusetts Historical Society; p. 170 (broadside) Courtesy, American Antiquarian Society; p. 173 (currency) Smithsonian Institution, Washington, D.C., photo by Douglas Mudd; p. 173 (Howitzer) West Point Museum, United States Military Academy, West Point, N.Y.; p. 193 (penny note) Library of Congress; p. 203 (inkwell) Independence National Historic Park; p. 215 (ballot box) Independence National Historic Park; p. 216 (barrel) Peabody Essex Museum, Salem, MA; p. 224 (kettle) Ohio Historical Society; p. 240 (compass) Smithsonian Institution, Washington, D.C.; p. 254 (telescope) Thomas Jefferson Memorial Foundation, Inc.; p. 266 (spittoon) Courtesy, The Henry Francis du Pont Winterthur Museum; p. 279 (bank note) Miriam and Ira D. Wallach Division of Art, Prints and Photographs, The New York Public Library, Astor, Lenox and Tilden Foundations; p. 280 (miniature log cabin) National Museum of American History, Smithsonian Institution, Behring Center; p. 292 (flag) Texas Memorial Museum; p. 299 (plow) Smithsonian Institution, Washington, D.C.; p. 303 (watch) Smithsonian Institution, Washington, D.C.; p. 303 (telegraph transmitter) Division of Political History, Smithsonian Institution, Washington, D.C.; p. 307 (sheet music) Special Collections, Milton S. Eisenhower Library, The Johns Hopkins University; p. 321 (cotton gin) Smithsonian Institution, Washington, D.C.; p. 323 (shoe) Valentine Museum, Cook Collection; p. 336 (fiddle) National Museum of American History, Smithsonian Institution, Washington, D.C.; p. 346 (poster) Courtesy, American Antiquarian Society; p. 358 (cane) Collection of McKissick Museum, University of South Carolina; p. 360 (shackles) Private Collection; p. 361 (revolver) Ohio Historical Society; p. 375 (jacket) Smithsonian Institution, Washington, D.C.; p. 387 (potholder) Chicago Historical Society; p. 402 (bible) Anacostia Museum, Smithsonian Institution, Washington, D.C.; p. 410 (ticket) Collection of Janice L. and David J. Frent; p. 416 (plow) Courtesy Deere & Company; p. 429 (watch) Union Pacific Museum Collection; p. 433 (*McClure's*) Special Collections, The Ida Tarbell Collection, Pelletier Library, Allegheny; p. 433 (telephone) Smithsonian Institution, Washington, D.C.; p. 441 (tobacco) Duke Homestead; p. 455 (silver bar) The Oakland Museum; p. 460 (bucket) Kansas State Historical Society; p. 470 (moccasins) Photo Addison Doty, Santa Fe, NM; p. 485 (sewing machine) National Museum of American History, Smithsonian Institution, Washington, D.C.; p. 487 (typewriter) National Museum of American History, Smithsonian Institution, Washington, D.C.; p. 493 (baseball and glove) Smithsonian Institution, Washington, D.C.; p. 495 (faucet) Picture Research Consultants & Archives; p. 512 (dagger) Library & Archives Division, Historical Society of Western Pennsylvania; p. 513 (paycheck) Chicago Historical Society, Archives and Manuscript Department; p. 520 (button) Collection of Janice L. and David J. Frent; p. 536 (postcard) Chicago Historical Society; p. 555 (IWW poster) Library of Congress; p. 567 (recruiting poster) Library of Congress; p. 569 (machine gun) National Museum of American History, Smithsonian Institution, Behring Center; p. 572 ("Save Wheat" poster) Herbert Hoover Presidential Library; p. 596 (refrigerator) From the Collections of The Henry Ford; p. 602 (Hughes book) Picture Research Consultants & Archives; p. 604 (button) Private Collection; p. 604 (*This Side of Paradise*) Matthew J. & Arlyn Bruccoli Collection of F. Scott Fitzgerald, University of South Carolina; p. 613 (movie poster) Collection of Hershenson-Allen Archives; p. 621 (wheelchair) FDR Library/photo by Hudson Valley Photo Studio; p. 623 (1932 buttons) Collection of Janice L. and David J. Frent; p. 653 (tank) U.S. Army Ordnance Museum Foundation, Inc.; p. 655 (Good Neighbor button) Collection of Colonel Stuart S. Corning, Jr./Picture Research Consultants, Inc.; p. 663 (Double V button) Private Collection; p. 674 (atomic bomb) National Archives; p. 682 (Truman and Churchill button) Collection of Janice L. and David J. Frent; p. 691 (Jackie Robinson) The Michael Barson Collection/Past Perfect; p. 692 (banner) Dr. Hector P. Garcia Papers, Special Collections & Archives, Texas A & M University, Corpus Christi, Bell Library; p. 696 (helmet) West Point Museum, United States Military Academy; p. 697 (button) Collection of Janice L. and David J. Frent; p. 705 (sign) NEW Traffic Safety; p. 719 (*The Feminine Mystique*) W. W. Norton & Company, Inc. N.Y.C. © 1963; p. 720 (album cover) Private Collection; p. 722 (NAACP button) Collection of Janice L. and David J. Frent; p. 734 (food stamps) Getty Images; p. 738 (pennant) Private Collection; p. 742 (Indian resistance button) Collection of Janice L. and David J. Frent; p. 745 (flag) Smithsonian Institution, Washington, D.C.; p. 750 (campaign poster) Collection of Janice L. and David J. Frent; p. 761 (beret) West Point Museum, United States Military Academy, West Point, N.Y.; p. 768 (Vietnam button) Picture Research Consultants & Archives; p. 769 (antiwar button) Collection of Janice L. and David J. Frent; p. 785 (magazines) Young Americans for Freedom; p. 791 (VW with sign) © Dennis Brack; p. 795 (bumper sticker) Courtesy, Christian Coalition; p. 799 (Yuppie handbook) Book cover from *The Yuppies Handbook: The State-of-the-Art Manual for Young Urban Professionals* by Marissa Piesman and Marilee Hartley. Copyright © 1984 Marissa Piesman and Marilee Hartley; p. 816 (piece of Berlin Wall) Patton Museum of Cavalry & Armor; p. 828 (Green Card document) Nolo; p. 829 (ballots) © Reuters NewMedia Inc./Corbis.

A Note to Students: This list of terms is provided to help you with the vocabulary of historians and economists. Many of these terms refer to broad, enduring concepts that you may encounter not only in further studies of history but also when following current events. The terms appear in bold at their first use in each chapter. In the glossary, the page numbers of those chapter-by-chapter appearances are provided so you can look up the terms' uses in various periods and contexts. For definitions and discussions of words not included here, consult a dictionary and the book's index, which will point you to topics covered at greater length in the book.

affirmative action Policies established in the 1960s and 1970s by governments, businesses, universities, and other institutions to overcome the effects of past discrimination against specific groups such as racial and ethnic minorities and women. Measures to ensure equal opportunity include setting goals for admission, hiring, and promotion, considering minority status when allocating resources, and actively encouraging victims of past discrimination to apply for jobs and other resources. (pp. 731, 787, 814)

agribusiness Farming on a large scale, using the production, processing, and distribution methods of modern business. Farming became a big business, not just a way to feed a family and make a living, in the late nineteenth century as farms got larger and more mechanized. In the 1940s and 1950s, specialized commercial farms replaced many family-run operations and grew to an enormous scale. (pp. 463, 712)

alliance system The military and diplomatic system formulated in an effort to create a balance of power in pre–World War I Europe. Nations were bound together by rigid and comprehensive treaties that promised mutual aid in the case of attack by specific other nations. The system swung into action after the Austrian archduke Franz Ferdinand was assassinated in Sarajevo on June 28, 1914, dragging most of Europe into war. (p. 566)

anarchist A person who rebels against established order and authority. An anarchist is someone who believes that government of any kind is unnecessary and undesirable and should be replaced with voluntary cooperation and free association. Anarchists became increasingly visible in the United States in the late nineteenth and early twentieth centuries. They advocated revolution and grew in numbers through appeals to discontented laborers. Anarchists frequently employed violence in an attempt to achieve their goals. In 1901, anarchist Leon Czolgosz assassinated President William McKinley. (pp. 488, 512, 540, 606)

antebellum A term that means "before a war" and commonly refers to the period prior to the Civil War. (pp. 289, 316, 386)

antinomian A person who does not obey societal or religious law. In colonial Massachusetts, Puritan authorities accused Anne Hutchinson of antinomianism because she believed that Christians could achieve salvation by faith alone; they further asserted, incorrectly, that Hutchinson also held the belief that it was not necessary to follow God's laws as set forth in the Bible. (p. 89)

archaeology A social science devoted to learning about people who lived in the past through the study of physical artifacts created by humans. Most but not all archaeological study focuses on the history of people who lived before the use of the written word. (p. 3)

Archaic America Various hunting and gathering cultures that descended from Paleo-Indians. The term also refers to the period of time when these cultures dominated ancient America, roughly from 8000 BP to between 2000 and 1000 BP. (p. 10)

artifacts Material remains studied and used by archaeologists and historians to support their interpretations of human history. Examples of artifacts include bones, pots, baskets, jewelry, furniture, tools, clothing, and buildings. (p. 3)

artisan A term commonly used prior to 1900 to describe a skilled craftsman, such as a cabinetmaker. (pp. 43, 94, 106, 164, 201, 298, 323, 485)

Bill of Rights The commonly used term for the first ten amendments to the U.S. Constitution. The Bill of Rights (the last of which was ratified in 1791) guarantees individual liberties and defines limitations to federal power. Many states made the promise of the prompt addition of a bill of rights a precondition for their ratification of the Constitution. (pp. 206, 213)

black nationalism A term linked to several African American movements emphasizing racial pride, separation from whites and white institutions, and black autonomy. Black nationalism gained in popularity with the rise of Marcus Garvey and the Universal Negro Improvement Association (1917–1927) and later with the Black Panther Party, Malcolm X, and other participants of the black power movements of the 1960s. (pp. 602, 741)

bloody shirt A refrain used by Republicans in the late nineteenth century to remind the voting public that the Democratic Party, dominated by the South, was largely responsible for the Civil War and that the Republican

Party had led the victory to preserve the Union. Republicans urged their constituents to "Vote the way you shot." (pp. 417, 440)

***bracero* program** A policy begun during World War II to help with wartime agriculture, in which Mexican laborers (*braceros*) were permitted to enter the United States and work for a limited period of time but not to gain citizenship or permanent residence. The program officially ended in 1964. (p. 716)

brinksmanship A cold war practice of appearing willing and able to resort to nuclear war in order to make an enemy back down. Secretary of State John Foster Dulles was the foremost proponent of this policy. (p. 708)

Calvinism The religious doctrine of which the primary tenet is that salvation is predestined by God. Founded by John Calvin of Geneva during the Protestant Reformation, Calvinism required its adherents to live according to a strict religious and moral code. The Puritans who settled in colonial New England were devout Calvinists. (p. 85) *See also* predestination.

checks and balances A system in which the executive, legislative, and judicial branches of the government curb each other's power. Checks and balances were written into the U.S. Constitution during the Constitutional Convention of 1787. (pp. 207, 788)

civil service The administrative service of a government. This term often applies to reforms following passage of the Pendleton Act in 1883, which set qualifications for U.S. government jobs and sought to remove such jobs from political influence. (pp. 418, 443) *See also* spoils system.

closed shop An establishment in which every employee is required to join a union. (p. 594)

cold war The hostile and tense relationship that existed between the Soviet Union on the one hand and the United States and other Western nations on the other from 1947 to 1989. This war was said to be "cold" because the hostility stopped short of armed (hot) conflict, which was warded off by the strategy of nuclear deterrence. (pp. 680, 703, 757, 804, 811) *See also* deterrence.

collective bargaining Negotiation by a group of workers (usually through a union) and their employer concerning rates of pay and working conditions. (pp. 572, 629, 692)

collective security An association of independent nations that agree to accept and implement decisions made by the group, including going to war in defense of one or more members. The United States resolutely avoided such alliances until after World War II, when it created the North Atlantic Treaty Organization (NATO) in response to the threat posed by the Soviet Union. (pp. 578, 594, 687) *See also* North Atlantic Treaty Organization.

colonization The process by which a country or society gains control over another, primarily through settlement. (pp. 31, 55, 80, 272, 381, 522, 565, 748)

Columbian exchange The transatlantic exchange of goods, peoples, and ideas that began when Columbus arrived in the Caribbean, ending the age-old separation of the hemispheres. (p. 34)

communism (Communist Party) A system of government and political organization, based on Marxist-Leninist ideals, in which a single authoritarian party controls the economy through state ownership of production in order to reach the final stage of Marxist theory, in which the state dissolves and economic goods are distributed evenly for the common good. Communists around the globe encouraged the spread of communism in other nations in hopes of fomenting worldwide revolution. At its peak in the 1930s, the Communist Party of the United States worked closely with labor unions and insisted that only the overthrow of the capitalist system by its workers could save the victims of the Great Depression. After World War II, the Communist power and aspirations of the Soviet Union were held to be a direct threat to American democracy, prompting the cold war. (pp. 581, 613, 620, 653, 679, 703, 733, 757, 783, 811) *See also* cold war.

conscription Compulsory military service. Americans were first subject to conscription during the Civil War. The Draft Act of 1940 marked the first peacetime use of conscription. (pp. 383, 481, 569) *See also* draft.

conservatism A political and moral outlook dating back to Alexander Hamilton's belief in a strong central government resting on a solid banking foundation. Currently associated with the Republican Party, conservatism today places a high premium on military preparedness, free-market economics, low taxes, and strong sexual morality. (pp. 382, 406, 436, 508, 541, 622, 665, 697, 704, 730, 773, 783, 812)

consumer culture (consumerism) A society that places high value on and devotes substantial resources to the purchase and display of material goods. Elements of American consumerism were evident in the nineteenth century but really took hold in the twentieth century with installment buying and advertising in the 1920s and again with the postwar prosperity of the 1950s. (pp. 488, 601, 704)

containment The U.S. foreign policy developed after World War II to hold in check the power and influence of the Soviet Union and other groups or nations espousing communism. The strategy was first fully articulated by diplomat George F. Kennan in 1946–1947. (pp. 680, 703, 758, 822)

covenant An agreement or pact; in American history, a religious agreement. The Pilgrims used this term in the Mayflower Compact to refer to the agreement among themselves to establish a law-abiding community in which all members would work together for the common good. Later, New England Puritans used this term to refer to the agreement they made with God and each other to live according to God's will as revealed through Scripture. (pp. 77, 106) *See also* Halfway Covenant.

cult of domesticity　The nineteenth-century belief that the place of women was in the home, where they should create a haven for harried men of the household working in the outside world. This ideal was made possible by the separation of the workplace and the home and was used to sentimentalize the home and women's role in it. (pp. 493, 516) *See also* separate spheres.

de-industrialization　A long period of decline in the industrial sector. This term often refers specifically to the decline of manufacturing and the growth of the service sector of the economy in post–World War II America. This shift and the loss of manufacturing resulting from it were caused by more efficient and automated production techniques at home, increased competition from foreign-made goods, and the use of cheap labor abroad by U.S. manufacturers. (p. 799)

democracy　A system of government in which the people have the power to rule, either directly or indirectly through their elected representatives. Believing direct democracy dangerous, the framers of the Constitution created a government that gave direct voice to the people only in the House of Representatives and placed a check on the voice of the people in the Senate by offering unlimited six-year terms to senators, elected by the state legislatures to protect them from the whims of democratic majorities. The framers further curbed the perceived dangers of democracy by giving each branch of government (legislative, executive, and judicial) the ability to check the power of the other two. (pp. 164, 189, 212, 248, 265, 337, 346, 373, 413, 434, 464, 490, 505, 539, 564, 622, 653, 681, 760, 791, 817) *See also* checks and balances.

détente　French for "loosening." The term refers to the easing of tensions between the United States and the Soviet Union during the Nixon administration. (pp. 773, 787)

deterrence　The linchpin of U.S. military strategy during the cold war. The strategy of deterrence dictated that the United States would maintain a nuclear arsenal so substantial that the Soviet Union would refrain from attacking the United States and its allies out of fear that the United States would retaliate in devastating proportions. The Soviets pursued a similar strategy. (pp. 687, 725)

domino theory　The assumption underlying U.S. foreign policy from the early cold war until the end of the Vietnam conflict that if one country fell to communism, neighboring countries would also fall under Communist control. (pp. 686, 708)

doves　Peace advocates, particularly during the Vietnam War. (p. 770)

draft (draftee)　A system for selecting individuals for compulsory military service. A draftee is an individual selected through this process. (pp. 167, 382, 569, 659, 687, 768, 793) *See also* conscription.

emancipation　The act of freeing from slavery or bondage. The emancipation of American slaves, a goal shared by slaves and abolitionists alike, occurred with the passage of the Thirteenth Amendment in 1865. (pp. 192, 250, 272, 309, 333, 369, 399, 581)

English Reformation　*See* Reformation.

Enlightenment　An eighteenth-century philosophical movement that emphasized the use of reason to reevaluate previously accepted doctrines and traditions. (p. 119)

evangelicalism　The trend in Protestant Christianity stressing salvation through conversion, repentance of sin, adherence to Scripture, and the importance of preaching over ritual. During the Second Great Awakening, in the 1830s, evangelicals worshipped at camp meetings and religious revivals led by exuberant preachers. (pp. 260, 307, 331, 443, 795) *See also* Second Great Awakening.

fascism　An authoritarian system of government characterized by dictatorial rule, disdain for international stability, and a conviction that warfare is the only means by which a nation can attain greatness. Nazi Germany and Mussolini's Italy are the prime examples of fascism. (pp. 622, 650)

federal budget deficit　The situation resulting when the U.S. government spends more money than it takes in. (p. 814)

feminism　The belief that men and women have an inherent right to equal social, political, and economic opportunities. The suffrage movement and second-wave feminism of the 1960s and 1970s were the most visible and successful manifestations of feminism, but feminist ideas were expressed in a variety of statements and movements as early as the late eighteenth century and continue to be expressed in the twenty-first. (pp. 218, 411, 555, 600, 719, 730, 783, 814)

flexible response　Military strategy employed by the Kennedy and Johnson administrations to match a wide range of military threats by complementing nuclear weapons with the buildup of conventional and special forces and employing them all in a gradual and calibrated way as needed. Flexible response was a departure from the strategy of massive retaliation used by the Eisenhower administration. (p. 758)

franchise　The right to vote. The franchise was gradually widened in the United States to include groups such as women and African Americans, who had no vote when the Constitution was ratified. (pp. 310, 412, 515) *See also* suffrage.

free labor　Work conducted free from constraint and in accordance with the laborer's personal inclinations and will. Prior to the Civil War, free labor became an ideal championed by Republicans (who were primarily Northerners) to articulate individuals' right to work how and where they wished, and to accumulate property in their own name. The ideal of free labor lay at the heart of the North's argument that slavery should not be extended into the western territories. (pp. 272, 305, 319, 345, 401)

free silver　The late-nineteenth-century call by silver barons and poor American farmers for the widespread coinage of silver and for silver to be used as a base upon which to expand the paper money supply. The coinage of silver created a more inflationary monetary system that benefited debtors. (pp. 446, 508) *See also* gold standard.

free soil   The idea advanced in the 1840s that Congress should prohibit slavery within western territories. "Free soil, free speech, free labor, and free men" became the rallying cry of the short-lived Free-Soil Party. (pp. 345, 381)

frontier   A borderland area. In U.S. history, the borderland between the areas primarily inhabited by Europeans or their descendants and the areas solely inhabited by Native Americans. (pp. 31, 63, 90, 132, 166, 243, 259, 286, 344, 507)

fundamentalism   Strict adherence to core, often religious beliefs. The term has varying meanings for different religious groups. Protestant fundamentalists adhere to a literal interpretation of the Bible and thus deny the possibility of evolution. Muslim fundamentalists believe that traditional Islamic law should govern nations and that Western influences should be banned. (pp. 607, 793, 812)

gender gap   An electoral phenomenon that became apparent in the 1980s when men and women began to display different preferences in voting. Women tended to favor liberal candidates, and men tended to support conservatives. The key voter groups contributing to the gender gap were single women and women who worked outside the home. (pp. 801, 820)

globalization   The spread of political, cultural, and economic influences and connections among countries, businesses, and individuals around the world through trade, immigration, communication, and other means. In the late twentieth century, globalization was intensified by new communications technology that connected individuals, corporations, and nations with greater speed at low prices. This led to an increase in political and economic interdependence and mutual influence among nations. (pp. 773, 812)

gold standard   A monetary system in which any circulating currency was exchangeable for a specific amount of gold. Advocates for the gold standard believed that gold alone should be used for coinage and that the total value of paper banknotes should never exceed the government's supply of gold. The triumph of gold standard supporter William McKinley in the 1896 presidential election was a big victory for supporters of this policy. (pp. 448, 506) *See also* free silver.

gospel of wealth   The idea that wealth garnered from earthly success should be used for good works. Andrew Carnegie promoted this view in an 1889 essay in which he maintained that the wealthy should serve as stewards and act in the best interests of society as a whole. (pp. 439, 535)

government bonds   Promissory notes issued by a government in order to borrow money from members of the public. Such bonds are redeemable at a set future date. Bondholders earn interest on their investment. (p. 173)

Great Awakening   The widespread movement of religious revitalization in the 1730s and 1740s that emphasized vital religious faith and personal choice. It was characterized by large, open-air meetings at which emotional sermons were given by itinerant preachers. (p. 119)

Great Society   President Lyndon Johnson's domestic program, which included civil rights legislation, antipoverty programs, government subsidy of medical care, federal aid to education, consumer protection, and aid to the arts and humanities. (pp. 729, 784)

guerrilla warfare   Fighting carried out by an irregular military force usually organized into small, highly mobile groups. Guerrilla combat was common in the Vietnam War and during the American Revolution. Guerrilla warfare is often effective against opponents who have greater material resources. (pp. 160, 357, 372, 470, 525, 708, 758, 833)

Halfway Covenant   A Puritan compromise that allowed the unconverted children of the "visible saints" to become "halfway" members of the church and to baptize their own children even though they were not full members of the church themselves because they had not experienced full conversion. Massachusetts ministers accepted this compromise in 1662, though the compromise remained controversial throughout the seventeenth century. (p. 91)

hard currency (hard money)   Money coined directly from, or backed in full by, precious metals (particularly gold). (pp. 173, 196, 217, 264)

hawks   Advocates of aggressive military action or all-out war, particularly during the Vietnam War. (p. 770) *See also* War Hawks.

holding company   A system of business organization whereby competing companies are combined under one central administration in order to curb competition and ensure profit. Pioneered in the late 1880s by John D. Rockefeller, holding companies such as Standard Oil exercised monopoly control even as the government threatened to outlaw trusts as a violation of free trade. (p. 433) *See also* monopoly; trust.

impeachment   The process by which formal charges of wrongdoing are brought against a president, a governor, or a federal judge. (pp. 410, 634, 789, 818)

imperialism   The system by which great powers gain control of overseas territories. The United States became an imperialist power by gaining control of Puerto Rico, Guam, the Philippines, and Cuba as a result of the Spanish-American War. (pp. 353, 419, 506, 566, 656, 688, 748, 824)

indentured servitude   A system that committed poor immigrants to four to seven years of labor in exchange for passage to the colonies and food and shelter after they arrived. An indenture is a type of contract. (pp. 54, 105)

iron curtain   A metaphor coined by Winston Churchill during his commencement address at Westminster College in Fulton, Missouri, in 1946, to refer to the political, ideological, and military barriers that separated Soviet-controlled Eastern Europe from the rest of Europe and the West following World War II. (pp. 682, 708, 760, 816)

isolationism A foreign policy perspective characterized by a desire to have the United States withdraw from the conflicts of the world and enjoy the protection of two vast oceans. (pp. 522, 578, 594, 651, 679)

Jim Crow The system of racial segregation that developed in the post–Civil War South and extended well into the twentieth century; it replaced slavery as the chief instrument of white supremacy. Jim Crow laws segregated African Americans in public facilities such as trains and streetcars and denied them basic civil rights, including the right to vote. It was also at this time that the doctrine of "separate but equal" became institutionalized. (pp. 415, 483, 557, 664)

Keynesian economics A theory, developed by economist John Maynard Keynes, that guided U.S. economic policy from the New Deal to the 1970s. According to Keynesians, the federal government has a duty to stimulate and manage the economy by spending money on public works projects and by making general tax cuts in order to put more money into the hands of ordinary people, thus creating demand. (p. 643)

laissez-faire The doctrine, based on economic theory, that government should not interfere in business or the economy. Laissez-faire ideas guided American government policy in the late nineteenth century and conservative politics in the twentieth. Business interests that supported laissez-faire in the late nineteenth century accepted government interference when it took the form of tariffs or subsidies that worked to their benefit. Broader uses of the term refer to the simple philosophy of abstaining from interference. (pp. 439, 506, 534, 609, 622, 824)

land grant A gift of land from a government, usually intended to encourage settlement or development. The British government issued several land grants to encourage development in the American colonies. In the mid-nineteenth century the U.S. government issued land grants to encourage railroad development and through passage of the Land-Grant College Act (also known as the Morrill Act) in 1863 set aside public lands to support universities. (pp. 55, 92, 167, 303, 353, 430, 460)

liberalism The political doctrine that government rests on the consent of the governed and is duty-bound to protect the freedom and property of the individual. In the twentieth century, liberalism became associated with the idea that the government should regulate the economy and ensure the material well-being and individual rights of all people. (pp. 509, 534, 587, 623, 692, 705, 731, 783, 814)

liberty The condition of being free or enjoying freedom from control. This term also refers to the possession of certain social, political, or economic rights such as the right to own and control property. Eighteenth-century American colonists evoked the principle to argue for strict limitations on government's ability to tax its subjects. (pp. 78, 132, 159, 189, 215, 238, 260, 319, 356, 373, 566, 831)

manifest destiny A term coined by journalist John O'Sullivan in 1845 to express the popular nineteenth-century belief that the United States was destined to expand westward to the Pacific Ocean and had an irrefutable right and God-given responsibility to do so. This idea provided an ideological rationale for westward expansion and masked the economic and political motivations of many of those who championed it. (pp. 287, 350, 522)

McCarthyism The practice of searching out suspected Communists and others outside mainstream American society, discrediting them, and hounding them from government and other employment. The term derives from Senator Joseph McCarthy, who gained notoriety for leading such repressive activities from 1950 to 1954. (p. 694)

mercantilism A set of policies that regulated colonial commerce and manufacturing for the enrichment of the mother country. Mercantilist policies ensured that the American colonies in the mid-seventeenth century produced agricultural goods and raw materials to be shipped to Britain, where they would increase wealth in the mother country through reexportation or manufacture into finished goods that would then be sold to the colonies and elsewhere. (p. 66)

Middle Passage The crossing of the Atlantic (as a slave destined for auction) in the hold of a slave ship in the eighteenth and nineteenth centuries. Conditions were unimaginably bad, and many slaves died during these voyages. (pp. 72, 112)

military-industrial complex A term first used by President Dwight D. Eisenhower to refer to the aggregate power and influence of the armed forces in conjunction with the aerospace, munitions, and other industries that produced supplies for the military in the post–World War II era. (p. 710)

miscegenation The sexual mixing of races. In slave states, despite social stigma and legal restrictions on interracial sex, masters' almost unlimited power over their female slaves meant that liaisons inevitably occurred. Many states maintained laws against miscegenation into the 1950s. (pp. 324, 441, 602)

monopoly Exclusive control and domination by a single business entity over an entire industry through ownership, command of supply, or other means. Gilded Age businesses monopolized their industries quite profitably, often organizing holding companies and trusts to do so. (pp. 29, 260, 422, 433, 463, 505, 630, 673, 687, 798) *See also* holding company; trust.

Monroe Doctrine President James Monroe's 1823 declaration that the Western Hemisphere was closed to any further colonization or interference by European powers. In exchange, Monroe pledged that the United States would not become involved in European struggles. Although Monroe could not back his policy with action, it was an important formulation of national goals. (pp. 251, 522, 546, 565)

nationalism A strong feeling of devotion and loyalty toward one nation over others. Nationalism encourages the promotion of the nation's common culture, language, and customs. (pp. 248, 385, 564, 708, 760, 812)

nativism Bias against immigrants and in favor of native-born inhabitants. American nativists especially favor persons who come from white, Anglo-Saxon, Protestant lines over those from other racial, ethnic, and religious heritages. Nativists may include former immigrants who view new immigrants as incapable of assimilation. Many nativists, such as members of the Know-Nothing Party in the nineteenth century and the Ku Klux Klan through the contemporary period, voice anti-immigrant, anti-Catholic, and anti-Semitic sentiments. (pp. 355, 466, 536, 606)

New Deal The group of social and economic programs that President Franklin Roosevelt developed to provide relief for the needy, speed economic recovery, and reform economic and governmental institutions. The New Deal was a massive effort to bring the United States out of the Great Depression and ensure its future prosperity. (pp. 508, 621, 651, 679, 704, 731, 806, 820)

New Right Politically active religious conservatives who became particularly vocal in the 1980s. The New Right criticized feminism, opposed abortion and homosexuality, and promoted "family values" and military preparedness. (p. 784)

New South A vision of the South promoted after the Civil War by Henry Grady, editor of the *Atlanta Constitution*, who urged the South to abandon its dependence on agriculture and use its cheap labor and natural resources to compete with northern industry. Many southerners migrated from farms to cities in the late nineteenth century, and northerners and foreigners invested a significant amount of capital in railroads, cotton and textiles, mining, lumber, iron, steel, and tobacco in the region. (pp. 400, 440)

North Atlantic Treaty Organization (NATO) A post–World War II alliance that joined the United States, Canada, and Western European nations into a military coalition designed to counter efforts to expand by the Soviet Union. Each NATO member pledged to go to war if any member was attacked. Since the end of the cold war, NATO has been expanding to include the formerly Communist countries of Eastern Europe. (pp. 680, 804, 816)

nullification The idea that states can disregard federal laws when those laws represent an overstepping of congressional powers. The controversial idea was first proposed by opponents of the Alien and Sedition Acts of 1798 and later by South Carolina politicians in 1828 as a response to the Tariff of Abominations. (pp. 229, 239, 278, 347)

oligopoly A competitive system in which several large corporations dominate an industry by dividing the market so each business has a share of it. More prevalent than outright monopolies during the late 1800s, the oligopolies of the Gilded Age successfully muted competition and benefited the corporations that participated in this type of arrangement. (pp. 437, 458)

paternalism The idea that slavery was a set of reciprocal obligations between masters and slaves, with slaves providing labor and obedience and masters providing basic care and direction. The concept of paternalism denied that the slave system was brutal and exploitative. While paternalism did provide some protection against the worst brutality, it did not guarantee decent living conditions, reasonable work, or freedom from physical punishment. (p. 323)

planters Owners of large farms (or more specifically plantations) that were worked by twenty or more slaves. By 1860, planters had accrued a great deal of local, statewide, and national political power in the South despite the fact that they represented a minority of the white electorate in those states. Planters' dominance of southern politics demonstrated both the power of tradition and stability among southern voters and the planters' success at convincing white voters that the slave system benefited all whites, even those without slaves. (pp. 59, 95, 112, 139, 161, 225, 244, 272, 321, 374, 402, 440)

popular sovereignty The idea that government is subject to the will of the people; before the Civil War, the idea that the residents of a territory should determine, through their legislatures, whether to allow slavery. (p. 346)

Populism A political movement that led to the creation of the People's Party, primarily comprising southern and western farmers who railed against big business and advocated business and economic reforms, including government ownership of the railroads. The movement peaked in the late nineteenth century. The Populist ticket won more than one million votes in the presidential election of 1892 and 1.5 million in the congressional elections of 1894. The term *populism* has come to mean any political movement that advocates on behalf of the common person, particularly for government intervention against big business. (pp. 506, 835)

predestination The idea that individual salvation or damnation is determined by God at, or just prior to, a person's birth. The concept of predestination invalidated the idea that salvation could be obtained through either faith or good works. (p. 85) *See also* Calvinism.

progressivism (progressive movement) A wide-ranging twentieth-century reform movement that advocated government activism to mitigate the problems created by urban industrialism. Progressivism reached its peak in 1912 with the creation of the Progressive Party, which ran Theodore Roosevelt for president. The term *progressivism* has come to mean any general effort advocating for social welfare programs. (pp. 485, 508, 534, 564, 591, 623, 745, 835)

Protestant Reformation *See* Reformation.

Protestantism A powerful Christian reform movement that began in the sixteenth century with Martin Luther's critiques of the Roman Catholic Church. Over the centuries, Protestantism has taken many different forms, branching into numerous denominations with differing systems of worship. (pp. 47, 64, 79, 106, 150, 249, 268, 307, 316, 355, 440, 536, 605, 623, 785)

Puritanism The ideas and religious principles held by dissenters from the Church of England, including the belief that the church needed to be purified by eliminating the elements of Catholicism from its practices. (pp. 64, 78, 105)

reform Darwinism A social theory, based on Charles Darwin's theory of evolution, that emphasized activism, arguing that humans could speed up evolution by altering the environment. A challenge to social Darwinism, reform Darwinism condemned laissez-faire and demanded that the government take a more active approach to solving social problems. It became the ideological basis for progressive reform in the late nineteenth and early twentieth centuries. (p. 538) *See also* laissez-faire; social Darwinism.

Reformation The reform movement that began in 1517 with Martin Luther's critiques of the Roman Catholic Church, which led to the formation of Protestant Christian groups. The English Reformation began with Henry VIII's break with the Roman Catholic Church, which established the Protestant Church of England. Henry VIII's decision was politically motivated; he had no particular quarrel with Catholic theology and remained an orthodox Catholic in most matters of religious practice. (pp. 46, 78)

republicanism The belief that the unworkable model of European-style monarchy should be replaced with a form of government in which supreme power resides in the hands of citizens with the right to vote and is exercised by a representative government answerable to this electorate. In Revolutionary-era America, republicanism became a social philosophy that embodied a sense of community and called individuals to act for the public good. (pp. 164, 186, 213, 237, 337, 355)

scientific management A system of organizing work developed by Frederick Winslow Taylor in the late nineteenth century to increase efficiency and productivity by breaking tasks into their component parts and training workers to perform specific parts. Labor resisted this effort because it deskilled workers and led to the speedup of production lines. Taylor's ideas were most popular at the height of the Progressive Era. (p. 538)

Second Great Awakening A popular religious revival that preached that salvation was available to anybody who chose to take it. The revival peaked in the 1830s, and its focus on social perfection inspired many of the reform movements of the Jacksonian era. (p. 268) *See also* evangelicalism.

separate spheres A concept of gender relations that developed in the Jacksonian era and continued well into the twentieth century, holding that women's proper place was in the private world of hearth and home (the private sphere) and men's was in the public world of commerce and politics (the public sphere). The doctrine of separate spheres eroded slowly over the nineteenth and twentieth centuries as women became more and more involved in public activities. (pp. 268, 442, 493, 601) *See also* cult of domesticity.

social Darwinism A social theory, based on Charles Darwin's theory of evolution, that argued that all progress in human society came as the result of competition and natural selection. Gilded Age proponents such as William Graham Sumner and Herbert Spencer claimed that reform was useless because the rich and poor were precisely where nature intended them to be and intervention would retard the progress of humanity. (pp. 438, 483, 517, 538) *See also* reform Darwinism.

social gospel movement A religious movement in the late nineteenth and early twentieth centuries founded on the idea that Christians have a responsibility to reform society as well as individuals. Social gospel adherents encouraged people to put Christ's teachings to work in their daily lives by actively promoting social justice. (pp. 535, 624)

social purity movement A movement to end prostitution and eradicate venereal disease, often accompanied by censorship of materials deemed "obscene." (p. 535)

socialism A governing system in which the state owns and operates the largest and most important parts of the economy. (pp. 491, 508, 536, 575, 613, 625, 665, 686, 744)

spoils system An arrangement in which party leaders reward party loyalists with government jobs. This slang term for *patronage* comes from the phrase "To the victor go the spoils." Widespread government corruption during the Gilded Age spurred reformers to curb the spoils system through the passage of the Pendleton Act in 1883, which created the Civil Service Commission to award government jobs on the basis of merit. (pp. 267, 418, 439, 458) *See also* civil service.

states' rights A strict interpretation of the Constitution that holds that federal power over states is limited and states hold ultimate sovereignty. First expressed in 1798 through the passage of the Virginia and Kentucky Resolutions, which were based on the assumption that states have the right to judge the constitutionality of federal laws, the states' rights philosophy became a cornerstone of the South's resistance to federal control of slavery. (pp. 202, 252, 277, 384, 403, 552)

strict constructionism An approach to constitutional law that attempts to adhere to the original intent of the writers of the Constitution. Strict construction often produces Supreme Court decisions that defer to the legislative branch and to the states and restrict the power of the federal government. Opponents of strict construction argue that the Constitution is an organic document that must be interpreted to meet conditions unimagined when it was written. (p. 786)

suffrage The right to vote. The term *suffrage* is most often associated with the efforts of American women to secure voting rights. (pp. 190, 268, 309, 337, 401, 441, 505, 534, 564, 748) *See also* franchise.

Sun Belt The southern and southwestern regions of the United States, which grew tremendously in industry, population, and influence after World War II. (pp. 715, 785)

supply-side economics An economic theory based on the premise that tax cuts for the wealthy and for corporations encourage investment and production (supply), which in turn stimulate consumption. Embraced by the Reagan administration and other conservative Republicans, this theory reversed Keynesian economic policy, which assumes that the way to stimulate the economy is to create demand through federal spending on public works and general tax cuts that put more money into the hands of ordinary people. (p. 795) *See also* Keynesian economics.

temperance movement The reform movement to end drunkenness by urging people to abstain from the consumption of alcohol. Begun in the 1820s, this movement achieved its greatest political victory with the passage of a constitutional amendment in 1919 that prohibited the manufacture, sale, and transportation of alcohol. That amendment was repealed in 1933. (pp. 271, 307, 442, 515, 535)

third world Originally a cold war term linked to decolonization, "third world" was first used in the late 1950s to describe newly independent countries in Africa and Asia that were not aligned with either Communist nations (the second world) or non-Communist nations (the first world). Later, the term was applied to all poor, nonindustrialized countries, in Latin America as well as in Africa and Asia. Many international experts see "third world" as a problematic category when applied to such a large and disparate group of nations, and they criticize the discriminatory hierarchy suggested by the term. (pp. 688, 748, 758, 784)

trickle-down economics The theory that financial benefits and incentives given to big businesses in the top tier of the economy will flow down to smaller businesses and individuals and thus benefit the entire nation. President Herbert Hoover unsuccessfully used the trickle-down strategy in his attempt to pull the nation out of the Great Depression, stimulating the economy through government investment in large economic enterprises and public works such as construction of the Boulder (Hoover) Dam. In the late twentieth century, conservatives used this economic theory to justify large tax cuts and other financial benefits for corporations and the wealthy. (p. 610)

Truman Doctrine President Harry S. Truman's assertion that American security depended on stopping any Communist government from taking over any non-Communist government — even nondemocratic and repressive dictatorships — anywhere in the world. Beginning in 1947 with American aid to help Greece and Turkey stave off Communist pressures, this approach became a cornerstone of American foreign policy during the cold war. (p. 680)

trust A corporate system in which corporations give shares of their stock to trustees who coordinate the industry to ensure profits to the participating corporations and curb competition. Pioneered by Standard Oil Company, such business practices were deemed unfair, were moderated by the Sherman Antitrust Act (1890), and were finally abolished by the combined efforts of Presidents Theodore Roosevelt and William Howard Taft and the sponsors of the 1914 Clayton Antitrust Act. The term *trust* is also loosely applied to all large business combinations. (pp. 433, 534, 633) *See also* holding company.

vertical integration A system in which a single person or corporation controls all processes of an industry from start to finished product. Andrew Carnegie first used vertical integration in the 1870s, controlling every aspect of steel production from the mining of iron ore to the manufacturing of the final product, thereby maximizing profits by eliminating the use of outside suppliers or services. (pp. 431, 464)

virtual representation The notion, propounded by British Parliament in the eighteenth century, that the House of Commons represented all British subjects — wherever they lived and regardless of whether they had directly voted for their representatives. Prime Minister George Grenville used this idea to argue that the Stamp Act and other parliamentary taxes on colonists did not constitute taxation without representation. American colonists rejected this argument, insisting that political representatives derived authority only from explicit citizens' consent indicated by elections, and that members of a distant government body were incapable of adequately representing their interests. (p. 142)

War Hawks Young Republicans elected to the U.S. Congress in the fall of 1810 who were eager for war with England in order to legitimize attacks on Indians, end impressment, and avenge foreign insults. (p. 244) *See also* hawks.

welfare capitalism The idea that a capitalistic, industrial society can operate benevolently to improve the lives of workers. The notion of welfare capitalism became popular in the 1920s as industries extended the benefits of scientific management to improve safety and sanitation in the workplace as well as institute paid vacations and pension plans. (p. 596) *See also* scientific management.

welfare state A nation or state in which the government assumes responsibility for some or all of the individual and social welfare of its citizens. Welfare states commonly provide education, health care, food programs for the poor, unemployment compensation, and other social benefits. The United States dramatically expanded its role as a welfare state with the provisions of the New Deal in the 1930s. (pp. 632, 705, 732)

Yankee imperialism A cry raised in Latin American countries against the United States when it intervened militarily in the region without invitation or consent from those countries. (pp. 760, 814)

yeoman A farmer who owned a small plot of land sufficient to support a family and tilled by family members and perhaps a few servants. (pp. 65, 116, 279, 334, 383, 412, 464)

A note about the index:

Names of individuals appear in boldface; biographical dates are included for major historical figures.

Letters in parentheses following page numbers refer to:
(i)   illustrations, including photographs and artifacts, as well as information in picture captions
(f)   figures, including charts and graphs
(m) maps
(b)   boxed features (such as "Historical Question")
(t)   tables
(n)   notes

colonial disputes over, 130(i), 132–138, 136(m), 137(m), 140(b)–141(b)
conflict between settlers and Indian tribes on, 54, 55, 57, 62, 64, 66–68, 97–98, 174–175, 222–225, 223(m), 251, 286. *See also* Native Americans
defense of, 134–138, 138(m), 140(b)–141(b), 222–225, 223(m), 224(i), 259
Farmers' Alliance on, 507
French, 132, 133–134, 133(i), 133(m), 140(b)
life on, 53–54, 54–56, 63, 67(i), 80–81, 84, 90, 99, 106, 108, 110, 111(i), 132–138, 459–461
in Proclamation of *1763*, 137(m), 138, 140(b)
settling, 54–56, 85(m), 92–95, 96(m), 105(m), 106, 110, 122(m)–123(m), 239, 243, 255, 286, 316–317, 317(m), 340(m), 344, 460(m)
Western (west of Mississippi River), 453–473. *See also* West, the
Whiskey Rebellion on, 221
Front Royal, Va., battle of (*1862*), 385(i)
Frowne, Sadie, 486
Fruit
commercial production of, 463
United Fruit controls "banana republics," 523
"Fruits of Amalgamation, The" (Clay), 320(i)
Fuel Administration, 572
Fugitive Slave Act (*1850*), 348, 348–349, 361
Fugitive slaves, 180, 199, 310, 332, 369
in Civil War, 369, 370, 381, 385
impact of *Uncle Tom's Cabin*, 348, 349–350, 349(i), 365
laws on, 348, 348–349, 365
on underground railroad, 310–311
Fulbright, J. William (*1905–1995*), 769
Fuller, Margaret (*1810–1850*), 308
Fulton, Mo., Churchill's iron curtain speech in, 682, 684(b)–685(b)
Fulton, Robert (*1765–1815*), 261
Fundamental Orders of Connecticut, quasi-constitution, 89
Fur trading, 107(m)
beaver hats and, 286(i)
British frontier forts and, 223(m), 225
Indian, 90, 121, 122(m), 225
international competition for, 107(m), 121, 122(m)
Lewis and Clark and, 240, 241
in Oregon Country, 287
smuggling, 137

Gabriel, slave leader, 237
Gadsden, James (*1788–1868*), 350
Gadsden Purchase (*1853*), 298(m), 350, 350(m), 266(b)
Gage, Thomas (*1721–1787*), 141(b), 150, 152–153, 154, 161
Galbraith, John Kenneth, on affluent society, 711

Galloway, Joseph, 151
Gama, Vasco da (*c. 1469–1524*), 29(m), 31
Gambian culture, 112
Games
baseball, 493–494, 501, 603, 691, 714
football, 603–604, 603(i)
lacrosse, 140(b)
Mexican ball court, 16(i)
Puritans ban, 86
soccer, 828
Gansevoort, Peter, 158(i)
Garcia, Héctor Peréz, 692
Garcia, Jerry, 744
Garfield, James A. (*1831–1881*), 444
assassinated, 445
on Fourteenth Amendment, 409
as president (*1881*), 444–445
Garland, Hamlin (*1860–1940*), 500
Garment industry, 535, 536, 811
dangerous conditions in, 536–537, 537(i)
globalization in, 826(b), 827(i)
ILGWU in, 536
mechanization of, 485–486
sweatshops in, 485–486, 486(i), 535
Triangle fire in, 536–537, 537(i)
women in, 387, 485–486, 486(i), 663, 826(b), 827(i)
Garnet, Henry Highland, 310
Garrison, William Lloyd (*1805–1879*), 272, 275(b), 315, 320(i), 347, 422
on abolition, 272, 361
on women's rights, 272–273
Garthwaite, Anna Maria, 104(i)
Garvey, Marcus (*1887–1940*), 601–602
Gary, Martin, 421
Gas. *See* Oil industry
Gas masks, in chemical warfare, 562(i)
Gaspée (British ship), 148
Gates, Horatio (*c. 1727–1806*), 169(m), 174, 177–178, 177(m), 178
Gates, John "Bet a Million," 461(i)
Gates, Merrill, 454
Gay American(s), 721
in military, 659, 820
persecuted under McCarthyism, 695
rights, 800, 802–803, 802(i), 802(m), 813
Gay and lesbian rights movement, 802–803, 802(i)
AIDS (acquired immune deficiency syndrome) and, 802
antidiscrimination laws and, 802–803, 802(m)
civil union and, 803
gay pride parades in, 802, 802(i)
politics and, 802, 803, 813
Stonewall riot sparks (*1969*), 802, 802(i)
Gaza Strip, 823, 823(m)
in Six-Day War (*1967*), 774, 774(m), 792(m)
Gender. *See also* Women
citizenship and, 441
discrimination, 739, 745–747, 750
gap in education, 718
gap in income, 663, 690, 713, 746, 799, 801
gap in politics, 801, 820

patriarchy and, 441–442
Title IX bans in all aspects of education (*1972*), 750, 752
voting. *See* Woman suffrage
wage differences by, 703, 718–719, 746, 747, 799, 801
General Agreement on Tariffs and Trade (GATT) (*1994*), 824, 825
General Court, in Massachusetts Bay Colony, 87
General Electric, 436, 499(b), 533, 715(b)
advertising, 598(b)
investment bankers and, 437
outsources research work to India, 826(b)
Generall Historie of Virginia (Smith), 53
General Managers Association (GMA), fights Pullman strike, 514
General Motors, 592(i), 702(i), 799
as biggest corporation in world, 702(i)
CIO strike at (*1937*), 636
sources parts globally, 824
unionized, 636
General Theory of Employment, Interest, and Money (Keynes), 643
Geneva, Switzerland, 708, 710
Geneva accords (*1954*), 708
divide Vietnam on 17th parallel, 708, 708(m), 763(m), 764(t)
mandate free elections, 708, 762
Genoa, Italy, 29, 29(m), 31
"Gentleman's Agreement" (*1907*), Japan restricts emigration, 549
Geography. *See also* Maps and mapping
exploration and, 29(m), 30–32, 32–34
George III, king of Great Britain (*r. 1760–1820*), 138, 138(i), 139, 164, 166, 171, 177, 179
Georgia, 122(m), 168, 346, 552, 638, 790
in American Revolution, 172(m), 177, 177(m), 178
black voters in, 740(m)
cession of western lands, 188(m)
Cherokee removal from, 193, 276–277, 276(m), 317(m), 467. *See also* Cherokee Indians
Civil War in, 381, 384, 389, 391(m), 394(t)
colony founded *1732*, 96(m), 112
Continental Congress and, 150, 166
in cotton belt, 216, 318(m), 321(m), 334(m)
farming in, 335, 335(m), 417(f), 507
government in, 189, 338, 338(t)
KKK in, 606, 691
plantations in, 321, 321(m)
population in, 112, 319(f), 421
railroads in, 430(m)
ratifies Constitution, 204, 205(m)
Reconstruction in, 400(i), 407, 417(f)
Redeemers in, 421, 421(m)
secedes, 364, 364(m), 370–371
sharecropping in, 417(f)
slaves in, 319(f), 331(i), 338(t)
Georgia, former Soviet state, 817(m)
Gephardt, Richard, 813

Hue, Vietnam, Tet Offensive in (*1968*), 763(m)
Huerta, Dolores, 743–744
Huerta, Victoriano, 565–566, 565(m)
Hughes, Charles Evans (*1862–1948*), 594, 642
Hughes, Langston (*1902–1967*), 602
Huia Indians, 468(m)
Huitzilopochtli, Mexica war god, 21
Hull, Charles, 533
Hull, Cordell (*1871–1955*), 651
Hull, John, 96(i)
Hull House, 535, 624
    opens in Chicago (*1889*), 533, 534
    settlement house movement and, 533–534, 534(i), 535
Human rights, 805
    Carter and, 784, 791–792, 793–794
    Soviet Union and, 773
    UN adopts declaration of (*1948*), 748(b)
    U.S. detention and, 831, 833–834
Humphrey, Hubert H. (*1911–1978*), 772
Hungary, 582(b), 681, 816
    agricultural rural domain in, 479(m), 480
    free elections (*1990*), 817(m)
    Germans occupy (*1941*), 654(m)
    immigration from, 479(m), 480–481, 480(f)
    republic (*1919*), 577, 578(m)
    revolt in (*1956*), 708
    Soviets control (*1944*), 668, 669(m), 670, 681, 683(m)
Hunkpapa Sioux Indians. *See also* Sioux Nation
    Sitting Bull as chief, 467
Hunter, David, 381
Huron Indians, 140(b), 198
    in Great Lakes region, 19(m)
Hurricanes, Katrina and Rita (*2005*), 830
Hurston, Zora Neale, 602
Hussein, ibn Talal, king of Jordan (r. *1953–1999*), 823
Hussein, Saddam (*1937–*), 832
    driven out of Kuwait by Operation Desert Storm, 814–816, 815(m), 822
    fails to comply with UN agreement, 815(m), 823, 832
    invades Kuwait (*1990*), 814
    turns weapons on Iraqi Kurds and Shiites, 815–816
Hutchinson, Anne (*1591–1643*), 88–89
Hutchinson, Thomas (*1711–1780*), 131–132, 132(i), 135, 142, 143, 147, 148, 150, 154, 171
    quoted, 131, 132, 143
Hydroelectric power. *See also* Electricity industry
    Aswan Dam, Egypt, 709
    on government lands, 543, 549
    Hoover Dam, 626
    monopoly of, 543, 549
    rising usage, 716, 745
    Tennessee Valley Authority (TVA), 627, 628(m)

Hydrogen bomb. *See also* Nuclear arms race.
    Soviets develop (*1955*), 687
    U.S. develops (*1950–1954*), 687

Ibos, 113(m)
ICBMs (intercontinental ballistic missiles), Soviets test-fire (*1957*), 710
Idaho, 578, 582(b), 831
    gold in, 455, 455(m)
    migrant workers in, 630
    populists in, 520
    railroad in, 430(m), 462(m)
    Territory, 455(m), 458
    unions in, 508
    woman suffrage in (*1896*), 516, 517(i), 573(m)
Igbo culture, 112
"I have a dream" speech (King), 738, 739(i)
Illinois, 276, 348, 407, 465, 487, 521
    anti-ERA campaign in, 797(b)
    auto industry in, 593(m), 596(m)
    cession of Indian land in, 289(i), 374
    farming in, 299, 302(i)
    free state, 250, 251(m), 252(i), 351(m), 357
    KKK in, 606
    Lincoln in, 285–286, 286(i), 359–360, 363
    railroads in, 304(m), 350, 430(m), 461, 462(m)
    Schlafly (Phyllis) in, 783, 797(b), 797(i)
    temperance movement in, 433
    Territory, 175, 176(m), 179, 243, 245(m)
I Love Lucy (TV show), 719
Imamo, Japanese pilot, 661(i)
"I'm Just Wild about Harry" (Truman's campaign song, *1948*), 693(i)
Immediate Not Gradual Abolition (Heyrick), 275(b)
Immigration and immigrants, 478(i), 607–608. *See also individual ethnic groups;* Slaves and slavery
    amnesty to illegal, 828
    in automobile industry, 592
    bracero program (*1941–1964*), 641(i), 716, 716(i)
    on Brooklyn Bridge, 477–478
    causes of, 108, 128(b), 300(b), 301(b), 307, 356–357, 478(i), 479–483, 479(m), 639(i), 825, 828
    citizenship and, 228, 300(b), 466–467
    civil rights for, 716
    colonial growth from, 104–105, 105(m), 108
    on Comstock, 300(b), 301(b), 456–457
    conditions on ships, 109, 112, 113, 115(i)
    Congress limits, 606, 734. *See also* Immigration policy
    Democrats court, 440
    discrimination against, 298–299, 300(b), 307, 411, 440, 638–639, 638(i), 639(i), 665, 831

    families of, 84, 302(i)
    German Jewish physicists in U.S. atomic program, 666(b)–667(b)
    Homeland Security controls (*2002*), 831–832
    illegal, 716, 716(i), 743, 828
    indentured servants, 62–64, 63(i), 65, 109, 112
    Jews denied asylum, 665
    Know-Nothings oppose, 355, 355(i)
    literacy test for, 483
    measuring, 306, 306(f), 322(f), 479–483, 479(m), 480(f), 481(m)
    merit exams and, 444(i)
    mixed population and neutrality (*1914*), 567
    nativism and, 355, 356, 466, 536
    new wave (after *1880*), 480–482, 480(f), 481(m)
    numbers fall in wartime, 573, 585
    old wave (before *1880*), 480–482, 480(f), 481(m)
    opportunities for, 305, 307, 444(i), 828
    patriotism campaign unites (*1917*), 572, 574–575
    political rights for, 362
    pushcarts, 482(i)
    racism and, 482–483, 606
    radicals, 491–492, 492(i), 512, 606
    on railroads, 466, 480
    religions of, 606
    restriction of, 463, 464, 466, 482–483, 585, 606
    surge in (*1990*s), 734, 812, 825, 828
    women voters, 600
    work of, 263, 300(b), 306–307, 455–457, 466–467, 479–483, 479(m), 480(f), 485, 573
Immigration and Nationality Act (*1965*), 734
    caps on all nationalities, 734
    enables *1990*s surge, 734, 812, 825, 828
Immigration policy
    amnesty, 828
    ban on Asians lifted (*1952*), 694
    bracero program (*1941–1964*), 641(i), 716, 716(i)
    caps on all nationalities (*1965*), 734, 812, 825, 828
    on Chinese, 463, 466, 483, 557, 585, 606, 639, 694
    Communists barred (*1952*), 694
    Congress restricts (*1924*), 606
    on Japanese, 606, 639, 694
    on Mexicans, 606, 716, 716(i)
    political pressure on, 300(b), 466, 483, 606
    quotas in, 606, 694, 734
Immigration Reform and Control Act (*1986*), 828
Immigration stations
    Angel Island, Calif., 483
    Castle Island, N.Y., 483
    Ellis Island, N.Y., 483, 586(i)
    El Paso, Tex., 586(i)

North Dakota, 241. *See also* Dakota
Territory
wheat farms in, 463
Northeast. *See also* New England; New
Jersey; New York
antiforeign sentiment against European
immigrants in, 411
antislavery movement in, 272–273,
273(i), 278, 293
coal shortages during *1902* strike, 541
cultural shifts in, 268–273
economy of, 303, 304(m)
energy consumption in, 803
Federalists in, 240(m), 242, 246–247
manufacturing in, 262–264, 299, 303
railroads in, 304(m)
shipping embargoes affect, 241–242,
244
society in, 305
temperance movement in, 443
in War of *1812*, 244, 245(m), 246–247
Northern Pacific Railroad, 430(m), 469
Northern Paiute Indians, 19(m)
on Comstock, 457–458
Northern Securities Company, 540–541
North Korea (People's Republic of North
Korea), 832
Communist Chinese intervene in, 697
Communist regime in (*1948*), 696,
696(m)
invades South Korea (*1950*), 696
in Korean War (*1950–1953*), 695–697,
696(m)
nuclear power in, 817–818, 834
as Soviet occupation zone (*1945*), 695,
696
Northrup, Solomon, 350
North Vietnam, 708(m), 763(m)
Communist regime (Vietminh) in, 708
constructs Ho Chi Minh Trail for
supplies and soldiers, 762, 763(m),
766(b)–767(b)
directs National Liberation Front fighting
in South Vietnam, 762, 767(b), 771
Gulf of Tonkin incident and (*1964*), 763
peace negotiations with, 771, 775, 776
takes over South Vietnam (*1975*), 776
U.S. bombing of, 763, 764(t), 765,
766(b)–767(b), 767(i), 768, 769, 771,
772, 775
Northwestern Farmers' Alliance, 507
Farmers' Alliance and, 506–508, 507(i)
Northwest Ordinance (*1787*), 197–199, 344
bans slavery north of Ohio River, 197,
199, 344
divides western land cessions into ten
future states, 197, 198(m)
Indian territory in, 197–198, 199
"Northwest Passage," search for, 33, 48, 92
Northwest Territory, 186, 188(m), 196,
223(m)
Indian conflict in, 197–198, 222–225,
222(i), 223(m), 224(i)
Indian lands in, 187, 188(m), 197–198,
198(m), 199, 222(i). *See also* Indian
Territory

land ordinances for (*1784–1787*), 186,
197–199, 344
land sales in, 197, 222, 238, 264, 267,
279, 279(f), 281, 302–303
maps of, 188(m), 198(i)
settlement of, 197, 198–199, 222
slavery prohibited in, 197, 199, 344
as solution to western lands issue, 186,
188(m)
Norton, Eleanor Holmes, 730(i)
Norway, 749(b)
Germans occupy (*1940*), 654, 654(m)
as NATO country, 683(m)
Nova Scotia, free blacks in, 154, 193(i)
Noyes, John Humphrey, 308, 309(i)
Nuclear arms race
antinuclear demonstrations in (*1982*),
804, 806(i)
arms limitations, 707(i), 758, 773, 793,
804, 817–818, 832
brinksmanship in, 707–708, 707(i),
761–762, 761(m), 804, 806
China enters (*1964*), 778
in cold war, 681, 687–688, 694, 699,
707–708, 707(i), 767(b), 804, 805–806
Cuban missile crisis in (*1962*), 758,
759(m), 761–762, 761(m)
defense spending in, 707, 710, 761, 763,
793, 804, 806
deterrence policy in, 687, 707–708, 725,
793, 804, 805–806, 832
disarmament in, 806
Eisenhower and Khrushchev discuss
test ban, 710
ICBMs in, 710
India enters (*1998*), 817, 818
INF agreement in (*1987*), 806
Iraqi weapons in, 823
mutually assured destruction (MAD)
in, 708
North Korea in, 817–818, 834
Pakistan enters (*1998*), 817–818
Polaris submarine in, 710
public fear of, 710, 711(i)
Reagan and Gorbachev disarm, 804,
806
SDI (Star Wars) in, 804, 832
Soviets in, 687, 694, 710, 758, 806
test ban treaties, 758, 762
U.S. bases in, 710
U.S. in, 666(b)–667(b), 681, 685(b), 687,
699, 707–708, 710–711, 758, 804,
806, 832
Nuclear power industry
Chernobyl explosion (*1986*), 803
first plant built (*1954*), 705
opened to commerce, 705
opposition to, 803
produces 11 percent of electricity in
U.S. (*1977*), 803
Three Mile Island accident (*1979*), 803
wastes from, 803
Nueces River, in Mexican-American War,
294, 295(m)
Nullification, doctrine of (in states' rights),
277–278, 347

Nurses and nursing, 387, 393(b), 535,
555, 573, 574(i), 601, 659, 663, 713,
765(i), 768
in Civil War, 387, 393(b)
public health, 535
training, 387
in Vietnam War, 765(i), 768
as "woman's job," 601
Nye, Gerald, 652
Nye committee, investigates why U.S.
went to war in *1917*, 652

Oahu, Hawaii, Japanese attack Pearl
Harbor on (*1941*), 649, 653,
656–657, 656(m), 658(i), 660,
672(m), 674
Oakland, Calif.
built on Peralta ranch, 465, 465(i)
draft protest in, 728(i)
Oakley, Annie (Phoebe Moses)
(*1860–1926*), 472
Oberlin College, 269
women in (*1855*), 269, 269(i)
O'Brien, Tim, on Vietnam War, 768
Occupational Safety and Health Act
(OSHA) (*1970*), 745, 798
O'Connor, Sandra Day (*1930–*), first
woman justice on Supreme Court,
800, 801
O'Dell, Jack, 695
Odessa, Tex., population in, 605(m)
O'Donnell, Hugh, 509, 512
Office of Economic Opportunity (*1964*),
733
Oglala band of Lakota Sioux, 452(i), 467,
469. *See also* Sioux Nation
Ohio, 401, 419, 518, 521, 586, 593
antiwar protesters in, 775
automobile industry in, 593(m), 596(m),
825
electoral votes in, 833
Hondas produced in, 825
industrial capitalism in, 432–433, 436
railroads in, 304(m), 430(m), 462(m)
temperance movement in, 443
Ohio Company of Virginia (*1747*), 136(m)
land speculation in Ohio Country, 133,
136(m), 138
Washingtons in, 133
Ohio Country. *See also* Ohio Valley
French in, 135, 136(m), 137
Indians in American Revolution, 141(b),
171, 174, 174–175, 176(m), 179
as Indian Territory, 132, 133–134,
140(b)–141(b), 171, 198, 222–225,
235–236
land speculators and settlers in, 133,
138, 222–225, 222(i), 223(m), 224(i)
Tecumseh in, 235–236, 236(i)
Ohio River, 141(i), 175, 176(m), 180, 197
as boundary of slavery, 197, 199, 344
Indian Territory and, 198, 222, 235. *See
also* Ohio Country
navigation on, 261, 261(m), 431
Northwest Territory and, 188(m),
197–199, 344

Progressivism *(continued)*
  limits of, 554–559
  moralism and idealism of, 566, 569, 573, 575–576, 578, 579, 582(b)–583(b), 592
  in New Deal coalition, 623–624
  Facism and, 557–559
  Roosevelt (T.) and, 540–549, 540(i), 542(i), 546(m), 547(i), 547(m), 548(m), 550–552, 559
  stalled, 549–550
  theory and practice, 538–540, 551–552
  urban industrialism and, 485, 532(i), 591
  for white men only, 555–559
  Wilson (W.) and, 552–553, 553–554, 555, 558
  woman suffrage and, 555–557
Prohibition *(1920–1933)*, 606, 607, 608(m). *See also* Temperance movement
  anti-immigrant feeling in, 493, 536, 573, 608
  begins *1920*, 573, 597
  bootleggers in, 597–600
  criminal gangs in, 598–600
  "dry" states, 536, 573
  ends *1933*, 600
  public resistance to, 597, 598–599, 600
  speakeasies in, 597–598, 614
Prohibition Party *(1869)*, 443
  in reform coalition, 516
Promontory Point, Utah, transcontinental railroad completed in *(1869)*, 429
Property owners, 144
  Iroquois and, 20
  Loyalists as, 143, 171, 172
  in Oneida community, 308, 309(i)
  pardons after Civil War, 401
  probate of, 162(b)
  in public office, 190, 337
  voting rights of, 65, 66, 98, 116–117, 190–191, 198, 265, 310, 337
  women as, 20, 172, 190, 191, 191(i), 248, 249, 306, 516
Property rights
  in bills of rights, 189–190
  state governments back over labor, 488, 489(i), 512, 513, 514, 515(i)
  Supreme Court elevates over all other rights, 439
Prophetstown, Indian village of regeneration, 235–236
  in battle of Tippecanoe *(1811)*, 244, 244(m)
Prosser, Thomas, 237
Prostitutes and prostitution
  Mann Act *(1910)* prohibits transporting, 535
  moral reform movement against, 271
  as "social evil," 535, 536
Protestant Reformation, 46, 46–47, 78–79, 85
Protestants and Protestantism, 64, 72, 99, 316, 556(i). *See also individual denominations*
  anti-Catholic backlash in, 307, 355, 355(i), 606, 608

evangelical, 119, 249–250, 260, 268, 270, 271(i), 272–273, 281, 307–311, 331, 333, 336–337, 336(i), 719, 795. *See also* Evangelical religion
  missionaries in, 270, 290(i), 308, 522–523
  persecution of, 79(i)
  political leanings in, 440
  progressives in, 535–536
  rural, 331, 333, 336–337, 336(i), 605–606
  sects of, 108–109, 119
  Sunday schools in, 270
  traditional morality in, 271, 281, 784, 785. *See also* New Right; Reform movements; Temperance movement
  women in, 88–89, 91, 92, 92(i), 120(i), 249–250, 249(i), 270–271
Public Enemy, The (movie), 613
Public Opinion, on immigration, 483
Public parks, 495, 501
  Central Park as first *(1873)*, 495
  Olmsted designs, 495
Public school system, 414–415. *See also* School(s)
  free, 268, 300(b), 305, 322, 336, 441, 496
  gender equality in (Title IX), 750, 752
  integration of, 722, 723(i), 751, 786, 786(i), 786(m), 788
  prayer and Bible reading banned in, 736, 785, 795
  segregation in, 638, 692, 722, 723(i), 738, 751
  teaching evolution banned in, 607
Public transportation. *See* Mass transit
Public works projects, in Great Depression
  Civilian Conservation Corps (CCC) *(1933)*, 626, 665, 819(i)
  Civilian Works Administration (CWA) *(1933)*, 626
  Congress authorizes *(1930)*, 610
  Federal Art Program and, 627(i)
  Hoover Dam as, 626
  Tennessee Valley Authority (TVA) as, 627, 628(m)
  Works Progress Administration (WPA) *(1935)*, 633, 633(i), 665
Publishing. *See also* Magazines; Newspapers; Printing; Writers
  abolitionist, 272, 315, 348, 349–350, 349(i), 365
  anti-anarchist, 492(i)
  in antilynching campaign, 441–442, 442(i)
  banned in Boston, 428
  books analyzing the American experience, 427, 428(i), 454, 596, 604, 711, 714, 720, 732
  business wizards as authors, 799
  censorship of, 381, 695
  feminist movement and, 719, 719(i), 746
  first book printed in America, 76(i)
  for freedmen, 414(i)
  free schoolbooks, 635(b)
  inflammatory, 492(i)

influential, 80–81, 82(b)–83(b), 103, 133(i), 164, 215(i), 218(b)–219(b), 219(i), 272, 275(b), 348, 349, 349(i), 350, 438, 441–442, 442(i), 538, 542(i), 643, 711, 719, 719(i), 720, 721, 732, 746, 747(i)
  muckrakers, 434(b)–435(b), 542, 542(i)
  slave narratives, 112–113, 114(i), 350
  on tenement conditions, 484, 544(b)–545(b)
  on Vietnam War, 757, 758(i), 765, 768, 777, 778
Pueblo Bonita, Chaco Canyon, N.Mex., 16(i)
Pueblo Indians, 126(i)
  revolt against Spanish, 69, 126(i)
  in Southwest, 19(m), 468(m)
Pueblo Revolt, in New Mexico *(1680)*, 69
  leaders of, 69, 126(i)
Puerto Rico, 759(m)
  ceded to U.S. *(1898)*, 526, 527, 527(m), 528(m), 565(m)
  manufacturing in, 826(b)
  as Spanish territory, 39(m), 71(m), 137(m), 525, 528(m)
Pulitzer, Joseph *(1847–1911)*, 525, 526(i)
Pulitzer Prize to Gwendolyn Brooks, black woman poet, 691
Pullman, George M. *(1831–1897)*
  as industrial capitalist, 513–515
  labor relations of, 513, 514, 515(i)
Pullman, Ill., as company town, 513, 515(b)
Pullman strike *(1894)*, 508, 513–515, 515(i), 529, 536
  Federal troops crush, 514, 515(i)
  newspapers misrepresent, 514
Punitive Expedition *(1916–1917)*
  Pershing leads to Mexico, 563, 565(m), 566
  pursues Pancho Villa, 566, 566(m)
Pure Food and Drug Act *(1906)*, 542, 542(i)
Puritans and Puritanism
  baptism in, 91
  beliefs of, 77–78, 80–81, 81(i), 82(b)–83(b), 84, 84(i), 85–86, 86(i), 88–89, 105
  Covenant, 77, 80–81, 85, 87, 88–89, 106
  in England, 64, 86(i), 89–90
  Great Awakening and, 119
  Halfway Covenant, 91
  as missionaries to Indians, 81, 82(b)–83(b)
  music and, 76(i), 86, 147
  persecution by, 77–78, 88–89, 91–92
  practices of, 76(i), 84(i), 85–86, 86–88, 88(i), 91–92, 97
  punishments of, 87(i), 91
  as settlers in New England, 76(i), 77–78, 80–81, 82, 84–92
  as slaveowners, 107
  splintering of, 88–89
  voting rights of, 87, 89, 97
  witch hunting by, 92, 92(i)
  zeal of, 64, 77, 78, 85, 87(i), 91

Instructor's Resources for *The American Promise: A Compact History,* Third Edition

See the preface for full descriptions of these supplements.

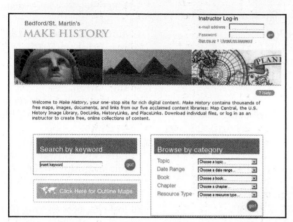

- **Make History** at **bedfordstmartins.com/makehistory**
  Provides access to Map Central, U.S. History Image Library, DocLinks, HistoryLinks, and PlaceLinks for one-stop searching by keyword, topic, date, or book chapter and easy downloading of the maps, images, documents, and Web links found.

- ***Instructor's Resource Manual,*** ISBN 0–312–44840–6
  Includes model answers for review questions, lecture strategies, a guide addressing common misconceptions and difficult topics, film suggestions, discussion starters, in-class activities, a survival guide for first-time teaching assistants, and more.

- **Transparencies,** ISBN 0–312–41737–3
  Includes over 160 full-color acetate transparencies of all full-sized maps and many images from both the full-length and compact editions of the text.

- **Book Companion site** at **bedfordstmartins.com/roarkcompact**
  Gathers all the electronic resources for the text, including the Online Study Guide and related Quiz Gradebook, at a single Web address. The resources on this Web site are also formatted for use with **course management systems** such as Blackboard, WebCT, Angel, and Desire2Learn.

- **Computerized Test Bank CD-ROM,** ISBN 0–312–44838–4

- **Instructor's Resource CD-ROM,** ISBN 0–312–44839–2
  Features PowerPoint presentations built around chapter outlines, maps, figures, and selected images from the textbook, plus the *Instructor's Resource Manual,* and more.

- ***Using the Bedford Series in History and Culture in the U.S. History Survey*** at **bedfordstmartins.com/usingseries**

- An assortment of **videos and multimedia** for qualified adopters

- ***The American Promise*** **for Distance Learning via Telecourse**